The Emerging Nation: A Documentary History
of the
Foreign Relations of the United States
under the
Articles of Confederation, 1780-1789

Mary A. Giunta
Editor-in-Chief and Project Director

J. Dane Hartgrove, Associate Editor

Norman A. Graebner, Peter P. Hill, Lawrence S. Kaplan
Consulting Editors

Volume III

Richard B. Smith
Project Publication Specialist, 1994

Mary-Jane M. Dowd
Editor and Project Director, 1985-1991

National Historical Publications and Records Commission
1996

The cover illustration is taken from a photograph of the die of the Great Seal of the United States, adopted in 1782 and engraved by Robert Scot of Philadelphia. For further information on the design, adoption, and use of the Great Seal, see Richard S. Patterson and Richardson Dougall, *The Eagle and the Shield: A History of the Great Seal of the United States* (Washington, 1976).

Library of Congress Cataloging-in-Publication Data

The emerging nation: a documentary history of the foreign relations of the United States under the Articles of Confederation, 1780-1789 / Mary A. Giunta, editor in chief; J. Dane Hartgrove, associate editor; Norman A. Graebner, Peter P. Hill, Lawrence S. Kaplan, consulting editors; Richard B. Smith, project publication specialist; Mary-Jane M. Dowd, editor and project director.

xxi, 1001 pps 150mm x 225mm
   Includes bibliographical references and index.
   Contents: v. 1. Recognition of independence, 1780-1784 — v. 2. Trials and tribulations, 1780-1785 — v. 3. Toward federal diplomacy, 1780-1789.
   ISBN 0-16-048498-7 (vol. 1: alk. paper). — ISBN 0-16-048499-5 (vol. 2: alk. paper). — ISBN 0-16-048500-2 (vol. 3: alk. paper).
   1. United States—Foreign relations—1783-1815—Sources. 2. United States—Foreign relations—1775-1783—Sources.
I. Giunta, Mary A. II. Hartgrove, J. Dane. III. Dowd, Mary-Jane M.
E303.E44   1996
327.73'009'033—dc20   96-10279
                                                              CIP

For sale by the U.S. Government Printing Office
Superintendent of Documents, Mail Stop: SSOP, Washington, DC 20402-9328
ISBN 0-16-048500-2

Preface

The Emerging Nation: A Documentary History of the Foreign Relations of the United States under the Articles of Confederation, 1780-1789, traces the battles of John Adams, Benjamin Franklin, John Jay, and others to establish a credible international presence for the United States of America as a new nation.

This is an extraordinary collection of documentary materials brought together from universities, libraries, historical societies, and private organizations, including the National Archives, the Library of Congress, and French, British, and other European repositories. The collection of diplomatic despatches, treaties, private letters, and other documents is an essential record of the formative years of United States diplomacy.

These documents provide teachers and students with a basic reference work. They brim with information and insights valuable to historians, political scientists, government officials, lawyers, and other individuals interested in the development of early United States foreign policy. They provide insight into how a new nation gains diplomatic stature and shapes a foreign policy out of the ashes of war and amidst divergent interests at home and abroad.

The National Historical Publications and Records Commission is proud to present this three-volume documentary record of the beginnings of United States foreign policy.

John W. Carlin
Archivist of the United States
and Chair, National Historical
Publications and Records Commission

General Introduction

We believe that God has hardened the heart of the
Pharaoh, so that he cannot let the people go, till the
first-born of his land are destroyed, 'till the hosts are
overthrown in the midst of the sea, and till poverty
and distress like the lice of Egypt shall have covered
the land.[1]

So declared the first Secretary for Foreign Affairs under the Articles of
Confederation, Robert R. Livingston, in a letter to John Jay as he attacked
King George III's refusal to make peace during the waning days of the
American Revolution. But through diplomatic negotiations peace did come,
a peace that challenged American leaders – John Jay, Benjamin Franklin,
John Adams, Thomas Jefferson, and Livingston, among others – to secure
the new nation, to forge in diplomatic arenas the freedom gained on the
battlefield. In the letters, despatches, and other documents that record their
actions, one can see their struggles to gain recognition from foreign powers,
to negotiate treaties and agreements with other countries, and to protect
the sovereign rights of the United States. One can see their efforts to
defend American claims to western territories in the face of attempts to
define U.S. borders in narrow terms, and one can see the intrigues that
aroused political jealousies and competitive interests among the American
states. In like manner, in letters, despatches, and other documents of their
European counterparts, one can see attempts to maintain authority and to
increase influence in world affairs through diplomatic schemes and
negotiations.

[1] *Robert R. Livingston to John Jay, 9 May 1782, National Archives, RG 360: Papers of
the Continental and Confederation Congresses and the Constitutional Convention, item
79, v. 1, pp. 714-723 (LBkC); M247, reel 105.*

The Emerging Nation: A Documentary History of the Foreign Relations of the United States under the Articles of Confederation, 1780-1789, presents significant historical documents in three volumes. Volume One, *Recognition of Independence*, covers the extensive peace negotiations leading to the Treaty of Paris of 1783; Volume Two, *Trials and Tribulations*, explores the frustrations in diplomacy associated in part with the inability of the government under the Articles to control commerce, to tax the states for needed revenues, and to enforce treaties; Volume Three, *Toward Federal Diplomacy*, reflects continued diplomatic efforts to reach foreign agreements to enhance United States security in the world community while political leaders established a federal union.

It is the goal of the editors of this publication to make available significant documents to serve as a starting point for the study of United States diplomacy for the years 1780 to 1789. The documents begin with John Adams' acceptance of his commission as minister plenipotentiary to negotiate peace with Great Britain, continue with United States efforts to seek treaties and financial aid from European nations, and end with United States diplomatic efforts at the opening of the First Federal Congress.

In order to present the historical richness of as many documents as possible, introductions, headnotes, and annotations have been used judiciously in support of a basic understanding of the events. This editorial philosophy reflects the goal of the editors "to let the documents speak for themselves." As gathered here, they have much to say.

Historical Overview

During the 17th and 18th centuries Great Britain and France engaged in a series of wars as they fiercely competed for territories in India, Africa, the West Indies, and North America. The capstone of these wars in North America came in 1754 when conflict over claims to land and trade west of the Appalachian Mountains by French and British colonials ignited the French and Indian War, 1754-1763, which became a worldwide conflict known as the Seven Years War, 1756-1763. At the close of hostilities, France relinquished to Great Britain its rights to Canada, Acadia, Cape Breton Island, the islands in the St. Lawrence River, and all territories east of the Mississippi River. It gave all French territories west of the Mississippi River and New Orleans to Spain. Although France retained fishing rights off the coast of Newfoundland by the terms of the Treaty of Paris of 1763, the result of defeat was virtual expulsion from the continent. Only Great Britain and Spain held colonies in North America.

But while the French were defeated, they remained undaunted. Some French leaders saw that the British in their victory had sown the seeds of future difficulties. The French presence in North America had made the American colonials dependent on British support. Now that the French presence was removed, the Americans were free to acquire additional territory, rely even more on their own local governing bodies, and in general pursue a more independent course.

Following the signing of the Treaty of Paris of 1763, postwar attempts by Parliament to enforce tighter controls and impose higher taxes on the colonies met with strong resistance. Disputes grew more serious from 1765 to 1775. In April 1775 open warfare erupted with the battles of Lexington and Concord in Massachusetts. In November of that year, the Continental Congress began to search abroad for financial aid and military stores to meet its obligations. A major, albeit clandestine, source was found in France. It was this secret aid that kept America's hopes for nationhood alive during the difficult years of 1775, 1776, and 1777.

America's victory at Saratoga in the fall of 1777 helped to precipitate formal French involvement in the war. France's leadership acted less from a conviction that the United States had demonstrated an ability to maintain its independence by force of arms, than from a concern that the Americans might accept a peace settlement with Great Britain. For its part, the United States was now prepared to ally itself with France, necessity having replaced earlier altruistic plans of minimal relations with foreign powers. American and French diplomats signed treaties of alliance and of amity and commerce on February 6, 1778. Congress ratified the treaties that Spring without substantive debate and proceeded to seek the assistance of other nations.

Spain's entry into the war as France's ally in June 1779 provided Congress with the opportunity to seek another alliance. Congress hoped for Spanish recognition of American independence and material aid in conducting the war. For its part, Spain was ready to provide assistance that might discomfit Great Britain, but regarded the American rebellion as a dangerous example for its own American colonies. In addition, the refusal of the United States to renounce its right to navigate the Mississippi River, or its claims to lands west of the Appalachians, gave Spain reason not to honor American requests. John Jay, who arrived in Spain in January 1780, spent two and a half years in negotiations with small success.

John Adams, who represented the United States in France, 1778-1779, returned to Europe in early 1780 as American commissioner to draw up a treaty of peace and a commercial agreement with Great Britain. Disputes with the Comte de Vergennes, the French Foreign Minister, over the proper timing of an announcement of his mission to London caused Adams to transfer his residence to Holland, where he might establish American credit with one or more of the Dutch banks. After many months filled with frustrations, Adams was successful in obtaining Dutch recognition and financial support in 1782.

Congress also sought aid from Russia. In late 1781, it sent Francis Dana, Adams' secretary, as minister plenipotentiary to the Court of St. Petersburg, with instructions to enroll the United States in the League of Armed Neutrality and to negotiate a treaty of amity and commerce with the Russian monarch. After spending almost two years in the Russian capital, Dana found that Catherine II had no intention of recognizing the United States. Thus his mission was a failure.

Peace negotiations with Great Britain, the most successful effort of United States diplomacy of the period, began in the spring of 1782. Under Lord Shelburne's direction, British representative Richard Oswald contacted Benjamin Franklin in April 1782 to begin talks. The negotiations culminated on November 30, 1782, with the American representatives (Adams, Franklin, Jay, and Henry Laurens) signing the preliminary articles. They agreed to terms without informing the French beforehand, thereby incurring the disapproval of Vergennes, whose own peace efforts were directed towards the negotiation of the European preliminary articles, signed in January 1783. The Anglo-American definitive treaty of peace signed on September 3, 1783, was basically the same as the preliminary treaty. Congress ratified the treaty on January 14, 1784, and Franklin and David Hartley exchanged instruments of ratification in June.

Following the signing of the preliminary treaty, the Anglo-American discussions continued in the hope of producing a commercial agreement in addition to the peace treaty. When Shelburne's ministry fell in February 1783, to be replaced by a Fox-North coalition, Richard Oswald was replaced by David Hartley as the British negotiator in Paris. Charles James Fox and Hartley at first seemed of one mind in their desire to resolve trade matters with the Americans. However, British public opinion quickly hardened against allowing the Americans to enjoy their prewar trade relationship with any part of the Empire. American withdrawal of all restrictions on trade with the former mother country in April 1783 accordingly met with no parallel British response. While American ships were permitted to bring American produce to Great Britain, an Order in Council in July 1783 banned all but small American ships from carrying produce to British possessions in the West Indies. Hartley spent several frustrating and unsuccessful months trying to change the British position on trade with the United States.

Failure to negotiate a trade agreement with Great Britain was but one difficulty in United States trade relations with the leading powers. The

Franco-American treaty of amity and commerce specified most-favored-nation status for each country's trade goods. French goods should therefore have had an advantage over British goods in any competition for American markets. However, French commercial practices made no allowance for credit, and French manufacturers did not adapt their products to the American market. Despite the lack of an Anglo-American commercial agreement, British goods were made available on credit, and with the removal of American trade restrictions, soon commanded a lion's share of sales.

In spite of overwhelming difficulties, Congress sought to negotiate commercial treaties with the other nations of Europe based upon principles of reciprocity. While John Jay, soon to become Secretary for Foreign Affairs, returned to New York in 1784, Thomas Jefferson joined Franklin and Adams that year to participate in the negotiations. These three American commissioners, working together in Paris, notified more than twenty European nations of their readiness to treat, but the response was meager. Franklin had already negotiated a treaty with Sweden, and Adams and Jefferson would complete a treaty with Prussia. Despite preliminary talks with Denmark and Portugal, the commissioners signed no other commercial treaties with European states in the 1780s.

Congress appointed John Adams its minister to Great Britain in February 1785. Adams diligently reported on his reception in London, but soon perceived that the British were disinterested in any commercial arrangements with the United States. His protests regarding Britain's failure to evacuate the Northwest posts, to settle the Northeast boundary in Passamaquoddy Bay, or to provide compensation for slaves removed from the United States, were met by British complaints of American failure to repay British creditors or compensate loyalists for confiscated property. In response, Adams advised Congress to retaliate against British commerce by establishing imposts and prohibitions, emphasizing that the British government otherwise would refuse to resolve its differences with the United States. He also counselled the American States to facilitate strict observance of peace treaty terms.

Jefferson's experience in France was certainly more pleasant than that of Adams, but only slightly more productive. France wished to promote an expansion of Franco-American trade, but without disrupting its economic system or suffering a decline in government revenues. France made L'Orient, Bayonne, Dunkirk, and Marseilles free ports for American trade, but navigation fees charged American ships at these ports eliminated any possibility of profitable commerce. French notions of most-favored-nation status did not extend to certain privileges, such as admission of American whale oil on the same basis as that admitted from the Hanse towns, until

Jefferson pointed out the anomaly. Jefferson also mounted a major effort to persuade the French to make the terms upon which the Farmers General (which collected taxes and duties on various categories of imported goods) purchased tobacco more congenial to American merchants. French officials were generally sympathetic to Jefferson's efforts, but France's antiquated economic system and precarious financial situation prevented a genuine Franco-American commercial rapprochement. The only really bright spot on America's trade horizon was its incipient China trade, which would yield handsome profits while stimulating America's shipbuilding industry and providing experience for future American naval officers.

Another difficulty that confronted the American envoys in Europe was the declaration of war on the United States by the Barbary pirates of North Africa. Congress authorized Adams and Jefferson to appoint agents to negotiate peace treaties with the North African rulers, setting aside $80,000 for use in this effort. The American diplomats sent Thomas Barclay, the U.S. Consul General in France, to handle the Moroccan negotiations. Morocco's ruler promptly released his American captives and signed a peace treaty. However, American efforts to negotiate with Algiers and Tripoli failed to reach a satisfactory conclusion. It is interesting to note that Jefferson favored building a fleet with which to suppress the Barbary corsairs, while Adams advocated raising adequate funds to meet the pirates' demands.

Congress had better success in matters relating to its authority regarding foreign diplomats and consuls in the United States. It refused to extradite a French adventurer calling himself the Chevalier de Longchamps for trial and punishment in France on the demand of the French government for his physical attack on the French Consul General, François Barbé de Marbois, on the principle of extraterritoriality, because the culprit had a valid claim to American citizenship. Longchamps was sentenced in an American court to an appropriate punishment for his crime, and the French government ultimately accepted the logic of the American position.

Congress had equal success in asserting its authority to approve the appointment of foreign consuls to posts in the United States, chiding Richard Soderstrom, the Swedish Consul at Boston, for proceeding to his post and soliciting an exequatur from the Governor of Massachusetts without first receiving congressional approval. When Sir John Temple, the British Consul General, overstepped his authority by approaching Secretary for Foreign Affairs John Jay in behalf of loyalists seeking redress of grievances in accordance with the terms of the definitive treaty of peace, Jay asked Adams to inform the British government that such requests were the province of a diplomat, not a consul.

As Secretary for Foreign Affairs, it fell to Jay to make a second effort to reconcile Spanish-American differences over the western lands and the navigation of the Mississippi. In mid-1785, Don Diego de Gardoqui, Spanish chargé d'affaires, arrived in the United States to negotiate a trade agreement and an arrangement regarding the river. Congress empowered Jay to negotiate, but not to sign any agreement without first submitting it for approval. A year passed, during which Jay allowed himself to be persuaded that a commercial agreement with Spain was worth closing the Mississippi to American navigation for 25 or 30 years. When Jay laid his proposal before Congress in late August 1786, the Eastern and Southern States formed voting blocs for and against it respectively. There would be no agreement with Spain under the Articles of Confederation.

A major theme during the period from 1778 to 1788 was French pressure for a consular convention with the United States to codify the powers, privileges, and immunities each side accorded to the other's consuls. Congress wanted consular officials to confine themselves to matters of navigation and commerce, without according them any extraterritorial qualities. The convention went through several drafts, one of which was signed by Franklin in 1784, but left unratified by Congress. Jefferson, commissioned to negotiate a convention in October 1787, achieved a practical agreement that minimized extraterritorial privileges. It was signed in August 1788, but not ratified by the United States until 1790.

Domestic upheavals in Massachusetts and elsewhere in the mid-1780s, fostered high glee in the reports of the British Consul General, who was convinced that the unrest marked the beginning of the end of the American experiment in self-rule. The British diplomat's view reflected the position of many foreign leaders toward the United States. Though it had succeeded in extricating itself from colonial rule and was, if ever so slowly, emerging as a new nation in the world community, its central government was considered weak and ineffectual. For prominent American leaders, this situation offered potential for change.

The need to strengthen the central government through an overhaul of America's fundamental law was a recurring theme in the correspondence of Jay and Adams, as it was in Madison's missives to Jefferson. For them, only by establishing a government with the power to control commerce, to raise revenues, and to force individual States to comply with federal laws and international agreements would the United States redeem itself in the eyes of Europe. The Constitution that emerged from the convention in Philadelphia in the summer of 1787 would win the general approval of America's principal diplomatic figures, although all would concede the need for a bill of rights.

When John Adams left Europe in 1788, he returned to a country in the throes of debate regarding ratification of the United States Constitution.

Some States were eager to adopt the charter, others were indifferent, and a few were hostile, given the absence of a bill of rights. The authors of the *Federalist Papers* (including John Jay) were quick to point out the advantages of the Constitution for American diplomacy and foreign trade. After much debate, ratification was successful and a new federal government was established.

Positive foreign response evolved over time. The Comte de Moustier, the French minister to the United States, was at first suspicious of the new measure, but by 1789 had come to accept and support it, as had the French Foreign Ministry in Paris, on the premise that a stronger central government in America would ultimately serve French interests. British leaders eventually favored the new Constitution and came to view its adoption as advantageous to their interests. While some feared that a strong federal government would discriminate against British commerce or shipping in retaliation for British restrictions on American trade, they also realized that such a government would be able to enforce compliance with the terms of the 1783 peace treaty regarding recovery of debts and confiscated property.

Of the major European powers, only Spain had reason to regret the adoption of the Constitution. Given increasing immigration from Europe and the shift of population westward beyond the Appalachians, a stronger federal government could only mean increasing pressure on Spanish lands east of the Mississippi and on Spain's control of the mouth of that river. Despite the machinations of Spain's representatives in Louisiana, the Old Southwest, Tennessee, and Kentucky became integral parts of the United States.

The experience gained by the American diplomats under the Articles of Confederation served the nation well when they were elected or appointed to federal positions under the Constitution. Adams became Vice-President of the United States, Jefferson, Secretary of State, and Jay, Chief Justice of the United States. When the federal government began functioning in March of 1789, a period filled with challenges had ended; a new era with the same or similar challenges, but filled with even greater potential, had begun.

Note on Sources

The major source for documents included in this three-volume edition is National Archives Record Group 360: Records of the Continental and Confederation Congresses and the Constitutional Convention. Other significant sources include copies of records from the Public Record Office of Great Britain and the Archives du Ministère des Affaires Etrangères of

France relating to the diplomacy of the 1780s in the Manuscripts Division of the Library of Congress; the papers of Richard Oswald, David Hartley, and Lord Shelburne in the William L. Clements Library of the University of Michigan; The Adams Papers in the Massachusetts Historical Society; and the John Jay Papers in the Columbia University Libraries. Additional materials are included from the George Bancroft Papers in the Rare Books and Manuscripts Division of the New York Public Library; the Benjamin Franklin Papers and the Thomas Jefferson Papers at the Library of Congress; and the Benjamin Vaughan Papers in the American Philosophical Society Library. Whenever possible, research has been conducted in modern documentary editions. These include: *The Papers of John Adams, The Papers of Benjamin Franklin, John Jay: The Making of a Revolutionary, Unpublished Papers, 1745-1780, John Jay: The Winning of the Peace, Unpublished Papers, 1780-1784, The Papers of Thomas Jefferson, Lafayette in the Age of the American Revolution, The Papers of James Madison, The Papers of Robert Morris, The Papers of George Washington, Letters of Delegates to Congress, 1774-1789, Documentary History of the First Federal Congress of the United States of America, March 4, 1789-March 3, 1791, The Documentary History of the Ratification of the Constitution,* and *The United States and Russia: The Beginning of Relations, 1765-1815.*

Note on Maps

The maps included in these volumes are extracted from "A Map of the British and French Dominions in North America with the Roads, Distances, Limits, and Extent of the Settlements, Humbly Inscribed to the Right Honourable The Earl of Halifax, And the other Right Honourable The Lords Commissioners for Trade & Plantations, By their Lordships Most Obliged and very humble Servant Jno. Mitchell," annotated "B. F. Stevens's Facsimile of the Red-Line-Map in the British Museum ... 1897" from R.G. 76: Records of Boundary and Claims Commissions and Arbitrations. Additional information was extracted from the maps included in Samuel Flagg Bemis, *The Diplomacy of the American Revolution*, copyright 1935 by The American Historical Association, and from Samuel Flagg Bemis, *Pinckney's Treaty*, copyright 1926 by The Johns Hopkins University Press. National Archives and Records Administration volunteer Dean Aurecchia, formerly a cartographer with the United States government, rendered the FRUAC maps. The American Historical Association and The Johns Hopkins University Press gave permission to use their maps in the preparation of the FRUAC maps.

Editorial Methodology

Document selection reflects the establishment of the United States as an independent nation in the world community. Selections are from the official papers of the United States Congress; British, French, and Spanish government records; and unofficial documents, including the papers of individuals who played a prominent role in United States foreign relations during this period. Where appropriate, selected documents, of significant value are included in their entirety. Where only part of a document contains significant diplomatic information, that portion has been excerpted. It was common to prepare multiple copies of letters and documents to defeat the accidents of 18th century travel and foreign interception. Whenever possible the editors have selected the recipient copy or record copy. When other copies have been printed, their selection is reflected in the citation. Headnotes were prepared to bridge documents or to present information necessary to understand the historical context of the documentation. Standard biographical reference works and modern documentary editions, including the *Dictionary of American Biography*, the *Dictionary of National Biography*, the *Biographical Directory of the United States Congress, 1774-1989, La Grande Encyclopédie: Inventaire Raisonné des Sciences, des Lettres et des Arts, Repertorium der diplomatischen Vertreter aller Länder, Enciclopedia Universal Ilustrada Europeo-Americana, The Papers of Thomas Jefferson, The Diary of John Adams, The Papers of John Adams, John Jay: The Making of a Revolutionary, Unpublished Papers, 1745-1780, John Jay: The Winning of the Peace, Unpublished Papers, 1780-1784*, and *The Papers of Benjamin Franklin*, along with other research sources, were used to identify historical figures.

With few exceptions, documents are in chronological order. To ensure textual accuracy in the preparation of documents for publication, stylistic characteristics, including spelling, capitalization, and punctuation are maintained. Encyphered documents are provided in plain script. Ship names have been placed in italics. Contractions, abbreviations, and diacritical marks are retained as written. Unintelligible text is indicated by asterisks. Crossed-out words have been indicated by canceled text. Crossed-out text which is unintelligible is indicated by asterisks placed in angle brackets. Interlineations and marginalia are placed on the line in the closest approximate position, as indicated by the writer. Significant docketing information is placed at the end of the document. Conjected words and dates are placed in brackets. Contemporary translations are indicated in the source citation at the end of the document. Translations provided by the

xiii

project staff are indicated at the beginning of the document. Dates written at the end of the document are placed at the beginning. Salutations and closings are included as written but are placed on a continuous line.

Textual Devices and Abbreviations

...	the deletion of a small amount of text completing a sentence or paragraph
....	the deletion of a larger section of text including one or more paragraphs
*******	unintelligible text
<*****>	unintelligible crossed out text
~~which~~	crossed out text in original
<than>	expanded text
[which]	conjected text
ACS	autograph copy signed
AD	autograph draft
AL	autograph letter
ALD	autograph letter draft
ALS	autograph letter signed
AN	autograph note
APS	American Philosophical Society
C	copy
CS	copy signed
DS	document signed
f	folio
ff	microfilm frames
FFAA	Archives du Ministère des Affaires Etrangères
HC	copy in hand of Hartley
JCC	printed Journal of the Continental Congress
LBkC	letterbook copy
LC	Library of Congress
LS	letter signed
M23	National Archives Microfilm Publication of the Despatches from the United States Consuls in Algiers, Algeria, 1785-1906
M40	National Archives Microfilm Publication of the Domestic Letters of the Department of State, 1784-1906
M61	National Archives Microfilm Publication of the Foreign Letters of the Continental Congress and the Department of State, 1785-1790

M247	National Archives Microfilm Publication of the Papers of the Continental Congress, 1774-1789
M332	National Archives Microfilm Publication of the Miscellaneous Papers of the Continental Congress, 1774-1789
MHS	Massachusetts Historical Society
NA	National Archives
NSDAR	National Society Daughters of the American Revolution
NYPL	New York Public Library
PCC	Papers of the Continental Congress
PRO: FO	British Public Record Office: Foreign Office Files
PRO: CO	British Public Record Office: Colonial Office Files
Pol. Corr.	Political Correspondence
(translation)	contemporary translation of document
[Translation]	translation prepared for this edition
v	volume
vo	verso
WTF	William Temple Franklin

List of Presidents of the Congress

Samuel Huntington (Connecticut)	elected September 28, 1779
Thomas McKean (Delaware)	elected July 10, 1781
John Hanson (Maryland)	elected November 5, 1781
Elias Boudinot (New Jersey)	elected November 4, 1782
Thomas Mifflin (Pennsylvania)	elected November 3, 1783
Richard Henry Lee (Virginia)	elected November 30, 1784
John Hancock (Massachusetts)	elected November 23, 1785
Nathaniel Gorham (Massachusetts)	elected June 6, 1786
Arthur St. Clair (Pennsylvania)	elected February 2, 1787
Cyrus Griffin (Virginia)	elected January 22, 1788

Maps

The Emerging Nation, 1783

Spain's Maximum Concession as Indicated in Floridablanca's Instructions to Gardoqui of September 1787

Illustrations

Benjamin Franklin by Joseph Siffred Duplessis. Courtesy of Independence National Historical Park.

John Adams by John Singleton Copley. Courtesy of Harvard University.

John Jay engraved by B.B.E., published by R. Wilkinson, 1783. Courtesy of the Library of Congress.

Charles Gravier, Comte de Vergennes, engraved by Vangelisti. Courtesy of the Library of Congress.

Marquis de Lafayette by Philiber Louis Debucourt. Courtesy of National Portrait Gallery.

Thomas Jefferson by Charles Willson Peale. Courtesy Independence National Historical Park.

Acknowledgements

In the fall of 1983, the National Archives decided to publish a documentary history of the foreign relations of the United States for the period 1783 to 1789. Later the period was expanded to include the years 1781 and 1782. The project, referred to as FRUS, was based on records in the National Archives. In 1986 the Department of State became a co-sponsor and provided financial assistance in the initial work of document transcription. In the early years of the project, some 6,000 documents were copied from the records of the National Archives. Several National Archives employees were assigned to work on this project. These included Mary-Jane M. Dowd, who served as editor and project director of FRUS, 1985-1991, Alec B. Kirby, and Angie Spicer VanDereedt. Under Ms. Dowd's direction some 2,600 documents from a base of some 6,000 documents primarily from Record Group 360: Papers of the Continental Congress and Confederation Congresses and the Constitutional Convention, were selected and transcribed for inclusion in the FRUS project. Three National Archives volunteers, Renée F. Cooper, Patricia D. Gray, and Mary S. Woods, also worked with Ms. Dowd. Each provided valuable service in document transcription, proofreading, and translation of French-language documents located in the National Archives.

In 1991, the Archivist of the United States placed the project under the administration and sponsorship of the National Historical Publications and Records Commission (NHPRC). NHPRC staff member Mary A. Giunta was appointed editor-in-chief and project director. A revised plan for the project was developed. The plan included an evaluation of the document database and an evaluation of documents located in significant archival and historical collections in the United States and Europe. Based on this plan, several important changes were made. The project name was changed to The Emerging Nation: A Documentary History of the Foreign Relations of the United States under the Articles of Confederation, 1780-1789, to reflect American attempts under the then operative plan of government to become a separate nation in the world community. Three distinguished historians, Norman A. Graebner, Peter P. Hill and Lawrence S. Kaplan, were invited to join the project as consulting editors. They participated in the selection of documents, wrote introductory essays, and provided essential advice on the work of the project. J. Dane Hartgrove, a diplomatic historian and records specialist of the Office of the National Archives, joined the project staff in 1992 as associate editor. He secured copies of documents located in significant manuscript and archival collections at the Library of Congress, in various repositories outside the Washington, DC, area, and from NHPRC project offices. Through his efforts some 1900 new documents, primarily copies of documents located in foreign repositories, were selected for consideration for inclusion in the volumes. In addition, Dr. Hartgrove played a significant role in the translation of French-language documents and the preparation of headnotes and annotations. Richard B. Smith, formerly of the staff of the National Archives, served as project publication specialist through most of calendar year 1994. The project benefited greatly from his interest, skills, and labors in scholarly publication. National Archives printing specialist Isabelle V. Saunders served as coordinator with the Government Printing Office staff in seeing the volumes through publication. Her efforts greatly facilitated the publication of these volumes. John A. Grier of the Government Printing Office has provided professional support and advice throughout the preparation of these volumes.

Beginning in 1991, volunteer participation was significantly expanded. Volunteers transcribed, translated, verified texts, conducted historical research, worked on document databases, located and copied documents in manuscript repositories, located copies of pictures, coded documents for publication, and drew maps. They visited libraries and worked at home and on vacation. Their many hours of labor, their commitment to work on

FRUAC, their sharing of their expertise, and their general desire to contribute were simply extraordinary. From student interns to retired individuals, volunteers played an extremely important role in this project. It is accurate to say that the day-to-day work of the project could not have been completed without them. They are: Carol S. Aiken, Patricia A. Alfredson, Dean Aurecchia, Nathanael Cavanaugh, Marjorie Cooper, Renée F. Cooper, Helen G. Cullinan, Mary H. Curzan, Elizabeth Drain Hardin, Yvette M. Fallin, Maria Flesher, Arthur L. Gamson, Sherry S. Harris, Norma S. Hoehndorf, Burt Knauft, Elizabeth S. Lourie, Lisa Mastney, Beatrice B. Meyerson, Betty Moore, Laurent Pion-Goureuau, William F. Reed, Jr., Peter Ringland, Renee Schick, Widajanti Soekarso, and Mary S. Woods. Patricia A. Eames, Coordinator of the NARA volunteer program, identified potential volunteers for the project. Her role deserves recognition.

The following individuals, dedicated to documentary scholarship, made our labors lighter: Paul H. Smith and Gerald W. Gawalt, Letters of Delegates project, Library of Congress Manuscript Division; Barbara Oberg, Jonathan Dull, Ellen Cohn, Karen Duval, and Kate Ohno, the Benjamin Franklin Papers project, Yale University; Ene Sirvet, John Jay Papers project, Columbia University; Elizabeth M. Nuxoll and Mary A. K. Gallagher, Robert Morris Papers project, Queens College, CUNY; C. James Taylor and Peggy J. Clark, Henry Laurens Papers project, University of South Carolina; and Richard A. Ryerson, Celeste Walker, Gregg L. Lint, Joanna M. Revelas, and Anne Decker, The Adams Papers project, Massachusetts Historical Society. It is with particular appreciation that we acknowledge the assistance of Ene Sirvet, Richard A. Ryerson, Kate Ohno, and Anne Decker. They provided document identification and verification of several important items which enhanced document selection of Jay, Franklin, and Adams materials. John P. Kaminski of the Ratification of the Constitution project produced our indexes. His acumen provides the user of these volumes with easy access to the documents. Kenneth R. Bowling, First Federal Congress project, shared his thoughts on the editing of documents, especially government documents of the period.

Members of the staffs of manuscript and archival repositories were most helpful in answering questions, providing copies of materials and arranging for interlibrary loans. These include: Frederick Bauman, Ernest Emrich, Jeffrey Flannery, Charles Kelly, Michael Klein, Kathleen McDonough, Joseph Sullivan, and Mary Wolfskill, Library of Congress Manuscript Division Reading Room; Beth Carroll-Horrocks, Associate Librarian and Manuscripts Librarian, American Philosophical Society Library; Deborah L. Sisum, Deputy Keeper, Catalog of American Portraits, Smithsonian Institution; Catherine H. Grosfils, Editorial Librarian, Audio-Visual Library, Colonial Williamsburg Foundation; Elizabeth Gombosi, Harvard University

Art Museum; Shirley A. Mays, Library Technician, Independence National Historical Park Photographic Library; Joanna Britto, Manager, Rights and Reproductions, National Portrait Gallery, Smithsonian Insitution; Jennifer Tolpa, Assistant Reference Librarian, Massachusetts Historical Society; Richard Salvato, Rare Books and Manuscripts Division, New York Public Library; Christine Nelson, Associate Curator of Autograph Manuscripts, Pierpont Morgan Library; Rob Cox and Arlene Shy, William L. Clements Library, University of Michigan; and Grace Eleazer, Manager, Museum Registration, and Jennifer Menson, Registration Assistant, Winterthur Museum. In particular, Dr. Shy provided detailed information on various manuscripts in the Shelburne, Hartley, and Oswald collections.

The volumes include documents from modern documentary editions sponsored by the NHPRC. The following publishers have granted permission to publish a number of documents included in Volume One, Volume Two and Volume Three: The University of Pittsburgh Press, *The Papers of Robert Morris, 1781-1784*, materials from Volume 4: January 11-April 15, 1782, E. James Ferguson, Editor, John Catanzariti, Associate Editor, copyright 1978; Volume 6: July 22-October 31, 1782, John Catanzariti, and E. James Ferguson, Editors, copyright 1784; Volume 7: November 1, 1782-May 4, 1783, John Catanzariti, Editor, copyright 1988; Princeton University Press, *The Papers of Thomas Jefferson*, materials from Volume 6, 21 May 1781 to 1 March 1784, Julian P. Boyd, Editor, copyright 1952; Volume 7, 2 March 1784 to 25 February 1785, Julian P. Boyd, Editor, copyright 1953; Volume 8, 25 February to 31 October 1785, Julian P. Boyd, Editor, copyright 1953; Volume 9, 1 November 1785 to 22 June 1786, Julian P. Boyd, Editor, copyright 1954; Volume 10, 22 June to 31 December 1786, Julian P. Boyd, Editor, copyright 1954; Volume 11, 1 January to 6 August 1787, Julian P. Boyd, Editor, copyright 1955; Volume 14, 8 October 1788 to 26 March 1789, copyright 1958; HarperCollins, *John Jay, The Making of A Revolutionary, Unpublished Papers, 1745-1780*, Richard B. Morris, Editor, copyright 1975, *John Jay, The Winning of the Peace, Unpublished Papers, 1780-1784*, Richard B. Morris, Editor, copyright 1980. We encourage the use of these and other modern documentary editions for a further understanding of history.

Curators, librarians, and directors of several collections and repositories have granted permission to include copies of a number of documents and pictures entrusted to their responsibility and care for inclusion in *The Emerging Nation* volumes: Richard A. Ryerson, Editor-in-Chief, The Adams Papers, Massachusetts Historical Society; Beth Carroll-Horrocks, Associate Librarian and Manuscripts Librarian, American Philosophical Society; John C. Dann, Director, William L. Clements Library; Jean Ashton, Director, The Rare Book and Manuscript Library, Columbia University; Sarah

Elliston Weiner, Curator of Art Properties, Low Library, Columbia University; François Renouard, Director of Archives and Documentation, Archives du Ministère des Affaires Etrangères; William A. Moffett, Director of the Library, The Huntington; Stuart M. Frank, The Kendall Whaling Museum; Judith Gardner-Flint, Librarian, John Work Barrett Library, Johns Hopkins University; Louis L. Tucker, Director, Massachusetts Historical Society; Georgane F. Love (Mrs. Dale Kelly Love), Historian General, National Society Daughters of the American Revolution; Margaret Heilbrun, Director of the Library and Curator of Manuscripts, New-York Historical Society; Wayne Furman, Director, Office of Special Collections, New York Public Library; Christine Nelson, Associate Curator of Autograph Manuscripts, The Pierpont Morgan Library; Patton Hash, Director, The South Carolina Historical Society; and Nancy M. Shawcross, Curator of Manuscripts, Van Pelt Library, the University of Pennsylvania. Materials from the British Public Record Office are included by permission of the Controller of Her Britannic Majesty's Stationery Office. Materials from the Royal Library, Windsor Castle, are included with the permission of Her Majesty Queen Elizabeth II.

John P. Kaminski, in addition to preparing the index for this volume, reviewed the typescript copy, and suggested changes that enhanced the presentation of the text. Mary A. K. Gallagher provided special assistance with our Spanish document translations. Patricia Violante-Cassetta, Translater/Intrepreter, the Italian Embassy, Washington, D.C., verified Italian translations. Volunteers Helen G. Cullinan, Irene Stoess and Howard Imbrey provided Latin translations.

Staff members of the National Archives Library, including Lida H. Churchville, Maryellen Trautman, Jeffrey T. Hartley, Samuel L. Anthony and David Lake, provided research assistance, filled interlibrary loan requests, and sought elusive identifications or facts. John A. Dwyer, Richard H. Smith, and Robert E. Richardson of the National Archives Cartographic and Architectural Branch provided reference service in the preparation of the maps.

Gerald W. George, executive director of the NHPRC, provided significant support for the project. Roger A. Bruns, former deputy executive director of the NHPRC, provided administrative support and assistance. NHPRC staff members Laurie A. Baty, Laurette O'Connor, Nancy Taylor Copp, Delores G. Taylor, and Sheneé Turner provided computer and administrative assistance.

With the publication of this final volume, it is appropriate for the editor-in-chief to recognize those individuals, although they may be acknowledged elsewhere, who have given their finest efforts, talents and intellectual capacities over the longest period of time in the daily work of the project or who have served in particularly critical roles. They have stayed the course, expended their energies extensively and intensively and by so doing, have made the completion of these volumes possible. J. Dane Hartgrove is diligent, conscientious and meticulous in his approach to documentary editing, historical research and foreign language translation. These qualities as well as his extensive knowledge of both United States and European history are reflected throughout these volumes. Mary H. Curzan, National Archives volunteer, became virtually a third staff member on the project. Her work in proofreading, transcribing and formatting most of the three thousand pages deserves special acknowledgement and a strong expression of gratitude. John P. Kaminski of the Documentary History of the Ratification of the Constitution project not only served as the indexer for these volumes but volunteered to serve in the additional role of reviewer and consultant. His vigilant review, historical knowledge and documentary editing acumen are sincerely and gratefully acknowledged.

These volumes are dedicated to all of the aforementioned.

Mary A. Giunta
Editor-in-Chief

Volume Three: Toward Federal Diplomacy, 1780-1789

> *But whatever may be our situation, whether firmly*
> *united under one national Government, or split into a*
> *number of confederacies, certain it is, that foreign nations*
> *will know and view it exactly as it is; and they will act*
> *towards us accordingly. If they see that our national*
> *Government is efficient and well administered – our*
> *trade prudently regulated – our militia properly organized*
> *and disciplined – our resources and finances discreetely*
> *managed – our credit re-established – our people free,*
> *contented, and united, they will be much more disposed*
> *to cultivate our friendship, than provoke our resentment.*[1]

It is fitting that these sentiments appeared in Federalist Number 4, among the earliest of the Federalist Papers.[2] These writings reflected the all-consuming preoccupation of the leaders of the Confederation, especially of John Jay,[3] the author of this piece, with the weaknesses of the Articles of Confederation and the vital need for the new Constitution. The perceived failure of the Confederation to maintain internal order, to meet its financial obligations, to defend its frontiers, and to control interstate commerce had led to the Mount Vernon Conference of 1785 and to the Annapolis Convention[4] of 1786. Indeed, even the most ordinary matters of business could not be conducted when fewer than seven of the thirteen states were available to provide a quorum.

Granting the urgency of domestic problems, the leaders responsible for the conduct of foreign relations – primarily Jay in New York as Secretary for Foreign Affairs and the two principal envoys in Europe, John Adams[5] in The Hague and London, and Thomas Jefferson[6] in Paris, were even more concerned about the state of America's relations with Europe, for despite modest advances, the pervading feeling was frustration over the weaknesses of the central government and the errant behavior of the States. As early as 1784, James Madison[7] wondered if it would be "...good policy to suspend further Treaties of Commerce, till measures shall have taken *place in America which may correct the idea in Europe of impotency in the foederal Govt. in matters of commerce....*[8] *It was obvious from the outset that the inability of Congress to control the behavior of States with respect to treaty obligations was a threat to the survival of the nation.*

Congress was powerless to prevent States from violating the terms of treaties with foreign governments. State laws preventing collection of debts by British creditors or refusing to return confiscated Loyalist property gave a patina of justification to Britain's refusal to evacuate the Northwest posts. Presumably, when the United States respected the treaty "in all particulars," Britain would fulfill its obligations, as its king claimed.

Jay, more than Adams or Jefferson, was conscious of the consequences of the impotence of the central government, and more aware too of the damage the intrusion of the States into foreign relations could do to American interests. Almost singlehandedly, he used his limited powers to project such authority abroad as the Confederation could muster. His reports to Congress became for the most part government policy; and if that policy went unheeded, it was not due to vacillation on his part. He displayed his concern impartially when he felt the nation's pride or sovereignty to be in jeopardy.

In the 1780s, Great Britain was primarily concerned with shoring up those aspects of its power that had been weakened by the American war, and with strengthening its military and naval potential. An interpretation of its Navigation Act in a manner that would bolster Britain's position in foreign trade and increase or maintain the pool of British seamen from which the Royal Navy would be manned was in Britain's best interests. American failure to comply fully with certain articles of the peace treaty was more a nuisance than a hostile action, but demanded a reciprocity in noncompliance which kept Anglo-American relations under stress throughout the period.

Jay's dealings with Spain evoked bitter criticism from Southerners and Westerners. The New Yorker's negotiations with Diego de Gardoqui,[9] Spain's Chargé d'affaires in the United States, appeared to bargain away the American right to navigate the Mississippi in exchange for compensatory advantages in Spanish ports. Aroused by the opposition of the Southern States, Congress in June 1787 directed Jay to reassert to Gardoqui, America's right to use the river. Jay claimed that he had never intended to surrender America's right to navigate the Mississippi; he regarded Spain's concession of American commerce with Spanish ports as equivalent to temporarily refraining from using the river.

The Confederation's lack of power was an even more significant factor in the abortive negotiations over American sailors held captive in Algiers. Unlike relations with Spain, in which both sides were vulnerable, Algiers held all the advantages. The guarantee of safe passage in the Mediterranean was always available: namely, to pay suitable tribute to the Dey.[10] This route was followed by the European powers, who found it less expensive to pay the pirates than to fight them. Such recourse was not open to Americans. Although the issue was never as vital to America's survival as other problems in foreign relations, none was more painful. For Jefferson, who was given the task of ransoming the American captives, the solution lay in arms. He wanted to join a federation that would sweep the pirates from the sea once and for all, and was distressed over France's submitting to Algerine demands. Jay's reaction was more cynical; he sensed that Europe had no interest in challenging the pirates, and would relish the prospect of a war between America and the Barbary States, from which Europe would benefit.

At the root of the troubles of the Confederation was the inability of Congress to raise funds from taxation or import duties to fulfill its responsibilities. Among the consequences of this impotence were creditors unpaid and bad credit among European bankers. Insolvency cast a shadow upon relations with Britain, France, and the Netherlands. The most embarrassing aspect of this situation was the failure to pay French creditors, French veterans of the American Revolution, and the French Crown itself.

For Jefferson, France was the linchpin to America's future security and prosperity. While Adams may have had less faith than the Virginian in the utility of a close French connection, he was more knowledgeable than his colleague about the desparate state of America's finances. Both statesmen recognized that the French creditors had to be paid, and in the absence of a government which could raise funds, new loans had to be negotiated with the bankers in Amsterdam.

France was the only European nation to have a military alliance with the United States. While the alliance potentially was a troublesome element in the Franco-American relationship, it was not a contentious issue under the Confederation. Neither government anticipated American involvement in a future European war. The threat of a general war in Europe loomed throughout most of the decade; France assumed that the United States would remain neutral.

There was considerable ambiguity in France's attitude toward the Confederation. On the one hand, French officials in the United States constantly expressed concern that the natural ties between Britain and America would damage French interests. But France continued to grant concessions to Americans throughout the period in the form of arrets disrupting the Farmers-General monopoly on tobacco imports, opening free ports for American shipping, and exempting Americans from whale oil duties applied against Britain.

On the other hand, France seemed to be complacent, even satisfied, with the continued weakness of America's central government. An insecure America, in this scenario, would be more dependent on France's good will and patronage, and more likely to defer to France's advice on foreign affairs. Versailles never expected the United States to serve a positive role as an ally in a future war, and had little expectation in 1787 that the Constitution would unify the disparate American States. To conclude from this evaluation that France preferred a weak America to a strong nation excessively minimizes the primary objective of all French ministers to separate the United States as best they could from what they considered a natural connection with Great Britain.

Jefferson viewed France as a potential counterweight to British predominance in America's foreign trade. The Franco-American treaty of amity and commerce should have been the instrument not only of expanding American trade with France, but also of encouraging France to replace Britain as the source of America's manufactures. Jefferson felt that it failed in both areas. The latter was never more than a chimera; France's economy, on the eve of revolution, could not have coped with British competition, let alone match the longstanding credit arrangements British suppliers had with American merchants. While it is questionable whether the circumstances of the time justified American skepticism of France's behavior, the ancien regime did make an effort to modify its commercial practices to accommodate American trade. Its actions were more than empty gestures; they represented a genuine, if abortive, effort to wean America away from British influence.

On balance, France in the early stages of its Revolution looked with benevolence on an American government that would be solvent enough to discharge its financial obligations and strong enough to confront British hegemony over its foreign commerce. In contrast, Britain and Spain both preferred a weak Confederation of thirteen divided States to a strong federal government that would challenge Britain's commercial and maritime dominance and assert its power on the frontiers. However, both powers expected to benefit from America's enhanced ability to liquidate its debts and to exert control over the actions of its citizens.

The federal government formed in 1789 took over the problems in foreign relations which Congress had been unable to solve under the Confederation. Machinery was now in place that could permit a growing nation to pay off its foreign debts, settle the Mississippi question, reach a peace with Algiers, and come to an understanding with Great Britain. America's three principal leaders in foreign affairs remained in positions from which they could bring their experience to bear on diplomatic problems – Jay as Chief Justice of the United States Supreme Court, Adams as Vice President, and Jefferson as Secretary of State. Those problems would all eventually be solved for, as *Federalist Number 4* had predicted, with the federal government "efficient and well administered," foreign powers would be "much more disposed to cultivate our friendship than provoke our resentment."

[1] Kaminski, John P. and Saladino, Gaspare J., eds., Commentaries on the Constitution: Public and Private, Volume I (21 February to 7 November 1787), p. 576, of The Documentary History of the Ratification of the Constitution, Volume XIII (Madison: State Historical Society of Wisconsin, 1981).

[2] A collection of eighty-five essays gathered and published as The Federalist (2 vols., 1788) urging the adoption of the Federal Constitution by stressing the inadequacy of the Articles of Confederation and expanding upon the principles of republican government. The authors were Alexander Hamilton, John Jay and James Madison.

[3] Jay, John (1745-1829). Political figure, diplomat and jurist. Member, Continental Congress, 1774-1777, 1778-1779; president, 1778-1779. Chief justice of the State of New York, May 1777-December 1778. Elected minister to Spain, September 27, 1779. With John Adams, Benjamin Franklin, and Henry Laurens, commissioner to negotiate peace, 1781-1784. Secretary for Foreign Affairs, 1784-1790. With Alexander Hamilton and James Madison, author of The Federalist. Chief Justice of the U.S. Supreme Court, 1789-1795. Minister to Great Britain, 1794-1795. Governor of New York, 1795-1801.

[4] Convention proposed by Virginia. In March 1785, at the suggestion of James Madison, delegates from Virginia and Maryland met at Alexandria and Mount Vernon, Virginia, to negotiate an agreement regarding commerce on the Potomac River. The Maryland legislature later called for another conference on commercial questions, to include Pennsylvania and Delaware. The Virginia legislature agreed, but Madison secured a broadening of the invitation to include all the States in a general trade convention to be held at Annapolis, Maryland, in September 1786. Delegates from five States (New York, New Jersey, Pennsylvania, Delaware, and Virginia) met as planned. The following year, another convention met in Philadelphia to revise the Articles of Confederation.

[5] Adams, John (1735-1826). Statesman, diplomat, political leader. Massachusetts delegate to the First and Second Continental Congresses, 1774-1778. Commissioner to France, 1778-1779; to negotiate peace, 1779-1783; to conclude a commercial treaty with Great Britain, 1779-1781; and to conclude treaties of amity and commerce with European nations, 1783-1786. Minister to the United Provinces of Netherlands, 1782-1788, and to Great Britain, 1785-1788. Vice President of the United States, 1789-1797. President of the United States, 1797-1801.

[6] Jefferson, Thomas (1743-1826). Political figure, diplomat, scientist, architect and author. Member, Virginia House of Burgesses, 1769-1775. Member, Continental Congress, 1775-1776, 1783-1784. Author, Declaration of Independence. Governor of Virginia, 1779-1781. Author, Notes on the State of Virginia, written at the behest of French Secretary of Legation François Barbé de Marbois. With John Adams and Benjamin Franklin, commissioner to negotiate commercial treaties in Europe, 1784-1786. Minister to France, 1785-1789. U.S. Secretary of State, 1790-1793. Vice President of the United States, 1797-1801. President of the United States, 1801-1809.

[7] Madison, James (1751-1836). Virginia political figure. Member, Continental Congress, 1780-1783, 1787-1789. Member, Virginia House of Delegates, 1784-1786. Delegate, Annapolis Convention, 1786, and Constitutional Convention, 1787. With Hamilton and Jay, author of The Federalist. Member, U.S. House of Representatives, 1789-1797. Secretary of State, 1801-1809. President of the United States, 1809-1817.

[8] James Madison to Thomas Jefferson, Orange [VA] April 25th. 1784, Rutland, Robert A. and Rachal, William M.E., eds., The Papers of James Madison (Chicago and London: The University of Chicago Press), Volume VIII, p. 21.

[9] Gardoqui, Diego Maria de (1735-1798). Spanish diplomat and political figure. Educated in England, a scion of the Bilbao-based commercial firm of Joseph Gardoqui and Sons, he sought a career in the Spanish Ministry of Finance, which used him as an interpreter in negotiations with the Americans. These resulted in Spanish aid to the United States, most of which flowed through Joseph Gardoqui and Sons or the commercial house established by Diego's brother James. Consul General at London, 1783-1784. Encargado de Negocios to the United States, 1784-1789. Minister of Finance in the ministry of Manuel de Godoy.

[10] Sidi Muhammad ibn Abd Allah. Muhammad III, Emperor of Morocco, 1757-1790.

The Franco-American Consular Convention: First Steps

With the signing of the Franco-American treaties of alliance and of amity and commerce on February 6, 1778, the United States acquired both an ally and a trading partner. In addition to military alliance and possible commercial agreements, each side had the right to have consuls, vice consuls, agents, and commissaries in the other's ports. The functions of these officials were to be defined by a separate agreement at a later date. The French government expressed its desire for such an agreement almost immediately following the signings. In contrast, Congress was uncertain as to a consular convention with France. There were several reasons for this uncertainty.

The consul, who represents the commercial interests of the country that appoints him, was an official previously unknown in the United States, where the British navigation system had prohibited the functioning of foreign commercial representatives. In addition, many Americans were suspicious of the political implications of allowing the representatives of a foreign government to exercise authority within the United States. France's insistence that French subjects should be subject to trial before French consular courts for violation of French laws while in the United States, or subject to extradition to France for such offenses, caused Americans further concern.

French and American consular practices also differed greatly. French consuls, who came under the administrative control of the Minister of the Navy, were salaried members of the French civil service, forbidden to engage in commerce. In contrast, most U.S. consuls were merchants who performed consular functions as an adjunct to their commercial careers.

Initial stirrings toward a Franco-American consular convention were made by the French in 1779. In June of that year, France's first minister to the United States, Conrad Alexandre Gérard de Rayneval,[1] submitted a plan of provisional regulations to Congress; it was rejected. French Naval Minister Gabriel de Sartine[2] and Foreign Minister the Comte de Vergennes[3] oversaw preparation of a new proposal in 1780. After determining that Benjamin Franklin[4] at Paris, had no powers to negotiate such a convention, Vergennes turned the task over to the Chevalier de la Luzerne,[5] Gérard's successor in the United States, who submitted the proposal to Congress in July 1781.

[1] *Gérard de Rayneval, Conrad-Alexandre (1729-1790). French diplomat. As undersecretary of state to Comte de Vergennes, he assisted in the treaty negotiations with Franklin, Deane, and Lee in 1777-1778. Minister to the United States, 1778-1779.*

[2] *Sartine, Antoine-Raymond-Jean-Gualbert-Gabriel de (1729-1801). French government official. Lieutenant general of police, 1759-1774. Minister of the navy, August 1774-1780. Emigrated at the outset of the Revolution.*

[3] *Vergennes, Charles Gravier, Comte de (1719-1787). French political figure and diplomat. Minister to the Elector of Trier, 1750-1754, also envoy to Hanover, 1752, and to the Elector Palatinate, 1752-1753. Ambassador to the Ottoman Empire, 1755-1768. Ambassador to Sweden, 1771-1774. Secretary of State and Minister of Foreign Affairs, 1774-1787.*

[4] *Franklin, Benjamin (1706-1790). Printer, author, philanthropist, inventor, statesman, diplomat and scientist. Deputy postmaster general for the colonies, 1753-1774. Pennsylvania representative, Albany Congress, 1754. Colonial agent, 1757-1762, 1764-1775. Member, Continental Congress, 1775-1776. With Silas Deane and Arthur Lee, commissioner to negotiate treaties with France, 1776-1778. Minister to France, 1778-1785. With John Adams, John Jay, and Henry Laurens, commissioner to negotiate peace, 1781-1784. With John Adams and Thomas Jefferson, commissioner to negotiate commercial treaties in Europe, 1783-1785. President, Executive Council of Pennsylvania, 1785-1788. Member, Constitutional Convention, 1787.*

[5] *Luzerne, Anne-César, Chevalier de la (1741-1791). French diplomat. Envoy extraordinary near the Elector of Bavaria, 1776-1778. Minister to the United States, 1779-1784. Ambassador to Great Britain, 1788-1791.*

Proposed Franco-American Consular Convention

[Philadelphia, 24 July 1781]

A Plan of a Convention between the Most Christian King[1] and the United States of North America for the purpose of determining and fixing the functions and prerogatives of their respective Consuls, vice consuls and agents. –

The most Christian king and the thirteen United States of North America having mutually granted to each other, by the 29 Article of the treaty of Amity and Commerce concluded between them, the power of keeping in their respective states Consuls, vice consuls and agents, and being willing in consequence thereof to determine and fix < * > in a lasting manner and on terms of equality the functions and prerogatives of the said Consuls, vice consuls and Agents, have agreed as follows. –

Article 1.

The Consuls and Vice Consuls named by the Most Christian King and the United States shall be obliged to present their appointments on their arrival in the respective states. And there shall be delivered to them the exequatur < * > necessary for the exercise of their functions. And upon the exhibition which they shall make of that exequatur, the governors, Presidents, commandants, Chief judges, magistrates < ** > of the place, tribunals and other officers exercising authority in the ports and places of their consulships shall < * > cause them to enjoy there immediately and without difficulty the preeminences, authority and privileges mutually granted without exacting from the said Consuls and vice consuls any duty or Emoluments under any pretext whatsoever. –

2.

The respective Consuls shall have power to establish vice consuls in the different ports and places within their Departments, where necessary: There shall in like manner be delivered to them the exequatur necessary for the exercise of their functions and upon the exhibition which they shall make of the said exequatur; they shall be admitted and recognized in the terms and according to the powers, authority and privileges stipulated by the 1. 5 & 6 Articles of this present Convention. –

3.

The respective Consuls and vice consuls shall only be taken from among the natural born subjects of the power nominating them. They shall all be appointed by their respective sovereign, *and in Consequence* of such appointment they shall not exercise any traffic or commerce whatsoever either ~~by~~ on their own account or on account of any other.

4.

The respective Consuls shall have power to establish Agents in the different ports and places within their department where necessary. These agents may be chosen from among the merchants of their nation or strangers and shall be furnished with a brevet Commission from one of the said Consuls and shall respectively be authorized/bound to render to their respective merchants, seamen and vessels all possible service and to inform the nearest consul or Vice Consul of the wants of the said merchants seamen and vessels; but the said agents shall not in any other respect participate in the immunities, rights and privileges granted to Consuls & Vice Consuls by the present Convention. Nor shall they exact any Duty by Virtue of their appointment under any Pretence whatsoever. –

[5.]

The Consuls and Vice consuls, the officers of the consulship and generally all persons attached to the consular functions shall respectively enjoy a full and entire immunity for their persons, papers and houses. They shall be exempted from all personal service and public offices from finding quarters for soldiers, from militia duties, from watch, ward, guardianship *curatelle* and from all duties, taxes, imposts and charges whatsoever save on real estates which they shall own/possess, which shall be subject to the taxes imposed on the estates of all other individuals. They shall be at liberty to fix upon the outer door of their house the arms of their Sovereign, provided always that this mark of distinction shall not give to the said house the right of asylum to any malefactor or criminal who shall take refuge there but he shall be immediately delivered up on the first requisition and without any difficulty. –

6.

The Most Christian King and also the United States shall give precise and effectual Orders in the ports and places within their jurisdiction, that no let < **** > or hindrance be given to the funeral rites & obsequies of any subject of the one or the other nation who shall die within the territories of the other.

7.

In all cases generally whatever respecting the police and administration of justice, where it shall be necessary to have a judicial declaration of the said consuls & vice consuls respectively, the governor President Commandant, Chief Judges < * > Magistrates of the place, tribunals or other Officers whatever at their respective residence or Consulate having authority there shall be bound to give them notice thereof by in writing or by sending to them a civil or military officer to inform them of the object in view and the necessity there is of going to them & demanding from them that declaration, and the said Consuls & Vice Consuls shall be bound on their part readily & bona fide to conform themselves legally to what shall be required of them on those occasions. –

8.

The respective Consuls and vice Consuls shall have power to establish a Chancery, for depositing the consular acts & deliberations, the effects left by persons deceased or saved from shipwreck, also the testaments, obligations, contracts and in general all the acts and proceedings made and done by or between people of their nation. They shall of Consequence have power to appoint capable persons to manage that chancery, to admit them into office to administer an oath to them, to give them the keeping of the seal and the right of sealing the Commissions, judgments and other acts of consulship and also to execute the office of notaries & scribes. –

9.

The respective Consuls and vice consuls shall have the exclusive right of receiving in their chancery or on board of vessels the declarations and all other acts which the captains masters seamen, passengers & merchants of their nation shall be willing to give there. And their testament and other dispositions of a last will, and the copies of the said acts duly authenticated by the said consuls or vice consuls and under the seal of their consulship shall be admitted in all courts of justice in France and the United States.

They shall also have the exclusive right of taking inventories & liquidating Accounts appraisements and of proceeding to the sale of the personal effects left by the subjects of their nation who shall happen to die in the respective states. They shall proceed therein with the assistance of two merchants of their said nation whom they shall chuse & shall cause to be deposited in their chancery the effects & papers of the said successions, nor shall any officer, civil or military, of justice, or of the police of the country be allowed to give them any interruption or disturbance whatever. But the said consuls & vice consuls shall not be at liberty to deliver up the effects/ property or the produce of them/thereof to the lawful heirs or their attorneys until they have caused to be discharged all the debts which the deceased may have contracted in the country by judgment by acts or by bills, the writing and signature of which shall be proved and certified by two noted merchants of the nation of the said deceased & in all other cases the payment of debts shall not be ordained but upon the creditor's giving sufficient and landed security by a Bondsman resident there to return the sums unduely received, both principal, interest and costs, which securities however shall be duely discharged after one year in time of peace & after two years in time of war if a demand in discharge cannot before that time ~~cannot~~ be made against the heirs who shall appear.

10.

The respective Consuls & vice consuls shall receive the declarations & consulats protests of all captains and masters of their respective nation on account of <*> damages at sea by leakage or throwing goods overboard even though foreign merchants are interested in the cargo; or the Captains & masters shall lodge in the chancery of the said consuls & vice consuls the Consulats protests, which they shall make in other ports on Account of the accidents that have happened to them during their voyage; and in both cases the said consuls & vice consuls respectively shall settle the damage <*> without delay by experienced persons of their nation whom they shall name *ex officio* and by experienced persons equally of each nation/partly of their own nation & partly strangers where a stranger is interested in the cargo.

11.

In case either by tempest or other accident the ships or vessels of France shall be wrecked on the coasts of the United States or the ships or vessels of the United States shall be wrecked on the coast of France, the consul or vice consul nearest to the place of shipwreck shall have power to do whatever he shall judge proper as well for saving the ship or vessel, her cargo and appurtenances as for storing & securing the effects & merchandize saved. He shall have power to take an inventory of them; nor shall any military officers nor officers of the Customs or Naval officers nor officers of justice or of the police of the country be allowed to interfere farther than by affording to the consuls & vice consuls, the captain & crew of the vessel wrecked or stranded all the assistance and favour required of them either for the speedily saving & securing the effects or for preventing the disorders which too frequently accompany such accidents. — To prevent all Interference of Jurisdictions/sorts of dispute and discussions in case of shipwrecks, it is agreed that where there is no consul or vice consul to assist in saving the wreck or when the residence of the said consul or vice consul not being at the place shall be farther distant than that of a competent territorial judge, of this latter shall immediately < * > promote with all expedition, the saving the wreck and the measures prescribed by their respective laws, provided always, that the territorial Judge shall retire upon the coming of the consul or vice consul to whom he shall transfer the whole & commit the farther prosecution of the measures by him taken & the Consul or vice consul shall reimburse him the expences incurred.

The merchandize saved shall be deposited in the nearest Custom house or other nearest Place of Security if there shall be no Custom House with an inventory made out by the Consul or vice consul or in their absence by the judge who shall have had Cognizance thereof/take an account of them in order that the said merchandizes may, after payment of the expence, be afterwards delivered without any formal process to the owners who being furnished with a Release/Replevin from the nearest consul or vice consul shall reclaim them in person or by attorney either for the purpose of reexporting the – merchandizes, in which case they shall not pay any kind of duties on exportation; or for the purpose of selling them in the country, if they are not there prohibited and in this case the said merchandize being damaged an abatement shall be made on the import duties proportioned to the damage suffered which shall be determined by the verbal process stated at the time of the wreck or stranding.

12

The Consul & vice consuls of the Most Christian King established in the United States and the Consuls & vice consuls of the United States in france shall there exercise the police over the all the vessels of their respective nations and shall have on board the said vessels all power and jurisdiction in all discussions which can arise there. They shall have the entire inspection of over the said vessels, their crews, the changes & the recompenses for making them and also for whatever shall concern their navigation & the observance of their respective laws ordinances & regulations respectively.

They shall be at liberty to go on board the vessels of their nation arriving in the respective ports havens & roads, and that as often as they shall judge necessary for the performance of their office nor shall any officers of the customs or of the police or any other persons whatever prevent them.

They shall be at liberty to <*> arrest & sequester all the vessels carrying the flag of their respective nation <**> and even to send them back respectively from France to the United States and from the United States to France; and to arrest without any difficulty every captain master, seaman or passenger of their respective nation.

They shall be at liberty to reclaim sailors, deserters and the vagabonds of their respective nation and to arrest and detain them in the country or to send them away & cause them to be transported out of the country: it shall be sufficient that the consuls or vice consuls respectively can prove that the sailors, deserters and vagabonds, of what nation soever they be, are inserted in the registers, or entered on the roll of the crew, and the one or other of these two pieces being sufficient to <*> establish the validity of the claim and detention and of the transportation of the said seamen, deserters and vagabonds, none of them whether french or Americans shall, in the res-pective countries, either by himself or others, be at liberty to claim the benefit of the laws or authority of the country, all tribunals, judges and officers whatsoever being interdicted from all cognizance thereof, In all these cases, the said seamen, deserters and vagabonds shall be delivered to the reclaimers, whatever may be their engagements, and they shall not be engaged, detained or withdrawn in any manner or by any person whatever, whether natives or foreigners, upon the requisition which the said consuls or vice consuls shall cause to be made by persons authorised by them and entrusted with the requisition signed by them.

And for the execution of all the regulations above mentioned the governors, commandants, chief judges, magistrates of the place, tribunals, and other officers of the respective countries having authority there, shall be held and bound to assist the respective consuls and vice consuls and upon a simple requisition signed by them, saving the power of arresting, to detain and keep in prison, at the disposal and cost of the said consuls & vice consuls, the sailors, deserters and vagabonds reclaimed, until they shall have an opportunity of putting them on board & sending them out of the country.

13.

In case the subjects respectively shall commit any crime against any inhabitants of the country, which deserves exemplary punishment, they shall be tried by the judges of the country. —

14

The consuls and vice consuls of the most Christian King established in the United States and the consuls and vice consuls of the United States established in france shall, to the exclusion of the tribunals of the country, have cognizance there of all differences and processes which shall arise on land between the captains, masters, crews, passengers and traders of their respective nation; They shall settle them in an amicable manner or decide them summarily & without costs, and the appeal from their judgments shall be carried respectively to the tribunals of France and the United States, that judge in the last resort & that ought to have cognizance thereof. They shall exercise these offices of private justice and of necessary police, nor shall any military officer, nor any officer of justice or of police in the country intermeddle or interpose in any manner whatever. –

In case any differences or suits on account of their commerce shall happen either between french merchants living in France and their countrymen settled under the protection of the most Christian King in the United States, or between the American merchants dwelling in the United States and their countrymen settled under the protection of the United States in the Kingdom of France, the said differences & suits shall be brought to trial & decided between them in a summary way & without expence by the consul or vice consul of their respective nation, and the appeals from their judgment shall be to the respective tribunals which judge in the last resort, whether in France or in the United States.

With respect to all other differences & suits that may arise between the subjects of the Most Christian King and those of the United States in the respective countries, either as plaintiffs or defendants one against another as well on account of dealings, bargains and traffic one with another & the payments to be made in consequence thereof, as for bills of exchange, insurances, damages at sea, bankruptcies, and all other causes civil & criminal relative to commerce, they shall be prosecuted in the country before the tribunals which ought to take cognizance thereof in the first instance and by appeal, nor shall the respective consuls & vice consuls under any pretence intermeddle therein in any manner. –

                              15.

The general advantage of commerce having given occasion to establish in France certain tribunals & particular forms for the speedy determination of commercial matters, the American merchants shall enjoy the benefits of those establishments in France and the United States shall procure equal advantages coinciding with the tribunals and forms in favour of the french merchants in matters of the same nature.

                              16.

The subjects of the most Christian King and those of the United States who shall prove that they are under the laws of their respective nation, the certificate of the consul or vice consul of the district mentioning their names, surnames and place of abode as inserted in the registers of the consulship shall not, for any cause whatever, lose in the respective dominions & States, the quality of subjects of the country ~~of~~ to which they originally belong, conformably to the 11 article of the treaty of Amity & commerce of the 6 feby 1778, of which this present article shall serve for an interpretation if < * > Occasion require, and the said subjects respectively shall consequently enjoy an exemption from all personal services in the place of their residence & moreover they shall not be subject to any tax relative to labour.

17.

All stipulations abovementioned being founded on an exact reciprocity shall < ** > henceforth serve for regulating, fixing and rendering invariable all the objects to which they relate. But if any other Nation enjoys, or acquires under any title or in virtue of any convention whatever a more favourable treatment either in france or in the United States with regard to Consuls vice consuls and Agents & their preeminences, powers, authority and privileges, the consuls & vice consuls & Agents of the most Christian King in the United States, and the consuls, vice consuls and agents of the United States in France shall participate therein agreeably to the terms of the 11 Article of the said treaty of Amity & Commerce concluded between the Most Christian King and the United States.

18.

The ratifications of this present convention shall be delivered in good form & exchanged by one party & by the other in the space of six months or sooner if possible.

In testimony whereof &c. agreeable to the original remaining with us.

Le chv. de la Luzerne

Philad[a] the 24 July 1781

July 28, 1781
Referred to   M[r] Randolph[2]
                   M[r] Van Dyke[3]
                   M[r] Ellsworth[4]

National Archives: Record Group 360: Records of the Continental and Confederation Congresses and the Constitutional Convention, hereafter cited as NA: PCC, item 25, v. 2, pp. 21-32 (translation); National Archives Microfilm Publication M247, hereafter cited as M247, reel 32.

[1] *Louis XVI (1754-1793). King of France, 1774-1793.*

[2] *Randolph, Edmund (1753-1813). Virginia lawyer, legislator and political figure. Aide-de-camp to George Washington, 1775. Member, Virginia Convention, 1776. Mayor of Williamsburg, 1776-1777. State attorney general, 1776-1786. Delegate, Annapolis Convention, 1786. Governor of Virginia, 1786-1788. Delegate, Constitutional Convention, 1787. U.S. Attorney General, 1789-1793. U.S. Secretary of State, 1794-1795.*

[3] Van Dyke, Nicholas (1738-1789). Delaware lawyer and political figure. Member, state constitutional convention, 1776. Member, state council, 1777; speaker, 1779. Member, Continental Congress, 1777-1781. Signer, Articles of Confederation, 1781. State president, 1783-1786.

[4] Ellsworth, Oliver (1745-1807). Connecticut lawyer and political figure. Member, State general assembly, 1773-1776. State attorney, 1777. Member, Continental Congress, 1778-1783. Member, Governor's council, 1780-1785, 1801-1807. Judge, State Superior Court, 1785-1789. Delegate, Constitutional Convention, 1787. United States Senator, 1789-1796. Chief Justice, United States Supreme Court, 1796-1800. With William R. Davie and William Vans Murray, commissioner to France, 1800.

∞ *Discussing the Consular Convention* ∞

On July 28, 1781, Congress appointed a committee composed of Edmund Randolph, Nicholas Van Dyke, and Oliver Ellsworth to meet with the Chevalier de la Luzerne in order to reconcile any disagreements regarding the wording of the consular convention which Luzerne had submitted to Congress the previous day. Meeting in the second half of August, the negotiators soon agreed upon acceptable compromises. However, Luzerne had to work hard to persuade Congress that it had the power to approve the consular convention, rather than submit it to the individual States for approval.

Congressional Resolution

Friday January 25. 1782

The plan of a convention respecting consular powers being reconsidered and amended was read over together with Instructions to the Minister plenipotentiary of these United States respecting it and the same were agreed to by nine states as follows

Resolved That the Minister plenipotentiary of the United States at the court of Versailles be and he is hereby authorised and instructed to enter into a Convention with his Most Christian Majesty, on the part of the United States for the establishment of Consular powers and privileges according to the scheme hereto subjoined, unless it shall be deemed by his most Christian Majesty more expedient that the same should be executed in the United States.

That the said Minister plenipotentiary use his discretion as to the words or arrangement of the convention, confining himself to the matter thereof in all respects except as to so much of the sixth article as relates to the erection of a chappel, taking care that reciprocal provision be made for the recognition of the Consuls & vice Consuls of the United States and for the admission of persons attached to the Consulate to the privileges stipulated in the 5 Article in a manner most conducive to expedition and freeest [sic] from difficulty.

NA: PCC, item 5, pp. 602-603 (Journal); M247, reel 19.

Approved Draft of
Franco-American Consular Convention

Jany 25. 1782

The draught of a convention between his Most Christian Majesty and the United States of North America for defining & regulating the functions and privileges of Consuls, vice consuls Agents and Commissaries.

The most Christian king and the United States of North America having, by the 29 Article of the treaty of Amity and Commerce concluded between them, granted mutually the liberty of having each in the ports of the other, consuls, vice Consuls, agents and commissaries and being willing in Consequence thereof to determine & fix, in a reciprocal and permanent manner the functions & prerogatives of the said Consuls, vice consuls Agents & commissaries respectively have agreed as follows. –

Art. 1. It shall be the duty of the Consuls of his most Christian Majesty to present their commissions in the first instance to the United States in Congress assembled, by whom an act shall be made recognizing them as such. This act shall be delivered by the Consuls to the Supreme executive power of the State or States to which they may be sent. Two copies of the exequatur, that is a public notification of the quality of the consuls shall thereupon issue from the Supreme executive power without fees or perquisites of office; one to be retained by the Consuls, the other to be published in one or more gazzettes. This being done, the pre eminences authority and privileges stipulated in this Convention shall be allowed to them in all places, before all tribunals & by all persons. –

Art. 2. The Consuls of his most Christian Majesty and of the United States may appoint any number of vice Consuls within their respective departments.

Upon the notification of their appointment by the Consuls to the Supreme executive power of the State to which they may be sent the exequatur shall be applied for and delivered by the several States to them in the same manner as to Consuls, and thereupon the pre eminences, authority and priviliges stipulated in this Convention in favour of vice Consuls shall be allowed in all places before all tribunals and by all persons.–

Art. 3 Consuls and vice consuls shall be subjects or citizens of the power appointing them and interdicted from all traffic or commerce for their own or another's benefit. –

Art. 4 Consuls may also appoint any number of Agents within their departments, who may be of their own nation or not at pleasure They shall receive a commission from the consul appointing. They shall not assume any pre-eminence, authority or privilege herein granted to Consuls or vice consuls, nor exact any fees or reward under any pretence whatever. But they shall confine themselves wholly to the assisting of Merchants, mariners and vessels and giving information respecting them to the nearest Consul or vice consul. –

Art. 5 There may be attached to the consulate at the will of the Consuls within their departments any number of persons. Neither the papers nor houses of Consuls or vice consuls shall be searched. Consuls and vice consuls shall enjoy full and entire immunities for their persons and be exempt from personal service, public Offices, finding quarters for soldiers, militia duty, watch, ward, guardianship, attorney-ship, committee-ship, and from all duties, taxes and imposts whatsoever on moveable property; but shall be liable in respect of real and landed property in the same manner as the subjects or citizens of the Country. The arms of his Most Christian Majesty or of the United States, as the case may be, shall be placed upon the outward door of their house and being so placed shall entitle the house to the exemptions aforesaid: But no Asylum shall be thereby obtained for malefactors or criminals, who shall be delivered up immediately on demand. The same privileges & immunities as those granted in this fifth article to consuls and vice consuls shall be granted to persons attached to the consulate and living under the same roof with the consuls or vice consuls, provided approbation shall be given of their number and appointment by the supreme executive power of the state, to which they may belong.

Art. 6. Consuls, and Vice consuls in places where there are no Consuls, may have a chappel in their houses for the celebration of divine service according to their religious profession. And his Most Christian Majesty and the United States shall cause particular care to be taken, that no obstacle or hinderance be thrown in the way of the funeral Obsequies or ceremonies observed towards the deceased of either nation

Art. 7. In all cases in which it may be necessary that the Consuls or vice-consuls should perform any juridical or official act, the public bodies or the persons in public Authority, who shall require such act, shall either inform them thereof in writing or send a military or civil officer, with a verbal message respecting it: And the Consuls or vice consuls shall on their part readily and *bona fide* do whatsoever may be demanded of them on these occasions.

Art. 8. The Consuls and vice consuls respectively may establish a chancery as a depository of the consular acts and deliberations, of effects left by the dead or saved from shipwreck, of testaments, obligations, contracts, and all other acts and things done by or between people of their nation. They may appoint the officers of the chancery, administer to them an oath of Office, intrust to them the keeping of the Seal and the right of affixing the same to commissions, judgments and other consular acts and empower them to discharge the functions of Notaries and registers. –

Art. 9. The Consuls and vice consuls respectively shall have the exclusive right of receiving in their chancery or on board of vessels of their nation all the declarations and other acts which the captains, masters seamen passengers and merchants of their nation shall think proper to make or lodge therein; and last wills and testaments & copies of any act duly authenticated by the Consuls or vice consuls and under the seal of their Consulate shall receive full faith and credit in all courts of Justice as well in France as in the United States. They shall also have the exclusive right of inventorying the effects of those of their nation, who may die within their Consulate, liquidating their accounts & selling their moveable property. They shall call to their assistance in this business two merchants of their own nation and of their own choice and cause to be deposited in the chancery the effects and papers of the deceased of their own nation, without being interrupted therein by any officer military judiciary or of the police. But neither the Consuls nor vice consuls shall deliver the effects of the deceased or the produce of their sales over to the heir or lawful successor or his representative or Attorney until all the debts which the deceased shall have contracted by judgment act or bill shall be discharged, the signature of the handwriting and genuineness thereof being first certified by two merchants of the same nation with the deceased and of reputation. In all other cases payment of no debt shall be made unless the creditor shall first enter into a bond with one sufficient surety at least, who is resident on the spot, for the return of all monies unduly received as well the principal as interest and costs. The Surety shall not be bound beyond one year in time of peace and two years in time of war. If however within those terms the creditor shall call upon the lawful representative or successor to the property of the deceased by a proper legal process and prove his title to the money so received, the surety shall stand discharged

Art. 10. The consuls and vice consuls respectively shall receive the declarations consulats or other consular acts of all captains & masters of their respective nations for damages received at sea by leakage, or the throwing of goods overboard. And all consulats or other consular acts made by them in foreign ports for accidents during the voyage shall be lodged in the chancery aforesaid. If a subject of France and a citizen of the United States be jointly interested in the cargo, the damage shall be settled by the tribunals of the country not by the consuls or vice consuls. But where subjects or citizens of their own nation are alone interested the Consul or vice consul shall then chuse experienced persons of their respective nations to settle the same.

Art. 11. In every case of a wreck, the nearest Consul, or vice consul may exercise his discretion in saving the vessel wrecked with her cargo and appurtenances and in storing and securing what is saved & may also take an inventory thereof. In this business no officers of the customs, of justice, of the police or naval Officer shall interfere, but upon application made to them for their assistance, in which case they shall exert themselves in the most effectual manner. To prevent all clashing of jurisdictions in case of shipwreck, it is agreed, that that where there shall be no consul or vice consul or they may be more distant from the place of the accident than a judge of the country having authority in such cases, this judge shall immediately proceed to the exercise of his authority according to law; but shall retire upon the coming of a consul or vice consul, into whose hands he shall put the whole business rendering an account of his transactions and receiving from the consul or vice Consul reimbursement for all expences. Whatsoever is saved shall be lodged in the nearest custom house or naval office or where there is no custom house or naval office in the nearest place of security with an inventory prepared by the Consul, vice consul or in their absence by the judge of the country as aforesaid. Upon the order of the nearest Consul or vice Consul and without any fees or perquisites for storage when lodged in public stores the owner may reclaim the property so saved in person or by attorney and may either reexport the same free from all duties of exportation or sell it in the country if goods of such a quality be not prohibited. In this latter case, of a sale of unprohibited goods, there shall be an abatement of the duties on importation in proportion to the damages sustained by the ship wreck to be determined by the account taken by the consul, vice consul or judge of the country, or any other competent officer at the time of the accident. –

Art. 12 The consuls and vice consuls shall have on board of the vessels of their respective nations all power and jurisdiction in matters of a civil nature. They shall have the power of causing the laws regulations and Ordinances of their respective nations concerning navigation to be observed on board of their said vessels. For this purpose they shall freely and without any molestation or hindrance from any officer or other person visit the said vessels. They may cause to be arrested & sequestered every vessel carrying the flag of their respective nations and even send them back to France or the United States, as the case may be, as well as arrest any captain, master, seaman or passenger of their respective nations. They may cause to be arrested and detained in the country sailors and deserters of their respective nations or cause them to be transported therefrom. It shall be sufficient evidence of the sailors and deserters belonging to their respective nations, if their names appear in the registers of the vessels or the roll of their crew. Proof being thus made concerning sailors & deserters all tribunals, judges and officers whatsoever shall be interdicted and disabled from taking cognizance in any manner of complaints exhibited by such sailors or deserters. But they shall be delivered up to an order signed by the consuls or vice consuls, without being detained engaged or withdrawn in any manner. That these powers vested in consuls and vice consuls may be compleatly executed, all persons in authority shall assist them, and upon a simple requisition made by the consuls or vice consuls in writing shall cause to be kept in prison at the disposal and cost of the consuls or vice consuls the sailors and deserters so arrested until an opportunity shall be presented of sending them out of the Country.

Art. 13. All offences committed in France by a citizen of the United States against a subject of his Most Christian Majesty shall be enquired into and punished according to the laws of France, and those committed in any one of the United States by a subject of his Most Christian Majesty against a citizen of the United States shall be enquired into and punished according to the laws of such State. But offences committed in France by a citizen of the United States against a citizen of the United States, or committed in any one of the United States by a subject of his most Christian Majesty against a subject of his most Christian Majesty shall be subject to the jurisdiction of the consuls and vice consuls of France or of the United States as the case may be

Art. 14 All differences and disputes between the subjects of his most Christian Majesty in the United States or between the citizens of the United States in France, and all differences and disputes concerning commerce between the subjects of his most Christian Majesty one party being resident in France or elsewhere and another in the United States; or between the citizens of the United States, one party being resident in the United States or elsewhere and another in France shall be heard tried and decided on by the Consuls or vice consuls of their respective nations either by referring the same to arbitrators or by making a decree summarily & without costs. No officers civil or military shall intermeddle or interpose herein in any respect. Appeals shall be carried to such courts as have been or may be appointed by his most Christian Majesty and the United States respectively. No disputes or differences between a subject of his most Christian Majesty and a citizen of the United States shall be determined or taken up in any manner by the consuls or vice consuls but shall be decided by the courts of the country in which the defendant shall be found. – Art. 15. The advantages to Commerce having caused the erection of certain tribunals in France and particular forms for the speedy determination of commercial matters, the merchants of the United States shall enjoy the benefits of those establishments in France, and the United States in Congress assembled will recommend to the legislatures of the several states to establish equal advantages in the speedy decision of causes in favour of french Merchants in matters of the same nature. Art. 16. The subjects of his Most Christian Majesty and the citizens of the United States shall be exempt from all personal services in the place of their residence either in France or the United States as the case may be. Whensoever any person in France or the United States as the case may be shall claim any privilege or exemption as a subject of his Most Christian Majesty or of the United States before any judge tribunal, or officer whatsoever, the certificate of the consul or vice consul of the district, containing his name, surname and the place of his residence and the affidavit of the person claiming such priviledge or exemption that he is a subject of his Most Christian Majesty or of the United States, as the case may be, shall be sufficient evidence thereof, unless the contrary shall manifestly appear. – Art 17. Conformably to the third and fourth articles of the treaty of Amity and Commerce between his most Christian Majesty & the United States if any other nation by virtue of any Convention whatsoever shall receive greater indulgence either in France or in the United States with regard to consular powers, privileges or Authority, the Consuls, vice consuls, agents and commissaries of France and of the United States as the case may be shall participate therein. –

Passed by nine States

NA: PCC, *item 25, v. 2, pp. 7-14 (C); M247, reel 32.*

Benjamin Franklin to Robert R. Livingston

Sir,[1]   Passy, June 25. 1782.

I have received your respected Letters of Jany 26 & Feby 13th. The first was accompanied with the form of a Convention for the Establishment of Consuls. M^r. Barclay[2] having been detained these 6 Months in Holland, tho' in continual Expectation of returning hither, I have yet done nothing in that Business, thinking his Presence might be of use in Settling it. As soon as he arrives I shall move the Completion of it. The second enforces some Resolutions of Congress sent me with it, respecting a Loan of 12,000,000 livres to be demanded of France for the current Year. I had already received the Promise of Six Million, together with the clearest and most positive Assurances, that it was all the King could spare to us, that we must not expect more; that if Drafts & Demands came upon me beyond that sum, it behov'd me to take Care how I accepted them, or where I should find Funds for the Payment, since I could certainly not be farther assisted out of the Royal Treasury. Under this Declaration with what Face could I ask for another Six Millions? It would be saying, you are not to be believ'd; you can spare more. You are able to lend us twice the Sum if you were but willing. If you read my Letter to Mr Morris[3] of this Date, I think you will be convinced how improper any Language capable of such a Construction would be to such a Friend. I hope, however, that the Loan Mr Adams has opened in Holland for three Millions of Florins, which it is said is likely to succeed, will Supply the Deficiency.

. . . . . .

The Ambassador from Sweden to this Court,[4] applied to me lately to know if I had Powers that would authorise my making a Treaty with his Master in behalf of the United States. Recollecting a general Power that was formerly given to me with the other Commissioners, I answer'd in the Affirmative. He seem'd much pleased, and said the King[5] had directed him to ask the Question, and had charged him to tell me, that he had so great an Esteem for me, that it would be a particular Satisfaction to him to have such a Transaction with me. I have perhaps some Vanity in repeating this; but I think too, that it is right the Congress should know it, and judge if any Use may be made of the Reputation of a Citizen, for the Public Service. In Case it should be thought fit to employ me in that Business, it will be well to send a more particular Power, and proper Instructions. The Ambassador added, that it was a pleasure to him to think, and he hop'd it would be remember'd, that Sweden was the first Power in Europe, which had voluntarily offer'd its Friendship to the United States, without being Sollicited. This Affair should be talk'd of as little as possible 'till compleated.

. . . . . .

Be pleased to present my Duty to the Congress, and believe me to be with great Esteem & Regard Sir, Your most obedient & most humble Ser^t
B. Franklin

NA: PCC, item 82, v. 2, pp. 164-172 (ALS); M247, reel 108.
  [1] Livingston, Robert R. (1746-1813). New York political figure and diplomat. Member, Continental Congress, 1775-1776, 1779-1780, 1784. Secretary for Foreign Affairs, 1781-1783. Chancellor of New York State, 1777-1801. Minister to France, 1801-1804.
  [2] Barclay, Thomas (1728-1793). Philadelphia merchant and diplomat. Vice-Consul (June-October 1781), then Consul in France. Commissioner to settle the accounts of the United States in Europe, 1782-1786. Agent to negotiate treaty of peace and commerce with Morocco, 1785-1786. Appointed Consul to Morocco in 1791, but died in Lisbon while en route to his post.
  [3] Morris, Robert (1734-1806). Merchant, financier, political figure. Member, Continental Congress, 1775-1778; member, Committee of Secret Correspondence, Committee of Foreign Affairs, Committee of Commerce. Superintendent of Finance, 1781-1784. Established Bank of North America, January 1782. Member, Annapolis Convention, 1786; Constitutional Convention, 1787. Member, U.S. Senate, from Pennsylvania, 1789-1795.
  [4] Creutz, Gustaf Philip, Graf von (1731-1785). Swedish diplomat. Minister to France, 1766-1772; ambassador, 1772-1783.
  [5] Gustav III. King of Sweden, 1771-1792.

Thomas Jefferson to James Madison

Dear Sir   Annapolis May 8. 1784.
I will now take up the several enquiries contained in your letter of Apr. 25 which came to hand yesterday.
'Will it not be good policy to suspend further treaties of commerce till measures shall have been taken place in America which may correct the idea in Europe of impotency in the federal government in matters of commerce?' Congress think such measures requisite, and have accordingly recommended them as you will perceive by my last. in the mean time they seem to think that our commerce is got & getting into vital agonies by our exclusion from the West Indies, by late embarrasments in Spain & Portugal, and by the dangers of the Mediterranean trade. these you observe form the aggregate of our valuable markets. they think that the presumption of one or two countries should not be a reason for suspending treaties with all countries: and that the prospect of effect from their recommendations on commerce will perhaps drive on the treaties. the present favourable disposition of the piratical states on the Barbary coast has been repeatedly urged by our ministers as a circumstance that may be transient & should therefore be seised to open the Mediterranean to us.
'Has Virginia been seconded &c. in her proposition for arming Congress with powers to frustrate the unfriendly regulations of Great Britain?' Pennsylvania & Maryland offered much larger powers. those of Virginia might have been defeated by the British king repealing his proclamation

one day & renewing it the next. yet the powers & plans from all these states were different: and it was visible they would authorize no single measure. therefore Congress recommended a uniform measure.

'Is the impost gaining or losing ground?' gaining, most certainly. Georgia, North Carolina, New York, Connecticut & Rhode island are yet to pass it. the three first are supposed to be willing to do it. Connecticut has held off merely to try whether Congress would not rescind the commutation. finding a firmness on this point it is said & beleived that at their next session they will come into it. Howell[1] has often told me that R.I. will not accede to it as long as any other state holds off: but when every other shall have adopted it, she will.

'Does the settlement of the public accounts make any comfortable progress?' they are going on, but slowly I beleive. however they go on, and of course approach their term.

'Has any resolution been taken by Congress touching the old Continental currency?' that question has been debated by a grand Committee upwards of a month. they yesterday came to the inclosed resolution. it was decided by only 6 votes against 5. I think it will gain strength in the House. the Southern & middle states I beleive are for it , & I think one or two of the Eastern may perhaps come over. yet there is far from being a certainty of this.

'Has ——— forborne to take any step in favor of ——— ?' their object was certainly not the same with ours. yet they have not openly set their faces against us. they have one delegate, honest & disinterested, who certainly will in no case do it?[2]

'Whether the war ceased in March or April?' I think no decision has taken place on that subject in our court of Appeals. our ministers write that it is no question on that side the water but that it ended in March.

the produce of our slave tax being nearly equal to the Continental requisitions, can you not get it appropriated to that purpose, & have it all paid in money? Virginia must do something more than she has done to maintain any degree of respect in the Union & to make it bearable to any man of feeling to represent her in Congress. the public necessities call distressingly for aid, and very ruinous circumstances proceed from the in-attention of the states to furnish suppplies in money. S. Carolina is the foremost state in supplies notwithstanding her distresses. whence does this proceed? from a difference of spirit solely; from a pride of character; from a rejection of the unmanly supineness which permits personal inconveni-ency to absorb every other sentiment. there is no man who has not some vice or folly the starving of which would not pay his taxes.

I am now to take my leave of the justlings of states and to repair to a feild where the divisions will be fewer but on a larger scale. Congress yesterday joined me to mr Adams & D⁷ Franklin on the foreign commercial negotiations. I shall pursue there the line that I have pursued here, convinced that it can never be the interest of any party to do what is unjust, or to ask what is unequal. mr Jay was to sail for America this month. his health has obliged him to return to try his native air. he is appointed Sec^y· for Foreign affairs.

I pray you to continue to favor me with your correspondence. at the close of every session of assembly a state of the general measures & dispositions, as well as of the subordinate politics of parties or individuals will be entertaining and useful. during recesses other objects will furnish matter sufficient for communication. on my part I shall certainly maintain the correspondence. if moreover you can at any time enable me to serve you by the execution of any particular commission I shall agree that my sincerity may be judged by the readiness with which I shall execute it. in the purchase of books, pamphlets &c. old & curious, or new & useful I shall ever keep you in my eye. whether I shall procure for you the books you have before desired at Philadelphia or Paris shall be decided according to circumstances when I get to Philadelphia, from which place I will write to you.

       ·   ·   ·   ·   ·

I think Colo. Monroe³ will be of the Committee of the states. he wishes a correspondence with you; and I suppose his situation will render him an useful one to you. the scrupulousness of his honor will make you safe in the most confidential communications. a better man cannot be....

May 11. Many considerations have determined me to go on to Boston & take shipping from thence. this was a conclusion of yesterday. all my letters dated previous to that will state me as purposing to sail from N. York. I leave this place to-day; expect to stay in Philadelphia till the 25ᵗʰ· and to be at Boston about the 3ᵈ· of June.

I am with the sincerest esteem, D⁷· Sir Your affectionate friend & ser^t·

                                       Th. Jefferson

LC: *Madison Papers*, microfilm reel 2 (ALS). See also Smith, Paul H., ed., *Letters of Delegates to Congress, 1774-1789* (Washington, DC: *Library of Congress*, 1976-   ), hereafter cited as Smith, *Letters of Delegates*, v. 21, pp. 600-603.

¹ *Howell, David (1747-1824). Rhode Island educator, jurist and political figure. Taught at Rhode Island College (later Brown University), 1766-1779; maintained his association with that institution until his death. Member, Continental Congress, 1782-1785. Justice, state supreme court, 1786-1787. Attorney general of Rhode Island, 1789. Commissioner to determine the northeastern boundary of the United States under the Jay Treaty. Judge, United States District Court for Rhode Island, 1812-1824.*

² *The two blanks in the first sentence of this paragraph represent "Maryland" and "George Town" respectively. The "honest & disinterested" delegate was probably Thomas*

Stone (1743-1787), who was a member of the State senate, 1779-1783, and a member of the Continental Congress, 1775-1776, 1778, and 1784.
³ *Monroe, James (1758-1831). Virginia military figure, diplomat and political figure. Military service, reaching staff rank of major, 1776-1778. Studied law under Thomas Jefferson, 1780-1783, who sent him, as a lieutenant colonel, to ascertain the military situation in the South. Member, Virginia House of Delegates, 1782, 1786, 1810. Member, Continental Congress, 1783-1786. U.S. Senator, 1790-1794. Minister to France, 1794-1796. Governor of Virginia, 1799-1802, 1811. Minister to Great Britain, 1803-1807. Assisted in negotiation of Louisiana Purchase, 1803, but failed in negotiation of West Florida boundary with Spain, 1804. U.S. Secretary of State, 1811-1817. Secretary of War, 1814-1815. President of the United States, 1817-1825.*

Benjamin Franklin to Comte de Vergennes

Passy, May 31. 1784

Some inconveniencies are Said to have arisen from a want of certainty in the powers of our Consuls. The articles respecting that matter have been some time prepared and agreed to between Mʳ de Rayneval and me. If there is no change of Sentiment respecting them, I beg leave to request Your Excellency would direct such steps to be taken as may be proper for compleating them. I am ready on the part of the United States to Sign them at any time.

With great Respect, I am Sir, Your Excellency's Most Obedient & most humble Servant   B. Franklin

French Foreign Affairs Archives: Political Correspondence, hereafter cited as FFAA: Pol. Corr., United States, hereafter cited as U.S., v. 27, f. 394 (C); LC microfilm reel 16.

∞ *The Franco-American Consular Convention:* ∞
Further Steps

After Congress approved a draft of the consular convention on January 25, 1782, the Chevalier de la Luzerne sent a copy to France's naval minister, the Marquis de Castries,¹ who was responsibile for consular arrangements. Robert R. Livingston, the Secretary for Foreign Affairs, sent a copy to Benjamin Franklin, together with instructions from Congress that gave him the discretion to change the draft after talks with French officials.

The years 1782 and 1783 were full ones for all concerned. The Marquis de Castries did not present a comparison of the original French proposal and the draft approved by Congress to the Comte de Vergennes,

France's Foreign Minister, *until May 1783. After some discussions on the French side, Vergennes presented a new draft of the convention to Franklin in September 1783.*

Meanwhile, Franklin had shown the draft approved by Congress to Thomas Barclay, the U.S. Consul in France, who strongly objected to its third article, which prohibited consular officials from engaging in trade. That article did not appear in the September 1783 draft. Franklin, working primarily with Vergennes' first secretary, Joseph Matthias Gérard de Rayneval,[2] made such good progress in reconciling the French and American positions that he could report to Congress in December that the convention was completed and the transcription process under way in preparation for its signing.

However, Vergennes still had to secure acceptance of the agreement by Castries, who was surprised by certain changes that had been made in the September 1783 draft. The French naval minister particularly objected to the omission of commissaries from the types of consular officials covered by the convention, since this had a direct impact on the provisioning of French naval vessels operating in American waters. Vergennes and Castries ultimately settled their differences (without the return of the commissaries), and the consular convention was ready to be signed by late July 1784.

---

[1] *Castries, Charles-Eugène-Gabriel, Marquis de (1727-1801). French military and government leader. Minister of the Navy, 1780-1787. Created marshal of France, 1783. Governor of Flanders and Hainaut, 1787-1790. Emigrated 1790, commanded forces opposing the revolutionary army in 1792, supported Louis XVIII in exile.*

[2] *Rayneval, Joseph-Matthias Gérard de (1736-1812). French diplomat. Undersecretary to the French Foreign Minister. French minister to Great Britain, early 1783.*

Franco-American Consular Convention

Versailles 29[th.] July 1784

Convention between his most Christian Majesty and the thirteen United States of North America, for the Purpose of determining and fixing the Functions and Prerogatives of their respective Consuls, Vice Consuls, Agents and Commissaries.

His Majesty the most Christian King and the thirteen United States of North America, having by the 29[th.] Article of the Treaty of Amity and Commerce, concluded between them, mutually granted the Liberty of having in their respective States and Ports, Consuls, Vice Consuls, Agents and Commissaries, and being willing in Consequence thereof to determine and fix in a reciprocal and permanent Manner the Functions & Prerogatives of the said Consuls, Vice Consuls, Agents and Commissaries, his most Christian Majesty has nominated the Sieur Charles Gravier, Count of Vergennes Baron of Welferding, &c. Counsellor of the King in all his Councils, Commander of his Orders, Head of the Royal Council of Finances, Counsellor of the State of the Sword, Minister and Secretary of State, and of his Commands and Finances; and the United States, the Sieur Benjamin Franklin, their Minister Plenipotentiary to his most Christian Majesty, who, after having communicated to each other their respective full Powers, agreed upon what follows: –

Art. 1st:

The Consuls and Vice Consuls nominated by his most Christian Majesty, and the United States, shall be bound to present their Commissions on their Arrival in the respective States, according to the Form, which shall be there established. There shall be delivered to them without any Charges the *Exequatur* necessary for the Exercise of their Functions; and, on the Exhibition they shall make of the said Exequatur, the Governors, Commanders, Heads of Justice, public Bodies, Tribunals and other Officers, having authority in the Ports and Places of their Consulates, shall cause them to enjoy, as soon as possible, and without Difficulty, the Préeminences, Authority, and Privileges, reciprocally granted, without exacting from the said Consuls and Vice Consuls any Duty, under any Pretext whatever.

Art: 2d:

The respective Consuls shall [have] Power to establish Vice Consuls in the different Ports and Places of their Departments where Necessity shall require. – There shall be delivered to them likewise the Exequatur necessary to the Exercise of their Functions, in the Form pointed out in the preceding Article, and, on the Exhibition which they shall make of the said Exequatur, they shall be admitted and acknowledged in the Terms, and according to the Powers, Authority, and Privileges stipulated by the 1st: 4th: and 5th: Articles of the present Convention.

Art. 3rd:

The respective Consuls and Vice Consuls may establish Agents in the different Ports and Places of their Departments, where Necessity shall require. – These Agents may be chosen among the Merchants, either national or foreign, and furnished with a Commission from one of the said Consuls – It shall be their Business, respectively, to render to their respective Merchants, Navigators, and Vessels, all possible Service, and to inform the nearest Consul, or Vice Consul of the Wants of the said

Merchants, Navigators, and Vessels, without the said Agents otherwise participating in the Immunities, Rights, and Privileges attributed to the Consuls and Vice Consuls, and without Power to exact from the said Merchants any Duty or Emolument whatever under any Pretext whatever.

Art: 4^{th:}

The Consuls and Vice Consuls, the Officers of the Consulate, and, in general all Persons attached to the consular Functions shall enjoy respectively a full and entire Immunity for their Person, their Papers, and their Houses. The List of the said Persons shall be approved and inspected by the Executive Power of the Place of their Residence. –

They shall be exempt from all personal Service and public Offices, from Soldiers Billets, Militia, *Watch-Guard, Guardianship and Trusteeship*, as well as from all Duties, Taxes, Impositions, and Charges whatsover, except *the real Estates* of which they may be Proprietors, which shall be subject to the Taxes imposed on the Estates of all other Individuals.

They shall place over the outward Door of their House, the Arms of their Sovereign: without this Mark of Distinction giving to the said House the Right of Assylum for any Malefactor or Criminal, so that in Case it should happen that any Malefactor or Criminal take refuge there, he shall be instantly delivered up on the first Requisition, and without Difficulty.

Art: 5th.

Generally in all Cases whatever which concern the Police or Administration of Justice, where it may be necessary to have a juridical Declaration from the said Consuls and Vice Consuls respectively, the Governors, Commandants, Chief Justice, Public Bodies, Tribunals, or other Officers whatever of their respective Residence there, having Authority, shall be bound to inform them of it, by writing to them, or sending to them a military or civil Officer to let them know, either the Object which is proposed, or the Necessity there is for going to them to demand from them this Declaration, and the said Consuls and Vice Consuls shall be bound on their Part to comply faithfully with what shall be desired of them on these Occasions.

Art: 6^{th:}

The Consuls and Vice Consuls respectively may establish a Chancery where shall be deposited the Consular Acts and Deliberations, all Effects left by deceased Persons, or saved from Shipwreck, as well as Testaments, Obligations, Contracts, and, in general, all the Acts and Proceedings done between, or by Persons of their Nation.

They may, in Consequence, appoint for the *Business* of the said Chancery capable Persons, receive them, administer an Oath to them, give to them the Keeping of the Seal, and the Right of sealing Commissions,

Judgments, and other Acts of the Consulate, as well as there to discharge the Functions of Notaries and Registers.

Art: 7th.

The Consuls and Vice-Consuls respectively shall have the exclusive Right of receiving in their Chancery, or on board of Vessels, the Declarations and all the other Acts which the Captains, Masters, Seamen, Passengers, and Merchants of their Nation would make there, even their Testaments and other Dispositions of last Will, and the Copies of the said Acts duly authenticated by the said Consuls or Vice Consuls, and, under the Seal of their Consulate, shall receive Faith in Law in all the Tribunals of France and the United States.

They shall have also and exclusively the Right to inventory, liquidate, and proceed to the Sale of the moveable Effects of the Estates left by Subjects of their Nation who shall die within the Extent of the Consulate. – They shall proceed therein with the Assistance of two Merchants of their said Nation, of their own choosing, and shall deposite in their Chancery, the Effects and Papers of the said Estates, and no Officer, military or civil, or of the Police of the Country, shall trouble them, or interfere therein, in any Manner whatsoever: but the said Consuls and Vice-Consuls shall not deliver up the same and their Product to the lawful Heirs, or their Attornies until they shall have discharged all the Debts which the deceased shall have contracted in the Country, by Judgment, by Acts or by Notes, the writing and signing of which shall be known and certified by two principal Merchants of the Nation of the said deceased, and in all other Cases the Payment of Debts cannot be ordered but, on the Creditors giving sufficient and local Security to repay the Sums unduly received, Principal, Interest and Costs, which Securities, however, shall remain duly discharged after a Year in Time of Peace and two Years in Time of War, if the demand in Discharge cannot be formed before these Delays, against the Heirs which shall present themselves.

Art: 8th.

The respective Consuls and Vice Consuls shall receive the Declarations "Consulats," and other Consular Acts from all Captains and Masters of their respective Nation, on Account of average Losses sustained at Sea, by Leakage, or throwing Merchandizes over board, and these Captains and Masters shall leave in the Chancery of the said Consuls and Vice Consuls, the "Consulats," and other Consular Acts which they may have had made in other Ports on Account of the Accidents which may have happened to them on their Voyage. If a Subject of his most Christian Majesty and a Citizen of the United States are interested in the said Cargo, the Average shall be fixed by the Tribunals of the Country and not by the Consuls or Vice Consuls; and the Tribunals shall admit the Acts and Declarations, if any should have been passed before the said Consuls and Vice Consuls; but when only the Subjects of their own Nation; or Foreigners shall be interested, the respective Consuls or Vice Consuls and in Case of their Absence or Distance, their Agents furnished with their Commission, shall officially nominate skilful Persons of their said Nation, to regulate the Damages and Averages.

Art: 9^{th:}

In Case by Storms or other Accidents, French Ships or Vessels shall *run ashore* on the Coasts of the United States, and the Ships and Vessels of the United States, shall *run ashore* on the Coasts of France, the Consul or Vice Consul nearest to the Place of Shipwreck shall do whatever he may judge proper, as well for the purpose of saving the said Ship or Vessel, its Cargo and Appurtenances, as for the storing and Security of the Effects and Merchandize saved. He may take an Inventory, without any Officers military, of the Custom House, Justices, or the Police of the Country interfering, otherwise than to facilitate to the Consuls, Vice Consuls, Captain and Crew of the Vessel shipwrecked, or run ashore, all the Assistance and Favor which they shall ask, either for the Celerity and Security of the Salvage, and Effects saved, or to prevent all Disturbances.

To prevent even any kind of Dispute and Discussion in the said Cases of shipwreck – It has been agreed, that where no Consul or Vice Consul shall be found to attend to the Salvage, or that the Residence of the said Consul (or Vice Consul (he not being at the Place of Shipwreck) shall be further distant from the said Place than that of the competent territorial Judge, the latter shall immediately there proceed therein with all the Celerity, Safety, and Precautions prescribed by the respective Laws, but the said Territorial Judge shall retire on the coming of the Consul or Vice Consul, and shall resign to him the Procedures by him done, the Expenses of which the Consul or Vice Consul shall cause to be reimbursed to him.

The Merchandize and Effects saved, shall be deposited in the Custom House, or other nearest Place of Safety, with the Inventory of them, which shall be made by the Consul or Vice Consul, or, in their Absence, by the Judge, who shall have had cognisance thereof, and the said Merchandizes and Effects shall be afterwards delivered, after levying therefrom the Costs, and without Form of Process, to the Proprietors, who, being furnished with a *Replevy* from the nearest Consul or Vice Consul, shall reclaim them by themselves, or by their Attornies, either for the Purpose of reexporting the Merchandizes, and, in that Case they shall pay no Kind of Duties of Exportation, or for the Purpose of selling them in the Country, if they are not prohibited, and in this latter Case, the said Merchandizes being averaged, there shall be granted them an Abatement of the Entrance Duties proportioned to the Damage sustained, which shall be ascertained by the verbal Process formed at the Time of the Shipwreck, or of the Vessels running ashore.

Art: 10^{th:}

The Consuls and Vice Consuls shall have on board of the Vessels of their respective Nations full Power and Jurisdiction in Matters civil – They shall cause to be executed, the respective Laws, Ordinances and Rules concerning Navigation, on board the said Vessels, and, for this Purpose, they shall go there without being interrupted by any Officer or other Person whatsoever.

They may cause to be *arrested* every Vessel carrying the Flag of their respective Nation – They may sequester them, and even send them back respectively, from the United States to France, or from France to the United States – They may cause to be arrested, without Difficulty every Captain, Master, Sailor, or Passenger of their said respective Nation.

They may cause to be arrested, or detained in the Country the Sailors and Deserters of their respective Nations, or send them back, or transport them out of the Country.

It shall be a sufficient Proof that the Sailors and Deserters belong to one of the respective Nations, that their Names be written in the Ship's Registers, or inserted in the Roll of the Crew.

One and the other of these Proofs concerning Sailors and Deserters being thus given, no Tribunals, Judges, and Officers whatsoever shall, in any Manner whatever take cognisance of the Complaints which the said Sailors and Deserters may make – but they shall, on the Contrary be delivered up on an Order signed by the Consul or Vice Consul without its being in any ones Power in any Manner to detain, engage, or withdraw them. And to attain to the complete Execution of the Arrangements contained in this Article, all Persons having Authority shall be bound to assist the said Consuls or Vice Consuls, and, on a simple Requisition signed by them, they shall cause to be detained and guarded in Prison at the Disposal and Expense of the said Consuls and Vice Consuls, the said Sailors and Deserters until they shall have an Opportunity to send them out of the Country.

Art: 11^{th:}

In Cases where the respective Subjects shall have committed any Crime, they shall be amenable to the Judges of the Country.

Art: 12^{th:}

All Differences and Suits between the Subjects of his Most Christian Majesty settled in the United States, or between the Citizens and Subjects of the United States settled in France, and all Differences and Suits concerning Commerce between the Subjects of his most Christian Majesty, and one of the Parties residing in France or elsewhere, and the other in the

United States, or between the Citizens and Subjects of the United States, one of the Parties residing in the United States, or elsewhere, and the other in France, shall be determined by the respective Consuls, either by a Reference to Arbitration, or by a summary Judgment and without Costs.

No Officer, civil or military shall interfere or take any Part whatever in the Affair – Appeals shall be carried before the Tribunals of France, or the United States to whom it may appertain to take Cognisance thereof. The Consuls or Vice Consuls shall not take Cognisance of Disputes or Differences which shall arise betwixt a Subject of his most Christian Majesty and a Citizen of the United States – But the said Disputes shall be brought before the Tribunals to which the Defendant shall be amenable.

Art: 13th:

The general Utility of Commerce having caused to be established in France, Tribunals and particular Forms to accelerate the Decision of commercial Affairs, the Merchants of the United States shall enjoy the Benefit of these Establishments in France, and the Congress of the United States shall recommend to the Legislatures of the different States to provide equivalent Advantages in Favor of the French Merchants for the prompt Dispatch and Decision of Affairs of the same Nature.

Art: 14th:

The Subjects of his most Christian Majesty and those of the United States who shall prove that they belong to the Body of their respective Nations, by the Certificate of the Consul or Vice Consul of the District, mentioning their Names, Surnames and Place of their Settlement, as inscribed in the Registers of the Consulate, shall not lose, for any Cause whatever, in the respective Domains and States, the Quality of Subjects of the Country of which they originally were, conformably to the 11th: Article of the Treaty of Amity and Commerce of the 6th: February 1778, of which the present Article shall serve as an Interpretation in Case of Necessity, and the said Subjects, respectively, shall enjoy, in consequence, Exemption from all personal Service in the Place of their Settlement.

Art: 15th:

If any other Nation acquires, by Virtue of any Convention whatever, either in France, or in the United States a Treatment more favorable with Respect to the Consular Préeminences, Powers, Authority, and Privileges, the Consuls, Vice Consuls and Agents of his most Christian Majesty, or the United States, reciprocally shall participate therein, agreeable to the Terms stipulated by the 2th: 3d: & 4th Articles of the Treaty of Amity and Commerce concluded between his most Christian Majesty and the United States.

Art: 16^{th:}

The Ratifications of the present Convention shall be given in proper Form and exchanged on both Sides within the Space of six Months, or sooner if possible.

In faith whereof We, the Underwritten, Ministers Plenipotentiaries of his most Christian Majesty and the United States of North America, have signed the present Convention, and have thereto affixed the Seal of our Arms.

Done at Versailles the 29^{th:} July one thousand seven hundred and eighty four.

Gravier de Vergennes   B. Franklin.

NA: PCC, *item 100, v. 2, pp. 243-255 (LBkC); M247, reel 127.*

Charles Thomson to John Jay

Dear Sir,   Philadelphia Sept 18. 1784

I should have answered your letter of 12 Aug. much sooner, had I not from the tenor of it flattered myself with the hopes of seeing you here in a very short time. I wish exceedingly to see and converse with you not only on the subject of your acceptance but on the general State of our Affairs. There is at present no person whose business or whole duty it is to attend to matters of national Concern. The Committee of the states have in my opinion very unwarrantably separated, and though the Chairman has written to the several States to send on a Delegate to form a Committee at Philadelphia, I have little hopes of their meeting. The Superintendant of Finance is busyly winding up his Affairs so as to quit his Office; ~~and~~ as to the department of foreign affairs our Ministers abroad are left wholly to themselves without the least information of what is passing here. And the several States seem to be acting as if there was nothing beyond their respective bounds which claimed their attention or deserved their notice. Our public credit is again verging to a precipice and the seeds of jealousy and internal commotion seem to be springing up while at the same time I am far from thinking we are secure from the insidious designs of our late enemy, or the deep rooted jealousy of our southern neighbour. Yet gloomy as the prospect appears it only wants a little common sense, & common attention in the states to brighten the scene, to ensure public tranquility & private happiness and to render our situation enviable; and on your Acceptance I greatly rely for these purposes –

The enclosed letter came by M^rs. Montgomery & was sent to me to be forwarded. Be pleased to make my most respectful compliments to M^rs. Jay and accept the assurance of the unfeigned affection of Dear Sir your friend & Servt   Chas Thomson[1]

Columbia University Libraries: John Jay Papers (ALS).
[1] Thomson, Charles (1729-1824). Pennsylvania political figure. His reputation as "the Samuel Adams of Philadelphia" caused conservatives to block his election to the First Continental Congress. As Secretary of the Continental Congress, 1774-1789, however, he was at the center of national politics throughout this period.

Congressional Resolution Regarding the Franco-American Consular Convention

December 14. 1784 –
On Motion of Mr Jay seconded by M^r. Gerry[1]
Resolved, Unanimously – Eight States only being represented, that his Excellency the President inform the Minister Plenipotentiary of the United States at the Court of France that it is the desire of Congress, in case the Convention proposed for regulating, and ascertaining, the Powers and Privileges of Consuls should not be already signed, that he delay signing it until he shall receive further Instructions on the Subject from Congress –

NA: PCC, item 5, p. 1010 (Journal); M247, reel 19.
[1] Gerry, Elbridge (1744-1814). Massachusetts political figure. Member, provincial congress, 1774-1776. Member, Continental Congress, 1776-1780, 1783-1785. Delegate, Constitutional Convention, 1787; opposed ratification of the Constitution. Member, U.S. House of Representatives, 1789-1793. Member, XYZ Mission, 1797-1798. Governor of Massachusetts, 1810-1812. Vice President, 1813-1814.

Benjamin Franklin to the President of Congress

Sir,[1]   Passy February 8th: 1785.
I received, by the Marquis de la Fayette,[2] the two Letters you did me the Honor of writing to me the 11th: and 14th: of December; the one enclosing a Letter from Congress to the King; the other a Resolve of Congress respecting the Convention for establishing Consuls. The letter was immediately delivered, and well received. The Resolve came too late to suspend signing the Convention, it having been done in July last; and a

Copy sent so long since that we now expected the Ratification. As that Copy seems to have miscarried, I now send another. I am not informed what Objection has arisen in Congress to the Plan sent me. Mr Jefferson thinks it may have been to the Part which restrained the Consuls from all Concern in Commerce. That Article was omitted, being thought unnecessary to be stipulated, since either Party would always have the Power of imposing such Restraints on its own Officers, whenever it should think fit. – I am, however, of Opinion that this or any other reasonable Article, or Alteration may be obtained at the Desire of Congress, and established by a Supplement.

Permit me, Sir, to congratulate you on your being called to the high Honor of presiding in our national Councils, and to wish you every Felicity, being with the most perfect Esteem, &c.   B. Franklin.

NA: PCC, item 100, v. 2, p. 230 (LBkC); M247, reel 127.

[1] Lee, Richard Henry (1732-1794). Virginia political figure. Brother of Arthur, William, and Francis Lightfoot Lee. Member, Virginia House of Burgesses, 1758-1775. Member, Continental Congress, 1774-1779, 1784-1785 and 1787; president, 1784. U.S. Senator, 1789-1792.

[2] Lafayette, Marie-Joseph-Paul-Yves-Roch Gilbert du Motier, Marquis de (1757-1834). French military officer and political figure. Inspired by the Declaration of Independence, this wealthy young aristocrat sailed for America in April 1777 without his government's approval. Congress commissioned him a major general in the Continental Army on July 31, 1777; he at first served on the staff of General Washington, who virtually adopted him, and later commanded a division of Virginia light troops. He spent the period from January 1779 to April 1780 in France working for American interests, then returned to America to make preparations for the arrival of Rochambeau's expeditionary force. He led an unsuccessful attempt to capture Benedict Arnold at Hampton Roads in March 1781, foiled a British attempt to capture Richmond, and retreated before Cornwallis until the arrival of reinforcements made it possible for him to press the British commander into making moves that became the initial stages of the Yorktown campaign. In December 1781 he returned to France, where he assisted the American commissioners in their negotiations with France and Spain regarding the western boundaries. Later in the 1780s, he worked diligently with Thomas Jefferson to simplify French trade restrictions that prevented a fuller blossoming of Franco-American commerce. During the initial stages of the French Revolution, he helped to convert the Estates General into a National Assembly; introduced the Declaration of the Rights of Man adopted by that body on July 11, 1789; and served as commander of the Paris National Guard, July 1789-October 1791.

John Jay to the President of Congress

Sir   [New York] Office for foreign Affairs 23$^{d.}$ June 1785
I have the Honor of transmitting to your Excellency herewith enclosed,
the Copy received from D$^{r.}$ Franklin of the Convention which appears to
be in the french Language between that and this Nation respecting Consuls
together with the Translation for which it was referred to me. –
To me it appears Expedient to provide, that in future every Treaty or
Convention which Congress may think proper to engage in, should be
formally executed in two Languages, Viz$^{.}$ the Language of the United
States, and such other Language as the Party contracting with them may
prefer. –
I also take the Liberty of observing that in my Opinion it is much to be
desired that some Limits may be assigned for the Duration of the
Convention in Question; and therefore that Measures be taken for
obtaining the Admission of an Article for that Purpose –
I have the Honor to be with great Respect & Esteem Your Excellency's
Most ob$^{t.}$ & very hble: Serv$^{t.}$ –   John Jay –

NA: PCC, *item 80, v. 1, pp. 225-226 (LS); M 247, reel 106.*

John Jay's Report on the
Franco-American Consular Convention

[New York] Office for foreign Affairs July 4$^{th.}$ 1785
The Secretary of the United States for the Department of foreign
Affairs to whom was referred a Copy of the Convention respecting
french and american Consuls Reports –
That the Convention, of which the above mentioned is a Copy, having
been formally executed by french and american Plenipotentiaries, nothing
is wanting to perfect that Compact, but the Ratifications specified in the
16$^{th.}$ Article. –
The only Question therefore that remains to be decided is, whether
Congress ought to ratify this Convention. –
To decide this Question properly, it appears necessary (1$^{st.}$) to recur to the
Powers and Instructions given to their Minister on this Subject, and enquire
whether he has pursued them essentially, and (2$^{d.}$) whether in Case of
Deviations, they are of such a Nature as to justify a Refusal to ratify. –
It is to be observed that on the 25$^{th.}$ January 1782 Congress –
"Resolved that the Minister Plenipotentiary of the United States at the

Court of Versailles, be and is hereby authorised and *instructed*, to enter into a Convention with His Most Christian Majesty, on the Part of the United States for the Establishment of consular Powers and Priviledges According to the Scheme hereunto subjoined; unless it shall be deemed by his Most Christian Majesty more expedient that the same should be executed in the United States. –

"That the said Minister Plenipotentiary use *his Discretion* as to the *Words or Arrangement* of the Convention; Confining himself to the *Matter* thereof in *All Respects*, except as to so much of the Sixth Article, as relates to the Erection of a Chapel, taking Care that reciprocal Provision be made for the Recognition of the Consuls and Vice Consuls of the United States, & for the Admission of Persons attached to the Consulate to the Priviledges stipulated in the 5th. Article, in a manner most conducive to Expedition and freest from Difficulty." –

This is the only Instruction as well as the only Authority given on the Subject, to the American Minister; that your Secretary finds.

Scheme	Convention
Title	Title
Convention between his Most Christian Majesty and *the United States of North America* for defining and regulating the Functions and Priviledges of respective Consuls, Vice Consuls, Agents & Commissaries. –	Convention between his Most Christian Majesty and the *thirteen United States of North America* for the Purpose of determining and fixing the Functions & Prerogatives of their respective Consuls, Vice-Consuls, Agents & Commissaries.

The Stile of the Confederacy being "the United States of America," the Scheme and the Convention are both erroneous so far as they both add the Word *North*. –

But the Title of the Convention departs essentially from that of the Scheme, inasmuch as it limits the Compact to the *thirteen* United States of America, and consequently *excludes* from it all such other States as might before the Ratification of it or in future be created by, or become Parties to, the Confederacy; Whereas the Words in the Title of the Scheme *United States of North America* would if used, have comprehended them all. –

Scheme–	Convention
1st. Article.	1st. Article
It shall be the Duty of the Consuls of his Most Christian Majesty *to present their*	The Consuls and Vice Consuls nominated by his Most Christian Majesty and the United States,

Commissions in the first Instance to the United States in Congress Assembled by whom an Act shall be made recognizing them as such. – This Act shall be delivered by the Consuls to the Supreme Executive Power of the State or States to which they may be sent. Two Copies of the Exequatur, that is, a public Notification of the Quality of the Consuls, shall thereupon issue from the Supreme Executive Power without Fees or Perquisites of Office, one to be retained by the Consuls, the other to be published in one or more Gazettes. This being done the Pre-eminences &ᶜ· shall be allowed to them &ᶜ· –

shall be bound to present their Commissions on their Arrival in the respective States according to the Form which shall be there established. There shall be delivered to them, without any Charges, the Exequatur necessary for the Exercise of their Functions; and on the Exhibition they shall make of the said Exequatur the Governors &ᶜᵃ· having Authority in the Ports and Places of their Consulates shall cause them to enjoy as soon as possible and without Difficulty the Pre-eminences &ᶜ·–

The Scheme expressly directs that their Commissions shall in the first Instance be presented to Congress, but the Convention by omitting this, seems to intend something else – it indeed directs that they shall present their Commission on their Arrival in the respective States according to the Form "qui s'y trouvera etablis"[1] which shall be there found established; but whether established by the State or by Congress is undecided.

The 2ᵈ· Articles in both appear to be alike in Substance.

  Scheme   Convention
  3ᵈ· Article
Consuls & Vice Consuls shall be Subjects or Citizens of the Power appointing them and interdicted from all Traffic or Commerce for their own or anothers Benefit.

This Article is wholly omitted in the Convention, and that Omission is an Essential though perhaps not in itself a very important Deviation from the Scheme.–

The 4ᵗʰ· Article in the Scheme and the 3ᵈ· in the Convention respecting Agents, differ essentially only in this, that the former has these Words "nor exact any Fees or Reward under any Pretence whatever" whereas the latter seems to limit that Prohibition, by these Words "and without Power to exact

from the said Merchants any Duty or Emolument whatever under any Pretext whatsoever." –
The 5ᵗʰ· Article in the Scheme and the 4ᵗʰ· in the Convention have no material Difference.

Scheme	Convention
6ᵗʰ· Article.	

Consuls and Vice Consuls, in Places where there are no Consuls, may have a Chapel in their Houses, for the Celebration of divine Service, according to their religious Profession – And his Most Christian Majesty & the United States shall cause particular Care to be taken that no Obstacle or Hindrance be thrown in the Way of the funeral Obsequies or Ceremonies observed towards the deceased of either Nation.

This Article is omitted in the Convention. By the Instruction given to the Minister, that Matter seems to have been left to his Discretion. The Omission however appears important to your Secretary from this Consideration, that although the Catholic Religion may be freely and publicly professed and exercised in the United States, yet the Protestant Religion has no legal Toleration in France. This Omission therefore is a Departure from the Line of Reciprocity. –
The 7ᵗʰ· Article in the Scheme and the 5ᵗʰ· in the Convention are much alike. –
The 8ᵗʰ· Article in the Scheme and 6ᵗʰ· in the Convention are similar.–
The 9ᵗʰ· Article in the Scheme and the 7ᵗʰ· in the Convention also correspond. –

Scheme	Convention
Extract from 10ᵗʰ· Article	Extract from 8ᵗʰ· Article
on Average	*on Average*

"If a Subject of France and a Citizen of the United States be jointly interested in the Cargo, the Damage shall be settled by the Tribunals of the Country, not by the Consuls or Vice

"If a Subject of his Most Christian Majesty and a Citizen of the United States are interested in the said Cargo, the Average shall be fixed by the Tribunals of the Country, and

Consuls. But where Subjects, Citizens of their own Nation are alone interested, the Consul or Vice Consul shall then chuse experienced Persons of their respective Nations to settle the same." –

not by the Consuls or Vice Consuls; *and the Tribunals shall admit the Acts and Declarations, if any should have been passed before the said Consuls and Vice Consuls.* But when only the Subjects of their own Nation *or Foreigners* shall be interested, the respective Consuls or Vice-Consuls, *and in Case of their Absence or Distance, their Agents furnished with their Commission, shall officially* nominate skilful Persons of their said Nation to regulate the Damages and Averages." –

The Convention here appears to differ materially from the Scheme in *three* Respects. – (1) As it provides for the Admission in Evidence by our Tribunals of Acts and Declarations passed before Consuls and Vice Consuls respecting the Matter in Controversy, and consequently opens a Door to *ex parte* Affidavits. (2) The Scheme confines the Jurisdiction of Consuls and Vice Consuls to Cases where none but their own People are concerned; Whereas the Convention extends it to *Foreigners.* – (3) The Scheme authorises none but Consuls and Vice Consuls to appoint Persons to settle the Damages in Question; but the Convention makes an ulterior Provision and authorises their Agents ex officio to do it in certain Cases. –

The 11$^{th.}$ Article in the Scheme and the 9$^{th.}$ in the Convention are not materially different. –

Scheme
Extract from 12$^{th.}$ Article.
"They" (Consuls and Vice Consuls) "may cause to be arrested & sequestered every Vessel carrying the Flag of their respective Nations. – They may cause to be arrested and detained in the Country, Sailors and Deserters of their respective Nations, or cause them to be transported therefrom."

Convention
Extract from 10$^{th.}$ Article
"They may cause to be arrested every Vessel carrying the Flag of their respective Nation. They may sequester them, *and even send them back* respectively from the United States to France or from France to the United States. They may cause to be arrested without Difficulty every *Captain, Master,* Sailor or *Passenger* of their said respective Nation. They may cause to be arrested and detained in the

Country the Sailors and Deserters of their respective Nations, or send them back or transport them out of the Country. –

These Articles differ in these Respects. The Scheme does not authorise the Consuls *to send Vessels back* but the Convention does. The Scheme does not authorise them to arrest *Captains and Masters* of Vessels, but the Convention does. The Scheme does not authorise them to arrest *Passengers*, but the Convention does. –

Scheme 13$^{th.}$ Article.	Convention 11$^{th.}$ Article
All Offences committed in France by a Citizen of the United States against a Subject of his Most Christian Majesty shall be enquired into and punished according to the Laws of France, those committed in any one of the United States by a Subject of his Most Christian Majesty against a Citizen of the United States, shall be enquired into and punished according to the Laws of such State. But Offences committed in France by a Citizen of the United States against a Citizen of the United States, or committed in any one of the United States by a Subject of his Most Christian Majesty against a Subject of his Most Christian Majesty shall be subject to the Jurisdiction of the Consuls and Vice Consuls of France or the United States as the Case may be. –	In Cases where the respective Subjects shall have committed any Crime, they shall be amenable to the Judges of the Country. –

These two Articles differ in this, that the one in the Scheme gives Cognizance of certain Offences to Consuls and Vice Consuls, but the one in the Convention gives that Cognizance to the Judges of the Country. –

The 14$^{th.}$ Article in the Scheme and the 12$^{th.}$ in the Convention differ only in this, that the former refers certain *Offences*, Disputes and

Differences to the Jurisdiction of the Consuls and Vice Consuls, whereas the latter is silent as to *Offences*, and omits making any mention of them.– The 15th. Article in the Scheme, and the 13th. in the Convention are alike. –

<table>
<tr><td>Scheme</td><td>Convention</td></tr>
<tr><td>16th. Article</td><td>14th. Article</td></tr>
</table>

The Subjects of his Most Christian Majesty and the Citizens of the United States shall be exempt from all personal Services in the Place of their Residence, either in France or the United States as the Case may be. Whensoever any Person in France or the United States as the Case may be, shall claim any Priviledge or Exemption of a Subject of His Most Christian Majesty or of the United States, before any Judge, Tribunal or Officer whatsoever, a Certificate of the Consul or Vice Consul of the District, containing his Name, Surname, and the Place of his Residence, and the Affidavit of the Person claiming such Priviledge or Exemption, that he is a Subject of his Most Christian Majesty or of the United States, as the Case may be, shall be sufficient Evidence thereof, unless the contrary shall manifestly appear. –

The Subjects of his Most Christian Majesty and those of the United States who shall prove that they belong to the Body of their respective Nations, by the Certificate of the Consul or Vice Consul of the District, mentioning their Names, Surnames and Place of their Settlement, as inscribed in the Registers of the Consulate, shall not lose, *for any Cause whatever*, in the respective Domains and States, *the Quality of Subjects of the Country of which they originally were*, conformably to the 11th. Article of the Treaty of Amity and Commerce, of the 6th. February 1778, *of which the present Article shall serve as an Interpretation* in Case of Necessity, And the said Subjects respectively shall enjoy in Consequence, Exemption from all personal Service in the Place of their Settlement. –

These two Articles vary from each other essentially – *first*, in that the Certificate of the Consul is by the Convention made the sole and conclusive Proof of Nationality, whereas the Scheme requires also the Affidavit of the Party, and makes that joint Evidence conclusive only in Cases where *the contrary shall not manifestly appear* – *Secondly*, in that the Convention declares that Persons having such Certificates *shall not lose for any Cause whatever the Quality of Subjects of the Country of which they originally were*, – whereas the Scheme by not giving such Operation to those Certificates, leaves such Persons within the Reach of Naturalization.

Thirdly, in that the Convention makes this Article Auxiliary to the 6ᵗʰ· Article of the Treaty, by declaring that it shall serve as an Interpretation in Case of Necessity – whereas the Scheme does not constitute any Connection between this Article and the Treaty.

There is no Difference between the 17ᵗʰ· Article in the Scheme and the 15ᵗʰ· in the Convention except that the former refers only to the 3ᵈ· and 4ᵗʰ· Articles of the Treaty, whereas the latter refers to the 2ⁿᵈ· 3ʳᵈ· and 4ᵗʰ·–

The Convention contains an Article Vizᵗ· the 16ᵗʰ·, which provides for the Exchange of Ratifications, but there is no such Article in the Scheme.

It appeared proper to your Secretary thus particularly to state the principal Variances between the Scheme and the Convention, that Congress may the more easily judge how far they correspond. The Deviations in Question tho' different in Degrees of Importance, yet seem to be alike in this, that they depart from the *Matter* of the Scheme, and not merely from the Verbage or Arrangement of it. –

As Sovereigns treat and act with each other by their Ministers, it becomes essential that the Acts of those Ministers should not be obligatory, until after they are ratified; it being reasonable that the Sovereigns should have an Opportunity of judging whether their Powers have not been exceeded, and whether their Instructions have been pursued. A Refusal to ratify can therefore be warranted only by one or other of these Principles, Vizᵗ· either that their Ministers have exceeded the Powers delegated by their Commission, or departed from the Instructions given them to limit and regulate the Exercise and Use of these Powers, which are commonly expressed in very general Terms. –

Hence it becomes important that the Sovereign refusing to ratify, should be in Capacity to shew clearly what the Powers and Instructions given were, and also that the Treaty or Convention in Question is not conformable thereto. –

In the present Case there can be no Difficulty, because all the Power and Authority delegated to the American Minister rest entirely on the Resolution of the 25ᵗʰ· of January 1782; which in a few Words, so blends his Authority and his Instructions that he could not communicate to the french Minister, the one without the other. –

Where an open and general Commission is given, accompanied by private and particular Instructions, the one may be shewn and the other reserved – And though a Departure from such Instructions is good Cause to refuse a Ratification; yet more Difficulties attend such Cases than the present, because the other Party being ignorant of the Instructions, and relying on the full Powers, treat in full Confidence and Expectation that the Proceeding will be ratified. –

But as the french Minister in this Instance knew exactly how far the American Minister could go, and saw plainly that he was not to depart from the *Matter* of the Scheme which accompanied, & was referred to in his Powers and Instructions; they could in Case of essential Deviations, only expect a Ratification *de Gratia*, and not *de Jure*; and consequently can have no Reason to be dissatisfied in Case it should be declined. –

Thus much appeared necessary to observe, in order to shew that Congress have a Right to refuse the Ratification in Question – but whether it would be politic and expedient to do it, are Questions which must be entirely referred to the Wisdom of Congress. Your Secretary however in Order fully to comply with what he conceived to have been the Intention of Congress in referring the Convention to him, will now proceed to state the several Objections to which in his Opinion it is liable. –

The Convention appears well calculated to answer several Purposes; but the most important of them are such, as America has no Interest in promoting. They are these

1$^{st.}$ To provide against Infractions of the french & american Laws of Trade. –

2$^{nd.}$ To prevent the People of one Country from migrating to the other.

3$^{rd.}$ To establish in each other's Country an influencial Corps of Officers, under one Chief, to promote mercantile and political Views.

The *first* of these Objects is clearly evinced, by the 10$^{th.}$ Article.

The *second* of these Objects though less explicitly, is still sufficiently evident from the 14$^{th.}$ Article. –

The *third* of these Objects as it respects *mercantile* Views is apparent from the general Tenor of the Convention, and it appears plain to your Secretary, that a Minister near Congress, Consuls so placed as to include every Part of the Country in one Consulate or other, Vice Consuls in the principal Ports, and Agents in the less important ones, constitute a Corps, so coherent, so capable of acting jointly and secretly, and so ready to obey the Orders of their Chief, that it cannot fail of being influencial in two very important political Respects; *first* in acquiring & communicating Intelligence, and *secondly* in disseminating, and impressing such Advices, Sentiments and Opinions, of Men or Measures, as it may be deemed expedient to diffuse and encourage. –

These being the *three* great Purposes which the Convention is calculated to answer; the next Question which naturally occurs is, whether the United States have any such Purposes to answer by establishing such a Corps in France. –

As to the 1$^{st.}$ – We have no Laws for the Regulation of our Commerce with France or any of her Dominions, and consequently we want no Provisions or Guards against the Infraction of such Laws. –

As to the 2$^{nd.}$ – We have not the most distant Reason to apprehend or fear that our People will leave us and migrate either to the Kingdom of France or to any of its Territories, and consequently every Restriction or Guard against it must be superfluous and useless. –

As to the 3$^{d.}$ – France being a Country in whose Government the People do not participate, where nothing can be printed without previous Licence, or said without being known, and if disliked followed with Inconveniences, such a Corps would there be very inefficient for political Purposes – Where the People are perfectly unimportant, every Measure to influence their Opinions must be equally so – For *political Purposes* therefore we do not want any such Corps in France.

As to assisting our Merchants, and such other Matters as properly belong to Consuls, they would answer all those Purposes just as well, without these extraordinary Powers, as with them. –

Hence it is clear to your Secretary that the *three* great Purposes which the Convention is calculated to answer, are such as the United States have no Interest in promoting. Whether France has any such Purposes to answer in the United States, and how far this Convention may facilitate the Pursuit of them, are Questions which the Discernment of Congress renders it unnecessary for your Secretary to discuss. –

Your Secretary also considers this Convention as greatly deficient in Reciprocity, inasmuch as by it we are to admit french Consuls into all our Ports and Places without Exception, whereas no Provision is made for the Admission of ours into any of the Ports, Places and Dominions of his Most Christian Majesty except the Kingdom of France only. He also thinks that the Omission of the Article securing to Consuls the Right of worshipping in their own Way in Chapels in their Houses, is a Deviation from Reciprocity, especially as that Liberty is not only permitted but established here.

But independent of these general Circumstances and Considerations your Secretary thinks the Convention is liable to several strong and *particular* Objections. –

When these States assumed a Place among the Nations of the Earth they agreed upon and published to the World the Stile and Title by which they were to be known and called, and your Secretary does not conceive that other Nations are more at Liberty to alter that Stile, than the United States are to alter the Title of his Most Christian, Most Catholic, or any other Majesty in Europe. He therefore thinks that no Act should be ratified by Congress until every Error of this Kind is corrected. Though these Matters are very unimportant in themselves, yet they become so as

Precedents; one little Liberty unchecked, often smoothing the Way for a greater. –

The Convention directs the Consuls on their Arrival in the respective States to present their Commissions according to the Forms which shall be there found established. Although the *Word respective* here used, relates to the two Countries, and not to the individual States of which our Confederacy is composed, yet it still is doubtful whether the Form alluded to is to be established by Congress or the State to which they may be sent and at which they may arrive. The like Remarks apply to the Case of Vice Consuls mentioned in the 2$^{nd.}$ Article. –

In Countries where the Laws alone govern, it should in the Opinion of your Secretary, be an invariable Maxim not to permit any civil Power to be exercised in it but by the Citizens of the Country legally and constitutionally authorised thereto; and that as few Persons as possible, should live exempt, in any Respect, from the Jurisdiction of the Laws. In his Opinion therefore none but the immediate Representatives of Sovereigns ought to have such Exemptions – A Consul is not of that Description. According to the Law of Nations Embassadors must be received – but that Law does not extend to Consuls and therefore, every Nation may admit them on their own Terms. It is not easy to assign a good Reason for granting them a full and entire Immunity for their Persons, Papers, Houses & Servants, other than such as the free Citizens of the Country enjoy – as they are protected by the Laws, they should be subject to them. –

But the Convention goes much further. It grants this Immunity not only to Consuls and also to Vice Consuls, but also to all their different Officers, and in general to all Persons attached to the Consulate. Various Abuses, difficult to detect, and still more difficult to correct, would naturally attend such extensive Exemptions from the Process and Jurisdiction of our Laws; which can only proceed in one open plain direct Path, without the Aid of those Detours and Expedients well known and daily practiced in absolute Governments. –

The 5$^{th.}$ Article, respecting calling upon them for Evidence, seems to be an unnecessary Departure from our Laws – Why should Consuls and Vice Consuls, be called upon to give Evidence in a Manner less formal and less coercive than the first and highest Officers of our Government are. –

The 6$^{th.}$ and 7$^{th.}$ Articles establishing consular and vice *consular Chanceries* create an *Imperium in Imperio*, which in several Respects must clash with the internal Policy of these States, and with which it is not clear that Congress can authorise any Persons to interfere – such as

(1)   Their Officers shall discharge the Functions of Notaries. If by Notaries be intended such as are known in this Country – they

are public Officers who can only be appointed in the manner prescribed by the Governments of the different States.

(2)   All Effects left by deceased Persons (of their Nation) are to be deposited there, and they are to have the *exclusive* Right to inventory, liquidate and sell the moveable Effects &ᶜ so left – so that with Respect to these Matters, not only the Executors of the deceased are to be excluded, but our Judge of Probates is to lose his Jurisdiction. And yet consular Copies of such Wills and Acts though unknown to our Laws, are to be admitted as Evidence in our Courts. –

(3)   If a french Merchant having many Goods in Possession and many Debts to pay, should die; his Creditors according to this System, are to have no other Dependence for Payment but the Integrity of the Consul or Vice Consul who alone can take Possession of his Goods. No Action can be brought against these Officers nor any Process touch any Thing in their Houses – so that our Courts are so far to lose their Jurisdiction, and american Creditors in effect – their Right of Action. –

(4)   Notes given by french Men dying here are put on another Footing from Notes given by our Citizens, with Respect to Evidence. For the Convention demands that the *writing and signing* of them shall be known and certified by *two principal Merchants of his Nation*; which very materially alters our Law on that Subject. –

From these and other Circumstances it appears that this Convention will make a strong Line of Separation between french and american Inhabitants in this Country. –

The 10ᵗʰ· Article needs no Comment. It gives to Consuls as complete Jurisdiction over french Vessels in our Harbours, as any of the King's Officers could exercise over them in the Harbours of France. One Circumstance however is very striking and merits much Attention Viz: their Power to *arrest Passengers*, which doubtless will be the Case whenever Passengers attempt to come here in a Manner and for Purposes not consistant with the Ordinances against Emigration. And the Power to arrest also the Captains and Masters, is doubtless intended to punish Neglect of those Ordinances, and to render them very circumspect in their Conduct relative to Passengers and Cargoes. –

How far the Power of arresting and reexporting Sailors and Deserters may operate on Emigrants is not difficult to foresee, as the Consuls are to be the only Judges, and our Courts are excluded from hearing the Complaints of any Persons whom the Consuls may describe by those Appellations. –

The 14ᵗʰ· Article makes the Certificate of a Consul conclusive Proof of a Man's being a Frenchman and declares that he who shall make *such Proof* shall not lose *for any Cause whatever* the Quality of Subject. –

That the Manifestation of so important a Fact should depend wholly on such a Certificate; that no counter Proof should be offered and prevail; is really to make the consular Chancery a Court of Record (and that not only for Judicial Acts, but also for Facts) against whose Records and even the Copies of them there can be no averment. This does not comport with the Genius and Spirit either of our Constitutions or our Laws, both of which secure to every Inhabitant and Citizen the inestimable Priviledge of offering in our Tribunals every Species of legal Evidence that may tend to elucidate the Merits of the Cause before them. –

But this is not the only Objection to which this Article is liable – one much more interesting is obvious. –

Where such Certificates appear the Person named in them is not to lose *for any Cause whatever* the Quality of Subject – so that even legal Naturalization is not to operate as a Cause. –

That this is the true Construction of that Clause is evident from its expressly referring to the 11$^{th.}$ Article of the Treaty, and declaring that it shall serve as *an Interpretation* thereof – Let us recur to that Article.

After stating the Priviledges which Persons of the two Nations shall enjoy in each others Country, it thus proceeds "But it is at the same Time agreed that its Contents shall not affect the Laws made or *that may be made hereafter in France* against Emigrations, which shall remain in all their Force and Vigour – And the United States on their Part, or any of them, shall be at Liberty to enact such Laws relative to that Matter, as to them shall seem proper." –

Now let us collect into one Point of View the different Parts of the System, from their dispersed Situation in the Treaty and in the Articles of this Convention, and see how it will operate –

The King has a Right to make what Laws he may think proper respecting Navigation and Emigration. –

Suppose a Law directing that every Passenger shall on his Arrival in America immediately report himself to the Consul or Vice Consul nearest the Place of his Arrival, to the End that his Name & Description be entered in the Consular Registers. –

The 10$^{th.}$ Article of the Convention declares that they shall cause to be executed the respective Laws, Ordinances and Rules concerning Navigation, on board the said Vessels – and that they may cause every Passenger to be arrested. –

Hence it will happen that every Passenger will be noted and described in their Books before such Passenger can obtain Naturalization – and if he should afterwards obtain it, the 14$^{th.}$ Article renders it avoidable by ordaining that "they who shall prove that they belong to the Body of their respective Nations by the Certificate of the Consul or Vice Consul of the District, mentioning their Names, Surnames and Place of their Settlement *as inscribed in the Registers of the Consulate*, shall not lose, *for any Cause whatever* in the respective States and Domains *the Quality of Subjects of the Country of which they originally were*" – and the same Article proceeds to declare, what is really not the Fact, that this is conformable to the 11$^{th.}$ Article of the Treaty; and as if conscious that the said Article does not admit of such Construction, it adds that it shall serve as an Interpretation of it – that is, that it shall be so construed in future. That 11$^{th.}$ Article does no more than declare the Right of the King to make what Laws he pleases against Emigration, but there is nothing in it which says or seems to say, that his Subjects producing the beforementioned Certificates *shall not for any Cause whatever lose that Quality* in our Country. –

Although the true Policy of America does not require, but on the contrary militates against such Conventions, and although your Secretary is of Opinion, that the Convention as it now stands ought not to be ratified, Yet as Congress have proceeded so far in the present Instance, he thinks that Instructions should be sent to their Minister at Versailles to state their Objections to the present Form, and to assure the King of the Readiness of Congress to ratify a Convention made agreeable to the Scheme beforementioned provided an Article be added to limit its Duration to eight or ten Years, in order that Practice and Experience may enable them to judge more accurately of its Merits, than can ever be done of mere theoretical Establishments however apparently expedient. –

All which is submitted to the Wisdom of Congress –

John Jay –

Read 6 July 1785
Wednesday 13 assessed for consideration
July 10. 1786 Referred back to the Secretary for foreign Affairs to report

NA: PCC, item 81, v. 1, pp. 275-304 (DS); M247, reel 107.
^{1} *which shall be there found established*

Louis Guillaume Otto to Comte de Vergennes

[Translation]

N⁰· 5.

New York, 6 September 1785.

My Lord.

We have had, M. de Marbois and I, a confidential talk with a Delegate who unburdened himself to us with much frankness on several points, of which it is my duty to render You an account.

We thought we should broach the matter of the ratification of the convention. We led him to it by communicating to him the draft of the Convention, Mr. Jay's principal observation on which rings false. We told him: "that it was a pity that not one of the Delegates with whom M. le Chevalier de la Luzerne had discussed this affair was in Congress, that this Minister had never sought to conceal from Congress that the convention was more favorable to us in some respects than it was to the Americans, although all its stipulations are perfectly reciprocal, that Congress in according us slight advantages had intended to show the King that the United States did not wish to increase their population at the expense of ours and that they also desired to help us introduce order among our Merchants in order to counterbalance as much as possible the advantages without number that the nature of things gives the English over us; that to refuse ratification of a convention was not, as Mr. Jay observes, a thing that should be taken lightly, especially if one considers that the draft agreed upon by Congress dates from the period in which the distresses of the United States were extreme, and which they refuse when they are fully at peace and think they no longer have need of us."

Moreover, Congress has hitherto neither adopted nor rejected Mr. Jay's report, and that is how this Assembly gets out of embarrassing difficulties; but I have observed that the 16ᵗʰ· article of the Convention makes mention of the exchange of ratifications, and that decency requires that they see to this subject or that reasons for not doing so be given. The Delegate to whom we spoke told us: "that he thinks it safer to defer until the next Congress, which will take this up again this November, that then Mr. Gerry of Massachusetts, one of the most active opponents, will leave Congress, and that this Assembly will then view the drawbacks of its refusal in a calmer manner, that Mr. Jay's report will not be adopted lightly, that this Minister, in whom much ability cannot be denied, nevertheless allows himself to be drawn into the party of the East, that he wishes to acquire popularity by proving himself the most zealous partisan of Democracy and the declared Enemy of all foreign influence, that nonetheless an inclination toward England is perceived on his part, which has been disagreeable to several delegations, and that his reports have not always been received as he might wish. "

I think, My Lord, that there will indeed be some change in Congress this November; but Mr. King,[1] another Delegate from Massachusetts, will remain there and will probably have a colleague as ill-disposed as he. The Delegation from Massachusetts or, more accurately, several prominent persons in office in that State and in the three neighboring States, have received the most erroneous representations in our regard from Mr. John Adams. He applies himself even in his Despatches to Congress to balance the services that we have rendered to the United States by an exaggerated exposition of the advantages that the revolution procures us; as a rule, he gives an account *by profits and losses*, and he concludes from this that it is we who thereby gain the most. It is certain that these constant efforts to deprecate us must produce their effect on an assembly which receives the opinions that it adopts concerning the various powers with which it deals principally from its Ministers in Europe. We cannot counteract them because we do not always know what they are writing and because we would not have great success in speaking in praise of ourselves, that moreover even the better-disposed Delegates do not, as a rule, have the right to respond to the artful insinuations of Mr. Adams with a speech when it is not a question of passing a resolution. Thus, My Lord, the surest means I know to destroy these false impressions would be that Mr. Jefferson be apprised in some indirect manner of what is happening here, and his reports be the Antidote to those of Mr. Adams. One could also take the position of abandoning these people to themselves, but I have no need to explain to You all the disadvantages of that system; the Americans owe us a great deal, and some would be very glad to find a reason not to pay us in our negligence; but what is more important still is that the Americans, in spite of their remoteness from Europe, the feebleness of their Government, and the little service we can expect from them, as a power perhaps have from day to day more indirect means to contribute to the prosperity of the Realm in time of peace and the conservation of our distant possessions in time of war. I therefore think it proper for us to humor them in large part, and if they neglect their own interests by neglecting us, we should treat them, if it is permitted for me to say so, as a wise teacher treats indocile and capricious children, by recalling them to him by dint of evenness and benevolence. It seems to me that I am only setting forth Your System here, My Lord, but You will at least be able to judge whether I have done it well.

Mr. Jefferson shares the same principles. He is very attached to the alliance. He enjoys an excellent and deserved reputation here, although his resolution is doubted. If he has knowledge of the difference of the two drafts, perhaps he will be able to take advantage of it with Congress to make known the disadvantages of delay of the ratification and to propose that the convention be worded in conformity with the draft communicated to M. le Chevalier de la Luzerne and ratified without delay. It would be embarrassing to press Congress ourselves, for it suffices with people as particular as these to ask them for something earnestly to make them think that he who asks has everything to gain and that they have everything to lose. I think the convention a thing extremely desirable, but we shall be much stronger by having M^r· Jefferson act and by not acting here ourselves except through our friends.

.   .   .   .   .

I am with a profound respect My Lord Your most humble and most obedient servant,   Otto.²

Received 16 Oct^ber·

FFAA: Pol. Corr., U.S., v. 30, f. 270-277 (LC transcription).

¹ King, Rufus (1755-1827). Political figure and diplomat. Delegate, Massachusetts General Court, 1783-1785. Member, Continental Congress, 1784-1787. Delegate, Constitutional Convention, 1787. Moved to New York City, 1788. U.S. Senator, 1789-1796, 1813-1825. U.S. Minister to Great Britain, 1796-1803, 1825-1826. Federalist candidate for Vice President, 1804, 1808. Federalist candidate for President, 1816.

² Otto, Louis Guillaume (1754-1817). French diplomat. Secretary to the Chevalier de la Luzerne, 1779-1784. Chargé d'affaires in the United States, August 1785-January 1788, October 1789-July 1791.

Louis Guillaume Otto to Comte de Vergennes

[Translation]

N^o· 22.   Philadelphia, 18 November 1785.

My Lord.

Mr. Franklin¹ having been unanimously elected President of the State of Pennsylvania, he has taken possession of his office, and the first messages that he has addressed to the general assembly have confirmed the public in the high opinion that it had conceived of his patriotism and his competence. The numerous affairs with which he is occupied render him a little less communicative than he had been previously, but the various conversations that I have had with him leave me no doubt concerning the sincerity of his attachment for France. I thought I should speak to him regarding the non-ratification of the convention for the establishment of Consulates; he appeared much astonished by it, and he assured me that he had never heard in this regard the least objection on the part of Congress, that the convention had conformed entirely to the draft which that

Assembly had sent him, with few changes directed only toward subjects of little importance, that moreover he was persuaded that when Congress had examined this business more particularly, it would make no difficulty in ratifying a convention which it had approved in draft. I have, My Lord, no instruction on this matter, I even left Versailles without knowing that there was a signed convention, I cannot speak of it to Mr. Jay, since he must not know that we have communication of his report, and I am pained not to be able to take a step to regulate an affair that is of the greatest importance for the safety of our Commerce and of our Consular establishments in America.

. . . . . .

I have received by a merchant Vessel, My Lord, the duplicate of a letter that you wrote to M. de Marbois,[2] to recommend to him a draft of a Treaty between M. d'Ogny[3] and the Director of the American post offices. I shall not fail to communicate this draft to Congress as soon as the States are assembled, and it does not appear to me that the stipulations which it contains can in any way displease the Americans. M. d'Ogny's eagerness to conclude this treaty as soon as possible is all the more justified, since it becomes more important from day to day to multiply the channels of communication between the two nations. I have learned with much regret, My Lord, that the packet boats have received orders to sail henceforth only every two months, and that the delay of the Courier we have long expected is due to this innovation. This arrangement, which from an economic point of view may appear advantageous, is essentially prejudicial to the political connection and to that of Commerce. Henceforth, to our packet boats will be preferred those of England and merchant Vessels, and communication will become so much the more irregular because the English will always be capable of intercepting our letters and of retaining those that appear to them too favorable to our connections with America. It appears moreover by the second article of M. d'Ogny's draft that the intention of the Court is to dispatch packet boats every month; this incongruity between the orders that appear to have been given at L'Orient and the words of the treaty would have persuaded me to delay the communication of this treaty if I did not have reason to hope that my representations, joined to the report that M. de la Forest[4] will send to the Department of the Navy, will persuade the Government to change nothing in the old packet boat schedule.

I am with a profound respect My Lord Your most humble and most obedient servant.   Otto.
Received 16 Jan.ʳ 1786.

FFAA: Pol. Corr., U.S., v. 30, f. 413-415vo. (LC transcription).
¹ Franklin arrived in Philadelphia on September 14, 1785.
² Marbois, François Barbé de (1745-1837). French diplomat and statesman. Secretary of legation in the United States, 1779-1785; chargé des affaires, 1784-1785. Consul at Philadelphia, 1781-1784; consul general at Philadelphia, 1784-1785. Intendant of St. Domingue, 1785-1789.
³ Ogny, Claude François Marie Rigoley, Baron d'. French government official. Intendant General of the Post Office.
⁴ Forest, Antoine René Charles Mathurin de la. French Vice Consul, later Consul, at New York.

Louis Guillaume Otto to Comte de Vergennes

[Translation]

Nᵒ· 23.   New York, 28 November 1785.

My Lord

. . . . .

I shall follow with so much the more exactitude, My Lord, the orders that you gave my Predecessor relative to the Frenchmen who are in this country, that they are rather generally bad subjects or at least unfortunate by their own fault. It is essentially necessary that we in no way appear to involve ourselves in the domestic affairs of the United States; they are very jealous of their rights, and even in the least important things they fear yielding to foreign authority. M. de la Forest and I are so impressed by this verity that we avoid with the greatest care everything that might induce a discussion of Consular prerogatives and other distinctions commonly accorded in Europe to members of the diplomatic corps. In America there are few Frenchmen who merit being protected, and these comport themselves so well and are so circumspect in their transactions that they have no need of any support. Moreover, I shall never refuse my assistance to Frenchmen who truly need it, and in that case I shall be all the more sure of succeeding, since my requests will be founded on the natural equity that should form the basis of all the Codes, and since I shall only employ the influence given me by my office to aid those who are worthy of it.

. . . . .

Your opinion, My Lord, of Mr. Jay's report relative to the convention is that which every impartial person should have. Dr. Franklin finds Mr. Jay's objections so superficial that he does not think them even worthy to be the subject of a negotiation. It is not the same with this Minister's general observations on the service which the Consular establishments and the convention can be to the United States. It would be difficult to respond to it in a satisfactory manner if this question were not at this moment out of place. It is no longer a question of knowing whether the Americans should make a convention, since Congress has approved the draft of it, but it is necessary to limit oneself to investigating whether the changes that were made in it in France are sufficiently important to warrant Congress to refuse ratification of it, and that is the weak point in Mr. Jay's reasonings, which appear dictated more by animosity than by justice.

.   .   .   .   .

Mr. Temple[1] arrived here several days ago, My Lord, with the title of Consul General of the British Court. He is the same one who played a role not very agreeable to the Americans during the war, although he was himself born in New England. The public in general has received him with much distinction, and everyone appears to be pleased to see a public officer charged to treat with the Americans in the name of the King of England finally arrive. But Congress is not a little embarassed by the conduct that it should hold on his account, and several members of this assembly do not know what kind of reception to give to a Consul whose sovereign has made no treaty of Commerce with the United States. Mr. Temple has been announced in the public papers with much emphasis, his friends take care to give out that he will live with all the pomp of a Minister Plenipotentiary and that, independently of his own fortune, he will spend annually 4,000 Louis that the King of England has accorded him. These reports make an impression on many persons who had at first viewed him with indifference; the Americans allow themselves to be easily dazzled by display, and if Mr. Temple has the means he is supposed to have, he will soon cause his previous conduct and the declamations the Gazettes contain against him to be forgotten. Moreover, he has the advantage of being the son-in-law of the present Governor of Massachussetts, a man of much influence, who will not fail to support him on all occasions.

This circumstance, My Lord, leads me to observe in general that it is important that His Majesty's Minister in America make a great expenditure. In the seven years that I have known the Americans, I have seen that they are very susceptible to judging the representatives of foreign nations according to the ostentation they display in their residences. Although the work of M. Gerard and of M. le Chevalier de la Luzerne has been of the greatest utility to the Americans, they subsist almost as much from their dinners as from their services, and it is only after having *toasted* well that one succeeds here in inviting a confidential conversation and in inspiring good dispositions. M. le Chevalier d'Annencour,[2] one of our Consuls who has best succeeded in America, has made himself a rule to propose nothing to the Leaders of the State of Maryland until after a long meal, and he has almost always obtained what he has asked for. I hope, My Lord, that you

will excuse these minute details, by considering that all that serves to paint
the character of the nation in which I reside should necessarily enter into
my reports.

I am with a profound respect My Lord Your most humble and most
obedient servant   Otto.
Recd 17 Jany 1786.

FFAA: Pol. Corr., U.S., v. 30, f. 425-428vo. (LC transcription).
^{1} Temple, Sir John (1731-1798). British colonial and consular official. Surveyor of
customs at Boston before 1771, when he emigrated to England. Loyalist, married to a
daughter of James Bowdoin. After obtaining a weak letter of recommendation from John
Adams, returned to America, 1781. British consul general at New York, 1785-1798.
^{2} Annemours (Anmours), Charles François, Chevalier d'. French government official.
Consul for Virginia and Maryland, resident in Baltimore, 1779-1791.

John Jay's Report on American Prisoners in Algiers

[New York] Office for foreign Affairs 2^d January 1786
The Secretary of the United States for the Department of foreign
Affairs to whom was referred a Letter to his Excell^y the President
dated 28th August 1785 from Richard OBryen[1] and others in
Captivity at Algiers; which Letter was transmitted enclosed in one
from James Wilkie[2] of Marseilles – Reports
   That this Letter states, that the Ship *Dauphin* Richard OBryen Master of
Philadelphia, bound from St Ubes was taken the 30th July last, having
fifteen Souls on Board.
   That the Schooner *Maria* Capt: Isaac Stephens[3] Master of Boston, bound
from that Place to Cadiz, was taken the 27th July last having six Persons on
board. –
   That they were carried to Algiers, and sent to work at the King's Places,
in a destitute Condition, and there kept to Labour with very scanty
Allowance of Provisions. –
   That Charles Logie Esquire[4] the british Consul there, afterwards took
them to his House, on becoming responsible for them at the Rate of 600£
Stel^g a Man, and engaging to pay monthly two Dollars for each of them to
the King. –
   Your Secretary is of Opinion that a Copy of this Letter should be sent to
the American Ministers charged with negociating Peace with the Barbary
Powers,[5] with orders to provide for the Redemption of these and all other
Americans detained there in Captivity, in the most speedy and least

expensive Manner, which the State of their Negociations and other Circumstances may admit. –

Your Secretary is further of Opinion that the American Minister at the Court of London be directed to signify to his britannic Majesty the Sense they entertain of the Humanity and Generosity of his Consul Charles Logie Esquire – That he also write a Letter to Mr Logie and inform him that the United States are exceedingly pleased with his Conduct, and will immediately provide for the Reimbursement of the Expences incurred by his Generosity to their captive Citizens – That he also make further Enquiries concerning the friendly and liberal Behaviour of Mr Logie, and transmit the Result of them to your Secretary without Delay. –

Your Secretary further Reports that in his Opinion it will be necessary to provide in Season, for supplying the Ministers directed to treat with the Powers in Question, with further Funds, it appearing very doubtful whether the Sum granted to them will be adequate to the Attainment of the Objects of those Negociations, especially as the Expence of purchasing Peace will naturally be enhanced by the Number and Value of the Captives to be liberated. –

All which is submitted to the Wisdom of Congress. –

John Jay

NA: PCC, item 81, v. 2, pp. 8-10 (LS); M247, reel 107.

[1] O'Bryen, Richard (1758-1824). American seafarer and consular representative. As master of the Philadelphia-owned merchant vessel Dauphin, captured by Algerine pirates, 30 July 1785. Conducted extensive correspondence with American officials, including John Adams and Thomas Jefferson, during his captivity, which lasted until September 1795. Assisted in negotiating and implementing the peace treaty with Algiers, 1795-1796. Concluded peace treaty with Tripoli, 1796. U.S. Consul General at Algiers, 1797-1803. Aided Commodore Preble in negotiations with Tripoli, 1803-1804. Changed spelling of name to O'Brien late in life.

[2] Wilkie, James. English merchant who represented the Turkey Company at Marseilles in the 1780s.

[3] Stephens, Isaac. American seafarer. As master of the Boston-owned schooner Maria, captured by Algerine pirates, 27 July 1785. Associated with Richard O'Bryen in correspondence with American officials. Released March 1796, after peace made with Algiers.

[4] Logie, Charles. British Consul at Algiers, ca. 1785-1793.

[5] Morocco and the Regencies of Algiers, Tunis, and Tripoli. The four states that controlled the North African coast from Egypt through the Straits of Gibraltar, also called the Barbary States or Powers, were nominally provinces within the Ottoman Empire. In practice, their locally-chosen rulers, the Emperor of Morocco, the Dey of Algiers, the Bey of Tunis, and the Pasha of Tripoli, while honoring the Sultan as head of their religion, for the most part pursued independent courses of action, declaring war, making peace and making treaties without obtaining the consent of Constantinople.

Thomas Jefferson to John Jay

Sir   Paris, January 2. 1786.
Several Conferences & Letters having passed between the Count de
Vergennes & myself on the Subject of the Commerce of this Country with
the U.S. I think them sufficiently interesting to be communicated to
Congress. They are stated in the Form of a Report & are herein inclosed....

.   .   .   .   .

I communicated to the Count de Vergennes according to your
Commands the Report of Capt Shaw's[1] Voiage to China, making at the
same Time those Acknolegements which were due for these new Proofs of
the Friendship of the French Nation towards us. I inclose you my Letter &
his answer, whereby you will see that he thought it a proper Occasion to
express the Dissatisfaction of this Court with the Acts of some of the
American Legislatures on the Subject of foreign Commerce, & to hint that
their Continuance would render Measures necessary here to countervail the
Inequalities they supposed us to be establishing. I also inclose my Reply, &
have now the Honor to submit those Transactions to the Consideration of
Congress, who are best able to calculate the Result of such a commercial
Contest, should it arise, & who will be so good as to instruct me as to their
Pleasure herein, as an Answer will be expected by this Court, within such
Time as they think reasonable....

.   .   .   .   .   .

When m^r Barclay was on the Point of setting out for Marocco, m^r
Beaumarchais[2] (who had hitherto declined settling with him) tendered him
a Settlement of his Accounts. The immense Amount of these Accounts,
with the Hope that they would not occupy much Time, and a Persuasion
that no Man on Earth could so well settle them as m^r Barclay, who is
intimately acquainted with many of the Transactions on which they are
founded, induced me to think the Interests of the U.S. would not suffer so
much by a short Delay of the Journey to Marocco, from whence nothing
disagreeable was to be immediately apprehended, as they would suffer by
leaving such Accounts as these to be settled by Persons less competent: I
advised m^r Barclay to proceed to the Settlement. I wrote to m^r Adams
asking his opinion thereon, & to m^r Carmichael[3] praying him to find
Means of making known to the Emperor of Marocco that a Negociator was
actually commissioned and would soon proceed to his Court. m^r Adams
concurred with me in Opinion, and those Accounts are now in such
Forwardness that m^r Barclay assures me he shall be able to set out the
ensuing Week. I inclose two Letters from Capt. Stevens one of our Captives

at Algiers to m^r· Harrison[4] of Cadiz, which were forwarded to me by m^r· Charmichael.

I have taken Opportunities of speaking with the Che^{vr}· de la Luzerne on the Subject of his Return to America, & to press it by all those Inducements which Assurances of the Esteem entertained for him there were likely to excite. He told me there was no Place he would prefer to America for the Exercise of his Functions, but he said with great Candor, that as in the diplomatic Line there are different Grades of Emploiment, & that an Advancement from one to the other of these was usual, he wished if possible to avail himself of < * > present Circumstances to obtain a Promotion. I suppose in Fact that if he can be sent to London in the Room of the Count d'Adhemar,[5] or to Holland in the Room of the Marquis de Verac,[6] who wishes to be translated to London, as these are Embassies, he will not in either of those Cases return to America. In the mean Time the Emoluments of his Office are, as I suspect, rendered necessary to him by the Expences he incurred in America.

· · · · ·

...I am Sir, your most obedient & most humble Servant

Thomas Jefferson

LC: *Jefferson Papers, microfilm reel 5 (press copy).*

[1] *Shaw, Samuel (1754-1794). Massachusetts military figure, merchant and consul. Artillery officer, aide-de-camp to General Henry Knox. Supercargo of the Empress of China, the first United States ship to trade at Canton, China, 1784-1785. Named U.S. Consul at Canton, 1786.*

[2] *Beaumarchais, Pierre-Augustin Caron de (1732-1799). French playwright, adventurer and government agent. A commoner who married well, Beaumarchais gained entry to French court circles as music teacher of Louis XV's daughters. His business sense made him several fortunes. Author, The Barber of Seville and The Marriage of Figaro. Served as secret agent in Austria and Great Britain. Organized the clandestine shipment of munitions and supplies to the American rebels, 1776-1778. Lost money on an edition of Voltaire's works, 1784-1790, and in selling Dutch muskets to France's revolutionary armies, 1792. Considered an emigré for a time, but returned to France.*

[3] *Carmichael, William (?-1795). Diplomat. Secretary to the American commissioners in France, 1777-1778. Member, Continental Congress, 1778-1779, from Maryland. Secretary of legation to John Jay in Spain, 1780-1782. Chargé d'affaires ad interim in Madrid, 1782-1790; en titre, 1790-1794.*

[4] *Harrison, Richard Hanson (1750-1841). Maryland merchant. With Richard Hooe, proprietor of Hooe and Harrison of Alexandria, Virginia. Proprietor of Harrison and Company, which represented Hooe and Harrison, at Cadiz, 1780-1791. Unofficial American agent at Cadiz, 1780-1791. Appointed U.S. Consul at Cadiz, June 1790, but declined appointment, January 1791. Auditor of the U.S. Treasury, 1791-1836.*

[5] *Adhémar, Jean Balthazar d'Azémar de Montfalcon, Comte d'. French diplomat. Ambassador to Great Britain, 1783-1787.*

[6] Vérac, Charles Olivier de Saint Georges, Marquis de (1743-1828). French diplomat. Minister to Russia, 1780-1783. Ambassador to the United Provinces of the Netherlands, 1785-1787.

John Jay to John Adams

Sir,   [New York] Office for foreign Affairs 2[d.] January 1786. I have the Honor of transmitting to you herewith inclosed a Copy of a Letter of the 21[st.] December from M[r.] Temple to me, which I laid before Congress. They have been pleased to direct that you communicate it to His Britannic Majesty – That you inform him, that the Complaint stated in it, being in general Terms, and unsupported by any particular Facts or Evidence, they do not think it necessary, or proper, to take any Measures in Con-sequence of it. And that you assure him, that as it is their determination the Treaty of Peace shall be punctually observed by their Citizens, and that His Majesty's Subjects shall enjoy here all the Rights which friendly and civilized Nations Claim from each other; so they will always be ready to hear every Complaint which may appear to be well founded, and to Redress such of them, as, on Investigation, shall prove to be so.

This Communication will give you an Opportunity of Remarking, that the Office of Consul General does not extend to Matters of this Kind – Neither the Rights of Commerce, nor of Navigation being in question, and therefore that it was Delicacy towards his Majesty, rather than a Sense of the propriety of such an Application from a Consul General, which induced Congress to treat it with this Mark of Attention.

It would perhaps be well to pursue the Subject, to intimate the Expediency, as well as Propriety, of sending a Minister here, and if Circumstances should so dictate, to accompany it with assurances that Congress expect a Minister and are ready to receive and treat him in a Manner consistent with the Respect due to his Sovereign.

The advantage alluded to in one of your Letters, if no other, would result from such an Appointment, viz: – That the British Court would then probably receive more accurate Representations of Affairs in this Country, than they are at present supplied with by Men, who Write and Speak more as their Wishes and Feelings, than as Truth and Knowledge dictate. –

I have the Honor to be, with great Respect, Sir, Your most obedient, and Very humble Servant,   John Jay –

· · · · · ·

Massachusetts Historical Society, hereafter cited as MHS: The Adams Papers, microfilm reel 367 (LS).

Sir John Temple to Lord Carmarthen

My Lord[1]   New York 5th of Jan: 1786.
I had the honor of writing to your Lordship on the seventh of last Month by the Halifax Packet, which saild the day after for Falmouth; since which, Nothing material or worthy your Lordships Notice hath occurrd in these states; except, that two more ships, of considerable burden, are now fitting out at Philadelphia for the East Indias, & will probably sail in about a Month. I know not what effect such adventurers to the East may have upon our East India Company's trade, but it is my duty to inform your Lordship of such enterprises as fast as they come to my knowledge.

The Trade & Navigation of these states appear to me to be now, in a great measure at a stand: the exclusion of their ships & Vessells from his Majestys Sugar Islands greatly deranged & decreased what commerce they had been accustomed to; and, a dread of the Barbary Rovers hath of late, struck a Palsey into what remained of their Trade to Spain Portugal & the Mediteranian: The Mercantile part of the people, in consequence thereof, begin to have their Eyes open to what they ought to have seen (rather than have indulged intoxication from their independance) immediately upon the restoration of Peace to their Country: "That Great Britain hath undoubtedly many commercial favors, to grant if she pleases to these states, while they, in return, have scarce a single favor or advantage to offer: The Vast debt owing to the British Merchants who unwisely gave too much Credit, together with high taxes, Poverty, and other concuring circumstances, have been the means of bring[ing] the Commercial part of these states in some measure to their reason; but, the landed people, still continue to hold high notions of "their rising importance among the Nations of the Earth," and talk seriously of entering into alliance *offensive & defensive* with france, upon condition that they be protected by the Sword or otherwise, from the depredations of Barbary Cruizers; and this, I beleive france with much Art & address, is now laboring to bring about with Congress! and, perhaps at the same time, are stimulating the Algerines in order to hasten on such a Treaty: from what hath been communicated to me, I apprehend there to be too much foundation for what I have thus written: & some of the best of the people, and of the most property here, seem pensive & thoughtfull upon the Occasion, justly apprehensive of the most banefull consequences to their country from such an Accursed alliance.

I have received a Letter from the Commissioners appointed to investigate the claims of the American loyalists, requesting that I would send them, compleat setts of all the Public Acts & laws in the several states of

America respecting the Persons & Property of the said Loyalists, which I shall do as soon as possible: The distance of many of the states from New York where I reside, with the present severe season of the Year, renders it impracticable for it to be done before the Spring: in the meantime, I have made application to the Congress's Secretary for foreign affairs, that the said Loyalists or their proper Attorneys, may have Access to all Public Records in these states, as expressed in my letter to him of the 21st ultimo: Copy of which, together with his Answer this instant received, I take the liberty of enclosing to your Lordship.

I have met with all due respect & Attention from Congress; & from the Government of this particular State, as well as unbounded civility from the Ministers residing here from foreign Courts; with the latter, I cannot however pretend to keep pace, in the expences of a Table &c$^{a.}$ Most of the Congress have already dined with me; &, upon her Majestys approaching Birthday, I purpose to have them all; together with the foreign Ministers, Consuls, &c^{a}: –

With the highest Ambition to merit your Lordships Approbation of my Conduct in office, I have the honor to be, my Lord, Your Lordships most faithfull, and Obedient Servant,   J. Temple.

R. 2$^{d.}$ Febry

British Public Record Office: Foreign Office Files, hereafter cited as PRO: FO 4/4, pp. 3-6
(LC transcription).
  [1] *Carmarthen, Francis Osborne, Marquess of (1751-1799). British political figure. Opponent of Lord North's Ministry. Appointed ambassador to Paris, February 1783, but did not serve, resigning upon the fall of Shelburne's administration. Secretary of State for the Foreign Department in Pitt's Ministry, 1783-1791. From March 1789, Duke of Leeds.*

Louis Guillaume Otto to Comte de Vergennes

[Translation]

N$^{o.}$ 32.   New York, 10 January 1786.

My Lord

Mr. Jay's political importance increases every day. Congress appears to govern itself only by his impulses, and it is as difficult to obtain anything without the concurrence of this minister as to have a measure that he has proposed rejected. The indolence of most of the members of Congress and the ignorance of some others occasion this Superiority. It is much more convenient to ask the opinion of the minister of foreign affairs regarding all current business than to resolve themselves into a Committee, so that Mr. Jay's prejudices and passions insensibly become those of Congress, and that without being aware of it this Assembly is no more than the instrument of its first Minister. Happily Mr. Jay is a patriot and generally well disposed, but his grievances against France render him highly inflexible regarding our most just requests. I have already had the honor to inform you that neither M. de Marbois nor I have received any response to the various memoranda that we have delivered for nearly a year. This minister always tells me that Congress is too busy to take them into consideration, but I know that this Assembly has not had anything very important to decide for a long time, and that these delays are due only to the ill will of Mr. Jay. I would not complain, My Lord, if I did not have reason to fear that the long silence of Congress may be attributed to my inactivity, but I am pained to see that for the simplest things, and what requires only two hours of discussion, this minister has put off responding for several months. Such is among others the Treaty proposed by M. le Baron d'Ogny. I have not yet obtained any response on this Subject, and I cannot importune Mr. Jay since his response is always ready; it is to say that he will seize the first occasion to bring this affair to the attention of Congress. Besides, this Minister has the character, for which the Quakers are reproached, of never responding directly to any question that is put to him. As he never makes his opinion known, it is impossible to rectify it, and although it may be he who inspires most of the resolutions of Congress, he always has the air of referring to this assembly for all the clarifications that are asked of him. It is very troublesome for us, My Lord, that for so important a position, the choice of Congress has justly fallen on a man who does not like us. The article of the fisheries is always on his mind, and it is impossible to make him see reason regarding a subject on which we have not really been prejudicial to the United States. Besides, whatever this minister's prejudices may be in our regard, I cannot deny that there are few men in America more able to fill the position that he occupies. The veneration that he has inspired in almost all members of Congress proves more than anything else that even the jealousy so inseparable from the American character has not found a hold on him, and that he is as circumspect in his conduct as he is firm and unshakeable in his political principles and in his coldness for France.

I have been aware for two months, My Lord, that the delegates from Massachusetts were beginning to draw nearer to me and to make demonstrations of amity towards me of which it was impossible for me to see the cause. The new delegates recently arrived have gone still further than their predecessors, and have not ceased to tell me with affection that the sentiments of their State towards France were always the same, and that they feared that our Court may have been given unfavorable impressions in their regard. I thought I should investigate the causes of this change, and having seized a moment when wine had gone to the Head of Mr. Gerry, one of the principal members of this Delegation, who has always played the primary role after the Adamses, I had no difficulty in rendering him communicative. He began by reminding me of the intercepted letters of M. de Marbois; we know very well, he told me, that his System with regard to the fisheries has never been that of your Court, but this circumstance has considerably diminished the popularity of that chargé d'affaires. All the difficulties that he has experienced since were personal to him, and in no way proceeded from a coldness of the Americans for France. However, we are not unaware that we have been portrayed in France in a very unfavorable manner, and we sincerely desire that your Court be disabused in that regard. I had no difficulty, My Lord, in recognizing in this conversation the malignity of M. de Marbois' Enemies in wishing to render him responsible for all the negotiations that have not succeeded; but what strikes me most is that it appears that the delegates from Massachusetts have been informed of the complaints that this chargé d'affaires has brought against them in his despatches, and that they are seeking to reestablish good relations by blaming everything on my predecessor. I do not understand how they could have been informed of his Sentiments in their regard, unless you have spoken of them to Mr. Jefferson, and that Minister has written about it to his constituents. Moreover, I am very pleased to see the confidence between this delegation and our Court reborn. Massachusetts will long play the principal role in the National Council; it is always represented by 4 or 5 delegates, all men of Merit and Hard-Working, while the other States are rarely represented by two. This State is distinguished besides by its inviolable attachment to fixed principles that it never abandons, and by dint of constancy and resolution, it is always sure of succeeding. It has the advantage of setting the rule, so to speak, in New Hampshire, Rhode Island, and Connecticut, and these 4 States, almost always in accord, rarely miss carrying all the votes. As for M. de Marbois, I can only repeat what I have already had the honor of writing you. All impartial persons have only one opinion with regard to him. His great merit, his attachment for the United States, his assiduity, and especially his equitable Sentiments and his remoteness from every kind of party have won him the respect and consideration of all Americans capable of judging without prejudice.

I am with a profound respect My Lord, Your most humble and most obedient servant   Otto.

FFAA: Pol. Corr., U.S., v. 31, f. 19-28 (LC transcription).

James Bowdoin to John Adams

Sir,   Boston January 12th 1786
 I am honored by your Excellency's Letter of the 2^{d} of Sept. by Mr Storer.
 The navigation Act of Massachusetts having been found to militate with the french treaty of commerce, & to exclude our fish from the Levant by excluding the Subjects of the italian & other States coming with their Vessels for it, when our own in attempting to carry it to them would be intercepted by the Algerines, it was judged expedient to repeal it in part: so that it now operates in full force, only against the Subjects of great Britain & their property. A Copy of the repealing Act will be sent to you, & also of an Act passed by the Legislature of Rhode Island at their last Session –
 I have transmitted copies of our repealing Act to the Executives of the Several States, & warmly urged a Similitude of measures, without which the United States cannot hope to bring about an alteration in the commercial System of Britain –
 That System, in my idea of it, is clearly opposed to her own interest considered in all its parts, & in a complex view of it. It is very true, their encouragement of their whale fishery, by suffering the alien duty on oil to depress ours, will encrease their Shipping in this branch, encrease their Seamen, & in several other ways be advantageous to them. To a person, that looks no further, it would appear, that this was good policy, & the goodness of it would be inferred from the advantages arising. But when he should extend his view, & see how that Stoppage of the American whale fishery, by depriving the Americans of so capital a mean of paying for the woolen Goods they used to take of Britain, must at the same time occasion the American demand to cease or be proportionately diminished, not to mention the risk of a change or deviation of the trade from the old channel, he will calculate the national profit & loss, that arises from that Stoppage –
 3000 tons of oil was the usual annual quantity produced by the Whalemen at Nantucket: all of which was Shipped to England at an average price of 35£ p[er] ton making about......£105,000 St$^{g.}$
The whole of which went to pay for & purchase a like amount of woolens & other british goods: nine tenths of the value of which are computed to arise from the labor of the manufacturer, & to be so much clear gain to the nation: the other tenth therefore being deducted gives the national gain arising from the industry of the Nantucket Whalemen, & the

American capital employed in that business: viz. £94,500.......... £10,500
                                                                        £94,500
without the nation's paying a shilling for the risk of insurance or any other risk whatever.

On the change of trade, pursuant to the new regulations, the british Merchants must employ a large capital in the Whale fishery, whose products we will Suppose, equal to that of the Nantucket....£105,000 St^{g.}

They will have made an exceeding good voyage if the whole of that Sum Should be equal to one half of the cost of the outfits: though from many of the vessels not meeting with Fish, & from a variety of accidents, to which such a voyage is Subject, it probably would not be a quarter. The whole of the product goes towards payment of the outfits & charges of the voyage, & a large Sum must be advanced for the Second Voyage &c. –

Now altho' this mode of commerce would be productive of some national benefits, yet considered in a comparative view with the benefits resulting from the former mode they would be found of little importance.

A like comparison may be made with other branches of commerce, particularly the british West Indian, & the result will be found the same: For the sake then of gaining pence & farthings, Britain is sacrificing Pounds by her new regulations of Trade. – She has a right to see for herself: but unhappily, resentment & the consequent prejudices have so much disordered her Powers of vision, that it requires the Skilful hand of a good political optician, to remove the obstructing films. If she will not permit the application of your couching instruments, or if applied they can work no effect, the old lady must be left to her fate, & abandoned as incurable. –

But it is to be hoped, not so much on her account as our own, that they may be successful. – One ground of hope is that private negotiation, which Mr Nathl. Barrett[1] is gone to France to perfect & execute, relative to their taking our whale oil duty free, & in lieu of it giving at an agreed rate, according to their quality, such french manufactures as are best Suited to our market: excepting a certain proportion of the oil, which must be paid for by bills of exchange, to raise money for the men engaged in the voyage. – About two months ago, Mr Barrett sailed for France, with letters for Mr Jefferson & the Marquis de la Fayette, & if he succeeds, a great revolution in trade will probably be the consequence: & France, on the principle of reciprocal benefit, exclude Britain from all trade with America. This appears to me so probable, that, if you could impress the british Ministry with the same idea, you would find little difficulty to bring about a commercial treaty with them, perfectly agreeable to your own mind, & to the wishes of the United States. An interchange of a few letters on this Subject with Mr Jefferson would give you the present State of the negociation. –

With the most perfect regard, I have the Honor to be, Sir, Your Excellency's Most Obed.ᵗˑ hble Servᵗ   James Bowdoin[2]

Ans.ᵈ May 9. 1786

MHS: *The Adams Papers, microfilm reel 367 (LS).*

[1] *Barrett, Nathaniel. Boston merchant who came to France in late 1785 as the representative of a consortium of Massachusetts merchants who wished to sell American whale oil. He provided Thomas Jefferson with much information on the American whaling industry, and considered applying for the post of consul at Rouen in 1789. He returned to America in 1791.*

[2] *Bowdoin, James (1726-1790). Massachusetts merchant and political figure. Beneficiary of a considerable inheritance, he was elected to the Massachusetts general court in 1753, serving three terms in that body. Member, Massachusetts council, 1757-1774. Recurring health problems caused him to decline positions that required travel, such as election to the Continental Congress. Member, Massachusetts executive council, 1775-1777. President, state constitutional convention, 1779. Governor of Massachusetts, May 1785-April 1787.*

John Jay to Thomas Jefferson

Dʳ Sir, –   New York 19ᵗʰ January 1786
    Since my last of 7ᵗʰ December last and indeed for some Time before that, Congress has been composed of so few States actually represented, as not to have it in their Power to pay that Attention to their foreign Affairs which they would doubtless otherwise have done – Hence it has happened that no Resolutions have been entered into on any of the important Subjects submitted to their Consideration. This obliges me to observe a Degree of Reserve in my Letters respecting those Subjects, which I wish to be free from, but which is nevertheless necessary lest my Sentiments and Opinions should be opposed to those which they may adopt and wish to impress.
    There is Reason to hope that the Requisition will be generally complied with – I say generally, because it is not quite clear, that every State without Exception will make punctual Payments. Although a Disposition prevails to enable Congress to regulate trade, yet I am apprehensive that however the Propriety of the Measure may be admitted, the Manner of doing it will not be with equal Ease agreed to. –
    It is much to be regretted that the Confederation had not been so formed as to exclude the Necessity of all such kind of Questions – it certainly is very imperfect, and I fear it will be difficult to remedy its Defects, until Experience shall render the Necessity of doing it more obvious and pressing.

Does France consider herself bound by her Guarantee to insist on the Surrender of our Posts? Will she second our Remonstrances to Britain on that Head? I have no Orders to ask these Questions but I think them important. Spain insists on the Navigation of the great River, and that renders a Treaty with her uncertain as yet. —

Among the public Papers herewith sent you will find the Speech of the Governor of New York, to the Legislature, and the Answer of the senate — a Spirit more foederal seems to prevail than that which marked their Proceedings last Year. You will also perceive from the Papers that Massachusetts begins to have Troubles similar to those which this State experienced from Vermont. North Carolina suffers the like Evils and from the same Causes. Congress should have recollected the old Maxim *Obsta principiis*.[1]

I wish the Negotiations with the Barbary Powers may prove successful, because our Country in general desires Peace with them — for my part I prefer War to Tribute, and that Sentiment was strongly expressed in my Report on that Subject. —

Our Indian Affairs do not prosper. I fear Britain bids higher than we do. Our Surveys have been checked, and Peace with the Savages seems somewhat precarious — that Department might in my Opinion have been better managed. —

With great and sincere Respect and esteem I have the Honor to be &c: John Jay. —

NA: PCC, item 121, pp. 167-170 (LBkC); M61, reel 1.
  [1] *resist the beginnings; stop it now.*

James Monroe to Thomas Jefferson

Dear Sir   New York Jany. 19. 1786
...It hath been matter of great surprise and concern here that the dispatches respecting the barbary powers should have been so long in reaching you. *This Mr. Lambe*[1] *was presented to some of the gentlemen* in *Congress by the late president Huntington.* At that time it was propos'd, and for which purpose a *report was* brought in, to carry on *these treaties* immediately from *the U.S.* and to *appoint the persons* and *dispatch them hence* to fit out *the* Alliance, *load her with naval stores* and *present her to the Emperor.* By this procedure it was presum'd we might, by telling these *powers that we were as yet unacquainted with them or their wants,* succeed *better than even under the mediation of France.* And the *secretary of foreign affairs having reported that this man was fit for the negotiation, the committee*

advised that *he be employed*. But it was rejected. We have since heard that *he was*, from *his station in life* and probable *talents*, by no means *worthy such a trust*. We have lately heard from Mr. Adams that Mr. Barclay with Franks[2] are sent to the Emperor and that Mr. Lambe and a Mr. Randall[3] to Algiers. *These pirates* have already made *a great impression upon our trade* and *unless these negotiations prove successful will materially injure it.* I am happy to receive your sentiments upon the subject of *commercial treaties* and will with pleasure communicate mine to you more fully than I heretofore have done. With great propriety you have in the first instance taken it up with reference *to the powers of Congress, for upon those does the whole depend* and I entirely agree with you that they have *no original inherent jurisdiction over the commerce of the states* and that it commences and can be exercis'd only *by treaties* with *other nations;* how then will this circumstance affect us? When we propose to them to *form treaties* they will inquire do we labor under any inconveniences which thereby we can remove; they will examine their situation in *our ports* to *ascertain whether treaties* can obtain fairer or more equal terms to them, are these *temporary* or so founded in the nature of *their government that they will be perpetual.* If then it shall appear that *we can give them nothing they* do not at present enjoy, and that we can *not deprive them of these advantages,* I think it will follow they will *lay themselves under no restriction.* It would not otherwise be their interest to do. To obtain *reciprocal advantages* then cannot possibly *be the object with other powers* in *treating* with us, for more than *this they now possess.* But nations are often benefited as much by obtaining *restrictions upon others* in *the ports of* a particular one *which* do not apply *to themselves* as by particular stipulations in *their own favor* and upon this principle *treaties are sometimes* form'd as was the case in that between *Britain and Portugal.* How stand the *powers of the union* and how *their interests* with respect to *a treaty* of this kind? For instance can they *stipulate with France that British goods shall pay ten per cent higher duties here than those of France in consideration for a free trade with her islands; this certainly does not come within the provisos* contained in the *confederation* and is of course within the *powers of Congress.* Nor have I any doubt of its expedience, if it could be obtain'd. *Treaties* of this kind would be more favorable to us and successful, as to the particular objects it might seek, than an entire *prohibition of commerce with the powers with whom we* [have] none. By seeking this *power* it would seem as if we were satisfied with our situation *with those with whom we have treaties,* that those with whom we have not *were culprit nations* and that we would exercise it immediately on them. If then we are dissatisfied with our *treaties* with *France* and *the Netherlands* this right *of prohibition* can never avail us with respect to them. And in its *exercise* upon other *powers* it may give a dangerous shock to our *commerce* and a *monopoly of* it *to other powers,* and if, holding *the power*, we proceeded wisely with it and endeavor'd to turn it to the best account we could and to make it a condition *with France* that we would put it in force *against* [h]er for such or such other considerations, yet could we not obtain the same ends for less expence, for instance for the imposition of *ten per cent* upon her *commerce*. Every expedient is unquestionably inferior to the complete and absolute *controul over commerce in the [hands] of the U.S.* but this *[plan]* of *a treaty* appears to me to be a better succedanium for the defect than any other I have heard, since it creates the restriction we would wish to effect *upon the offending nation* and brings us at the same time upon *the ocean as a commercial people*. They might be of short duration. Those *treaties* which stipulate to each other *the rights of the most favored nation* obtain none of these ends and appear to me to fetter us as to the powers with whom they are made. It fetters us as to the imposition of *higher duties* [on] them than we impose on *others*, or subjects us to a variance, while it admits on their part of a constant deviation from the spirit of *the treaty* by the explication which it authorises th[em] to make of *the compensation*. Nothing hath been done on the subject since my last. In my next I may add something fur[ther] on it. The *commission* will *expire* soon but another may be given or instructions form'd respecting it. I beg you to give me furt[her] your sentiments on it.

.   .   .   .   .

...I am with my best wishes for your health and happiness yr. affectionate friend & servant,   Jas. Monroe

Julian P. Boyd, editor, The Papers of Thomas Jefferson (Princeton University Press, 1950-), v. 9, pp. 186-191.

[1] *Lamb, John. Norwich, Connecticut, sea captain and merchant who served as U.S. agent for the negotiation of a treaty with the Regency of Algiers, 1785-1786. Lamb, who claimed to have five years of commercial experience in the Barbary States, was recommended to Congress by Samuel Huntington and other prominent men of Connecticut, and had the support of Alexander Hamilton and John Jay for his appointment, which was linked to political and financial machinations involving the two remaining ships of the Continental Navy.*

[2] *Franks, David Salisbury (c. 1740-1793). Montreal resident who joined the Continental Army in late 1775, subsequently serving in various capacities, including aide-de-camp to General Benedict Arnold with the rank of lieutenant colonel. After Arnold's defection, Franks sought and received a court of inquiry, which absolved him of any complicity in Arnold's treason. Diplomatic courier, 1781-1784. Vice-Consul at Marseilles, 1784. Assistant to Thomas Barclay in Moroccan treaty negotiations, 1786; carried treaty to the United States, early 1787.*

[3] *Randall, Paul R. Secretary to John Lamb, U.S. agent to negotiate peace with the Regency of Algiers, early 1786.*

John Jay to the President of Congress

Sir[1]   New York 20th January 1786
     As the Attention of american Merchants begins to turn to the China
and India Trade, and several of their Vessels will probably be employed in
it in the Course of this Year; I take the Liberty of submitting to the
Consideration of Congress the Propriety of appointing a Consul and Vice
Consul General for Canton and other Ports in Asia – Such Officers would
have a Degree of Weight and Respect which private Adventurers cannot
readily acquire, and which would enable them to render essential Services
to their Countrymen on various Occasions – more Credit would be given
by Strangers to Men who bring such Evidence of their Merit, than to others
whose Characters cannot be so soon and so certainly known, and their
Commission would give them more ready Access to and greater influence
with Princes, Governors and Magistrates than private Merchants can in
general expect. –
     I have the Honor to be with great Respect Y[r] Excellency's most ob[t.] &
very hble: Serv[t]   John Jay –
Read 23 Jan[y] 1786

NA: PCC, item 80, v. 2, pp. 125-126 (LS); M247, reel 106.
     [1] John Hancock was elected president of Congress on November 23, 1785, but never
served because of illness. He resigned on May 29, 1786. Since Hancock was not present
in Congress at the time of his election, David Ramsay was elected president pro tempore,
also on November 23, 1785. Ramsay continued in that position until the election of
Nathaniel Gorham as president on June 6, 1786.
     Ramsay, David (1749-1815). South Carolina political figure, physician, and historian.
Member, state house of representatives, 1776-1783, 1784-1790. Surgeon to state militia
artillery battalion during siege of Charlestown, 1780; prisoner of war, 1780-1781.
Member, Continental Congress, 1782-1783, 1785-1786; president pro tempore from
November 23, 1785, to June 6, 1786. State senator, 1792-1798; president during those
years. Author of several historical works, including History of the American Revolution,
1789, and Life of George Washington, 1807.

John Adams to John Jay

Dear Sir   Grosvenor Square Jan. 21. 1786
     On Wednesday, the Chevalier De Pinto[1] informed me that he had
written to Lisbon, for Explanations from his Court upon certain Points: that
he expected an Answer, in a few days, and that as soon as he should
receive it, he would call upon me and proceed in the Negotiation. that in

the mean time he would not disguise from me, the Solicitude of his Court to Send a Minister, to Congress. Ettiquette forbid, that the Court of Portugal should Send an Ambassador, Minister Plenipotentiary or Envoy, to America, untill the United States would agree to Send one of equal Rank to Lisbon. – But if Congress had any Reasons for not sending Ministers of so high an Order, they might send a Resident or Chargé D'Affaires. – I answered him that I had heard it was the Intention of Congress to Send a Consul, but that I could Say no further.

Lord Carmarthen on Thursday told me, he was at work upon an Answer to my Memorial concerning the Posts, and should compleat it, as soon as he could collect some further Information concerning the Debts, of the Obstructions to the Payment of which the Ministry had rec^d Complaints from Persons in this Country who were interested in them. – You may conclude from this as well as I, what kind of Answer it will be. – I am very glad that I am to have an Answer. Whatever it may be, it will lead to further Ecclaircissement and a final Accommodation. Yet I think the Answer will not come before the Spring. – It will take Eighteen Months more to settle all Matters, exclusive of the Treaty of Commerce.

Mr Eden[2] has said within a few Days, that he believed there would be a Treaty of Commerce with the United States of America, within a Year or two. He may wish to be employed in it, for however Sanguine he may be of his success at Versailles I shall loose my Guess if he ever accomplishes a commercial Treaty with that Court. – He may however. – This Nation would now crouch to France for the Sake of being insolent to Us. The Disposition to crush the weak is almost always attended with that of cringing to the Strong. Arrogance to Inferiours is ever servile to superiours. But a Treaty with France, Such as She would accept, would be hurtfull to such Numbers and raise such an Opposition that I cannot yet believe Mr Eden will be permitted to sign one. The Term of two Years is expired and Del Campo has done nothing. – Crawford[3] is returned without doing any Thing as I suppose.

The true Secret of the Appointment of Eden, as I conceive is the Court of Versailles was offended, that Crawford was not allowed to do any Thing and used Some Sharp Expressions, which intimidated the Ministry. Eden was appointed for two Ends first to appease the Wrath at Versailles and Secondly to keep up a misterious delusive hope in the English Nation. Perhaps too the Ministry are afraid of commercial Speculations between France & Ireland. These Conjectures are precarious, and no great Stress should be laid upon them.

With great Respect, I have the Honour to be, dear Sir, your most obedient and most humble Servant   John Adams

NA: PC, *item 84, v. 6, pp. 75-78 (ALS); M247, reel 113.*

[1] *Pinto de Balsamão, Luis, Chevalier de. Portuguese diplomat. Minister to Great Britain, 1774-1789.*

[2] *Eden, William (1744-1814). British political figure and diplomat. Member of Parliament, 1774-1793. Member, Carlisle Commission, 1778. Chief secretary to the lord lieutenant of Ireland, 1780-1782. Vice-treasurer of Ireland, April-December 1783. Special envoy to negotiate commercial treaty with France, 1785-1786, and further agreements with France, 1787. Special ambassador to Spain, 1787. Special envoy to the United Provinces of the Netherlands, 1790; ambassador, 1791-1793. From 1793, Lord Auckland. Postmaster general, 1798-1804. President of the board of trade, 1806-1807.*

[3] *Craufurd (Crawford), George. British diplomat. Envoy sent to negotiate an Anglo-French treaty of amity and commerce, 1785.*

John Adams to John Jay

Dear Sir   Grosvenor Square Jan. 26. 1786

Give me Leave to introduce to you John Anstey Esq[1] Barrister at Law and a Member of Parliament, who goes out by Authority to verify the Claims of the Loyalists, as they call themselves. – I believe it to be the Design of M[r] Pitt[2] to pay their Demands which shall be found to be Supported, and withdraw their Pensions and then leave them to seek their Fortunes. in such a Case if our States repeal their Laws against them, they will generally return, to their old homes, or to some other Part of the United States, where they must become good Citizens or be compleatly insignificant.

By M[r] Anstey, I Send you, the Kings Speech and the Debates upon it. The most remarkable Thing in them, is, that the King and every Member of each House, has entirely forgotten that there is any such Place upon Earth as the United States of America. –...

.   .   .   .   .

In the meantime it is much to be wished, that a friendly Settlement could be made with Spain, and that a Minister might be sent to Holland, whose Inhabitants are the most cordial Friends we have in Europe.

I have had an opportunity this Week of Conversation with the Marquis of Lansdown[3] and Lord Abbington[4] his Friend and Admirer. They appear to me, to be as far from having adopted any decisive System relative to Us, as M[r] Pitt or M[r] Fox.[5] This Conversation has removed every Expectation that there will be any Party or even any Individual in Parliament in favour of a liberal Commerce with us.

The United States therefore have no Choice left. They must Support their own navigation, or have none.

With great and sincere Esteem, I have the honour to be, Sir, your most obedient and most humble Servant   John Adams.

NA: PCC, item 84, v. 6, pp. 79-82 (ALS); M247, reel 113.

[1] Anstey, John (d. 1819). British barrister and poet. Commissioner for auditing public accounts relating to loyalist claims.

[2] Pitt, William (1759-1806). British political figure. Second son of William Pitt, Earl of Chatham (1708-1778). Member of Parliament, 1781-1782; a supporter of Lord Shelburne. Chancellor of the exchequer in Shelburne's cabinet, July 1782-March 1783; viewed recognition of American independence as implicit and irrevocable from the outset of peace negotiations. Prime minister, as first lord of the treasury and chancellor of the exchequer, December 1783-March 1801, and May 1804-January 1806.

[3] Shelburne, William Petty, Lord (1737-1805). British political figure. President, Board of Trade and Foreign Plantations, under Bute, 1763. Secretary of state for the southern department (which included the American colonies until January 1768) under Chatham, July 1766-October 1768. Opposed Lord North's American policy, but favored reconciliation with the American colonies rather than recognition of American independence. Secretary of state for home and colonial affairs under Rockingham, March-July 1782. Chief minister and first lord of the treasury, July 1782-February 1783. Created Marquis of Lansdowne, December 1784.

[4] Abingdon, Willoughby Bertie, Earl of (1740-1799). British nobleman of strong democratic tendencies who supported the American cause throughout the Revolutionary War. A friend of the Marquis of Rockingham, he voted with the Rockingham Whigs in the House of Lords, and later supported Lord Shelburne's ministry. He was an advocate of Irish conciliation, sympathized with the French Revolution and opposed the war with France.

[5] Fox, Charles James (1749-1806). British political figure. As member of Parliament, a vocal opponent of Lord North's American policy. Secretary of state for foreign affairs in Rockingham's Ministry, April-July 1782, and in a coalition with Lord North, April-December 1783. Thereafter, steadfast opponent of the policies of William Pitt.

Congress to Samuel Shaw

[New York, January 27, 1786]

The United States of America in Congress Assembled.

To Samuel Shaw Esq[r.] Greeting

We reposing especial Trust and Confidence in your abilities and Integrity have constituted and appointed And by these presents do constitute and appoint you the said Samuel Shaw our Consul to reside at Canton in China, and there to exercise the Functions, and to enjoy all the Rights, Preeminences, Priviledges and Authorities to the said Place or office of Consul appertaining you demanding and receiving no Fees or perquisites of office whatever And we do hereby enjoin it upon all Captains Masters and

Commanders of Ships and other Vessels, armed or unarmed sailing under
our Flag as well as all other of our Citizens to acknowledge and obey him
the said Samuel Shaw in his Consular Capacity and we do hereby pray and
request his Imperial Majesty the Emperor of China, and his Governors and
Officers to permit the said Samuel Shaw fully and peaceably to enjoy and
exercise the said office without giving or suffering to be given any
molestation or Trouble to him, but on the contrary to afford him all
Countenance and assistance We offering to do the same for all those who
shall be in like manner recommended to us by his said Majesty.

In Testimony whereof we have caused the Seal of the United
States of America to be hereunto affixed – Witness the Honble
David Ramsay Chairman of Congress in the absence of his
Excellency John Hancock President this 27$^{th.}$ Day of January in the
year of our Lord 1786 and of our Sovereignty and Independence
the tenth.   David Ramsay

John Jay Secretary of the U$^{d.}$ States for the Depart$^{t.}$ of foreign affairs –
Cha$^{s.}$ Thomson Sec$^{y.}$

NA: PCC, item 120, v. 2, pp. 76-77 (LBkC); M40, reel 2.

Thomas Jefferson to John Jay

Sir   Paris, Jan. 27. 1786
I had the honor of addressing you by the way of London on the 2$^{d.}$
instant. since that yours of Dec. 7. has come to hand. I have now the
pleasure to inform you that mr Barclay, having settled as far as depended
on him the accounts of Monsieur de Beaumarchais, left Paris on the 15th
instant to proceed to Marocco. business obliged him to go by the way of
l'Orient and Bourdeaux, but he told me he should not be detained more
than a day at either place. we may probably allow him to the last of
February to be at Marocco.

The imperial Ambassador[1] some days ago observed to me that about
eighteen months ago Doctor Franklin had written to him a letter proposing
a treaty of commerce between the Emperor and the U. S. that he had
communicated it to the Emperor & had answered to Doctor Franklin that
they were ready to enter into arrangements for that purpose, but that he
had received no reply from him. I told him I had been informed by Doctor
Franklin of the letter making the proposition, but that this was the first I
had ever heard of an answer expressing their readiness to enter into
negociation. that on the contrary we had supposed no definitive answer had

been given, and that of course the next move was on their side. he expressed astonishment at this & seemed so conscious of having given such an answer that he said he would have it sought for and send it to me for my inspection. however he observed that the delay having proceeded from the expectation of each party that the other was to make the next advance, and this matter being now understood the two parties might now proceed to enter into the necessary arrangements. I told him that Congress had been desirous of entering into connections of amity and commerce with his Imperial majesty, that for this purpose they had commissioned mr Adams, D^r· Franklin & myself or any two of us to treat, that reasons of prudence had obliged them to affix some term to our commissions, & that two years was the term assigned: that the delay therefore which had happened was the more unlucky as these two years would expire in the ensuing spring. he said he supposed Congress could have no objections to renew our powers, or perhaps to appoint some person to treat at Brussels. I told him I was unable to answer that, & we remitted further conversation on the subject till he should send me his letter written to Doctor Franklin. a few days after his secretaire d'Ambassade[2] called on me with it. it was the letter of Sep. 28. 1784. (transmitted in due time to Congress) wherein he had informed D^r· Franklin that the Emperor was disposed to enter into commercial arrangements with us and that he would give orders to the government of the Netherlands to take the necessary measures. I observed to Monsieur de Blumendorff (the secretary) that this letter shewed we were right in our expectations of their taking the next step. he seemed sensible of it, said that the quarrel with Holland had engrossed the attention of government, and that these orders relating to the Netherlands only it had been expected that others would be given which should include Hungary, Bohemia & the Austrian dominions in general, and that they still expected such orders. I told him that while they should be attending them I would write to mr Adams in London, my collegue in this business, in concert with whom I must move on it. I think they are desirous of treating, and from questions asked me by Monsieur de Blumendorff, I suspect they have been led to that decision, either by the resolutions of Congress of Apr. 1784. asking powers from the states to impose restraints on the commerce of states not connected with us by treaty, or else by an act of the Pennsylvania assembly for giving such powers to Congress, which has appeared in the European papers. in the mean time I own myself at a loss what to do. our instructions are clearly to treat, but these made part of a system, wise and advantageous if executed in all it's parts, but which has hitherto failed in it's most material branch, that of connection with the powers having American territory. should these continue to stand aloof, it may be necessary for the U.S. to enter into commercial regulations of a defensive nature. these may be embarrassed by treaties with the powers having no American territory, and who are most of them so little commercial as perhaps not to offer advantages which may countervail these embarrassments. in case of a war indeed these treaties will become of value, and even during peace the respectability of the Emperor, who stands ~~at present.~~ at the head of one of the two parties which seem at present to divide Europe, gives a lustre to those connected with him, a circumstance not to be absolutely neglected by us under the actual situation of things. I attend a letter from mr Adams on this subject. not trusting the posts however, and obliged to wait private conveiances, our intercommunication is slow, & in the mean while our time shortening fast.

...[I] have the honour to be with the most perfect respect & esteem, Sir your most obedient & most humble servant   Th: Jefferson

NA: PCC, *item 87, v. 1, pp. 225-228 (ALS); M247, reel 115.*

[1] *Mercy d'Argenteau, Florimond-Claud, Comte de (1727-1794). Austrian diplomat. Ambassador to France, 1766-1790. Governor general of the Austrian Netherlands, 1790-1794. Ambassador to Great Britain, 1794.*

[2] *Blumendorf, Franz Paul von. Imperial diplomat. Secretary of Embassy in Paris, 1786. Chargé d'affaires, France, 1790-1792.*

Conde de Floridablanca to Don Diego de Gardoqui

[Translation]

Confidential   El Pardo, 28 January 1786
My dear sir:

I would like to respond to Your Excellency's secret despatches numbers 3, 4, 5, and 6 as extensively as you desire, but neither my activities nor my poor health permit it, and I shall have to restrict myself to assuring Your Excellency that the King is very satisfied with your conduct, and has sent me official documents in which he imparts the terms we can offer for our arrangements with those people, since it appears to me that, given what is said to Your Excellency on this occasion, and the instructions imparted to you, Your Excellency has sufficient means to draw these people into a reciprocally useful Convention which will serve as the basis for those which time and experience may reveal to be most convenient for both parties; moreover, I expect that by the time of the receipt of this letter, Your Excellency will have achieved some results from the plan which you told me you had developed with Jay and the other friend, and from Your Excellency having been able to assert our good offices for peace with Morocco, and those which we might have offered in Algiers if the States had not contested our just demands.

On this point it is advisable that they understand that with little trouble, we can frustrate for the Americans all commerce on the Western seas, and even in the Azores and the Canary Islands and in the Mediterranean, since we hold at our disposition the Moroccans and even the Algerines, who come out into the Ocean as far as the islands and will not allow any merchant ship to pass.

The King has been so generous that out of his goodness, he has protected the Americans, and he continues to protect them by freeing them from this piracy and evil, and I think their conduct and ingratitude should provoke the indignation of His Majesty.

I shall only reply in particular to the point regarding boundaries of which Your Excellency speaks in your secret despatch number 3, by informing Your Excellency that the letter from the Marquis de la Fayette which Your Excellency cited, and which was produced by Mr. Jay, is not significant. This French cavalier was insistent that the King adopt the boundaries set by England for the Floridas in her treaty with the Americans. I told him repeatedly that this was impossible, because they had made a Treaty concerning something that was not theirs; but that until there was a definitive Treaty with England herself and we had acquired other knowledge and understanding, those boundaries would be followed for the time being. In fact, we were thinking here of some retrocession of part of Florida to England by the definitive Treaty, if this lent itself to other things; and in such case it was of course useless to alter what had been established and to excite chimeras. On the other hand, we thought to settle this point amicably with Congress, acquiring information, and meanwhile that condescension was exercised, as my paper explained; but we never thought that Congress would consider it a Treaty, nor that they would do us the injustice of thinking we were so stupid or weak that in something which concerns us we would accept the injustice which they and the English wished to impose. Endeavor, Your Excellency, to stay well, and be certain of my desire to please you, and that of my wish that God keep you many years.   Floridablanca[1]

Miguel Gómez del Campillo, editor, Relaciones Diplomaticas entre España y los Estados Unidos, *v. I (Madrid: Consijo Superior de Investigaciones Cientificas Instituto Gonzalo Fernandez de Oviedo, 1944), hereafter cited as Gómez y Campillo,* Relaciones Diplomaticas, *pp. 506-508.*

[1] *Floridablanca, José Moñino y Redondo, Conde de (1728-1808). Spanish diplomat. Chief minister and secretary for foreign affairs, 1776-1792.*

John Jay to Samuel Shaw

Sir   New York 30 Jany 1786

I have the Honour of transmitting to you herewith enclosed a Commission constituting you Consul of the United States at Canton in China. You have my best wishes that you may derive advantages from this office equal to the Honour and Propriety with which I am persuaded it will be exercised. Altho neither Salary nor Perquisites are annexed to it, yet so distinguished a mark of the Confidence and Esteem of the United States will naturally give you a Degree of weight and Respectability, which the highest personal merit cannot very soon obtain for a Stranger in a foreign Country.

It will not be necessary for me to dwell on the advantages your Country may derive from the Information you may acquire – Permit me however to request the Favour of your Correspondence, and that you will transmit to me by proper Conveyances whatever Intelligence and observations you may think conducive to the public good. The mercantile and other Regulations at Canton respecting Foreigners, the Number and size of foreign Vessels and of what Nations which annually enter there – their Cargoes and what articles of Merchandize answer best, are matters which merit attention. It might also be useful to know whether Foreigners do or can carry on a circuitous Trade in that part of the World, either on their own account or by being Carriers for others whether asiatic or European. Accurate Information on all these points will probably require Time to collect and as accurate Information only can be useful, I cannot flatter myself with receiving ample Details from you very soon after your Arrival, unless on such of these Subjects as may not require much Time to investigate.

I shall not omit writing to you by every opportunity, and will do myself the Pleasure of sending you such Information respecting our Country as though perhaps not very essential to you either as a Consul or a Merchant, cannot fail of being interesting to an American Citizen early and strongly attached to his Country.

With sincere Esteem and the best Wishes for your Health and Prosperity I am &$^{ca.}$ John Jay

NA: PCC, item 120, v. 2, pp. 74-75 (LBkC); M40, reel 2.

Samuel Shaw to John Jay

Sir   New York 30th Jany 1786

Will you allow me to beg the favour of you to convey to the Honourable the Congress my most humble and grateful acknowledgments, for the honour they have been pleased to confer upon me, in their appointment of me to be their Consul for Canton in China and to assure them, that nothing on my part shall be wanting to discharge faithfully the Trust reposed in me, and to render the appointment as much as possible a public benefit.

May I, Sir, be permitted to observe, that while the United States have judged proper to make this appointment, there appears to be no provision against any casualties, which are always possible, and in so long a voyage as that which I am about to undertake, may by no means be improbable. This consideration joined to that of the loss time which would attend a new appointment, should any casualty prevent me from reaching that distant Country, induces me to submit to your consideration, and to that of the Honourable Congress, the propriety of appointing a Vice Consul, who, in case of the Death or absence of the Consul, should be invested also with his Powers. Perhaps such appointment may also be judged proper, from the probability that my inquiries in the commercial line, which I trust would not be uninteresting to our Country, might lead me to go from Canton to visit the European establishments and other settlements on the coast of India, in which case the powers of Consul to devolve on the Vice Consul, who should remain at and in the neighbourhood of Canton. should this Idea meet your concurrence, I would request the indulgence of mentioning Mr. Thomas Randall,[1] as a Gentleman properly qualified for the appointment. He is a native of the Country, whose commission he has had the Honour of supporting with reputation during a trying period of the late war. He has been in China with me, and is now about to return there again.

As Wednesday next is the Day appointed for the sailing of our Ship, I flatter myself you will see the necessity of an application being made to Congress as early as possible and that you will, with your usual goodness excuse the trouble I cause you in this business.

Be pleased, Sir, to accept my sincerest thanks for the obliging manner in which you have afforded me your good offices, and believe me to be with most respectful attachment &^{ca.}   Samuel Shaw

NA: PCC, *item 120, v. 2, pp. 81-83 (LBkC); M40, reel 2.*

¹ Randall, Thomas. *Military officer and merchant, originally from Boston. Continental artillery officer, 1775-1779. Close friend of Samuel Shaw. Involved in privateering ventures and West Indian trade during last years of the war, sometimes in partnership with Thomas Truxtun. Second supercargo of the* Empress of China, *1784-1785. Shaw and Randall established the first American commission house in Canton. It was Randall who handled the sale of the sea-otter skins which the* Columbia *brought to Canton in 1789.*

John Jay's Report on Anglo-American Relations

[New York] Office for foreign Affairs 31ˢᵗ January 1786

The Secretary of the United States for the Department of foreign Affairs to whom was referred his Letter of 28ᵗʰ December 1785 < ***** > enclosing Mʳ Adams of the 15ᵗʰ, 17ᵗʰ, 21ˢᵗ, 25ᵗʰ, & 27ᵗʰ October last – Reports,

That in his Opinion it should be

Resolved, That Congress approve of the Manner in which Mʳ· Adams appears from his several Letters to have executed the Duties of his Legation to the Court of Great-Britain, and that they are greatly pleased with the Diligence, Attention and Intelligence he has manifested therein. –

Resolved, That ways and means should be seasonably devised for placing such further Funds in Europe as will probably be necessary as well for the Support of the public Servants there, as for supplying any Deficiency in the Sum appropriated for the Negociations with the Barbary Powers – Ordered, That this Resolution be referred to the Treasury to report. –

From the Tenor and Complection of all Mʳ· Adams Letters it appears evident to your Secretary

1. That general and full Powers to regulate the Trade of the United States both foreign and domestic should be vested in Congress. –

2. That the United States should be put in a very respectable Posture of Defence, by forming ample Magazines of military Stores, and by having a considerable Part of the Militia always well prepared to take the Field.

3. That proper Measures should be devised to cause a punctual Compliance with and Payment of the Requisitions of Congress, and to prevent unconstitutional Dismemberments of any of the States which manifestly tending to weaken the Force and impair the Union by creating domestic Contention & affording Objects for foreign Manoeuvres are highly impolitic.

4. That M$^{r.}$ Jefferson should be directed to communicate to the Court of France the exact State of the United States with Great Britain relative to the Posts, to urge the Guarantee of France as a Reason for their friendly Interference, and to ascertain how far the United States may expect his Most Christian Majesty's good Offices and Aid on that Subject. –

5. That pursuant to the 8th Article in the Treaty with France it would be proper to request his most Christian Majesty's good Offices with the Barbary Powers to promote the present Negociations with them. –

Your Secretary is also induced to believe as well from Conversations with M$^{r.}$ Gardoqui as from M$^{r.}$ Carmichaels Letter, that Spain would if applied to very sincerely endeavour to exert her Influence with the Emperor of Morocco in favor of the United States, Wherefore he thinks that Application should be made to his Catholic Majesty for that Purpose. –

Your Secretary sees many good Consequences that might result from communicating M$^{r.}$ Adams Letters to the Executives of the different States, and accompanying them with a Letter from Congress urging the Necessity of ordering all the general Concerns of the Union by a stable, well digested System, and to that End of delegating such Powers as may be adequate to the great Objects of duly regulating the Commerce protecting the Union, and of drawing forth & directing its Resources both of Wealth and Power, as Exigencies may require. Your Secretary nevertheless has great Doubts of the Prudence of communicating M$^{r.}$ Adams Letters, lest Copies of them should return to England and place him there in a Situation neither agreeable to himself nor advantageous to the Public. –

Your Secretary has reason to believe that too much of their Contents has already slipped out – He having been lately told by a Person, who ought not to have had such Information, that M$^{r.}$ Adams had written that the Situation of the british Debts was made an Objection to the Evacuation of our Posts. He is however of Opinion that a Letter from Congress cautiously stating the general State of our Affairs and strongly impressing the Necessity of Efficiency and Vigour in the foederal Government would be very expedient. –

All which is submitted to the Wisdom of Congress.   John Jay –
read 1 feb^y 1786

NA: PCC, item 81, v. 2, pp. 27-30 (DS); M247, reel 107.

John Jay's Report on a Draft Anglo-American Treaty of Amity and Commerce

[New York] Office for foreign Affairs 2ᵈ· Febʸ 1786
The Secretary of the United States to whom was referred the Draft
of a Treaty of Amity and Commerce between his Britannic
Majesty and the said States, which was transmitted by Mʳ Adams,
together with his Letters that accompanied it, Reports

That in his opinion the United States may safely enter into Treaty with
Britain on the Terms and agreeable to the Tenor of the said Draft; and
therefore that it should be

Resolved That Congress approve of the said Draft and that in the Blank
left for the Term of the Duration of the Treaty be inserted twenty years.

Your Secretary thinks it would be expedient to refer the Letters abovementioned to the same Committee to whom other Letters from Mʳ· Adams
were yesterday committed

All which is submitted to the Wisdom of Congress –

John Jay –

NA: PCC, *item 81, v. 2, p. 31 (DS); M247, reel 107.*

William Carmichael to the American Commissioners in Europe

Gentlemen   Madrid 3ᵈ· Febʸ· 1786
On the 4ᵗʰ of December last Mr Lamb delivered me the Letter which
Your Excellencies did me the honor to address me dated from London the
1ˢᵗ· & from Paris the 11ᵗʰ of October. At the Same time that Gentleman
communicated to me his Instructions & I all the Intelligence I had been
able to procure relative to the negociation between this Country & the
Regency of Algiers.

The Cᵗ· D'Expilly[1] whose friendship I cultivated had returned to Algiers
long before Mʳ Lambs arrival & a Secretary whom he had dispatched from
that Place After his return with Letters for the Minister had also set off for
Alicant. From these Gentlemen I had obtained an account of the State of
the Negotiation. The Principal Articles proposed by Spain had been agreed
to by the Dey and his Ministers; But as the Former wished to include the
Courts of Naples and Portugal in the Pacification, the Cᵗ de Florida Blanca
had instructed the Cᵗ· d'Expilly to prevail on the Latter to Admit & receive
Ministers from these Courts & was actually waiting the Answer from

Algiers at the period when Mr Lamb came hither. It was evident to me that should this proposition be accepted, of which I had no doubt with respect to the first mentioned court, the Nomination & Voyage of these Ministers would occasion delay & Until the Treaty between Spain & the Regency should be concluded, I had reason to think that this Court would not interfere directly in our favor. The Manner in which his Exc^y the C^t de Florida Blanca had explained his Sentiments to me on this Subject, induced me to form this opinion. For as soon as I knew the probable success of D'Expillys Negotiation I insinuated to the Minister how acceptable the good offices of his Majesty to accommodate the States with the Barbary powers would be to the People at large in America, and his Excellency then Assured me that as soon as their own Affairs were arranged with Algiers, His Catholic Majesty[2] would employ all his influence to accelerate a peace for the United with that and the other Barbary States, & authorized me to inform Congress of the Kings intentions. Having received these Assurances I engaged the C^t D'Expilly to prepare by every favorable insinuation the Deys Ministers & favorites to support any overture which might be made by the States, which he promised me to do & the proofs of Confidence he gave me, induce me to rely on his promises. He also engaged to give me the earliest Information with respect to the Intentions of those People & since his return has proved by his behavior to our Captives & his correspondence with me, that he will avail himself of all the means which he can employ with propriety to fulfil his promises. When Mr Lamb arrived, The Royal Family had just come to this Capital from the Escurial & during its residence here it is extremely difficult to have Access to the Minister. The King in a few days after went to Aranjuez on a hunting Party & the C^t de Florida Blanca Accompanied him & none but the Family Ambassadors follow the Court on this Occasion. However as I was desirous to have a conference with the Minister as soon as possible on the Subject of your Excellencys Letter, I wrote to the Undersecretary in the Department of Foreign Affairs charged with the Correspondence to the United States to know whether If I came to Aranjuez I should have an opportunity of speaking with his Excellency to whom I wished to make a communication in Person of some Advice I had received lately. N° 1 is a copy of the Answer I rec^d from that Gentleman. On the Return of his Majesty to this Capital I procured an audience from the Minister to whom I communicated Mr Lamb's arrival & the Object of his Mission, making use of such Arguments & Insinuations as I thought most likely to Induce his Excellency to contribute to its Success. I received from him the Strongest Assurances to the same purport as those beforementioned. At the Same time however he added, that Until he should receive further Advice from Algiers it was impossible for him to take an open part in the Negotiation & advised me to detain my Countrymen until the Court went to the Pardo when he hoped to have it in his power to give me a more explicit Answer. During this Audience I took an occasion of mentioning without Affectation Your Excellencies Sentiments with respect to his Generous Interference in the Affair of Morrocco, with which he appeared much pleased & told me it should not be his fault, nor did he think it would be mine if Spain & the United States were not as good friends as they were near Neighbours in America –...

I communicated to Mess.ʳˢ· Lamb & Randall what passed on this occasion & these Gentlemen consented to wait without reluctance here until the period mentioned by the Minister. Four Days after the Court had been fixed at the Pardo, I again Waited on the Minister who received me very well, but on explaining the Motive of my visit His Excellency declared to me that it was not in his power to be more explicit as he had not yet rec^d the Letters he expected from Algiers – that until he received the Intelligence he expected he could not order the C^t D' Expilly to employ the Kings Interference in our Affairs, repeating his former Assurances & hinting the Obstacles we must expect to encounter in this Negotiation; At the same time he observed to me that we must not be discouraged. He told me that the first Objection made by the Algerines would Arise from our not having a Treaty with the Grand Seigneur,[3] as this circumstance occasioned Great Difficulties to Portugal in the Actual Negotiation – I intreated his Excellency to pardon my importunity and Anxiety on this subject as they proceeded as much from my wish to cement an Amicable intercourse by reciprocal good Offices between the two Countries of Spain & America as from my apprehension that Unless Mr Lamb should arrive at Algiers before their Cruisers were sent to Sea, further Hostilities on their part might render an accommodation still more difficult: I also urged the nature of Mr Lambs instructions & the necessity of Congress being early informed of the Disposition of the Regency Expressing a hope that by the time M^r· Lamb could arrive at a Sea Port & prepare for his Departure from thence it might be in his Excellencys power to Afford him all the Assistance necessary to insure the Success of his Mission. To these reflections I added the Loss that would accrue to Spain from the Difficulties to which we should be exposed in our Intercourse with a Country whose produce found a ready sale in America & from which Country Spain could be supplied with so many Articles that it now takes from the Northern Nations of Europe, whose Consuls his Excellency knew did every thing in their power to obstruct the peace which he was endeavouring to make for the commercial & Political Interests of a Country the Councils of which he directed – The C^t de Florida Blanca replied that he acquiesced in my reasons for the Departure of Mr Lamb & repeated to me & Authorized me to write your Excellencies that "*the Day after their own Affairs should be arranged with Algiers his Catholic Majesty would employ all his Influence to facilitate our Accommodation"* to which he added many assurances of his desire to give a preference to the Commerce of the United States ~~over~~ to that which Spain at present carried on with the Northern part of Europe, particularly with Sweden & Denmark. The Freedom with which this Minister has spoken to me on several Occasions his Sentiments with respect to the Northern powers hath not less surprized than convinced me of his wish to diminish their Commerce & Influence In the Mediterranean. In the course of this Conversation He appealed to my own Experience on the reliance that might be placed on his word to which I made the proper Answer & acknowledgements & concluded by asking passports & letters for Mess.rs Lamb & Randall which his Exc.y promised to send me. On my Return to this City from the Pardo I rec.d letters from Algiers of which N.o 2 3 are Copies. They were brought by a courier Extraordinary & the Arrival of that Courier induced me to hope that the Minister might have rec.d such information as might enable him to act openly in our favor, Altho in fact this hope arose more from my Wishes that such might be the Case, than from the reasons which ought to Induce a contrary sentiment in consequence of the Information which I had rec.d with respect to their negotiation previously. Your Excellencies will easily conceive that the first efforts of this court must be employed to procure a peace for those Nations to which they are allied by the tyes of Family connections, Engagements to which these Connections have given rise, & the mutual Aids which they have rec.d from these Nations during their late Operations against Algiers – However notwithstanding these considerations, I took the Liberty of reminding his Excelleny the C.t de Florida Blanca of the Passports & Letters he had promised me; to insinuate my expectations of being able to Obtain all that might be Necessary for Mr Lamb on his arrival at Algiers – To this Application I rec.d a reply of which N° 5 is a copy as also a Letter to the C.t de Assalto Capt.n General of Catalonia of which I also annex a Copy N.o 6 – as I do of the several Letters which I have rec.d from Algiers since the Arrival of Mess.rs Lamb & Randall in Madrid –

The Latter set off for Barcelona the 26.th Ult.o in Company with Mr Harrison a Native of Virginia who will have the honor to deliver your Excellencies Letters from me. Mr Lamb did not leave this until the first inst.t but as he travels post he will arrive at Barcelona Before the Gentlemen Abovementioned. I refer your Excellencies to the acc.t these Gentlemen may render you of my Conduct in this Business. I have procured Bills for Mr Lamb on Barcelona for the Am.t of which he has drawn agreable to his Instructions. I have established a credit for whatever he may chuse to draw. I have given him Letters to the C.t D Expilly & have given him all the Advice that I thought might be useful to him – On his Arrival at Algiers He will find Letters of Introduction to Most of the Consuls employed by Foreign Nations there from their Ministers at this Court. I did not to chuse to expose his mission to these Gentlemen Until his Departure from Barcelona renders it public. Having rendered to your Excellencies an acc[t] of my proceedings in consequence of the Letter which you did me the honor to address me by Mr Lamb it may be necessary to add for your information & that of Congress to which Body I take the Liberty of requesting you to forward a copy of this Letter, that the Peace negotiating at present between this Country & the Regency of Algiers will cost this Country near one million & a half of Dollars – & I beg leave to add that my information is so circumstantial & derived from such a source as leaves me not the Smallest reason to doubt its Authenticity – The Dey of Algiers is now more than Eighty years old & his Ministers all press a conclusion of the Treaty in order that While they are in power they may participate [in] the presents made on this Occasion – The Durability of this peace is uncertain or of any other made in the present Moment with these Pirates. If I am rightly informed, as soon as their Treaty is concluded with Spain & Naples, They mean to declare war Ag[st.] Denmark the Venetians & perhaps the Dutch – I shall not fail to inform you of all I can learn upon these points, Because there may be circumstances on which may depend your future Instructions to Mr Lamb & the Measures which Congress may think proper to Adopt.

...with the highest sentiments of gratitude for the Confidence your Excellencies have been to accord me I have the honor to be with great Respect & Regard Your Excellencies Most Obed[t.] & Humble Ser[t]

W[m.] Carmichael

LC: *Jefferson Papers,* microfilm reel 5 (ALS).

[1] *Expilly, Conde d'. Spanish diplomat. Plenipotentiary charged with peace negotiations with Algiers, 1785-1787.*

[2] *Charles III (1716-1788). King of the Two Sicilies (as Charles VII), 1734-1759. King of Spain, 1759-1788.*

[3] *i.e., the ruler of the Ottoman Empire.*

Sir John Temple to Lord Carmarthen

My Lord,   New York 4[th.] Feb: 1786.

The Members of Congress are now sitting in this City: I do not learn that they, at present, have any important matter under their consideration;

but, it is whisper'd, a business of great Magnitude will in the course of the Session be deliberated upon by their body, & for that purpose, circular letters have, it is said, been written to the Supreme power of each state requesting that their respective delegates may be order'd to attend in their places at Congress before the expiration of the present Month: much industry is exercised by french incendiaries, & by Americans under their influence to inflame both Congress & the people at large against his Majestys holding the Western Posts of Oswego, Niagara, & Detroit; & some have even proposed the taking those places by force early in the Spring: Whether this be the Important business said to be soon coming on in Congress; or Whether it be a proposal from france, of canceling the debt owed to her by these states, and to free its commerce (either by money or Arms) from the Barbary Cruizers, in consequence of a proposed aliance *offensive and defensive* with that insidious Artfull Nation, I know not, but if it be the latter, I trust, notwithstanding their deep corruption in these states, that their plan will fail, it being seen through & known, to all honest and sensible men, that such an Alliance would compleat the ruin of this Country.

...you will believe me to be with all deference and Respect, My Lord, Your Lordships most faithfull, and Obedient Servant.   J. Temple.

The Congress have this day Appointed a Consul to the East Indias.
R. 15^(th:) March.

PRO: FO 4/4, pp. 43-46 (LC transcription).

Louis Guillaume Otto to Comte de Vergennes

[Translation]

N°· 36 Duplicate.   New York, 10 February 1786.
My Lord

The Americans have seen with much satisfaction the Treaty of alliance that You have signed with the Dutch Plenipotentiaries; this recent proof of His Majesty's wise policy inspires a new confidence in them, and persuades them more and more that the King has no other design than to assure the happiness and the repose of Europe after having given peace to the new world. Mr. Temple, who had announced several months ago that England and Holland were going to be united more closely than ever, is a little embarrassed at this moment; he does not know what direction to give to his past assertions, and in order to hide his confusion he affects to congratulate the Dutch minister and me with all his heart for the happy alliance that exists between our two nations. Mr. Van Berkel,[1] whose family has continually been of the French party in Holland, rejoices greatly at this event, and he seizes every occasion to indicate his joy of it to Mr. Temple.

This Consul, My Lord, generally has reason to be little satisfied with his situation. Instead of a rapprochement between the two Nations, he sees only repeated attacks against the Commerce of England. Massachusetts and Rhode Island have already excluded English navigation from their ports; the Delegates from New Hampshire assure me that their State will follow the same course. North Carolina has just published an Act by which Vessels from all Nations that have not made a treaty of Commerce with the United States will pay double duties. The State of Virginia explains itself still more clearly in a law entitled *An Act to place a special impost on English Vessels.* It establishes a duty of five shillings per ton on all British navigation, and for fear of being deceived by the Captains, it gives orders to the Officers of the Ports to go on board all English ships, and to measure with precision the number of tons that they can hold; I am enclosing here a translation of that act. Several other States are on the point of adopting analogous means, and English Commerce will soon find itself exceedingly constrained throughout the United States.

Virginia has just taken another step equally important for the commerce and navigation of the United States. By an Act,[⊗] a translation of which I have the honor to address to You, it names eight Commissioners to regulate, with Delegates from the other States, in an Assembly convoked for this purpose, the commercial interests of the United States, and to make their report of it in order to place Congress in a position to make general commercial regulations for the entire United States. This measure appears indispensable to give this Assembly knowledge of the true interests of its Constituents. Most of the members of Congress are either lawyers or cultivators, consequently little versed in the business of Commerce; it will therefore be important, as soon as all the States have given it powers concerning commercial regulations, to follow the various reports of the committees of the respective States, to combine the principles in them, and to form from them an ensemble that may be equally agreeable to the North and to the South of the United States. This great work will require time and much prudence and impartiality, and perhaps another year will pass before all the States can agree on a uniform plan. The Chambers of Commerce established in the various States are beginning to correspond very punctually. In a circular letter from that of New York, I find the following passage: "Although according to our late treaty with Great Britain we may have the air of living in peace, we find ourselves effectively engaged in a war all the more dangerous because our enemies are less visible and in greater number than of old. It is true that all Europe had desired to see us independent, but at this moment there is not a power that does not dream of sacrificing our interests to its commercial policy. Our situation should teach us to seek resources at home without having our Eyes fixed unceasingly on Europe." This spirit of jealousy and reprisals which reigns throughout the United States makes me foresee, My Lord, that it will be very difficult for us to preserve our Treaty of Commerce intact. I beg You to send me Your orders in this regard so that I may make them known to Congress when the occasion presents itself.

I am with a profound respect, My Lord, Your most humble and most obedient Servant.   Otto.

Received 23 June.

⊗ of 21 January

FFAA: Pol. Corr., U.S., v. 31, f. 81-83vo. (LC transcription).

¹ Van Berckel, Pieter Johan (?-1800). Dutch government official and diplomat. Burgomaster of Rotterdam. Older brother of Engelbert François van Berckel, pensionary of Amsterdam. Minister to the United States, 1783-1788.

Louis Guillaume Otto to Comte de Vergennes

[Translation]

Nᵒ· 38. Duplicate.   New York, 14 February 1786.

My Lord

                            .   .   .   .   .

The Committee which Congress had charged with making a report on the measures to take in consequence of the delay of the States in the payment of their various quotas rendered an account of its deliberations on the 3ʳᵈ of this month. It began with a general recapitulation of the annual expenditures, amounting to 2,508,327 Dollars or 13,168,716 Livres tournois, inclusive of the interest on the public debt. It explained that in the course of the next year, the reimbursement of two portions of capital was due in conformity with the Contracts, that a great part of the domestic debt was not yet liquidated, and that the auditing of these accounts would further increase the annual expenditure considerably; that the expenses of the Government of the United States were very modest, and little susceptible of reduction; that the War Department had not been very extravagant at a time when appearances of peace had rendered all armament prodigiously useless, and when seven hundred men composed the whole military force of the United States; but that circumstances had changed, and that the hostile movements of the Savage Nations and of the Barbary Corsairs rendered at least the establishment of some storehouses indispensable and consequently increased the annual expenditure of this Department; that it resulted from these various observations that not only would the Quotas of the respective States not be diminished, but that it would even be necessary to increase them; that the Confederation authorized Congress to levy contributions in three ways: 1$^{st.}$ by requisitions, 2$^{nd.}$ by loans, 3$^{rd.}$ by the emission of paper money; that the first of these methods had hitherto produced only very little results, since it had not even sufficed for the payment of the interest; that it would be imprudent to dream of making new loans at a moment when one had not even the means to pay the old interest; that the emission of paper money would only make the public calamity increase, and render the situation of the domestic creditors of Congress infinitely more unfortunate, without satisfying in any way the foreign creditors; that the sale of lands would not increase the resources of the Treasury, since it would only call in old bills, such as certificates and old paper money; that after having considered the insufficiency of all these means, the Committee was of the opinion that it was necessary to find some other expedient to remedy the destitution of the Treasury; that although Congress might have proofs without number of the generosity of its ally and of the patience of its domestic creditors, and especially of the Army, it would be contrary to the interest and to the honor of the United States longer to postpone satisfying their engagements; that the Committee thought that the recommendations of 18 April 1783 could alone fulfill this objective, if all the States wished to pay deference to it; that these recommendations turned on two subjects: 1$^{st.}$ the power of Congress to levy a duty on importations throughout the United States. 2$^{nd.}$ another power to levy, independently of the aforesaid duty, in the manner that it judges most efficacious, the sum of 1,500,000 Dollars; that in examining the conduct which the various States have pursued with regard to these recommendations, the Committee found that with the exception of New York and Georgia, they had all granted the first part of it, and that the second had only been approved by a small number; finally, that one could hope to put an end to the public difficulties if all the States would concur in so salutary a measure.

This report, My Lord, appeared imperfect to Congress for all that regards the States that have not adopted the impost of 5 percent. It has named a new Committee with orders to discuss the matter of the impost very precisely, and to make its report thereon as soon as possible.

I am with a profound respect, My Lord, Your most humble and most obedient Servant   Otto.
Received 23 June.

FFAA: Pol. Corr., U.S., v. 31, f. 96-99 (LC transcription).

John Adams to John Jay

Sir   Grosvenor Square Feb. 16. 1786 –
   The Expences of Insurance on American Vessells, the Obstructions of
their Commerce with Spain Portugal and Italy: and Compassion for our
Fellow Citizens in Captivity: all occasioned by Apprehensions of the
Barbary Corsairs, must excite Solicitude in every Man capable of thinking
or Feeling. it is nevertheless certain that too great an alarm has been
Spread, since no more than two vessells have been taken by the Algerines,
and one by Morocco. Artificial allarms might be diminished, by discontinuing the Practice of insuring in England. Loyds Coffeehouse has made a
great and clear Profit, because no Vessell has yet been taken, which has
been there insured. if the American Merchants would open offices at home
the Praemium would be saved to the Country, and they would find a large
Ballance in their favour. The Ballance of Trade with the English is so much
against us, that we ought not unnecessarily, to make ourselves tributary to
them.
   Mr Lamb drew upon me Bills for 2000£, at Madrid the 24$^{th.}$ of January,
and assures me in his Letter of Advice that I shall hear from him soon at
Barcelona. This Gentlemans Motions are slow: what can have detained him
so long, I know not. – an entire Stranger to him < ******* > having never
seen him, nor heard of him untill he was announced in your Letter, I can
say nothing of his Character or Conduct. Mr Jefferson understood him to
be recommended by Congress and he was certainly the Bearer of their
Orders, and I could not but concur in the Sentiment of my excellent
Colleague, and in his Construction of the Intentions of Congress. – Since
the Appointment was made and became irrevocable, I have heard such
Opinions and Reports of him, as have astonished me. he has with him in
M$^{r.}$ Randall an ingenious worthy Man, who, may Supply any deficiencies,
as we hope, and we must now wait with Patience, untill they inform us of
their Proceedings.
   Mr Barclay, and Mr Franks are at length departed from Paris. Their Delay
was occasioned by Mr Beaumarchais. – It will be so late before these
Gentlemen can arrive at Morocco, that the Emperor may be out of Patience
and send out his Frigates.
   If the Agents were arrived, there would be little reason for Confidence
in their Success. The Sum of Eighty Thousand Dollars, it is much to be
feared will not be Sufficient to procure Treaties of Peace. We may find the
whole Sum consumed, and the Difficulty of making Peace augmented.
Congress will take all these Things into Consideration, and transmit their
Orders both respecting the Sums to be given as Presents, and the Funds

from whence they are to be drawn. without a fresh Loan in Holland, the Treasury of the United States in Europe will soon be exhausted.

The american Commerce can be protected from these Affricans only by Negotiation or by War. if Presents should be exacted from us, as ample as those which are given by England, the Expence may amount to Sixty Thousand Pounds Sterling a Year, an enormous Sum to be sure, but infinitely less than the Expence of fighting. two Frigates of 30 Guns each would cost as much, to fitt them for the Sea besides the accumulating Charges of Stores, Provisions, Pay and Cloathing. The Powers of Europe generally Send a Squadron of Men of War, with their Ministers, and offer Battle at the same time that they propose Treaties and promise Presents. Mr Barclay and Mr Lamb are armed only with Innocence and the Olive Branch: and there is some reason to expect, that the Emperor, and Dey will feel their Dignity hurt by the *Appearance* of Deputies not immediately appointed by Congress. Time will clear up all doubts, and Subsequent Arrangements may be taken accordingly.

an Envoy from Tripoli is here at present. I saw him at Court but have not made him a Visit. He wishes to see me, as is supposed from what he said yesterday to a Gentleman. He said "that most of the foreign Ministers had left their Cards, but the American had not. We are at War with his Nation, it is true, and that may be the Reason of his not calling. We will make Peace with them however for a tribute of an hundred Thousand Dollars a Year. Not less." He Speaks no European Language, unless except a little of the Lingua Franca, and perhaps a little Italian. to go with an Interpreter would occasion Speculation, and Suggest to him Schemes which he might not otherwise think of. to treat with him before any Measures are taken with Moroco and Algiers might offend them.

With great Respect, I have the Honour to be, Sir your most obedient and most humble servant.   John Adams.

NA: PCC, *item* 84, *v.* 6., *pp.* 95-100 (ALS); M247, *reel* 113.

John Lamb to John Adams

Sir   Barcelona Febr^y· 16th 1786
   on the 11$^{th·}$ Day we ariv^d here I have Drawn on my credit for Twenty six hundred pounds Sterling in all, Two thousand of which I shall receive on munday next. I hope that, and the small trinquets which I brought from Paris will introduce me to an audience at Algiers. have mett maney little Disapointments since we left france which hath Detaind us untill this time.

hope to Sail from this next week. must refer your Excellency to m^{r.} Harrison for the Particulars of my present situation, he is fulley acquainted
   I am with Due Respect, your Excellencyes most obt Hm^{le.} Servt.

                                                        John Lamb

NA: PCC, item 92, pp. 53-54 (ALS); M247, reel 120.

John Adams to John Jay

Sir   Grosvenor Square Feb. 17. 1786
   At a late Levee, the King, in conversation with one of the foreign Ministers, was pleased to say "that the Tripoline Ambassador,[1] refused to confer with his Ministers, and insisted on an Audience: but that nothing had been said at it, more than that Tripoli and England were at Peace, and desirous to continue so. His Majesty added, all he wants is a Present, and his Expences borne to Vienna and Denmark."
   If nothing more was said, at the Audience, there are not wanting Persons in England, who will find means to Stimulate this African to stir up his Countrymen against american Vessells. it may reasonably be suspected that his present Visit is chiefly with a View to the United States: to draw them into a Treaty, of Peace, which implies Tribute, or at least Presents: or to obtain Aids from England to carry on a War against us. feeling his Appearance here to be ominous, like that of other irregular Bodies, which from their horrid hair "Shake Pestilence and War" I thought at first to avoid him but finding that all the other foreign Ministers had made their visits, and that he would take amiss, a longer inattention it was judged necessary to call at his Door, for the form. but when the Attempt was made, which was last Evening so late that there was no Suspicion of his being visible, the Ambassador was announced at home and ready to receive the Visitant. it would Scarcely be reconcileable to the Dignity of Congress to read a Detail of the Ceremonies which attended the Conference: it would be more proper to write them to Harlequin for the amusement of the Gay at the New York Theatre. It is Sufficient to say, that His Excellency made many inquiries concerning America; the Climates, Soil, Heat and cold &c and observed "it is a very great Country; but *Tripoli is at War with it.*" in return, it was asked, how there could be War, between two nations, when there had been no Hostility, Injury, Insult or Provocation on either Side? His Excellency replied, that Turkey Tripoli, Tunis, Algiers and Morocco, were the Sovereigns of the Mediterranean, and that no nation could navigate that Sea, without a Treaty of Peace with them. that America must make such Treaties, with Tripoli, first, then with Constan-

tinople, then with Algiers & Morocco, as France, England, and all the other Powers of Europe had done. A Secretary brought him some Papers, one of which was put into my hand. it was a french Translation of a Full Power from the Pacha, Dey and Regency of Tripoli, to treat with all the Powers of Europe, and to manage all the foreign concerns of his Country, without limitation of time or Place. The original Commission in his own Language was also produced and shewn. it was observed that America was not named in it: but it was replied that the Power was universal to manage every Thing and that a Treaty might be made at once, or at least that Conferences might be held, and the Result written to Tripoli and America for further Instructions. "What time was required to write to Congress, and receive an Answer?" Three months, at least. "That was too long, but he should remain here, Sometime. You may call here tomorrow or next day, with an Interpreter, and we will hear and propose Terms"

As his Excellency expected to gain by the Negotiation, as much as the American knew he must loose you will perceive the former was the most eager to promote it. When Mr Jeffersons answer to a Letter upon this subject shall arrive, it will be proper to learn his Terms, but there is reason to believe they will be too high, for your Ministers to accept, without further Instructions.

This is the Substance of a Conference, which was carried on with much difficulty, but with civility enough, on both Sides, in a Strange mixture of Italian Lingua Franca, broken French and worse English.

This Minister appears to be a Man of good Sense and temper.

With great Respect, I have the Honour to be, Sir, your most obedient and most humble servant   John Adams.

NA: PCC, item 84, v. 6, pp. 103-107 (LS); M247, reel 113.

[1] Abdurrahman Adja, Sidi Hadji. Tripoline Ambassador to Great Britain, 1786-1787.

Paul Randall to John Adams

Barcelona February 17$^{th.}$ 1786 –

I should have paid the highest respect to your Excellency's Injunction of writing by every safe oppertunity – but that I conceived such Information as I could have communicated hitherto, would have been only a reiteration of M$^{r.}$ Carmichaels Letters – at present – as M$^{r.}$ Lamb does not write nor has directed me thereto – I think it my duty to manifest an early disposition of complying in every respect with your Excellency's directions. –

On the 11$^{th.}$ Ins^t we arrived here after an Expeditious Journey from Madrid, & on the next Morn presented a Letter of Recommendation from the Count De Florida blanca, to the Captain General of this Province to forward Mr. Lamb in every thing expedient for his Embarkation for algiers – Mr. Lamb applyed to this Capt General for Leave to extract the £2.000 St^g – being his last draught & which your Excellency we trust is advised of – the Capt. General replyed, that it was not within his department to grant the Licence & referred Mr. Lamb to the Intendant, who likewise refused, notwithstanding which – I believe Mr. Lamb upon the Explanation of his Business to the proper officers, superintending this Branch of the revenue is in Hopes of obtaining a Dispensation – and permission to effect the same

The Business remaining in this Dilemma is an unfortunate period for me to address your Excellency – however as Mr. Lamb thinks his Expectations pretty well grounded, I conceive it my indispensable Duty to mention the situation of these affairs, altho a few days or even hours may make a considerable alteration in them –

The advanced season renders it very embarrassing to await the express authority of the Court for effectuating that Design – so that the present Course of the Business is deemed the most expedient –

It may be impertinent in me to offer my Conjectures on the propriety of proceeding immediately to algiers, and making a Dependance on the Count De Espilly – who has endeavoured to convince Mr. Carmichael that his utmost Exertions shall in no wise be wanting to assist this Negotiation; more especially as Mr. Lamb is hourly expecting to accomplish his purpose here – Mr. Harrison who is Bearer of this Letter is as perfectly acquainted with the progress already made in every respect during our Residence in Madrid & the little continuance here, as I myself am – as well as the Councils & Designs which have been agitated relative to Mr. Lamb's Mission – to him therefore I refer your Excellency, in the highest Confidence on his Judgement & discretion – as the particular friend of Mr. Carmichael, & a Gentleman who has had an oppertunity on many occasions of discovering a generous intention to serve his Country –

I shall consider myself entirely devoted to this service, notwithstanding the stipulation of six months & shall remain at algiers, or elsewhere to accomplish my duty – unless absolutely directed by your Excellency to return – tho' perhaps Mr. Lamb may be desirous of my coming forward with some Dispatches – in which case I shall think myself at Liberty of considering in what Manner I may be of most service to my Country, in completing my Commission & the Confidence your Excellency have done me the Honor to repose in me – As I am not to consider this as an official Letter, I have written with a less scrupulous Caution than the Uncertainty of all Events might render prudent – tho' I wish to consider myself more a Candidate for your Excellency's particular good opinion, than as seeking a future Employment in the publick Service – which I find myself very inadequate to at present –

In a full & grateful dependance I rest with the honor of naming myself your Excellency's most devoted, obed$^{t \cdot}$ Serv$^{t \cdot}$ P R Randall

NA: PCC, item 92, pp. 55-58 (C); M247, reel 120.

John Adams to John Jay

Sir   Grosvenor Square Feb. 20. 1786
Yesterday the Tripolitan Ambassador sent a Message by a Doctor Benamor, an English Jew most probably, who has formerly resided in Barbary, and Speaks the Arabic Language as well as the Italian and Lingua Franca, to inform me, that he wished to return < *** > his visit, in the same friendly and respectfull manner, and that as he had much at heart a Treaty between the Barbary and American States, he wished it might be soon. It was agreed that he should be received at noon.

At twelve His Excellency came in Ceremony, accompanied with his Secretary, and Benamor for an Interpreter, "whom he had chosen in Preference to the Interpreter assigned him by the Court, because he was sorry to See, that this nation was not so Steady in its Friendship to America as the French. The French Consul at Tripoli congratulated him upon his Appointment and hoped he would meet in England with a Minister with whom he might make a Treaty of Peace with America: but he was sorry to say he found here much Ill Will to the Americans and a Desire to prevent him from Seeing the American Minister. For this Reason he would have nothing to do with the Court Interpreter. It was the delight of his soul and the whole pleasure of his Life to do good: and he was zealous to embrace an opportunity which now presented itself, of doing a great deal. The Time was critical, and the sooner Peace were made the better for from what passed before he left home, he was convinced if the Treaty should be delayed another Year, it would after that, be difficult to make it. If any considerable Number of Vessells and Prisoners should be taken, it would be hard to perswade the Turks especially the Algerines to desist. a War between Christian and Christian was mild and Prisoners on either Side were treated with Humanity but a War between Turk and Christian was horrible, and Prisoners were sold into Slavery. Although he was himself a Mussulman he must still say he thought it a very rigid Law, but as he could not alter it, he was desirous of preventing its operation, or at least of softening it, as far as his Influence extended. "The Algerines were the most difficult to treat. They were eager for Prizes, and had now more and larger ships than usual. if an Application should be made first to Algiers they would refuse. but when once a Treaty was made by Tripoli or any one of the barbary States, they would follow the Example. There was such an intimate Connection between all, that when one made Peace, the rest followed. Algiers had refused to treat with Spain, in defyance of all her Armaments, untill Tripoli interposed, "and then they relaxed at once. He called God to witness, that is to say, he swore by his Beard, which is a Sacred Oath with them, that his Motive to this Earnestness for Peace, although it might be of some benefit to himself, was the Desire of doing good."

When he was informed that Congress had received some friendly Letters from the Emperor of Moroco, and that an Agent was gone to treat with his Majesty, "he rejoiced to hear it and doubted not that the Agent would succeed, as the Emperor was a Man of extensive Views, and much disposed to promote the Commerce of his subjects." As it was now apparent that his principal Business here was to treat with the United States, and that no Harm could be done by dealing frankly with him, the Commission of Congress to treat with Tripoli was shewn him, as well as those to Morocco, Algiers and Tunis. He "was rejoiced to see them, and although he could not answer for Algiers, he would undertake for Tunis and Tripoli, "and he would write in favour of any Person who might be sent or go with him in Person to assist in the completion of Peace with all the States of Barbary, which was more than he had ever before said to any Ambassador or Minister in Europe." It was then proposed that His Excellency should mention the Terms which he might think proper to propose, but he "desired to be excused, at present, and that tomorrow Evening at his House he might have an Opportunity of explaining himself more particularly." This was agreed to. –

It was then observed, that although America was an extensive Country the Inhabitants were few in Comparison with France, Spain and England, nor would their Wealth bear any Proportion to that of these Nations or of Holland; that we were just emerged from the Calamities of War, and had as yet few ships at Sea, especially in the Mediterranean, so that the Barbary Corsairs could not expect to make any considerable Number of Prizes. "God forbid, was his reply that I should consider America upon a Footing at present, in Point of Wealth with these nations. I know very well that she has but lately concluded a War which must have laid waste their Territories, and I would rather wish to leave to her own Generosity, the Compliments to be made upon the occasion, than Stipulate any Thing precisely."

This Man is either a consummate Politician in Art and Address, or he is a benevolent and wise Man. Time will discover whether he disguises an interested Character, or is indeed the Philosopher he pretends to be. if he is the latter Providence seems to have opened to us an Opportunity of conducting this thorny Business to a happy Conclusion. Col. Smith will go to Paris to communicate the whole to M^r. Jefferson and entreat him to come over to London in order to finish as much as possible of it, immediately, and to agree with the Portuguese Minister at the same time. M^r. Jefferson has long projected a Visit to England, and this will be a good Opportunity. No Notice will be taken of it, publickly in America, and his real Errand will be concealed from the Public here.

If the Sum limited by Congress should be insufficient we shall be embarrassed, and indeed a larger sum could not be commanded unless a new Loan should be opened in Holland. I doubt not a Million of Guilders might be obtained there, upon the same terms with the last two Millions. This would enable Congress to pay their Interest in Europe and to pay the French officers, who are uneasy.

With great Respect and Esteem, I have the Honour to be, Sir your most obedient and most humble servant   John Adams. –

NA: PCC, item 84, v. 6, pp. 111-117 (ALS); M247, reel 113.

John Jay's Report on
a Franco-American Postal Convention

[New York] Office for foreign Affairs 21st. February 1786 The Secretary of the United States for the Department of foreign Affairs to whom was referred a Letter to him of the 28th. November last from the Chargé des Affaires of France enclosing a Plan of a Treaty for the Correspondence of Letters between the Post Offices of France and those of the United States – Reports That he has submitted the said Plan to the Consideration of the Post Master General of the United States, whose Opinion thereon appears in the following Letter Viz^t.

"General Post Office February 16. 1786
"Sir
"I have had under Consideration the proposed "Plan of a Treaty for the Correspondence of Letters between the Post Offices of France, and those of the United States of North America," and observe but one Defect in it;

and that is, *it is left optional with the Writers to pay the Postage or not;* and, if we may judge from Experience, they will not pay it. The Consequences will be

> 1st. That a Receipt must be given by the American Office, which will make the United States accountable for the Amount of the Postage. –
>
> 2nd. The Letters must then be distributed from New Hampshire to Georgia; and the dead or (refuse) Letters returned to New York, at *the Risque of the United States;* which will, evidently, be very great, if we consider the Distances to which the Letters must travel, the Size and Situation of many of our Ferries, and our Seasons, especially the Winter. –
>
> 3rd. Accounts must be kept between the American and French Offices, which, in their very nature, must be complex & intricate, both Nations being interested in the Postage of each Letter; and that Postage being marked, partly in french Money & partly in Pennyweights and Grains of Silver; the former, not being sufficiently understood by us, will occasion many Errors, and be the Source of much Confusion. –

We were exactly upon the above Plan with Respect to the british Packets at their first Establishment, as you will observe from the enclosed Advertisement; but the Inconveniences attending it were so great that it was found necessary to make an Alteration; and the whole Business was amazingly simplified by providing that *all the Packet Postage should be paid in England.* By this small change in the System every Difficulty is removed; and, as Experience has evinced it's Utility, I beg leave to recommend the Adoption of the same Mode in the present Case. Indeed, it will be more advantageous to *France* than the Plan now proposed, because the Number of refuse Letters will be lessened by it, as *all* the Letters put into the Offices in France will then be paid for, and the refuse Letters from this Side of the Water will not be more numerous upon this Plan than upon the other: there will also be a Saving of the Commissions allowed to the Deputy Post Masters for transacting the Business. –

The other Regulations, such as giving the Captains Receipts for the Mails, sending Invoices of the Letters &^{ca.} are equally proper upon either Plan."

"I have the Honor to be &^{ca.}"   "Eben^r Hazard"[1]

Your Secretary thinks the Observations of the Post Master General are well founded, and therefore is of Opinion, that he the said Post Master General should be duly authorised to conclude the said Treaty with the Director of the french Posts vested with equal Powers on the part of his Most Christian Majesty provided the Alterations in question are admitted, and provided further that the Duration of the said Treaty shall not exceed the Term of ten Years. Your Secretary is also of Opinion that the said Treaty should be engrossed and executed in both Languages. –

All which is Submitted to the Wisdom of Congress-   John Jay–
Read 25. feb' 1786

NA: PCC, item 81, v. 2, pp. 35-38 (DS); M247, reel 107.

[1] Hazard, Ebenezer (1744-1817). Surveyor General of the United States Post Office, 1776-1782. Postmaster General of the United States, 1782-1789.

John Adams to Thomas Jefferson

Dear Sir   Grosvernor Square Feb. 21. 1786.

I have desired Colonel Smith[1] to go Express to Paris, to intreat you to come here without loss of Time. The Portuguese Minister has received his Instructions from his Court, and We may here together conduct and finish the Negotiation with him, I suppose in three Weeks. But, there is another Motive more Important. There is here a Tripolitan Ambassador with whom I have had three Conferences. the Substance of what passed Colonel Smith will explain to You. – Your Visit here will be imputed to Curiosity, to take a Look at England and pay your Respects at Court and to the Corps Diplomatick. There is nothing to be done in Europe, of half the Importance of this, and I dare not communicate to Congress what has passed without your Concurrence. What has been already done and expended will be absolutely thrown away and We shall be involved in a universal and horrible War with these Barbary States, which will continue for many Years, unless more is done immediately. I am so impressed and distressed with this Affair that I will go to NewYork or to Algiers or first to one and then the other, if you think it necessary, rather than it should not be brought to a Conclusion. Somebody must go to NYork, one of Us, or Humphries or Smith in order to perswade Congress of the Necessity of doing more. Then Somebody must go to Holland to obtain the means, and then Somebody perhaps to Algiers to make Use of them. The Tripolitán might be perswaded to go with him. I refer you to the Bearer for all other Particulars, and have the Honour to be, with great Esteem your Friend

John Adams

LC: *Jefferson Papers, microfilm reel 5* (ALS).

¹ *Smith, William Stephens (1755-1816). Military officer, diplomat and political figure. Continental Army officer, 1776-1783, with service under John Sullivan, Israel Putnam, and the Marquis de Lafayette. Appointed aide to Washington, July 1781. Supervised British evacuation of New York, 1783. Secretary of legation in Great Britain, 1785-1788. Son-in-law of John Adams. Federal marshal, supervisor of the revenue, and surveyor of the port of New York. Prosecuted, but acquitted, for helping Francisco de Miranda with his filibustering expedition to South America, 1806. Member, U.S. House of Representatives, 1813-1816.*

John Adams to John Jay

Sir   Grosvenor Square Feb. 22. 1786

On Monday Evening another Conference was held with the Tripolitan Ambassador, attended with his Interpreter Benamor, who is a decent Man, and very ready in the English as well as Arabick and Italian. The Foreign Ministers here say it is the Custom of all the Ambassadors from Barbary to be much connected with Jews to whom they are commonly recommended. It may be supposed the Jews have interested Motives, and therefore although their Interference cannot be avoided, they ought to be Objects of Jealousy. Benamor soon betrayed Proofs enough, that he had no Aversion to the Ambassadors obtaining large Terms.

The Ambassador who is known to many of the foreign Ministers here is universally well spoken of. When he began to explain himself concerning his Demands, he said "they would be different, according to the Duration of the Treaty. if that were perpetual, they would be greater, if for a Term of Years less. His Advice was that it should be perpetual. once signed by the Bashaw, Dey and other Officers, it would be indissoluble and binding forever upon all their Successors. but if a temporary Treaty were made, it might be difficult and expensive to revive it. for a perpetual Treaty, such as they had now with Spain, a sum of Thirty Thousand Guineas must be paid, upon the Delivery of the Articles signed by the Dey and other Officers. if it were agreed to he would Send his Secretary by Land to Marseilles, and from thence by Water to Tripoli, who should bring it back by the same rout signed by the Dey &c. He had proposed so small a sum, in Consideration of the Circumstances, but declared it was not half of what had been lately paid them by Spain. if we chose to treat upon a different Plan, He would make a Treaty perpetual, upon the Payment of Twelve Thousand five hundred Guineas for the first Year and three Thousand Guineas annually untill the Thirty Thousand Guineas were paid. It was observed that these were large sums, and vastly beyond Expectation. but his

Excellency Answered, that they never made a Treaty for less. Upon the Arrival of a Prize, the Dey and the other officers were entituled by their Laws to large shares, by which they might make greater Profits than these Sums amounted to, & they never would give up this Advantage for less.

He was told that altho there was a Full Power to treat the American Ministers were limited to a much smaller sum. So that it would be impossible, to do any Thing untill we could write to Congress and know their Pleasure. Col Smith was present at this as he had been at the last Conference And agreed to go to Paris to communicate all to Mʳ· Jefferson and perswade him to come here, that we may join in further Conferences and transmit the Result to Congress. The Ambassador believed that Tunis & Morocco would treat upon the same terms, but could not answer for Algiers. They would demand more. When Mʳ· Jefferson arrives we shall insist upon knowing the Ultimatum and transmit it to Congress.

Congress will perceive that one hundred and Twenty Thousand Guineas will be indispensible, to conclude with the four Powers at this Rate, besides a Present to the Ambassadors, and other incidental Charges. besides this a Present of five hundred Guineas is made upon the Arrival of a Consul in each state. No Man wishes more fervently that the Expence could be less, but the Fact cannot be altered and the Truth ought not to be concealed.

It may be reasonably concluded, that this great Affair cannot be finished, for much less than two hundred Thousand Pounds Sterling. – There is no Place in Europe or America where Congress can obtain such a sum, but in Holland. Perhaps a loan for two Millions of Guilders might be filled in Amsterdam upon the terms of the last.

If it is not done, this War will cost us more Millions of Sterling Money in a short time. besides the miserable Depression of the Reputation of the United States ~~and~~ the cruel Embarrassment of all our Commerce, and the intollerable Burthen of Insurance, added to the Cries of our Countrymen in Captivity.

The probable Success of Mʳ· Barclay and Mʳ· Lamb, need not be pointed out. If a perpetual Peace were made with those States, the Character of the United States would instantly rise, all over the World, our Commerce and Navigation and Fisheries would extend into the Mediterranean, to Spain & Portugal, France and England. The Additional Profits would richly repay the Interest, and our Credit would be adequate to all our Wants.

Col Smith is gone to Paris, he departed yesterday. By the Sixth Article of the Confederation "No State, without the Consent of the United States in Congress assembled shall send any Embassy to or receive any Embassy from, or enter into any Conference, Agreement Alliance or Treaty with any King, Prince, or State." All the States are so deeply interested in this Case, that surely no Seperate State can have occasion to move for the Consent of Congress upon this Occasion, but if unexpectedly Congress should not agree to treat, there are Several States in the Union So deeply interested in Navigation that it would richly compensate each of them, to go to the whole Extent of two hundred Thousand Pounds to obtain Peace. Nevertheless a Single State might obtain Peace and Security for its ships at a much cheaper rate.

With great and sincere Esteem, I have the Honour to be, Sir your most obedient and most humble servant   John Adams

NA: PCC, item 84, v. 6, pp. 119-124 (LS); M247, reel 113.

John Jay's Report on the Navigation of the Mississippi River

[New York] Office for foreign Affairs 25[th.] February 1786
The Secretary of the United States for the Department of foreign Affairs to whom was referred a Letter to him from A. Fowler[1] of 1[st.] October last, complaining that a Boat which he had sent down the Mississipi was stopped at the Natches by the Spaniards – Reports

That there is good Reason to believe that the King of Spain is resolved if possible to exclude all Nations from the Navigation of that Part of the Mississippi which runs between his Territories. –

That therefore the United States will not have that Navigation open to their Citizens unless by *Arms* or by *Treaty* That in the Opinion of your Secretary the Time for the *former* is not yet come – that the free Navigation of that River is now the Subject of Discussion between the spanish Encargado de Negocios and himself – and that great Difficulties oppose their agreeing on that Head. But that however doubtful the Success of these Negociations may be, it appears to him most prudent that they should not be precipitated; and therefore thinks that the Letter which he has written to M[r.] Fowler and of which a Copy is subjoined prevents the Necessity of taking further Measures for the present. As the Country adjacent to the River becomes filled with People, and the Affairs of the Confederacy become regulated and arranged, the Attainment of that and every other Object will daily and proportionably become more probable and easy. –

All which is submitted to the Wisdom of Congress.

John Jay–

NA: PCC, item 81, v. 2, pp. 39-40 (DS); M247, reel 107.

[1] *Fowler, Alexander. Originally an army auditor at Fort Pitt, he later ran a store there. He presumably also attempted to trade down the river by boat in 1785.*

Paul R. Randall to John Adams

Barcelona Feb. 25$^{th.}$ 1786 –

The last letter I had the Honor to address to your Excellency was of the 17$^{th.}$ instant – conveyed by Mr Harrison, who has resided in Cadiz, I believe in Quality of Consul – in which I suggested some small Difficulties embarrassing Mr Lamb's Embarkation – but as I had not received Intelligence of their Removal until Mr Harrison was on the Point [of] Setting out – he will supply to your Excellency, that Permission is granted to Mr Lamb for extracting the sum of £2,000 st[erling] out of the Kingdom upon giving Caution to abide the Directions of the Court thereupon. —

Mr Lamb has since purchased a Vessel, instead of freighting, which was perhaps rendered necessary considering a full Quarantine, and that he was demanded half the Price of a Small Vessel – for the Freight of a few Months. In three or four days the Vessel will be rendered fit for Sea – at the End of which Time, I know of no further Obstacles to impede our Progress to Algiers. We have no late Intelligence from thence, and are not acquainted or even informed: — whether the Spanish Peace is absolutely concluded or not – tho' we are in the presumption that it must be e'er this.

My Industry should not be wanting in Seeking every Occasion to advise your Excellency upon each individual Step, could my Services be equal with my Intentions – but that crude Information might rather obscure than reflect Light upon the Business — especially as we have not always safe Conveyances to command at this distance.

Mr Jefferson will conclude from M. Harrison that Mr Lamb will Shortly proceed – therefore it may not be of much Importance to offer this Letter for his Inspection – rather than take a more unsuspicious Method of forwarding it to your Excellency inclosed to my Brother — but as I conceived it might be in some Measure satisfactory to your Excellency to be ascertained in these trifling particulars in a Business so interesting; – I have taken the Liberty to write, and at the same Time to evince, that in Matters of more Consequence my Attention shall not be wanting.

With Sentiments of the highest Respect, your Excellency will permit me to consider myself Your most Obedient & hum Ser^t PR Randall

. . . . . .

MHS: *The Adams Papers, microfilm reel 367 (ALS).*

John Adams to John Jay

Sir   Grosvenor Square Feb 26. 1786

The Envoy from Portugal, has received from his Court an Answer to his Dispatches relative to the Treaty with the United States, and the enclosed Extract from it, which has been delayed some time by the Sickness of the Chevalier de Freire, the Portuguese Secretary of Legation, that Minister did me the Honour to deliver [it] to me two days ago, with his request that it might be transmitted to Congress. at the same time he delivered me the enclosed State of the Trade between the United States and Portugal the last Year.

When M^r· Jefferson arrives we shall endeavour to finish this Business.

The Proposition of Sending and receiving a Minister has been many times made before. – Congress will no doubt answer this which is now made formally and officially. The Regard which is due from one Sovereign to another, and indeed common Decency seems to require it. to refuse it would be thought Surprizing. indeed according to all the Rules of Politeness between Nations and Sovereigns, it ought to be left to the Option of her most faithfull Majesty to Send what Species of public Minister She shall judge proper, and Assurances should be given of the most amicable Disposition of Congress to receive him with all the respect due to his Sovereign and to send a Minister to her Majesty of equal Character.

The United States are at this moment Suffering Severely for Want of an equitable Adjustment of their affairs with the Powers of Europe, and Affrica which can never be accomplished, but by conforming to the Usages established in the World.

If the United States would come to the Resolution to prohibit all foreign Vessells from coming to their Ports, and confine all Exports and Imports to their own Ships and Seamen they would do, for any thing that I know, the wisest Thing which human Prudence could dictate. But then the Consequence would be obvious. They must give up the most of their Commerce, and live by their Agriculture. in this Case They might recall their Ministers and Send no more.

on the other Hand, if the United States would adopt the Principle of the French Oeconomists, and allow the Ships and Merchants of all Nations equal Privileges with their own Citizens, they need not give themselves any further Trouble about Treaties or Ambassadors. The Consequence nevertheless would be the Sudden Annihilation of all their Manufactures and Navigation; We should have the most luxurious set of Farmers that ever existed, and should not be able to defend our sea Coast against the Insults of a Pirate.

As these are two Extreams that we know Americans will never consent to, we must vindicate our own Manufactures and Navigation, by Legislation at home and Negotiation abroad, and therefore, the Prejudices against Exchanges of Public Ministers will be found some of the most pernicious that ever have arisen among American Citizens. Laws at home must be made in Conformity to the State of Affairs abroad, which can never be known to Congress but by Ambassadors.

With great Respect, I have the Honour to be, Sir your most obedient and most humble Servant   John Adams

NA: PCC, item 84, v. 6, pp. 127-130 (ALS); M247, reel 113.

John Adams to John Jay

Sir   Grosvenor Square Feb. 27. 1786
At the last Conferences, as they call here what is understood in Paris by Ambassadors Days the Marquis of Carmarthen was pleased to make an Apology for not having yet answered the Memorial requiring the Evacuation of the Posts. "It would sound oddly to say that he had delayed his answer, to prevent Delays, but it was true. He had drawn up his answer, but as he was obliged to Say Something, concerning the old Debts, he had been obliged to wait for a little further Information, that he might State in one View all the Acts of the Assemblies which had interposed Impediments." – As this is some kind of Respect to the Memorial, it ought to be communicated to Congress as no doubt it was intended and expected, that it should be.

The publick Prints will inform you, that the Newfoundland Bill[1] and the American Intercourse Bill[2] is revived. it would be sufficient to convince every American what the system is, to say that M[r] Jenkinson[3] was the Member of Administration and the House of Commons, Selected to conduct this Business. comparing his well known Character with what he said, you will believe that the same Men and the same Principles which have governed this Nation in their Conduct towards America these twenty Years, prevail to this hour as far as the Circumstances will admit; and that M[r] Pitt is either a convert to their sentiments, or is only an ostensible Minister.

It remains with the States to determine what Measures they will take to discourage a Commerce the most impoverishing and ruinous, that can be imagined, to promote a more beneficial Intercourse with the rest of Europe, and to support their own Manufactures and navigation, for on such Measures alone can they have any Dependence, in future.

With Sincere Esteem I have the Honor to be, Sir your most obedient and most humble servant   John Adams.

NA: PCC, item 84, v. 6, pp. 142-144 (ALS); M247, reel 113.

¹ The Newfoundland Act (25 George III, c. 1) permitted the importation of American produce to Newfoundland in British ships. Designed to rectify a situation in which poor Canadian harvests had left many in Newfoundland hungry, it was renewed on an annual basis until 1788, when it was believed that Canada was more capable of meeting the needs of Newfoundland.

² A reference to the American Intercourse Bill proposed by the Shelburne ministry in early 1783. The bill was an effort to keep the United States within the British economic sphere; its opponents charged that it would effectively repeal Britain's Navigation Act. It was defeated in 1783.

³ Jenkinson, Charles (1727-1808). British political figure. Member of Parliament, 1761-1786. Undersecretary of state, 1761-1763. Joint secretary to the treasury, 1763-1765. After Lord Bute's retirement, leader of the "King's Friends" in the House of Commons. A Lord of the Admiralty in Grafton's administration. A lord of the treasury, 1767-1772. Secretary at war under Lord North, 1778-1782. After the war, primarily interested in commercial affairs. President, council for trade and the plantations, 1786. Named Baron Hawkesbury, 1786. Played a principal part in negotiation of the Jay Treaty. Named Earl of Liverpool, 1796.

Lord Carmarthen to John Adams

Sir   St James's Feb 28. 1786

In answer to the Memorial you did me the Honour to deliver to me, on the 8ᵗʰ Decʳ, I have to observe to you, Sir, that it is His Majesty's fixed Determination, upon the present, as well as every other Occasion to Act in perfect Conformity to the strictest Principles of Justice and good Faith.

The seventh Article both of the Provisional and of the Definitive Treaties between His Majesty and the United States clearly Stipulates the withdrawing with all convenient Speed, His Majestys Armies, Garrisons and Fleets, from the said United States, and from every Port, Place and Harbour within the same; and no doubt can possibly arise respecting either the Letter or Spirit of such an Engagement. The fourth Article of the same Treaties as clearly Stipulates that Creditors, on either Side, shall meet with no lawful Impediment to the Recovery of the full Value in Sterling Money of all bonâ fide Debts, heretofore contracted.

The little Attention paid to the fulfilling this Engagement on the Part of the Subjects of the United States in general and the direct Breach of it, in many particular Instances, have already reduced many of the Kings Subjects to the utmost degree of Difficulty and Distress: nor have their Applications for Redress, to those whose Situations in America naturally pointed them out as the Guardians of public Faith, been as yet successfull in obtaining them that Justice to which, on every Principle of Law, as well as of Humanity, they were clearly and indisputably entitled.

The Engagements entered into by Treaty, ought to be mutual, and equally binding on the respective contracting Parties. It would therefore be the Heighth of Folly, as well as Injustice, to suppose, one Party alone obliged to a strict Observance of the Public Faith, while the other might remain free to deviate from its own Engagements, as often as Convenience might render such Deviation necessary, though at the Expence of its own national Credit and Importance.

I flatter myself however, Sir, that Justice will speedily be done to British Creditors; and I can assure you, Sir, that whenever America shall manifest a real Determination to fulfill her Part of the Treaty, Great Britain will not hesitate to prove her sincerity, to cooperate in whatever Points depend upon her for carrying every Article of it, into real and compleat Effect.

The inclosed Paper[1] contains a State of the Grievances complained of, by Merchants and other British Subjects, having Estates Property and Debts due to them in the several States of America

I am Sir your most obedient humble Servant   Carmarthen

NA: PCC, item 84, v. 6, pp. 151-154 (C); M247, reel 113.

[1] See JCC, 1786, pp. 784-797. For a contemporary copy, see NA: PCC, item 84, v. 6, pp. 155-176; M247, reel 113.

Lord Carmarthen to Sir John Temple

Sir,   St James's February 28th 1786.

I have received the Favor of your Letters dated the 7th Decr and the 5th Jan^{ry}, and I am sorry to find, that you had suffered so much from the bad Weather which had rendered your Voyage to North America so very tedious. I have laid your Letters before The King, and as I have the Satisfaction to acquaint you, that the Information which they contain has met with His Royal Approbation, I am persuaded you will continue to convey from Time to Time such farther Observations and Intelligence as you may be able to collect, and as may appear to you to be of use to His Majesty's Service.

I am also to desire you will procure and transmit to me with as much Expedition as possible, Copies of all Acts of Congress, and of all Acts of the Legislatures of the several Provinces of the said United States, any ways relating to or affecting the Commerce, or Shipping of His Majestys Dominions, with such Information or observations as may, in your Judgment, throw any Light thereupon.   Carmarthen

.   .   .   .

PRO: FO 4/4, pp. 107-108 (LC transcription).

Don Diego De Gardoqui to John Jay

Dear Sir   New York 28th Feby. 1786

You may remember that in one of the conversations which we had soon after I arrived here, you said that if you had returned directly from Spain to America you would have asked for a Permit to export a Spanish Horse for Breed, and that I offered to write and request such a Permit. I accordingly did write in June last to his Excellency Count de Florida Blanca who was pleased to mention it to the King; but his Majesty instead of Granting the Permit ordered a Horse to be sent to me for you. one was chosen afterwards and sent to Cadiz where he has been many months expecting a Vessel that might carry him to this Place. He has arrived at last after a voyage of 75 Days, and will be disembarked as soon as part of the Cargo is taken out – all which I communicate to you for your Information, repeating that I have the Honour to subscribe myself &ca.

Diego de Gardoqui

NA: PCC, item 97, p. 132 (translation); M247, reel 125.

John Adams to Matthew Robinson-Morris

Sir[1]   Grosvenor Square March. 2d 1786 –

You have obliged me very much by your kind Letter of 27th Feb. The Americans are indeed Englishmen, and will continue such in Language & sentiments and manners whether they are allowed to be friends or Compelled to be Ennemies of those other Englishmen who inhabit these Islands Great Britain and Ireland. The priviledges of purchasing inheriting exercising Trades, voting or being chosen into Offices of all kinds, if declared by Act of Parliament would no doubt be considered in a friendly light, but give me leave to Say would have no material effect, While embarrassments are either studiously or ignorantly thrown in the Way of Commerce – The United States are willing to throw Wide Open every Port [in] their dominions to British Ships and Merchants and Merchandizes, and I am ready in their behalf to pledge their Faith in a Treaty to this Effect; upon the reciprocal Stipulation of this Nation that her Ports Shall be equally open to our Ships, Merchants and Produce But the United States must repel Monopolies by Monopolies, and answer prohibitions by Prohibitions. I may be uninformed respecting the East Indies But although the E. I. Company have by their Charter and Act of Parliament An exclusive Priviledge of Importing East India Goods into the Port of London only, I dont know that Americans or any other Foreign Nation are Prohibited to Trade with the British Factories and Settlements in Asia: This nevertheless is not a Point with us. The Ministry might except the Charter of the rights of the East India Company. But the American Commerce is a System and a free Intercourse between the United States and Canada Nova Scotia Newfoundland, and the West India Islands as well as a Markett for their Oyl and Fins and Sperma Caeti Candles and ready Built Ships is so Essential to it, that if One Nation will not another must If England will not Germany Holland France &c. will – & this commerce is even more necessary to your Colonies than it is to us, and the Present Policy is Sowing the Seeds of disquiet and discontent in the Minds of your Colonies that will alienate them all if persisted in. this Uneasiness has already broke out in Barbadoes into Violence which Occasioned the Troops to fire upon the People by which a Number were Killed as the Public Prints inform us, and it will increase from day to Day: the 5$^{th:}$ of March 1770 ought to be an eternal Warning to this Nation on that Night the foundation of American Independance was laid. I have the Honour to agree perfectly with you in opinion that England might receive more benefit from a liberal Commerce with America, than She would if We had remained under her Government. and I may be permitted to say that having been from 1774 to this day either in Congress or in her Service Abroad I have been fully acquainted with every Step and Motive of her Conduct towards the Powers of Europe, and it has been her Constant Rule to conceed no Preferences to France or any other Nation, that She might be at Liberty to Settle a Commercial Plan with England upon the Fairest Terms. Little did She expect or foresee that England would refuse the favours intended her. — I must say the Ministry appear to have no idea of the Principles on which Congress have acted. The consequence must be that the Trade of America must Leave this Country and go to her rivals — The Ministry and the Nation too seem to Consider the United States as a Rival and we know very well What in English Lexicography, is the meaning of the Word Rival. it is an Ennemy to be beat down by every means but it may be depended on that if the United States are treated in this manner, they will make Common Cause with the other rivals of British Commerce which at this day are almost as numerous as the Nations of Europe.

It is the Earnest desire of the United States to live in friendship with this Country, and to have no other Contention but in reciprocal good offices.

it seems to be your opinion that the People of England have the same disposition. I beg you to explain yourself on this Head, as I must confess I have not met with any Symptoms of it excepting in a few a very few Individuals, much fewer than I expected when I first arrived here. to what purpose is the universal Industry to represent the Commerce of the United States as of no Importance? Where would have been the Stocks – the Exchange and the revenue of this Country without it! there has been a Constant Stream of Produce Cash and Bills flowing into this Country Since the Peace from the U.S. Remittances to an immense amount have been made and even a large Sum through France Spain Portugal and Holland, which has contributed in no Small degree to turn the Ballance of Exchange so much in your favour as well as to throw a Surplus into the Exchequer, and raise the stocks. and these Remittances might have been nearly doubled if Common Sense had dictated to the British Poli[ti]cians to receive from us in Payment Such things as we have.

The Americans are at this day a great People and are not to be triffled with their Numbers have increased fifty per Cent since 1774. a People that can Multiply at this rate amidst all the Calamities of such a War of Eight years, will in twenty years more be too respectable to want Friends. they might sell their friendship at this time at a very high Price to others however lightly it may be Esteemed here.

I have the Misfortune to differ widely from your opinion in the address that the "Independance of America happened a Century too Soon" it would be easy to show that it happened at the best point of time. there is no imaginable Period past or future, at which it could have been brought into Event to so much Advantage for America but this would lead me too far. the Information you may have received concerning the Confusions Distresses &c of the U. S. are of a piece with those misrepresentations which have constantly misguided this Nation for five and twenty years. The Inconveniences now felt are confined to those who have been deceived into an Excess of Trade with this Country, by Expectations which have been disappointed that the Usual Remittances would have been received; and have arisen from a desire to Live and Trade in friendship with England. The Country in General is in a thriving and flourishing Condition and this Country alone will finally be the sufferer by the Impediments they have thrown in the Way of their own Interest.

You will perceive Sir that I have written too freely and too largely. in my Situation it may be imprudent. But the Subject is of Great Importance and deserves your closest attention. you will Greatly Oblige me by Communicating your Sentiments with equal Frankness.

With Great Esteem I have the Honour to be yours &c &c –

John Adams

MHS: *The Adams Papers, microfilm reel 113 (LBkC).*

[1] *Robinson-Morris, Matthew (1713-1800). British scholar and political figure. A devout Whig, he opposed Lord North's American policy in four pamphlets published between 1774 and 1777. From 1794, Baron Rokeby.*

Charles Thomson to John Jay

Sir   [New York] Office of Secretary of Congress 3^{d} March 1786
    Your Letter of the 1$^{st.1}$ has been laid before the United States in Congress assembled and I have it in charge to inform you that Congress have no objection against your accepting the Spanish Horse presented to you by his Catholic Majesty.
    With much respect I have the Honor to be &$^{ca.}$ Cha$^{s.}$ Thomson

NA: PCC, item 120, v. 2, p. 124 (LBkC); M40, reel 2.
[1] *See NA: PCC, item 80, v. 2, pp. 169-170; M247, reel 106.*

John Jay to Louis Guillaume Otto

Sir   [New York] Office for foreign Affairs 6$^{th.}$ March 1786
    Various Considerations arising from the local and other Circumstances of the United States induce me to think that the 4$^{th.}$ and 5$^{th.}$ Articles in the proposed Convention for regulating the intercourse between the Post offices of France and the United States will not be expedient – I have the Honour of enclosing a Plan, which being less complicated would in my opinion be more easily executed.
    It will give me pleasure to confer with you on this subject whenever it may be convenient to you, for it is my wish that this and every other measure interesting to both Countries may be so concerted and conducted as to promise the most satisfaction to each.
    I have the Honour to be &$^{ca.}$ John Jay

NA: PCC, item 120, v. 2, pp. 125-126 (LBkC); M40, reel 2.

[Enclosure]
Draft Franco-American Postal Convention

Plan of a Convention between the Post office of France and that of the United States of America for regulating their mutual Intercourse and correspondence –

His most Christian Majesty having authorized   The Director of the Post office of France – and the United States having authorised Ebenezer Hazard Esq[r.] their postmaster General to form and conclude such Convention, they have accordingly agreed upon the following Articles Viz[t.]

1

There shall be maintained on both sides a good, constant, and mutual Correspondence for the Transmission, Reception, and Distribution of Letters, Dispatches, and Packets.

2

All Imposts, Postage, and Charges which may be due on Letters passing from the post offices of France to those of the United States, shall be paid in France and on the other Hand, all Letters passing from the post offices of the United States to those of France, shall be paid in the United States. That is to say, no french or other Postage due on Letters coming from that Kingdom to the United States shall be demanded or received in the United States; nor any american postage due on Letters going from the United States to France shall there be demanded or received – The Packet postage on Letters passing by Packets to or from France and the United States to belong to the Sovereign whose Packet shall carry such Letters.

3

And as his most Christian Majesty has in order to promote and facilitate the Intercourse and Correspondence between the two Countries, been pleased to establish Packets at L'Orient which sail once a month from that Place to New York. It is agreed that all Letters intended to be transmitted from L'Orient to New-York by the said Packets shall be put up into a Mail by the Post office at L'Orient, which Mail sealed with the known and acknowledged Seal of that Post Office, and directed to the Post Office at New York, shall on its arrival at New York be immediately delivered to the said Post office, where the same shall be opened by the Post Master, in the presence of the Consul or vice Consul of France there residing, or of the french agent for the said Packets, and all such Letters as may be found therein franked by the french Ministers of either of the great Departments, shall be immediately delivered to the said Consul, Vice Consul, or Agent, to be forwarded and transmitted in such manner as he or they may think proper – And further that whenever and as often as the post master at

New York shall receive from a Captain of one of the said Packets a Mail so put up and directed, and being in good order, he shall give to the said Captain a Receipt for the same, mentioning therein the name of the Captain and Packet who brought it, the Time when received and that the same was in good order.

4

That all Letters intended to be transmitted from New York by one of the said Packets to L'Orient shall be put up into a Mail by the Post Office at New York, which mail sealed with the known and acknowledged seal of the said Office and directed to the Post Office at L'Orient shall at the stated Times appointed for the sailing of a Packet, be delivered by the said Post Master to the Captain thereof who shall thereupon give him a Receipt for the same specifying when he received it and that it was in good order.

5

That whenever one of the said mails shall arrive at L'Orient and be delivered to the post Office there it shall be opened in the Presence of the Consul Vice Consul or Agent of the United States there residing, to whom all such Letters found therein as may be franked by the President of Congress or either of the Ministers of the great Departments shall be immediately delivered, and they shall be forwarded and transmitted in any manner that the said Consul, Vice Consul, or Agent may think proper. But they or such one of them to whom the said Letters shall be so delivered shall without Delay give a proper Receipt for the same to the Post Office—

6

The Director of the Post Office at L'Orient and the Post master at New York shall with every Mail send to each other a Letter of advice specifying the number of Letters enclosed in it; which said Letters shall be counted on the opening of the mail to determine whether the number received be the same with the number sent. –

NA: PCC, *item 120, v. 2, pp. 126-130 (LBkC); M40, reel 2.*

Louis Guillaume Otto to Comte de Vergennes

[Translation]

N°· 41. Duplicate.   New York, 6 March 1786.
My Lord

The Draft of the Convention between M. le Baron d'Ogny and the Director of American Post Offices has been in Mr. Jay's hands for several months. In vain have I reminded him of the necessity of settling a matter so interesting for the Commerce of the two Nations as soon as possible; instead of having our plan adopted as You had desired it, he has at last just sent me a Draft entirely different from that which I had communicated to him. I have the honor to send You the enclosed translation of it; I could not prevent myself from showing my surprise at it to Mr. Jay; I observed to him that this new plan did not in any way fulfill our object, that the purpose of this convention was to prevent letters from remaining in the post office for lack of franking, and to give to the respective managements of the post offices the facility to recover what was due them; that moreover the individuals who sent letters were only too disposed to defraud the packet boats by transmitting their correspondence by other opportunities, but that in the event that letters would be paid for only upon their reception, the packet boat would be preferred to any other ship; that with regard to the postage due to the Administration of the packet boats, it was unjust to have it supported solely by the French while the Americans never paid it, since the expenses of the packet boat were in all cases discharged only in France. Mr. Jay insisted on his plan; he told me that it was founded on a complete reciprocity and that local circumstances did not permit Congress to adopt our draft; that moreover the Director of Post Offices would explain to me much better than he the reasons that render our arrangement impracticable. I have since had a conference with this Officer, who assured me that the same Convention had taken place with England: but that several reasons had obliged the United States to cancel it. "It is not," he continued, "that we are not persuaded that such an arrangement is perfectly just and reciprocal, but we do not have the same means as the old Governments of Europe for executing a plan of administration. By the projected Convention we would engage ourselves to pay the Management of the French post offices for all the letters that we would receive from it, but a great part of those letters could be lost by the inadvertence of subordinate Clerks or by accidents which the rigor of winters and the dangerous passages of rivers render only too frequent. In these cases the United States would be held to pay France for letters which they would not have received in total. Moreover, it happens rather often that during the absence of the Postmaster, letters are lost or removed gratis by individuals; negligence that has hitherto occasioned only a negative loss for the Management of post offices, but this loss would become positive if we engaged ourselves to pay France for the letters that we would have received. Besides, the difference of the charges marked on the back of the letters would give rise to much prejudicial defiance towards our administration. We have against us a rather troublesome experience. In the space of one year we have returned to England refused letters for the sum of 500 Pounds Sterling, without reckoning what has been mislaid or lost. We do not have enough employees to handle so many details, and my advice is to leave things on the old footing." The reasoning of this Director of Post Offices appeared sufficiently satisfactory to me; I promised him, My Lord, to send You Mr. Jay's new plan.

If I am permitted to express my sentiment on this latter project, I cannot refrain from observing that it is not only inadmissible but entirely useless; *inadmissible* because it engages us without any compensation to do a thing that should depend only on our will, because it submits us to formalities incompatible with the dignity of the King, who should be completely free to stipulate to his packet boats the course that appears to him the most advantageous, and because we would appear to share a favor while we confer a very extravagant and absolutely gratuitous one; *useless* because the principal points of this Plan have hitherto been executed by order of the Court, the letters have been franked in France, the mail carried to the Post Office and fastened with the Seal of the Consulate. Moreover, Mr. Jay has not yet made his report to Congress on it, and I am sure that I will have the time to receive Your orders before this Secretary of State sends his new plan to me officially. I beg You, My Lord, to stipulate for me the response that I shall make to him.

I am with a profound respect, My Lord, Your most humble and most obedient Servant,   Otto.
Received 23 June ——
Sent copy to M. d'Ogny on 15 August 1786.

FFAA: Pol. Corr., U.S., v. 31, f. 164-167 (LC transcription).

Board of Treasury to John Adams

Sir,   Board of Treasury March 7th, 1786. —
We do ourselves the honor of transmitting to you the Resolves of Congress of the 15th Day of February last, from which you will observe the embarrassments under which the United States labor to comply with their Foreign Engagements through the want of Exertions in the several States to Pay in their Quotas of the annual Requisitions. – The present State of the Treasury is in consequence so reduced, that we are apprehensive it may not perhaps be in our power to Remit to the Commissioners of the Dutch Loans in Europe sufficient Funds in Season to discharge the whole Interest which will become due on the Dutch Loans on the First day of June next if the Sum of Eighty thousand Dollars, which has been appropriated by the Resolves of Congress of the 15[th.] February 1785, for the purpose of Forming

Treaties with the Barbary Powers should be drawn out of the hands of the Dutch Commissioners before that day. – We are using our endeavours to make Arrangements so that our Remittances may arrive in Season; but as they may be prevented by some casualty from coming to hand by the first of next June, it becomes our duty to request the favor of you to avoid (if it possibly can be done) drawing out of the hands of the Dutch Commissioners, the Monies appropriated for the purpose of making Treaties with the Barbary Powers, before the first of June next, and to direct it (if our Remittances should not arrive in Season) to be appropriated to the Payment of the June Interest. –

You may rest assured, Sir, that every exertion will be made by this Board that the Remittances may arrive in Season, without placing any dependence on this resource; and that at all events, the Sum of Seventy thousand Dollars, shall be Remitted to the Dutch Commissioners on or before the first Day of August next to wait your Orders.

To your Excellency who knows so well the importance of preserving the Publick Faith with Foreign Nations, and particularly with the Dutch Money Lenders, it would be unnecessary to use any Arguments to shew the propriety of our Application on this Subject. – We are satisfied that if the State of the Negotiations will possibly admit of it, you will permit this Money to remain for the purposes we have mentioned. –

On examining the Abstract of the Distribution of the Obligations on the Five Million Loan to the 30[th.] September last, we find that there remained Undistributed on that Day One hundred and thirty eight Obligations, equal to 138,000 Florins. It is much to be wished that this Loan may be completed with all the dispatch possible. Without it we have too much reason to fear we shall experience difficulties in remitting sufficient Sums to Europe to Pay the Interest of the Foreign Loans, and the Salaries of the Foreign Ministers and Agents during the present Year. – Samuel Osgood[1]
Walter Livingston[2]
Arthur Lee[3]

MHS: *The Adams Papers, microfilm reel 367* (C).

[1] *Osgood, Samuel (1748-1813). Massachusetts political figure. Delegate, Essex County convention, 1774, and Provincial Congress, 1775. Continental Army officer, attaining rank of colonel. Member, state constitutional convention, 1779, and state Senate, 1780. Member, Continental Congress, 1781-1784. One of three commissioners of the U.S. Treasury, 1785-1789. Postmaster General of the United States, 1789-1791. Later served in New York state assembly and held minor federal posts in New York.*

[2] *Livingston, Walter (1740-1797). New York political figure. Member, provincial convention and first provincial congress, 1775. Commissary of stores and provisions for New York, and deputy commissary general of the Continental Army's northern*

department, 1775-1776. Member, state assembly, 1777-1779; Speaker, 1778. Member, New York-Massachusetts boundary commission, 1784. Member, Continental Congress, 1784-1785. Commissioner, United States Treasury, 1785-1789.

³ Lee, Arthur (1740-1792). Colonial agent, diplomat, political figure. Practiced law in London, 1770-1776. Commissioned agent of Massachusetts, 1770. Appointed correspondent of Congress in London, 1775. Appointed correspondent of Congress in London, 1775. With Silas Deane and Benjamin Franklin (whom he subsequently accused of malfeasance), commissioner to France, 1776-1779. Commissioner to Spain, 1777. Returned to America, 1780. Member, Virginia House of Delegates, 1781-1783, 1785-1786. Member, Continental Congress, 1782-1784. Member, U.S. Board of Treasury, 1785-1789.

John Jay's Report on British Consuls

[New York] Office for foreign Affairs 8ᵗʰ March 1786
The Secretary of the United States for the Department of foreign Affairs to whom was referred his Letter of 28ᵗʰ February enclosing one to him from the british Consul General with two Memorials presented to him one by Wᵐ Hunt,¹ and the other by Richᵈ Laurence² to report on the *Propriety of the Application* and the *Expediency of a Reply* – Reports –

That the Cognizance of Consuls being confined to Matters arising within their Consulates respecting the Trade and Navigation of their Nations, with the one to which they are sent, direct or official Applications from them to the Sovereign of the Country on Subjects foreign to the Objects of their Commissions, would certainly be irregular, and unless under very particular Circumstances improper. –

Mʳ· Temple's Letter does not appear to your Secretary to come within the Description of such a *direct* and *official* Application. It contains nothing official in Stile, Matter or Subscription, it is silent as to the Treaty, and makes no Complaint. Your Secretary views it in no other Light than that of conveying Information respecting Matters in which public Justice *may be* concerned, and Humanity certainly is. –

In the Judgement of your Secretary therefore, it is not necessary that any Answer should be given by Congress to Mʳ· Temple, nor any Notice taken of *these Papers particularly.* –

But your Secretary thinks, that Policy as well as Justice, demands that Infractions of the Treaty of Peace should not pass unnoticed, especially when the Evidence of them exists in the Laws of either of the States, which, being matters of Record and of public Notoriety, must be supposed to come officially to the Knowledge of Congress. –

Your Secretary apprehends from the Silence, which Britain has hitherto observed respecting this Subject, that she is well content these Infractions should remain uncorrected, that they may hereafter serve to justify such Measures as she may wish or find it convenient to pursue, under the Pretext of Retaliation; either by continuing to detain from us our frontier Posts and Countries, or by any other Plans which Resentment or Policy may suggest. Your Secretary takes the Liberty further to remark, that in any such Event France will probably not think herself obliged to fulfil her Guarantee of the Countries acknowledged to be ours by the Treaty of Peace, unless we on our Part fulfil the Terms of that Treaty. And as it is not to be presumed that these Infractions will never be drawn into Question or Discussion, your Secretary thinks it would redound more to the Honor as well as Advantage of the United States, to do Justice while unpressed, than at a Season when every Thing they may do of that Kind, may be imputed to less meritorious Motives. –

All which is submitted to the Wisdom of Congress –   John Jay –

Ent^d· read 8 March 1786

NA: PCC, item 81, v. 2, pp. 53-56 (DS); M247, reel 107.

[1] *Hunt, William. New York loyalist jailed at Westchester, NY, in August 1784 for depredations committed while a member of a loyalist military unit during the war. With other loyalists in similar circumstances, he appealed to British Consul General Sir John Temple in February 1786 and to Congress in August of that year. The Papers of the Continental Congress do not record the final disposition of this case.*

[2] *Lawrence, Richard. Loyalist imprisoned in New York after November 1784 trial in which he was convicted of depredations against private citizens during the war. His failure to plead the Sixth Article of the peace treaty in his defense, which would have absolved him of responsibility for actions performed under orders from British military and civilian commanders, was cited by John Jay in reports to Congress as the reason for Lawrence's continued incarceration.*

Louis Guillaume Otto to Comte de Vergennes

[Translation]

N^o· 42. Duplicate.   New York, 8 March 1786

My Lord

By the 8th· article of our Treaty of Commerce, the King engages himself to employ his good offices with the Emperor of Morocco and the regencies of Algiers, Tunis, and Tripoli to protect the United States from all insults on the part of the Barbary Corsairs. A Gazetteer has taken the opportunity to make public that Congress has fulfilled all its engagements towards France, but that the piracies of the Algerians sufficiently prove that His Majesty has not been equally faithful to his promises. It has occurred to me, moreover, that the public was rather disposed to believe that, very far from concerning ourselves for the Americans with the Barbary powers, we secretly favored their hostilities against the flag of the United States. I thought I should have an explanation of this with Mr. Jay and with several members of Congress; I told them that I was persuaded that as soon as His Majesty was requested to interpose his good offices in their favor, he would execute this part of the Treaty with as much exactitude as he had fulfilled his other engagements. They all answered me that Congress had never shared the opinion of some ill-intentioned persons regarding France, and that it was so convinced of His Majesty's good dispositions, that it has given Mr. Jefferson orders to implore his interposition with the Barbary States. Mr. Jay took the opportunity to assure me that the little jealousy that we have hitherto displayed in India and the cordiality with which we have received Americans there had produced an excellent effect, that he perceived not only from his private conversations but by the letters that are sent to him from various parts of the Continent, that his compatriots would not know how to praise enough the disinterest of France in admitting the flag of the United States to its ports in India; that the Dutch minister, who had refused the Captains letters of recommendation, had lost a great deal of his popularity, and that the Americans would always be sensible of all that would be done for or against their interests in that part of the world, that they could not do without this Commerce, and that no obstacle could vanquish their penchant for these perilous but profitable expeditions. Among many other grievances, My Lord, the Americans cannot pardon England for the overt opposition and the underhanded schemings that she permits herself in order to exclude them from India.

Not a week goes by without some State of the Union giving proofs of its aversion to that power. The *Test* law, or the form of the oath of allegiance, has occupied the Pennsylvania Assembly for some time. Some members of this Legislature, and especially Mr. R. Morris, wished to strike from this law an Article relative to the abjuration of allegiance to the King of England. Their arguments were rather specious: "To abjure formally the Sovereignty of England is to suppose that this power is still in a position to assert its title to this country, it is to doubt the absolute independence of Pennsylvania and the validity of the treaty by which the King of Great Britain renounces all his rights. The Oath of allegiance taken to the Sovereignty of this State contains an implicit renunciation of the dominion of all powers whatsoever, and consequently of England." It was difficult to respond in a satisfactory manner to this reasoning, but the wish of the people was too strongly pronounced for the Assembly to dare contravene it. During the debates, several menacing addresses were presented to it, and among others those from the County of Dauphin, whose expressions were so incautious that the Speaker ordered these addresses to be thrown under the table. The Bill was approved by a great majority, and this formality of solemnly renouncing the Sovereignty of England will be forever perpetuated in this State, the reminder of a revolution that time could have effaced.

I am with a profound respect, My Lord, Your most humble and most obedient Servant,   Otto.
Received 23 June.

FFAA: Pol. Corr., U.S., v. 31, f. 168-170 (LC transcription).

John Jay Report on the Treaty with Prussia

[New York] Office for foreign Affairs 9th. March 1786
The Secretary of the United States for the Department of foreign Affairs to whom was referred the Treaty lately concluded with Prussia, and transmitted with a Joint Letter from Mr. Adams and Mr. Jefferson – Reports

That on considering the several Articles in the said Treaty, he observes that each Party is to enjoy in the Dominions of the other the same Rights and Privileges as to Commerce &c as are or shall be granted to the *most favored Nation*. –

On this Point your Secretary adheres to the same Opinion which he heretofore communicated to Congress in his Report of 17th. May last, on the Draft of a Treaty of Amity and Commerce transmitted by the American Ministers. He also thinks that much of the reasoning in that Report applies to certain other Articles in the Treaty under Consideration.-

Your Secretary suspects that the following Article is a little equivocal Vizt.

"more especially each Party shall have a Right to carry their own Produce, *Manufactures & Merchandize* in their own or any other Vessels, to *any Parts* of the Dominions of the other, *where* it shall be lawful for all the Subjects or Citizens of that other freely to purchase them; and thence to take the Produce, Manufactures, & Merchandize of the other which all the said Citizens or Subjects shall in like Manner be free to sell them paying &ca." –

Altho the Meaning of this Article appears obvious, yet it might perhaps be construed to imply that there are or will be *certain free* Ports, *where* every

Thing brought by or belonging to either Party may be freely sold and bought, in Contradistinction to other Ports and Places in the same Dominion *where* such Liberty is not allowed. The Intention of the Article doubtless is that such Liberty is to be enjoyed at *every* Port and Place. –

The latter part of the 10 Article is not quite reciprocal. Viz:

"And where on the Death of any Person holding real Estate within the Territories of the one Party, such real Estate would by the Laws of the Land descend on a Citizen or Subject of the other, were he not disqualified by Alienage, such *Subject* shall be allowed a reasonable Time to sell the same and to withdraw the Proceeds without Molestation &c: *But this Article shall not derogate in any Manner from the Force of the Laws already published or hereafter to be published by the King of Prussia to prevent the Emigrations of his Subjects.*"

This latter Clause reserves to the King of Prussia the Right of making Laws to prevent Emigrations, but does not so limit the Extent of those Laws, as that they shall not operate against the Right to Sell &c· granted in the preceding one; for instead of saying that such Laws shall not derogate in any Manner from the true Intent and Meaning of this Article, it says that this Article shall not derogate in any Manner from the Force of his Laws &ca· Besides the like Right is not reserved to the United States. –

Upon the whole Matter, and particularly considering that the Duration of this Treaty is limited to *ten* Years, your Secy· thinks that it will be prudent and best to ratify it. –

A Year from the Day of the Signature is allowed for the Exchange of Ratifications – It appears to have been signed by

Baron Thulemeir[1]	10 September 1785
Mr· Adams	5 August 1785
Doctr· Franklin	9 July 1785
Mr· Jefferson	28 July 1785

This Term of a Year is doubtless to be computed from 10 September last, for as the Prussian Minister appears to have signed it last, and it was not until then compleat, there can be no Room for the Questions that might have otherwise arisen on the Subject. –

All which is submitted to the Wisdom of Congress. –

John Jay –

read 10 March 1786

NA: PCC, item 81, v. 2, pp. 57-60 (DS); M247, reel 107.
[1] *Thulemeyer, Friedrich Wilhelm, Baron von. Prussian diplomat. Envoy to the United Provinces of the Netherlands, 1763-1788.*

Thomas Jefferson to John Jay

Sir –   London Mar. 12. 1786.

The date of a letter from London will doubtless be as unexpected to you as it was unforeseen by myself a few days ago. on the 27th of the last month Col^{o.} Smith arrived in Paris with a letter from mr Adams enforming me that there was at this place a minister from Tripoli, having general powers to enter into treaties on behalf of his state and with whom it was possible we might do something in our commission to that power; and that he gave reason to believe he could also take arrangements with us for Tunis. he further added that the minister of Portugal here had received ultimate instructions from his court, and that probably that treaty might be concluded in the space of three weeks, were we all on the spot together. he therefore pressed me to come over immediately. the first of these objects had some weight on my mind because as we had sent no person to Tripoli or Tunis, I thought if we could meet a minister from them on this ground our arrangements would be settled much sooner & at less expence. but what principally decided with me was the desire of bringing matters to a conclusion with Portugal before the term of our commission should expire, or any new turn in the negociations of France & England should abate their willingness to fix a connection with us. a third motive had also it's weight. I hoped that my attendance here & the necessity of shortening it might be made use of to force a decisive answer from this court. I therefore concluded to comply with mr Adams's request. I went immediately to Versailles & apprised the count de Vergennes that circumstances of public duty called me hither for three or four weeks arranged with him some matters, & set out with Col^{o.} Smith for this place where we arrived last night, which was as early as the excessive rigour of the weather admitted. I saw mr Adams immediately, and again to-day. he informs me that the minister of Portugal was taken ill five or six days ago, has been very much so, but is now somewhat better. it would be very mortifying indeed should this accident, with the shortness of the term to which I limit my stay here, defeat what was the principal object of my journey, & that without which I should hardly have undertaken it. with respect to this country, I had no doubt but that every consideration had been urged by mr Adams which was proper to be urged. nothing remains undone in this way. but we shall avail ourselves of my Journey here as if made on purpose just before the expiration of our commission to form our report to Congress on the execution of that commission, which report they may be given to know, cannot be formed without decisive information of the ultimate determination of their court. there is no doubt what that determination will be: but it will be useful to have it, as it may put an end to all further expectations on our side the water, & shew that the time is come for doing whatever is to be done by us for counteracting the unjust & greedy designs of this country. we shall have the honour before I leave this place, to inform you of the result of the several matters which have brought me to it.

A day or two before my departure from Paris, I received your letter of January   . the question therein proposed How far France considers herself as bound to insist on the delivery of the posts, would infallibly produce another, How far we consider ourselves as guarantees of their American possessions, and bound to enter into any future war in which these may be attacked? the words of the treaty of alliance seem to be without ambiguity on either head. yet I should be afraid to commit Congress by answering without authority. I will endeavour on my return to sound the opinion of the minister if possible, without exposing myself to the other question. should any thing forcible be meditated on those posts, it would possibly be thought prudent previously to ask the good offices of France to obtain their delivery. in this case they would probably say we must first execute the treaty on our part by repealing all acts which have contravened it. now this measure, if there be any candour in the court of London, would suffice to obtain a delivery of the posts from them, without the mediation of any third power. however if this mediation should be finally needed I see no reason to doubt our obtaining it, and still less to question it's omnipotent influence on the British court.

I have the honour to be with sentiments of the highest respect & exteem Sir your most obedient & most humble serv.ᵗ·   Th: Jefferson

NA: PCC, *item 87, v. 1, pp. 243-245 (ALS); M247, reel 115.*

John Jay to George Washington

Dear Sir[1]   New York 16 March 1786

.   .   .   .   .

Altho you have wisely retired from public Employments, and calmly view from the Temple of Fame, the various Exertions of that Sovereignty and Independence which Providence has enabled you to be so greatly & gloriously instrumental in securing to your Country; yet I am persuaded that you cannot view them with the Eye of an unconcerned Spectator.

Experience has pointed out Errors in our national Government, which call for Correction, and which threaten to blast the Fruit we expected from our "Tree of Liberty." The Convention proposed by Virginia[2] may do some good, and would perhaps do more, if it comprehended more Objects. – an opinion begins to prevail that a general Convention for revising the articles of Confederation would be expedient. Whether the People are yet ripe for such a Measure, or whether the System proposed to be attained by it, is only to be expected from Calamity & Commotion, is difficult to ascertain. I think we are in a delicate Situation, and a Variety of Considerations and Circumstances give me uneasiness. It is in Contemplation to take measures for forming a general convention – the Plan is not matured – if it should be well concerted and take Effect, I am fervent in my Wishes, that it may comport with the Line of Life you have marked out for yourself, to favor your Country with your Counsels on such an important & single Occasion. I suggest this merely as a Hint for Consideration, and am with the highest Respect & Esteem Dear Sir Your most ob$^{t.}$ & very h'ble. Servant

John Jay –

LC: *George Washington Papers, microfilm reel 96.*

[1] *Washington, George (1732-1799). Virginia political figure and military leader. Militia officer, 1752-1758. Member, Virginia House of Burgesses, 1759-1775. Member, Continental Congress, 1774-1775. Commander-in-Chief, Continental Army, 1775-1783. President, Constitutional Convention, 1787. President of the United States, 1789-1797.*

[2] *Convention proposed by Virginia. In March 1785, at the suggestion of James Madison, delegates from Virginia and Maryland met at Alexandria and Mount Vernon, Virginia, to negotiate an agreement regarding commerce on the Potomac River. The Maryland legislature later called for another conference on commercial questions, to include Pennsylvania and Delaware. The Virginia legislature agreed, but Madison secured a broadening of the invitation to include all the States in a general trade convention to be held at Annapolis, Maryland, in September 1786. Delegates from five States (New York, New Jersey, Pennsylvania, Delaware, and Virginia) met as planned. The following year, another convention met in Philadelphia to revise the Articles of Confederation.*

John Jay's Report of Instructions
to the Ministers to France and Spain

[New York] Office for foreign Affairs 22$^{d.}$ March 1786

The Secretary of the United States for the Department of foreign Affairs to whom was referred his Report of 31$^{st.}$ January last on certain Letters from M$^{r.}$ Adams, in order that he might prepare Drafts of the Instructions therein proposed –

Reports

That in his Opinion the Minister Plenipotentiary of the United States at the Court of Versailles should be instructed in Manner following Viz$^{t.}$

Sir

It is the pleasure of Congress that you represent to his most Christian Majesty –

That by the 11th. Article of the Treaty of Alliance between his said Majesty and the United States, they guaranty to each other as follows –

"The two Parties guaranty mutually from the present Time and for ever, against all other Powers, *to wit*, the United States to his most Christian Majesty, the present Possessions of the Crown of France in America, as well as those which it may acquire by the future Treaty of Peace; and his most Christian Majesty guarantys on his part to the United States, their Liberty, Sovereignty and Independence, absolute and unlimited, as well in Matters of Government as Commerce, and also their Possessions, and the Additions or Conquests that their Confederation may obtain during the War, from any of the Dominions now or heretofore possessed by Great-Britain in North-America, conformable to the 5th. and 6th. Articles abovewritten; the whole *as their Possession shall be fixed and assured to the said States, at the Moment of the Cessation of their present War with England.* –

That the United States consider all the Countries, Dominions and territorial Rights ascertained and assured to them at the Conclusion of the late War, by the Treaty of Peace between them and Great Britain, to be comprehended within the Terms and the true Intent and Meaning of the said Guarantee. –

That among other Obstacles to their full and perfect Enjoyment of the said Countries and territorial Rights, Great Britain continues to withold from them the Possession of their frontier Posts and Places occupied by them during the late War within the Boundaries of the United States, as ascertained & fixed by the said Treaty of Peace – Altho' by the 7th. Article of the said Treaty it was stipulated and agreed, that his britannic Majesty should *with all convenient Speed,* withdraw all his Armies and Garrisons from the said United States and from *every Post and Place within the same* &^{ca.} –

That as near three Years have since elapsed, the United States consider the Detention of those Posts and Places as being contrary to the Terms of the Treaty, and inconsistent with the good Faith with which it ought to have been observed. –

That they have by their Minister at the Court of London remonstrated to his britannic Majesty on this Subject, but that no satisfactory Answer has as yet been given to them. –

That from the defensive State in which those Posts and Places are kept, as well as from the Number of Forces stationed in the Province of Quebec, the Intention of his britannic Majesty to evacuate them has become problematical. –

That being thus circumstanced, the United States think it their Duty to lay these Facts before their good Friend and Ally and to request that in the first Instance, he will be pleased to join with them in making such further Remonstrances to his britannic Majesty, as it is to be hoped may render any less pacific Proceedings unnecessary. –

That the Confidence which the United States repose in the Justice and Good Faith of his Majesty, leaves them no Room to doubt of his Readiness to join with them in the Measure proposed; and therefore that they have instructed their Minister at the Court of London, as soon as he shall be informed thereof, to confer freely and fully with his Majesty's Minister at the same Court; and in Concert with him, to make such Remonstrances on the Subject to his britannic Majesty, as they may jointly think most Expedient and conformable to their respective Instructions. –

It is also the Pleasure of Congress that you represent to his most Christian Majesty

That by the 8th. Article of the Treaty of Amity & Commerce subsisting between him and the United States it is stipulated that "The most Christian King will employ his good Offices and Interpositions with the King or Emperor of Morocco or Fez; the Regencies of Algiers, Tunis and Tripoly, or with any of them; and also with every other Prince, State or Power, of the Coast of Barbary in Africa, and the Subjects of the said King, Emperor, States and Powers, and each of them, in order to provide as fully and efficaciously as possible for the Benefit, Conveniency and Safety of the said United States, and each of them, their Subjects, People and Inhabitants, and their Vessels and Effects, against all Violence, Insults, Attacks or Depredations, on the part of the said Princes and States of Barbary, or their Subjects. –

That the United States have found it necessary to commence Negociations with the above named Powers for the Purpose of forming such Treaties and Arrangements with them, as may prevent their committing any future Depredations on the American Vessels and Trade – You are to communicate to his Majesty an exact State of the Measures taken for that Purpose, and to request that he will, agreeable to the said Article, interpose his friendly Aid and good Offices to promote the Success of those Negociations – which Negociations Mr. Adams and You will conduct in such a Manner, as you and he may think best calculated to give them all the Advantage that can result from his Majesty's Interposition. –

Your Secretary further Reports that the Chargé des Affaires at the Court of Spain should be instructed as follows – Vizt.

It is the Pleasure of Congress that you present their Thanks to his Catholic Majesty for the very friendly Manner in which he interposed his good Offices with the Emperor of Morocco in Behalf of the american Vessel and Crew captured by one of his Corsairs; as well as for the kind Disposition he has expressed of his Readiness to promote a good Understanding between the United States and that Prince. –

You will communicate to his Majesty that Congress have taken Measures for negotiating a permanent Peace with the Emperor, and that they would esteem themselves greatly obliged by his Majesty's Endeavours to promote the Success of those Negociations, by exerting his Influence at that Court in their Favour. –

You will assure his Majesty that his friendly Attention to the United States will always make a correspondent Impression on them, and that they will always be happy to embrace every Occasion of testifying the Sense they entertain of it, as well as of manifesting their sincere Disposition to unite the two Nations by the strongest Ties of mutual Affection and reciprocal Advantage. –

Your Secretary takes the Liberty of observing, that as their High Mightinesses have agreed by the 23$^{d.}$ Article of the Treaty between them and the United States, to second and aid the Negociations of the latter with the African piratical States, it would in his Opinion be proper for Congress to avail themselves of this Article, and apply to their High Mightinesses accordingly. –

All which is submitted to the Wisdom of Congress –   John Jay –
Ent^d read 22 March 1786

NA: PCC, item 81, v. 2, pp. 65-72 (DS); M247, reel 107.

Thomas Barclay to Thomas Jefferson

Dear Sir   Madrid 23 March 1786 –
I had the pleasure of addressing you twice since my Arrival here, and though I had nothing worth the attention of you or M. Adams to Communicate, I thought I wou'd wish to know how I am employ'd and to be able to say to him that I have made some progress in my Journey –

Yesterday I was Introduced to the Count of Florida Blanca at the Parto, he received and treated me like a Man of Business extremely well disposed to serve our Country. his Manner was frank and easie – He said the Emperor of Morocco proposed making the King negociater of the Peace, but that he wou'd inform the Emperor it wou'd be better the Business shou'd be done in Morocco. and he Called in his Secretary, and gave him directions to prepare the letters for me against Saturday next.

He added, that he wou'd propose to the King to write to the Emperor himself, and I have no Doute but I shall have the Honor of Carrying this Powerful Recommendation –

We are again to wait on the Count of Florida Blanca on Sunday, and probably I may have it in my power to write you more particularly by Mondays Post. I am with great respect and great Esteem Dear Sir your most obed Humb Servant   Tho' Barclay

Mr Lamb sailed the 11th from Barcelona

NA: PCC, *item 87, v. 1, pp. 265-266 (ALS); M247, reel 115.*

French Government Report on the Tobacco Trade

Resolves of a Comittee held at Berni[1]

24th. March 1786.

The comittee resuming their former deliberations respecting a treaty made with M^r. Morris, informed of the circumstances in w^h. it was made; also informed of the dispatch of twelve thousand Hogsheads of tobacco, the approaching arrival of which has been announced by M. Couteulx[2] the correspondent of Mr Morris, have unamimously thought, that the execution of the treaty ought to extend untill the 1st of Janu^y 1788, saving the right of annulling, in case of failure of execution on the part of the said M^r. Morris, the conditions of the said treaty, taking afterwards into consideration the interest of the national commerce with that of the U^d States, have agreed on the resolutions hereafter enumerated.

1^t. After the expiration of the treaty with M^r. Morris there shall be made no more bargains of the same kind.

2^d. The Farmer General shall always have in his Magazines a necessary supply for the exercise of his priviledge; which supply shall be formed, as well by What shall be furnished by the contract with M^r. Morris, as by what he shall procure by means of commerce.

3^d. To secure this supply the Farmer General shall purchase during the continuation of the contract with M^r. Morris only the tobacco which can be furnished by trade & brought in French or American vessels to amount of *12 to 15 thousand Hogsheads* every year at the same price & on the same conditions stipulated with the said M^r. Morris.

4th. In cases where cargoes shall not be assorted the tobacco shall be paid for at the following prices.

1^t. Quality, James & York River Tobacco, N^t. Cwt.–   38 livres

2^d. d^o. Potomack & Rappahanna   36 livres

3$^{d.}$ d$^{o.}$ Maryland Tobacco   34 livres
All the first qualities of each kind proper for France.
5$^{th.}$ In case of difficulty respecting the quality samples shall be sent to the
Council, & it shall be determined by a commission which shall be
authorized to have the samples examined by such person ~~to whom it~~ as may
be proper.
6$^{th.}$ When the Tobacco furnished by the Americans shall not be delivered
in a manufacturing port, there shall be deducted from the stipulated prices,
thirty sols p^r c. wt quintal for expences of transportation.

Faithfully translated from the Original by John Pintard.
Letter 31 May 1786 Hon: T. Jefferson –

NA: PCC, item 87, v. 1, pp. 512-513 (translation); M247, reel 115.
    ^{1} Enclosed in Jefferson to Jay, May 31, 1786 (NA: PCC, item 87, v. 1, p. 498 (ALS);
M247, reel 115).
    ^{2} Probably one of the partners in the merchant-banking firm of Le Couteulx &
Compagnie, which consisted of Laurent-Vincent le Couteulx de la Noraye, Jacques-Jean
le Couteulx du Moley, and Barthélemy-Jean-Louis de la Noraye in Paris; Antoine le
Couteulx de Verclives and Jean-Barthélemy le Couteulx de Canteleu in Rouen; and branch
offices in Havre-de-Grâce and Cadiz.

John Lamb to William Carmichael

                    Algiers – Without date but supposed the 26$^{th.}$ of March 1786 –
Dear Sir.
    We arrived here the 25$^{th.}$ March & on the same day were admitted on
Shore & received with every attention & politeness that could be expected
by C$^t.$ D'Espilly & the French Consul – This day had liberty to land our
trunks unsearched, but cannot write you with any certainty of the business
we have come here upon as I have not yet been before the Dey: as soon
as that matter comes to pass shall send forward immediately. please to
forward the acc$^t.$ of our arrival to Paris. I have not yet wrote M$^r.$ Jefferson
& M$^r.$ Adams as I expect tomorrow to have a more direct way to our
Ministers
    do not leave me in this Country & not write me
    I am your friend
                                                        John Lamb.

NA: PCC, item 98, p. 17 (C); M247, reel 125.

Thomas Barclay to John Adams

Dear Sir   Madrid 27th. March 1786 –
I arrived here the 10th. and expect to be able to proceed to Cadiz in a
few days, the Copys of three short Letters which I wrote to Mr. Jefferson,
will place before you our Progress untill this day, when I had the pleasure
of receiving through the hands of Mr. Carmichael the King's Letter to the
Emperor; informing him that it would be better the Peace should be made
in Morocco than in Spain, and recommending the Object of the Mission
to His Majesty's Attention. The Count De Florida Blanca has also sent me
Letters to General O-Reily at Cadiz, to the Consul General of Spain at
Morocco, & to one of the Spanish Fathers placed at Mequinez for the
Redemption of Captives; In short I have the greatest Reasons to be pleased
with the Part this Court has taken in the Affair which I think reflects
much honor on Mr. Carmichaels Influence and Attentions. To shew you at
once the State in which I found the Business with Morocco Situated on my
arrival here, I send you Copy of a Letter written by the Count De Florida
Blanca to Mr. Carmichael offering the intervention of His Catholic Majesty
on the Idea of the Business being done here, with Mr. Carmichaels Reply,
And I have now to add that I shall Set forward with the most flattering
prospects of Success, hoping soon to be able to give you a Satisfactory
Account of the Business being finished; It will not perhaps be in my Power
to write you very often, There are at this Place and at Vitoria, persons
appointed to translate or decypher every Suspicious paper & from them
little can escape. Nothing new of consequence will probably arrise untill I
reach Morocco. If I am able to close the treaty to my satisfaction, I shall
Send it to you by Land and remain in Africa or Spain untill you return it
with the Ratification, and I embrace this Opportunity of offering my
Services, if you want them, at Tunis & Tripoli, where I am certain this
Court will on application give its weight to the Person employed at those
places — If you should think my going farther than Morocco necessary, let
me know as soon as possible your Intentions, that I may arrange Matters
accordingly, and avail myself of the Disposition which this Court Shews to
Serve us; Please to put your Letters under Cover to Mr. Carmichael
unsealed that he may be at once Master of the Subject; Situated as we are,
we cannot leave this without being presented, which will be done I expect
in a few days by the French Ambassador, When we will continue our
Journey; but the Roads to Cadiz are in Such Shocking order that the
Gentleman by whom I now write has been twenty four days coming from
thence.

M^r· Lamb purchased a Vessel of about 50 Tons at Barcelona, and Sailed for Algiers the Eleventh with a Wind capable of placing him in Port the next day; He went under Spanish Colors which I hope may protect him, tho' there is no Peace hitherto Signed between the two Countries.

A Person is expected every hour from Algiers who will be able to give a particular Account of M^r· Lamb, if I am so lucky as to see him, I will transmit you what I can learn and M^r· Carmichael will give you all the information he can collect —

I am with great respect Dear Sir Your Most obed Serv.

Thos· Barclay

rec^d 24. Nov. 1786 by Post.

MHS: *The Adams Papers, microfilm reel 367 (ALS).*

American Commissioners in Europe to John Jay

Sir   Gros^r· Square March 28th 1786

Soon after the arrival of M^r· J. in London, we had a conference with the Ambassador of Tripoli, at his House.

The amount of all the information we can obtain from him was that a perpetual peace was in all respects the most adviseable, because a temporary Treaty would leave room for increasing demands upon every renewal of it, and a stipulation for annual payments would be liable to failures of performance which would renew the war, repeal the negociations and continually augment the claims of his Nation and the difference of expence would by no means be adequate to the inconvenience, since 12,500 Guineas to his Constituents with 10 p^r C^t upon that sum for himself, must be paid if the Treaty was made for only one year.

That 30,000 Guineas for his employers and £3,000 for himself were the lowest terms upon which a perpetual Peace could be made, and that this must be paid in Cash on the delivery of the Treaty signed by his Sovereign – That no kind of merchandises could be accepted.

That Tunis would treat upon the same terms, but he could not answer for Algiers or Morocco.

We took the liberty to make some inquiries concerning the grounds of their pretentions to make war upon Nations who had done them no injury, and observed that we considered all mankind as our friends who had done us no wrong, nor had given us any provocation.

The Ambassador answered us that it was founded on the Laws of their Prophet, that it was written in their Koran, that all Nations who should not have acknowledged their authority were sinners, that it was their right and duty to make war upon them wherever they could be found, and to make Slaves of all they could take as Prisoners, and that every Mussulman who should be slain in battle was sure to go to Paradise.

That it was a law that the first who boarded an Enemy's Vessel should have one Slave, more than his share with the rest, which operated as an incentive to the most desperate valour and enterprize, that it was the practice of their Corsairs to bear down upon a ship, for each Sailor to take a dagger in each hand and another in his mouth, and leap on board, which so terrified their Enemies that very few ever stood against them – that he verily believed the Devil assisted his Countrymen, for they were almost always successful. We took time to consider and promised an answer, but we can give him no other, than that the demands exceed our expectation, and that of Congress, so much that we can proceed no further without fresh instructions.

There is but one possible way that we know of to procure the money, if Congress should authorize us to go to the necessary expence, and that is to borrow it in Holland. We are not certain it can be had there – But if Congress should order us to make the best terms we can with Tunis, Tripoli, Algiers and Morocco, and to procure this money wherever we can find it, upon terms like those of the last Loan in Holland, our best endeavours shall be used to remove this formidable obstacle out of the way of the prosperity of the United States.

Inclosed is a copy of a letter from P. R. Randall esquire at Barcelona, the last from Mr. Barclay was dated Bayonne. It is hoped we shall soon have news from Algiers and Marocco, and we wish it may not be made more disagreeable than this from Tunis and Tripoli

We are &c.   John Adams
                                                       Thomas Jefferson

The aforegoing Letter was taken from a Copy furnished by Mr. Jefferson for the purpose, the original having been communicated to Congress and referred by them to a Committee, which never reported on nor returned it.–   H. Remsen junr.[1] –

NA: PCC, item 86, pp. 369-371 (C); M247, reel 114.
  [1] Remsen, Henry, Jr. Under-Secretary of the Department of Foreign Affairs, 1784-1790. Chief Clerk of the Department of State, 1790-1792. Named first teller of the Bank of the United States, 1792.

John Lamb to John Jay

Algiers March 28th. 1786

Your Excellency will have this handed to you by Mr. Randall, therefore I shall not be so perticular as I should have been by Aney Other hand, After Our Arrival here and admittence on Shore thought but to wate Sum Days before we Desired an Audience on the bussiness on which we came here About. this Day Sent and Desired one to be hear^{d.} on our Subject, had for Answer that if we Came for Peace Should not be hear^{d.} but for aneything Else we might have a hearing. we Desired to Ask of our Slaves, and the Day Readily granted that. in Consequence of the Denyal of Peace, thought Proper to Send in Randall to give the earlyest notice So that your Excellencys might take Such steps as were proper: As to the unfortunate People I am assured and by good Authority that they will cost Upward of thirty five thousand Dollars: I Shall Stay here as long as prudence will permitt me then Sail for Carthagena and wate your Excellencys further Commands: for this present time must begg leave to refer you to Mr. Randall for my Reasons for sending him Away, by this Opertunity and for further Perticulars which I have not mention^{d.} Naturally wish Your Excellencys Aprobation of my Conduct and am with Due Respect Your Excellency most obt & hm^{bl.} Servt.　　　　John Lamb

NB it will not be long before I shall Give a more Perticular acc^{t.}

NA: PCC, item 91, v. 2, p. 483 (ALS); M247, reel 119.

John Jay's Report on British Control of the Northwest Posts

[New York] Office for foreign Affairs 30th. March 1786

The Secretary of the United States for the Department of foreign Affairs to whom was referred Mr. Adams Letters of the 2^{d.} 6th. 9th. 12th. & 15th. December 1785 and 4th. January 1786 with the Papers enclosed with them, and also a Motion founded on Mr. Adams Memorial demanding the Evacuation of the frontier Posts &ca: – Reports

That in his Opinion the Instructions proposed by the Motion in Question would be proper & expedient – Because

　　1. A categorical Answer in the Negative would involve the United States either in War or in Disgrace – They are not prepared for the former, and should if possible avoid the latter. –

2. It would not be expedient to press that Answer while the Intentions of the Court of France on the Subject remain doubtful.–

Your Secretary therefore thinks that M^r· Adams should be immediately instructed in the Words of the said Motion Viz^t· "to protract *his* Negociations with the Court of Great-Britain respecting the Posts which should have been before this surrendered to the United States and other Infractions of the said Treaty by that Power, so as to avoid demanding a categorical Answer respecting the same until the further Orders of Congress. –

All which is submitted to the Wisdom of Congress –

John Jay –

NA: PCC, *item 81, v. 2, pp. 79-80 (DS); M247, reel 107.*

Comte de Vergennes to Louis Guillaume Otto

[Translation]

N. 2.   Versailles, 31 March 1786.

I have received, Sir, the despatches that you have taken the trouble to write me from N^o· 9 to 33 inclusively.

We are very pleased, Sir, that the regulations of commerce of which we had complained have been revoked; there remains not another thing for us to desire except that they not be revived sooner or later: we shall be certain in that regard only when we see the affairs of commerce confided exclusively to the Care of Congress. Besides, if something official on this matter reaches you, you will limit yourself to taking it ad referendum. As for the reflections which the delegate with whom you conversed regarding commerce made to you, they are so absurd that they do not merit the trouble of being raised again.

.   .   .   .   .   .

I have not given you instructions, Sir, relative to the convention concerning the Consuls, because you had nothing to negotiate on that subject. I presume that you will have delivered a note to Congress conformably to what I have sent you by my despatch N^o· 1.

Mr. Van Berkel had reason to complain concerning the conduct of the Sheriff who entered his house to arrest a domestic there: but I think at the same time that this Minister would have done well to content himself with the declaration that was made to him by the Judge, instead of opening a discussion on the immunities associated with the character of foreign Ministers. These immunities are for the most past arbitrary: it is up to the

Court or the Nation that receives a representative from another Sovereign to regulate them, save that it is up to the latter to accept them, or to reject them and to recall its Minister: That, Sir, is the sole reflection that I have to make on the memorandum that you have written on this matter. I shall only add that you should abstain from any conduct either relative to the etiquette or relative to the prerogatives that foreign ministers accredited to Congress can claim: If difficulties in this regard present themselves, you will limit yourself to reporting them, and to awaiting instructions.

. . . . . .

[De Vergennes]

FFAA: Pol. Corr., U.S., v. 31, f. 202-204vo. (LC transcription).

Paul R. Randall to His Father

House of Quarantine Alicant April 2ᵈ 1786

. . . . . .

After a Passage of fifteen Days from Barcelona ten of which we lay embayed at Majorca, and the remainder through two successive Storms brought us on the Coast of Barbary; we were under Necessity of entering the Harbour under full Sail, as there was too much Sea to stay without & ask Permission.

Off the Mole we were met by the Captain of the Port who conducted us into Security until the Dey should be advised of our Arrival. He at first refused to admit us on shore, but upon the representation of the Count D'Expilly, that we were come in a Spanish Vessel & had a disagreeable Passage also insisting upon a Article of the Spanish Treaty, that every Person coming in these Vessels should not be prevented landing – he at length withdrew his Refusal. We were conducted to the House of the Consul of France,[1] to whom we had official Letters, where was also lodged the Count D'Expilly the Spanish Ambassador (who is a Frenchman) negociating for Spain. We were recieved with the utmost Politeness, & entertained at the Consul's House during my Stay from the 25ᵗʰ· of March to the 30ᵗʰ·

They both rendered their Services from the friendly Disposition of the Count towards America & particularly to mʳ· Carmichael our Chargé des Affaires at Madrid.

On the 27ᵗʰ· they advised mʳ· Lamb to request an Audience from the Dey through the French Consul but he returned this Answer.

"That if we came on the Subject of Peace he would not see us, but if we wished to visit him & talk to him on other Matters he would be glad to see us" These are his Words from the Druggerman or Interpreter, all Business being done by these Machines who are Turks, having generally been Prisoners & have Learnt the European Languages in foreign Countries. It may readily be supposed, that he would wish to sell those unfortunate Captives & would therefore give an Opportunity for offering a Price.// This was the Opinion of the Count, Consul & Mr Wolfe.// [2]

Sent the next Day, but raining the Dey who values himself on his Politeness answered the Message by saying – "As it was bad Weather then, he would send for us the next Day – that it might be more agreeable to us." – But to my Mortification it did not clear until my Departure from thence. A Spanish Vessel of War being in the Port awaiting the Count's Orders, & ready to sail I thought best to propose to m^{r.} Lamb that I should take a Passage on her as he insisted on my going to Paris with this Answer or rather Refusal of the Dey supposing (as he said) that I could carry better Information than he could write. // I asked m^r Lamb what I could say to the Minister except that the Dey had refused to treat of Peace & most earnestly requested it as a Favor – but he would make me no Reply or give me any Instructions //

I therefore concieved it more expedient to embark in this Vessel than to go to Marseilles – as I am in hopes of attending the Count's Secretary who is charged with his Despatches & may obtain a considerable Diminution of the Quarantine besides the disagreeable Passage I should have had in a wretched Jentau.

The Conjecture on the Dey's Denial is: – that the United States have not a Peace with the Porte – besides there is an Article in the Spanish Treaty that the Dey will not treat, nor even speak with any Minister on the Subject of Peace until the Power he represents, or for whom he negociates, is in Peace or Treaty with the Ottoman Court. // This I am not perfectly ascertained in. // This Article was inserted by the Dey to prevent the Spanish Court interceding for Portugal & Naples whose King is Son to his Majesty of Spain. Whether this Reason or Intelligence is well founded it is not for me to determine, from the short Stay I made & the many Difficulties accruing in procuring Information. Certain it is that the Algerines must be at War with some Nation, it is a Government of Rapine.

The Ministers from Portugal & Naples are now on their Way to Algiers – // They are still at Carthagena May 15th. // a Person on the Spot from the Manner these Gentlemen proceed might discover this interesting particular, but as I am sent out of the Way, my Knowlege ends here however I will make as many Observations for your Information as I can at present conveniently, not having had it in my Power to take Notes.

It is generally supposed by the Politicians at Algiers that the Portuguese will not succeed in their Application but if they should that the Dey will break with some other Nation & the Danes are looked upon as the next Object, under Pretext that they sell their Mediterranean Passes to the Merchants of Lubeck otherwise the Venitians must experience the Fury of these Barbarians, not having it in their Power to make as ample Presents as their Rivals for Dey's Favor. // One of the commanders of the Cruizers told a Spanish Officer he expected to cruize against the Danes. //

The Manner of declaring War is simply by sending Home the Consul, saying they have no further Need of his remaining at Algiers.

The present Dey is advanced to the Age of 80 well beloved by his Subjects & has increased the publick heap to a great Pinnacle of Riches – his Avarice is unbounded – He lays out no Wealth on his own Person – lives no better than his Officers of Government – & as Provisions are extremely cheap in this Country what he can spend is a mere trifle – He has elevated himself by his own Industry from the Degree of Shoemaker which he has carried on in Algiers ever since he came from the Levant his Life has ever been abstemious never indulging in any Pleasure whatever.

As his Ships are built with Timber recieved in Presents & fitted out with naval Stores in like Manner, no Expenditures accrue therein & they are Christian Slaves who employ these Materials.

The Pay of the Soldiers is in three Degrees of 4 1\2 Chequins every two Moons or Months of 28 Days to the principal Troops, in which Number the Dey & his Officers recieve no more than the meanest of them Three chequins to the more inferior & the remainder have only two Chequins – each chequin is about two Spanish Dollars.

This is the chief outlet to the Treasury. The civil List may be supposed very inconsiderable when the Honor is the only Pay. His Revenues are little known – he has five p. C.· on all Importations, & for exporting Wheat he demands what he pleases – it generally amounts to one third the Value.

The Regency is divided into three Provinces, the two more distant are ruled by Beys or Viceroys who are obliged to account to the Dey in large Contributions – which they make up by extorting from the Peasantry or Moors – this is the greatest Revenue properly so called – as the Tribute he recieves from foreign Nations varies so frequently.

The Dutch besides paying him 200,000 Dollars for their Peace, // I am not confident whether the Dutch or the Danes paid this Sum. // yield him a Tribute of 20,000 p An. – The Venitians pay as much in Gold annually. I believe it cost the Danes much more to make their Treaty. The Venitian Peace was broke within two Years & renewed shortly after with considerable Presents.

The English although they boast to have the best Treaty, have paid (as I have discovered from a Person who has inspected the Consul's Books) £28,000 Stlg. in Presents since the Year 1759.

Every Consul on his Arrival pays in Presents as a Matter certainly expected to the Amount of several thousand Dollars – besides some Consuls who are under the Necessity of giving in like Manner every two Years four five to seven thousand Dollars. I think they are the Venetian & Danish. Whenever Business is to be done, one must not apply without Presents, even to the most inferior Officers & yet they have no Control. The Dey is absolute.

The Salary of the English Consul is £800 Stlg. p An. but the Infinity of Fees with which Offices are loaded in England reduces it to about £650. // I hardly think an American Consul necessary at Algiers. // The French has about as much, but he lays up very little, as he is very generous. The Venitian Consul has the most being £800 & not nominal with Respect to Presents. I should observe that if they displease the Dey's Officers they return them & demand others instead. If a Present is offered at a certain Value, as is commonly the Case for they will ask you if you do not tell them at first, the Donee sends it to a Jew who to ingratiate himself will often say it is not worth half the Sum put upon it, which being returned another is required amounting to the Price set.

Thus you see there is a Difficulty in every Thing, even in throwing away Money. The Presents must be at least double the Value formerly given – to such a Pitch of Insolence are they arrived. A remarkable Instance of this avaricious Spirit has been related to me there by a Merchant, who was employed by one of the principal Officers to procure him a Watch from London – which being furnished a Present was made to the same great Man of another Watch by a Person some Time after at a certain Price – by not pleasing him it was returned – The Person who sent it not knowing how to procure another immediately was advised by the Merchant to commission him to purchase the said English Watch – upon which he applied to the Owner & offered a great Sum – he objected to parting with it at first, saying it went well & was very valuable – however the Merchant telling him that he would receive it back in a short Time as a present – this Man who is the second or third in the Kingdom – & may probably succeed the Dey – delivered it over & had it again in a half hour as a Present – so little Delicacy prevails – & Money that Source of Misery in luxurious Kingdoms poisons their Happiness even here, where they cannot enjoy it.

One would suppose Money the best Present – but still Caution must be observed – otherwise it may be returned hoping to recieve greater Value than the specifick Sum.

I should have mentioned that a principal Production of the Dey's Revenue is a Tithe or Tenth on every Thing raised in his Kingdom & if Liberty reigned in this abundant Clime there would be no Necessity of

Recourse to Rapine & Piracy – He also succeeds to the Estates of those Officers who are not permitted to marry – this produces much.

The Spaniards have made their Peace at length at the round Sum of a million of Dollars – but by bad Management in a Spanish General (Mazerado) who was sent to supersede the present French Count it has cost them two million & an half – besides the Purchase of the Captives. This Man was the Occasion of the Algerine Cruizers sailing so speedily last Year that the Spanish Court could not advise their Allies whereby many Portuguese fell into their Hands, & perhaps our unfortunate Americains because the Spaniards having always a Number of Ships cruizing for them – there was greater Security in the Mediterranean & the Borders of the Straights. – This ill Conduct reflects Honor on the present Ambassador who has superseded him since. The General promised the Value of 200,000 Dollars in naval Stores, but the King disapproving of it, the Count D'Expilly more wisely effected a Commutation for them in Money.

As the Money is paid according to the Treaty – the Dey has set the Sum of 3600 Dollars on every Spanish Captain – 2000 for each Mate or Pilot, and $1200 for the private Seamen & Soldiers – but a difference is made with Respect to those who have escaped from Oran where the Spaniards have a Garrison – being Delinquents banished for various crimes. I myself have seen a Servant exiled from Barcelona to that Place for seven Years – for no other Charge than having passed the Gates with two Oz of French Snuff found upon him – such as he is hope a milder Fate among these Barbarians but they are mistaken as they are all made Slaves – Whether a Sum should have been stipulated for the unfortunate Captives I leave to Ministers of State & Plenipotentiaries.

The Captives as near as I ~~can~~ could ascertain are

> 1100 Spaniards – 400 of which are properly redeemable
> 110 Neapolitans
> 50 Genoese – who are most frequently redeemed by the
> Charity of Individuals
> 120 Portuguese
> 60 Italians – including some Imperialists taken with
> them
> 20 Malthese
> <u>21 Americans</u>

About 1500 in all when properly distributed. There are some
Women
Of the latter but eight are born in America – the rest are British Subjects except one French Boy, for whom all the Interest of the French Consul cannot avail to release him, one Swede.

There is an Article in the English Treaty, that all British Subjects taken in any Vessel whatever, shall not be deemed a real Captive – however the present Consul not thinking proper to make Application – they lie at the Mercy of the Americans to redeem them. ∥ I doubt whether the French would really interest themselves, one of the Divan has said we might possibly succeed if they were really in earnest ∥ This Privilege is lost by the Negligence of the present Consul – never to be recovered without a new Treaty. As there are two Englishmen otherwise made Prisoners that this Man has neglected – it is not much to be wondered at that those should suffer whose Fate may affect the Politicks of America in Relation to Great Britian.

As the Generosiy of m^r Logie has been much applauded by rescuing the American Captives from the Maine (a Place where Persons in their Stations are employed in making & mending Sails) I made particular Enquiry into the Matter.

These Captains as soon as they landed were sent to the said Place and had been there but a short Time when they recieved a Letter from m^r Logie offering the most friendly Aid & invited them to his House but only to the greater Misery of being one of his Slaves & one of them actually served at his Table – where some British Captains were dining who insulted his Distress – & yet when I was in London this Man was spoken of as a Prodigy of Humanity. They have since been taken under the Patronage of the Count d'Expilly & walk about the Streets he being responsible for them. ∥ They wear the Badge of Slavery but are not necessitated to do it. It is rather a Protection to them. ∥ The French Consul is really a good Man & would have been assisting to them, but as he thought that they had put themselves under the Protection of the English Consul – he did not care to embroil himself with m^r Logie who keeps himself at a Distance from all other Consuls even in Algiers where Society is so much wanted.

All Captains & Boys are the Dey's Privilege & six of the American Captives who are Lads are now in his Palace & very great Favorites (but only one of them indeed is an American) their Price will be very high as there will be so great a Want of Christian Slaves in the Dey's Service after the Spaniards are released.

The French Treaty terminates within six Months so that many Difficulties may arise should a Sum be demanded on the Renewal. ∥ I should suppose the French might assist on the Occasion. ∥

The Algerines were sadly beaten by Lewis 14th who might have imposed any Terms on them as might also the English in the Reign of Queen Anne – but the immortal Charles the 5th Emperor of Germany & King of Spain lost his crown in the Bay of Algiers.

The Spaniards would have succeeded in one Campaign had their Fleet persevered another half hour – the Turks demanded the Dey to put out a Flag but he prevailed on them to continue a little longer when they repulsed the Enemy. Six Ships of the Line & 5 or 600 Men well disciplined would drive them all to Destruction. // This I am since confirmed in by the Opinion of a Spanish Colonel a good and experienced Officer. // I think four Frigates would be a Match for all their Cruizers. There may be 12,000 Turks in Algiers – but a Force to attack them should not wait as the Spaniards did in the last Campaign until all the Strength of the Kingdom might be collected.

The Bay & Harbour are immensely strong – but the Art of Gunnery is little known by them. Their Fortifications are constructed under the Direction of a Greek & their Ships by a Frenchman. The Moors or Militia are the poorest Animals ever in Battle-array. they are truly Barbarians – The Turks are most civil but no-body must oppose them.

Algiers may be taken by Storm in a regular Siege when those Militia would be the Destruction of this Enemy & might produce every Disorder fatal to an Army. The Turks have no Discipline, much less the Peasantry who are only armed on an Invasion – they are debased to the lowest Ebb of human Misery under tyrannical Oppressors.

Although Algiers is environned with Fortifications, yet one Hill is neglected of considerable Importance, commanding the Town.

The Government of Tunis is continually afflicted by the Bey of Constantine, who from Time to Time threatening it with War obliges the Tunisians to submit to great Contributions. Their naval Force is only five or six small Vessels. Tunis has suffered so much by the Plague as to lose half its Inhabitants in one Year near 500,000 Souls.

Tripoli happily for it is at a sufficient Distance from the Oppression of Algiers. No Nation has made Peace with Algiers which was not in Treaty with the Porte – but the particular Dependance of the Algerines on this Court is hard to determine. The Grand Seignor is Head of their Church to be sure – & Algiers was settled from his Dominions – he permitting them to assume a Form of Government they admitting for the Superior – perhaps it yielded a Revenue, but at present they are too strong for the Turk to enforce it. However the Mischief he can do them most fatal to their Existence in their present State is in preventing the Turks re-inforcing Algiers & this may be the only Dependance.

I believe the Emperor of Germany & Empress of Russia had their Peace with Algiers effected through the Mediation of the Porte – However I seem to think the Grand Seignor was obliged to pay the Dey of Algiers for some Imperialists taken by him – which he had engaged to procure from Algiers.

As I have not looked into Books for my Observations but was under the Necessity of asking Questions in French I was greatly at a loss to ascertain the Information I picked up from various Persons – indeed I had no Idea of being hurried off in such a Manner as to prevent my writing on the Subject before this Time.

If possible the Dey of Algiers should have been sounded before our Approach but who to have employed is not easy to determine, perhaps a Person on the Spot would have purchased the American Slaves at a much lower rate than I fear they will at present be held at – percieving the Americans to take such early Steps for the Liberation of their Citizens

I hardly think the English Politicks have done us any Mischief in this Quarter, but the Consul taking Notice of the Captives immediately on their landing would make the Dey suppose a full Price could be procured for them at some Time – so that it cannot be imagined their Freedom will be purchased at a lower Consideration than the Spaniards what they are redeemed at we may suppose the Measure of the Sum to offer at least although I fancy more will be demanded // I have seen a Spanish slave a private Seaman which cost 1000 Dollars since I left Algiers. //

The only Means of insuring better Terms is in taking their Cruizers // The Spanish Peace will render it more difficult as their Harbours will afford a Shelter // but they rarely exchange, though there are Instances of two or three being recieved for one Christian

The Dey has demanded two for one for the Prisoners the Spaniards have taken – they amount to four or five hundred.

The Price of Slaves has been enhanced to double within a few Years. A Person employed by one of the Baltic Powers purchased some Slaves at three or four hundred Chequins – perhaps five or six Years ago (which my Memory cannot ascertain) and it was thought he had them at a low Price. He is an English Gentleman (m^r· Wolfe)[3] who has been Chargé des Affaires for the British Court – and whose Services have been grossly neglected, without paying him even his Disbursements. // He is since appointed Consul for Spain but conditionally until another may be sent if thought proper. // this Gentleman has tendered himself to forward the American Interest in every Respect, & would have been extremely useful – but his Merit was not known. // He offered his Services to D^r· Franklin. // The Count & French Consul recommended him particularly to m^r· Lamb. I had but little Opportunity of seeing him – however on another Negociation – if I am at Liberty to give my Opinion – I think this Gentleman should be associated with some American to be hereafter sent on the Business – he appears to have a great Knowlege of the Country & is so well with the Dey, that he has requested the King of Spain to name him as Consul but I doubt if the Spainards know sufficiently their Interest to ~~appoint him~~ prefer him.

The Count professes great Obligation to him. Thus have I given you as circumstantial a Detail of the Information I could procure with the greatest Industry in two or three Days – upon discovering that m^r Lamb was absolutely bent upon sending me to Paris trusting merely to my Memory. // In a secret Expedition little preparatory knowlege can be acquired by Information. //

I shall subjoin a Detail of their Marine Force – mostly procured from the Captains – I fear the Description will not be clear – indeed I hardly think their Cruizers distinguishable from the Mediterranean Vessels.

One sollicitous of Applause & future Employment might perhaps give himself Credit for adventuring on this tempestuous Sea at this Season – as a Proof which we might have run from Algiers to this Place in 18 Hours – but it was not prudent at Night & besides we did not care to enter the Road even the next Day – besides appearing before such an Enemy without any previous ~~Notice~~ Steps taken to ensure us against the Rapacity of those Barbarians who have so little Regard for Treaties that the Crews of French & Swedish Vessels quarrelling in the Harbour – the Captain of the Port went on board with some Attendants & ordered them all severely bastinadoed – & no Complaint I believe was ever made. A Gentleman who has been there 19 Years told me at Algiers that he never saw a Moor he could trust or a Turk whose Word he might depend on. Such is this People & those are the Ideas my Voyage has furnished me with.

April 3^d – As I write at the House or rather Chamber of Quarantine where seven or eight Spanish Officers are making all Kinds of Noise – it is impossible for me to arrange my Ideas – but as I am not writing a History but only scribbling for your Amusement, you will excuse the imperfect Manner they are delivered in.

Notwithstanding what Historians have said of the Divan or Dey's Council the Form is scarcely preserved – it was composed of the five principal Officers of his Government to whom he submits his Sentiments like all other Tyrants merely for their Approbation & to flatter him that he does right.

The Minister of Marine has had the same Occupation of Shoemaker with the Dey – & the Admiral has been a Fisherman. The meanest Turk aspires to the Succession but no Moor is admitted to any Employment, & there is but one Instance in an half-blooded Turk enjoying any Office – It is the Bey of Constantine whose Mother was a Moorish Woman.

The Wealth of the Treasury is supposed to exceed in Value ten Millions of Dollars, concieve what a Prize the Spainards would have had in taking Algiers by Storm.

I imagine the Dey will demand at least 200,000 Dollars from us – besides the Purchase of the Captives which is computed by the French Count at

40,000 Dollars – Likewise it will cost 100,000 Dollars in Presents and other Charges incident.

The only Truce to be obtained is in the Dey's Promise – he never grants a Cessation of Hostilities formally.

Detail of Marine Force Of Algiers.

1. Vessel of 32 Guns & 450 Men – 24. nine 2. eighteen & 6. four pounders

1.	28 d°·	400	24. d°· 2. twelves 2. sixes
2.	24 d°·	350	20 sixes 4 fours
2.	20 d°·	300	20 d°·
2.	18 d°·	260	18 d°·
1	16 d°·	250	16 d°·

Two small Craft described like the American Refugee boats – 55 Gun-boats carrying each a twelve pounder built since the last Campaign but one of the Spaniards & which annoyed them exceedingly in OReilys Expedition.

It is said these Corsairs carry Cannon of a great Variety of Callibers. The Dey has it in Contemplation to build two Frigates. One third of the Crews are Turks who are Marines, the rest are Moors his best Seamen much esteemed by the Dey, who can have very little Opportunity of procuring Sailors as no Commerce is carried on by the Algerines. However the Fleet can be manned in one Day by absolute Command.

The Vessels are well found but weak & slight built, not differing much in their Hulls from Bermudian-built Sloops. They have no foreign-built Vessels at present.

They have all black Sides & white Bottoms. They are not shy nor make any Preparations for Action – have indifferent Quarters – are barricadoed but depend much on boarding – therefore Vessels to oppose them should be well defended by nettings & strong close Quarters.

They never cruize together but when they go out separate within two Days. In the Straights their principal Object is the Fisherman along Shore.

Care should be taken not to be within the Bay of Algiers in Summer. Calms being frequent, in which Case those Gun-boats might be of dangerous Consequence. The Algerines think they sail faster than any Vessels whatever & indeed they have much the Appearance of it – though the Commodore of 32 Guns chased an American built Ship deeply laden a whole Day before he came up with her. As soon as they take a Prize the Prisoners are immediately removed as the most valuable Part of it. The Prizes sometimes perish by being intrusted to the most indifferent Seamen – but they seldom lose their own Vessels. They have Compasses from Marseilles regulated with the proper Variations – so that they are not at a Loss for Calculation.

Notwithstanding their Vessels may be so well supplied I think the Commodore not equal with a twenty-Gun Ship of any European Power I have seen if regularly fitted out. I should therefore concieve the Sloops of War of twenty Guns to be the proper Cruizers, especially in the Mediterranean where there is so frequent Necessity of putting into Harbours. // I was since told at Carthagena that the King of Naples is constructing six on those Dimensions //

Although I concieve they do not materially differ from the Mediterranean Vessels, yet I will add a Description procured from those Captains.

The Commodore has no Galleries but a long Quarter-Deck running over his Stern about twelve feet. None of them have Heads but long Prows: four of them have Galleries & Sterns like Merchantmen. // Their light Sails are made of very bad Canvass. // All of them Xebecque-rigged with the Mizzen Mast close aft. They are all three masted & have no Gib Booms. The two largest are rigged about the Main-mast as our Ships & all the rest have slender fore-masts & top-masts in one as Polacres. Their mizzen & foremasts like Ships. The six smallest carry latteen Yards & square Sails likewise. All of them have large & small Mizzens. Their foretacks hawl out two thirds the Bow Sprit – which is in one & but a small Spar.

They are fitted for Sea in a few Days so that no Calculation can be made that they will not sail in some Time from their being totally unfitted as I saw them.

They will not certainly sail before the middle of May, as the Count has given me Reason to believe & perhaps not before the first of June.

Their Course on the Atlantic is generally along the Coasts of Spain & Portugal, & sometimes even to Cape Finisterre – & very rarely towards the Western Islands – as many in America have imagined.

They are the Christian Slaves who prepare them for Sea, which induces me to suppose they differ but little in their rigging from the Straights Vessels. Those to have more Merit with their Owners exert all their Talent – & they have the best Materials I should imagine.

The American Slaves are engaged at present in carrying Stone Mortar &c. for constructing a Building to secure the Gun-boats in Winter – They have had the same Allowance from the Count D'Expilly as the Spanish Slaves.

The Algerines are not satisfied with the late Peace – as every Thing goes into the Treasury & they lose their Hope of further Plunder from so near an Enemy.

· · · · · ·

P. R. Randall

NA: PCC, item 87, v. 1, pp. 389-420 (Extract/C); M247, reel 115.

[1] *Kercy (Kersey), Jean Baptiste Mercy Guyot de. French Consul at Algiers.*

[2] *Material enclosed in double slashes (//) indicates text written in the margins by the author.*

[3] *Wolfe (Wolf, Woulfe), John. British vice consul at Algiers, 1777-ca. 1785. Described in different sources as a "respectable Irishman" who had long lived in Algiers, a Jewish merchant who had converted to Christianity, and an English merchant born in Ireland, John Wolfe resigned as vice consul when Charles Logie was given the consulate, which had been promised to Wolfe. He stood well with the Dey, who joined the Count D'Expilly in recommending him to be the Spanish consul at Algiers, but that appointment also went to another individual.*

Congressional Committee Report
on the Barbary Negotiations

[New York, April 5, 1786]

The Committee...to whom was referred to [sic] report of Secretary of the United States for the Department of foreign Affairs relative to negociations, and other measures to be taken with the Barbary Powers,

Report that in their opinion the Negociations now on foot with those powers must be conducted according to the plans hitherto adopted, until Congress can be better informed of the effects and Events of them. –

But the Committee are of opinion that the monies heretofore appropriated, and means provided for obtaining peace with those powers will be found inadequate for effecting that object; and that therefore Congress ought immediately to make further provision and to procure by loan or otherwise further and considerable sums of money for the express purposes of procuring peace with those powers, which further provision and sums of money (if the overtures of the United States for peace shall be rejected) shall be employed in protecting the Commerce of these States –

And that the United States may be prepared for the latter Event the Committee are of opinion that the attention of the federal Government, ought to be turned to the marine Department, and an ordinance be passed as soon as may be for organising and arranging the same. Wherefore they submit the following resolves –

Resolved that the Commissioners of the Treasury devise ways and means to Obtain by loan, or otherwise, a sum not exceeding   Dollars for the purposes of securing the Commerce of the United States against the Depredations of the Barbary States, and if by loan, ways and means to secure the repayment thereof – and report

Resolved that it is proper and expedient for the federal Government to turn their ~~Ear~~ earliest attention to the Marine Department, and that a Committee be appointed to frame and report an ordinance for organising the same

NA: PCC, *item 25, v. 2, p. 459 (C); M247, reel 32.*

Thomas Barclay to Thomas Jefferson

Dear Sir   Madrid 5th. April 1786

I had the pleasure of writing to you the 31st. of last Month by a gentleman going to Paris & of sending you a Copy of what I wrote Mr. Adams the 27th. I now, by the spainsh Courier, send you Copies of both those Letters. This day the Spanish dispatches arrived from Algiers by which Mr. Carmichael, who writes you by this Opportunity, received a Letter from Mr. Lamb, with another from Mr. Randal, the last dated the 26th. of March. Mr. Randal writes that they did not arrive at Algiers untill the 25th. when the Dey refused them permission to land, but on the representation of the Count D'Espilly, the Minister employed by this Court to negotiate with Algiers (who is an intimate acquaintance of Mr. Carmichael & to whom Mr. Lamb & Mr. Randal had Letters of introduction) they were permitted to land, & were received by the french Consul with great attention. The Count D'Espilly has mentioned his fears of Mr. Lambs success, "As the United States have not treaty with the Porte, & that the most that can be expected will be a Truce untill Congress can send a Minister to Constantinople." The Deys fleet is not ready for Sea, nor has any steps been taken towards fitting it out. Our people who were carried into Algiers have behaved with the utmost decorum & were made extreamly happy by the arrival of Mr. Lamb. To the above I have little to add but that the Truce between Spain & Algiers expired with the last month, and that as there are no preparations making by the Dey to send out the Cruizers, tho' the season is advancing fast, the probable Consequence is, that the Peace will be made with Spain; In the mean time the Count D'Espilly has demanded a Truce of another Month. The Ministers from Portugal and Naples to Algiers, are waiting at Carthagena to see the Event of the Spanish negotiations; if they are terminated to the wishes of this Court, they will proceed to Algiers under the sanction of Spain, and in that Case I am certain Mr. Lamb may be provided with the same recommendations to the Dey, that were so kindly given me to the Emperor.

I shall set out for Cadiz in a few days, the Roads are very near being impassable. I am, with great Respect & Esteem Dear Sir, Your most Obedient, humble servant   Tho⁵· Barclay

NA: PCC, item 87, v. 1, pp. 271-272 (LS); M247, reel 115.

Board of Treasury to John Adams

Sir.   Board of Treasury April 6ᵗʰ· 1786
    We do ourselves the Honor of transmitting to you a Duplicate of our Letters to yourself, and the Commissioners of the Dutch Loans of the 7ᵗʰ⁚ and 22dᵈ⁚ March last. The latter together with one of this Date addressed to the same Gentlemen & Enclosing a Bill in their Favor on Messʳˢ· Wilhem, and Jan Willink[1] of Amsterdam, we Request the Favor of you to forward by the first Mail – Our Letter to the Commissioners is left open for your Perusal, by which you will find, that our Directions to those Gentlemen are to Appropriate the Proceeds of this Bill for the Purpose specified in the Resolve of Congress of the 14ᵗʰ⁚ Febrʸ· 1785 relative to the proposed Treaties with the Barbary Powers, in Case the monies appropriated for this Object have not been drawn out of their hands previous to the Receipt of this Bill – but in Case this Event has taken Place our Orders are to discount the Bill, and to apply the Proceeds for the Payment of the Dutch Interest, which becomes due on the first of June next – This Remittance, added to the Sum of Thirty thousand Dollars, which will be remitted to them for the same Purpose by Messʳˢ· Constable Rucker & Cº· in pursuance of a Contract made with this Board will very nearly Compleat the whole Sum of Interest which will become due on that day; the Deficiency we trust will be made up by additional Subscriptions to the Loan; but should this not be the Case, we must request you not to draw the whole Monies appropriated for the Barbary Treaties out of the hands of the Commissioners (if not already done) relying on our taking Measures to remit, with all possible Dispatch to those Gentlemen a further Sum of twenty thousand Dollars, with Directions to apply it in the first Instance to make up any Deficiency arising on this Account on the Sum of Eighty Thousand Dollars, appropriated for the Purpose above mention'd –
    We have the Honor to be with great Esteem, Your Obedᵗ⁚ Humᵇˡᵉ⁚ Servᵗˢ⁚   Samuel Osgood
                                                         Walter Livingston

MHS: The Adams Papers, microfilm reel 367 (LS).
    [1] Willink, Jan and Wilhem. Proprietors of one of the four Amsterdam banking houses that handled the Dutch loans contracted by the United States. The others were (1) Nicolaas and Jacob van Staphorst, (2) Jacobus de la Lande, and (3) Hendrik Fynje.

John Jay to Sir John Temple

Sir   New York 7th. April 1786

The Letters you did me the Honor to write on the 25th February and 17th. March last, together with the Papers they enclosed, were immediately communicated to Congress. Although I am not directed to say any thing officially on the Subject, yet wishing that the Irritation left in both our Countries by the War, may not be increased, by mistakes and Misapprehensions, I take the Liberty of mentioning to you one or two Circumstances which place the Complaints in Question, in a point of view in which I believe they have not been generally seen.

That certain Individuals do complain of Infractions of the Treaty is evident, and it is equally true that not one of them have thought proper to apply to Congress for Redress either by Petition, Memorial or otherwise – Whether these Individuals or any, and which of them are British Subjects, are Questions which merit accurate Inquiry for a variety of important Reasons which are too obvious to require minute Enumeration – but be that as it may, it certainly is more natural and more proper, that they who want Redress should apply for it, than that Government should inquire after them, and take pains to seek for and decide upon Cases which the Parties interested shew no Disposition to bring before them. Whatever may be the cause of this Disinclination, I think it fair to conclude that they who will not apply for redress in the ordinary and established manner, have no Right to be dissatisfied if they do not receive it.

The Information you have been pleased to convey to Congress, respecting the Persons who applied to you, cannot be deemed such an application as the Forms of business in all Countries require.

In cases where complaints arise from a supposed violation of Treaty, I think there can be but two proper modes of applying for Redress. The one is by the Direct application of the Party interested, and the other is by the Sovereign affected by such Infraction.

In the present case the Parties interested have made no direct application, and it is much to be regretted that your Commission, which is understood to extend only to matters respecting Trade and navigation, does not enable you supposing it to be proper to apply officially on the Part of his britannic Majesty. If this opinion should be erroneous it would give me Pleasure to be better informed.

Such being the State of things, the Silence of Congress appears to me very natural, for the self respect observed by *all* Governments must oppose their interfering in those matters which ------ however proper for their Cognizance are only so when regularly brought before them, especially too when the Regular way is plain, known and open, and when no necessity or accidental Circumstances render a Deviation from it unavoidable.

I assure you Sir, it gives me pain to see any obstacles retarding the Return of good Humour and mutual Content between our two Countries, for although all minds are not superior to the Influence of the Irritation before spoken of, yet I am persuaded the wisest and best men on either side think it more consistent with the Dignity and Happiness of both People to repress rather than to cherish that Irritation.

With great Respect &ᶜᵃ·   John Jay

P. S. Congress have lately ordered me "to report particularly and specially how far the several States have complied with the Proclamation of Congress of the 14ᵗʰ· January 1784 and the Recommendation accompanying the same pursuant to the Definitive Treaty of Peace, between the United States of America and Great Britain." –

NA: PCC, item 80, v. 2, pp. 203-205 (C); M247, reel 106.

John Temple to Lord Carmarthen

My Lord,   New York 9 April 1786.
Since I had the honor of writing to your Lordship on the 2ᵈ· of last Month by the Shelburne Packet, I have had various applications for releif from persons avowing themselves to be British Subjects now confined in the jails of this state for transactions that took place during the late War in this Country! conceiving such Imprisonment of his Majestys subjects to be a direct violation of the Treaty of Peace, I transmitted the several Memorials (of which the enclosed are copies) to Congress through their Secretary for Foreign affairs; and, from the enclosed correspondence between the said Secretary & my self, it will appear to your Lordship, how fruitless have been my Endeavours for the enlargement of those unfortunate people.

As I had no Instructions for the Government of my Conduct in such business, I have done the best that my Judgment suggested to me upon the Occasion, and I hope that my Conduct will meet with your Lordships Approbation.

The Idea of Confining my Appointment of Consul General in these states, *merely* to Matters of Trade & Navigation, I have no doubt was suggested to Congress by their selfsufficient uncourtly Minister in London, who enviously apprehending, and perhaps truely apprehending, that, if I could enter upon business in general with Congress, I might possibly ripen

Matters to a tolerably good understanding between his Majestys Ministers & these states, much sooner than it is probable he, with his Mulish Obstinacy, will be able to do it in London.

The Trade & Navigation of this Country hath declined & is declining beyond what anyone could have imagined it would have done, in so short a time after the Peace; This, with the heavy Taxes, Extreeme Poverty, & unpromising prospects, of the States in general, hath put the Inhabitants into very ill humor; They will not however look to the *real cause* of such their unhappy conditions (their seperation from G^t Britain, that protected & Cherrished their Commerce) but attribute it entirely to Animosity & revenge in their Mother Country the excluding their Ships & Vessells from the Sugar Islands, & subjecting their Whale Oyl to heavy duties. Though many sensible people see the Matter in quite another light, the Majority entertain the sentiments I have mentioned; & they are encouraged in them & their ill humor fann'd, by corrupt Americans & french Inscendiaries, in this Country.

The Mercantile part of the people already sharply *feel* the distresses that a Seperation from Great Britain hath brought upon *them*; & the landed men, who are *still intoxicated* with their Independence, will soon find that the Necessary supplys to pay even the Interest of their Public debt, & the support of an Independent Government, will be too great & Weighty for their Purses; & perhaps be the Means of their recovering their Senses, sooner than they otherwise would do.

I am personally upon very social easey Terms with all the Members of Congress, & with all others in Power & influence here; They all dine with me, & I dine with them & with the foreign Ministers, frequently: The being upon such a footing, will enable me I apprehend, to execute the Trust reposed in me, with greater ease & facility than if I kept myself at a distance from them.

I am, with great deference & Respect, My Lord, Your Lordships most faithfull, and Obedient Servant.   J. Temple.
R. 16$^{th:}$ May.

PRO: FO 4/4, pp. 177-180 (LC transcription).

Thomas Barclay to John Adams and Thomas Jefferson

Gentlemen   Madrid 10$^{th.}$ April 1786
The day before yesterday Mr Carmichael received Letters from Algiers from Mr Lamb dated the 24$^{th.}$ of last month and from Mr Randal the 26$^{th.}$ (which I think a wrong date) with a Postcript from on board a Vessel in the

Bay of Alicante of the first instant after a Passage of twenty Six hours, He cannot come on shore without a Permission from Court to shorten his Quarantine, which Mr. Carmichael has applied for, & probably Mr. Randal will soon be at Paris – Though Mr. Carmichael will write to you on this Subject, & though I have no information from Africa but what I derive from him, I think it a Part of my Duty to give you the outlines of what Intelligence I can collect, though it should prove a work of supererogation. Mr. Lamb's Letter is short and obscure nor do I understand the whole of it. However he says, no peace can be made untill Congress grant a larger Sum to pay for it, and that he will return to Spain to wait for Orders, Mr. Randal says, the Dey has refused to treat with Mr. Lamb, without assigning any reason for it. It does not appear by either Letter that Mr. Lamb has had any audience of the Dey, But I shall think it very strange if he returns to Europe without knowing on what terms a treaty may be made, & should I find that to be the Case, unless I have your directions to the contrary, I shall hold myself justifiable at the Expence of some time & Money, to attain that knowledge. The removal of the Court, the compliance with necessary forms, and the intervention of the Holy week (during some days of which I need not pretend to set forward) have detained me some time longer than I expected; But the delay can be of no Consequence, as the Count de Florida Blanca was so condescending as to apprise the Spanish Consul at Morocco of my being thus far on the way – Indeed the attention shewn here to the Business in which I am engaged, far surpasses my warmest expectations. It will give me great Pleasure to receive a Letter from you if an opportunity to Cadiz should offer, please to put it under Cover to Messrs. Lynch & Bellew of that Place who will take Care of it.

I am Gentlemen Your most ob^{t.} humble Servt.　　　　Thos. Barclay

NA: PCC, *item 91, v. 1, pp. 119-120 (C); M247, reel 119.*

Louis Guillaume Otto to Congress

at New York the 18th. April 1786

The Undersigned Charges des Affairs of france has received express orders to remind Congress that a convention relating to the functions of the respective Consuls was signed between his Majesty and the U:S: on the 29th of July 1784 – And that the ratifications have not as yet been exchanged. The King being desirous that this formality should be no longer deferred, on account of the inconveniences resulting from the delay it has met with, requests that Congress will send their ratification to M^r· Jefferson as soon as possible to be exchanged for that of his Majesty –

The undersigned takes the liberty to observe that there has not as yet been any answer returned to the memorial which he had the honor to present to Congress in the name of his Majesty the 30th of November last of the Interests of which he has received orders to remind this Assembly –

Otto –

report Sec^y f: Afairs – May 1st· 1786.

NA: PCC, *item 81, v. 2, pp. 92-94 (translation);* M247, *reel 107.*

Count d'Expilly to William Carmichael

Sir & very dear Friend   [Algiers, April 20, 1786]

I have expressed my regret to your countrymen at their unseasonable arrival, & assured them on their coming that they would effect nothing; The Dey had some days before declared to me & that publicly in presence of his Divan that he would treat with no power about peace that had not previously made it with the Sublime Port. The mode I pointed out would have answered infinitely better, Congress must leave you perfect master of this business, & you must allow M^r· Wolf to act for you, as the measure is actually adopted, Congress must use another mode, that of beginning with Constantinople. You will find inclosed a letter for my old & good friend M^r· Timoni call on him & deliver it to him, he is the only person capable of facilitating the means for making your peace with the Port, that with Algiers will afterwards be easy, more especially should you be so fortunate as that the Corsairs of the Regency shall return without having made any American prizes, & more particularly if they should meet with any of your Frigates that would drub them a little, consult M^r· Timoni he is a very good man & no one in the world can render you greater services than he. M^r· Lamb will do me the justice to say that I have not trifled with him a moment, he goes away quite chagrined with not being able even to redeem his unfortunate countrymen, who are the more to be lamented as every body loves them here, the Moors even cannot avoid pittying them, so well do they know how to bear with their captivity. My wife departs for Alicant in company with M^r· Lamb on board a French vessel that I have   he has let me have the Spanish Brig which brought him here, by doing which he rendered me a service; M^r· Randall having gone with my secretary I could not deliver him your letter which I return to you. Follow M^r· Timonis advice who will enable you to succeed at Constantinople & you will soon have peace with Barbary more assuredly as it knows the interest which the House of Bourbon takes in the concerns of your Republic.

I recommend Sir & dear friend my wife to you, she will go to Madrid as soon as her quarantine is ~~out~~ performed, I hope that she will find a sincere friend in you. You have M$^{r.}$ Woulf here who can serve you, & who loves the U$^{d.}$ States. If you succeed in making peace with the porte you will want no One here at Algiers.

This departure has been so hastened that I have been obliged to write this letter in a hurry, I hope my dear friend that you will excuse any disorder in it, I conclude with repeating my sincere & tender attachment for you, with which I shall ever be my dear Carmichael Your most humble and most obedient servant   Count d'Espilly.

If you cannot see M$^{r.}$ Timoni directly, I beg that you will seal the letter & forward it to him instantly – ...

Faithfully translated from the Original by John Pintard.

NA: PCC, *item 84, v. 6, pp. 283-284 (translation); M247, reel 113.*

Thomas Jefferson to Richard Henry Lee

Dear Sir   London Apr. 22. 1786.

I expect to leave this place in about three days. our public letters, joint & separate, will inform you what has been done, and what could not be done here. with respect to a commercial treaty with this country be assured that the government not only has it not in contemplation at present to make any, but that they do not conceive that any circumstances will arise which shall render it expedient for them to have any political connection with us. ~~them.~~ they think we shall be glad of their commerce on their own terms. there is no party in our favor here, either in power, or out of power. even the opposition concur with the ministry & the nation in this. I can scarcely consider as a party the Marquis of Lansdowne, and a half dozen characters about him, such as D$^{r.}$ Price.[1] &c. who are impressed with the utility of a friendly connection with us. the former does not venture this sentiment in parliament, and the latter are not in situations to be heard. the Marquis of Lansdowne spoke to me affectionately of your brother, Doct$^{r.}$ Lee, and desired his respects to him, which I beg leave to communicate through you. were he to come into the ministry (of which there is not the most distant prospect) he must adopt the king's system, or go out again, as he did before, for daring to depart from it. when we see that through all the changes of ministry which have taken place during the present reign, there has never been a change of system with respect to America, we cannot reasonably doubt that this is the system of the king himself. his obstinacy of character we know; his hostility we have known, and it is embittered by ill success. if ever this nat[ion,] during his life, enters into arrangements with us, it must be in consequence of events of which they do not at present see a possibility. the object of the present ministry is to buoy up the nation with flattering calculations of their present prosperity, and to make them believe they are better without us than with us. this they seriously believe; for what is it men cannot be made to believe! I dined the other day in the company of the ministerial party. a General Clarke sat next to me, a Scotchman & a ministerialist. he introduced the subject of American affairs, and in the course of the conversation told me that were America to petition parliament to be again received on their former footing, the petition would be very generally rejected. he was serious in this, & I think it was the sentiment of the company, and is the sentiment of the nation. in this they are wise, but for a foolish reason. they think they lost more by suff[er]ing us to participate of their commercial privileges at home & abroad, than they lose by our political severance. the true reason however why such an application should be rejected, is that in a very short time we should oblige [th]em to add another hundred millions to their debt in unsuccesful attempts to retain the subjection offered to them. they are at present in a frenzy, and will not be recovered from it till they shall have leaped the precipice [they] are now so boldly advancing to. writing from England, I write you nothing but English news. the Continent at present furnishes nothing interesting....being with great esteem Dear Sir Your most obedient and most humble servant   Th: Jefferson

LC: *Jefferson Papers*, microfilm reel 5 (Press Copy).
[1] *Price, Richard (1723-1791). British philosopher and financial specialist. He provided advice on the retirement of the British national debt, and his studies of probability theory led to the establishment of life insurance and old-age pension systems. A friend of Benjamin Franklin, Lord Shelburne, and Lord Chatham, he was an enthusiastic supporter of both the American and the French Revolutions.*

John Adams and Thomas Jefferson to John Jay

Sir   Grosvener Square April 25ᵗʰ· 1786 –
Soon after our meeting together in London, We had a Conference with
the Secretary of State for foreign Affairs,[1] in which we communicated to
him, the joint Commission of Congress, for negotiating a Treaty of
Commerce with Great Britain, and left an attested Copy of it in the hands
of his Lordship. At the same time his Lordship was informed that as the
Commission was limited to two years duration which would expire on the
twelfth of May, We should be ready to confer upon the subject of it with
his Majesty's Ministers; but as one of us would be obliged to return in a
short time to Paris, it was wished that an early opportunity might be taken
to see upon what points we could agree, and to discuss those in which at
first we might differ. his Lordship after harping a little on the old string, the
insufficiency of the powers of Congress to treat and to compell Compliance
with Treaties, said he would lay the Matter before the Ministry and the
King. in a few day's his Lordship meeting one of us, proposed in his own
name and that of Mʳ· Pitt, that, as the Project already Communicated
contained many political Regulations, we should prepare a Project of a
Treaty merely commercial. The next day at the office, it was said to the
under Secretary of State, Mʳ· Frasier,[2] his Lordship not being there, that the
Project already proposed, was in our opinion the best that could be
proposed, for the mutual interest of the two Nations: but if any parts of it
were objectionable in the Minds of the Ministry, we were ready to enter
into a candid disquisition of them, and to receive any counter project,
which might contain the sense of the Cabinet; but untill we knew which
Articles were objected to, it would be in vain for us to attempt a new
draught: We could only repeat the proposition of the former one. Mʳ·
Frasier reported this conversation to his Principal, who directed him to
write us, that as the former Project contained many political Regulations,
his Lordship wished to receive a Plan of a Treaty merely commercial. We
accordingly sent five or six Articles of the former Pland [sic] and proposed
them as a Treaty of Commerce, which we suppose would be a good one,
and except in one point as compleat as we can expect. The point we mean
is the Priviledge of ships built in the United States. It is much to be wished
that such Ships might enjoy in the British Dominions as ample Previledges
as British built Ships, whether owned or navigated by Americans or not,
and we should now add an Article to that Purpose, if there was the smallest
symptom of an Inclination to treat at all. But there is not. There is no
party, nor Individual here in favour of a Treaty, but upon the Principle that
the United States will retaliate, if there is not one. all agree that if America

will suffer England to pockett (that is their Expression) all her navigation, England would be unwise not to avail herself of the advantage.

The Negotiation with Portugal is brought to a Conclusion as far as her Minister here has authority to proceed. We propose to execute the treaty, and hope to receive the Counterpart executed by the Chevalier De Pinto, before our Commission expires. The treaty itself shall be transmitted to Congress as soon as it is finished and we shall not trouble you with a tedious detail of Projects and Counter projects. yet the enclosed Copies of parts of a Letter, concerning flour and Privateering and contraband, may be necessary for our justification.

We have the honor to inclose copies of Letters from Mr Carmichael of the 5th. April, from Mr Barclay of the 5 April from the Comte D'Espilly & Mr Lamb to Mr Carmichael dated Algiers 26th. of March.

We have every reason to fear that the negotiations with the Turks will be very tedious and expensive, upon the present plan, and without success. Our Commission to Constantinople expires in a few Days and we have no new Commission to this power which enables us to send Agents. And indeed the Sublime Porte is so great a Power that its dignity would be offended, if such a measure were attempted. There are reasons to expect that a Minister to that Court would be well received and that our Commerce and Naval Stores would be there an object.

With great respect we have the honor to be Your Excellency's most Obedient Humble Servt's –

John Adams.
Th: Jefferson

NA: PCC, item 86, pp. 373-375 (LS); M247, reel 114.

^1 Lord Carmarthen

^2 Frazier (Fraser, Frazer) William. British government figure. Under Secretary of State to Lord Carmarthen.

John Jay to John Adams

D^r. Sir   [New York] Office for foreign Affairs 1st May 1786.

it is the Pleasure of Congress that you protract your Negociations with the Court of great Britain Respecting the posts which should have been before this surrendered to the U. S and other infrac[t]ions of the said treaty By that power so as to avoid demanding a categorickall Answer Respecting the same untill the further orders of Congress.

I have the Honor to be with great Respece D^r. Sir Your most ob^t. & very Hble: Servt.

John Jay –

Rec^d 24th. June 86

MHS: The Adams Papers, microfilm reel 368 (LS).

Thomas Jefferson to the Comte de Vergennes

Sir   Paris May 3. 1786.

· · · · ·

Information lately received relative to the Barbary States has suggested
that it might be expedient, and perhaps necessary for us to pave the way to
arrangements with them by a previous application to the Ottoman porte.
Your Excellency's intimate acquaintance with this Subject would render
your advice thereon equally valuable and desireable. if you would be pleased
to permit me to wait on you any day or hour which shall be most
convenient for yourself, I should be much gratified by a little conversation
with you on this Subject.

I have the honour to be with Sentiments of the highest respect and
esteem your Excelllency's most obedient and most humble Servant.

Th. Jefferson

FFAA: Pol. Corr., U.S., v. 31, f. 282-283 (LC transcription).

Rufus King to John Adams

Sir,   New York 4. May 1786.

· · · · ·

Although it is admitted by every one, that the Duties of your legation
have been ably discharged, yet it seems to be as generally allowed, that
little good can be expected, in the present disposition of the British
ministry from the continuation of a minister from our country at the British
Court – on this Subject congress will be very temperate, and nothing will
be decided hastily – there certainly was a time since the war when there
existed a very general disposition in America, to be intimately allied with
the country of your present Residence – that disposition has since changed,
is now universally weakened, and in several parts of America does not now
exist –

Whether the measures pursued in the British Cabinet, and which have
produced this change in America, were best calculated to advance the
prosperity of Great Britain or America, a short futurity will determine –
certain it is, that they have a tendency to produce that Unanimity in
America so much to be desired, as the Basis of those national Regulations,
which alone can establish our commerce, and make our country respectable
– indeed they have in some sort already produced this good Object – the
Arrets of France relative to the Cod Fishery tend to the same purpose –

America begins to learn, that she must depend upon herself, for Prosperity & Happiness –

With perfect respect – I have the honor to be your ob^t & very Hble Serv$^{t:}$ Rufus King

Ans$^{d.}$ 14. June. 1786

MHS: *The Adams Papers, microfilm reel 368 (ALS)*.

John Jay's Report on Relations with Great Britain

[New York] Office for foreign Affairs 8th May 1786
The Secretary of the United States for the Department of foreign Affairs to whom was referred a Letter from the Honble M$^{r.}$ Adams of December last in Cyphers – Reports

That the Contents of this Letter may be classed under three Heads.

(1).   The Characters of the british King and his Ministers, which for the Reasons assigned by M$^{r.}$ Adams should be kept secret. –

(2).   The restrictive and unfriendly System of Trade with Respect to America, which the british Government, and the Nation in general, appear to prefer and will probably adopt – of this System the United States have much Reason to be apprehensive, and their Inability to meet it by general and proper Regulations, will doubtless encourage and promote it. –

Congress at present can do nothing on the Subject except in the way of Recommendations; which being a very ineffectual Way, had better not be tried; lest non Compliance should diminish their Respectability, and impair the little Authority they possess. In the Opinion of your Secretary Recommendations should be avoided as much as possible, and every constitutional Requisition impartially enforced, with uniform Punctuality and Decision. –

(3)   The Probability that the Posts will be detained on Pretence of the Treaty of Peace having been violated by american Acts relative to british Debts & the Tories –

On this Point your Secretary can only repeat what has been suggested in other Reports Viz$^{t.}$ that what wrongs may have been done, should be undone; and that the United States should, if it were only to preserve Peace, be prepared for War. –

M$^{r.}$ Adams Advice in this and many of his other Letters is just, but until Congress shall be put, by further Powers, in Capacity to act upon it, there would be a little Use in particular Reports on Subjects which to them are at present rather Matters of Speculation than Provision.

All which is submitted to the Wisdom of Congress. –

John Jay –

NA: PCC, item 81, v. 2, pp. 99-101 (DS); M247, reel 107.

John Adams to James Bowdoin

Sir   London May 9. 1786

Your Excellencies Letter of the 12. of January I have had the Honour to receive, and am much obliged to you for the Information in it

Your opinion of the Policy of this Country, will be found in the Result of Things to be just, and your Reasoning in Support of it is so conclusive and at the sametime, So obvious, that it is astonishing it has not its Effect upon the Cabinet. Every Consideration has been repeatedly urged to no Effect. Seamen, the Navy, and Power to Strike an awful Blow to their Ennemies at Sea, on the first breaking out of a War, are the Ideas that prevail over all others. Mr Jenkinson, an old Friend of the British Empire, is still at his Labours. He is about establishing a Bounty upon fifteen Ships, to the Southward and upon two to double Cape Horn for Sperma Caeti Whales. Americans are to take an oath that they mean to Settle in England, before they are entitled to the Bounty. I have long since informed Congress, that nothing is to be expected from this Country, but Poverty, Weakness and Ruin. if after all our People will carry on a ruinous Trade, it is their own Concern. But no Man can do them a greater Injury, than by holding up to their View a hope, that We shall receive any Relief, by taking off the Duty on oil, or by admission to the West India Islands. They will infallibly be deceived if they entertain any such Expectations.

I have been circumstantially informed from time to time and Step by Step, from Mr Jefferson the Marquis de la Fayette and Mr Barrett of all the Negotiations for exchanging our oyl for the Produce, Manufactures and Sugars of France. The great Revolution in Trade, which you mention ought to be promoted by every Friend of America, and it must take Place. I have made use of all these Considerations. But if an Angel from Heaven Should declare to this Nation that our States will unite, retaliate, prohibit or trade with France, they would not believe it. There is not one Man in the Nation, who pretends to believe it, and if he did he would be treated with Scorn. Let me intreat you, Sir, and every other Citizen of the United States to extinguish all hopes of relief to their Trade from this Country.

Peace with the Turks, comprehending under this Term Constantinople Tunis, Tripoli, Algiers and Morocco, is essential to our Navigation and Commerce and political Consideration in Europe. Two or three hundred Thousand Guineas, and nothing less will obtain it. it will be miserable Policy and Oeconomy, to loose two or three millions in Trade, Insurance &c and still worse to add two or three millions more in fitting out a Navy to fight them, in order to Save that Sum in customary Presents. We are now limited to a Sum that will be worse than thrown away.

Intrigues of Individuals are said to be on foot, to Sett South America free from Spain, and not improbably the Pulse may be felt in the United States. But I hope the States will not only be prudent themselves, but oblige Individuals to be so too. – Portugal & Spain are bound by a Treaty of 1778 to Support each other in such a Case, and all the World will be in flames. We had better avoid the fury of them.

Three great Objects agitate the Cabinets of Europe in Secret. The Passage of the Dardinells and navigation of the Danube, I consider as one, a free Commerce with all the East Indies is a Second, and the Independence of South America is the third. They will all be pursued untill they are obtained, as I fully believe. But as all know the Contest will be Sharp, extensive and long, all are afraid to begin. This is all confidential, between you and me and a few of our discreet Friends.

God bless our Country, but I still tremble for its Safety.

With great Respect, I have the Honour to be your Excrellencys most obedient and most humble Servant   John Adams.

MHS: *Winthrop Papers* (ALS).

Don Diego de Gardoqui's Memorial to Congress

New York. May 11[th.] 1786

The Underwritten Encargado de Negocios of his Catholic Majesty, has the Honor to represent to the Honorable Congress, that having observed in none of their Requisitions to the respective States for the Money necessary to make the Payments due up to the 31[st.] December 1785, on the Loans made in the last War, any mention made of the considerable Sums which their Agent M[r.] Oliver Pollock[1] received from his Excellency Sen[r.] Count de Galvez,[2] and various other Subjects of New Orleans and *Havana*, which amount to one hundred and thirty two thousand, Seven hundred and Seventy four Hard Dollars, and six Reals of Plate, on which Account the said Agent was detained at the last mentioned Port, from whence, by the Generosity of his Excellency, his Creditors permitted him to go to his own Country, under a judicial writing, whereby he bound himself to pay the said Sum to this Encargado, as soon as he should arrive in this Country – and although a year has since elapsed, it has not been performed, nor has any thing been paid. He finds himself therefore obliged to remind the Honorable Congress of the Necessity of taking proper Measures for the Payment of the beforementioned Sum.

The Encargado de Negocios of the King flatters himself That the seasonable Friendship which very consistently with the Principles of the War, his Excellency manifested towards the United States, will induce the Honorable Congress to pay the most speedy Attention to this Representation, and to provide that the Persons interested may be reimbursed without Delay.   Diego de Gardoqui

NA: PCC, item 120, v. 2, pp. 301-302 (translation); M40, reel 2.
¹ Pollock, Oliver (1737-1823). American merchant residing in New Orleans. Intermediary between Spanish colonial officials and American military leaders in the West, 1776-1778. U.S. commercial agent at New Orleans, 1778-1783. Principal source of credit for George Rogers Clark after the capture of Kaskaskia in 1778, which put him heavily in debt. Appointed U.S. commercial agent at Havana, 1783, but arrested and kept in custody for 18 months at the instigation of his creditors. Released at the behest of Governor Bernardo de Gálvez, he eventually recouped his fortune through trade in the West Indies and New Orleans, and had his claims reimbursed by Virginia and the federal government.
² Gálvez y Gallardo, Bernardo Vicente Polimar de (1746-1786). Spanish military leader and colonial administrator. Named colonel of Spain's Louisiana regiment in 1776, he served as governor of Louisiana, 1777-1783. Brigadier, 1779. Captured Baton Rouge and Natchez, 1779; Mobile and Pensacola, 1780. Captain general of Louisiana, the Floridas, and Cuba, 1784-1785. Viceroy of New Spain, 1785-1786.

Thomas Jefferson to John Adams

Dear Sir   Paris May 11. 1786.

I do myself the honour of inclosing to you letters which came to hand last night from mr Lamb, mr Carmichael and mr Barclay. by these you will perceive that our peace is not to be purchased at Algiers but at a price far beyond our powers. what that would be indeed mr Lamb does not say, nor probably knows. but as he knew our ultimatum, we are to suppose from his letter that it would be a price infinitely beyond that. a reference to Congress seems hereon to be necessary. till that can be obtained, mr Lamb must be idle at Algiers, Carthagena or elsewhere. would he not be better employed in going to Congress? they would be able to draw from him & mr

Randall the information necessary to determine what they will do. and if they determine to negotiate, they can reappoint the same, or appoint a new negotiator, according to the opinion they shall form on their examination. < * > I suggest this to you as my first thoughts; an ultimate opinion should not be formed till we see mr Randall, who may be shortly expected. in the mean time, should an opportunity occur, favour me with your ideas hereon, that we may be maturing our opinions. I shall send copies of these three letters to mr Jay by the packet which sails from l'Orient the 1ˢᵗ· day of the next month.

On my return to Paris the Imperial ambassador informed me he had received full powers for treating with us. I repeated to him the information that ours would expire the 12ᵗʰ· of this month. he said he supposed Congress would have no objections to renew them, proposed that I should write to them on the subject, and in the mean time desired our project and observed that we might be proceeding to arrange the treaty, so as that it should be ready for signature on the arrival of our powers. I gave him a copy of our project, in which, taking the Danish one for the ground work, I made the alterations noted on the within paper: being such as had occurred & met our approbation during the Prussian Tuscan & Portuguese negotiations. I write to Congress an information of what has passed, and in the mean time shall take no other step till you favor me with your opinion whether we should proceed to prepare terms according to Count Merci's proposition.

I inclose you a copy of the queries of which I had put an illegible one into your hands when in London.

...I have the honor to be Dear Sir your most obedient and most humble servant   Th: Jefferson
ansᵈ 23. 1786

MHS: *The Adams Papers, microfilm reel 368 (ALS).*

Comte d'Estaing to Thomas Jefferson

Sir   Paris 17. May 1786.

In giving you an account of an opinion of Mʳ· Massiac's,[1] and which absolutely corresponds with my own, I cannot too much observe how great a difference may take place in the course of forty years between the means which he required and those which political circumstances that I cannot ascertain may exact.

This Secretary of State afterwards Vice Admiral, had the Modesty when a Captain to propose a means for the reduction of Algiers, less brilliant to himself, but more sure and economical than the one Government was about to adopt. They wanted him to undertake a bombardment, he proposed a simple blockade. All the force he required was a single man of war, two strong Frigates, and two Sloops of war.

I am convinced that by blocking up Algiers, cross-anchoring and with a long tow, that is to say, with several cables spliced to each other, and with iron chains, one might if necessary always remain there, and there is no Barbarian power thus confined which would not soon sue for peace.

During the war before last the English remained even in winter at anchor before Morbian on the coast of Brittany, which is a much more dangerous coast. Expeditious preparation for sailing of the vessels which form the blockade, which should be of a sufficent number to prevent any thing from entering or going out while the rest remain at their stations, the choice of these stations, skilful manoeuvres, strict watch during the night, every precaution against the element which a seaman ought to be acquainted with; also against the enemy to prevent the sudden attack of boats, and to repel them in case they should make an attack, by *bastingages* prepared for the purpose, frequent refreshments for the crews, relieving the men, an unshaken constancy and exactness in the service are the means which in my opinion would render the event indubitable.

Bombardments are but transitory. It is if I may so express myself, like breaking glass-windows with guineas. None have produced the desired effect against the Barbarians – even an imperfect blockade were one to have the patience and courage to persist therein, would occasion a perpetual evil, it would be insupportable in the long run, to obtain the end proposed no advantage ought to be lost. If several powers would come to a good understanding and pursue a plan formed on the principles of humanity; if they were not counteracted by others, it would require but a few years to compel the Barbarians to cease being pirates, they would become merchants in spite of themselves. It is needless to observe that the unsuccessful attempts of Spain, and those under which the Republic of Venice perhaps hides other views, have increased the strength as well as the self love of all the Barbarians. We are assured that the Algerines have fitted out merchantmen with heavy cannon, this would render it necessary to block the place with two ships so that one of the two might remain moored near the bar, while the other might prepare to support such of the Frigates as should give chace. But their chebecks, even their Frigates and all their vessels although overcharged with men are moreover so badly armed and manoeuvred that assistance from without would be most to be feared. Your Excellency has told me the only and true means of bringing to terms the only people who can take a pleasure in disturbing *our* commerce. You see I speak as an American Citizen, this title dear to my heart, the value of which I fully prize, affords me the happy opportunity of offering still more particularly the homage the sincere attachment and respect with which I have the honor to be, Sir, your Excellency's most humble & most obedient Servant.   Estaing[2]

NA: PCC, *item 107, v. 1, pp. 241-243 (translation); M247, reel 133.*

[1] *Massiac, Claude Louis, Marquis de. French naval officer. While a captain, successfully blockaded the port of Algiers with a small force, bringing about Algerine acquiescence to French peace terms. Later, vice admiral and Minister of the Navy.*

[2] *D'Estaing, Jean Baptiste Charles Henri Hector (1729-1794). French naval officer. Vice admiral commanding the French fleet of 17 ships of the line that blockaded New York and attempted to capture Newport, 1778. Captured St. Vioncent and Grenada, wounded in failed Franco-American effort to capture Savannah, 1779.*

John Adams to Lord Carmarthen

My Lord –   Grosvenor Square May 18. 1786 –
I do myself the Honour of transmitting to your Lordship herewith inclosed, an Act of the United States of America in Congress assembled, the 13th. of October 1785. together with Sundry other Papers relative to the Boundary Line, between the United States, and his Majestys late Province of Nova Scotia, part of which is now called New Brunswick – It is Still fresh in the Recollection of every Person who was concerned in the Negotiation of the late Peace, that Mitchells Map,[1] was made use of by the British and American Plenipotentiaries; and the River St Croix, was marked out on that Map as there delineated for the Boundary: which Circumstance alone, it is hoped, will be Sufficient to determine all questions which may have been raised, concerning so recent a Transaction. In former Controversies between the Crowns of Great Britain and France, concerning the Boundary between the late Province of Massachusetts Bay and Nova Scotia, it has been often contended by the British Ministers and Commissaries that the River St Croix, was a River Still further Eastward, than the Easternmost of those three which fall into the Bay of Passamaquaddi; but never once admitted to be a River more westerly. So that the Plenipotentiaries at the Peace, on both Sides had Reason to presume, that when they fixed on the St. Croix Surveyed by Mitchel, and laid down by him on his Map, there never could afterwards arise any Controversy concerning it. Yet it Seems, My Lord, that a Number of his Majestys Subjects have crossed over this River, and Settled in the Territory

of the United States, an Encroachment, in which they cannot be supposed to be countenanced by his Majestys Government.

Difficulties of this kind, if early attended to, are easily adjusted, and I shall be ready at all times to enter into Conferences, that every Point may be discussed and all Uneasiness prevented. but while new Maps are every day made and old ones coloured according to an erroneous Idea, a foundation may be laid, for much future Evil, both to Nations and Individuals

I am, my Lord, your Lordships most obedient, and most humble Servant
John Adams.

PRO: FO 4/4, f. 271-273 (ALS); LC Acc. No. 10, 693, microfilm reel 2.

[1] *Mitchell's map.* The reference is to A Map of the British and French Dominions in North America With the Roads, Distances, Limits, and Extent of the Settlements, Humbly Inscribed to the Right Honourable The Earl of Halifax, And the Other Right Honourable The Lords Commissioners for Trade & Plantations, By Their Lordships Most Obliged and Very Humble Servant Jno. Mitchell (*London: Andrew Millar, 1755*). *John Mitchell (d. 1768), a physician, botanist, and cartographer, practiced medicine in Virginia, 1735-1746, thereafter residing in or near London.*

William Carmichael to Thomas Jefferson

Sir   Aranjuez, May 18[th.] 1786

The Courier by whom I did myself the Honor to address your Excellency the 16[th.] inst. having been detained a Day longer than I expected, I avail myself of this Circumstance to advise you of M[r] Lamb's Arrival at Madrid, last Night. This morning I received a Letter from him by one of my Servants whom he dispatched for that purpose: He therein requests me to send him "any Orders or Letters on acc[t.] of our Affairs" that I may have received for him, and complains that he has had no Answers to the Letters he has written. He added that should he have no Instructions in my Hands for him. – he must send an Express to Paris & London in a Day or two as he must soon set out again for Alicant – intimating that the Money he has to command will fall short by twenty thousand Dollars of the Sum necessary to redeem our Captives.

As his Motives are entirely unknown to me & as I wish to spare every Expence to the publick that is not absolutely necessary, I immediately dispatched the Servant advising him of the Hour the Spanish Courier would set out and requesting him to take post & repair hither, that by consulting together we might convey immediate Information to your Excellency & thro' you to M[r.] Adams of the Situation of our Affairs.

I am now awaiting his Arrival. Since I came hither I am informed that the Court of Versailles has very lately offered its good Offices to terminate the Differences between this Court and that of Naples. The Answer made to this proposition is said to be the following. After the usual Acknowlegements &ᶜ &ᶜ the Count de Florida Blanca assured the french Ministry that there was no Difference or Rupture between Spain & Naples, that the Misintelligence was merely of a domestick nature, a Coolness between the Father & Son consequently could not with Propriety be submitted to Arbitration of a third Party.

I have no further Intelligence of or from Mʳ· Barclay, but I this Day was shewn a Letter from an European Consul in Morocco mentioning that the Emperor was much irritated against the british Nation. His Manner of manifesting his ill Humor is somewhat singular. He desired all the Europeans to have inserted in their Gazettes that he looked upon Spain & Portugal as his best Friends in Europe — and that the Chests of Cocao sent by the former were worth more than all the british presents. That the english Nation was false and perfidious & entirely void of all Principles of Religion. This is no bad Omen for the Success of Mʳ Barclay's Mission. Mʳ Randall writes you by this Conveyance. His Information joined to the Letter from the Count D'Expilly of which I enclosed a Copy in my last will best explain the State of our Negotiation with Algiers unless Mʳ· Lamb Should have other Information than he has communicated to me hitherto.

I am Your Excellency's Most obedient & humble Servant

Wᵐ· Carmichael

LC: *Jefferson Papers, microfilm reel 5 (LS).*

John Lamb to Thomas Jefferson

Madrid May 20ᵗʰ 1786

After maney little Disapaintments, I arrᵈ at Algiers the 25ᵗʰ of March and within the term of three or four Days I found That the whole amᵗ· of the money in my hands belonging to the publick would not purchas the people who are the unfortunate in consequence of which I Dispatchᵈ· Mʳ· Randall so that your Excellencyes might have the earlyest notice of our matters in that Quarter: in a short letter to your Excellencyes I stated our affairs accordingly mʳ· Randall saild the 29ᵗʰ or 30 march. with my desire to him to proseed with all posible Dispatch, to give the earlyest notes that was in my power, but when I came here I found mʳ· Randall was in Aranjuez. I recᵈ· a line from him at nine the next evening in consequence of which I wrote him, and desired him to Proceed. he answerᵈ· my letter, the three letters I herein inclose so that your Excellencys will naturally excuse me for the detention, m^r Randall the bairer of this therefore I have not inclos^d his letters. It seems he hath been unwell.

On the 3^d Day of April was admitted to an Audience with the Day. but would not speake of Peace, set the Slaves a most Exorbitent price far beyond my limitt, the Seventh I had a second intervue. but still he was of the Same mind. about the Seventeenth I had the third and last intervue he fell sumthing of his first Price and I here inclos the Last Price, which is enormous as your Excellencys will see, my next vues were to have an Acquaintance with their Principal minister which I soon braught to pass, by sum presants to this ministers confident, and he was our interprater. he told me it was his Greatest Desire that our peace might be made with their Regency and that for his part he would use his utmost indeavours for the purpose. but untill the affaires of Spain were Settled, could be little Done on our matter, and further told me not to mind the little Putoffs by the Day nor the enormous price ask^d for our slaves, that the price that was set on our people was ondly to Put a more modest face on the Price that they intend to make the Spaniard pay for their People, and advis^d me to go to Spain and wate untill they had Done with Spain, and that I migth rest assured that he would at all apertunitys write to me. I beg^d him to write mr Carmichael. he Did. I beg^d him to Give me a free pass to come to Algiers and to go when I pleas^d he likewise Did, but told me that if the letter was exposd that he had wrote m^r Carmichael, he should loose his life, and when I returnd that I might expect the Same. I had several intervues with this minister and the above is the purport and substanc, Exepting that they had an intire rite to make Peace or war, without the Voyce of the Grand Seynor, and that they were under no controle by the ottoman port. he told me that it would not be long after my arival in Spain before he should let me know what steps it would be best to take, and when for me to return if I was orderd back. and as I found it was of no consequence to Tarrey longer their untill I had further Orders took his advize and returnd. Their is no Doubt but I shall here from him soon: after wating in Spain a long time for the infuluence of that court, was oblig^d to leve Madrid without my wishes on that. for I got no letter alltho mr. Carmichael *took* the utmost pains. About four or five Dayes before I left Algiers I rec^d Two Letters from m^r Carmichael. inclos^d in one of those was an open letter from the court of Spain In favour of our mission to the That Regency and Directed to Count De Expelly. but Previous to the reception of the letter he told me if shuch a letter came to him he could not make any use of it neither did he. the reasons he best knows. but this is sure that he cares verry little about our peace in that Quarter: the letter I carry^d from france was of no consequence. if your Excellency could procure a letter from the court of

France and Directed to the Day with their Desires to him for a Peace with the United States of America it would give Greater wate but such a letter I Dare say would be heard to be Procured: The treatement I rec^d from the french consul was Polite indeed he paid me Greate atention. m^r Logie Likewise rec^d me as an ould friend and Declared to me that he had no orders to counter act my mission from his court, which I am sure of – I left the Packett in the hands of Count De Expelly who hath employ^d her for Spain untill I call for her – and have the Counts riceet for the Vessell: Thought Proper to leave my owne Stores which I Carry^d over, in Algier and left them with m^r Woulf whome is a very honest good Gentelman, and I belive a friend to our Cause in that Quarter. and by the Desire of Count De Expelly have left the care of our unfortunate People Likewise in his hands, to gather with four hundred Dollars to Pay their Post Expence, and buy them such things as will make them comfortable which money I am sure will be frugally Expended. I shall wate your Excellencyes further orders at Alicant, hopeing that my conduct may be Approv^d of And Am with Due Respect your Excellencyes Most Obedient Hm^le Servt.

John Lamb

NB The Plaegue is within the limites of the Regency of Algiers in consequence of which it will make Verry Long Quarantines in Spain. the Vessel that I have bought for the conveniancy of our busyness I believe will be orderd to Mahone to Proforme Quarantine. to Purchase this Vessel was unavoyadle as I could not Get to Algier well without I here Give your Excellencys an acc^t of the Prices of our unfortunate people and it as Followes Viz

3 Capts	@ 6 m Dollars Each Pr. head	18000
2 mates	@ 4 m Ditto Each Pr head	8000
2 Passengers	@ 4 m Ditto Each Pr head	8000
14 Saylors	@ 1400 Ditto Each Pr head	19600

Numb^r 21 amts To the inormous Sum of   53600
Elevenen Per cent to be added according to custom   5896
is Spanish milled Dollars   59496

So that your Excellencys See how far be yound your Expetations the Sum amts which renders me incapible of acting *untill* further orders. the price the Spaniards are Giveing for their peoples is little Short of what is charg^d us and they have Eleven hundred men & Sum upwards in Algiers it will cost Spain more than one million and one half of Dollars for their Slaves ondely the Peace of Spain and their Slaves will am^t to more than three million of Dollars. I have ondley to add that their Cruizers will in all Probability be at Sea by the Sixth of June at farthest. I am of Opinion that if we follow our Pretention for Peace this summer that they will here Propossals but not at the price we Expected. nor by the open way we first went to work. if

France will Give nothing but Seald letters we had better have none: To fight those People the first year will cost us more than half a million Pounds Sterling. I have by Experience of a long Daet a Perfect knowledg of the cost of arm$^{d.}$ Vessels and at the Distance we are from those people and foreign Ports to make use of it will be a heavey Tax on us and without the least Prospect of Gain. I hope I shall be Excus$^{d.}$ in Speaking my mind so freely. it is out of Zealus Desires for the Good of the Country I belong To. And it is my Opinion that for a less Sum than the first year would cost us to fight we can make Peace and if we intend it at all now is the ondley time to Pursue as the way is Seemingly open for a Tryal. I hope their is no more of our People will be So unhappy as to fall into those peoples hands this Summer and in that case in a Measure it will discourage them in their Expectations: Spain is our Sure friend in our Peace with Algiers: but they have not finish$^{d.}$ their Peace at Presant. we shall have their assistance at the conclusion of their peace.

With Due Respect as above   J. Lamb

I have no Objections of their being a Tryal made at Constantinople but it will be of no Consequence as to Peace with Algiers. as the Count mentions in his letter his Vues are to have m$^{r.}$ Woulf appointed in Our peace with Algiers, and m$^{r.}$ Woulf is a very Good man but it is well to take time before larger power is Given Strangers. The Count kept me as much in the Dark as he Could on all acc$^{t.}$: my advice is if we should arme against those people to unite our selves with those Nations that are not at Peace with Algiers and that will lessen our Expence much on the Ocation.

NA: PCC, item 87, v. 1, pp. 522-531 (ALS); M247, reel 115.

John Adams to Thomas Jefferson

Dear Sir   London May 23. 1786
    I am honoured with yours of the 11$^{th.}$ with the enclosures from Mr Lamb, Mr Carmichael and Mr Barclay. I am not Surprized that M$^{r.}$ Lamb, has only discovered that our means are inadequate, without learning the Sum that would be Sufficient. *It faut marchander avec ces Gens la.*[1] – They must be beaten down as low as possible. but We Shall find at last the Terms very dear. The Algerines will never make Peace with Us, untill We have Treaties finished with Constantinpole, Tunis Tripoli, & Morocco. They always Stand out the longest. Mr Barclay will have no better fortune and I dont believe it worth while for him to wait a Moment to discover what Sum will do.

I think with you, that it is best to desire Mr Lamb immediately, to return to Congress, and Mr Randal too. it is Surprizing that neither of them, has given Us more circumstantial Information, and that Mr Randal has not come on to Paris and London. – I think you will do well to write him to come forward without loss of time. and am glad You Sent Copies of all the Letters to Mr Jay. I concur with you entirely in the Propriety of your going on with the Comte de Merci, in the Negotiation and in transmitting to Congress the Plan you may agree upon, that they may Send a new Commission if they judge proper.

I have a Letter from Mr Randal at madrid 4 May, but shall not answer it as I wish you to write him in behalf of both of Us to return immediately to Paris and London. I have a Letter too from Isaac Stephens at Algiers the 15. of April. He says the Price is 6000 Dollars for a Master 4000 for a Mate, and 1500 for each Sailor. The Dey will not abate a 6^d,[2] he Says and will not have any Thing to Say, about Peace with America. He Says "The People" i.e. the Sailors I Suppose, are carrying Rocks and Timber on their backs, for nine miles out of the Country, over Sharp Rocks and Mountains. That he has an Iron round his Leg. &c He begs that We would pay the Money for their Redemption, without Sending to Congress but this is impossible.

With great Regard I am Sir your affectionate   John Adams

LC: *Jefferson Papers, microfilm reel 5 (ALS).*
[1] *One must bargain with those People.*
[2] *sixpence*

Thomas Jefferson to John Jay

Sir   Paris May 23. 1786.

Letters received both from Madrid & Algiers while I was in London having suggested that treaties with the states of Barbary would be much facilitated by a previous one with the Ottoman porte, it was agreed between mr Adams and myself that on my return I should consult on this subject the Count de Vergennes, whose long residence at Constantinople rendered him the best judge of it's expediency. various circumstances have put it out of my power to consult him till to day. I stated to him the difficulties we were likely to meet with at Algiers and asked his opinion what would be the probable expence of a diplomatic mission to Constantinople, & what it's effect at Algiers. he said that the expence would be very great, for that presents must be made at that court, and every one would be gaping after them; and that it would not procure us a peace at Algiers one penny the cheaper. he observed that the Barbary states acknoleged a sort of vassalage to the Porte, & availed themselves of that relation when any thing was to be gained by it: but that whenever it subjected them to a demand from the Porte they totally disregarded it: that money was the sole agent at Algiers, except so far as fear could be induced also. he cited the present example of Spain, which tho' having a treaty with the Porte, would probably be obliged to buy a peace at Algiers at the expence of upwards of six millions of livres. I told him we had calculated from the demands & information of the Tripoline Ambassador at London that to make peace with the four Barbary states would cost us between two & three hundred thousand guineas, if bought with money. the sum did not seem to exceed his expectations. I mentioned to him, that considering the uncertainty of a peace when bought, perhaps Congress might think it more eligible to establish a cruise of frigates in the Mediterranean & even to blockade Algiers. he supposed it would require ten vessels great & small. I observed to him that Mons.ᵣ de Massiac had formerly done it with five; he said it was true, but that vessels of relief would be necessary. I hinted to him that I thought the English capable of administering aid to the Algerines. he seemed to think it impossible, on account of the scandal it would bring on them. I asked him what had occasioned the blockade by m.ᵣ de Massiac: he said, an infraction of their treaty by the Algerines. I had a good deal of conversation with him also on the situation of affairs between England & the United states: & particularly on their refusal to deliver up our posts. I observed to him that the obstructions thrown in the way of the recovery of their debts were the effect & not the cause as they pretended, of their refusal to deliver up the posts: that the merchants interested in these debts shewed a great disposition to make arrangements with us, that the article of time we could certainly have settled, & probably that of the interest during the war: but that the minister shewing no disposition to have these matters arranged, I thought it a sufficient proof that this was not the true cause of their detaining the posts. he concurred as to the justice of our requiring time for the paiment of our debts, said nothing which shewed a difference of opinion as to the article of interest, and seemed to beleive fully their object was to divert the channel of the fur trade before they delivered up the posts, and expressed a strong sense of the importance of that commerce to us. I told him I really could not forsee what would be the event of this detention, that the situation of the British funds, & desire of their minister to begin to reduce the national debt seemed to indicate that they could not wish a war. he thought so, but that neither were we in a condition to go to war. I told him I was yet uniformed what Congress proposed to do on this subject, but that we should certainly always count on the good offices of France, and I was sure that the offer of them would suffice to induce

GrBritain to do us justice. he said that surely we might always count on the friendship of France. I added that by the treaty of Alliance, she was bound to guarantee our limits to us, as they should be established at the moment of peace. he said they were so *"mais qu'il nous etoit necessaire de les constater."*[1] I told him there was no question what our boundaries were, that the English themselves admitted they were clear beyond all question. I feared however to press this any further lest a reciprocal question should be put to me, & therefore diverted the conversation to another object. This is a sketch only of a conference which was lengthy. I have endeavored to give the substance, & sometimes the expresssions where they were material. I supposed it would be agreeable to Congress to have it communicated to them, in the present undecided state in which these subjects are. I should add that an explanation of the transaction of Monsieur de Massiac with the Algerines, before hinted at, will be found in the inclosed letter from the Count d'Estaing to me, wherein he gives also his own opinion. the whole is submitted to Congress, as I conceive it my duty to furnish them with whatever information I can gather which may throw any light on the subjects depending before them. I have the honour to be with the most perfect esteem & respect Sir Your most obedient & most humble serv$^{t.}$

Th: Jefferson

NA: PCC, *item 87, v. 1, pp. 367-370 (ALS); M247, reel 115.*

[1] *but that it would be necessary for us to ascertain them.*

Report of the Committee of the French Controller General of Finances on the Purchase of American Tobacco

[Translation]

[Berni,] 24 May [1786]

Report of the Committee established at Berni, under the Controller General,[1] in the presence of M. le Comte de Vergennes, and attended by Messieurs de St. Amand, Paulze, and La Perrière, representing the farmers general.[2]

The committee taking up its prior deliberations relative to the agreement made with Mr. Morris; informed of the circumstances in which it was accepted, and what rendered it necessary; informed also of the shipment of twelve thousand Hogsheads of tobacco, of which M. le Couteulx, a correspondent of Mr. Morris, has announced the impending arrival, thought unanimously that the agreement should run until 1 Jan$^{y.}$ 1788, save for the right of cancellation in case of nonexecution on the part of Mr. Morris of the conditions of the agreement; taking then into consideration the interest of national Commerce with that of the United States, the Committee agreed on the following stated dispositions:

1ˢᵗ· At the expiration of the agreement of Mr. Morris, no contract of the same kind will be made.

2ⁿᵈ· The farmers general will continuously have in its storehouses the provisions necessary for the exercise of its privilege; which provisions will be formed as much from the supplies resulting from Mr. Morris' contract as from those that it will procure for itself by means of Commerce.

3ʳᵈ· To assure these provisions, the farmers general have accepted an engagement to buy, for the duration of Mr. Morris' contract only, tobaccos that may be furnished by Commerce and carried on French and American ships, to the amount of *12 to 15 thousand hogsheads* each year, at the same price and conditions stipulated by the agreement made with Mr. Morris.

4ᵗʰ· In the event that the shipments furnished are not suitable, tobaccos will be paid for at the following prices:

1ˢᵗ· quality; James River and York River tobaccos, per hundredweight net...............................	38 livres
2ⁿᵈ· quality; Potomack and Rapanack tobacco..............	36 livres
3ʳᵈ· quality; Maryland tobacco.........................	34 livres

The whole 1ˢᵗ· qualities of each type appropriate for France.

5ᵗʰ· In case of difficulty regarding the qualities, samples of them will be sent to the Council, and it will be resolved by a Commission that will be authorized to have the samples examined by such person as it shall seem fit.

6ᵗʰ· When the tobaccos furnished by the Americans are not delivered to a port of Manufacture, the agreed price will be lowered the amount of thirty sous per hundredweight net for costs of transportation.

7ᵗʰ· Communication of the above agreed-upon articles will be made to the Americans.

Sent to Mr. Jefferson on 30 May 1786.

FFAA: Pol. Corr., U.S., v. 31, f. 378-379 (LC transcription).

¹ *Calonne, Charles Alexandre de (1734-1802). French government figure. Controller General of Finances, November 1783-April 1787.*

² *The three representatives of the Farmers General on the Franco-American trade committee were Alexandre Victor de Saint Amand, Jaques Paulze, and Jacques Joseph de Brac de la Perrière.*

John Adams to John Jay

Dear Sir   Grosvernor Square May 25. 1786
   I have not presented a formal Memorial in the Name of our Sovereign
concerning the Negroes carried off contrary to the Treaty, although it has
been frequently and constantly, insisted upon with the British Ministry, for
several Reasons. one was a desire to confine the first Memorial to one
point, the frontier Posts that the real Motives and Intensions of the
Cabinet might be the more distinctly laid open to Congress. another reason
was the Frankness of Ministers to own in Conversation, that the Negroes
must be paid for, as a clear Point. Another was, that time might be allowed
to you Sir, to transmit me, the whole Amount & Evidence of the Claim.
and lastly that I might have the explicit Instructions of Congress to demand
Payment for the Negroes in Money, and especially at what Prices they
should be stated. By the Answer of Lord Carmarthen to the Memorial of
the 30th. of November, Congress will see, that the Detension of the Posts
is attempted to be justified, by the Laws of certain States impeding the
Course of Law for the recovery of old Debts &c. Were another Memorial
to be now presented relative to the Negroes, the same Answer would
undoubtedly be given or more probably a reference only to that Answer.
   It is my Duty to be explicit with my Country, and therefore I hope it will
not be taken amiss, by any of my fellow Citizens, that when they are told,
that it is in vain to expect the Evacuation of Posts, or Payment for the
Negroes, a Treaty of Commerce, or Restoration of Prizes, Payment of the
Maryland or Rhode Island Demand, Compensation to the Boston Merchants, or any other relief of any kind, untill these Laws are all repealed.
Nor will the Ministry ever agree to any Explanation concerning the Interest
during the war, or Payments by Installment. The old Creditors have formed
themselves into a Society, and have frequent Meetings, send Committees
to Mr. Pitt and Lord Carmarthen, and I am well informed oppose even a
Treaty of Commerce, upon this ground, and the Ministers know them to
be so numerous, that they could raise a Clamour, a Consideration which
has always had more Weight at this Court and in Parliament than the
Interest of America or the British Empire.
   What then is to be done? The States it may be said will not repeal their
Laws? If they do not, then let them give up all Expectations from this
Court and Country, unless you can force them to do as you please by
investing Congress with full Power to regulate the Trade.
   I will run the Hazard, Sir of all the Clamour that can be raised against
me, by my Friends or by my Ennemies, if any such there are, and of all the
Consequences that can befall me, for writing my Sentiments freely to

Congress on a Subject of this Importance. It will appear to all the World, with an ill grace, if we complain of Breaches of the Treaty, when the British Court have it in their Power to prove upon us Breaches of the same Treaty of greater Importance. My Advice then, if it is not to impertinent to give it, is that every Law of every State, which concerns either Debts or Royalists, which can be impartially construed contrary to the Spirit of the Treaty of Peace, be immediately repealed. And the Debtors left to settle with their Creditors, or dispute the Point of Interest at Law. I dont believe a Jury would give the Interest. I beg Leave to suggest another Thing, if Congress are themselves clear, that Interest ~~was no Part~~ during the war was no Part of that bonâ fide Debt which was intended by the Contracting Parties. they may declare so by a Resolution or the Legislatures of the seperate States may declare so, and then the Courts of Justice, and the juries will certainly give no Interest during the war. But even in this Case, those States who have few Debts and have made no Laws against the recovery of them will think it hard that they should be subjected to Dangers, by the Conduct of such as have many, and have made Laws inconsistent with the Treaty both respecting Debts and Tories. You will give me leave Sir to suggest another Idea. Suppose the States should venture to do themselves Justice. for Example. Suppose Maryland should undertake to pay herself, for her Bank Stock, and Negroes, carried off, after the Treaty by accepting Security for it from her own Citizens who are Debtors to British subjects and giving Discharges to those Debtors or engaging to stand between them and the Claims of the Creditor. Suppose the Carolinas Virginia and all the other States who had Negroes carried off after the Peace, should do the same. Suppose the Massachusetts should make up the Losses of the Inhabitants of Boston in Goods carried off by General How in the same way at least those of them who were promised Compensation by General How, for these are undoubtedly Creditors of the British Government. Suppose farther that each State should undertake in the same way to compensate, the owners of Vessells taken after the Commencement of the Armistice. I throw out these Hints ~~and~~ as Possibilities and Speculations only, sensible that they might open a Door to much altercation. But I will not fail to add that I think it would be much sounder Policy and nobler Spirit, to repeal at once every Law of every State which is in the smallest degree inconsistent with the Treaty, respecting either Debts or Tories, and am well persuaded that no Inconvenience would be felt from it. neither Law Suits, nor Bankruptcies nor Imprisonments would be increased by it, on the Contrary the Credit and Commerce of all the States would be so increased, that the Debtors themselves in general would find their Burthens lighter.

With great Esteem, I have the Honour to be Sir your most obedient and humble Servant   John Adams.
P.S. inclosed are two Acts of Parliment and the Kings last Proclamation. The other Acts which affect America shall be sent as soon as they are passed and I can obtain them.

NA: PCC, item 84, v. 6, pp. 183-190 (ALS); M247, reel 113.

Don Diego De Gardoqui to John Jay

Sir   New York 25 May 1786
    The Period is arrived that we have wished for many months when there w$^{d.}$ be a full Meeting of Congress, that you might refer to them the Difficulty which you have manifested to me respecting the Claim to navigate the River Mississippi which is ill founded. I request the Favor of you to do it as soon as possible, and that you will be persuaded of what I have always assured you, that the King will not permit any Nation to navigate between the two Banks belonging to his Majesty, from the Extent of his Conquests made by his royal arms over the English in East & West Florida, according to the Dominion formerly held by the English, and the Jurisdiction exercised by the Commandant of Pensacola on which it depended, as well as the Countries to the East of the Mississippi, of which formal possession was taken by Captain Don Baltazar de Villers,[1] commandant of the post of Arkanzas, for his Majesty on the 22 Nov$^{r.}$ 1780
    His Majesty does not consider the Regulation made between the United States & Great Britain, respecting the Territories conquered by his arms, but as a conditional agreement in which they *tacitly* leave safe the territorial Rights which he possessed in those parts.
    Those Territories were in that same State of Conquest and in the possession neither of England nor the United States, when they disposed of them. There can be no Doubt but that Treaty of 30 Nov. 1782, when the War between Spain & England continued, could not fix the Limits of Countries [of] which [they] were not in possession. His Majesty therefore understands those Stipulations as conditional, and dependent on the Situation in w^{h} things might be left by a general peace.
    The Honble Congress cannot be ignorant of the good and generous Disposition of his Majesty towards the United States, and the Importance of his powerful Friendship – his Majesty having been pleased to give so many strong proofs of favor to the Americans, captive in Barbary; and those

he afterwards afforded for aiding their Commissioners for negociating and obtaining peace with those powers.

They should also be persuaded that the King enjoys so great Consideration with those powers, that as being a Nation which possesses the friendship of his Majesty, they may be sure of that of the Emperor of Marocco, and in a great Degree of that contracted with the Regency of Algiers. America has Reason to fear the evil Consequences which all their Commerce w^d experience if his royal Mediacion should be withdrawn, for she w^d not only be deprived of that in the Mediterranean, but would also be much interrupted in that which she carries on thro' the Western Islands and Canaries, & even on her own Coasts

It appears to me equally just to remind the Honble Congress of the Generosity with which his Majesty has delayed requesting till now the paym$^{t.}$ of the Principal of the Debts contracted by the United States both in Spain & America, being so delicate as not to apply even for the Interest due thereon notwithsanding the Difficulties with which he provides for his Treasury

These facts appear sufficient to remove the Difficulties you have manifested to me respecting the limits, and the navigation of the said River – but I contemplate in its greatest Latitude the Risque which the United States would run, by not yielding without Delay to the just Rights of the King, of losing *the only Trade* whose Ballance is in their favor; exposing themselves to the Danger of enjoying it but illy, and of frustrating other Compacts reciprocally useful w^h Time and Experience may bring about.

The Importance of this Object is evident in all the States, for it is well known that all their Productions meet with a ready Sale in the Markets of Spain, where they are paid for in Gold and Silver, whereas all other Nations pay with Manufactures (in great part articles of Luxury) with which they impoverish this Country.

Spain in its present State is a Consumer both in Europe and America. There is not a Nation but what earnestly desires the Friendship and Favor of the King, and as he has no occasion for the Codfish *oil* Salmon, Grain, Flour, Rice, nor other Productions he may, considering the Right which obliges his Subjects to provide themselves by their own industry or other useful & important Means, find it convenient to prohibit them, to remind this Nation at present as a friend, that they have no Treaty – whereas in Case they generously comply, the King will consider them in Comerce as being the most favored nation, making reciprocal Regulations, so that whenever one is made here favorable to Spain in Regard to Imports & Exports, another equivalent to that of the United States shall there be made –

No one is ignorant of the great Advantages w^h the United States derive from their Trade with Spain, from whence they yearly extract Millions, as well by their Productions, as by their Navigation w^h so much promotes the Growth & Maintenance of their marine.

Spain has no occasion for foreign Commodities to become very brill[i]ant in its proper Dominions, and to find an advantageous Consumption for its Products & manufactures; so that the Generosity & Friendship w^h she manifests proceed solely from the benevolent Attentions which with a liberal Hand the King wishes to distinguish the United States.

In Consideration that nothing be said of such Difficulties, I believe that his Majesty will consent to guarantee to the United States their Rights & Dominions as they shall be left by our Treaty – I will do my best Endeavours on this & other points, and will interpose my Prayers that his Majesty may adopt the most favorable Measures in order that the Satisfaction of the Debts due from the United States to Spain may be made with such Relaxations as may be convenient to them

The Honble Congress will well percieve the Importance of the Guarantee and Friendship of one of the first Sovereigns in Europe, which will give Consistency to their Confederacy, and whose Magnanimity desires only to proceed by Equity, Justice, and sincere Desires of a constant friendship, and good Neighbourhood –

I ought not therefore to doubt but that such an illustrious Confederacy will entertain correspondent Dispositions, and I hope that you will not delay to promote it, and to advise me as soon as possible, that so salutary a work may not be deferred, to which for my part I shall contribute with the greatest good Will for the Benefit of both Nations

I have the Honor to be &c^a·   Diego de Gardoqui

NA: PCC, item 97, pp. 166-169 (translation); M247, reel 125.

[1] Captain Baltazar de Villiers, the Spanish commandant at Arkansas Post, landed on the east bank of the Mississippi and formally took possession of the British colony of West Florida on November 22, 1780.

Jean Jacques Bérard to Comte de Vergennes

[Translation]

My Lord   Paris, 25 May 1786

I have just attested to you all the gratitude that I owe you, and that Commerce in general owes you for the decision that you pronounced yesterday on the Commerce of America. However good the cause that you have rightly wished to sustain, I sense, more than ever, how much the enlightened protection that you have accorded to it was necessary. This will be a new right to add, My Lord, to those you have already acquired regarding the American Nation and regarding French commerce.

I should take the liberty of observing to you, My Lord, that it seems to me indispensable not to insert into the decision the clause that only those tobaccos that come by American or French ships will be received.

1$^{st.}$ This serves to destroy the perfect equality that you have wished to establish between commerce and Mr. Morris, seeing that the latter has the liberty by the agreement to employ ships from all nations.

2$^{nd.}$ The shipments of the Americans would perhaps be greatly impeded thereby. Since their difficulties with the Barbary pirates, they have sought to procure other destinations for their ships, in such a way that few American ships perhaps being without employment, & certainly having very few French ones there, Mr. Morris could, by availing himself of neutrals, ship his tobaccos, and private individuals would not be able to do so.

3$^{rd.}$ The prohibition on employing foreign Vessels for the transportation of tobaccos to France should occasion complaints from the Swedes, the Dutch, and other nations with whom we have treaties of commerce. One such measure appears to me therefore of the greatest importance, & to merit a particular examination.

When our reciprocal relations with America are very well established, one will be able, I think, only then to propose an arrangement of this type. I presume that at this time, My Lord, you will find it dangerous, & its suppression in yesterday's decree of the Committee necessary. Although no one has ruled on the tobaccos that are at present in the ports, you will doubtless find it agreeable, My Lord, to remind the Controller General that they should be included in the decision.

I dare also to ask you the favor of pointing out to him how necessary it is that the Farm, following other principles than those that have merited your just reproaches to him, henceforth be equitable towards Commerce, & that no motive may make it treat one merchant more favorably than another. I dare to repeat to you, however, My Lord, that I do not think that such a change can be hoped for from the current Committee of the Farm.

I am with a profound respect My Lord Your most humble & most obedient Servant.   J. Berard[1]

FFAA: Pol. Corr., U.S., v. 31, f. 282-284 (LC transcription).

[1] Bérard, Jean Jacques. French merchant. Proprietor of J.J. Bérard & Company, a L'Orient mercantile house heavily involved in the tobacco trade with America.

Thomas Jefferson to John Jay

Sir   Paris May 27. 1786.

. . . . .

The fur trade is an object of desire in this country. London is at present their market for furs. they pay for them there in ready money. could they draw their furs into their own ports from the U. S. they would pay us for them in productions. nor should we lose by the change of market, since, tho the French pay the London merchants in cash, those merchants pay us with manufactures. a very wealthy & well connected company is proposing here to associate themselves with an American company, each to possess half the interest & to carry on the fur trade between the two countries. the company here expect to make the principal part of the advances; they also are solliciting considerable indulgences from this government from which the part of the company on our side the water will reap half the advantage. as no exclusive idea enters into this scheme, it appears to me worthy of encouragement. it is hoped the government here will interest themselves for it's success. if they do, one of two things may happen: either the English will be afraid to stop the vessels of a company consisting partly of French subjects & patronised by the court; in which case the commerce will be laid open generally; or if they stop the vessels, the French company, which is strongly connected with men in power, will complain in form to their government, who may thus be interested as principals in the rectification of this abuse. as yet however, the proposition has not taken such a form as to assure us that it will prosecuted to this length.

As to the article of tobacco, which had become an important branch of remittance to almost all the states, I had the honour of communicating to you my proposition to the Court to abolish the monopoly of it in their farm; that the C^t· de Vergennes was I thought, thoroughly sensible of the expediency of this proposition, and disposed to befriend it, that the renewal of the lease of the farms had been consequently suspended six months and was still in suspence; but that so powerful were the Farmers general, and so tottering the tenure of the Minister of finance in this office, that I despaired of preventing the renewal of the farm at that time. things were in this state when the M de la Fayette returned from Berlin. on communicating to him what was on the carpet, he proposed to me a conference with some persons well acquainted with the commercial system of this country. we met. they proposed the endeavoring to have a committee appointed to enquire into the subject. the proposition was made to the C^t· de Vergennes, who befriended it & had the M. de la Fayette named a member of the committee. he became of course the active and truly zealous member for the liberty of commerce, others tho' well disposed, not chusing to oppose the farm openly. this committee has met from time to time. it shewed an early and decisive conviction that the measure taken by the farm to put the purchase of their tobaccoes into monopoly on that side the water, as the sale of them was on this, tended to the annihilation of commerce between the two countries. various palliatives were proposed from time to time. I confess that I met them all with indifference. my object being a radical cure of the evil by discontinuing the farm and not a mere assuagement of it for the present moment which, rendering it more bearable, might lessen the necessity of removing it totally & perhaps prevent that removal. in the mean time the other branches of the farm rendered the renewal of the lease necessary: and it being said to be too far advanced to have the article of tobacco separated from it & suspended, it was signed in the month of March, while I was in England, with a clause, which is usual, that the King may discontinue when he pleases on certain conditions. when returned, I found here a Memorial from the merchants of l'Orient complaining of their having 6000 hhds. of tobacco on hand, and of the distresses they were under from the loss of this medium of remittance. I inclosed it to the Count de Vergennes and asked his interference. I saw him on the 23. inst. and spoke to him on the subject. he told me there was to be a committee held the next day at Berni; the seat of the Comptroller General, & that he would attend it himself to have something done. I asked him if I was to consider the expunging that article from the farm as desperate. he said that the difficulty of changing so antient an institution was immense, that the king draws from it a revenue of 29 millions of livres, that an interruption of this revenue at least, if not a diminution, would attend a change, that their finances were not in a condition to bear even an interruption, and in short that no minister could venture to take upon himself so hazardous an operation. this was only saying explicitly, what I had long been sensible of that the Comptroller general's continuance in office was too much on a poise to permit him to shift this weight out of his own scale into that of his adversaries. and that we must be contented to await the completion of the public expectation that there will be a change in this office, which change may give us another chance for effecting this desirable reformation. incidents enough will arise to keep this object in our view, and to direct the attention to it as the only point on which the interests & harmony of the two countries (so far as this article of their commerce may influence) will ultimately find repose. the Committee met the next day. the only question agitated was how best to relieve the trade under it's double monopoly. the committe found themselves supported by the presence & sentiments of the Count de Vergennes. they therefore resolved that the contract with mr Morris, if executed on his part, ought not to be annulled here, but that no similar one should ever be made hereafter. that, so long as it continued, the farmers should be obliged to purchase from twelve to 15,000 hhds of tobacco a year, over & above what they should receive from mr Morris, from such merchants as should bring it in French or American vessels, on the same conditions contracted with mr Morris; providing however that where the cargo shall not be assorted, the prices shall be 38. 36. & 34. livres for the 1$^{st.}$ 2$^{d.}$ & 3$^{d.}$ Qualities of whichsoever the cargo may consist. in case of dispute about the quality, specimens are to be sent to the council, who will appoint persons to examine & decide on it. this is indeed the least bad of all the palliations which have beem proposed: but it contains the seeds of perpetual trouble: it is easy to foresee that the farmers will multiply difficulties & vexations on those who shall propose to sell to them by force, and that these will be making perpetual complaints, so that both parties will be kept on the fret. if, without fatiguing the friendly dispositions of the ministry, this should give them just so much trouble as may induce them to look to the demolition of the monopoly as a desireable point of rest, it may produce a permanent as well as temporary good. this determination of the committee needs the king's order to be carried into effect. I have been in hourly expectation of receiving official information that it is ultimately confirmed by him. but as yet it is not come, and the post will set out to-day. should it arrive in time, I will inclose it. should it not arrive, as I do not apprehend any danger of it's being rejected, or even altered materially (seeing that M. de Vergennes approved of it, & M. de Calonnes acquiesced) I have supposed you would wish to be apprized of it's substance for a communication of which I am indebted to the M. de la Fayette. tho' you cannot publish it formally till you know it is confirmed by the king yet an unauthoritative kind of notice may be given to the merchants to put them on their guard. otherwise the merchants here, having first knowlege of it, may by their agents purchase up all the tobaccoes they have on hand, at a low price, &d thus engross to themselves all the benefit.

. . . . .

...with sentiments of the most perfect esteem & respect, Sir, your most obedient & most humble servent   Th: Jefferson

August 3. 1786 The injunction of Secresy taken off from the letter of 27 May from Mr Jefferson & the papers accompanying it as far as relates to the tobacco Contract –   Chas Thomson Sec^y.

NA: PCC, item 87, v. 1, pp. 478-485 (ALS); M247, reel 115.

John Jay's Report on Relations with the Barbary States

[New York] Office for foreign Affairs 29th. May 1786

The Secretary of the United States for the Department of foreign Affairs to whom was referred a joint Letter from M^r. Adams and M^r. Jefferson of 28th March last, together with a Motion of the Honble M^r. Pinckney on the Subject of it   Reports

That those Gentlemen in this Letter mention, that in a Conference with the Ambassador of Tripoli he informed them, "that 12,500 Guineas to his Constituents, with five per cent on that Sum for himself, must be paid if the Treaty was made for only a Period of one year.

That thirty thousand Guineas for his Employers, and three thousand for himself, were the lowest Terms, on which a *perpetual* Peace could be made.

That *Tunis* would treat on the same Terms, but that he could not answer for Algiers or Morocco.

They further observe, that if Congress should order them to make the best Terms they can with Tunis, Tripoli, Algiers and Morocco, and to procure the money wherever they can find it upon Terms like those of the last Loan in Holland, their best Endeavours should be used &^ca."

The Motion in question proposes an Instruction conformable to the above Suggestion.

Two questions seem to arise on this Letter.

(1)   whether those Ministers shall be authorized and instructed to make the best Terms they can with those Powers.

(2)   whether they shall be authorized and instructed to endeavour to borrow money in Europe for the Purpose.

Your Secretary thinks full confidence may be reposed in the Integrity and Discretion of those Ministers, and therefore is of opinion that it would be expedient to leave the Terms of the proposed Treaties to their Prudence.

As to authorising and Instructing them to endeavour to borrow money for the purpose in Europe, your Secretary much doubts the Policy of it.

The Probability of their borrowing so much money appears questionable—

Because those Nations to whom our war with the Barbary States is not disagreeable, will be little inclined to lend us money to put an End to it.

Because no Funds are yet provided for paying even the Interest of our former Loans, either foreign or domestic.

Because the Payments due to France though pressed have not been compleated. –

Because the reluctance of the States to pay Taxes, or to comply with the economical Requisitions of Congress, or to give Efficacy to their Federal Government, are Topics of common Conversation in Europe.

If a Loan should be attempted and not succeed, the Credit and Respectability of the United States would be diminished by the attempt.

Your Secretary thinks that neither Individuals nor States should borrow money without the highest Probability at least of being able punctually to repay it, and that States should never attempt a Loan without having previously formed and arranged adequate Funds for its Discharge.

It appears to your Secretary improper to open such a Loan, even if the Success of it was certain.

> Because as the federal Government in its present State is rather paternal and persuasive, than coercive and efficient, Congress can make no certain Dependence on the States for any specific Sums to be required, and paid at any given periods, and consequently, are not in Capacity safely to pledge their Honor and their Faith for the repayment of any specific Sums they may borrow, at any given periods, which must be the Case if they should make this or any other Loan.

> Because as the People or Generality will never provide for the public Expences, unless when moved thereto by constitutional Coercion, or by the Dictates of Reason, or by their Feelings; and as the first of these three motives is here out of Question; your Secretary thinks it probable that the States on being applied to, will be more disposed to supply money to purchase these Treaties of Peace, while they feel the Evils resulting from the War, than they will to supply money to repay borrowed Sums, when all their Fears and Dangers from Salee Rovers,[1] Algerine Corsairs, and the Pirates of Tunis and Tripoli are vanished and gone.

For these Reasons your Secretary is much inclined to think that a fair and accurate State of the matter, should be transmitted to the States – that they should be informed that the Sum of   will be necessary to purchase Treaties from the Barbary States, and that until such time as they furnish Congress with their respective proportions of that Sum, the Depredations of those Barbarians will in all Probability continue and increase.

All which is Submitted to the Wisdom of Congress.

John Jay

NA: PCC, item 124, v. 2, pp. 16-20 (DC); M247, reel 141.

[1] *Salee or Sallee rovers, also known as salleemen, were corsairs who sailed from the Moroccan port of Salé. Sallee rovers were more prominent in the 17th century, when the port and its environs were an independent entity.*

John Jay to the President of Congress

Sir   [New York] Office for foreign Affairs 29 May 1786
    In my Negociations with Mr. Gardoqui I experience certain difficulties
which in my Opinion should be so managed, as that even the Existence of
them should remain a Secret for the present.
    I take the Liberty therefore of submitting to the Consideration of
Congress whether it might not be adviseable to appoint a Committee with
power to instruct and direct me on every point and Subject relative to the
proposed treaty with Spain –. In Case Congress should think proper to
appoint such a Committee, I really think it would be prudent to keep the
appointm^{t.} of it secret, and to forbear having any Conversations on Subjects
connected with it, except in Congress, & in Meetings on the Business of
it –
    With great respect I have the Honor to be Your Excellencys most ob^{t.} &
very h'ble Servt.   John Jay –
Read 30th. –
Aug 3. 1786 Referred to Com^{ee} of the Whole which is to sit on thursday
10.

NA: PCC, *item 81, v. 2, pp. 185,188 (ALS); M247, reel 107.*

Thomas Jefferson to Comte de Vergennes

Sir.   Paris May 31. 1786.
    I have been honored with your Excellency's Letter of Yesterday, inclosing
a Copy of the Resolutions of the Committee on the Subject of Tobacco, &
am bound to make my Acknolegements for this Attention to the Commerce between this Country & the United States, which will I hope by this
Measure be kept alive till more Simple & permanent Arrangements become
practicable. I have communicated it to Congress by an Opportunity which
offered this Morning. Perhaps it is for Want of Information that I
apprehend it possible for the London Merchants, availing themselves of
their early Notice of this Regulation & their Proximity to the Ports of
France, to run in French Vessels the whole 15,000 hhds of the first Year
before the French or American Merchants can possibly bring them from
America. This might defeat the End of the Regulation as those Merchants
would take Paiment in Cash & not in Merchandize. I Suppose the Committee had in View *tobaccoes coming last from a Port of the United States,* &
that it may not be yet too late to restrain the Order to such only. Of this

your Excellency is the best Judge, to whom I have the honor of Submitting the Doubt; and am with Sentiments of the most profound Respect & Esteem Your Excellency's most obedient & most humble Servant

Th: Jefferson

FFAA: Pol. Corr., U.S., v. 31, f. 400-400vo. (LC transcription).

John Adams to James Bowdoin

Sir.

London June 2. 1786

. . . . .

The Representations of the Encroachments on the territory of the United States, have been laid before the British Ministry: but I presume, they will, like many others be little attended to. – in short Sir, I must be so free as to say to you, that by every thing I have seen & heard in this Country, nothing of any material Consequence will ever be done, while there remains in force, a Law of any one State impeding the recovery of *bona fide* Debts contracted before the 30[th.] of Nov[r.] 1782 or inconsistant with the Article of the Treaty of Peace respecting the tories –

It is very true that Mitchels Map governed the American & British Plenipotentiaries, in Settling the Line between the two Nations. There is upon that Map but one River, which is marked with the Name of S[t.] Croix, and that was the object undoubtedly fixed upon.

There is no river upon that Map that I remember marked with the Name of Schooduck or Megacadava. Next to the great river S[t.] Johns, proceeding westward upon that Map, is a little River inscribed Mechior R. next to that is another Stream running between the words < * > Carriage Harbour, next to that we come to a larger River, running from Kousaki L. into the Bay of Passimaquoddi and inscribed with the name of R. S[t.] Croix next to that Still proceeding Westward is Passamaquade R. But that inscribed R. S[t.] Croix running from the Sea, or what I call Passamaquoddi Bay, up to the Kousaki L. was marked with the Pencil for the Boundary — It is impossible for me to say more – if the true S[t.] Croix cannot be discovered by these marks, there is no remedy, but by an Ulterior agreement, or the Law of the Strongest — It is astonishing that to this hour, no Man can produce a Map of all the Bay's Harbours, Islands, & Rivers in that neighbourhood, that can be depended on, If the ministry will meet me, in a fair discussion of the Question, or in any of the Methods pointed out to me by my Superiors for a Settlement, I Shall be glad, they have it under Consideration, & as soon as they give me an answer, I shall transmit it to Congress — but as they dont love pains & trouble as well as you & I do, I fear they will leave it all to Sir Guy Carleton, who is no more of a friend to the United States than any other British Knight and will be guided by the Royalists more than by Maps or Surveys. Why any of my Countrymen Should choose to give to these Royalists so much Importance as they do, I know not, We Should recollect that all Parties in this Country are pledged to support them, & Party faith is a Stronger tye than national Faith –

.   .   .   .   .

Your   John Adams

MHS: *The Adams Papers, microfilm reel 113 (LBkC).*

Sir John Temple to John Jay

Sir,   New York 7 June 1786.

I have this day been informed that British Mediterranean Passes are & have been Counterfited at Philadelphia! and that, many Ships & Vessells belonging to the American states, have already saild with such Passes! If this be a fact, and I think I can depend upon the information given me, I cannot but lament the Misery that such of your Mariners will probably meet with, sh^d they, with such counterfit Passes, fall into the hands of the Barbary Corsairs, who are now become so Nice & exact with regard to British Mediterranean Passes of the last Cut & form, that I am really of Opinion, not one of such Counterfits will Escape detection; & then, over & above the *disgrace* of an unpardonable Crime (that of Counterfiting) the people who meant or mean, to avail themselves of such Counterfits would, it is more than probable, meet with severity in the Extreeme, sufficient to make humane Civilized people Shudder at even the Mentioning of it!

I have the honor to be, with great Regard & Esteem, Sir, Your most Obedient, & most humble Servant,   J. Temple.

NA: PCC, *item 92, pp. 561-562 (ALS); M247, reel 120.*

Richard O'Bryen, Zaccheus Coffin and Isaac Stephens to Thomas Jefferson

N° 1   Algiers June 8th 1786
Honoured Sir

I take the Liberty of addressing these letters to you hoping you will excuse the freedom of an American &c. and unfortunate captive at present. No doubt but a Mr Lamb has given you and m^r Adams every particular information respecting the state of affairs in Algiers. I am much surprized when I look at the date of your letter to us being the 4th of November & with orders to Mr Lamb to redeem us Americans. I am surprized that from the 4th of November until the 20th of March that m^r Lamb did not get our redemption ascertained by some person in Algiers. But he retarding the time until he could make it convenient to come himself and not informing himself of the method generally used towards the redemption of captives, but on the contrary comes to Algiers and gives out that he came to redeem the Americans.

It was immediately signified to the Dey that m^r Lamb had brought money for that purport, it became such a town talk that the Dey hardly knew what sum to ask. after a few days the Dey asks what sum m^r Lamb would give. Mr Lamb signified he would give ten thousand dollars. the Dey then said 50,000. I think the demand was very apropos to the offer of m^r Lamb. Mr Lamb tried to get the Dey to lower his price, but the Dey was determined not to lower his price any thing worth mentioning.

We are much surprized that m^r Lamb should bring so trifling a sum as five or six thousand dollars to redeem 21. Even if the Dey had let us go agreeable to your calculation he could not have redeemed us. But m^r Lamb when he first arrived told us he would get us along in a few days, which much disappointed us, for he afterwards told us he had no money to redeem us. what he had was for presents if he succeeded in a cessation of hostilities with this Regency. one time he would say his funds were in Holland – then in Spain, and then that you & m^r Adams had given no power only to draw for £3300 st^{lg} & that m^r Randal must write the order. so that in his own language his hands were tyed by the ministers. I believe the Dey of Algiers was well convinced that Americans would give the sum he asked. I have reason to suspect that the Dey had a hint conveyed to him by the British Consul, who you may be assured is an inveterate enemy to the Americans. about 5 months ago I wrote m^r Carmichael that the British Consul had put himself to great trouble in sending expresses to his court. about that time was the first time that he knew that it was the intention of the Americans to sue for a peace with the Barbary States. It is not the interest of any commercial nation that the Americans should obtain a peace with the Barbary States, whilst they reap such benefits in being the carriers of our commerce, particularly the English, French & Spanish being jealous of us. Consider Sir what great insurance we pay in getting our vessels insured. in a short time the great insurance we pay would obtain us a peace, or our ships obliged to be sold or with the greatest difficulty in procuring English registers and passes – if not soon remedied our trade must fall into some other channel. and with the greatest difficulty we shall retrieve it again, our seamen having no longer employment in the United states but must through necessity seek a living in some other country. The British Consul I think informs his court respecting the time when the Algerine cruisers generally go out. by that means the people of England take the greatest advantage on insuring American property. and is their policy & benefit to spread the alarm much greater than it really is. there is no danger of our commerce being prevented by the Algerines if we keep clear of the streights, coasts of Spain &ᶜ· Portugal and the Madeiras. we may trade to France, England, Holland, Sweden and any where to the N. of 44°· N. Latᵈᵉ·

The Algerine cruisers generally go out in April, but uncommon they went out the 25ᵗʰ· of May this year. they generally make three cruises a year. finish about the 20ᵗʰ· November & then unrig & ly by until the next year. the Algerines have no merchant ships or vessels for trade excepting a few coasting craft which go along shore with wheat &c. the French being their carriers in commerce & nothing great. their marine strength is nine sail of xebecs, one of 32 guns, one of 30. three of 24 and three of 18. and one of 12. guns – the vessels are small to the metal they carry. 1/8 of the crews are Turks, the remainder Algerine Moors.

A war with the Algerines would be a very expensive war. they having no merchant men it would be attended with a very great expence, on our side the expence of building a force adequate to the Algerines to get men to keep that force in commission, and still it would be a great risque to trade, you are fully sensible the sum it would take to redeem a few: and then it would alter the insurance but trifling.

The United States should use every means to obtain a peace with the Barbary States, although it would cost vast sums, for until all obstacles are removed that prevent commerce we cannot expect to be a commercial nation. it is bad policy to use any threats or make any parade with cruisers if we intend suing for a peace, but on the contrary let those people see that we are inclinable for a peace – no doubt but it was great policy in the Dey to refuse mʳ· Lamb at first on the terms of peace. consider Sir the policy of this Regency in all their transactions with the Christian nations. but I believe they are inclinable to a peace with the Americans but should for political views be negociated very private, particularly by the Americans. I believe they gave Mʳ· Lamb sufficient reason to believe so. they seem well inclined to a peace with us, and I believe would take some naval stores as masts, yards, planks, scantling, tar & turpentine. the English, French, Dutch, Danes & Swedes and I may say all nations are tributary to them – making them valuable presents & supplying them. The Algerines would never redeem or make an exchange with any nation they should be at war with. the Dey of Algiers cares not about his people particularly the Moors. the Turks he sets a little store by. those nations that he has been at war with for ages have experienced it. it is the policy of Christian nations to keep those nations of Turks & Moors at war with other Christian Nations, and the people in general here wish for a war with those nations in the streights, for I am sure that nothing but so great a sum as the Spaniards are to give would reconcile those people to the Spaniards, They having such an inveteracy against them for persecuting the Mahometan religion but money is the God of Algiers & Mahomet their prophet. they like those nations that they are afraid of & that give them most. But should the Algerines be influenced by the commercial Christian nations not to make a peace with the United States, then we should exert ourselves & fit out ships mounting about 24. guns, nine of that force and two brigs, a schooner also – fast sailing vessels & have them coppered for the sooner we would harrass those people the better for we should if so lucky as to take two or three of them they would be inclinable to a peace and on easier terms for us. To rendezvous at Mahon & Gibraltar, and often to come in sight of Algiers, and I make no doubt when they found a spirited nation against them they would alter their opinion. not to be afraid of them like unto those dastardly nations, that have given them such reason to boast of a superiority in courage to Christians. The Algerines have 55. gun boats in case of an invasion or attack on the city which is very strong being well fortified & I think they are a tolerable smart active people, spirited in an attack, but with any thing of a warm reception easily repulsed. They put great confidence in boarding therefore ought to be well barracked. if they can avoid an action it is their choice to be off.

The Algerines do not expect to derive any great advantage by being at war with the Americans, our country being so far situated from them, they will not attempt to approach our coasts. they have very little Idea of America and I believe the British Consuls used their influence in signifying to the Algerines the unjustness of our cause, but since we arrived here we used our influence to convince them of the justness of our quarrel which they say that if they were in our situation they would do the same. There is a great difference between negociating with these people and a Christian nation. The foundation of all treaties should be laid by some person or Consul in Algiers that knows how to treat with them for there are certain times & seasons for those affairs. The Dey's sentiments always ought to be well sounded and the sentiments of his ministers and headmen for it is by them all business is transacted with him – for they have the Dey's ear at command particularly the Causennage who is head minister. the Micklassha is the next. he is son in law to the Causennage and is Generalissimo of all the Fortifications – entire direction of the Marine – a particular favorite of the Dey, and I think no man fills his office better. a valuable present to the Micklassha & Causennage chosen by some man that is well acquainted with what suits those men best. I am sure it would be very requisite & not hove away. The Dey is well advanced in years, and I am sure when he goes to his long home that there will be a very great change in the state of affairs in this Regency. The Causennage will be his successor & the Micklassha will be the prime minister. If anyone knows those peoples policy I should think the Count D'Expilly does; being a year here negociating the Spanish peace & has had so many conferences with the Dey & his ministers. he has got the great men in office on his side. Give a Turk money with one hand & you may take his Eyes out with the other.

Since the Brig arrived from Tunis which is the brig which mr. Lamb came to Algiers in, the brig was overhauled & the Captain examined by the Micklassha respecting the property. I am credibly informed by a Gentleman by the name of Capt. Bassline,[1] who is a great favorite of the Micklassha's, that the Micklassha was well convinced by the information he had that the brig was an American property, which I heard the evening the brig arrived in Algiers. but the Micklassha despised any such mean action but signified to the Dey that the report was false. I hope this particular favor shewn the Americans by the Micklassha will not escape your notice but by every prudent step cultivate the friendship of so great & so good a man. The information by all I can learn & I have every reason to believe was given by the British Consul, mr. Lamb's bosom friend. it is said & I have been credibly informed that mr. Logie had the information from a mr. Gregory[2] British Consul in Barcelona, and I should think it a very dangerous affair for the brig to come to Algiers again particularly with money for a redemption as there is no knowing the policy and political views of these people in Algiers. Permit me to mention to you that if it was not convenient to redeem us, when the time is advanced which mr. Lamb signified to the Dey that it would be good policy to get us on the Spanish list as the Spaniards have not yet agreed on the price for their people; and in as much as the Count D'Expilly may get us for less than what the Dey asks, and as we were taken on the time when the Spaniards were about settling a truce unknown to the Americans. Delays breed danger & opportunity once lost is not easily recovered, and our captivity will become an old affair and here we shall remain.

The American peace hangs on a thread, but I make no doubt if well planned but the United states will obtain it.

The Neapolitan & Portuguese Ambassadors are shortly expected here, it is uncertain that they will obtain a peace, but if they do I will engage the Portuguese particularly will pay well for it. The Spaniards have not surmounted all their difficulties yet with those people, but I believe it will take some time yet – a few days ago arrived a Venitian & a French Vessel with shot &c. for the Dey. The Venitian brought their tribute which was about 10,000 Algerine sequins and about 5,000 dollars worth of presents, but they accepted the tribute & I believe would not accept the presents. so that it is supposed when the Algerines settle with the Spaniards that they will be apt to commit hostilities on the Venitians. such tricks are very common to them.

It is believed M[r] John Wolfe will not get to be Spanish Consul in Algiers, but I am very sure he is a very good man; no one in Algiers better acquainted with the ways & policy of this Regency and would be a very fit man to transact any business for any nation. I refer you to m[r] Carmichael & m[r] Randall for his character and must observe that there is no doing anything among those people without money. all the crowned heads in Europe to write to the Dey of Algiers would avail but very little. to negotiate a peace with the Algerines should be a statesman well acquainted with the different languages. but as I have said before the foundation should be laid by some Consul in Algiers whom the United States could depend on and then an American to come & conclude it. A good Consul is very requisite here.

We are much surprized at m[r] Lamb's ungentleman like behaviour whilst he was in Algiers & could hardly believe Congress would [have] sent such a man to negociate so important an affair as the making a peace with the Algerines where it required the most able Statesman & Politician.

The Count disapproved of his behaviour much & said he was a very uncapable man to treat for the redemption of us & worse for making the peace. A man that has no regularity in small affairs will have none in great ones. There is no Consul or man that has the least friendship for the Americans but says he was a very unable man & not the gentleman, which I believe Sir, when we can make such an observation on him we are sensible that a man of your abilities can have no great opinion of him.

M[r] Lamb's unguarded expressions, his hints, threats &c despising the French & Spaniards, signifying their deciet & in fact every thing that he possibly could utter in the most vulgar language that it was with pain we see him so unworthy of his commission & the cloth he wore. his particular intimacy with m[r] Logie the British Consul, m[r] Lamb's bosom-friend who I believe got all his secrets from him said often that the Americans had taken two forts on the Mississippi from the Spaniards and often in the hearing of some servants who spoke English that if the Spaniards did not assist the Americans in making their peace that we should take some of their territory from them. no doubt but the Count was informed of all this, for one of m[r] Lamb's servants is servant to the Count at present, & m[r] Lamb often said in my presence to m[r] Wolfe that he (meaning m[r] Wolfe) or the Count would have all the honor of laying the foundation of the peace.

Sir we are very sensible of your particular attention to us, and through your & m^r· Carmichaels care of us, we are indebted for the particular civility & attention of the C^t· D'Expilly & French Consul. But still it is impossible for us to be content whilst we are under the character of slaves, so disagreeable is confinement to the men of the Land of Liberty. My crew go through the severities of slavery that is possible for men to endure. Capt^s· Stevens & Coffin³ have families & at present unknown how provided for. I have an aged mother, brother & sisters. that their whole dependance & subsistance was on me. certainly the longer we stay here the greater expence we shall incur on our country. If we do not make our grievances known to you Sir I am sure who can we apply to we have wrote to America when we were first taken, but not one of us has recieved a letter & cannot tell what our country has resolved on respecting us. we must submit to our hard fate & trust to God & our country to extricate us from Algiers. I hope m^r· Barclay will succeed with the Maroccians – their situation being more in the way of annoying us than the Algerines. I am surprized m^r· Lamb did not pay m^r· Logie the small sum of about 5 guineas which m^r· Logie paid to the marine for excluding us from it. M^r· Lamb often insisted m^r· Logie to make some charge but at last Logie made a charge & m^r· Lamb did not pay him.

A Gentleman of the name of m^r· Basseline who rendered m^r· Lamb many services and lies much in his power to do many more he being on the most friendly footing with the Micklassha &c. is here at present. when m^r· Lamb was on his return to Spain being confused in his affairs & wanted to leave m^r· Wolfe some money Bassaline gave m^r· Lamb about four hundred dollars in gold which m^r· Lamb gave to m^r· Wolfe to defray some expences. but as Bassaline was called to Spain he went on board the same vessel that m^r· Lamb did & during 17. days which they were together m^r· Bassaline signified to M^r· Lamb that he wanted the money. but m^r· Lamb evaded the matter from day to day and has not paid Bassaline or given him an order on any person for the money. Capt. Bassaline has returned to Algiers mentioned this affair to m^r· Wolfe &c. which has much surprized him of the behaviour of m^r· Lamb & I make no doubt but m^r· Bassaline wanted the money in Spain. His unpolitical behaviour in all his transactions is much against the honor and dignity of the United states. no doubt but m^r· Randall gave you a sketch of his behaviour. not that I have any particular inveteracy against m^r· Lamb but prompted by a principle of honor & esteem for my country I mention m^r· Lamb's behaviour to you hoping that what I have mentioned will not escape your notice.

M^r· Wolfe will have occasion to write m^r· Carmichael respecting money he having orders from m^r· Lamb to supply the captives & nothing to do it with. also m^r· Wolfe will give an account of our expenses &c. The Cruisers

are out at present. we are treated with the greatest civility by all the French
& Spaniards here.

An account how we are situated & where.

4. of us at the house of Monsr. Ford

7. in the Dey's palace

9. in the marine

1. at the Swedish Consul's.

I am with the greatest Respect & Esteem your most obedient & humble
Servant   Rich^{d.} O'Bryen
Zach^{s.} Coffin
Isaac Stevens

NA: *Record Group 59 (General Records of the Department of State), hereafter cited as
RG 59, Consular Despatches, Algiers, v. 1(C); National Archives Microfilm Publication
M23, hereafter cited as M23, reel 1.*

[1] *Bassline, Basseline, Bassaline. Evidently a sea captain who frequently called at Algiers.*

[2] *Not further identified.*

[3] *Captains Isaac Stephens and Zaccheus Coffin. Coffin, the supercargo of Stephens'
vessel, would die of tuberculosis in the winter of 1787-1788.*

Thomas Barclay to John Adams and Thomas Jefferson

Gentlemen   Mogadore 10th. June 1786

I arrived here after an agreeable Passage of Five days and was very well
received by the Governor & by the People who seem pleased to see Persons
from a Country at so great a distance come to compliment their Sovereign;
As the Governor had no orders concerning our going forward, I was obliged
to Send a Courier to Morocco to demand that Permission, and at the same
time write Mr. Chiappi[1] of that Place, desiring him to lay my Request
before the King, that no greater Guard might be sent here, than would be
Sufficient to render the road safe & the Journey comfortable. To this Letter
an answer was returned the Day before yesterday, that the King desired that
I might depend on a most gracious Reception, & Yesterday the Governor
of Morocco with thirty Soldiers arrived here to conduct us to Court. His
Majesty wrote to the Governor of Mogadore to furnish me with every thing
I want, & to send me from hence satisfied, and has given orders at two
places on the Road that we may be furnished with his own Mules.

The Governor of Mogadore was so polite as to request I would return on
board the Vessel to give him an Opportunity of receiving us at the Head
of his Soldiers, & has since proposed making an Entertainment in the
Country, but I declined both Offers on account of the Parade and of the
unavoidable expence that would have attended them. It is in vain to be

troubling you at present with any Opinion about the probability of our Success, which indeed I think somewhat uncertain. there are some prejudices to be obviated and one Matter of Moment stands in the way. We have fixed on the day after tomorrow for our departure and I shall as soon as possible have the pleasure of addressing you from Morocco. In the mean time I am with the greatest esteem & Respect, Gentlemen, Your most ob^{t.} humble Servt,   Thos. Barclay

.   .   .   .   .

MHS: *The Adams Papers, microfilm reel 368 (LS).*

¹ *Chiappe, Francisco. Italian merchant resident in Morocco who, styling himself "Secretary of his I.M. for Foreign Affairs," represented the Emperor of Morocco by sending and receiving communications to and from U.S. diplomatic representatives. He and his brothers Girolamo and Giuseppe later served as U.S. commercial agents in Morocco, Tangier, and Mogador.*

John Jay to Thomas Jefferson

Dr Sir   New York 16th. June 1786

.   .   .   .   .

...I always wished, and that very sincerely, that on the Return of Peace, France might derive essential Advantages from our Commerce – I regret that this has not been the Case, and that the Causes which occasioned the Disappointment have not sooner been investigated and removed. In my Opinion you have done it candidly and ably; and it would give me great Pleasure to hear that France has so regulated her Commerce as that the People of this Country may indulge their Desire of giving the Productions of this Country in Exchange for those of that. There is certainly much Wisdom and Knowledge in France, but the Interests of Commerce do not appear to be as well understood in that Country as in England. However the System of farming and Monopoly may comport with the Views of Government in some Points, the Experience of Ages bears Testimony to the Injuries they have done to Commerce. Governments however like Individuals sometimes become too strongly attached by long continued Habit even to what daily does them Harm – so that we may apply to Errors in Politics what was wisely remarked of Errors in Morals, it is hard for those who are *accustomed* to do Evil to learn to do well. When I was in France I heard that System censured by almost every Gentleman whom I heard speak of it, and yet it seems so firmly fixed, perhaps by golden Rivets, even on Sovereignty itself, as that the speedy Destruction of it seems rather to be wished for than expected. –

.   .   .   .   .

I am impatient to receive the Orders of Congress on the Subject of your Negociations with the Barbary Powers. As yet that Business remains under Consideration – as to further Loans – I have long thought that they should be preceded by proper Arrangements for the Payment of Interest and Principal; so that the public Faith may be punctually kept – national Character depends upon it, and I for my part think national Character is of more Importance, than even Peace with those Pirates. –

Your Reasons for going to England appear to me as they did to you, cogent and conclusive, and I make no Doubt but that Good will result from it, altho' perhaps not all that might have been expected. The Affair of our Posts is a serious Business, and the more so as in my Opinion Britain has too much Reason on her Side – They who ask Equity, should do it. –

. . . . .

With great and sincere Esteem and Regard I have the Honor to be &^{ca}

John Jay –

NA: PCC, *item 121, pp. 188-190 (C); M61, reel 1.*

John Adams to John Jay

Dr Sir   Grosvenor Square June 16. 1786.

Two days ago, I was honoured with your Letter of the 4. of May, in which another of the first of the same month is referred to, and as I hear there is a Passenger expected from the Packet, I hope to receive it from him when he arrives in town.

Lord Carmarthen told me yesterday, "that he had Letters from Mr Anstey, mentioning his civil reception: His Lordship said, too, that a Minister Plenipotentiary would certainly be sent to Congress: that it was not from any Coldness or Want of Respect to the United States that it had not been already done; but merely from the difficulty of finding a proper Person: that he had received many Applications, but they had been generally from Persons who he was sure would not be agreable in America: and in some Instances from Persons more suitable for a Place in the Customs, than in the Corps Diplomatique."

A long Conversation ensued upon the Subject of the Posts Debts &c little of which being new, is worth repeating. The Policy of giving up the Interest during the War, and of agreeing to a Plan of Payment by Installments, was again insisted on, from various considerations, particulary from the evident Injustice of demanding Interest for that Period. it was urged that the Claim of Interest in most Cases was grounded upon Custom, and the mutual Understanding of the Parties: but that it never had been the Custom, nor had it ever been Understood or foreseen, that an Act of Parliament should be passed, casting the American Debtor out of the Protection of the Crown, cutting off all Correspondence and rendering all Intercourse criminal; for that was the Result and the legal Construction during the whole War. Here his Lordship fully agreed with me and even outwent me, saying that "it was very true that by construction of the Law of this Land, it was High Treason in a Creditor in Great Britain to receive a Remittance from his Debtor in America during the War. His Lordship added some slight Expressions concerning the Interest and wished that the Courts were opened for recovering the Principal. We might leave the Interest for an After Consideration. in short they waited only for some Appearance of a disposition." "The Answer to my Memorial of 30. Nov. contained their true Intentions. They sincerely meant to fullfill every Engagement, whenever they saw a Disposition on our Part." These Expressions you see are somewhat oracular but they conveyed so much meaning to me that I will no longer hesitate to recommend to Congress to to take up this matter and decide it at once. it would be going too far to point out the Mode, but it may be suggested whether it is not expedient for Congress to require of all the States who have made Laws irreconcileable to the Treaty, immediately to repeal them. declaring at the same time, that Interest upon Book Debts and simple Contracts, during the War, cannot be considered as any Part of the Bona Fide Debts intended in the Treaty. as to Specialties, there may be in some Cases more Difficulty. Yet I dont see but the same Reasoning is applicable to all. The Legal Contract was dissolved by throwing us out of the Protection of the Crown and our subsequent Assumption of Independence, and had no Existence untill revived by Treaty. private honour and Conscience are out of this Question. those who think themselves bound by these Ties, will do as they please. but I believe under all the Circumstances, few Persons even of the most delicate Sentiments will be scrupulous. if such a Declaration should be made by Congress Candour will require that it should extend to both Sides, to the British and Refugee Debtor to American Creditors as well as Vice Versa. If Congress should choose to avoid involving themselves in such a Declaration, it would not be proper for individual States to do it; and in this Case, I humbly conceive the Laws ought to be repealed, and the Question left to *Judges* and *Juries*, who upon the strictest Construction of Law Equity and the treaty may in my opinion in most Cases if not in all, deny the Interest during the War to the Creditor. in some of these Ways relief must be had, or in none, for the Ministry here will never intermeddle in the Business.

If any one should ask what was the Intention of the Contracting Parties at the Treaty? The Answer must be, the Treaty itself must determine, and any one who reads it may judge as well as one of the Plenipotentiaries. The Word "heretofore," was not used in Preference to the words "before the War," with any View to the Interest but to comprehend Debts which had been contracted during the war. The Intention was, no doubt that whatever Judges and Juries should find to be a Debt, should be recovered. and I believe that any Man acting in the Character of either, will find it difficult to say upon his oath, that Interest during the War, is bonâ fide due. — did any Debtor, foreseeing the War, contract a Debt, and pledge his Faith to pay Interest during the Continuance of it? Let this be proved and a Judge or Juror would compell Payment. But probably there is not one such Case. – The War may be considered as one of those Accidents, bona fide not expected or foreseen, against which Equity will always give Relief.

With great and sincere Esteem, I have the Honour to be, Sir your most obedient and most humble Servant   John Adams.

NA: PCC, item 84, v. 6, pp. 299-304 (ALS); M247, reel 113.

James Monroe to Thomas Jefferson

Dear Sir –   N. York June 16. 1786.

. . . . . .

What shall finally be done with Spain respecting the Mississipi becomes an interesting question, and one pres[sed] on us for a decision. Gardoqui has been long labouring it's occlusion with Jay. for sometime I have been perfectly satisfied the latter required no arguments to bring him into the same sentiment; the proposition that it be shut for thirty years in consideration for which Spain will admit us into her ports upon a footing with her own subjects we reciprocating: this you may recollect was rejected at Annapolis upon its own merits only: It is however magnified here as a great advantage & equivalent to the consideration requir'd. we are also threatned with the prospect of a treaty between Spain (in case this fails) and Britain yet I cannot comprehend upon what principle it can take effect. Jay stated difficulties in the management of this bus[in]ess with the minister & proposd, without bringing any of these circumstances to view that a committee be appointed with power to controul all circumstances respecting the treaty with a view of evading his instructions & concluding the treaty before they were known – but as they were known to some who had mark[ed] the progress of the business each proposition was discuss'd on its own particular merits in the first instance – a Committee was appointed to report – Jay attended it. of this I was ~~of it~~ a member – To us he cod make no communication we did not already know – so that the plan fail'd in not carrying a committee in the first instance for the purpose. This was a fortnight past & as yet we have made no report – I have given circumstantially the state of this business [as] it has appear'd to me, not on evidence absolutely presu[mptiv]e only – I intended to have wrote you more fully but am [ju]st advis'd the packet will sail immediately – with my sincerest wishes for yr. health & happiness I am dear Sir yr. friend & servant   Ja⁵· Monroe

LC: *Jefferson Papers, microfilm reel 5 (ALS).*

Louis Guillaume Otto to Comte de Vergennes

[Translation]

N. 52.   New York, 17 June 1786.
My Lord

The abasement into which Congress has fallen since the peace begins to arouse the attention of all true patriots. It is felt that it is impossible for the federal Government to remain in its current inaction without placing the esteem of the United States and its very independence in danger. Indeed, the most pressing recommendations of this Assembly are treated by most of the States with an indifference that causes people less susceptible to taking part in public affairs to groan. The Department of Finances has never been as destitute as it is at this moment, and one of the Commissioners has assured me that it has nothing more with which to meet current expenses. The most important members of Congress do all that is in their power to have several articles added to the act of the Confederation that the current situation of affairs appears to render indispensable. It is proposed to give Congress executive powers, and the right exclusively to make emissions of paper money and to regulate commerce, it is desired moreover that this assembly be divided into two Chambers in order to prevent an eloquent and ill-intentioned member from carrying all the votes. As for the executive power, My Lord, the Confederation will always be unsteady as long as Congress has not obtained this important point. The idea of a sovereign Body that has only the right to deliberate and to recommend is repugnant to reason, and in spite of the jealousy of a great number of individuals in America, one cannot conceal from oneself the inconsequence of such a system of government. The continual rotation of members of Congress is another inconvenience whose baneful effects are felt more and more; it is difficult for men who only make a journey from one end of the Continent to the other and who only stay a few weeks in New York to be familiar with affairs. Be that as it may, My Lord, much time and many negotiations will be necessary to have these defects corrected, and it is impossible to foresee the end of the current difficulties.

. . . . .

I am with a profound respect, My Lord, Your most humble and most Obedient Servant,   Otto.
Received 1 August

FFAA: Pol. Corr., U.S., v. 31, f. 412-414vo. (LC transcription).

Thomas Jefferson to John Lamb

Sir   Paris June 20. 1786.
Having communicated to mr Adams the information received at different times from yourself, from mr Randall & mr Carmichael, we find that the sum likely to be demanded by Algiers for the ransom of our prisoners as well as for peace is so infinitely beyond our powers & the expectations of Congress, that it has become our duty to refer the whole matter back to them. whether they will chuse to buy a peace, to force one, or to do nothing, will rest in their pleasure. but that they may have all the information possible to guide them in their deliberations, we think it important that you should return to them. no time will be lost by this, & perhaps time may be gained. it is therefore our joint desire that you repair immediately to New-York for the purpose of giving to Congress all the information on this subject which your journey has enabled you to acquire. you will consider this request as coming from mr Adams as well as myself, as it is by express authority from him that I join him in it. I am of opinion it will be better for you to come to Marseilles & by Paris: because there is a possibility that fresh orders to us from Congress might render it useful that we also should have received from you all possible information on this subject. and perhaps no time may be lost by this, as it might be long before you would get a passage from Alicant to America. I am Sir your most obedient & most humble servant   Th: Jefferson

NA: PCC, item 91, v. 2, p. 500 (ALS); M247, reel 119.

Thomas Barclay to
John Adams and Thomas Jefferson

Gentlemen   Morocco 26th. June 1786

Gentlemen   Morocco 26$^{th.}$ June 1786

This day week we arrived here, since which I have had two audiences
from his Majesty, the first a public one & the second a private one of
yesterday. It is but a few minutes since I heard that a Courrier would depart
this Evening for Daralbeyda, & I have not time to enter into particulars.
It will be agreable however for you to know, that the last draught of the
Treaty is made & will probably be signed in a few days, & that our stay
here will not exceed that of a week from this time. I believe you will be
satisfied on the whole, as there is only one article more I could wish to see
inserted, & that I really think, in all human probability will never prove of
the least Consequence.

I shall proceed to Tangiers and take an early Opportunity of sending you
a more detailed account of my proceedings; In the mean time I recommend
your transmitting as soon as possible, through Mr. Carmichael the Powers
to treat with Tunis & Tripoli, & (if Mr. Lamb has declined all further
concern) for Algiers: If you had a Treaty with the Porte I flatter myself the
rest would follow, & at all events Tunis and Tripoli Should be invited to
our friendship.—

There is a young man now under my Care, who has been a Slave some
time with the Arabs in the Desart, his Name is James Mercier, born at the
Town of Suffolk, Nansimond County Virginia. The King sent him after the
first Audience, & I shall take him to Spain. I have not time to add, but
that I am, Gentlemen Your most obedient, humble Servant,

Tho' Barclay

Rec^d and a Copy Sent to Mr Jay 23^{d.} August 1786 –

MHS: The Adams Papers, microfilm reel 368 (LS).

John Adams to John Jay

Sir   London June 27. 1786

The Chevalier De Pinto, the Envoy of Portugal, informed me, this Day
that he had received Instructions from his Court, to inform me, "that the
Queen[1] his Mistress has sent a Squadron to cruise in the Mouth of the
Streights with orders to protect all Vessells belonging to the United States
of America equally with those of her own Subjects and that She would
continue those orders as long as they should be agreable to Congress."

The Reply, was, that it could not be doubted that so signal a Mark of her Majesties friendly Attention to the Interest and Safety of the Citizens of America, would be very agreable to Congress, and that the first Opportunity should be embraced to make the Communication to them.

So much Notice will probably be taken of this by Congress, as to return the Compliment, at least i[t]s Thanks.

If the United States should ever think themselves able to pay Taxes, and begin a Navy, this War of the Algerines would be a good Opportunity. I have never dared however to recommend it: because, that as Negotiation and customary Presents, and Redemption of Captives, must finally terminate the War, whatever Sums are spent in it whatever time is spent, or lives lost in it, it has ever appeared to me, that all this would be thrown away.

It would employ our Shipwrights, and make various Branches of Business brisk, to order half a Score Frigates of thirty six Guns to be built, and it would give us an Ecclat; but it would cost Money.

With great Regard yours   John Adams

Sept 29. 1786 The injunction of Secresy taken off — ref.^{d.} to report.

NA: PCC, *item 84, v. 6, pp. 307-310* (ALS); M247, *reel 113.*
¹ *Maria I, Queen of Portugal (1734-1816), ruled 1777-1816.*

Louis Guillaume Otto to John Jay

Sir   New York 27th. June 1786

On the Occasion of the Letter which I had the Honor to write to you on the 18th April last you was pleased to promise me verbally to solicit with Congress the Ratification of our consular Convention as soon as there should be nine States represented – all the Members of this assembly with whom I have conversed have assured me that the Delay which this Ratification has experienced was principally owing to this – that Congress had not received a Copy of this Convention until long after its signature, and that since that Time this assembly has never found itself sufficiently numerous to take it into Consideration. I have transmitted this Answer to my Court, and Mr. Jefferson has received analagous Instructions to inform the Minister of the Reasons of the long Silence of Congress respecting an Object on which the Plenipotentiaries of the two Nations had solemnly agreed. Since that Period the Congress have not only been found compleat, but they have ratified the Treaty of Commerce with Prussia, although the Signature of that Treaty was a good deal more recent than that of the consular Convention. The United States being again sufficiently represented I beg the Favour of you to submit this affair to their Consideration

– whatever may be their Resolution in this Respect, it is to be desired, to facilitate the Business with which the respective Consuls are charged, that they may be informed of the Extent of their Powers, and that they may know in a clear and precise manner the Limits which their Sovereigns have assigned to their Authority.

I am &^{ca.}   Otto

NA: PCC, *item 120, v. 2, pp. 374-376 (translation); M40, reel 2.*

Henry E. Stanhope to Philip Stephens

Sir¹   *Mercury*, Long Beach June 27th. 1786

I have the honor to obey their Lordships directions of the 15th. Instant relative to the Complaint made by the Governor of Boston upon my Conduct while at that Port –

Having received orders from Commodore Sawyer² to receive the Agent to the Contractor for supplying the Navy (or His Clerk) and proceed to Boston, and pay all possible attention to the Vessel he might provide for the reception of the Cattle he should purchase there. Upon my arrival in Nantasket Road I sent the 2^{d.} Lieutenant Philips to the Governor with a Letter communicating my Arrival and Intention of Proceeding with the Ship to the Town so soon as the Wind would allow me to pass the Narrows, when I should pay my compliments to Him: The Officer returned with his Answer of civility, and reported that the People at the wharf where he landed had cut away the Boat's Pendant; The succeeding day I arrived off the Town and was informed by Lieutenant Stoven of the 17th. Reg^{t.} who was a Passenger (and had remained in Boston where he had gone with Lieu^{t.} Philips) that the People were much enraged I had not saluted the Castle in passing it. Knowing that I could not comply with the object of my Order without much management, I sent the 1st. Lieutenant Nash to the Governor to communicate my Intentions of Saluting upon his Assurance of returning an equal N^{o.} of Guns, to this he replied (after much futile evasion, and wish to receive a Gun less) that he would consider of it; however, notwithstanding this very extraordinary rudeness, and unparralleled Indignity to the Flag, I waited upon him, where after many enquiries about the object of my arrival (which I evaded) the size of the Ship, N^{o.} of Guns & Weight of Metal, he said my Lieutenant had mentioned to him something relative to a Salute desiring to know what would be the N^{o.} of Guns fired, and whether the largest, expressing a wish for thirteen. I told him the N^{o.} was discretional but that in all Points the

Salute would be the same to him as any similar Power, he said he was thinking of a Gun or two less, and upon my declaring the impossibility, he asserted that the French had always been content to receive such a return, which I communicated to the French Consul then present, who denied it, observing that he knew not what the Policy of the Nation might require, but in any other Case the Captain of the Ship would suffer severely, however after much Language to this Purpose, I took my leave of the Governor who promised to give me an answer the next Morning, which he did about Noon, in consequence of which I waited upon him with my Officers to be very effectually assured of his intention in this point, & embraced that opportunity of communicating to him the loss of my Boat's Pendant, observing I should consider the return of the Salute as a Declaration of his absolute Protection in it's fullest extent, as well for our persons, as for any Property we should purchase of whatever kind it should be, to which he assented in the most explicit Terms, observing that he did not conceive there was any cause of Apprehension – The Salute was accordingly given, and returned, some Days after I applied to him for my Boy that had run from me, upon which he referr'd me to a Magistrate whose assistance was ineffectual – During our stay every sort of Indignity that could be conceived either thro' the Press, or by personal application was offered to me and my officers, the Sunday after our arrival a German informed that two men (whom he described) were employed to assassinate us in the Mall, one of which was a Deserter from General Burgoyne's Army whom we actually saw there with every appearance of the worst purpose, as also that an attack was intended upon the Ship by Boats, with which during the Night we were surrounded and I firmly believe with the design suggested to us, which was prevented by our vigilance – The Day on which we dined with the Governor a Jack Ass was brought near to his house by a Mob for our accommodation, but we had fortunately quitted it some Minutes before tho' in going on board we were very ill treated and narrowly escaped with our Lives of which he took not the least Notice, nor yet evinced any Inclination to suppress such rudeness – On the 31$^{st.}$ of July while walking in the Public Walk, Lieu$^{t.}$ Stoven came to me with information that at the head of the Mall were many People Armed who he was well assured intended an Attack, and that he had come to my assistance. I therefore quitted the Place, and passed them about 60 in N$^{o.}$ all furnished with Swords, or Sticks, one brushed against me as I suppose to provoke me. I walked on however without noticing it, and was soon followed, and overtaken by the Mob which had considerably increased, when the nearest Man made a Blow at me; I told him to desist, and upon another Man making a second attempt, I drew my Sword and made a Pass at him, two Gentlemen of the Town whom we met (Mess$^{r.}$ Lovell & Newman) exerted themselves even to striking one of them for our Protection, but to little purpose, when finding they got in our Rear we ran with all expedition till we gained the House of M^r· Moretow a Gentleman of the Law who tho' strongly attached to his Government, extended his protection to us, and harangued them, we placed our Backs to the Wall in which situation we continued previous to the Door being opened, parrying the Blows threatened us, when the Sherriff was passing, and ordered them to disperse which however did not take place for some hours, during which time many Gentlemen offer'd their assistance –

I cannot but observe from my general acquaintance at Boston, and private civilities, that independant of my public Character I should have considered myself and was assured my Person would be safe, but such was the Inveteracy as well of the Governor as M^r· Samuel Adams[3] to whom his Excellency alludes, that I do not conceive any Conduct but the most humiliating and consequently disgracefull to the honor of the British Flag would have been a protection from their Insults, and I earnestly hope that their Lordships Report of my Conduct in this Instance will be approved by His Majesty, as my Intention was to support the Dignity of the Nation, to which I flatter myself their Lordships will be the more particularly inclined, from the very peculiar Order I had received from Commodore Sawyer of which I enclose a Copy. I am &c.   H. E. Stanhope.[4]
In the Lords of the Admiralty's July 11th· 1786

PRO: FO 4/4, pp. 477-480, 482 (LC transcription).
  [1] Stephens, Philip. British government official. Secretary of the Lords Commissioners of the Admiralty.
  [2] Sawyer, Herbert (1731?-1798). British naval officer. Commodore and commander-in-chief at Halifax, 1785. Rear admiral, 1788. Vice admiral, 1793. Admiral, 1795.
  [3] Adams, Samuel (1722-1803). Massachusetts political figure. A leading proponent of the revolutionary cause. Member, Continental Congress, 1774-1781. President, state senate, 1781-1788. Lieutenant governor of Massachusetts, 1789-1793, governor, 1794-1797.
  [4] Stanhope, Henry E. British naval officer. Captain, frigate Mercury.

Emperor of Morocco to the
President of the Congress

[Morocco, 28 June 1786]
In the Name of the most merciful God – No power can exist on the earth without the will of the powerful & almighty God.

From the servant of God Mohamed Ben Abdallah, may God be with him. Amen.

To His Excellency the President of the Congress of the United States of America. Peace to him who follows the right way of God.

This is to acquaint you that we recieved your letter by the hands of your Ambassador Thomas Barclay who delivered to us likewise another from the King of Spain. From the contents of these letters we learned that you were disposed to establish a treaty of peace and commerce with us, such as we have with other Christian powers; to which having agreed, we have completed a treaty by sea & land on the terms desired of us and the articles are inserted in a book confirmed by our Royal seal being affixed thereto.

We have ordered all our servants who command at our sea-ports to recieve your vessels & citizens who shall come to our dominions, and treat them as we do the Spanish nation, and all our ports from Tetuan to Wadnoon are open to you, at any of which your Vessels may anchor in safety, and your people transact their business at their own pleasure. In answer to His Majesty the King of Spain, we have acquainted him with what has been done, and we remain in perfect peace and tranquillity with you.

Concluded the first of the blessed month of Ramadan in the year one thousand two hundred.

I certify the above to be a true copy of the translation made by Isaac Cardoza Nunes Interpreter at Morocco, of a letter from the Emperor of Morocco to the President of Congress, which was dated on the first day of Ramadan 1200 – being the 28[th.] of June 1786

Tho' Barclay

NA: PCC, item 91, pp. 261-262 (C); M247, reel 119.

John Adams and Thomas Jefferson to John Lamb

Sir –   London June 29[th.] 1786 –

The Importance of Peace with the Algerines, and the other Inhabitants of the Coast of Barbary, to the United States, renders it necessary that every information which can be obtained should be laid before Congress: And as the demands for the Redemption of Captives, as well as the amount of Customary Presents, are so much more considerable than seem to have been expected in America, it appears to us necessary that you should return without loss of Time to New York there to give an account to Congress of all the Particulars which have come to your Knowledge, as well as of your own Proceedings, and of the Monies which have been paid on account of the United States in consequence of your draughts upon their Minister in London –

From Congress when you arrive there you will receive orders for your future Government, and in the meantime we have no further occasion for your services in Europe – If you Know of a certain passage immediately from any Port in Spain, we advise you to avail yourself of it: if not, we think it most adviseable for you to come to Paris; and from thence, after having consulted with M[r.] Jefferson – to repair to L'Orient and embark for New York in the first Packett –

As the Instructions we send to M[r.] Randal are to come on to Paris in his Way to America, unless he should choose to accompany you from some port in Spain, we desire you to furnish him with Money for his Expences to Paris & London out of the Cash already in your hands and we recommend to him as well as to you all reasonable attention to Economy –

We are   J A & [TJ]

LC: *The Adams Papers,* microfilm reel 113 (LBkC).

Don Diego de Gardoqui to Congress

New York 30[th.] June 1786

The underwritten Encargado de Negocios of his catholic Majesty has the Honor to remind the Honble Congress, that on the 14[th.] October last he received assurances that they would adopt all posssible means that the public Tranquility should not be interrupted in the Territories mentioned in his Paper of Complaints of 23[d] September in the same year – Soon after the worthy Delegates of the State of Georgia returned to assist at the assembly of their Government, they confirmed in its Name the same pacific Dispositions, promissing [sic] to repress all Excess, and concurring in the very salutary Intentions of his Majesty. Relying on this superior security, and on the Promises of such respectable Individuals this Encargado flattered himself with seeing the good Effects thereof; when contrary to his Hopes, he finds himself obliged to call the attention of this Honorable Body to the Continuation of the reiterated Complaints against the Proceedings of many Americans in that Quarter, and to shew the imminent Risque which threatens, if they do not provide without Delay that the State of Georgia repress the Invasions of those who are called its Inhabitants.

The Encargado of his Majesty will explain succinctly the principal Complaints of the various Nations of Indians, which anciently, and since the late Cessions and Conquests by the Spanish Arms, have been under the immediate Protection of his Majesty.

They complain bitterly that being at the Conclusion of the War (in which the English ceded all the Lands they possessed) at the Distance of fifteen Days Journey from the Frontiers of Georgia, they used that intermediate Patrimony for their Huts and subsistence, but that those Agressors have usurped their Lands with such immoderate Ambition as that they have encroached within two Days Journey, depriving them of all the rest and of their only Subsistence.

That since the last War they have made repeated Representations to induce the Georgians to desist from extending themselves over their Lands, solemnly protesting that if they continued their unbounded Intrusions they would be obliged to repel them by force.

That there have been several who insidiously have prevailed upon every wandering Indian they met with, to sign what they called a Deed of Cession, against which and similar absurd Deceptions the Chiefs and principal Indians have made Representations.

That they have loudly demanded certain Lands and Places respecting which the Indians say with Truth, that they were ceded in Times past to the English and conquered by the Spaniards, whose Monarch was then Lord Sovereign and Protector.

Lastly all the Chiefs and principal Warriors of those Nations of Indians have resorted to the Spanish Commandants, representing that in Consideration of the repeated pacific Admonitions which their well known Humanity had inculcated into them – They had 'till then restrained themselves, bearing it with a Degree of Moderation without Example, but that having been disppointed like many others, in the Hopes with which the State of Georgia had amused them, promising that, in the Session of their last Assembly they should be redressed, they could not dissemble nor permit their Goodness to be longer abused – That considering the terrible Circumstances to which they were reduced, they hoped they would not give offence by having resolved to defend their Patrimony, and oblige the Invaders to retire within their Limits, assuring them faithfully that it was not their Intention to make war on the United States, but only to recover what those Trespassers had usurped.

The said Encargado of his Majesty has been also informed of various undue Practices with some principal Indians who were rightfully bound under the Protection of his Majesty –

On considering these Facts he cannot see with Indifference certain Pieces lately Published in several Papers, and particularly in those of this City dated the 1st May last.

He has good Reasons to consider these Persons as aggresors, for he is firmly persuaded that the refined Justice of Congress could not authorize such a notorious violation of the Rights of Cession and Conquest, of the Territories belonging to his King his Master; and in the actual possession of his royal Arms. But he much regrets that the Evils which may thence result to the Public, are not obviated by undeceiving them with Respect to such Errors. –

The said Encargado has no doubt but that the Honble Congress will take care to give the most express orders that no Geographer nor assistant Surveyor do enter into the Territories ceded to his Majesty, or conquered by his arms, that the evil Consequences to which they would be exposed may be avoided.

Urged by the purest Zeal & anxious to avoid the like uneasinesses, the Encargado of his Majesty has the honor to intimate to Congress the pressing necessity of ceasing to delay the Settlement of the Boundaries between the two Nations. And I hope that in the mean time they will adopt without the least Delay the efficacious measures which the important Object of this note requires – and that they may be communicated to him that on his part he may pacify the Complainants, and represent to the King his Master the continuance of the pacific Disposition of this Honble Body.

Diego de Gardoqui

NA: PCC, item 120, v. 2, pp. 382-386 (translation); M40, reel 2.

John Adams to Thomas Jefferson

Dear Sir   London July 3. 1786.

Yours of the 23 of June is come to hand, with a Copy of Mʳ Lamb's of 6 June from Aranjuez.

There is no Intelligence from America of Armies marching to take the Posts from the English. The News was made as I Suppose against the opening of the Three Per Cents, and it had the intended Effect to beat down the Stocks a little.

Altho the Posts are important, the War with the Turks is more So. I lay down a few Simple Propositions.

1.   We may at this Time, have a Peace with them, in Spight of all the Intrigues of the English or others to prevent it, for a Sum of Money.

2.   We never Shall have Peace, though France, Spain, England and Holland, Should use all their Influence in our favour without a Sum of Money.

3.   That neither the Benevolence of France nor the Malevolence of England, will be ever able materially to diminish or Increase the Sum.

4.   The longer the Negotiation is delayed, the larger will be the Demand.

From the Premises I conclude it to be wisest for Us to negotiate and pay the necessary Sum; without Loss of Time. Now I desire you and our noble Friend the Marquis, to give me your opinion of these four Propositions. which of them do you deny? or doubt? if you admit them all, do you admit the Conclusion? Perhaps you will Say, fight them, though it should cost Us a great Sum to carry on the War, and although at the End of it We should have more Money to pay as presents. if this is your Sentiment, and you can persuade the Southern States into it, I dare answer for it that all from Pensylvania inclusively northward, would not object. it would be a good Occasion to begin a Navy.

at present, We are Sacrificing a Million annually to Save one gift of two hundred Thousand Pounds. This is not good Oeconomy. – We might at this hour have two hundred Ships in the Mediterranean, whose Freight alone would be worth two hundred Thousand Pounds, besides its Influence upon the Price of our Produce. our Farmers & Planters will find the Price of their Articles, Sink very low indeed, if this Peace is not made. The Policy of Christendom has made Cowards of all their Sailors before the Standard of Mahomet. It would be heroical and glorious in Us, to restore Courage to Ours. I doubt not We could accomplish it, if We should set about it in earnest, But the Difficulty of bringing our People to agree upon it, has ever discouraged me.

You have seen Mr. Randall before this no doubt, if he has not fallen Sick on the Road.

This Letter is intended to go by Mr Fox. The Chev. De Pinto's Courier unfortunately missed a Packet, which delayed him and consequently the Treaty a Month. The Queen his Mistress, as I wrote you a few Days Since, has given orders to her Squadron cruising in the Streights to protect all Vessells belonging to the United States. This is noble and Deserves Thanks.

Accept the Sincerest Assurances of Esteem and Affection from dear Sir your most obedient   John Adams

LC: *Jefferson Papers,* microfilm reel 5 (ALS).

John Jay to Sir John Temple

S^r·   [New York] Office for foreign Affairs 5$^{th·}$ July 1786

I have received and laid before Congress the letter you did me the honor to write on the 7$^{th·}$ Ul$^t·}$ – On returning to Town from Philadelphia last Saturday I found that this letter had during my absence been referred to me; and I shall without Delay report upon it as soon as some preceding References shall be dispatched. –

Forgery of every kind is doubtless base as well as criminal, & Governments which connive at or encourage it, impair their own Dignity and corrupt the Morals of their People. –

Whether your Information respecting the Practice of counterfeiting Mediterranean Passes at Philadelphia is well or ill founded, merits Enquiry. I wish it had been accompanied with some Evidence, if only such a degree of it as might create strong Probability, and afford Ground for just Suspicion. Public and extraordinary Measures for detecting and punishing Crimes, always imply a Presumption that they exist, and tend to establish Imputations which may prove unjust and injurious. In my Opinion therefore Government should observe Caution and Delicacy on such Occasions. Mere Suspicion is very slender Proof of Guilt, and tho' perhaps it should sometimes prompt silent Enquiry, yet I think it can very rarely be a proper Foundation for such open and decided Proceedings, as must naturally cause and diffuse an Opinion that there was at least strong circumstantial if not direct Proof of Criminality. –

I am persuaded that you credit the Intelligence you have received, and it is very probable that the same Circumstances which lead you to credit it would if known have the same Influence on others. But, Sir, I really and sincerely think that no Government ought to presume, that criminal Practices of any particular kind prevail in any particular Place, until some circumstantial or other Indications and Symptoms of it appear.

I can easily conceive that your Information may be very direct and particular, and yet so received and circumstanced as not to permit you to communicate it in Detail. It is not my Wish to learn from you more Particulars than you can with Propriety communicate; but I assure you, Sir, it would give me Pleasure to pursue and co-operate in any proper Measures that may be calculated to detect and suppress the Practice you mention–

With great Esteem and Regard I have the Honor to be S$^r·}$ Your most obed^t and hble: Serv$^{t·}$ John Jay. –

NA: PCC, item 80, v. 3, pp. 253-254 (C); M247, reel 106.

Sir John Temple to John Jay

Sir,   Wednesday Evening,
                                                           New York 5 July 1786 –
I have just had the Honor to receive your Letter of this date, in which
you inform me that mine of the seventh of last Month, concerning the
counterfeiting British Mediterranean Passes at Philadelphia, had been laid
before Congress; – that it had, by that honorable Body, been referred to
you; and that, you should in the Course of your Business, report upon it. –
Your following Sentiments upon the Criminality of Forgeries; that such
Crimes, if encouraged or connived at by Government, would impair its
Dignity, and corrupt the Morals of the People; are certainly very honorable,
just, and proper upon the Occasion; and I am sorry that I cannot with
Propriety impart to you, the ample Information I have had, of the Forgery
in Question; but, in the present Instance, it would neither be wise, prudent,
nor honorable in me, to communicate to you in Detail, the full and
sufficient Intelligence I have faithfully received, that British Mediterranean
Passes have been, for some time past, counterfeited and sold at
Philadelphia, and that, Ships and Vessels belonging to the Subjects of these
States have sailed on Foreign Voyages with such Passes. – Would you be
pleased Sir to make Enquiry of any of your reputable Merchants, or Masters
of Ships, either here or at Philadelphia, I am persuaded the Fact would be
established to your compleat Satisfaction, for I do assure you I have every
Reason to expect that I shall be able to transmit to his Majesty's Ministers,
by the Packet to sail on Friday, one of those Counterfeit Passes, purchased
by my Desire at Philadelphia.
    I am sorry that the Information given you at the begining of last Month,
concerning such Forgeries, was not thought of Importance enough to merit
an earlier Attention; for, as I before mentioned to you, these Counterfeit
Passes, will only render such Subjects of your States as have gone to Sea
with them, still more wretched and miserable than they otherwise would
have been, should they happen to fall into the Hands of the Barbary
Corsairs; for, from Measures lately adopted by his Majesty's Ministers to
defeat all such Attempts, not one of those forged Passes will, in my
Opinion escape Detection, when *Proofs*, that may give you pain to receive,
and myself to be made further acquainted with (of such an atrocious Forgery
of National Documents!) may be furnished you from Tunis, Tripoli, Algiers,
and other Barbary States, who will undoubtedly consider themselves as
principally intended to be injured, by such Counterfeits. I, however Sir,
have done my Duty, and shall, by the Packet to sail on Friday, transmit
Copies of our Correspondence upon this Business, to his Majesty's Principal

Secretary of State at St. James; in the mean time, I have the Honor to be, with great Consideration and Respect, Sir, Your most faithfull & Obedient Servant,   J. Temple.

NA: PCC, *item* 92, *pp. 565-566 (LS); M247, reel 120.*

Sir John Temple to Lord Carmarthen

My Lord,   New York 7th. of July 1786.

Inclosed is duplicate of the letter I had the honor of writing to your Lordship on the 7th. of last month by the *Tankerville* Packet; since which, I have had an Answer from the Congress's Secretary for foreign affairs concerning the counterfeiting Mediterranean Passes at Philadelphia! Congress however have not yet taken any steps either to detect or punish those who have been guilty of such an unpardonable forgery: and although the fact is beyond all doubt, your Lordship will perceive by the inclosed Letter from Mr. Secretary Jay, what little room there is to expect, that the matter will be taken up & prosecuted to the National honour of these states. Seeing it in this light, I have been ballancing in my Mind, Whether or not to offer a reward immediately, in His Majesty's Name, of One hundred pounds sterling money of Great Britain to any person or persons who can & will give such information as that those concerned in said forgery may be fairly convicted of the Crime: but having no Instructions for my Government on such Occasions; and, as I have not any discressionary Power or Authority, to offer or dispose of even a Shilling in any way whatsoever, I was apprehensive it might be disapproved, & the hundred Pounds become a loss out of my own purse; for a Similar case precisely, happened when I was formerly Surveyor General of his Majestys Customs in this Country: I gave 30 Pistoles for a Blank Clearance granted by a Collector of the Customs to cover an infamous fraud, the Collector was detected by the Clearance so purchased, but the 30 Pistoles was disallowed by the Commissioners of the Customs, & never to this day hath it been repaid to me.

These forged Mediterranean Passes have been sold at Philadelphia at Nine & ten guineas each: I employed a trusty person to purchase one of them for me; but some how or other it became suspected who the Pass was for! the Gentleman therefore made no further attempts to Obtain one; I do not however dispair of Obtaining one through some other Channel; sh^d I be successfull, it shall be immediately forwarded to your Lordship.

In Obedience to your Lordships directions I have now the honor of enclosing (under a flying seal) a Letter to the Board of Admiralty, together with a List of such Ships & Vessells as have Arrived & departed from this Port, with Mediterranean Passes, since I entered upon the Employment of Consul General.

The *Imperial* Ship from Canton, loaded principally with Tea & China Ware (which I had the honor of Mentioning in my last) finding the Markets bad, & very little money to be had, does not dispose of her Cargo here, but will proceed to Ostend as soon as she can be refited for the Sea.

It is with Pleasure that I can inform your Lordship, what Silver & Gold is to be had in this Country, goes in his Majestys Packet boats to England, The last Packet, the *Tankerville*, carried upwards of Three hundred Thousand Spanish Mill'd dollars! and the *Carteret* Packet, to sail tomorrow, will I believe, carry home near as much more. The french Packets carry none.

With all deference, I have the honor to be, My Lord, Your Lordships most faithfull, and Obedient Servant,   J. Temple
R 1ˢᵗ: Augˢᵗ:

PRO: FO 4/4, pp. 449-452 (LC transcription).

Thomas Jefferson to John Adams

Dear Sir   Paris July 9. 1786.

. . . . .

Have you no news yet of the treaty with Portugal? does it hang with that court? my letters from N. York of the 11ᵗʰ· of May inform me that there were then 11 states present & that they should ratify the Prussian treaty immediately. as the time for exchange of ratifications is drawing to a close, tell me what is to be done, and how this exchange is to be made. we may as well have this settled between us before the arrival of the ratification, that no time may be lost after that. I learn through the Marechal de Castries that he has information of New York's having ceded the impost in the form desired by Congress, so as to close this business. corrections in the acts of Maryland, Pennsylvania &c. will come of course. we have taken up again the affair of whale oil, that it they may know in time in America what is to be done in it. I fear we shall not obtain any further abatement of duties; but the last abatement will be continued for three years. the whole duties paiable here are nearly 102 livres on the English ton, which is an atom more than four guineas according to the present exchange.

The monopoly of the purchase of tobacco for this country which had been obtained by Robert Morris had thrown the commerce of that article into agonies. he had been able to reduce the price in America from 40/ to 22/6 lawful the hundred weight,[1] and all other merchants being deprived of that medium of remittance the commerce between America & this country, so far as it depended on that article, which was very capitally too, was absolutely ceasing. an order has been obtained obliging the farmers general to purchase from such other merchants as shall offer, 15,000 hogsheads of tobacco at 34, 36, & 38 livres the hundred according to the quality, and to grant to the sellers in other respects the same terms as they had granted to Robert Morris. as this agreement with Morris is the basis of this order I send you some copies of it which I will thank you to give to any American (not British) merchants in London who may be in that line. during the year this contract has subsisted, Virginia & Maryland have lost 400,000£ by the reduction of the price of their tobacco.

...be assured of the friendship & esteem with which I have the honor to be Dear Sir Your most obedient and most humble serv^t

Th: Jefferson

MHS: *The Adams Papers, microfilm reel 368* (ALS).

[1] *That is, from 40 shillings to 22 shillings, 6 pence, per hundred pounds.*

Thomas Jefferson to John Adams

Dear Sir   Paris July 11. 1786.

Our instructions relative to the Barbary states having required us to proceed by way of negotiation to obtain their peace, it became our duty to do this to the best of our power. whatever might be our private opinions, they were to be suppressed, and the line marked out to us, was to be followed. it has been so honestly, & zealously. it was therefore never material for us to consult together on the best plan of conduct towards these states. I acknolege I very early thought it would be best to effect a peace thro' the medium of war. tho' it is a question with which we have nothing to do, yet as you propose some discussion of it I shall trouble you with my reasons. of the 4. positions laid down in your letter of the 3^d instant, I agree to the three first, which are in substance that the good offices of our friends cannot procure us a peace without paying it's price, that they cannot materially lessen that price, & that paying it, we can have peace in spight of the intrigues of our enemies. as to the 4th. that the longer the negotiation is delayed the larger will be the demand, this will depend on the intermediate captures: if they are many & rich the price may be raised; if few & poor it will be lessened. however if it is decided that we shall buy a peace, I know no reason for delaying the operation, but should rather think it ought to be hastened. but I should prefer the obtaining it by war. 1. justice is in favor of this opinion. 2. honor favors it. 3. it will procure us respect in Europe, and respect is a safeguard to interest. 4. it will arm the federal head with the safest of all the instruments of coercion over their delinquent members, & prevent them from using what would be less safe. I think that so far you go with me. but in the next steps we shall differ. 5. I think it least expensive. 6. equally effectual. I ask a fleet of 150. guns, the one half of which shall be in constant cruise. this fleet built, manned & victualled for 6. months, will cost 450,000£ sterling. it's annual expence is 300£ sterl. a gun, including every thing: this will be 45,000£ sterl. a year. I take British experience for the basis of my calculations, tho' we know, from our own experience, that we can do, in this way, for pounds lawful, what costs them pounds sterling. were we to charge all this to the Algerine war it would amount to little more than we must pay if we buy peace. but as it is proper & necessary that we should establish a small marine force (even were we to buy a peace from the Algerines,) and as that force laid up in our dockyards would cost us half as much annually as if kept in order for service, we have a right to say that only 22,500£ sterl. per ann. should be charged to the Algerine war. 6. it will be as effectual. to all the mismanagements of Spain & Portugal urged to shew that war against those people is ineffectual, I urge a single fact to prove the contrary where there is any management. about 40. year ago, the Algerines having broke their treaty with France, this court sent Monsʳ de Massac with one large & two small frigates, he blockaded the harbour of Algiers three months, & they subscribed to the terms he dictated. if it be admitted however that war, on the fairest prospects, is still exposed to incertainties, I weigh against this the greater incertainty of the duration of a peace bought with money, from such a people, from a Dey 80 years old; & by a nation who, on the hypothesis of buying peace, is to have no power on the sea to enforce an observance of it.

So far I have gone on the supposition that the whole weight of this war should rest on us. but 1. Naples will join us. the character of their naval minister (Acton[1]) his known sentiments with respect to the peace Spain is officiously trying to make for them, and his dispositions against the Algerines give the greatest reason to believe it. 2. every principle of reason tells us Portugal will join us. I state this as taking for granted, what all seem to believe, that they will not be at peace with Algiers. I suppose then that a Convention might be formed between Portugal, Naples & the U.S. by which the burthen of the war might be quartered on them according to their respective wealth; and the term of it should be when Algiers should subscribe to a peace with all three on equal terms. this might be left open for other nations to accede to, and many, if not most of the powers of Europe (except France, England, Holland & Spain if her peace be made) would sooner or later enter into the confederacy, for the sake of having their peace with the Pyratical states guarantied by the whole. I suppose that in this case our proportion of force would not be the half of what I first calculated on.

These are the reasons which have influenced my judgment on this question. I give them to you to shew you that I am imposed on by a semblance of reason at least, & not with an expectation of their changing your opinion you have viewed the subject, I am sure in all it's bearings. you have weighed both questions with all their circumstances. you make the result different from what I do. the same facts impress us differently. this is enough to make me suspect an error in my process of reasoning tho' I am not able to detect it. it is of no consequence; as I have nothing to say in the decision, and am ready to proceed heartily on any other plan which may be adopted, if my agency should be thought useful. with respect to the dispositions of the states I am utterly uninformed. I cannot help thinking however that on a view of all the circumstances, they might be united in either of the plans.

Having written this on the receipt of your letter, without knowing of any opportunity of sending it, I know not when it will go: I add nothing therefore on any other subject but assurances of the sincere esteem and respect with which I am Dear Sir your friend & servant   Th: Jefferson ans^d. July 31. 1786

MHS: *The Adams Papers, microfilm reel 368 (ALS).*
¹ *Acton, Sir John Francis Edward (1736-1811). As an expatriate Englishman serving as an officer in the Tuscan navy, Acton was asked to reorganize the Neapolitan navy in 1779. To the post of minister of the navy, he subsequently added those of minister of war, minister of finance, and prime minister of Naples.*

James Bowdoin to John Adams

Sir,   Boston July 11th. 1786

In addition to the papers I some time ago sent you, relative to the encroachments made upon our Eastern boundary by our Neighbours of New Brunswick, I have the honor of transmitting to your Excellency copies of other Letters & papers upon the same Subject –

By Messrs Smith & Bowles's Deposition it appears, that the Province of New Brunswick is by its Charter bounded on the Western Shore of Passamaquoddy, & that the Seventh Town or Parish, beside other islands, includes Moose, Fred^k & Dudley Islands, which lie on the West Side of Passamaquoddy bay, & are & have been for some time possessed by our people.

The proceedings of the Sheriff of the County of Charlotte, relative to those Islands & some of the people upon them, you have already been informed of.

The Papers now sent, respecting the Seizure of the two Vessels mentioned in them, shew that it is the intention of the Government of New Brunswick, said to be founded on Letters or Instructions from Lord Sidney, to exclude us from the Navigation of that Bay: on the Western Shore of which, & of the River Schooduck, running into that bay, a number of Townships have been by order of this Government laid out, & some of them sold. These Townships must for a long time be inaccessible, & of no value, if we are to be excluded from navigating that Bay: to the use of which, if the territory of the two nations bounds upon it, they have each, by the Treaty of peace, an equal right: the Seizure of those Vessels must therefore be considered as a violation of the Treaty: especially as they were when Seized on the Western side of the Bay.

You will observe by the Deposition & by Col^o· Allan's[1] Letter it is said, that Lord Sydney[2] had wrote to the Governor of New Brunswick,[3] that M^r· Adams in April last had not mentioned anything to the British Ministry, respecting the boundary lines of that territory or our claims to it: from whence the people there concluded, though very erroneously, that the territory or themselves were to be abandoned. It is hoped your Excellency has by this time had instructions from Congress to remonstrate to the British Ministry on that head; & that you will be able at least to procure orders to the Governor of New Brunswick, that our people on those Islands be not in future molested, & that no interruption be given to our vessels with regard to the navigation of that bay –

You will also observe by one of M^r· Delesdernier's[4] letter[s], that the seizure of the vessels was in retaliation for a vessel taken at the Westward. If this respects a vessel lately seized at Martha's Vineyard, & I do not know of any other it can relate to, She was seized in the breach of our navigation Act, & the trial I am informed will be had at the next Court for that County. This however can be no justification of their Seizures within the jurisdiction of this Commonwealth –

At the late Session of the General Court that Act was suspended until the other States should adopt similar ones: Rhode Island & New Hampshire having suspended or repealed their Navigation Acts.

I lately received your Letter with the Enclosures relative to the Whalefishery &c & this day had the honor of your Letter of the   of May – The former I have communicated to a number of Gentlemen in the mercantile line; & hope they will profit by the communication: & the latter will be shewn to confidential friends only – The Vessel being on the point of departure, I have only time to acknowledge the receiving of them, & to thank you for the information contained in them –

With real & the most respectful regard, I have the honor to be Sir, Your Excellencys Most ob^t· hble Servt·   James Bowdoin

.   .   .   .   .

PRO: FO 4/4, pp. 487-490 (LC transcription).

[1] Allan, John (1746-1805). Soldier and merchant. Nova Scotian who, having received part of his education in Massachusetts, favored the American cause. Member, provincial assembly, 1770-1776. Upon learning of his impending arrest for treason, he fled to Machias, Maine, 1776. Continental Congress agent to the Eastern Indians, 1777-1783. Colonel of Machias militia, 1777-1783. Merchant on Allan's Island in Passamaquoddy Bay, 1784-1786.

[2] Parr, John (1725-1791). British army officer and colonial administrator. Served with the 20th Foot, 1745-1776, attaining rank of lieutenant-colonel. Major of the Tower of London, 1778-1782. Governor of Nova Scotia, 1782-1786; after Dorchester's appointment as Governor General of British North America, lieutenant governor of Nova Scotia, 1786-1791.

[3] Townshend, Thomas (1733-1800). British political figure. Member of Parliament, 1754-1783; a Whig. A lord of the treasury under Rockingham, 1766, and Grafton, 1766-1767; joint paymaster of the forces under Grafton, 1767-1768. Opposed Lord North's policies. Secretary of state for war in Rockingham's administration, March-July 1782. Secretary of state for home affairs under Shelburne, July 1782-April 1783. From March 1783, Baron Sydney. Secretary of state for home affairs under Pitt, December 1783-June 1789.

[4] Not further identified.

Philip Stephens to Henry E. Stanhope

Sir   Admiralty Office 11th· July 1786

Having communicated to my Lords Commissioners of the Admiralty your Letter of the 27th· Ultimo, in answer to the complaint made against you by the Governor of Boston respecting your conduct there in August last, which was transmitted to you in my Letter of the 15th· of last Month; I am directed by their Lordships to inform you, that they observe the Assault which you met with at Boston was a consequence of your own reprehensible indiscretion in being on shore, and suffering any of your officers to be so, unnecessarily, after you had been apprized, as you relate, of the malevolent disposition, and had experienced the Insults, of the lower Class of the Inhabitants at that Place; and more especially while you had reason to believe, as you alledge, that attempts were meditated even on the Ship you commanded; under which circumstances you should not upon any account have been absent from your duty on board her.

Their Lordships having taken these particulars into their consideration, together with the very improper tenor of your correspondence with the Chief Magistrate of the State with whom it was requisite for you to communicate for the purpose of executing the Commission with which you were charged, and of whose disregard, as you saw reason to complain, you should have reserv'd yourself to have reported the particulars to your Commanding Officer, command me to acquaint you that they are highly displeased with your very injudicious and intemperate conduct therein.

I am &C.   Php Stephens.

PRO: FO 4/4, pp. 483-484 (LC transcription).

John Jay's Report Regarding Negotiations with Spain

[New York] Office of foreign Affairs 12th July 1786
The Secretary of the United States for the Department of foreign Affairs to whom was referred a Note of the 30th Day of June last from the Encargado de Negocios of his Catholic Majesty
Reports,
That in his Opinion it should be

Resolved. That the United States are sincerely disposed to conduct their Negociations with his Catholic Majesty with the greatest Candor and good Humour, and if possible to terminate them by such a Treaty as may preserve and perpetuate the Peace and Friendship which happily subsists between him and them, and between his Subjects and their Citizens.

Resolved therefore that unless all Questions, relative to the true Boundaries of Florida shall (as they hope will be the Case) be settled by mutual Agreement, the United States will chearfully consent and be ready to refer the same to the ultimate Decision of three or more impartial Commissioners. And as it is their earnest Wish and Desire that these Negociations and Proceedings may be carried on in the most friendly Manner, and may not be interrupted or impeded by any offensive or irritating Measures on either Side – It is further

Resolved, That a Copy of the abovementioned Note be transmitted by the Secretary for foreign Affairs to the Governor of the State of Georgia; and that he be informed that Congress have received with Regret repeated

Complaints of the Conduct of some People in that State towards the Spaniards, and that they desire and expect that such Measures will be immediately taken as may prevent the like in future.

Resolved, That the State of Georgia be further informed that the Liberality and Friendship of his Catholic Majesty, manifested in many recent Instances, towards the United States, leave no Room to apprehend that he wishes to adhere to any Claims of Territory which on Examination may appear ill founded, or to extend his Dominion at the Expence of that Justice and Magnanimity for which he is signalized. That as the United States, (however tenacious of, and determined to assert their just Rights) have full Confidence in the Integrity, and set a high Value on the Friendship, of his Catholic Majesty, they are exceedingly anxious to evince the Reality of these Sentiments by a correspondent Conduct, and to restrain and punish all such Excesses of rash and inconsiderate Adventurers, as may give just Cause of Umbrage to the spanish Government.

Ordered, That a Copy of the aforegoing Resolutions be given to the said Encargado de Negocios. –

All which is submitted to the Wisdom of Congress –   John Jay –
read July 13. 1786
Reported – Sepr 11$^{th.}$ 1786 –

NA: PCC, *item 81, v. 2, pp. 119-122 (DS); M247, reel 107.*

Richard O'Bryen to Thomas Jefferson

Sir   Algiers July 12$^{th.}$ 1786

Since the arrival of m^r Lamb at Algiers I wrote you several letters informing you of some particulars which came within my observation. Mr Lamb has actually agreed with the Dey of Algiers for the redemption of us unfortunate captives. it is near three months since m^r Lamb left Algiers and was to get the money in four months. I hope for our sakes, & the honor of his country, that he will not deviate from his word with the Dey of Algiers. We recieved a few lines from m^r Lamb by the Spanish Brig. Mr Lamb says he had stated our situation to you some months ago and that he had not recieved any answer from you or from Mr Adams and therefore can not tell what will be determined on on our behalf.

He mentions in his letter that it was not in his power to redeem us as his orders were not to go higher than 200 dollars per man. I never blamed him for not redeeming us as there was so small a sum appropriated for that use, as he repeatedly told me & others. It is near one year since we are in the fetters of slavery without having any account from the Continent, and lately within the time that m^r· Lamb arrived here without any assurances from our Country or Countrymen, and m^r· Lamb's letter has struck us with the most poignant grief so that our gloomy unfortunate situation affects us beyond our expression or your Imagination. we try to administer consolation to our unfortunate crews: but poor fellows endure the severities of slavery. I am confident our Country must have resolved on something respecting us before this time. certainly Liberty that is the basis of America will never let twenty one unfortunate citizens remain slaves to the Turkish yoke.

The other day when I was in the Dey's palace to see the boys that belonged to my vessel, the next man to the Dey asked me when I had heard from M^r· Lamb, and asked me if I did not expect to go clear soon. I said I did not know, and he said that the American Ambassador had agreed with the Dey to give 50,000 dollars & to get the money in four months time which he often tells the boys.

The Algerines have taken several prizes this cruise. They went out the 27th· of May & to day the last of them returned into port.
A Russian ship of 700 ton loaded with wine – 15 Men
A Leghorn ship of 20 Guns & – 44 men
Two Genoa barks of the Coast.
One Neapolitan, but is returned being taken in a Spanish bay.
One Spaniard taken but the vessel returned.
A Brig under Imperial colours – all Genoese on board. a hard task to clear her but is given up, those people being much afraid of the Emperor. – Four Portuguee fishing boats taken off Cape S^t· Vincent – 15 Portuguese fishermen.

One of the Algerines went out of the coast of Portugal where they took the Fishermen – off Cape S^t· Vincents.

We should be happy in hearing from you respecting our redemption or if it is our hard lot here to remain we must make the best of it. –

I remain your most obedient & very unfortunate

Rich^d OBryen

NA: RG 59, *Consular Despatches, Algiers, v.1 (C)*; M23, reel 1.

Treaty of Peace and Friendship Between Morocco and the United States

[Morocco, July 15, 1786]
To all Persons to whom these Presents shall come or be made known –
Whereas the United States of America in Congress assembled by their Commission bearing date the twelvth day of May One thousand Seven

hundred and Eighty four thought proper to constitute John Adams, Benjamin Franklin and Thomas Jefferson their Ministers Plenipotentiary, giving to them or a Majority of them full Powers to confer, treat & negotiate with the Ambassador, Minister or Commissioner of His Majesty the Emperor of Morocco concerning a Treaty of Amity and Commerce, to make & receive propositions for such Treaty and to conclude and sign the same, transmitting it to the United States in Congress assembled for their final Ratification, And by one other Commission bearing date the Eleventh day of March One thousand Seven hundred & Eighty five did further empower the said Ministers Plenipotentiary or a Majority of them, by writing under their hands and Seals to appoint such Agent in the said Business as they might think proper with Authority under the directions and Instructions of the said Ministers to commence & prosecute the said Negotiations & Conferences for the said Treaty provided that the said Treaty should be signed by the said Ministers: And Whereas, We the said John Adams & Thomas Jefferson two of the said Ministers Plenipotentiary (the said Benjamin Franklin being absent) by writing under the Hand and Seal of the said John Adams at London October the fifth, One thousand Seven hundred and Eighty five, & of the said Thomas Jefferson at Paris October the Eleventh of the same Year, did appoint Thomas Barclay, Agent in the Business aforesaid, giving him the Powers therein, which by the said second Commission we were authorized to give, and the said Thomas Barclay in pursuance thereof, hath arranged Articles for a Treaty of Amity and Commerce between the United States of America and His Majesty the Emperor of Morocco, which Articles written in the Arabic Language, confirmed by His said Majesty the Emperor of Morocco & seal'd with His Royal Seal, being translated into the Language of the said United States of America, together with the Attestations thereto annexed are in the following Words, To Wit:

In the Name of Almighty God,

This is a Treaty of Peace and Friendship established between Us and the United States of America, which is confirmed, and which we have ordered to be written in this Book and sealed with our Royal Seal at our Court of Morocco on the twenty fifth day of the blessed Month of Shaban, in the Year One thousand two hundred, trusting in God it will remain permanent.–

.1.

We declare that both Parties have agreed that this Treaty consisting of twenty five Articles shall be inserted in this Book and delivered to the Honorable Thomas Barclay, the Agent of the United States now at our Court, with whose Approbation it has been made and who is duly authorized on their Part to treat with us concerning all the Matters contained therein. –

2.

If either of the Parties shall be at War with any Nation whatever, the other Party shall not take a Commission from the Enemy nor fight under their Colors.

.3.

If either of the Parties shall be at War with any Nation whatever and take a Prize belonging to that Nation, and there shall be found on board Subjects or Effects belonging to either of the Parties, the Subjects shall be set at Liberty and the Effects returned to the Owners And, if any Goods belonging to any Nation, with whom either of the Parties shall be at War, shall be loaded on Vessels belonging to the other Party, they shall pass free and unmolested without any attempt being made to take or detain them –

.4.

A Signal or Pass shall be given to all Vessels belonging to both Parties, by which they are to be known when they meet at Sea, and if the Commander of a Ship of War of either Party shall have other Ships under his Convoy, the Declaration of the Commander shall alone be sufficient to exempt any of them from examination –

.5.

If either of the Parties shall be at War, and shall meet a Vessel at Sea belonging to the other, it is agreed that if an examination is to be made, it shall be done by sending a Boat with two or three Men only, and if any Gun shall be fired and injury done without Reason, the offending Party shall make good all damages.

.6.

If any Moor shall bring Citizens of the United States or their Effects to His Majesty the Citizens shall immediately be set at Liberty and the Effects restored, and in like Manner, if any Moor not a Subject of these Dominions shall make Prize of any of the Citizens of America or their Effects and bring them into any of the Ports of His Majesty, they shall be immediately released as they will then be considered as under His Majesty's Protection.–

.7.

If any Vessel of either Party shall put into a Port of the other and have occasion for Provisions or other Supplies, they shall be furnished without any interruption or molestation.

.8.

If any Vessel of the United States shall meet with a Disaster at Sea and put into one of our Ports to repair, she shall be at Liberty to land and reload her Cargo without paying any Duty whatever.

.9.

If any Vessel of the United States shall be cast on Shore on any Part of our Coasts, she shall remain at the disposition of the Owners and no one shall attempt going near her without their Approbation, as she is then considered particularly under our Protection, and if any Vessel of the United States shall be forced to put into our Ports, by Stress of weather or otherwise, she shall not be compelled to land her Cargo, but shall remain in tranquillity untill the Commander shall think proper to proceed on his Voyage.

.10.

If any Vessel of either of the Parties shall have an engagement with a Vessel belonging to any of the Christian Powers within Gun shot of the Forts of the other, the Vessel so engaged shall be defended and protected as much as possible untill she is in safety; And if any American Vessel shall be cast on shore on the Coast of Wadnoon or any Coast thereabout, the People belonging to her shall be protected and assisted untill by the help of God, they shall be sent to their Country.

.11.

If we shall be at War with any Christian Power and any of our Vessels sail from the Ports of the United States, no Vessel belonging to the Enemy shall follow within twenty four hours after the Departure of our Vessel and the same Regulation shall be observed towards the American Vessels sailing from our Ports – be their Enemies Moors or Christians –

.12

If any Ship of War belonging to the United States shall put into any of our Ports she shall not be examined on any Pretence whatever, even though she should have fugitive Slaves on Board, nor shall the Governor or Commander of the Place compel them to be brought on Shore on any pretext, nor require any payment for them.

13.

If a Ship of War of either Party shall put into a Port of the other and salute, it shall be returned from the Fort, with an equal Number of Guns, not with more or less –

.14.

The Commerce with the United States shall be on the same footing as is the Commerce with Spain or as that with the most favored Nation for the time being and their Citizens shall be respected and esteemed and have full Liberty to pass and repass our Country and Sea Ports whenever they please without interruption –

.15.

Merchants of both Countries shall employ only such interpreters, & such other Persons to assist them in their Business, as they shall think proper. No Commander of a Vessel shall transport his Cargo on board another Vessel, he shall not be detained in Port, longer than he may think proper, and all persons employed in loading or unloading Goods or in any other Labor whatever, shall be paid at the Customary rates, not more and not less—

.16.

In case of a War between the Parties, the Prisoners are not to be made Slaves, but to be exchanged one for another, Captain for Captain, Officer for Officer and one private Man for another; and if there shall prove a difficiency on either side, it shall be made up by the payment of one hundred Mexican Dollars for each Person wanting; And it is agreed that all Prisoners shall be exchanged in twelve Months from the Time of their being taken, and that this exchange may be effected by a Merchant or any other Person authorized by either of the Parties –

.17.

Merchants shall not be compelled to buy or Sell any kind of Goods but such as they shall think proper; and may buy and sell all sorts of Merchandise but such as are prohibeted to the other Christian Nations.

.18.

All goods shall be weighed and examined before they are sent on board, and to avoid all detention of Vessels, no examination shall afterwards be made, unless it shall first be proved that contraband Goods have been sent on board, in which Case the Persons who took the contraband Goods on board shall be punished according to the Usage and Custom of the Country and no other Person whatever shall be injured, nor shall the Ship or Cargo incur any Penalty or damage whatever –

.19.

No Vessel shall be detained in Port on any pretence whatever, nor be obliged to take on board any Article ~~whatever~~ without the consent of the Commander who shall be at full Liberty to agree for the Freight of any Goods he takes on board –

.20.

If any of the Citizens of the United States, any Persons under their Protection, shall have any disputes with each other, the Consul shall decide between the Parties and whenever the Consul shall require any Aid or Assistance from our Government to enforce his decisions it shall be immediately granted to him –

.21.

If a Citizen of the United States should kill or wound a Moor or on the contrary if a Moor shall kill or wound a Citizen of the United States, the Law of the Country shall take place and equal Justice shall be rendered, the Consul assisting at the Tryal, and if any Delinquent shall make his escape, the Consul shall not be answerable for him in any manner whatever. –

22^d

If an American Citizen shall die in our Country and no Will shall appear, the Consul shall take possession of his Effects, and if there shall be no Consul, the Effects shall be deposited in the hands of some Person worthy of Trust untill the Party shall appear who has a Right to demand them, but if the Heir to the Person deceased be present, the Property shall be delivered to him without interruption; and if a Will shall appear, the Property shall descend agreeable to that Will, as soon as the Consul shall declare the Validity thereof. –

.23.

The Consuls of the United States of America shall reside in any Sea Port of our Dominions that they shall think proper, And they shall be respected and enjoy all the Privileges which the Consuls of any other Nation enjoy, and if any of the Citizens of the United States shall contract any Debts or engagements the Consul shall not be in any Manner accountable for them, unless he shall have given a Promise in writing for the payment or fulfilling thereof without which promise in Writing no Application to him for any redress shall be made –

.24.

If any differences shall arise by either Party Infringing on any of the Articles of this Treaty, Peace and Harmony shall remain notwithstanding in the fullest force, untill a friendly Application shall be made for an Arrangement, and untill that Application shall be rejected, no appeal shall be made to Arms. And if a War shall break out between the Parties, Nine Months shall be granted to all the Subjects of both Parties, to dispose of their Effects and retire with their Property. And it is further declared that whatever indulgences in Trade or otherwise shall be granted to any of the Christian Powers, the Citizens of the United States shall be equally entitled to them. –

.25.

This Treaty shall continue in full Force, with the help of God for Fifty Years. –

We Have delivered this Book into the Hands of the before-mentioned Thomas Barclay on the first day of the blessed Month of Ramadan, in the Year One thousand two hundred. –

I Certify that the annex'd is a true Copy of the Translation made by Isaac

Cardoza Nuñez, Interpreter at Morocco, of the Treaty between the Emperor of Morocco and the United States of America. –

Tho⁸ Barclay

Translation of the additional Article

Grace to the only God

I the underwritten the Servant of God, Taher Ben Abtelhack Fennish do certify that His Imperial Majesty my Master (whom God preserve) having concluded a Treaty of Peace and Commerce with the United States of America has ordered me the better to compleat it and in addition of the tenth Article of the Treaty to declare "That, if any Vessel belonging to the United States shall be in any of the Ports of His Majesty's Dominions, or within Gunshot of his Forts, she shall be protected as much as possible and no Vessel whatever belonging either to Moorish or Christian Powers with whom the United States may be at War, shall be permitted to follow or engage her, as we now deem the Citizens of America our good Friends" –

And in obedience to His Majesty's Commands I certify this Declaration by putting my hand and Seal to it, on the Eighteenth day of Ramandan in the Year One thousand two hundred.

The Servant of the King my Master whom God preserve.

Taher Ben Abdelhack Fennish[1]

I do Certify that the above is a True Copy of the Translation made at Morocco by Isaac Cardoza Nunes, Interpreter, of a Declaration made and Signed by Sidi Hage Tahar Fennish in Addition to the Treaty between the Emperor of Morocco and the United States of America which Declaration the said Tahar Fennish made by the Express Directions of His Majesty.

Tho⁸ Barclay

Note, The Ramadan of the Year of the Hegira, 1200 Commenced on the 28ᵗʰ· June in the Year of our Lord 1786 –

Now know Ye that We the said John Adams & Thomas Jefferson Ministers Plenipotentiary aforesaid do approve & conclude the said Treaty and every Article and Clause therein contained, reserving the same nevertheless to the United States in Congress assembled for their final Ratification.

In testimony whereof we have signed the same with our Names and Seals, at the Places of our respective residence and at the dates expressed under our signatures respectively. –   John Adams.

London January 25. 1787.
Th: Jefferson
Paris January 1. 1787.

NA: PCC, item 91, pp. 215-229 (C); M247, reel 119.

[1] Fennish, Tahar ben Abdelhack. Moroccan government official charged with negotiating the treaty of peace and commerce between the United States and Morocco.

John Adams to John Jay

Sir   London July 15. 1786

On Wednesday, the 13. the Marquis of Carmarthen informed me, that, Captain Stanhope of the *Mercury* Man of War, to use his Lordships own Words "had received a Severe Rap over the Knuckles, from the Lords of the Admiralty, for his Conduct at Boston." His Lordship had received a Letter from Lord How, accompanied with a long dull Letter from Captain Stanhope which instead of being a justification of his Conduct was rather an Aggravation of it." – His Lordship then called in his Under Secretary of State, Mr Fraser, and ordered the Letter from the Admiralty to be brought to him, which he read to me. – It informed him, that the Lords of the Admiralty, had called upon Captain Stanhope, for his justification of his Conduct to Governor Bowdoin and had received from him the Letter, inclosed for the Information of his Majesty, which their Lordships however thought no Apology. That their Lordships had accordingly, Signified to Captain Stanhope *their Sensible Displeasure* at his Conduct; and as the *Mercury* had been ordered home from the American station, their Lordships would take Special Care, that he should be no longer continued in that Service.

The Secretary of State was pleased to say farther that he would speak to Lord Sidney, concerning the Affair of the Eastern Line, that Sir Guy Carleton might have Instructions concerning it before he went out.

His Lordship was asked if any Appointment had been made of a Minister Plenipotentiary to the United States, and answered "Not yet."

With great Respect I have the Honour to be, Sir your most obedient and most humble servant   John Adams.

Read 19 Septr 1786

NA: PCC, *item 84, v. 6, pp. 339-342 (ALS); M247, reel 113.*

William Carmichael to John Jay

Sir   Madrid 15th July 1786

As I presume Mr Barclay may not have it in his power to forward to Congress or to their Ministers at Paris & London, an account of the Success of his mission in Morocco, I do myself the honor of transmitting the inclosed copies, N$^{o.}$ 1 & 2. of papers which I received yesterday from his Excel^y the Ct de Florida Blanca. that Minister had the goodness to permit me to see the originals from which these extracts are made & I am happy to find by the conduct of the Court of Spain in this Instance, that

I have not been deceived in the Ideas which I have long entertained of the sincere disposition of the present Minister to establish a mutual good understanding on the basis of reciprocal Candor & good offices –

Mr Lamb will have informed you of the Situation of our affairs at Algiers. I have given their Excellencies Messrs Adams and Jefferson, to whom Congress hath judged proper to confide that negotiation, all the intelligence in my power to afford them. I make no doubt those Gentlemen will have transmitted to you copies of the essential part of my Letters as well as of various papers I have forwarded for their Information. My Duty will not permit me to conceal that the Ct D'Expilly who negotiates on the part of this Country at Algiers appears dissatisfied with the Conduct of Mr Lamb. But as the Latter asserts that neither the Consul of France nor the C˙ D'Expilly manifested an Inclination to contribute to his success, I shall refrain from making any other Observation on this subject, than that even if the Complaints of the Count were well founded – they ought not to have been rendered notorious. Their publicity thro' the channels above indictated, hath occasioned to myself in particular much anxiety & some trouble to remove the prejudices to which the circumstance gave rise. It appears that this Court was determined to finish the negotiation with Algiers as soon as possible & I have reason to beleive that the C˙ D'Expilly was directed to sign the treaty without insisting on former pretensions even to leave to a distinct negotiation the ransom of the Spanish Slaves. –

I am apprehensive the Treaty will not answer the Expectations of this Ministry nor compensate for the sum expended to procure it. Portugal & Naples will not be included in the Treaty in question. Their peace with the regency is problematical –

. . . . .

I have the honor to be with the sincerest Respect Sir Your most Obed˙ Humble Ser˙ W™˙ Carmichael

NA: PCC, item 88, pp. 428-431 (ALS); M247, reel 116.

Francisco Chiappe's Commission as United States Agent at Morocco

[Morocco, July 15, 1786]

Copy of a commission given to Don Francisco Chiappe at Morocco with the names of the Agents at Mogadore & Tangiers to whom commissions have also been given.

I the underwritten Thomas Barclay Agent for the United States of America at Morocco, having received from his Imperial Majesty a treaty of peace &

commerce between his Majesty & the said United States dated on the first day of the Ramodan in the present year of the Hegera one thousand two hundred, & thinking it necessary that an Agent residing at Morocco should be appointed to take proper care of all matters relative to such of the citizens of America as may possibly arrive in any part of the empire of Morocco & shall have occasion to apply for aid or assistance to such agent. As also that a fit & proper chanel may be formed, whereby all public papers relative to America may be transmitted to His Majesty; until the will and pleasure of Congress be known, I do hereby with the consent & approbation of his Imperial Majesty the Emperor of Morocco, constitute & appoint Mr· Francis Chiappi of the City of Morocco, Agent for the United States, ~~touching~~ until the pleasure of the Honorable the Congress of the United States touching this matter shall be known.

In testimony whereof I hereunto put my hand & seal, dated Morocco the fifteenth day of July in the year of our Lord 1786.   Thos Barclay
Agent at Morocco.................   Francis Chiappi
      at Magadore   Joseph Chiappi – who is Consul for
                                   Genoa & Vice-consul for Venise
      at Tangiers   Girolamo Chiappi – who is Consul for
                                   Venise & vice-consul for Genoa.

NA: PCC, item 91, pp. 322-323 (C); M247, reel 119.

James Monroe to Thomas Jefferson

Dear Sir   New York July 16th· 1786
...In my last I advis'd you of an intrigue on foot under the management of Jay to occlude the Missisipi supported by the delegation of Massachusets – since my last no further measures have been openly taken in the business yet it is not relinquish'd – as yet there hath not been a fair tryal of the sense of Congress on the subject. I have a conviction in my own mind that Jay has manag'd this negociation dishonestly. on the other hand I am persuaded that the minister here has no power on the subject – yet I am firmly persuaded that he has conducted himself in such manner in this business as to give him & his court hopes which the sense of Congress nor his instructions authorise. Having been on all foreign business laterly, indeed since you left us, I have had a[n] opportunity of knowing him well, & this communication is founded in circumstances this opportunity hath given me....I am Dear Sir yr. affectinate friend & servant
                                            Jas· Monroe

LC: Jefferson Papers, microfilm reel 5 (ALS).

Thomas Barclay to John Adams and Thomas Jefferson

Gentlemen   Morocco 16th. July 1786.

I wrote you on the 26th. of last Month and expected to have followed my Letter in a Week, but Several unforeseen Matters have hitherto detained us; however I expect we shall set out tomorrow or the day following. The 13th. Instant the Treaty was sent to me by the Effendi Since which some important alterations have been made which the Villainy & carelessness of the Talbe Houdrani (to whom the drawing was committed) made necessary; and yesterday it was again delivered from Tahar Fennish, to whose hands the King committed the arrangement of the Matter. It still wants an additional Article, or rather a Declaration which His Majesty has permitted to be made in his Name, but which he desired might not make a Part of the Treaty: when this is done, it will stand as I described it in my last Letter Viz^{t.} "There is only one Article more I wish to see inserted & that I think will never prove of any Consequence." When I send you the Treaty it will be necessary to accompany it with some Remarks, with which I will not now trouble you, & the only one I shall make is, that the King throughout the whole has acted in a Manner the most gracious and condescending, and I really believe the Americans possess as much of his Respect & Regard as does any Christian Nation whatever. If you should think my Services at Algiers, Tunis or Tripoli necessary, I hope your Commands will meet me in the South of Spain, for after returning to Paris it will be utterly impossible for me to engage further in the Business. A peace with the Barbary Powers is absolutely essential to the Commerce of our Country, and I think a general one might be made notwithstanding the impediments that appear. The Emperor has ordered five Frigates on a Cruize in the Atlantic Ocean; He is now at Peace with all the World except Russia, Malta, Hamburg and Dantzick – A Treaty with the first of these Powers was concluded on, and the Articles drawn; but it was afterwards broken off. The Emperor complains much of the Treatment he receives from England, & Mr. Duff, who came here some time ago as Pro-Consul, returned the day before we arrived, highly offended at his Reception, the Emperor having refused to receive the Letter which Lord Sydney wrote, Saying he would read no Letters from England but Such as were written by the King – I had a Letter yesterday from Mr. Carmichael and was in great hopes it would have cover-ed one from you, but I am hitherto without the Pleasure of hearing from you:

I am allways, Gentlemen Your most obet. humble Servant.

Rec^{d} 1st. Sept^{r.}   Thos Barclay

MHS: *The Adams Papers*, microfilm reel 368 (ALS).

Thomas Jefferson's Estimate of American Exports and Imports

[Paris, July 17, 1786]

Estimate of the Exports of the United States of America

	to Europe	to West Indies	Total
	Louis	Louis	Louis
Fish	107,000	50,000	157,000
Fish oil	181,688	9,562	191,250
Fish-bones	8,400		8,400
Salted meats		131,500	131,500
Live stock		99,000	99,000
Butter & cheese		18,000	18,000
Flour, bread, 660,000 barrels			
	330,000	330,000	660,000
Wheat, 2,210,000 bushels			
	331,000		331,000
Indian corn pulse	30,000	61,000	91,000
Rice 130,000 barrels	189,350	70,650	260,000
Indigo	51,700		51,700
Tobacco 87,000 hogsheads			
	1,305,000		1,305,000
Potash 20,000 barrels	49,000		49,000
Peltry	184,900		184,900
Flax-seed	79,500		79,500
Hemp	21,000		21,000
Iron, copper	84,000	6,000	90,000
Turpentine &c. 60000 barrels			
	29,410	1,840	31,250
Timber, lumber	82,000	164,000	246,000
Ships, 300	216,500		216,500
Miscellanies	22,000		22,000
	3,302,448	941,552	4,244,000

Estimate of the Imports of the United States of America
From Europe & Africa

Woolen cloths of every description
Linens of every description
Hosiery hats
Gloves, shoes, boots, Saddlery & other things of leather.
Silks, gold & silver lace, jewellry, millinery, toys

East India goods –
Porcelain, glass, earthen ware.
Silver, copper, brass, tin, pewter, lead, steel, Iron in every form
Upholstery, cabinet work, painter's Colours
cheese, pickles, confitures, chocolate
Wine – 2000 Tons @ 100 Louis 200,000 Louis. brandy, beer
Medicinal drugs, snuff, bees-wax
Books, stationary, mill stones & grind stones, marble
Sail cloth, cordage, Ship chandlery, fishing tackle, Ivory, ebony, barwood,
    dyewood
Slaves salt, 521,225 bushels at 24 sous   <u>Louis 26,062.6</u>
                                    Louis 3,039,000.00

From the West Indies

	Louis.	liv.	s.
Salt 500,484 bushels @ 24 sous	25,024	4	16
Fruits	2,239	12	00
Cocoa 576,589^{lb} at 12 sous	25,798	12	00
Coffee – 327,360^{lb} at 16 sous	15,249	14	5
Sugar 10,232,432^{lb}	168,007	00	00
Molasses 3,645,464 gallons at 24 sous	186,281	19	4
Rum 3,888,370 gallons at 2$^{#}$ 14s	437,441	15	00
Ginger, pimenta	1,395	1	4
Cotton 356,591^{lb} at 24 sous	17,829	13	4
Skins	7,870	6	00
Indigo 4,352^{lb} at 5^{f} 8 sous.	979	4	16
Ivory, turtle shell	247	4	16
Lignum vitae, sarsaparilla, fustic, annetas	5,170	00	00
Logwood	13,624	21	00
Mahogany	23,280	00	00
			927,438-8-8
	[Total]		3,966,438 8 8

NA: PCC, *item 87, v. 1, pp. 703-704* (C); M247, *reel 115*.

William Carmichael to Thomas Jefferson

Dear Sir   Madrid 18 July 1786
    I have just rec^d the inclosed Letters from Mr Lamb which I forward by
the Same Courier to whom I intrusted my last for Your Exc$^{y.}$ Mr Lamb
writes me that his health not permitting him to journey by land he has
resigned his commission & means immediately to close his public acc$^{nts.}$

The C^t DExpilly & Another Agent of Spain employed at Algiers & at Tunis are now here –

The first is much attached to me, & the Other I shall cultivate – & thro' their means be enabled to obtain intelligence with respect to the situation of Affairs on the Barbary Coast & make such Insinuations as Yourself and Mr Adams may judge proper for the Public interest. Whatever may be the decision of Congress I think it necessary to induce the Algerines to beleive that the United States are more disposed to be at peace than at war with them –

Their Minister of Marine desires peace with us. & appears apprehensive of seeing American Cruisers in the Mediterranean – I have ways of cultivating his Friendly disposition & exciting his apprehensions – The C^t Expilly informed me of a circumstance that marks Strongly the Rancor of the British in all parts of the world to us. I omitted mentioning it to you, because I wished to have previously an exact detail of the Transaction in writing from the C^t himself – He tells me that After Mr Lambs departure from Algiers, The British Consul at Barcelona Mr Gregory advised Mr Logie Consul at Algiers, that the Spanish papers procured by Mr Lamb for his Vessel were not regular, – that Mr Lamb had taken with him 80000 P^s &c & that the Dey might seize the vessel as american property – Mr Logie immediately communicated this information to the Dey; The Vessel having been sent by the C^t D'Expillys desire to Tunis on public business – The Dey replied That he had permitted the American Officers to Land, that they were gone Away & as he supposed, had taken their money with them. That the vessel was now under his protection & Concluded by telling the Consul to mind his own business & not intermeddle in future with what did not concern him. This Conduct of the British Consuls must arise from the Court, for their private Characters are good & they are men of Liberal and humane principles – As soon as the Treaty is published I will send you a copy of it. D'Expilly will return in a few weeks to Algiers to terminate the ransom of the Slaves & to aid the Neopolitan & Portuguese envoys in their Negotiation. The Success of which is doubtful — These Pirates will have Russia & the Emperor on their hands as in the last cruise They have taken a Russian Vessel worth 80000 P^s & a Tuscan ship with forty Prisoners. The Russian Minister at this court,[1] to whom I gave the first information of this capture, tells me that he will write to the Dey as a Pacha of the Turkish Empire & inclose him a copy of the Article of their Treaty with the Port, demanding an immediate restitution of the Vessel & People with damages – He added, that he is sure of the approbation of his Sovereign, who will be pleased to see one of her Ministers writing in a haughty Stile to a Power that all Europe courts at present. When shall we be in a situation to do this?...

I have the honor to be With Great respect Your Exc^{ys.} Obed^{t.} Hb^{le.} Ser^t
Wm. Carmichael

. . . . .

LC: *Jefferson Papers, microfilm reel 5 (ALS).*
¹ Zinov'ev, Stepan Stepanovich. Russian diplomat. Minister to Spain, 1771-1792.

John Lamb to Thomas Jefferson

Alicant July 18th. 1786.
July 15th I for^{dd.} to your Excellencys a letter of which this is nea[r]ly a
Duplicate as my first may not come to hand, I find your Excellency had not
rec^d my letters I wrote by Mr. Randall in them I gave an Exact acc^{t.} of
Algiers as I could collect whilst I stay^d in that place and likewise how we
were situated ther, and sent Duplicates of the Same to Congress, & by safe
opertunityes, one Via Cades under cover to Mr. Gardoqui, Directly to new
york, and m^{r.} Randall writes me of the 20th. June Bourdeaux that he hath
forwd the other Emediately to Philadelphia, So that their is not the least
Doubt of Congress haveing a full acc^{t.} of all my Proceedings as I ware
present myself, for I can add nothing to the acc^{t.} I have given to your
Excellency, neither to Congress ware I presant. I have forw^{dd.} a Coppy of
all my letters to Congress, Since I have been on this business, at the time
I wrote to Excellencys: my Indisposition will not permitt me to undertake
the Journey that Your Excellencys has pointed out. therefore I am under the
necessity to begg a Settlement of my Reasonable Acct^{s.} Since I have been
on this Journey, and Returne the letter of Credite to Your Excellencys
Orders. I had Comm^{d.} an Acquaintance with one of the princaple officers
at Algiers, and from him I had Greate Expectations of a Settlement with
that Regency by next Season, Or at least to have the last price for Our
unfortunate people, and what they would have for a peace, and to Strive
for hostile proceeding to sease for one year, so that Congress might have
more time to prepare, and suppos^d that in case I brought to pass the above
which I had every Incouragment of, it would at least be worth the Expences
we have allreadi been at. these ware my reasons and these my Prospect and
in consequence of the same thought best to Porseveor. and Exiboted as
Soon as I possible Could to ministers and Likewise to Congress, As I well
know how far Short the Apropriation was for the peace and that none
could be Added to it by gentlemen Abroad; it is my Opinion that it is out
of the Power of the united States to force those people to a compliance of
a peace, and to have them Going on in the manner they Do it is not so
well. to buy a peace will no Doubt cost a considerable Sum; but however
notions of a Strong navy hath Given the preference a purchase &c

I am Sencoble that your Excellency have rec^d. maney letters from Gentlemen on my mission, and I think they wrote without consideration as in fact when they wrote they know^d. nothing of the matter. a coppy hath been Sent to your Excellency from algiers or rather forw^dd. from Madrid. the Gentleman whome wrote that letter know^d. nothing of my business in Algiers and of Course Could not write the Truth. I find Some of the Sentances in his letter speaking of my Business, is entirely false: it is necessary to have Sum order given on Acc^t. of our people in Algiers. they ware Strip^d. of their cloathing and had maney necessary Debts against them when I came to Algiers. out of humanity I paid for their Cloaths and the Rest of their Obligation I paid, looking on them but Reasonable, and they amounted with what money I left to Upwards of Eight hundred hard Dollars, leaveing Sum money with them: now they write me it is Allmost out and Verey soon they will be in a Verey miserable Condition indeed.

I am with Due Respect Your Excellency most Obedient Hm^le. Servt.

John Lamb

LC: Jefferson Papers, microfilm reel 5 (ALS).

John Adams to John Jay

Dear Sir   London July 30. 1786

I have received, the Letter you did me the Honour to write me, on the Sixth of June, with the Ratification of the Treaty with Prussia. As the Term limited, is near expiring, I shall go over to Holland or send Col Smith, to make the Exchange.

.   .   .   .   .

I cannot but lament from my inmost Soul, that Lust for Paper Money which appears in some Part of the United States: there will never be any Uniform Rule, if there is a Sense of Justice, nor any clear Credit public or private, nor any Settled Confidence in publick Men or Measures, untill Paper Money is done away.

It is a great Satisfaction to me, to learn that you have rec^d in my Letter of the fourth of March the Answer of this Court to the Memorial respecting the Posts. As that is a Dispatch of more importance than all others you have rec^d from me. I shall be anxious to know your Sentiments upon it. You will not expect me to answer Lord Carmarthens Letter, nor to take any further Steps concerning it untill I shall receive the orders of Congress.

I wish for the Instructions of that August Body concerning a Requisition in their Name for the Negroes. Whether I am to demand Payment for them, at what Prices, and for what Number.

With great Regard I have the honour to be &c   John Adams

NA: PCC, item 84, v. 6, pp. 343-344 (ALS); M247, reel 113.

John Adams to John Jay

Dear Sir   London July 31. 1786

Paul Randall Esqʳ, who has been with Mʳ· Lamb to Algiers will have the Honour to deliver this Letter. in order to lay before Congress the earliest Information of all that has come to his Knowledge, in the Course of his Journeys and Voyages he proposes to return, without loss of Time to New York. He has conducted, as far as I can judge, with Prudence and Fidelity, and has merited a Recommendation to Congress.

His Salary, will be paid him by Mʳ Lamb if arrived in New York, out of the Monies remaining in his Hands. Mʳ Lamb has drawn upon me for Three Thousand two hundred and twelve Pounds twelve Shillings Sterling, and his Bills for that Sum have been accepted and paid. He will account with Congress for the Expenditure of it, and pay the Ballance into their Treasury. Mʳ Randal was at some Small Expence for Cloathing, which it will be but reasonable to allow him.

There are, it seems, at Algiers, one and twenty Prisoners taken on board the two American Vessells. Mʳ Lamb has left some Money for their Benefit, but however anxious they may be to be redeemed from Captivity, there is reason to fear, that all that Money will be expended before they obtain their Liberty, in which Case they will probably write to me for more. I should therefore be happy to receive the Instructions of Congress, whether I may be permitted to releive them and how far, or whether they must be left to the Care and Expence of their Friends in America. if the last should be the Determination of Congress, I should think it will be necessary that some publick Advertisement should be made that those Friends may know their Duty according to their Abilities. The Provision that is made, for the Subsistence and Cloathing of Captives either by the Government or their Masters is said to be very inadequate to their Comfort and Necessities.

With great Respect and regard I have the Honour to be, dear Sir your most obedient and most humble Servant   John Adams.

Read 18 Sept 1786

NA: PCC, item 84, v. 6, pp. 347-350 (ALS); M247, reel 113.

William Carmichael to Thomas Jefferson

Madrid 31 July 1786

. . . . .

...The Court of Spain has conducted itself so generously in our affair with the Emperor of Morocco, I have so many reasons to be assured of the King's & Minister's desire to serve us in promoting our accomodation with the other Barbary powers, that if my advice could have the least weight, I should counsel our Ministers to sollicit the good offices of his CM to further the views of the States on this head. I will stake my reputation on the best endeavours of Spain & forfeit all confidence if the Ct de Florida Blanca doth not act as efficaciously as circumstances will permit him to effect what he hath already promised me. You Sir, ought to know our present situation – particularly with GB. Have just learned *positively* what I suspected long ago that the British ministry would accomodate their disputes with respect to the Mosquito shore with Spain. This has been done to the satisfaction of this Court. Campo at London has the merit of this act of convention, tho' the minister of G.B. here has had the whole trouble. I have not seen the articles of this arrangement but I know that the British are to evacuate the Mosquito shore & that they think themselves recompensed by cessions more extensive in another quarter.

. . . . .

The Ct de F.B. has been indisposed for some time. This is a public misfortune but still more to me personally. Mr. Barclay mentions to me that the English are in disgrace in Morocco. If your powers from Congress are so extensive as to admit mr Barclay's negociating in Barbary, if even you can conjointly with Mr Adams take upon you what certainly I would do to consult the public interest without orders, you will allow that gentleman to make overtures in order to prevent hostilities at least to give time to Congress to adopt such measures as they may judge proper. Be assured that all that I can do to second the operations of a man proper to be employed, as he is, I shall do cheerfully....

NA: PCC, *item 87, v. 1, pp. 646-649 (C); M247, reel 115.*

John Adams to Thomas Jefferson

Dear Sir   London July 31. 1786
   I have rec^d, the Ratification of the Prussian Treaty, and next Thursday Shall Sett off for the Hague in order to exchange it with the Baron De Thulemeyer.

Your favour of the 11th. instant I have rec^{d.} There are great and weighty Considerations urged in it in favour of arming against the Algerines, and I confess, if our States could be brought to agree, in the Measure, I Should be very willing to resolve upon external War with them. But in Such a Case We ought to conduct the War with Vigour, and protect our Trade and People. The Resolution to fight them would raise the Spirits and Courage of our Countrymen immediately, and We might obtain the Glory of finally breaking up these nests of Banditti. But Congress will never, or at least not for Years, take any Such Resolution, and in the mean time our Trade and Honour suffers beyond Calculation. – We ought not to fight them at all, unless we determine to fight them forever. This thought is I fear, too rugged for our People to bear. to fight them at the expence of Millions, and make Peace after all by giving more Money and larger Presents than would now procure, perpetual Peace, Seems not to be Oeconomical. – Did Monsieur De Massac, carry his Point without making the Presents. Did Louis 14. obtain his Point without making the Presents? has not France made Presents ever Since? Did any Nation ever make Peace with any one Barbary State, without making the Presents? is there one Example of it? I believe not, and fancy you will find that even Massac himself made the Presents.

I agree in the Opinion of the Wisdom and Necessity of a Navy for other Uses, but am apprehensive it will make bad worse with the Algerines. I will go all Lengths with you in promoting a Navy, whether to be applied to the Algerines or not. but I think at the same time We should treat. Your Letter however has made me easier upon this Point. – Nevertheless I think you have rather under calculated the Force necessary to humble the Algerines. They have now fifty Gun Boats, which being Small Objects in Smooth Water against great Ships in rough Water are very formidable. None of these existed in the time of Monsieur Massac. The Harbour of Algiers too is fortified all round, which it was not, in Mr Massacs time, which renders it more difficult and dangerous to attempt a Blockade.

I know not what dependence is to be put upon Portugal and Naples, in Case of a War with the Barbarians. perhaps they might assist us, in some degree. –

Blocking Algiers would not obtain Peace with Morocco Tunis or Tripoli, So that our Commerce would still be exposed.

After all, tho I am glad We have exchanged a Letter upon the Subject, I perceive that neither Force nor Money will be Applied. Our States are so backward that they will do nothing for Some Years. if they get Money enough to discharge the Demands upon them in Europe, already incurred, I shall be agreeably disappointed. – A Disposition Seems rather to prevail among our Citizens to give up all Ideas of Navigation and naval Power, and lay themselves consequently at the Mercy of Foreigners, even for the Price of their Produce. – It is their Concern, and We must Submit. for your Plan of fighting will no more be adopted than mine of negotiating. – This is more humiliating to me, than giving the Presents would be. I have a Letter from Mr Jay of 7. July, by Packet, containing nothing but an Acknowledgment of the Receipt of our Letter of 25. of April. –

N. Hampshire and R. Island have Suspended their Navigation Acts and Massachusetts now left alone will suspend theirs, So that all will be left to the Convention, whose System if they form one, will not be compleated adopted and begin to operate under Several Years. –

Congress have rec^d the Answer which you Saw, to my Memorial of 30 Nov. and Mr Ramsay writes me, he is not distressed at it, because it will produce a repeal of all the Laws, against recovering private Debts.

With every Sentiment of Friendship I am yours   John Adams

LC: *Jefferson Papers, microfilm reel 6 (ALS).*

Louis Guillaume Otto to Comte de Vergennes

[Translation]

N$^{o.}$ 56   New York, 1 August 1786.
My Lord.

In a brief visit that I made to Boston, I took care to go back to the source of the opposition that we have always found in the Delegates from Massachusetts with regard to our Consular Convention. I saw with astonishment that the faith of a people who at this moment is generally attached to us had been surprised by the false representations of Mr. Gerry. That Delegate went to Boston in March 1785, and after having requested an extraordinary session of the Senate, he explained to it with much vehemence the disadvantages that would result from a number of French Consuls spread through the continent and *enjoying all the same privileges and prerogatives as the Ambassadors*. The Senate, without taking cognizance of the draft of the convention, and excited by Mr. Gerry's clamors, immediately sent its Delegates the following instructions: "The Legislature is informed that Congress has concluded or is on the point of concluding a convention with the Court of France, declaring that any Consul named by that Court to reside in the United States of America would enjoy all the powers and privileges that are commonly accorded to Ambassadors, and being impressed by the dangerous consequences of such an arrangement, it stipulates to You in the most positive manner for You to oppose the ratification of any convention of this tenor and to take the measures that You think most proper *to prevent the extension of the powers and privileges of the Consuls beyond their customary limits.*" Although this last expression, My Lord, is very vague, the Delegates have taken care to interpret it in the sense that most suited their passions, and knowing that the majority of their Colleagues were not in their favor, they have found means to defer from day to day the deliberations that were to take place on this matter. The present delegation being composed of able men, but who are attached to Mr. Bowdoin, the Governor of Massachusetts and father-in-law of Mr. Temple, the Consul of England, I have reason to believe that the warmth that they put into this discussion comes in great part from the desire of Mr. Bowdoin not to let the French Consuls enjoy greater prerogatives than his son-in-law. This conjecture is confirmed, My Lord, by the great coolness of this Governor for France; he is sprung from a family that the revocation of the Edict of Nantes forced to leave the Kingdom, and we have constantly found in America an implacable hatred among the descendants of these refugees. The talents and the fortune of Mr. Bowdoin render him very powerful in his State; however, he can only act secretly against our interests, and he would risk losing his popularity by showing too much animosity or even indifference to France. Be that as it may, the Delegates from Massachusetts will not be sufficiently strong to counterbalance the dispositions of Congress to conform to His Majesty's desire.

. . . . .

I am with a profound respect My Lord Your most humble and most obedient servant,   Otto.
Received 22 Sept^(ber.)

FFAA: Pol. Corr., U.S., v. 32, f. 32-33vo. (LC transcription).

John Jay to the President of Congress

Sir   N. York 3 Aug^t· 1786
   Every Person to whom is committed the Management of a Negociation, from which many good or ill Consequences will probably result, must find himself placed in a very delicate and responsible Situation. In that Point of Light I consider our present Negociations with Spain, and that my Sentiments on the Subject may be conveyed to Congress with Precision, and authentic Evidence of them preserved, I have reduced them to Writing as concisely and accurately as I could find Leisure to do since I received Notice to attend this Day. –

It appears to me that a proper commercial Treaty with Spain, would be of more Importance to the United States, than any they have formed, or can form, with any other Nation. I am led to entertain this Opinion from the Influence which Spain may, and will have, both on our Politics and our Commerce. –

France whom we consider as our Ally, and to whom we shall naturally turn our Eyes for Aid in case of War &c: is strongly bound to Spain by the family Compact, and the Advantages she derives from it are so various and so great, that it is questionable whether she could even remain neuter in Case of a Rupture between us and his Catholic Majesty. Besides, we are well apprized of the Sentiments of France relative to our western Claims, in which I include that of freely navigating the River Missisipi. I take it for granted that while the Compact in Question exists, France will invariably think it her Interest to prefer the good Will of Spain to the good Will of America, and altho' she would very reluctantly give Umbrage to either, yet if driven to take Part with one or the other, I think it would not be in our Favor. Unless we are Friends with Spain, her Influence whether more or less, on the Counsels of Versailles, will always be against us. –

The Intermarriages between Spain and *Portugal* which have taken place in this and the late Reigns, have given the former a Degree of Influence at the Court of the latter, which she never before possessed; and leading Men in both those Kingdoms, seem disposed to bury former Jealousies and Apprehensions in mutual Confidence and good Offices. How far this System may be perfected, or how long continue, is uncertain; while it lasts, we must expect Good or Evil from it, according as we stand well or ill with Spain. –

Britain would be rejoiced to find us at Variance with Spain on any Points – she remembers that we were once her Subjects, and loves us not – she perceives that we are her most important Rivals in the Spanish Trade, and that her Nursery of Seamen on the Banks of Newfoundland, will prosper or otherwise as ours of the like kind shall increase or diminish, and it will encrease or diminish in Proportion as we may or may not undersell them at foreign Markets, among which that of Spain is the most advantageous.–

If Spain should be disposed to sink that Scale in Favor of Britain, there is little Reason to doubt but that the latter will offer her powerful Inducements to grant and perpetuate valuable Preferences to her. –

It is hard to say how far these Inducements may extend, or how far they might *both* think it their Interest to join in every Measure tending to impair our Strength, and thereby quiet those Fears with which uneasy Borderers and discontented Neighbours, usually inspire each other. –

Recent Transactions tell us that the Influence of Spain in Barbary is not contemptible. When Time shall have cast a thicker Veil over the Memory of past and long continued Hostilities – when the Convenience of Spanish Money and Spanish Favors shall become better known and more felt at Fez, Algiers &c: it is more than probable that those Powers will be little inclined to disoblige a Nation, whose Arms have given them much Trouble, and from whose Gratuities they derive more Wealth and Advantages than they have ever been able to reap from Depredations, and from Plunder often hardly gained. –

The Influence which the Catholic King will and must have, in greater or lesser Degrees in Italy, with several of whose Sovereigns he is allied by Blood as well as by Treaties, merits some Consideration. The Trade of the Mediterranean deserves our Notice, and Spain has convenient Ports in that Sea. –

In various Ways therefore may Spain promote or oppose our political Interests with several other Countries – and we shall I think either find her in America a very convenient Neighbour, or a very troublesome one. –

They who are acquainted with the Commerce of that Country, can be at no Loss in perceiving or estimating its Value. –

It is well known that they consume more than they export, and consequently that the Balance of Trade is and must be against them – hence it is that the Millions they yearly bring from the Mines of America, so soon disappear, flying out of Spain by every Road and Port in it. –

Details would be tedious, and considering where I am, unnecessary – it is sufficient to observe, that there is scarcely a single Production of this Country but what may be advantageously exchanged in the Spanish European Ports for Gold and Silver. These Advantages however must depend on a Treaty – for Spain like other Nations may admit Foreigners to trade with her or not, and on such Terms only, as she may think proper. –

The Conclusion I draw from what has been said is, that on general Principles of Policy and Commerce, it is the Interest of the United States to be on the best Terms with Spain. This Conclusion would be greatly strengthened by a Review of our present local and other Circumstances – but they are well known, and their Language is strong and intelligible. –

Sir, I do really believe that Spain is at present sincerely disposed to make Friends of us – I believe this, not because they have repeatedly *told* us so – for in my Opinion little Reliance is to be made on the Professions of Courts or Courtiers – they will say what they may think convenient, but they will act according to what they may think their Interest. –

It appears to me that the Independence, Situation, Temper, Resources and other Circumstances of the United States, lead the Court of Spain to regard them with much Attention, & I may add, with Jealousy and Apprehension. –

Their Conduct induces me to think that their present Policy and Design is, to cultivate our Friendship, and ensure the Continuance of it, by such Advantages in a Treaty, as may prevent its becoming our Interest to break with them.

To this Cause I ascribe the Civilities shewn to the United States, by the Release of their Citizens at the Havanna, and by the Interposition of his Catholic Majesty in their Favor at Morocco &c: –

To the same Cause I ascribe the very liberal and beneficial Articles which their Plenipotentiary here is willing to have inserted in the Treaty I am now negociating with him, and which are specified in the following Notes of them Viz.ᵗ –

1. That all commercial Regulations affecting each other shall be founded in perfect Reciprocity. Spanish Merchants shall enjoy all the commercial Privileges of native Merchants in the United States, and American Merchants shall enjoy all the commercial Privileges of native Merchants in the Kingdom of Spain and in the Canaries and other Islands belonging and adjacent thereto. The same Privileges shall extend to their respective Vessels, and Merchandize consisting of the Manufactures and Productions of their respective Countries. –

2. Each Party may establish Consuls in the Countries of the other (excepting such Provinces in Spain, into which none have heretofore been admitted, Viz.ᵗ Bilboa and Guipusca) with such Powers and Privileges as shall be ascertained by a particular Convention. –

3. That the bona fide Manufactures and Productions of the United States (Tobacco only excepted, which shall continue under its present Regulations) may be imported in American or Spanish Vessels, into any Parts of his Majesty's European Dominions and Islands aforesaid, in like Manner as if they were the Productions of Spain. And on the other Hand, that the bona fide Manufactures and Productions of his Majesty's Dominions may be imported into the United States, in spanish or american Vessels in like Manner as if they were the Manufactures and Productions of the said States. And further that all such Duties and Imposts as may mutually be thought necessary to lay on them, by either Party, shall be ascertained and regulated on Principles of exact Reciprocity, by a Tariff to be formed by a Convention for that Purpose to be negociated and made, within *one* Year after the Exchange of the Ratification of this Treaty; and in the mean Time, that no other Duties or Imposts shall be exacted from each others Merchants and Ships, than such as may be payable by Natives in like Cases.

4. That inasmuch as the United States, from not having Mines of Gold and Silver, may often want Supplies of Specie for a circulating Medium, his Catholic Majesty as a Proof of his good Will, agrees to order the Masts &

Timber which may from time to time be wanted for his royal Navy, to be purchased, and paid for in Specie, in the United States Provided the said Masts & Timber shall be of equal Quality, and when brought to Spain, shall not cost more than the like may there be had from other Countries.– 5. It is agreed that the Articles commonly inserted in other Treaties of Commerce for mutual and reciprocal Convenience shall be inserted in this, and that this Treaty and every Article and Stipulation therein shall continue in full Force for   Years to be computed from the Day of the Date thereof. –

These Articles need no Comment. – It is easy to perceive that by them we gain much, and sacrifice or give up nothing. They will not indeed permit our Tobacco to be vended in their Country – but that Prohibition now exists, and will probably continue, whether we do or do not make a Treaty with Spain. –

It is also certain that by Means of the Canaries, our Flour and other Commodities will find the Way to Spanish America, and the Supply of that Market even by a circuitous Route, cannot fail of affording a very lucrative Vent for those Articles. –

Mr Gardoqui is not personally averse to our visiting the Phillipines, but his Instructions do not reach that Point. –

I have Hopes that this may be carried, and in that Case it is obvious we should be the better for the Acapulco Trade. –

I forbear to dwell minutely on these commercial Subjects, because nothing I could say respecting them would be new. –

My Attention is chiefly fixed on two Obstacles, which at present divide us Viz.t the Navigation of the Missisippi and the territorial Limits between them & us.

My Letters written from Spain, when our Affairs were the least promising, evince my Opinion respecting the Missisippi, and oppose every Idea of our relinquishing our Right to navigate it. I entertain the same Sentiments of that Right, and of the Importance of retaining it, which I then did. –

Mr. Gardoqui strongly insists on our relinquishing it. We have had many Conferences and much Reasoning on the Subject, not necessary now to detail – His concluding Answer to all my Arguments has steadily been, that the King will never yield that Point, nor consent to any Compromise about it – for that it always has been and continues to be one of their Maxims of Policy, to exclude all Mankind from their American Shores. –

I have often reminded him that the adjacent Country was filling fast with People, and that the Time must and would come, when they would not submit to seeing a fine River flow before their Doors without using it as a Highway to the Sea for the Transportation of their Productions – that it would therefore be wise to look forward to that Event, and take Care not to sow in the Treaty any Seeds of future Discord – He said that the Time alluded to was far distant, and that Treaties were not to provide for Contingencies so remote and future – for his Part he considered the rapid Settlement of that Country as injurious to the States, and that they would find it necessary to check it. Many fruitless Arguments passed between us, and tho' he would admit that the only way to make Treaties and Friendship permanent, was for neither Party to leave the other any Thing to complain of, yet he would still insist, that the Missisippi must be shut against us. The Truth is, that Courts never admit the Force of any Reasoning or Arguments but such as apply in their Favor; and it is equally true, that even if our Right to that Navigation, or to any Thing else, was expressly declared in Holy Writ, we should be able to provide for the Enjoyment of it no otherwise than by being in Capacity to repel force by force. –

Circumstanced as we are, I think it would be expedient to agree that the Treaty should be limited to twenty five or thirty Years, and that one of the Articles should stipulate that the United States would forbear to use the Navigation of that River below their Territories to the Ocean. Thus the Duration of the Treaty and of the Forbearance in Question, would be limited to the same Period. –

Whether M$^{r.}$ Gardoqui would be content with such an Article I cannot determine, my Instructions restraining me from even sounding him respecting it – I nevertheless think the Experiment worth trying for several Reasons –

> 1. Because unless that Matter can in some way or other be settled, the Treaty however advantageous will not be concluded. –
>
> 2. As that Navigation is not *at present* important, nor will probably become much so, in less than twenty five or thirty Years, a Forbearance to use it while we do not *want* it, is no great Sacrifice.–
>
> 3. Spain now excludes us from that Navigation, and with a strong Hand holds it against us – she will not yield it peaceably, and therefore we can only acquire it by *War* – now as we are not prepared for a War with any Power, as many of the States would be little inclined to a War with Spain for that Object, at this Day; and as such a War would for those and a variety of obvious Reasons be inexpedient, it follows, that Spain will for a long Space of Time yet to come exclude us from that Navigation. Why therefore should we not (for a valuable Consideration too) consent to forbear to use, what we know is not in our Power to use. –
>
> 4. If Spain and the United States should part on this Point – what are the latter to do? Will it after that be consistent with

their Dignity to permit Spain forceably to exclude them from a Right, which at the Expence of a beneficial Treaty, they have asserted? They will find themselves obliged either to do this and be humiliated, or they must attack Spain. Are they ripe and prepared for this? I wish I could say they are. –

It is possible that such an Article if agreed to might lessen one of the Arguments urged to enhance the Value of western Lands: but would not the Spaniards continuing by Force to exclude us from the Navigation, soon have the same Effect? In either Case that Argument must lose some of its Force, but in the one Case America would also lose some of its Dignity – it can be no Question therefore which of the two Cases would be least desirable. –

If such a Compromise should be attempted and not succeed, we shall lose nothing by it for they who take a Lease admit the Right of the Lessor. –

I have some Hope that it would succeed, for I suspect Spain would argue that as we are tempted to this Forbearance now by other Articles in the Treaty, the like Temptations will again induce us to prolong it – besides, I much doubt whether the Minister extends his Views far beyond the Limits of his own Life or Administration – if he can render that easy and satisfactory, he may perhaps without much Reluctance, leave future Disputes to be settled by future Ministers. It is hard to say whether this will or will not be the Case – I am for trying the Experiment, because it can in my Opinion do us no Injury and may produce much Good. –

With respect to territorial Limits, it is clear to me, that Spain can justly claim nothing East of the Missisippi but what may be comprehended within the Bounds of the Floridas. How far those Bounds extend, or ought to extend, may prove a Question of more Difficulty to negociate than to decide. Pains I think should be taken to conciliate and settle all such Matters amicably, and it would be better even to yield a few Acres than to part in ill Humour. If their Demands when ascertained, should prove too extravagant, and too pertinaciously adhered to, one Mode of avoiding a Rupture will still be left Viz.ᵗ referring that Dispute to impartial Commissioners. I do not mean by this, that any third Sovereign should be called in to mediate or arbitrate about the Matter – They make troublesome Arbitrators, and not always the most impartial – I mean private Men for Commissioners – and to me there appears little Difficulty in finding proper ones – for not being prepared for War, I think it much our Interest to avoid placing ourselves in such a Situation, as that our forbearing Hostilities may expose us to Indignities. –

It is much to be wished that all these Matters had lain dormant for Years yet to come – but such Wishes are vain – these Disputes are agitating – they press themselves upon us, and must terminate in Accommodation, or

War, or Disgrace. The last is the worst that can happen, the second we are unprepared for, and therefore our Attention and Endeavours should be bent to the first. –

Permit me, Sir, to make one or two Observations more. If the System of Spain respecting us, really is, what I suppose it to be, then it follows that this is the best Season for making a Treaty with her that can be expected.–

The late War has left her new commercial Engagements to make, particularly with Britain, whose Attention to Commerce leaves us no Room to suppose her indifferent to that with Spain – She is now able & willing to grant us Favors – other Treaties and other Dispositions and Views may render her in future both unable and unwilling to do the like. –

At a Time when other Nations are shewing us no extraordinary Marks of Respect, the Court of Spain is even courting our Friendship by strong Marks not merely of polite and friendly Attention, but by offering us Favors not common for her to hold out or bestow – for I consider the Terms she proposes as far more advantageous than any to be found in her commercial Treaties with other Nations. –

If after all her Endeavours to take us by the Hand, we should hold it back, every Disposition and Passion opposite to kind and friendly ones, will undoubtedly influence her future Conduct. Disappointed in her Views, and mortified by Repulse, and that in the Sight of Europe, we may easily judge what her Feelings would be – nor is it difficult to foresee that those Feelings stimulated by the Jealousies and Apprehensions beforementioned, will naturally precipitate and keep her in a System of Politics from which the United States cannot expect to derive Advantage. –

The Missisippi would continue shut – France would tell us our Claim to it was ill-founded – the Spanish Posts on its Banks, and even those out of Florida in our Country, would be strengthened, and that Nation would there bid us Defiance with Impunity – at least until the American Nation shall become more really and truly a Nation than it at present is. For unblessed with an efficient Government, destitute of Funds and without public Credit either at Home or abroad, we should be obliged to wait in Patience for better Days, or plunge into an unpopular and dangerous War, with very little Prospect of terminating it by a Peace either advantageous or glorious. Supposing this Spanish Business out of Question, yet the Situation of the United States appears to me to be seriously delicate and to call for great Circumspection both at Home and abroad – nor in my Opinion will this cease to be the Case, until a vigorous national Government be formed and public Credit and Confidence established. –

These, Sir, are my Sentiments on these important Subjects: and whether they accord with, or vary from those which may here prevail, yet I shall always remember that I am to be governed by the Instructions, and that it is my Duty faithfully to execute the Orders of Congress. –

John Jay –

NA: PCC, *item 81, v. 2, pp. 193-210 (LS); M247, reel 107.*

Don Diego de Gardoqui to John Jay

[Read in Congress, New York, August 3, 1786]

Spain being by far the greatest consumer of all the European Kingdoms, & haveing besides extensive territories of Consume in her West Indies, it is of course of the greatest ymportance to any foreign nation in all Commercial ynterests. –

England is very contious of the advantages that may be gott by a freindly commerssial Treaty, & leaves no pains to bring it to a happy conclussion as soon as possible. She well Knows that Spain's annual consume of Cod fish, brings her in from 4. to 5. millions of dollars, by which she employs between 5. to 6000 Seamen.

That great quantities of pickled Salmon & Trayn oyl are besides pouring annualy into the Spanish Marketts from her ports.

To this must be add, her great woollen Manufactures, but as Spain is advancing fast in the latter, & will probably stop the ymportation of them, England wants to secure the Fisheries which sees no prospectt of Spain's haveing any at all. –

Under the above principals, England exerts to the utmost to prevent that the American States shou'd come to a freindly good understanding with Spain, fully assur'd that no other nation can out rival them in the valuable branches of fisheries.

She well Knows that the local situation of the United States & other advantages render a much better fish than that of Newfoundland, & that the Spanish marketts afford 1. to 1 1/2 dollars p quintal more to the former. She is besides fully persuaded that the Trade of the States with Spain must rise them amazingly, as their Flour, grain, Rice, Tabaco, & several other smaller articles, such as Lumber, Masts, yards, Bees Wax, &^{ca} are valuable. If it be added to this, the consideration that Spain & the States, are the almost only Masters of this vast Continent, who if well joyn'd may deffy the other powers or at least Keep them in Etternal peace, there can be no doubt of it's being a mutual Interest.

NA: PCC, *item 97, pp. 170-171 (translation); M247, reel 125.*

Sir John Temple to Lord Carmarthen

N⁰· 9.   New York 4th of August 1786
My Lord,

.   .   .   .   .

...I have at last & within these few days been able to procure from
Philadelphia, one of the Counterfeit Mediterranean Passes, Mentioned to
your Lordship in my last! it was Obtained by a person who had it partly
fill'd up as for his own Vessell, in order to prevent suspicion that it was for
me! I have compared it with the true passes, & think it much better done
than I could have supposed! Nevertheless, upon close examination, it is
clearly to be discovered, that it was not struck off from the same plate with
the true Passes. The Lords of the Admiralty & their Secretary, will, I
believe, think their Signatures but too well counterfeited! This Pass cost me
ten guineas, which I trust your Lordship will cause to be repaid into the
hands of my Agent Mr Sneyd. – ...

.   .   .   .   .

With all deference, and Respect, I have the honor to be, My Lord, Your
Lordships most faithfull and Obedient Servant   J: Temple
R Sept· 6th

PRO: FO 4/4, pp. 561-564 (LC transcription).

Congressional Resolution on Slaves Carried Off by the British

[New York] August 9th· 1786.
On a Report of a Committee to whom was referred a letter from the
Secretary for foreign Affairs. –
Resolved That the Secretary for foreign Affairs cause to be made out
Separate lists of the numbers, Names, and owners of the Negroes belonging
to the Citizens of each State and carried away by the British in Contra-
vention of the late Treaty of peace, and that he transmit the said lists to
the Executives of the States to which they respectively belong. –
                                                    Chaˢ Thomson Secʸ·
NA: PCC, item 122, p. 63 (DS); M247, reel 140.

Charles Alexandre de Calonne to Comte de Vergennes

[Translation]

Paris, 9 August 1786.

I had the honor, Sir, to write to you in the month of April last to ask you whether you did not see any disadvantage in having executed the disposition of the decree of 1701, which prohibits receiving by English Ships other Merchandise than that grown or made in England, the entry of which into the Kingdom is particularly permitted.

You desired, Sir, that the execution of that Law be suspended for the duration of the Conferences relative to the Treaty of Commerce under consideration with that power, and you added that the Treaty of 1713 having abrogated in some Manner this disposition of the Decree of 1701, you thought that it was appropriate to wait, whether the Treaty would take place or not, before changing anything in the present state of affairs.

Although the Stipulations of the Treaty of 1713 that are supposed to be reciprocal have not been executed by England, and although She has maintained towards us, as towards the other Powers, her act of Navigation, I have allowed the former state of affairs to stand, as you proposed.

However, Sir, the interest which we have, and of which you were so very conscious, to increase our connections of Commerce with the United States, made me think that one could without disadvantage prohibit the Farmers General from receiving any leaf Tobaccoes that would not be carried directly from the Place of origin to the Ports of the Kingdom by French or American Ships, if the Tobaccoes are of American growth.

I shall wait, Sir, for you to inform me of your opinion in this regard in order to give the Farmers General the order to conform to these dispositions.

I have the honor to be with a most Sincere and inviolable attachment, Sir, your most humble and most obedient Servant.   de Calonne

FFAA: Pol. Corr., U.S., v. 32, f. 37-38 (LC transcription).

John Jay to the President of Congress

Sir   [New York] Office for foreign Affairs 10th August 1786
I have this Moment received an Order of Congress in the following Words viz.t "That the Secretary for foreign Affairs state to Congress without Delay any Information he may have received respecting the Sentiments of the Court of France touching our Right of navigating the Missisippi, also

that he state to Congress the territorial Claims of Spain on the east Side of the Missisippi."

Permit me Sir to observe that it is impossible to execute this Order instantly – because the Sentiments of the Court of France touching our Right to navigate the Missisippi, are to be collected from Paragraphs and Documents so mixed with the Mass of Papers in this Office as to require Time to select and copy. The Evidence we have of the territorial Claims of Spain on the east Side of the Missisippi is in the same Predicament, and some Time will be necessary to extract and arrange it. –

It would be rash in me to attempt making this Statement from Memory, especially as Omissions and Mistakes however accidental and unintentional might give Occasion to unpleasant Doubts and Conjectures. –

I shall immediately lay aside other Business, & diligently apply myself to preparing this Statement; there shall be on my part no avoidable Delay, and the Moment it is finished it shall be transmitted to your Excellency.

I have the Honor to be with great Respect Your Excellency's Most ob^{t.} and very hble: Servt.   John Jay –
Read 10th. –

NA: PCC, item 81, v. 2, pp. 213-214, 216 (LS); M247, reel 107.

James Madison to Thomas Jefferson

Dear Sir   Philad^{a.} Aug: 12^{th:} 1786
...The States which have appointed deputies to Annapolis are N. Hampshire, Mass^{ts.} R. Island, N. Y., N. J. Pen^{a.} Delaware & Virg^{a.}...Many Gentlemen both within & without Cong^{s.} wish to make this Meeting subservient to a plenipotentiary Convention for amending the Confederation. Tho' my wishes are in favor of such an event, yet I despair so much of its accomplishment at the present crisis that I do not extend my views beyond a Commercial Reform. To speak the Truth I almost despair even of this. You will find the cause in a measure now before Congress of which you will receive the details from Col° Monroe. I content myself with hinting that it is a proposed treaty with Spain one article of which she shuts the Missisipi for twenty five or thirty years. passing by the other southern States figure to yourself the effect of such a stipulation on the assembly of Virginia already jealous of northern politics and which will be composed of about thirty members from the western waters, of a majority of others attached to the western country from interests of their own of

their friends or their constituents and of many others who though indifferent to the Mississipi will zealously play off the disgust of its friends against federal measures. Figure to yourself its effect on the people at large on the western waters who are impatiently waiting for a favorable result to negociation with Guardoqui & who will consider themselves as sold by their Atlantic brethren. Will it be an unnatural consequence if they consider themselves as absolved from every federal tie and court some protection for their betrayed rights? This protection will <**> appear more attainable from the maritime power of Britain than from any other quarter; and Britain will be more ready than any other nation to seize an opportunity of embroiling our affairs. What may be the motive with Spain to satisfy herself with a temporary occlusion of the Mississipi at the same time that she holds forth a claim to it as absolutely inadmissible is matter of conjecture only. The patrons of the measure in Congress contend that the Minister who at present governs the Spanish Councils means only to disembarrass himself at the expence of the successors. I should rather suppose he means to work a total separation of interest and affection between the western & eastern settlements and to foment the jealousy between the <*> Eastern & southern States. By the former the population of the western country it may be expected will be checked and the Mississipi so far secured: and by both the general security of Spanish America be promoted. As far as I can learn the assent of <*> nine states in Congress will not at this time be got to the projected treaty. but an unsuccessful attempt by six or seven will favor the views of Spain and be fatal i fear to an augmentation of the federal authority if not to ~~that~~ the little now existing. My personal situation is rendered by this business particularly mortifying. Ever since I have been out of Congress I have been inculcating on our assembly a confidence in the equal attention of Congress to the rights and interests of every part of the republic and on the western <*> members in particular, the necessity of making the Union respectable by new powers to Congress if they wished Congress to negociate with effect for the Mississipi....Wishing you every possible happiness I remain D^r· Sir your affectionate friend & Servt·   J^s· Madison Jr.

.   .   .   .   .

LC: *Madison Papers, microfilm reel 2 (C).*

Louis Guillaume Otto to Comte de Vergennes

[Translation]

Nᵒ· 58.   New York, 13 August 1786.

My Lord.

The commercial convention that is supposed to take place in Annapolis at the beginning of next month now occupies all the Legislatures of America. The Delegates have been named, but one doubts the punctuality of their assembling and their dispositions to concur regarding the general principles of their operations. Everyone is impressed with the need to establish a general plan for the Commerce of the Continent as soon as possible, and the most notable persons from almost all the States assure me that they desire to accord exclusive favors to France and to place extraordinary duties on the Commerce of Great Britain.

Mr. Jay himself has just spoken of it to me with much warmth; I beg You, My Lord, to permit me to quote his very words here. It is not for me to determine the justice of his observations, but it is my duty to transmit to You the opinions of the Americans best informed regarding a matter which is so intimately linked with the prosperity of our Commerce. "We are very much conscious," Mr. Jay told me, "that the Commerce of America is so reduced that extraordinary efforts are necessary to extract it from its present difficulties. We appear to be neglected in Europe because we have scant means, but our situation is such that we should necessarily become a rich and formidable power as soon as a numerous population has caused our industry to develop. Based on these reflections, it would be good policy to cultivate us while we are young and have need of assistance from the European nations; but among all the powers there is none with whom we more eagerly desire to maintain ties of amity and Commerce than France. I am even persuaded that the people in general, and especially Congress, are disposed to accord Your Commerce exclusive favors and to dissolve all the ties by which we still adhere to England. Your wines, your brandies, your manufactures of all kinds suit us better than what we can obtain from other nations; but there are two things that continually oppose themselves to the success of our speculations. They are the difficulty of remittances and the little probity of Your merchants in the shipments they make to America. I could also mention the impediments placed on our exports by Your privileged companies, but we have reason to believe that these difficulties will be dispelled at once. We do not have as much hope with regard to the remittances that we could make in France of various objects which the Kingdom has hitherto obtained from the north of Europe. In according particular favors to our ship timbers and naval stores, a very great service would be rendered to both nations, and Americans would be furnished with a means to pay for the goods they obtain from France. As for the Commerce of the Antilles, it cannot be denied that by facilitating the provisioning of the planter, one will necessarily cause the price of sugars to fall, and that the merchants of Bordeaux, in losing a part of the Trade of their flour, would gain on the other hand a much more considerable exportation of their wines and the other goods which they are in a position to furnish us. Moreover, it is certain that before buying the produce of other nations, it is necessary to sell our own commodities. If Portugal receives our flour, it will pay us for it in wines. In like fashion, all the provisions that we import into St. Domingue or Martinique will serve to pay for the wines of Bordeaux and the other products of the Kingdom. All good Citizens see with chagrin that the impediments placed on the Commerce of the Antilles have hitherto furnished a few ill-intentioned persons with arms against France. One is even persuaded, and I cannot avoid thinking it myself, that there is a secret convention between Your minister and that of Great Britain to exclude us from the islands. If, in place of these difficulties, France would apply herself to attract us by all sorts of favors, I know too well the dispositions and the taste of my compatriots not to assure You that she could possess herself almost entirely of the Commerce of the United States. An object of this importance demands all the attention of Your Court at a time when Congress is about to occupy itself with a general act of navigation; all the attentions will be keenly felt and will produce the best effect."

These reflections, My Lord, have been made to me successively by the principal members of Congress and especially by the influential men of New England. The sentiments of Mr. King, which I have had the honor to report to You, are shared by only a few persons interested in the Newfoundland fisheries. In general, My Lord, I have found in the Northern States the most favorable dispositions in our regard and much animosity against England. It appears that the scant success of the American Commissioners in Barbary, the response made to Mr. Adams by Lord Carmarthen, and the repeated hostilities of the savages have reconciled the heads of all the Governments to us. Mr. Jefferson's despatches, in which he makes mention of several salutary recommendations that You have given him, My Lord, have also produced an excellent effect, and the public has been very content with the resolutions passed by the Committee concerning the supply of tobaccoes. The Contract made with Mr. Morris had alarmed all the planters of Virginia, and I had the honor to inform You at the time of all that had come to me on that subject.

I transmit these details to You, My Lord, with all the more confidence because I see by a letter from M. le Marshal de Castries to M. de la Forest that the Court is not averse to listening to overtures concerning means to facilitate the commerce of the two nations. Permit me to add here that all the favors that can be reconciled with the true interests of our commerce will be received by the Americans with much gratitude. The enthusiasm easily spreads throughout the country by means of the public papers which are found in everyone's hands, and the official letters of Mr. Jefferson or some decree of the Council that favors any branch of America's Commerce make the greatest sensation.

I am with a profound respect My Lord Your most humble and most obedient servant   Otto.

Received 22 Sept[ber.]

FFAA: Pol. Corr., U.S., v. 32, f. 39-42 (LC transcription).

William Carmichael to John Jay

Sir   S[n.] Ildefenso, 14 Augt 1786

.   .   .   .   .

...It seems Mr Lamb's bad state of health will not permit him to leave Alicant where he is at present. He informs me that He means to send to America a vessel which he purchased on public Accpt to convey him to Algiers; But as the C[t.] D'Expilly & others Assure me that this vessel is not properly cleared out as Spanish Property, I declined risquing my Letters. This Vessel might have been sold to this Government at first cost & with all reasonable Incidental charges. In the transaction of these Affairs I have had much vexation, have incurred considerable Expence & I shall have little credit, as measures have been adopted. Our Peace with Morrocco was certain last year, that with Algiers is probable in the course of this year & perhaps still to be attained if proper Methods are pursued. I have given my sentiments to our Ministers on this head & I hope I shall be excused for repeating that if the C[t.] de F. B. lives I will answer for the best endeavours of this Court to contribute to our Pacification with Algiers & the other Barbary Powers. Permit me to observe that hostilities ag[st.] these Pirates without previous arrangements taken in Europe & particularly with the powers who have no Treaties with them, will be attended with much Expence & with little probability of success adequate to the Disbursement: which these hostilities will occasion.

I have the honor to be with great respect Sir Your Most Obed[t.] Hb[le.] Ser[t]   W[m] Carmichael

.   .   .   .   .

NA: PCC, item 88, pp. 456-461 (C); M247, reel 116.

Comte de Vergennes to Charles Alexandre de Calonne

[Translation]

M^r· de Calonne

Versailles, 15 August 1786.

I have received, Sir, the Letter which you did me the honor to write me on the 9th of this month. It has as its object the question of knowing whether, in spite of the treaty of Commerce that we are negotiating with England, we can prohibit the Farmers General from receiving other tobaccoes from America than those brought into our ports by French or American vessels.

You surely recall, Sir, that it was agreed at the Conference held in Berny that the Farmers General would take, at the price agreed upon in the contract made with Mr. Morris, tobaccoes that would come from America in French or American ships, and that tobaccoes coming from England would no longer be admitted.

My opinion is, Sir, that we could not take the execution of this disposition too strictly in hand: our mercantile interest with America imperiously requires it; and we can do it without inconvenience, because the exploitation of the exclusive privilege of Tobacco has nothing in common with the treaty that we are negotiating with Great Britain.

[De Vergennes]

FFAA: Pol. Corr., U.S., v. 32, f. 43-43vo. (LC transcription).

John Jay's Report on the Mississippi River

[New York] Office of foreign Affairs, 17th August 1786

The Secretary of the United States for the Department of foreign Affairs in obedience to the Order of Congress directing him to state to them without Delay the territorial Claims of Spain on the east Side of the Missisippi, and the Sentiments of France touching our Right to navigate that River, Reports –

That the time allotted for this Report must necessarily render it concise and summary. –

It is well known that Spain claims the two Floridas, and contends that West Florida extends higher up the River Missisippi than is admitted by our Treaty with Britain, but how much higher *exactly*, your Secretary is uninformed, and has Reason to think that Spain has not yet made up her own Mind on that Point.

Spain also claims certain Posts & Places on the Missisippi of which she divested the English during the War, but how far they mean to stretch their

Claims over the adjacent Country, the Negociations between Mr Gardoqui and your Secretary have not as yet extended so minutely to that Point, as to enable him to determine.

. . . . .

As to the Sentiments of France touching our right to navigate the Missisippi, your Secretary began at an early period to believe and still thinks that the Court of France will not admit it. –

. . . . .

Whether they have adopted new Opinions on that Point your Secretary can not decide – He has however no Reason to believe that has been the Case, for he can perceive no Reason why such an Alteration in their Sentiments should have taken place. On the contrary it seems from Mr Jefferson's letter of 23^d May last that the Minister is not ready to admit all our Claims as ascertained by the Treaty of Peace to be within their Guarantee. He intimated that all our Limits were not fixed, and your Secretary thinks that the Minister could have meant to allude only to our western Limits and Claims. Britain disputes no Boundaries with us unless perhaps part of our Eastern – and those Disputes had not yet been brought before the french Court – but Spain still adheres to Pretensions of which France had been long and well informed and therefore your Secretary supposes the Minister then had those in View. –

Your Secretary sincerely wishes that the Event may not confirm his Opinion, and that the Court of France may clearly admit all our Claims and paticularly that to navigate the Missisippi to be well founded, and to be within the Terms, Intent & Meaning of the Guarantee. –

All which is submitted to the Wisdom of Congress. –   John Jay –
Read. 22 Aug. 1786

NA: PCC, item 81, v. 2, pp. 217-238 (DS); M247, reel 107. See also item 124, v. 2, pp. 220-244 (C); M247, reel 141.

John Jay's Report on the
Franco-American Consular Convention

[New York] Office for Foreign Affairs 18 August 1786
The Secretary to the United States for the Department of Foreign Affairs, to whom was referred back his Report of 4 July 1786 on the Consular Convention between France and the United States – Reports

That in his opinion a Copy of *that Report* should be transmitted to the Minister Plenipotentiary of the United States at Paris, in order that he may thereby become fully informed of the objections to which the Convention is liable –

That a certified Copy of *the Act of Congress* of the 25 day of January 1782 authorizing and directing the Honble. Dr. Franklin to conclude a Consular Convention be also sent to him.

That a certified Copy of *the Scheme* of such Convention, referred to in the above Act of Congress, be also sent to him –

That he be instructed to communicate the said Act of Congress, and the said Scheme, to his most Christian Majesty, and to point out to him the instances in which the Convention deviates from the said Scheme –

That he be also instructed to propose to His Majesty, that the said Convention be so amended, as perfectly to correspond with the Scheme in every part where a deviation from the same is not permitted by the said Act – And further that he represent to his Majesty, the desire of Congress to make the said Convention *probationary* by adding a Clause for limiting its duration to eight or ten Years –

That he assure his Majesty of the determination of Congress to observe on all occasions the highest Respect for Candour and good faith in all their proceedings, and that on receiving the Convention so amended, and with such a Clause, they will immediately ratify it –

Your Secretary thinks it should also be Resolved – That the Honble Thomas Jefferson Esq, the Minister Plenipo: of the United States at the Court of Versailles be, and he hereby is authorised and directed, to conclude and sign on the part of the United States, with the Minister of his most Christian Majesty having equal Powers, a Convention for the regulation of their respective Consuls, conformably to the Scheme abovementioned, in every respect except where deviations from it are permitted by the said Act of Congress of the 25 day of January 1782, and with a Clause limiting the duration of the said Convention to any term of years not exceeding ten.

Your Secretary thinks he should be directed to write the following Letter to Mr. Jefferson

Sir

I have the honor of transmitting to you herewith enclosed the following Papers to wit –

N°. 1. A Copy of the Consular Convention signed by the French and American Plenipotentiaries –

2. A Copy of the Act of Congress under which the American Plenipotentiary signed the same –

3 A Copy of the Scheme of a Convention mentioned and referred to in the said Act –

4. A Copy of a Report on the said Convention –

5. A Copy of an Act of Congress containing instructions and giving authorities to you on the Subject of the said Convention.

These Papers will possess you fully of the whole business. I am persuaded that it will appear to you as it does to Congress, to be a delicate one, and to require delicate management. –

The original Scheme of the Convention is far from being unexceptionable, but a former Congress having agreed to it, it would be improper now to recede; and therefore Congress are content to ratify a Convention made conformable to that Scheme, and to their Act of the 25 day of January 1782, provided a Clause limiting its duration be added –   It will be proper therefore to press on the Court, *only* such objections to the Convention, as arise from its departure from the Scheme. On making an accurate comparison, such departure will appear manifest to his Majesty; and there is reason to expect from his candour, that he will readily consent to remove the objections occasioned by it –

As it certainly is wise to try the merits of Institutions entirely new, by actual experience, before Nations adopt them forever, the propriety of rendering, this Convention Probationary in the first instance, is unquestionable – Congress cannot therefore ~~cannot~~ presume that his most Christian Majesty will object to a Clause for limiting, its duration. The design of this Convention being, for mutual and reciprocal benefit and Convenience, it would be doing injustice to his Majesty, to suppose that he would wish to provide for its existing longer than it should prove useful and satisfactory, If after the experience of a few years it should be found to answer the purposes intended by it, both Parties will have sufficient inducements to renew it, either in its present form, or with such alterations and amendments as time, experience and other circumstances may indicate.

I have the honot &c: &c: &c: –   John Jay
Read 12 Sept

NA: PCC, *item 81, v. 2, pp. 145-148 (C); M247, reel 107.*

John Jay to Thomas Jefferson

Dr Sir   New York 18th August 1786

. . . . .

It has happened from various Circumstances, that several Reports on foreign Affairs still lay before Congress undecided upon. The want of an adequate Representation for long Intervals, and the Multiplicity of Business which pressed upon them when that was not the Case, has occasioned

Delays and Omissions which however unavoidable are much to be regretted. It is painful to me to reflect that altho' my Attention to Business is unremitted yet I so often experience unseasonable Delays and successive Obstacles in obtaining the Decision and Sentiments of Congress, even on Points which require Dispatch. But so it is, and I must be content with leaving nothing undone that may depend upon me. –

The consular Convention is now as it has long been, under the Consideration of Congress, and I have Reason to hope they will soon enable me to send you full Instructions on that Subject. –

I have long thought and become daily more convinced that the Construction of our foederal Government is fundamentally wrong. To vest legislative, judicial & executive Powers in one and the same Body of Men, and that too in a Body daily changing its Members, can never be wise. In my Opinion those three great Departments of Sovereignty should be for ever separated, and so distributed as to serve as Checks on each other. But these are Subjects that have long been familiar to you and on which you are too well informed not to anticipate every Thing that I might say on them. –

.   .   .   .   .

I am, Dʳ Sir, with great Esteem & Regard &c: John Jay –

NA: PCC, *item 121, pp. 199-201 (LBkC); M61, reel 1.*

James Monroe to Thomas Jefferson

Dear Sir   New York Augt. 19. 1786.

My last advis'd you of the progress of Spanish negotiation. Until that time the reference of Jay's letter to a committee was, I believe, the point at which it rested; but to enable you to form a satisfactory opinion of the object of that letter I transcribe you [the] only operative paragraph in it. "I take the liberty therefore of submitting to the consideration of Congress whether it might not be adviseable to appoint a committee with power to instruct and direct me on every point and subject relative to the proposed treaty with Spain." You are to observe his only ultimata were respecting the Mississippi and the boundaries; the committee, consisting of a member from Massachusetts, Pennsylvania, and myself, kept it about two months and at length two of them reported that they be discharged, the letter referred to a committee of the whole and himself ordered to attend. It was agreed to with this alteration that he attend Congress to explain the difficulties stated in his letter and to lay before them a state of the negotiation. He accordingly came and being aware objections would be made to his entering into debate, produced a long written speech which he read by virtue of his office and which was in substance as follows. France against our right of the navigation of the Mississippi and, in case of a variance with Spain upon that point, against us. Well to be on good terms with Spain therefore on that account as well as to avail ourselves of her influence in the councils of Portugal, the Italian States and the Barbary Powers, as also in those of France herself. That Great Britain would rejoice to see us at variance with Spain, and therefore would foment dissentions between us that in case this treaty failed, Spain, mortified and disappointed in the eyes of all Europe would enter into engagements with Britain (or in resentment) so as to exclude us from her ports. For these reasons and fully to obtain the confidence and good wishes of that power, as also her good services in the lines abovesaid, he thought it wise to forebear the use of the navigation of the Mississippi for twenty-five years or thirty, if necessary, as a condition to obtain at the same time the following liberal articles as the basis of a commercial treaty. – 1. All commercial regulations shall be reciprocal, Spanish merchants in the ports of [America] and American merchants in those of Spain and the Canaries to have the rights of native merchants of the two countries. 2. To establish consuls in their respective countries. 3. The *bona fide* manufactures and productions of both parties, tobacco excepted, to be admitted in the ports aforesaid in the vessels of both parties upon the same footing as if they were their own manufactures and productions; and further that all such duties and imposts as may mutually be thought necessary to lay on them by either party shall be regulated on principles of exact reciprocity by a tariff to be form'd within one year after the ratification of this treaty, and in the mean time they shall severally pay in the ports of each other those of natives only. 4. Masts and timber for the navy to be bought, provided they be as cheap as in other countries. This was the amount of his communications as to the project which he urged our adopting by all the arguments he could think of, such as, we cant obtain the use, and therefore of no consequence; we must now decide; must terminate in accomodation, war, or disgrace, the last the worst, the second unprepar'd for, the first the preferable course; that we should avail ourselves of the moment or Britain would; therefore no time to lose with others of the same kind. This subject hath, since the above communication, engaged the attention of Congress for ten days past. The delegates of Massachusetts who are his instruments on the floor moved in committee to repeal his ultimata with a view of suffring him to proceed at pleasure, and upon this point hath the debate turn'd. It hath been manifest they have had throughout seven states and we five. They, to Pennsylvania inclusive, and Delaware being absent, the rest against him. We deny the right in seven states to alter an instruction so as to make it a new one but they will proceed, be that as it may, the treaty in that event be form'd and soon presented for ratification. To prevent this we have told them we would give notice to the secretary of the incompetency of his powers as also to the resident of Spain to justify Congress in refusing to ratify, if they should chuse it. In this state it remain'd without any new proposition untill yesterday, being friday. We stated however in the close of the day that we would agree that a treaty be form'd upon the following conditions. That exports be admitted thro the Mississippi, paying at New Orleans a duty of two and half per cent ad valorem to Spain, to be carried thence in Spanish American and French bottoms. That imports be prohibited in that line. If this should be adopted we propose to change the scene of negotiations and to carry it to Madrid, to take it out of the present and put it into yours and Adams's hands. We fear however and with too much reason that this will fail. Nothing could have been more unfortunate than even the agitation of this subject. It hath lessen'd the ground on which we stood and given Spain hopes she had no reason to calculate on. What prospects to the general interest might be calculated on as resulting from the deliberations of the convention at Annapolis must be diminished. In short the measure strikes me as every way highly injurious. I am sorry to inform you that our affairs are daily falling into a worse situation, arising more from the intrigues of designing men than any real defect in our system or distress of our affairs. The same party who advocate this business have certainly held in this city committees for dismembering the confederacy and throwing the states eastward the Hudson into one government. As yet this business hath not gone far but that there should be a party in its favor, and a man, heretofore so well respected but in my opinion so little known, engag'd in it is to me very alarming....I am Dear [Sir] very affectionately yr. friend & servant,

Jas. Monroe

Boyd, Jefferson Papers, v. 10, pp. 274-277. See also LC: Jefferson Papers, microfilm reel 6 (ALS) for encyphered copy.

Louis Guillaume Otto to Comte de Vergennes

[Translation]

N⁰· 59.   New York, 20 August 1786.
My Lord.

Congress has just published the new requisitions for the expenses of the current year. The interest and the partial reimbursements owed to France are still included in these requisitions, and although they are little efficacious, they at least serve to establish on the books of the treasury the sums owed by the individual States in proportion to the annual deficit of their contributions. These last demands, which amount to almost four million piastres either in cash or in Government paper, were drawn up on the second of this month, and the 1ˢᵗ· of January of next year has been fixed for the payment of the entire Sum. As almost half of this amount is destined for the reimbursement of the domestic debt, Congress is permitting the various States to pay a large portion of their Shares in Loan Office interest certificates, and to set this interest, Citizens are supposed to address themselves to the Bureaus established in their States, and foreigners to any Bureau. This favor, which principally concerns His Majesty's subjects, had already been accorded by the previous requisitions, and I took care at the time to give our merchants notice of it through the *Gazette de France.*

An object equally important, My Lord, has occupied Congress and various legislative Assemblies for some time. I had the honor to render You an account of the hostile dispositions of the savages, and I see with anxiety that their animosity is being more and more inflamed, and that the United States find themselves in the unfortunate necessity of arming troops in order to restrain their audacity. This course is not only very onerous for the finances of Congress, but it contributes to maintain an implacable hatred between the savages and the inhabitants of the frontiers. Several persons, and particularly Mr. Jay, are of the opinion that there has been too much haste in concluding bargains for wilderness areas that can only be useful to the confederation a hundred years from now, the acquisition of which has hitherto served only to inspire jealousy in the savages. It would be much more prudent not to take advantage of the great cessions which England made so adroitly in its treaty of peace and to wait until a superabundant population can push back the nomadic hordes that infest the frontiers of the United States. But the destitution of finances having brought about the consideration of these lands as a source of wealth for Congress, treaties have been made with perfidious nations that remember their promises only so long as the presents they have been given are not consumed. Several companies have orders to march to the falls of the Ohio in order to join the local militia and to push back the savages, and as the finances of Congress do not permit it to make greater efforts, it has requested the State of Virginia to send reinforcements to the banks of the Ohio and to show the expenses of this armament as a deduction from its annual contributions.

Although this circumstance, My Lord, is most unfortunate, it nevertheless contributes to disaffect the Americans more and more against the English Ministry, which is regarded as the prime mover of these difficulties. No one is unaware that the Commandants of the forts have continually assured the savage leaders that there never was any treaty between Great Britain and the United States, and that the latter availed themselves of this pretext in order to possess themselves of all the lands situated between the Mississippi and the Ocean. The failure of the negotiations with the regencies of Barbary forms another very powerful grievance against England, and Mr. Temple is so convinced of the animosity of the Americans that he does not have the courage to leave the city of New York, where England has more partisans than throughout the entire extent of the United States. That Consul being obliged to visit Philadelphia, he had his passport from the King of England, drawn up in Latin, placed in the gazettes; a measure which appeared most ridiculous, and which could only be attributed to his fear of being insulted en route.

Lord Carmarthen's response to Mr. Adams' memorial concerning the surrender of the posts has doubtless been transmitted to You, My Lord, by another channel; however, I think I should enclose it here because it is essentially a part of my correspondence and because it sets forth the point of view from which the English Ministry considers a subject which has occupied Congress, and particularly the State of New York, for a very long time. The fur trade, which formerly was very considerable, is absolutely lost to the Americans, and as it is impossible to fulfill the conditions proposed by the English Ministry, there is no hope of recovering posts so important by negotiations. All these circumstances, My Lord, have tilted the balance considerably in our favor for several weeks. A parallel has been drawn between the frank and generous conduct of our Ministry and the insidious policy of England, and at this moment, when the Americans have need of Your support and Your counsels, they are more pleased than ever with the happy alliance which they have contracted with His Majesty. The Gazetteers neglect no occasion to eulogize the King and his Ministers, and if we are interested in concluding any new commercial arrangements with the United States, I think that this moment will be more favorable than any other.

I am with a profound respect My Lord Your most humble and most obedient Servant   Otto.

Received 22 Sept^ber.

FFAA: Pol. Corr., U.S., v. 32, f. 50-52vo. (LC transcription).

Louis Guillaume Otto to Comte de Vergennes

[Translation]

N°· 60.   New York, 23 August 1786.

My Lord.

It has been more than a year that M. Gardoqui has been negotiating a Treaty of Commerce with Mr. Jay, without being more advanced today that he was on arriving here. This delay is related to several circumstances which I think I should explain. The Northern States, which in all commercial negotiations recognize no other interest than that of their fisheries, would be tolerably disposed to finish with Mr. Gardoqui if the Southern Delegates did not propose the opening of the Mississippi as a condition *sine qua non*. In consequence of this difference of sentiments and interests, the Delegates of the five Southern states have combined to break off all negotiations with Mr. Gardoqui entirely. They say publicly that this Minister has no powers, that this whole affair is in the hands of M. de Galvez, and that in general a negotiation of this importance should not be opened in America, since the facility one has in a republic of knowing the dispositions of the Sovereign body gives great advantages to a foreign minister, who on his part conceals his instructions and the Ultimatum of his Court with the greatest care. Moreover, they fear that the indifference of the Northern States regarding the navigation of the Mississippi may make them accelerate the negotiation, and that they may find no means to prevent votes to the detriment of the Southern States; they have asserted in the full Congress that France alone can succeed in procuring them a treaty of Commerce with Spain, and that they would negotiate with that power in vain without the mediation of their great Ally. Amidst this fermentation, the principal leaders of this league came to me to explain the necessity of having recourse to Your good offices, My Lord, and to put this negotiation entirely in His Majesty's hands. "The navigation of the Mississippi," they told me, "is perhaps the most important object for the United States. The inhabitants of the vast and fertile countries of Kentucky and the neighboring lands have no other outlet than New Orleans; if Congress cannot procure an entrepot for them in that city, they will regard its protection as entirely useless, and we are informed in the most positive manner that they are disposed to disengage themselves from the Confederation and to throw themselves into the arms of England in order to procure themselves by the lakes and the St. Lawrence River the outlet they are refused by way of the Mississippi. In that case, it will be easy for Great Britain to exchange Gibraltar for East Florida and to place the whole interior of America in its dependence. We ardently desire to be intimately linked with Spain, but we are persuaded at the same time that without the help of France, we will never be able to negotiate with success. Several Northern delegates, and especially Mr. Jay, have wished to persuade us that France was against the opening of the Mississippi, but we know that the peace has brought about a new order of things, and that the objections which Your Court had made to our claims can no longer turn on the same principles. Only the Comte de Vergennes can procure for us the advantages we desire; we have written to Mr. Jefferson, enjoining him to secrecy thereon, and we wish our treaty to be made by Your Court or that it not be made at all."

— After having explained to me, My Lord, several other motives that make them want this course, they communicated the following articles to me in writing, which should serve as the basis for the negotiation:

1.) All commodities and products of the interior of America are allowed to descend the Mississippi in flatboats to New Orleans, which will be the entrepot for these commodities and will only be used for exports.

2.) Upon their arrival at New Orleans, the Americans will pay a duty of 2 1/2 % of the value of the said commodities, which duty will take the place of compensation for the favour requested of Spain.

3.) An American consul will reside in that city and will be personally responsible for the smuggling that could take place.

4.) The said commodities can only be re-exported from New Orleans in French, Spanish or American ships.

5.) Imports of all kinds will be prohibited, and no ship may reascend the Mississippi, with the exception of the flatboats that have served to transport the commodities, and which will reascend empty and will carry only passengers.

6.) Spain will permit French and Americans merchants to reside in New Orleans to handle the Commerce in the said commodities.

7.) France will take part in this Commerce on account of her mediation.

In communicating all these details to me, My Lord, the Delegates earnestly requested me to transmit them to You; they enjoined me at the same time to the most profound secrecy vis-à-vis M. Gardoqui and all persons who may speak to me of this negotiation.

Without giving them any hope, and conforming to the orders You were so good as to give me not to interfere in the affairs of Spain, I told them that they could be sure of my discretion and that I would render You an account of the confidential conversation that they had had with me. They would like to give Mr. Jefferson powers to negotiate the treaty in Madrid, but to stipulate to him in the most positive manner to govern himself entirely according to Your Counsels and not to take a step without Your consent. They already have seven States on their side, and if they can win over two more, which is very likely, Mr. Jefferson will receive his instructions immediately.

I had this conference, My Lord, only a few hours before the departure of the packet boat; it is possible that the passion of the Delegates who spoke with me made them exaggerate some of the details; I shall take care to return later to the points which seem to me susceptible of correction without losing sight of the reserve and circumspection which you have been so good as to prescribe for me.

I am with a profound respect My Lord Your most humble and most obedient servant   Otto.
Received 22 Sept^{ber.}

FFAA: Pol. Corr., U.S., v. 32, f. 58-60vo. (LC transcription).

William Stephens Smith to John Jay

Sir   London August 24th 1786
...In the absence of Mr Adams it becomes my duty to make every communication, which in my opinion, may be of the least service to my Country, upon this principle your Excellency will excuse me if I should trouble you with Minutia – From the earliest moment that I had an oppertunity of attending to their public proceedings and the Conduct of their officers, subsequent to the preliminary articles of the Peace, & during my residence at New York superintending the evacuation &c. I was fully convinced that this Government, was under the most pressing necessity to sign that and the definitive Treaty – on the first view of it, it shew a liberality and extention of policy, which if properly persued, would soon have relieved both Countries from the inconveniencies they laboured under, from the expence and calamities of the war – with this impression your Excellency must suppose, I view'd with astonishment the Conduct of their officers, so diametrically opposite to the ostensible Spirit of the treaty – but it was so evident to me at that time, that I did not hesitate to declare by Letter to General Washington, that a breach of treaty was their object – this they have in my opinion since, sufficiently shewn – and have been steady in the pursuit of a favourite object, viz – another war with us independent of our allies. the first question which will arise on this subject is, what can be their object in a war with us? the simplest answer which occurs to me at present is – another treaty – wherein they without doubt flatter themselves, they will be able to make some better provision for their Loyalists and embrace more of the trade of the back-Country, than if they

were quietly to regulate themselves by the articles of the late treaty – in a Conversation the day before yesterday with the Commanding officer of the Guards, (whose duty is in the palace, and about the person of the King; and of course in the way of forming *his* opinions, on the current opinions of the Court) on the subject of the frontier posts and the boundary Line, (which appears to be coming forward as a subject of consideration) – he gave me to understand, that the fur-trade was considered of vast importance to this Country – and upon my getting the map, & ~~by~~ pointing out the course of that trade and the particular situation of the posts which ought to be occupied by each agreable to the articles of the Peace, & endeavouring to convince him that they would by no means be excluded from the trade of the natives – he said, "*dam* it I don't know any thing about it, only that the Gentleman who made that Peace, was said to be a fool, & not only overreached in the making of the Treaty – but totally unacquainted with the Geography of the Country he gave away – and of the importance of the trade of it to his own, and that he did not believe the posts would be given up without some further explanation" – but my good Sir, reply'd I – what becomes of the faith & Honour of your Nation pledged for the fulfilment of that treaty, in this case – he swore he knew nothing about it, "but this was the talk amongst them" – I was satisfied with his candour but did not then think it proper to put it to a further test – It may not be improper to examine their ability on the Subject of another war; they have with some address made the establishment of a Colony on our left, hostile to our Country and governments; in making this lodgement, they also took care to make every very considerable deposits of warlike stores and ammunition, they have in addition to the regular military Regiments which accompanied them, since made some reinforcements, and they feel themselves in some degree competent to the defence of their territories – while they trust to the activity of their fleets to carry on a Maritime War, as of itself calculated to produce every effect they wish – the Minister has bent the whole force of his Abilities to the payment of the Navy debt of the last War, which he has accomplished, of course notwithstanding the immense debt of the Nation, administration have a resource should they choose to step forward with naval hostilities, for on the Credit of the Navy bills, they can run into the war, to the tune of eight, ten or twelve Millions – without making it a Parliamentary question, or committing themselves to their debates for supplies, it will be answering their ends full as well, to let the ways & means be pointed out for the absorption of the Debt after it is contracted as to make it a National question in the first instance – indeed much better – for in case that the question should be brought forward in the first instance, I believe the Nation at large would revolt at the Idea of another American War, unless Government could hold out some irritating ostensible reason, at once to justify their intentions, and to exasperate the Nation – indeed I have some doubt whether the People at large would at present submit to it on any principle, but it can do no injury for us to attend closely to their proceedings and hold ourselves as *guarded as possible.*

I still seriously think that we have it in our power to regulate the system of this Court – that is, if we have the power amongst ourselves – of bringing our foedral abilities to a point of dignified opperation – their present pursuits, not being friendly and perhaps hostile to us is founded on our supposed disunion, and the want of those foedral systems which is necessary to check and counter act their plans, – we promise ourselves (here) much from the rivision of the Laws of the particular States, and the wisdom of the Commerical Convention, which I am informed is to meet at Annapolis in the course of next month – The first if it should lessen the pressure on the Loyalists will shake their settlements in Nova Scotia, and the last have it decidedly in their power to lay the foundation of a liberal Commercial Treaty in some degree essential to the trading interests of both Countries – Mr Bond[1] a young gentleman from Philadelphia, is to be appointed to reside there in quality of Commercial Agent, his Commission is not yet made out, so that I am not clear as to his title, line of Duty, or appointments – but I expect in a few days to be able to give your Excellency a fuller account respecting him & his pursuits, in the mean time, you'll excuse the length & freedom of this & believe me – your Excellency's most obed^t Servt W. S. Smith

NA: PCC, *item 92, pp. 118-125 (ALS); M247, reel 120.*

[1] *Bond, Phineas (1749-1815). British government official. Born in Philadelphia, he studied law in London in the early 1770s, but was in Philadelphia when it was occupied by British forces in 1777, and withdrew with them in June 1778. Practiced law in London, 1779-1786. Appointed consul for the States of New York, New Jersey, Pennsylvania, Delaware and Maryland, April 1786; recognized by Congress, May 3, 1787. His concurrent appointment as commissary for commercial affairs in the United States was never recognized. Consul General for the Middle and Southern States, 1793-1812. Chargé des affaires, 1795-1796.*

Enclosure: General Advertiser

London August 10. [1786]

    The state of the United Provinces, may be truly said to be very alarming. A civil war there is looked upon as inevitable. The Aristocratic party have been supported by the Court of France, against the Prince of Orange.[1] On the contrary, the Prince has received marks of friendship, from his relations, the Kings of England and Prussia. But there has very lately, a *third* party started up in Holland. This is the *Democratic*. This party seems to declare strongly against the Aristocratic; but however, is not in favour of the Prince. The commotions and fears occasioned by these divisions, are the *true* causes of the late rise of our funds; for the monied people in the Provinces, dreading the consequences of these divisions, have sent their property here to be vested in our Stocks.

The dispute between this country and America, is unquestionably become exceedingly serious. Mr. Adams, the American Minister at our Court is gone. His return, whatever may (for certain reasons) be said, is nevertheless very doubtful. His declaration to the Secretary of State, before he went, viz. "That if the forts, in the back settlements, were not given up to Congress according to the terms of the Treaty, he had it in charge from Congress to say, *That America would most assuredly make* Reprisals upon the British trade, in North America, and in the West-Indies." This declaration means, and says too much, to be treated, like former declarations, from the same hand, with cold indifference.

It is also a fact, that a considerable number of American ships and vessels, have *lately* been taken by the British cruizers in the West Indies. And it is equally true, that the French have likewise lately taken a considerable number of American ships and vessels, near their islands in the West Indies.

So true is the *mutability* of Courts, and so *flexible* are the politics of Ministers, that in case of a *rupture* between Great Britain and America, which is considered as *unavoidable*, it may, upon as good foundation as it is possible for human wisdom to divine, be asserted, That France will be perfectly *neuter* in the dispute.

France will, however, most probably exceedingly rejoice at a quarrel between England and America. And there is not a doubt that Mr. Eden and the Duke of Dorset,[2] have [been] sent the strongest assurances, from the French Ministry, that the Court of France will take no part in it. France undoubtedly sees, by this time, that her interference in the late American war was unnecessary, and expensive to herself. She is now satisfied and convinced, that England can never make an internal impression upon America; and therefore, that she need not give that assistance, which she once thought America wanted. It is a fact, with which our Ministers are not unacquainted, that the *present* politics of the French Cabinet are, to observe a strict *neutrality*, in whatever relates to Great Britain and America.

There are two *parties* in America, as well as in England; but there is a wonderful difference between them. In America the parties are, one *violent* for a rupture with England, on account of not delivering up the forts in the back settlements; the other party is *moderate*, and say, that before they quarrel with England, they ought to cast the beam out of their own eye, which figurative expression, alludes to the non payment of their debts; and if they had permitted this subject to remain as a *private* matter between individual and individual, no notice in a *national sense* could have been taken of it; but the legislatures of Carolina and New York, having passed laws to make such refusals *legal*, notwithstanding the words of the treaty are, "That the creditors on either side, shall meet with *no lawful impediment* to the recovery of all *bona fide* debts; heretofore contracted." The non-payment became, from the moment of passing these laws, a *national* question; and therefore the moderate party say, that whenever the treaty is *fulfilled* on their part; and is not at the same time fulfilled on the part of Great Britain, that war is both proper and necessary. – This is the true state of *parties* in America.

In England the state of parties, upon the American question, is this: – The Court, that is, the *interior cabinet*, are certainly for a war with America; and they believe, to a certainty, all the assurances they receive from France, of the *neutrality* of that power. These form one party; the other party is the people at large, who are perfectly *asleep*. The tricks of a lunatic, the size of a hat, or the cut of a coat, are subjects which engage the public attention more ardently, than the blundering dash of a minister's pen, which may involve two nations in blood.

We have thus related the state of the dispute with impartiality and accuracy. The public will judge for themselves on the priciple of *right*.

NA: PCC, *item 92, p. 130 (printed text): M247, reel 120.*
[1] *Willem V, Prince of Orange and Nassau (1748-1806). Stadhouder of the United Provinces of the Netherlands, 1751-1795.*
[2] *Dorset, John Frederick Sackville, Duke of (1745-1799). British diplomat. Ambassador to France, December 1783-August 1789. Lord steward of the royal household, October 1789-February 1799.*

Comte de Vergennes to Louis Guillaume Otto

[Versailles] August 25, 1786[1]
You can assure the Congress that the King will seize with Eagerness all Occasions to facilitate their good Intelligence with the Barbary Powers. This Assembly without Doubt have been informed of the Support that his Majesty affords to the American Commissioners who negociate at Algiers and at Morocco; the Treaty which has been recently signed with this last Power, and which will probably be published in America, will be the best

refutation of the Suspicions which many public Papers are willing to inspire against our System of Policy.

NA: PCC, item 120, v. 2, pp. 478-479 (translation); M40, reel 2.
   ¹ This extract from Vergennes' despatch to Otto of 25 August 1786 was enclosed in a note from Otto to Jay dated 23 October 1786.

Congressional Resolutions Regarding the Spanish Negotiations

[New York] Tuesday Aug 29. 1786 In Congress

. . . . .

...The Secretary hath united the project of a commercial treaty with Spain, with the interfering claims of the two powers respecting the boundaries and the Mississippi, and proposes that to obtain what he calls liberal terms in commerce, we should by compact forbear the use of the navigation of the Mississippi for the period of the treaty – that the claims of the parties respecting the boundaries remain as they are, to be the subject of future discussion and compromise. – The project is a plain and simple one – it proposes to give the merchants, the vessels, and the productions and manufactures of each country in the ports of each other – viz – those of Spain in the ports of the United States, & those of the United States in the ports of Spain & the Canaries the same privileges as if they were those of the Country itself. It behoves us therefore in the first instance to enquire what alteration this will make in those instances from the condition on which we now stand – 2dly Whether this alteration, if there should be any will be beneficial to the United States?
1st As to Merchants – we cannot suppose (and believe the contrary to be the case) that the King of Spain makes any discrimination in the ports aforesaid between Merchants his subjects and those of other nations; the laws of Spain distinguish only articles of commerce, and those into *such as are* and *such as are not contraband*; and the penalties and privileges are precisely the same in both instances in their application to foreigners and subjects. If discriminations therefore in this line can be beneficial, we tie up our hands from extending them to our citizens without obtaining any consideration for it –
2dly As to vessels engaged in the carriage of the manufactures of both countries – Spain hath no navigation Act – to the ports which are open the vessels of all countries are admitted, and in the carriage even of her own productions and manufactures upon the same footing with those of her

own subjects; here we bind up ourselves again without a valuable consideration for it.

3dly As to productions &c – The two Nations engage to receive those of each other into the ports aforesaid as if they were there own; with respect to Spain and the Canaries this is certainly the case at present. The productions &c of the United States (Tobacco excepted, which is hereby excluded) are admitted into the ports aforesaid in the most liberal manner that the Article will admit a construction of, and precisely upon the same terms with similar Articles, the growth of the Colonies of Spain, in different quarters of the globe: so that this treaty will not open to us a single port, nor admit us into those now open upon better terms than those we now enjoy. Can these positions be controverted, that neither our Merchants, our vessels, nor our productions will be received into the ports of Spain and the Canaries, upon different terms from those on which they are now received? if this is not the case let the contrary be shewn –

But how will the Secretarys project affect us? The merchants of Spain shall have in our ports the rights of the native merchants of America. When we consider that our commerce is subjected in every Article to the most severe restrictions in almost every foreign port, that under the necessary encouragement given by France & Britain to their own fisheries, that Article is excluded from their ports – that the Mediterranean Sea is shut against us – & that it is the interest of those powers, as it would after this treaty be that of Spain also, it should be so always – that the West India Islands are also occluded almost altogether – that the wheat and rice trade is from these causes greatly injured – that the Tobacco is a monopoly in the hands of the farmers General in France in Spain contraband – thus banished from the European countries and their dependencies one would suppose it the duty of every wise American Statesman to secure our rights and interests at home – to give in our own ports to our own citizens exclusive privileges, but of this advantage the project would deprive them. – Spain shall be admitted into the carriage of our productions &c upon the same footing that we are into that of hers. If the materials of both parties were such as to employ the same number of vessels in the carriage, such a compact would on the part of these States in their circumstances be unwise; but when we consider how few ships will be employed in the carriage of the productions &c of Spain, how unimportant they are in point of bulk and proportion to that of the productions of these States, the disadvantage of the stipulation must obviously occur. How contrary would such a stipulation be to the policy of Great Britain – To the policy of her navigation Act, an Act which gives to her own Subjects in their intercourse with all other nations, high privileges and immunities they do not enjoy – To the wisdom of this Act and her other regulations in commerce, it is owing that she hath attained to such a height of power and grandeur on the Seas, as to be at the same time the terror and the admiration of the world; that her Subjects have obtained such commercial wealth and astonishing resources as to be able to support her in the most splendid enterprizes, and the longest and most difficult wars, that her councils could devise, or the change of fortune expose her to; yet of the right of adopting and pursuing such a system of policy, or in any degree discriminating in favour of our own carriage, would the project deprive us –

Spain shall have a right to bring her Manufactures &c here and take off our own (Tobacco excepted) in the same manner as they were her own – It is difficult to understand the nature of this engagement – If by this it is meant that productions &c of the one shall of right be admitted into the ports of the other independent of the will of the other, after this treaty for that term, the duties remaining as they are (Tobacco only excepted) its operation is very extensive & important. The parties have in that instance given up the right of prohibition or restriction on Imports or exports, which do not apply at the time to similar Articles of their own. The case is perhaps without a precedent, and one would suppose it never could have one, unless the family compact between the different branches of the house of Bourbon may be considered as such, which was even between those Nations found inconvenient, and afterwards by the treaty of Paris in 1763 annulled.   Independent Nations have always heretofore retained to themselves the right of regulating their own interior police, which they could not do if thus connected, and made dependent on that of others, and by that means of securing to themselves a reciprocity in their intercourse with other nations – many are the purposes to which the exercise of this power in different countries is made subservient, depending in each on a variety of circumstances – the nature of the Government – the manners of the people – state of population – resources and the purposes to which it might incline to turn them, with others, that upon examination might occur; but here they might be defeated – If for instance the object was to promote virtue & frugality, by prohibiting the importation of foreign luxuries – if to encourage Manufactures and to countenance the mechanical Arts at home, by prohibiting imports from other countries, the right by this treaty would be adrogated – In short the police of these States would be so interwoven with that of Spain, and the management of her own System made so dependant on her will that we should not be able to act on it afterwards – Such a stipulation would also be contrary to the federal compact, for by it each State retains the right of prohibiting the importation or exportation of any species of goods or commodities whatever." – If such then is its purport, it is in direct violation of the compact itself, and of course void – If it is our intention to merit &

preserve the confidence of our constituents, we should hold this compact sacred: and if to support any Character among the Nations of the Earth, we should enter into no engagements we cannot fulfil; it is sufficiently low already, we need not debase it further. If on the other hand they retain the right of prohibiting or of encouraging Imports and exports by emposing what duties they may from time to time think proper, under this restriction only, that their Subjects and Citizens respectively, shall pay in the ports of each other, the duties of Natives only, the effect will be very confined and unimportant. It is still within the power of each Nation to suspend all commercial intercourse with the other; for by prohibiting the importation of the Manufactures and productions of the other, by its own Subjects or Citizens, the prohibition is extended to those of the other, and the commerce at an end; each party still retains the right of contracting with others and without restraint – for instance Spain might covenant with France to admit her flour or fish into her ports, paying the duty of five pr Cent ad valorem, and afterwards impose twenty pr Cent on similar Articles from these States: if the same duty on our commodities was emposed equally on her own and our citizens there would be no violation of the treaty, and thus while she preserved her faith with us, she would give a monopoly in these Articles to France. So that in either view, this stipulation which the Secretary holds to be so liberal and advantageous, will not bear a close examination; it presents at first view in appearance, plausible colours, but when investigated will be found to be either mischievous, or at best of no advantage to these United States –

Our treaties with France, the United Netherlands, Sweeden, Prussia &c stipulate to each "the right of the most favoured Nations." These nations therefore coming into the terms of Spain, will be entitled to these benefits, and that they will cannot be questioned, for in so doing they give up little or nothing – The evils of this project will therefore be almost universal & of course without remedy – They will also of right require a consideration for so doing, equivalent to the value of the occlusion of the Mississippi. In addition to which the Article of Tobacco will by compact be excluded from all their ports, as well as from those from Spain –

Spain is of all countries the one from whose commercial restrictions we have the least to fear, and of course the one with whom there is the least necessity for our binding ourselves under any engagements to. Her exports are but few, and her commerce with all Nations against her. Encumbered with her immense & opulent colonies, the great exertion of the Spanish Monarchy is to keep them together – the price of an Alliance with Britain is exclusive advantages in trade – This separates her from France, and in the superiority of her fleets, puts her commerce and her Colonies together into the Arms of Britain. Spain will therefore maintain her connexions

with France, from whose superiority by Sea she hath less to fear, &
cultivate the friendship of the United States. A connexion with Britain
turns the scale against the other powers in favour of Britain, and makes her
a british colony – A connexion with France and the allies of France
preserves things as they now stand: we may therefore safely conclude that
as the friendship of the United States, must form an essential part of her
system; that if she fails in the present object, which from the disposition of
the United States (made known to her by the Secretary himself at the
Court of Spain, in the midst of the war, and while surrounded with
difficulties) she must calculate on; she will either come forward and grant
fully the terms we require, or at least still seek an accommodation by the
most friendly and conciliating attention to our Interests – by
procrastination she will still court our commerce, and continue to exert her
influence with the regency of Algiers &c for the relief of our prisoners, and
with other powers in our favour by bargain unless these advantages become
a part of the treaty we lose them.)

As to the surrender or forbearance of the use of the navigation of the
Missisippi for the term proposed, for the consideration proposed (the right
of the United States to dismember the government being out of the
question) it is inadmissible for the reasons above stated – but it is also
inadmissible upon the principle of the right, and independent of the right,
upon the highest principles of national expedience, which apply even if the
commercial project were an advantageous one. In the present state of the
powers of Congress, it should be the policy of every wise Statesman to
pursue such a System of conduct as shall be best calculated to gain the
confidence of the several States in the federal councils and thereby an
extension of their powers – but this measure we apprehend would tend to
defeat that object. – The States who have ceded it and the confederacy at
large look up to the western lands as a substantial fund for the discharge of
the public debt – the value of these lands will depend in a great measure
on the navigation of the Mississippi – by suspending this right, we
depreciate this fund, unnecessarily burden the confederacy with an
additional weight, and proportionally injure the publick creditors. – By the
compact with Virginia it is stipulated that the western country shall be
divided into States, and admitted with the rights of the original States into
the confederacy. The spirit of this compact is, that the territory should
retain all its rights, and have them promoted under the patronage of
Congress. This Act would therefore be a direct violation of it, and have a
tendency to fix the weight of population on one side of the Continent only
– But the dismemberment of the Government which this unquestionably
is, without the consent of the State interested, one would suppose, would
prevent even the consideration of the Subject by Congress. That the

United States have a right to the free navigation of the Mississippi, and the boundaries as established in the treaty with Great Britain, is a truth too well established in the Journals of Congress, and too fully supported by their Acts on the subject, to require any thing to be said at this day in its favour – to proceed on a contrary principle would manifest such a contradiction to their former Acts, and be such a subversion of the rights of nature and the States, as to lessen them throughout the world. It would also be such a sacrifice for particular purposes, as would be obvious to even the most undiscerning. The right therefore cannot now be called in question, nor can it be a principle on which we are to act – ...

. . . . .

By the second Art: of the Confederation of these United States, each State retains its sovereignty, freedom & independence and every power, jurisdiction & right which is not therein expressly delegated to the U.S in Congress Assembled. This is a fundamental law of the Nation and the powers granted in the 9th Article to make treaties must be construed in subordination to it; no treaty even of peace entered into by the U.S in Congress Assembled extending to a cession or suspension of the rights of any of the states without their consent can therefore be valid; much less can such a treaty of commerce, which in point of political necessity can never be so pressing.

How then shall we proceed in the present critical circumstances with Spain? An honorable arrangement with the court of Spain upon these points & an advantageous treaty of commerce, though indeed whilst our trade is so restrained by the piratical powers it will be of less consequence than it otherwise would be, are certainly desireable objects. A continuance of the negotiation in the hands of the Secretary alone, as his sentiments are now known in Congress & differ so widely from the Opinions of several States in this Confederacy, especially upon the points relative to the Mississippi & the boundaries would not be adviseable. Upon the first point therefore it will be proper to instruct our chargé des affaires at the court of Spain to agree with that court on the principles – the treaty ultimately to be concluded here – that it be negotiated under the mediation of France. Upon the 2^{d} it will be proper agreeably to the arrangement at Annapolis that two other commissioners be appointed with Mr Jay, the consent of the majority of whom shall be necessary to conclude the treaty.

It is to be observed that the Secretary hath no power to treat on the subject of Commerce – being confined solely to the interfering claims of the two parties as above, The power to form such a treaty with Spain having been committed to Mr Adams, Franklin & Jefferson at Annapolis on 7th May 1784 under a commission which had then near one year to run, with all the other powers of Europe upon principles then agreed on as applying to all. This must be the more obvious from the care the US have always taken to establish the principles in Congress upon which their treaties should be formed & making their ministers the instruments only of their will, especially at Annapolis in 1784 when their system of commercial policy to be established in treaties was after mature consideration agreed to and men appointed from different quarters of the Union as being necessary to concentre a representation of the different interests. Can it be supposed then, that the commission of these gentlemen with respect to Spain without even mentioning it or agreeing on the principles in the instructions to the Secretary or even mentioning the subject of trade in said instructions, were repealed, and he thus loosely authorised to form a treaty of commerce? That their interfering claims however may be amicably settled and that the two nations may enjoy reciprocal advantages in trade it is hereby resolved—: That the Charge des affaires of the US at the court of Spain be instructed to assure his Catholic Majesty of the high regard the US entertain for his friendship & of their earnest desire to cultivate & preserve always the best understanding between his Majesty & the said States: That as an evidence of this disposition they are willing to settle their interfering claims respecting the Mississippi & the boundaries upon the following principles. 1. That New Orleans be made an Entrepot for the reception of the bonâ fide produce of the US brought down the river Mississippi by the Citizens of the said States — such produce to be landed at s^d port for exportation — that the s^d citizens be at liberty to return with their boats empty or with passengers only up the Mississippi to the places from whence they came. 2. That such produce aforesaid shall pay there or the merchants exporting it give bond for the payment within six months from the date of a duty not exceeding   per cent ad valorem at the time of exportation to the crown of Spain. That such produce aforesaid shall be exported thence in Spanish, American or French vessels those in the bottoms of Spain under the regulation of Spain, and those in the bottoms of America & France under the regulations of the two countries by treaty or otherwise. That imports of every kind & country to the said port & up the said river in American & french bottoms be prohibited and that all vessels engaged in Transportation of said exports shall come to such port in ballast only. That the US be authorised to appoint a consul to reside at New Orleans who shall be responsible for any violation of these stipulations by the citizens of the U.S. That American factors be permitted to reside at said port for the management of the business of exportation only. That as to the boundaries they must insist on those established in their treaty with G Britain. And further to assure his Cath: Majesty that so soon as instructions shall be given to his Minister in these states to this effect the US will authorise their Minister, to conclude a treaty in conformity herewith — But that they cannot enter into any treaty or compact whatsoever with his Cath: Majesty on the said subjects upon any other terms or conditions whatsoever

That the hon^ble M Jefferson be furnished with a copy of these instructions & directed to make known to his M C^n Majesty the sincere regard they have for his person & family, the gratitude they bear for his former good offices & of the earnest desire they have of his friendly Mediation with the Catholic King that by his interposition the interfering claims of the two nations may be amicably settled.

That the resolutions of the 20 July 1785 & the 25 of August following authorising the Secret^y of foreign Affairs to treat with Don Diego de Gardoqui respecting the boundaries & the Mississippi in the words above recited be and they are hereby repealed.

That two Commissioners be appointed & associated with the Sec^y of foreign Affairs with powers to enter into a treaty with Don Diego de Gardoqui or such other person as his CM shall appoint upon the following principles – Upon the Mississippi & the boundaries as above, but that they receive no proposition on the said points until he shall be authorised by his said Majesty to accede to the said terms

That they be authorised to enter into a commercial Treaty with Spain upon the following principles. 1 That each party shall have a right to carry their own produce manufactures & merchandize in their own bottoms to the ports of the other paying in both cases such duties only as are paid by the most favoured nations, freely where it is freely granted to such nation or paying the compensation where such nation does the same....

NA: PCC, item 5, pp. 1175-1201 (Journal); M247, reel 19.

Congressional Resolution Regarding the Spanish Negotiations

[New York] Thursday Aug 31st. 1786

Whereas under the 9th. of the Articles of Confederation it is declared "The United States in Congress assembled shall not enter into treaties or alliances unless nine States assent to the same" And whereas by resolutions of the 20 July and 25 day of August 1785 the hon^ble. John Jay Sec^y for Foreign Affairs was authorised with the assent of nine States to negotiate with Don Diego de Gardoqui under certain instructions, the last clause of which was in the words following viz "And that the following be substituted that the Secretary to the United States for the department of foreign

Affairs be and hereby is instructed in his plan of a treaty with the Encargado de Negocios of his Catholic Majesty particularly to stipulate the right of the United States to their territorial bounds and the free navigation of the Mississippi from the source to the Ocean established in their treaties with Great Britain and that he neither conclude or sign any treaty, compact or convention with the said Encargado de Negocios until he hath previously communicated it to Congress and received their approbation" from which qualifications and restrictions the said John Jay could not depart without a violation of his instructions. And as the repeal, by seven States, of the said recited last clause has the effect of enlarging the powers of the said negociator and granting him an Authority he did not posses under the former instructions to which the assent of nine States is alone constitutionally competent under the Confederation, as the removal of a positive restraint confers a positive authority; And as a delegate cannot exceed the authority delegated to him, nor delegate to another a greater power than he himself possesses it follows that the right of entering into treaties being delegated by the confederation to the concurrent assent of nine States in Congress assembled this power cannot be delegated to others or any alterations made in instructions upon this subject but by a similar concurrence of nine States. The right of entering into treaties comprehends an absolute & exclusive right of admitting or rejecting every Article of such Treaty as well as the whole collectively. This right cannot be exercised by seven states, consequently it cannot be delegated by them to any other person or description of persons without an absolute violation of the principles of the Confederation If a treaty entered into in pursuance of instructions be not ratified by the law of Nations it is *causa belli*. If only seven States repeal the said last recited clause of Mr Jay's instructions & he thereupon proceeds to enter into a treaty upon different principles than those under which he was formerly authorised by nine States the said treaty cannot be considered as formed under instructions constitutionally sanctioned by the Authority required under the confederation nor are the United States under the laws or usage of nations bound to ratify & confirm the same Therefore resolved that the Sec^y for foreign Affairs be informed that as the said recited clause of his instructions restraining him from entering into any treaty or compact with the encargado de Negocios of his Catholic Majesty which did not fix the territorial limits of the United States agreeable to the definitive treaty with G Britain & the right of the United States to the free navigation of the Mississippi from its source to the Ocean was repealed by the assent of seven states when nine were alone competent to such alteration & enlargement of his powers the United States in Congress assembled do not consider him as authorised to negociate upon different principles than those under which he was formerly instructed by the said resolutions of the 20th

July & 25 August 1785, nor, should he proceed to enter into a treaty upon other principles, do they conceive the United States bound under the law of Nations to ratify & confirm a compact formed under powers thus unconstitutional and incompetent"

.   .   .   .   .

NA: PCC, item 5, pp.1213-1216 (Journal); M247, reel 19.

Assumptions and Draft Instructions
for Don Diego de Gardoqui Regarding
Boundaries and Exclusive Navigation of the Mississippi

[Translation]

San Indefonso, 1 September 1786

Assumptions

1ᵒ· It appears from Gardoqui's despatches up to 4 July that there has been no progress, nor is progress expected, on these two subjects because the Americans propose to occupy all the lands they can outside the boundaries of the Floridas, in accordance with their agreement with the English; the same lands that we claim to include within our demarcation, or that are occupied by various nations of Indians that have Treaties with us or with the Americans, or with both parties.

2ᵒ· The tenacity of the Americans in claiming the navigation of the Mississippi is equally apparent because, having allotted immense tracts of land in the upper reaches of the river to many of their leaders, and formed the new State of Kentucky, they anticipate great advantages and benefits from cultivating them if their commodities have an outlet. And as those same States, or interested individuals, are the ones that must discuss our claims in Congress, there is no doubt that they will be strongly opposed thereto.

3ᵒ· Gardoqui informs us, enclosing despatches from our Governors of Florida and copies of American gazettes, that the Creek Indians were getting ready and had begun to harass the Georgians in order to drive them back and to force them to evacuate the lands that they had occupied, and that the actions of these Indians are attributed to the Spaniards.

4ᵒ· By reason of the Treaties that we have made with several of those nations, we are obliged to protect them; and we should do it out of decency and in our own interest, because they serve us as a barrier against the Americans.

5ᵒ· The most advantageous thing that Gardoqui has heard from some members of Congress is that a Treaty could be negotiated in which there would be no mention of the navigation of the Mississippi. But he rejected that proposition, and with reason, for the basic difficulty would remain, and they would think themselves authorized by our very silence to do whatever they want.

6°· The Americans now find themselves in the position of being under great obligations to the King for the Treaty of Peace that he has helped them obtain with Morocco and for the assistance that His Majesty has given them, and that he may yet give them in also achieving peace with the other regencies of Africa. They also owe much gratitude to His Majesty for the generous succor he gave them in their need, and of which he has hitherto not asked repayment, no less than for the respect and appreciation with which he treats them and the warm reception that their subjects and commerce have received in Spain.

Plan

Considering all these circumstances and reducing our own claims regarding boundaries almost to those that the Americans do not dispute with us, and to a short tract of land from the bank of the Mississippi and the mouth of the Yazoo to the confluence of the Flint and the Apalachicola, which divides the Floridas; although with some clause which allows the Indian nations who may reside in this land to be watched over by His Majesty, whose royal intention is not to banish them from their established holdings, but to shelter them under his dominion and protection, it might be agreed that the rest of the lands which the Indian nations occupy today (which would be enumerated) would remain neutral, so that neither the Spanish nor the Americans could legally take possession of them, nor establish themselves within their boundaries, in perpetuity or at least until a formal survey is made by Commissioners that both parties name, and all these boundaries are arranged otherwise through a separate communication; in the same way, it could be stipulated that it is not lawful for Americans to descend the Mississippi beyond the Ohio river or at least the Yazoo, and that neither they nor any other nation may ascend it from its mouths to the same Ohio or Yazoo rivers, at least so long as this point is not settled in another manner by a specific convention, made after the proper investigation and with an exact survey of those lands and of the settlements on both banks of the river.

The forgiveness of the loans made by His Majesty, explained in respectful terms and with generosity, could be a recompense for these concessions, which the Americans would consider as effective losses and of great interest. All the States will benefit from this, since all, pro rata, would have to contribute to the repayment.

And by these means, it appears that we may withdraw with decency from the engagement of the day, and postpone for a time the events that eventually appear inevitable: that the Americans will take possession of all those countries up to the Mississippi and the Ocean, not excepting the Floridas, objectives which we cannot doubt that they have in mind without deceiving ourselves. And in any case, we would be able to take advantage of this truce to put ourselves in a better position to contain them than we are today.

San Idlefonso, 1st of September 1786.

Gómez del Campillo, Relaciones Diplomaticas, *v. 1, pp. 380-383.*

William Carmichael to John Jay

Duplicate   S$^{n.}$ Ildefonso 2$^{d.}$ Sept$^{r.}$ 1786
Sir

. . . . .

The ill state of health of the C^t de Florida Blanca for some time past hath until a few days ago prevented him from giving audience to the Corps Diplomatic, for which reason I have not had until the 1$^{st.}$ instant an opportunity of any personal communication with that Minister. on that Day I paid him my compliments on his recovery & congratulated him on the peace just ratified with Algiers. I seized the opportunity which the Latter circumstance afforded me, to remind his Excellency of the former assurances he had been pleased to make me of employing the good offices of his C.M. to facilitate our pacification of the Barbarisque powers, & begged him once more to authorize me to reiterate to Congress these Assurances of his Majestys amicable sentiments. After concisely recapitulating the Conduct of the King in the Negotiation with Morrocco He assured me that the United States might depend on the continuance of the good Offices of his Majesty with respect to the other Barbary States But at the same time with much apparent Candor owned that a treaty with the Port, which he thought Attainable, was a preliminary Step absolutely necessary to pave the way for our Treaty with Algiers. On this Subject I have conveyed my sentiments to our Ministers at Paris & London as well as the information I have rec^d Relative thereto – I have cultivated & shall continue to cultivate the friendship and correspondence of those whose services may be useful to the United States by their Connections at Constantinople Algiers & Tunis. I have now before me a long Letter from the C$^t.$ D'Expilly who will set out from hence for Algiers with Presents for the Dey and his Ministers. This Letter containing severe strictures on the conduct of another I mean to Submit by the first safe occasion to our Ministers intrusted with the management of this business.

...Notwithstanding a positive order I obtained from the Minister of the Indies in the month of March 1785 to pay the Americans to whom his C.Majestys Government at the Havanna was indebted & to facilitate the recovery of their private Debts, I have been again obliged to have recourse to the same Minister in behalf of M[r] Plunket[1] of Baltimore whose case is attended with very aggravating Circumstances. Promises have been repeatedly made me of redress. But the fact is that there are so many demands for repayment of Sums due to their own & French Subjects & the Treasury is so Low, that much patience & perseverance is necessary to procure the principal of Money due & very favorable Occasions must occur to obtain an Indemnification of Losses sustained by the Tardy or oppressive measures of the Servants of the Crown at a distance. L[t] Governor Unzaga[2] whose tyrannical proceedings gave rise to those complaints, is in disgrace, in part owing to the strong representations I made of his Conduct. He has not been permitted to come to the Court since his return to Europe. I hope, before I leave this Residence to obtain a satisfactory determination of the Ministry all Circumstances considered –

It is probable Mr Gardoqui will shortly receive ulterior propositions of the court relative to the object of his Mission – but as I have no information of the Situation in which the Negotiation rests, It is as impossible, as it would be improper for me to sound the Ministry on the Subject. I must beg leave to take the Liberty of repeating my wishes that Congress would [take] some notice of the gratious Interference of his Catholic Majesty, which facilitated our peace with Morrocco. The Slightest mark of Attention & Respect to this Monarch will be well Received & contribute to remove prejudices which are entertained more or less of the Disposition of the United States, which the British in particular represent as hostile to Spain–

I have the honor to be With great Respect Sir Your Most Humble Ser[t]

W[m.] Carmichael

NA: PCC, item 88, pp. 468-472 (ALS); M247, reel 116.

[1] *Plunket, Thomas. Baltimore merchant who did business in Havanna during and immediately after the Revolution.*

[2] *Unzaga y Amézaga, Luis (1717-1793). Spanish military and political figure. Governor of Cuba, 1783-1785.*

Doctor Edward Bancroft to William Fraser

Sir   London 2ᵈ Septʳ· 1786.

. . . . .

On my arival in France I found that the intercourse between that Kingdom & the United States had lately declined rather than increased; the imports from the Latter, consisting of little more than the Tobacco sent by Mʳ Robᵗ Morris, to fulfil his Contract with the Farmers General, and the Exports from France to the United States being confined almost wholly to Brandy, Wine, Cambric & a very few Silk Goods, and not amounting altogether to one half even of the imports from them. But the French Government though disappointed, have not relinquished the hope of creating a more extensive commercial Intercourse, with the United States, & have lately instituted a Committee to devise means for effecting this purpose, which Committee is composed of I think two Councillors of State, and the Same number of Intendants of Commerce; the Intendant of the Marine the Lieutenant General de Police, the two Inspectors General of Commerce, & the Marquis de La Fayette who are occasionally assisted by three Deputies of the Farmers General & by Mʳ Berard, an Eminent merchant of Port L'Orient. The principal & most important Object hitherto discussed by this Committee, is a plan offered & supported by the Marquis de La Fayette (at the desire of Mʳ Jefferson) for suppressing the monopoly of the Farmers general so far as it relates to Tobacco and sending that Article "*Marchand*" throughout the extent of their exclusive Priviledge, by substituting a Duty of 32 Sols and a half upon its importation *in the Leaf only*, and leaving the sale & manufacture of it afterwards free to every one. – To this Proposition, & the several reasons alledged by M. de la Fayette in Support of it, The Farmers General, were required to make distinct written Answers, & the Marquis having replyed to them, he sent a Statement of the whole to the Press, but caused only 10 or 12 Copies to be printed, one of which I obtained from him, and as it contains some important Facts respecting a very considerable object of the revenue of France I shall inclose it herewith, not only for your personal, but for that of Lord Carmarthen & Mʳ Pitt or any other of the Kings Ministers who may think it worthy of Notice.

The Plan itself though secretly approved and favoured by Count de Vergennes, was not adopted; partly because of the influence opposed to it by the Farmers General and partly because the Comptroller General was apprehensive that it might facillitate the Smuggling of Tobacco, and thereby endanger this important Branch of the Revenue. M. de La Fayette flatters himself however, that it may hereafter be resumed with more

Success; and in the meantime, to obviate the Complaints which Mr Jefferson had made of the Contract subsisting between the Farmers General & Mr Robt Morris of Philadelphia, for 60,000 Hogsheads of Tobacco to be delivered in France within the Space of three years, at 36 Livres p 100 lb. (whereby Mr Morris was not only tempted but enabled to keep down the Price of that Article in the United States), it was determined, that during the Continuance of this Contract, the Farmers General should be held to purchase over and above the Tobacco contracted for, as far as 15000 Hogsheads annually, from other persons indiscriminately who may import it into France in French or American Bottoms *only*, at the same Price, as that contracted for with Mr Morris; and that no other Contract for Tobacco should be made by the Farmers General after the Expiration of that now subsisting.

It had been Mr Jeffersons expectation that the 15000 Hogsheads to be annually purchased from others beside Mr Morris, should be imported *directly* from the United States, but on examining the Terms of the Settlement made with the Farmers General on this Subject, he found that it permitted the Tobacco in question to be brought from Great Britain or any other Country to France, provided it were brought in French or American Vessels, and he thereupon applied for an Alteration of the Settlement in this respect, but the Ministers of France tired as he supposes of the subject, declined resuming the Consideration of it.

The Subject of American Fish Oil is the only other matter of any consequence, hitherto Acted upon in the New Committee, and on this Subject it was decided that the Oil of the United [States] should hereafter be admitted into France on the Same terms as that of the Hans Towns, who in this particular are the most favoured in France where their oil as I understand Pays only a Duty equal to between three & four Pounds Sterling.

The great Subject of the Commerce of the United States & other foreigners with the French West india islands is likely to remain as it was Settled by the Edict of the 30th of August 1784.

.   .   .   .   .

I have the honor to be with great Truth & respect Sir Your most faithful & most Obedient Servant   Edwd Bancroft[1]

PRO: FO 4/4, pp. 595-599 (LC transcription).
[1] *Bancroft, Edward (1744-1821). Naturalist, chemist, physician and spy. Born in Massachusetts, he studied medicine in England before the war. There he became acquainted with Benjamin Franklin, for whom he later acted as a spy, making frequent trips between London and Paris. At some point, he became a double agent, and used his knowledge of secret affairs to speculate on the London Stock Exchange. After the war, he used his knowledge of chemistry to make important discoveries relating to the dying of fabrics.*

William Stephens Smith to John Jay

Sir –   London September 4th 1786 –
The enclosed paper will inform your Excellency of the departure of Lord
Dorchester – (late Sir Guy Carleton)[1] for his Government in Canada; he
is said to be possessed of powers to settle the disputes, relative to the
boundaries &c. as you will note on perusing the Paragraph – This sentence
corresponding with, Lord Carmarthens promise to Mr Adams, as stated in
Mr Adams's dispatches of the 15th July Ul^{to} (viz. "That the Secretary of
State was pleased to say further, that he would speak to Lord Sidney,
concerning the affair of the Eastern Line, that Sir Guy Carleton might have
instructions concerning it before he went out" –) furnishes a line
explanatory of the System of Administration, consistant with what I have
stated in my last Letters to your Excellency – If they had a disposition to
explain and settle that point, I suppose Mr. Adams's powers are sufficient
on our part, and Mr Hartley[2] the Minister on their part is here; those two
Gentlemen by stating their Ideas when they fixed the Boundary, previous
to their signing the Definitive Treaty, might produce sufficient grounds for
positive orders on that Subject, which might save a great deal of trouble on
both sides – but I think from this, and many other circumstances, we may
conclude, they will not yet listen to, or decide on, any question we may
propose – least their Consular plan might not have a fair chance, for
operation – I do not think it improbable, after they have established as
many Consuls as they think will answer their ends, but those Gentlemen,
if closely attended to, will be found coming gently forward, with seperate
proposals to the states or districts where they may respectively reside, for
the establishment of a commercial intercourse independent of foedral
systems, and thus by holding out seperate advantageous plans to the several
States, they expect it will be unnecessary to trouble Congress, & our foedral
Government on the Subject – Is it possible, Sir, that my Country can
submit, to the operation of their projects? I flatter myself it is impossible –
and that they soon will be convinced of the folly of their Plans, and begin
to believe, that in their negotiations with *our Country*, they must change
their old systems and instead of the bad side of the human Character, step
upon the fair Theatre, and for once deal with honor and integrity – it will
be new grounds to them it is true – but I have this opinion of my Country,
that it is the only Grounds on which *this People* can expect, any advantageous establishments –
I shall acknowledge myself under great obligation to your Excellency, for
the earliest information of the result of the commercial Convention, I

promise myself great things for my Country in consequence of it, and shall be anxious untill I am informed of its happy termination –

I am with every sentiment of respect Your Excellency's most Obed^t Servt W. S. Smith

NA: PCC, item 92, pp. 144-146 (ALS); M247, reel 120.

^{1} Carleton, Guy (1724-1808). British military officer. Lieutenant governor of Quebec, 1766-1775; governor, 1775-1778. Heavily involved in formulating Quebec Act, 1774. Commander of British troops in Canada, 1775-1777; knighted, 1776, for defense of Quebec. Commander-in-chief in America, 1782-1783. Created Baron Dorchester, 1786. Governor of Quebec, 1786-1796.

^{2} Hartley, David (1732-1813). British statesman and scientist. Friend of Benjamin Franklin. Member of Parliament, 1774-1780, 1782-1784; a consistent supporter of Rockingham. Opposed American war and African slave trade. Plenipotentiary to negotiate definitive Anglo-American peace treaty, 1783.

Peter Allaire: Occurrences from 8 August to 7 September 1786

[New York, September 7, 1786]^1

. . . . .

[August] 19$^{th.}$ Advices has been Received by the last French Packet, which arrived the 16th Ins^t that the American Merchants, had obtained from the Court of France an Order, that all the Tobacco. (to the Amount of thirty thousand Hogsheads) Merchantable that should be imported into any of the Ports of France, either in American or French Vessells navigated by Americans or Frenchmen, that the Farmers General should pay from thirty four Livres to 38 Livres p^r Hundred, on their Refusing the Merchant to have Liberty to sell his Cargos to any other; and Inspectors appointed to Examine it, & certify wether it is of the first Second or third Quality, if the Cargoe will not stand their Inspection, to be permitted to sail for any other port. Every American Vessell so Loaded from any of the Ports of America, to be obliged to produce a certificate from the french Consul, or Vice Consul Certifying, that the said Vessell is American property, saild from such a Port, with such a Quantity of Tobacco, Also a Certificate from the American Custome House & the Governour of the State from whence the Vessell sailed, in default of which, not to be permitted to Enter – and liable to Confiscation.

. . . . .

The Masts, Bowsprits & Yards purchased by the French Consul at Boston, are now shiping, as he left this City a few days ago for Boston, to have them put on Board one of his Majesties Vessells. there are about five hundred Masts, of the largest size that were to be procured, for the French Navy, the Frigate built at Boston had Orders to take some on board, but they were too large.

.   .   .   .

[August 21] One & Twenty Sail of Nantucket Vessells have Returned from the Whaling fishery, the least has brought home Six hundred Barrells blubber which are great Voyages, One Ship & one Brig has arrived into this port, with good Success. – all of which is intended for the French Market.

.   .   .   .

Congress finding the Indian Affairs increase, and the many applications from the different States to Regulate the Indian Trade & Treaties have come to the Resolution the 10th of this Month to divide the Trade into two Districts, North & South: the Southern shall comprehend within its Limits, all the Indian Nations in the Territory of the united States who reside Southward of the River Ohio, Northern shall Contain all the Indian Nations within the said Territory and Westward of Hudsons River &c. And be it further Ordained that none but Citizens of the United States, be suffered to reside amongst the Indian Nations or to Trade with any of the Indian Nations within the Territory of the United States under the penalty of 500 Dollars, that no Person Citizen or others shall reside amongst or Trade with any of the Indian nations without a Licence from one of the Superintendants, under the penalty of 500 Dollars....

.   .   .   .

PRO: FO 4/4, pp. 623-638 (LC transcription).
¹ Allaire, Peter (1740-1820). New York merchant. Employed by the British espionage service during the Revolutionary War, he subsequently provided regular intelligence reports on happenings in the United States to the British Foreign Office through his friend Sir George Yonge, with whom he engaged in land speculation.

Thomas Barclay to
John Adams and Thomas Jefferson

Gentlemen.   Tangier 10th September 1786.
    I am at present waiting for a fair wind to embark for Ceuta to avoid the quaranteen in Spain, and I embrace the Delay occasion'd by the strong Easterly Winds that have prevail'd for some time, to reply to the Queries with which you honour'd me at parting. – You put them respecting the Barbary States generally but as my business has been with the Emperor of Morocco only, I shall confine myself to what relates to his Dominions – and will State the answers in the order you put the Queries. –

Commerce. The articles exported from this Country are the Gums arabic, Sandrach and Senegal – Bees-wax, Copper in Blocks, Morocco leather, Almonds, Dates, Figs and Walnuts, and Lemmons and Oranges might be had, was there wood in the Country to make boxes to pack them in – Great quantities of olive oil and oil of Argan (a fruit somewhat resembling an olive) are exported particularly to Marseilles, where it is used in making Soap, – Mules are exported to Surinam and to other parts of America both on the Continent and among the Islands – many of these Animals passing from Constantina to Mogadore by land being a Journey of 1000 miles – Elephant's teeth, Gold Dust and Ostrige feathers are brought from the Southward by the People who trade as far as to the River Nigre, and are Sold and Shipped at Mogadore the most Southerly Port in the Empire except Santa Cruis, from which last place the Emperor has forbid any foreign Trade to be pursued, and from Mogadore and Daralbeyda the export of wheat is very great. Morocco imports from Spain, Portugal, and Italy Several of the manufactures of these Countries, particularly Silks, Linnens, and woolen Cloths – with England and Holland the trade is more general and comprehends not only the same kind of Goods, but a variety of others, such as Iron ware of various Sorts, including tools made use of by Workmen, Tinware, Steel, Iron in bars Copper Utensils, Ship Chandlery and Cordage for the repairing Deficiencies in merchant Vessels. Wine and Spirituous Liquors for the use of the Christians may be Imported from any part of the World Duty free, but the use is forbidden to the Mahometans, nor is there any thing in the Country sold by measure but Grain – They import Rice from the Levant which is of an inferior quality to the American Rice, and I believe a little of this article might answer and perhaps the Consumption increase – but this is conjecture for there is no answering for the taste of the Moors – Flour they have much cheaper than the price at which we could supply them. They raise a good deal of Tobacco themselves, and some pretty good about Fez and Mequinez, none of it however is equal to our's but the Consumption of american tobacco wou'd be confin'd to the Europeans and consequently it wou'd not prove of much consequence – Furs are not used here and they want neither fish nor oil, provisions of all kinds are Cheap and their Sea coast furnishes with abundance of fish for common use, and their Ramadan or Lent do's not permit the use of Fish more than of Flesh, being a Strict abstinence from all kind of food or Drink for about sixteen hours of the Twenty four – There is no demand for tar or turpentine, each Merchant Ship brings as much as is likely to be wanted for the Voyage, and the Emperor is Supply'd from the Baltic. Ship timber wou'd certainly be a most agreeable Object to the Emperor, but he is the only person in his Dominions who wou'd purchase it – and the price wou'd be made by himself, he was anxious to know whether we had this article in America – Ready built Ships, that is Frigates properly fitted out for Sea and arm'd, wou'd prove the most acceptable article that cou'd be sent to him, but his making a purchase of any wou'd depend on the opinion he had of the value – He some time ago encouraged the building of one at Genoa and when she arrived at one of his Ports, He rejected her on account of the price. –

The Duties of Goods imported with a few exceptions is a tenth part of the Goods – foreign Hides pay 3 Dollars and Iron and Steel four Dollars p. quintal – Cochineal and alkermes are monopolized by the Emperor, and Sold at a great advance on the Price the former is used in Dying the Morocco Skins and the latter in Dying the Caps such as the Soldiers and many of the inhabitants wear – Ostrige feathers are a monopoly in the hands of a Jew at Mogadore without whose permission none can be exported – Offences committed against the interest of the Revenue are punish'd by fine impos'd by the Emperor sometimes with great Severity – never with less than the crime deserves. All Countries pay the same Duties but the King will sometimes favor an Individual by the remission of part of the ordinary Duties in return for some Service, or as a mark of his approbation – The Moors are not their own carriers, nor is there any trading Vessels under the Colours of the Emperor. From this Short State it will appear that few of the articles produced in Morocco are wanted in our parts of America – nor cou'd any thing manufactur'd here find a Sale there except a little Morocco Leather, which is very fine and good and the consumption of it in the Empire almost incredible – They make some Gold and Silk thread at Fez – and in various parts of the Country coarse and fine Stuff for Alhaiques – a good many Carpets, some coarse Linnen and a Great many red woolen Caps, and these articles I think compose the whole of their manufactures, which from the unskilfulness of the People who work at them, the Leather excepted, are too Dear for Exportation – Still this Country holds out objects to the Americans, Sufficient to make a treaty of Peace and commerce a matter of consequence – Our Trade to the Mediterannean is render'd much the Securer for it – and it affords us Ports where our Ships may refit if we shou'd be engaged in an European War, or in one with the other Barbary States – Our Vessels will certainly become the Carriers of Wheat from Morocco to Spain, Portugal & Italy – and may find Employment at times when the navigation of our own Country is stop'd by the winter Season – and we shall resume our old mule trade from Barbary to Surinam and possibly to some of the West India Islands. with respect to the prices of the exports of this Country I will add a list of them together with one of the Duties.–

Ports. I will enlarge a little on this Subject by giving you a General Idea, not only of the best ports in the Empire, but of all that are of any consequence omitting Waladia Azumor and some others which in no Degree, in my Opinion, deserve to be ranked in the number. I will begin with the most Southerly which is the only one of them which I have not seen. – *Santa Cruz*. Is the only Seaport in Sus, and is Situated about Ninety miles to the Southward of Mogadore and Six from the western extremity of Mount Atlas, being between the end of that mountain and the Sea, from which it is distant half a mile. It is placed on the declivity of a Hill and cannot be injur'd by any Shipping. There are no Fortifications nor any Guns mounted except two for Signals – The Road for Vessels is open but the anchoring good – being a hard sandy Bottom – and the depth of water so gradual that Ships may anchor in such as suits them best. There are about Two thousand Houses in the Town and the Trade was very considerable until the Emperor order'd the Port to be Shut up – it was the mart for all the Commodities of Tafilet and Sus, and is the thoroughfare through which the Inhabitants of the Sea Coast pass to those Kingdoms, or to the Sahara. The trade is now remov'd to

Mogadore. A Town built by order of the present Emperor containing two thousand Houses and Eleven thousand Inhabitants, as appears by an account taken previous to a Distribution of Corn being made a few months ago by order of the Emperor – about a mile from the Shore runs a tongue of Land called the Island of Mogadore, and between the Land and the Island the Ships anchor and may pass in Safety if they draw no more than fifteen feet water – some say sixteen feet – The Island proves a considerable Shelter for them, but a Strong Southerly or Southwest wind incommodes them much – occasioning a swell in the Channell which is sometimes dangerous – the Bottom is hard and rocky and it is necessary to put Buoys to the Cables to prevent them from Cutting – The Town is defended by Two Batteries, one of 9 Iron and 33 Brass cannon, 20. of which are fine Spanish Guns left at Gibraltar, in the last Seige, the other of either five or six Iron guns and 20 Brass, and 33 more may be mounted – On a rock to the Northward of the Town is a Battery of ten guns, and on the main Land to the Southward, one of 16, another for ten Guns is now building, and on the Island are five little forts of five Guns each – The Moors consider Mogadore as a strong place though some people think that all the Batteries being of Stone is a great disadvantage – Many of the Guns, all of which are about eighteen pound Cannon, are yet unprovided with carriages, But the Town being a place much esteem'd by the Emperor, He is doing every thing in His Power to Strengthen and improve it – the number of Guns actually mounted is 118 or 119. –

Safia. This town is Situated on the Side of a Hill, about 2 miles from the Southerly point of Cape Cantin – It was once a place of importance, but it is now decaying fast, and at present the inhabitants are interdicted from

all foreign trade. The anchoring ground is very good in water which varies
in depth from 25 to 40 fathom, but there is little Shelter (indeed almost
none) and if it blows hard, as it Sometimes do's in Winter, Ships must put
out to Sea for Security. - The Principal fortification is founded on a Rock,
and capable of mounting a Great number of Cannon, there are three iron
& five Brass Guns mounted of about 18 pound Shot, the Brass Guns were
made at Constantinople, and ten or twelve small Guns lye unmounted. It
is a place of little Strength as it now Stands, and is reduced from 4000
Houses which it is said to have contain'd - to about eight hundred. -

Masagan. Was one of the Strongest places in Barbary, when in the hands
of the Portuguese about eithteen [sic] years ago. The Emperor learning that
orders were come from Lisbon that the Town shou'd be evacuated, and the
fortifications destroy'd, marched with a considerable Army and train of
Artillery, and while the Inhabitants were executing the instructions from
their Court, bombarded the place, so that between the two parties it was
left in a State of Desolation, of 1500 houses, it retains about 400 of the
meanest that were most easily repair'd. The Ruins, however shew that it
was a place of Consequence. Ships of any Draught of water may lye at
Some Distance from the Town, the Soundings being gradual and the
anchoring Ground good. but there is no Shelter and if it blows hard the
Ships must run out to Sea. -

Daralbeyda. Is at present remarkable for the great export of Wheat which
has taken place there within twelve months, and which has amounted
perhaps to half a Million of Bushells - It is a poor place, containing four
or five hundred miserable Huts - The anchoring ground is good in some
parts with a sandy Bottom, in twelve fathom water, in other parts the
Bottom is Stoney and rocky and in winter it is dangerous. -

Rabat. Is built on the Banks of the Buragrag where that River enters the
Sea, and divides it from Salè which is on the opposite Shore at about a
mile Distance - Rabat contains about 2500 Houses, and is one of the best
looking Towns I have seen in Barbary. The entrance into the River is much
obstructed by a Bank of Sand which runs Across the Mouth of it, and
which is constantly Shifting - At ordinary Tides vessels drawing 8 feet
water may pass and at Spring Tides those of twelve, but sometimes loaded
vessels in the River are oblig'd to remain there three or four months for a
Passage out, which they can only have by the Shifting of the Sands -
There are three forts at this place. One on a point which commands the
entrance of the River of 10 Guns, and two on the Sea Shore, one of which
is of eight, and the other intended for 16 Guns, of which three only are
mounted - There is also a Castle or Fort without Guns upon the Hill on
which the Town is built. -

Salè. Is Built on an Eminence on a Point of the Burregreg at its entrance into the Ocean opposite to Rabat, it is defended towards the Sea by a Battery of 8 pieces of Cannon – and is Surrounded by a double Wall. The Streets are narrow and dirty and the Houses mean the number being about 2500 – As the Navigation is in common with Rabat what has been Said in the last article need not be repeated. This Place which has been long famous for its depredations against the Christians, seems to be declining fast, but the same observation was made on it some Centuries ago. –

Mamora. Is Situated on a high rock on the Southern Side of the River Cebu, a mile above its entrance into the Sea and where the River is about a half a mile broad. It was formerly a place of considerable importance, but is now in the last Stage of Desolation – There are the remains of two fortifications almost entire, and which Seem to be built Since the Town has been destroy'd. One of them is near the Sea Shore and on the declivity of the Rock, once mounted 12 Guns, and at present has three of Brass and one of Iron mounted – The other Fort stands higher up, was once of the same Strength with the former but is now without Guns. The remains of the walls – ditches and Defences, Shew that this was once deem'd a place of consequence, though a Bar runs across the mouth of the River that prevents the entrance of large Vessels as the Portuguese experienced in an expedition which they made against it in the year 1515. –

Laracha. Is a strong place but not of considerable extent situated on the Top and Declivity of a Hill facing the Port where the Ships lye, It is a Bar harbour with a narrow Channell sufficient for one Vessel to pass – and Ships bound in must keep the Shore as a Seaman wou'd term it, close on board on the Starboard hand – At common tides there are 12 feet water on the Bar, and in Spring tides Depth sufficient for any Vessel – which can lye Safe in the Port, well Defended from any Winds and where 60 or 80 Sail may take the Ground in Soft mud without Injury – The Channell is defended by three forts – the one farthest from the Town of 8 Guns, the next of 9, and the other of three – and every vessel going into the Harbour must pass along close by these Guns – On the entrance into the Harbour is a Pile of Batteries rais'd over each other in three Stories – each Battery consisted of 20 Guns, but the only ones mounted are 16 Brass of about 16 pound ball which Guns are in the middle Battery – This pile has an Air of Great Strength, but part of the middle Battery having sunk near 2 feet, I think the whole work must be greatly weaken'd by this misfortune – On a parallel with this middle Battery runs a small one of three Guns, on an Angle one of eleven, and below nearly on a level with the Sea, one of nine; so that the number of Batteries are nine, and that of Guns, if all were mounted wou'd be 103, but of these perhaps 50 are wanting – there are, however, a considerable number of Guns Scatter'd about without Carriages, and from appearances there seems to be little apprehension of a necessity of using any – The last attack on this Place was made by the French in 1768 or 1769 – when they forced their way in Boats under the cover of their Ships into the harbour, with a Design to destroy the Shipping, but the Tide going out, left them a prey to the Moors who never make prisonrs on such occasions – I think the French lost 413 men being about one half of their whole number – the rest remaining on board the Ships and the Emperor order'd their heads to be sent to Morocco, where he paid 2 Ducats a piece for about 200 that were preserv'd for him. I saw ten or twelve Moors at Laracha who assisted in repelling this Invasion – and who spoke of it with great seeming pleasure; The people suppos'd the French were come to possess themselves of the Country, and took up arms very generally to oppose them – A Strong Citadel once commanded the Harbour – it is Situated on a Hill with a Ditch Surrounding a part of it, but it is tumbling to Ruins – The inside of the Walls contain nothing but narrow alleys across which a great number of low arches are turn'd, the use of which I cou'd neither learn nor conjecture, – and a great many miserable Huts. – *Arzilla.* Is a little wall'd Town that has seen better days. The houses in number two or three hundred, are going fast to decay, as well as the fortifications. the Walls have been Strong and are encompassed with a Ditch – there are three or four guns mounted, and on a fort which lyes some distance from the town, six or eight, over one of the Gates is the Arms of Spain. – A Reef or ledge of Rocks runs along the coast, but it is broken so as small Vessels may pass in, and large ones may anchor on the outside in ten fathom water, but there is neither Port nor Shelter.

Tangiers. Is one of the most ancient Cities in Barbary, it has undergone many revolutions, and was once a place of Splendor and commerce. The whole Country distinguishing itself from the name of the City. –

The King of Portugal took it in 1471, and in 1662 it was deliver'd to Charles the Second of England as part of his Wifes Dowry and it was by that Monarch improv'd at an expence of two millions Sterling. in 1684 it was Destroy'd and abandon'd by the English. The Mole where a first rate Man of War coud ride in Safety, was with incredible labour destroyed – the fortifications and walls were not only blown up, but the ruins tumbled into the Harbour. In Short in about 6 months the English made a considerable progress in the destruction of the Port, which has since remain'd in the quiet possession of the Moors. – The town is placed on the right hand Side of the entrance into the Bay on a Hill two miles from the Sea and about 5 miles distant from an opposite point on which a Battery of ten guns is placed – The form of the Bay is that of the third part of a Circle, and the number of Houses in the Town about 800, said to be half as many as were in it when the English had possession At present small vessels may come in, and lye ashore on a Soft Beach, without danger. but large ones must anchor at a Distance in the Bay, and in case of blowing weather put to Sea for Safety. The Batteries here are, one almost level with the Sea, and consisting of 13 Guns of 12 or 14 pound ball, the rest are on the Hill viz̄ – One of 9 Brass Guns, of about 24 pound Shot cast in Portugal and three more may be mounted. a Second of 12 new iron Guns of 24 pound Shot, cast in England, and seven more may be mounted, and another of seven Iron Guns, of 12 or 14 pound Shot; exclusive of these are two little Batteries of two Guns each. The Battery which was Situated on the top of the Hill near the Castle where the Basha resides, and which contain'd 18 Guns of 16 pound ball, was totally destroy'd about twelve months ago by the blowing up of the Magazine where the Emperor's Powder was stor'd. All the fortifications are going to Decay – and seem very unequal to a Contest of any consequence. Tangier is about 7 miles from Cape Spartel and consequently may be said to be within the Streights leading to the Mediterannean. –

Tetuan. Is Situated to the eastward of Ceuta, which lyes between Tangier and that place, but being in the hands of the Spaniards (as well as Melila and Peñon de Velez) does not come under my notice. – Tetuan lies on the River Marteen, about 6 miles from the Mediterannean Sea. the Custom House at Marteen being about halfway between the City and the Sea, across the mouth of this river also runs a Bar on which there is only Six feet water, and as there is little tide here, the Depth never exceeds 8 feet, and seldom is so much, Vessels must therefore lighten on the outside of the Bar, and can then pass up the Bay and River three miles to the Custom House, and from thence to Town. no boats but small ones with fruit can go, owing to the Shallowness of the River. The Town is built on a Hill, at the foot of a Mountain, and has only one fort or Citadel flank'd with four towers, and mounting 20 Cannon to defend it – The Houses are said to be about two thousand five Hundred – and the Inhabitants exclusive of Jews twenty thousand – but the estimation a few years ago was Double this number – No Christian is permitted to enter the City, and therefore this account of it depends on the Veracity and Knowledge of some jews, who visited me at my encampment near it. On the River Marteen, within half a mile of the Mediterannean, is a Square Castle, at which Five Guns of Sixteen pound ball are mounted. –

From this view of the Ports belonging to the Emperor, it will be seen that none of them are good, that Laracha is the best, next to which are I think Salè and Tetuan, but I believe the place from whence I write, might, with great abilities and Industry, and at a great Expence, be made a most Valuable Seaport – I think also that Masagan might be made a place of great Importance. –

Naval force, The whole naval force of this Country consists of ten Frigates carrying 170 Guns; which at present are employ'd in this manner,

1. at Daralbeyda of 18 Guns, six pound ball.
4. Sail'd from Laracha for Daralbeyda of 16 Guns to load Corn and Barley for the Emperor to distribute among his Subjects –
1. at Laracha of 22 Guns,   6 pound Shot –
1. at   D° of 14 d°   d°
1. at   D° of 12 d° –   4 pound d° –
2. gone to Constantinople, with presents of Salt Petre and Silver, to the Grand Seignior, of 20 Guns each. –

This is the State of the Emperor's fleet at present, and the five frigates which are to take on Grain at Daralbeyda are those the Commodore inform'd me some time ago were to go on a Cruize. His Ten half Galleys which I saw at Marteen are laid up on Shore irrecoverably perish'd – He has however given orders for building some Galleys and half Galleys; two of which are on the Stocks here – The number of Seamen Employ'd is about 798 men, and 1000 apprentices and he can encrease the number as much as he pleases by ordering his Governors to put others on board his Vessels. A few days ago he made a general request to all the foreign Consuls, that each of their Nations shou'd send ten Seamen to improve his people in the Art of Navigation, promising to pay each Person who will come half as much more as he receives in his own Country – He has not any Treaty of Peace with Russia, Hamburg, Dantzic or Malta – but he wrote some days ago to the Sea Ports that he was not at Hostilities with any Nation whatever except the United States. The resources for encreasing his Navy are not internal, at least they depend chiefly on his Neighbours. He has a good deal of Small live oak and Corkwood, which last is esteem'd very good Wood when cut in a proper time and Season'd – and the properties of the former are well known. The Prizes that are brought in, also furnish Timber for building and are broke up for that purpose – The Rigging, Sail Canvas, Anchors, Ship Chandlery, Tar, Pitch & Turpentine, are furnish'd by Holland, England, and Sweden, and His Frigates are often repair'd at Gibraltar without any expence to Him, and one return'd from thence since we left Morrocco, the fitting out of which cost the British seven thousand pounds Sterling. – The Season for cruizing is in the Summer or rather from April to September, and the Grounds to the Northward as far as the Coast of Portugal to the westward off the Canary, and Western Islands – and in the Mediterannean. His frigates are in good order and his Seamen neither very excellent nor despicable. –

Prisoners. There are not any Prisoners or Christian Slaves in the Empire of Morocco – except Six or Seven Spaniards, who are in the Sahara or Desert, and which the Emperor is endeavouring to procure that they may be deliver'd to their Country. This Part is not in Strict obedience to the King, though govern'd by his Son Abderhammon, from whom it is somewhat difficult to procure the release of Europeans that are cast away in those parts – and his Majesty has no way to get them but by encouraging the Southern Traders to purchase and bring them to Morrocco, or to prevail on his Son to Send them – And here it will be doing a piece of justice to the Emperor which he well Deserves to Say that there is not a man in the World who is a greater Enemy to Slavery than He is. He Spares neither money nor pains to redeem all who are so unfortunate as to be cast away, whom he orders to be fed and cloth'd, untill they are return'd to their Country – The Venetian Consul told me that the King being some time ago posses'd of Sixty Christians the Consul had a commission sent to him to redeem them, at an expence of 1000 Dollars each, but when his Majesty was applied to, he answer'd that he woud not Sell them, but that the Grand master of Malta (with whom he was *not* at Peace) having liberated some Moors these Christians Shou'd be deliver'd up as a Compliment to him – At another time his Majesty made a purchase of Moorish Slaves, who were in the Possession of the Christian Powers on the Coast of the Mediterannean for which he paid 160 thousand Dollars, without ~~paying~~ Shewing any regard to wch of the Barbary States they belonged and set them all at liberty without any condition whatever – The Expence of redeeming Slaves in the days of Muley Ishmael and Muley Abdallah was about 1000 Dollars a Head or three Moors for 1 Christian.

Treaties. I do not think there is any danger of the present Emperor's breaking any of his Treaties intentionally or in matters of Consequence. He Some time ago however Settled the Duty on the export of Barley by treaty with the British and soon after encreas'd it. The English Merchants at Mogadore intended representing this matter to the Emperor, and did not Doubt but it wou'd be put to rights. – He said not long ago that if an European Vessel took on board any of his Subjects who went on a pilgrimage to Mecca, and landed them any where but in his Dominions He wou'd go to war with the nation to whom the Vessel belong'd – and on being told that there was nothing in any of the treaties to prevent a European vessel from doing this – He reply'd if that was the case, he wou'd not break the peace, but it wou'd be a Peace without friendship – When this Emperor dies, there will probably be great Contentions, and I Suppose treaties will avail little either at Sea or Land until these contentions are adjusted –

Land Forces. The Grandfather of the present King rais'd an army of 100,000 Negroes from whose Descendents, the Army has ever since been recruited. But these Standing forces at different times and for various reasons have been reduced to the number 14767 – four thousand of whom are station'd at Morocco and the remainder in Seven Regiments in the different Provinces – their pay including the maintenance of a Horse is one Ducat p. month, 10 Fanegas of Wheat, 14 of Barley and 2 Suits of Cloaths annually and the King frequently makes distributions among their families, and whenever he Sends any of them on particular business, such as Conducting foreigners through the Country, they are well paid. At the Commencement of a Campaign, He generally gives them ten Ducats, and at the end of it five and it is His Inclination and endeavours to keep them Satisfy'd. All his Male Subjects are born Soldiers, and in case of Necessity, all who are able are oblig'd to attend him in the field. – I suppose the Emperor has fifty thousand Horses and Mules distributed through his Dominions – which he recalls when he pleases and places at pleasure in the hands of Others. These are all consider'd as obliged to take the field at a moments warning, and I have often heard, and I believe it to be true that in a few weeks, Shou'd an Invasion from the Christians be dreaded, (the fear of which is always accompanied by an Idea that they come to take Possession of the Country) the Emperor cou'd bring into the field two hundred thousand men – but I doubt much whether He cou'd equip half the Number – The Strength of this Country certainly lyes in his Land Forces, on their own Ground which wou'd ever prove formidable in case of an invasion – Both Regular troops and Militia are extremely expert in manuvring on horseback, at Skirmishing, at Sudden attacks and at Sudden Retreats – but I apprehend they wou'd cut but a bad figure in an open field against European troops. on this Subject I can only add that when the Emperor wants Soldiers, He orders Such of the Bashas to join him as he thinks proper with the Number of men wanted – The present Emperor has not had much occasion to call forth the Strength of His Country – In 1774 he went against Melilla with 80000 Militia, which I think was the greatest Draught he ever made. –

Revenue. The amount of this article is very fluctuating, and uncertain, it consists of the following Articles. –

Duty on Exports which varies according to the Will of the Emperor. –

Duty on Imports which is in the Same State, but at present taking them generally is 10 p Cent.

Tax of 10 p. Cent. on all the Grain rais'd in the Country, on the Cattle and other moveable Property – which however is rated so much in favour of the proprietors that it does not produce one half the Value. –

Tax on each City according to its abilities

Tax on Tobacco brought into the Cities – of little consequence being farmed at 3000 Dollars p. annum. –

Fines on the Bashas or rather public Officers for Offences of any kind.

Fines for Smugling Goods which are arbitrary. –

Fines impos'd on Towns or Provinces for revolting, quarreling with each other, or for offences commited by Individuals when the offenders are not discover'd. –

Property – which falls into the hands of the Emperor at the Death of any Public Officer whose account with the public is unsettled. –

Proportion of Prizes made at Sea. –

Profit on Cochineal and Alkermes. –

Presents from Foreign Nations and from his own Subjects. –

There are a few other articles, such as coining money &cᵃ, not worth enumerating. Nor does my knowldge of these which I have mention'd enable me to write as particularly about each as I cou'd wish – The Sum of four Millions of Mexican Dollars is by many thought a high rate to State his annual revenue at, but Mogadore and Daralbeyda will pay between them one million of Dollars in Duties for the last year, and I think the other places and other articles will certainly produce three times as much, though he receives no taxes from Tafilet and little from Sus. –

Language. The common Language Spoken in the Sea Ports is the Moorish which is a Dialect of the Arabic the differences either in Speaking or writing between the two being very little. A Language is Spoken in the mountains and in the Eastern part of the Empire, called Berebere (or as it is usually pronounced, the Breber) tongue – and the European language that is the best known is the Spanish, for all the Jews, who are very numerous, Speak it. French, Italian and English are pretty equally understood and rank after the Spanish. –

Government. The Government is that of Absolute Monarchy without limitation. The Emperor is the Supreme executive Magistrate, in whom is united all Spiritual and temporal Power – and his People hold their lives and Property totally at his will and pleasure. The life of the meanest of his Subjects cannot be touch'd, except in an emergency, but by his own order, or by the Order of some Basha to whom he has delegated the power of life and Death – a Power he rarely places out of his own hands, – Criminals from the most distant provinces are sent to Morocco, where the King hears the Complaints against them, and as soon as he pronounces Sentence it is executed on the Spot, and this is always at an audience. when we left Morocco no execution had taken place for four months. – This Court do's not depend in any degree on the Ottoman Porte, nor on any other Power whatever – But there is a Strict friendship between the Grand Seignior and the Emperor, and as there is a possibility of a war between the Turks and Russians – the Emperor thinking it a kind of common cause, being between Christians and Muslemans has Shewn his disposition lately to aid the Grand Seignior by Sending him two twenty Gun frigates with Saltpetre and Silver to a very considerable amount. –

Religion. The Moors of the Empire of Morocco profess the Mahometan religion and obedience to the precepts of the Koran – but the Emperor holds the power of dispensing occasionally with such as he thinks propper. thus the exportation of Corn which is prohibited by the Koran, is permitted by the King. – With respect to their Piracies – I beleive they do not proceed from any religious principle – It Seems to be the general opinion that they took rise on the expulsion of the Moors from Spain in the reign of Phillip the 3^d when 700,000 were banish'd from that Country. – that necessity and Revenge first instigated them to commit depredations on the Europeans – and their hands were strengthen'd and hatred encreas'd by the final Expulsion in the Reign of Ferdinand and Isabell when 17000 families join'd their friends on the Sea Coast of this side of the Mediterannean – A Piratical War, begun against the Spaniards, was extended to the other Christian Powers, And all the Barbary States have been enabled to support this War from the Supplies given them by the Maritime Powers of Europe, many of which seem contending with each other which shall enable the Moors most to injure the Trade of their Neighbours. –

What I have said on this article, I give as the best information I can procure but it is not Satisfactory – and I am persuaded the Origin, of these Depredations, is of a much older date, for early in the Seventh Century, the Spaniards made a Decent on the Town from which I write to revenge the Piracies committed by the People of this Country. –

Captures. No American Vessel has been taken by the Emperor but one, which was commanded by Captain Irwin,[1] and bound from Cadiz to Virginia – She lyes on the Beach at this Place, and the Emperor order'd the Basha to deliver her and the Cargo to me, but as I understood She had been Insur'd in Spain, I did not chuse to take her under my care. – The Emperor has no Treaty with Russia, Germany Hamburg Dantzic or Malta – But there seems to be a Cessation of Hostilities with all the world – He had order'd five frigates to be fitted for Sea, and I think it more than probable they were intended to Cruize against the Americans. –

Having thus answer'd the Queries which you were pleas'd to make – I shall at present conclude with the assurance of my being always with great respect and Esteem. Gent^n Your most obed^t hble Servt –

Tho' Barclay

NA: PCC, item 91, v.1, pp. 171-186 (ALS): M247, reel 119.

[1] *Erwin, Captain James. American seafarer. In October 1784, Erwin's vessel, the brig Betsey, outward bound from Philadelphia to Teneriffe, was captured by a Moroccan corsair and taken into Tangier. Erwin and his crew were not enslaved, but allowed to remain at large in the town of Mogadore. They were subsequently released with their vessel as a sign of the Emperor of Morocco's desire for friendly relations with the United States. The Betsey arrived at Cadiz on July 18, 1785.*

John Adams to Thomas Jefferson

Dear Sir   Grosvenor Square Sept.ʳ 11. 1786
   On my Return from Holland, on the Sixth instant I found your Favours of the 8. and 13. Aug. – on my Arrival at the Hague The Exchange of Ratifications was made on the 8 August with The Baron De Thulemeier, and I had it Printed. it is only in French. – Copies Shall be Sent you as Soon as I can find an Opportunity....

·   ·   ·   ·   ·

   As to Mʳ Lambs Settlement, I still think he had better embark forthwith for New York from Spain. if he cannot he may transmit to you and me his Account, and remit to Us the Ballance in favour of U.S.
   Mʳ Barclays Proposal, of going to Tunis and Tripoli, I Suppose appears to you as it does to me, from what We learned from the Ambassador from Tripoli in London, to be unnecessary at least till We hear farther from Congress. It Seems to me too, very unlikely that any Benefit will be had from a Journey to Algiers. – I wish to See the Treaty with Morocco, and to know the Particulars of that Affair, first. – At present I believe We are taken in, and that We shall be plagued with Demands for annual Presents. I confess, I have no Faith in the Supposition that Spanish Interference has counted for Money, or, at least that it will pass long for it.
   If however you are clearly in favour of Sending Mʳ Barclay to Algiers, I will make out a Commission, and Send it to you, for your Signature Signed by myself, because I would not Set up my own Judgment against yours, Mʳ Charmichaels and Mʳ Barclays: but I confess, at present I cannot see any Advantage in it, but on the contrary Several Disadvantages. Mʳ Randal is gone to Congress, and We may expect further orders, e'er long.
   With Sincere Affection I am, dear Sir, your Friend and Servant
                                                        John Adams

·   ·   ·   ·   ·

LC: *Jefferson Papers, microfilm reel 6 (ALS).*

Thomas Barclay to John Adams and Thomas Jefferson

Gentlemen.   Tangier 13ᵗʰ September 1786 –
   Though in a letter written at this place – dated 10ᵗʰ instant, I gave you a long answer to the questions with which you charged me, I will now add some farther particulars on the Subject of this Country, which you will possibly be inclined to know. –

The Emperor is on the most cordial and friendly footing with Spain, the presents, made him from that Court, have been uncommomly great, and among other valuable articles lately sent, were 80 thousand Dollars in Specie. –

It was, some time ago, debated in the Council at Versailles whether war should not be declared against Morocco for the treatment which the Emperor gave M^r· Chinie[1] the french Consul when he was last at Morocco. The fact was that the Emperor wrote to Rabat desiring to see the Consul at the Court from which M^r· Chinie excus'd himself on account of his health, which the Emperor was inform d was very good – Some time after the Consul went up to Morocco, with a letter from M^r De Castries, in answer to one which the Emperor had written to the King of France, but the Emperor was so much offended at the letter not being from the King himself, and at Mr Chinie for not complying with his Desire to go to Morocco, that, He wou'd not look at it, but ordered it, at the Public Audience, to be tied round the Consul's neck, and dismissed him – The late proConsul of France has been very successful in reconciling matters, and the present Consul was very well receiv'd while I was in Morocco, – the Emperor however strongly advising him to avoid the ways of his Predecessor. –

The Swedes are bound by treaty to Send an Ambassador once in two years, and the presents are considerable and very usefull to the Emperor. –

The Danes are bound by treaty to pay an annual tribute of 25 Thousand Dollars. –

The Venetians, by treaty also, are bound to pay ten thousand Chequins being about Twenty two thousand Dollars. –

The presents from Holland are more considerable than those from any of the three last mention'd Powers, but they are not stipulated. –

The English pay also very high without being bound to do so by treaty and they enjoy at present very little of the Emperor's friendship or good wishes – There is not a Nation on earth of which he has so bad an opinion, and I have heard him say they neither minded their Treaties nor Promises. – It wou'd be going into too long a Detail to mention all the particulars that gave rise to these prejudices which may very possibly end in a war. –

The Emperor of Morocco has no Treaty with the Emperor of Germany, and has given notice to the Imperial Consul at Cadiz that unless the Emperor of Germany sends him Three frigates, He will cruize against his Vessells. –

With the Portugueze, He is very friendly their Men of War come into this bay to get Supplies of Provisions and other necessaries, During their cruizes against the Algerines – and a Man of War of 64 Guns which is lying at Anchor here for that purpose will Sail in a few days to join the Portuguese Squadron of Six Vessels that are now in the Mediterannean to prevent the Algerine Cruizers from getting into the Atlantic. – By the treaty between Portugal and Morocco the Emperor is not to allow his Vessels to Cruize to the Northward of Cape Finistre. –⊗

I have already mentioned the Situation of the Emperor with the Porte – With Tunis and Tripoli he is on very good terms – but a Coolness has subsisted between Him and the Dey of Algiers for some time, which began I believe upon the Emperor's having made Peace with Spain without communicating with the Dey. I am told, however, that some late friendly overtures have been made from Algiers which will probably reinstate the Countries in their old Situation. –

The Dominions of the Emperor consists of the Kingdoms of Fez, Morocco, Tafilet and Sus, and his influence extends a great away into the Desert; Fez and Morocco are in many parts very fertile in Corn, fruit and oil, and any quantity of Wine might be rais'd but the use of it is prohibited – The last Harvest has produced an encrease of 40 for one, an asertion which from examination I know to be true, and 30 for one is not deem'd extraordinary – The resources of the Country are great – but the cultivation of those resources slovenly to a Degree. – All the Arts and Sciences are buried in Oblivion, and it appears almost impossible that these are the Decendants of the people who conquer'd Spain, ruled it for Seven hundred years, and left Some very Striking memorials behind them in that Country – The Streets and Houses in the City of Morocco are despicable beyond belief, with here and there the remains of Something that, with the Mosques, shews the City was one of more consequence – There are Schools in all the Towns where reading and writing are taught and in some places arithmetic, and very rarely a little astronomy and these branches comprehend the learning of the Moors – The people seem to be warlike, fierce avaritious and Contemners of the Christians. The Arabs, who dwell in Tents, despise the Inhabitants of the Cities, but unite with them in their attachment to the Sovereign. – The Emperor is 66 years of age according to the Mahometan reckoning which is about 64 of our years. He is of a middle Stature inclining to fat, and has a remarkable cast in his right eye which looks blacker than the other; His Complexion is rather dark owing to a small mixture of Negro blood in him – He possessed in his early years all the fierceness of his ancestors, but being entrusted by his father in Public matters, He turned his throughts on the art of Government, and during his father's life time obtain'd absolute Dominion not only over the Country, but over his father who entrusted everything to his management, approving even of those acts which he did contrary to his instructions and the most perfect friendship always subsisted between them. It is about 28 years since he ascended the Throne without a Competitor, Since which he has taken the Utmost Pains to conquer those habits and prejudices in which he was educated – One of his people, not long ago, making a Complaint of some ill treatment he had receiv'd, and not meeting such reddress as he expected broke out into some language that the Emperor was not accustom'd to hear. His Majesty, with great temper, said "Had you spoke in such terms to my Father or Grandfather, what do you think wou'd have been the consequence" – The King is fond of accumulating wealth and of distributing it – The Sums he sends to Mecca are so extraordinary that they occasion conjectures that He may possibly retire there one Day Himself. He is religious and an observer of Forms, but this did not hinder him on a late Journey from Salè to Morocco to strike out of the direct road and go to a Saints House, where a number of Villians [sic] (about 300) had taken sanctuary, every one of which he order'd to be cut in pieces in his presence. He is a just man according to his Idea of Justice, of great personal Courage – liberal to a Degree – A Lover of his People, Stern, and rigid in distributing justice, and though it is customary for those people who can bring presents never to apply to him without them, yet the poorest Moor in his Dominions, by placing himself under a Flag which is erected every Day in the Court where the public Audiences are given, has a right to be heard by the Emperor in preference to any Ambassador from the first King upon earth, And to prefer his complaint against any Subject be his rank what it may. – His families which are in Morocco, Mequinez, and Tafilet consist of, 4 Queens. –

40 Women who are not married, but who are attended in the same manner as if they were Queens. –

243 Women of inferior Rank, and these are attended by,

858 Females who are shut up in the Seraglios, and the number of Eunuchs is great. – The last Queen which He married two years ago, is now about 14 or 15 years of age – and his children are Sixteen Sons and Seven Daughters. –

I shall conclude this letter with a short account of the two audiences I had, the first was a public one at which there were about one thousand people present. The Emperor came out on horseback, and we were presented by the Basha of Morocco. After enquiring what kind of Journey we had and whether we came in a frigate, He asked the Situation of America with respect to Great Britain, and the Cause of our Separation. He then question'd me concerning the number of the American Troops during the war and Since the peace – Of the religion of the white Inhabitants and of the Indians – Of the latitudes of the United States and remarked that no person had sail'd farther, than the 80th Degree of North Latitude, and enquired whether our Country produced Timber fit for the construction of Vessels. He then asked for the letters, and ordering that from the King of Spain to be open'd, He examin'd it and said He knew the writing very well, He then looked at an alarm Watch which happened to Strike, and asked several questions about it, he concluded by saying "Send your Ships and trade with us. I will do every thing you can desire," – at which he looked Round to his Great Officers and People, who all cried out, God preserve the life of our Master. He then ordered his Gardens to be shewn us and the American boy to be sent to me. –

The second audience was in the Garden, when the King was again on horseback and as soon as we bowed to him he cried, bona, bona, and began to complain of the treatment he had receiv'd from the English. He examin'd a watch that was among the Presents, and an Atlas with which he seemed very well acquainted, pointing out to me Different parts of the World and Naming them, though he cou'd not read the names as they were printed. He asked to see the Map of the United States, which was among the others, and after examining it, called for a pen and paper and wrote down the latitudes to which his Vessels had Sail'd – after which he put down the latitudes of the Coasts of America, desiring to know which were the best ports, and said he wou'd probably send a Vessel there – I presented him with a book containing the constitutions of America and other public papers, and one of the Interpreters told him it also contained the reasons which induced the Americans to go to war with Great Britain – Let these reasons, said he, looking over the book, be translated into Arabic and sent to me as soon as possible. After some talk about Tobacco, the Day of the Month and the Sun's Declination, and saying he wou'd order a Bag of herbs of Great and peculiar qualities to be sent me, I inform'd him that I wou'd appoint Mr· Francis Chiappi of Morrocco, as an Agent to act in behalf of any American Citizens, who coming to this Country may have occasion for his Service – or to transmit to His Majesty through Mr· Tahar Fenish any letters or papers from the Congress of the United States Untill the farther pleasure of Congress shall be known –

In this account of the Audiences I have omitted some particulars which were of no consequence, and what I have related Serves only to shew the turn of thinking which the Emperor possesses, and the Objects that engross his attention. – I have the honor to be Gentn· Your most obedt h'ble Servt·–   Tho' Barclay

⊗ My Information says Cape Finistre, but Really it ought to be Cape Sr Vincent. I Cannot at present be Certain about it –

NA: PCC, item 91, v. 1, pp. 189-193 (ALS); M247, reel 119.
^{1} Not further identified.

Richard O'Bryen to William Carmichael

Sir,   Algiers Sept. the 13th 1786

Your letter dated in St Ildefenso of the 29th Aug. I recieved yesterday by the Spanish packet-boat, & am much obliged to you for writing to me. We are very sensible of your particular attention in every respect to serve us unfortunate Americans, & we are confident that, it is through your means & the particular humanity of the Count D'Expilly that we & our crews are comfortably provided for.

I am exceeding sorry that the longer we stay here the more we lose sight of our liberty. Ever since Mr Lamb made his appearance in Algiers we have found our redemption to be farther off. I am sorry that our redemption cannot take place without the approbation of Congress which I assure I did not think the ministers would take on them to redeem us at so great a price as the Dey has asked without orders from Congress.

Four weeks ago we learned by the master of a Swedish Ship from Alicant that Mr Lamb had sent the brig with his despatches for Congress & that he expected an answer shortly. We recieved a letter from him yesterday dated in Alicant of the 7th Inst. he informs us that matters turned out so that he sent the brig for America, & that he expected shortly to have new orders. I am very confident that Mr Adams & m^r Jefferson acted for the best, but I take the liberty of mentioning to you that it was badly planned & worse executed, but I am much surprized that they were not better informed respecting affairs in Algiers. From m^r Jefferson's letter he expected that we would be redeemed & wished us a happy sight of our country. Mr Lamb said & shewed me his orders that Mr Lamb's limits were only 100 dollars for a sailor. I am sure no man could think we possibly could be redeemed at that price. Mr Lamb declared he had but 6000 dollars, & that was not appropriated for us, but for presents to these people. I have mentioned you in the proper manner to Mr Wolfe. he has been unwell these five weeks. Mr Wolfe also has mentioned you in very friendly language to us, & has a very great opinion of your abilities & that you had behaved with great zeal to serve your country.

We are losing a very favorable opportunity in Algiers respecting paving the way towards our peace which is of very great importance to the United

States. perhaps the ministers have some other plan in view. Mr Lamb's plan was to set all Europe a fighting or, to take some of the Spanish territory in America & thereby oblige the Spaniards to make our peace. he ought not to have thought it much more say it. Mr Lamb informed me shortly after his arrival in Algiers respecting the letter you wrote him to keep up the honor of the United-States. he told me he was more tenacious of it than any man, but shortly I found much to the contrary. Mr Wolfe is of opinion that we will be redeemed for less money than the Dey has asked for us. I cannot see into that part. I lately had a discourse with Mr Logie. he says that the Dey has not agreed on the price of the Spanish slaves as yet. what the Dey said to the Count was to go & bring the rest of the money for the peace & that he would make no great difficulty respecting the price of the slaves. I think that when the Algerines get the remainder of the money for the peace that they will extort on the price of the slaves. I believe the Spaniards will find more difficulty in Algiers & the Barbary States than is generally thought in Madrid. Mr Logie told me that he had the best information in Algiers & the other States; that lately he learned that the Tunisians had ordered the Spanish agent there to signify to the court of Spain that they must have nearly as much as they are to give this Regency. Tunis being a kingdom tributary to this regency the Algerines can influence them, & as there are but few cruisers belonging here but what belong to Individuals the Spanish commerce will intice the vessels & those sailors to go to Tunis. The first article in a treaty with this regency should be a peace, the 2^d the price of the slaves & the 3^d respecting Tunis as it is tributary to this regency equally as Ireland is to England. The peace with the Tunisians should be well provided for in the treaty with this Regency.

I am informed that m^r Barclay has effected a peace with Morocco. I hope it may be so, their situation being more detrimental to our commerce than the Algerines. The Algerine cruisers of nine sail of chebecks sailed the 14th of August and to this date has but sent in one prize which was a small vessel of 40 ton belonging to Sardinia. the number on board was 14 men & a woman, supposed of some rank. I hope no American will be so unlucky as to fall in their way as nothing would be more detrimental to the peace & our redemption. I am informed by the master of a vessel lately from Gibraltar that there had been a ship belonging to Baltimore or Philadephia there loaded with flour & that after discharging her cargo, she sailed for Malaga. I wish they would be more sparing of their American colours in the streights. It is well known in Algiers that such vessels are in Spain.

Respecting the Portuguese & Neapolitan negociation I cannot well learn much about it, there being no stranger here but a French gentleman which came from the Levant & stays at the French Consul's. he is said to be a merchant but I cannot say I know. he brought some presents such as clocks

&c. but they are not approved of. they give the British the preference. I have asked m^r Logie respecting this stranger. he says he believes he is in no public business. I have remarked that all the other consuls have moved out to their country-houses excepting the French consul but m^r Logie told me without asking him any thing about him that he is endeavouring to renew the French peace & that he is confident he has not effected it. that if he had Logie would know every article in it in twenty-four hours after it had been concluded. It is given out at the French consul's that he stays in town expecting the Count D'Expilly's arrival.

Respecting the Portuguese m^r Logie says the Dey would not listen to any proposition the Count made, for he said & they generally say here that they have made too much peace, & that if they were to make a peace with the Portuguese that they would have no nation worth cruising against. It seems reasonable to me this regency will be always at war with some nations that they are not afraid of being invaded by, & it is greatly in favor of the American peace that we are so far situated from them that they cannot go on our coasts, not like those nations in the streights that the Algerines in 36 hours are on their coasts & successful in taking prizes. The Dey said to the Count when he asked for a peace for the Neapolitans that he would miramus, or see about it. Those people will not have many negociations on hand at one time; they want to get done with one thing first, before they begin another. I am told that a difference has happened between the courts of Spain & Naples, and I think if the Spaniards do not make the Neapolitan peace that they will be puzzled to do it themselves. The Neapolitans, Genoese, Leghornese & Portuguese being so handily situated for the regency of Algiers, that I think if any of them should obtain a peace that their terms must be very high. I cannot say what great sums may do – but Money is the God here & Mahamet their Prophet.

They are generally very inquisitive here respecting our marine strength & what the produce of the country may be, & what was the occasion of our dispute with the English. My carpenter is taken as a servant to the Micklassha who has said that he was informed that there were some American Frigates in the Streights but we have told them that we knew nothing of any vessel of American Cruisers being in the Streights. The Micklassha about four weeks ago asked if we had heard any thing respecting or from our Embassador. we told him we had not but we believed the sum for our redemption was so great that we were much afraid that we should not be redeemed, the Dey asking so great a price for us. but he told us that soon our Embassador would arrive. We are particularly noticed by the Micklassha & hope that the character of the Americans will by no means depreciate with him. Notwithstanding their wish is to make more American prizes. the Micklassha owns two of the cruisers. The Dey owns one, & the

Causenase or prime minister another, & Bylick or the public three of the rest. others belong to Individuals. I had a man of my crew very ill with sore eyes in the hospital under the care of the Spanish Doctor, who told me that the sailor would certainly lose his eye sight, which alarmed me much I went to the Micklassha with the man to get permission for the man to go & see what the English Doctor could do for him. The Micklassha told me to take him to the English Doctor for him to use his endeavours to cure him & that he would pay for him. The man is much better. The greatest news here is expecting the Count with the money. The Danish consul was called before the Micklassha & asked respecting they were informed that the Danes had sheltered the Hamburgh vessels under their flag. I believe the cruisers will be very troublesome to the Danes. The Venitians had committed something upon the eastern part of his kingdom having a Malthese galley with their fleet and which destroyed three craft of this regency in a small port. The Algerines have signified to the Venitian consul to make good the damage. The Swedes have their peace with this regency guaranteed by the Grand Seignor which is greatly in their favor as on the death of the Deys here the successor will have all treaties renewed. they not being bound by any principle of national honor to any treaty. The capture of the Russian ship here will afford some speculation next spring in the Levant & Mediterranean sea.

We are treated with a great deal of civility by the French consul and M[r] Gimong a French merchant here. Mons[r] Ford the gentleman we are boarded with is a worthy respectable character & does every thing in his power to make our situation agreeable. I hope the French & Spanish will experience the like return & be treated with much lenity in America. We are four at M[r] Ford's, five in the Dey's house and one at the Swedish consul's and eleven in the marine, where the poor men endure the severities of slavery. I wrote a long letter by the Count to M[r] Jefferson, but have no answer as yet. The 27th of July arrived a vessel from Alicant or Malaga by which m[r] Lamb wrote to consul Logie, and did write him since his arrival in Spain three letters which m[r] Logie informed me of. M[r] Lamb did not write to us by any of those opportunites. M[r] Lamb informed m[r] Logie that the commercial treaty between England & America was broke off. I was much surprized how consul Logie knew that m[r] Jefferson & m[r] Adams would not take it on them to redeem us without the approbation of Congress. But m[r] Logie told some of my people that he had letters from m[r] Lamb and afterwards Logie told me the same vessel M[r] Logie informed the Micklassha that the vessel was not Spanish property he knowing six months ago that the vessel & master was under English colours, but the property being gone away the English took her pass from her. The Capt. was examined & Don Pedro the Spanish Agent called on, but I believe those people let it pass telling the

Capt. not to come in their way again. Logie is a proper mischief- maker, a good spy for the Algerines. We have recieved no letters from any part of America which is strange. I think that m^r Jefferson & m^r Adams are at too great a distance to act on this Barbary affair. it requires they were more handily situated. as to being in London to negociate a peace here it reminds me of the sun going to the northward and a long time before it returns to the southward again. but Congress know best. You will oblige me in writing me a few lines by the Count D' Expilly when he leaves Madrid, if possible you can tell me your opinion about our redemption. Mr Wolf's compliments to you – a steady, sensible man. Logie and he are at a great difference. Logie views m^r Wolfe as an enemy to the interests of Great-Britain. You will please return our thanks to the Count for the many particular favors shewn us by him whilst he was in Algiers. I remain with much esteem & respect your most obedient very humble servant

Rich^d O'Brien

I shall write you when I have any thing particular.

NA: RG 59, *Consular Despatches, Algiers* (C); M23, reel 1.

Thomas Barclay to John Adams and Thomas Jefferson

Gentlemen   Ceuta 18th Septr 1786
     As you will probably wish to know the particulars of the Negotiations of the Treaty with the Emperor, and as the perusal will not take up a great deal of time I shall lay them before you –
     After the first Audience was over, Mr Tahar Fennish, in whose Hands the Negotiation was placed, came from the Emperor and informed me that His Majesty had read the Translation of the Letters – That he had made a Treaty with Spain very favorable for that Country, that he would write to His Most Catholic Majesty to give a Copy of that Treaty, from which, one, with United States might be formed & that he would either request the King of Spain to order it to be signed at Madrid, or it might be sent to Morocco for Signature by Express – I replyed, that, "I had taken a long Journey in order to make this Treaty, and that I would be very sorry to return untill it was finished. If Mr Fennish would give a Copy of the Spanish Articles I would point out such as would be necessary for us, and I doubted not but we would soon agree upon them.
     Mr Fennish said that some of the Papers were at Mequinez and some at Fez, and that it would be impossible to collect them so as to make them

useful on this Occasion. I answered that If permission was given to me I would lay before the Emperor through him the Heads of such a Treaty as I imagined would be perfectly agreeable to both Countries; that if any objections should appear, we would talk them over, and after due Consideration, do what would seem right. To this Mr Fennish agreed, promising his best Offices to forward and settle every thing on good and reasonable Terms. The next day but one, the Heads of the Treaty in Arabic, were put into the Hands of Mr Fennish, who shew'd them to the Effendi; by whom Seven of the Articles were objected to as highly unreasonable; They were however read before His Majesty and some of the principal Officers of the Court, when all the Articles except four were admitted without hesitation, and the next Morning I received a Message from one of the Persons who was present at the reading, with Compliments upon the Progress I had made, and taking to himself entirely the Merit of removing three of the Objections. –

When the proposition for an Exchange of Prisoners was read The King said "This is not right, why are the Christians Powers so averse to go to war with me? It is the Fear of their Subjects falling into Slavery." To which the Kings Preacher replyed, These People deserve more indulgence from you than many others with whom you are in Alliance. They are nearer our Religion, and our Prophet mentions those who profess their manner of Worship with Respect. Upon which the Emperor said, Let this Article be admitted – The next day I put the Treaty at full length into the Hands of the Interpreter to get it translated into Arabic and in a few days, a rough draught in Arabic formed from my draught but much curtailed was delivered to me by the Talbe who has drawn it up by His Majesty's Instructions, and who though he had altered it in the Form preserved the Substance; I caused this draught to be translated into English by one Person, and into French by another and agreed to receive the Treaty as it then stood; And I was the more anxious not to differ upon points of Form merely, because I knew the Effendi, who is the chief Officer at Court wanted to embarrass me and to draw the Affair into a length of time, and to get it into his own Hands, and this disposition had appeared on various Occassions, indeed on all that offered.

In the opening of the Affair I was asked by the Interpreter what I had to offer on the side of the United States by way of Presents in future, or by way of Tribute, to which I replyed (supposing the Question might come from Mr Fennish on the Part of the Emperor) that I had to Offer to His Majesty the Friendship of the United States and to receive his in Return, to form a Treaty with him, on liberal and equal Terms. But if any engagements for future Presents or Tributes were necessary, I must return without any Treaty. I took Care that these Sentiments should be conveyed to M^r

Fennish, and nothing was afterward said about it, nor a hint droped that any thing was expected. While the last draught of the Treaty was making, I was told it would be proper that the Delivery to me in behalf of the United States should be inserted, to which I very readily acquiesced, and wrote on a piece of Paper what I wished should be added; when the Treaty was finally put into my hands, seald by the King, and not 'till then, did I see or suspect in what Manner that Insertion is made, and which I wish with all my Heart was extinguished, at least one of the two.

Mr Fennish being confined to his Chamber our Papers fell into the Hands of the Effendi, who notwithstanding the Emperor had ordered them to be delivered, detained them under various pretences, But at length (without our coming to an open Quarrel) He sent them, when on examination we found the Talbe had omitted a Matter of some Consequence in one of the Articles, the rectifying of which and the getting a Declaration made by Mr Fennish by order of the King, took up a Day or two. I was asked to sign an Acceptation of the Articles on the Part of the United States but as the Treaty was not drawn up in the Form I expected, I excused myself without however giving any Offence, referring Mr Fennish to Congress and the Ministers. It is a Friendly well intended Treaty given by the Emperor without much being demanded on his Part; If it proves satisfactory it will be proper for you Gentlemen to give your Sentiments of it to Mr Fennish and that Congress ratifies it – And here perhaps it may not be unnecessary to say, that Mr Fennish throughout the whole as far as I can judge, has acted with the Utmost Candor and veracity, and I thought myself very happy in having been put into his hands. When the Business was over, the Emperor sent a Message to me by Mr Fennish, desiring to know whether I had any thing to ask and (to be repeat the Words in which it was delivered) if I had, not to be ashamed or backwards in doing it. I was prepared for this Compliment before I left Spain and was advised to request a Permission to export twenty thousand Fanegas of Wheat without Duty by which I should probably gain as many Dollars, and with great Truth I assure you that I am persuaded it would have immediately been granted. But I did not chuse to end an Embassy, begun avowedly on disinterested Principles, by making such a Request, especially as I was informed he would look on the United States as under some Obligations for such an Indulgence shewn their Servant: And as the Professions of an Inclination to give a mark of his Approbation of the transactions were repeated, I accepted them and pointed out a Manner in which he might shew the friendly disposition he had expressed; This was by his giving Letters to Constantinople, Tunis, Tripoli and Algiers recommending to these several States to enter into an Alliance with the United States and by advising them to receive in the most friendly manner such Agents and propositions as should be sent them from America. The Emperor immediately came into these Views and Mr Fennish desired that I would draw up the Form of a Letter such as I wished should be written, which I did and the indisposition of this Gentleman, was the Reason given why I did not get them at Morocco. I wrote twice to the Emperor and waited in Tangiers for an Answer, which I received from Mr Fennish saying the Letters were not prepared, & at present I shall add no more than that the Emperor is perfectly well informed that I had no orders to ask such Letters and that if there is any thing wrong in having done it, it is entirely an act of my own. The Treaty having been compleated His Majesty gave a written Paper not only describing our Rout but the time we should remain at the principal Towns. We came to this place to avoid a Quaranteen in Spain, and have been detained by some tempestuous weather. The Commandant of the Marine at S^n Roque hearing we were at Tangiers and at a Loss how to reach Spain without performing a Quaranteen sent a Vessel for us, directing the Commander to attend us wherever we should choose.

I think it probable, that you will not judge it necessary for me to go up the Mediterranean as Mr Lamb I hear has returned to Algiers, a Circumstance that will make me very happy, for though I was not backward in offering my Services, I was influenced only by the necessity I thought there was of doing something. Therefore if I do not receive your decided Orders at Cadiz to pursue these African Objects, I will embrace the first Opportunity of embarking from Spain for America.

I beg leave to assure you of my being with every Sentiment of Esteem and Respect Gentlemen Your most ob^t humble Servant –

Tho' Barclay

NA: PCC, *item 91, v. 1, pp. 197-205 (LS); M247, reel 119.*

Thomas Jefferson to John Jay

Sir   Paris Sep. 26. 1786

·   ·   ·   ·   ·

It being known that M. de Calonne the Minister of Finance for this country is at his wit's end how to raise supplies for the ensuring year a proposition has been made him by a dutch company to purchase the debt of the United States to this country for twenty million of livres in hand. his necessities dispose him to accede to the proposition, but a hesitation is produced by the apprehension that it might lessen our credit in Europe & perhaps be disagreeable to Congress. I have been consulted hereon by the Agent for that company. I informed him that I could not judge what effect it might have on our credit & was not authorized either to approve or disapprove of the transaction. I have since reflected on this subject & if there be a danger that our payments may not be punctual, it might be better that the discontents which would thence arise should be transferred from a court of whose good will we have so much need to the breasts of a private company. but it has occurred to me that we might find occasion to do what would be grateful to this court & establish with them a confidence in our honor. I am informed that our credit in Holland is sound. Might it not be possible then to borrow there the four & twenty millions due to this country & thus pay them their whole debt at once. This would save them from any loss on our account; nor is it liable to the objection of impropriety in creating new debts before we have more certain means of paying them: it is only transferring a debt from one creditor to another, & removing the causes of discontent to persons with whom they would do us less injury. Thinking that this matter is worthy the attention of Congress I will endeavour that the negociation shall be retarded till it may be possible for me to know their decision, which therefore I will take the liberty of praying immediately.

...I...have the honor of being with sentiments of the most perfect esteem & respect Sir, your most obedient & most humble Servt

Th: Jefferson

NA: PCC, item 87, v. 1, pp. 650-553 (C); M247, reel 115.

John Adams and Thomas Jefferson to John Lamb

Sir   [Paris, September 26, 1786]

We have recieved your two letters of the 15 & 18 July from Alicant and are sorry to learn that your indisposition discourages you from travelling by land or by sea.

We still think it most advisable both for your own interest and that of the United States that you should return to Congress for their further instructions as soon as possible, & we again propose to you to embark from Spain by the first opportunity.

Congress have never informed us of any promise made or encouragement given you that you should be settled with in Europe & we think it best you should settle with their board of Treasury. nevertheless if you transmit to us your account we will adjust it as far as lies in us subject to the revision of Congress. Your letter of credit we wish you to return to one of us by the first opportunity as you will not have occasion to draw again by virtue of it.

Mr Randal is gone to New-York and it is our wish that you might be there with him that Congress might have an opportunity of recieving from both together as much Information as possible, that you might mutually aid each other in settling your accounts.

We have the Honor &c.   John Adams
                                                                   [Th: Jefferson]

NA: PCC, *item 87, reel 1, pp. 658-659 (C); M247, reel 115.*

John Jay to Thomas Jefferson

Sir   [New York] Office for foreign Affairs 3^d October 1786
    I have the Honor of transmitting you herewith enclosed the following Papers Viz$^{t.}$

N$^{o.}$ 1. a Copy of the Consular Convention signed by the french and american Plenipotentiaries. –

N$^{o.}$ 2. a Copy of the Act of Congress under which the american Plenipotentiary signed the same. –

N$^{o.}$3. a Copy of a Scheme of a Convention mentioned and referred to in said Act. –

N$^{o.}$ 4. a Copy of a Report on the said Convention. –

N$^{o.}$ 5. a Copy of an Act of Congress containing Instructions and giving Authorities to you on the Subject of the said Convention. –

These Papers will possess you fully of the whole Business. I am persuaded that it will appear to you as it does to Congress, to be a delicate one, and to require delicate Management.

The original Scheme of the Convention is far from being unexceptionable, but a former Congress having agreed to it, it would be improper now to recede; and therefore Congress are content to ratify a Convention made conformable to that Scheme, & to their Act of the 25th Day of January 1782, provided a Clause limiting its Duration be added. It will be proper therefore to press on the Court, *only* such Objections to the Convention, as arise from its Departure from the Scheme. On making an accurate Comparison, such Departure will appear manifest to his Majesty; and there is Reason to expect from his Candor, that he will readily consent to remove the Objections occasioned by it. –

As it certainly is wise to try the Merits of Institutions entirely new, by actual Experience, before Nations adopt them forever, the Propriety of rendering this Convention probationary in the first Instance, is unquestionable. Congress cannot therefore presume that his most Christian Majesty will object to a Clause for limiting its Duration. The Design of this

Convention being for mutual and reciprocal Benefit and Convenience, it would be doing Injustice to his Majesty to suppose that he would wish to provide for its existing longer than it should prove useful and satisfactory.

If after the Experience of a few Years, it should be found to answer the Purposes intended by it, both Parties will have sufficient Inducements to renew it, either in its present Form, or with such Alterations and Amendments as Time, Experience and other Circumstances, may indicate.-

With great Respect and Esteem I have the Honor to be &^{ca.}

John Jay –

NA: PCC, item 121, pp. 207-209 (LBkC); M61, reel 1.

John Adams to John Jay

Dear Sir   London October 3. 1786
    An Event has taken Place, of too much Importance to the United States, to be omitted, in Dispatches to Congress. A Messenger arrived at the Secretary of States Office, last night, with a Treaty of Commerce between France and England, Signed by the Comte De Vergennes and Mr Eden. it cannot be supposed that the Contents can be fully known: but it is suggested that England has stipulated, to reduce the Duties upon French Wines, to the Sum which is now paid upon Portugal Wines, reserving at the same time a Power of reducing those upon the latter, one third lower than they are if necessary. A Minister Mr Faukner,[1] is in the mean time, Sent off to Lisbon, to negotiate there, both this Point and another in dispute with Ireland.

England has Stipulated that France shall enjoy, all the Priviledges in Trade of the most favoured Nation in Europe; So that a Reservation is made of a Right to allow the United States of America, Some Superiour Advantages.

It is Supposed that France is to admit, British Manufactures, and that all the Commerce is to be carried on in British Bottoms. The Treaty is probably Subject to the Ratification, or Consent of Parliament, and will be kept as Secret as possible till the Meeting of that assembly.

The Consequences of this Treaty cannot be indifferent and Time alone can reveal who is the gainer. but this is clear that if either obtains any considerable Advantage a War must eer long be the Consequence of it, for neither of these nations can bear to be outwitted by the other in commercial affairs.

.   .   .   .   .   .

With great and sincere Esteem, I have the Honour to be, Sir your most obedient and most humble servant   John Adams

NA: PCC, item 84, v. 6, pp. 351-354 (ALS); M247, reel 113.
[1] Fawkener, William. British diplomat. Envoy charged with special mission to negotiate a commercial treaty with Portugal, October 1786-January 1787.

Sir John Temple to Lord Carmarthen

N° 11. –   New York 4th of October 1786.
My Lord,

. . . . .

...Mobs, Tumults, & bodies of Men in arms, are now on tiptoe in various parts of this Country! all tending to the Dissolution of, not only what is called the Supreme power (Congress) but to bring into Contempt & disregard, the Legislatures & Governments of the several States! at this hour, while I am writing, I have undoubted Intelligence that at Springfield, (a County Town in the State of Massachusetts) more than 1,500 Men in Arms are there assembled to stop the proceedings of the Courts of Justice, until the Constitution of Government be altered and reformed to their approbation! and that about 1,000 Militia (horse & foot) by order of the Governor, are there also assembled to Support Government against the said Insurgents! In the mean time, the Governor of that State hath, by Special Proclamation, called the Legislature to meet as upon last Thursday; and upon the proceedings & doings of that Legislature; it Seems to depend, whether or not Arms shall decide the matter between the contending Parties! Public Affairs are much the same in the State of New Hampshire: The whole Legislative body of that State, were, for four hours, Prisoners, in the hands of a tumultuous Assembly in Arms! indeed dissatisfaction and uneasiness prevails more or less throughout this Country, the Greater part of the People (poor, and many in desperate Circumstances) do not, it seems, want any Government at all, but had rather have all power & property reduced to a Level, and it is more than probable that general Confusion will take place, before any permanent Government be established in this unhappy Country; perhaps in the hour of their Confusion and distress, some or all of the States may seek for European friendship Council and advice, if they do, my most hearty wish is, that wisdom may lead them to look up to that Sovereign, to whom they once happily belonged! and who only of all Sovereigns upon Earth, hath or can have any unfeigned regard for their real welfare & happiness: My Voice, and my utmost influence in this

Country, still guided by Prudence, shall stedfastly & faithfully correspond
with such my wishes.

.   .   .   .   .

I have the honor to be with great Deference & Respect, My Lord, Your
Lordship's most faithfull, and Obedient Servant   J. Temple

.   .   .   .   .

R. 24ᵗʰ Novʳ·
PRO: FO 4/4, pp. 653-656 (LC transcription).

Peter Allaire: Occurrences
from 7 September to 4 October 1786

New York 5ᵗʰ October 1786.

The Northern States have begun again to shew their Restless and
turbulent disposition, the same Spirit Actuates them as did before the
beginning of the Rebellion, and they have far exceeded the Southern States
in Acts of Riot & disobediance, they have appointed Several Committees,
held many meetings, all tending to the Altering and Subverting their
present Constitution, the abolishing of Officers and Offices, as an
unnecessary burthen and Greivance to the People – on the Second of
September at the Town of Northampton when Judge Ward went there to
Open the Courts of Judicature, the Inhabitants to the Numbers of about
1600 of which Six hundred were compleatly Arm'd and Officer'd, met the
Judge, and forewarned him at his peril to open the Courts, and forbid any
and all judicial proceedings, took possession of the Courthouse for twenty
four hours, on Judge Wards going to the Courthouse, Several presented
their Bayonets to his Breast, and prevented his entry: he then proceeded to
a Tavern, opened the Court and Immediately adjourned; & sent express to
inform the Governour and Council. the Rioters being Persons of property
and Supported by fifty Townships and Six Counties, nothing legal can be
done with them, Judge Ward askd the Leaders their Names, they directly
gave them in without the least hesitation. since the above the Counties of
Worcester & Berkshire have acted in a Similar manner, and prevented all
juditial Proceedings. Governour Bowdoin Ordered the Militia to the
Assistance of the Judge, but before they Arrived the Judge had quitted the
Town & the Rioters returned to their habitations without committing the
least Violence or Injury....

.   .   .   .   .

Congress finding themselves incapable of transacting any material
Business with any foreign nation, or even their own Domestic matters,

untill all the States have agreed to the impost Act, And as Several of the States have granted the Impost Conditionally, that is, that the Impost Law shall not take place in any of those States which have granted it, until all the States in the Union have fully consented thereto, have come to the Resolution of sending Delegates to confer with the following States, Viz, New York, Philadelphia, New Jersey, Connecticut, North Carolina, Maryland and New Hampshire: *To explain to them more fully the embarrassed State of the Publick finances, and to urge to them the Necessity of a full and Immediate compliance with the Requisitions of Congress &c.* part of their Instructions

The Delegates appointed for New York waited on Gov' Clinton shewed him their Instructions from Congress, and endeavoured to make him sensible of the absolute necessity there was of a Speedy Compliance of the State of New York to the Requisitions of Congress, that the Impost Act as it was passed last Assembly was by a Vote of Congress, deemed *inadmissible*, that the State of N York was the only one that Impeaded all public matters, and that untill they had complyed with the desires of Congress, all foreign and Domestic business were absolutely at a Stand &c &c. Desired he would Immediately Issue his Proclamation & Convene the Senate & Assembly, that they might more fully explain themselves, *Answer*, he did not think the matter of Importance enough to comply with their Request. the Assembly meet in November.

Philadelphia.

This Day (15th September) the Honor Rufus King & James Monroe a Committee of Congress are to have an Audiance of this State to make certain Communications Relative to the Situation of the finances of the United States, (the Doors are to be shut:) Those Gentleman [sic] are returned & have Reported to Congress, that they had laid before the Assembly of the State of Pensilvania their Instructions and had communicated to them the urgent Necessity of a speedy Compliance of the desires of Congress, (with a particular Acc^t of their Argument &c) and that the Assembly had given them for Answer: They had considered of the Arguments made use by the Hon: Gentleman [sic] appointed by Congress, and would Immediately take the same into Consideration.

Old Franklin the President of Philadelphia State, made a Speech at the Head of the Assembly and Senate to the Philadelphia Militia. *That he was directed by the Members present, to express their perfect approbation of their true military appearance and Evolutions. That Liberty and Independance was Established. But that the Peace of the United States might be interuped, that some appearances of late indicated a change, that it was the duty of freemen to Arm, and know how to use their Arms, and asked them, if they did not feel a Superiority of Character & Confidence in themselves, which they knew not before.*

The Commissioners from the Different States which were appointed to take into Consideration the Trade of the United States and to report an Act for that purpose, to the united States in Congress Assembled, as when agreed to by them, & afterwards confirmed by the Legislators of each particular State, will Effectually provide for the same, met at Anopolis [sic] the 7th September and have concluded on an Address to their Respective States, Recommending a General Convention of Deputies to meet the Second Monday in May next for a final Adjustment of that Business.

.   .   .   .   .

The Eastern part of the State of Massachusets (the Counties of York, Cumberland & Lincoln) sent Delegates from Twenty Two Townships to Portsmouth Casco Bay, they met the ninth September to consider on a seperation from the Government of Masssachusets after Enumirating their Grievances, they came to the following Resolution – Resolved that the grievances they laboured under, were such as could not be removed in their present connection with the Government of Massachusets on taking the Votes for a Seperate Government they were 18 for: 4 Against, they have accordingly drew up a Petition to the Legislature desiring leave to be made a Seperate Government.

.   .   .   .   .

PRO: FO 4/4, pp. 657-672 (LC transcription).

John Jay to Don Diego de Gardoqui

Sir   Office for foreign Affairs 6th October 1786
    The Letter you did me the Honor to write the 25th May last was immediately laid before Congress. The Subjects of our Negociation have frequently since engaged their Attention and Consideration, and I have now the Pleasure to inform you that in consequence of some recent Acts I find myself more in Capacity than I was, to make and receive Propositions relative to certain Matters in Difference between our Countries. I shall be happy if our Negociations should be so fortunate as to terminate in a Treaty satisfactory to both.
    As soon as some Business which I must immediately Dispatch shall be completed, which will be in the Course of a few Days, it will give me Pleasure to renew our Conferences, and I will do myself the Honor of giving you Notice of it without Delay.
    With great Consideration and Esteem I have with Honor to be &$^{c.}$
                                                        John Jay

NA: PCC, item 81, v. 3, pp. 227-228 (Extract/C); M247, reel 107.

Louis Guillaume Otto to Comte de Vergennes

[Translation]

N°· 64.   New York, 10 Oct^{ber.} 1786.

My Lord.

The Commissioners named by various States to propose a general plan of Commerce and to give to Congress the powers necessary to execute it were meeting in Annapolis over the last month. But, only five States being represented, they did not think they should broach the principal question, and they limited themselves to addressing to Congress and to the various Legislatures a report that characterizes the present spirit of this country's politics. In translating this report, I have taken care not only to put it into French but to render it intelligible. They endeavored to give the original an obscurity that the people will see through with difficulty, but which the powerful and enlightened Citizens will not fail to turn to account.

For a very long time, My Lord, they have felt the necessity of giving the federal Government more energy and vigor, but they have also felt that the excessive independence accorded to the Citizens with regard to the States, and to the States with regard to Congress, is too dear to individuals for them to be divested of it without great precautions. The people are not unaware that the natural consequences of a greater power accorded to the Government will be a regular collecting of taxes, a strict administration of justice, extraordinary duties on imports, strict actions against debtors, and lastly a marked preponderance of the rich men and the great proprietors. It is therefore in the interest of the people to preserve, as much as possible, the absolute liberty that was accorded to them at a time when they knew no other law than necessity, and when an English army laid, so to speak, the foundations of the political Constitution. It is in these tempestuous times that it was necessary to agree that all power should emanate only from the people, that everything be submitted to its supreme will, and that the Magistrates be only its servants.

Although there were no Patricians in America, there is a class of men known under the denomination of *Gentlemen*; who by their wealth, by their talents, by their education, by their families, or by the positions that they fill, aspire to a preeminence that the people refuse to accord them, and although several of these men have betrayed the interests of their class in order to acquire popularity, there reigns among them a liaison all the more intimate, since they fear almost all the efforts of the people to despoil them of their possessions, and since they are in addition creditors, and consequently interested in strengthening the Government and attending to the execution of the laws. These men ordinarily pay the highest taxes, while the small proprietors escape the vigilance of the Collectors. Most of them being merchants, it is important to them to solidly establish the credit of the United States in Europe by the exact payment of debts and to have Congress given sufficiently extensive powers to make the people contribute thereto.

They have tried in vain, My Lord, by pamphlets and by other publications, to propagate notions of justice and of integrity, and to divest the people of a liberty of which they make such bad use. In proposing a new organization of the federal Government, they would have caused all minds to rebel. Ruinous circumstances for the Commerce of America have happily chanced to furnish the reformers a pretext to introduce some innovations. They represented to the people that the name American had become a disgrace among all the nations of Europe; that the flag of the United States was everywhere exposed to insults and vexations; that the farmer, no longer being able to freely export his produce, would soon be reduced to the last misery; that it was time to employ reprisals and to prove to foreign nations that the United States would not suffer this violation of the freedom of Commerce with impunity, but that vigorous measures could only be taken by unanimous Consent of the thirteen States and that, Congress not having the necessary powers, it was essential to form a general assembly charged to present it with the plan that it should adopt, and to indicate to it the means to execute it. The people, generally discontented with the difficulties of Commerce, and little suspecting the secret motives of their Antagonists, embraced this measure with ardor, and named Commissioners who were supposed to meet in Annapolis at the Commencement of September.

The authors of this proposition, My Lord, had no hope or even any desire to see this Assembly of Commissioners, which should only prepare a question much more important than that of Commerce, succeed. The measures were so well taken that at the end of September, there were no more than five States represented in Annapolis, and the Commissioners of the Northern States were held up for several days in New York in order to delay their arrival. The assembled States, after having waited almost three weeks, had broken up on the pretext that they were not numerous enough to enter into the matter, and to justify this dissolution, they sent the various Legislatures and Congress a report, of which I have the honor to send You the enclosed translation. In this document, the Commissioners make use of an infinity of circumlocutions and ambiguous phrases to explain to their constituents the impossiblity of taking into consideration a general plan of Commerce and the powers relative thereto without touching at the same time on other objects intimately connected with the prosperity and the national importance of the United States. Without naming these objects, the Commissioners elaborate on the present crisis of public affairs, on the dangers to which the confederation is exposed, on the discredit of the United States in foreign countries, and on the necessity of reconciling under a single point of view the interests of all the States. They conclude by proposing for the month of May next a new Assembly of Commissioners charged not only with deliberating on a general plan of Commerce, but *on other matters that might interest the harmony and the well-being of the States and on the means of adapting the federal Government to the needs of the union.* In spite of the obscurity of this document, You will perceive, My Lord, that the Commissioners do not wish to take into consideration the grievances of Commerce, infinitely interesting to the people, without perfecting at the same time the fundamental constitution of Congress. It is hoped that new Commissioners will be named with powers sufficiently extensive to deliberate on these important subjects and to put Congress in a position not only to approve resolutions for the prosperity of the union, but to execute them.

I am with a profound respect My Lord, Your most humble and most obedient servant   Otto.
Rec 5 Dec^ber.

FFAA: Pol. Corr., U.S., v. 32, f. 88-89vo., 94-95vo. (LC transcription).

John Jay's Report on the Franco-American Consular Convention

[New York] Office for foreign Affairs 12th October 1786
The Secretary of the United States for the Department of foreign Affairs, to whom was referred a Letter to him of the 6th Instant from the Chargé des Affaires of France, requesting that the Resolution of Congress concerning the Consular Convention may be communicated to him. –

Reports

That in his Opinion it would not be expedient to establish a Precedent of communicating to a foreign Minister here, any Acts of Congress committing Business or giving Instructions to their Minister at his Court; for as such a Practice would doubtless be inconvenient in *some* Instances, it had better be avoided in *all*; lest if Congress should sometimes do it, and sometimes not, they would become exposed to the Necessity either of explaining the Reasons of such Diversity, or to the Risque of giving Offence by apparent Partiality. –

Your Secretary therefore thinks it adviseable that he be ordered to inform the Chargé des Affaires of France that as their Communications to his Most Christian Majesty will be officially made by their Minister resident at his Court, they do not think it necessary to accept his polite Offer of conveying any they may direct respecting the consular Convention. –

All which is submitted to the wisdom of Congress.   John Jay –

NA: PCC, item 81, v. 2, pp. 179-180 (DS); M247, reel 107.

James Monroe to Thomas Jefferson

Dear Sir   New York Octr. 12. 1786

Since my last I have receiv'd yours of the 9. of July. I advis'd you therein of the progress that had been made by Mister Jay in the Spanish negociation, that he had brought a project before Congress for shutting the Mississippi and not for opening it for the term of twenty five or thirty years combin'd with some commercial stipulations, the latter to be the price of the former, although admitted they opened no new port nor admitted us into those now open upon better terms than those we now enjoyed. Since this project was presented, the negociation has been more with Congress to repeal the ultimata than with Spain to carry the instructions into effect. I inform'd you of the proposition from Massachusetts for the repeal in Committee of the Whole. This was carried by Pennsylvania inclusive eastward, Maryland inclusive southward being against it. Delaware was absent. In the house we mov'd to postpone the report of the Committee in order to take up propositions to the following effect. That the negotiation as to the Mississippi and the boundaries be taken out of the hands of the Secretary and committed to Carmichael. The following points to be agreed on there and afterwards concluded here. 1st that New Orleans be made an entrepot for exports, that they be shipp'd thence in the bottoms of America, Spain and France under the regulations of each party. 2d. That they pay at said port a duty of 2 1/2 pr. centm. ad valorem to the crown of Spain as a compensation for port duties. 3d. That imports be prohibited. 4th. That the instructions of Annapolis be reviv'd as the basis of a treaty of commerce. 5th. That two additional commissioners be appointed with equal powers with the secretary to conclude the same. Upon this there was precisely the same division. The question was then taken on the report and carried by 7. states. Upon this the following proposition was mov'd, "is the repeal constitutionally carried by 7. states so as to give a new instruction materially different than the former" and set aside by the previous question.

We are told he will proceed, but of this have no certain information. It is extraordinary that he should have taken up the subject of trade, as powers upon principles that applied to all nations alike had already been given under a commission which had at the time his were, near one year to run to form a treaty with Spain, which were not repeal'd by these nor the subject mention'd except by a distant implication. I do suspect the business rests for the present untill the new Delegates take their seats, in which he will be govern'd by circumstances. I suspect the point will ultimately be carried, but this is yet doubtful. I forgot above to mention the negotiation was to have been carried on in our propositions under the mediation of France....I am affectionately your friend and servt.,

Jas. Monroe

Boyd: Jefferson Papers, v. 10, pp. 456-458.

John Jay's Report on State Laws
Contrary to the Treaty of Peace

[New York] Office for Foreign Affairs 13th October 1786
The Secretary of the United States for the Department of Foreign Affairs to whom was referred a Letter of the 4th March last, from the Honbl. John Adams Esquire together with the Papers that accompanied it –

Reports

That as the Subject of these Papers and of this Report appears to Your Secretary in a very important point of light, he thinks they should be so incorporated, as that the Record of the latter in this Office may always exhibit an entire and compleat view of the whole business – He therefore Reports –

.   .   .   .   .

On considering the before recited Papers[1] these important Questions present themselves –

1st. Whether any individual State has a right, by Acts of their own internal Legislature, to explain and decide the Sense and meaning, in which any particular Article of a National treaty shall be received and understood within the limits of that State?

2nd. Whether any & which, of the Acts enumerated in the List of Grievances do violate the treaty of peace between the United States and Great Britain? –

3d. In case they or any of them should be found to violate it, what measures should be adopted in Relation to Great Britain? and

4th. What measures should be adopted in Relation to the State or States which passed the exceptionable Acts?

Of these in their Order, and

        1st. Of the right of an individual State to enact in what Sense a National treaty shall be understood within its particular Limits –

Your Secretary considers the thirteen independent Sovereign States as having, by express delegation of Power, formed and vested in Congress a perfect though limited Sovereignty for the general and National purposes specified in the Confederation. In this Sovereignty they cannot severally participate (except by their Delegates) or have concurrent Jurisdiction, for the 9th Article of the Confederation most expressly conveys to Congress the sole and *exclusive* Right and Power of determining, on War and *Peace* and of entering into *treaties* and Alliances &c. &c. –

When therefore a treaty is constitutionally made, ratified and published by Congress, it immediately becomes binding on the whole Nation, and superadded to the laws of the land, without the intervention, consent or fiat of State Legislatures. It derives its obligation from its being a compact between the Sovereign of this, and the Sovereign of another Nation, but Laws or Statutes derive their force from being Acts of a Legislature competent to the passing of them. Hence it is clear that treaties must be implicitly received and observed by every Member of the Nation; for as State Legislatures are not competent to the making of such Compacts or treaties, so neither are they competent in that capacity, authoritatively to decide on or ascertain the construction and sense of them. When doubts arise respecting the construction of State Laws, it is common and proper for the State Legislatures by explanatory or declaratory Acts to remove those doubts; but when doubts arise respecting the construction of a treaty, they are so far from being cognizable by a State Legislature, that Congress itself have no authority to settle and determine them. For as the Legislature only which constitutionally passes a law has power to revise and amend it, so the Sovereigns only who are Parties to the Treaty have power by posterior Articles and mutual consent to correct or explain it –

All doubts, in cases between private individuals, respecting the meaning of a treaty, like all doubts respecting the meaning of a law, are in the first instance mere judicial Questions, and are to be heard and decided in the Courts of Justice having Cognizance of the causes in which they arise; and whose duty it is to determine them according to the Rules and Maxims established by the laws of Nations for the interpretation of treaties –

If this Reasoning and these Principles be right, as Your Secretary thinks they are, it follows of consequence, that no individual State has a right by legislative Acts to decide and point out the sense in which their particular Citizens and Courts shall understand this or that Article of a treaty. A

Contrary doctrine would not only militate against the common and received principles and ideas relative to this Subject, but would prove as ridiculous in practice, as it appears irrational in theory; for in that case the same Article of the same treaty may by law mean one thing in New Hampshire, another in New York, and neither the one nor the other in Georgia. –

It would be foreign to the object of this Report to inquire how far such legislative Acts are valid and obligatory even within the limits of the State passing them. Much might be said on that head – certain however it is, that they cannot bind either of the contracting Sovereigns, and consequently cannot bind their respective Nations –

2$^{nd.}$ Whether any and which of the Acts mentioned in the list of Grievances, do violate the treaty with Great Britain?

It is to be observed that the violations complained of are confined to three Articles of the treaty Viz^t the 4$^{th.}$ 5$^{th.}$ and 6$^{th.}$ – Your Secretary will therefore proceed to arrange and consider these Acts in that order.

The 4$^{th.}$ Article of the treaty is in these Words. – "It is agreed that the Creditors on either side, shall meet with no lawful impediment to the recovery of the full value in Sterling money of all bona fide debts heretofore contracted." –

This Article in the opinion of your Secretary establishes this point viz$^{t.}$ that the bona fide debts theretofore contracted remained unextinguished by the War. The propriety of making this remark will appear from adverting to the distinction there is between cases where the Rights of Creditors survived the War, and cases where Creditors having been divested of their rights in the course of the War, are restored to them by the treaty of Peace. In the former case, his Right remains precisely as it was, but in the latter case, it *may* sometimes be *questionable* whether the treaty *restores that right* wholly, or *only in part*; and such questions are only to be decided by recurring to the Article of Restoration. This distinction is introduced for the purpose of casting light on the question whether interest is, or is not payable on or comprised in the *bona fide* debts mentioned in the Article before us: For if the Article considers these debts or Contracts as being in their original state of extent and obligation, there can be little doubt but that when a stipulation to pay interest makes a part of the Contract, every attempt to invalidate that particular part must be in opposition to the treaty. But on the other hand, if the Article is to be considered as restoring Creditors to rights they had lost in the War, then inasmuch as it provides only for the Recovery of the *bona fide debts* without making mention of the interest accrued on them, it may be a question with some, whether the right to recover the interest is so attached to the right of recovering the principal, as that a restoration of the latter necessarily implies and restores the former – for nothing being said in the Article to exclude interest, the only question is whether the revival of the Principal debt does or does not operate as a revival of the interest? – but this is only a secondary Question and to be asked only in case it should appear that both principal and interest were lost in the War, and restored by the treaty under the denomination of *bona fide debts* which words some construe as including both principal and interest, and others think can intend only the principal–

They who consider this Article as being *restoratory* must insist and ought to shew, that the debts said to be *restored* were actually lost to the Creditors in the course of the War. If that was the case they must have been so lost either by extinction, remission or Confiscation, and that either tacitly and silently by the laws of War, or expressly by National Acts –

Your Secretary is not informed of any laws of War among civilized nations whereby all debts before subsisting between the people of belligerent Nations are immediately and silently, either extinguished, remitted or confiscated; and it would he conceives be useless to adduce the obvious reasons which induce him to think that there neither are nor ought to be any such Laws. If this be so, it follows that the 4th Article cannot be considered as *Restoratory* on the Principle that the debts in question were lost by the silent operation of such Laws. –

The next enquiry then is whether belligerent Powers have a right by express Acts to extinguish, remit or confiscate such debts. Your Secretary thinks that the Laws of Nations strictly and rigidly considered will authorize it; but that since Mankind have become more enlightened and their Manners more softened and humanized it has not been common as well for those reasons, as for others suggested by the interest of Commerce and mutual intercourse, to practice such severities –

But admitting that the United States had a right to extinguish, remit or confiscate debts due from their Citizens to british Subjects, it still remains to be required whether, and in what manner, and by what Acts they exercised that Right – for if they did not exercise this right at all, then it will follow that these debts were neither extinguished, remitted nor confiscated, and consequently that the Article cannot be considered as *restoratory*, nothing being more clear than that Restoration always implies previous deprivation. –

Here a very important question presents itself vizt whether the State Legislatures can derive a right from the existence of War between their Sovereign and a foreign one, to extinguish, remit or confiscate, by their Acts, debts due from their Citizens to the Subjects of that foreign Sovereign. –

The rights to make War, to make Peace, and to make treaties appertaining *exclusively* to the National Sovereign, that is, to Congress, Your Secretary is of opinion that the thirteen State Legislatures have no more authority to exercise the Powers, or pass Acts of Sovereignty on those points, than any thirteen individual Citizens. To execute the laws or exercise the rights of War against a National enemy belongs only to the National Sovereign or to those to whom the National Sovereign may constitutionally delegate such authority – so that whatever right each State individually considered, may have to sequester or confiscate the property of their own proper Citizens, yet with respect to the common enemy of the Nation they can separately do no Act of National Sovereignty; for surely a thirteenth part of a Nation can with no propriety assume a power of doing National Acts proper only to the National Sovereign. However recent may be the date of the Confederation, yet an Union founded in Compact and vesting the Rights of War and Peace in Congress preceded it, and Your Secretary is exceedingly mistaken if there ever was a period since the Year 1775 to this day when either of the then Colonies, now States, were in Capacity to pass State laws for Sequestering or confiscating the debts or property of a National enemy. It was then and afterwards, by virtue of National Commissions, that the Enemy's property on the Sea was liable to be captured and confiscated, and equal authority was necessary to justify the confiscation of their property found on the land. Whatever State Acts therefore may have been passed during the War, exercising Rights accruing to the Sovereign from the Laws of Nations respecting War, they cannot in the opinion of Your Secretary be obligatory on either of the belligerent Sovereigns, and consequently not on any of their respective Citizens or Subjects. –

Your Secretary would not have it inferred from these remarks, that the States have passed *general* laws for confiscating british debts due from their Citizens – His design in these remarks is to obviate any arguments that might be drawn from certain other Acts less general and direct, but in his opinion equally improper such for instance as those whereby certain british Subjects were declared Traitors, and whereby, as a consequence of treason the debts due to them became payable to the State to which those british Subjects were declared to be Traitors – for such laws, however absurd, do exist. There are also certain other Laws authorizing the payment of debts due to certain Individuals to be made at the State treasury in Paper Money &c. &c:. –

The Question then again recurs, did *Congress* do any Act for extinguishing, remitting or confiscating debts due from Americans to British Subjects?

.   .   .   .   .   .

In short your Secretary does not know of any Act of Congress whereby debts due from Americans to Britons were either extinguished, remitted or confiscated, and therefore he concludes that the 4th Article of the treaty must be understood not as reviving, or restoring, those debts, but as considering them to be and remain exactly and precisely in their pristine and original State, both with respect to extent and obligation – If this conclusion be just, Your Secretary can perceive no ground for the singular reasonings and questions that have prevailed respecting the payment of interest claimed by british Creditors in virtue of express Contracts between them and their American debtors. However harsh and severe the exaction of this interest, considering the War and its effects, may be and appear, yet the treaty must be taken and fulfilled with its bitter as well as its sweets, and although we were not obliged to accept peace on those terms, yet having so accepted it, we cannot now invalidate those terms or stipulations, nor with honor or Justice refuse to comply with them. Much better would it be for the United States either severally or jointly, by their bounty, to relieve those suffering and deserving Individuals on whom the Performance of this Article may press too hard, than by Reasonings and Comments which neither Posterity or impartial Co[n]temporaries can think just, to permit our National Reputation for probity, candor and good faith to be tarnished. –

Your Secretary will conclude what he has to say on the Subject of interest with a few short remarks – It appears to him that there are only *three* Cases in which interest can with justice be demanded; and that in the *first* of the three the Courts of Justice are not, and ought not, to be at liberty to refuse it – Viz.

> 1st. In all cases where interest is fairly and expressly contracted and agreed to be paid. In such cases the debtor is unquestionably bound to pay it, and ought not to be absolved or excused from it by any Act of Legislature. In the opinion of your Secretary every Legislature deviates from the reason and limits of their institution, when they assume and exercise the power of annulling or altering *bona fide Contracts* between Individuals –
>
> (2) Interest may be claimed in certain cases by Custom – viz. in Cases where it has long been usual for Merchants to expect, and to allow interest on debts after the stipulated term and time of Credit and payment has expired. This Custom in the ordinary course of things is reasonable, for equity demands that he who does not pay at the appointed day, should thereafter pay interest to his Creditor, as well by way of compensation for the disappointment as for the use of the money. Whether the Reason of this custom can apply in time of War, or whether the equity of the demand of

interest in virtue of the Custom, is or is not overbalanced by the equity of refusing it by reason of the effects of the War, are questions proper for the consideration of the Jury, and your Secretary sees nothing in the treaty to prevent their deciding as to them shall appear just and right –

(3) Interest may be demanded and is often given under the idea of damages for wrongful and vexatious delays of payment. Every case of this kind must stand on its own merits, and the treaty leaves the Jury at Liberty to give such a verdict as their opinion of those merits may dictate –

. . . . .

...It is much to be wished, that the executive of each of the States could be prevailed upon, at the conclusion of every session, to transmit to Congress Copies of all the Acts passed by the Legislature during the course of it – or that Congress would be pleased to direct that such Copies be regularly purchased and sent to them at the public expence –

There are other matters mentioned in the List of Grievances relative to the performance of the 4th. Article, which merit some consideration: They may be comprized under two Heads

(1st) Popular and improper Opposition to the Recovery of debts

(2nd) The Payments in Paper made into State Treasuries, on Account of debts due to british Creditors, pursuant to certain Acts of some of the States requiring, or authorizing the same

With respect to the *first* of these, Your Secretary thinks the following observations are applicable to such cases, when and wherever arising. –

Although popular reluctance and opposition to pay debts may, and probably does, in some instances retard and embarrass the recovery of them, yet while the course of Justice continues steadily to bear down that opposition, and to execute the laws with punctuality and decision, such vanquished opposition rather does honor than discredit to the Government, and therefore however inconvenient and temporary commotions or improper combinations may have been, yet the vigorous and effectual interposition of Government must forever acquit it of blame –

But if from the imbecility and relaxation, or from the connivance of Government, it should so happen, that the ordinary course of Justice becomes and continues so obstructed, as that Foreigners claiming the benefit of treaties with the United States, cannot avail themselves of rights secured to them by such treaties, then in his opinion the delinquent State cannot be without blame; for as every Government is and must be presumed to have sufficient power and energy to exact from its own Citizens a compliance with their own Compacts and Stipulations, a failure or omission to do it, will naturally be imputed to the want of inclination, and not to the want of Means. Whenever such Cases happen, they must excite the notice of Congress to whom it appertains, to see that National treaties be faithfully observed throughout the whole extent of their jurisdiction. –

.   .   .   .   .

From the principles stated in the preceding part of this Report your Secretary infers that the treaty of peace does consider the debts mentioned in the 4th. Article as being exactly in their original state of obligation and extent, leaving the Contracts on which they depend to be executed according to the tenor, true intent and meaning of them. If so, british Creditors have no sort of concern with any payments (made on account of the debts due to them) other than such as they either accepted, directed or approved, for in relation to the Creditor all such payments are, as if they had never been made, and he is justifiable in proceeding against his debtor accordingly. But between the debtor so paying into a State Treasury, and the State directing, inviting, or authorizing him to do it, an account should be opened, and the State is, in your Secretary's opinion, bound in justice to repay him the then real value of such Money as he so put into the treasury, together with lawful interest for the use of it. –

But violations of the 4th. Article are not the only ones alledged in the list of Grievances – It expressly charges that as little respect has in certain instances been paid to the 5th. and 6th. Articles. Of these, in their Order.–

The 5th. Article is in these Words. – "It is agreed, that Congress shall earnestly recommend it to the Legislatures of the respective States, to provide for the Restitution of all Estates, Rights and Properties, which have been confiscated, belonging to real british Subjects; and also of the Estates, Rights and Properties of Persons resident in districts in possession of his Majesty's Arms, and who have not borne Arms against the said United States; and that Persons of any other description shall have free liberty to go to any part or parts of the thirteen United States, and therein to remain twelve Months unmolested in their endeavours to obtain the Restitution of such of their Estates, Rights and Properties, as may have been confiscated; and that Congress shall also earnestly recommend to the several States, a Reconsideration and Revision of all Acts or Laws respecting the Premises, so as to render the said Acts or Laws perfectly consistent, not only with justice and equity, but with that Spirit of Conciliation, which, on the return of the blessings of Peace, should universally prevail: and that Congress shall also earnestly recommend to the several States, that the Estates, Rights and Properties of such last mentioned Persons shall be restored to them, they refunding to any Persons who may now be in possession, the *bona fide* Price (where any has been given) which such Persons may have paid on purchasing any of the said lands, Rights or Properties, since the Confiscation. And it is agreed, that all Persons who may have any interest in confiscated lands, either by debts, Marriage settlements, or otherwise, shall meet with no lawful impediment in the prosecution of their just rights." –

．　　．　　．　　．　　．

On the 4th July 1776 all british Subjects became Aliens to the United States – thenceforth to the end of the War they were not only Aliens, but Alien enemies – as such they were during that period under legal disabilities either to acquire or convey lands in this Country. On these principles therefore it was right and just that the Act should consider all those lands to be still the lands of the british Subjects in Question, of which they were Proprietors on the 4th. July 1776. –

The next enquiry is, whether the like retrospect in the Cases of offending *Citizens* was justifiable?

On this point Your Secretary thinks it not improper to observe, that if it shall appear that the Complainants are not interested in nor affected by such Retrospect that then it is a matter which they being Foreigners have no right to meddle with nor to complain of –

By their own shewing it appears that the Complainants are and were british Merchants that is british Subjects, who during the War when they were Alien enemies accepted grants of land lying in this Country in payment of debts. No point is more indisputable or more clearly established both by the law of this Country and of England than that Alienation of land to an Alien operates a forfeiture of it to the Sovereign, and if such be the law respecting alien friends, with how much greater force does it apply to the Case of alien Enemies? It follows then that the british Merchants in question not being capable of purchasing and holding lands in this Country, nothing passed to them by the said Grants from their debtors and if they thereby acquired no right or title to the Lands in Contemplation, they can with no propriety complain of or reprehend the Legislature of South Carolina for passing that or any other law respecting those lands –

As Your Secretary considers this reasoning as being conclusive, he thinks it unnecessary to swell this report by any further remarks on the retrospect in this Act. –

There remains but one further question on this head – Vizt. Whether the 5th. or the 6th. Articles of the treaty contain any thing to validate the titles which these british Merchants claim to have to these lands?

By the 5th. Article "It is agreed that all Persons who may have any interest in Confiscated lands either by debts, marriage settlements or otherwise shall meet with no lawful impediment in the prosecution of their just Rights."–

The obvious meaning of which is that all fair lawful Contracts touching land, to which the Parties were at the time competent, shall continue in full force and be executed in favour of innocent Persons claiming the benefit thereof, notwithstanding the said lands may have been confiscated. The Article clearly relates to Grants or Contracts which at the time they were made were valid, and not to Grants or Contracts which at the time they were made conveyed no rights to the Grantees or Contractees. The Article expressly removes impediments to the prosecution of just or legal rights, and that idea excludes the supposition of its meaning to confer validity to Claims not warranted by law, or to create Rights which at no prior period had even existence –

If therefore these british Merchants never had nor could have title to or interest in these lands by any Grants made during the War and subsequent to July 1776 Your Secretary cannot perceive the most distant Reason for blaming the conduct of the Commissioners in paying no respect to such fruitless Grants –

As to the 6$^{th.}$ Article, it gives no Colour to the Complaint. It provides

(1) That there shall be no *future* Confiscation. The Confiscation in question was *prior* and not *future* to the treaty –

(2nd) It forbids the Commencement of Prosecutions against any person for *the part he may have taken during the War*

The Sale of land long before vested in the State by Confiscation, can with no more propriety be called a *Commencement of a Prosecution*, than the leasing, or tilling or fencing it can be –

(3^{d}) It declares that no Person shall *on that Account* suffer any *future* loss in his Person, liberty or property –

If there was any *loss* in the present Case it arose from the Confiscation that took place during the War which being in point of time before the treaty, cannot be easily construed to have been *posterior* or *future* to it –

Thus your Secretary has considered this complaint as resting on the facts and principles stated and assumed by the Complainants, and he presumes that nothing further need be added to manifest its futility – He cannot however dismiss it, without remarking the want of Candor observable in the statement of this Complaint –

.   .   .   .   .

From the aforegoing review of the several Acts complained of, it is manifest that the 4th and 6th Articles of the treaty have been violated by certain of them –

The next enquiry in order, seems to be whether these violations can be justified or excused by any prior ones on the part of Britain?

There is no doubt but that Britain has violated the 7[th.] Article, which provides that "his Britannic Majesty shall with all convenient speed, and without causing any destruction or carrying away any Negroes or other property of the American Inhabitants, withdraw all his Armies, Garrisons and fleets from the said United States, and from every Port, Place and harbour within the same" –

The Violations of this Article alluded to, are these Viz[t.] –

1[st.] That on the evacuation of New York, Negroes belonging to American Inhabitants were carried away –

2[nd.] That his Britannic Majesty's Garrisons have not been withdrawn from, but still keep possession of certain Posts and Places within the United States –

With respect to the Negroes it may be proper to distinguish them into *three* Classes –

1[st.] Such as in the course of the War were captured and disposed of as booty, by the Enemy –

2[nd.] Such as remained with and belonged to American Inhabitants within the british lines –

3[d.] Such, as confiding in Proclamations and Promises of freedom and protection, fled from their Masters without, and were received and protected within the british Camps and lines –

The Stipulation, "not to carry away any Negroes or other property of the American Inhabitants" cannot in the opinion of Your Secretary be construed to extend to, and comprehend the *first* Class. By the laws of War all Goods and Chattels captured and made booty *flagrante Bello* become the property of the Captors. Whether Men can be so degraded as under any circumstances to be with propriety denominated Goods and Chattels, and under that idea capable of becoming booty, is a question on which opinions are unfortunately various even in Countries professing Christianity and respect for the rights of mankind. Certain it is that our Laws assert, and Britain by this Article as well as by her practice admits, that Man may have property in Man. If so, it is fair reasoning to conclude that this like other moveable property is capable of changing Owners by Capture in War. The Article places "Negroes and other property of the American Inhabitants" on the same footing; so that if it means, that Captured Negroes shall not be carried away, it must also mean that no other captured property shall be carried away – which would in other words amount to an agreement that the british fleet and Army should leave behind all the booty, then in this Country, which they had taken from American Inhabitants at any period of the War. It would be a task beyond the abilities of your Secretary to raise such a Construction of the Article on any principles capable of supporting it. –

As to the *Second* Class, to wit, such as belonged to and remained with American Inhabitants within the british lines, they seem clearly to be within the design and meaning of the Article; for as the enemy had never taken them from their Masters nor treated them as booty, the property remained unchanged; and the like reasoning applies to all other Negroes kept as Slaves within their lines, and respecting whom the enemy had done no Act which divested their Masters of the property –

Your Secretary also thinks that the *third* Class are clearly comprehended in the Article and for the same reason Viz.^t because they still remained as much as ever the property of their Masters. They could not by merely flying or eloping extinguish the right or title of their Masters nor was that title destroyed by their coming into the enemy's possession, for they *were received, not taken*, by the enemy – they were received not as Slaves but as friends and freemen, by no Act therefore either of their own or of their friends was the right of their Masters taken away, so that being the property of American Inhabitants, it was an infraction of the 7th Article of the treaty to carry them away. –

Whenever the conduct of Nations or of Individuals becomes the Subject of investigation, truth and candor should direct the enquiry. The circumstances under which these last mentioned Negroes were carried away make a strong impression on the mind of your Secretary, and place that transaction before him in a point of view less unfavourable to Britain, than it appears in to his Countrymen in general. He is aware he is about to say unpopular things, but higher motives than personal considerations press him to proceed. –

If a War should take place between France and Algiers, and in the course of it France should invite the American Slaves there to run away from their Masters, and actually receive and protect them in their Camp, what would Congress and indeed the World think and say of France, if on making peace with Algiers she should give up those American Slaves to their former Algerine Masters? Is there any other difference between the two Cases than this Viz.^t that the American Slaves at Algiers are *white* People, whereas the African Slaves at New York were *Black* People?

It may be said that these remarks are made out of Season, for whether they be well or ill founded, the fact is that Britain expressly agreed to give them up, and therefore ought to have done it. –

How far an obligation to do wrong may consistent with morality be so modified in the execution as to avoid doing injury and yet do essential Justice, merits Consideration. By this agreement Britain bound herself to do great wrong to these Slaves, and yet by not executing it she would do great Wrong to their Masters. This was a painful dilemma, for as on the one hand, she had invited, tempted and assisted these Slaves to escape from their Masters, and on escaping had received and protected them, it would have been cruelly perfidious to have afterwards delivered them up to their former bondage, and to the Severities to which such Slaves are usually subjected – so on the other hand, after contracting to leave these Slaves to their masters, then to refuse to execute that Contract and in the face of it to carry them away, would have been highly inconsistent with justice and good faith. But one way appears to your Secretary in which Britain could extricate herself from these embarrassments; that was to keep faith with the Slaves by carrying them away, and to do substantial justice to their Masters by paying them the value of those Slaves. In this way neither could have just cause to complain, for although no price can compensate a Man for bondage for life, yet every Master may be compensated for a runaway Slave.–

In the opinion therefore of Your Secretary, Great Britain ought to stand excused for having carried away these Slaves, provided she pays the full value of them; and on this he thinks the United States may with great propriety and justice insist. Indeed there is an intimation in one of M\(^{r.}\) Adams Letters that the British Minister did not object to it –

But however capable of palliation the conduct of Britain respecting these Negroes may be, it unquestionably was an infraction of the 7\(^{th.}\) Article –

It is equally clear that her continuing to hold the Posts from which by that Article she agreed to withdraw her Garrisons, is also a decided Violation of the treaty. –

It appears then that there are violations of the Treaty justly chargeable on both Parties, but as the present enquiry is whether our violations can be justified by antecedent ones on the part of Britain, their respective dates must be ascertained –

It is but just to observe that Britain withdrew her fleet and Army from New York before the treaty was ratified. She evacuated that place on the 25 November 1783, and it was not until the next Year that the treaty was ratified –

    .   .   .   .   .

In whatever light therefore deviations from the Treaty prior to its final conclusion and Ratification may be viewed, it is certain that deviations on our part preceded any on the part of Britain, and therefore instead of being justified by them, afford excuse to them. –

As to the detention of our Posts, your Secretary thinks that Britain was not bound to surrender them until we had ratified the treaty. Congress ratified it 14\(^{th.}\) January 1784 and Britain on the 9\(^{th.}\) April following. From that time to this the 4\(^{th.}\) and 6\(^{th.}\) Articles of the treaty have been constantly violated on our part by legislative Acts then and still existing and operating–

Under such circumstances it is not a matter of surprize to your Secretary that the Posts are detained, nor in his opinion would Britain be to blame in continuing to hold them, until America shall cease to impede her enjoying every essential right secured to her, and her People and Adherents by the treaty –

Your Secretary has heard another reason or excuse assigned to justify deviating from the 4th. article and restraining british Creditors in the recovery of their debts, Viz:t. that by giving time to the Debtor, he became more able to pay the debt; and as that additional ability was a benefit to the Creditor, the latter ought not to complain of the restraint which produced it –

Although this argument may be somewhat ingenious, it unfortunately proves too much. By the treaty a british Creditor has a right to sue when he pleases, and by the common law a Farmer has a right to plough when he pleases, a Merchant to send out his Vessels when he pleases, and every Man to eat and drink when he pleases –

Admit that a british Creditor would do better to delay his Suits, that a Farmer was about to plough in an improper manner or season – that a Merchant had ordered his Vessels to sea when a hurricane was expected or that a certain Gentleman injured his health by intemperance, – admit these facts – Would it thence follow that every or any good natured officious Man, who might think himself more judicious and prudent, has a right to hinder the Creditor from Suing, the Farmer from ploughing, the Merchant from dispatching his Vessels, or the *bon vivant* from indulging his Appetite? Surely not.

In short as your Secretary is uninformed of any facts or matters that can justify the violations on our part, the only question which seems to remain to be considered is

What is to be done?

The United States in Congress Assembled have neither committed, nor approved of any violation of the treaty. To their conduct no exceptions are taken, but to their justice an appeal is made relative to the conduct of particular States. The United States must however eventually answer for the conduct of their respective Members, and for that and other reasons suggested by the nature of their Sovereignty and the Articles of Confederation Your Secretary thinks they have good Right to insist and require that National faith and national treaties be kept and observed throughout the Union; for otherwise it would be in the power of a particular State by injuries and infraction of treaties to involve the whole Confederacy in difficulties and War –

In his opinion it would highly become the dignity of the United States to act on such occasions with the most scrupulous regard to justice and

Candor towards the injured Nation, and with equal Moderation and decision towards the delinquent State or States. –

In the present case he thinks it would be proper to resolve –

1st. That the Legislatures of the several States cannot of right pass any Act or Acts, for interpreting, explaining or construing a National treaty or any part or Clause of it; nor for restraining, limiting, or in any manner impeding, retarding or counteracting the operation and execution of the same, for that on being constitutionally made, ratified and published they became in virtue of the Confederation part of the law of the land, and are not only independent of the will and power of such Legislatures, but also binding and obligatory on them –

2nd. That all *such* Acts or parts of Acts as may be now existing in either of the States repugnant to the treaty of Peace ought to be forthwith repealed, as well to prevent their continuing to operate as violations of that treaty, as to avoid the disagreeable necessity there might otherwise be of raising and discussing questions touching their validity and obligation. –

3d. That it be recommended to the several States to make such repeal, rather by describing than reciting the said Acts, and for that purpose to pass an Act declaring in general terms that all such Acts and parts of Acts repugnant to the treaty of Peace between the United States and his britannic Majesty or any Article thereof shall be, and thereby are repealed, and that the Courts of law and equity in all Causes and Questions cognizable by them respectively and arising from or touching the said treaty shall decide and adjudge according to the true intent and meaning of the same, any thing in the said Acts or parts of Acts to the contrary thereof in any wise notwithstanding –

The two first of these proposed Resolutions do not appear to your Secretary to require any Comments –

He thinks the third would be expedient for several Reasons –

As it is general and points at no particular State, it cannot wound the feelings of any –.

The general Law it recommends he thinks preferable to a minute enumeration of the exceptionable Acts and Clauses because either omissions might accidentally be made in the enumeration or questions might be agitated and perhaps improperly determined respecting this or that Act or Clause which some may think exceptionable and others not. By repealing in general terms and obliterating all exceptionable Acts and Clauses as it were by one stroke of the pen, the whole business will be turned over to its proper department, Vizt. to the judicial, and the Courts of law will find no difficulty in deciding, whether any particular Act or Clause is or is not repugnant to the treaty. When it is considered that the Judges in general are Men of Character and learning, that they stand in responsible situations, and feel as well as know the obligations of Office and the value of Reputation, there is reason to presume that their conduct and judgments relative to these as well as other judicial Matters will be wise and upright –

Your Secretary also thinks that in case these resolutions should be adopted it would be proper that a circular letter from Congress should accompany Copies of them to the States, but as the forming a draft or Plan of such a Letter, seems not to belong to the department of *foreign* Affairs, he forbears to report one –

He is further of opinion that a Copy of this report should be transmitted to the Minister Plenipotentiary of the United States at the Court of London for his information; and that he be instructed candidly to admit that the 4$^{th.}$ and 6$^{th.}$ Articles of the treaty have been violated in America, as well as the 7$^{th.}$ has on the part of Great Britain. –

That he inform his britannic Majesty that the United States are taking effectual measures for removing all cause of complaint on their part. –

That he also be authorized to propose and conclude in the name and behalf of the United States a Convention with his Majesty whereby it shall be agreed that the value of the Negroes or other American Property, carried away contrary to the 7$^{th.}$ Article, be estimated by Commissioners and paid for, and that the said Payment together with a surrender of all the Posts and places now held by his Majesty within the limits of the United States shall be within   Months after all the Acts and parts of Acts existing in the several States and which violate the treaty are repealed, and due notice thereof given –

That he be also instructed to assure his Majesty that it will always give pleasure to Congress fairly and candidly to discuss and accommodate every difference or Complaint that may arise relative to the construction or to the performance of the treaty. That they are determined to execute it with good faith, and that as this is the only instance in which any Complaints of that kind have ever come regularly before them, they flatter themselves that the frankness and Candor of their Conduct on this Occasion will create in him the same confidence in the purity of their intentions, which they repose in his assurance "that whenever America shall manifest a real determination to fulfil her part of the treaty Great Britain will not hesitate to co-operate in whatever points depend upon her for carrying every Article into real and complete effect." –

It might also be well to instruct M$^{r.}$ Adams to endeavour to have an Article inserted in the Convention for the remission of the interest or a proportion of it which became due on private Contracts during the War, but your Secretary apprehends from the general and great impropriety of such interference with private Contracts, that his endeavours would be fruitless –

He also thinks it might be proper to instruct Mr Adams to obtain if possible an Article, to fix the true construction of the declaration for ceasing Hostilities, and stipulating that compensation be made for all Captures contrary to it, but he likewise fears that as this may be considered as a judicial Question, and as the balance of the Captures so circumstanced is in favor of Britain, that her consent to such an Article would not be easy to obtain –

It appears to Your Secretary that this System ought to give perfect satisfaction to the Court of London unless perhaps in one point, vizt that the Individuals who have suffered by our violations are left without compensation for their losses and sufferings. –

Although strict justice requires that they who have wrongfully suffered should as far as possible receive retribution and Compensation, yet as it would be very difficult if practicable to prevail on the States to adopt such a measure, he thinks it best to be silent about it, especially as the United States have neither the power nor the means of doing it, without their concurrence –

Besides as the detention of the Posts has been and continues injurious to the United States, the Consequences of the respective Violations may be set against each other, and although the account may not be exactly balanced, yet it cannot be well expected that in Affairs of such magnitude the same regard can be had to minutiae as in transactions between Individuals –

This report is on a Subject no less new and singular than important – Your Secretary is not conscious of any errors in it, and yet there may be some. He hopes the facts are not mistaken or misstated – he believes his reasoning on them to be just, and he flatters himself whatever mistakes relative to either, may be discovered, that they will be treated with Candor, and ascribed neither to want of attention, nor of Care, but to that fallibility, from which few, if any even of the wisest and most able, are wholly exempt. –   John Jay

NA: PCC, item 5, pp. 1251-1355 (C); M247, reel 19.

[1] See John Adams' memorial to the British Ministry, 30 November 1785, Volume 2, and Lord Carmarthen to John Adams, 28 February 1786, enclosing a statement of grievances of British creditors of the same date, supra.

Louis Guillaume Otto to Comte de Vergennes

[Translation]
N°· 66.   New York, 16 Oct^{ber·} 1786.

My Lord.

Mr. Jay's first report concerning our Consular convention having been rejected, that Minister limited himself in a second report to proposing two conditions under which this convention could be accepted without any prejudice for the United States. –

One of these conditions consists of adopting without any change the Counterdraft sent to Mr. Franklin in 1782 and approved by Congress; the powers given to that Minister not having been sufficiently extensive to permit him a considerable deviation from the principles contained in that document. The other condition relates to the duration of the convention; Mr. Jefferson will receive the order to entreat His Majesty to add to it a separate article by which its execution is limited to a certain number of years, so that at the end of this time the articles that appear prejudicial to the interest of the two nations may be changed. This report has been unanimously approved by Congress, My Lord, and Mr. Jay is supposed to send analogous instructions to Mr. Jefferson by the packet boat that will bring You this letter. The five Southern States were of opinion to ratify the convention contingently as it is and to entrust the small changes that remain to be made therein entirely to His Majesty's disposition, but fearing to occasion new delays, they preferred to yield to the entreaties of Mr. Jay and the Northern Delegates and to wait until Mr. Jefferson has terminated this negotiation with the Court. They particularly recommend to this Minister to treat this subject in the most respectful manner and to observe to You, My Lord, that this convention being a thing completely new for the United States, they could not foresee the effect that it would produce, and that in this uncertainty it was important for them to limit the duration of it to a certain term.

The details, of which I have just had the honor to render You an account, My Lord, have been transmitted to me verbally by several Members of Congress and by Mr. Jay, but they did not wish to officially communicate to me the response of this Assembly, under the pretext that, the United States having a Minister Plenipotentiary residing near His Majesty, communications of this nature should be made by him. The care taken to leave me ignorant of a part of the contents of the resolution of Congress, makes me believe that it includes secret instructions that they are interested in concealing from us. The prompt departure of the packet boat does not leave me any hope of enclosing a copy of it in this Despatch; but I shall do everything possible to procure it eventually.

I congratulate myself the more, My Lord, for having finally, in spite of all the intrigues of some Northern Delegates, obtained a response from Congress, that there come to me from several parts of the Continent the complaints concerning the desertion of crews and other abuses that the Consuls are not in a position to prevent, since their powers are still not recognized.

I am with a profound respect My Lord, Your most humble and most obedient servant   Otto.

FFAA: Pol. Corr., U.S., v. 32, f. 103-104vo. (LC transcription).

Charles Alexandre de Calonne to Thomas Jefferson

Sir   Fontainebleau 22ᵈ· October 1786

As it is the intention of the King to favor as much as possible the commerce of the Uᵈ States, I have the honor to communicate to you the measures that have been taken on this subject.

By a letter of the 9ᵗʰ· January 1784 to the Marquis de la Fayette I informed him that instead of two free ports promised by the Treaty with the Uᵈ States the King had determined to grant them four, which has been done, and I promised him that I would direct my attention to the custom House duties which are prejudical to Commerce, observing however that this object demanded long investigations, which are not yet compleated. By another letter I informed him, that his Majesty had suppressed the duties upon the exportation of Brandy, and I expected this suppression would be useful to the American Commerce; I likewise promised him that the duties of the King & the Admiralty payable by an American vessel on her Arrival in a French port, should be diminished & reduced to a single duty, & regulated according to the number of masts & draught of water, & not by the uncertain estimations of measurement. This reduction requires a perfect knowledge of all the duties paid in our ports; & as they are of various kinds, the statements which I have ordered to be made are not ready.

You know Sir that the King has appointed a Committee for the particular purpose of examining our Commercial Connexions with the Uᵈ States & that the Marquis de la Fayette has presented a project, conformable to the ideas contained in your letter to the Count de Vergennes: But you will consider how imprudent it would be to hazard by a change of system the product of a branch of revenue which amounts to 28 Millions upon an article which is not of the first necessity. After a long discussion of every means that can be at present adopted to encourage the importation of American Tobacco it has been resolved not to break the agreement made with Mr. Morris but that after the expiration of this contract no similar one shall be made; that in the meanwhile the Farmers General should be obliged to purchase annually about Fifteen thousand Hogsheads of American Tobacco imported directly from the U^d States in French or American Vessels at the same price on the same conditions which have been stipulated by the Contract with M. Morris.

You will remember Sir that before a regulation could be made in favor of the importation of Whale Oil, the M. de la Fayette had taken a particular arrangement with M^r· Sangrain[1] for the Sale of this Article to the Acc^t· of 800,000 Livres & that I had granted him passports in order to render this first importation free from all duties whatsoever. The same M^r· Sangrain afterwards made an agreement with some merchants of Boston to the yearly amount of 400000 Livres to last during six years for which his Majesty has granted the same favors which are enjoyed by the Hanse Towns.

This matter having been lately more extensively examined, the Administration to whom the Committee communicated their wish, agreable to the Marquis de la Fayette's demand & your opinion, entirely to abolish all duties upon Oil have found that at present they could not consent to it on account of the engagements made with other powers. All that could be done was to grant, during ten years to the Whale Oil, Spermaceti & whatever is comprehended within these denominations, imported from the U^d States in French or American Vessels, the same favors, the same diminution of duties which the Hanse Towns enjoy.

His Majesty hopes that the commercial connections between the U^d States & France will become so considerable as to engage him to continue the effect of this provisional determination, & it has been observed by the committee that a great duty of fabrication has been hitherto paid upon the most favored Whale Oil & even upon the national, His Majesty consents to abolish the duty of fabrication with respect to the whale Oil & Spermaceti directly imported from the U^d States in French or American Bottoms so that this oil & Spermaceti shall not pay during Ten Years any other duty but 7 livres 10 sols & 10 sols per livre, this last Augmentation of ten sols per livre shall cease in 1790.

It has also been determined that particular information be taken concerning the consumption of Carolina Rice in France & that means be devised to encourage the importation of this article.

Representations having been made concerning the considerable duties laid upon the importation of Pot Ash & pearl Ash, also upon Beaver Skins & Hair, & raw Leather, His Majesty has suppressed all duties whatsoever upon those articles, if imported of the growth of the U^d States in French or American Vessels – He is likewise desirous of encouraging every Article of American Fur.

His Majesty has moreover consented to abolish all duties upon Masts, Yards, Keels for Ships, Red Cedar, green Oak & in a word all kinds of wood fit for ship building imported from the U^d States in French or American Vessels.

The Committee having likewise represented that there was a duty of 5 p C^t on the purchase of foreign built Ships & that this duty was prejudicial to the sale of American Vessels, His Majesty has been pleased to exempt from all duties the purchase of Ships which shall be proved to be built in the U^d States.

Great duties having been formerly laid upon all shrubs, trees & seed, His Majesty has abolished these duties when the above articles shall be imported in French or American vessels.

It having been represented that the State of Virginia had ordered the arms for her militia to be made in France, an order is passed that the prohibitions which hitherto have prevented the exportation of arms & gunpowder, as well as the duties laid upon these articles when exported by permission, shall be abolished; & that whenever the U^d States shall think it expedient to export from France, Arms, guns & gunpowder, they shall have full permission, provided these articles are exported in French or American Vessels, & they shall be liable only to a very small duty in order to facilitate the calculation of exports.

Lastly His Majesty has received with the same favor, the applications made to the Committee for the suppression of the heavy duties actually paid upon books, & papers of all kinds: – the King abolishes all those duties when above articles shall be exported to the U^d States in French or American vessels.

It is with great pleasure Sir that I inform you of the dispositions of His Majesty, they are a new testimony of his great desire to establish the most intimate commercial connection between the two nations & of the favorable attention he will always pay to any proposal made in the name of the United States of America.

I have the honor of being with sincere attachment Sir Your most humble and most obedient Servant   De Calonne

Your nation will undoubtedly receive with pleasure the information of the facilities which the King has just granted to the exportation of the wines of Bourdeaux, Guyenne & Touraine & the suppression of the duties granted by different Arrets of Council of which the Marquis de la Fayette will give you notice. –

Faithfully translated from the Original by John Pintard.

NA: PCC, item 87, v. 1, pp. 714-717 (translation); M247, reel 115.
[1] *Sangrain, Pierre Tourtille. French entrepreneur with a contract for the nighttime illumination of 30 French cities for a period of 15 years. Interested in procuring whale oil for this purpose at the lowest possible price, he became involved in the negotiations of Lafayette and Jefferson for the admission of American whale oil into the French market.*

Congressional Resolutions on Expanding Control of Foreign Commerce

[New York] Monday Oct 23. 1786

The Committee consisting of Mr Pinckney,[1] Mr Smith[2] and Mr Henry[3] to whom was referred an act of the legislature of the State of Georgia, passed in consequence of the Resolution of the 30: April 1784, respecting Commerce and the subject of the said recommendation, – having reported

"That it appears by the said resolutions, the United States in Congress Assembled recommended to the Legislatures of the several States to vest them for the term of fifteen Years with power to prohibit any goods, wares or merchandize from being imported into or exported from any of the States in Vessels belonging to or navigated by the Subjects of any Power with whom these States shall not have formed treaties of Commerce. That they also recommended to the Legislatures of the said States to vest the United States in Congress Assembled for the term of fifteen Years with the Power of prohibiting the Subjects of any foreign State, Kingdom or Empire unless authorised by treaty from importing into the United States any goods, wares or merchandize which are not the produce or manufacture of the dominions of the Sovereign whose Subjects they are: Provided that to all Acts of the United States in Congress Assembled in pursuance of the above powers the assent of Nine States shall be necessary. – The Committee have carefully examined the Acts passed by the several States in pursuance of the above recommendation and find – That the State of Delaware has passed an Act in full compliance with the same.– That the Acts of the States of Massachusetts, Rhode Island, New York, New Jersey, Virginia and Georgia are in conformity to the said recommendations, but restrained in their operation until the other States should have granted powers equally extensive. – That the States of Connecticut, Pensylvania & Maryland have passed laws agreeable to the said resolution, but have fixed the time at which the Powers thereby invested shall begin to operate, and not left the same to commence at the time on which Congress shall begin to exercise it – which your Committee conceive to have been the intention of the same. – That South Carolina by an Act passed the 11th March 1786, have invested the United States in Congress Assembled with the power of regulating the trade of the United States with the West Indies and all other external or foreign trade of the said States for the term of fifteen Years from the passing of the said Act. – That New Hampshire by their Act of the 23d of June 1785, invested the United States in Congress Assembled with the full power of regulating trade for fifteen Years by restrictions or duties, with a Proviso suspending its operation until all the other States shall have done the same. – That North Carolina by their Act of the 2d June 1784, have <******> authorised their delegates to agree to & ratify an article or articles by which Congress shall be empowered to prohibit the importation of all foreign goods in any other than vessels owned by citizens of the United States or navigated by such a proportion of seamen citizens of the United States as may be agreed to by Congress, which when agreed to by all the States shall be considered as a part of the Articles of Confederation and perpetual Union. – From the above review of the Acts passed by the several States, in consequence of the said recommendation, it appears that though in order to make the duration of the Powers equal, it will be necessary for the States of Connecticut, Pensylvania, Maryland and South Carolina so far to amend their Acts as to permit the authorities therein granted to commence their operation at the time Congress shall begin to exercise them, yet still, the powers granted by them and by the States of Massachusetts, Rhode Island, New York, New Jersey, Delaware, Virginia & Georgia, are otherwise in such compliance with the recommendation, that if the States of New Hampshire & North Carolina had conformed their Acts to the said resolution, agreeable to the urgent recommendation of Congress of the 3d March last, the Powers therein requested might immediately begin to operate. – The Committee however are of opinion that the Acts of the States of New Hampshire and North Carolina manifest so liberal a disposition to grant the necessary Powers upon this subject, that their not having complied with the recommendation of March last, must be attributed to other reasons than a disinclination in them to adopt measures similar to those of their sister States – the Committee therefore conceive it unnecessary to detail to them the situation of our Commerce languishing under the most ruinous restrictions in foreign Ports, or the benefits which must arise from the due and equal use of Powers competent to its protection and support, by that body which can alone beneficially, safely and effectually exercise the same" – Whereupon

Resolved That it be again earnestly recommended to the Legislatures of the States of New Hampshire & North Carolina at their next session to reconsider their Acts and pass them in such conformity with the resolutions of the 30 April 1784, as to enable on their part, the United States in Congress assembled to exercise the Powers thereby invested as soon as possible

Resolved That as the extent and duration of the Powers to be exercised by the United States in Congress Assembled under the recommendation abovementioned ought to be equal, it be recommended to the Legislatures of Connecticut, Pensylvania, Maryland & South Carolina, so far to amend their Acts, as to vest the Powers therein contained for the term of fifteen Years from the day on which Congress shall begin to exercise the same –.

NA: PCC, item 1, v. 38 (Journal); M247, reel 14.

[1] Pinckney, Charles (1757-1824). South Carolina political figure and diplomat. Military service, 1779-1780. Member, state house of representatives, 1779-1780, 1786-1789, 1792-1796, 1805-1806, and 1810-1814. Member, Continental Congress, 1785-1787. Member, Constitutional Convention, 1787. Governor of South Carolina, 1789-1792, 1796-1798, and 1806-1808. U.S. Senator, 1798-1801. Minister to Spain, 1802-1804. Member, U.S. House of Representatives, 1819-1821.

[2] Smith, Melancton (1744-1798). New York merchant, lawyer, and political figure. Member, First provincial congress, 1775. Commander, Dutchess County home guard, 1775-1777. Sheriff, Dutchess County, 1777-1779. Moved to New York City, ca. 1785. Member, Continental Congress, 1785-1787.

[3] Henry, John (1750-1798). Maryland political figure. Member, Continental Congress, 1778-1780, 1785-1786. U.S. Senator, 1789-1797. Governor, 1797-1798.

Thomas Jefferson to John Jay

Sir   Paris Oct. 23. 1786.

In a letter of Jan. 2. I had the honor of communicating to you the measures which had been pursued here for the improvement of the commerce between the U.S. & France, the general view of that commerce which I had presented to the C. de Vergennes, the circumstance of the renewal of the farms which had obliged me to press separately & in the first place, the article of tobacco, & that which had also brought forward that of whale oil: & in my letters of May 27. & 31. I informed you of the result on the first of these articles. during the course of these proceedings a Committee had been established for considering the means of promoting the general commerce with America, and the M. de la fayette was named of that committee. his influence in obtaining that establishment was valuable, but his labors & his perseverance as a member of it became infinitely more so. immediately after the committee of Berni, of which my letter of May 27. gave an account, we thought it expedient to bring the

general subject of the American commerce before the Committee; & as the
members were much unacquainted with the nature & value of our
Commercial productions, the Marquis proposed that in a letter to him as
a member I should give as particular details of them as I could, as a ground
for the committee to proceed on. I did so in the letter, a copy of which I
have now the honour to inclose. the committee were well disposed and
agreed to report not only the general measures which they thought
expedient to be adopted, but the form of the letter to be written by the
Minister of finance to me, for the communication of those measures. I have
received his letter this morning & have now the honour to inclose it. I
accompany it with the one proposed by the committee, of which you will
perceive that it is almost a verbal copy: it furnishes a proof of the
disposition of the king & his ministers to produce a more intimate
intercourse between the two nations. indeed I must say that, as far as I am
able to see, the friendship of the people of this country towards us is cordial
& general, & that it is a kind of security for the friendship of ministers who
cannot in any country be uninfluenced by the voice of the people. to this
we may add that it is their interest as well as ours to multiply the bands of
friendship between us. as the regulations stated in the minister's letter are
immediately interesting to those concerned in our commerce, I send printed
copies of it to the seaport towns of France. we may consider them as an
ultimate settlement of the conditions of our commerce with this country:
for tho the consolidation of ship duties & the encouragement for the
importation of rice are not finally decided, yet the letter contains a promise
of them so soon as necessary facts shall be known. with a view to come at
the facts relative to the two last objects, I had proposed whenever I should
receive the final decision now inclosed, to avail myself of the pause which
that would produce, in order to visit the seaport towns with which we trade
chiefly, and to collect that kind of knowledge of our commerce, & of what
may be further useful to it, which can only be gathered on the spot, &
suggested by one's own inspection, but the delay which has attended the
obtaining the final determination has brought us to the entrance of winter
and will oblige me to postpone my journey to the spring. besides the objects
of public utility which induce me to make a tour of this kind, that of health
will oblige me to pay more attention to exercise and change of air than I
have hitherto done since my residence in Europe: and I am willing to hope
that I may be permitted at times to absent myself from this place, taking
occasions when there is nothing important on hand nor likely to arise.

The assistance of the M. de la Fayette in the whole of this business has
been so earnest & so efficacious, that I am in duty bound to place it under
the eye of Congress, as worthy their notice on this occasion. their thanks,
or such other notice as they should think proper, would be grateful to him,

without doubt. he has richly deserved and will continue to deserve it whenever occasions shall arise of rendering service to the U.S. these occasions will continually occur. tho the abolition of the monopoly of our tobaccoes can not be hoped under the present circumstances, changes are possible which may open that hope again. however jealous too this country is of foreign intercourse with their colonies, that intercourse is too essential to us to be abandoned as desperate. at this moment indeed it cannot be proposed: but by watching circumstances, occasion may arise hereafter, & I hope will arise. I know from experience what would in that case be the value of such an auxiliary.

I have the honour to be with sentiments of the most perfect esteem & respect Sir your most obedient & most humble servant

Th: Jefferson

NA: PCC, item 87, v. 1, pp. 694-696 (ALS); M247, reel 115.

John Jay to Thomas Jefferson

Dr Sir   New York 27th. October 1786

. . . . . .

The inefficacy of our Government becomes daily more and more apparent. Our Credit and our Treasury are in a sad Situation, and it is probable that either the Wisdom or Passions of the People will produce Changes. −

A Spirit of Licentiousness has infected Massachusetts, which appears more formidable than some at first apprehended; whether similar Symptoms will not soon mark a like Disease in several other States, is very problematical. −

The public Papers herewith sent contain everything generally known about these Matters. A Reluctance to Taxes, an Impatience of Government, a Rage for Property, and little Regard to the Means of acquiring it, together with a Desire of Equality in all Things, seem to actuate the Mass of those who are uneasy in their Circumstances; to these may be added the Influence of ambitious Adventurers, and the Speculations of the many Characters who prefer private to public good, and of others who expect to gain more from Wrecks made by Tempests, than from the Produce of patient and honest Industry. As the Knaves and Fools of this World are forever in Alliance, it is easy to perceive how much Vigour and Wisdom a Government from its Construction and Administration should possess, in Order to repress the Evils which naturally flow from such copious Sources of Injustice and Evil. −

Much I think is to be feared from the Sentiments which such a State of Things, is calculated to infuse into the Minds of the rational and well intentioned. In their Eyes the Charms of Liberty will daily fade, and in seeking for Peace and Security, they will too naturally turn towards Systems in direct Opposition to those which oppress and disquiet them. –

If Faction should long bear down Law and Government, Tyranny may raise its Head, or the more sober part of the People may even think of a King. –

In short, my Dr Sir, we are in a very unpleasant Situation – Changes are necessary, but what they ought to be, what they will be, and how and when to be produced, are arduous Questions. I feel for the Cause of Liberty and for the Honor of my Countrymen who have so nobly asserted it, and who at present so abuse its Blessings. If it should not take Root in this Soil little Pains will be taken to cultivate it in any other. –

I have the Honor to be with great Respect & Esteem &c.

John Jay

NA: PCC, *item 121, pp. 211-215 (LBkC); M61, reel 1.*

John Adams to John Jay

Dear Sir   Grosvenor Square October 27. 1786.
When the Ratification of Congress, of their Treaty with the King of Prussia,[1] arrived here, the Term limited for the Exchange of it was near expiring. as a few Members of the States general, had discovered Uneasiness at my coming to London without going to the Hague to take Leave, it seemed a convenient Opportunity to go over and Shew them as much of the Respect they required as remained in my Power. accordingly I went, and making the customary Visits to the President, Pensionary and Secretary, renewed the assurances of the Friendship, Esteem and Respect of the United States for their High Mightinesses and the Republic, and the Visit appeared to be kindly received. The Exchange of Ratifications was soon made with the Baron De Thulemeier who had time to transmit the Act of Congress to the great Prince, who first proposed the Treaty, Some days before he expired. The Ratification under the Signiture of Frederic the great is here inclosed.

at the same time, Sir, you will receive so much of the Substance of a Treaty of Commerce, between France and England, as the Ministry have thought fit to publish. This is so great an Event, and must have Consequences so extensive, that I feel myself incapable of forming any Judgment of it upon the whole. Every Treaty of Commerce between these nations, for three hundred Years, has been found benefical to France and hurtful to England.

But at present, this Nation is very Sanguine, the Advantage will be theirs. They boast of the Superiour skill of their Manufacturers the Superlative Excellence of their Manufactures; the Multitude of Inventions and Machines peculiar to themselves, by which Time and Labour is Saved, and Productions Sold cheaper than in any other Country. A Markett like France, where five and Twenty Millions of people have occasion for English Fabricks must be a valuable acquisition. Commercial Connections by softening Prejudices, may lessen the Disposition to War, and a Friendship, even an Alliance with France, would enable the two nations to govern the World. This is at present the style of Conversation, and the Treaty appears to be popular.

France and England, are both endeavouring, at this moment to impose upon each other by professing Desires of Friendship which they never felt. The secret Motive of both is to impose upon the United States of America. The English imagine that by assuming an Appearance of Friendship for France, they shall excite a Jealousy of France in America, and provoke Congress to break their Faith with her. The French are in hopes that by putting on a shew of Familiarity with England they shall stimulate Congress to make them proposals of closer Connections. The whole at Bottom, is a Farce of political Hypocrisy. – The United States will continue Steadily, it is to be hoped, on the Reserve.

.   .   .   .

The present appearances of Friendship, are forced and fained. The time may not be far distant, however, when we may see a Combination of England and the House of Bourbon, against the United States. it is not in gloomy Moments only, but in the utmost Gaiety of Heart, I cannot get rid of the Persuasion that the fair Plant of Liberty in America must be watered in Blood. You have seen enough in Europe, to know that these melancholy forebodings are no chimeras. There is such a Disposition, in the principal Powers who have Possessions in the Indies, that our Country will find no other Resource, but to swear her Children on the holy Altar, to fight them all at once in defence of her Liberties. – it may have some tendency, to save us from such Extremities if we enter into Treaties with the two Empires, for these will soon be jealous of any Connection between France and England.

.   .   .   .

I hope our Country in every part of it, will cherish their Militia as the Apple of their Eyes, and put every Thing in as good a Posture of defence as possible, and keep up a constant Expectation of War. This is the best and the most Serious Advice that can be given, by, Dear Sir, your most obedient and most humble Servant   John Adams

NA: PCC, *item 84, v. 6, pp. 355-358 (ALS); M247, reel 113.*
   [1] *Frederick II (1712-1786). Frederick the Great. King of Prussia, 1740-1786.*

Board of Treasury to John Adams

Sir: Board of Treasury October 31ˢᵗ 1786.

In your Letter of the 19ᵗʰ May last you were pleased to inform us that you had already accepted Bills which had been drawn on you to a considerable amount by Mʳ· Barclay and Lamb, in consequence of the appropriation which had been made by Congress for forming Treaties with the Barbary Powers; but as we have no advice from you since that date, we are at a loss to know whether the whole or what part of the appropriation has been drawn for on the Dutch Commissioners to the present day – The Accounts transmitted by those Gentlemen to the first of June last do not specify the particular disbursements for this object; but as far as we are able to form an Estimate from the Accounts transmitted, we presume that out of the various drafts you have made on them to the first of June last, 76.000 Florins have been on Account of the Barbary Negociations – If this is the Case 114.000 Florins remained after that day, subject to the appropriation above mentioned. –

The Embarrassments of the Government for want of a Steady and operative System of Revenue are daily growing more distressing; and such commotions have of late prevailed in the States of Massachusetts and New Hampshire, that we cannot promise ourselves that the complexion of our Affairs will soon change for a Better. Thus circumstanced it has not been in our power since the remittance of the last sum of 144,000 Florins, through your hands to make any considerable remittance to the Dutch Commissioners – We wish therefore most anxiously that the whole of the Monies appropriated by Congress may not have been exhausted by an unsuccessful attempt to form Treaties; as we are Extremely apprehensive that in this case there may not be Sufficient funds in the Month of February next, in the hands of the Dutch Commissioners to enable them to discharge the Interest which will then be due; and it is not in our power to remit in Season any Funds to make up a deficiency. –

If therefore you can possibly avoid drawing out of the hands of Messʳˢ· Willinks the whole of the Monies which have been appropriated for the Barbary Treaties till the February Interest is discharged, we must request the favor of you to do it; and no time shall be lost on our Part in making such further remittances, as may complete any part of the sum of 200.000 Florins, which may have been applied towards the Payment of Interest. – We are with great Respect & Esteem Sir Your Obed^t Hum^e Serv^{ts}

Samuel Osgood
Walter Livingston
Arthur Lee

MHS: *The Adams Papers, microfilm reel 369 (LS).*

John Jay to John Adams

Dr Sir   New York 1st November 1786.

. . . . .

My Report on the Answer of the british Minister to your Memorial respecting our frontier Posts is under the Consideration of Congress. Your Ideas and mine on those Subjects very nearly correspond, and I sincerely wish that you may be enabled to accommodate every Difference between us and Britain, on the most liberal Principles of Justice and Candor. The Result of my Enquiries into the Conduct of the States relative to the Treaty is that there has not been a single Day since it took Effect on which it has not been violated in America by one or other of the States – and this Observation is equally just whether the Treaty be supposed to have taken Effect either at the Date or [of] Exchange of the provisional Articles, or on the Day of the Date of the definitive Treaty, or of the Ratifications of it.–

Our Affairs are in a very unpleasant Situation and Changes become necessary and in some little Degree probable. When Government either from Defects in its Construction or Administration, ceases to assert its Rights, or is too feeble to afford Security, inspire Confidence and overawe the ambitious and licentious, the best Citizens naturally grow uneasy and look to other Systems. –

How far the Disorders of Massachusetts may extend or how they will terminate is problematical; nor is it possible to decide whether the People of Rhode Island will remain much longer obedient to the very extraordinary and exceptionable Laws passed for compelling them to embrace the Doctrine of the political Transubstantiation of Paper into Gold and Silver.

I suspect that our Posterity will read the History of our last four Years with much Regret. –

. . . . .

There is Reason to believe that the People of Vermont are in Correspondence with Canada. This Hint by calling your Attention to that

Subject may possibly suggest Modes of Inquiry and further Discoveries on your Side of the Water. Some suppose that the eastern Insurgents are encouraged if not moved by Expectations from the same Quarter but this is as yet mere Suspicion. –

. . . . .

With great and sincere Esteem and Regard I have the Honor to be Dr Sir Your most ob$^{t\cdot}$ & very hble: Serv$^{t\cdot}$　　　　　　　John Jay

MHS: *The Adams Papers, microfilm reel 369 (LS).*

Louis Guillaume Otto to Comte de Vergennes

[Translation]

N$^{o\cdot}$ 69.　　　　　　　　　　　　　　　　New York, 10 Nov. 1786.
My Lord.

. . . . .

The resolutions of the Annapolis *convention,* My Lord, of which I have had the honor to render You an account, have yet been adopted only by Virginia. The other States are little disposed to introduce a new system of confederation, and Congress itself appears to wish to reserve for itself the right to propose the changes necesssary to consolidate the union. It is in this view that it has named a grand Committee, composed of one Member from every State, and charged with submitting to that Assembly the alterations to make in the old system. They are all included in the following articles:

1. Congress shall have the exclusive right to regulate the commerce of the United States both with foreign nations and among themselves, to prohibit imports or exports that appear to it susceptible thereof, to order imposts on any merchandise whatever, and to determine the manner of collecting them.

2$^{o\cdot}$ When Congress shall send the various States requisitions concerning their respective Quotas, it will at the same time fix the period within which the States shall be required to pass acts conforming to these requisitions, and in the event that a State shall neglect to pass these laws, it shall pay one tenth above its Quota.

3$^{o\cdot}$ When a State shall have continued in its refusal for ten months, Congress shall have the right to raise the Quota which is owed to it in the said State itself, by seizing funds that are in the hands of the tax Collectors, to the extent of the Sums set forth in the requisitions, and in the event of opposition on their part, Congress shall be able to dismiss them and to name others to replace them. If the State itself wishes to oppose such a measure, it shall be considered as having violated the federal contract.

4. The States shall pay annually the interest on the arrears due to Congress on their Quotas.

5. In the event that Congress shall judge it appropriate to adopt a new system of finance, this change shall become obligatory for the United Sates when the Legislatures of eleven States have consented to it.

6. Congress shall have the exclusive right to determine what action should be considered a crime of high treason; it may establish a sovereign Court of Appeals that is especially versed in affairs of commerce, and in cases in which an article of a treaty concluded with a foreign nation shall have been violated by a law of an individual State, and generally in all proceedings that shall have reference to subjects the administration of which has been reserved to Congress. This court shall be composed of seven Judges, of which one shall be from New Hampshire, from Rhode Island, and from Connecticut, one from Massachusetts, one from New York and from New Jersey, one from Pennsylvania, one from Delaware and from Maryland, one from Virginia, and one from the two Carolinas and from Georgia.

7. The Delegates from each State shall return to Congress punctually at the beginning of November, and those who leave this assembly without having obtained its permission shall lose their seats in Congress and shall be disqualified from holding any position under the United States.

If these articles were adopted, My Lord, they would infallibly give Congress an exorbitant power, the Confederation would recover a new vigor, taxes would be paid punctually, foreign debts acquitted, and the credit of Congress would be restored. But I can only regard the execution of this plan as a chimera, and I would not even have thought I should render You an account of it if this assembly had not long been occupied with it as with a practicable matter. The necessity of the existence of this Sovereign body is not sufficiently obvious at this moment; the individual States do not see in it a Sovereign that protects, but a creditor who does not cease to demand money from them. A great number of Citizens would not even be displeased to see the entire dissolution of the confederation, since Congress alone appears to them responsible for the domestic and foreign loans, and since at the time of the destruction of this assembly, they would think themselves discharged from all their debts.

. . . . .

I am with a profound respect My Lord, Your most humble and most obedient Servant   Otto.
Received 23 Jan.ʸ 1787.

FFAA: Pol. Corr., U.S., v. 32, f. 131-135 (LC transcription).

Edward Rutledge to John Jay

My dear Sir   [Charleston, S.C.] Nov 12. 1786

After a disagreeable Passage & a variety of Weather Tincker has at last safely landed Us in Charleston, where I have reassumed the Character of a busy Man, & have a clear Prospect of passing an active Winter between my Professional, & Political Occupations. But altho' my Exertions shall be equally great, the individual, & the Public will not be equally benefited. That Spirit of Faction which is prevalent in other States, has extended her Influence to this; & is too manifest not to be discerned, even where she assumes, the Shape of Instruction. It is really very curious to observe, how the People of this World, are made the Dupes of a Word; "Liberty" is the Motto; & every attempt to restrain Licentiousness or give efficacy to Government is charged audaciously on the real Advocates for Freedom as an attack upon Liberty. On my Return home, I found several of my Compatriots so highly disgusted with the artifices of some unworthy Characters, that they had determined to withdraw, from the Theatre of Public Action, to Scenes of Retirement, & ease. But I have the Pleasure to think that, I have prevailed on them, to change their Resolutions, & to continue in responsible Stations: for indeed my Friend, if the Field is to be abandoned by Men of Virtue, either from the Clamor of the worthless, or the ingratitude of the foolish part of the Creation, the Condition of Humanity would be wretched indeed. Whereas, if Men who have given decided, & repeated Proofs, of their Love to their Country, unite together, & shew a firmness, similar to that which they displayed thro' the war; I am convinced that sooner or Later they will vanquish their Enemies & secure to themselves, & their posterity, all the Ends of good Government.

The Subject of the Western Waters I found was in the Possession of many of our People on my arrival – Various are their Opinions; the majority of those, with whom I have conversed, believe we should be benefited by a limited Cession of it to Spain; or rather a Cession for a limited time. But then, we must take Care, to be explicit on one Head. We must not be called on by Spain, at a future day, to guarantee the Cession. That will be absolutely inpracticable; & she should understand clearly, the extent of our Engagement. If, from our Relinquishment at present, she can retain for a Number of Years, the exclusive Navigation of the River, it is well; – it will stop Migration, it will concenter Force, because the Settlers can have no vent for the Productions of that Country, but down the Mississipi, & therefore, I think they will not be fond of immediately inhabiting her Banks. But when the Time shall arrive, when the Inhabitants shall be very numerous, will it not be worth the while of Spain to permit them the Navigation of the River, give them the Benefits of their Labor, encourage them in the Spirit of Agriculture, & divert their Minds from Conquests? – I should suppose it would. It will behoove Spain to consider this Affair with much Attention; consider too the Genius, as well as the Interest of those Western Settlers and ever carry in her Remembrance that, in her Cessions of American Territory, Great Britain cherished an Idea that, she was sowing the Seeds of Discord, between the States and Spain – Again, suppose at some future day G:B: should set on foot by the way of Canada & the Lakes, a negociation with these Western People, & assist them, in opening not only the passage of the River, but the way to the Southern World, how is this to be counteracted? Would it not become Spain to put on the Spirit of accommodation with the Settlers of this distant Country, & prevent by such a Measure, such an injurious union? – I am too little acquainted with the Wisdom of that Court, to say what they will do; & after all, the Changes in Men & Measures leave a vast Field for Speculation into distant Ages – What is the Wisdom of the most wise to day, is depreciated into nothing Tomorrow. But we must nevertheless act, & acting from the best of our Judgment endeavour to justify Wisdom of her Children –...Adieu my dear Friend & believe that I am warmly attached to your Family & yourself.   Ed: Rutledge[1]

.   .   .   .   .   .

Columbia University Libraries: John Jay Papers (ALS).

[1] Rutledge, Edward (1749-1800). South Carolina political figure. Member, Continental Congress, 1774-1776. Signer, Declaration of Independence. Member, state assembly, 1778-1779, 1782, 1786, 1788 and 1792. Militia officer, 1779-1780; captured at Charlestown, 1780. Prisoner of war, 1780-1781. Governor, 1798-1800.

Samuel Osgood to John Adams

Dear Sir –   New York, Nov.ʳ 14.ᵗʰ 1786
   I have to acknowledge the Rec.ᵗ of your Favor, which I should have answered Sooner, had any Thing within the Compass of my Knowledge occurred, of Sufficient Consequence to inform you of. – The present Secretary for foreign Affairs, I have no Doubt, keeps you well informed of all the political Occurrences here. –
   But in a Government, where expedients only keep up its Existence; it is impossible to foresee what Sudden & unexpected Changes may take Place–
   The federal Government Seems to be as near a Crisis as it is possible for it to be – The State Governments are weak & Selfish enough; & they will of Course annihilate the first – Their Stubborn Dignity will never Permit a federal Government to exist – There are however a few Men in every

State, who are very Seriously impressed with the Idea, that without a proper federal Head, the Individual States must fall a Prey to themselves, or any Power that is disposed to injure them – with this Idea, they are thinking very Seriously in what Manner to effect the most easy & natural Change of the present Form of the federal Government, to one more energetic; that will at the Same Time create Respect, & secure properly, Life, Liberty & Property – It is, therefore not uncommon to hear the Principles of Government Stated in common Conversation – Emperors, Kings, Stadholders, Governors General, with a Senate, or House of Lords, & House of Commons, are frequently the Topics of Conversation. Many are for abolishing all the State Governments, & for establishing Some Kind of general Government, but I believe very few agree in the general Principles; much less in the Details of Such a Government.

How to effect a Change is the Difficulty – The Confederation provides that Congress shall make the Alterations, & that they Shall be adopted by the Several Legislatures – Yet the Idea of a Special Convention appointed by the States to agree upon, & propose Such Alterations as may appear necessary, Seems to gain Ground – But the Danger is that neither Congress nor a Convention will do the Business – for the Situation of the United States, & of Some of the particular States, is Such, that an Army must be kept up – And the Probability is at present, that, that Army, will be Seriously employed – And in Case of a civil War – The Men of Property will certainly attach themselves very closely to that Army; the final issue of which, it is feared, will be, that the Army will make the Government of the united States. – Many Say already, any Change will be for the better – And are ready to Risque any Thing to effect it – The Disturbances in Massachusetts Seem most likely to produce Some very important Event. It is a little Surprising to Some, how they come to break out in Such a Manner there. – It is said that the Insurgents have two Objects in View – One to reduce their State Debt, & those Securities given by the united States to Citizens of that State for their Services, or Monies loaned, to their current Value in the Market – the other, to annihilate private Debts. – Perhaps this may be in Part true – And the greater Number may have nothing farther in View but to remedy some supposed Grievances, yet as it affords a fine Opportunity for the restless Enemies of this Country to sow Dissensions, we have too much Reason to believe, that they are not only looking on as Spectators, but that they are industriously employed in disseminating Disaffection to the present Form of Government – If these Enemies are british, or their old Adherents among us, which seems to be the Case, because they are traced from Hampshire & Berkshire, to Vermont, & from thence to Canada. If they are british, their Object must be something farther than mere Revenge – And that Object can be nothing Short of establishing a monarchical Government in this Country, & placing some one of ~~the~~ George's Sons on the Throne – If this Object is worth to the british, from five to ten Millions Ster.ᵍ & they can advance the Money – they can & will effect it. Not by Force of Arms, for if they should come out openly against us we should fight again – But be assured, this Country is extremely poor, as well as extravagant – And I have no doubt but ten Millions artfully applied would secure nearly the whole Country. – That the british will, & do cherish all their old Adherents is not to be doubted – And that those Adherents never will be Americans, is a Principle founded in Nature –

That the french will not be silent, inoperative Spectators in these Negotiations, if they should happen, is most certainly to be expected – They wish to keep us Just where we are; or if a little more insignificant quite as well; they will therefore View without Emotion any civil Commotions that tend to weaken us: But if there should be any Danger of the Scale's preponderating in favor of any other foreign Power, they will act with their usual Address. –

The British Party is, & will be great – The french Party also – The genuine Americans few. – The Speculators numerous, who care not what the Government is, so that they can speculate upon & spunge it.

Mʳ· Jay will probably have furnished you with the News Papers of this Country, which will contain much with Respect to the Hostile Disposition of the Indians – That the british instigate them to make Depredations on us, is very natural – But why they are reinforcing Canada, which by the public Papers appears to be the Case, is not so easy to determine.

All Things are operating here to bring the Cincinnati into Vogue. – I cannot say, I think they are all for supporting Government; but they are for having Government.

The Leader of the Insurgents in Massachusetts is entitled to the Ribbon & Eagle – He left the Army in the Fall of 1780 being then a Captain of good Reputation; his Name is Shays. – A Man without Education – But not without Abilities. – He is privately involved – which may be the Reason why he has adopted such violent Measures. It is generally supposed that he cannot Retreat. –

As to the Situation of the Finances of the united States they can scarcely be in a worse Condition – As to making any farther Attempts to discharge any Part of the Principal or Interest of our Foreign Debt it is in vain – The thirteen States do not pay enough to keep the civil List together; which do not require more than one hundred thousand Dollars a Year. – I have enclosed you a Schedule which will give you a full View of the Requisitions of Congress – the Payments & Balances due. –

I am Sir with great Respect Your most obedient Servant

Samuel Osgood

MHS: *The Adams Papers, microfilm reel 369 (ALS).*

Phineas Bond to Lord Carmarthen

My Lord   Philadelphia Nov.ʳ 26.ᵗʰ 1786.

I have the Honor to inform your Lordship, I arrived at New York on the 15ᵗʰ of this Month: – I immediately waited upon the Consul General, and communicated my Appointments, of which He had been already informed, in your Lordship's Dispatches.

While I remained at New York, there was not a sufficient Number of Delegates collected, to form a Congress; I therefore deliver'd my Commissions, to the Secretary for Foreign Affairs, for the Purpose of having them duly notified to the different States, when a Congress should be formed: my Stay at New York was very short; – I took the earliest opportunity of proceeding from thence to this Place: as soon as my Commissions are forwarded to me, I shall enter upon the Duties of my Appointments.

When I had the Honor of an Interview with the Consul General, He expressed some Doubts as to the Construction of my Commission, as Consul, founded upon the Circumstance of the State of New York being comprehended in my District; – conceiving his Powers, as to that State, must cease, while I remained upon the Spot: I explained the Motive, which induced Goverment to extend my Commission to New York; which I presume was in Consequence of an Idea, prevailing in England, that the Congress was about to establish foederal Towns in two different Parts of the Continent, as the occasional Residence of that Body, & as the terms of the Commission of the Consul General, confined his Residence to the Place where the Congress might assemble, it was deemed improper to leave a State of so much Importance as that of New York, unprotected, if the Removal of the Congress from thence, should occasion the Consul General to change his Place of Residence: that State was therefore included in the District I have the Honor to superintend: but I consider it to have been the Sense of Goverment, that I should refrain from the Exercise of all Powers, as Consul, in that State, while his Majesty's Consul Gen.ˡ remained there: tho' under my Commission as Commissary for commercial Affairs, I am enabled to make any Representations to the Legislature of that State, in common with the other individual States, thro' out the Continent of North America. –

I trust, my Lord, I have properly conceived the Intention of Goverment upon this Occasion; as it is my most earnest Wish to pursue that Line of Conduct which may secure a perfect Harmony, as the best means of effecting the important Objects of our Appointments.

I have great Pleasure in assuring your Lordship, that I have much Reason to be satisfied with the very polite Reception I met with, from the Consul General; who added to great personal Civility, the warmest Assurances of his Readiness & Desire, to contribute his Advice & Assistance towards facilitating any measures which might be deemed expedient to promote the commercial Interests of Great Britain.

I shall take the Liberty, from Time to Time, to communicate whatever may occur of sufficient Importance to call for your Lordship's Attention. I have the Honor to be, my Lord, with Sentiments of the greatest Respect, Your Lordship's faithful & most obd^t Servt P. Bond
R. 8th Jan$^{ry.}$

PRO: FO 4/4, pp. 763-765 (LC transcription).

Instructions to the Virginia Delegates to Congress Regarding Navigation of the Mississippi River

In the House of Delegates Wednesday the 29thof November 1786
Resolved unanimously that a copy of the Memorial of sundry inhabitants of the western Country be transmitted to the Delegates representing this State in Congress.

Resolved unanimously that the common right of navigating the Missisippi and of communicating with other nations through that Channel, be considered as the bountiful gift of Nature to the United States as proprietors of the Territory watered by the said River and it's Eastern branches.

Resolved unanimously that the Confederacy having been formed on the broad basis of equal rights in every part thereof to the protection and guardianship of the whole, a sacrifice of the rights of any one part to the supposed or real interests of another part, would be a flagrant violation of Justice, a direct contravention of the end for which the foederal Government was instituted, and an alarming Innovation of the System of the Union.

Resolved therefore unanimously that the Delegates representing this State in Congress be instructed in the most decided terms to oppose any attempt that may be made in Congress to barter or surrender to any nation whatever the right of the United States to the free and common use of the river

Missisippi, and to protest against the same as a dishonorable departure from that comprehensive and benevolent Policy, which constitutes the vital Principle of the Confederacy, as provoking the just resentments and reproaches of our Western brethren, whose essential Rights and Interests would be thereby sacrificed and sold, as destroying that confidence in the Wisdom, Justice and liberality of the foederal Councils, which is so necessary at this Crisis to a proper enlargement of their authority, and finally as tending to undermine our repose, our prosperity and our Union itself, and that the said Delegates be further instructed to urge the proper negotiations with Spain for obtaining her concurrence in such regulations touching the mutual and common use of the said river as may secure the permanent harmony and affection of the two Nations, and such as the wise and generous Policy of his Catholic Majesty will perceive to be no less due to the Interests of his own Subjects than to the just and friendly views of the United States.

1786. December 6th   Teste John Beckley[1] C.H.D^s
Agreed to by the Senate. –
John Beckley C. h. d   A copy, John Beckley, C. h. d

NA: PCC, item 75, pp. 407-409 (C); M247, reel 88.
  [1] *Beckley, John (1757-1807). Virginia political figure, lawyer and government official. Between 1775 and 1789, at various times he served as clerk of the state senate, house of delegates, high court of chancery and ratification convention, as well as mayor of Richmond. Clerk, U.S. House of Representatives, 1789-1797, 1801-1807.*

John Temple to Lord Carmarthen

N° 13. –   New York 7th Decr 1786.
My Lord,

              .   .   .   .   .

...Your Lordship in Letter N° 3 of the 7th June, desired that I would endeavour to learn what resolution Congress may have taken upon "The State of Grievances complained of by his Majesty's Subjects." which your Lordship put into the Hands of Mr Adams in London. It is with Satisfaction & pleasure that I have lately been successful in my Endeavours upon this Subject – The Statement of those Grievances was transmitted by Mr Adams to the Congress, who refered it to Mr Jay their Secretary for Foreign Affairs, with Orders for him to report what, in his Judgement, was fit & proper for them to say or do upon the occasion, which Mr Jay it seems has had under consideration for a considerable time. I am upon such a footing of Acquaintance with Mr Jay as that the other Evening, when by ourselves at his own House I asked him what Resolution Congress had come to, if any, concerning the State of grievances drawn up and given to Mr Adams, by My Lord Carmarthen? When he frankly told me (but with desire that I would not mention it in this Country) that he had reported fully upon the matter, that his report consisted of many Sheats of paper to make it plain & clear to common Understanding. That his Report upon the whole was, a full acknowledgement that many of the most important Articles in your Lordships Statement were just. Must be admitted as fact – and consequently a violation of the subsisting Treaty. That His Majesty was every way justifiable in still holding the Western Posts untill these States should Manifest a fair & honorable disposition to fulfill their part of the said Treaty. That he also in his report entered largely into the Complaint on the American side the question, particularly of the Negroes being carried off contrary to an Article in the Treaty, & upon the whole, as far as I could judge from his verbal acco^t of *the Report* (which will doubtless be adopted by Congress) it seems he has stated matters in such a light as will I trust be more pleasing to his Majesty & to his Ministers than I expected it would be. The Report is I understand upon the Table of Congress, but nothing can be done concerning it till the begining of next Month, when they will meet, choose a President, & then proceed to Business; soon after which, 'tis probable their Resolution & doings upon this Business will be transmitted to their self sufficient, wrong headed Minister in London, who by his Mulish disposition, has lost ground in every respect, with Congress as well in the particular state he belongs to: It is more than probable that both himself & his useless Secretary will soon be called Home, at any Rate, that after the expiration of their three Years appointment (12 Months hence) they never will be reappointed to the Court of London. It is now pretty generally thought that had a Man of a Modest conciliating disposition been sent to London a much better understanding would have long before this have subsisted between His Majesty & these States –

.   .   .   .   .

I have the honor to me [sic] My Lord Your Lordships most faithfull & obedient Servant   J. Temple
R. 8th Jan^{ry}

PRO: FO 4/4, pp. 811-814 (LC transcription).

John Jay to Thomas Jefferson

Dr Sir   [New York] Office for foreign Affairs 14th Decem^r 1786

My last to you was dated the 27th October by the Way of London, since which I have been honored with yours of the 11th and 13th August. They both arrived the 23^d Novem^r last, but Congress not having made a House since the 7th of that Month, they have not yet been officially communicated.

The Information relative to Sir Guy Carleton's Instructions, is in direct Opposition to Intelligence I have received on the same Subject from Persons in London, who have Opportunities of knowing the Truth, and whose Credit is unquestionable. It is possible however that they may have been either accidentally or designedly deceived. A Variety of Considerations and some Facts afford Room for Suspicions, that there is an Understanding between the Insurgents in Massachusetts and some leading Persons in Canada, but whether with or without the Consent or Connivance of the british Government, is still to be ascertained. There is so much Evidence of their having sent Emissaries to Quebec, and of Propositions made to, and received by them from a Character of Distinction there, that I am induced to think there is at least some Truth in it. A Report has also circulated that the Insurgents have Money, and pay not only for Supplies and Ammunition, but also for personal Services. This Fact is as yet supported by slender Proof, so much so that my Judgment remains undecided and in Suspence about it. Intimations have been given that the People of Vermont are less and less anxious to be admitted into the Confederacy, and that they rather incline to a Connection of some kind or other with Britain than with us. This also remains to be proved. Two Circumstances however give it some Appearance of Probability, Viz^t it is said and believed that they talked with Sir Guy Carleton during the War, and they know that by remaining separate from the States, they will also remain uncharged with our Debts. –

An Idea that may do Mischief has been very incautiously dropped where it should never have entered; that the Interests of the Atlantic and Western Parts of the United States are distinct, and that the Growth of the latter tending to diminish that of the former, the western People have Reason to be jealous of the northern. If Britain really means to do us Harm, she will adopt and impress this Idea. –

You will perceive from the public Papers, that the Government of Massachusetts has behaved with great Moderation and Condescension towards the Insurgents – more so that [sic] in my Opinion than was wise. *Obsta Principiis*[1] always appeared to me to be a Maxim very applicable to such Cases. Those Malcontents undoubtedly mean more than the Redress of the Grievances which their Leaders complain of, and there is little Doubt but that those Leaders have more extensive Views than their Followers suspect. During the Winter they may perhaps continue quiet, but if during the Course of it they should be able to bring their Affairs into System, and either obtain or be promised foreign Countenance and Aid, they will probably give us Trouble in the Spring. These People bear no Resemblance to an English Mob – they are more temperate, cool and regular in their Conduct – they have hitherto abstained from Plunder, nor have they that I know of committed any Outrages but such as the Accomplishment of their Purpose made necessary. I hear to Day that some of their Leaders in one of the Counties have certainly been taken by a Party of Horse from Boston. –

. . . . .

The public Papers will tell you how much Reason we have to apprehend an Indian War, and to suspect that Britain instigates it. In my Opinion our Indian Affairs have been ill managed – Details would be tedious – Indians have been murdered by our People in cold Blood and no Satisfaction given, nor are they pleased with the Avidity with which we seek to acquire their Lands. Would it not be wiser gradually to extend our Settlements, as want of Room should make it necessary, than to pitch our Tents through the Wilderness in a great Variety of Places, far distant from each other, and from those Advantages of Education, Civilization, Law and Government which compact Settlements and Neighbourhood afford? Shall we not fill the Wilderness with white Savages, and will they not become more formidable to us than the tawny ones who now inhabit it? –

As to the Sums of Money expected from the Sale of those Lands, I suspect we shall be deceived, for at whatever Price they may be sold, the Collection and Payment of it will not be easily accomplished. –

I have the Honor to be &ᶜᵃ·   John Jay. –

NA: PCC, item 121, pp. 224-230 (LBkC); M61, reel 1.
¹ Resist the beginnings; stop it now.

Thomas Jefferson to John Adams

Dear Sir   Paris Dec. 20. 1786.
    Colᵒ· Franks will have the honor of delivering to you the treaty with the emperor of Marocco, & all it's appendages. you will perceive by mr Barclay's letters that it is not necessary that any body should go back to Marocco to exchange ratifications. he sais however that it will be necessary

that Fennish receive some testimony that we approve the treaty: and as, by the acts of Congress, our signature is necessary to give validity to it, I have had duplicates of ratification prepared, which I have signed, & now send you. if you approve & sign them send one back to me to be forwarded to Fennish thro' mr Carmichael. perhaps a joint letter should be written to Fennish; if you think so, be so good as to write & sign one & send it with the ratification & I will sign and forward it. the other ratification is to go to Congress. Col⁰· Franks wishes to proceed with the papers to that body. he should do it I think immediately, as mr Jay in a letter to me of Oct. 26. says that Congress has heard thro' the French Chargé des affaires that the treaty was signed, & they wonder they have not heard it from us.

I inclose you a copy of a letter from mr Lamb. by which you will perceive that he does not propose to quit Alicant. I will forward the resolution of Congress to mr Carmichael which was inclosed of yours of Nov. 30. to see if that will move him. as the turn of this resolution admits a construction that Congress may think our original appointment of him censurable, I have, as in justice I ought, in a letter to mr Jay, taken on myself the blame of having proposed him to you, if any blame were due. I have inclosed him a copy of my letter to you of Sep. 24. 1785. mr Barclay has proposed to go to Alicant to settle Lamb's accounts, & has asked to be strengthened with our authority. if Lamb will obey the resolve of Congress it will be better to let him go & settle his account there. but if if he will not go back, perhaps it might not be amiss for mr Barclay to have instructions from us to require a settlement, those instructions to be used in that case only. if you think so, be so good as to write a joint letter & send it to me. but this, if done at all, should be done immediately. how much money has Lamb drawn? – I have suggested to mr Jay the expediency of putting the Barbary business into Carmichael's hands, or sending some body from America, in consideration of our separate residence & our distance from the scene of negociation.

I have seen, without alarm, accounts of the disturbances in the East. but Mr Jay's letter on the subject had really affected me. however yours sets me to rights. I can never fear that things will go far wrong where common sense has fair play....I must conclude here with assurances of the sincere esteem of Dʳ Sir your friend and servant　　　　　　Th: Jefferson

·　　·　　·　　·　　·

ansᵈ· Jan. 25. 1787

MHS: *The Adams Papers*, microfilm reel 369 (ALS).

Thomas Jefferson to John Jay

Sir   Paris Dec. 31. 1786

I had the honor of addressing you on the 12th of the last month, since which your favor of Oct. 12. has been received, inclosing a copy of the resolution of Congress for recalling m$^{r.}$ Lamb. my letter by m$^{r.}$ Randall informed you that we had put an end to his powers & required him to repair to Congress....

I am happy to find that m$^{r.}$ Barclay's mission has been attended with complete success. for this we are indebted unquestionably to the influence & good offices of the court of Madrid. Col^{o} Franks, the bearer of this will have the honor to put into your hands the original of the treaty with other papers accompanying it. it will appear by these that m$^{r.}$ Barclay has conducted himself with a degree of intelligence & of good faith, which reflects the highest honor on him.

.   .   .   .   .

...I have the honour to be with the most perfect esteem & respect, Sir your most obedient & most humble servant.   Th: Jefferson

NA: PCC, item 87, v. 1, pp. 790-792 (LS); M247, reel 115.

Samuel Shaw to John Jay

Sir   Canton in China 31$^{st.}$ December 1786

I have the honour to avail myself of this opportunity, which the return of our Ship to America affords me, for communicating to you such information respecting the Commerce carried on with China by the other Nations of the World, as my situation and circumstances, after a second Voyage to this Country, have enabled me to obtain. It will not I presume be expected that this communication should be altogether perfect; but as the nature of the Commerce here is exceedingly uniform and not liable to many alterations, a competent knowledge of it can never fail to be the result of a moderate share of attention and application. I shall therefore only say that I have every reason to believe the following accounts, as far as they extend, are authentic; and I shall consider myself happy if they should be in the least satisfactory on the several points recommended to my attention, in the Letter of instructions with which you have been pleased to honor me.

The Commerce of the Europeans with China appears to be as simple perhaps as any in the known World. The Danes, Spaniards, Imperialists,

Swedes, French, English and Dutch have regular establishments at Canton and trade by Companies. The Portuguese, although they are in possession of Macao, do not in the manner of the other Nations, keep a public establishment, but carry on this trade by Agents sent from Europe, who also return in their Ships. As the business of unloading and loading their Ships is by particular indulgence, transacted at Macao, a considerable saving thence accrues on the duties which the other Nations are obliged to pay.

The English Ships bring out from Europe lead and large Quantities of Cloth; which latter the Company are obliged by their Charter to export annually to China, for the encouragement of their home woollen Manufacture. The remainder of their Cargoes is made up with supplies for the Company's establishments in India, and such European commodities as will answer the various Markets on the Coasts. After having disposed of these, they take onboard Cotton, with which, their lead & Cloth they proceed to China. The English derive considerable advantage from the permission granted to private Ships, owned by their subjects in India, to trade with China. These Vessels, besides the Cotton, Sandal wood, putchosh root, ebony, opium, sharks-fins, and birds-nests they bring from the Coasts, drive on a smuggling trade with the Dutch settlements in and about Malacca, and with the Natives, whom they supply with Opium, Cloathing, fire Arms, &ᶜ· in return for which they receive pepper, block tin and spices. The proceeds of these, with the silver and other articles they bring from India, are about one third carried back in such Merchandize as will suit the India markets, and the remainder, either in Cash or transfers on the Chinese Merchants, is paid into the Company's Treasury, for which they receive bills on the Company in England, at the Exchange of five shillings and six pence sterling for a Dollar, payable twelve months after sight. This fund has for a number of years rendered it unnecessary for the Company to export from Europe any specie for carrying on their Commerce with the Chinese.

With respect however to this advantage derived by the English from their subjects in India, as well as from their Credit with the Chinese, it must be observed that both have been pushed as far as they would bear. Last year their ships depended greatly on the Latter of these resources for their homeward Cargoes, and the Company have sent from England, the present year, upwards of three millions of Dollars, in specie alone.

Besides the trade to China, these Country Ships (so called because they are not suffered to pass westward of the Cape of Good Hope) sometimes make very good Voyages to Batavia, the Capital of the Dutch settlements in India. They carry there all kinds of Cotton piece Goods – a variety of silk manufactures, and large quantities of salt petre. In return those that come to Canton take pepper and block tin, and such as go back to the Coast generally carry sugar, which pays a handsome freight.

The Dutch by their resources from their Settlements on Java, Sumatra, Malacca, and their other possessions in India, are enabled to manage their trade with China under equal if not superior advantages to any other People.

The other Companies depend principally upon their Lead and Silver brought from Europe; though sometimes the English Captains from the Coasts of India furnish them with the latter in return for bills. This exchange is forbidden by the English Company and any person detected in it forfeits his privilege and may be sent prisoner to England. However this penalty as it is seldom if ever inflicted is but little regarded. British Subjects in India, who wish to remit their property to Europe, will find means of doing it through other Channels than that of the Company's Treasury. They get a penny and sometimes two pence more on a Dollar, and bills payable at a shorter sight.

There being no french Company at the Conclusion of the late War, several essays have been made for conducting the trade of that nation with China. In the year 1783, the King made the expedition on his own Account with four Ships. In 1784, he lent three large ships to a company of Merchants, who were obliged to sell a certain number of shares to such individuals as chose to become adventurers; and the last year there was only one ship. The result of these experiments very probably induced the forming a new Company, and the present year they employ eight Ships; six for India and two for China; one of which last, having been late in the season off the Cape of Good Hope, has gone to the Mauritius. Their China Ships depend chiefly for their return Cargoes on the specie they bring from Europe. Their India Ships carry out Stores and Merchandize to the Islands of Mauritius and Bourbon, and to their settlements on the Indian peninsula, whence they return to France with pepper, Coffee, drugs, saltpetre and piece Goods, such as muslins, Calicoes, Chintzes, and the other various manufactures of that quarter, as well in silk as in Cotton. A Consul of France, part of their former establishment, is still retained here. He has a House and Table found him by the King, with a Salary of six thousand Livres per annum. Should any disputes arise among the subjects of France, his decision, in a Court of Chancery, where he presides, is final unless an appeal be made to the King and Council.

The Commerce of the Imperialists is closed. The German Dominions are not well situated for prosecuting it. The Company have had no ship here since 1783, and are one hundred and fifty thousand Dollars in Arrears to the Chinese for the Cargoes then supplied. Their agent, Mr. Reid,[1] returns this Season to Europe.

The establishments of the Swedes and Danes have hitherto been supported principally by the smuggling trade they carried on in the Channel and upon the Coast of Britain. But as the British parliament have taken off the duties on Teas imported in their own Ships, it is expected this policy will very considerably prevent the advantages that were reaped by those Nations, and not a little injure that branch of their Commerce. The general opinion seems to be, that the trade of both these nations with China must therefore be on the decline.

The Spaniards, after conducting their trade in private ships, have formed a Company at Manilla, whose fund is said to be eight millions of Dollars. They have now two Ships here, which return to Manilla, where their Cargoes are disposed of. Part is retained for the market there – such parts as will suit their settlements in America are sent by the way of Acapulco – and the residue to Europe, in other Ships. This nation must depend principally on its silver.

The Portuguese scarcely retain the Shadow of their former consequence. A few ships, owned by individuals at Macao and their remaining settlements in India, are kept in the Country trade, which is managed by them in much the same manner as by the English. Their trade to Europe, as has been observed is also conducted by private persons, and so little do they now derive from their possessions in India, that they are obliged to depend in a great measure on a credit from the Chinese for their homeward Cargoes. Scarcely one of their Ships brings from Europe sufficent funds – and were it not for this Credit, and the aids they receive from such European Company servants in India as are desirous of sending home their property not subject to the scrutiny of their Masters, the Commerce of this Nation with China would undoubtedly fail.

Besides the Europeans, the Armenians and Moors drive a considerable trade with China in pearls & other Merchandize, which they freight, in Portuguese and English bottoms, from the red Sea, the Persian Gulph, and the Peninsula of India.

Since the year 1783, some small Vessels have been fitted out by private persons in India and at Macao, for the fur trade to Kamchatka and the North-West Coast of America. Their success has answered the expectations of the adventurers, and not a little reduced the price of furs brought here from Europe.

Such are the outlines of the commerce carried on by the Europeans with China. The national establishments are on a liberal footing. The supercargoes are provided with elegant factories, and every accommodation they can wish. All expences are paid, and a commission allowed them for transacting the business, which is divided among them according to seniority. In the English Factory a young Gentleman (whose Father perhaps or other near relation is one of the Company) comes out at fourteen or fifteen years of Age, as a writer with all expences paid and one hundred pounds Sterling per Annum. At the expiration of five Years, he commences super Cargoe, when his Salary ceases, and he is included for part of the Commission; What may be the Amount of this depends on the number of Ships The present Year twenty five have already arrived, and five more are expected [four of them have since arrived. Jan^{yr} 4th 1787 –]. The proportion to the Chief and second, who share alike, will it is supposed be from twelve to fifteen thousand pound sterling each.

The English Captains in the Company's Service and all the Officers are allowed the privilege of private trade, on which account, as soon as their Ships are moored at Wampo [fourteen miles below Canton], the Captains take each his own factory at Canton. Their adventures consist chiefly of clock work of all kinds, (of which the Chinese are extremely fond) cutlery ware, glass, furs, some silver, and genseng, besides articles from the Coast of India. The Captain's privilege in the Ship is about sixty tons measurement; this he commonly fills up with fine Teas, Cassia, Silks, porcelain &^{c} which on his entering the English Channel, are disposed of to smugglers, between whom and the Custom House Officers there is always a clear understanding. The ships are built and equipped by private Merchants, who charter them to the Company at a certain tonnage. They are generally from eight hundred to a thousand tons burthen, and no ship is suffered to perform more than four voyages. A Captain must have great Interest to get one of these Ships, or pay from five to seven thousand pounds for the Command. In this case, he may sell again, and if he should Die during the Voyage, the privilege is filled up for the benefit of his heirs or assigns. This arrangement extends to the subordinate Officers. The Country Captains also take factories at Canton, and for privilege make the best bargain they can with their Employers.

Other Nations, instead of privilege to their Officers for private trade, allow a certain gratuity to each, according to his rank. Every Captain has an appartment in the factory and a place at the Company's table, where there is also a plate for any other Officer who may come to Canton.

No Europeans are suffered to remain at Canton throughout the year. After their Ships are gone, and they have settled their Accounts with the Chinese, they repair to Macao, where they continue till the Arrival of their Ships the next season, when they return to Canton.

As soon as a Ship, whether public or private, arrives at Wampo, a Fiador or security, must be engaged before she can discharge any part of the Cargo. This person is one of the principal Merchants, and generally him with whom the trade is made, though it does not hinder from dealing with others. He is answerable to the Custom House for payment of the Emperor's

Customs of entrance which average between four and five thousand Dollars p. ship. Besides this tax, there are duties on every other Article, whether of import or export; but with these there is no trouble, it being understood in all bargains with the Chinese, whether buying or selling, that they pay them.

The trade on the part of the Chinese is conducted by a set of Merchants, who style themselves the Co-hoang; a word expressing our idea of a trading Company. This cohoang consists of ten or twelve Merchants, who have the exclusive privilege of the European and Country trade, for which they pay a considerable Sum to Government; and no other dealers, if we except the petty shop keepers, who are also licensed by Government, can be concerned in it but by their permission. The cohoang assemble as often as is necessary – communicate the information they have obtained respecting the Commodities at market – agree on the prices at which they will purchase – and fix those of their own Goods in return. When it happens that a Ship has but a small Cargo, an individual of the Cohoang is unwilling to be its fiador, as perhaps his profits will not pay the duties. In this case a person is nominated in the Cohoang, and the Vessel's business done on their joint Account. There is generally no material variation from the prices fixed by the Cohoang.

Each ship and factory must also have a comprador. This is a person who furnishes provisions and other necessaries for which he contracts at certain prices. There is much imposition in this article; and if the Ship is small, the Comprador, besides being paid for all supplies, will have a doceur of an hundred or an hundred and fifty taels [one hundred dollars are equal to Seventy two taels]. This must be submitted to, as the Government derive a stated revenue for every ship of whatever Size, which the Comprador has permission to supply.

All the Company Ships on coming to Wampo have each a banksal on shore for the reception of their water Casks, Spars, sails, and all the lumber of the Ship, besides appartments for the sick. The french have theirs separate from the other Europeans, on an Island thence called french Island. The others are on the Main, on the opposite side, and confined to the Ground they occupy; for the remainder being rice fields, and constantly watered, renders it impossible to go beyond the limits of the banksal: Whereas french Island is a delightful situation, and the resort of the Gentlemen of all Nations, who go off and on at pleasure. Excepting those of the French and the Americans, no common sailors are allowed to go there. For the exclusive privilege of this Island, every french Ship adds an hundred taels extra to the Hoppo's present [The Hoppo is the Chief Officer of the Customs]. The banksal is a large building framed with bamboo reeds and covered with mats and Straw. They are erected by the Chinese, who pull them down immediately on their being left, in order that they may have the advantage of setting up new ones. The expence for a banksal is about two hundred dollars.

Besides a fiador and Comprador, each Ship must also have a linguist, which costs about an hundred and twenty taels. This person is absolutely necessary, as he is employed in transacting all business with the Custom House, which is in the City, where no European can be admitted – provides boats for unloading and Loading, and is always at call.

When the Hoppo goes to measure the shipping at Wampo, which he does when ever there are three or four that have not been visited, he is attended by the Cohoang. On these occasions the Captains produce their Clock work and other Curiosities, of which the Hoppo lays by such as he likes, and the fiador for the Ship is obliged to send them to him. sometime after the Hoppo demands the price, for he will not receive them as a present, when the Merchant, who understands matters perfectly, tells him about one twentieth part or less of their Value, and takes the money.

As soon as the Ship is measured the fiador takes out a permit for unloading, and the Linguist provides two boats to receive the Goods, which are hoisted out of the Ship in presence of two Mandarines, who live in their boat along side. When the Goods arrive at Canton, one of the principal mandarines, with his assistants, attends to weigh, measure, and take an Account of every thing, after which liberty is granted to sell. Such Articles as the fiador or the Cohoang do not want may be disposed of to any other purchaser, from whom the linguist collects the duty and settles with the fiador. When the return Cargo is to be sent on board, the Mandarines attend as before, examine and take an Account of every thing. Each package must have the sellers mark upon it, in order that the linguist may know where to apply for the Duties. No fees are paid to those Officers either by the buyer or seller, their Salaries being fixed by the Emperor. The expence of unloading is paid by the Europeans, and the Chinese deliver the return Cargoe along side the ship, free of all duties & Charges whatever. All Merchandize must be unloaded and loaded by Chinese boats.

In the Customs of Canton, as in other parts of the World, instances of knavery sometimes occur. The duty on Silks may be compromised with the mandarine, who will accept a present of about one half for letting them go free. In these cases the ships boat carrying the flag of its Nation, attends at the time and place appointed, takes in the Goods, and receives the mandarine's permit, which passes her without further examination. All boats are searched in coming to and going from Canton, and must have a permit; besides which they must, unless carrying the national flag, be stopped and examined at three different houses on the River.

The factories at Canton, occupying less than a quarter of a mile in front, are situated on the bank of the River. The Key is inclosed by a railed fence, which has Stairs and a Gate opening from the Water to each factory, where all Merchandize is received and sent away. The limits of the Europeans are extremely confined, there being, besides the Key, only a few streets in the Suburbs occupied by the trading people, which they are allowed to frequent. Europeans, after a dozen years residence, have not seen more than what the first month presented to view. They are sometimes invited to dine with the Chinese Merchants, who have Houses and Gardens on the opposite side of the River; but even then no new information is obtained. Every thing of a domestic concern is strictly concealed; and though their wives, mistresses, and Daughters are commonly there, never one of them is visible.

The Europeans at Canton do not associate together so freely as might be expected; the Gentlemen of the respective factories keeping much by themselves, and excepting in a few instances, observing a very ceremonious and reserved behaviour. At the Danish factory, there is every Sunday evening a concert of music, performed by Gentlemen of the several Nations, where every body attends that it pleases. This is the only occasion where there appears to be any thing like a general intercourse. On the whole, the situation of the Europeans is not enviable; and considering the length of time they reside in this Country – the restrictions to which they must submit – the great distance they are from their connections – the want of society & of almost every amusement, it must be allowed that they dearly earn their money.

Much has been said respecting the knavery of the Chinese, particularly those of the trading Class, but there is no general rule without an exception. The small dealers are many of them indisputably Rogues, and require to be very narrowly watched. But the Merchants of the Cohoang are a set of as respectable men as are commonly found in other parts of the world. They are intelligent exact accomplants – punctual to their engagements, and, though not worse for being well looked after, value themselves much upon maintaining a fair Character. The concurrent testimony of all the Europeans justifies this remark.

The ships employed in this trade are on an average seven hundred tons each – some as many as fourteen but none less than five, and for the last three years the numbers have considerably varied. In 1783, exclusive of the Country Ships returning to India, there sailed from Canton and Macao forty five ships for Europe, sixteen whereof were English. In 1784, there were eleven English, four french, including one chartered at the Mauritius, five Dutch, three Danes and four Portuguese, which sailed for Europe; eight English and one Danish Country Ships that returned to the Coasts, and one American. The Swedish Ships lost their Season that year. In 1785, there were eighteen English, four Dutch, one French, four Spanish, three Danish, four Swedish. one English American under Imperial Colours, Sailed for Europe and America – and ten English Country Ships that returned to the Coast – and the present Season the list is as follows – twenty nine English, five Dutch, one French, two Spanish, two Danish, one Swedish, five American for Europe and America – twenty three English Country Ships that return to the Coast – and five Portuguese from Macao to Europe.

Having been thus particular respecting the manner in which other Nations conduct their commerce with China it will not, I trust, be improper to make a few observations on the nature of our own.

The inhabitants of America must have Tea, the consumption of which will necessarily increase with the increasing population of our Country; And while the Nations of Europe are for the most part obliged to purchase this Commodity with their ready money, it must be pleasing to an American to know that his Country can have it upon more easy terms, and that the otherwise useless produce of its Mountains and forests will in a considerable degree supply him with this elegant Luxury. The advantages peculiar to America in this instance are striking, and the manner in which her Commerce has commenced, and is now going on with this Country, has not a little alarmed the Europeans. They have seen, the first year, a single Ship, one fifth part of whose funds did not consist of ready money, procure a Cargo of the same Articles, & on equally good terms as those of their own Ships, purchased as has been observed, for the most part with specie. They have seen this ship again here on her second Voyage, and four others in addition. They see these Ships depending, and that too with sufficient reason, upon the productions of their own Country to supply them with the Merchandize of this; and though a very small proportion of their funds consisted in specie, they see them all returning with full and valuable Cargoes. Such are the advantages which America derives from her Genseng.

With respect to the demand in this Country for the Genseng of America, which might perhaps be rendered as beneficial to her Citizens as her mines of Silver and Gold have been to the rest of Mankind, the world has been much mistaken. Until the American flag appeared in this quarter, it had been generally supposed that forty or fifty peculs [a pecul is 133 1/3 lb. English] were equal to the Annual consumption; But experience has proved the contrary. Upwards of four hundred and forty peculs were brought here by the first American Ship in 1784, which did not equal the quantity brought from Europe the same season; the greatest part of which must have been previously sent there by Citizens of the United States. The present year more than eighteen hundred peculs have been sold, one half of which came in the American Vessels. Notwithstanding this increased quantity since 1784, the sales have not been materially affected by it; and it is probable there will always be a sufficient demand for the Article to make it equally valuable.

On a consideration of the subject of Genseng the enquiry seems naturally to arise, whether it cannot be rendered more beneficial to the Country which produces it than it is at present? How far the culture of this Commodity is practicable – in what manner it may be best promoted, and whether it would be for the interest of America to prevent the exportation of it in any but American bottoms directly to this Country, may be objects not unworthy of national attention.

Besides the advantages which America may derive from her Genseng, in the Commerce direct with China, others would also accrue by making the Voyage circuitous, which could be performed without loss of time. The ship in which I have made my second Voyage to China, stopped at Batavia, the Capital of the Dutch establishments in India. we were well received there and allowed to trade on the same terms as other Nations. Iron and naval Stores, the produce of our Country, found a ready Sale; and besides these, we disposed of articles, which, though not immediately productions of our own, had been received from other Countries in exchange for them. A profit may be sometimes made on Merchandize carried from Batavia to Canton. No doubt similar advantages might result to the Americans, in circuitous Voyages to China by the Coasts of Malabar and Coromandel, and through the streights of Malacca.

On the whole it must be a most satisfactory consideration to every American, when he finds that his Country can carry on its Commerce with China under advantages, if not in many respects superior, yet in all cases equal with those possessed by any other People.

I have thus, Sir, used my best endeavours to communicate to you every information I have been able to obtain of the means by which the other nations of the world carry on their Commerce with China. should these remarks be found in any degree interesting to my Country, it will afford me the most heartfelt satisfaction. The matter of this communication I believe may be relied on; but for the manner in which it is made, I must request that indulgence which I have been so happy as to experience on a former occasion.

I must not omit mentioning that the death of M^r· Sears,[2] our late worthy friend and partner, renders it necessary that M^r· Randall should return to America, in order to attend to our private concerns. This step I hope will not be disagreeable to you. He will be able to give any farther information respecting the aforegoing particulars that may be necessary. I shall in the meantime go to Bengal, and return here the ensuing Season. If in this Tour any new information should be obtained, I will do myself the pleasure of transmitting it to you. I have the Honor to be &^c·

Samuel Shaw

NA: PCC, *item 120, v. 3, pp. 227-243 (LBkC); M40, reel 3.*

¹ *Not further identified.*

² *Sears, Isaac (1730-1786). New York merchant and political figure. After commanding merchantmen in the coasting trade, Sears won a reputation for bravery as a privateersman during the French and Indian War. A principal leader of popular unrest against British rule in New York City. After that city's fall in 1776, he moved to Boston, where he promoted privateering throughout the war. He returned to New York in late 1783, resumed his mercantile career, and became involved in the incipient American China trade. In 1786, he accompanied Samuel Shaw and Thomas Randall to Canton, where he died of a fever and was buried on French Island.*

Sir John Temple to Lord Carmarthen

N° 14. –   New York 4ᵗʰ Jan: 1787.
My Lord,

Herewith is duplicate of the Letter I had the honor of writing to your Lordship, by the *Swallow* Packet, on the 7ᵗʰ of last Month, since which, I have received a Letter from Mʳ Fraser of the first of Novʳ informing me that your Lordship was then much indisposed; I hope & trust that the December Mail (which I expect will arrive in about three Weeks) may bring me Intelligence of your Lordships perfect recovery.

Public affairs in this Country have not much altered their complexion since the date of my last Letter: the Winter having set in uncommonly early & severe hath caused a pause in the Opposers to Government in the New England states, when the Moderate seasons of the Year return, the rising of the people will, I am of Opinion, return also.

There is at present No Congress sitting, and it is altogether uncertain when, or whether ever, a Congress will set again under the present flimsey federal Government of this distracted Country.

This Packet I understand carries home between thirty & forty thousand pounds sterling, mostly in Spanish Mill'd dollars.

I have the honor to be My Lord Your Lordships most faithfull and Obedient Servant   J: Temple
R. 2ᵈ Febry

PRO: FO 4/5, *pp. 19-20, 22 (LC transcription).*

Dutch Bankers to John Adams

Amsterdam 5 January 1787

We had the honor to receive in due time Your Excellency's ever respected Favor of   advising us to pay in Specie the premiums of 6 p C for 60000 F drawn last October at the charge of the United States. We shall immediately publish the same, together with the Payment of the Interest due 1 proximo on the Loan of Two Millions Which will we trust have the good effect upon the Credit of America Your Excellency and we promise ourselves. Such a Measure is the best possible Refutation of the exaggerated Reports published with avidity by Persons, thro malice or Ignorance of the Confidence and Respect due to the Government of the United States.

.   .   .   .   .

We...have the honor to be most respectfully Your Excellency's Very obedient humble Servants   Wilhem & Jan Willink
Nic° & Jacob van Staphorst.

NA: PCC, *item 84, v. 6, pp. 375-376 (LS); M247, reel 113.*

Phineas Bond to Lord Carmarthen

My Lord   Philadelphia Jany. 5th 1787

In my letter of the 1st inst. by the Jan. packet, I had the honor to inform your Lordship "I had not yet been able to enter upon the duties of my appointments, as a congress was not then assembled at New York;" nor have I since heard a sufficient number of delegates is yet collected there to form a congress.

In the usual course of intelligence, your Lordship has most probably been informed of the contents of the letter contained in the enclosed paper: if genuine it manifests plainly the disposition of the French Court to establish and secure as much as possible, a commercial connection with the United States; for which purpose, exemptions and indulgencies to a most liberal latitude seem to be in contemplation. Whether the disposition of France extends as far as the letter seems to imply, your Lordship will be best able to decide: certain it is the contract alluded to *now* exists; and so favorable is it to the importation of tobacco into France, that it has been and will be the means of diverting that very considerable subject of remittance from its just and honest channel, viz, the making good the very important engagements entered into and depending between the American merchants and their British correspondents; an object of no small consequence to them, when it is considered how few resources, in the way of remittance, this country possesses in the present confined state of its trade.

I conceive it to be my duty to submit this matter to your Lordship's consideration, and shall as often as occasion may offer, take the liberty of communicating whatever affects the interests of the commercial part of the nation.

I have the honor to be, my Lord, with sentiments of the highest respect, Your Lordship's most faithful and obedient servant   P. Bond. Rec$^{d.}$ 15$^{th.}$

Annual Report of the American Historical Association for the Year 1896 (Washington: Government Printing Office, 1897), hereafter cited as AHA 1896, v. 1, p. 518.

Thomas Jefferson to John Jay

Sir   Paris Jan. 9. 1787.

.   .   .   .   .

I will certainly do the best I can for the reformation of the Consular Convention, being persuaded that our states would be very unwilling to conform their laws either to the Convention, or to the scheme, but it is too difficult, & too delicate to form sanguine hopes. however that there may be room to reduce the convention as much as circumstances will admit, will it not be expedient for Congress to give me powers, in which there shall be no reference to the scheme? the powers sent me, oblige me to produce that scheme, & certainly the moment it is produced, they will not abate a tittle from it. if they recollect the scheme & insist on it, we can but conclude it: but if they have forgotten it (which may be) and are willing to reconsider the whole subject, perhaps we may get rid of something the more of it. as the delay is not injurious to us, because the Convention whenever & however made is to put us in a worse state than we are in now, I shall venture to defer saying a word on the subject till I can hear from you in answer to this. the full powers may be sufficiently guarded by private instructions to me not to go beyond the former scheme. this delay may be well enough ascribed (whenever I shall have received new powers) to a journey I had before apprised the minister that I should be obliged to take to some mineral waters in the South of France....I shall return by Bourdeaux, Nantes, & lorient to get the necessary information for finishing our commercial regulations here. permit me however to ask as immediately as possible an answer either affirmative or negative as Congress shall think best, and to ascribe the delay on which I venture to my desire to do what is for the best.

.   .   .   .   .

...I have the honour to be with sentiments of the most perfect esteem & respect, Sir, your most obedient & most humble servant

Th: Jefferson

LC: *Jefferson Papers, microfilm reel 6 (press copy).*

Louis Guillaume Otto to Comte de Vergennes

[Translation]

N⁰· 74.   New York, 10 January 1787.

My Lord

Since the negotiations for the peace, M. le Chev⁻ᵉʳ· de la Luzerne and M. de Marbois have often had occasion to observe to You that the Despatches of the American Plenipotentiaries had inspired in Congress suspicions of our sincerity and of our political views. Independently of the intercepted Letters which the English wished to turn to so great an account, M. le Chev⁻ᵉʳ· de la Luzerne has informed You in his N⁰ˢ· 323, 340, & 345 that Congress had received reports that were infinitely prejudicial to us, but that it was impossible for him to investigate the details thereof. In Your Despatch N⁰· 50, My Lord, You suspect Mr. Jay, with much foundation, of having accused us of wishing to diminish the great concessions that Great Britain proposed to make to the United States. This conjecture is today confirmed in the most incontestable manner.

I have often tempered, My Lord, the ardor of the Members of Congress who discussed the fisheries and the intercepted Letters with me. One of my conversations with a Delegate who is very attached to us induced him to tell me that it was not only these letters that had made Congress doubt our sincerity, but that there was in the repository of foreign affairs an authentic document that justified the American Negotiators only too well in having signed the preliminary articles without consulting us. I answered him that far from having acted against the interest of the States, we had always treated them with a generosity and a candor of which there was perhaps no example. I had him consider how many times we had exceeded the obligations of an ally to alleviate the distress of the United States and to reduce the claims of England to just limits, that we had only wished to take part in their negotiations in order to give more harmony and energy to the common measures of the two allies and to prevent a separation of interests that would have necessarily plunged the States into the greatest confusion, that the two parties that ruled then in Congress had need of a disinterested and generous mediator to guide the revolution to a glorious end, but that the American Plenipotentiaries had represented our policy in an odious light because they wished to justify a step that was clearly contrary to the instructions that Congress had given them. This response produced a complete confession on the part of my adversary: "We know very well," he told me, "that the jealousy of Messrs. Adams and Jay may have irritated them against a Court that appeared to protect Mr. Franklin, but their mistrust was not completely without foundation. Mr. Oswald[1] communicated to our Plenipotentiaries the draft of a treaty much more favorable than the one we obtained; this treaty was on the verge of being approved, when Your Minister made every effort to have it rejected. An authentic copy of this document is in our repository of foreign affairs; it establishes the frontier of the United States well beyond Montreal and the Lake of the Woods; it extends our fisheries and our southern borders and anticipates in general all the difficulties that have since arisen. But we know that Your Court sent a Plenipotentiary to London only to prevent the success of this negotiation."

This grievance, My Lord, relates so little to what you were so good as to write to M. le Che^r· de la Luzerne in Your Despatch N^o· 50 that I thought I should thoroughly respond to it. I am especially interested in demonstrating that Mr. Oswald had the greatest interest in inspiring the American Plenipotentiaries with distrust in our regard in order to engage them to conclude a separate peace, and that the personal character of the latter had them only too disposed to give credence to the insidious and false communications of the English Negociator, that the jealousy of these Plenipotentiaries against Mr. Franklin had been all the less founded, since we should naturally have more regard for the Minister of the United States accredited to His Majesty than for Commissioners who were not invested with the same dignity, that moreover the conduct of this Minister had fully justified the good opinion that His Majesty had conceived of his talents, of his zeal, and of his prudence. It was easy for me to convince the Delegate with whom I was conversing that the measure of which we were accused would have been very imprudent, since we should have foreseen that the English Minister could turn it to account; that it would have been very bad policy to place reliance in our common enemies at so delicate a conjuncture; that at the moment when we were wresting from England the most painful sacrifice that she had ever made, we would have looked very inconsistent, to say no more, to hinder her good intentions with regard to the Americans; that moreover we had no interest in rendering the negotiations of the United States less advantageous; that with regard to the fisheries and the Western lands, we had always articulated our way of thinking with much candor; that we had always offered up sincere prayers for the success of the demands of Congress, but that we had refused to prolong the war in order to procure for it advantages that were not essentially related to the independence of the United States; that if we had wished to lend an ear to all the exaggerated claims of some States, we would have put down our arms only after having vainly attempted the conquest of Canada, of Acadia, and even of Newfoundland; that we had known the true interests of the States better than the Americans themselves; that the Western lands had always appeared to us a useless and dangerous posssession, and that the result today justified the predictions of M. le Chev$^{er.}$ de la Luzerne; that the modest finances of the States were going to be entirely exhausted by continual wars with the Savages, and that if the reports of Messrs. Adams and Jay were founded, the Americans could not refrain from agreeing that by placing limits on the perfidious generosity of England, we would have rendered the confederation the most signal service." The Delegate agreed with the justice of this reasoning, but he added nevertheless the most implicit faith in Mr. Jay's Despatches, of which several volumes accompany and explain the draft of the treaty that I have just mentioned: "It is hard," he told me, "for our contemporaries to decide so complicated a question; posterity and history will judge it better than we."

This discovery, My Lord, finally explains to us the secret motive of the distrust that several members of Congress have shown us since the peace; we know the grievances that they have against us, and we are in a position to respond to them. I await Your orders before entering into any explanation with other Delegates. As they all have the right to instruct themselves in the Repository of foreign affairs, they mysteriously imbibe in the correspondence of Messrs. Adams and Jay principles that are very unfavorable to us.

The order that Mr. Jay has introduced in his department facilitates the research that members of Congress often make for their private instruction, and I see that with the exception of the Delegates from Virginia and from Carolina, the most assiduous among them are precisely those who speak to me with the most circumspection and who are the most strongly opposed to the ratification of our Consular convention and to the motion that the Southern States have made to treat with Spain only under His Majesty's mediation. Unfortunately, Mr. Franklin, who more than any other American is in a position to render justice to us, is too far from New York to rectify the false reports of his Colleagues, and although there has never been a Minister charged with longer and more important negotiations, he has rendered no account of his mission; he was named upon his arrival to

America to the Presidency of Pennsylvania without having other relations with Congress than those that result from his present position.

I am with a profound respect My Lord Your most humble and most obedient Servant   Otto
r. 23 March.

FFAA: Pol. Corr., U.S., v. 32, f. 178-181vo. (LC transcription).
  [1] Oswald, Richard (c.1705-1784). British merchant and political figure. Consulted by North Ministry because of his knowledge of American commercial affairs. Friend of Benjamin Franklin and Lord Shelburne. Plenipotentiary to negotiate peace with the American commissioners in Paris, April-November 1782.

Thomas Jefferson to John Adams

Dear Sir   Paris Jan. 11. 1787.
Mr. Jay, in his last letter to me, observes they hear nothing further of the treaty with Portugal. I have taken the liberty of telling him that I will write to you on the subject, & that he may expect to hear from you on it by the present conveyance. the Chevalier del Pinto being at London, I presume he has or can inform you why it is delayed on their part. I will thank you also for the information he shall give you.

There is here an order of priests called the Mathurins, the object of whose institution is the begging of alms for the redemption of captives. about 18 months ago they redeemed 300, which cost them about 1500 livres a peice. they have agents residing in the Barbary states, who are constantly employed in searching and contracting for the captives of their nation, and they redeem at a lower price than any other people can. it occurred to me that their agency might be engaged for our prisoners at Algiers. I have had interviews with them, and the last night a long one with the General of the order. they offer their services with all the benignity & cordiality possible. the General told me he could not expect to redeem our prisoners as cheap as their own, but that he would use all the means in his power to do it on the best terms possible, which will be the better as there shall be the less suspicion that he acts for our public. I told him I would write to you on the subject, & speak to him again. what do you think of employing them, limiting them to a certain price, as 300 dollars for instance or any other sum you think proper? he will write immediately to his instruments there, & in two or three months we can know the event. he will deliver them at Marseilles, Cadiz, or where we please, at our expence. the money remaining of the fund destined to the Barbary business may I suppose be drawn on for this object. write me your opinion if you please, on this subject, finally, fully, & immediately, that, if you approve the proposition, I may enter into arrangements with the General before my departure to the waters of Aix, which will be about the beginning of February.

I have the honour to be with very sincere esteem and respect Dear Sir your most obedient & most humble serv.^{t.} Th: Jefferson ans^{d.} Jan. 25.

MHS: *The Adams Papers, microfilm reel 369 (ALS).*

Louis Guillaume Otto to Comte de Vergennes

[Translation]

N°. 75.   New York, 19 Jany. 1787.
My Lord.

The false news of the exchange of Louisiana for a French possession in the Antilles was almost forgotten when an alleged treaty by which France is placed in possession of the two Floridas under the condition of closing the navigation of the Mississippi to the Americans and continually maintaining a considerable body of troops to prevent future invasions of the Spanish possessions by inhabitants of the South was printed the same day in two different Gazettes. It was easy to divine the purpose and the authors of this fabrication, but the most well-informed Americans and even those who are the most attached to us were deceived by the authentic form that was given to the various articles of the treaty. I have endeavored in vain to assure the members of Congress and the principal Citizens of New York that this treaty was entirely forged in England and that there has never been a question of an exchange of the Floridas; they have answered me that this news has been repeated so often and has been accompanied by such plausible circumstances that they could no longer doubt its authenticity; that before the publication of this document, the Southern States had eagerly desired this exchange because they must expect to live on better terms with a French Colony than with the Spanish; but that the article concerning the navigation of the Mississippi proved to them only too well that His Majesty's sentiments in their regard were altered for the worse; that the treaty of commerce between France and England must necessarily increase their alarms, because it implied a great rapprochement between the two Courts; that the United States would henceforth have two neighbors so much the more formidable, in that they appeared to want to combine against them by closing to them not only the islands, but also the most important channels of their commerce and their industry on the Continent. I have hitherto limited myself, My Lord, to verbally communicating to the Members of Congress the orders which You were so good as to give me in Your Despatch N°· 3, but seeing that all my assurances could not calm the humors, I sent to Mr. Jay, at his request, an extract from the passage relative to the exchange of Louisiana. This Minister had nothing more pressing than to have it printed. The clamors ceased at once, they were astonished that they could believe for one moment news so little probable, they commend the wisdom and the good policy of France, upon which they had allowed themselves reflections little considered some days before, and they no longer have the least doubt regarding the fabrication of the alleged treaty of cession. – Although the publicity that Mr. Jay gave to my communication has produced the most prompt and salutary effect, I could not refrain from complaining with respect to this Minister, and from telling him that his conduct would henceforth constrain me to an extreme reserve in his regard. He answered me that the ferment was so great that no less than the name of M. le Comte de Vergennes was necessary to discredit the false news that the English Emissaries did not cease to propagate in America, that he was persuaded that there was always a very considerable party in favor of England in the United States, that it was by inspiring hatreds and mutual animosities that it expected to succeed in detaching the United States from France, and that in order to render the cession of Louisiana still more odious, they have given out that His Majesty, having in vain expected the punctual reimbursement of the American debts, had decided to recover Louisiana in order to have a foothold on the Continent and to be able at leisure to make himself master of Georgia or of Carolina so as to recoup his losses. In addition, Congress has strongly disapproved of the precipitancy of Mr. Jay, who has no right to publish the information that was sent to him. But I shall henceforth have no less than the greatest care in making only verbal communications to that Minister whenever You shall not have expressly ordered me to treat with him in writing.

Mr. Jay's apprehensions, My Lord, concerning the underhanded schemings of some few English Emissaries appeared to me well-founded. I perceive especially that since the arrival of Mr. Temple, the Consul of England, the public papers very often contain insinuations injurious to France or at least prejudicial to the alliance. I at first scorned these publications, but seeing that they became more insidious day by day, I decided to respond to them without relying on anyone for the translation of my paragraphs. The moderation that I employed therein gave no suspicion of their author, and I have reason to be content with their effect. Mr. Temple's purpose is not only to alienate the Americans, but to irritate our Government, since he knows that the American gazettes are read in

France, and he hopes that the sentiments contained in his publications will be attributed to Congress or to people in office. On the other hand, that Consul knows the Americans too well not to have perceived that the least rapprochement between France and England gives them the most violent alarms. He has therefore seized very adroitly the moment of publication of our treaty of Commerce to inundate the gazettes with paragraphs concerning the intimacy and good understanding which exist between the two nations; at the same time, he did not neglect to deplore the fate of the United States, which will not fail, according to him, to be the victims of this coalition sooner or later. These lamentations come to us alternately from Boston, from Rhode Island, from Philadelphia, but I always recognize in them the pen or at least the policy of Mr. Temple. He affects, especially in public and in the presence of Members of Congress, to make me the most amicable and obliging welcome, to speak to me with emphasis of the important consequences which must necessarily result from our treaty of Commerce, and to infer therefrom that the system of Europe had entirely changed and that the united forces of the two most powerful nations would henceforth lay down the law for the entire Universe. In order not to increase the fears of the Americans, My Lord, I am obliged to be extremely circumspect in my responses and to see Mr. Temple as seldom as decency permits me.

I am with a profound respect My Lord Your most humble and most obedient servant   Otto.
r. 23 March

FFAA: Pol. Corr., U.S., v. 32, f. 182-184vo. (LC transcription).

Charles W. F. Dumas to Thomas Jefferson

[Translation]

Sir,   The Hague, 23 Jan. 1787

Upon my return from Amsterdam, I hasten to respond to the confidential question which your Excellency directed to me in his Letter of 25 Dec. last.

If there were a way to negotiate in Holland Money for the United States to reimburse the 24 million livres tournois that they owe to France?

I consulted some intimate friends there on whom I can rely, not only with regard to Discretion, which will be scrupulously observed, but also with regard to ability, honesty, and perfect sufficiency for the execution even of such an enterprise: – And here is the Result of our conversations, written down in Amsterdam the 20th & 21st, although I am transcribing and dating it as above.

As for the Credit of Congress, it is certain that it will establish itself little by little on a solid footing: What contributes greatly thereto is the regular receipt of the Interest at the exact time of its falling due, & especially also the receipt in money of the Premiums on the Negotiation of two Million florins, which Congress had the choice of making in new obligations. – It is also thought that this Credit henceforth will have reached the point that one could, in full assurance, give encouragements to further Negotiations, and promises concerning their success, if the English Papers did not continue to spread, regarding the state of affairs in America, Opinions very suitable to give the fever to Men of Property, & certain Gazetteers in this country adopt them eagerly in their papers. These latter belong to the Faction of those who, in thwarting as much as they can the efforts made to establish civil Liberty in this country, fancy that continual reproduction of imagery that represents popular disturbances and commotions (which, according to them, take place in America) should disgust minds here with the notion of thinking of a Constitution in which the People have some influence in the Government. – Although one scarcely fears that these reprobates are attaining their goal thereby, it is no less unfortunate that their artifice makes enough of an impression on a number of little-educated persons to make them suspect that, given such troubles, such confusion, such feebleness of the Government in America, it is not prudent to grant it a large Credit. – It is possible to recall the more sensible to sounder ideas; but the great number of Men of Property is little so, & gives way to prejudice rather than to reason.

It is therefore impossible to assert positively that a new Negotiation would meet with success, nor to determine the sum & the conditions thereof. – What adds to the uncertainty & makes one fear that in any event these conditions would be very onerous is that here they are not unaware that the internal Debt of Congress in America can be purchased *at a price** such that the Purchasers find incomparably more profit therein than would be granted them here, while the soundness of this internal Debt is quite as good as that of the external Debt.

What it would therefore be best to do, according to my friends, would be to undertake France's pretension here on conditions that could be stipulated, accompanied by a small sacrifice on the part of that Kingdom, with the Liberty to negotiate the money here for a limited number of years on the *Credit of Congress* & under the *Guarantee of France*. – This last condition, in which one sees nothing but the honorable for Congress, would have much influence *on the Interest*, of which one would obtain *less* in this case than otherwise. It could not be done in the present circumstances for the reasons cited above: & in this manner one could at the same time *defer for several years the times of reimbursement* that are going to fall due soon, which, it seems to me, would be very agreeable to Congress. – It is also thought that the sacrifice which France would be making thereby would not constitute an obstacle: for this operation would allow her to pour a considerable sum into her Treasury which she would in no way be obliged to return, & which in consequence would in no way turn to the charge of the Kingdom. – So not the least difficulty is expected on France's part in granting that Guarantee, since that Court is very exactly informed on the state of American affairs, & since it has an interest in maintaining them.

If there is some inclination for this Plan, my Friends will voluntarily enter into negotiations thereon, & will in that case examine the degree of possibility of finding the entire Sum in a limited time: which is a point which one can only set about determining by broaching it and treating thereon with other people. – They think that if conditions were at the least established in an acceptable manner, access would promptly be found to 3 to 4 Million Holland Florins (6 to 8 Million Liv. tourn., or 12 to 16 hundred thousand Dollars).

P.S. We spoke later on, and under the seal of secrecy, on the above question with one of the most expert men in the matter. He confirmed our opinion absolutely, adding only that if something was decided on *promptly*, the *sacrifice* in question would be *very small*, & even that it could be *improved* by a diminution of the Interest. The reason for this is the present abundance** of money. But as this can change in a short time, it is necessary to decide as soon as possible.

In reflecting on all this during my return, it seemed to me that Your Excellency & M. le Marquis De la Fayette could, since it is only a question of purchasing the Debt due to France, render a great service both to France & to the United States by supporting & favoring this sale, so as to reserve to Congress the *Option* of deferring the Reimbursement for several years, without it being necessary to lose precious time, perhaps irrevocable, in consulting Congress in advance: For in this manner, France being free to sell or to endorse the Debt in order to fill its treasury, & Congress to profit from the Option, no injury whatever would be done to anyone, they would profit from the good occasion, and each would be helped, since the *Option* would be equivalent to the *Loan* in question, & would be even more advantageous. If Your Excellency appreciates my opinion, & wishes to give me his orders after having conferred & agreed, if not Ministerially, at least personally, with the Ministers in France, I shall immediately go to Amsterdam to execute them, & shall inform Your Excellency of the House consulted, against which I know in advance that neither the said Ministers nor Your Excellency will have any objection.

I am with the most respectful devotion, Your Excellency's most humble and most obedient servant   C.W.F. Dumas[1]

* They have assured me & have promised to show me that one can have it in Amsterdam at 9% net profit per year.

** Proceeding from the *ordinary* payment of Interest here, & from the still *extraordinary* event of Reimbursements made by Russia, & from the fact that neither the English nor the French have yet opened any new Loan.

LC: *Jefferson Papers, microfilm reel 6 (ALS).*
   [1] *Dumas, Charles William Frederick (1721-1796). Swiss scholar and translator residing at The Hague. American agent in the United Provinces of the Netherlands, 1775-1792; unofficial American chargé d'affaires, 1785-1792. He was pro-Patriot, pro-French during the 1787 Dutch unrest.*

William Stephens Smith to John Jay

Sir –   London, Jany. 24th. 1787.
   I had the honor of addressing your Excellency from Bath on the 3^d inst, which Doctor Mitchel, a young Gentleman of New York took charge of, accompanied with several Letters from France, which I had very fortunately received the day before – perhaps they mention the King of France having called an *Assemblee des Notables* to meet at Versailles on the 29th. inst. – but least it should have been omitted, I take the liberty of informing you, that it is to consist of 140 members – viz a Number of Arch-Bishops & Bishops for the Clergy – 36 members of the *Noblesse*, among whom are the Count de Estaing – Duke de la Rochefaucauld[1] – & the Marquis de Lafayette – the first President & Solicitors General from every Parliament some Councillors of State & Intendents – 30 Cities will send their mayors and the Princes of the Blood close the Council –...the Kings Letters to his *Noblesse* states that *he* wishes to communicate to *them*, his views relative to *relieving the Burthens of his People* – to *arrange his Finances* & to *reform many abuses* – they are great objects & worthy of a patriotic King – the last *Assemblee des notables* was in 1626 and as they now have recourse, to this extraordinary means it seems fair to conclude that there is an extraordinary Embarrassment somewhere – or that the King has a mind (extraordinary for despotic monarchs) capable of examing the affairs of his kingdom, for the purpose of promoting the happiness of his people – should the progress of improvement ever enlighten the Nation at large, so as to teach them how to derive all the advantages from that variety of soil & Climate and happy

Geographical Situation, of which their Country is capable – thousands will be rendered happy, who now groan under the burthen of existance – I am flattering myself with expectations to hear that my Country is rising superior to the late shocks of internal Commotion, and that our Countrymen will recollect, that the Eye of the World is upon them, & that it is a duty, that they, not only owe, themselves and their posterity – but mankind in general – to give a dignified example of the happiness and the advantages to be derived, from the establishment of human rights on an immoveable Basis....I...am with the most perfect respect Your Excellency's most Obed^{t.} Humble Servt.   W. S. Smith

NA: PCC, *item 92, pp. 180-182 (ALS); M247, reel 120.*
  ¹ *Rochefoucauld-d'Enville, Louis Alexandre, Duc de la Roche-Guyon et de la (d. 1792). French nobleman. A liberal thinker with whom Thomas Jefferson maintained close ties during his stay in France.*

Preliminary Ratification of the Treaty of Peace and Friendship with Morocco

London January 25. 1787.
Paris January 1. 1787.
Now know Ye that We the said John Adams & Thomas Jefferson Ministers Plenipotentiary aforesaid do approve & conclude the said treaty and any Article and Clause therein contained, reserving the same nevertheless to the United States in Congress assembled for their final Ratification.

In testimony whereof we have Signed the same with our Names and Seals, at the Places of our respective residence and at the dates expressed under our signatures respectively. –   John Adams.
                    Th: Jefferson

NA: PCC, *item 91, v. 1, p. 229 (LS); M247, reel 119.*

John Jay's Report Regarding Queen Maria I of Portugal

[New York] Office for foreign Affairs 25th January 1787
The Secretary of the United States for the Department of foreign Affairs, to whom was referred a Letter to him from the Honorable J. Adams, of 27th. June last informing that the Queen of Portugal

had ordered her Squadron in the Streights to protect the Vessels of the United States equally with those of her own Subjects

Reports

That in his Opinion, as this is a particular Mark of her Majesty's friendly Disposition, it should be acknowledged in the Manner most likely to be pleasing and acceptable. He therefore thinks it would be proper for Congress to write her a Letter of the following Tenor. –

Great and good Friend

We take the earliest Opportunity since our annual Election of presenting to your Majesty our sincere Acknowledgments for the friendly Regard you have manifested for us, in having ordered your Squadron in the Streights to protect our Vessels equally with those of Portugal. –

Permit us to assure you that we shall retain this Mark of generous Attention in grateful Remembrance, and shall omit no Opportunity of testifying our Desire to establish and perpetuate between our two Countries an Intercourse of Commerce and good Offices, which may prove no less beneficial than agreeable to both. –

We pray God to bless and preserve your Majesty. Done by the Congress of the United States convened at the City of New York the   Day of 1787. –

As this Communication was made by the Queen's Envoy in London to M^r· Adams, your Secretary thinks this Letter should be transmitted to him, and that the Compliment would be more delicate if his Secretary was commissioned to carry and deliver it. Perhaps too, so striking a Proof of Respect might, among other Consequences, promote the Conclusion of the Treaty. –

M^r· Adams in the same Letter takes Notice of the Question whether it would not be expedient for the United States to wage War with the hostile Powers of Barbary; but as your Secretary submitted his Sentiments on that Subject to Congress in his Report of the 20th· Day of October 1785 he forbears to repeat them in this. –

All which is submitted to the Wisdom of Congress. –   John Jay –

Read – Feb^y· 3^d· 1787 –
Order taken – returned Feby 10th 1787

NA: PCC, *item 81, v. 3, pp. 181-182, 184 (DS); M247, reel 107.*

John Adams to Thomas Jefferson

Dear Sir   Grosvenor Square Jan. 25. 1787
   I have received your Letters of December 20. and Jan. 11. by Coll.
Franks. – The whole of the Business shall be dispatched, and Coll Franks
sent to Congress as you propose, as soon as possible. I have prepared a
Draught of a joint Letter to Mr Barclay, and signed it, concerning Mr Lamb,
and shall inclose it to you with this. As to the Treaty with Portugal, the
Chevalier De Pinto's Courier whom he Sent off when you were here, is
Still in Lisbon. He is a confidential Domestick of De Pinto and calls every
day, at the Ministers Office in Lisbon but can get no Answer. – De Pinto
is very uneasy, makes Apologies when he Sees me, but can do no more. He
Says M^r De Melo[1] has been Sick and the Queen in the Country, and that
Falkner[2] could obtain no Audience for these Causes till December. – I
Suppose the Treaty of Commerce between France & England has
astonished Portugal, and divided the Court into Parties, So that neither
Administration can be Settled, nor a System adopted relative to Spain
France, England or America. – Congress are always informed of Facts as
Soon as they happen, and it is not to be expected that We Should write
Letters every Day to tell them, that Events have not happened. as to the
Reasons why the Treaty is not Signed, they know at New York as well as
You and I know, or even as De Pinto knows them.
   The charitable, the humane, the Christian Mathurins deserve our kindest
Thanks, and We Should be highly obliged to them if they could discover
at what Price, our Countrymen may be redeemed: but I dont think We
have Authority to advance the Money without the further orders of
Congress. There is no Court, or Government, that redeems its Citizens
unless by a Treaty of Peace. This is left to private Connections and
benevolent Societies. <**> if Congress redeem these, it will be a
Precedent for all others, and although I ~~would~~ might in Congress vote for
Setting the Precedent, and making it a Rule, Yet I dont think that as
Subordinate Ministers We have a Right to do it. The Money remaining,
must in February be applied to the Payment of Interest, and We must
absolutely come to a full Stop in all Expences relating to Barbary Matters
untill further orders of Congress. Lamb has drawn on me for ~~Two~~ Three
thousand and ~~Nine~~ two hundred & twelve Pounds, twelve Shillings. M^r
Barclay has drawn a great Sum. 4020£:0:0. according to the Minutes
inclosed.
   If Congress thought the original Appointment of Lamb censurable they
had reason. but You and I were not censurable. We found him ready
appointed to our hands. I never Saw him nor heard of him. – He ever was

and Still is as indifferent to me, as a Mohawk Indian. But as he came from Congress with their Dispatches of such importance, I Supposed it was expected We should appoint him. – There is no harm done. – if Congress had Sent the Ablest Member of their own Body, at Such a Time and under Such pecuniary Limitations he would have done no better.

With great and Sincere Esteem I have the honour to be, dear Sir, your most obedient and most humble Servant   John Adams

LC: *Jefferson Papers, microfilm reel 6 (ALS).*
[1] *Mello e Castro, Martinho de. Prime Minister of Portugal and Secretary of State to Queen Maria I.*
[2] *William Fawkener.*

Louis Guillaume Otto to Comte de Vergennes

[Translation]

N⁰. 76.   New York, 25 January 1787.
My Lord.

The Northern Delegates and Mr. Jay having done everything possible to them to obtain from Spain a Treaty of Commerce by sacrificing the right that the United States claim to have regarding the navigation of the Mississippi for 25 years, those from the South have not only protested against this measure, but they have written very strongly to their States to request from them particular instructions on a subject that appears to them to be of major importance. Virginia immediately passed a resolution "of being opposed in the most decided manner to any treaty or convention that could tend to exchange or cede to any nation whatever the right of the confederated States to the free and common navigation of the Mississippi, and to order its Delegates to protest against such a treaty as dishonorable and diametically opposed to the general policy of the confederation; as offensive to the inhabitants of the West, whose interests and dearest rights would be shamefully sacrificed and sold; as prejudicial to confidence in the justice, wisdom, and magnanimity of the great federal Council, confidence so necessary in the present crisis; lastly, as fitted to undermine the repose, the prosperity, and even the union of the Confederation." In transmitting these resolutions to its Delegates, the Virginia Assembly enjoins them moreover "to conduct the negotiations with Spain in a manner to obtain the free navigation of that river, to ensure an affection and a permanent harmony between the two nations, and to make His Catholic Majesty understand that it would be a generous policy not to have less regard for the just and amicable demands of the United States than for the interests of his own subjects." – These strict instructions prove only too well, My Lord, that the Southern States would rather detach themselves from the Confederation than consent to the renunciation demanded of them.

I should observe here that since the emancipation of the district of Kentucky, Virginia does not appear to have any direct interest in the navigation of the Mississippi, but this State yielded to the views of independence that Kentucky had long manifested only because it found it impossible to keep it by force; by vigorously taking up its interests on all occasions, it hopes to bring it back under its laws and to make it understand that it would prosper only under the protection of a powerful State. – This navigation, so little important to most of the States, has for some time been developing into a subject of discussion among the various Delegates; those from the South have been so active that they have attracted Jersey into their party, and I have just been informed that that State has given its representatives secret instructions analogous to those of Virginia. – The Delegates from the South still insist, My Lord, on their first motion, their confidence in Your good offices is limitless, and they only wish to accept a treaty with Spain under His Majesty's mediation. They often speak to me about it with an enthusiasm that leaves me no doubt regarding their sincerity, but I do not think that they can succeed. The votes are currently divided, and they are only waiting for Delaware to make the balance shift to one side or the other; in this same situation, there would only be 7 States against 6, while the confederation requires the consent of nine States for all affairs of this type.

. . . . .

I am with a profound respect My Lord Your most humble and most obedient servant   Otto.
r. 23 March:

FFAA: Pol. Corr., U.S., v. 32, f. 186-188vo. (LC transcription).

John Adams and Thomas Jefferson
to John Jay

Sir: London Jan. 27. 1787.

We had the honour of transmitting to Congress, Copies of the Commission and Instructions, which in pursuance of the Authority delegated to Us, were given to Mr Barclay, to conduct a negotiation with ~~Algiers~~ Morocco

Mr Barclay has conducted that Business to a happy Conclusion, and has brought with him Testimonials of his prudent Conduct, from the Emperor of Morocco and his Minister, So clear and full, that We flatter ourselves Mr Barclay will receive, the Approbation of Congress. Mr Barclay has received Somewhat more than four Thousand Pounds Sterling, for the Expences of Presents and all other Things. Colonel Franks, who accompanied Mr Barclay in his tedious Journeys, and difficult Negotiations, in the Character of Secretary, will be dispatched to Congress, and will have the honour of delivering this Letter, together with the Treaty, the Emperors Letter to Congress, and a variety of other Papers, relative to this Mission, a Schedule of which is annexed.

The Resolution of Congress, vacating Mr Lambs Commission and Instructions, has been forwarded to him, and We have repeatedly advised him to return to New York. that Gentleman has received Somewhat more than three thousand Pounds Sterling of the public Money for which he is accountable to Congress.

We beg Leave to recommend Mr Barclay and Colonel Franks, to the favourable Consideration of Congress.

It is no Small Mortification, not to be able to communicate any Intelligence concerning the Treaty with Portugal. The Chevalier De Pinto is equally uninformed. – His own confidential Domestick dispatch'd to Lisbon last Spring has been constantly waiting on the Minister for an Answer, but has obtained none, and is not yet returned to London. The Treaty between France & England, has probably excited Parties and Surprize in Portugal, and the System of Men and Measures is not yet Settled. The Apologies are the Queens Absence in the Country and the Prime Ministers Indisposition.

The Article of Money is become so Scarce and precious that We Shall be obliged to Suspend all further Proceedings in the Barbary Business, even for the Redemption of Prisoners untill We shall be honoured with fresh Instructions from Congress.

With great Respect We have the Honour to be, Sir, your most obedient and most humble Servants   John Adams

     [Thomas Jefferson]

NA: PCC, item 84, v. 6, pp. 403-406 (ALS by Adams); M247, reel 113.

John Adams to John Jay

Sir   Grosvenor Square Jan. 27. 1787.

.   .   .   .   .

There is a Practice, beginning to be talked of, if not practised, for British Merchants to procure Some American Merchant to metamorpose a British into an American Bottom to trade to the East Indies. This Practise appears to me to be infamous and destructive, and to merit the immediate Consideration of Congress. – of the particular Case, I know nothing: but Congress can have full Information.

I am, dear Sir, with great Regard &c   John Adams

NA: PCC, *item 84, v. 6, p. 407 (ALS); M247, reel 113.*

Thomas Jefferson to James Madison

Dear Sir   Paris Jan. 30. 1787.

My last to you was of the 16th of Dec, since which I have received yours of Nov. 25. & Dec. 4. which afforded me, as your letters always do, a treat on matters public, individual & oeconomical. I am impatient to learn your sentiments on the late troubles in the Eastern states. so far as I have yet seen, they do not appear to threaten serious consequences. those states have suffered by the stoppage of the channels of their commerce, which have not yet found other issues. this must render money scarce, and make the people uneasy. this uneasiness has produced acts absolutely unjustifiable; but I hope they will provoke no severities from their governments. a consciousness of those in power that their administration of the public affairs has been honest, may perhaps produce too great a degree of indignation: and those characters wherein fear predominates over hope may apprehend too much from these instances of irregularity. they may conclude too hastily that nature has formed man insusceptible of any other government but that of force, a conclusion not founded in truth, nor experience. societies exist under three forms sufficiently distinguishable. 1. without government, as among our Indians. 2. under governments wherein the will of every one has a just influence, as is the case in England in a slight degree, and in our states in a great one. 3. under governments of force: as is the case in all other monarchies & in most of the other republics. to have an idea of the curse of existence under these last, they must be seen. it is a government of wolves over sheep. it is a problem, not clear in my mind, that the 1st condition is not the best. but I believe it to be inconsistent with any great degree of population. the second state has a great deal of good in it. the mass of mankind under that enjoys a precious degree of liberty & happiness. it has it's evils too: the principal of which is the turbulence to which it is subject. but weigh this against the oppressions of monarchy, and it becomes nothing. *malo periculosam, libertatem quam quietam servitutem.*[1] even this evil is productive of good. it prevents the degeneracy of government, and nourishes, a general attention to public affairs. I hold it that a little rebellion now and then is a good thing, & as necessary in the political world as storms in the physical. unsuccessful rebellions indeed generally establish the incroachments on the rights of the people which have produced them. an observation of this truth should render honest republican governors so mild in their punishment of rebellions, as not to discourage them too much. it is a medecine necessary for the sound health of government. if these transactions give me no uneasiness, I feel very differently at another peice of intelligence, to wit, the possibility that the navigation of the Missisipi may be abandoned to Spain. I never had any interest Westward of the Alleghaney; & I never will have any. but I have had great opportunities of knowing the character of the people who inhabit that country. and I will venture to say that the act which abandons the navigation of the Missisipi is an act of separation between the Eastern & Western country. it is a relinquishment of five parts out of eight of the territory of the United states, an abandonment of the fairest subject for the paiment of our public debts, & the chaining those debts on our necks *in perpetuum*. I have the utmost confidence in the honest intentions of those who concur in this measure; but I lament their want of acquaintance with the character & physical advantages of the people who, right or wrong, will suppose their interests sacrificed on this occasion to the contrary interests of that part of the confederacy in possession of present power. if they declare themselves a separate people, we are incapable of a single effort to retain them. our citizens can never be induced, either as militia or as souldiers, to go there to cut the throats of their own brothers & sons or rather to ~~have their own throats cut by them~~ be themselves the subjects instead of the perpetrators of the parricide. nor would that country quit the cost of being retained against the will of it's inhabitants, could it be done. but it cannot be done. they are able already to rescue the navigation of the Missisipi out of the hands of Spain, & to add New Orleans to their own territory. they will be joined by the inhabitants of Louisiana. this will bring on a war between them & Spain; & that will produce the question with us whether it will not be worth our while to become parties with them in the war, in order to reunite them with us, & thus correct our error? & were I to permit my forebodings to go one step further, I should predict that the inhabitants of the U. S. would force their rulers to take the affirmative of that question. I wish I may be mistaken in all these opinions.

We have for some time expected that the Chevalier de la Luzerne would obtain a promotion in the diplomatic line, by being appointed to some of the courts where this country keeps an Ambassador. but none of the vacancies taking place which had been counted on, I think the present disposition is to require his return to his station in America. he told me himself lately, that he should return in the spring. I have never pressed this matter on the court, tho' I knew it to be desireable and desired on our part: because if the compulsion on him to return had been the work of Congress, he would have returned in such ill temper with them as to disappoint them in the good they expected from it. he would for ever have laid at their door his failure of promotion. I did not press it for another reason, which is that I have great reason to beleive that the character of the Count de Moutier,[2] who would go were the Chevalier to be otherwise provided for, would give the most perfect saisfaction in America. – As you are now returned into Congress it will become of importance that you should form a just estimate of certain public characters; on which therefore I will give you such notes as my knowlege of them has furnished me with. you will compare them with the materials you are otherwise possessed of, and decide on a view of the whole. you know the opinion I formerly entertained of my friend Mr. Adams. yourself & the governor were the first who shook that opinion. I afterwards saw proofs which convicted him of a degree of vanity, and of a blindness to it, of which no germ had appeared in Congress. a 7 months intimacy with him here and as many weeks in London have given me opportunities of studying him closely. he is vain, irritable and a bad calculator of the force & probable effect of the motives which govern men. this is all the ill which can possibly be said of him. he is as disinterested as the being which made him: he is profound in his views: and accurate in his judgment except where knowledge of the world is necessary to form a judgment. he is so amiable, that I pronounce you will love him if ever you become acquainted with him. he would be, as he was, a great man in Congress. mister Carmichael is I think very little known in America. I never saw him & while I was in Congress I formed rather a disadvantageous idea of him. his letters, received then, shewed him vain & more attentive to ceremony & etiquette than we suppose men of sense should be. I have now a constant correspondence with him, & find him a little hypocondriac and discontented. he possesses very good understanding tho' not of the first order. I have had great opportunites of searching into his character & have availed myself of it. many persons of different nations coming from Madrid to Paris all speak of him as in high esteem & I think it certain that he has more of the Count de florida b's friendship than any diplomatic character at that court. as long as this minister is in office Carmichael can do more than any other person who could be sent there. you will see franks and doubtless he will be asking some appointment. I wish there may be any one for which he is fit. he is light indiscret [act]ive honest affectionate. tho' Bingham[3] is not in diplomatic office yet as he wishes to be so I will mention such circumstances of him as you might otherwise be deceived in. he will make you believe he was on the most intimate footing with the first characters in Europe & versed in the secrets of every cabinet. not a word of this is true. he had a rage for being presented to great men & had no modesty in the methods by which he could effect it. if he obtained access afterwards, it was with such as who were susceptible of impression from the beauty of his wife. I must except the <***> marquis de bouilli[4] who had been an old acquaintance. the marquis de la fayette is a most valuable auxiliary to me. his zeal is unbounded, & his we[ight] with those in power great. his education having been merely military, commerce was an unknown feild to him. but his good sense enabling him to comprehend perfectly whatever is explained to him his agency has been very efficacious. he has a great deal of sounder genius is well remarked by the king & rising in popularity. he has nothing against him but the suspicion of republican principles. I think he will one day be of the ministry. his foible is a canine appetite for popularity and fame. but he will get above this. the Count de Vergennes is ill. the possibility of his recovery renders it dangerous for us to express a doubt but he is in danger. he is a great minister in European affairs but has very imperfect ideas of ours, no confidence in them. his devotion to the principles of pure despotism render him unaffectionate to our government but his fear of England makes him value us as a make weight. he is cool reserved in political conversation, free & familiar on other subjects and a very attentive agreeable person to do business with. it is impossible to have a clearer, better organised head, but age has chilled his heart. nothing should be spared on our part to attach this country to us. it is the only one on which we can rely for support under every event. it's inhabitants love us more I think than they do any other nation on earth. this is very much the effect of the good dispositions with which the French officers returned....I shall...set out in a fortnight for the waters of Aix in Provence....it will give me an opportunity of examining the canal of Languedoc & of acquiring knowlege of that species of navigation which may be useful hereafter: but more immediately it will enable me to take the tour of the ports concerned in commerce with us, to examine on the spot the defects of the late regulations respecting our commerce, to learn the further improvements which may be made on it, and, on my return, to get this business finished. I shall be absent between two & three months, unless any thing happens to recall me here sooner, which may always be effected in ten days, in whatever part of my route I may be. in speaking of characters I omitted those of Reyneval and Hening[5] the 2 eyes of m. de ver. the former is the most important character because possessing the most of the confidence of the Count, he is rather cunning than wise, his views of things being neither great nor liberal. he governs himself by principle which he has learnt by rote ~~without~~ and is fit only for the detail of execution, his heart is susceptible of little passions but not of good. he is brother in law to M. Gerard from whom he received disadvantageous impressions of us which cannot be effaced. he has much duplicity. Hening is a philosopher sincere friend, liberal, learned, beloved by every body the other by nobody. I think it a great misfortune that the U.S. are in the department of the former. as particulars of this kind may be useful to you in your present situation, I may hereafter continue the chapter. I know it safely lodged in your discretion.

·   ·   ·   ·   ·

[Thomas Jefferson]

LC: *Madison Papers, microfilm reel 2 (AL).*

[1] *I prefer an endangered freedom to a peaceful servitude.*

[2] *Moustier, Eléonore-François-Elie, Comte de (1754-1817). French diplomat. Minister to the Elector of Trier, 1778-1785. Minister to Great Britain, February-May 1783. Minister to the United States, February 1788-October 1789. Minister to Prussia, 1790-1791. Refused the position of Minister of Foreign Affairs, 1791. Emigrated; did not return to France until 1814.*

[3] *Bingham, William (1752-1804). Philadelphia merchant, government agent, banker, and political figure. British Consul at St. Pierre, Martinique, 1770-1776. Continental Congress agent in the West Indies, 1777-1780. Derived great wealth from trade and joint ownership of privateers. A founder and director of the Bank of North America. During European travels, 1784-1786, wrote pamphlet refuting trade theories of Lord Sheffield. Member, Continental Congress, 1786-1788. Member, Pennsylvania House of Representatives, 1790-1791; speaker, 1791. Pennsylvania state senator, 1794-1795, and also president of state Senate. United States Senator, 1795-1801.*

[4] *Bouillé, François Claude Amour, Marquis de (1739-1800). French general. Captured Barbados and Tobago, 1781. Commander at Metz, 1789. Plotted with Louis XVI to secure his escape from France, but failed and fled to England, 1791.*

[5] *Hennin (Henin), Pierre Michel. French government official. One of the Comte de Vergennes' two undersecretaries of state, the other being Joseph-Matthias Gérard de Rayneval.*

Thomas Jefferson to John Jay

Sir   Paris Feb. 1. 1787.

. . . . .

In some of my former letters I suggested an opportunity of obliging this court by borrowing as much money in Holland as would pay the debt due here, if such a loan could be obtained; as to which I was altogether ignorant. to save time, I wrote to Mr. Dumas, to know whether he thought it probable a loan could be obtained, enjoining him the strictest secrecy, and informing him I was making the enquiry merely of my own motion & without instruction. I inclose you his answer. he thinks purchasers of the debt could be found, with a sacrifice of a small part of the capital, and a postponement be obtained of some of the first reimbursements. the proposition for an immediate adoption of this measure by me, was probably urged on his mind by a desire to serve our country more than a strict attention to my duty & the magnitude of the object. I hope on the contrary that, if it should be thought worth a trial, it may be put into the hands of mr Adams who knows the ground & is known there, and whose former succesful negociations in this line would give better founded hopes of success on this occasion.

. . . . .

...I inclose you a letter from one of the foreign officers complaining of the nonpaiment of their interest. it is only one out of many I have received. this is accompanied by a second copy of the Moorish declaration sent me by mr Barclay. he went to Alicant to settle with mr Lamb: but, on his arrival there, found he was gone to Minorca. <****> a copy of his letter will inform you of this circumstance, <**> and of some others relative to Algiers, with his opinion on them. whatever the states may enable Congress to do for obtaining the peace of that country, it is a separate question whether they will redeem our captives, how, & at what price? if they decide to redeem them, I will beg leave to observe that it is of great importance that the first redemption be made at as low a price as possible, because it will form the future tariff. if these pyrates find that they can have a very great price for Americans, they will abandon proportionably their pursuits against other nations to direct them towards ours. that the choice of Congress may be enlarged as to the instruments they may use for effecting the redemption, I think it my duty to inform them that there is here an order of priests called the Mathurrins, the object of whose institution is to beg alms for the redemption of captives. they keep members always in Barbary searching out the captives of their own country, and redeem I beleive on better terms than any other body, public or private. it occurred to me that their agency might be obtained for the redemption of our prisoners of Algiers. I obtained conferences with the General & with some members of the order. the General, with all the benevolence and cordiality possible, undertook to act for us if we should desire it. he told me that their last considerable redemption was of about 300 prisoners, who cost them somewhat upwards of 1500 livres apeice, but that they should not be able to redeem ours as cheap as they do their own; & that it must be absolutely unknown that the public concern themselves in the operation, or the price would be greatly enhanced. the difference of religion was not once mentioned, nor did it appear to me to be thought of. it was a silent reclamation & acknowlegment of fraternity between two religions of the same family, which historical events of antient date had rendered more hostile to one another than to their common adversaries. I informed the general that I should communicate the good dispositions of his order to those who alone had the authority to decide whatever related to our captives. mr Carmichael informs me that monies have been advanced for the support of our prisoners at Algiers which ought to be replaced. I infer from the context of his letter, that these advances have been made by the court of Madrid. I submit the information to Congress.

.   .   .   .   .

...assuring you of those sentiments of perfect esteem, & respect with which I am Sir your most obedient & most humble servant

Th: Jefferson

LC: *Jefferson Papers, microfilm reel 6 (press copy).*

Phineas Bond to William Fraser

Sir,   Philadelphia Feb. 4[th.] 1787.
   I had the honor to receive your letter of the 1st of Nov. at this place: I return you many thanks for your polite attention in forwarding the late act of Parliament, for the further increase and encouragement of shipping and navigation; tho' I was so fortunate as to bring one of them from England with me; and found it particularly useful immediately upon my landing, in directing the mode of proceeding in the repairs of a British ship, then in some part of New England, about which the Consul-General had been applied to: as he was not in possession of the Act he was at a loss what to direct, and I was happy in the opportunity of communicating my sentiments upon the subject, which I presume to hope was the means of obviating the difficulties which had arisen.

I take the liberty of mentioning this circumstance for the purpose of suggesting the necessity of furnishing us as speedily as possible with all Acts of Parliament, which, in any degree, prescribe rules of conduct for us; or which have a tendency to correct or reform the laws of navigation and commerce applied to the United States.

Perhaps this may be the only essential line in which we may be immediately useful, in our respective appointments; for such is the present state of this country that I cannot discover any prospect of speedy or effectual relief for the many inconveniences the British merchants labor under. Happy shall I be if a longer residence will enable me to see things thro' a clearer medium, and tend to dissipate those clouds which at present hang over the trading interests of Great Britain, as far as they are connected with this continent.

I am weary of repeating to the Marquis of Carmarthen the situation in which I still continue to stand: there has not been a congress assembled since I arrived, and when that body will meet again seems quite uncertain: in the present state of the federal powers, little efficacy can attend their deliberations: how far those powers are to be extended, or whether they will be extended at all are matters of great doubt, and involved in great perplexity.

I most sincerely hope the Marquis of Carmarthen is perfectly recovered from his late indisposition.

I beg you to accept my best wishes that you may long enjoy health and happiness, and am with great truth Sir, Your most faithful and obed: servant   P. Bond

P. S. An opportunity, for London, will offer shortly from hence; by which I hope I shall be able to write; in order chiefly to represent the necessity of establishing agents in the different States conformable to the plan we conversed about, previous to my departure from England

AHA 1896, v. 1, pp. 519-520.

Peter Allaire: Occurrences
from 5 January to 2 February 1787

New York 6 february 1787.
A Gentleman[1] is arrived here, sent by the Emperor of Germany,[2] under the Title of Commissioners of Commerce; his intentions are to apply to

Congress for a commercial Treaty, between the Emperor and Grand Duke of Tuscany,[3] with the United States. he Arrived at Philadelphia the middle of December last, in a Vessell belonging to a New Company lately Established there, called The Trieste American Company, who have advanced the Sum of One Million of florins (about Seventy five thousand Pounds Sterling) to put this Scheme in Execution, and he came passenger in the first of their Vessells, they propose Sending four Ships Yearly, two in the fall, and two in the Spring. should this Ship answer their expectation, her Cargo consists of the following Articles, Small Red & White Wines, Raisins, Oil, Olives, Currants, Sweatmeats, Perfumes, Baskets in Nests, Silk Hankercheifs, Slight wearing Silks, Coarse Linnens, Dowlass, Sheeting, Damask linnen, Table Cloths, Napkins, Lookinglass, Window Glass, Chip Hats, Red & White Vinagar, Almons, Sheet Copper, Copper Kettles, Sause pans, &c. Copper bottoms for large Kettles, Striped Cottons, Check Linnen, Silk & Cotton striped Linnens, all kind of Iron hollow ware, and hard ware, Spades Hoes, Shovels, Brandy, Coarse Cloths, Sithes, fryin Pans, and a great many Trinkits, in Wax & flowers &c.

As the Emperor is owner of all the Copper Mines in Germany, his cheif design is, to furnish America, with wrought Copper & Sheet Copper, but it will not Answer, for the following Reasons, (I have seen the Invoice & argue from facts) their Copper in Sheets & Copper Utensils, are about three p Cent dearer then the English their Navigation longer, & more expensive, they must have ready money, the English Copper Company gives Six Months Credit, therefore they never can Rival England in that Article, their Iron Ware, are not adapted to the American taste, nor is it cheaper. (he intends sending by the Return of the ship, English Iron ware for them to copy After) the only Article that I find in the above Cargoe, wherin they can undersell England, is in Glass Ware, Lookin Glass, and Window Glass, which they purchase at thirty p Cent cheaper, then the London or Bristol Glass, but the Sizes he has brought, are not adapted for this Country & the expence of cuting them, is equal to the price of the Glass, the Dowlass, Sheeting & Coarse linnens, come within Seven p Cent of those Imported from England, therefore until the ballance Trade is in favour of America, they cannot Rival you in any thing except Glass & Glass Ware; as the Americans would rather pay Ten p Cent advance, then pay ready money.

I have been thus particular, that you may fully Answer every proposition & Assertion, that may be made with respect to this New Established American Company

When the Cargoe is Sold he proposes, sending back the following Articles, viz, Tar, Pitch, Turpintine, Oil of Turpintine, Tobacco, Indigo, Pickled & dry'd Codfish, Herrings & Mackrell in Casks, furs, Wax, Whale

Oyl, Brown & Havanah Sugars, Logwood, Mohogany, sassaparella, Rice, and a few Casks Rum, that part of the Cargoe which has been Sold, he seems contented with, & the Ship returns in the spring.

I have conversed several times with him, with respect to the Americans trading up the Miditeranian, & Convinced him, no American would adventure in those Seas, when they could get nearly as good a price for their Goods in France & England, for fear of the Algerines and Moors, but if he could point out a safe and Secure method, I made no doubt, but the Americans, would be glad to Trade with the American Trieste Company. he then shewed me full powers from the Emperor & Grand Duke of Tuscany, to Grant Imperial flags, to every American Merchant who would load a Vessell, and consign her to the Trieste Comp^y, paying the same duties, as other foreigners, until a Treaty of Commerce should be concluded between the parties.

As I am to have the perusal of his propositions, before they are laid before Congress, shall send you a Copy thereof at present, there is a dispute between the United States, & the Great Joseph, (he says in his Instructions to his Embassadore,) I *will* Acknowledge the Independance of the United States; the President of Congress, informed Baron Beleen Bertholf, that he could not be Received untill the Emperor *had* Acknowledged their Independance; this affair is not as yet setled, between the Imperial & American Embassadores at Paris, and until it is, nothing can be done with respect to the proposals of this Gentleman, they are expected by the first french Packet.

.   .   .   .   .

The Insurgents on the 30 December last at Plymouth (State of Boston) County of Grafton, set fire to the Court House, and burnt it to the ground being the shortest method of puting a final Stop to all further proceedings, they having Received intimation, that the Judges would be protected by an Armed force, part of the Militia have been ordered to Attend them.

.   .   .   .   .

Commissioners have been appointed by every State in the Union, to meet at Philadelphia in May next, to consult & form a New feuderal Union the present one being found defective (General Washington is one appointed by the state of Virginia), with Orders, to draw up such Articles, as they shall think Requisite, that a Copy be given to the Commissioners of each State Signed by the President, which Articles must be passed unto a Law before they can be binding and Congress have the Requisite Power they now want.

With Respect to the Loan for the raising of the Troops for the Indian War, not a Single Dollar has been subscribed in this State.

24$^{th.}$ Capt Shays[4] & Days,[5] have prevented the Quarter Sessions at

Springfield & Rehoboth, the Judges & Justices, politely invited those Gentlemen to dine with them, agreed to hold no Court until a new representation had taken place, and returned peacable home.

31[th.] This day an Express Arrived from Governour Bodoin of Boston to Congress (there being no house as yet or President) M[r] Thompson Secretary to Congress calld all the Members together & informed them, that, the Insurgents had met at Springfield to the Number of 2200 Men Commanded by Shays, that he had Ordered General Shepard[6] with about 1200 Men Militia to go & disperse them, that they met the 28th Instant near Springfield, that Gen. Shepard desired them to lay down their Arms & return home, that the Insurgents, insulted him, & came on in Order of Battle, that he then sent a flag, & forbid them coming nearer then a line drawn at this Pint; on which Shays gave the word of command to March, and Attack him, that the two first fires Gen Shepard Ordered his Men to fire above their heads, not finding any of themselves hurt, they boldly Marched on, that then he Ordered two field peices to be fired, which killed five & wounded Nine, the Insurgents then Retreated about a Mile, that he waited for General Lincoln,[7] who was on his March, with 1700 Men and within thirty Miles, that he should when joined, Attack the Insurgents, & made no doubt of his dipersing them, & bringing the Ringleaders Prisoners to Boston

.   .   .   .   .

Several of the Members of Congress waited on Mos[r.] Otto the French Consul to know if there was any truth in the Report, that Spain had ceeded to France the Floridies, Ans[r.] that his Orders from Mon[r.] Vergennes were, that there was no truth in the Assertion.

.   .   .   .   .

R. 12th March 1787.

PRO: FO 4/5, pp. 73-94 (LC transcription).

[1] *Beelen-Bertholff, Baron de.* Austrian agent sent to the United States in 1783 to determine prospects for trade between the republic and the lands subordinate to the Holy Roman Empire. Although authorized to initiate trade relations, he was not accredited to the Continental Congress. Trade prospects being unpromising, nothing came of Beelen-Bertholff's mission.

[2] *Joseph II (1741-1790).* Holy Roman Emperor, also known as Emperor of Austria, 1765-1790. Ruled jointly with his mother, Empress Maria Theresa, until her death in 1780.

[3] *Grand Duke of Tuscany.* The reigning monarch was Grand Duke Leopold I (1747-1792), ruled 1765-1790. The third son of Maria Theresa and Emperor Francis I, he became grand duke upon his father's death and emperor upon his brother Joseph II's death. As Leopold II, Holy Roman Emperor, King of Hungary, and King of Bohemia, 1790-1792.

[4] *Shays, Daniel (c. 1747-1825). Military officer and insurgent. Served in Massachusetts militia and Continental Army, 1775-1780; captain, 5th Massachusetts. Emerged as leader of insurgents who prevented state courts from sitting, August-September 1786, in order to prevent the authorities from inflicting more hardship on common people overburdened with debts. Lost battles against state forces under General Benjamin Lincoln, January-February 1787, and fled to Vermont. Pardoned, June 1788. Moved to western New York, where he received a pension for his wartime service.*

[5] *Day, Luke. Military officer and insurgent. A resident of West Springfield, Mass., he returned from the war a captain, with a brevet as major. A demagogue and public speaker, the guiding spirit of Shays' Rebellion, he and his men were not present to support Shays' attack upon the Springfield arsenal. Day's force disintegrated after its retreat was blocked by Benjamin Lincoln, and its leader fled.*

[6] *Shepard, William (1737-1817). Massachusetts political figure, military officer. Served in French and Indian War, ending as a captain. Lieutenant colonel, state militia, 1775-1776. Colonel, 4th Massachusetts Infantry, 1776-1783. Member, state house of representatives, 1785-1786. Major general, state militia, during Shays' Rebellion, 1786-1787. Member, governor's council, 1792-1796. Member, U.S. House of Representatives, 1797-1803.*

[7] *Lincoln, Benjamin (1733-1810). Massachusetts political and military figure. Brigadier general, February 1776, and major general, May 1776, of Massachusetts provincial forces. Major general, Continental Army, February 1777. Operated successfully against Burgoyne's lines of communication with Canada, 1777. Assigned to command of Southern Department, September 1778. Failed in operations before Savannah; captured, with his entire army, in Charleston, May 1779. Exchanged, November 1779. Served under Washington, 1780-1781. Secretary at War, 1781-1783. Commanded Massachusetts troops sent to suppress Shays' Rebellion, early 1787. Lieutenant governor of Massachusetts, 1788. Collector of the Port of Boston, 1789-1809.*

Sir John Temple to Lord Carmarthen

N[o.] 15.   New York February 7th 1787
My Lord

$$\cdot \quad \cdot \quad \cdot \quad \cdot$$

Since my last, the insurgents in the Massachusetts collected at and near Springfield in larger numbers and apparently more determined to overthrow the government of that State, than at any time before: Upon which the governour and commander in chief ordered a large body of militia with artillery, under the command of General Lincoln, to march with all possible expedition into Hampshire, to suppress the rebellion, but before he could arrive at Springfield a party of the Berkshire and Hampshire militia, commanded by General Sheppard, in support of government, had a small trial with the insurgents, who disputed the ground with him, but upon the discharge of only one piece of artillery with grape shot, which killed four or five, the whole body (supposed to be about twelve hundred) fled in all directions, without firing even a single shot! Sheppard did not attempt to pursue, but thought proper to keep his ground, and his possession of the magazines and continental stores, until General Lincoln should arrive. Lincoln halted but a short time at Springfield, and then pressed forward to Northampton Hatfield, Hadley, and other towns where he had information the insurgents were, in a dispersed condition: and by the last accounts it is said he had taken many of them prisoners. I will not trouble your Lordship with anything further in detail upon this business, as the narrative in the enclosed News-papers is, I beleive, nearly correct. I do not however think, notwithstanding Lincoln's success, that peace and quietness will soon take place in that part of the country. When Lincoln returns with his troops to Boston, the insurgents will, it is more probable renew their hostile attempts, & with cruel revenge, against the adherents to government; and keep the country in such a state of distress, as government cannot prevent without stationing troops in Hampshire and the neighbouring counties.

. . . . .

I have the honour to be with all deference and respect, My Lord Your Lordship's most faithful and Obedient servant.   J. Temple

P.S. Yesterday arrived in this port the Spanish Ship St Antoni from Carthagena said to have a very large sum in Silver on board. Her business, I am told, is to purchase a full cargo of flour &c, and to smuggle it into the Spanish dominions. In one view I am glad she is come, for every farthing of the money she leaves here, will find its way to England, in the course of the year.
R. 6th March

PRO: FO 4/5, pp. 69-72 (LC transcription).

John Jay to Thomas Jefferson

Dr Sir   New York 9th February 1787
Since my last to you of the 14th December I have been honored with yours of the 26th September last, which with the Papers that it enclosed have been laid before Congress, but neither on that nor any of your late Letters have any Orders as yet been made. –
The annual Election produces much Delay in Affairs – from that Time to this scarcely any Thing has been done. It was not until last Week that, seven States being represented, a President was elected – the Choice fell on Major General St Clair.[1] They have much back Business to dispatch –

several Reports on important Subjects from the different Departments, are to be considered and decided upon. A Form of Government so constructed has Inconveniences, which I think will continue to operate against the public or national Interest, until some Cause not easy to be predicted shall produce such a Modification of it, as that the legislative, judicial and executive Business of Government, may be consigned to three proper and distinct Departments. –

The Struggles for and against the Impost remain, but promise little. The States in general pay little Attention to Requisitions, and I fear that our Debts foreign and domestic will not soon be provided for in a Manner satisfactory to our Creditors. The Evils to be expected from such Delays are less difficult to be foreseen than obviated. Our Governments want Energy, and there is Reason to fear that two [sic] much has been expected from the Virtue and good Sense of the People. –

You will receive herewith enclosed a Letter from Congress to his most Christian Majesty, with a Copy of it for your Information. It is in Answer to one received from him, and should have been of earlier Date had Congress sooner convened – be pleased to explain this Circumstance to the Minister. –

The public Papers herewith sent contain all we at present know respecting the Troubles in Massachusetts. Whether they will soon be terminated, or what Events they may yet produce, is perfectly uncertain; and the more so as we are yet to ascertain, whether and how far they may be encouraged by our Neighbours. –

I enclose a Copy of a Letter from M^r· Otto, formally contradicting the Report of an Exchange between France and Spain for the Floridas. That Report had excited Attention, and given Pleasure to Anti-Gallicans. –

Our Apprehensions of an Indian War still continue, for we are at a Loss to determine, whether the present Continuance of Peace is to be ascribed to the Season, or their pacific Intentions. –

We have not yet received the Morocco Treaty – as soon as it arrives I am persuaded that Congress will take the earliest Oopportunity, of making their Acknowledgments to the friendly Powers that promoted it. M^r· Lamb is still absent – He doubtless has received the Order of Congress directing his Return, either from you and M^r· Adams, or directly from me. –

Congress has not yet given any Orders respecting further Negociations with the Barbary States, nor can I venture to say what their Sentiments will be on that Head. I am equally at a Loss to judge what they will direct, respecting Treaties of Commerce with the Emperor and other European Powers. For my part I think and have recommended, that Commissions and Instructions should be sent to you and M^r· Adams for those Purposes. In my Opinion such Treaties for short Terms might be advantageous – The Time is not yet come for us to expect the best – The Distance of that Period will however depend much on ourselves. –

With very sincere Esteem and Regard, I am D.ʳ S.ʳ &c:

John Jay –

NA: PCC, item 121, pp. 238-240 (LBkC); M61, reel 1.

¹ St. Clair, Arthur (1736-1818). Soldier, Pennsylvania political figure, government official. Born in Scotland, he served as an officer in the British army during the French and Indian War. Resigning in 1762, he became the largest landowner in western Pennsylvania. Colonel with the American forces in Canada, 1775-1776; brigadier general at Trenton and Princeton, 1776-1777; as a major general, he gave up supposedly impregnable Ft. Ticonderoga, 1777. Exonerated by court-martial, 1778, but held no important commands thereafter. Member, Continental Congress, 1786-1787; president, 1787. Governor, Northwest Territory, 1787-1802.

Louis Guillaume Otto to Comte de Vergennes

[Translation]

N.º 78.   New York, 10 Feb. 1787.
My Lord.

.   .   .   .   .

... M. Van Berkel is disgusted with his situation, and he very often wishes to request his recall. He openly says that it is useless for the States General to maintain a Minister Plenipotentiary near a Government which has no regard for the most legitimate and pressing demands. That Minister has been soliciting the restitution of a Dutch Ship¹ taken during the war for two years without having received any decisive response. – Some other circumstances are contributing to excite his resentment. A member of Congress sent to Boston to request subsidies said before the whole Assembly "that His Most Christian Majesty was too generous to insist immediately on the payment of the sums that are owed to him, but that the Dutch, *schooled in the understanding of money matters*, would not be so indulgent." This discourse has been reprinted all over the continent. M. Van Berkel was so much shocked by this that he has never taken any step toward recovery of the Dutch debt. He thought he was in a position officially to demand Satisfaction in Congress, but his friends pointed out to him that in a country in which the Sovereign and the Secretaries of State are themselves treated with the greatest thoughtlessness by orators and Gazetteers, a foreign Minister could scarcely hope to obtain justice. Don Diego de Gardoqui has still more reasons to be discontented, but he conceals his dislikes under the most insinuating appearances, and the more he encounters obstacles in the negotiation of his treaty of commerce, the more he affects to be satisfied with his situation.

But if external affairs, My Lord, experience delays without number, one should not infer therefrom that Congress has been entirely idle since the peace. The various departments have been set up in the most perfect manner, regularity is introduced in all the branches of the general administration, and the United States lack only permanent funding to be one of the better organized Governments. Foreign affairs, the War Department, the Treasury are entrusted to reliable and capable men whose integrity, wisdom, circumspection are fully proven. Secrecy is much better guarded here than it was during the war; one notes especially that the various branches of the Treasury Department overlap each other so artfully that it is impossible for it to commit the least embezzlement. But this fine edifice unhappily becomes useless through the exhaustion of the treasury.

. . . . .

I am with a profound respect My Lord Your most humble and most obedient servant   Otto.
r. 23 March

FFAA: Pol. Corr., U.S., v. 32, f. 194-197 (LC transcription).
  ¹ Presumably a reference to the sloop Chester, which was captured by an American privateer and condemned by the South Carolina court of admiralty in July 1777. On July 24, 1786, Congress authorized the sloop's owners to request a new trial before a court of appeals, the outcome of which is unknown.

Richard O'Bryen and Others to John Adams

Sir,   Algiers February the 13ᵗʰ· 1787.
   Your three Letters to us, dated London the 29ᵗʰ· September, we received the 7ᵗʰ· Instant, and is [are] exceeding sorry to find by the Tenor of your Letters to us that you can give us no comfortable Hopes or Assurances of speedy Relief.
   Respecting the erroneous Report you suppose we might have heard of what Mʳ· Lamb said to the Dey, and that it is not likely that he made any promises to the Dey, we shall mention to you what Mʳ· Lamb used to tell us, when he used to return from the Dey's Palace after having his different Audiences.
                   Extract from our Journals in Algiers.
   Saturday the 25ᵗʰ· of March arrived a brig from Barcelona with John Lamb, Esquire, and Mʳ· Randall, Commissioners from the United States of America to treat with Lord Prince Mahomet Bashaw Dey of the warlike

City and Kingdom of Algiers. At 11 A.M. the Captain Port went on board the Brig and returned on Shore to the Mickelhadge or third Great Man, informing him there was two Americans on board the Brig, & came to redeem their People. Immediately the Dey was informed, and at one P.M. they were admitted to land. Mr. Lamb's Message to the Dey was to admit him to the Honor of kissing his Hand on the Terms of Peace. The Dey answered that he would not but if he came to redeem his People he would give him &c audience. On the 29th. Mr. Randall left Algiers on board a spanish Brig of War bound to Alicant. On the first of April Mr. Lamb was introduced to the Dey by the French Consul and attended by Mr. Wolfe Mr. Lamb asked the Dey his Price for the Americans the Dey said he would see about it of the Marine Officers. On the 3^{d.} of April Mr. Lamb had his 2^{d.} Audience. The Dey asked Mr. Lamb what he would give – Mr. Lamb offered ten thousand Dollars. The Dey said his Price was fifty thousand Dollars. Mr. Lamb said the Price was great, but would see about it or consider. On the 5th. Mr. Lamb had his 3^{d.} Audience. The Dey would not lower his Price, but said he wanted us in the Marine. Mr. Lamb offered to take us at thirty thousand Dollars. The Dey turned Angry and said he had Bread and Olives enough for us. On the 7th. Mr. Lamb had his fourth Audience. The Dey would not lower his Price but seventeen hundred Dollars. Mr. Lamb said the Price was great – he would see what he could do in four Months Time. The Dey sent his Druggeroman to Mr. Lamb after he returned to the French Consul's and asked Mr. Lamb if he was content with the Bargain. Mr. Lamb said the Price was great, but he must be content. Ever since it is considered in Algiers that Mr. Lamb made a regular Bargain with the Dey. Often since Cidy Ally, the Dey's Lord of his Bedchamber, has told a young Lad one of our Crew. That the American Embassador had agreed to take us at the Dey's Price. The Lad is one of the Dey's Chief Attendants. And the other Day the Mickelhadge or third great Man to the Dey asked my Carpenter who is a Servant or Slave to the Mickelhadge where was the American Embassador saying he had promised to come or return in four Months.

Sir, we would not wish to be understood that we write so urgent on Mr. Lamb's Contracts with the Dey to facilitate our Redemption, but it is to give you a true Representation of Mr. Lamb's Proceedings for the Good and Honor of our Country – As we are fearful that if another American Embassador came here it would be a very great Detriment to his Proceedings, and should not be much surprised if the Dey told him that he had made one Bargain already with the Americans, which they did not keep or fulfil.

As Mr. Jefferson wrote us that Mr. Lamb was to make no Bargain respecting our Redemption without our Consent when Mr. Lamb told us of the Dey's Price we begged of him to make no further Proposition on our Account, as it was not in his Power to redeem us, but he went on his own Way & did as I mention so that you see the considering Part of the Bargain was always on Mr Lamb – When the Dey mentioned so great a Price, why was he not decisive and say it was intirely out of his Power to give any such Price, better to say so than to make Promises that he was not empowered to do, not to deceive the Dey and dishonor his Country.

If we are not to be redeemed until the Dey let us go as cheap as others, we think we never shall be redeemed, for those People do what they have a Mind to let the Slaves go for what they will or not let them go on any Terms. We confess it would be setting a bad Example to pay so great a Sum for a few and other unfortunate Captives would feel the ill Effects of it. It is the Duty of our Country to redeem us on the best Terms they can. Our unfortunate Crews are employed on the most laborious Work. We are not Prisoners of War – we are Slaves – the Consideration of which will induce our Country to consider our lamentable Misfortune, hoping they will adopt some effectual Plan of extricating us from Slavery and not suffer a Remnant of their Countrymen to die in Slavery in this barbarous Country. We hope Mr Lamb has not told us one Story and wrote the Ministers in Europe another but from the Tenor of your Letters we believe he has misrepresented his Proceedings in Algiers to you.

Redeeming the Slaves is one Thing and making the Peace is another, two different Bargains. Witness the Spaniards – we cannot see that redeeming us would be any Detriment to the making a Peace or that we shall be got for less –

If Mr Lamb in having four Audiences with the Dey could not prevail on him to lower his Price – what will induce the Dey to it on the Terms of Peace or Conclusion of Treaties? Forty or fifty thousand Dollars can be no great Object to so great and rich a Prince as the Dey of Algiers to induce him to a Treaty with the United States.

Permit us to observe to you, & our Country, That it has been the Custom from Time immemorial for all Nations to redeem their People on the best Terms they could. The Spaniards and other Nations used to redeem every three Years until they were all led away with an erroneous Opinion that the Sums paid for the Redemption used to enable the Algerines and the other Barbary States to continue their Depredations of Piracy. Time, which reveals all Things, has shewn the Spaniards & other Nations, how erroneous their Judgment was. No Nation in the World can fit an equal Number of Cruisers half so cheap as the Algerines can.

Mr Lamb declared to us that he did not bring any Money to redeem us, and even told us that if the Dey would let us go at ten thousand Dollars, he could not redeem us. The six thousand Dollars he had, was for Presents to pave the Way towards a Peace, in Case he brought them on a Truce. Why was M^r. Lamb so anxious with his Propositions to the Dey when he declared to us that he had no Money appropriated towards our Use?

We hope you will consider our lamentable Misfortune and not extinguish entirely our Hopes of being once more in the Land of Liberty.

Your most obedient and very h^ble. Servants   Richard OBryen.

Zacch^s. Coffin.

Isaac Stephens.

And^w: Montgomery Mate[1]

Alexander Forsythe Mate[1]

NA: PCC, item 104, v. 6, pp. 314-320 (C); M247, reel 131.

[1] Not further identified.

Thomas Jefferson to John Jay

Sir   Paris Feb. 14. 1787.

In the letter of the 8th instant which I had the honour of writing you, I informed you that the Count de Vergennes was dangerously ill. he died yesterday morning, and Count de Montmorin[1] is appointed his successor. your personal knowlege of this gentleman renders it unnecessary for me to say any thing of him.

...I have the honour to be with sentiments of the most perfect esteem & respect, Sir, your most obed^t. & most humble serv^t.

Th: Jefferson

LC: Jefferson Papers, microfilm reel 6 (Press Copy).

[1] Montmorin-Saint-Hérem, Armand-Marc, Comte de (1745-1792). French political figure and diplomat. Ambassador to Spain, 1778-1784. Minister of foreign affairs, 1787-1791. Accused of pro-Austrian sympathies and killed in the massacre of September 1792.

John Jay to the Marquis de Lafayette

D^r. Sir   New York 16th. February 1787

Congress being again convened, I have communicated to them the Letter you did me the Honor to write on the 28th. October last. The Paper it enclosed had been laid before M^r. Gardoqui, and made known to his Court, but it seems the Count De Florida Blanca does not consider it in the same point of Light that that we do, Viz^t as a conclusive Approbation of, and Consent to the Limits fixed by our Treaty with Britain – on the contrary, he extends the Claims of Spain higher up the River. That and the Navigation of the River present serious Points of Opposition between us.

I think with you that Spain deviates from the Line of true Policy respecting those Objects; but in this as in other Cases, it is often more easy to perceive Errors than to correct them. –

You have heard long before this that the Convention you allude to miscarried. Another is now in Contemplation, and some of the States have delegated distinguished Characters to represent them at it. Whether all or how many of the States will adopt that Measure is uncertain, the People being divided in Sentiment respecting the Expediency of it. –

Our Frontiers yet enjoy Peace, but whether owing to the Season of the Year, or the pacific Disposition of the Indians, is problematical. –

The Insurrection in Massachusetts appears to be suppressed, but Time only can discover whether that Suppression is radical or temporary. The public Papers herewith enclosed will give you the Details. –

What Plan or System Congress will adopt relative to the hostile Barbary States is not yet decided. The one you suggest has Advantages. The great Question I think is, whether we shall wage War or pay Tribute? I for my Part prefer War, and consequently am ready for every proper Plan of uniting and multiplying their Enemies. –

Mʳˢ· Jay joins with me in requesting the favor of you to present our Compliments and best Wishes to the Marchioness. –

I have the Honor to be &c: John Jay

NA: PCC, item 121, pp. 243-245 (LBkC); M61, reel 1.

Louis Guillaume Otto to Comte de Vergennes

[Translation]

Nº· 79.   New York, 16 Feby. 1787.
My Lord.

From a description of the active and passive navigation of the State of New York, it appears that English ship arrivals last year amount to 67, while only 7 ships arrived from France. This great disproportion is due in part to the English not admitting any American vessel into their islands and to they themselves carrying on the Commerce in cattle and timber which the United States furnishes to their Antilles. It is nonetheless very true that Great Britain still directly maintains very considerable commercial connections with America.

By combining, My Lord, the discourses of Sir John Temple with all that takes place every day under my eyes, I cannot keep from thinking that the English Minister is only showing himself to be so tenacious with regard to the Commerce of his Islands, and maintains his Navigation Act with such rigor, in order to procure a favorable treaty with the United States at a given time. This time will come when Congress has unanimously received powers to regulate Commerce. The more England has adhered to its exclusive system, the more she will be able to turn to account the sacrifices she makes, and the more exacting she will be with regard to compensations. The revolutions which are daily being effected in the commercial policies of Europe prove to us the possibility of such a result. The Commerce of the United States is of too great an importance for England to neglect the means of possessing herself of it almost exclusively. By suddenly abandoning to the United States the provisioning of its Antilles and the free exportation of sugars, necessary for the consumption of these States, she could place a very high price on a sacrifice that will be felt the more acutely, as it will be sudden and unexpected. Some extraordinary favors will be the natural consequence thereof, and the allies of the United States could not complain, since these favors will not have been *gratuitous* and will consequently not be extended to the nations which have concluded treaties of commerce with the United States. England cannot be unaware that its Navigation Act is at this time very unfavorable to the Antilles; her Colonies are rarely provisioned, while ours abound in everything necessary for their subsistence, and very often furnish the English the surplus of their cattle and produce. However, that power, very far from relaxing in the execution of its prohibitive laws, is excluding all American vessels from its ports more severely than ever. Not even the numerous petitions of the planters are taken into consideration by Parliament; it appears to fear gratuitously granting the United States any advantages that it could sell them for a very high price when the American Government has all the vigor necessary to pass and to execute resolutions favorable to English Commerce. The Lake forts, although formally ceded by the treaty of peace, could be another compensation for advantages which Congress grants to English commerce, and these two enticements will render the negotiations of England very easy in America.

The latest arrangements made in Paris, My Lord, concerning the Commerce in tobaccos have given the greatest satisfaction here. Rice henceforth becomes the most important subject of our commercial negotiations, not only because its consumption is very considerable in France, but because Carolina presents an immense outlet for our valuable merchandise, as well as for the most common woollen goods for the negroes. But that subject should depend in large part on our present position with regard to seaports in the Levant.

I am with a profound respect My Lord Your most humble and most obedient servant,   Otto.
r. 23 March

FFAA: Pol. Corr., U.S., v. 32, f. 198-199vo. (LC transcription).

Louis Guillaume Otto to Comte de Vergennes

[Translation]

N° 80.   New York, 17 Feby. 1787.
My Lord.

A Company of Dutch Merchants having had transmitted to Congress a plan to immediately reimburse the debt of the United States to France and to secure itself with His Majesty's credit, that Assembly has sent it back to the Office of the Treasury for examination. This Office, My lord, is very far from approving the proposition of the Dutch. In the report that it delivered to Congress, it begins by analyzing the views that these merchants may have in burdening themselves with a debt that at this moment is almost hopeless. It appears probable to it that the Dutch have only made this offer because they hope to be repaid in commodities and to secure themselves a type of monopoly in America for several years. The Commissioners think that Congress has no interest in changing the nature of a debt that has always been regarded by Americans as sacred, since it was contracted not only with their benefactor, but to supply the most pressing needs of the confederation; that by transferring this credit to the Dutch, it would cease to be so respectable, and the people would feel the necessity of paying it off much less; that it is very fortunate for Congress to have a great debt to pay, because without this common link the confederation would soon lose all its importance by the refusal of the people to meet the needs of the general Government, but that the consideration of the great services rendered by France would always furnish powerful motives to dispose the people to fulfill the engagements made by Congress; that in addition, it does not appear that His Most Christian Majesty is informed of this proposition, and that he might be offended by such an important step, which must in all events have his approbation before producing any effect; that His Majesty appears to make allowance for the present confusion of affairs in America, and that He will probably await a more favorable time to demand the arrears that are owed him. The Commissioners therefore propose to reject the plan of the Dutch entirely. This affair, My Lord, is still very secret, and it is only with much difficulty that I have been able to procure the details that I have the honor to transmit to You. Congress has not yet passed a resolution. The State of Frankland, My Lord, that broke away from North Carolina several years ago, having perceived that it was impossible for it to govern itself, has just become reconciled to its metropolis. In consequence of this step, the legislative Assembly has granted a general amnesty and a deferral of all taxes payable since the secession. The Delegates who have informed me of this important news assure me that tranquility is perfectly reestablished in their State.

An American Captain, My Lord, has just found on an island, the name of which he conceals, very precious and very abundant furs, with which he formed a cargo for China. His ship is supposed to depart within a few days. These furs resemble those that Captain Cook's[1] crew sold in Canton at a very high price, and that he had carried from the west coast of America. The cargo in question is composed of 8600 sea Otter pelts, an immense number when one considers that pelts of this species were sold by Cook's crew at the rate of 120 piastres apiece. Two of Captain Cook's sailors are on board this Ship. As the Shipowners maintain the most profound silence, there is as yet only very vague information on the Island in question. I am tempted to think that it is one of the Malvinas or Falklands, since various navigators, and among others Wallis[2] and Carteret,[3] make mention of Otters that they found there. Whaling attracts many Americans to these islands, and the whalers of Nantucket have even made some temporary establishments there. This discovery could become a great source of riches.

I am with a profound respect My Lord Your most humble and most obedient servant   Otto.
r. 23 March

FFAA: Pol. Corr., U.S., v. 32, f. 200-201vo. (LC transcription).

[1] Cook, James (1728-1779). British mariner and explorer. Surveyed St. Lawrence Channel, 1759, and coasts of Newfoundland and Labrador, 1763-1767. Conducted three expeditions of exploration in the Pacific, 1768-1771, 1772-1775, and 1776-1779.

[2] Wallis, Samuel (1728-1795). British circumnavigator. Discovered Tahiti and the Wallis Islands in the Pacific, 1767.

[3] Carteret, Philip (d. 1796). British navigator. Commanded second vessel in Samuel Wallis' expedition to explore the Southern Hemisphere, 1766. After becoming separated from Wallis in the Straits of Magellan, he discovered Pitcairn Island and the Queen Charlotte Islands and explored St. George's Channel.

Pieter Johan Van Berckel to Congress

New York 20th February 1787

The undersigned Minister Plenipotentiary from their High Mightinesses the Lords States General of the United Netherlands to the Congress of the U^d States of America has the honor of representing;

That he is informed, that the State of Virginia has in the last session of their Legislature passed an Act laying an additional Impost of Two per Cent ad valorem on such Articles Commodities & Merchandizes as shall be imported into that State, & that it is expressly declared in one of the Articles of this Act, that an Additional Impost of Two pence per Gallon shall be paid by all Liquors heretofore subject to any Impost which shall be imported into that State after the 20th. January 1787 Excepting French Brandies imported from any port in the dominions of the King of France in Vessels belonging to the Subjects of the said King or to the Citizens of the U^d States, which Brandies imported in the aforesaid manner after the 20th. January 1787 shall be exempted from every duty.

The undersigned in the first place observes that this Act is of that nature whose operations take effect before those who are concerned in it can have the smallest information about it; But what is of more importance is, that the Act is directly contrary to the Second Article of the Treaty of Amity & Commerce between Their High Mightinesses & the United States, importing "That the Subjects of the said States General of the United Netherlands shall not pay in the ports, Roads, Countries, Islands, Towns or places belonging to the U^d States of America or any of them, other or greater duties or impositions whatever, than such as the most favored nations are or shall be obliged to pay"

The words of this Article are so plain & clear that they do not require the least interpreation or comment, But it seems, that the Assembly of Virginia, in passing their Act, have either not recollected, or perhaps have not honored this Subject with the necessary attention, As otherwise there can be no doubt, but they would have noticed that this Act interfered with the Treaty, by not only leaving their High Mightinesses Subjects charged with former Imposts, but also by subjecting them to an additional Impost of two pence per Gallon on Brandies which they may import after the 20th. January 1787, While the Subjects of the King of France are eased & declared entirely exempted from every Impost whatever on the same Article, imported in the same manner specified in the Act.

As it is evident that this immunity granted to French Subjects cannot but be very prejudicial to the Dutch Subjects, who cannot hereafter import Brandies upon the same terms with the French, it is incontesable that this

Branch of Commerce & Navigation is indirectly taken from them & that they have reason to complain that they are by no means treated as the most favored nation.

These are the complaints which the Undersigned conceives himself indispensably bound to represent to Congress, to whom alone the power of Concluding & executing Treaties has been delegated by the U^d States. He requests that they will consider the foregoing & see that the Infraction made by the State of Virgina on the Second Article of the abovementioned Treaty be fully redressed & that the Dutch Subjects may enjoy uninter-ruptedly the immunities & priviledges which are granted & gauranteed [sic] to them by the faith of a Treaty, which the undersigned claims in their behalf.

Done at New York the 20$^{th.}$ February 1787

P. J. Van Berckel.

Faithfully translated from the Original by John Pintard.

NA: PCC, item 99, pp. 283-284 (translation); M247, reel 126.

Congressional Resolution Calling for a Convention to Revise the Articles of Confederation

[New York] February 21st 1787 –

Whereas there is provision in the Articles of Confederation and perpetual Union for making alterations therein by the Assent of a Congress of the United States, and of the Legislatures of the Several States; And Whereas experience hath evinced that there are defects in the present Confederation, as a means to remedy which Several of the States, and particularly the State of New York by express instructions to their delegates in Congress have Suggested a Convention for the purposes expressed in the following Resolution, and such Convention appearing to be the most probable means of establishing in these States a firm National Govern-ment. –

Resolved That in the Opinion of Congress it is expedient that on the second Monday in May next a Convention of Delegates who shall have been appointed by the Several States, be held at Philadelphia for the sole and express purpose of revising the Articles of Confederation, and reporting to Congress and the Several Legislatures such alterations and provisions therein as shall when agreed to in Congress, and confirmed by the States render the federal Constitution adequate to the exigencies of government and the preservation of the Union. –   Cha⁣ᵗ Thomson Secʳʸ·

NA: PCC, *item* 122, *p.* 74 (LBkC); M247, *reel* 140.

John Jay to John Adams

Dʳ Sir   New York 21ˢᵗ· February 1787
    I had the Pleasure of receiving two Days ago your Letter of the 30ᵗʰ· November by Mʳ· Mitchel – it was the next Morning laid before Congress.
    Nine States are now represented, but as yet little Progress has been made in the Business before them. My Report on the Infractions of the Treaty complained of by Britain, has been referred to a new Committee, and I think a very good one; various Opinions prevail on the Subject and I cannot conjecture what the ultimate Decision of Congress on it will be. –
    The Insurrection in Massachusetts seems to be suppressed, and I herewith enclose the Papers containing the Details we have received since the 6ᵗʰ· Instant, when I wrote to you by the Packet – Your Sentiments on that Business prove to have been just. I ought to write to you fully on many Subjects, but I am not yet enabled – when I shall be cannot be predicted. Our Government is unequal to the Task assigned it, and the People begin also to perceive its Inefficiency. The Convention gains Ground – NewYork has instructed her Delegates to move in Congress for a Recommendation to the States to form a Convention; for this State dislikes the Idea of a Convention unless countenanced by Congress. I do not promise myself much further immediate Good from the Measure than that it will tend to approximate the public Mind to the Changes which ought to take place. It is hard to say what those Changes should be exactly – there is one however which I think would be much for the better, Viʒᵗ· to distribute the foederal Sovereignty into its three proper Departments of executive, legislative and judicial; for that Congress should act in these different Capacities was I think a great Mistake in our Policy. –
    This State in their present Session has greatly moderated their Severities to the Tories; a Law having been passed to restore a very great Majority of those resident here to the Rights of Citizens. I hope all Discriminations inconsistent with the Treaty of Peace will gradually be abolished, as Resentment gives place to Reason and good Faith. But, my Dear Sir, we labour under one sad Evil, the Treasury is empty though the Country abounds in Resources, and our People are far more unwilling than unable to pay Taxes. – Hence result Disappointment to our Creditors, Disgrace to

our Country, and I fear Disinclination in too many to any Mode of Government that can easily and irresistably open their Purses. – Much is to be done, and the Patriots must have Perseverance as well as Patience.

I am, Dr Sir, Your aff^t· Friend amd Servt·   John Jay –

MHS: *The Adams Papers, microfilm reel 369 (LS)*

Phineas Bond to Lord Carmarthen

My Lord   Philadelphia Feb. 21st 1787

I have frequently informed your Lordship that my commissions have not yet been recognized by the congress: Within the last fortnight that body assembled for the first time since my arrival; they proceeded to the election of a president, and, in the usual course of business, my commissions were referred to a committee, but by reason of the indisposition of one of the members, no report has yet been made thereon.

I have been in so uncertain a state, I could do little more than take measures to collect from the different States an accurate account of all duties imposed by the respective legislatures, on British goods, and of the tonnage of British bottoms; and also to obtain full information of all the Acts of Assembly which have been passed to limit or restrain the recovery of British debts, or which, in any degree, affect British property: I hope shortly to be fully satisfied upon these important objects of inquiry, for the purpose of informing Government, how far the Treaty of Peace has been violated, and the better to enable me to take fit measures to obtain such redress as justice and the faith of nations call for.

In such an extensive continent, my Lord, I have found it rather tedious and difficult to accomplish my purpose at this season; the roads being almost impassable, render all communication between State and State very dilatory; and the great obstruction of navigation, by the severity of the frosts impedes that intercourse, which, at other seasons of the year, is by means of the coasting vessels, not only frequent but certain.

Thro' the interests of some English merchants in the different States, to whom I have applied, I trust I shall, e'er long, be enabled to transmit to your Lordship, a precise and accurate detail of whatever respects the important duties of my Commissions: when they are recognized by Congress, and when I have materials to act upon I mean to make every decent and suitable representation which may, at all, tend to remove the existing grounds of complaint: for the present, I shall forward such representations to confidential persons in the remote States, to be, by them presented to the different legislatures; but I shall not dispense with my own attendance even in the most remote State, where my personal interference may be deemed expedient to promote the commercial interests of the nation.

I am very apprehensive, however, my Lord, the accidental delay I have met with from the Congress respecting my Commissions will postpone the opportunity of applying to any of the distant States this Winter; the fixed seasons of dispatching business will probably be over, before I could properly digest and represent the subjects of complaint; in the mean time, my Lord, I beg leave to assure your Lordship substantial reasons now exist to render the appointment of discreet agents for proper districts thro' this continent, absolutely and immediately necessary: new and important objects of duty and attention arise out of the late Act for the further increase and encouragement of shipping and navigation, every endeavor will be used to elude the purposes the Legislature had in view and it will require some address and industry to detect and correct the schemes which will be practiced to defeat the extensive operation of law, the effect of which if properly pointed, must inevitably cramp the little remnant of commerce now enjoyed by this country.

This circumstance will give additional weight to the representation I had the honor to make to your Lordship in my letter of the 8th of Aug. last, previous to my departure from England; in which I took the liberty of suggesting to your Lordship, the expediency of appointing agents for the different ports, to check and prevent the frauds committed respecting Mediterranean Passes and to enforce his Majesty's proclamations and the orders of Council thereupon made: a copy of that letter I have now the honor to enclose to your Lordship and beg leave to observe it will not be possible for a consul to superintend every port in the district, to which he is, or may be, appointed: and in my own particular case my second commission, as commissary for commercial affairs, may carry me to very remote States, out of my consular district where particular exigencies may require my personal inquiry and attendance.

Your Lordship I understood clearly saw the extent of the mischief arising from the frauds now practiced and the necessity of defeating such practices: – the mischief is become more alarming, as the fraud is become more general: as far as I can learn most American vessels, sailing in the track of the Algerine cruizers, carry forged passes; – the Lords of the Admiralty will know how closely the false resembled the genuine passes: and perhaps to destroy the evil completely, their lordships may deem it necessary to call in the present passes and to emit new ones with suitable devices to guard as much as possible against imitation: – but for the present, my Lord, the nomination of fit agents seems to be only expedient to correct a matter of great national consequence; – their appointment may combine the important duties to which I have alluded: they may enforce the regulations of the new Act of Navigation, they may check the indirect practices now prevailing in respect to Medit$^{n.}$ Passes; and moreover they may act as deputies to the commissions at present existing; and in distant States, at least, they may take the charge of conducting such representations as may be thought advisable. – As the trade of this country is now restricted within very narrow bounds: and will be more confined Government may conceive such agencies competent to every purpose of commercial regulation and their appointment may, for a time, or perhaps wholly, supersede the necessity of appointing consuls to other districts; especially as the commission of the consul-general extends to every case, where resort is to be had to the Executive Body of the United States assembled in Congress, and my second commission as commissary for commercial affairs comprehends every application which may be requisite to the individual Legislatures, thro'out this continent.

I have the honour to enclose to your Lordship a list of the ports or rather districts which seem to require the superintendence of agents, and have annexed my remarks upon their importance, in point of trade and the probable duty of each agency.

The Revolution which has happened in North America, called for new and peculiar Regulations for commerce; and the frauds which have been practiced evince the necessity of enforcing them by due diligence and strict attention.

There can be no better test, my Lord, of the importance of the new act, and its tendency to increase the carrying trade of G$^{t.}$ Britain as far as it respects this country, than the alarm and perplexity it has occasioned here. Hitherto the practice of providing American ships with double papers has been very successfully managed; and the fraud has not only prevailed, to the detriment of the revenues in British ports but has even operated to elude those duties which the Legislatures of the States have imposed upon British Bottoms: by an ingenious collusion between partners in trade residing in different countries, ships have enjoyed the advantages of British bottoms in harbours within his Majesty's dominions, and the privileges of American Bottoms in the ports of America. – The attention recommended by government to their different officers to adhere to the provisions and regulations of this new and salutary Act, in their full extent, will it is to be hoped effectually prevent the further progress of these and similar deceptions –

I shall hope to be favored with your Lordship's instructions, upon the subjects to which I have now alluded, as soon as your Lordship's important engagements will admit

With sentiments of the greatest respect, I have the honor to be, my Lord Your Lordship's very faithful and most obed: servant   P. Bond. Rec^d. April 8th.

AHA 1896, v. 1, pp. 521-525.

Thomas Jefferson to John Jay

Sir   Paris Feb. 23. 1787.
  The assemblée des Notables being an event in the history of this country which excites notice, I have supposed it would not be disagreeable to you to learn it's immediate objects, tho no ways connected with our interests. the assembly met yesterday; the king in a short but affectionate speech informed them of his wish to consult with them on the plans he had digested, & on the general good of his people, and his desire to imitate the head of his family, Henry IV,[1] whose memory is so dear to the nation. the Garde des Sceaux[2] then spoke about twenty minutes, chiefly in compliment to the orders present. the Comptroller general in a speech of about an hour opened the budget, and enlarged on the several subjects which will be under their deliberation. he explained the situation of the finances at his accession to office: the expences which their arrangement had rendered necessary, their present state with the improvements made in them, the several plans which had been proposed for their further improvement, a change in the form of some of their taxes, the removal of the interior customhouses to the frontiers, and the institution of Provincial assemblies. the assembly was then divided into committees, with a prince of the blood at the head of each. in this form they are to discuss separately the subjects which will be submitted to them. their decision will be reported by two members to the Minister, who on view of the separate decisions of all the committees, will make such changes in his plans as will best accomodate them to their views without too much departing from his own, and will then submit them to the vote (but I believe not to the debate) of the General assembly, which will be convened for this purpose one day in every week, and will vote individually.
  The event of the count de Vergennes' death, of which I had the honour to inform you in two letters of the 14th. inst. the appointment of the Count de Montmorin, & the propriety of my attending at his first audience which will be on the 27th. have retarded the journey I had proposed, a few days. I shall hope on my return to meet here new powers for the Consular convention as under those I have it will be impossible to make the changes

in the convention which may be wished for. I have the honor to be with
sentiments of the most perfect esteem & respect, Sir, your most obedient
& most humble servant   Th: Jefferson

LC: *Jefferson Papers, microfilm reel 6 (Press Copy).*
 ¹ *Henry IV (1553-1610). As Henry III, King of Navarre, 1572-1589.*
 ² *Keeper of the Seals*

Sidi Hassan to Congress

Algiers 25ᵗʰ· February 1787
I cannot omit writing to your Excellencies, to inform you that Mʳ· Lamb
has been here at Algiers, and having treated and spoken on certain Points
respecting Peace and Captives, went away and has not returned; and to
assure you that he is a Gentleman of good Deportment, and I really like
and esteem him for his good Qualities, as I have also written to Mʳ·
Carmichael at Madrid; and I shall be well content with the said Mʳ· Lamb
in preference to any other Person, whenever it shall be proposed to treat
on any Point.   And this I have the   Honor to communicate to your
Excellencies for your Information and Satisfaction. –
May God preserve your Excellencies many Years.
                                        Sidij Assan Nickillange
                            (Superintendant) of the Marine of Algiers
NA: PCC, *item 91, v. 2, p. 533 (translation); M247, reel 119.*

Virginia State Council Report on
the Seizure of Spanish Property
by George Rogers Clark

In Council, February 28, 1787
The Board resumed the consideration of several Letters bearing date the
22ᵈ day, of december, 1786 and addressed to the Governor¹ from Danville,
by Thomas Marshall² and others, which said Letters with the inclosures had
been laid before them on Saturday last. –
The Board lament that those dispatches pregnant as they are with
subjects, deeply interesting to our national character and quiet, and
intended for the last assembly, should for the first time, on the fifth day of
this instant, have been handed to the governor in Willamsburg on his late
journey to Norfolk on public business. –

From the respectability of the names subscribed to those letters, they confide in the following facts;

1. That the prosecution of the treaty proposed to be held with the indians under the authority of Congress, will tend to the safety of our Western Settlements;

2. That the success of the treaty would be forwarded by the appointment of some Commissioners at least who are resident in the parts of the Country likely to be exposed to the incursions of the Savages.

3. That General Clarke[3] has been, and perhaps is now employed, in levying recruits, in nominating officers and in impressing provisions for the support of the post at Saint Vincennes. and

4. That General Clarke hath made a seizure of Spanish property without any authority for such an act.

The Board therefore advise,

1. That copies of the letters aforesaid, and their inclosures be forthwith transmitted to our delegates in Congress; with an earnest request to communicate them, in whole or in part, according to their discretion, immediately to that body: to urge the speediest arrangements for a treaty to be holden with the indians in april next under the sanction of the federal government; and to propose as Commissioners, General James Wilkinson,[4] Colonel Richard Clough Anderson,[5] and Colonel Isaac Shelby.[6]

2. That it be notified to general Clarke, that this Board disavow the existence of a power derived from them to the said Clarke to raise recruits, appoint officers, or impress provisions.

3. That as the seizure of Spanish property was never authenticated to this Board before the receipt of the said letters, so had it been known at a period sufficiently early for prevention, it would have been prevented. But that this offence against the law of nations having been committed, it becomes the Executive to declare their displeasure at the act, and to cause the national honor to be vindicated by the institution of legal proceedings against all persons appearing to be culpable: That the attorney general be consulted on the documents aforesaid, and requested to take himself, or to call upon the attorney general of Kentucky, as the case may require, to take such steps as may subject to punishment all persons guilty in the premises: That the said seizure of Spanish property be disclaimed by government in a special proclamation: That a Copy of this order be also sent to our delegates, in order that they may, if it shall seem expedient, acquaint the minister of his catholic majesty with these Sentiments of the Executive: And that another copy be forwarded to Thomas Marshall, esquire, and the

other gentlemen who concurred in the letters aforesaid. – All which several matters so advised the Governor orders accordingly. –

Attest. A. Blair & C. C.[7]

NA: PCC, item 71, v. 2, pp. 491-493 (C); M247, reel 85.

[1] Edmund Randolph

[2] Marshall, Thomas (1730-1802). Surveyor, legislator and soldier; father of John Marshall. Engaged by George Washington as assistant surveyor of the Fairfax estate. Member, Virginia house of burgesses, 1761-1767, 1769-1773, 1775. Officer, Virginia Continental Army regiments, 1775-1781. Appointed surveyor for part of Kentucky, November 1780. Commissioned to settle public accounts in Kentucky, 1781. Moved to Kentucky, 1783. Represented Kentucky in Virginia legislature. Surveyor of Revenue for the District of Ohio.

[3] Clark, George Rogers (1752-1818). Military leader and surveyor. Secured Virginia's commitment to the defense of Kentucky against British-inspired Indian attacks, 1776. Captured Kaskaskia, Cahokia, and Vincennes, 1778; recovered Vincennes after its recapture by the British, 1779. Frustrated British efforts to control Kentucky and the Northwest, 1779-1783. With Richard Butler and S.H. Parsons, commissioner to treat with the Indians of the Northwest, who in January 1786 at Ft. McIntosh acknowledged U.S. sovereignty over former British territories.

[4] Wilkinson, James (1757-1825). Soldier. Officer, Continental Army, 1775-1778, serving as secretary of the board of war, 1778. Forced to resign from the army because of his involvement in the Conway Cabal, he served as its clothier-general, 1779-1781. Moved to Kentucky, 1784, where he advocated separation from Virginia. Made trading voyage to New Orleans, 1787, where he acquired a trading monopoly after having convinced the Spanish that he was working to separate Kentucky from the United States. Rejoined army, 1791. Commissioned brigadier general, 1792. Took over Detroit from the British, 1796. With William C.C. Claiborne, represented the United States in taking over the Louisiana Purchase, 1803. Governor, Louisiana Territory, 1805-1806. Involved in the Burr conspiracy, but found not guilty by a court martial, 1811. Made a major general, 1813, and commanded failed effort to capture Montreal that fall. Left army, 1815. Later involved in efforts to obtain Texas land grant from Mexico.

[5] Anderson, Richard Clough (1750-1826). Soldier. Officer, Virginia Continental Army and militia regiments, 1775-1781. Surveyor-general to locate the lands Virginia reserved for its veterans in Kentucky. Settled near Louisville. Served in Kentucky constitutional convention, 1788.

[6] Shelby, Isaac (1750-1826). Soldier, Kentucky political figure. As Virginia militia officer, prepared military surveys in Kentucky and served as commissary of supplies for frontier post garrisons. Provided boats for George Rogers Clark's Illinois campaign, 1779. Member, Virginia legislature, 1779. Appointed to command the escort for commissioners to determine western boundary between Virginia and North Carolina, he became a North Carolina militia colonel, 1780. A leader of militia forces at battles of King's Mountain and Cowpens. Member, North Carolina legislature, 1781-1782. Surveyed lands granted to

North Carolina veterans, 1782-1783. Moved to Kentucky, 1783. Member of Danville convention on separation from Virginia, November 1784, and of succeeding conventions, 1787-1789. Governor, 1792-1796, 1812-1816. Led Kentucky volunteers in invasion of Canada, 1813.

[7] *Blair, Archibald. Clerk of the Virginia state council.*

John Sullivan to Don Diego de Gardoqui

State of Georgia, Frontier of the Creek Nation 1st of March 1787

May it please your Excellency,

Having waited thus far in expectation of permission to join the spanish Troops in South America, and having expressed to your Excellency an ardent inclination to obtain the mere honor of serving in any spanish Regiment as a Volunteer, which requisitions as they were not complied with in due time, I beg leave to decline the acceptance of any rank or degree in the service of his Catholic Majesty....Being a Soldier of fortune, as I profess – and having studied from my infancy the science of Arms, *practical* war is now my pursuit, as a profession most congenial with my principles and disposition; and thousands of Americans (Officers in the late war) pant for an opportunity to serve this Country. The banks of the Ohio and Missisippi, are actually alive with the first American Characters of this stamp – and called upon from thence by my heroic brethren of the Army – honor, virtue, and the bias of an antient intercourse, and former habits incline me to assist them. From the Natches to the Kaskaskies – from Pittsburg to S$^{t.}$ Mary's River, they are prepared to pour forth with the greatest ease 50,000 Veterans in Arms, in defence of their *commercial* Rights, throughout the navigable Rivers of the southern parts of this Empire. The grain is actually germinating, sown by the pride, avarice, and folly of a certain extern. power, which the pure air of Liberty working at the root, and the Laws of nature, superior to the narrow policy of any foreign Court, must finally and very speedily raise into a host of myrmidons, the children of Enachim; the Sons of the Earth; irresistable in this Land, at least by any force that may obstruct their pretentions or assail them.

The important Drama, may it please your Excellency, is now approaching; a new Drama, in which the Tragedians of the *west* are to appear in the military Buskin – and I am invited to Act as a Character of some consequence among them. Time will tell how decisively *my part* shall be performed. Of this I am sure, that I shall exhibit to my utmost the part of a Soldier. A very inconsiderable time must inevitably call forth to trial, the mighty energy of the Ohio and Missisippi, and incidents and events are gradually teeming into birth, which will shortly open a spacious field for a daring spirit to explore.

May it please your Excellency, the States of Georgia, Franklin, and Kentucky, confederated; the Counties of Bourbon, &$^{c.}$ on the Natches; the settlements on Cumberland, Kaskaskies, and the Wabash, and the Governments of Pittsburg, Westmoreland, &$^{c.}$ abound with the seeds of War; nor will any obstruction from New Orleans to the Blaise, impede the overwhelming inundation preparing to pour down along the waters of the Missisippi, into the Bay of Mexico. The torrent will be irresistable; the Crop is actually in the ground; harvest is ready for the hook, and the hook for the harvest, the reaper has introduced his Sickle, combustibles are laid into a pile; nay, the very brand is already applied and the fire only requires to be fanned. The permission of Congress will not be solicited on this Occasion. In Congress this people are not represented. I am now on my way to the western waters, where people too long confined to unnatural boundaries, are ready to float with the Current of the Missisippi into the Sea, and with irresistable irruption and impetuosity to burst over every artificial barrier and mound which may obstruct their free passage into the ocean. The Americans are amphibious animals; they cannot be confined to the Land alone: Tillage and Commerce are their elements – both or neither will they enjoy, both they will have or perish. I have the honor to remain, with the utmost deference, your Excellency's most obedient & most hble. Serv$^{t.}$

John Sullivan late Captn 4th Reg^t American Light Dragoons[1]

. . . . .

NA: PCC, *item 120, v. 3, pp. 276-279 (LBkC); M40, reel 3.*
[1] *Not further identified.*

William Bingham to Lord Lansdowne

My Lord[1]							Philadelphia March 4th 1787
I did myself the Honor of writing to your Lordship immediately after my Return to America, to request your Lordship to accept my warmest Acknowledgments for the polite Attentions which your Lordship & Lady Lansdown were So obliging as to pay to Mrs Bingham & myself, during our Residence in London.

As Your Lordship once expressed a Desire of being acquainted with the political Events of this Country, & as it was during your Lordships Administration that Peace & Tranquillity were restored to the United States & their Independance confirmed, it must certainly be more than

Matter of curious Speculation to be informed, what has been the Result of this important Secession of one Country from the other.

It is found from the Experience of Several Years, that the System of Confederation, which formed the Bond of Union betwixt the Thirteen States, tho fully competent to answer the Purposes for which it was instituted during the War, is not endowed with sufficient Powers to compell, & carry into Effect, the general Interests of America in Times of Peace, when the political Objects are more extensive & complicated –

To derive those Advantages from Commerce, which a Country, furnishing Provisions & raw Materials is entitled to, & whose Connection from these Circumstances will be courted by all manufacturing Nations, there must be Power lodged Somewhere, to form Commercial *Regulations*, whose Effects must be general & pervade every Part of the Union

The Disposition of the European Powers is to monopolize their own carrying Trade, & Secure as much as they can, of that of other Nations America, Since the Peace has found herself excluded from most of the Ports that She formerly had liberty of resorting to, & has indiscriminately admitted all Nations to repair to her Ports, & bear off the bulky Productions of her Country, which furnish such abundant Employment for Shipping; The Powers of Congress are not Sufficient to restrain this pernicious Intercourse, nor to form a *Retaliating* System, which would operate to the Exclusion of the Ships of those Powers who would not permit Similar Indulgencies –

This has been a principal focus of the Complaints that exist in America–

Another, & a very essential one, is the immense Quantity of Manufactures that flowed into America, immediately after the Peace, more in Value than the Productions of the Soil, for many Years, would pay for; more especially as the Agriculture of the Country had been neglected during the War, & would require Some Years of Tranquillity to restore it–

Besides this unfavorable Circumstance; there was another Drain on the Country, arising from the old Claims of British Creditors to an immense Amount, & which by the Treaty, there was to be no lawfull Impediment in the Recovery of

The Merchants & Factors of the British, Soon accumulated the greatest Portion of Specie in the Country, in Return for their Merchandize, & Shipped it to Europe; This deprived the Country of a Sufficient Circulating Medium, & arrested the hands of Industry both in Agriculture & Commerce.

As Soon as Judgments were awarded in the Courts in favor of the Claims of British Creditors, Executions were taken out, & the real Estate of the Debtors, exposed to Sale – In many Cases, they did not Sell for one third of their intrinsic Value, owing to the Scarcity of Money, which was not

Sufficient to discharge but a Small Proportion of the Duties required of it, for the purpose of Alienation – Hence the Legislatures of *Several* of the States, were under the Necessity of interposing & favoring the Debtors, by authorizing them to extinguish their Debts by distant Installments –

This was certainly violating the Treaty; but if any Palliation can be offered for departing from the rigid Line of Justice, it is admissible here, for the Specie & Productions of the Country were not Sufficient to discharge the Demands upon it; there was therefore a moral Impossibility to oppose to the fulfillment of the Obligations prescribed by this Treaty; *Summum Jus*[2] would in this Case have been *Summa Injuria*[3]; for the Creditors to have exacted the Engagements that the literal construction of the Treaty justified, would have been to require of this Debtor, that he Should "make Bricks without Straw;" – This in a great Measure, occasioned the Revolt in Massachusets, which has been lately suppressed. At the Same Time, I do not believe that the Principles of Justice are more inherent in the People of any Country, than in those of America, & I am confident that the Claims of the British Merchants will be extinguished to their Satisfaction – They are in some Measure to blame for the Distresses we experience, as the immense Credits they incautiously gave to an exhausted Country immediately after the Peace is one great Cause of our present Calamities.

However, there are no Lessons so instructive, as those taught in the School of Adversity, both for Nations as well as Individuals, & America has greatly benefited therefrom – Instead of those Habits of Luxury & Dissipation which the Appearances of Plenty & Prodigality brought upon her, we find Industry, Oeconomy, & public Spirit prevail; She has recovered from her Delusion, & finds it Folly to expect to Rest without the fatigue of Exertion, to procure the Means. She wants Nothing now but a strong efficient Government, which will command Respect & Confidence abroad, & act with Vigor & Energy at home –

The Defects of the Confederated System are So glaring, & the Necessity of a Speedy & effectual Revision & Amendment So generally acknowledged, that Congress have recommended to the States to appoint, & many of the States have accordingly (& all will,) come to the Resolution of appointing Delegates to a general Convention, to be held in May next at Philadelphia, for the purpose of forming, & making a Report to Congress of, Such a foederal Constitution, as may be Suited to the Exigencies of the Union, & which when approved of by Congress, & ratified by the Several Legislatures, is to have full Force & Efficacy –

Having the Honor of a Seat in Congress, as Representative of the State of Pennsylvania, I was very active in promoting this Measure, as I am convinced that all our political Misfortunes flow from the Weakness of our foederal Government

As your Lordships Administration gave Independance to this Country, your Lordship may possibly take an Interest in its Welfare, & in its Progress towards that State of political Improvement, that can alone ensure its Happiness; Should this be the Case, I Shall be happy in being honoured with your Lordships Commands, & Shall take a pleasure in making every important Communication

Tho' G. Britain & the United States have at present no very good Understanding, yet I am convinced they would find a mutual Interest in a more intimate Connection –

The Extension of her Commerce Since the Peace, the flourishing State of her Funds & of her transatlantic Possessions have opened Such abundant Sources of Wealth, as to make her disregard Objects of inferior Consequence –

But the Time may come, & I believe it not far distant, when America by the Establishment of a high toned Government, by the Improvement of her natural Advantages & by an increasing Population & Commerce, may make herself more respectable, & have more Enfluence on the political System of G. Britain, than She can now pretend to –

I am fearfull that the United States will Soon find it a Duty they owe to the Dignity of the Sovereign Power, to recall their Minister at the Court of Sᵗ James, as the present Administration has not thought proper to appoint a Corresponding Character, to reside in this Country –

Permit me to request your Lordship to present my Respectfull Complements to Lady Lansdown, & to believe me with the most profound Respect My Lord Your Lordships most obedᵗ & very h'ble Servant

Wᵐ Bingham

University of Michigan, William L. Clements Library: Shelburne Papers, v. 88, f. 110-113vo. (ALS).

¹ *Formerly Lord Shelburne.*
² *extreme law*
³ *extreme injustice*

Louis Guillaume Otto to Comte de Montmorin

[Translation]

Nᵒ· 82.   New York, 5 March 1787.

My Lord,

The situation of Congress in regard to the treaty with Spain daily becomes more embarrassing. The inhabitants of Kentucky and Frankland are insisting not only on the free navigation of the Mississippi, but they threaten to commit hostilities against the inhabitants of Louisiana unless Spain renounces its exclusive system. They quite recently detained two

Spanish Bateaus that were carrying on Commerce at Fort St. Vincent on the Wabash. "If the Spanish," they say, "do not permit us to go down the river, we shall in our turn prevent them from coming up it." They propose to arm ten thousand men and to force their way through the Colony of Santa Fe. The enclosed authentic letter, addressed to a North Carolina Delegate, contains all the plans, either illusory or practicable, of those people. One of their Deputies in the Assembly of Pennsylvania has just expressed his thoughts publicly with an animosity and dishonesty which has astonished everyone. He proposed to have this State's Delegates in Congress given instructions analogous to those of Virginia and Jersey, but the Assembly has refused to take up a subject that appears to it to be exclusively the province of Congress.

In the meantime, the two parties which divide this latter Assembly are doing their best to gain a majority. Some New England Delegates are beginning to declare themselves for the opening of the Mississippi: "Although we are persuaded," one of the more moderate among them told me, "that these Western territories will gradually absorb our population, a very great misfortune, the fear that these vast regions may submit to England in order to obtain from Her the protection which we refuse them, makes us desire the free navigation of the Mississippi as the only means of keeping these people under the laws of Congress. It would be better that an earthquake had swallowed this territory, the inhabitants of which, friends or enemies, will always raise obstacles to the political measures of the United States; but inasmuch as they exist, it will be in our interest to render them favorable to us by every kind of good offices." – It appears, My Lord, that since the revolt of a County in Massachusetts, all minds are struck with apprehension that the interior regions would be joined to Canada. The encouragements given to the Insurgents by Lord Dorchester, the hostilities of the savages, and a conspiracy to kidnap the geographer of the United States charged with surveying the lands of Ohio have increased these anxieties. One could not imagine all the difficulties which that Geographer has experienced; he has communicated to me his report, of which I have the honor to enclose a Copy.

The particular situation, My Lord, in which England and Spain find themselves with regard to the United States, requires very serious reflections by the patriotic and French party.

If Congress cannot procure the free navigation of the Mississippi for the inhabitants of the West, it will necessarily come about either that the latter make a passage across Louisiana by force under the secret protection of England, or that, in order to procure themselves an outlet by the St. Lawrence river, they submit completely to this latter power, or indeed that a coalition of interests be made between Spain and England, and that all the territory of the West becomes a dependency of Louisiana and Canada. "It is not in vain," say the Kentuckians, "that nature has raised immense ranges of mountains between us and the United States; its intention was to separate us forever; our interests differ as much from theirs as our fertile plains differ from the sands of the Chesapeake; even our rivers, by flowing toward the Mississippi or the St. Lawrence, indicate the route we should take to make our commerce flourish." – Those who fear that Spain and England are secretly acting in concert in order to divide this territory think they have for some time caught glimpses of a very good understanding between these two Courts; they are especially struck by the great moderation which Great Britain has shown in evacuating her posts on the Mosquito Coast, of which she had always appeared very jealous. They think that she would not have abandoned the Indians, who had been her most faithful allies, if she had not had a mind to be reconciled with Spain and turn her sacrifices to account in some future negotiation.

The Spanish Plenipotentiary, My Lord, appears not in the least affected by the reports which have just reached us from the West; he tells us that New England has nothing to fear, and that even though the inhabitants of Kentucky should make an expedition West of the Mississippi toward New Mexico, they would be repulsed very easily by the Colonists of Santa Fe and its environs. I do not know to what extent this confidence can be justified.

I am with a profound respect My Lord Your most humble and most obedient servant.   Otto.
rec. 28 May

FFAA: Pol. Corr., U.S., v. 32, f. 207-209vo. (LC transcription).

Peter Allaire: Occurrences
from 7 February to 6 March 1787

New York 7ᵗʰ March 1787.
The State of Virginia have passed an Act to impose a duty on all Spiritous liquors imported into that State of Two pence p Gall after the 20ᵗʰ January 1787, *Except French Brandies* imported from some port within the dominions of the King of France, in Vessells belonging to Subjects of the King, or to Citizens belonging to the United States which Brandies so imported after the 20 January 1787 shall be duty free.

Also, three pence p pound on Cheese, six pence p pound on all Teas, four p Cent on Cordage, Vessells to pay Two Shillings p Ton, owned wholly by Citizens of this & the United States Three Shillings p Ton on all Vessells, owned by all Nations who *are in Commercial Treaty with the United States*. And Six *Shillings p Ton* on all Vessells, owned by Subjects of any foreign power, *not* in Commercial Treaty with the United States, which tonage shall be in lieu of all former Tonage heretofore imposed except Six pence p Ton for the support of the Light House.

. . . . .

Generals, Lincoln & Shepard, surprised Shays on Sunday 4 February took 150 Prisoners. Shays fled with about 100 Horse into Northampton then into the State of Vermont, and it is generally beleived that he has gone to Canada to Lord Dorchester for Assistance & what confirms the above report, is, that Major Beckwith[1] is arrived express from Canada with dispatches, to go in this Packet, his lodgings are closely watched, to know who goes to him and those that have, are lookd on with suspicion.

A few Nights ago, the States Powder House, situated about two Miles from this City, was broke open, & Robed of forty three barrels Gun Powder, it is Imagined to be done by some of the Insurgents, as the Track of many feet were traced in the Snow down to the Water, where a New England Sloop, had Anchored the Evening before, and had sailed again before day, there are many parties of the Insurgents, still in Arms.

. . . . .

The State of Massachusets, on the 3ᵈ of February their Legislature met, approved of what the Executive had done with Respct to the suppression of the Insurgents, and declared a Rebellion existed in that Commonwealth, and requested the Executive to adopt the most Vigorous measures to bring the promoters to condign punishment.

. . . . .

The Legislature of the State of Massachusets, have Ordered a Number not exceeding fifteen hundred Men to be raised for four months, to be Quartered in such parts of the State as the Executive think necessary for securing the Peace & quelling the present Rebellion.

They have Also Voted forty thousand pounds for defraying the Expences of the Militia Employed against the Insurgents.

A Pitition from the inhabitants of the Western frontiers back of Virginia & North Carolina to congress, complaining that the Spaniards have refused them the free Navigation of the Mississipi, and desire their interference, as they are intituled to it by treaty, that should the Spaniards refuse them, they will certainly be provoked to explore other Paths which do not lead to such desireable Riches, as cultivation And perhaps would be extreemly inconvenient to the Spanish nation & desire Congress to procure an Order for a free Navigation from the Spanish Minister here, until one can be procured from Spain. that they had sent a Vessell down the Mississpi [sic] in June last, which Vessell had been seized by the Spaniards and Sold: that the Spaniards had sent a Vessell up the River into their Territory, which they had seized & sold she had Ten thousand Dollars on board to purchase furs.

March 4...Shays & Days [sic] have taken Shelter in Vermont & have about 1600 Men with them, for the State of Vermont has repealed the Act they passed two years ago, which Authorised their Governour to deliver up any Offenders who had taken shelter in their State, on proper application being made by any of the United States, wherein such Offence had been committed, so that the Insurgents have not only a Place of Safety, but friends to Assist them, in which the united States dare not March their Army. Men that will bear the inclemency of the present Season & suffer hunger & Cold, must have greater designs, then the not paying the present Taxes the back part of this State with Connecticut & Massachusets in all Appearance will be in Arms by May or June.

Inclosed I send you the particular Acco^t between each of the United States & Congress, which I took from Authentic Copies, and had them published, which will at one View convince you of their punctuallity.

I Remain with Respect   P.A.

PRO: FO 4/5, pp. 133-144 (LC transcription).
[1] *Beckwith, George (1753-1823). British military officer and government official. After regimental and staff service, assigned to reorganize British intelligence network in America, early 1781. Remained in military intelligence work throughout the 1780s; principal British agent in the United States, 1787-1791. Appointed governor of Bermuda, 1797, of St. Vincent, 1804, and of Barbados, 1809. As full general, commanded troops in Ireland, 1816-1820.*

Benjamin Hawkins to Thomas Jefferson

Dear Sir   New-York 8th. March 1787
                    .   .   .   .   .
We are not here in so profound a calm as in Europe. The uneasinesses which have existed in Massachusets for some time past grew into a serious opposition to that Government, and they are now by the vigorous though not timely opposition of the government put in train of adjustment. The Southern States are more tranquil, and are emerging fast into order; and if the Foederal Government can be made efficient the revolution will be a blessing to them. Virginia taking the lead for this most desirable object proposed a convention to be in may next at Philadelphia. North Carolina and some other States have followed her example and Congress on the

21st. of February recommended it to all as the most probable mean of establishing a firm national Government.

Spain availing herself of probable conjectures bids far to be the first power who will strengthen our bonds of Union. Unmindful of her true interest, she seems determined to oppose her partial contracted policy, to that generous reciprocity of mutual good offices, which being the basis of our friendship would be a never failing guarantee to both Nations. She has seized some of our boats on the Mississipi and refuses us absolutely the navigation thereof. Our citizens view this as an infraction of their rights. The States of Virginia, North Carolina, New Jersey and some others have expressed it in strong terms; the words of North Carolina are "That their delegates be instructed to oppose in the most unequivocal terms any attempt that may be made to barter or to surrender to any Nation the right of this State to the free and common Navigation of the Mississipi, and in case any such surrender should take place, that they should be instructed to protest against the same, as an unjust depravation of the right of this State, and one which Congress are not authorized to make by the articles of confederation."

This arose from this additional circumstance. Seven states only counting from the east have repealed the article in favor of the Missisipi in the instructions to Mr. Jay and he is now at full liberty to shut up or not the Missisipi and he appears to me to approve of it for the period of twenty years. Should this take place, I know not what consequences may ensue. Our Western citizens will feel much alarmed for their situation. They will have less confidence in the justice of Congress and be disposed to carve for themselves. They are already numerous and daily increasing. For a violation of a treaty Congress would be immediately responsible and probably our western citizens might skirmish for some years without bringing about an open rupture and within eight or ten we would be able to support our right. What can be done? You may eventually be able to do something. If the French court had the Floridas and would establish an entrepôt at New-Orleans or some other place equally convenient on a liberal scale, it would certainly be of the first consequence to them, in a commercial point of view, as we should consume their manufactures principally, in return for the raw materials which we could supply them with in abundance. With Spain somthing could be done if we had a man of great abilities and prudence at Madrid there to treat; here I am sure we have nothing to hope as I conjecture Mr. Gardoqui has duped himself and consequently given such an impression of things here as to lead his court to be very sanguine in their expectations. And he does not appear to me to be a man of a noble mind enough to acknowledge his error and to give that true complexion which he has certainly learnt to discover.

. . . . .

I am with sincere esteem & regard & Friendship Dear Sir your most obedient hle. Servt.,   Benjamin Hawkins

Boyd, Jefferson Papers, v. 11, pp. 201-203.

John Jay's Report on a Dutch Import Duty Complaint

[New York] Office for foreign Affairs 14th March 1787
The Secretary of the United States for the Department of foreign Affairs, to whom was referred a Letter to him from the Minister of the United Netherlands of the 20th Day of February last enclosing a Note of the same Date, complaining of an Act of the Legislature of the Commonweath of Virginia, exempting french Brandies imported in french and american Vessels from certain Duties, to which the like Commodities imported in dutch Vessels are left liable; as being contrary to the 2d Article in their Treaty with the United States, stipulating that they shall be treated as the *most favored Nation*

Reports

That although he has no official Knowledge of the said Act, yet from the Account given of it in the said Note, and from other Information, he believes that such an Act exists. –

The *second* and *third* Articles in the Treaty with France respect this Subject – the second is in these Words. –

"The most Christian King and the United States engage mutually not to grant any particular Favor to other Nations in respect of Commerce and Navigation, which shall not immediately become common to the other Party, who shall enjoy the same Favor *freely*, if the Concession was freely made, or on allowing the same *Compensation* if the Concession was conditional." –

The second Article in the Treaty with the United Netherlands on the same Subject is in these Words Viz^t

"The Subjects of the said States General of the United Netherlands shall pay, in the Ports, Havens, Roads, Countries, Islands, Cities or Places of the United States of America, or any of them, no other nor greater Duties or Imposts of whatever Nature or Denomination they may be, than those which the Nations the *most favored* are or shall be obliged to pay: And they shall enjoy all the Rights, Liberties, Privileges, Immunities and Exemptions in Trade, Navigation and Commerce which the said Nations do or shall enjoy, whether in passing from one Port to another in the said States, or in going from any of those Ports to any foreign Port of the World, or from any foreign Port of the World to any of those Ports." −

It is observable that this Article takes no Notice of Cases where *Compensation* is granted for Privileges. −

Reason and Equity however in the Opinion of your Secretary will supply this Deficiency, and give to both Articles exactly the same Construction and Operation in those Cases. Where a Privilege is *gratuitously* granted, the Nation to whom it is granted, becomes in respect to *that Privilege* a favored Nation, & from that Circumstance *both* the Articles in Question deduce Claims to the like Favor − but where the Privilege is *not* gratuitous, but rests on *Compact*, in such Case, the Favor, if any there be, does not consist in the *Privilege* yielded, but in the *Consent* to make the Contract by which it is yielded; for Bargains may from their Objects & Circumstances be sometimes so made, as that the *Consent* to make them, may be deemed a Favor. The Favor therefore of being admitted to make a *similar* Bargain, is all that in such Cases can reasonably be demanded under the Article; Besides, it would certainly be inconsistent with the most obvious Principles of Justice and fair Construction, that because France purchases at a *great Price* a Privilege of the United States, that therefore the Dutch shall immediately insist, not on having the like privilege, at the like Price, but *without any Price at all.* −

Supposing that this Reasoning is just, and that the Article ought to be so construed, then the first Question that presents itself in the present Case is − Whether the Grant by Virginia to France of the Privilege in Question is gratuitous or not? −

From the Tenor of the Act it does appear to your Secretary to be gratuitous, and not to partake in the least of the Nature of Compact. −

If this be the true Construction of the Act, then in the Opinion of your Secretary, France did thereupon become, in respect to *the Privilege* granted, a favored Nation, and the Dutch having a Right to be treated as the most favored Nation, have a just Claim to be favored *in like Manner.* −

But they are not favored in like Manner, and they complain of it; and hence arises another Question, Viz$^{t\cdot}$ What is to be done?

According to the present State of our national Government, the Act of Virginia will doubtless continue to exist, and the Dutch will continue to pay more Duties than the French, on Brandies imported there, until the Act is repealed. −

However well disposed Virginia may be, and doubtless is, to correct every Mistake, yet some Time must elapse before the next Session of their Legislature, and therefore the Repeal of the Act cannot take place immediately. −

Your Secretary thinks the two following Resolves would be proper, Viz^{t}

Resolved that whenever any of these States shall think proper to grant a Favor to any foreign Nation, such State ought to extend it to such other foreign Nations, as by Treaties with the United States are to be treated as the most favored Nations.⊗

Resolved that a Copy of the above Resolution and of the Representation of the Minister of the United Netherlands be transmitted to the Commonwealth of Virginia, to the End that the Legislature of that Commonwealth may take the earliest Opportunity of revising the Act of which the said Minister complains, and rendering the same perfectly consistent with the Treaty subsisting between the United States and the United Netherlands; and of causing to be repaid whatever extra Duties may in Virtue of the said Act, be exacted on the Brandies there imported in dutch Vessels, during the Operation of the same. −⊗

As the United States have at present no Minister or Representative at the Hague, through whom it would be most proper to convey whatever Congress might think proper to communicate to their High Mightinesses on the Occasion; your Secretary thinks it would be well to quiet the Minds of the States General on this Subject, by directing that Copies of the aforegoing Resolutions be given to their Minister, and that he be requested to assure their High Mightinesses, that Congress are well persuaded that the Omission of Virginia, in not extending to them the Favor granted to France, was entirely inadvertent and not designed, and they flatter themselves that the said Resolutions, and the Respect with which they will be treated by Virginia, will fully manifest to their High Mightinesses, the good Faith and Friendship of the United States in general and of Virginia in particular. −

Your Secretary thinks he ought not to close this Report without adding a few Remarks which the Consideration of this Subject suggests, and which make a strong Impression on his Mind. −

If individual States go into the Practice of granting Favors to foreign Nations, of what Nature will those Favors be, & what Tendency will such a Practice have? −

By the 6th. Article of the Confederation no particular State can send nor receive Ambassadors, enter into Negociations, contract Engagements, form Alliances, nor conclude Treaties with any Kings, Princes or States whatever, without the Consent of the United States assembled in Congress.−

This Article appears to have been calculated to preserve Uniformity, not only in our political, but also in our commercial Systems. −

If no individual State can contract with a foreign Power, it follows that the States individually can grant no Privileges otherwise than gratuitously.−

But would not such a Practice naturally tend to introduce a Commerce of Favors and of Privileges, and encourage private Intrigues, and Influence to promote and direct it? – Would not the Uniformity and Equality of our commercial System be thereby insensibly deranged? Would not the Balance of foreign Privileges, in Time, become in favor of some States, and against others; and would not the latter be often constrained to grant Favors as Inducements to obtain others? Thus by Degrees there would be *favored*, and *favorite* States – Thus by Degress the foederal Head would become less and less important, and the Bands of the Union become more and more loose and ineffectual. –

Your Secretary in making these Remarks has no particular State in his Eye, he means them as general Remarks, and hopes they will be so received and understood. –

All which is submitted to the Wisdom of Congress. –

John Jay –

read 15 March 1787
Passed. Octr 13th 1787.
⊗ *In the left margin: Agreed Oct. 13.*

NA: PCC, *item 81, v. 3, pp. 193-200 (DS); M247, reel 107.*

John Jay's Report on the Petition of Richard Lawrence

[New York] Office for foreign Affairs 14$^{th.}$ March 1787
The Secretary of the United States for the Department of foreign Affairs to whom was referred the Petition of Richard Lawrence, complaining that he is confined in the Gaol of the City of New York on Actions and Judgments at Law, commenced and had against him according to the Form of an Act of the State of New York, passed the 17$^{th.}$ March 1783, entitled an Act for granting a more effectual Relief in Cases of certain Trespasses –
Reports
That as the said Act is recited at Length in his Report of the 13$^{th.}$ Day of October last, and which also contains his Reasons for considering it as being a direct Violation of the Treaty of Peace, he hath until now postponed reporting on this Petition, in Expectation that the Resolutions of Congress on the Complaints stated in that Report; would reach every Case of the like Nature. But as that Report still remains under Consideration, and as the said Richard Lawrence and other Petitioners still remain confined in Prison, He thinks it his Duty for the Reasons specified in that Report briefly to observe, that in his Opinion the said Act and all

Prosecutions under it for military Damages committed during the late War, are Violations of the Faith of the Treaty of Peace, and as such ought to be done away. –

He forbears reporting any Resolution as proper in his Opinion to be taken on this Head, because he thinks that considering how the national Government is circumstanced, the Resolutions contained in his former Report are the most expedient that he is able to devise. –

All which is submitted to the Wisdom of Congress. –

John Jay –

read 15. March 1787

NA: PCC, *item 81, v. 3, pp. 189-190, 192 (DS); M247, reel 107.*

James Madison to Thomas Jefferson

Dear Sir   N. York. March 19$^{th.}$ 1787.

. . . . . .

The appointments for the Convention go on auspiciously. Since my last Georgia, S. Carolina, N. York, Mass$^{ts.}$ and N. Hampshire have come into the measure....What may be the result of this political experiment cannot be foreseen. The difficulties which present themselves are on one side almost sufficient to dismay the most sanguine, whilst on the other side the most timid are compelled to encounter them by the mortal diseases of the existing constitution....

Congress have continued so thin as to be incompetent to the despatch of the more important business before them. We have at present nine States and it is not improbable that something may now be done. The report of M$^{r.}$ Jay on the mutual violations of the Treaty of peace will be among the first subjects of deliberation. < *** > He favors the British claim of interest but refers the question to the court. The amount of the report which is an able one is that the treaty should be put in force as a law and the exposition of it left like that of other laws to the ordinary tribunals.

The Spanish project sleeps. A perusal of the attempt of seven states to make a new treaty by repealing an essential condition of the old satisfied me that M$^{r.}$ Jay's caution would revolt at so irregular a sanction. A late accidental conversation with Guardoqui proved to me that the negociation is arrested. It may appear strange that a member of Congress should be indebted to a foreign minister for such information. yet such is the footing on which the intemperance of party has put the matter that it rests wholly with M$^{r.}$ Jay how far he will communicate with Congress as well as how far he will negociate with Guardoqui. But although it appears that the

intended sacrifice of the Missisipi will not be made, the consequences of the
intention and the attempt are likely to be very serious. I have already made
known to you the light in which the subject was taken up by Virginia. M^r
Henry's disgust exceeded all measure and I am not singular in ascribing his
refusal to attend the Convention to the policy of keeping himself free to
combat or espouse the result of it according to the result of the Missisipi
business among other circumstances. N. C. also has given pointed
instructions to her delegates, so has New Jersey. A proposition for the like
purpose was a few days ago made in the legislature of Pennsylvania but
went off without a decision on it's merits. Her delegates in Congress are
equally divided on the subject. The tendency of this project to foment
distrusts among the atlantic states at a crisis when harmony and confidence
ought to have been studiously cherished has not been more verified than
[by] it's predicted effect on the ultramontane settlements. I have credible
information that the people living on the Western waters are already in
great agitation & are taking measures, for uniting their consultations. The
ambition of individuals will quickly mix itself with the original motives of
resentment and interest. A communication will gradually take place with
their British neighbors. They will be led to set up for themselves, to seize
on the vacant lands, to entice emigrants by bounties, and an exemption
from federal burthens....It is hinted to me that British partisans are already
feeling the pulse of some of the Western settlements. Should these
apprehensions not be imaginary Spain may have equal reason with the U.S.
to rue the unnatural attempt to shut the Miss: Guardoqui has been
admonished of the danger and I believe is not insensible to it tho' he
affects to be otherwise and talks as if the dependance of Britain on the
commercial favors of his court would induce her to play into the hands of
Spain. The eye of France also can not fail to watch over the Western
prospects. I learn from those who confer here with Otto and delaforest that
they favor the opening of the Miss: disclaim^g at the same time any authority
to speak the sentiments of their court. I find that the Virginia delegates
during the Miss: discussions last fall entered into very confidential
interviews with these gentlemen. In one of them the idea was
communicated to Otto of opening the Miss: for exports but not for imports
and of giving to France and Spain some exclusive privileges in the trade.
He promised to transmit it to Vergennes to obtain his sentiments on the
whole matter and to communicate them to the delegates. Not long since
Grayson[1] called on him and revived the subject. He assured G. that he had
received no answer from France and signified his wish that you might pump
the count de Vergennes < *** > *observing that he would deny to you his
having received any information from America.* I discover thro several channels
that it would be very grateful to the French politicians here to see our

negociations with Spain shifted into your hands, and carried on under the mediating auspices of their court.

Van Berkel has remonstrated against the late acts of Virginia giving privileges to French wines and brandies in French bottoms, contending that the Dutch are entitled by their treaty to equal exemptions with the most favored nation without being subject to a compensation for them. Mr Jay has reported against this construction but considers the act of Virginia as violating the treaty, first because it appears to be gratuitous not compensatory on the face of it. Secondly because the states have no right to form tacit compacts with foreign nations. No decision of Congress has yet taken place on the subject.

...Adieu. Y$^{ns.}$ Af^y Js. Madison Jr

LC: *Madison Papers, microfilm reel 2 (ALS).*
[1] *Grayson, William (ca. 1740-1790). Virginia lawyer and political figure. Aide-de-camp to General Washington during Revolutionary War. Member, Virginia house of delegates, 1784-1785, 1788. Member, Continental Congress, 1785-1787. U.S. Senator, 1789-1790.*

Congressional Resolutions on State Observance of the Treaty of Peace

[New York]   March 21st 1787
On the Report of the Secretary to the United States for the department of foreign Affairs to whom was referred a Letter of the 4th March 1786 from M^r J Adams, minister plenipotentiary of the United States of America at the Court of London, together with the Memorial of the said Minister dated the 30th November 1785 and presented by him on the 8th of December following to his Britannic Majesty's Secretary of State; and the Answer received by Mr Adams to the said Memorial, and contained in a letter from the said Secretary of State dated at St. James's "February 28th 1786," and other papers accompanying the same. –
Congress unanimously agreed to the following Resolutions.
Resolved That the Legislatures of the Several States cannot of right, pass any Act or Acts for interpreting, explaining or construing a National Treaty, or any part or clause of it; nor for restraining, limiting or in any manner impeding, retarding or Counteracting the operation and execution of the same, for that on being constitutionally made, ratified and published they become in Virtue of the Confederation part of the Law of the Land,

and are not only independent of the will and power of such Legislatures, but also binding and obligatory on them. –

Resolved That all such Acts or parts of Acts as may be now existing in any of the States, repugnant to the Treaty of peace, ought to be forthwith repealed, as well to prevent their continuing to be regarded as violations of that Treaty, as to avoid the disagreeable Necessity there might otherwise be of raising and discussing questions touching their Validity and obligation.–

Resolved That it be recommended to the several States to make such Repeal rather by describing than reciting the said Acts, and for that purpose to pass an Act declaring in general terms that all such Acts and parts of Acts repugnant to the Treaty of Peace between the United States and his Britannic Majesty or any Article thereof, shall be and thereby are repealed, and that the Courts of law and equity in all causes and questions cognizable by them respectively, and arising from or touching the said Treaty, shall decide & adjudge according to the true intent and meaning of the same, anything in the said Acts or parts of Acts to the Contrary thereof in any wise nothwithstanding. –   Cha⁵ Thomson sec^y

NA: PCC, *item 122, pp. 75-77 (C); M247, reel 140.*

William Carmichael to Thomas Jefferson

Sir   Madrid March 25th. 1787

I received somewhat later than I should have expected from its date, the Letter you did me the honor to write me the 18th. Ult^o. I have forwarded the duplicate of the recall of Mr Lamb to that Gentleman & have also transmitted to Mr Barclay the joint confirmation of the Morrocco treaty together with the Letter to Fennish which however is without your signature.

Mr Barclay writes me from Barcelona, where he is at present, that he chuses to forward it thro' my channel & that he intends to return it [to] me for that purpose. It is not probable that he will meet Mr Lamb who writes me from Minorca that he means shortly to proceed to N. York. The Latter has occasioned me much chagrin....

· · · · ·

With the highest sentiments of respect & Esteem I have the honor to be Your Excellency Obliged & H^ble. Ser^t.   W^m. Carmichael

LC: *Jefferson Papers, microfilm reel 7 (ALS).*

John Jay's Report on the Status of Phineas Bond

[New York] Office for foreign Affairs 28th March 1787
The Secretary of the United States for the Department of foreign
Affairs, to whom was referred his Letter of 8th December last to his
Excell' the President with two Commissions from his britannic
Majesty dated the 5th Day of April last, the one constituting
Phineas Bond Esq' his Consul for New York, New Jersey
Pensylvania, Delaware and Maryland, the other constituting him
his Majesty's Commissary for commercial Affairs throughout the
United States

Reports

That as his britannic Majesty has no Treaty of Commerce with the
United States, the Admission of his Consuls and Commissaries by them, is
Matter of Favor and not of Right, and therefore that the Propriety of
granting it must turn on Considerations of Expediency. –

Your Secretary perceives one Objection which operates against the
Admission both of the Consul and Commissary in Question, Viz' That it
will add to the Number of official Foreigners in this Country, who considering the present State of our Commerce serve too much to watch and
to circumscribe it. –

How far Britain may have a Right to expect this Mark of Respect and
Civility from the United States, is a Question, respecting which Prejudices
rather too strong, and Opinions not sufficient examined, seem to be
entertained by many of our Citizens. Your Secretary has (he thinks with
Candor and Impartiality) investigated the Causes of the Complaints
subsisting between the two Countries, and he would not be candid were he
not to confess that in his Opinion Britain has more Reason to complain of
the United States than the United States of Britain since the Peace. He is
happy in the Reflection that he serves a Government to whom he can
reveal this Opinion without Offence, and only regrets that Facts oblige him
to entertain it. –

When he considers that it is the Interest of this Country to be on good
Terms with Britain, and how little Advantage can result from cherishing
the Irritation which subsists between them, he thinks it would be wise to
avoid Asperities, and by some Acts of good Humor on our part cultivate
the like Disposition on theirs. –

He finds that all our commercial Treaties provide for the Reception both
of Consuls and Commissaries &ca by express Articles. The french one adds
these words "whose Functions shall be regulated by a particular Agreement."[1]
The Dutch one adds these Words "whose Functions shall be regulated by

particular Agreements, when either Party chooses to make such Appointments."[2]
The Swedish one adds these Words *"whose Functions shall be regulated by a particular Convention."*[3] The Prussian one adds these words *"whose Functions shall be regulated by particular Agreement whenever either Party shall choose to make such Appointment."*[4]

Your Secretary conceives that according to the true Sense and Construction of all these Treaties and Articles, the United States are not bound to receive any Consuls or Commissaries until after their Powers shall have been ascertained by Agreement. –

Although the United States have already received Consuls without such previous Agreement and thereby set a Precedent for receiving more, yet they have not received a single Commissary, and therefore may with Propriety refuse to receive any without such previous and preparatory Convention. And in the Opinion of your Secretary it will be best not to receive any Commissaries from any Nation on other Terms. –

If those ideas should be approved then he thinks it would be well to Resolve as follows

> Whereas Phineas Bond Esq[r] has presented to the United States in Congress assembled a Commission in due Form bearing Date the 5th April 1786 from his britannic Majesty constituting and appointing him the Consul of his said Majesty in the States of New York, New Jersey, Pensylvania, Delaware and Maryland, and although no commercial Treaty or Convention subsists between his Majesty and the United States, whereby either have a perfect Right to establish Consuls or Commissaries in the Dominions of the other, Yet as the United States are disposed by every proper Mark of Liberality and Attention to promote a good Correspondence between the two Countries, and particularly as amicable Negociations are now depending between them – Therefore

> Resolved that the said Phineas Bond Esq[r] be and he hereby is received and recognized as the Consul of his britannic Majesty throughout the States of New York, New Jersey, Pensylvania, Delaware and Maryland, and that his Commission be registered in the Secretary's Office. –

> Resolved that all the Privileges, Pre-eminences and Authority which the Laws of Nations and of the Land give to a Consul received by the United States from any Nation with whom they have no commercial Treaty or Convention, are due to and shall be enjoyed by the said Phineas Bond as Consul for the five States abovementioned, and that certified Copies of these Resolutions be transmitted to the Executives of the said five States for their Information. –

With Respect to Mr Bonds other Commission constituting him a Commissary for commercial Affairs, your Secretary observes that Commissions of this kind are not usual, That the precise Limits of the Authority conferred by it are not easy to ascertain – that the Power it gives him in these Words, Viz^t *"to protect our Merchants and others our Subjects trading to or residing in the said States, or that may have Pretensions depending therein"* is a Power that seems to place him in the Capacity of a Minister in those Respects, and in the Exercise of which it is not improbable that he will make official Applications to Congress. Your Secretary suspects that this Appointment was made to supply in some Sort the place of a Minister; and in his Opinion it will be most prudent not to let it take Effect. –

He thinks it would be advisable for your Secretary to write the following Letter to Mr Adams on the Subject. –

Sir

In Obedience to the Orders of Congress I have the Honor of informing you, that Phineas Bond Esqr has presented to Congress a Commission from his britannic Majesty constituting him Commissary for all commercial Affairs within the United States, and another Commission constituting him Consul for the States of New York, New Jersey, Pensylvania, Delaware and Maryland. –

Congress being desirous on this and every other Occasion to manifest their Disposition, to cultivate a friendly Correspondence with Great Britain, have received Mr Bond in his latter Capacity, although no Treaty or Convention subsists between the two Countries, whereby either have a Right to establish Consuls in the Dominions of the other. –

As yet Congress have not received any Commissaries for commercial Affairs, and they think it most prudent not to receive them from any Nation, until their Powers shall have been previously ascertained by Agreement; lest as those Appointments are seldom made, and both Parties may not have precisely the same Ideas of the Extent of the Powers and Privileges annexed to them, disagreeable Questions and Discussions might and probably would otherwise take place on those delicate Subjects. –

You will be pleased to submit these Reasons to his Majesty, and to assure him that Congress regret the Objections which oppose their complying with his Wishes in this Instance, but that they are ready to join with his Majesty in such Agreements or Conventions as may be necessary to remove them, and which may also tend to promote and establish a friendly and satisfactory commercial Intercourse between the two Countries. –

All which is submitted to the Wisdom of Congress. –   John Jay –

read 29 March 1787

Passed May 3^d 1787 –

¹ In the right margin: "29. Art:"
² In the right margin: "21 Art:"
³ In the right margin: "26. Art:"
⁴ In the right margin: "25. Art:"

NA: PCC, item 81, v. 3, pp. 201-208 (DS); M247, reel 107.

Louis Guillaume Otto to Comte de Montmorin

[Translation]

N°. 84.   New York, 30 March 1787.

My Lord.

M. Van Berkel, Minister of the States General, has delivered to Congress an official note to complain of the exclusive advantages that Virginia has granted to our Commerce, and of which I have had the honor to render You an account in my Despatch N°. 78. This assembly referred its examination to the Virginia Delegates, who came to me to confer on it. We agreed to keep to the letter of the treaty of Commerce with Holland and to respond that the favors granted to our commerce in Virginia were not *gratuitous*, but that they were a compensation for the advantages mentioned in M. de Calonne's letter to Mr. Jefferson. This explanation, although a little forced, will nevertheless produce the good effect of rendering inefficacious Mr. Van Berkel's remonstrances. That Minister has lost his popularity since one of his letters was published in which he exhorts his masters to suppress the smuggling that the Americans conduct with impunity in Surinam and in the other Dutch colonies.

The Virginians, My Lord, do not limit themselves to the favors that they have granted to our brandies and our wines; they propose to extend them to our silks and our cloth. Mr. Grayson, one of their Delegates, who is the most devoted to us, has just told me that he regards this measure as indispensable in order to emancipate his State from the shackles of English Commerce. He himself wants to make the motion concerning it in the next Assembly, and he asked me if a duty of 100 sous per ell on English fabrics would not be equivalent to a prohibition. I pointed out to him that it would be dangerous to carry this measure so far, for fear of having it annulled by a subsequent assembly, but that a modest duty would suffice to place the French Merchant above the competition, which would in addition have the advantage of not exciting the clamors and intrigues of the English party.

He appreciated this reasoning, and he is going to look for ways to get his motion passed. I am entering into these details, My Lord, because Virginia, as well as Carolina, offers the greatest outlet to our Commerce without any comparison. You will see by the enclosed letter from Mr. Jefferson that that Minister infinitely desires to attract the Carolinians to France. The last paragraph of this Letter contains a testimony so evident of his good dispositions towards us that it serves as proof of what I have had the honor to send You previously in this regard.

I am with a profound respect My Lord Your most humble and most obedient Servant   Otto.
rec. 28 May

FFAA: Pol. Corr., U.S., v. 32, f. 230-230vo. and 233 (LC transcription).

Lord Carmarthen to George Miller

Sir.[1]   White hall April 1787.

His Majesty having been graciously pleased, upon the humble Representation and Request of the Merchants of London & Liverpool, trading to South Carolina North Carolina and Georgia, to appoint you to be Consul to those States, and also Deputy Commissary, for Commercial Affairs, to the united States of America, and you having received His Majesty's Commissions accordingly, I have received The King's Commands to direct you to proceed to your Station with as little Delay as possible. On your Arrival in America, you will take the necessary Steps for obtaining the approbation of Congress of your Commissions, in order to your entering on the Duties of your respective Offices. After which you will make the following Points the Objects of your utmost Care and Attention.

You will, from Time to Time make proper Representations to the executive Branches of the Legislature of those States against the Impolicy & Injustice of such Laws and Ordinances as have passed therein, tending to counteract the Endeavours of His Majesty's Subjects in the Recovery of their Debts, in conformity to the 4th Article of the Treaty of Peace.

You will particularly attend to such Representations as may be communicated to you by the Committee of the Merchants interested in the Trade between His Majesty's Dominions and the United States of America, affecting the Property, Navigation and Commerce of British Subjects; and endeavour to obtain such Redress as the Nature of the several Cases will admit of.

You will receive herewith the necessary Instructions which have been transmitted to His Majesty's other Consuls, with the Orders of Council relative to Mediterranean Passes, as well as several Acts of Parliament lately passed, and His Majesty's Proclamation of the 4th Instant for the Regulation of the Trade between Great Britain, America and the West Indies. You will particularly attend to the several Orders & Restrictions therein contained, and use your utmost Endeavours to detect whatever Frauds may be practiced in America with respect to false Registers Passes and other Documents, so as to mask and cover Ship[s] not British, and thereby gain them Admission unto His Majesty's Plantations and Colonies. And you will carefully report to me from Time to Time the Names & Descriptions of all such British Ships as may come within the Limits of Your Consulship, the Masters of which shall refuse to comply with the Whole or any Part of the Regulations contained in the several Acts and Orders of Council above mentioned

You will constantly correspond with His Majesty's Consul General and with the other Consuls and Commissaries residing in America upon all such Points as may be necessary for your mutual Information & Assistance in the Execution of your respective Functions; and you will also from Time to Time communicate to the Merchants of Great Britain all such Information upon Commercial Matters as may appear to affect their Concerns, and transmit to them as well as to me, Copies of all such Acts passed in the several Legislatures within Your District as may appear repugnant to the Commercial Interests of His Majesty's Dominions

You will also transmit to me from Time to Time a particular Account of all such Occurrences as may happen within the District of your Consulship the Knowledge of which you may judge to be in any shape conducive to His Majesty's Service, or interesting to His Majestys Subjects in general.

Carmarthen

PRO: FO 4/5, pp. 203-208 (LC transcription).

^{1} Miller, George. American loyalist who served as British Consul for North Carolina, South Carolina and Georgia, resident in Charleston, beginning in 1787.

Congressional Order to John Jay on the Spanish Negotiations

[New York] April 4th 1787

Ordered That the Secretary for foreign affairs give information to Congress of the State of his Negotiation with the Encargado de Negocios of Spain, and that an actual State of that business be laid before Congress. –

Chas Thomson Sec^y

NA: PCC, item 122, p. 80 (C); M247, reel 140.

Peter Allaire: Occurrences
from 7 March to 5 April 1787

Sir,   New York 5 April 1787
    In my last I informed You that a Person in Congress would do business
with your house on a liberal plan, how I came to propose it I have Already
communicated to You, since which we have fully canvassed the matter, and
will send such samples as lays within the line of his business, every Packet
directed to such Person as shall be named in England, neither the Contents
or the Packet am I to be trusted with, he taking on himself to send them,
as my detaining one letter, would for ever put it in my power to ruin him.
he leaves me in about a fortnight to meet the Delegates at Philadelphia, he
being one Appointed by his State for the forming of the New federal Union
And proposes Returning in October or November next by which time I
expect Your Answer, his proposals are to have his Commissions paid on
being Employed. I think he may be trusted, should he Accept of your
proposal, if you think such a Person Requisite for I am convinced he could
be of more Real Service than half doz Tem— & B–ds, the first thinks the
Post beneath him, Since his being a Baronet & the other not bred up, or
knows anything of the Mercantile line, he has been ever since his Arrival
here endeavouring by the Assistance of his friends, to get his Attainder
Repealed by the Interest of that Old Rascal Franklin, but nothing is yet
done. Several of the Congress have Assured me they do not think that B–d
will be Acknowledged Commercial Agent, suppose they do, he can be of
very little Utility to his Employers, & no benefit to the Commercial
Interest. nor has either T–p–le or B–d the Spirit of an Englishman tamely
to see English Subjects deprived of their liberty and property without
Remonstrating, they do not know their Duty, nor the power invested in
them, nor how to protect their Masters Subjects – An Englishman has
been imprisoned on a charge of Murder for having during the War, gone
into Jersey & killd a Man, having met with Opposition on a forageing
party, & a Bill has passed the Assembly to grant Relief to Merchants
Against British Creditors only; yet those Gentlemen sit quiet and tamely
bear the Insult.

                        .   .   .   .   .
I Remain with Respect   P. A.

Occurrences from 7 March to [5] April 1787.
March 7. A Report having prevailed that the Boston Insurgents had taken
shelter in this state, the Senate & Assembly met, & Ordered the Governor,

Adjudant General & Attorney General, up to Pokeepsie (about 120 Miles above N York on the North River) with Orders to call out the Militia, on their Arrival there the Insurgents retired to the State of Vermont, a few days before the Governor arrived, a M[r] Hindman[1] with a party of Eighty Insurgents, Attacked a party of Lincolns Army of about 90, neither side came of Victorious, they both retired, Government lost Six Men & Twelve Wounded, the Insurgents left 4 Killed & carried off their wounded, supposed about Twenty....

.   .   .   .   .

The Army of the Insurgents have gone into the State of Vermont until the weather will permit them to take the feild, their Leaders, Shays, Days, and Wheeler,[1] are gone to Canada to endeavour to procure Assistance from Lord Dorchester, General Lincoln by Order of the Executive of Boston, has sent an Express to his Lordship, desiring him to deliver up the Rebels, Days, Shays & Wheeler, the Executive of Boston, have also Issued a Proclamation forbiding all persons from purchasing any of the landed property of any of the Insurgents, until they have been acquitted by due course of Law, also, ordering the Civil and Military power to prevent any Person or Persons from moving out of the States (many families since the Troubles have removed with their goods & Chatels into the State of Vermont, exceeding Two thousand Souls.)

.   .   .   .   .

The State of New York has granted Relief to Certain Merch[ts] Against British Creditors (freeing their Persons from Arrest &[c] a pointed Insult to Great Britain, as all other Nations have the priveledge of Recovering their Debt by the common Course of Law. Yet neither of the Above Gentlemen have thought proper to put in a Memorial against such unjust proceedings, M[r] B— is solely intent on pleasing and geting into favour of that Jessuit Franklin, in hopes through his means, to be admitted to stay in the State of Pensilvania he (being proscribed by that State as a Rebel) tho it is generally said that Congress will not Receive him.

Your Navigation Act, is felt more & more every day And a few proper Persons Appointed in this Country, with those You have in the West Indies would in a few Years make the British Carriers for Almost all America.

.   .   .   .   .

The last Acco[ts] received, are that Days & Shays are at Vermont enlisting Men, having Returned from Canada that the State of Rhode Island has granted protection to the Insurgents & that Wiley[1] & Parsons[1] are enlisting Men in that State, the Weathers being uncommonly cold has prevented them from Assembling, what their intent is, time only can discover.

I have the honor to be   P. A.

PRO: FO 4/5, pp. 173-177, 179-186 (LC transcription).
[1] Hindman, Wheeler, Wiley and Parsons. Presumably subordinate leaders in Shays' Rebellion.

Louis Guillaume Otto to Comte de Montmorin

[Translation]

N 85   New York, 10 April 1787.

My Lord

The insufficiency of the present Confederation and the absolute necessity of remodeling it completely are so well perceived that most of the states have without delay named Delegates charged to assemble in Philadelphia in order to agree on a new system of Government less defective and less precarious than that which exists at this moment, or rather what *should* exist.

Congress is really only a phantom of sovereignty destitute of powers, of energy, and of consideration, and the edifice that it should support is falling into ruin. This Assembly, fearing to lose the little renown that remains to it, at least wished to seem to suggest the idea of a new *General Convention*; it is in these lights that it published the enclosed resolution. Rhode Island is hitherto the only State that has positively refused to send Delegates to Philadelphia; this conduct, joined to several other equally uncivil and imprudent measures, has rendered it completely contemptible in America. The public papers are filled with sarcasm against that little republic, and unfortunately it appears to merit all the evil that is said of it.

If all the Delegates named for this Philadelphia convention attend, there will never have been seen, even in Europe, an Assembly more respectable for the talents, knowledge, disinterest and patriotism of those who compose it. General Washington, Dr. Franklin, and a great number of other distinguished personages, although less known in Europe, are named to it. It cannot be doubted that the interests of the confederation will be more solidly discussed there than they have ever been. A sad experience of several years proves only too well that it is impossible for things to remain on the present footing. During the war Congress borrowed, so to speak, its strength from the English armies that infested the States from all parts; the paper money that it could create infinitely, the subsidies from France, the enthusiasm and the patriotism of individuals, the confiscations, the numerous troops gave it an importance that vanished at the moment of the peace. It is therefore a question of adopting a new plan of confederation, of giving to Congress coercive powers, considerable imposts, an army, the right to exclusively regulate the Commerce of all the States. — But this new general Assembly itself only has the power to propose. Would the States wish to allow themselves to be divested of a part of their Sovereignty? Would they consent to be no more than provinces of a great Empire? Could the Majority of the States make the law for those who do not wish to sacrifice their current independence? — That is what one has reason to doubt; but I must endeavor, My Lord, to present to You facts and not conjectures.

I cannot however refrain from observing to You, that although this new Convention may be the sole means of reconciling the scattered members of the Confederation, the most educated Americans are very far from regarding it as sufficient. There prevails in the formation of these States a radical flaw that will perhaps always be opposed to a perfect union; it is that the States really have no pressing interest to be under a single leader. Their politics, which are limited to their commercial speculations, inspire them even reciprocally with aversion and jealousy: passions that were absorbed during the war by the enthusiasm of liberty and of independence, but that begin to recapture all their force. – These republicans no longer have Philip at their portals, and as they threw off the yoke of England in order not to pay taxes, they bear with impatience that of a Congress that can only charge them imposts without offering them any protection against enemies that no longer exist. The confederation is really supported only by the Aristocratic party, and that party weakens daily. The Cincinnati and all the public Creditors are in this class, but in proportion as they are ruined by the intrigues of the opposite party or by the exhaustion of the continental treasury, they become plebeians to obtain positions of confidence or at least to have the wherewithal to live; others are going to carry their industry and the feeble debris of their fortune into the western districts; a small number of them go to England.

I am with a profound respect My Lord Your most humble and most obedient servant   Otto.
rec. 28 May

FFAA: Pol. Corr., U.S., v. 32, f. 237-238vo. and 240 (LC transcription).

John Jay to the President of Congress

Sir   [New York] Office of foreign Affairs 11th April 1787
   In obedience to the Order of Congress directing me to give Information
of the State of my Negociation with the Encargado de Negocios of Spain
&c., I have the Honor of informing your Excellency that on the 6th
October last I wrote the following Letter to M[r] Gardoqui, Viz[t1]

.   .   .   .   .

   That I have since had several Conferences with M[r] Gardoqui on the well
known Points in Difference between us, Viz[t] on the Navigation of the River
Missisippi and on the Limits. –
   With Respect to the first Point we have had repeated Conversations
which produced nothing but Debate and in the Course of which we did not
advance one single Step nearer to each other. He continued and still
continues decided in refusing to admit us to navigate the River below our
Limits on any Terms or Conditions, nor will he consent to any Article
*declaring our Right in express Terms, and stipulating to forbear the Use of it for
a given Time.* But he did not appear to me so decidedly opposed to the same
Ideas in the Way of *Implication* – though he did not say so. I drew that
Inference from a Number of Circumstances, but yet he said nothing so
unequivocal to warrant it, as to commit himself. I thought it therefore
advisable to try how far he would silently yield to that Idea; and therefore
drew up Articles in a Variety of Shapes, *clearly implying the Right,* and
expressly forbearing the Use during the Term of the Treaty. These Drafts he
positively refused to admit; and finding that Arguments in Support of them
rather irritated than convinced him, we parted without doing any Thing.
Subsequent Conferences took place, and he continuing inflexible in refusing
the Articles as they stood, we gradually but very cautiously talked of
Amendments. It was my Business to endeavor to change the *Dress* but
retain the *Spirit and Sense* – many Difficulties and Questions unnecessary
to detail, occurred – It was however finally so adjusted as in my Opinion
to save the *Right* and only suspend the *Use* during the Term of the Treaty;
at the Expiration of which this and every other Article in it would become
null and void. It is as follows Viz[t]
   "And to the End that this Treaty may the more effectually provide for
the Continuance of that perfect Harmony which at present happily subsists
between his Catholic Majesty and the United States; and that all
Differences and Questions which might otherwise arise respecting the
Navigation of the River Missisippi may be avoided & obviated by an
amicable Stipulation on that Subject. As his Catholic Majesty's System of
Government & Policy prohibits all foreign Trade, Intercourse and Com-

merce within his Territories, and as the United States are desirous as far as possible to meet the Wishes of his Majesty, and to evince the Sense they entertain of his friendly Disposition towards them, and of the recent Proofs he has been pleased to give them of it, Therefore it is expressly stipulated and concluded that his Catholic Majesty and the United States are freely, and in common, and without receiving any Interruption from each other, to use and navigate the said River from its Source down to the southern Boundary of the said States; And that the United States will faithfully observe that Limitation, and not navigate or use the said River below, or further down than the said Boundary in any part of its Course therefrom through his Majesty's Countries to the Mouth thereof." –

Congress will doubtless observe that the Reasons assigned in this Article for Forbearance, militate against a Supposition of his Majestys having an exclusive Right; for it does not either admit *his* Right or relinquish *ours*, but on the contrary, in Order to avoid and obviate Differences and Questions, to suit his Majesty's System of Government and Policy, to meet the King's Wishes, and to evince our Sense of his Friendship – it only stipulate *not to use &ca:* –

On that and every other Occasion I thought it best to be very candid with Mr Gardoqui – I told him that he must not conclude that what I might think expedient would also be deemed so by Congress, and hoped that when he considered they were sitting in the same Place with us, he would see the Propriety of my observing the greatest Delicacy and Respect towards them. –

As to the Limits, I have Reason from him to believe that notwith-standing the Extent of their Claims, he would in Case all other Matters were satisfactorily adjusted, so far recede as to give up to us all the Territories not comprehended within the Floridas as ascertained by our separate and secret Article with Great Britain, of which I early perceived that he was well informed. –

As he could not in any Manner be drawn lower down than this Line, it struck me that it would be prudent to confine if possible all Questions of Limits to the Land between the two Lines; and therefore hinted the Expediency of settling the Dispute so limited by Commissioners – He expressed no Reluctance to this, and I believe he has written for In-structions on that Point but am not certain. He seemed very cautious of committing himself; and I cannot now say that he admitted our Right to extend down to the first Line, but only gave me to understand that, all other Things being agreed, his Majesty from Motives of Accommodation might be content with that Limitation. –

These are the Facts, and so Matters at present stand between him and me. A Variety of Circumstances and Considerations which I need not mention, render this Negociation dilatory, unpleasant and unpromising; and it is much to be wished that the United States could jointly and unanimously adopt and pursue some fixed and stable Plan of Policy in Regard to Spain, especially during the Residence of Mr Gardodqui, who I do verily believe is sincerely disposed to do every Thing useful and acceptable to America, that his Instructions and the essential Interests of his Country, as understood by him and his Master, will permit. –

I have the Honor to be with great Respect & Esteem Your Excellency's Most Ob^t and hble: Servant   John Jay

NA: PCC, *item 81, v. 3, pp. 227-232 (DS); M247, reel 107.*
^{1} *See Jay to Gardoqui, 6 October 1786, supra.*

John Adams to William Stephens Smith

[Grosvenor Square London 11 April 1787]^1

The Secretary of the United States of America for the department of foreign Affaires, His Excellency John Jay to whom was referred a letter to him from the Honourable John Adams of the 27th of June last, informing that the Queen of Portugal had ordered her Squadron in the Straits to protect the Vessels of the United States, equally with those of her own Subjects; on the 25th day of January last reported, that in his opinion, as this is a particular mark of her majesty's friendly disposition, it should be acknowledged in the manner most likely to be pleasing and acceptable. He therefore thought it would be proper for Congress to write her a letter of the following tenor – Great and good friend –

We take the earliest oppertunity, since our annual election, of presenting to your Majesty our sincere Acknowledgements, for the friendly regard you have manifested for us, in having ordered your Squadron in the Straits to protect our Vessels equally with those of Portugal – Permit us to assure you that we shall retain this mark of generous attention in grateful Remembrance, and shall omit no opportunity of testifying our desire to establish & perpetuate between our two Countries, an intercourse of Commerce and good offices which may prove no less benefical than agreable to both.

We pray God to bless and preserve your Majesty. Done by the Congress of the United States convened at the City of New York the   Day of 1787.

As this Communication was made by the Queens Envoy in London to Mr Adams their Secretary thought this Letter should be transmitted to him, and that the Compliment would be more delicate if his Secretary was commissioned to carry & deliver it. –

The United States in Congress assembled on the third day of February 1787 ordered that the report of the secretary of foreign affairs dated 25th January 1787 on a Letter of 27th June last from Mr Adams, be referred to the said Secretary to take order for the transmission of the Letter to the Queen of Portugal, when signed by the President, in the manner suggested in said Report.

These therefore, are to authorise and require, you in pursuance of the instructions of Congress to proceed to Portugal and deliver their Letter, herewith presented to you, to Her Faithfull Majesty, either with your own hand in an audience to be obtained for that purpose, or by the hand of her Majesty's Minister of State for foreign affairs as you shall find upon enquiry to be most proper

You are first to consult with Her Majestys Minister of State for foreign affairs, deliver him a Copy of this Commission which contains a Copy of the Letter of Congress to Her Majesty, and follow his advice, concerning the manner of delivering it – Done at Grovenor Square in London this Eleventh Day of April. A.D. 1787.   John Adams

NA: PCC, item 92, pp. 320-321 (C); M247, reel 120.

[1] Smith, William Stephens (1755-1816). Military officer, diplomat, and political figure. Continental Army officer, 1776-1783, with service under John Sullivan, Israel Putnam, and the Marquis de Lafayette. Appointed aide to Washington, July 1781. Supervised British evacuation of New York, 1783. Secretary of legation in Great Britain, 1785-1788. Son-in-law of John Adams. Federal marshal, supervisor of the revenue, and surveyor of the port of New York. Prosecuted, but acquitted, for helping Francisco de Miranda with his filibustering expedition to South America, 1806. Member, U.S. House of Representatives, 1813-1816.

John Jay's Report on George Rogers Clark's Seizure of Spanish Property

[New York] Office for foreign Affairs 12th April 1787 The Secretary of the United States for the Department of foreign Affairs, to whom was referred certain Papers communicated to Congress by the Honorable the Delegates of Virginia and North Carolina,

Reports –

That he presumes the Designs of Congress in referring these Papers to him was, that he should report only on such Matters stated in them, as respect foreign Affairs. –

It appears from the Act of the Council of Virginia of 28th February last, "that General Clarke hath made a Seizure of spanish Property without any Authority for such an Act," and that the Executive of that Commonwealth hath with great Propriety, directed such Steps to be taken "as may subject to Punishment all Persons guilty in the Premises." – They also ordered a Copy of the Act to be sent to their Delegates, that they might if it should seem expedient, acquaint the Minister of his Catholic Majesty with the Sentiments of the Executive expressed in it. –

From the Temper visible in some of the Papers sent from the Western Country, as well as from the Intelligence they convey, your Secretary apprehends that the Period is not distant when the United States must decide either to wage War with Spain, or settle all Differences with her by Treaty, on the best Terms in their Power. But as his Sentiments on this Head have already been candidly and explicity submitted to Congress, a Repetition of them would be improper, because unnecessary. –

He thinks that on the present Occasion the following Resolutions would be adviseble Viz^t –

> Resolved that the United States in Congress assembled learn with Concern and Displeasure, that certain Citizens of the Commonwealth of Virginia, have in Violation of the Laws of Nations, and of the Peace and Dignity of that State, and of the United States, violently seized the Property of certain Subjects of his Catholic Majesty at Fort St Vincennes ~~Resolved~~ and that Congress approve of the Act of the Executive of Virginia, directing proper Measures to be immediately taken for punishing the Offenders, – And further that the Secretary at War be and he hereby is directed, to order the commanding Officers of Detachments in the Western Country to afford the Government of Virginia such Aid as the Governor may from time to time require and specify, for keeping the Peace, and duly executing the Laws of that Commonwealth throughout its western Jurisdiction; and further that they be careful, on due Proof, to apprehend and deliver to the Government of Virginia, all such of the said Offenders as may be in the Dominions of the United States, without the proper Limits of either of the States. –

> Resolved that although no Representations on this Subject have as yet been made to Congress by, or on the Part of his Catholic Majesty, yet as their ready Attention to whatever may affect the

Friendship happily subsisting between him and them, will manifest the Sincerity of their Desire to maintain it, the Secretary for foreign Affairs be and he hereby is directed, to transmit Copies of this and the aforegoing Resolutions to the Encargado de Negocios of his Catholic Majesty now here, and also to the Chargé des Affaires of the United States at Madrid. –

It appears to your Secretary to be most consistent with the Principles of the Confederation, and with the Dignity of Congress, that individual States forbear to make formal Representations or Communications to foreign Ministers or Powers, but through and by Means of the federal Sovereign.

The Papers communicated to Congress by the Honorable the Delegates of North Corolina, shew

That on the 6th June 1786 Thomis Amis of that State arrived at the Natches on the Missisippi, with sundry Articles of Merchandize which he purposed to carry down, and out of the River – And that he was stopped, and his Merchandize taken from him by the Spanish Officer commanding there. –

It is well known that Spain will not permit our People to navigate that part of the River which runs through their Countries, and such of them as make the Experiment must expect Consequences similar to those which Mr Amis experienced. –

Your Secretary is convinced that the United States have good Right to navigate the River from its Source to, and through its Mouth; and unless an Accommodation should take place; that the Dignity of the United States and their Duty to assert and maintain their Rights, will render it proper for them to present a Memorial and Remonstrance to his Catholic Majesty, insisting on their Right, complaining of its being violated, and demanding in a temperate, inoffensive but at the same Time in a firm and decided Manner, that his Majesty do cease in future to hinder their Citizens from freely navigating that River, through the part of its Course in Question. Your Secretary is further of Opinion, that in Case of Refusal, it will be proper for the United States then to declare War against Spain. –

There being no reputable middle Way between Peace and War, it will be expedient to prepare without Delay for the one or the other; for Circumstances which call for Decision seem daily to accumulate. –

If Congress conceive that a Treaty with Spain on the Terms proposed is eligible, the sooner such Sentiments are communicated to your Secretary the better. If an Idea of obtaining better Terms should be entertained, the sooner that Question can be decided the better; and for that Purpose your Secretary thinks it would be well, either to place some other Negociator in his Stead, or to associate one or more Persons with him in the Business –

any Manner of conducting it most advantageous and most satisfactory to his Country, will always be the Manner most pleasing and agreeable to him. –

With Respect to prescribing a Line of Conduct to our Citizens on the Banks of the River, your Secretary is embarrassed. If War is in Expectation, then their Ardor should not be discouraged, nor their Indignation diminished – but if a Treaty is wished and contemplated, then those People should be so advised and so restrained as that their Sentiments & Conduct may as much as possible be made to quadrate with the Terms and Articles of it. Your Secretary cannot forbear to express his Solicitude that this very important and consequential Business may not be left in its present Situation – the Objects involved in it are of great Magnitude, and Effects must and will result from it, by which the Prosperity of America will be either greatly advanced, or greatly retarded. He also takes the Liberty of observing, that a Treaty disagreeable to one half of the Nation had better not be made, for it would be violated – and that a War disliked by the other half, would promise but little Success, especially under a Government so greatly influenced and affected by popular Opinion. –

All which is submitted to the Wisdom of Congress. –

John Jay –

read. April 13th. 1787 –
Assigned – for Wednesday 18th April – 1787 –

NA: PCC, item 81, v. 3, pp. 235-240, 242 (DS); M247, reel 107.

President of Congress to the State Governors

Sir, [New York April 13, 1787]

Our Secretary for foreign affairs has transmitted to you Copies of a letter to him from our Minister at the Court of London of the 4th day of March 1786, and of the papers mentioned to have been enclosed with it.

We have deliberately and dispassionately examined and considered the several facts and matters urged by Britain as infractions of the Treaty of peace on the part of America; and we regret that in some of the States too little attention appears to have been paid to the public faith pledged by that Treaty. –

Not only the obvious dictates of Religion, Morality and National honor, but also the first principles of good policy, demand a candid and punctual compliance with engagements constitutionally and fairly made. –

Our National constitution having committed to us the management of the National concerns with foreign States and powers; it is our duty to take care, that all the rights which they ought to enjoy within our Jurisdiction by the Laws of Nations, and the faith of Treaties remain inviolate. And it is also our duty to provide that the essential interests and peace of the whole confederacy be not impaired or endangered by deviations from the line of public faith into which any of its members may from whatever causes be unadvisedly drawn. –

Let it be remembered that the Thirteen Independent Sovereign States ~~has~~ have by express delegation of power formed and Vested in us a general, though limited Sovereignty, for the general and National purposes specified in the Confederation. In this Sovereignty they cannot severally participate (except by their delegates) nor with it have concurrent Jurisdiction; for the 9th Article of the Confederation most expressly conveys to us, the sole and exclusive right and power of determining on War and peace, and of entering into Treaties and Alliances &c. –

When therefore a Treaty is Constitutionally made – ratified and published by us, it immediately becomes binding on the whole Nation, and superadded to the Laws of the land, without the intervention of State Legislatures. Treaties derive their obligation from being compacts between the Sovereign of this, and the Sovereign of another Nation, whereas Laws or Statutes derive their force from being the Acts of a Legislature competent to the passing of them. Hence it is clear that Treaties must be implicitly received and observed by every member of the Nation; for as State Legislatures are not competent to the making of such Compacts or Treaties, so neither are they competent in that capacity, authoritatively to decide on, or ascertain the construction and Sense of them. When doubts arise respecting the construction of State Laws, it is not unusual nor improper for the State Legislatures by explanatory or declaratory Acts to remove those doubts – but the case between Laws and Compacts or Treaties, is in this widely different, for when doubts arise respecting the sense and meaning of a Treaty they are so far from being cognizable by a State Legislature that the United States in Congress Assembled have no authority to settle and determine them. For as the Legislature only which constitutionally passes a Law has power to revise and amend it, so the Sovereigns only who are parties to the Treaty have power by mutual consent, and posterior Articles to correct or explain it. –

In cases between Individuals all doubts respecting the meaning of a Treaty, like all doubts respecting the meaning of a Law are in the first instance mere Judicial questions, and are to be heard and decided in the Courts of Justice having cognizance of the causes in which they arise, and whose duty it is to determine them according to the Rules and maxims established by the laws of Nations for the interpretation of Treaties. From these principles it follows of Necessary consequence that no individual State has a right by Legislative Acts to decide and point out the sense in which their particular Citizens and Courts shall understand this or that Article of a Treaty. –

It is evident that a contrary doctrine would not only Militate against the common and established maxims and ideas relative to this subject, but would prove no less inconvenient in practice than it is irrational in Theory; for in that case the same Article of the same Treaty might by Law be made to mean one thing in New Hampshire, another thing in New York, and neither the one nor the other of them in Georgia. –

How far such Legislative Acts would be Valid and obligatory even within the limits of the State passing them, is a question which we hope never to have occasion to discuss. Certain however it is that such Acts cannot bind either of the contracting Sovereigns, and consequently cannot be obligatory on their respective Nations. –

But if Treaties and every Article in them be (as they are and ought to be) binding on the whole Nation, if individual States have no right to accept some Articles and reject others, and if the impropriety of State Acts to interpret and decide the sense and construction of them be apparent; still more manifest must be the impropriety of State Acts to controul, delay or modify the operation and execution of these National compacts. –

When it is considered that the several States Assembled by their delegates in Congress have express power to form treaties, surely the Treaties so formed are not afterwards to be Subject to such alterations as this or that State Legislature may think expedient to make, and that too without the consent of either of the parties to it – that is in the present case without the consent of all the United States who collectively are parties to this Treaty on the one side and his Britannic Majesty on the other. Were the Legislatures to possess and to exercise such power, we should soon be involved as a Nation in Anarchy and confusion at home, and in disputes which would probably terminate in hostilities and War with the Nations with whom we may have formed Treaties. Instances would then be frequent, of Treaties fully executed in one State, and only partly executed in another, and of the same Article being executed in one manner in one State, and in a different manner or not at all in another State. History furnishes no precedent of such liberties taken with Treaties under form of Law in any Nation. –

Contracts between Nations like Contracts between individuals should be faithfully executed, even though the Sword in the one case and the Law in the other did not compel it – honest Nations like honest men require no constraints to do Justice; and though Impunity and the Necessity of Affairs may sometimes afford temptations to pare down contracts to the measure of Convenience yet it is never done but at the expence of that esteem, and confidence, and credit, which are of infinitely more worth than all the momentary advantages which such expedients can extort. But although contracting Nations cannot like individuals avail themselves of Courts of Justice to compel performance of Contracts; yet an appeal to heaven and to Arms is always in their power, and often in their inclination. –

But it is their duty to take care that they never lead their people to make and support such appeals, unless the Sincerity and propriety of their conduct affords them good reason to rely with confidence on the Justice and protection of Heaven. –

Thus much we think it useful to observe in order to explain the principles on which we have Unanimously come to the following Resolution Viz^t "Resolved That the Legislatures of the several States cannot, of right pass any act or acts for interpreting, explaining or construing a National Treaty, or any part or clause of it, nor for restraining, limiting or in any manner impeding, retarding or counteracting the operation and execution of the same, for that on being constitutionally made, ratified and published they become in Virtue of the Confederation part of the Law of the Land, and are not only independent of the will and power of such Legislatures but also binding and obligatory on them." –

As the Treaty of peace so far as it respects the matters and things provided for in it, is a law to the United States which cannot by all or any of them be altered or changed, all State Acts establishing provisions relative to the same objects which are incompatible with it must in every point of View be improper. Such Acts do nevertheless exist, but we do not think it Necessary either to enumerate them particularly, or to make them severally the subjects of discussion. – It appears to us sufficient to observe and insist that the Treaty ought to have free course in its operation and execution and that all obstacles interposed by State Acts be removed. We mean to act with the most Scrupulous regard to Justice and Candor towards Great Britain, and with an equal degree of delicacy, ~~and~~ Moderation, and decision towards the States who have given occasion to these discussions. –

For these reasons we have in general terms "Resolved That all such acts or parts of Acts as may be now existing in any of the States repugnant to the Treaty of peace ought to be forthwith repealed, as well to prevent their continuing to be regarded as Violations of that Treaty as to avoid the disagreeable Necessity there might otherwise be of raising and discussing questions touching their Validity and obligation." –

Although this Resolution applies Strictly only to such of the States as have passed the exceptionable Acts alluded to, yet to obviate all future disputes and questions, as well as to remove those which now exist, we think it best that every State without exception should pass a law on the Subject. We have therefore "Resolved That it be recommended to the several States to make such repeal rather by describing than reciting the said Acts, and for that purpose to pass an Act declaring in general terms that all such Acts and parts of Acts repugnant to the Treaty of peace between the United States and his Britannic Majesty or any Article thereof shall be and thereby are repealed, and that the Courts of Law and equity in all cases and questions cognizable by them respectively, and arising from or touching the said Treaty shall decide and adjudge according to the true intent and meaning of the same, any thing in the said Acts or parts of Acts to the contrary thereof in anywise notwithstanding." –

Such Laws would answer every purpose, and be easily formed – The more they were of the like tenor throughout the States, the better. They might each recite that, Whereas certain Laws or Statutes made and passed in some of the States, are regarded and complained of, as repugnant to the Treaty of peace with Great Britain, by reason whereof, not only the good faith of the United States pledged by that Treaty, has been drawn into question, but their essential Interests under that Treaty greatly affected. And whereas Justice to great Britain, as well as regard to the honor and Interests of the United States, require that the said Treaty be faithfully executed, and that all obstacles thereto, and particularly such as do or may be construed to proceed from the Laws of this State, be effectually removed – Therefore:

Be it enacted by   and it is hereby enacted by the authority of the same that such of the Acts or parts of Acts of the Legislature of this State, as are repugnant to the Treaty of peace between the United States and his Britannic Majesty or any Article thereof, shall be and hereby are repealed; and further that the Courts of Law and equity within this State, be and they hereby are directed and required, in all causes and questions cognizable by them respectively, and arising from or touching the said Treaty, to decide and adjudge according to the Tenor, true intent and meaning of the same, any thing in the said Acts or parts of Acts to the contrary thereof in anywise notwithstanding –

Such a general Law would we think be preferable to one, that should minutely enumerate the Acts and clauses intended to be repealed; because Omissions might accidentally be made in the enumeration, or Questions might arise, and perhaps not be satisfactorily determined respecting particular Acts or clauses about which contrary opinions may be entertained. By repealing in general terms all Acts and clauses Repugnant to the Treaty, the business will be turned over to its proper department Viz.ᵗ the Judicial, and the Courts of Law will find no difficulty in deciding whether any particular Act or clause is, or is not contrary to the Treaty. Besides when it is considered that the Judges in general are men of Character and Learning and feel as well as know the obligations of Office, and the Value of Reputation, there is no reason to doubt, that their conduct and Judgments relative to these, as well as other Judicial matters will be wise and upright.

Be pleased Sir to lay this letter before the Legislature of your State without delay. We flatter ourselves they will concur with us in Opinion that candor and Justice are as Necessary to true policy as they are to sound Morality, and that the most honorable way of delivering ourselves from the embarrassment of mistakes is fairly to correct them. It certainly is time that all doubts respecting the public faith be removed and that all questions and differences between us and Great Britain be amicably and finally settled. The States are informed of the reasons why his Britannic Majesty still continues to occupy the frontier posts which by the Treaty he agreed to evacuate: And we have the strongest assurances that an exact compliance with the Treaty on our part shall be followed by a punctual performance of it on the part of Great Britain. –

It is important that the several Legislatures should as soon as possible take these matters into consideration, and we request the favor of you to transmit to us, an authenticated copy of such Acts and proceedings of the Legislature of your State as may take place on the Subject, and in pursuance of this Letter. –

By order of Congress

A. St. C. President
Chas Thomson Secy

NA: PCC, *item* 122, *pp.* 81-88 (C); M247, *reel* 140.

James Madison's Motions Regarding Negotiations with Spain

[New York April 18, 1787]

Resolved that the present State of the negociations with Spain, and of the Affairs of the United States, renders it expedient that the Minister Plenipotentiary at the Court of France, should proceed under a special Commission to the Court of Madrid, there to make such representations, and to urge such negociations, as will be most likely to impress on the said Court the friendly disposition of the United States, and to induce it to make such concessions and arrangements touching the Southern limit of the U.S. and their right to navigate the Mississippi below the same, and to enter into such commercial Stipulations with the United States, as may most effectually guard agst. a rupture of the subsisting harmony, and promote the mutual interests of the two nations.

Resolved that the Secretary for the department of Foreign Affairs prepare and report the instructions proper to be given to the said Minister

Plenipotentiary, with a proper commission and letter of Credence; and that he also report the communications and explanations which it may be advisable to make to Mr Guardoqui relative to this change in the mode of conducting the negociations with his Court.

NA: PCC, *item 81, v. 3, p. 95 (AD)*; M247, reel 107.

John Adams to John Jay

Dear Sir   London April 19. 1787
    I do myself the Honour to inclose the New Act of Parliament for regulating the Trade between the Territories of the United States of America and the Dominions of the King of Great Britain, by which Congress will see that the Same System continues, and is fortified with fresh Provisions. Provisions & Lumber, the Growth or Production of the United States are now, prohibited, from any foreign Island. The West India Planters and Merchants complain, to no purpose.
    The Canada Merchants give out, that there is some Negotiation on foot between Lord Dorchester and Vermont, the Object of which is to give Vent to the Productions of that Territory, thro Canada and the River St Lawrence, that the West Indies may derive some Assistance, from that Source.

                          .   .   .   .
    With great Regard, I have the Honour to be, Sir your most obedient and most humble Servant   John Adams

NA: PCC, *item 84, v. 6, pp. 443-444 (ALS)*; M247, reel 113.

John Jay's Report on Moving Negotiations with Spain to Madrid

[New York] Office for foreign Affairs 20 April 1787
The Secretary of the United States for the Department of foreign Affairs to whom was referred a Motion made the 18th April Instant, by the Honble Mr Madison in these words, Viz^t "Resolved that the present State of the negociations with Spain and of the Affairs of the United States, renders it expedient that the minister Plenipotentiary at the Court of France, should proceed under a Special Commission to the Court of Madrid, there to make such

Representations, and to urge such negociations, as will be most likely to impress on the said Court the friendly Disposition of the United States, and to induce it to make such concessions and arrangements touching the Southern Limit of the United States and their Right to Navigate the Missisippi below the same, and to enter into such Commercial Stipulations with the United States, as may most effectually guard against a Rupture of the subsisting Harmony and promote the mutual Interests of the two Nations.

"Resolved that the Secretary for foreign Affairs prepare and Report the Instructions proper to be given to the said Minister Plenipotentiary, with a proper Commission and Letter of Credence, and that he also report the communications and explanations which it may be adviseable to make to Mr Gardoqui relative to this change in the mode of conducting the negociations with his Court."

Reports

The first Question that his motion presents, is whether it will be expedient to endeavour to carry the Spanish negociation from New York to Madrid.

It is generally and with Reason held to be more honorable to a Nation that foreign Powers should send Ambassadors to Treat with their Sovereign at his own House, than that they should send Ambassadors to treat with a foreign Sovereign at his Court.

It is also, and with equal Reason generally deemed more advantageous to negociate at Home than in a distant Country; because in the latter case, much must be confided to the Discretion of the negociator, and because the Distance prevents his consulting and being directed by his Sovereign on unexpected occasions and Events as they rise, and which sometimes require immediate Decision.

As these Considerations afford strong and weighty Reasons for continuing the present negociation at the seat of Congress those for carrying it to Madrid should clearly preponderate before they are permitted to operate that change.

Two Reasons are assigned for the proposed Change: one of them is exceedingly indefinite, Viz^t the *present State of our affairs* – what particular Facts and Circumstances in the present State of our Affairs are alluded to, your Secretary is at a loss to discern; for he does not know of any that would in his opinion be meliorated by the Change.

The other Reason is the *present state of the negociation* with that he is perfectly well acquainted; but if the negociation goes to Madrid, he does not conceive that it will leave behind it any of the Difficulties, Questions, or Embarrassments which perplex and retard it at New York.

The Reasons therefore assigned in the motion for the measure in Question, do not appear to him adequate to the consequences drawn from them.

Should such a measure be adopted, the Court of Spain will doubtless view it as very singular, and from that Circumstance be disposed to suspect that it originated in other than the avowed Inducements – why should Congress forego the Honor and Convenience of treating with us at Home? If discontented with their own negociator, why this circuitous way of changing him? if with ours, how has it happened that no Symtoms of it have appeared? on the contrary we are well informed that he is esteemed and respected in America: as to the Differences between us – how are they diminished by this measure? These and a variety of other Questions will more readily occur to the Spanish Court, than satisfactory answers to them and your Secretary apprehends that all these Investigations will terminate in a firm belief that a design to gain Time and to amuse was the true Reason. Whether such a suspicion would be well or ill founded, would be unimportant; for its operation would be exactly the same in the one case as in the other. The only Question is whether it is not highly probable, nay almost certain that they would impute it to that cause?

Your Secretary has Reason to believe that Mr Gardoqui as well as some others, are not ill informed of interesting Debates in Congress, and that the Conversation of members out of Doors does not always remain *sub Rosa*. How or in what point of Light, the Design of such a measure would strike him, your Secretary can only conjecture. It is however natural to suppose that he would take no pains to prevent its proving abortive, and that his Representations of it to his Court would not be calculated to give it a welcome Reception there, nor to impress them with a favourable opinion of the Purposes intended by it.

When too the Court of Spain finds that Mr Jefferson is only empowered to *confer* about the Missisippi and the Boundaries, but not to *conclude*; their suspicions of a Design to Delay and amuse would be confirmed, for it is observable that the Motion proposes only to authorize him to *enter into commercial Stipulations* – on the other topics he is to *make Representations*, to urge such negociations as will be most likely to *impress* on the Court the friendly Disposition of the United States, and to *induce* it to make Concessions &^{c} – but not a word that gives him power to *conclude* a Treaty on those Points. Perhaps this may only be an inadvertent Inaccuracy in the Motion, if not it gives much Colour to the Inferences above suggested.

All these Considerations and Circumstances combined induce your Secretary to think it highly probable that his Catholic Majesty will not consent to treat at Madrid, that his opinion of the Candor of the United States will be diminished by the measure in question, and that he will direct his Minister here to state his ultimate propositions explicitly to congress, and to insist on a speedy and Categorical answer.

If such would be the *probable* Consequence of the measure proposed, your Secretary thinks it would be hazarding too much to adopt it.

If Congress should notwithstanding think it expedient to transfer the negociation to Madrid your Secretary is convinced that it cannot be confided to a Person better qualified to manage it than M͏ͬ Jefferson; and in that case your Secretary will with alacrity and Zeal do whatever may depend upon him to promote the success of it.

All which is submitted to the Wisdom of Congress

John Jay –

NA: PCC, *item 81, v. 3, pp. 243-248 (DS); M247, reel 107.*

John Jay's Report on Anglo-American Relations

[New York] Office for foreign Affairs 23ᵈ April 1787

The Secretary of the United States for the Department of foreign Affairs in obedience to the Order of Congress directing him to report Instructions to their Minister Plenipotentiary at the Court of London, on the Subject of his Letter of 4ᵗʰ March 1786, and of the Papers which accompanied it. Reports the following

Resolved That the Minister of the United States at the Court of Great Britain, be, and he hereby is, instructed to inform his britannic Majesty, that Congress do candidly admit, that the 4ᵗʰ and 6ᵗʰ Articles of the Treaty of Peace have been violated in America, and that they consider the 7ᵗʰ Article as having been violated on the part of Great Britain. That he do also inform his britannic Majesty, that Congress are taking effectual measures for removing all Cause of Complaint on their part, and that he communicate to his Majesty their Resolutions of the 21ˢᵗ day of March last, together with their Circular Letter to the States of the 13ᵗʰ Day of April I̶n̶s̶t̶a̶n̶t̶.

Resolved That the said Minister be, and he hereby is authorized and directed, in the name and Behalf of the United States to propose and conclude a Convention with his Majesty, whereby it shall be agreed that the Value of the Slaves or other American Property carried away contrary to the 7ᵗʰ Article, be estimated by Commissioners and paid for, and that the said Payment, together with a Surrender of all the Posts and Places now held by his Majesty within the Limits of the United States shall be made within   Months after the several States shall each have passed such a Law for repealing all the Acts or parts of Acts existing in the same and repugnant to the said Treaty, as is specified in the Circular Letter above mentioned, which   Months shall be computed from the Time that formal Notice, of all the States having passed such Laws, shall be duly given to his britannic Majesty.

Resolved That the said Minister be, and he hereby is, further instructed to assure his Majesty that it will always give pleasure to Congress fairly and candidly to discuss and accommodate every Difference or Complaint that may arise relative to the Construction or to the Performance of the Treaty. That they are determined to execute it with good Faith, and that as this is the only Instance in which any Complaints of that kind have ever come regularly before them, they flatter themselves, that the Frankness and Candor of their Conduct on this occasion will create in him the same Confidence in the Purity of their Intentions, which they repose in his Assurances "that whenever America shall manifest a real Determination to fulfil her part of the Treaty, Great Britain will not hesitate to Cooperate in whatever points depend upon her, for carrying every Article into real and compleat Effect."

Resolved That the said Minister be, and he hereby is, further instructed to endeavour to have an Article inserted in the Convention for the Remission of the Interest or a proportion of it, which accrued on private Contracts during the war. And that he also endeavour to obtain an Article to fix the true Construction of the Declaration for ceasing Hostilities, and to stipulate, that Compensation be made for all Captures contrary to it.

And to the End that the said Minister may have the more ample Information on these several Subjects, Ordered that a Copy of the Report of the Secretary for foreign Affairs on his said Letter be transmitted to him by means of some proper and confidential Person that may be going from Hence to London.

All which is submitted to the Wisdom of Congress   John Jay –

NA: PCC, item 81, v. 3, pp. 97-99 (DS); M247, reel 107.

James Madison to Thomas Jefferson

Dear Sir   April 23. 1787.

·   ·   ·   ·   ·

The Spanish negociation is in a very ticklish situation. You have been already apprized of the vote of seven states last fall for ceding the Missisipi for a term of years. From sundry circumstances it was infered that Jay was not proceeding under this usurped authority. A late instruction to him to lay the state of the negociation before Congress has discovered that he has adjusted with Guardoqui an article for suspending the use of the Miss. by the citizens of U.S. The report however leaves it somewhat doubtful how far U.S. are commited by this step and a subsequent Report of the secretary on the seisure of Spanish property in the western country: and on information of discontents, touching the occlusion of the Miss. shews that the probable consequences of the measure perplex him extremely. It was nevertheless conceived ~~that~~ by the instructed delegations to be their duty to press a revocation of the step taken in some form which would least offend Spain and least irritate the patrons of the vote of seven states. Accordingly a motion was made to the following effect – that the present state of the negociation with Spain and of the affairs of U.S. rendered it expedient that you should proceed under a special commission to Madrid for the purpose of making such representations as might at once impress on that court our friendly disposition and induce it to relax on the contested points, and that the proper communications and explanations should be made to guardoqui relative to this change in the mode of conducting the negociation. This motion was referred to <*> M^r· Jay whose report disapproves of it. In this state the matter lies. Eight states only being present no effective vote is to be expected. It may notwithstanding be incumbent on us to try some question which will at least mark the paucity of states who abet the obnoxious project. Massachusets and New York alone of the present states are under that description; and Connecticut & New Hamp. alone of the absent. Maryland and S. Carolines have heretofore been on the right side. Their future conduct is somewhat problematical. The opinion of New Hamp. is only ~~known~~ conjectured. The conversion of Rhode Isl^d· countenances a hope that she too may in this instance desert the New England standard.

...In the mean time with my fervent wishes for your happiness I remain Y^r· Affect^e friend   Js. Madison Jr

LC: *Madison Papers, microfilm reel 2* (ALS).

Richard O'Bryen to Thomas Jefferson

Sir   Algiers April the 28th 1787
   It is my unfortunate lot to write you many letters from Algiers but since the pest rages so much, I take the liberty of informing you of the lamentable situation of my crew in the marine where they are employed on the most laborious work & so much exhausted that if some speedy measure is not adopted to redeem them from slavery I am afraid they will all be

carried off by the pest, as it rages much, on the 22$^{d.}$ of this month there died 215 people in Algiers, & in those three months past there have died 200 christian slaves. The Spaniards & Neapolitans having redeemed their people there are at present but 800 slaves belonging to Bylicke[1] & about 120 slaves belonging to private property. therefore we expect to be called to the marine as there is a scarcity of slaves at present to do the requisite duty on board the Algerine cruisers. One of my crew is dead and another after having the pest 14 days with two large buboes on him it has pleased God that he should recover. By considering our present unfortunate situation, we hope it will induce our country & countrymen who are charged with Barbary affairs to adopt some speedy & effectual measure for our release, hoping they will never suffer a remnant of their countrymen to die in slavery in Algiers. Certainly it can answer no good end of keeping us in slavery, if nothing concerns a peace, for redeeming the slaves & making a peace are two different things in Algiers. It is my sincere opinion that the Dey & his Ministers consider that they made a regular bargain with Mr Lamb for our ransom, & I believe it is recorded so on the public books of this regency, & should not be surprized if another American Ambassador was to come to Algiers, at the Dey's telling him he had made one bargain already with the Americans, which they did not fulfill.

It seems the Neapolitan Ambassador had obtained a truce with this Regency for three months, & the Ambassador wrote his court of his success, but about the 1st of April when the cruisers were fitting out the Ambassador went to the Dey & hoped the Dey would give the necessary orders to the Captains of his cruisers not to take the Neapolitan vessels. the Dey said the meaning of the truce was for not to take the Neapolitan cruisers, but if his chebecs should meet the Neapolitan merchantmen to take them & send them for Algiers. The Ambassador said that the Neapolitan cruisers would not want a pass on those terms. The Dey said if his chebecks should meet either men of war or merchant vessels to take them, so gave orders accordingly. The Algerines sailed the 9th inst. & are gone I beleive off the coast of Italy. This shews there is very little confidence to be put in the royal word. no principle of national honor will bind these people & I believe not much confidence to be put in them in treaties. The Algerines are not inclinable to a peace, with the Neapolitans. I hear of no negociation. when the two frigates arrive with the money for the ransom of the slaves I believe they are done with the Neapolitans. The being so handily situated to them, in 24 hours the cruisers are on the coasts of Italy, which is a great inducement for not making a peace. On the 23^d inst. arrived a Neapolitan prize to the Algerines, & on the 25th arrived a Neapolitan Jittan a prize. They were taken near the gulph of Genoa. The crews of them escaped with their boats. This is a great inducement to the

Algerines not to make a peace with the Neapolitans, & the Algerines being under no dread of a bombardment on their city, therefore if they should obtain a peace, the terms will certainly be very high. It certainly makes a great difference with those people, a making peace with Naples or America. for they well know we are situated at a great distance from them, & if we do not come in their way they will not go on our coasts being a great distance & navigation that they are not acquainted with. The Neapolitans are very handy to them & having many merchant vessels, the Algerines are generally attended with success in taking some every cruise.

The Spaniards have paid a great sum for their peace 1,200,000 dollars is the sum paid in Algiers. The Government is very rich & the Dey is very political. No nation can fit out an equal number of cruisers so cheap as the Dey of Algiers. In Algiers the cruisers are not all public vessels, there are about three out of the nine that belong to Bylic, the rest belong to head-officers as Prime minister, General of the Marine, & General of the County, Lord of the Bedchamber &c. Those great men owning the cruisers, they do not wish for peace with those nations in the Streights. The present Dey is very old, & I believe cannot live many years. when he goes to his long home I dare say there will be a great change in the policy of this Regency, making war on some & making peace with others. It is a great thing in a peace with Algiers to make the treaty with the Dey that has just got the government in his hands as it may be more likely he might keep to the treaty he made himself & they generally do not mind what treaties the former Deys make. It is customary with every Dey to renew all treaties. Tunis being tributary to Algiers it would be requisite in the treaty with Algiers to notice Tunis. It is not very easy to know the proper way of laying the foundation of a treaty with those Algerines. Be assured that the foundation of all treaties should be laid by some person that could be depended on in Algiers, & then a wise man to come & conclude the treaty. I should not put much confidence in any Consul in Algiers to have the managing of the American treaty, for it is well known that those nations that are at peace with the Barbary States do not wish that any other nation should obtain a peace, that they should not reap part of those advantageous branches of commerce in the Mediterranean. Before the war the Americans used to employ 200 sail of merchantmen in the streights trade, & used to reap great advantages by it, but at present our trade is but small being cramped on all quarters, which must certainly hurt the Americans much, & when once commerce gets into another chan[n]el, it is a long time before it is brought back again. Certainly the Indies of the French is their trade in the Mediterranean. The French are too knowing to admit us to be sharers of this valuable trade. they & many more trading nations will leave many obstacles in the way of the Americans obtaining a peace with the Barbary States. The Algerines are in no measure depending on the Grand Seignor. They reverence him on account of his being the head or protector of their religion. a little [letter] from him to the Dey of Algiers has some weight in favor of the nation whom the Grand Seignor writes about. but letters from the Christian Kings have no weight. Money is their God & Mahomet their Prophet. The Dey of Algiers must conduct himself agreeably to the Parliament or the Soldiery, he not being absolute in every affair. Those great men here must give their voice, & it must be attended to by the Dey. The Causnagee, that is the prime minister & second Dey, it is believed will succeed the Dey, in the government of this regency. The Mickelhassee, or general of the marine & fortifications, is son in law to the Causnagee, & it is supposed will be prime minister. This man has very great influence & no man can fill his office better than he does, it is he who directs the cruisers where to cruise, & I believe that any thing he mentions or advises the Dey to has much weight. Amongst all those great men the Mickelhassee I believe is most in favor of the Americans. There should some man that could be depended on here have power to lay the foundation of the American treaty & those great men should be paid much attention to that have the Dey's ear at command. A few valuable presents given in a proper season to these great men would not be hove away, as I am sure no nation can obtain a peace here without they gain some of those great men in their favour. When Mr Lamb asked for a peace the Dey undoubtedly said he would not treat, the Dey not knowing the minds of his ministry then had some of those great men been in favour of America, they would have shewed the Dey that a war with America could not be attended with any advantage to the Algerines as we were so far off & they would have courted the Dey to make a peace with America, & once you get those great men in favour of a nation as they rise in office, they have the more influence & are more apt to keep the treaties that it was their wish the former Dey should make than to keep treaties that they wished the Dey had never made.

There are other good men the Aujar or general of the county, & there is the Lord of the Bedchamber Cidy Ally which is the Dey's companion & much in his good graces. this Cidy Ally was a Georgian or Greek who turned & is thought much of with the Dey but not on a very friendly footing with the other great men.

I shall mention to you a Mr Woulf who is an English merchant here, & is exceeding well acquainted with the policy of this country. This man told me he had wrote four years past to Dr Franklin respecting this Barbary affair. He is much esteemed here & in good repute. Also a Mr Fauri who is watchmaker to the Dey & his ministers these 25 years. These are proper men for sounding these Algerines on any subject, but if an American comes here before some step has been taken as I have mentioned he will perhaps meet with as much success as Mr Lamb did.

Your most obedient & very humble Servant

Rich^d O'Bryan, Slave to the Regency of Algiers

NB. There have arrived three Neapolitan & one Genoese prize to the cruisers.

NA: RG 59, *Consular Despatches, Algiers* (C); M23, *reel 1.*

¹ *Bylicke (Bylic) presumably refers to the government or public administration of the Regency of Algiers.*

John Jay's Report on American Captives in Algiers

[New York] Office for foreign Affairs 1st May 1787

The Secretary of the United States for the Department of foreign Affairs to whom was referred a Petition from Hannah Stephens praying that her Husband¹ be redeemed from Captivity at Algiers, and also a Letter from the Honble T. Jefferson proposing that a certain Order of Priests be employed for such Purposes.

Reports

That in his Opinion Resolutions of the following Tenor would be expedient, Viz^t

Resolved that the Honorable T. Jefferson Esquire the Minister of the United States at the Court of Versailles be, and he hereby is authorized to take such Measures as he may deem most adviseable for redeeming the American Captives at Algiers, and at any Expence not exceeding that which European Nations usually pay in like Cases. –

Resolved that the Board of Treasury be and they hereby are directed to provide Ways and Means for enabling Mr Jefferson to defray the said Expences, either by remitting Money from hence or by a Credit in Europe.–

All which is submitted to the Wisdom of Congress –   John Jay –

Read 2 May 1787

Passed July 18, 1787

NA: PCC, *item 81, v. 3, pp. 105, 108* (DS); M247, *reel 107.*

¹ *Captain Isaac Stephens*

John Jay to the President of Congress

Sir   [New York] Office for for[eign] Affairs 1ˢᵗ May 1787

M͗ P. Bond has applied to me repeatedly about the Business of his Commissions now before Congress. His anxiety relative to it has brought him to this City; and he earnestly requests that it may be concluded with as little Delay as may consist with the Convenience of Congress. –

As it is natural that not only M͗ Bond but also his Court should experience some Solicitude on the Subject, I take the Liberty of mentioning these Circumstances to your Excellency; and to observe that it would be a Pity the Influence of your late circular Letter on general Opinion and on british Prejudices and Complaints, should be weakened by any Measure less liberal, especially if in *itself* not very important to either Country. –

I have the Honor to be with great Respect and Esteem Your Excellency's Most obᵗ and very hble: Servᵗ   John Jay –

NA: PCC, *item 81, v. 3, pp. 101-102 (LS); M247, reel 107.*

Phineas Bond to Lord Carmarthen

My Lord   New York, May 1ˢᵗˑ 1787.

Having in vain attempted by letters to obtain the determination of the congress respecting my commissions, I found it expedient to come hither, my Lord, under a hope I should be able to accomplish by personal attendance what my corespondence with the secretary for foreign affairs could not effectuate.

Upon my arrival here a few days since, my Lord, I waited upon Mr. Jay and received an assurance that he would take the earliest opportunity to submit my commissions to the consideration of the congress; but the meeting of that body is so irregular, that I cannot possibly judge whether I shall have it in my power, to transmit to your Lordship the result of their determination by this packet.

Every transaction in Congress, my Lord, that regards foreign affairs is conducted with great secrecy so that I have not yet learned with any degree of accuracy what the opinion of the members is, upon this subject: I have reason to think there have been some objections to the receiving of consuls, on the score of there being no commercial treaty existing with Gt. Britain; and it is very probable this circumstance would stand in the way of the recognition of my commissions, if there were not a palpable inconsistency in acknowledging a Consul-General, and rejecting consuls for particular departments.

Appointments of this sort, my Lord, are viewed here, with a very jealous eye: – they are considered as having a tendency to abridge the little trade this country now enjoys, and which a strict attention to the commercial regulations of Gt. Britain must be the means of confining within more narrow limits.

It may be necessary your Lordship should be informed of the difficulties I have met with, in endeavoring to obtain a determination of the Congress, and of the uncertain footing upon which my commissions now stand, to prevent the progress of my further arrangements in the line of consuls or agents for districts which I understand were in the contemplation of Government and which as far as the nomination of agents went, I lately presumed to recommend to your Lordship as a matter of expedience.

I have now the honor to enclose to your Lordship a newspaper which contains a circular letter transmitted to the governors of the respective States by the Congress: It manifests a disposition to remove every cause of complaint on the part of Gt. Britain and recommends a uniform acquiescence in the terms of the Treaty of Peace, which certainly, my Lord, in many instances have been most grossly violated.

The enclosed Acts of Assembly point out the expediency of such a recommendation and plainly indicate the disposition of the States of Virginia and S. Carolina to avoid a compliance with what Justice Integrity and Good faith, independent of the solemn stipulations of treaties so plainly enjoin, it seems therefore rather problematical whether those States will adopt the recommendation.

The Congress are well aware, my Lord, of the firm ground on which Government stands: it cannot be expected that Gt. Britain can comply with the terms of the treaty while the U. S. A. so far from fulfilling their positive engagements, are ever counteracting the stipulations of the Treaty, by municipal laws.

From the recommendation of the Congress, my Lord, I fear little is to be expected; tho' nominally the great executive body of the continent, each individual State claims and exercises sovereign and independent rights over itself, consequently each State may adopt or reject whatever is consistent with local convenience, or interferes with particular advantages: there is a defect of energy in the Congress, they want means to enforce their requisition and tho' they claim "a general tho' limited sovereignty, for the general and national purposes specified in the confederation," yet, my Lord, each State may resist every federal measure, and the dissent of any one State may effectually mar the success of the most important recommendation; unless therefore the hands of the Congress be strengthened, by the enlargement of their powers and unless they be enabled to conduct the affairs of the Union, by a system of uniform measures, and are vested with the means of enforcing such measures, foreign powers can have no reliance upon the engagements of the Federal Government, nor can the Confederation exist.

I have the honour to be, my Lord, Your Lordship's most faithful and most obed: servant   P. Bond
Rec.ᵈ June 11.ᵗʰ

AHA 1896, v. 1, pp. 528-530.

Louis Guillaume Otto to Comte de Montmorin

[Translation]

N.ᵒ 87.   New York, 1 May 1787.
My Lord.

          .   .   .   .   .

... Communications with the province of Quebec have just been opened by order of Lord Dorchester, and will give rise to a mutually advantageous Commerce. All kinds of goods can be exchanged, with the exception of furs, of which England reserves the monopoly to herself. In spite of the treaty of peace, it appears that the forts on the Lakes must remain in the hands of that power, which is building immense entrepots of pelts there. Since the United States has not restored the confiscated properties to the refugees, and since England finds herself obliged to give them compensations, she thinks herself authorized on her part not to fulfill the articles of the treaty which are onerous to her. For more than a year, an English Commissioner has resided in America in order to conduct a survey of the wealth of all the Royalists whose properties were confiscated, and to order reimbursement for it in Europe. This expense, although generous, is in reality the price which England is paying for the posts of Michillimakinac, Detroit, and Niagara....

I am with a profound respect My Lord Your most humble and most obedient Servant   Otto.
rec. 11 July

FFAA: Pol. Corr., U.S., v. 32, f. 252-253 (LC transcription).

Congressional Resolution Recognizing
Phineas Bond as Consul

[New York May 3, 1787]

Congress proceeded to the consideration of the report of the Secretary of the United States for the department of foreign Affairs to whom was referred his letter of the 8th December last to His Excellency the President with two Commissions from his Britannic Majesty dated the 5th day of April last, the one constituting Phineas Bond Esqr his Consul for New York, New Jersey, Pensylvania, Delaware and Maryland, the other constituting him his Majestys Commissary for commercial Affairs throughout the United States, and Congress approved of the said Report and agreed to the following Resolutions, to wit,

Whereas Phineas Bond Esqr has presented to the United States in Congress Assembled a Commission in due form bearing date the 5th of April 1786 from his Britannic Majesty constituting and appointing him the Consul of his said Majesty in the States of New-York, New Jersey, Pensylvania, Delaware and Maryland, and although no Commercial Treaty or Convention subsists between his Majesty and the United States whereby either have a perfect right to establish Consuls or Commissaries in the dominions of the other, yet as the United States are disposed by every proper mark of liberality and attention to promote a good correspondence between the two Countries, and particularly as amicable Negotiations are now depending between them,

Resolved That the said Phineas Bond Esquire be and he hereby is received and recognized as the Consul of his Britannic Majesty throughout the States of New-york, New Jersey Pensylvania, Delaware and Maryland, and that his Commission be registered in the Secretary's Office.

Resolved That all the privileges, pre-eminences, and authority which the Laws of Nations and of the land give to a Consul received by the United States from any Nation with whom they have no Commercial Treaty or Convention are due to and shall be enjoyed by the said Phineas Bond as Consul for the five States above mentioned, and that certified Copies of these Resolutions be transmitted to the Executives of the said five States for their information. –   Chaª Thomson secʸ

NA: PCC, item 122, pp. 92-93 (C); M247, reel 140.

John Jay to John Adams

Sir   Office for foreign Affairs 3^{d.} May 1787

In Obedience to the Orders of Congress I have the Honor of informing you, that Phineas Bond Esqr. has presented to Congress a Commission from his britannic Majesty, constituting him Commissary for all commercial Affairs within the United States, and another Commission constituting him Consul for the States of New York, New Jersey, Pensylvannia, Delaware and Maryland. –

Congress being desirous on this and every other Occasion, to manifest their Disposition to cultivate a friendly Correspondence with Great Britain, have received Mr. Bond in his latter Capacity, although no Treaty or Convention subsists between the two Countries, whereby either have a Right to establish Consuls in the Dominions of the other. –

As yet Congress have not received any Commissaries for commerical Affairs, and they think it most prudent not to receive them from any Nation, until their Powers shall have been previously ascertained by Agreement, lest as those Appointments are seldom made, and both Parties may not have precisely the same Ideas of the Extent of the Powers and Privileges annexed to them, disagreeable Questions and Discussions might and probably would otherwise take place on those delicate Subjects. –

You will be pleased to submit these Reasons to his Majesty, and to assure him that Congress regret the Objections which oppose their complying with his Wishes in this Instance, but that they are ready to join with his Majesty in such Agreements or Conventions as may be necessary to remove them, and which may also tend to promote and establish a friendly and satisfactory commercial Intercourse between the two Countries. –

I have the Honor to be with great Respect & Esteem, Sir Your most ob^{t.} and very hble. Servt. –   John Jay

MHS: *The Adams Papers, microfilm reel 370 (LS).*

Sir John Temple to Lord Carmarthen

(N° 18)   New York May 3^d 1787.
My Lord,

Herewith is duplicate of the letter (N° 17,) which I had the honor of writing to your Lordship on the 5th of April by the *Speedy* Packet, since which nothing material hath occurred in these States worthy your Lordship's particular attention, except the inclosed circular letter from

Congress to the several States, recommending (they should have said *requiring*) that all acts or clauses of acts in the several States, repugnant to the treaty of peace with His Majesty, be repealed as soon as may be. This circular letter and the resolves of Congress on which it is grounded, fairly acknowledge a violation of the treaty on the part of these States! I can lay claim to no merit, for when I do the utmost in my power it is no more than my duty in the station His Majesty hath placed me here, but I believe I have been considerably instrumental in this business being taken up and acted upon by Congress: Nevertheless, I am of opinion that the respective States who have violated the treaty, will not comply with the said recommendation, which will shew to the world that Congress is not a power competent for Sovereigns to transact business with. The troops raised by Congress a few months ago are almost all disbanded, and I beleive, because they have no money to feed, cloath, or pay them.

A few days ago a small Sloop arrived at this port from Canton. She brings information that all the Ships and vessels that sailed from these States last year, had safely arrived at Canton, were there loaded, and about returning home. The general reports are, that these vessels will have made profitable voyages, particularly in the article of spices, abundance of which they have on board; and that the naval stores they carried out, sold at Batavia at a vast price. For my own part I am still of opinion that this trade to India will not long be successful; nevertheless, as all other attempts at trade and navigation have, in a great measure, failed in these States, the people I hear are about to become further and greater adventurers to India.

Since the date of my last the packets with the February and March mails have arrived from England, but I had not the honor of receiving any commands from your Lordship by them. I am with all deference, My Lord, Your Lordship's Most faithful & Obedient Servant   J. Temple
R. 11th June

PRO: FO 4/5, pp. 239-240 (LC transcription).

Peter Allaire: Occurrences
from 5 April to 3 May 1787

New York 3^d May 1787

.   .   .   .   .

The Payment in Return made for British Goods through the whole Continent, is cheifly Bullion, which is procured from the Spanish West Indies, Flax Seed (sent to Ireland) Pot and Pearl Ashes, Pig Iron, Ginsang

&c from the Northward of New York; Cask, Rice, Indigo, Pitch, Tar, Turpentine, Tobacco and Bills procured from the west Indies of the English & Dutch for Flour Lumber &c. from the Southern States; and always in British bottoms, the proportion at least is three British Vessells to one of all other Nations, that Enter & Clear within the United States. The Fur Trade, while you keep possession of the frontier Posts you command nine tenths of that Valuable commerce, and by moderate calculation made by the Fur Merchants and presented this session to the Assembly this State alone suffers One hundred thousand pounds a Year in being deprived of the furr Trade, besides the difficulty for the Merchants making Returns for debts due in England.

.   .   .   .

I Remain with the greatest Respect Sir Your Mo H S   P. A. R. 13ᵗʰ June 1787

PRO: FO 4/5, pp. 247-262 (LC transcription).

John Adams to John Jay

Dʳ Sir   Grosvenor Square, London May 8. 1787
    I am honoured with your letter of April 2ᵈ, and am happy to receive the Resolutions of Congress, inclosed in it, especially those of the twenty first of March 1787. The Convention at Phyladelphia, is to consist of Members, of Such Ability, Weight, and Experience, that their Result must be beneficial to the United States.
    The Settlement of So many great Controversies Such as those between the Massachusetts and New York Pensilvania and Connecticut, New York and Vermont &c Show that the Union has great Weight in the Minds of the People. It is indeed an Object of Such Magnitude, that great Sacrifices ought to be made to its Preservation. The Consequences of a Division of the Continent cannot be foreseen fully, perhaps by any Man: but the most short sighted must perceive such mannifest danger both from foreign Powers, and from one another as cannot be looked upon, without terror. The Navigation of the Missisippi, in the South and the Fisheries in the North have ever appeared to me, Objects without which the Union cannot be preserved. And therefore Whether the free *Use* of them be obstructed, for a time or not, it has ever appeared a dangerous Policy, to cede the *right* even for a moment. inclosed is a Letter from our unfortunate Countrymen in Captivity at Algiers, which must be sent in the original as there is not time to transcribe it.

I hope Sir, eer long to receive your orders in Consequence of the Resolutions of Congress preparatory to my Return home in the next Spring. The Conduct of this Court in so imprudently as well as uncivilly, neglecting to Send a Minister to America, renders it impossible for Congress, consistently with their own Dignity, to renew my Commission. When the American Minister shall leave this Country, they will begin to think it necessary to send one of their own to New York. They may, for what I know wish, in this Way to get rid of one, whom they have not been able to mould to their Views, in hopes of obtaining another of a more ductile temper. Let them try the Experiment. I dare Say they will be disappointed. for if Congress appoints another, he will not be found more to their Taste. This Country is in a shocking Situation. its Royal Family its Administration and its Opposition, are all such, as will never Seduce an American Mind from his Duty. He will only be shocked at the sight, and confirmed in his natural Principles and native Feelings. With great Respect &c

John Adams.

Read July 6.

NA: PCC, *item 84, v. 6, pp. 472-474 (ALS); M247, reel 113.*

John Jay to the President of Congress

Sir   Office for foreign Affairs 9th May 1787
   A Variety of obvious Circumstances and Considerations induce me to request the Favor of Congress to give me their express Instructions on the Points in Difference between the United States and the Crown of Spain.-
   With great Respect and Esteem I have the Honor to be Your Excellency's most ob^t and very hble: Servt·   John Jay –

NA: PCC, *item 25, v. 2, p. 469 (LS); M247, reel 32.*

John Jay's Report Regarding
the Franco-American Consular Convention

[New York] Office for foreign Affairs 10th May 1787
The Secretary of the United States for the Department of foreign Affairs, to whom was referred that Part of Mr Jefferson's Letter of the 9th January last which relates to the Consular Convention, Viz^t "I will certainly do the best I can for the Reformation of the

Consular Convention, being persuaded that our States would be very unwilling to conform their Laws either to the Convention or to the Scheme, but it is too difficult and too delicate to form sanguine Hopes; however, that there may be Room to reduce the Convention as much as Circumstances will admit, will it not be expedient for Congress to give me Powers in which there shall be no Reference to the Scheme?..." Reports,

.   .   .   .   .

As he perceives no Inconvenience likely to result from giving Mr Jefferson a Commission, authorizing him in general Terms to negociate and conclude a Convention with his Most Christian Majesty, for ascertaining the Authority and Powers of french and american Consuls, your Secretary thinks it will be adviseable to send him such a Commission, that he may thereby have an Opportunity of endeavoring to realize the Advantages he expects from it, and which under a new Administration (perhaps not well advised of what has passed) may be attainable.

In the Opinion of your Secretary it will therefore be expedient to send Mr Jefferson a Commission of the following Tenor, Viz^t

We the United States of America in Congress assembled at the City of New York. To our well beloved Thomas Jefferson Esquire our Minister Plenipotentiary at the Court of his Most Christian Majesty &c: &c: Send Greeting. Being desirous to promote and facilitate the Commerce between our States and the Dominions of his said Majesty, and for that Purpose to conclude with him a Convention for regulating the Privileges, Powers and Duties of our respective Consuls, Vice Consuls, Agents & Commissaries; and having full Confidence in your Abilities and Integrity, We do by these Presents authorize & empower you the said Thomas Jefferson in our Name & Behalf, to treat with any Person having equal Powers from his most Christian Majesty of and concerning such a Convention, and the same in our Name and Behalf to conclude, sign and seal; And We do promise to ratify & confirm whatever Convention shall in Virtue of this Commission be by you so concluded, provided the Duration of the same be limited to any Term not exceeding twelve Years. Witness our Seal and the Signature of his Excellency Arthur St Clair our President this Day of   in the Year of our Lord one thousand seven hundred and eighty seven and the eleventh of our Independence. –

Your Secretary thinks it would be proper to write the two following Letters to Mr Jefferson, the *first* of which he might communicate to the Court. –

Sir

Congress being desirous that the Commerce between the United States and France may be promoted by every reciprocal Regulation conducive to that End, wish that no Time may be lost in ascertaining the Privileges, Powers and Duties of their respective Consuls, Vice Consuls and commercial Agents and Commissaries.

They regret the Circumstance which calls you to the South of France, but are perfectly satisfied that you should make that or any other Journey which your Health may require. It is their Wish and Instruction that on your Return to the Court, your Attention may be immediately directed to the abovementioned Subject. Considering that Conventions of this Nature however apparently useful in Theory may from some Defects or unforeseen Circumstances be attended with Inconveniences in Practice, they think it best that they should be probationary at least in the first Instance, and therefore that the Term to be assigned for the Duration of the one in Question should not exceed   Years. They also think it adviseable, in Order to obviate any Difficulties that might arise from your not having been more formally authorized to complete this Business, to give you an express and special Commission for the Purpose, which I have now the Honor to enclose.

Sir

You will herewith receive another Letter from me of this Date, together with the Commission mentioned in it – both of them are in pursuance of the Ideas suggested in your Letter of the 9th January last. If the whole Subject should be reconsidered, and a new Convention to be formed, it is the Pleasure of Congress that the Duties, Powers and Privileges of Consuls, Vice Consuls, Agents and Commissaries be accurately delineated, and that they be as much circumscribed and limited as the proper Objects of their Appointment will admit and the Court of France consent to. How far it may be in your Power to obtain a Convention perfectly unexceptionable, must depend on several Circumstances not yet decided. Congress confide fully in your Talents and Discretion, and they will ratify any Convention that is not liable to more Objections than the one already in part concluded; provided an Article limiting its Duration to a Term not exceeding   Years be inserted. –

All which is submitted to the Wisdom of Congress   John Jay –
Read May 11th 1787
Passed 27 July 1787

NA: PCC, item 81, v. 3, pp. 113-118, 120 (DS); M247, reel 107.

Act of Connecticut General Assembly
Repealing Laws Contrary to the Treaty of Peace

[Hartford, 10 May 1787]

At a General Assembly of the State of Connecticut holden at Hartford on the second Thursday of May Anno. Dom. 1787 –

Whereas the United States in Congress Assembled have by their Resolution of the 13th of April 1787 Recommended to the several States, to repeal all such Acts, and parts of Acts of their several Legislatures, as may be now Existing, in any of the said States, repugnant to the Treaty of Peace between the United States, and Great Britain; and that each State pass such Act of Repeal whether any such exceptional Act is Existing in such State, or not, and that rather by describing than reciting such Act, for the purpose of obviating all disputes and Questions between the United States and Great Britain relative to said Treaty; and alltho' there hath been no Complaint, or suggestion Officially, or otherwise, that there is any Act, or part of an Act Existing, in this State, repugnant to said Treaty, Yet this Assembly being at all Times disposed to conform to the true intent, and Spirit of the Articles of Confederation, and to prevent and remove (so far as to this Assembly doth appertain) all Causes of dispute, and Contention, and every Just Ground of Complaint, have thought fit to Enact, and,

Be it Enacted by the Governor, Council, and, Representatives in General Court Assembled and by the Authority of the same, That such of the Acts, or parts of Acts of the Legislature of this State as are repugnant to the Treaty of Peace between the United States, and his Britannick Majesty, or any Article thereof shall be, and hereby are repealed –

And be it further Enacted by the Authority aforesaid that "the Courts of Law, and Equity within this State be, and They hereby are directed, and required in all Causes and Questions cognizable by them respectively, and arising from, or touching said Treaty to decide, and adjudge according to the Tenor, true intent, and meaning of the same any thing in the said Acts or parts of Acts, to the contrary thereof in any wise notwithstanding[1] –

A true Copy of Record. Examin^d. By   George Wyllys[2] Secret^y.

NA: PCC, item 66, v. 2, pp. 324-326 (C); M247, reel 80.

[1] For another example of state repeal of such laws, see that of Maryland (NA: PCC, item 75, p. 342; M247, reel 88).

[2] Wyllys, George, Secretary of the Connecticut General Assembly, 1775-1787.

Don Diego de Gardoqui to Conde de Floridablanca

[Translation]

N⁰· 174.   New York, 12 May 1787

Your Excellency:

My dear Sir: In my N⁰· 153 of 31 December, I informed Your Excellency of the tenacity with which the State of Virginia has opposed the loss of navigation on the Mississippi river, as its resolutions show.

Since that time, its delegate Madison has arrived at this Congress, and having reciprocally exchanged visits and initiated a friendship, which seems sincere, I have had occasions to enter upon this matter in a civil manner.

I have frankly expressed the urgent necessity of proceeding with such firmness as will not arouse suspicion in the inhabitants of Kentucky, and will give them a motive that will hasten that which they frequently threaten with regard to separation and allying themselves with Great Britain in the quality of an Independent State.

During the past two months, the attacks on me by various members of Congress have been fierce and continuous, especially by those from North Carolina and Virginia, so that they might contrive some means of facilitating Communication between their New settlements and New Orleans; but I have resisted openly and with vigor, and they have finally concluded that they should not entertain the least hope of obtaining such permission.

This clarity has not been sufficient to make the Delegates from Virginia abandon this claim, since I have just concluded having a most intense debate in this house with them all, which lasted more than three hours, in which they left no argument or pretext to convince me unused.

I shall recount the substance to Your Excellency, because to relate it all, even though I would be glad to do so, would be bothersome.

It should be noted that since my arrival, I have formed the plan of not giving cognizance to the right which they claim regarding that navigation, stating that the King's right was indisputable; so that after infinite bother, they desisted because of the inconveniences and the consequences.

It is said, then, that even if the Treaty were ratified with that exclusion, the inhabitants of Kentucky would not observe it; that Spain would complain with reason, and would have recourse to the United States to enforce the agreement; that distance and other factors make it impracticable to compel them by force, and even if it were attempted, they would raise the country in rebellion, and if it were possible to harass them, they would resort to the favor of Great Britain; that whatever the case, its population would greatly increase because of the large number of destitute persons who would emigrate to free themselves from the taxes that are paid here; that this same thing has happened in the territory of Vermont which, since seceding from the Government of New York, has grown extraordinarily for the same reason; and that ultimately we would end up by fomenting a formidable enemy like England, either by its acquisition of a number of subjects or allies, or also by the large increase by which its fur trade would be strengthened.

They reiterated to me the uneasiness caused in those new Settlements just by the mere rumor that Congress was thinking of ceding it for some years, and the fear they have that some excesses may be committed regarding the Mississippi, because the people are insubordinate.

We nevertheless maintained our respective points of view with the greatest tenacity, and this Conference was very intense, even though we conducted it in a rational and mannerly way. But before we separated, it seemed appropriate to me to disillusion them with a final refusal, and to assure them that His Majesty would not permit the least communication or passage through his possessions; and that they should be persuaded that even if they were to send the most eminent subject of the States to Madrid, he would not be granted an audience for such a claim.

I have well-founded reasons to believe that they have made the most painstaking efforts with my particular confidants to reduce them to their mode of thinking, and as for Mr. Jay, they have succeeded in intimidating him to such an extent that he has become insufferable to me and in the end does not dare even to discuss the matter.

I candidly confess to Your Excellency that it does not surprise me, in view of what has been aired in some Assemblies, the various documents that have been written, and the liveliness of the representations from the inhabitants of Kentucky, Westmoreland, and others which, even though little grounded in the truth, make a bad impression on the common people, because no one dares to rebut them, so that I have had to argue with skill in conversations and to rebut their false suppositions anonymously, overcoming a thousand difficulties by using another's hand to find a printer who would publish them.

I always thought that there would be great opposition on this point; but I confess that I did not imagine how much; and so I fear, in all seriousness, that it will not be possible to arrange matters as we wish; I should at least frankly assure Your Excellency that the prospect is very bad, because in addition to what has already been stated, I have received secret information regarding the inhabitants of Kentucky, that they complain bitterly of the rumor that Congress would think of consenting to give up that navigation, and that it is openly said that, if this takes place, all Collection of Imposts and taxes for the United States will be suspended; that if the subjects of His

Catholic Majesty should confiscate their ships which navigate the river below, they will do the same to the Spaniards who attempt to trade on the river above, and that in time force will open the path to the sea for them; and that if Congress attempts to punish them, or permits Spain to exact justice, they will form an offensive and defensive alliance with Great Britain.

These are, Your Excellency, the conversations of those people, among whose leaders are infinite numbers who had a military career in the last war.

For proof that these rumors are not idle, I further report to Your Excellency that on the 19th of February, Mr. Jay came to communicate to me the news that those settlers, without any reason, have seized a Spanish ship loaded with furs in a place called Port Vincent, which is said to be a small village of French settlers situated about one hundred and thirty miles upriver from the mouth of the Wabash river. I questioned him repeatedly and very carefully regarding the circumstances of this incident; but he assured me he did not know them, because he had had no official notice, and had only come to inform me, since it appeared to him that we should work in mutual openness, and that Congress, as did he, infinitely regretted this occurrence.

Later, the Delegates from Virginia sought me out here to confirm this same attack and the regret it has caused that Government, corroborating it with the enclosed translation, which is said to be a copy of the resolution of that Council in which such conduct is condemned.

For this reason, I not only showed my regret, but also explained to them very forcefully the consequences to which they would be exposed if they did not set about curbing such disorders.

Up to the present hour, I have not had the least notice of this incident from any of the King's possessions; so that I lack any basis to take any measures; and I fear that even when the matter is brought up, no reparation will be made, beyond a reiteration that Congress and the States disapprove of the conduct of General Clark, adding to me, perhaps confidentially, that the perpetrator of the attack has few sober hours during the day, which weakness is notorious throughout the country.

These circumstances, along with the present state of Congress, the authority of which has declined visibly for want of executive power, make my Commission difficult and very delicate, because, since I am unable to count on the energy of this body, the work is made suspect, since if anything is attempted, it can be discovered, with no guarantee that the result will be beneficial. Each State suspects its neighbor, varies in its principles, is divided by domestic parties, and has no public or private credit.

Some favor the division of Sovereignties, forming two or three closely linked defensive and offensive ones.

Others incline toward a General Confederation, with the appointment of one Chief who, together with a Parliament, would hold executive power for seven years, and there is no lack of those who would embrace a Chief who would end up as the Sovereign.

This diversity, and the decline which they have noted, have resulted in what Virginia has proposed, which is a Convention or General Meeting of Delegates from all the States, which was called for the second Monday of May in the city of Philadelphia *to revise and amend the Confederation.*

The first appointed by that State was General Washington, with other notables.

Pennsylvania followed her example, and the rest have adopted it also, and it will soon have taken place.

For this reason, I have inquired confidentially, and have devoted myself to investigating the mode of thinking of many of my confidants who have been appointed to it, with the idea of forming some judgment in order to inform Your Excellency of what may result, but I doubt that human understanding can predict it. For my part, I recognize my limitations, and will restrict myself to saying that the most able men have frankly confessed to me that it is absolutely impossible to predict the results of a compromise to which necessity has obliged them; but that even if it can serve as the basis to promote a solid Confederation, they fear that it will require years, because there is much disunity of purpose and a great number of destitute people who, since they have nothing to lose, might venture to better their fortunes by a disruption of all the machinery.

Each State in particular is exquisitely jealous of its Independent Sovereignty. Those who govern them, who find their self-interest and convenience in the predictable, staunchly oppose the slightest cession of their prerogatives, with which jealousy they carry the vote of their respective States, ascribing bad faith to those who govern the Confederation, so that if one had to judge by the present state of things, and even by what some prudent men say, one would deduce that this country is moving rapidly toward an Anarchy that should produce a general convulsion, and that it would not be strange if some person appears who might seize for himself what they now watch so scrupulously.

General Washington maintains a mysterious silence, perhaps prudent and politic, because he has neither accepted nor refused his appointment, reserving himself, according to my confidants, until he sees whether the States bestow powers ample and without limitation on their respective Representatives, allowing it to be known that if they do so, he will attend the aforementioned Convention.

There is no lack, nevertheless, of those who think that he will not come, because he has foreseen that things have not matured so as to produce the good effect of consolidating the Confederation, and believe that he will excuse himself because of his ailments.

The complicated circumstances of all this in general make me extremely worried, and I am kept awake many nights by the reflection that if, as I expect shortly, I were to receive His Majesty's orders to conclude the Treaty, and could persuade Mr. Jay to approximate these terms, there remains for me the apprehension that the Confederation could be altered this summer and not ratify the accord.

I assure Your Excellency that my perplexity is great since, not being at a distance to consult with Your Excellency without, on the other hand, exposing myself to losing the occasion; but, trusting in my intention, I promise Your Excellency to do whatever appears to me most conducive to the King's service, and if I fail, I hope for His Majesty's compassionate tolerance.

In order to proceed with more certainty, I shall go to Philadelphia when the Convention assembles, shall endeavor to sound the hearts and to examine, if possible, what happens, in order to form my appreciation of what it may produce and, bearing in mind the whole of the King's Instructions and orders, I shall proceed with what appears to me may result in the best service of His Majesty.

I greatly fear that Mr. Jay will not dare to continue the negotiation until he sees the results of the abovementioned Convention.

I shall take care to inform Your Excellency without losing an opportunity, and if it is urgent, I shall make use of them. Meanwhile, I impatiently await His Majesty's first orders, and I request those of Your Excellency, asking God to guard Your Excellency's life for many years.

New York, 12th of May of 1787.   Gardoqui

Gómez del Campillo, Relaciones Diplomaticas, *v. 1, pp. 374-380.*

John Adams to John Jay

Dear Sir   London May 14. 1787
Last Thursday, according to your Advice, I communicated to Lord Carmarthen, not officially but as private, tho authentic Intelligence, the Resolutions of Congress of the twenty first of March. – His Lordship appeared to be Sincerely and highly pleased. And Said that those Resolutions did the highest honour to Congress, and he wished I had Authority to communicate them formally. The Reason was explained to his

Lordship, that there had not been time for the Secretary of State to prepare Instructions but that they might be expected, to arrive in a few Weeks. The Measure is as well founded in good Policy as it is in Justice and Honour and must produce a good Effect. With great Respect I have the Honour to be, Sir, your most obedient and most humble Servant   John Adams. read 23 July 1787

NA: PCC, *item 84, v. 6, pp. 476-477 (ALS); M247, reel 113.*

Phineas Bond to Lord Carmarthen

My Lord   Philadelphia. 14th May 1787.
    I have already in a former letter taken the liberty of suggesting to your Lordship, the strategems used by the inhabitants of the United States, to elude the operations of the new Act of Navigation: the devices they have adopted are various, but none seem to have so dangerous a tendency as the prevailing practice of joint concerns in vessels entitled to the privileges of British Bottoms, which, by the connivance of British houses affords American traders the benefit of participating in those advantages, which the Act of Navigation meant to confine to British subjects alone.
    My Lord there is much reason to believe many cases now exist, where British ships are owned jointly by British and American traders; and, as long as oaths are treated with so much levity, it may be difficult to contrive a remedy to meet the mischief.
    It might however excite some dread of discovery, in those who are engaged in such illicit practices, if encouragement were held out to such as might give information to Government, in cases where vessels having British registers, are jointly owned by British and American traders, and perhaps a clause of this nature added to the late Act might have a good effect in checking this evil
    Your Lordship will be best able to judge how far it may be fit to adopt this idea.
    I have the honour to be, my Lord, Your most faithful and obed. servant
                                                              P. Bond.
Rec[d] 2nd July.

AHA 1896, v. 1, pp. 530-531.

Dutch Bankers to John Adams

Amsterdam 15 May 1787

We have Your Excellency's esteemed favor of 7[th.] and two of 8 Instant transmitting us Letters from the Board of Treasury. The detention whereof later than others we received p the April Packet, has retarded the Business of a new Loan during a whole Week. A delay of utmost consequence at the eve of the June Interest falling due. –

We sincerely lament the Necessity M[r.] John Rucker[1] was in to leave England, and hope the Discredit such an Event must occasion will be but temporary. Your Excellency acted very properly in forwarding Protests only of the drafts upon him, but we recommend Duplicates should be sent.

Notwithstanding we adopted the Payment of the Sixty Thousand Guilders Premiums in pursuance of Your Excellency's Advice, Had this been the only Deficiency in the Remittance for the June Interest, Our Zeal for the Credit and Interest of the United States, would have induced us to advance it; But the late considerable disposals of Your Excellency and His Excellency Tho' Jefferson Esq[r.] have exhausted the Funds in our Hands much below the Statement of the Treasury Board, exclusive of the 75000 livres Bills on M[r.] John Rucker contrary to its expectation not proving good, So that the Sum required is of such a Magnitude as to preclude all thoughts of supplying it, by any other means than a fresh Loan, for effecting which the Time is very short indeed, besides the Bonds of the Former Loans being now at a very low rate and People uncommonly sollicitous to sell them. A Panic we cannot account for, any other wise than by the Payment of the June Interest not being yet advertised. We have assembled the principal Brokers and opened the matter to them. Under all the actual disadvantageous circumstances, they have promised to second our Exertions to raise Money by a new Loan, Which we shall be obliged to pay dear for and make of no less Sum than a Million, Whereof the Undertakers will however engage to receive only a certain Sum, that we shall endeavour may be sufficient for Payment of the June and February Interests and the Sums Your Excellency may want for his Salary and ordinary disbursements, the remaining Bonds to lie by us for Account of the United States. Thus the Board of Treasury would not have to attend to any Remittances for this Country previous to the June Interest of 1788, by which Period we trust the Measures that will be devised by the Assembly of Delegates at Philadelphia, will have had the Operation necessary to secure punctual Remittances for the future Payment of the Interest on the Dutch Loans. We cannot yet flatter Your Excellency of Success, but if we should be so fortunate, We rely upon Your Excellency's readiness to pass immediately the requisite

Instruments, and to strain all your Influence, that the Ratification of Congress may take place and be transmitted to us without any Procrastination.

We are respectfully Your Excellency's Most obedient and very humble Servants   Wilhem & Jan Willink
                                    Nic⁵· & Jacob van Staphorst.

Gentleman   May 21, 1787.
In answer to your of the 15ᵗʰ, I have only to say I shall leave all to your Judgment   John Adams

MHS: *The Adams Papers, microfilm reel 370 (LS).*

¹ *Rucker, John. German-born American merchant with commercial experience in Great Britain and ties to the French banking house of I. L. and C. Le Couteulx. In 1784, he and William Constable organized the New York mercantile firm of Constable, Rucker and Company, which served as Robert Morris' agents for commercial activities in Europe and the Far East. Rucker ran the London branch of this firm. In May 1787, when remittances from the French Farmers General for tobacco supplied them by Morris failed to arrive in London in timely fashion, Rucker was forced to allow Morris' bills submitted to him for payment to be protested for lack of funds. Rucker sailed to New York that same month in an attempt to set matters straight.*

Phineas Bond to Lord Carmarthen

My Lord   Philadelphia May 16ᵗʰ 1787.
I have the honor to inform your Lordship, the Congress entered upon the consideration of my commissions, on the 3ʳᵈ of May, and resolved to admit the commission I hold as consul but to suspend my recognition as commissary for commercial affairs until the powers and extent of this latter appointment should be settled and defined by Convention, between Gt. Britain and the U. S. A.

As far, my Lord, as I could collect from the conversation I had with the secretary for foreign affairs, the resolution formed by the Congress, on this occasion, resulted from a disposition to prevent any future differences and discussions that might arise from the exercise of my commission as Comʸ for comˡ affairs. In strictness it is conceived by the Congress, that consuls or agents in the comˡ line were not admissible until treaties of commerce took place, and there is a particular clause in all the treaties formed between the United States and foreign powers to admit consuls etc, under the limitations and restrictions contained in those treaties: – this principle might have gone the length of rejecting both the commissions I have the honor to hold: but as the powers of a consul are well-known and defined by the laws of Nations, the rule was relaxed in this instance, with respect to my commission as consul, and I shall be permitted to exercise the duties of that appointment as soon as the forms of proceeding admit of my being announced to the 5 States to which the commission extends.

The Com^n as com^y for com^l affairs being considered as new, and out of the ordinary course of things, the adjusting and defining the extent of the powers will be referred by Congress to the Minster of the United States in London, and will, probably e'er long, be submitted by him to your Lordship's consideration:

I took pains, my Lord to explain to the Secretary for Foreign Affairs the objects which the commission as Com^y for Com^l affairs were particularly meant to embrace – but it seems necessary such objects should be defined thro' the medium of ministerial intervention however reasonable and just they may appear.

Your Lordship must well remember the grounds upon which this latter commission was recommended to the adoption of Government by a great body of the merchants of London engaged in the American trade: – they had experienced the severity of existing laws throughout this continent, made, not only in direct contravention of the Treaty of Peace, but in violation of those contracts, which are universally deemed sacred among nations, – they knew too, my Lord, the relaxed situation of the Federal Government and found the recommendations of Congress, in cases when recommendations had been made, ineffectual and incompetent to the purpose of obtaining adequate relief: it was therefore, my Lord, deemed necessary that some person should be cloathed with the authority of Government to represent the existing causes of complaint to each State, in the hope of obtaining from the justice of the individual legislatures a repeal of those laws which militate against their interests, and thereby to facilitate the security of their extensive concerns.

As the recommendations of Congress, my Lord, have proved ineffectual to obtain a compliance even with the stipulations of treaties, this mode of application to the different States seemed to be the only resort and such applications could alone be made under my second commission, as the duty of a consul is not deemed competent in matters of this sort: the suspension therefore of this commission, my Lord, puts by, for the present, the exertion of the only means from whence effectual relief could result: – but my Lord I presume to hope a conference with the American minister may place the reasonableness and expediency of this 2nd commission in so conspicuous a point of view as to promote the immediate recognition of it.

I have the honor to be, your Lordship's Most faithful and obedient servant
                                                          P. Bond
R: 2ⁿᵈ· July.

AHA 1896, v. 1, pp. 532-534.

Phineas Bond to Carmarthen

My Lord,   Philadelphia May 17ᵗʰ· 1787.
   Being concious how much the revenue of Gt Britain has been defrauded by illicit practices and knowing how anxiously and how successfully the attention of his Majesty's ministers has been applied to correct the prevailing abuses, I conceive I cannot do a more essential service; than to endeavour to promote this great object of Government by attempting to discover the methods used to elude the payment of duties imposed upon such articles as apply to the commerce of the United States with Gt. Britain and Ireland: and, my Lord, I am the more sollicitous to discover those methods, since they have a tendency to discourage every fair trader, and to divert the great means of remittance, from those channels in which they ought justly and naturally to flow.
   Tobacco is one of the articles transported from the middle States to Europe: the heavy duty it bears, encourages the practice of every artifice to avoid the payment of it and exposes the revenue to every possible deception.
   I hope shortly my Lord to be in possession of papers, which will furnish a clew to government, by which it may be discovered to what extent these frauds are practiced, and it is to be hoped measures may be devised effectually to defeat them.
   In the meantime, my Lord, I beg leave to say it has been confidently asserted here, that in the year 1784, 5200 hds. of tobacco were cleared from the port of Philadelphia for Ireland, and in the next year (1785) 4700 hds. of tobacco were cleared from Philadelphia for Ireland. The duty on the export of tobacco in 1784 ought to have yielded a revenue of upwards of £300,000, and the export of 1785 ought to have yielded nearly that sum: the returns of the customs of Ireland will show how much of that revenue has been produced: – if a deficiency appears, it may be reasonably considered that a quantity of tobacco, equal to that deficiency has been run into that kingdom. The price given for tobacco here, my Lord, is of itself a convincing proof of this illicit traffic, and of the success with which it is conducted: Peterboro' tobacco in Virginia sells so low as 22/6 Virgⁿ curry: (dollars 6/) pr. cwt. – in Philadelphia that sort of tobacco sells from 40/ to

45/ Pennsylv* Curry: (dollars at 7/6) pr. cwt. there is a difference of near 100 p. cent in the price between this port and Virginia besides the addition of freight: but the saving of 16^d duty upon each lb. of tobacco will amply compensate for the increase of expense and afford abundant profit to the adventurer.

But, my Lord, the Ministry does not stop here; the encouragement the Americans have met with in their trade to China has induced them to enter largely into this speculation; the number of ships already employed in that trade must overstock the American market; of course means will be used to establish a communication, not only with the W. India Islands but with Europe, to promote a ready and profitable sale for the excess of teas and piece goods, imported into this continent from China.

I shall endeavor, my Lord, to obtain accounts of the two cargoes already arrived, this spring, at New York and to transmit them to your Lordship as soon as possible.

I have the honor to be, my Lord, Your Lordship's most faithful and obed: servant.   P. Bond

R. 2nd July.

AHA 1896, v. 1, pp. 534-535.

Dutch Bankers to John Adams

Amsterdam 18 May 1787

Agreeably to what we had the honor to acquaint Your Excellency the 15 Instant, We have exerted ourselves to procure Money for Payment of the Interest due the First Proximo by the United States; A Matter very difficult to be accomplished as we had against us the late News from America, no immediate flattering Prospects and an excessive Scarcity of Money here at present. We have however been successful enough to persuade the Undertakers, to subscribe to a New Loan for One Million of Florins, upon the following Condition –

One Thousand Bonds for One Thousand Guilders each, to be issued upon the same Conditions as the preceeding Loan of Five p Cent, the Interest commencing the First of June. –

Of which Thousand Bonds, Two Hundred and Forty to be immediately negotiated to the Subscribers; The one Half of their Amount to be paid, upon delivery of the Bonds, The Undertakers reserving to themselves the Faculty of taking One Months Credit for Payment of the remaining Half.

The Surplus Seven Hundred and Sixty Bonds, are to remain in our Custody, subject to be delivered to the Undertakers, Each one in proportion to his Subscription, at the same rate of those actually negotiated. At the expiration of which Period, those on hand will be at the free disposal of Congress. –

Congress shall not be at liberty to make any farther Money Negotiations in this Country, until the surplus Seven Hundred and Sixty Bonds shall be placed, or before the End of the Eighteen Months they are to lie at the Choice of the Undertakers to purchase them. –

Such are the best Conditions we have been able to obtain, and altho' the Money will cost the United States Eight p Cent including Premium, Our Commission, Brokerage and Charges, We deem ourselves fortunate to have been thus able to face the June Interest; An object Your Excellency justly views of the highest Importance to the Credit and Interest of the United-States. By this Arrangement, we shall be obliged to advance Part of the Interest, until the Undertakers shall have compleated Payment for the engaged Bonds; Upon which Advances we do not doubt the United-States will most readily admit our Charge of Interest.

We endeavoured all in our Power, that the Money should be received by us in Recepissees, and thus leave you the time to visit this Country at your conveniency to pass the Bonds. But the Undertakers have insisted as an absolute condition, that they should be liable to pay only on receipt of the Bonds signed and perfected by you; So that there is an indispensable Necessity for Your Excellency's setting out for this Country, with the full Power you have from Congress, by the Packet that will leave Harwich next Wednesday or at latest on Saturday the 26th instant, when we will have every thing ready, that Your Excellency may be able to return by the next or following Packet: We request Your Excellency to be assured, nothing in our Power was left untried to spare you this Jaunt so suddenly; But since the Payment of the June Interest entirely depends upon this Exertion of your Excellency, We are confident it will be undertaken with Alacrity; And upon this conviction we have assumed to advertise, the Payment of the Interest on the First of June, Which is in all our News-Papers of this day.-

We are respectfully Your Excellency's Most obedient and very humble Servants   Wilhem & Jan Willink.
                                                  Nic⁵ & Jacob van Staphorst.

MHS: *The Adams Papers, microfilm reel 370 (LS).*

William Stephens Smith to Thomas Jefferson

Dʳ Sir –   Bourdeaux May 19ᵗʰ 1787.

Mʳ Short[1] having informed you from Paris of my intention of being here about the 14ᵗʰ and of the prospect of my remaining 2 or 3 day's – I doubt not but I should have had the pleasure of a line from you had that Letter reached you in time – I shall leave this place in the morning for Madrid – where I should be happy to hear from you – I move by order of Congress to Portugal on temporary business –...

I have left the Letters which m^r· Short gave me in the care of Messrs· French & Nephew[2] of this place, who will wait on you with them the moment they are informed of your arrival – you will encounter a very disgreable Circumstance at this place – you will find M^r· Barclay confined in the prison at the suit of the above mentioned Gentlemen for a debt of 75.000 Liv^rs· – he has been here about a fortnight and was taken on Wednesday last, when he will get out, I know not – the Creditors expect that Congress will release him, I have put my face against the Idea, as the circumstance arises from M^r· B's negotiations as a merchant & in his private capacity and not as Consul General from the United States – am I right or wrong? – M^r· B on the other hand expects present reliefe from the order of the parliament of Bordeaux – or from the King at Versailles, but I think this cannot be done, for there is no Consular treaty ratified between our Countries – & with respect to his being on his return from his mission to Morrocco – and in that point of light might be considered under the protection of the laws of Nation, if it does opperate, it will be but a temporary affair, as on his arriving at Paris – the same Game may be played over there – I am very apprehensive that the storm will thicken from all quarters & that he must sink under the accumulated weight – I have been with him & shall see him again to-day – I immagine this will render your stay here very short unless you see a prospect of serving him – M^r· Stephen Sayer[3] is in the same situation in London – and Mr Lamb is about to embark from Minorca with a load of Jack-asses for America. *Sic transit gloria mundi*[4] –...

Thus far I had wrote & it was 1/2 past 2 °Clock when M^r· Barclay entered my apartments, – I have received him as one risen from the dead – the parliament have liberated him upon the principle of his being on his return to Paris on a public Embassy – & having the papers relative to it in his possession – you will find him at the Hotel 'Angletere near the palace Gardens – I am D^r· Sir – with the greatest respect –

W.S. Smith

MHS: *Thomas Jefferson Papers* (ALS).
    [1] Short, William (1759-1849). *Virginia landowner, diplomat. Member, Virginia executive council, 1783-1784. Private secretary to Thomas Jefferson, secretary of legation at Paris, 1785-1789. Chargé des affaires ad interim, 1789-1790; en titre, 1790-1792. Minister to the United Provinces of the Netherlands, June-December 1792. Appointed joint commissioner with William Carmichael to negotiate treaty with Spain, 1793. Minister to*

Spain, 1794-1795. Cooperated in negotiation of Pinckney Treaty, signed October 27, 1795. Nominated Minister to Russia, 1808, but not confirmed by Senate.

[2] English mercantile firm in Bordeaux.

[3] Sayre, Stephen (1736-1818). American merchant, banker and unofficial diplomatic agent. Arrested in London on charges of plotting to overthrow the government, October 1775, but released for lack of evidence. Secretary to Arthur Lee's mission to Prussia, 1777. Attempted to interest Denmark and Sweden in commercial treaties with the United States, 1777-1779, but without success. Solicited post of agent to negotiate peace with the Barbary Powers, 1785, also without success.

[4] So passes the glory of the world.

Decree of the Bordeaux Parliament
Rescinding the Imprisonment of Thomas Barclay

[Translation]

[Bordeaux,] 19 May 1787.

Today the King's Attorney General[1] entered & said:

Messieurs,

The Investigation that we have made of the Request presented to the Court by Mr. Thomas Barclai does not permit us to think that we have fulfilled all the duties of our Ministry by responding to this Request in the ordinary form.

A new order of things prescribes a new course for us; & when the law of nations is concerned, it is not by authorized forms for civil & purely judicial actions that it can be defended & avenged.

Mr. Thomas Barclai is invested with the double title of Consul General of the United States of America in France, & of their Agent extraordinary to the Emperor of Marocco. In this quality, he has just fulfilled the mission with which he was charged by His Republic; he enjoyed in that Nation, so recently emerged from the shadows of Barbarity, the plenitude of the law of nations. He returned to France, joining to the honor of Treaties His Majesty's particular passports, & he was imprisoned in Bordeaux, at the request of Messrs. French Nephew & Company, by virtue of a judgment obtained against Him before the Judges & Consuls of Paris.

The principles of a predominant order exempt us, Messieurs, from discussing the nature of the debt, & from endeavoring to understand the operations of commerce of which it was the Result.

We must only consider at this time the public character with which Mr. Thomas Barclay is invested. In this respect, the King's Attorney General can see in the request presented to the Court to obtain the Abrogation of this imprisonment only a denunciation, made to His Ministry, of the most revolting violation of the Law of Nations.

Were we to consult the Publicists, they would all unite to teach us how sacred is the person of those who are sent from Nation to Nation, in whatever Capacity, & History coming to the support of their principles, we see from age to age, even in the most distant Centuries, this character of Ambassador, of Envoy or of Representative, respected by all Peoples, of torrents of Blood shed to avenge the insult made to one of these men invested with a national Ministry.

.   .   .   .   .

And we, Messieurs, refer you to a fact unheard of in a civilized Nation; the Representative of a Republic in irons; a Negotiator arrested on the pretext of a private debt; all the papers relative to his mission sequestered by a Bailiff, with them all the Instruments that can justify his character and his rights.

It would therefore be with reason that we resolve on penalties against both the Bailiff & the Party in whose name he was acting; but this Party, Messieurs, is also a foreigner, & enjoys in Bordeaux that freedom of the City which the King has just accorded to Peoples to whom he has given peace: we therefore prefer to believe that he is unaware of those Laws that bind all peoples, rather than to think that by this very deed he may have wished to offend both France & the Allies.

But a New Nation that owes its existence to His Majesty's protection & to the powerful Aid of French Arms, experiencing in France, in the person of its Representative, a type of outrage of which all the Powers are jointly and severally concerned in making a complaint, has the right to expect from you a signal Satisfaction.

The King's word in the Treaties establishes a national engagement which binds his Subjects, & which is added to the Sum of the Laws entrusted to your custody.

Accordingly, the King's Attorney General has requested the imprisonment made on the 15th Instant, of the person of Mr. Thomas Barclai, to be abrogated and annulled; the Jailer to be enjoined to open the gates for him, & the Clerk of the Court to expunge his name from its records; the effects seized to his prejudice to be restored to him; cautions and prohibitions to be issued to all Bailiffs & Sergeants within the jurisdiction of the Court to respect his person; lastly, that the Decree that will be issued be ordered to be printed, published, & proclaimed.

Du Don fils

The Court, granting the request of the King's Attorney General, has abrogated & abrogates the imprisonment made the fifteenth of this month of the person of Thomas Barclai; in consequence, enjoins the Jailer to open the gates to him, & the Bailiff to expunge his name from the records; restores to him the effects seized to his prejudice; issues cautions & prohibitions to all Bailiffs & Sergeants within the jurisdiction of the Court to respect his person; moreover, orders that the present decree be printed & proclaimed. Done at Bordeaux, in Parliament, on the nineteenth of May one thousand seven hundred and eighty-seven.

Mr. De Pichard, President
Collated. Signed, Lafargue.

FFAA: Pol. Corr., U.S., v. 32, f. 260-261vo. (LC transcription).

[1] *Jean Baptiste Pierre Jules Dudon fils (junior), whose French title was* Procureur Général du Roi.

Louis Guillaume Otto to Comte de Montmorin

[Translation]

My Lord.   New York, 19 May 1787.

. . . . .

However, there is one subject, My Lord, regarding which I still cannot offer any hope; this is the reimbursement of the considerable sums which His Majesty advanced to the United States during the war. In looking over the reports which I have had the honor to submit to the Court, You will easily comprehend that in the present confusion of finances it is impossible for Congress to fulfill its engagements, and that all our requests, however pressing they may be, will be inefficacious until the federal Government has completely altered its posture.

That Government, My Lord, is so little stable that, in spite of the precaution which I shall take of transmitting to You only reliable news, You will still find many contradictions in my reports. I hope that You will be so good as to attribute this apparent inexactitude to the inconceivable vacillation of affairs to which I am witness. Frequently a law is repealed, a political plan rejected, a resolution of Congress annulled by another resolution, before the Despatches which are supposed to inform You of them can reach Versailles.

I am with a profound respect My Lord Your most humble and most obedient Servant.   Otto

rec. 11 July

FFAA: Pol. Corr., U.S., v. 32, f. 262-263 (LC transcription).

John Lamb to Thomas Jefferson

Alicante bay May 20th 1787.

...I hope by this time that your Excellency is fulley persuaded of that Vile of that man De Expelley, *whome I have often warn^{d.} of before this,* his letters have been too freely handed to your Excellency, and to Congress likewise, for the benefit of our peace At Algiers. I most Heartily hope Congress will not be led to thank a man whome was Turn^{d.} Out of Algiers for the Most Atrotious crimes, and Sum Say Confined at present, and I make no Doubt of the Truth of the Same, if Your Excellency Can come at the Truth from Madrid, I am of opinion that you will think as I Do on the matter. I add that we have not had a wors Enemy than the above mentioned De Expelley. How far he Deceiv^{d.} Mr. Carmichael whilst he was holding him up to Our publick Vew I cannot pretend to Say. but if Mr. Carmichael was not Descive in the Man he had a Desire to baffle my efforts whilst on my Late Mission to make room for a more favourite plan. with news I can give your Excelency no lite at present, but that the number of our wretched people in Algiers are reduced by the Plague. Unhappy men indeed. I have had a Verey Disagreable winter, but am Sumwat Recruted. I hope to be at Congress by the begin^g August nex. I am Excedingly Sorrey that m^{r.} Barklay missed me that he had Authority to Settle my acc^{ts.} he writes me

I Am your Excellencys Most Hm^{le.} Servt.   John Lamb.

LC: Jefferson Papers, microfilm reel 7 (ALS).

John Adams to John Jay

Dear Sir   Grosvenor Square May 23. 1787

. . . . . .

Inclosed also are Copies of Letters from the Commissioners of Loans at Amsterdam, which render it necessary for me, to go to Amsterdam. I Shall Set off, on Fryday the twenty fifth, and hope to return in three Weeks, or less. it is with great regret that I find myself reduced to the necessity, of opening a new Loan, without the explicit ~~orders~~ and particular orders of Congress. But there is no Alternative but this or immediate and total Ruin to the Credit of the United States. Such is the nature of Money trans-actions in Holland, that if the punctual Payment of the Interest is not advertised, a Panick arises & spreads the Stock falls, and every one is eager to get rid of what he has in his hands. In Consequence of a delay only of a few days, to advertise the Payment of our Interest in June, my Obligations fell to ninety five Per Cent, as I am informed. But immediately upon the Advertisement appearing they rose again to ninety Nine, which is as high as they have been for several Years.–

Mr Barclay has drawn upon me for more Money than I expected to pay the Expence of Presents and other Things in the Morocco Negotiation, and has made Several draughts after I had Supposed, or at least hoped that the Payments were all made. – But I could do no other than presume, that the Demands were necessary, and accept his Bills. He will render his Account to Congress or the Board of Treasury. But if I am not mistaken he has drawn upon me for, near five thousand Pounds Sterling a Sum considerably, more than, one quarter Part of the Eighty thousand dollars, appropriated by Congress to Treaties with four Powers though it was always expected that Algiers would be more costly than all the other three.

The Expences of Coll Franks's Journeys and Voyages, and that of Coll Smith's Tour to Lisbon as well as mine to Portsmouth and Holland, will amount to Something, tho not very considerable. What Draughts upon the Bankers in Holland, Mr Jefferson has made, as mentioned in their Letter I know not, unless it be to pay for honourary Swords and Medals, ordered by Coll Humphreys[1] in obedience to the orders of Congress, for which I gave a Letter of Credit before I left France. Possibly Congress may have Authorised Mr Jefferson to draw upon their Commissioners in Holland. if they have I am glad of it, but had not been informed of it.

I regret very much, that I have not yet a Letter of Recall, which I might upon this my last tour to the Hague present to their High Mightinessess and take my Leave, in order to my Return home, upon the Expiration of my Commission to St James's. – But Altho this is now impossible I hope, Sir, soon to receive Such a Letter of Recall, that I may, have time to transmit it with a Memorial, which must answer the End of an Audience of Leave. With great Respect, I have the Honour to be &c

                                                            John Adams
Read 23 July 1787

NA: PCC, item 84, v. 6, pp. 481-484 (ALS); M247, reel 113.
[1] Humphreys, David (1752-1818). American military officer, diplomat, and poet. Served with the Continental Army, 1776-1783. Lieutenant colonel, aide-de-camp to George Washington, with whom he remained closely associated. Served as secretary to the American commissioners for negotiating treaties of amity and commerce in Europe. As a poet, associated with the "Hartford Wits" in composing The Anarchiad, 1786-1787. Served as secret agent in Europe during the Nootka Sound controversy, 1790-1791. U.S. Minister to Portugal, 1791-1797. U.S. commissioner to negotiate with the Dey of Algiers, 1793. U.S. Minister to Spain, 1797-1801. Imported Merino sheep into Connecticut, 1802, where he established a successful woolen mill.

Louis Guillaume Otto to Comte de Montmorin

[Translation]

N⁰· 88.   New York, 25 May 1787.
My Lord.

The attempt of the Southern States to transfer the residence of Congress to Philadelphia has just failed in such a way as to throw much ridicule on the authors of the motion. They were already sure of the consent of 7 States, the proposition was formally made, and the President was about to collect the votes, when a Delegate from Jersey, who had given his word to vote for Philadelphia, suddenly regretted it and left the chamber; some of his Colleagues vainly followed him in order to call him back; he embarked immediately and left his party in the greatest consternation. It is thought that one of the secret reasons for the activity of the Southern Delegates is their desire to force Mr. Jay, an inhabitant of New York, to resign from the position of Minister of Foreign Affairs, since his personal interests would probably not permit him to follow Congress to Philadelphia. Many other infinitely less important motives are also mentioned. Mr. Jay and the Northern Delegates, although of the minority party, have triumphed over their adversaries; they have on their side firmness, intelligence, and talents.

While the weakness of the general Government diminishes the importance of the United States in foreign countries, the activity of individuals makes the American flag known in the farthest reaches of Asia. Most of the ships sent to China last year have just arrived here with rich cargoes that are sold with an inconceivable rapidity. There is among these ships a little Sloop of fifty tons which astonished the Chinese, accustomed to seeing the great Vessels of the European Companies arrive in their port. This audacity, and the Ginseng that the Americans carry there in abundance, has already given them some celebrity, and they have formed very solid liaisons with Chinese merchants. The cargoes of five ships that have just arrived are valued at some two and a half million Livres tournois, and the profits amount to 33 percent. Several merchants are now involved in a commerce from port to port; this year they have sent three ships that are supposed to go first to France and load there for India, from which they will proceed to Canton. It appears that we shall see American ships more frequently at Isle de France and at Pondichery. The English, who in former times exclusively furnished the merchandise of China to these States, show much jealousy of this new Commerce, and when one considers the great consumption here of tea, porcelain, Nankins, and silks, the profits of England must be appreciably diminished. It is from this point of view, My Lord, that it appears that we should not be displeased to find United States ships in the seas of India, since it is demonstrated that the more the Americans augment their navigation, the more they make that of Great Britain fall.

That power is still treated by Congress with the same coldness. The equivocal reception of Sir John Temple has not however prevented the English ministry from sending Mr. Bond here to reside in the quality of Consul in the State of Pennsylvania. The resolution of Congress holds "that although it is not the custom to receive Consuls without having previously concluded a treaty of Commerce, Mr. Bond will enjoy all the prerogatives accorded by the law of nations and the laws of the country *to the Consul of a nation that has not made a treaty with the United States."* These prerogatives are entirely imaginary, and Sir John Temple, although invested with the title of Consul General, has neither jurisdiction, nor the power to negotiate any matter with Congress. Mr. Bond has, in addition to the quality of Consul, a Commission as Agent of Commerce, of which this Assembly has not wished to take any notice.

I am with a profound respect My Lord Your most humble and most obedient servant   Otto.
rec. 11 July.

FFAA: Pol. Corr., U.S., v. 32, f. 266-267vo. (LC transcription).

Contract for Dutch Loan

[Amsterdam June 1, 1787]

On the first Day of June in the Year one thousand Seven hundred and eighty Seven, appeared before me Pieter Galenus van Hole, Notary of Amsterdam, admitted by the hon^ble Court of Holland. –

His Excellency The Honble John Adams Esqr Minister plenipotentiary on the part of the united States of America, &^a &^a in quality as especially empower'd and authorized by the abovementioned States of America in Congress assembled, for and in behalf of Said States of America to raise a Loan with any Person or Persons, States or Companies, with Subjoined Assurance in good faith to ratify and fulfill all that Shall be done in this Respect by him hon^ble Appearer according to authentick Copy and Translation of the original commission or Power exhibited to me Notary and deposited in my Custody in behalf of the joint Money Lenders. –

The hon^ble Appearer residing in London but being now in this City.–

And the hon^ble Appearer acknowledged himself in his aforesaid quality and thus in the name and in behalf of the abovementioned States of

America to be duly and lawfully indebted to and in behalf of Sundry Persons or Money Lenders, in all a Sum of one Million of Guilders dutch curr^t money arising from and on account of so much ready Money received by him – the hon^{ble} Appearer in his aforesaid quality to his perfect Satisfaction from the Said Money Lenders pursuant the Receipt here after mentioned to be Signed by the hon^{ble} Appearer under the authentick Copies hereof, expressly and formally disavowing the Excuse of untold Moneys. –

And the hon^{ble} appearer promised in his aforesaid quality to repay and reimburse in this City the Said Sum of one Million of Guilders free from all Costs, Charges and Dammages to the abovementioned Money Lenders or their Assigns, at the expiration of fifteen years after the first Day of June 1787 and that, in the following manner, to Wit

That the abovementioned Principal Shall remain fixed during the Space of ten years and that with the eleventh year and thus on the first day of June 1798 a fifth Part or two hundred thousand Guilders of the Said Principal of one million Shall be redeemed and in the Same Manner from year to year untill the first day of June 1802 inclusive – So that the whole Principal Shall be redeemed and discharged within the abovementioned Space of fifteen years. And that mean while for Said Principal at first for the Whole and afterwards for the Residue, at the Expiration of every year, Interest Shall be paid, at the Rate of five Pr Cent in the year, Commencing the first Day of June 1787 and to continue untill the final accomplishment and that on Coupons to be Signed by or on the Part of Said hon^{ble} Appearer in his aforesaid quality. – That the abovementioned Redeeming Shall be performed by drawing in the presence of a Notary and Witnesses in this City after the Expiration of the firstmentioned ten years in Such a manner that the N^{os} of the Bonds or Obligations drawn, Shall be betimes made Known in the publick Papers. That the Payment of the Interests as also the Redeeming of the respective periods Shall be made at the Compting houses of the hereafter mentioned Gentlemen Directors or at Such other Places within this City as Shall likewise be advertized in the publick Papers. – That the Directors of this Negotiation Shall be Messieurs Wilhem and Jan Willink and Nicolaas and Jacob van Staphorst of this City Merchants, who are by these presents thereto named and appointed by the hon^{ble} Appearer in his aforesaid quality. –

. . . . .

NA: PCC, *item 145, pp. 271-295 (translation); M247, reel 156.*

Peter Allaire to Sir George Yonge
with Occurrences from 3 May to 4 June 1787

Sir[1]   New York 4 June 1787
...I have anticipated partly your Orders, with Respect to the procuring
the Arrivals & departures of all Vessells to the Imports, Exports, what
Cargoes, produce in return, & what part of the American Traffic, is carried
on by Great Britain, to send them, quarterly to your house with an Acco[t]
of what Laws relate to commerce Authenticated from the Different States,
will cost about fifty pounds a State, that is Twenty five to some Clerk in
the Custome house & £25 to the Governors private Secretary, a year....

· · · · ·

The Convention, Congress, and meeting of the Clergy of all
denominations, is now at Philadelphia, the old Proverb – great cry & little
wool, when your house settles business with us it must, (at *least it ought*) to
have an authentic information of the Trade carried on, at present *you are
intirely the carriers of the British plantation Trade*, and from this *State* you have
a full *one third of its commerce*. it is no desire or wish of mine to engage in
the procuring those informations from the different States as I shall have
my labour for my pains. if you order, I will Endeavour to Obey and it gives
me particular Satisfaction to find, that my mode of proceeding here, is
approved of by your house. I shall endeavour to merit their good Opinion.
M[r] Bond has been acknowledged as British Consul & Commercial Agent,
& all the privileges &c allowed him, with whom they have no Treaty.
there are none here, but those with whom they have Treaties. I have the
honor to be with the Greatest Respect   [P.A.]

Occurrences from 3[d] May to [4] June 1787
· · · · ·

With respect to the Power, Credit, Confidence and flourishing Situation
of the United States in Congress Assembled, as has been *Roundly asserted
to Your house*, I beg leave to quote the following Resolve of theres, passed
the 27th April 1787

Whereas the committee...to whom was referred a Motion of the
Delegates of New York for directing the Secretary at War, to Issue
Instructions Imediately to the Officers in the Recruiting Service, to suspend
any future Inlistments of Troops under the Resolution of Congress of 20th
October 1786 until the further direction of Congress, have Reported, That
in their Opinion the *present* Circumstances of the United States, makes it
prudent to postpone the further Inlistment of Troops &c &c. Therefore
Resolved, that as *neither of the Requisitions* of the 20 October 1786, nor the

Loans which the Board of Treasury were directed to make in Consequence thereof, for paying and subsisting the Troops directed to be Raised by the Resolves of the 20 October 1786 last, have yielded the sums expected from the same, and on the prospect of Obtaining which the additional Number of thirteen hundred & forty Men was determined to be raised, and as the *present Critical and Embarassed situation of the Funds of the United States* are such as not to permit the raising & Equiping the whole Number of Troops, mentioned in the said Resolve, without interfering with the more Necessary & Important purposes of Collecting supplies for the Maintenance of the Civil List, and the Contingencies of the Federal Government, the payment of the Interest, and such part of the Capital as are, and will become due on the foreign loans, and as it would be highly dangerous and Impolitic, either to apply the Sums appropriated to these purposes, to the Maintenance of an additional Military Establishment, in itself not Necessary, to the full extent or to place Arms, in the hands of a body of diciplined Troops, for whose pay & subsistance the united States *are not at present, nor will soon probably be in a Situation to provide for,* therefore Resolved, that the Secretary at War, be, And he is hereby Ordered to Issue, Imediately Instructions to the Officers in the Recruiting Service to suspend any further inlistments, under the Resolve of Congress of 20 October 1786 until further directions, except so far as to compleat the Corps now in Service, on the Ohio, or its Neighbourhood, that he direct the Troops already raised, with a suitable Number of Commissioned Officers to Rendeavous at fort Pitt, and that he report to Congress the Arrangement necessary, for compleating the said Corps, and for discharging the Officers who may have been commissioned, but whose Services, are by this Resolution considered unnecessary. NB the Military Establishment of Congress is Seven hundred & Eighty Men, non commissioned Officers included, nor have they funds sufficient to keep up that Number, without they can obtain more power, and be enabled to compel the delinquent States to pay up their Quota's of their federal Debt, and to lay such Taxes on the different States, as they shall think Necessary for the support of the federal Government, which they expect to have delegated to them, from the *Commissioners,* now *sitting at Philadelphia.* on the breaking up of which every State will Imediately call their legislatures, to Confirm by Law, whatever power maybe agreed on, *without which our Independency must fall to the ground,* and we become an insignificant Republic, consisting of thirteen petty Kingdoms for the Jealosies of the different States, *have increased, are Increasing and must be restrained, or Ruin'd.*

By the above Resolve, you will please to judge, what *Regard, or Attention,* should be paid to those Gentlemen, *who Roundly Assert, that every thing is Harmony & Concord with us.*

Three of the Members of the Assembly of Boston have been convicted of Seditious Practices in aiding and Abeting the Insurgents, Cap^n Moses Harvey Member from Montague fined fifty pounds, and to set one hour on the Gallows with a Rope round his Neck & to find Security for one Years good behaviour, Eli Parker Member from Amherst & James Fowler Member from Southwick fined Twenty pounds each, & find Security for good behaviour for 9 Months and *Seven* convicted of Treason and received sentence of Death

The above Sentence has exasperated the Insurgents & they have began their March into the state of Massachusets, they increase daily, and where the mischeif will end, is Difficult to say. I do not think they will put their Sentence into Execution, 790 of the Insurgents, have Accepted Pardons.

The Ship *Empress of China* from this port to Canton is arrived, has been out thirteen Months, the profits of which has induced the Merchants of Boston to fit out two Brigs & a Brig from this port for Canton, (about Six of those Vessells would about make, one of Your East India Ships, that is, carry about as much.)

.   .   .   .   .

Congress have just received an Acco^t from the Com^d Officer on the Ohio, that a Body of Insurgents, have taken possession of Fort St Vincent, and refuse any Obedience & connection, with the federal Troops, and who live in a lawless manner, having taken the above information, into Imediate consideration, they came to the following Resolution, Resolved That the Secretary at War, direct the Commanding Officer of the United States, on the Ohio, to take Imediate & Efficient measures, for disposessing a body of Men, who have in a Lawless and unauthorised manner taken possession of Fort St Vincent in defiance of the proclamation of the united States, and that he Employ the whole, or such part of the force under his Command as he shall judge Necessary to Effect the object.

Shays, Days, Wheeler and Parkins, are by advertisement to meet at Lake Champlain the first of May. we have the Insurgents from North to West, we only want the Southern States, to follow the Example to be compleatly surrounded by them, the East being the Ocean.

Congress have adjourned the 27th May to meet the 5th June at Philadelphia, the General Convention are now seting there their Object is, as soon as the Convention, have setled and Arranged the new federal Constitution, that a Congress be Imediately formed to put the same into Execution, and to inform those members who are not appointed to the General Convention what occurs daily, as most of the Convention are Members of Congress; so that they alternately Sit in Convention & in Congress, it is expected no material business will be transacted by Congress before November next,) by which time I expect your Answer, with Respect to the Gentlemans doing business with Your house, and what I am to do, with regard to the Imports & Exports of the United States, Number of Vessells, & Tonage of the different Nations trading therewith, and what proportion of trade is carried on by Great Britain; it is a labourious, and extensive undertaking, yet such as I humbly think your House ought to have, before a Treaty of commerce is entered into, without which you go, *en tatant*, as to a treaty of Amity, my Opinion is, *your Interest consists in disuniting them*, and that *they do not agree to fullfill the Preliminaries of Peace*, or fully to Enter into a Commercial negotiation; for by those means, you secure to yourselves the whole of the fur trade, and keep the people of the Six Nothern States in a continual ferment, you may depend *your party gains ground daily*, and should there ever be a War between the united States and Great Britain, I can assure you, that where you had one friend the last War, you would find three now, for the People at large, have been deceived, cheated, and ruined by Congress. The individual States have tenfold taxes to pay, and nine tenths of their Commerce deprived them, which they enjoyed before the Rebellion, nor should I be surprised, that in the space of few years, we should send you deputies, to take us on the same footing as Ireland, a glorious transaction to be performed by your house.

. . . . .

June 4   General Washington has been Elected President of the General Convention, now held at Philadelphia, Nine States are represented, letters have been wrote to those States that are not Represented to send their Delegates Imediately. Rhode Island still continues Refractory, they refuse sending delegates

I remain with Respect   [P.A.]

PRO: FO 4/5, pp. 303-326 (LC transcription).
   [1] Yonge, Sir George (1731-1812). British government official. Member of Parliament, 1754-1761, 1763-1796. One of the Lords of the Admiralty, 1766-1770. Vice-treasurer for Ireland, April-July 1782. Secretary for war, July 1782-April 1783, December 1783-July 1794. Master of the mint, July 1794-February 1799. Governor of the Cape of Good Hope, 1799-1801.

Louis Guillaume Otto to Comte de Montmorin

[Translation]

N°· 90.   New York, 8 June 1787.
My Lord.
   North Carolina having passed a resolution to remit to Congress some 80 thousand piastres for the payment of interest due in Europe, the Delegates of that State secretly arranged with M. Van Berkel to have this Sum sent

to Holland. Although this reimbursement is not very considerable, I thought I should evince to the Commissioners of the Treasury my surprise that without their consent a remittance had been arranged to the prejudice of the claim that we have on the United States; I made them understand that this measure would appear all the more extraordinary in France, that the interest of the loan from Holland last year had been charged to the Royal Treasury, and that it would have been much more appropriate to have transmitted to France whatever funds the United States could dispose of to meet the payment of that interest, which amounts to 80 thousand piastres annually. The Commissioners have given me their word that they knew nothing of this arrangement and that they would do whatever was possible to prevent the execution of it, all the more because it was very irregular and contrary to the articles of Confederation.

The English, My Lord, are no happier than the Dutch and His Majesty's subjects with regard to the recovery of their debts. Upon the request of Mr. John Adams, Congress has again sent the various States a circular letter to engage them to religiously fulfill the article of the treaty relative to the English creditors, and to make them understand that no Legislature has the power to make laws contrary to a treaty ratified by Congress. Only Maryland has adopted this principle by a solemn resolution; the other States will have difficulty in subscribing to it, and I even have reason to believe that Congress does not expect it. In addition, Mr. Adams appears to have renounced the hope of making a treaty of Commerce with England, although he has done everything in his power to gain the good will of the Ministry and the people of England....

It is probable, My Lord, that before his return to America, Mr. Adams will succeed in concluding a treaty of Commerce with Portugal. It is a trophy that is missing from the monument of a Minister who in his letters has had the vanity to call himself the *Washington of diplomacy*. Congress has already named an agent to reside at Lisbon. The present chill between that Court and that of St. James could be favorable to the negotiations of the United States, which are naturally partial to the Commerce of Portugal, to which they were long accustomed before the revolution, and which is for them the most lucrative and even the most indispensable, when one considers the immense quantity of Madeira wine that is consumed annually in America. Mr. Adams could therefore be honored for having made a much more useful treaty than those with Sweden and Prussia.

I am with a profound respect My Lord Your most humble and most obedient servant   Otto.
rec. 11 July

FFAA: Pol. Corr., U.S., v. 32, f. 273-274vo. (LC transcription).

Louis Guillaume Otto to Comte de Montmorin

[Translation]

N°· 91.   New York, 10 June 1787.

My Lord.

In my Despatch N°· 85 I limited myself to submitting to the Court a general idea of the changes which should be made in the federal Constitution by the Philadelphia *Convention*. The plans for reform which have been communicated to me since then enable me to inform You more amply of the innovations which the Deputies propose to introduce. – As it is a question of entirely recasting the American Constitution, I hope, My Lord, that You will excuse the lengthiness which it will be impossible for me to avoid. One is rarely a spectator at a political operation more important than this one, and it is difficult to confine to a few pages matters which should determine the good fortune, the power and the future vigor of a rising Empire.

The chief defect of the present Constitution, My Lord, is inequality of representation. Each of the States has one voice in the federal Council, but their populations, their areas, their riches differ tremendously. Georgia, Rhode Island, and Delaware have the same importance in Congress as Virginia, Pennsylvania, and Massachusetts, even though these latter States are at least fifty times more populous and wealthy than the others. It is a question therefore of dividing the States into districts composed of a certain number of inhabitants, and of giving each district the right to send a Deputy to Congress. By this method Virginia would have fifty votes for one of Georgia's, and a resolution of Congress would express the will of the *majority of the inhabitants*, and not of the *majority of a fortuitous division of the States*. The Deputies of all the districts would then form a political body similar to the House of Commons in England. The votes there would be counted by head and not collectively by States, and Bills concerning finances could only be proposed in this chamber.

But the intrigues of an enterprising man, the gold of a foreign power, the fatal eloquence of an accredited member, or perhaps the greed of a merchant could form a party there contrary to the general good. To avoid this inconvenience, they propose another Legislative branch which could be called the *Senate*, and which would resemble the upper Chamber of the English Parliament in its functions. The Senators would be elected by the Chamber of Deputies in proportion to the votes of each State. A resolution could only have the force of law after having been approved by a majority of the two Chambers.

However, it would still be possible that the press of business might precipitate important resolutions. A President elected for six years, and his Council, composed of various Ministers of State, would therefore have the right to examine these resolutions before they were made public and to send them back for reconsideration by the two chambers. In this case a majority of two thirds of the representatives would be necessary to pass a law.

But despite all these precautions, one could still only be certain of good *Legislation*, of which Congress, even in its present form, has acquitted itself well enough. It is not the same with the *executive* branch, since that Assembly has hitherto only had the right to *recommend* to the various States measures which appeared to it to be the most advantageous. According to the new plans, the President and his Council would have the right to execute by force the resolutions of the federal Council in somewhat the same manner as the Emperor carries out the decrees of the diet of Ratisbon, by calling out the troops or by ordering several neighboring States to invade a Government which refused to submit to the collective will of the States.

This last part of the plan, My Lord, will meet with the greatest difficulties, and even though several Deputies believe that they can assure its passage, it is impossible for me to put my trust therein. The interests of the small States would soon be sacrificed to the ambitious plans of their neighbors who, having the advantage of a much larger representation in Congress, would always be sure of a majority.

The reformers then observe how difficult it is to obtain the consent of the thirteen States to any innovation whatsoever, as ordained by the old Constitution. The opposition of a single State has prevented for four years the establishment of an impost of 5 percent on imports, an impost which would have sufficed for all the needs of the confederation. This faculty, almost as ruinous to the United States as the *liberum Veto* has been to the republic of Poland, is entirely incompatible with a well-ordered Government. Consequently, it is proposed that henceforth the vote of ten States be sufficient for any alteration that circumstances might render necessary in the general system, and that any State which refuses to conform thereto be excluded forever from the confederation.

To put an end to the contradictions which are sometimes found between the laws of particular States and those of the general Government, they propose to appoint a Committee of the two Chambers, charged with examining all the laws of the individual States and with rejecting all those that are contrary to the maxims and views of Congress. The States will particularly be deprived of the power to regulate commerce or to pass a law on any subject relating to the law of nations, and Congress reserves that branch of Legislation exclusively to itself.

The two Chambers of Congress, in concert with the Council of revision, would have the exclusive right to determine the number of troops and ships necessary to sustain the Majesty of the American People and, without asking for the particular consent of the States, they could allocate the taxes and the imposts in the manner which to them appeared most equitable, and in case of refusal by a particular State, Congress could levy double its quota on it by means of its own officers, in order to punish it for its opposition.

The Deputies, My Lord, who have communicated to me these various plans, are determined to sustain them with vigor in the Philadelphia Assembly. I shall not repeat here the doubts which I have expressed elsewhere regarding their success; but it is my duty to submit to You the opinion of another class of men, whose party will be equally strong and perhaps more obstinate in the Assembly in question.

These men observe that in the present state of affairs, it is impossible to unite under a single head all the members of the confederation. Their political interests, their commercial views, their customs, and their laws are so heterogenous that there is no resolution of Congress that can be equally useful and popular in the South and in the North of the Continent; even their jealousy appears to be an insurmountable obstacle. During the war the States had a common interest in repulsing powerful and cruel enemies; this interest exists no longer, why repair a building that no longer even has a foundation? Commerce henceforth becomes the principal basis for the political system of these States: The inhabitants of the North are fishermen and navigators, those of the center farmers, those of the South Planters. Their legislation should encourage, ameliorate, and perfect the various branches of their industry. To say that Congress will be able to make regulations that are specific and useful for each of these branches is to say that Congress will suffer from no passions at all, that intrigue will never play a part in its measures, that the interests of the North will never be sacrificed to those of the South: a thing theoretically impossible and known to be false from experience. "In this crisis," continue the partisans of this system, "there remains only one way to give each State all the power of which it is susceptible. That is to divide the Continent into several confederations, each of which would have a general Government independent of the others. This division is not difficult; nature appears to have indicated it. The confederation of the North could be composed of New Hampshire, Massachusetts, Rhode Island, Connecticut, Vermont, and the State of New York up to the Hudson River. The confederation of the Center would contain all the land situated between that river and the Potomac, and that of the South would be composed of Virginia, the two Carolinas, and Georgia. – The products, the interests, the laws, even the manners of the inhabitants would thus be classed according to their various nuances, and the three Governments would be fortified by reason of their proximity and of the identity of their political views. To those who say that one of these divisions might easily fall under the yoke of a foreign nation, has it not often been seen in Europe that several powers unite against another power which threatens to invade them? Treaties of alliance among the various States would serve as a common bond and would produce the same effect as a general confederation."

The Cincinnati, that is to say, the former officers of the old American Army, are interested in the establishment of a strong Government, since they are all creditors of the public, but considering the weakness of the national Council and the impossibility of being paid by the present administration, they propose to throw all the States into a single mass and to place General Washington at their head, with all the prerogatives and powers of a crowned head. They even threaten to bring about this revolution themselves with arms in hand as soon as they are convinced of the uselessness of the present *Convention*. This plan is too extravagant to merit the least discussion. The Society of the Cincinnati, which was formed without any public sanction, today thinks of adjusting the political constitution without having been authorized to do so by the people; but it is too weak and too unpopular to make any impression.

A fourth party, and perhaps the one that will triumph over all the others, proposes to leave things on their present footing. The State of Rhode Island, the Governor and the principal administrative leaders of New York, Mr. John Adams, and a great number of individuals in the various States are of this party. "We do not find," they say, "that the situation of the United States is as bad as some would have us to believe. Our cities and our population grow daily, our vast territories are being cleared, our Commerce and our industry are being extended prodigiously. If some districts lack gold and silver, we will give them paper that will replace it for them. If we are not respected in Europe, we will not be the more so after having sacrificed to a sovereign body a part of our liberty. Our foreign creditors will be paid when we have the means, and until then they cannot do us any harm. Why change a political system which has made the States prosper and whose only inconvenience is that it defers the payment of our debts? A government more absolute would expose us to the despotism of an Aristocratic Assembly or to the caprice of a single man; for how can it be imagined that the members of Congress, allowed to dispose freely of an army, a navy, a treasury swollen by contributions from all the States, will be willing to return to the ordinary class of Citizens at the end of a year and exchange public administration for that of a farm? It is important to our liberty that Congress be only a simple diplomatic body and not a sovereign and absolute Assembly."

It will be very difficult for the Philadelphia Assembly to adopt a plan from among this great variety of projects that will be agreeable to all the parties and all the States. If I may be permitted to have an opinion, My Lord, I would range myself on the side of those who propose not to change anything in the present confederation; not that I think that it will render justice sooner to the foreign and domestic creditors, nor that it will enhance the standing of the United States, nor even that it will preserve union and good understanding among its members longer, but because it is better suited than any other political system to the spirit of the people. Rich men, merchants, public officials, the Cincinnati are all in favor of a more absolute government, but their number is very small when it is compared to the whole mass of Citizens.

Whatever may transpire, the General Convention has just begun its sessions after having unanimously elected General Washington as its President. This nomination will certainly give more prestige to everything that emanates from this important and respectable assembly. It is hoped that its resolutions will bear the seal of the wisdom, moderation, and farsightedness, which are the General's principal traits of character.

I leave it, My Lord, to persons more clever than I to sort out what type of Government would be most agreeable to our interests in America, and I limit myself to furnishing them the raw materials.

I am with a profound respect My Lord Your most humble and most obedient servant   Otto.
recd. 11 July

FFAA: Pol. Corr., U.S., v. 32, f. 275-280vo. (LC transcription).

Thomas Barclay to Thomas Jefferson

Dear Sir   Bordeaux 12 June 1787 –
After you left this place My Fever Encreased upon me and Confined me two Days to my Bed, I am Now pretty well and I think I shall proceed home tomorrow, But I have Not given M$^{rs.}$ Barclay any hopes of seeing me soon lest I shou'd Disapoint her. – I Never stood so much in Need of your advice as I Do at this Moment, The House of French & Nephew have Refused Every accommodation that I have had in My Power to offer, and all the attempts that I Cou'd make to satisfy them have produced nothing But the Most Malignant and Malicious answers that Nothing but the Money or security in this City wou'd be Received, with the strongest asseverations that wherever I Go, thither will they Pursue Me. – Under

these Circumstances I Confess I am Very ill at Ease – and indeed somewhat Bewildered, The Idea of another attack being Made on my Person, perhaps in the Moment of My Joining my Family, is a Very unpleasing object for Contemplation, and it seems in some Degree Necesary that I should get among my Papers before I proceed to America – My Embarrasments arise from a Very unfortunate Connection that I Formed at L'Orient with a M. Moylan there, who Dying suddenly left Me a Great Debt to strugle with, and after paying about Two thirds of it, I was on the point of proceeding to America, from whence in Eighteen Months I have Not Received a livre but Fifty Pounds, and I think have not Mess. French & Nephew in the Most Treacherous Manner thrown this Dificulty in my way, In twelve or fifteen Months I shou'd have Discharged the Remainder of My Engagements – Wou'd you Beleive that those People in the last letter which they wrote to me at Madrid, said that I was, in going to America, proceeding as Any honest good man in my Circumstances ought to Do. It is a very Common thing for the Minister at Versailles to give to People in my situation a safe Conduct for six or twelve Months, and I wrote to the Marquis De la Fayette, upon this subject from the Prison, and twice afterwards, but to none of those letters have I Received any answer whatever – Nor do I Pretend to form any Conjecture from this silence – All I Can say is that it will be Utterly Impossible for Me to Pay Mess. French or any Body Else without going to America – and that Every Attempt made to Prevent Me will answer no End but that of Injuring all Parties Concerned – If my Person is at Risk I Cannot Attend to the settlement of My affairs – I Propose leaving My family behind Me, and M. Zachriah Loreilhe, who is Equally Bound with me in all the Engagements, will stay at Lorient untill they are liquidated. After having thus stated to you my Condition, any appology for the Trouble I give you will be Unnecessary. If my Office of Consul is sufficient to Protect My Person, a safe Conduct will be Unnecessary – But then one will be wanted for M. Loreilhe – If this security Can be obtained Even for Six Months, it will Give time to look about, and make some Exertions, But in Seven Years of the Present situation, nothing of Consequence Cou'd be Effected – I Beg you will take such steps as you shall Judge necessary to Releive Me from the shocking situation in which I am placed, and if you Judge proper Communicate with the Marquis De La Fayette – I hardly think I shall leave Bordeaux until there is time for a line from You in answer to this – therefore please to put one under Cover to M. Bondfield,[1] some of My Friends hold forth the Danger that I may Run as soon as I get out of the Jurisdiction of the Parliament of Bordeaux. You will wonder perhaps at my undecidedness on the point of going from hence – I Cannot help it, I have

so much to Risk, and the Issue is so uncertain, I am Ever Dear Sir Your
Most Obed & Obliged   Tho⁴ Barclay

.   .   .   .   .

LC: *Jefferson Papers, microfilm reel 7 (ALS).*
  ¹ *Bondfield, John (fl. 1775-1790). Montreal merchant who provided supplies to
American forces retreating from Canada in early 1776. He resettled at Bordeaux in 1777,
and the following year was appointed American commercial agent for Bordeaux and several
other French ports. Although he never held a formal diplomatic or consular position, he
remained a strong supporter of American interests throughout the 1780s.*

Congressional Committee Report
Regarding the Spanish Negotiations

[New York June 13, 1787]
  Committee to whom the letter from Mʳ Jay of the 9ᵗʰ of may was
referred for the "Express instructions of Congress on the points in difference
between the United States and the Crown of Spain" Report
  That any material departure from the Original intentions of Congress as
expressed in their resolutions of the 25th of august 1785, would be
obviously disagreeable to a large majority of the Citizens of the United
States.
  That Congress being desirous of conciliating between his Catholic
Majesty and these United States the most happy and lasting friendship
should so conduct themselves as to merit and preserve the confidence of
their constituents: As well as to convince his Catholic Majesty by a fixed
and stable plan of policy of their determination to preserve inviolate the
rights of their citizens, and in no case whatever to enter into engagements
which would be violated.
  That the Secretary for the department of Foreign affairs be directed in a
decent but firm decided and candid manner to State to Don Diego de
Gardoqui the embarrassments Congress are involved in, their desire of
conciliating with his Sovereign a lasting friendship, And indispensable
obligation to preserve the right of the United States to their Territorial
bounds and the free Navigation of the Mississipi from its source to the
Oceans as established in their treaties with Great Britain

NA: PCC, item 25, v. 2, p. 467 (C); M247, reel 32.

John Adams to John Jay

Sir   Grosvenor Square, London June 16. 1787
    Inclosed is a Copy of the Translation from the Dutch into the English, of the Contract, entered into by me in behalf of the United States by Virtue of their Full Power for a Millon of Guilders. This Measure became absolutely necessary, to prevent the total Ruin of their Credit, and the greatest Injustice, to their former Creditors, who are possessed of their Obligations: for the failure in Payment of the Interest, but for one day, would in holland cause those Obligations to depreciate in their Value like Paper Money.
    It is of great Importance that this Contract Should receive a prompt Ratification in Congress, and be retransmitted to Amsterdam as soon as possible. Whether this Loan may not enable Congress, or their Board of Treasury, to raise the Credit of their own Paper at home in some degree, is for them to consider, and whether the Board of Treasury may not purchase Produce to Advantage and contract to have it delivered free of all Risque & Charges at Amsterdam, and pay for it in Bills of Exchange I know not. – If they do this I should Advise them to send one Cargo to the House of Willinks, and another to the House of Vanstaphorsts, instead of consigning the whole jointly to both Houses. This would not only excite an Emulation between the two Houses, to make the most Advantage for the Interest of the United States: but would prevent delays and other Inconveniences, which must arise from two Houses meeting to consult and dispose of a Vessell and Cargo.
    As the Brokers, or Money Lenders, were pleased to insist upon my Signature to all the Obligations, I was obliged to make a Tour to Amsterdam, for that Purpose, and happened to enter the City the Day after the First Riots, which continued two nights while I was there. The Proceedings of the Prince of Orange have at last brought on a Crisis, and the English are holding out an Appearance, as if they thought it possible they might be obliged to take a Part in it. – if no foreign Power interferes, the Patriotic Party, is so much Stronger than the other, that I think the Prince must give Way, in the principal Points in Controversy. if any one foreign Power interferes, many others must follow the Example. This being well known and France and England, weary of War for the present, I hope the Dutch will be left alone to Settle their own disputes. With great Respect I have the Honour to be, dear Sir your most obedient and most humble Servant
Read 20 Sep^cr –   John Adams
Sept 28 Referred with the contract to the Sec^y for foreign Affairs to report

NA: PCC, item 84, v. 6, pp. 501-502, 504 (ALS); M247, reel 113.

Duke of Dorset to Comte de Montmorin

[Translation]

Paris, 16 June 1787

I have the honor, Monsieur le Comte, to inform you that, Mr. Thomas Barclay having been imprisoned in Bordeaux on the 15th of last month at the request of Messrs. French and Nephew, English merchants established in the said city, for a debt of 67,000 livres contracted four years ago & accompanied by several circumstances of fraud, the imprisonment was rescinded on the 19th of the same month by the Parliament of Bordeaux on the grounds, "That the said Mr. Thomas Barclay is Consul General of the United States of America & also their agent extraordinary near the Emperor of Morocco."

As to the first of these considerations, I pray Your Excellency to inform me whether the privileges of consuls established in France give protections against legitimate debts contracted between merchants, & also before the appointment to the office of consul; & moreover, even though the debt was accompanied by fraudulent circumstances.

In regard to the second consideration, I agree that a foreign minister, returning to his residence from the place of his negotiation, ought not to be detained on his journey; but, without examining whether the said Mr. Barklay has been invested with the alleged character of "agent extraordinary of the United States near the court of Morocco," it is reputed that he left Morocco several months since, that he remained some time in Cadiz; I have been assured that he has also been here in Paris, his alleged place of residence; & it is understood that at the present time he is living in Bordeaux, & not at all like a traveler who is going to his place of residence.

Regarding these facts, I leave it to Your Excellency to take such measures as you judge appropriate, whether by ordering the immediate cancellation of the decree that set Mr. Barclay at liberty to refuse payment of the debt, or by obliging him to give the necessary sureties so that Messrs. French and Nephew are not improperly defrauded of payment of a legitimate debt.

I have the honor to be most sincerely, Monsieur le Comte, Your Excellency's most humble and most obedient Servant   Dorset.

FFAA: Pol. Corr., U.S., v. 32, f. 286-286vo. (LC transcription).

Thomas Jefferson to Thomas Barclay

Dear Sir   Paris June 19. 1787.

Your favor of the 12$^{th.}$ came to hand two days ago. your adversary had been busy here in endeavoring to have your privilege examined & withdrawn. they had, as I think, interested mr Eden, the British minister, & thro' that or some other channel conveied a story to the ear of some of the ministers, very unfavorable to you. they had particularly represented some circumstance attending the original contracting of the debt as contrary to good faith, that it was for wines (I believe) sold, & to be paid for by a particular cargo of tobacco; that the wines being received, the cargo was otherwise applied. I mention these circumstances which I have heard vaguely, meerly to suggest to you the propriety of sending me a short state of the real transaction. I am this moment returned from the Count de Montmorin to whom I have spoken on the subject of your letter of safe conduct. I told him I knew nothing of the original transaction which I knew to have been represented to your disadvantage, but that from my personal knowledge of you I would pledge my own honour, either that nothing wrong had attended that transaction, or that you had no hand in it. we proceeded then to speak on the subject of your privilege. he said it was a settled point that the character of Consul does not privilege any person in this country against their creditors: that as to your character to the court of Marocco, 1. it might admit of question whether it could be a protection at all as it was not derived from Congress immediately: 2. that it would only have been a protection back to the place where you had received it had you come thither immediately; but that the long stay you had made at Bourdeaux seemed to have terminated it there. I told him you were arrested immediately almost on your arrival at Bourdeaux. but, says he, that arrest was annulled in a few days: yes, I replied, but the same creditors threatened to arrest you again the moment you should go out of the jurisdiction of Bourdeaux; & that tho' the second arrest might be annulled also, yet it was not a pleasant thing to be imprisoned & remain till a parliament could order the doors open. this seemed to make an impression, & we spoke of the safe conduct. he said he thought he could obtain a letter of safe conduct which should protect you till you should get to Paris, but that you would be liable to arrest the moment you should arrive. I asked if a Safe conduct could not be obtained to bring you to Paris, back again to Bourdeaux, & even to America. he thought it would be very doubtful & difficult: that you must in that case obtain the consent of the principal mass of your creditors, & furnish me with it: that tho he could not be sanguine as to the success, he would do what should depend on him: but he doubted the issue. you will be so good therefore as to decide on this view of the subject. the dates of your arrival at Bourdeaux, arrest, & discharge will be material. be assured that no endeavors shall be spared on my part, if you conclude to ask a Safe-conduct. if you should find it more eligible to proceed from Bourdeaux to Congress directly, I know of nothing relative to your office which need prevent it. I have the peasure to inform you that M^r· Barclay & your family are well; and pray you to accept assurances of the sincere esteem & respect with which I have the honor to be Dear Sir Your friend & servant   Th: Jefferson

P. S. I could wish a state of the treacherous conduct of French & co. of their letter to you advising you to go to America, &c. in case it should be necessary for me to apply to the minister.

LC: Jefferson Papers, microfilm reel 7 (press copy).

Thomas Jefferson to James Madison

Dear Sir   Paris June 20. 1787.

.   .   .   .   .

...I am uneasy seeing that the sale of our Western lands is not yet commenced. that precious fund for the immediate extinction of our debt will I fear be suffered to slip thro' our fingers. every delay exposes it to events which no human foresight can guard against. when we consider the temper of the people of that country, derived from the circumstances which surround them, we must suppose their *separation possible* at every moment. if they can be *retained til* their governments *become* settled & wise, they will *remain* with us always, and be a precious part of our strength & of our virtue. *But* this affair of *the Mississippi* by shewing that *Congress is capable* of hesitating on a question which proposes a *clear sacrifice* of the *western* to the *maritime states* will with difficulty be *obliterated.* the proposition of *my going to Madrid* to *try* to *recover* there the ground which has been *lost* at *New York* by the *concession* of the vote of *seven states* I should think desparate. with respect to *myself,* weighing the pleasure of *the journey* & bare possibility of *success* in one scale, and the strong *probability* of *failure* and the public *dissapointment directed* on *me* in the other, the latter preponderates. add to this that *jealousy* might be *excited* in the *breast* of a *person* who could find occasions of making *me uneasy.*

The late changes in the ministery here excite considerable hopes. I think we *gain in them all.* I am particulary happy at the *reentry of Malsherbes*[1] into the *council.* his knolege, his integrity render his value inappreciable, and the greater *to me* because while he had no *view* of *office we* had established together the most unreserved *intimacy.* so far too *I am pleased* with Montmorin. *His* honesty proceeds from *the heart* as well as *the head* and therefore may be more surely *counted on. The king* loves *business, oeconomy, order & justice.* He wishes sincerely the good of *his people.* He is *irascible, rude &* very *limited in his understanding, religious* bordering only on *bigotry.* He has no *mistress, loves his queen* and is too much *governed by her. She is capricious* like *her brother and governed* by *him,* devoted to *pleasure and expence, not remarkable* for any other *vices or virtues. Unhappily the king* shews a propensity for the *pleasures of the table.* that for *drink has increased lately* or at least it is *become more known.* for European news in general I will refer you to my letter mr Jay. is it not possible that the occurrences in Holland may excite a desire in many of leaving that country & transferring their effects out of it? may make an opening for shifting into their hands the debts due to this country, to it's officers & farmers? it would be surely eligible. I believe Dumas, if put on the watch, might alone suffice: but surely if mr Adams should go when the moment offers. *Dumas* has been in the habit of sending his *letters open* to *me* to be *forwarded* to Mr Jay. during my absence they passed through Mr *Short's* hands who made *extracts* from them by which I see he has been recommending himself and *me* for the *money negociations in Holland.* it might be thought perhaps that *I have* encouraged *him in* this. be assured my dear Sir, that no such idea ever entered my head. on the contrary it is a *business* which would be the most *disagreeable to me* of all others, & for which *I am* the most *unfit person living. I do* not understand *bargaining* nor possess the *dexterity* requisite to *make* them. on the other hand Mr *A.* whom I expressly and sincerely recommended, stands already on ground for that business which I could not gain in years. pray set *me* to rights in the minds of those who may have supposed *me privy* to this proposition. en passant, I will observe with respect to Mr. *Dumas* that the death of the C. de V. places *Congress* more at *their* ease how to dispose of *him.* our credit here has been ill treated here in public debate, and our *debt* deemed *apocryphal.* we should try to transfer this *debt* elsewhere, & leave nothing capable of exciting ill thoughts between us. I shall mention in my letter to mr Jay a disagreeable affair in which Mr. *Barclay* has been thrown into at *Bordeaux.* an honester man cannot be found, nor a *slower* nor more *indecisive one. His affairs* too are so *embarrassed and desparate* that the *public reputation* is every moment in danger of being *compromitted* with *him.* he is perfectly amiable & honest with all *this.*

·   ·   ·   ·   ·

I am with sentiments of the most sincere esteem Dear Sir Your friend &
serv^t   Th: Jefferson.

LC: *Madison Papers,* microfilm 2 (ALS); Boyd, *Jefferson Papers,* v. 11, pp. 480-484. *Italicized passages from printed edition.*

¹ *Malesherbes, Chrétien Guillaume de Lamoignon de (1721-1794). French political figure and writer. Instrumental in securing publication of* L'Encyclopédie, *1751-1752. Minister of the interior, 1775-1776. Minister of state, 1787-1788. Defended Louis XVI, 1792. Executed for treason, 1794.*

Thomas Jefferson to John Jay

Sir   Paris June 21. 1787.

. . . . . .

Mr Barclay has probably informed you of his having been arrested in
Bourdeaux for a debt contracted in the way of his commerce. he immediately applied to the parliament of that place who ordered his discharge. this
took place after five days actual imprisonment. I arrived at Bourdeaux a few
days after his liberation. as the Procureur general of the King had interested
himself to obtain it with uncommon zeal, and that too on public principles,
I thought it my duty to wait on him and return him my thanks. I did the
same to the President of the Parliament for the body over which he
presided: what would have been an insult in America being an
indispensable duty here. you will see by the inclosed printed paper on what
grounds the Procureur insisted on m^r Barclay's liberation. those on which
the Parliament ordered it are not expressed. On my arrival here I spoke
with the minister on the subject. He observed that the character of Consul
is no protection in this Country against process for debt: that as to the
character with which m^r Barclay had been invested at the Court of
Morocco, it was questionable whether it could be placed on the diplomatic
line, as it had not been derived immediately from Congress; that if it were,
it would have covered him to Paris only, where he had received his
commission, had he proceeded directly thither, but that his long stay at
Bourdeaux must be considered as terminating it there. I observed to him
that m^r Barclay had been arrested almost immediately on his arrival at
Bourdeaux. but says he that arrest was made void by the Parliament, and
still he has continued there several weeks. true, I replied, but his adversaries
declared they would arrest him again the moment he should be out of the
jurisdiction of the Parliament of Bourdeaux, and have actually engaged the
Marechaussée on the road to do it. this seemed to impress him. he said he
could obtain a letter of *sauf conduit*¹ which would protect him to Paris, but

that immediately on his arrival here he would be liable to arrest. I asked him if such a letter could not be obtained to protect him to Paris, and back to Bourdeaux and even to America? he said that for that the consent of the greater part of his creditors would be necessary, and even with this it was very doubtful whether it could be obtained. still if I would furnish him with that consent, he would do what should depend on him. I am persuaded he will, and have written to mʳ Barclay to obtain the consent of his creditors. This is the footing on which this matter stands at present. I have stated it thus particularly that you may know the truth, which will probably be misrepresented in the English papers, to the prejudice of mʳ Barclay. this matter has been a great affliction to him, but no dishonor where its true state is known. indeed he is incapable of doing any thing not strictly honorable.

.   .   .   .   .

...I have the honor to be with sentiments of the most perfect esteem and respect &ᶜ·   Th: Jefferson

NA: PCC, item 107, v. 2, pp. 16-26 (LBkC); M247, reel 133.
¹ safe conduct

Dutch Bankers to John Jay

Sir   Amsterdam the 30 June 1787
    We have the honour to transmit you the Copy of a Letter Received from his Excellʸ· John Adams, and to accompany the Obligations of the Negotiation of One Million Guilders Opened here by Order of Sᵈ· Excellʸ· We beg kindly to Receive them back Again as Soon as possible Ratifyed in due form by Congress for the Security of the Money Lenders We Refer to what We wrote on the Subject to the board of Treasury & have only to add, that tho We have used all possible pains in Setting of the Obligations, it has not Succeeded as to place more than 240000 livres – of Said Loan for the Payment of the Intrest Which fell due on the 1ˢᵗ June, Notwithstanding this disappointment will Continue our best Care to place the Remainder as Soon as possible, and your Excellʸ· may be assured of Our utmost endeavours and Zeal in the fullfilling of Sᵈ Loan and for the Intrest and Welfare of the United States.
    We have the honour to Remain Respectfully Sir Your most obᵗ most humb Servants   Wilhem & Jan Willink
                            Nichᵉ & Jacob van Staphorst & Co.
NA: PCC, item 145, p. 233 (LS); M247, reel 156.

Thomas Jefferson to John Adams

Dear Sir   Paris July 1. 1787.

...I am now occupied with the new ministry here to put the concluding hand to the new regulations for our commerce with this country, announced in the letter of M. de Calonnes which I sent you last fall. I am in hopes in addition to those, to obtain a suppression of the duties on Tar, pitch, & turpentine, and an extension of the privileges of American *whale* oil to their *fish* oils in general. I find the quantity of Cod fish oil brought to Lorient is considerable. this being got off hand (which will be in a few days) the chicaneries & vexations of the farmers on the article of tobacco, and their elusions of the order of Bernis, called for the next attention. I have reasons to hope good dispositions in the new ministry towards our commerce with this country. besides endeavoring on all occasions to multiply the points of contact & connection with this country, which I consider as our surest main-stay under every event, I have had it much at heart to remove from between us every subject of misunderstanding or irritation. our debts to the king, to the officers & the farmers are of this description. the having complied with no part of our engagements in these draws on us a great deal of censure, & occasioned a language in the Assemblées des notables very likely to produce disatisfaction between us. Dumas being on the spot in Holland, I had asked of him some time ago, in confidence, his opinion on the practicability of transferring these debts from France to Holland, & communicated his answer to Congress, pressing them to get you to go over to Holland and try to effect this business. your knowlege of the ground & former successes occasioned me to take this liberty without consulting you, because I was sure you would not weigh your personal trouble against public good. I have had no answer from Congress, but hearing of your journey to Holland have hoped that some money operation had led you there. if it related to the debts of this country I would ask a communication of what you think yourself at liberty to communicate, as it might change the form of my answers to the eternal applications I receive....

...I have the honour to be with sentiments of the most perfect friendship & esteem Dear Sir your most obedient & most humble servant

Th: Jefferson

ans^d. 10. 1787.

MHS: *The Adams Papers, microfilm reel 370* (ALS).

Pierre Charles Laurent de Villedeuil
to Thomas Jefferson

[Translation]

Paris, 2 July 1787

I have just, Sir, accounted for the causes that prevented the farmers-general from executing the arrangements contained in the letter that M. de Calonne addressed to you on 22 October last.

I have been informed, Sir, that the farmers-general, who had no knowledge in principle of the arrangements in that letter, received the order the first of last April to conform to them, & that on the 5th of the same month they sent their directors & other employees in the ports of the Kingdom instructions to collect on the oils and other products of the American fishery only the duties mentioned in M. de Calonne's letter.

I shall be careful, Sir, to maintain these arrangements & to render justice to the merchants from whom the farmers-general might have exacted heavier duties.

I have the honor to be &c.   de Villedeuil[1]

NA: PCC, item 107, v. 2, p. 58 (C); M247, reel 133.

[1] Villedeuil, Pierre Charles Laurent de. French government official. Intendant of Rouen until 1787, then Comptroller General of Finance, May 1787-July 1789.

Phineas Bond to Lord Carmarthen

My Lord.   Philadelphia July 2nd. 1787

.   .   .   .   .   .

The deliberations of the Convention, my Lord, are conducted with vast secrecy; and nothing is known with accuracy but that their drift is to endeavour to form such a federal constitution, as will give energy and consequence to the union. Whether this is to be done by improving the old governments or by substituting new ones – whether by continuing a power in each State to regulate its internal policy, or to abolish all separate establishments, and to form one grand federal authority, is a matter of consideration which creates much doubt and animadversion.

The task in which this assembly is engaged, my Lord, is attended with no small difficulty: wise and discreet as their determinations *may* be, they have no power to enforce their measures – they *may* recommend such plans as may seem eligible but who are to ratify them? Thirteen different States each claiming and exercising sovereign and independent powers, with various forms of government – great mutual jealousies and interests evidently clashing and interfering with each other. Even in this crisis my Lord when the sober part of the continent looks up to the Convention to prescribe some mode competent to remove existing evils, there is not a complete delegation of the States in Convention – two of the thirteen are not represented, New Hampshire did appoint delegates, but as no fund was provided for their expenses and support they declined attending – The Assembly of Rhode I positively refused to appoint, and when the motion was again lately agitated, it was negatived by a majority of 17 members.

It is plain my Lord, things cannot long remain as they are; there is an universal relaxation of laws and justice, and a total want of energy throughout the States.

. . . . .

In a former letter, my Lord, I made some mention of a trade carried on between this country and China; and expressed my apprehension it might, e'er long, be extended and directed to such channels as might prove greatly detrimental to the Revenue and commerce of Gt Britain.

I have the honor to enclose to your Lordship a list of the vessels employed, and fitting for this trade, from the different ports of this continent, and also an amount [account?] of some of the cargoes which have arrived in the course of this Spring.

In the restricted state of the American trade it is natural for men of enterprize to engage in such speculations, as are open to them and which afford a prospect of profit: the China trade may not hitherto have been very productive to this country; most of the articles brought from thence are of an inferior quality, particularly the teas: – It was at first thought, my Lord, the delays of the voyage, the necessary expense of the outfit the difficulty of making suitable remittances to obtain the proper investments, would soon have discouraged this undertaking: – but if one may judge from the present rage, it should seem as if new sources of profit appeared, and that the means of investment were facilitated so as to secure the future extension of the trade.

Independent of the ship which lately arrived here, and which it is said to return to Canton, one house in Philadelphia lately fitted out a ship called the *Alliance*, one of the largest ships ever built in N. America, supposed to be nearly as large as a 50 gun ship. – This ship sailed from hence about a fortnight ago, said to be bound to Canton; tho' it is presumed at least an endeavour will be made, to open a communication, if not to enter the ports of India, where articles of more value and more certain profit, can be had, than those they have already dealt in.

A company of merchants in Philad[a.] is at this time in a train of being established to engage in this trade – considerable sums (upwards of 100000 dollars) are already subscribed, a ship of between 300 and 400 tons now on the stocks and nearly finished, is contracted for and will be ready to sail in the Autumn.

Hitherto the remittances made from hence my Lord, have consisted of dollars Ginseng and a small quantity of furs: the remittance of silver can now be depended upon as this trade and the vast quantity sent to England must soon drain the country of all its circulating specia which at this time depend [on] a precarious illicit commerce carried on with the Spaniards. Nothing very considerable can result from Ginseng as a remittance; tho' it is an article of general consumption, a small quantity will stock the markets: but my Lord the want of the means of remittance will be amply supplied by the encouragement given to this American trade by the European agents and factors who had already assisted in lading their vessels and have given considerable credit and made great advances to those who are engaged in it. To this assistance the Americans now look with a certainty of support, the agents and factors of the European companies counteract the restriction laid upon their remitting their earnings to their own countries in this way. They give a credit and confidence to the American traders upon the faith of getting their property thro' them, circuitous to Europe, and it is said here, my Lord, that a large sum was advanced at Canton at a moderate premium upon Bottomry on the ship *Canton*, Captain Truxton[1] lately arrived here.

The Americans, my Lord, at first apprehended every sort of impediment would have been thrown in their way by the European Factors and Agents; who it was supposed very naturally would have inveigled their seamen and have monopolized the fit articles of investment; but the very reverse has happened: – the Americans have deserved [derived] assistance and encouragement from the very quarter from whence they expected opposition, and do not fail to boast of the civility and kindness they have experienced.

The encouragement the Americans have met with will certainly induce them to prosecute this trade with much vigor; and to extend their views at least to an intercourse with those settlements from whence they can be furnished with valuable silk and cotton piece goods, of which they have hitherto had but a scanty supply: if they can contrive to make large investments in those rich articles which are in demand in Europe, and which lie in a small compass, they will not confine their speculations to an import into America merely adequate to the consumption of this country which two or three well-freighted vessels might furnish, but they will contemplate an illicit trade to Europe, particularly to Ireland, which is, perhaps, no inconsiderable part of their plan.

This country, my Lord, is so restricted by the regulations of trade of other nations that this traffic seems to be the only expedient they can adopt and so weak are the resources of the merchants *here*, that if an early check or restraint can be thrown in their way, either by thwarting their credit, or by withholding the articles suitable to their commerce, I am convinced they would never rally; and then, my Lord, they would be confined to their coasting trade and to an illicit communication with the Spaniards: These come, in a secret manner, into the ports of America, and bring specie to a large amount, in return for which they carry away printed linens, hosiery thread, tapes, boots, shoes, etc; the amount of specie furnished to America thro' this channel is enormous – at least 500,000 dollars were brought into this port last year; and within a few weeks lately, 60,000 dollars were lodged in the bank here, by the Spanish traders.

Many people, my Lord, well-disposed to the interest of Gt. Britain are of opinion the establishing a free port, in the Bahama Islands under proper regulations from whence the Spaniards could draw the supplies they want, would effectually divert this profitable commerce from hence, thither.

...I have the honor to be, your Ldp's most faithful and obedient servant

P. Bond

Rec^d. Aug. 4th.

AHA 1896, v. 1, pp. 538-542.

[1] *Truxtun, Thomas (1755-1822). U.S. naval officer, seafarer. Successful privateeersman during Revolutionary War. Captain of the ship Canton, the first Philadelphia vessel sent to China, 1786. Appointed captain, U.S. Navy, 1794. Commanded frigate Constellation in victorious actions against French frigates L'Insurgente and La Vengeance, 1799-1800.*

Thomas Jefferson to Thomas Barclay

Dear Sir   Paris July 4. 1787.

I wrote you a fortnight ago an account of what had passed on your subject that day. yesterday I had a long conference with M. de [Rayneval][1] It is impossible for a person to be more cordially disposed than M de Montmorin but opposition from another quarter of the [sea] and the difficulty of the case [trouble] him. [Rayneval] observed to me that there was no country in Europe but France which took any notice of the character of a minister en passage between two other nations: but France doing it for other nations, I observed, & he agreed she should do it for us. but he repeated the objection of your long stay at Bourdeaux, & I the answer which I had given before on that subject, & which admits no reply. he added what I had never heard before: that France does not permit even a minister to her own court to depart without paying his debts, or giving either private or public security for them. I denied that this could be justified by the law of nations. he said he would send me a copy of the memoir on that subject which his court had sent to all the ~~nations~~ courts of Europe in the case of the landgrave of Hesse, and ended by pressing the distress in which M de Montmorin found himself, and how much they should be relieved by an amicable arrangement. I am afraid they are pressing on the other side a reversal of the decision of Bordeaux. I always suppose that most honest way of acting for another is to give a true state of things without disguise. I therefore told you in the first moment at Bordeaux what I thought of it. as soon as I found that the practice of this country relative to a minister en passage allowed an opening in your favor, I pushed it & still push it on that point. but they oppose their practice as to the debts even of a minister to their court. I make it a point to remove from the minds of those with whom I speak all doubts as to your conduct, & I believe I satisfy them, as I am satisified myself of it's perfect rectitude. I shall not fail to urge for you whatever their usage will admit; but acknolege that I apprehend for the event, and that an amicable arrangement should be pressed on your part. it is some days since I heard from your family. they were then well. I am in daily hopes of receiving a letter from you in answer to my last, & beg you to count on any service I can render you in this or any other matter as well as on the sentiments of esteem & friendship with which I have the honour to be Dear Sir Your most obedient & most humble serv^t

Th: Jefferson

LC: *Jefferson Papers, microfilm reel 7 (press copy)*.

[1] *For deciphered portions of document, see Boyd, Jefferson Papers, v. 11, pp. 544-545. The words in brackets are conjectured because the cypher list is incomplete.*

John Jay to William Short

Sir   New York 5th July 1787

•   •   •   •   •

It seems from the Arret respecting the Bounty and Duty on Fish, that the absolute Prohibition of foreign Fish is in Contemplation – a Circumstance of much Importance to the United States. "*Local Circumstances*" will however always operate in our Favor, and if wisely improved must in Time more than rival any Fishery not so circumstanced even though aided by Bounties. –

The Business of Finance appears to occupy the Attention of France and Britain as well as America, and doubtless with much Reason. I wish we made more Progress in it; but among other Reasons, the Sitting of the Convention at Philadelphia has called so many Members from Congress, that a sufficient Number of States are not represented to enable them to advance in that or any other Business, which requires the Presence of nine States. Hence it happened that I have not yet been enabled to write to Mr Jefferson on a certain Subject mentioned in his Letters, and on which I reported agreeably to his Ideas. I regret this Delay especially as it is uncertain how much longer it may continue. –

I have the Honor to be &c: John Jay –

NA: PCC, *item* 121, *pp. 262-264 (LBkC); M61, reel 1.*

Peter Allaire: Occurrences from 7 June to 5 July 1787

New York 5 July 1787

Congress have Appointed Six Commissioners to settle the Accounts of the United States, with each individual State and orders to allow them Six pCent for all advances made during the War, that the Domestic Debt of the United States may be liquidated, and that each State may pay their Ballance into the Federal Treasury, and that the Commissioners report the same in Twelve months, none of the delinquent States will pay their Quota, till compel'd.

The Insurgents of Massachusets, have again taken the field, (in Number about 6 or 700 Men,) they have made Prisoners of two Select Men, and keep them as Hostages to Retaliate should any of the Insurgents be hanged, that have been found guilty of Treason by the State of Massachusets, and wrote to the Legislature that for the first two Men they hang, they will retaliate on the two Select Men, and to the Sherif that if he attends the Execution of any of those Men, he shall be the third, what is remarkable, they wrote to the Select Men, and put the Letter into a Coffin, and laid the Coffin at each Mans Door, ten days previous to their being taken. the back part of Massachusets State, is in a state of Warfare, the Militia are Ordered out, and must keep the feild at least Six months, if they do not grow Refractory, in my Opinion they will; as the allowance made by Government, is not adequate to the time lost &c.

Congress have received Intelligence that the Southern Indians (back of G[e]orgia & the Carolina's) have held a grand Council, and declared War, against the United States, as they have not kept the Treaty made with them, and have sent Commissioners to take their hunting ground from them. since their declaration, they have Murthered five families; the

No[r]thern Indians have sent two of their Warriours to Congress (they are now here) to brighten the Chain of friendship and to desire them not to send Commissioners into their hunting ground, if they do their Young Warriors will kill them.

The Convention, now seting at Philadelphia to form a New federal Union, are so very secret in their proceedings that nothing has transpired, (Ten States are Represented,) or wether they will be able to accomplish their design, is a great doubt; for the first federal Union, was entered into precipitately under false Assertions, & misrepresentations, having an Enemy at their very Doors, fear compelled them to Unite, But now when Peace is Established, no Enemy near, a large Domestic and Foreign Debt to provide for (if they consent to the Union,) little Trade, no Manufactories, heavy Taxes layd on, both by Congress and their particular States, with a mutinous disposition pervading the thirteen United States, makes it a very doubtfull matter, wither all the States will confirm, what their Delegates may have Assented to, in the General Convention, more Especially as the Assemblies that Appointed them, are more then half, not returned, and others appointed, who are more inclined to please the People (no Assembly is bound to abide by what the proceeding one has done, which creates a continual delay & confusion, for if you obtain an Act this Session, very often the next repeals it.) nor are Congress held, in that repute and Respect, they were formerly, our present President, is an Auctioneer, and many of the Members after having made laws for the United States in the morning, will in the Afternoon, sell You, a pound of Sugar & half pound Tea: [unreadable] this our present Situation.

with respect to the English West India Trade, it is intirely carried on, by English Vessells, for almost every American Vessell that goes to any of your Islands, are seized under some pretence or other, and if acquitted, the expences attending the acquital, eats up all the profits, therefore until we enter into some commercial Treaty, you Enjoy the whole Trade, and are the carriers for America, for we have not a single Hhd$^{\text{f.}}$ Rum or Sugar, but was it is imported in English Bottoms from the English Islands. if your present Navigation Act continues, you will put a final stop to all American Ship Building, the Consequences of which are to[o] well known to Your house, to need any comment....

.   .   .   .   .

I Remain with Respect Yours   PA
R: 9$^{\text{th:}}$ Aug$^{\text{st:}}$ from Sir G. Yonge.

PRO: FO 4/5, pp. 421-436 (LC transcription).

George Miller to Lord Carmarthen

My Lord, Charleston, South Carolina, 10 July, 1787.

In Obedience to His Majesty's Commands, which Your Lordship did me the honour to signify under date of the 19th April, I embarked for this place on the 24th of the same month, where I only arrived the 8th Instant. –

Yesterday morning I waited upon the Governour, & exhibited my Commission, when his Excellency told me he believed it must be Recognised by Congress, before the Executive of the State, could do so, but that he would examine precedents, & take the opinion of this Council upon the subject: This day he favoured me by a visit, & informed me, that, both in point of regularity & precedent, it was his own & the opinion of the Privy Council, application for Recognition must in the first instance be made to Congress.–

. . . . .

I have the honour to be with the greatest Respect, My Lord, Your Lordship's most Obedient, and very humble Servant Geo: Miller

PRO: FO 4/5, pp. 441-444 (LC transcription).

Thomas Barclay to John Adams and Thomas Jefferson

Gentlemen Lorient 13th July 1787

I Do my self the honor to Inclose you two Books of 82 Pages Containing All my Accounts respecting My Mission to Morocco, by which You will see that the amount of the Expences attending the Negociation Including the Presents and all the Travelling Charges of M. Franks and myself amount to Livres 95179.10. which sum I shall place to the Debit of the United States.

The Particulars of the Purchases made, and of the Appropriation of all the Presents, together with an Account of the Articles remaining on hand make a part of these Accounts, and I do not know that any thing is left unexplained when I have told you that my reason for leaving the Lawns and Cambricks in the hands of M. Champion of this place for Sale, was because the Farmers' General would not permit Me to Carry them out of the Town by Land,...

I annex an Account of Bills Drawn on M. Adams amounting to £4645 Sterling – £100 of which in Favor of M Grand,[1] he writes to me, was Never sent forward for Acceptance, in which Case I have promised to account with him for it and then the amount: will be £4544 Sterling, which supposing the Exchange to be on an average 24 livres the pound

Sterling Clear of Negociating fees in Paris, the sum will be 109080 liv So that upon this Account I shall Remain indebted to the United States (untill I make a Settlement with them, and untill I know what I am to Charge for my Voyage) 13901.10 Livres –...

The Necessity I am under of hastening out to America shou'd not have prevented my waiting on M. Adams in London for his Commands, had not M. Jefferson given me a full Dispensation, on that head, and therefore I know M. Adams will Excuse Me –

Before I take leave permit me to thank you Both for the Many Marks of Esteem and Attention with which you have honord me, and to Request earnestly a Continuance of that Regard which I sincerely assure you is very Precious to Gentlemen

Your most obedient and obliged servant   Tho⁸ Barclay

MHS: *The Adams Papers, microfilm reel 370 (ALS).*
¹ *Grand, Roldolphe Ferdinand (1726-1794). Paris banker who handled U.S. accounts.*

Louis Guillaume Otto to Comte de Montmorin

[Translation]

Nᵒ· 94.   New York, 15 July 1787.
My Lord.

Mr. Jay, feeling himself too weak to contend against all the Southern States while treating with Spain, and fearing to lose the Department of Foreign Affairs by renouncing the navigation of the Mississippi for a limited time following the Ultimatum that Congress gave him, has finally changed parties. He has just sent that Assembly a letter in which he explains the inconveniences of concluding a treaty prejudicial to the claims of the southern States. He observes that it would be dangerous to push the Colonies of the interior to extremities by formally sacrificing a navigation that appears indispensable to them, that this treaty would occasion not only coolness among the various States, but that it could induce Kentucky and Frankland to throw themselves into the arms of England; that in spite of the interruption of negotiations with His Catholic Majesty, it was meritorious of the United States formally to disavow the hostilities committed by the inhabitants of Kentucky, who had seized two Spanish ships. – This letter, My Lord, gave general satisfaction, and it has restored calm in Congress. For fifteen days that Assembly has been exempt from factions, and therein reign a harmony and a unanimity that augur well for its future deliberations. It is certain that the negotiations with Spain have exposed the confederation to the greatest danger and that several Southern

Delegates have received secret orders to quit Congress in the event that ratification of a treaty by which the United States would have renounced the navigation of the Mississippi was proposed.

Since Mr. Jay's letter, My Lord, Mr. Gardoqui has requested the Ultimatum of Congress from that Minister, in order to transmit it to his Court; Mr. Jay answered him that his masters had not yet passed a definitive resolution, and that he would not fail to inform him thereof as soon as he received it.

The politics of Congress will consist henceforth in putting off the dispatch of its Ultimatum under various pretexts; this conduct is justified by the delicate situation of the United States. They fear that by sacrificing the interests of the western districts, the people will throw off the yoke of Congress in order to submit to Spain or to England. The most enlightened inhabitants of these Regions do not cease to write menacing letters to members of Congress and to give them some idea of the impossiblity of existing without the navigation of the Mississippi. On the other hand, Congress has reason to apprehend that by supporting the claims of the Kentuckians with too much vigor, it will indispose Spain against the United States and will induce her to approach England in order to devise the conquest of all the lands situated beyond the Allegheny Mountains.

It follows that by protracting the negotiations and by alternately giving hopes to Spain and to the Kentuckians, Congress prevents the two parties from taking violent measures and still leaves itself the option of adopting the system least prejudicial to its interests in the end. Meanwhile, these regions are becoming populated with a prodigious rapidity, and several districts will soon be able to undertake the boldest expeditions. The Southern Delegates had previously proposed to negotiate with Spain under the mediation of France, but they are beginning to think, with those of the North, that the true policy of the United States is not to encourage the Western settlements too much by the opening of the Mississippi, since they would not only become populated to the detriment of the maritime States, but always have the appearance of being propped up in order to prevent their defection.

Mr. Gardoqui occupies himself in the meantime, My Lord, in sending a great number of Colonists to Trinidad, which His Catholic Majesty has just made a free port. Emigrants are given the most enticing encouragements. The Governor of Tobago will probably be in a position to give the Court more particular details regarding this measure, which may interest us.

The Spanish Minister, My Lord, having lost all hope of concluding a treaty of Commerce with the United States, speaks of leaving America within the space of two months. He is generally esteemed here, and several Delegates have told me that they were pained to thwart his negotiations, and that duty alone induced them to disappoint a man for whom they had the most sincere attachment. Whatever may be the secret views of the Court of Madrid, it could not have sent here a minister more zealous and more popular.

I am with a profound respect My Lord Your most humble and most obedient servant   Otto.

rec. 1ˢᵗ· Septᵇᵉʳ·

FFAA: Pol. Corr., U.S., v. 32, f. 304-306 (LC transcription).

Thomas Jefferson to John Adams

Dear Sir   Paris 17 July. 1787.

I have been duly honoured with yours of the 10ᵗʰ· inst. and am happy to hear of the success of your journey to Amsterdam. there can be no doubt of it's ratification by congress. would to heaven they would authorize you to take measures for transferring the debt of this country to Holland before you leave Europe. most especially is it necessary to get rid of the debt to the officers. their connections at court are such as to excite very unfavorable feelings there against us, and some very hard things have been said (particularly in the Assemblée des Notables) on the prospects relative to our debts. the paiment of the interest to the officers would have kept them quiet: but there are two years now due to them. I dare not draw for it without instructions, because in the instances in which I have hitherto ventured to act uninstructed, I have never been able to know whether they have been approved in the private sentiments of the members of Congress, much less by any vote. I have pressed on them the expediency of transferring the French debt to Holland, in order to remove every thing which might excite irritations between us & this nation. I wish it may be done before this ministry may receive ill impressions of us. they are at present very well disposed. I send you by mr Appleton some pamphlets and have the honour to be with sentiments of very cordial esteem & respect Dear Sir Your affectionate humble servant   Th: Jefferson

ansᵈ Aug. 25. 1787.

MHS: The Adams Papers, microfilm reel 370 (ALS).

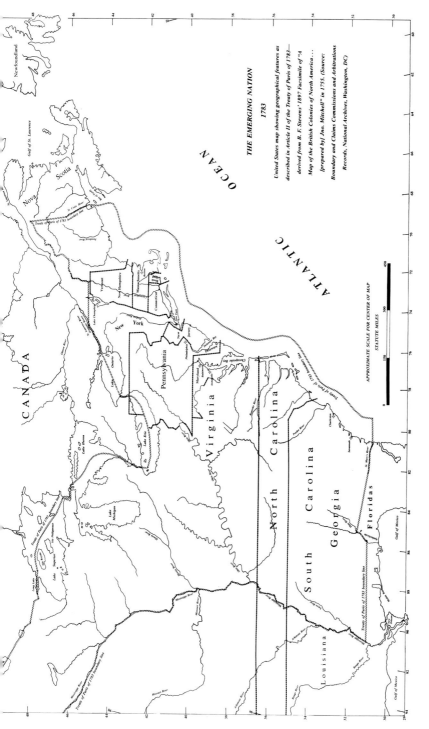

The Emerging Nation, 1783.

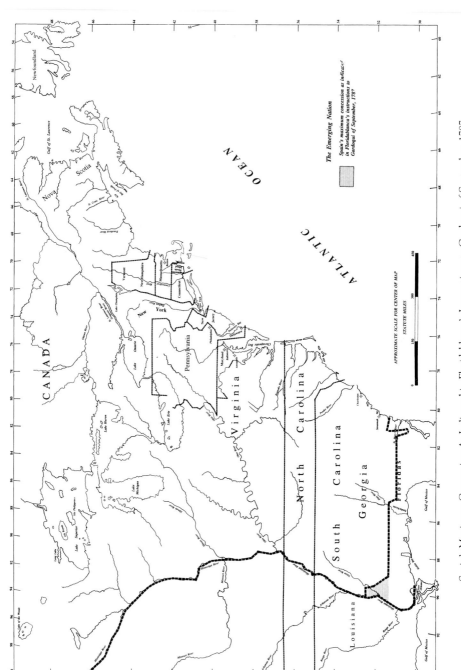

Spain's Maximum Concession As Indicated in Floridablanca's Instructions to Gardoqui of September, 1787.

Benjamin Franklin by Joseph Siffred Duplessis. Courtesy of Independence
National Historical Park.

John Adams by John Singleton Copley. Courtesy of Harvard University.

John Jay engraved by B.B.E., published by R. Wilkinson, 1783. Courtesy of the Library of Congress.

Charles Gravier, Comte de Vergennes, engraved by Vangelisti. Courtesy of the Library of Congress.

Marquis de Lafayette by Philiber Louis Debucourt. Courtesy of National Portrait Gallery.

Thomas Jefferson by Charles Willson Peale. Courtesy Independence National Historical Park.

Congressional Ratification
of the U.S.–Moroccan Treaty

[New York] July 18th 1787. –

On a report from the Secretary for foreign Affairs to whom was referred a treaty lately concluded with the Emperor of Morocco, Congress ratified the said treaty in the manner and form following.

The United States of America in Congress Assembled – to all who shall see these presents – Greeting

Whereas the United States of America in Congress Assembled by their Commission bearing date the twelfth day of May one thousand seven hundred and eighty four, thought proper to constitute John Adams, Benjamin Franklin and Thomas Jefferson their ministers plenipotentiary giving to them, or a majority of them full powers to confer, treat and Negociate with the ambassador, Minister or Commissioner of his Majesty the Emperor of Morocco concerning a treaty of Amity and commerce, to make and receive propositions for such treaty and to conclude and sign the same, transmitting it to the United States in Congress Assembled for their final ratification; and by one other Commission bearing date the eleventh day of March one thousand seven hundred and eighty-five, did further empower the said ministers plenipotentiary, or a majority of them, by writing under their hands and Seals to appoint such agent in the said business as they might think proper, with authority under the directions and instructions of the said Ministers, to commence and prosecute the said Negociations and Conferences for the said treaty, provided that the said Treaty should be signed by the said Ministers: And Whereas the said John Adams and Thomas Jefferson two of the said ministers plenipotentiary, (the said Benjamin Franklin being absent) by writing under the hand and Seal of the said John Adams at London October the fifth One thousand seven hundred and eighty five, and of the said Thomas Jefferson at Paris October the eleventh of the same year, did appoint Thomas Barclay agent in the business aforesaid giving him the powers therein, which by the said second Commission they were authorised to give, and the said Thomas Barclay in pursuance thereof, hath arranged Articles for a Treaty of Amity and commerce between the United States of America, and his Majesty the Emperor of Morocco, which Articles written in the Arabic language, confirmed by his said Majesty the Emperor of Morocco, and Sealed with his Royal Seal, being translated into the Language of the said United States of America, together with the attestations thereto annexed are in the following words, to wit.

(Here insert the Treaty and the Additional Article)

And whereas the said John Adams and Thomas Jefferson ministers plenipotentiary aforesaid, by writing under their respective hands and Seals, duly made and executed by the said John Adams on the 25th January 1787, and by the said Thomas Jefferson on the 1st day of January 1787, did approve and conclude the said Treaty and every Article and clause therein contained, reserving the same nevertheless to the United States in Congress Assembled for their final Ratification. Now Be it Known that we the said United States of America in Congress assembled, have accepted, approved, ratified, and confirmed, and by these presents do accept, approve, ratify, and confirm the said Treaty and every article and clause thereof.

In Testimony whereof we have caused our seal to be hereunto affixed – Witness his Excellency Arthur St Clair our President at the City of New-york, this 18th day of July in the year of our Lord one thousand seven hundred and eighty seven ,and in the twelfth year of our Sovereignty and Independence. –

NA: PCC, item 122, pp. 95-97 (C); M247, reel 140.

Congressional Resolution Regarding Redemption
of American Captives in Algiers

[New York] July 18, 1787

On a report of the Secretary of the United States for the department of Foreign Affairs to whom was referred a petition from Hannah Stephens praying that her Husband be redeemed from Captivity at Algiers, and also a Letter from the honble. T. Jefferson proposing that a Certain Order of Priests be employed for such purposes –

Resolved That the honble. T. Jefferson Esqr. the Minister of the United States at the Court of Versailles be, and he hereby is authorized to take such measures as he may deem most adviseable for redeeming the American Captives at Algiers and at any expence not exceeding that which European Nations usually pay in like cases –

Resolved That the Board of Treasury be and they hereby are directed to provide ways and means for enabling Mr. Jefferson to defray the said expences, either by remitting money from hence or by a Credit in Europe.–

NA: PCC, item 5, v. 3, pp. 1612-1613 (Journal); M247, reel 19.

John Paul Jones to John Jay

Sir,   New-York July 18. 1787

. . . . .

I should act inconsistently if I omitted to mention the dreadful situation of our unhappy Fellow-Citizens in slavery at Algiers. Their almost hopeless Fate is a deep reflection on our National Character in Europe. I beg leave to influence the Humanity of Congress in their behalf, and to propose that some expedient may be adopted for their Redemption. A Fund might be raised for that purpose by a duty of a Shilling p month from Seamen's wages throughout the Continent, and I am persuaded that no difficulty would be made to that requisition. I have the honor to be Sir, with great esteem, Your most Obedient and most humble Servant

Paul Jones[1]

NA: PCC, item 168, v. 2, pp. 351-354 (LS); M247, reel 185.

[1] Jones, John Paul (1747-1792). Seafarer and naval officer. Commissioned a lieutenant in the Continental Navy, 1775; captain, 1776. Commanded Providence, 1776-1777; Ranger, 1777-1778; Bonhomme Richard, 1779; Alliance, 1780; Ariel, 1781; and America, 1781-1782. After 1783, agent to solicit payment in Europe for prizes taken by his ships. Rear admiral, Russian navy, 1788-1790. Appointed commissioner to ransom prisoners and negotiate peace with Algiers, 1792, but died before he received commission.

Congressional Committee Report on Efforts to Fulfill the Terms of the Treaty of Peace

[New York July 20, 1787]

The Com^ce...to whom was referred the report of the Secretary for foreign affairs of the 23^d April last, respecting instructions to the Minister of the US at the Court of London submit the following resolves –

Resolved that the Minister of the US at the Court of ~~London~~ Great Britain be & he is hereby instructed to inform his Britannic Majesty that Congress have taken measures for removing all cause of complaint ~~against them~~ relative to the infraction of the 4th & 6th articles of the Treaty of Peace & that he communicate to his Majesty their resolutions of the 21st March last together with their circular letter to the states of the 13 day of April.

R. That the s^d Minister be & he hereby is authorized & directed in the name & behalf of the US to propose & conclude a convention with his Britannic Majesty whereby it shall be agreed that the Value of the Slaves or other American property carried away contrary to the 7th Article of the Treaty of Peace, be estimated by Commissioners & paid for & that the s^d

Payment together with a surrender of ~~the~~ all the Posts & places now held by his Majesty within the limits of the U S shall be made within ____ months after the several States shall have passed an act or Acts in conformity to the resolutions beforementioned – Which ____ months shall be computed from the time that formal notice shall be given his Majesty that all the States have passed an act or Acts as above mentioned – And that he also endeavour to obtain an article to fix the true Construction of the declaration for ceasing hostilities & to stipulate that compensation be made for all captures contrary to it –

Resolved that the s^d Minister be & he hereby is further instructed to assure his Majesty that it will always give pleasure to Congress fairly to discuss & accomodate every difference or complaint that may arise relative to the construction or to the performance of the Treaty – That they are determined to execute it with good Faith – And, that as this is the only instance in which any complaints have come regularly before them, they flatter themselves that the readiness with which they have taken measures to remove these complaints will create in him a full confidence in the purity of their intentions – And that he assure his Majesty, that they fully repose & confide in his assurances, "that whenever America shall manifest a real determination to fulfil her part of the Treaty Great Britain will not hesitate to co-operate in whatever points depend upon her, for carrying every article into real & compleat effect" –

read 19 July 1787
passed 20 July –

NA: PCC, *item* 25, *v.* 2, *pp.* 473-476 (D); M247, *reel* 32.

Congressional Resolution Regarding Thomas Barclay's Conduct in the Moroccan Negotiations

[New York July 23 1787]

The Secretary having further reported that from the papers N6 and others it appears that Thomas Barclay esq^r has in the conduct of the negociation with the Emperor of Morocco manifested a degree of prudence address and disinterestedness which in the Opinion of the Secretary merit the approbation of Congress,

Thereupon

Resolved That Congress are well pleased with the conduct of Thomas Barclay esq^r in the course of the Negociations on the part of the United

States with his Imperial Majesty of Morocco as detailed & represented in his and other letters & papers transmitted to them

NA: PCC, item 5, p. 1624 (Journal); M247, reel 19.

Thomas Jefferson to Comte de Montmorin

Sir   Paris July 23. 1787

    I had the honor a few days ago of putting into the hands of Your Excellency some observations on the other articles of American produce brought into the ports of this country. that of our tobaccoes, from the particular form of their administration here & their importance to the king's revenues, has been placed on a separate line, & considered separately. I will now ask permission to bring that subject under your consideration.

    The mutual extension of their commerce was among the fairest advantages to be derived to France & the United States from the independance of the latter: an exportation of eighty millions; chiefly in raw materials is supposed to constitute the present limits of the commerce of the U.S. with the nations of Europe, limits however which extend as their population increases to draw the best proportion of this into the ports of France, rather than of any other nation is believed to be the wish & the interest of both. of these eighty millions, thirty are constituted by the single article of tobacco. could the whole of this be brought into the ports of France, to satisfy first its own demands, & the residue to be revended to other nations, it would be a powerful link of commercial connexion. but we are far from this. even her own consumption, supposed nine millions, under the administration of the monopoly to which it is farmed, enters little as an article of exchange into the commerce of the two nations. when this article was first put into farm, perhaps it did not injure the commercial interests of the kingdom; because nothing but British manufactures were then allowed to be given in return for American tobaccoes. the laying the trade open then to all the subjects of France could not have relieved her from a paiment in money. circumstances are changed, yet the old institution remains. the body to which this monopoly was given was not mercantile. their object is to simplify as much as possible the administration of their affairs. they sell for cash: they purchase therefore with cash. their interest, their principles & their practice seem opposed to the general interest of the kingdom, which would require that this capital article should be laid open to a free exchange for the productions of this country. so far does the spirit of simplifying their operations govern this body that relinquishing the advantages to be derived from a competion of sellers, they contracted some time ago with a single person (M^r· Morris) for three years supplyies of American tobacco to be paid for in cash. they obliged themselves too, expressly, to employ no other person to purchase in America during that term. in consequence of this, the mercantile houses of France concerned in sending her productions to be exchanged for tobacco, cut off for three years from the hope of selling these tobaccoes in France, were of neccesity to abandon that commerce. in consequence of this too a single individual, constituted sole purchaser of so great a proportion of the tobaccoes made, had the price in his power. a great reduction in it took place; & that not only on the quantity he bought, but on the whole quantity made. the loss to the states producing the article did not go to cheapen it for their friends here. their price was fixed. what was gained on their consumption was to enrich the person purchasing it; the rest, the monopolists & merchants of other countries. the effect of this operation was vitally felt by every farmer in America concerned in the culture of this plant. at the end of the year he found that he had lost a fourth or a third of his revenue; the state, the same proportion of its subjects of exchange with other nations. the manufactures of this country too were either not to go there at all, or to go thtough the chanel of a new monopoly, which, freed from the controul of competition in prices & qualities, was not likely to extend their consumption. it became necessary to relieve the two countries from the fatal effects of this double monopoly. I had the honor of addressing a letter on the fifteenth day of august one thousand seven hundred & eighty five to his late Excellency the Count de Vergennes upon this subject. the effectual mode of relief was to lay the commerce open. but the King's interest was also to be guarded. a committee was appointed to take this matter into consideration; & the result was an order to the Farmers general that no such contract should be made again. And to furnish such aliment as might keep that branch of commerce alive 'till the expiration of the present contract they were required to put the merchants in general on a level with Mr Morris for the quantity of twelve or fifteen thousand hogsheads a year. That this relief too might not be intercepted from the merchants of the two suffering nations by those of a neighbouring one, & that the transportation of so bulky an article might go to aliment their own shipping, no tobaccoes were to be counted of this purchase but those brought in French or American Vessels. Of this order, made at Bernis, his Excellency Count de Vergennes was pleased to honor me with a communication, by a letter of the thirtieth of May one thousand seven hundred & eighty-six, desiring that I would publish it as well in America as to the American merchants in France. I did so; communicating it to

Congress at the same time. This order thus viewed with the transactions which produced it, will be seen to have been neccesary: & its punctual & candid execution has been rendered still more so by the speculations of the merchants entered into on the faith of it. otherwise it would become the instrument of their ruin instead of their relief. a twelve month has elapsed some time since: and it is questioned whether the farmers general have purchased, within that time, the quantity prescribed, & on the conditions prescribed. it would be impossible for the merchants to prove the negative: it will be easy for the farmers general to shew the affirmative if it exists. I hope that a branch of commerce of this extent, will be thought interesting enough to both nations, to render it the desire of Your Excellency to require, as it makes it my duty to ask, a report of the purchases they have made according to the conditions of Bernis, specifying in that report. 1. the quantities purchased. 2. the prices paid. 3. the dates of the purchase & paiment. 4. the flag of the vessel in which imported. 5. her name. 6. her port of delivery; & 7. the name of the seller. the four first articles make part of the condititions required by the order of Bernis; the three last may be neccesary for the correction of any errors which should happen to arise in the report.

But the order of Bernis was never considered but as a temporary relief. the radical evil will still remain. their will be but one purchaser in the kingdom, & the hazard of his refusal will damp every mercantile speculation. it is very much to be desired that before the expiration of this order some measure may be devised which may bring this great article into free commerce between the two nations. had this been practicable at the time it was put into farm, that mode of collecting the revenue would probably have never been adopted: now that it is practicable it seems reasonable to discontinue this mode, & to substitute some of those practised on other imported articles on which a revenue is levied without absolutely suppressing them in commerce. if the revenue can be secured, the interests of a few individuals will hardly be permitted to weigh against those of as many millions, equally subjects of His Majesty, & against those too of a nation allied to him by all the ties of treaty, of interests & of affection. the privileges of the most favored nation have been mutually exchanged by treaty. but the productions of other nations, which do not rival those of France, are suffered to be bought & sold freely within the kingdom. by prohibiting all His Majesty's subjects from dealing in tobacco except with a single company, one third of the exports of the United States are rendered uncommerciable here. this production is so peculiarly theirs, that its shackles affect no other nation. a relief from these shackles will form a memorable epoch in the commerce of the two nations. it will establish at once a great basis of exchange, serving like a point of union to draw to it other members of our commerce. Nature too has conveniently assorted our wants & our superfluities to each other. each nation has exactly to spare the articles which the other wants. we have a surplus of rice, tobacco, furs, peltry, potash, lamp oils, timber, which France wants; she has a surplus of wines, brandies, esculent oils, fruits & manufactures of all kinds which we want. The governments have nothing to do but *not to hinder* their merchants from making the exchange. the difference of language, laws & customs will be some obstacle for a time; but the interest of the merchants will surmount them. a more serious obstacle is our debt to Great Britain. yet since the treaty between this country & that, I should not despair of seeing that debt paid in part with the productions of France, if our produce can obtain here a free course of exchange for them. the distant prospect is still more promising. a century's experience has shewn that we double our numbers every twenty or twenty-five years. no circumstance can be foreseen at this moment which will lessen our rate of multiplication for centuries to come. for every article of the productions or manufactures of this country then, which can be introduced into habit there, the demand will double every twenty or twenty-five years. and to introduce the habit we have only to let the merchants alone. Whether we may descend by a single step from the present state to that of perfect freedom of commerce in this article, whether any, and what, intermediate operation, may be neccesary to prepare the way to this, what cautions must be observed for the security of His Majesty's revenue, which we do not wish to impair, will rest with the wisdom of his Ministers, whose knowlege of the subject will enable them to devise the best plans, while their patriotism & justice will dispose to the pursuit of them. to the friendly dispositions of Your Excellency, of which we had such early & multiplied proofs, I take the liberty of committing this subject particularly, trusting that some method may be devised of reconciling the collection of His Majesty's revenues with the interests of the two nations: and have the honour of assuring you of those sincere sentiments of esteem and respect with which I am Your Excellency's Most obedient & most humble servant   Th: Jefferson

Papers inclosed.
1. letter of M. le comte de Vergennes of May 30. 1786.
2. the order of Berni.
3. the contract with mr Morris referred to in the order of Berni.

FFAA: Pol. Corr., U.S., v. 32, f. 314-316 (ALS); LC microfilm reel 19.

Board of Treasury to John Adams

Sir.   Board of Treasury July 25[th:] 1787.

We are favored with your Letter of the 8[th:] of May last, transmitting Protests for Non Acceptance of the two Bills of Exchange for 75,000 Florins; drawn by Constable Rucker & C[o.] of New York on their Partner M[r.] John Rucker of London. From the Solidity of the House by whom the Bill was drawn (being in Partnership with M[r.] Robert Morris of Phil[a.]) we had not the most distant Apprehension of any Disappointment on this Remittance; you may therefore judge of our Surprise, and Mortification; when previous to the Receipt of your Letter, we heard of M[r.] Rucker's Arrival in this City – It gives us Pleasure to inform you that this Gentleman is returned by Direction of M[r.] Morris, to take up the Bills drawn on him; and that we have the fullest Assurance from the House, that Effectual Measures will be adopted for Paying the Bills remitted to You when they become due – We are glad you changed your first Intentions of transmitting the Original Bills; you will be pleasd to have them presented for Payment, when at Maturity. –

Your Communications to Congress on the Subject of the Loan you have Effected, in Consequence of this and other Circumstances for one Million of Florins, having been referred to this Board; we have agreed on a Report, approving of the same, and recommending an Immediate Ratification – As soon as the Determination of Congress is made known to us, you shall be acquainted with the Result –

We have the Honor to be with Esteem, Your Obed[t:] Humble Serv[ts:]

Samuel Osgood
Arthur Lee

MHS: *The Adams Papers, microfilm reel 370 (LS).*

John Jay to John Adams

My dear Sir   New York 25 July 1787

.   .   .   .   .

Your Experience in affairs, your Knowledge of Characters, and your intimate Acquaintance with the concerns and Interests of this Country, together with other circumstances & Considerations, induce me to wish that all Questions between us & the Court of London, as well as other affairs in Europe, could be arranged and adjusted before You leave it. The Manner however in which You mention your Intention to return is decisive, and as the Prospect of your doing much good here, is fair &

promising, perhaps it may upon the whole be best that you should be with us, especially considering the actual situation of our affairs. You have my good Friend deserved well of your Country, and your Services and Character will be truly estimated, at least by Posterity, for they will know more of you than the People of this Day.

I have collected your public Letters and Despatches, and a good Clerk has already recorded a large Volume of them. It is common you know, in the Course of Time for loose & detached Papers to be lost, or mislaid, or misplaced – It is to Papers in this office that future Historians must recur for accurate accounts of many interesting affairs respecting the late Revolution. it is best therefore that they should be recorded regularly in Books; and altho it will take much Time and Labor, which some may think unnecessary, I shall nevertheless persevere in the Work.

.   .   .   .   .

Be assured of my constant Esteem & Attachment, and believe me to be Dear Sir your affect$^{t\cdot}$ Friend & Servt John Jay – rec^d 21. Sept. ans^d 22. 1787.

MHS: *The Adams Papers, microfilm reel 370* (ALS).

John Jay's Report on Anglo-American Relations

[New York] Office for foreign Affairs 26th July 1787
The Secretary of the United States for the Department of foreign Affairs, to whom was referred two Letters from the Honorable Mr Adams of the 24th & 27th January last –
Reports. –
The first of these Letters gives Occasion to several Questions.
Shall Mr Adams return after the Expiration of his Commission to the Court of London, vizt 24th Feby 1788?
Your Secretary is persuaded that Mr Adams really wishes and means to return next Spring, and therefore thinks it would be proper for Congress to Resolve, that the Honble John Adams Esqr, the Minister Plenipotentiary of the United States at the Court of London, be permitted (agreeably to his Request) to return to America at any Time after the 24$^{th\cdot}$ February in the Year of our Lord 1788; and that his Commission of Minister Plenipotentiary to their High Mightinesses do also then determine. –
Resolved, that Congress entertain a high Sense of the Services which Mr Adams has rendered to the United States in the Execution of the various important Trusts which they have from time to time committed to him, and that the Thanks of Congress be presented to him for the Patriotism,

Perseverance, Integrity and Diligence with which he has ably and faithfully served his Country

       The second Question arising from this Letter is, whether it will be expedient for the United States to appoint another Minister to take the place of Mr Adams at the Court of London? –

On this Head your Secretary is of Opinion that it will be expedient to appoint another, because there do exist Differences between the United States and the Court of London which cannot too soon be adjusted, which must become the Subject of occasional Explanations and Negociations, and which on the part of the United States cannot be so well managed and conducted, as by means of an intelligent and discreet Minister on the Spot. Your Secretary's Feelings strongly prompt him to retaliate the Neglect of Britain in not sending a Minister here; but as he conceives that such Retaliation would eventually produce more Inconveniences than Advantages, he thinks it had better be omitted; especially as he is persuaded that this Neglect will cease the Moment that the American Government and the Administration of it shall be such as to impress other Nations with a Degree of Respect, which various Circumstances deny to Congress the Means of imposing at present. He thinks it should be the Policy of the United States at present to keep all Things as smooth and easy, and to expose themselves to as few Embarrassments as possible, until their Affairs shall be in such a Posture as to justify and support a more nervous[1] Stile of Conduct and Language. –

Britain disputes the Eastern Boundary of the United States, she holds important Posts and Territories on the Frontiers, and she complains that the Treaty of Peace has been violated by America. These Affairs are important, and the Management of them requires Prudence and Temper, especially considering how little the actual State of our national Affairs tends to repress the Influence, either of unfriendly Dispositions and Passions, or of that kind of Policy which the Weakness of Neighbours is very apt to suggest and promote. If Congress should concur in the Opinion that a Minister to succeed Mr Adams should be appointed, a Resolution like the following would perhaps be the most proper. –

       Whereas divers important Affairs still remain to be arranged and adjusted between his britannic Majesty and the United States, which on their part cannot be so well conducted as by means of a Minister Plenipotentiary at the Court of London. – therefore

Resolved, that a Minister Plenipotentiary to reside at that Court be appointed, and that his Commission take Effect on the 25th day of February 1788 and continue in Force for the Space of three Years thereafter unless sooner revoked. –

Your Secretary conceives it would be best that this Minister should be appointed so early as that he might have Time to reach London by the first of February, in Order that he may have an Opportunity of receiving Information from Mr Adams respecting Characters and Affairs, and that the Progress of the Business of the Legation may not be stopped by the Expiration of Mr Adams Commission. –

But if Congress should either not incline to appoint another Minister, or should think proper to postpone it so long as that he will not probably be in London in February, then he thinks it would be right to consider another Question arising from the Letter, vizt

       Whether it would be expedient to constitute Col^l Smith Chargé des Affaires? –

On this Head your Secretary finds himself embarrassed; for on the one Hand he esteems Col^l Smith as a Gentleman of acknowledged Merit, who has uniformly deserved well of his Country; and on the other, the Light in which the Duties of his Office have hitherto been viewed, gives the Colour of Propriety only to his reporting on the Expediency of *Appointments*, and not on the *Persons* most proper to be appointed – And as the Letter referred to him and now under Consideration, does nevertheless raise the Question relative to the *Person* as well as the *Place*, he thinks it proper to make these Remarks, lest (if not adverted to) his omitting to report on the *former* as well as the *latter*, might be ascribed to other than the true Reasons. He thinks that, if when Mr Adams quits the Affairs of the Legation, they are not to pass immediately into the Hands of a Successor, there can be little Doubt of the Expediency of appointing a proper Person to *take Charge* of them. –

In that Case therefore, it would in his Opinion be proper to *Resolve*, That a Person be appointed to take Charge of the Affairs of the American Legation at the Court of London, from the Expiration of the Commission of the present Minister, to the Arrival there of another Minister to succeed him, or until the further Order of Congress. –

       The next Question that arises on this Letter is, what should be done respecting the Commissions granted jointly to Mr Adams and Mr Jefferson? –

One of two Things may be done, vizt either appoint a Successor to Mr Adams and associate him with Mr Jefferson, or commit the Execution of those Commissions solely to Mr Jefferson.

Your Secretary further reports, that the Courts of London and the Hague will naturally be desirous to know the Intentions of Congress relative to their appointing Ministers to succeed Mr Adams at both; and he wishes to be directed on this Subject, in order that his Letters to Mr Adams may perfectly correspond with the Views of Congress. –

All which is submitted to the Wisdom of Congress. –

John Jay –

Read 26 July 1787

NA: PCC, *item 81, v. 3, pp. 127-132, 134 (DS); M247, reel 107.*
[1] In the eighteenth century, *nervous* could mean strong, spirited, robust or vigorous.

John Jay to Thomas Jefferson

Sir   [New York] Office for foreign Affairs 27th July 1787

You will herewith receive another Letter from me of this Date together with the Commission mentioned in it – both of them are in Pursuance of the Ideas suggested in your Letter of the 9th January last. If the whole Subject should be reconsidered, and a new Convention formed, it is the Pleasure of Congress that the Duties, Powers and Privileges of Consuls, Vice Consuls, Agents & Commissaries be accurately delineated, and that they be as much circumscribed and limited as the proper Objects of their Appointment will admit, and the Court of France will consent to. How far it may be in your Power to obtain a Convention perfectly unexceptionable, must depend on several Circumstances not yet decided. Congress confide fully in your Talents and Discretion, and they will ratify any Convention that is not liable to more Objections than the one already in part concluded, provided that an Article limiting its Duration to a Term not exceeding twelve Years be inserted. –

I have the Honor to be &c: John Jay –

NA: PCC, *item 121, pp. 270-271 (LBkC); M61, reel 1.*

John Jay's Report Opposing Formation of a Confederacy Against Algiers, Tripoli and Tunis

[New York] Office for foreign Affairs 2[d] August 1787

The Secretary of the United States for the Department of foreign Affairs, to whom was referred a Motion made the 27th of last Month in the Words following, Viz[t] "That the Minister Pleni-potentiary of the United States at the Court of France be directed to form a Confederacy with the Powers of Europe, who are now at War with the piratical States of Algiers, Tripoli and Tunis, or may be disposed to go to War with them, for the Purpose of protecting and securing the Citizens and Subjects of the contracting Parties in the free Navigation of the Mediterranean Sea: That it be an Article in the said Confederation, that none of the contracting Parties shall make Peace with any of the said piratical States, in which the whole Confederacy shall not be included; and in Case a general Peace shall be concluded between the belligerant Powers, that the whole Confederacy shall be Guaranties of the same, and in Case of an Aggression on the part of the said piratical States, they shall be obligated to have Justice done by recommencing Hostilities and continuing the same until this End is effected. That there be an Article stipulating the Quotas of the different Powers in Men and Shipping, ascertaining their Stations at different Periods, and fixing the general Command, in such Manner as may best secure the desired Object."-

Reports. –

That in his Opinion it would always be more for the Honor and Interest of the United States to prefer War to Tribute. –

That his Sentiments on this Subject are stated in a Report he had the Honor to make to Congress on the 20th October 1785, to which he refers.–

That the Measures proposed in that Report were founded on an Opinion, that the Resources of the United States in Seamen and Money were sufficient to execute and support them; but from Causes originating in the Inefficiency of the national Government our Navigation has since rapidly declined, and the public Revenue, depending on the Effect of Requisitions, has become inadequate to the ordinary Exigencies of the Union. –

That in his Judgment a vigourous Effort to revive our Navigation and meliorate our Finances, should at least accompany any Exertions to establish naval Force; for otherwise that Force will be languid and incompetent to its Object. –

It is with great Regret therefore that he is obliged to consider the Motion in Question as rendered unseasonable by the present State of our Affairs.–

If the Nations at War with the three States of Barbary should agree to confederate in the Manner proposed, he thinks it highly probable that the Quota of Force expected from the United States will be much greater than it would be in their Power to supply – nor would it become their Dignity to take the Lead in forming such a Confederation, unless they were prepared to support such spirited Propositions by spirited and important Operations. –

As Things now are your Secretary much doubts whether Congress could find the Means of building and keeping even three Frigates well manned and provided in that Service; and if such be the Case, he thinks it will be most prudent for Congress to delay entering into the proposed, or indeed any other Engagements, until the Means of executing them appear clearly to be within their Reach. –

All which is submitted to the Wisdom of Congress. –

John Jay –

Read 2 Aug. 1787

NA: PCC, item 81, v. 3, pp. 139-142 (DS); M247, reel 107.

Queen Maria I of Portugal to Congress

Lisbon 2^d August 1787

Dona Maria[1] by the grace of God, Queen of Portugal and of the Algarves on this and the other side of the Sea in Africa Governing Guinea, and the conquest, Navigation and Commerce of Ethiopia, Arabia, Persia, and India, &c^a – Salute the United States of America – whom I much esteem and prize –

I received your Letter with very particular satisfaction; and it was equally very agreable to me, that the orders I sent to the Commander of my Squadron, cruising in the mouth of the ~~Streights~~ straits, to protect your vessels in the same manner as those of Portugal, should evince you of the particular contemplation (or regard) and distinguished Value, I set on the United States.

The same orders, as the precedent were & shall be repeated, while the Portuguese fleets shall Cruise on those Seas And I hope that these demonstrations will convince you of the efficacious propensity and sincere desire I have of cultivating with you the best intelligence and of establishing between the two States a perfect friendship and Union promoting and consolidating their common interests, by the efficacious and permanent means of an Alliance that may ~~promote~~ procure to the two Nations the most solid and mutual advantages. – United States of America

God keep you under his holy Guard. – Written in the Palace of Lisbon the 2^d of August 1787.

NA: PCC, item 92, pp. 300-301 (translation); M247, reel 120.
[1] Queen Maria I (1734-1816), ruled Portugal 1777-1816.

Thomas Jefferson to Thomas Barclay

Dear Sir   Paris Aug. 3. 1787.

. . . . .

With respect to French's affair, being perfectly satisfied myself, I have not ceased, nor shall cease endeavoring to satisfy others that your conduct has been that of an honest & honourable debtor, & theirs the counterpart of Shylock in the play. I inclose you a letter containing my testimony on your general conduct, which I have written to relieve a debt of justice pressing on my mind, well knowing at the same time you will not need it in America. your conduct is too well known to Congress, your character to all the world, to need any testimonials.

. . . . .

I beg you to accept assurances of the sincere esteem & respect with which have the honor to be Dear Sir your friend & servant

Th: Jefferson

LC: Jefferson Papers, microfilm reel 7 (press copy).

Marquis de Lafayette to John Jay

My dear Sir   Paris August the 4ᵗʰ 1787

. . . . .

With Great Anxiety, My dear friend, I Wait for the Result of the Convention – No Circumstance Can Ever Be More Interesting to A Heart that Prides in the Glory of America, and is Happy of Her Happiness – indeed, my dear Sir, it is Time for the United States to take those Measures which Have long Been Talked of by their abler, and More zealous Citizens – I Can only pretend to Be Ranked Among the lat[t]er – But am so deeply Wounded by Any Circumstance that does Not Come Up to My ideas Of the future Greatness, prosperity, and Internal Happiness of the United States that I don't only Wish them to be first, but as perfectly Work as it is possible for A Nation to Do – and as they did Set me as their Rule, I pray to God they May Not Relax

...Have the Honour to be Dear Sir, Your   Lafayette

Columbia University Libraries: Special Collections, Iselin (ALS).

John Lamb to John Jay

Boston August 5th 1787

I Arived here this Day, but not Able to Set forw^d At prest on Acc^t my Eyes which Are bad. Shall proceed as Soon As may be Accord to the reso. of Congress Septr last

I am with Due Respect Your Excellencys Obedient Hm^{le} Servt

John Lamb

Read 20 Sept

NA: PCC, *item 91, v. 2, pp. 539, 542 (ALS); M247, reel 119.*

Thomas Jefferson to John Jay

Sir   Paris Aug. 6. 1787.

The last letter I had the honour of addressing you was dated June 21. I have now that of inclosing you a letter from the Swedish Ambassador praying that enquiry may be made for a vessel of his nation pyratically carried off, & measures taken relative to the vessel, cargo & crew. also a letter from William Russell & others citizens of America, concerned in trade to the Island of Guadeloupe, addressed to the Marechal de Castries, & complaining of the shutting to them the port of Point a Petre, and receiving them only at Basse-terre. this was inclosed to me by the subscribers to be delivered to the Marechal de Castries. but the present is not the moment to move in that business: & moreover I suppose that wherever parties are within the reach of Congress, they should apply to them, and my instructions come through that channel. matters arising within the kingdom of France, to which my commission is limited, & not admitting time to take the orders of Congress, I suppose I may move in originally. I also inclose you the copy of a letter from mr Barclay, closing his proceedings in our affairs with Marocco. before this reaches you, he will have had the honour of presenting himself to you in person. after his departure, the parliament of Bourdeaux decided that he was liable to arrest. this was done on a letter from the Minister informing them that mr Barclay was invested with no character which privileged him from arrest. his constant character of Consul was no protection, and they did not explain whether his character to Marocco was not originally diplomatic, or was expired. mr Barclay's proceedings under this commission being now closed, it would be incumbent on me to declare, with respect to them, as well as his Consular transactions, my opinion of the judgment, zeal, & disinter-

estedness with which he has conducted himself; were it not that Congress
has been so possessed of those transactions from time to time, as to judge
for themselves. – I cannot but be uneasy, lest my delay of entering on the
subject of the Consular convention may be disapproved. my hope was, &
is, that more practicable terms might be obtained: in this hope, I do
nothing till further orders, observing by an extract from the Journals you
were pleased to send me, that Congress have referred the matter to your
consideration, & conscious that we are not suffering in the mean time, as
we have not a single Consul in France, since the departure of mr Barclay.
– I mentioned to you, in my last, the revival of the hopes of the Cheval'·
de la Luzerne. I thought it my duty to remind the Count de Montmorin,
the other day, of the long absence of their minister from Congress. he told
me the Chevalier de la Luzerne would not be sent back, but that we might
rely that in the month of October a person would be sent, with whom we
should be content. he did not name the person, tho' there is no doubt that
it is the Count de Moustier. it is an appointment which, according to the
opinion I have formed of him, bids as fair to give content, as any one
which could be made.

· · · · ·

...I have the honor to be with sentiments of the most perfect esteem &
respect, Sir Your most obedient & most humble serv^t·

Th: Jefferson

· · · · ·

LC: *Jefferson Papers, microfilm reel 7 (press copy).*

President of Congress to Five State Governors

Sir　　　　　　　　　　　　　　　　　　New York [August 13, 1787]

　The want of a due Representation in Congress, so frequently as it has
happened, and for a length of time together, has very greatly embarrassed
the Affairs of the Union, and given much dissatisfaction to the States
which generally keep their Representations up, as well as disgust to the
Members who attend from those States. – It has been very often complained of and the States not represented pressed to send their Delegates
forward; too often, I am sorry to be obliged to observed [sic] Sir, with very
little Effect, although it must be obvious that, independent of the great
national Concerns which thereby suffer an inconvenience at least, if not a
disgraceful Delay, their own particular Interests run some risque from public
Measures being adopted without the Aid of their Counsels.

　What, Sir, must the Nations of the World think of Us when they shall
be informed that we have appointed an Assembly and invested it with the

sole and exclusive power of Peace and War, and the management of all national Concerns, and, during the Course of almost a whole Year, it has not been capable, except for a few Days, for want of a sufficient number of Members, to attend to these matters. Since the first Monday in Novr last so this time there has been a representation of nine States only thirty Days, and of ten States only three Days. And, as the Representation of most of the States has consisted of only two Persons, no great Business could be done without the unanimous Consent of every individual Member.

We are now Sir reduced to six States altho' matters of the highest Importance are pressing for a Decision, and cannot be long delayed without committing the Dignity of the Government, and exposing the Peace and safety of several of the States. Besides, Sir, the national Convention, to which the People look up for much good will soon rise, and it appears to be of great Consequence that, when their Report comes under the consideration of Congress, it should be a full Congress and the important Business which will be laid before them meet with no unnecessary Delay.

The Secretary wrote, not long ago to the unrepresented States, but no Effect has yet appeared to follow from it. I must therefore again repeat the Request, and on the most pressing terms, that your Excellency must use every means in your power to hasten forward the Delegates of your State.

With great Respect and Esteem I have the honor to be &c

A. S^t· Clair, Pres^t

A Copy of this Letter was sent to the Governors of Georgia, Maryland, Connecticut, Rhode-Island and New Hampshire.

NA: PCC, *item* 16, *pp. 326-328 (LBkC); M247, reel 24.*

Sir John Temple to John Jay

Sir,   New York 16th August 1787.

A relation at Canton sent me, in the *Hope* lately arrived from thence, a small box of Tea and a piece of Silk for Lady Temple's use. The ship hath been arrived more than a fortnight: I sent for the Tea and Silk several days ago, but the answer returned, by the Customer or Collector, was, that, "as there is not treaty of commerce subsisting between His Britannic Majesty and these States, I must pay the impost or duties charged upon such articles by the government of the State of New York." Will you be so obliging as to inform me whether or not it be right and proper for me to pay the duties so demanded? and I shall govern myself accordingly, for I have not even the most distant wish or desire for any favour or indulgence upon the occasion.

I am sorry Sir, to give you any trouble about so triffling a business, at the same time I am persuaded you will not think the saving a meer triffling impost or duty, upon the necessaries of my family, any object with me in thus applying to you.

I have the honor to be, with great respect, Sir, Your most obedient servant   J. Temple

NA: PCC, *item 92, p. 516 (LS)*; M247, *reel 120.*

John Marsden Pintard to John Jay

Sir   New York 18ᵗʰ August 1787
In my late tour to Boston I engaged with Messʳˢ Joseph Barrell, Crowel Hatch of Boston and Mʳ John Derby of Salem on a Voyage to the Northwest coast of America on discoveries and for which we are preparing two Vessels, the Ship *Columbia* about 220 Tons burthen, and the Sloop *Lady Washington* of about 90 Tons burthen, under the Command and direction of Captain John Kendrick. As there is the greatest prospect that this undertaking will turn out greatly to the advantage of the Commerce of the United States, and perhaps open a new source of Trade for their adventrous Merchants and a Nursery for their Seamen, as none but Americans are concerned in the Voyage, and the owners are determined that none but such shall go in any capacity whatever in the Vessels, we hope for the encouragement and patronage of the Honorable Congress. Will you therefore permit me Sir, to request the favour of you to procure a Sea Letter for the said Vessels from Congress, which will lay the owners under an obligation that shall always be acknowledged. I have the honor to be with the most perfect Esteem &ᶜ   John M. Pintard[1]

NA: PCC, *item 120, v. 3, pp. 270-271 (LBkC)*; M40, *reel 3.*
[1] *Pintard, John Marsden. Merchant. U.S. commercial agent to Madeira, 1783-1790. U.S. Consul at Madeira, 1790-1799.*

John Adams to Thomas Jefferson

Dear Sir   Grosvenor Square, London, Aug 25 1787
On my return from an Excursion to Devonshire with my Family, where We have been to fly the Putrefaction of a Great City in the Summer heat, I had the Pleasure to find your favours of the 17. & 23. of July.

A million of Guilders are borrowed on a new Loan in Holland, and I went over lately to Subscribe the Obligations, a Punctillio which the Brokers were pleased to think indispensible, to gratify the Fancies of the Money Lenders. But as I had no fresh Authority from Congress, nor any particular new Instructions, I have been and am Still under Serious Apprehensions of its meeting with Obstacles in the way of its Ratification. – if it is ratified, Congress may if they please, pay the Interest and Principal too, out of it, to the French officers. – I presume, that if Mr Grand, Should refuse your Usual draughts for your Salary Messrs Willinks and Vanstaphorsts, will honour them to the amount of yours and Mr Short's Salaries without any other Interposition than your Letter. But if they Should make any difficulty, and if it Should be in my Power to remove it, you may well Suppose, I shall not be wanting. – to be explicit, I will either advise or order the Money to be paid, upon your Draught as may be necessary. So that I pray you to make your Mind perfectly easy on that Score.

Mr Barclay, I agree with you, took the wisest Course, when he embarked for America, tho it will lay me under Difficulties in Settling my affairs finally with Congress.

The French Debt, and all the Domestic Debt of the United States might be transferred to Holland, if it were judged necessary or profitable, and the Congress or Convention would take two or three preparatory Steps. All the Perplexities, Confusions and Distresses in America, arise not from defects in their Constitutions or Confederation; not from a Want of Honour or Virtue, So much as from downright Ignorance of the Nature of Coin, Credit and Circulation. – While an annual Interest of twenty, thirty and even fifty Per Cent, can be made, and a hope of augmenting Capitals in a Proportion of five hundred Per Cent is opened by Speculations in the Stocks, Commerce will not thrive. Such a State of Things would annihilate the Commerce, and overturn the Government too in any nation in Europe.

.   .   .   .   .

With perfect Esteem, your sincere Friend   John Adams.

LC: *Jefferson Papers, microfilm reel 8 (ALS).*

Don Diego de Gardoqui to John Jay

Sir   New York 28th Augt 1787
    As I have a sincere desire that there may subsist the most perfect friendship and good correspondence between the King my master and the

United States, every incident which tends to the contrary occasions me an equal degree of concern.

I have read with pain for a year past, various articles in the American Gazettes, which, in Countries where every body is not well informed of the Latitude permitted here to the Press, will appear very extraordinary, but especially in the Court of Madrid, to which, trusting to the assurances of Congress, I have represented very different Ideas from those which many of those Prints may inspire.

A disinclination to trouble Congress with these Complaints, has induced me to omit them until now, for while the public disposition is confirmed by the Acts of the Government, it did not appear necessary nor perhaps regular to take notice of such ill advised anonymous writers. but a certain Letter of a distinct nature has been printed in the Gazette of Charleston of the 6th of the current Month, and reprinted a few days since in those of this City – the same (of which it is a Copy) was left at my House by a servant unknown; and even that would perhaps have been passed over in silence, if the author had not published it and put his name to it.

Consider then Sir, if the Circumstances, Reasonings, and Threats which it contains, are directed to excite uneasinesses, create Jealousies and prepare Minds to think and Act seditiously, and if it deserves to be taken notice of by the Government – it is certain that there is in it very high want of the Respect which is due to his Catholic Majesty and to the United States, since it endeavours to sow and nourish certain seeds of discord between both Nations, and wounds the Laws of civilized ones. I abstain from particularizing the Paragraphs of the said Letter, being persuaded that the many and very extraordinary Passages in it will not escape the observation of Congress – but it may be proper to observe that the Ideas he would give to understand of his having had any connection with me are not founded in fact. I believe it is a year ago that there came to my House a person, without any body to introduce him – he said it seems to me that his name was Sullivan[1] – that he had been an Officer in the American Army, that he was an Irishman and a Catholic, that he was without Employment, that he desired to go into the service of Spain in America, and that he came to supplicate me to procure him an Officer's Commission in one of our Regiments – I received him with proper politeness, and I answered him with all Candor that I was without power to gratify him, and that I was very much persuaded that whatever means he might employ he would not succeed in his pretension. He went away and from that day to this nothing more has occurred between us, until the receipt of the extraordinary Letter in question. I enclose you the Gazette of Charleston which contains that Letter, it appearing to me to be much my Duty to request the Attention of Congress to its Contents. I desire with earnestness and sincerity that I may be enabled to represent to the King my Master that this point with all its Circumstances instead of diminishing adds new proofs to those which affiance the assurances and Friendship of the United States.

I reiterate to you &ᶜ   Diego de Gardoqui

NA: PCC, item 97, pp. 198-199/1 (translation); M247, reel 125.

¹ *Lieutenant John Sullivan was a Leader of the Pennsylvania soldiers who surrounded the State House in Philadelphia in June 1783 to demand their back pay. When the mutiny collapsed, Sullivan fled to England. He returned to the United States in 1786, and was in Georgia in March 1787 when he wrote the letter to Gardoqui. He later sailed from Georgia for England without endeavoring to put his plans for Tennessee and Kentucky into effect.*

Comte de Montmorin to Louis Guillaume Otto

[Translation]

Nº· 4   Versailles, 31 August 1787.

·   ·   ·   ·   ·

It appears, Sir, that there is in all the American provinces more or less of a tendency towards democracy, and that in several this latter form of government will prevail in the end. The result will be that the confederation will have little solidity, and that by degrees the various states will live in perfect independence with regard to each other. (This revolution will mean nothing troublesome for us: we have never aspired to make a useful ally of America: we have had no other goal than to take this vast continent away from Great Britain. Thus we can view with indifference both the movements that trouble several provinces and the fermentation that reigns in Congress.) That should not prevent you from continuing to report on all that happens, and I can only give praise to the exactitude that I have remarked in your despatches in this regard.

I very much fear, Sir, that the discussions relative to the Mississipi are becoming serious, and that they will cause us difficulties: Spain may misunderstand her interests: but this does not give the Americans the right to force that power's hand. The mouth of the Mississippi belongs to her; consequently, she has the right to open it or to keep it closed, and the Americans can only obtain favor on her part by way of negotiation. The Court of Madrid would not be difficult if it had the same principles as we have on this subject.

·   ·   ·   ·   ·

De Montmorin

·   ·   ·   ·   ·

FFAA: Pol. Corr., U.S., v. 32, f. 350-351vo. (LC transcription).

Phineas Bond to Lord Carmarthen

My Lord   New York. Sep. 2$^{nd.}$ 1787

After waiting here a considerable time I have at length received an assurance from the Secretary for foreign affairs, that the resolution of Congress adopting my commission as his Majesty's consul, is now transmitted to all the five States, and that I may proceed to the exercise of my duty, in those States to which that commission extends.

I was the more anxious to have this matter arranged, as I conceived it probable I might be honored with your Ldp's instructions (respecting the appointment of agents) by the July Mail.

The packet arrived on the 30$^{th.}$ of Aug: and as I have not been favored with any directions from your Ldp. on that subject, I mean to return immediately to Philadelphia.

Shortly after the last packet sailed from hence, my Lord, the Ship *Hope*, Cap$^{t.}$ Magee[1] arrived here from China: I have obtained an account of her cargo, at Wampo which I have the honor to enclose to your Ldp. I am in a train of procuring a copy of the return of this ship's cargo delivered in at the Custom House here, and was in hopes I should have been able to have forwarded it to your Ldp. by this conveyance, but all the public offices are become very secret and jealous and it is with difficulty any vouchers are obtained from them.

The enclosed return of the cargo of the ship, *Empress of China*, Cap$^{t.}$ Green[2] may be depended upon, as it came directly from the Custom House. It may probably differ from the amount of this ship's cargo, which I lately forwarded to your Lordship; as the one I then sent was taken from a letter from a merchant in this place to his friend in Philadelphia

The Americans, my Lord, are using every possible endeavour to render this trade as productive as possible; and to extend it to more valuable articles, than they have hitherto dealt in.

About the time the *Hope* left Canton Mr Shaw[3] the American consul there was preparing to go to Bengal to open some communication for piece goods and such merchandize as may not only produce a good price here, but also supply the markets of Europe, – particularly Gt. Britain and Ireland.–

The letters I have the honor to enclose to your Ldp. directed to the Lords of the Admiralty and the Com: of the Customs will discover to government some of the practices now carried on to elude the operation of the Acts of Trade – I have the honor to be your Ldp's. most faithful and most obed. servant   P. Bond.

Rec^d 3$^{rd.}$ Oct.

AHA 1896. v. 1, pp. 544-546.

[1] Magee, James, who had commanded Massachusetts privateers during the war.

[2] Green, John (1736-1796). Pennsylvania seafarer, U.S. Navy captain. Master of several merchant vessels owned by the Philadelphia firm of Willing & Morris prior to the American Revolution. Commanded Continental Navy vessels Queen of France, Retaliation, and Lion, as well as Pennsylvania letter of marque brig Nesbitt, 1778-1781. Inmate, Old Mill Prison, Plymouth, England, 1781-1782. Commanded Continental Navy vessel Duc de Lauzun, 1782-1783. Captain, Empress of China, the first American ship to trade in China, 1784-1785.

[3] Shaw, Samuel (1754-1794). Military figure, merchant, and consul. Artillery officer, aide-de-camp to General Henry Knox. Supercargo of the Empress of China, the first United States ship to trade at Canton, 1784-1785. Named U.S. Consul at Canton, 1786.

Lord Carmarthen to Sir John Temple

Sir,   Whitehall Sept[r] 5[th:] 1787
    Your Letters to N° 21 have been received and laid before the King
    I send you inclosed the Petition of Richard Lawrence a Loyalist stating that his Property has been confiscated, and that he has been for upwards of Sixteen Months closely confined in the common Jail at New York in Violation of the Sixth Article of the Definitive Treaty of Peace; and I am to desire You will make Enquiry into the Circumstances of this Case and if you find the Petitioner justly entitled to the Benefit he claims under the Stipulations of that Treaty, that You will make the strongest Representations to Congress for his being immediately set at Liberty and full Restitution made to him of such Property as he may have been unjustly deprived of, together with such further Satisfaction as you may be able to obtain in his Behalf, and as the Nature of the Case will justify You in solliciting   Carmarthen

PRO: FO 4/5, pp. 507-508, 510 (LC transcription).

[Enclosure]

Richard Lawrence's Petition to King George III

To the King's most excellent Majesty.
    The humble petition of Richard Lawrence a Loyalist, and late a Master-Ship-Carpenter in the British service, but now a prisoner in the new Goal [sic] of the city of New York, in North America.
                            Sheweth,

That previous to the commencement of the unhappy contest betwixt Great Britain and America, your petitioner resided at Staten Island in the then Colony of New York, following his trade of a Ship-carpenter, and being zealously attached to your Majesty's government. After the rebellion began his loyalty remained unshaken, and as soon as the British troops landed upon Staten Island, he repaired to the Royal Standard.

That your petitioner was afterwards appointed by Sir William Howe[1] Commander in Chief of your Majesty's forces, Master-Carpenter of the Ship Yards at Staten Island and New York, and continued in that employment until the year one thousand seven hundred and eighty. And receiving an order from the said Commander in Chief, a true copy whereof is hereunto annexed, your petitioner in obedience to such order, did seize and take under his charge, several boats and vessels, and also large quantities of Ship-timber, and other naval Stores &c, belonging to the Rebels; and having received an appointment from his Excel[y] William Tryon Esquire,[2] then governour of New York, a copy whereof is also annexed, your petitioner did take upon himself the direction and management of the woods in the said appointment mentioned and by like orders from the Commander in Chief did take upon himself the direction and management of divers other woods upon Estates in Staten Island aforesaid, and large quantities of timber were under the inspection of your petitioner cut down from the said Woods and used in your Majesty's service, but your petitioner never made any advantage or profit thereof or converted any part to his own use or emolument, but the said Timber was entirely applied to the Public service.

That upon the evacuation of New York, your petitioner intended to have withdrawn into some part of your Majesty's dominions, but having several considerable sums of money due to him, and relying upon the sixth Article of the definitive treaty which declares "That there shall be no future confiscations made, nor prosecutions commenced against any person or persons for or by reason of the part which he or they may have taken in the present War; and that no person shall on that account suffer any future loss or damage either in his person, liberty or property." Your petitioner remained in New York after the evacuation thereof to manage and settle his affairs, but before he could effect the same, in manifest violation of that Treaty, and of national faith, several actions at law were commenced against him by the proprietors of the said Estates at Morisania and Staten Island for the damages they sustained by their timber being cut down and used in your Majesty's service, and by the owners of the boats & vessels, ship-timber and other Stores, which your petitioner seized by virtue of the annexed order; And although he pleaded the said treaty in Bar of such actions, yet judgement was given against him, and he was arrested and has been for upwards of sixteen months closely confined in the Common Goal

[sic] of New York, which has not only reduced him to poverty, but (being far advanced in years) hath also nearly put a period to his miserable existence, his health being greatly impaired, and having almost lost his sight by his long imprisonment, And his unfortunate wife and family reduced from competency to a state of indigence and distress.

That in hopes of relief your petitioner has laid his unfortunate case before the Congress of the United States of America, and the Governour and Assembly of the now State of New York, but no attention has be[en] given by any of them to his petitions. He therefore with the greatest humility ventures to lay his unfortunate situation before your Majesty, encouraged by the professed inclination your Majesty has shewn to alleviate the misfortunes of those persons who since the late War suffered for their loyalty and attachment to your Majesty's person and government; And as your petitioner from the aggravated wretchedness, which the loss of his liberty, and ruin of his fortune, has entailed upon him, is totally unable to satisfy the large damages recovered against him in the said actions, he must without some powerful interposition end his days in misery and wretchedness, confined to a loathsome prison, destitute of the common necessaries of life, deprived of the free use of the air, and cut off from all possibility of maintaining his unfortunate family, who are now reduced to beggary and dispair.

Your petitioner therefore most humbly hopes that your Majesty in your great goodness will be pleased to take his unfortunate case into consideration, and by your Royall interposition with the Congress of the said United States of America prevent his suffering the most dreadful, the most horrid of all human punishments, perpetual Imprisonment.

Richard Lawrence

NA: PCC, item 92, pp. 527-529 (C); M247, reel 120.

[1] Howe, Sir William (1729-1814). British general. Brother of Admiral Lord Richard Howe. Arrived in North America with reinforcements for General Thomas Gage, May 1775; commanded the British force in the Battle of Bunker Hill, June 17, 1775. Succeeded Gage in command of British troops in American colonies, October 1775; withdrew from Boston to Halifax, Nova Scotia, March 1776. With his brother, commissioned to treat with the American rebels and to attempt a reconciliation with the American colonies, May 6, 1776; Congress refused to treat on these terms. Captured Long Island (August 1776), New York (September 1776), and Philadelphia (September 1777). Victorious at White Plains (October 28, 1776), Brandywine (September 11, 1777), and Germantown (September 26, 1777). Submitted resignation in October 1777, complaining of not being properly supported at home. Left America, May 24, 1778.

[2] Tryon, William (1725-1788). British colonial official. Appointed lieutenant governor of North Carolina, 1764; governor, 1765-1771, during which time he put down the revolt of the Regulators. Governor of New York, 1771-1778. Commanded loyalist and British military forces in New York and Connecticut, 1777-1780.

Chevelier de Pinto to John Adams

Sir   London 7th September 1787

I have received orders from my Court to inform you that notwithstanding no Answer has hitherto been made to the project of a Commerical Treaty, which we conferred about in London nevertheless Sir the inclinations of Her Most Faithful Majesty are not less ardent nor less disposed to conclude this same treaty with the U^d States of Am^a on suitable terms & conditions, & I am moreover directed to add Sir that my Court will not delay to give you the most convincing & immediate proofs thereof. –

I am desired at the same time to observe to you that it would be very useful & suitable to appoint Ministers as soon as possible on the part of the two powers, & my Court expressly orders me to endeavour to arrange this important point with you Sir & to Agree definitively on the Character these Ministers are to bear in their Missions. It is ~~necessary~~ essential to inform on this head that it will be necessary to fix (at least) on the Title of Resident Minister, on account of reception at the Court of Lisbon, which is never granted either to simple Agents or to Consuls General: And as soon as this point shall be fixed I have orders to assure You Sir that the Court of Lisbon will lose no time to appoint & send to America the person that shall be chosen to reside with the Congress of the U^d States. I have the honor of being with much esteem & respect Sir Your m° hm. & m°· ob^d Serv^{t·}   Le Ch^{r·} de Pinto.

Faithfully translated from the Original by John Pintard.

NA: PCC, item 84, v. 6, p. 513 (translation); M247, reel 113.

John Jay to Thomas Jefferson

Dr Sir   New York 8th September 1787

. . . . .

The Convention will probably rise next Week, and their Proceedings will probably cause not only much Consideration, but also much Discussion, Debate and perhaps Heat; for as *docti indoctique scribimus*,[1] so *docti indoctique disinterested Patriots and interested Politicians will sit in Council and in Judgment, both within and without Doors. There is nevertheless a Degree of Intelligence and Information in the Mass of our People, which affords much Room for Hope that by Degrees our Affairs will assume a more consistent and pleasing Aspect. For my own part, I have long found myself in an awkward Situation, seeing much to be done and enabled to do very little. All we can do to persevere – if Good results our Labor will not be in vain, if not we shall have done our Duty, and that Reflection is valuable. –*

With the best Wishes for your Health and Happiness, and with very sincere Esteem and Regard, I am &c: John Jay –

NA: PCC, item 121, pp. 278-280 (LBkC); M61, reel 1.
¹ We, learned and the unlearned, write.

John Adams to the Chevelier de Pinto

Sir –   Grosvʳ· Sqʳ· Septʳ· 10ᵗʰ· 1787.

I have received the Letter, which you did me the honor to write me on the 7ᵗʰ of this month, & have observ'd with great Satisfaction, the assurances of her most Faithfull Majesty's desire, to conclude with the United States of America a treaty of Commerce upon convenient conditions –

I am very well convinced Sir, of the Utility & Convenience which would be found in the nomination of ministers between the two Powers & if it depended upon me, I flatter myself there would be no difficulty in concerting with your Excellency both that important point & the Character those Ministers should bear in their missions – But as I have neither instructions nor authority from my Sovereign to justify me in entering into such negotiations, I can only transmit to Congress copies of your Excellency's Letter & of my Answʳ· This I shall have the honor to do the first oppertunity – the earnest desire of the Citizens of the United States of America to shew their respects to Her Most faithful majesty & to live in perfect friendship with all her Majesty's dominions, will undoubtedly induce Congress to transmit as soon as possible their ansʳ to Her Majesty's friendly proposition

I have the honor to be &c &c –   John Adams

NA: PCC, item 84, v. 6, p. 515 (C); M247, reel 113.

William Stephens Smith to John Jay

Sir.   London Septʳ 12ᵗʰ 1787.

·   ·   ·   ·   ·

I have then the pleasure of informing your Excellency, that I entered the Kingdom of Portugal, on the 11ᵗʰ of July at Elvas, a Garrison town on the Gaudiana, where my reception was particularly polite, and after dining with the Commanding General (who immediately on my arrival, honoured me with a visit and an invitation) I proceeded on my Journey in the evening, at which time, the General had ordered a Dragoon to be ready to attend me to Lisbon, assuring me, that it was not only necessary as a security thro' the Country, but would facilitate my passage thro' the Towns & Villiages on my way, and he would serve also as a Guide on the road. I experienced many conveniences in this arrangement, and arrived at Lisbon on the afternoon of the 15th. on the 16th in the morning I wrote a Letter to the Minister of State for foreign Affairs, of which the enclosed No. 3. is a Copy, and on the evening of the 18th I had the honor of being introduced to him at a Ball given by the Marquis De Bombelles,[2] the Ambassador of France when his Excellency, was pleased to appologize, for not answering my Letter before, but observed, that this meeting, would render it unnecessary, and he would be very happy to see me at his office, in the morning at 11 °Clock – I waited on him agreable to appointment, and being immediately admitted, after a few prelimenaries, presented my Commission, which being read I delivered a Copy of it – he said, that he would lay it before Her Majesty and inform me of her pleasure – I then rose to take my leave – but His Excellency in a very friendly way requested me to keep my seat, & said, he had made his arrangements to pass the hour with me, – he then took the lead in a conversation, and touched upon the commerce of Portugal and the United States. I took the liberty of observing, that I once expected an intercourse between our two Countrys would have taken place before this, and was sorry to find, that the treaty which had been signed by the Portuguese & American Ministers at London, was not permitted to operate. – he said that tho' the treaty which was pending between us, was not yet finished, it would give Her Majesty, and himself, great satisfaction to have it arranged upon proper principles – that Her Majesty had had it in possession for some time, & had made some remarks and observations on it, which were of weight and required consideration – that she was much interested in my Country, and wished to be better acquainted with it – that she considered it as a great Empire, rising from wise and liberal establishments, and looked to it, with expectations, in favour of its future dignity and importance that the exchange of Ministers would be very agreable, and that a Gentleman of a respectable Character, Sent from my Country in that line, would be received with every mark of respect, and would have an opportunity of personally knowing the regard Her Majesty had for my Country & the favourable dispositions of her Ministers towards it – and in return, a Gentleman of equal grade & Character would be sent to reside with Congress, who would turn his whole attention to the cultivation of every friendly disposition, and from time to time, would give her Majesty every necessary information of the Country, its Inhabitants –

establishments, present situation, and future prospects that after such an exchange of Ministers, and the agreable advances to friendship & intimacy, there was not the least doubt, but a treaty might be readily concluded, which would be mutually advantageous – that Ministers being acquainted with the arrangements of Countries, might soon digest a treaty, upon principles consistant with the establishments in each, and he did not doubt, that when the Americans and the Portuguese became better acquainted, (which Her Majesty much wished) both would be satisfied, on every subject that it was in the power of Ministers to arrange, for the accommodation of their commercial Interests – but, that the mode of negotiating by Ministers resident in London, was tedious, and might not answer the good purposes, both parties might wish. — that the Chevalier De Pinto, a very able and good Minister, having been absent from his Country many years, was not acquainted with the little domestic arrangements, which were necessary to be attended to, in the Arrangements of a Commercial treaty – but that all these difficulties, might be overcome by an exchange of ministers, and America would find every favourable disposition existing respecting her, which she could wish – I expressed myself, much flattered by the polite reception with which I had been honoured, and particularly pleased to find Her Majesty, & His Excellency, disposed to view my Country & its establishments thro' so favourable a medium, and observed, that it would give Congress great pleasure, to have those favourable Sentiments conveyed to them, and that I did not doubt, but their future Conduct would convince Her Majesty, & His Excellency, how much obliged they were, by their good opinions – that a liberal Commercial intercourse with the Kingdom of Portugal, was among the first of their wishes & that it would afford them great satisfaction, if the present dispositions, should be nourished, & be productive of lasting friendships –

I took the liberty of further observing, that it would be satisfactory, to be made acquainted, with the objections to the treaty in its present garb – he said, it was still in her Majesty's possession and seemed disposed to wave the subject, I did not interfere with this disposition, but permitted myself to be led into a less pointed conversation, at the close of which, & as I was taking my leave, His Excellency, was pleased to say, that if I would wait on him the day after the next, he would inform me of Her Majesty's decision on the subject of my Commission – On the day appointed for this interview, I was confined to my bed by a very high fever, and was under the necessity of sending my excuse to the Minister, the enclosed N° 4. is a copy of my note on that occasion, – The next day, the Honourable Mr Fonseca, under Secretary of State, waited on me (being still confined) at the request of the Minister, to inform me, that my Commission had been submitted to her Majesty in Council, and as it was not issued by the

Sovereign, it was not consistant with the etiquette of Courts, that I should present the Letter from Congress (in Person) to Her Majesty, but that, His Excellency the Minister would present it the next day, if I would permit, – I observed, that I could not have a wish on this subject, separate from her Majesty's pleasure, and not being able to wait on the Minister, I delivered the letter to Mr Fonseca, to be conveyed to him – he then observed, that Her Majesty would be glad to see me at Court, where, tho', upon my Comission, I could not be presented, I might be admitted, as a foreigner of distinction – I expressed myself complimented by her Majesty's saying she would be glad to see me at Court, but was rather apprehensive, that as there was but one drawing room within the Month, that my indisposition might deprive me of that honor. – but this, Sir, I wished to avoid being sensible that my appearing at Court without being introduced to the Royal family, would make an unfavourable impression, and perhaps, furnish grounds for unpleasant observations, particularly, as my reception at the Court of Madrid & the attentions of the prime Minister the Comte de Floridablanca and the Corps diplomatic to me, there, had reached Lisbon before me, aided by a consciousness of the awkerdness [sic] of the Situation of being in a public drawing Room, as a simple, or a Curious traveller; I became anxious rather to avoid it, if it could be done with delicacy & without giving offence, – this I was enabled to do, & the day of audience having passed during my indisposition, my mind was rendered easy on the Subject – and when Mr Fonseca some few days after, repeated his visit – I begged him to present my respects to His Excellency the Minister of State, and as the business with which I was charged, was compleatly finished, I should only request the honor of another interview, and take my leave, it being my intention to embark in the Packett, which was to sail on the 7th for Falmouth, and that, I should be happy to take charge of any commands Her Majesty, or His Excellency had for Congress. – he expressed himself somewhat surprized, that I should think of going, without having seen the Court, & observed that even upon principles of curiosity it was worth a Gentleman's while, to see the Court of the Country thro' which he was passing, and pressed my waiting for the next Packett, within which time, her Majesty would give another audience –

I acknowledged the propriety of his remarks, but observed, that considering my Station at the Court of London and that the whole weight of the business, during my absence rested upon Mr Adams, I did not think, I could justify my staying a month longer, having no other object in view, but the gratification of my curiosity – particularly as it would be only entering the appartments of the Palace, walking round and out again – that if my visit to the Court, could be considered, as carrying with it the least degree of respect towards Her Majesty, I would willingly remain any space of time, but as that, did not appear to be the case & I could have nothing but the gratification of my curiosity in view, I did not doubt, but both himself and the Minister, as Gentlemen of business, would excuse and even approve of my decision – he was pleased to be very complimentary & further pressed my stay, but said he would communicate what I requested, to the Minister & he would agreable to my request, inform Her Majesty of my intentions and know if she had any commands

The next day, I received the enclosed N° 5 from him. he came agreable to the appointment, & said, that he had communicated my intentions to the Minister, & that he had intimated them, to her Majesty, that her reply to the Letter which I had brought, would be ready for me, & that Her Majesty, (tho' not a day of audience) had appointed the next at 1/2 past 4 in the afternoon, when in the Audience Chamber of the palace, it was her pleasure to receive me, & that the Prime Minister would introduce me to Her Majesty, & the Royal family, previous to my departure. – I acknowledged myself much complimented by Her Majesty's condesention, and at the hour appointed, the next day, I met the Minister at the Palace, who informed me it would be necessary to say a few words, on my introduction to Her Majesty

I was soon admitted, & having advanced with the usual ceremonies I was received by Her Majesty & the Prince and Princess of Brazil, and being presented to the former, I addressed her agreable to the contents of N° 6, and N° 7. is the answer she was pleased to return (which as I expressed my apprehension to the minister, that I should not be able fully to recollect, when I attempted to make a minute of it, he was so polite as to give it me in his own hand writing) – after which, the Minister taking me by the hand, introduced me to the rest of the Royal family, and the ceremony being finished, I retired with the accostomed formes – the Minister having followed me, gave me the inclosed Letter, addressed to the United States in Congress, from Her Majesty, in reply to the Letter with which I was charged, N° 8 is a certified Copy of its Contents, and N° 9 its translation – His Excellency then said, that if I was not otherway's engaged, he would accompany me to the Arsenal & Park of Artillery, & shew me some improvements & Curiosities in those departments, not unworthy the attention of a Soldier, to this unexpected and remarkable polite proposition, I consented, in a way which fully conveyed, the Sense I had, of His Excellency's condescension; we went from the palace together & passed the remnant of the day in the way proposed – As we were on the point of seperating – I beged permission to say one word more on the subject of the treaty, which rested between our Courts, and stated; that it would be particularly satisfactory to me, if His Excellency, would enable me, to make some communications, relative to the existing objections, and whether there was a prospect of their being overcome – he observed, that from what had already passed between us on that subject, I could not doubt but an adjustment of it, would be agreable to Her Majesty, and himself, and that he should employ the first leisure time he had, in revising it, & Her Majesty's observations on it, and after connecting them, he would forward a Counter-project to the Minister in London – but observed, that a Minister on the spot, would save a great deal of trouble, & on this Subject he said that he was obliged candidly to tell me, that Her Majesty, was not much pleased, that she had not been noticed by Congress, in the same way, that her friends and Neighbouring Nations had, that her majesty was not attached to any particular grade of Ministers, that Congress might take their choice whether to send an Ambassador – a Minister Plenipotentiary or Envoy – or a Resident – that she would regulate her choice and appointment by that of Congress – but she wished a communication between the two Countries in this line, and he, himself was conscious, it would tend to remove many obstructions, in the way of a proper intercourse, and that the only point in which her Majesty wished to be particular, was, that if Congress should think proper to send a Gentleman to reside at Lisbon, in the Character of their representative, he might not be commissioned as *Chargé des affaires*, as the etiquette of the Courts of Europe, in some degree, shut the door of Society against that grade, and would not admit at her Court, of that freedom of Communication, which would be agreable to Her Majesty, should exist, between the representative of Congress – herself & her Ministers – on this subject His Excellency was pleased to be very polite & complimentary to me, the particulars of which, your Excellency I doubt not, will excuse me from detailing – I then took my leave, & the day after, embarked for Falmouth – It must be superfluous for me, to enter into a detail of the Circumstances, which to my mind, places the Kingdom of Portugal, in such a Situation, as to become an object worthy of the attention of Congress; her Geographical Situation – the convenience of having her ports open to receive American Vessells, in case of War or peace, and the dispositions she nourishes relative to the Barbary powers, & the facilities America may experience from a connection, in favour of an exchange of produce, with her, and other European Nations – are Subjects on which Congress are so fully competent to decide, that an attempt to elucidate them on my part, must be unnecessary – Anxious for the approbation of my Country on this, and every other Subject, in which they think proper to honor me with their commands –

     I have the honour to be with great respect Your Excellency's most Obedient & very Humble Servant   W. S. Smith

NA: PCC, item 92, pp. 304-319 (ALS); M247, reel 120.

¹ Bombelles, Marc Marie, Marquis de. French diplomat. Minister to the German Reichstag at Regensburg, 1775-1782. Ambassador to Portugal, 1786-1788. Ambassador to Venice, 1789-1791.

Thomas Jefferson to John Jay

Sir   Paris Sep.ʳ 19. 1787.

...I shall proceed on the redemption of our captives at Algiers as soon as the Commissioners of the treasury shall enable me, by placing the money necessary under my orders. the prisoners redeemed by the religious order of Mathurins cost about 400 dollars each, and the General of the order told me that they had never been able to redeem foreigners on so good terms as their own countrymen. supposing that their redemption, clothing, feeding & transportation should amount to 500. dollars each, there must be at least a sum of 10,000 dollars set apart for this purpose. till this is done I shall take no other step than this preparatory one of destroying at Algiers all idea of our intending to redeem the prisoners. this, the General of the Mathurins told me was indispensably necessary, and that it must not on any account transpire that the public would interest themselves for their redemption. this was rendered the more necessary by the declaration of the Dey to the Spanish consul that he should hold him responsible, at the Spanish price, for our prisoners, even for such as should die. three of them have died of the plague. by authorising me to redeem at the prices *usually* paid by European nations, Congress, I suppose, could not mean the Spanish price, which is not only unusual but unprecedented, and would make our vessels the first object of those pyrates. I shall pay no attention therefore to the Spanish price, unless further instructed. hard as it may seem, I should think it necessary not to let it be known even to the relatives of the captives that we mean to redeem them.

. . . . .

...the King of Prussia, urged on by England, has pressed more and more the affairs of Holland, and lately has given to the states general of Holland four days only to comply with his demand. this measure would of itself have rendered it impossible for France to proceed longer in the Line of accomodation with Prussia. in the same moment an event takes place which seems to render all attempt at accomodation idle. the Turks have declared war against the Russians, and that under circumstances which exclude all prospect of preventing it's taking place. the King of Prussia having deserted his antient friends, there remain only France & Turkey, perhaps Spain also, to oppose the two empires, Prussia & England. by such a peice of

Quixotism France might plunge herself into ruin with the Turks & Dutch, but would save neither. but there is certainly a confederacy secretly in contemplation, of which the public have not yet the smallest suspicion: that is between France and the two empires. I think it sure that Russia has desired this, and that the Emperor, after some hesitation has acceded. it rests on this country to close. her indignation against the king of Prussia will be some spur. she will thereby save her party in Holland, and only abandon the Turks to that fate she cannot ward off, and which their precipitation has brought on themselves by the instigations of the English Ambassador[1] at the Porte, and against the remonstrances of the French Ambassador.[2] perhaps this formidable combination, should it take place, may prevent the war of the Western powers, as it would seem that neither England nor Prussia could carry their false calculations so far as, with the aid of the Turks only to oppose themselves to such a force. in that case the Patriots of Holland would be peaceably established in the powers of their government, and the war go on against the Turks only, who would probably be driven from Europe. this new arrangement would be a total change of the European system, and a favourable one for our friends....

The Count de Moustier is nominated minister plenipotentiary to America: and a frigate is ordered to Cherburg to carry him over. he will endeavor to sail by the middle of next month, but if any delays should make him pass over the whole of October, he will defer his voiage to the spring, being unwilling to undertake a winter passage. Monsr de St. Priest[3] is sent Ambassador to Holland, in the room of Monsr. de Verac appointed to Switzerland. the Cheval^{r.} de la Luzerne, might I beleive have gone to Holland, but he preferred a general promise of promotion, & the possibility that it might be to the court of London. his prospects are very fair. his brother the Count de la Luzerne[4] (now Governor in the West Indies) is appointed minister of the marine in the place of Monsr. de Castries who has resigned. the Archbishop of Toulouse[5] is appointed Ministre principale, and his brother Monsr. de Brienne[6] minister of war in the place of Monsr. de Segur.[7] the department of the Comptroul has had a very rapid succession of tenants. from M. de Calonne it passed to M. de Forqueux,[8] from him to Villedeuil, & from him to Lambert,[9] who holds it at present, but divided with a M. Cabarrus[10] (whom I beleive you knew in Spain) who is named *Directeur du tresor royal,* the office into which mr Necker[11] came at first. I had the honour to inform you that before the departure of the Count de la Luzerne to his government in the West Indies, I had pressed on him the patronage of our trade with the French islands, that he appeared well disposed, and assured me he would favor us as much as his instructions & the laws of the colonies would permit. I am in hopes these dispositions will be strengthened by his residence in the islands, and that his acquaintance among the people there will be an additional motive to favor them. probably they will take advantage of his appointment to press indulgences in commerce with us. the ministry is of a liberal complection, and well disposed to us. the war may add to the motives for opening their islands to other resources for their subsistence, and for doing what may be agreeable to us. it seems to me at present then, that the moment of the arrival of the Count de la Luzerne will be that moment for trying to obtain a freer access to their islands. it would be very material to do this, if possible, in a permanent way, that is to say by treaty. but I know of nothing we have to offer in equivalent. perhaps the paiment of our debt to them might be made use of as some inducement, while they are so distressed for money. yet the borrowing the money in Holland will be rendered more difficult by the same event, in proportion as it will increase the demand for money by other powers.

The gazettes of Leyden and France to this date are inclosed, together with some pamphlets on the internal affairs of this country.

I have the honor to be, with sentiments of the most perfect esteem and respect, Sir, Your most obedient & most humble servant

Th: Jefferson

LC: *Jefferson Papers, microfilm reel 8 (press copy).*

[1] *Ainslie, Sir Robert Sharpe. British diplomat. Ambassador to Turkey, 1776-1794.*

[2] *Choiseul-Gouffier, Marie Gabriel Florent Auguste, Comte de. French diplomat. Ambassador to Turkey, 1784-1792.*

[3] *St. Priest, François Emmanuel Guignard, Comte de. French diplomat. Ambassador to Turkey, 1768-1784. Ambassador to the United Provinces of the Netherlands, June 1788-February 1789.*

[4] *Luzerne, César Henri, Comte de. French government official. Governor of St. Domingue, 1785-1787. Minister of Marine, 1787-1790.*

[5] *Loménie de Brienne, Etienne Charles (1727-1794). French clergyman and political figure. Archbishop of Toulouse and Sens, 1763-1788. Chief, Royal Council on Finance, 1787-1788. Chief Minister, August 1787-August 1788. Named Cardinal, December 1788.*

[6] *Not further identified.*

[7] *Ségur, Philippe Henri, Comte de (1724-1801). French military leader, marshal of France. Minister of War, 1781-1787.*

[8] *Fourqueux, Michel Bouvard de. French government official. Minister of Finance, April-May 1787.*

[9] *Lambert, Claude Guillaume II. French government official. Comptroller General of Finances, August 1787-August 1788.*

[10] *Cabarrus, Francisco, Comte de. Financial specialist who refused appointment as director of the French royal treasury, 1787.*

[11] *Necker, Jacques (1732-1804). Swiss banker who served as France's controller general of finance, 1776-1781, 1788-1789, 1789-1790.*

Phineas Bond to Lord Carmarthen

My Lord,   Philadelphia Sep 20[th.] 1787
   I have the honor to inform your Ldp. the meeting of the Convention of the United States closed on the 17th inst. and I now enclose to your Ldp. the Constitution of Government recommended to the consideration of Congress. As far as I can judge the sober and discreet part of the community approve of the plan in its present form, and when due consideration is paid to the democratic temper of the times, it is perhaps the best shape in which it could have been handed forth to the people.

. . . . .

   I have the honour to be, my Lord, your Ldp's. most faithful and obedient servant
                                     P. Bond.
Rec[d] 3rd Nov.

AHA 1896, v. 1, p. 546.

John Adams to John Jay

Dear Sir   Grosvenor Square, London Sept. 22. 1787
   ...This Country is now in a critical Situation. The Courts of London and Berlin, have been advised by their Ministers at the Hague, to hold their heads very high, and Speak in a high Tone, in favour of the Prince and Princess of Orange, in order to encourage their Friends and intimidate the Opposition to them, in full Confidence that the internal State of Politicks and Finances in France, will not permit the Court of Versailles to interfere. in this Sanguine Expectation they may possibly be dis approved, and by their precipitate Proceedings find themselves involved in a War, they never intended. The Probability if not Certainty of a War, between the three Empires, and the Romantick quarrel to revenge an Irreverence to a Princess, as Silly a Tale as the Trojan Wars on Account of Hellen, have opened So Serious a Prospect to this nation that there is room to hope, that the Ministry will be more attentive and more equitable towards America. The French Court are Sending out the Comte De Moutier, as Minister to Congress. You will have no difficulty to believe that this Movement has been dictated by Wisdom and prudent Foresight. if the British Cabinet have equal Circumspection, they will See the Same Necessity. But no dependence can be placed upon the Judgment of the present Cabinet. The United States of America will take the coolest Precautions, while they fulfill their Engagements with honour, to maintain

their Neutrality inviolate. if a general and lasting War in Europe Should ensue, and America preserve her Peace, She will be, at the close of it, the first Country in the World, in Point of Affluence and Prosperity if not in real Power. – in Case of a War, my Situation here, will be extreamly delicate. The United States and their Ministers Stand in certain Relations to France and Holland, from whence result Duties which must in all Events be fullfilled. There are other Duties too towards England. to reconcile these among all jarring Interests and inflamed Passions in a State of War will be Somewhat difficult. But I flatter myself it may be done, for the few Months that remain before the Expiration of my Commission. With the truest Esteem and Regard, I have the Honour to be, dear Sir your most obedient and most humble Servant   John Adams.

NA: PCC, item 84, v. 6, pp. 519-521 (ALS); M247, reel 113.

John Adams to John Jay

Dear Sir   London Sept.ʳ 22. 1787
    There was Yesterday in the River, an Impress of Seamen, and Several American Vessells had their Men taken from them. An Application was made to me this Morning by a Master of a ship from New York, and I instantly wrote the inclosed Letter to Lord Carmarthen and went in Person to White Hall to deliver it. His Lordship read the Letter, and the Representation to me from the Captain and after some Conversation on the Subject assured me that he would take Measures to have the Men restored and Precautions against Such Mistakes in future. This opportunity was a favourable one, for some Communication of Sentiments upon the present Posture of Affairs, and his Lordship was invited to talk upon the Subject by Several Questions, which were proposed to him. His Lordships answers were civil enough, "He hoped there would not be War." "He should be very sorry for a war," &c &c But Nothing was to be learn'd from him, if he knew any Thing. – one fact indeed his Lordship assured me of, viz.ᵗ that War is in truth declared by the Port against Russia, that the Count De Montmorin, had sent him an Extract of a Dispatch of Monsieur De Choiseul the French Ambassador at Constantinople containing an Account of it. and that the French Ministry had done him the Justice to believe that the English Ambassador and Ministry, had done nothing to excite this declaration. His Lordships last Dispatches from Constantinople assured him of every Appearance of Peace, so that the Declaration must have been some Sudden Emotion of the Mufti or Jannizaries, &c It is easy to believe that the English did not excite the Turks to declare, for that Step excuses

France from any obligation to aid the Port. The present Conjuncture appears the most critical and important in Europe, of any that has ever happened in our Times. Mankind Seems impatient under the Yoke of Servitude that has been imposed upon them, and disposed to compell their Governors to make the Burthen lighter. But the Wars that now threaten, have no Tendency that Way or but a remote one. and what dependance can be placed upon the common People, in any Part of Europe?

Upon my Return home another American Master of a Vessell from Alexandria in Virginia came with his Complaint that the Press Gang had taken all his Men – I will demand every Man, as fast as I shall be informed of his being pressed: but I am much afraid of Pretences, Excuses &c &c – I expect to hear that one Sailor is Irish, another Scotch and a third English. – All in my Power however shall be done and you shall be informed of the Result. With great Respect, Sir, your most obedient and most humble Ser^t John Adams

NA: PCC, *item 84, v. 6, pp. 523-525* (ALS); *M247, reel 113*

John Adams to John Jay

Private   Grosvenor Square Sept^r· 22. 1787
Dear Sir

Your private Letter of the twenty fifth of July is very friendly and obliging as usual. give yourself no concern about my Apprehensions of your Want of Attention. I know too well your constant and assiduous Application to the Duties of your public offices, as well as to the just concerns of your private friends, ever to suspect you of failing in either. – I shudder when I think of your next Volume of my Dispatches. I shall appear before Posterity, in a very negligent Dress and disordered Air. in Truth I write too much to write well, and have never time to correct any Thing. – Your Plan however of recording all the Dispatches of the foreign Ministers is indispensible. Future Negotiations will often make it necessary to look back to the past, besides the Importance of publick History. – The true Idea of the Negotiation with Holland, particularly will never be formed, without attending to three Sorts of Measures. those taken with the Stadtholder and his Party, those taken with the Aristocratical People in the Regencys, and those taken with the popular Party. if any one of these had been omitted, that Unanimity could never have been effected, without which the United States could not have been acknowledged nor their Minister admitted.

.   .   .   .   .   .

Whether it would be in my Power to do most Service in Europe or at home, or any at all in either Situation, I know not. – My determination to go home was founded in a fixed opinion that neither the Honour of Congress nor my own, nor the Interest of either could be promoted, by the Residence of a Minister here, without a British Minister at Congress, and in that opinion I am still clear....The Convention at Philadelphia is composed of Heroes, Sages and Demigods, to be sure who want no Assistance from me, in forming the best possible Plan. but they may have Occasion for underlabourers to make it accepted by the People, or at least to make the People unanimous in it and contented with it. One of these Underworkmen, in a cool Retreat, it shall be my Ambition to become. With invariable Esteem and Affction, I am, dear Sir, your most obedient Servant and real friend

John Adams.

Columbia University Libraries: John Jay Papers (ALS).

Thomas Jefferson to John Jay

Sir   Paris. Sept. 22. 1787.
    The letters of which the inclosed are copies, are this moment received, and as there is a possibility that they may reach Havre before the packet sails, I have the honor of inclosing them to you. they contain a promise of reducing the duties on tar, pitch & turpentine, and that the government will interest itself with the city of Rouen to reduce the local duty on Potash. by this you will perceive that we are getting on a little in this business, tho', under their present embarrassments, it is difficult to procure the attention of the ministers to it....I have the honour to be with the most perfect esteem and respect, Sir, your most obedient & most humble servant   Th: Jefferson

LC: Jefferson Papers, microfilm reel 8 (press copy).

John Adams to Lord Carmarthen

My Lord –   Grosv.r· Square Sept.r 22.d 1787.
    I do myself the honor to inclose to your Lordship a Letter this moment received, from the Master of a Vessell belonging to the United States of America – His name is John Douglass, commander of the Ship *Four Friends* – American built & the property of Andrew Van Tuyl merch.t of New York – He informs me, that as two of his people were going on shore for pro-

vision for the day they were seized by the press gang and forced on Board His Majesty's Brig *Dispatch* then laying at execution dock – that the gang then came on board his Vessell and attempted to open the Hatches, when his cheif mate opposed them, and informed the officers that they were American Citizens – That altho the officers of the press then went away there is reason to believe, that another disagreable visit will be made before morning, which will distress him exceedingly as his ship is compleated for Sea & bound for New York.

The Names of the two men pressed, are Joseph Cowley, a Native of the City of New York, the other is a Negro Man called Primus the property of Mʳ Andrew Van Tuyl Merch of New York, but a Native of the City – It is my duty my Lord to make this representation to His Majesty's ministers and to request that orders may be given for the restoration of these Men to the Master of their Vessell, & further to propose to your Lordships Consideration, whether it be not expedient that some general order should be given, upon this occasion to the officers of His Majesty's Navy, to give a particular attention to American Vessells & Seamen least perplexities & inconveniencies of this kind should be multiplied.

With great respect I have the Honor to be – Your Lordships Most Obedient Humble Servᵗ   John Adams

NA: PCC, *item 84, v. 6, pp. 527-528 (C); M247, reel 113.*

John Adams to John Jay

Dear Sir   London Septʳ 23. 1787

The Accounts from Holland and France are very discouraging: So much so that it would be imprudent to enter into a detail of Evils that are inevitable. The Republick of Holland is in the Utmost danger of being extinct: and if the old Forms are hereafter preserved, the Prince will be so much Master, in Reality that the Friends of Liberty must be very unhappy, and live in continual disgrace and danger. The English are arming, with all the Affectation of Spirit and Firmness, and France neither moves nor negotiates with the least Appearance of Fortitude or Understanding. To do the former Justice, they have had the Prudence to Send both to Versailles and the Hague, Men of Sense and Business. England will rise in Consideration and Power, and France will Fall, in the Eyes of all Europe. This will make the former overbearing, and her People insolent, and France will soon, in my poor opinion at least, be obliged to go to War, or sink very low. The United States of America instead of being more courted by the English as they would probably be in case of a War, will rather be more neglected, perhaps treated cavalierly. – it is easy to see, however, that the Peace cannot long continue between the two European Nations. The Philosophical Visions of Perpetual Peace, and the Religious Reveries of a near Approach of the Millenium, in which all Nations are to turn the Weapons of War into Implements of Husbandry will in a few Years be dissipated. The Armaments now making in England, will disarrange Mr Pitts boasted Plans of Economy: and in short, there is every Appearance that the Peace of Europe will be for Years but an armed Truce. The Surplus of Revenue so ostentatiously displayed to the Public, is but an Artful Deception. Oh Fortunate Americans, if you did but know your own Felicity! instead of trampling on the Laws the Rights the general Plans of Power delivered down from your remote Forefathers, you should cherish and fortify, those noble Institutions, with filial and religious Reverence. – instead of envying the Rights of others, every American Citizen has cause to rejoice in his own. instead of violating the Security of Property, it should be considered as Sacred as the Commandment "thou shalt not Steal." instead of trampling on private honour and public Justice, every one who attempts it should be considered as an impious Parricide, who seeks to destroy his own Liberty and that of all his Neighbours. what would have become of American Liberty if there had not been more Faith, Honour and Justice in the Minds of their common Citizens, than are found in the common People in Europe? Do We see in the Austrian Netherlands, in the United Netherlands, or even in the Parliament in France, that Confidence in one another, and in the Common People, which enabled the People of the United States to go through a Revolution? Where is the Difference? it is a Want of Honesty, and if the Common People in America loose their Integrity, they will soon set up Tyrants of their own, or court a foreign one. Laws alone, and those political Institutions which are the Guardians of them, and a Sacred Administration of Justice, can preserve Honour Virtue, and Integrity in the Minds of the People. With great Respect, I have the Honour to be Sir your most obedient and most humble Servant   John Adams.

February 5th. 1788. Referred to the Secretary for foreign Affairs *to report*.

NA: PCC, *item 84, v. 6, pp. 531-534 (ALS); M247, reel 113.*

Congressional Committee Report
on the Dutch Protest of Import Duties

[New York, September 24, 1787]

The Committee...to whom were referred a report from the Secretary for the Department of foreign affairs, and a note from the minister of the United Netherlands – report –

that the said minister, in his note aforesaid, complains that, by an Act of the State of Virginia, French brandies imported into that State, in French or American vessels, are exempted from certain Duties, to which the like Commodities imported in Dutch vessels are left liable, as being contrary to the Second Article in their treaty with the United States

the Committee find that the State of Virginia, in her last Session, by a legislative Act, made the distinction complained of; and tho the reasons, that induced her to make the distinction, are not recited in the Act, yet, from various circumstances ~~and good information,~~ it appears, that the State granted the exemptions or favors complained of to France, in compensation,~~or in return~~ for certain favors and exemptions in commerce, enumerated in Mr Calonne's letter to Mr Jefferson dated the 22^d of October 1786, which, in the Opinion of the State, France had liberally granted to the United States, and especially to Virginia –

these proceedings of Virginia do not appear to have a precedent in the affairs of the United States, and give rise to several important questions, – they bring into view Articles in the treaties, which are not easily understood, as well as parts of our national system which hitherto appear only to have come generally into consideration.

the Second and third Articles in the treaty with France, and the Second in the treaty with the United Netherlands respect this Subject – The Second in the treaty with France is " – The Most Christian King and the United States engage mutually not to grant any particular favor to other Nations in respect of Commerce and navigation, which shall not immediately become Common to the other party, who Shall enjoy the same favor freely, if the concession was *freely* made, or on allowing the same Compensation if the concession was conditional"

By the Second Article in our treaty with the United Netherlands, it is Stipulated, that their Subjects shall pay in our ports, &c. no other ~~or~~ nor greater duties or imposts, than those which the Nations, *the most favored* are or shall be obliged to pay; and that they shall enjoy therein all the rights, liberties, privileges, Immunities, and exemptions in trade, navigation, and commerce which the said nations do or shall enjoy – but this Article takes no notice of Cases where compensation is granted for privileges – the

Committee conceive however – that reason and equity will give both Articles exactly the same Operation. – Where a privilege is gratuitously granted, the Nation to whom it is granted, becomes in respect to that privilege, a favored Nation, and from that Circumstance *both* the Articles in question deduce claims to the like favor – but where the privilege is not gratuitous but rests on compact, or where the privilege is yielded by one party as a Consideration, or as a compensation for a privilege yielded by the other, the favor, if any there be, consists only in the power of making the compact, or the exchange of privileges, and the favor, in this Case, due to the third Nation entitled to the benefits of the most favored Nations from either party, consists only in the right such third Nation has to make a compact or exchange of privileges with the party so in treaty with her, on the same terms as that party stipulated with the other – This construction is, in the opinion of the Committee, founded in the highest reason and propriety – and the contrary doctrine must be productive of confusion and Injustice – If France should, therefore, purchase at a certain price, a privilege of the United States, it would be evidently unreasonable that the Dutch should have a like privilege without any price at all – the Dutch would in this Case have better terms than the most favored Nation, France, and, therefore, more than is stipulated for, in the treaty, – and France clearly would have reason to complain, that she was not treated on so good terms as the most favored Nation, the Dutch –

But another question arises in this Case, < ****************** > , and that is, in what manner shall a privilege gratuitous, or not, be granted –

It is to be observed that the extent of most Commercial privileges granted by modern treaties, must be ascertained by a reference to those yielded by the grantors, to the most favored Nations, and, therefore, a variation in the privileges allowed by any one Nation to another, may Justly give occasion to vary the privileges allowed by the former to all other Nations, and thus by any change of privileges several Nations may become immediately interested, and each entitled to claim for itself whatever may be yielded to any one by such change or variation – The terms also of national treaties are, in general, indefinite and ought to receive a liberal and rational construction – The Committee, on carefully considering this part of the subject, are clearly of opinion, that whenever a privilege is yielded by a Nation which has stipulated to yield to other Nations the benefits allowed to the most favored, that the nature of the privilege, whether gratuitous or to be paid for, ought to be known and expressed at the time it is yielded; and if such privilege be intended as a compensation, or a compensation is to be received for it, the privilege and compensation form the inseparable parts of a compact, which, in the nature of things, must Stand connected together – a little attention to this Subject must fully evince that when a treaty has been formed by parties circumstanced as above supposed, that no privilege not merely gratuitous, can, with propriety, pass from one to the other, without compact; and that in nature of an additional Article to the subsisting treaty – the contrary position must be absurd both in Theory and practice – if France, for instance, which has Stipulated with several Nations to allow each of them the benefits of the most favored, can yield a privilege to any one of them, and it can remain uncertain for any longer or shorter time, whether that privilege was yielded gratuitously or not, how are the said other Nations to come at their rights in the mean time – but the Case in question goes further. France seems to have yielded the privileges and exemptions mentioned in the said Note, without herself knowing whether they would be gratuitous, or eventually be paid for: – for it appears to have been left to the option of the United States to make them the one thing or the other – besides if among Nations, all put on an equal footing by treaty, every privilege loosly granted is to be the foundation of distinctions, most modern treaties will be useless, and a total uncertainty must take place in the system of commerce

thus < ****** > it appears clear that even the nation itself can make no such distinctions in so loose and uncertain a manner < *** >

but a third question arises, and that is, what constitutional power has a State, a part of the nation, to Judge of the privileges yielded to her, or to the United States, and to deal out compensation for them? – By the articles of Confederation, it is agreed, that Congress shall have the sole and exclusive right and power of entering into treaties and alliances; provided that no treaty of Commerce shall be made, whereby the legislative powers of the respective States shall be restrained from imposing such imposts and Duties on foreigners, as their own people are subject to pay, or from prohibiting the exportation or importation of any Species of goods – it is also agreed that no State, without the Consent of the United States, shall enter into any Conference, Agreement, Alliance or treaty with any King, prince or State

thus by the federal compact, it is wisely and properly established that no State, or part of the nation, shall have any part in making a treaty, &c. between the nation and a foreign power, but by its Delegates in the national Council – the power of Congress to bind the Nation by treaty is complete, with these two exceptions only 1st. no treaty can authorise a foreigner to pay less duties than the Citizens of the State pay – 2d. no treaty can prevent the State from prohibiting the importation and exportation of goods – and whatever treaty, therefore, is made by Congress, not infringing these rights of the several States, is binding on all parts of the Nation; and it appears that the States in all Cases, except the present, have in laying duties, making Commercial regulations, &c. regarded treaties accordingly, and in this, they have conducted according to the obvious dictates of reason and propriety – the contrary conduct, the Committee conceive would be attended with infinite inconveniences – if one State can at discretion make distinctions between the Subjects of powers put on an equal footing by national treaties, Judge of privileges yielded, and of compensation for them, another State may make other distinctions, and thereby those Subjects be put into various Situations totally different –

contemplating this subject in every point of view it appears to the Committee so clear that a state cannot constitutionally make the distinctions alluded to that they should think it unnecessary to adduce any arguments, had not the Act complained of been passed by a very respectable state in the Union – the Committee are inclined to believe that it passed not having received the attention which that State usually pays to important laws which may effect the national system and public treaties, and that on the earliest notice the said State will do away [with] the distinction complained of – whereupon the Committee submit the following Resolutions –

Resolved – that no individual State can constitutionally, without the Consent of the United States in Congress Assembled, make any compensation for privileges or exemptions granted in trade Navigation or Commerce by any foreign power to the United States or any of them, and that whenever any of the States shall think proper to grant any privileges or exemptions in trade, Navigation, and Commerce, to any foreign Nation gratuitously, such State ought to extend them to such other foreign Nations as by treaties with the United States are to be treated as the most favored Nation

Resolved that a copy of the above resolution and of the representation of the minister of the United Netherlands be transmitted to the State of Virginia, to the end that the legislature of that State may take the earliest Opportunity of revising the Act of which the said Minister complains, and rendering the same perfectly consistent with the treaty subsisting between the United States and the United Netherlands; and of causing to be repaid whatever extra Duties may by virtue of the said Act, be exacted on brandies there imported in Dutch vessels, during the Operation of the same –

Resolved that copies of the foregoing resolutions be given to the said minister of the United Netherlands and that he be requested to assure their High Mightinesses that Congress are well persuaded that the Omission of Virginia, in not extending to them the favor granted to France, was entirely inadvertent and not designed; and they flatter themselves that the said resolutions, and the respect with which they will be treated by Virginia, will fully manifest to their High Mightinesses the Good faith and friendship of the United States in General and of Virginia in particular –

NA: PCC, *item 25, v. 2, pp. 477-481 (C); M247, reel 32.*

John Jay's Report on British Seizure
of the American Sloop *Little Robert*

[New York] Office for foreign Affairs 24th Septem[r] 1787
The Secretary of the United States for the Department of foreign Affairs, to whom was referred a Letter of 1st of last Month from Reade & Bogardus,[1]

Reports.

That the Object of the said Letter is to represent the Case of William Cannon, late Master of the Sloop *Little Robert* from New York, belonging to Mess[rs] Reade & Bogardus, Peter Mesier and William Cannon, which Case they state as follows, Viz[t] –.

"A Statement of Facts that happened to W[m] Cannon, late Master of the Sloop *Little Robert* from New York, belonging to Reade & Bogardus, Peter Mesier and William Cannon. –

"On the 26th of May 1787 he was lying at Anchor at the Island of Heneauga, where he had been about thirty Hours, when the Captain of a Schooner called the *Vigilant*, belonging to the Custom House of the Island of New Providence, came in his Boat with a Number of Men on board the said Sloop, and made Search for supposed Goods, Merchandize or Produce of the Island of Heneauga, when not finding any he left the Sloop and directed said Cannon not to lay longer than 48 Hours at said Island or he would seize his Vessel and Cargo; and in less than one Hour after said Cannon got under Way and left the Island aforesaid, and on the 30th May he returned there again in company with a french Schooner, who came from the Aux Cayes and had on board Sugar, Coffee, Cotton and Cocoa of the Produce of Hispaniola for the said Sloop *Little Robert*, when both of them came to an Anchor at about 9 O'Clock and began shifting the Cargo from the Schooner on board said Sloop – That about 11 O'Clock she was boarded by the said *Vigilant's* Boat with loaded Muskets, Pistols and Cutlasses, and in boarding they killed one Man named John Rodan, and much wounded another named William Bryan of said Cannon's Crew, without any previous Notice – after which they took Possession of both Vessels, got up their Anchors and directly proceeded to New Providence, where said Vessels and Cargos were condemned and sold. The whole of Captain Cannon's Stay at the Island of Heneauga did not exceed 34 Hours, and the Officer of the *Vigilant* had declared to Captain Cannon that he would allow him 48 Hours to do any Thing he might want to do to his Vessel. The *Vigilant* at the Time this Seizure was made had not a british Register nor never was made a Prize, and is now for Sale on that very Account, being an american built Vessel since the Peace. —"

Two Causes of Complaint result from these Facts, Viz^t the unnecessary Violence committed in the Act of seizing the Sloop, and secondly the Illegality of the Seizure and Condemnation of her. —

As the Facts on which the first Complaint is grounded are not supported by any Affidavits or Proofs, that Complaint does not as yet appear sufficiently authenticated to render a Remonstrance to the british Court on that Head adviseable; but your Secretary having Reason to believe that Capt Cannon, who is now in Town, is ready to depose to the Truth of those Facts, he thinks it might be well for him to take the Captain's Affidavit, and in Case it should fully support the Facts above stated relative to that Violence, then to transmit a Copy of the Letter and of the Affidavit to Mr Adams, to the End that he may communicate the same to the british Court, and urge their taking proper Measures for bringing the Offenders to Punishment, and prevent the like Excesses in future. —

With respect to the Illegality of the seizure and Condemnation, it is to be observed that the Sentence of the Court was not final — on the contrary the Party aggrieved might have appealed. Until the Proceedings of the Court are seen, an adequate Judgment cannot be formed either of their Regularity or Conformity to Law and Justice; nor can any Nation become chargeable with Failure of Justice, while Redress for the Grievance complained of may be had by pursuing the Course indicated and provided by their Laws for the Purpose. —

Hence your Secretary is of Opinion, that with Respect to the Merits of the Seizure and Condemnation Congress cannot in the present Stage of the Business, interpose, but must leave the Parties to pursue their Remedy in the ordinary and well known Course of judicial Proceedings. —

All which is submitted to the Wisdom of Congress.   John Jay — read 26 Sept. 1787

NA: PCC, *item 81, v. 3, pp. 155-158 (DS); M247, reel 107.*
¹ *Presumably a New York commercial house.*

John Sullivan to William Brown

Dear Major[1]   Charleston 24th. September 1787
    The receipt of your kind favour by Mr. Barrell afforded me the greatest satisfaction, and can assure you that I should have been happy in obliging not only that Gentleman, but any person whom you would please to recommend to my attention. The disgust he has taken at the southern Country and his consequent short stay among us deprive me of the pleasure of serving him as I would wish. Not many days have elapsed since my arrival from the western waters on particular business to this City. My intention is to return immediately to the State of Franklin, in which case I hope to see you before long. I have informed Mr. Barrell that I should have been happy in his Company, but he is totally unprepared either in Baggage or Horses for a march beyond the Alleghany mountains. Though a good young man he seems not only to be unfit for *such a service*, but is totally unacquainted with the Country in general. I thank you for your opinion concerning *certain matters*. There is no part of the Continent where you could live more at your ease than in Franklin. I would advise you therefore (previous to bringing on your family) to come southward by the first opportunity and secure a body of Land for yourself on the Tenassee River. There will be work cut out for you in that Country. I want you much – by God – take my word for it that we will be speedily in possession of New Orleans. I particularly request that this Letter may not extend beyond your perusal. Adieu   John Sullivan
P. S. Write me immediately what you mean to do and enclose your Letters to Major Washington of Savannah.

NA: PCC, *item 120, v. 3, pp. 298-299 (LBkC); M40, reel 3; see also, though practically unreadable, item 78 v. 21, pp. 477-480 (ALS); M247, reel 102.*
  [1] *Not further identified.*

John Jay's Report Regarding
Exemption of Consuls from Import Duties

[New York] Office for foreign Affairs 25th September 1787
The Secretary of the United States for the Department of foreign Affairs, to whom was referred a Letter of the 16th August 1787 from Sir John Temple the british Consul General,
Reports. –

That this Letter states, that a Relation at Canton, sent him in the *Hope*, lately arrived at this Port, a small Box of Tea and a Piece of Silk for Lady Temple's Use – that he sent for them, and that the Collector returned for Answer that as there was no Treaty of Commerce subsisting between his britannic Majesty and these States, Sir John must pay the Impost or Duties charged upon such Articles by the Government of the State of New York. Sir John requests to be informed, whether or not it be right and proper for him to pay the Duties so demanded. –

Two things in this Letter merit Attention – *first* the implied Claim of the Consul to an Exemption from Duties, and *secondly* the Reason assigned by the Collector for demanding the ordinary Duties in the *present* Case. –

The Respect due from Nation to Nation and from Sovereign to Sovereign, has introduced among civilized Nations the general Custom and Usage of exempting Ambassadors and public Ministers from Duties and Imposts. The only Question on this Point which merits Attention is, whether Consuls are to be considered in this Light? –

In the Opinion of your Secretary Consuls are not by the Laws or Usage of Nations considered or treated as public Ministers, and therefore that they are not entitled to the Exemptions in Question either here or elsewhere. –

It would seem from the Collector's Answer that he considers the *other* Consuls, between whose Nations and the United States Treaties of Commerce exist, as entitled to such Exemptions; and therefore your Secretary is inclined to think it would be expedient for Congress to correct that Mistake. It appears from general Experience that this Privilege to Ambassadors and Ministers has produced many Inconveniences, and is daily attended with great Abuses; in so much that some Nations have found it necessary to take Measures to guard against and check them. In France it is usual for Ministers to report the Articles intended to be introduced, and the Government pays the Duties to the Farmers – and a late Instance of an Ambassador at the Court of London, importing 800 Dozen of Wine at one Time for the Use of his Table, and shortly after disposing of 500 Dozen of them to Grocers, has called the Attention of the Ministry to the Necessity of establishing Regulations on the Subject; but what they will be, is not yet decided. If such Inconveniences result from such a Privilege to a few Ambassadors and Ministers, Men high in Office and Reputation, and whose Situations render such Practices particularly indecent and improper; it is easy to foresee how much greater and more extensive Evils would result from similar Indulgencies to the numerous Consuls to be found in every commercial Country disposed to admit them. –

It is submitted therefore to the Consideration of Congress whether (without taking any particular Notice of Sir Johns Case) it would not be proper to resolve as follows.

Whereas Doubts have in certain Instances arisen whether foreign Consuls residing in the United States are entitled to an Exemption from such legal Imposts and Duties on Merchandizes by them imported for their own Use, as are payable by other Subjects of their respective Nations –

Resolved that no Consuls of any Nation are entitled to such Exemptions in the United States. –

All which is submitted to the Wisdom of Congress. –   John Jay –

NA: PCC, item 81, v. 3, pp. 159-161 (DS); M247, reel 107.

John Jay's Report on the Petition of Valentine and Patrick French and Nephew

[New York] Office for foreign Affairs 26th Septem^r 1787

The Secretary of the United States for the Department of foreign Affairs, to whom was referred a Petition of Messrs Val. & Pat. French & Nephew,

Reports

That this Petition states, that the Petitioners had arrested Thomas Barclay Esquire, the american Consul General in France and Agent for negociating the Treaty lately concluded with Morocco, for the Recovery of a Debt due from him to them; and that the Parliament of Guienne from Respect to his official Character had released him. The Petitioners pray, in Substance, that the Law may have free Course against him. –

A late Letter from Mr Jefferson, now before Congress, mentions that the Obstacle in Question had been removed by the Interference of the french Minister, and in the Opinion of your Secretary very properly, for in his Judgment Mr Barclay, at least after his Return from Morocco, had no official Character to which the Laws of Nations annex such a Privilege. –

It is not necessary therefore that any *particular* Order on the Subject of this Petition be now made; but in the Opinion of your Secretary it would not be improper to take this Opportunity of obviating the Necessity of similar Applications in future by some *general* Resolution like the following, Viz^{t.} –

On a Report from the Secretary for foreign Affairs to whom was referred a Petition from Messrs French & Nephew –

Resolved that the Consuls of the United States in foreign Parts, as well as the Consuls of foreign Nations residing in the United States, may be prosecuted like private Citizens and Subjects, for their proper Debts, in the Manner prescribed by the Laws of the Land where they reside. –

Your Secretary will be much mistaken if the United States do not always experience more Inconveniences from the Residence of foreign Consuls here, than they will ever experience Advantages from the Residence of american Consuls abroad. These foreign Gentlemen already embarrass our Commerce, and that, as well as a Variety of other Circumstances and Considerations, should in his Opinion render it the Policy of America to allow them only that Degree of official Weight and Pre-eminence, which may be strictly due to them by the Laws of Nations. –

All which is submitted to the Wisdom of Congress. –   [John Jay]

NA: PCC, item 81, v. 3, pp. 1-2 (D); M247, reel 107.

Congressional Resolution Denying Consuls Exemption from Import Duties

[New York] September 28th 1787

On a report from the Secretary for Foreign Affairs

Whereas doubts have in certain instances arisen whether foreign Consuls residing in the United States are entitled to an exemption from such legal imposts and duties on Merchandizes by them imported for their own use as are payable by other Subjects of their respective Nations –

Resolved that no Consuls of any nations are intitled to such exemptions in the United States –   Cha' Thomson Sec'

NA: PCC, item 122, p. 99 (CS); M247, reel 140.

Thomas Jefferson to John Adams

Dear Sir   Paris Sep. 28. 1787.

...you know all that has happened in the United Netherlands. you know also that our friends Van Staphorsts will be among the most likely to become objects of severity, if any severities should be exercised. is the money in their hands entirely safe? if it is not, I am sure you have already thought of it. are we to suppose the game already up, and that the Stadtholder is to be reestablished, perhaps erected into a monarch, without the country lifting a finger in opposition to it? if so, it is a lesson the more for us. in fact what a crowd of lessons do the present miseries of Holland teach us? never to have an hereditary officer of any sort: never to let a citizen ally himself with kings: never to call in foreign nations to settle domestic differences: never to suppose that any nation will expose itself to a war for us &c. still I am not without hopes that a good rod is in soak for Prussia, and that England will feel the end of it. it is known to some that Russia made propositions to the emperor & France for acting in concert; that the emperor consents and has disposed four camps of 180,000 men from the limits of Turkey to those of Prussia. this court hesitates, or rather it's premier hesitates; for the queen, Monmorin & Breteuil[1] are for the measure. should it take place, all may yet come to rights, except for the Turks, who must retire from Europe: and this they must do were France Quixotic enough to support them. we I hope shall be left free to avail ourselves of the advantages of neutrality: and yet much I fear the English, or rather their stupid king, will force us into out of it. for thus I reason. by forcing us into the war against them they will be engaged in an expensive land war as well as a sea war. common sense dictates therefore that they should let us remain neuter: ergo they will not let us remain neuter. I never yet found any other general rule for foretelling what they will do, but that of examining what they ought not to do....I have the honor to be with my best respects to mrs Adams, & sentiments of perfect esteem & regard to yourself dear Sir your most obedient & most humble servant

Th: Jefferson

. . . . .

ans^d Oct. 9. 1787

MHS: *The Adams Papers, microfilm reel 370 (ALS).*
 [1] *Breteuil, Louis-Charles-Auguste le Tonnelier, Baron de (1730-1807). French ambassador to Austria, 1778-1783. Minister of State, 1783-1787. Strong supporter of the royal prerogative, opponent of fiscal reforms proposed first by Charles Alexandre de Calonne and then Jacques Necker. Chief minister at the time of the storming of the Bastille, 14 July 1789, he resigned, emigrated, and subsequently withdrew from politics.*

Phineas Bond to Lord Carmarthen

My Lord   Philadelphia Sep. 29. 1787.

. . . . .

The rumor of war, my Lord, has inspired the Americans with new spirits: they anticipate the benefits of a free trade, and already calculate upon the profits of being the carriers to all the belligerent powers. Much as they may affect to have subdued their prejudices against England, their animosities still continue and are palpable upon every occasion: – tho' it is probable my Lord, this country would not take a decided part in a war, if such an event should happen, she would be ready, at all times to show preference

to her "great and good ally": the ports of America would be very convenient to the fleets of France and the opportunities of harassing the W. India
trade from hence would give their cruisers great advantages over our
merchant ships – Your Lordship's decernment will immediately perceive
the necessity of paying the strictest attention to every port of consequence
on this Continent and of obtaining the most precise information of the
arrival and departure of the fleets and cruisers of foreign powers which
could be well arranged in the hands of a very few confidential persons. –

My last letter to your Lordship enclosed the Constitution of Government
recommended to the Consideration of Congress by the Convention of the
States which terminated on the 17th. inst. – Yesterday, my Lord, the
Congress in which there was a full representation from 11 States – (1
member from Maryland, Rhode I unrepresented) the report of the Convention and their letter and resolutions were by an unanimous resolve
ordered to be transmitted to the several States, for the purpose of being
submitted to a Convention of each, conformable to the recommendation
of the Conventoin: so that, as far as the power of Congress goes this
amounts to a compleat adoption, on their part, of the new consitiution.

Much, my Lord, as the discreet part of the citizens of America seem to
approve of this new form of Government which (as I have heretofore
observed to your Ldp. considering the democratic spirit of the times is
perhaps the most eligible shape in which it could have been handed forth
to the people, a faction has already appeared to throw obstacles in the way
of its establishment.

. . . . .

I have the honor to be, my Lord, Your Lordship's most faithful and most
obed. servant   P. Bond.
Rec. Nov. 6th.

AHA 1896, v. 1, pp. 546-549.

Louis XVI, King of France,
to the President and Members of Congress

Very dear Great Friends and Allies   Versailles September 30, 1787
Particular Reasons relative to the good of our Service have determined
us to appoint a successor to the Chevalier de la Luzerne our Minister
Plenipotentiary with You. We have Chosen the Count de Moustier to take
his place in the same Quality. The marks of Zeal which he has hitherto
given us persuade us that on this new occasion he will conduct himself in

such a manner as to render himself agreeable to you, and more and more worthy of our good will. We pray you to give full faith to whatever he may say to you on our part particularly when he shall assure you of the sincerity of our wishes for your prosperity, as well as of the constant affection and friendship which we bear to the United States in general, and to each of them in particular. We pray God that he will have you very dear Great friends and Allies in his holy keeping. Written at Versailles the 30 Sept' 1787   your good friend and Ally

Louis

Cte de Montmorin

NA: PCC, *item 96, pp. 382-383 (translation); M247, reel 124.*

Congressional Resolution Opposing Dutch Purchase of U.S. Debt to France

[New York] Oct 2. 1787

The board of treasury to whom was referred an extract of a letter from the honorable Mr Jefferson Minister plenipotentiary to the Court of France having reported –

That the said Minister states – "That a proposition has been made to Monsieur De Calonne, Minister of the Finances of France, by a Company of Dutch Merchants to purchase the debt due from the United States to the Crown of France; giving for the said debt, amounting to Twenty four million of Livres, the sum of Twenty million of Livres. That information of this proposition has been given to him by the Agent of the said Company, with the view of ascertaining whether the proposed Negociation should be agreeable to Congress" –

That the said Minister suggests – "That if there is a danger of the Public Payments not being punctual, whether it might not be better that the discontents which would then arise should be transferred from a Court, of whose good will we have so much need, to the breasts of a private Company."

"That the Credit of the United States is sound in Holland; and that it would probably not be difficult to borrow in that Country, the whole sum of money due to the Court of France; and to discharge that debt without any deduction, thereby doing what would be grateful to the Court, and establishing with them a confidence in our honor."

On a mature consideration of the circumstances abovementioned, the Board beg leave to observe

That at the time the debt due from the United States to the Crown of France was contracted, it could not have been foreseen, that the different Members of the Union, would have hesitated to make effectual provision for the discharge of the same; since it had been contracted for the security of the Lives, Liberties and Property of their several Citizens, who had solemnly pledged themselves for its redemption; and that therefore the honor of the United States cannot be impeached for having authorised their Minister at the Court of France to enter into a formal Convention acknowledging the amount of the said debt, and stipulating for the reimbursement of the principal and interest due thereon. –

That should the United States at this period, give any sanction to the transfer of this debt, or attempt to make a Loan in Holland for the discharge of the same, the Persons interested in the transfer, or in the loan, would have reason to presume that the United States in Congress would make effectual provision for the punctual payment of the principal and interest. –

That the prospect of such provision being made within a short period, is by no means flattering; and though the Credit of the United States is still sound in Holland, from the exertions which have been made to discharge the interest due to the Subscribers to the Loans in that Country; yet in the opinion of this Board it would be unjust, as well as impolitic, to give any public sanction to the proposed negotiation. – Unjust – because the Nation would contract an engagement, without any well grounded expectation of discharging it with proper punctuality. – Impolitic – because a failure in the payment of Interest accruing from this Negotiation, (which would inevitably happen) would justly blast all hopes of Credit with the Citizens of the United Netherlands, when the exigencies of the Union might render new Loans indispensibly necessary. –

The Board beg leave further to observe, that although a grateful sense of the services rendered by the Court of France would undoubtedly induce the United States in Congress to make every possible exertion for the reimbursement of the Monies advanced by His Most Christian Majesty; yet that they cannot presume, that it would tend to establish in the mind of the French Court, an idea of the National honor of this Country to involve Individuals in a heavy Loan at a time when Congress were fully sensible, that their resources were altogether inadequate to discharge even the Interest of the same; much less the installments of the principal which would from time to time become due. – How far the idea of transferring the discontents which may prevail in the French Court, for want of the punctual payment of Interest, to the breast of the private Citizens of Holland, would be consistent with sound policy, the Board forbear to enlarge on.

It may be proper however to observe that, the public integrity of a Nation is the best shield of defence, against any Calamites, to which in the course of human events, she may find herself exposed. –

The principle so far as it respects the conduct of the United States in contracting the Loans with France cannot be called in question: The reverse would be the case, should the Sanction of the United States be given, either to the transfer of the French debt, or to the Negotiation of a Loan in Holland for the purpose of discharging it. –

If it be further considered, that the consequences of a failure in the punctual payment of interest on the monies borrowed by the United States, can by no means be so distressing to a Nation (and one powerful in resources) as it would be to Individuals, whose dependence for support is frequently on the interest of the Monies loaned, the Board presume that the propos'd Negotiation cannot be considered at the present juncture in any point of view, either as eligible or proper. – Under these Circumstances they submit it as their Opinion

That it would be proper without delay to instruct the Minister of the United States at the Court of France not to give any sanction to any Negotiation which may be proposed for transferring the debt due from the United States, to any State or Company of Individuals who may be disposed to purchase the same. –

Resolved That Congress Agree to the said report.

NA: PCC, *item 5, v. 3, pp. 1649-1653 (Journal); M247, reel 19.*

Martin Oster to
Governor Edmund Randolph of Virginia

Sir   Norfolk, 2$^{d.}$ October 1787.

I have the honor to inform Y^r Excellency that on the 26th July last there entered this port the Brig *David* Capt Joseph Marie Anne Ferrier of the City of Cette in Languedoc, under pretence of distress, & that on examination of the conduct of the Captain by myself, he being now in my power, as also from the depositions made in my Chancery it appears & is proved,

That Capt Ferrier sailed the 1st July last from the Cape for Nantes with a Cargo on Freight of above One Hundred Thousand Weight of Coffee belonging to different persons.

That he had not above 15 days provision for his passage which evidently proves that it was not his intention to go to the place of his destination.

That the evening before his departure from the Cape whilst in the road he sold & clandestinely delivered in the night a great part of his Cargo.

That a few days after he also sold at Sea another part of his Cargo to a Captain of a Sloop who followed him, & with whom he had agreed at the Cape.

That to accomplish this collusion, he together with his Mate named *Bastard* corrupted the Crew, & forced a passenger to participate in his robbery.

That to excuse his stopping & to cause damage in order to oblige his Vessel to be sold, he made two leaks one in the Hold & the other in the Gun-room which occasioned 40 inches water & damaged 12,000^{wt} Coffee, which I ordered to be sold at public Sale in order to avoid a total loss.

That in order to give a better appearance to his fraudelent & affected stopping, he wickedly threw into the Sea an Anchor of 750^{wt} a large Cable of 120 fathoms, topmasts, Yards & a quantity of other things belonging to his Brig.

And in short to cover his misconduct with some show of speciousness he kept at Sea two Journals one true the other false, And he also fabricated a false verbal process which he dared to affirm as true, & signed it & caused it to be signed by his crew with intent to prove that he had been obliged to renounce his Voyage to Nantes & to put in wherever he could.

All these facts being authentically proved Sir, I propose with Y^r Excellencys consent to send the criminal to France in his own Vessel with the instructions of his process agreable to the ordonnances, to be judged according to the exigency of the case, by the Officers of the Admiralty of Nantes where the Vessel will be discharged.

As the sending of him away ought immediately to take place, as also the punishment of his Crime being necessary for the support of good order & the public confidence, I hope that Y^r Excellency & the Honorable Council will Approve of the same & that You will be pleased Sir to acknowledge as soon as possible the receipt of this letter.

.   .   .   .   .

I have the honor to be &c^a Oster[1]

Faithfully translated from the Original by John Pintard

NA: PCC, item 96, pp. 454-456 (translation); M247, reel 124.

[1] Oster, Martin. French consular official. Vice Consul for Pennsylvania, 1778-1783. Vice Consul for Virginia, resident at Norfolk, 1783-1792.

John Adams to Lord Carmarthen

My Lord   Grosv.ʳ Sqʳ octⁿ 3ᵈ 1787.

It is with concern, that I do myself the Honour to inclose to your Lordship a Letter which I received this morning from Charles Baldwin a Citizen of the United States of America who represents, that on the 22ᵈ of last month he was involuntarily taken out of the Ship *Favorite* Henry Cooper Commander belonging to New York by a Pressgang and taken without any of his Property but the Cloaths he had on, & Sent on board of the Dispatch tender – Where he remained till next day when he was Sent on board the *Vestal* Frigate at long reach, which 2 days after Sailed for Sheerness when arrived there he was Sent on board the *Conqueror* Guardship – he remained there one day, and was then Sent on board the *Scipio* of 64 Guns, which sailed the next day for spithead – This Letter is dated on board the *Tryumph* of 74 Guns at Spithead under the Command of Lord Hood, where probably this Charles Baldwin, (whose father & Family are well known to the Secretary of Legation of the United States) now is –

According to his representation there are Six of 7. others, American Citizens on board the Same Ship, in Similar Circumstances

It is my duty my Lord to remonstrate against this practice, which has been too common of impressing American Citizens, and especially with the aggravating Circumstances of going on board American vessells, which ought to be protected by the flagg of their Sovereign – It is my duty also to request Your Lordships interposition, to obtain for this < ** > Person and his Companions their Liberty –

With great respect I have the honor &c &c   J A –

MHS: *The Adams Papers, microfilm reel* 112 (LBkC).

Sir John Temple to Lord Carmarthen

Nº 24.   New York 3ᵈ of October 1787
My Lord,

.   .   .   .   .

The Convention of delegates, from twelve of the Thirteen states, which have been sitting so long at Philadelphia is at last dissolved, and the form of a supreme Government agreed upon by them, is gone forth to the people at large to be approved or disapproved. – Nine states approving, will render it Valid agreably to the tenor of said new Constitution, which I have also the honor now to inclose to your Lordship: before it was sent forward to be deliberated upon by the several states, there were some debates in Congress upon its Merits, but a great Majority of that body were in its favor, and I suppose there will be the same throughout all the states. Your Lordship will at once see, that by this New Constitution, which I have no doubt will be adopted, Great Powers will indeed rest with the President General of Congress, and Washington will undoubtedly be the first elected to that high station! but, sh^d there be elected, at any time hereafter, an aspiring able man, the *patronage* & *influence* such a station would afford him, would be very great indeed! but I beg pardon for making any observation upon a business of such magnitude, and which is now before your Lordship: though it appears as if the said Constitution had passed *Unanimously* in Convention, I understand that three Gentlemen dissented, vizt. Mr Gerry a delegate from Massachusetts, Mr Randolph and Mr Mason[1] from Virginia, & that, two out of the three New York delegates, designedly left the Convention, just before the Constitution was agreed upon to be signed.[2]

. . . . . .

I am with all deference, My Lord, Your Lordships most faithfull, and Obedient Servant   J. Temple
R. 6^{th:} Nov^r

PRO: FO 4/5, pp. 585-588.
   [1] *Mason, George (1725-1792). Virginia planter and political figure. Member, House of Burgesses, 1759. Author, Fairfax Resolves, 1774, and Virginia Declaration of Rights, 1776. Member, state assembly, 1775-1781, 1786-1788. Delegate, state constitutional convention, 1776; author of major portions of the resulting document. Active in organization of state military affairs, especially George Rogers Clark's conquests. Worked on state plan to cede Northwest Territory to the United States. Member, Constitutional Convention, 1787.*
   [2] *Robert Yates and John Lansing, Jr., left the convention on 10 July 1787.*

John Jay's Report on John Sullivan and Spanish-American Relations

[New York] Office for foreign Affairs 4th October 1787
The Secretary of the United States for the Department of foreign Affairs, to whom was referred a Letter of the 28th Day of August last from the Encargado de Negocios of his Catholic Majesty, enclosing a Charleston Paper in which was published a Letter to him, dated the 1st Day of March last, signed John Sullivan late Capt 4th Regiment american light Dragoons –

Reports.

That in his Opinion the said John Sullivan has by writing and publishing the Letter in Question, committed an Offence against the Peace and Dignity of the United States, for which he ought to be punished. –

That the very imperfect Provision as yet made for the judicial Cognizance of such Cases, renders it difficult to point out the Manner most proper for Congress to proceed in the present. –

The Expediency of calling upon the Executive of any State to apprehend and cause this Man to be tried according to the course of the Laws of the State is questionable, because unless done with a Degree of Vigor and Spirit, the Consideration of Congress would be still more diminished. –

Your Secretary has been informed that Mr Sullivan is really a Deserter from the late american Army, and was concerned in very seditious Practices at Philadelphia about the Time that Congress removed from thence. –

Perhaps it might be well to direct the Secretary at War to report the Facts respecting the Desertion and his Opinion what Measures can and ought to be taken in consequence of them. –

His Report together with the Letter abovementioned, would probably render it expedient to order the Secretary at War to cause the said Sullivan to be arrested in the Western Country, and sent under Guard to Philadelphia, where such of his Offences as might be cognizable by the Laws of that State would be properly tried, and where such further Proceedings might be had against him, as Facts and Circumstances may render proper. –

In the mean Time your Secretary thinks it would be prudent to – Resolve

That the Encargado de Negocios of his Catholic Majesty be informed, that Congress consider the Conduct of John Sullivan in writing and publishing the Letter of which the said Encargado de Negocios complains, as being very reprehensible, and that they will cause such Proceedings to be had against the Writer, as the Laws of the Land prescribe in such Cases – And further, that Congress will on this and every other Occasion, interpose their Authority to frustrate and punish all such Designs and Measures, as may be calculated to interrupt and disturb the Peace and good Understanding which happily subsist between his Catholic Majesty and the United States.–

All which is submitted to the Wisdom of Congress. –

John Jay –

NA: PCC, item 81, v. 3, pp. 9-12 (DS); M247, reel 107.

Congressional Resolutions on John Adams' Recall and Future Relations with Great Britain

Friday Oct 5[th.] 1787.

The Secretary of the United States for the department of foreign Affairs to whom was referred two letters from the hon[ble.] John Adams of the 24 and 27 of January last having reported as follows.

"The first of these letters gives occasion to several questions. 1. Shall M[r] Adams return after the expiration of his commission to the court of London viz 24 feb[y] 1788? Your Secretary is persuaded that M[r] Adams really wishes & means to return next spring and therefore thinks it would be proper for Congress to Resolve the the hon[ble.] John Adams the Minister plenipotentiary of the United States at the court of London be permitted (agreeably to his request) to return to America at any time after the 24 february in the year of our Lord 1788 and that his commission of Minister plenipotentiary to their High Mightinesses do also then determine" and having also reported a resolution approving his Conduct & giving him the thanks of Congress. Both resolutions < ****** > were agreed to as follows

Resolved That the hon[ble.] John Adams the Minister plenipotentiary of the United States at the Court of London be permitted, agreeably to his request, to return to America at any time after the 24 day of february in the year of our Lord 1788 and that his commission of Minister plenipotentiary to their High Mightinesses do also then determine

Resolved That Congress entertain a high sense of the services which M[r] Adams has rendered to the United States in the execution of the various important trusts which they have from time to time committed to him and that the thanks of Congress be presented to him for the patriotism, perseverance integrity and diligence with which he has ably and faithfully served his Country"

The Sec[y] having farther reported

The second question arising from this letter is Whether it will be expedient for the United States to appoint another Minister to take the place of M[r] Adams at the Court of London? On this head the Secretary is of Opinion that it will be expedient to appoint another, because there do exist differences between the United States and the Court of London which cannot too soon be adjusted, which must become the subject of occasional explanations and negotiations and which on the part of the United States cannot be so well managed and conducted as by means of an intelligent and discreet Minister on the spot. Your Secretary's feelings strongly prompt him to retaliate the neglect of Britain in not sending a Minister here; but as he conceives that such retaliation would eventually produce more inconveniences than advantages, he thinks it had better be omitted, especially as he is persuaded that this neglect will cease, the moment that the American govenment and the administration of it shall be such as to impress other Nations with a degree of respect which various circumstances deny to Congress the means of imposing at present. He thinks it should be the policy of the United States at present to keep all things as smooth and easy and to expose themselves to as few embarrassments as possible, until their affairs shall be in such a posture as to justify and support a more nervous stile of conduct and language – Britain disputes the eastern boundary of the United States; she holds important posts and territories on the frontiers and she complains that the treaty of peace has been violated by America. These affairs are important and the management of them requires prudence and temper especially considering how little the actual state of our National affairs tends to repress the influence either of unfriendly dispositions and passions or of that kind of policy which the weakness of neighbours is very apt to suggest and promote. If Congress should concur in the Opinion that a Minister to succeed Mr Adams should be appointed, a resolution like the following would perhaps be the most proper. Whereas divers important affairs still remain to be arranged and adjusted between his britannic Majesty and the United States which on their part cannot be so well conducted as by means of a minister plenipotentiary at the court of London therefore resolved that a minister plenipotentiary to reside at that court be appointed and that his commission take effect on the 25 day of feb^y 1788 and continue in force for the space of three years thereafter unless sooner revoked: Your Secretary conceives it would be best that this minister should be appointed so early as that he might have time to reach London by the first of february in order that he may have an Opportunity of receiving information from Mr Adams respecting characters and affairs and that the progress of the business of the legation may not be stopped by the expiration of Mr Adams Commission."

On the question

Resolved That this part of the report be postponed.

The Secretary having proceeded in his report – "But if Congress should either not incline to appoint another minister or should think proper to postpone it so long as that he will not probably be in London in Feby then he thinks it would be right to consider another question arising from the letter viz Whether it would be expedient to constitute Col. Smith Chargé des Affaires? On this head your Secretary finds himself embarrassed. For on the one hand he esteems Col. Smith as a gentleman of acknowledged merit who has uniformly deserved well of his Country and on the other the light in which the duties of his Office have hitherto been viewed gives the colour of propriety only to his reporting on the expediency of Appointments and not on the persons most proper to be appointed. And as the letter referred to him and now under consideration does nevertheless raise the question relative to the person as well as the place he thinks it proper to make these remarks lest if not adverted to his omitting to report on the former as well as the latter might be ascribed to other than the true reasons. He thinks that if when Mr Adams quits the affairs of the legation they are not to pass immediately into the hands of a successor there can be little doubt of the expediency of appointing a proper person to take charge of them. In that case therefore it would in his opinion be proper to resolve That a person be appointed to take charge of the affairs of the American legation at the court of London from the expiration of the commission of the present Minister to the Arrival there of another Minister to succeed him or until the further Order of Congress

On this part of the report a question was taken to agree thereto and was lost

NA: PCC, item 5, v. 3, pp. 1656-1660 (Journal); M247, reel 19.

Peter Allaire: Occurrences from 5 August to 5 October 1787

N. York 5 October 1787

Coll Alexander[1] of Georgia with three hundred Men, went against the Creek Indians, to revenge the Murder of Mr Michell & Jones, they killed Eighteen Indians, burnt two Towns, and was the 25 July on full march for their grand settlement to destroy it.

Express from Kentucky, that the Indians have murdered forty three families in Cumberland County, burning their houses, and distroying all the Grain, Horses, Cattle &c. they intend Attacking fort St Vincents and we are affraid the Fort cannot hold out until relief be sent them, the Western people intend sending 300 Men on horseback to their Assistance, we have now a kind of War with the Indians, from Georgia to the Ohio, we have at present the Chiefs of the Cherokees, Chactaws and Chickasaws, now making Peace with Congress, their Reception have not been much to their liking, having received no presents & pretty rough language, such as treatning them with a War, if not peaceable for while they were here an express Arrived, that a Boat on the Ohio with 14 Men & loaded with furrs was fired on & 13 Men killed, another Boat coming up Armed with a Swivel saved the Boat & the one Man

The Western People have taken a Track of Land belonging to the Chicksaws, called the Bluffs on the river Mississippi, to form a Town it is Six hundred Miles from the mouth of said River.

The Wyomin People have Erected a new State, on Tiago Point they muster about 2000 fighting Men, have refused obedience to the Laws of Pensilvania & adopted their own, (they say Shays is there) Congress are so much displeased with the Indians, that they came to the following Resolve, that no person should conduct any Indians to Congress, but their Commissioners for Indian Affairs, and should any Trader conduct any Indians, he shall be obliged to pay their Expences, and his licence as a Trader be taken from him, that the Secretary at War be directed to pay the Expences of the three chiefs now here (those Indians were conducted by a private Trader)

You may form some Opinion of the Western People from the following Letter from a Cap[t.] Sullivan, to his Excellency, Don Diego Gardoqui printed in the daily advertiser of the 17 August, herewith inclosed, Don Diego, went Imediately and layd the above Letter before Congress, their Answer, not being satisfactory he went to Philadelphia to make the matter known to General Washington President of the Convention but my Opinion is, there is no Executive Power existing in America, that can prevent those people from putting their Plan in execution.

The Insurgents in the State of Massachusets have dwindled away. Coll Lyman[2] with two hundred Men keeps them in Subjection.

.   .   .   .   .

The State of Massachusets, have Reprieved & permitted to Escape out of Jail, those persons that were found guilty of high Treason & the State have passed an Act of Amnesty: except Shays & Wheeler.

.   .   .   .

Sep[t.]...23...In Congress, Resolved that the Superintendant of Indian Affairs for the No[r]thern department, in his Absence Coll. Josiah Harman[3] to proceed to Fort S[t] Vincents & take such possessions as shall afford the most Effectual protection to the frontier Inhabitants from the Incursions of the Indians, and that they give notice to the Wabash, Shawanese & other hostile Tribes, to come in & inform them of their complaints, & to know their Reasons for making war against the United States, and to make Peace with them, if it can be done on Terms Consistent with the honor & dignity of the United States.

.   .   .   .   .

28...The Chevalier Longchamp,[4] who struck the French Consul two Years ago, and was sent to Gail, all kind of Bail & Security being Refused by the Chief Justice (Mc Kean)[5] and whom the King of France by his Consul demanded of Congress to be sent to France to Receive punishment, but by their acknowledging, they had no power or Authority over any of the Subjects of the united States, they got rid of the Affair, was Killed Yesterday in a Duel, By a French Officer, who sailed the same day for the French west Indies, it is supposed he came on purpose to take Satisfaction for the insult done that Nation, (Monsr Longchamp having married an American & had been Naturalized;

The Complection of the People at large of Pensilvania, Jersey and N York, seem to approve of the New Federal Constitution, But when the leading Men in Each State (who are of the lower Class) begin to think, that every individual State, will be reduced to a meer Corporation Town, and their subsistance taken from them, they will in my Opinion, make every Effort, to keep the Government as it is, if they succeed, nothing can prevent a Civil War in three or four years at farthest, as all New England are ripe for any thing, to avoid paying Taxes.

29...Congress Yesterday approved of the plan sent them by the Convention, and every Member has Received Orders to lay the same before their Respective Assemblies, and to Endeavour all in their power to obtain a Ratification of the same, by having delegates appointed from Each State with full powers to settle the federal Constitution on a permanent and Solid foundation.

I have the honor to be with Great Respect   P A
R. 8$^{th:}$ Novr 1787.

PRO: FO 4/5, pp. 637-651 (LC transcription).

[1] Not further identified.

[2] Not further identified.

[3] Harmar, Josiah (1753-1813). Military officer. Served as major or lieutenant-colonel of various Pennsylvania regiments, 1776-1783. Colonel, September 1783. Carried ratification of definitive treaty of peace to Paris, 1784. As commander of the army, 1784-1791, engaged in Indian warfare on the Ohio frontier. Adjutant general of Pennsylvania, 1793-1799.

[4] For information on the Longchamps Affair, see the previous volume of this publication.

[5] McKean, Thomas (1734-1817). Jurist and political figure. Member, Delaware House of Assembly, 1762-1775; speaker, 1772. Member, Continental Congress, 1774-1776, 1778-1782; president, 1781. Chief justice of Pennsylvania, 1777-1799. Governor of Pennsylvania, 1799-1808.

John Bondfield to Thomas Jefferson

Sir   Bordeaux 6 October 1787

. . . . .

Should hostilities take place the American Navigation if Neutre will reap great advantages but great abuses will take place which it will be difficult to prevent. the conections betwixt England and America will facilitate the means to obtain Cover for British bottoms under American Registers. france cannot enjoy the like advantages. difference of Language & other striking objects will make any attemps of false papers subject to more rigeurous scrutin. the Courts of both Nations will have employment from the contests that will arise nothing less than an Act of Navigation carrying protection to *American Built* Ships only with other partial cloggs can free the Americans from lending their names & transfering to other Nations the advantages which circumstances would give them exclusively.

. . . . .

with due respect I have the honor to be Sir Your very hble Servant
                                                    John Bondfield

LC: *Jefferson Papers, microfilm reel 8* (ALS).

Congressional Resolution
Condemning John Sullivan

October 8[th.] 1787 –
By The United States in Congress assembled.
Resolved that the Encargado de Negocios of his Catholic Majesty be informed, that Congress consider the Conduct of John Sullivan in writing and publishing the Letters of which the said Encargado de Negocios complains, as being very reprehensible, and that they will cause such Proceedings to be had against the Writer, as the Laws of the Land prescribe, and farther, that Congress will on this and every other Occasion interpose their Authority, to frustrate and punish all such Designs and Measures, as may be calculated to interrupt and disturb the Peace and good Understanding, which happily subsist between his Catholic Majesty and the United States. –   Cha[s] Thomson Secretary.

NA: PCC, *item 125, p. 152* (LBkC); M247, reel 142.

John Adams to John Jay

Dear Sir   Grosvenor Square October 9. 1787

France appears at this Moment, in the Light of a Simple People Sincerely disposed to Peace, benevolence and Humanity, and judging of the dispositions of others by her own. She Seems by her late Glory and Prosperity to have been Soothed into a Security and Tranquility, out of which it is Scarce possible to awaken her. England on the other hand appears, like a Nation Smarting under her Wounds, but covering her designs with a Veil of deep Dissimulation, while she was exerting her utmost Craft to obtain an opportunity of Gratifying her Resentment. We need not look farther for the Cause of the present Strange Appearances than the Diplomatic Arrangements of the two Nations. – Never was there a Time, when able and Attentive Men were So necessary for France at the Courts of London, and the Hague as at the late Peace. The Comte de Vergennes should have Sent to both Places, Men of the most enlarged Capacities, and dilligent Attention to the whole System of Europe. The Marquis de Verac, is as honest a Man, and as well intentioned, as he could have found. But I believe every Man who knows him will agree with me that a Gentleman more unqualified for his Mission could not have been found. The Comte D'Adhemar, has an elegant Figure, an handsome Face, and is a Favourite of the Ladies but whether from his unfortunate paralitical Stroke, or from his having no Turn for the Business of State, he appears to have been inattentive, not only to the affairs of Europe in General but to those of England and Holland. The Spanish Minister[1] has been extreamly attentive to make his Court to the Royal Family and the Minister here, and has been so successful as to obtain the Kings request, that he might be promoted to the Rank of a Marquis at home, and to that of Ambassdor here; but to Speak freely to you as I ought, he does not appear to me to know or care much about the System of Europe. – The French Chargé too, who is an ingenious Man and well behaved, has had the good fortune to recommend him Self to this Court so as to be, promoted to the Rank of Min. Plen. at their Instance.[2] – I have ever been upon good terms with all these Gentlemen, and have no personal dislike to any of them: but I cannot but See and lament the Causes, which appear to have contributed to a Catastrophy, So outrageous to the Rights of Mankind, and so humiliating, to the best Friends We have or ever had in France Holland and Spain. – I must confess that Favouritism, at the Court where he resides, in an Ambassador, of any denomination, is in my Opinion a fatal Objection against him: because I know it to be impossible to be obtained without the most criminal Simulation on one hand, or Negligence, or something worse, of the Interests of his Constituents on the other. There is a great difference between being esteemed and beloved: between being upon decent, civil and respectable Terms, and being taken into the Arms and embraced. Whenever and Wherever this is seen in Negotiations, Something may justly be suspected to be amiss. – unfortunately too Monsr de St Priest, who has been long in Constantinople, and had a great Reputation for ability and Success, in former Negotiations, was recalled at a most critical Time. – England on the Contrary, appears to have been meditating a Blow, even when the Nation were generally expecting the Commencement of the Millenium from the Operation of the Commercial Treaty. – She has Sent her Shrewdest Men to Versailles and the Hague. She appears to have been intriguing at Constantinople as well as in South America. She has been forming a League in Germany: and maintaining her Navy on a formidable Footing. – France may be as indifferent as she will about Holland, but that will not Secure her Peace. The English cannot See, without inward Rage and Fury, I might say without Terror and dismay, the works at Cherbourg. and Let Hollands fate be what it will. Let the Turks be disposed of as you please, in my Opinion France must demolish Cherbourg and Spain Set South America at Liberty, or there will be War. The Passions of this Nation are at present in a Flame. I hear Such a Language even in the Streets, and in Booksellers Shops, the only Scenes of popular Politicks into which I think it prudent to venture, that I am confident a War is not far off. – The Rage of this nation amazes me. – With a Gulph and a Precipice of public Ruin before their Eyes they are ready to take the Leap with Joy. The most interesting Question for Us is, whether We shall be neutral? This is undoubtedly our Wisdom, and Congress and the States will take the most decided Measures to prevent our People from giving any Provocation. They will no doubt forbid in the most effectual Manner any of their Citizens from Serving on board the Ships of either Nation, much less from taking Commissions and committing depredations. But will all this preserve our Neutrality? It is my Duty to be explicit upon this occasion, and to say, that Although the British Government may pretend and even Sincerely endeavour, to avoid a quarrel with the United States at the Commencement of the War, yet if they Should obtain any Signal Successes at first, which it is not improbable they may, there will arise such a Spirit of Domination and Insolence in the Nation, as will Stimulate Hostilities, against Us. It is my duty therefore, to advise, that the best Preparations, for our own defence and Security be made, that are in our Power. The Detail of Affairs in Holland is too dismal, to be repeated. The News Papers contain Accounts melancholly enough. The Plebeians and the Monarch are too closely connected, in Holland, to be overcome by the Patrician Aristocracy, and no rational Plan of a Reformation of their Government has been concerted by the People or their Leaders. It is a repetition of the Catastrophy of all ill constituted Republicks, and is a living Warning to our United States.

With great Regard I have the Honour to be, dear Sir your most obedient and most humble Servant   John Adams

NA: PCC, item 84, v. 6, pp. 535-538 (ALS); M247, reel 113.
¹ Campo y Pérez de la Serna, Bernardo del. Spanish diplomat. Floridablanca's English-speaking undersecretary, authorized to treat with John Jay, September 1781-May 1782. Minister to Great Britain, 1783-1795; Ambassador from 21 September 1787. Created Marqués del Campo, 17 August 1786.
² Barthélemy, François. French diplomat. Minister to Great Britain, 1787-1792.

Louis XVI, King of France: Instructions for Comte de Moustier

[Translation]

[Versailles, 10 October 1787]

The Zeal and prudence with which the Comte de Moustier has discharged the two missions which the King has successively entrusted to him has determined His Majesty to appoint him His Minister Plenipotentiary near the United States of North America. This mark of confidence is so much the more flattering for the Comte de Moustier, as His Majesty attaches a great value to the maintenance of His alliance with the United States, and as the conduct of His representative can essentially have an influence on their affections and their proceedings.

The Comte de Moustier will judge from this that he should apply himself to confirm the Americans in the principles which have induced them to join together with France: he will impress them to this effect, that they can have no more natural Ally than the King, whereas they can be certain that England is jealous of their prosperity, and that she will harm them as often as she finds occasion to do so. This matter will necessarily lead the Comte de Moustier to have conversations regarding Commerce, the subject which almost exclusively attracts the attention of the Americans. They will probably complain of the lack of favor which they will claim to meet with in France and particularly in our Islands. The Comte de Moustier will find a Memoir enclosed that will enable him to discuss this matter with complete knowledge of the subject. This document will furnish him with more than sufficient means to convince the Americans of the King's good intentions in their regard, and of His desire to make their Commerce prosper in so far as it can be done without prejudicing that of his own subjects. In addition, the Comte de Moustier will neglect nothing to acquire as much information as he can on every subject that may contribute to render our Commerce with the United States as advantageous as the nature of things will permit it. The Administration has not been sufficiently enlightened heretofore on this important matter; and it is to be feared that the Americans follow usages that will be prejudicial to us, and from which France will no longer be able to deter them. There is reason to believe that this is the principal object of the Court of London; and it is evident that France will lose everything that Great Britain will gain.

It would be wrong willfully to suppose that this power does not seek to diminish the sentiments which should attach the United States to France, and gradually to bring about their reconciliation with their late Mother-country. It will be useful for the King's Minister to follow the English agents' way of proceeding, and for him to do what depends on him, but without pretence, so as to render their insinuations of no account.

The Comte de Moustier will surely find the Americans very taken up with the ferment which reigns at this moment in Europe, and there is considerable likelihood that they will endeavor to talk with him thereof, and to learn through him the true state of things. In this event, the Comte de Moustier can say, relative to the affairs of Holland, that they have unexpectedly taken a decided turn in favor of the Stadhouder through one of those hazards that it is impossible to foresee, and which neither the Court of Berlin nor that of London expected, and that the resolutions passed by the States of Holland, as by the States-General under the influence of Prussian troops, have prevented His Majesty from making demonstrations in favor of the Patriots, and that He has resolved to leave things in their present state rather than to expose the Republic to the horrors of civil war, and to provoke a general war at the same time. To this reflection the Comte de Moustier can add that the same Sentiment that induced the King to save the United Provinces from the war with which they were menaced, likewise induced him to do what depends on him to prevent, as much as will be compatible with His dignity and with His interest, the outbreak of war between France and Great Britain. As it is very probable that they will speak to the Comte de Moustier of the armaments that are being made in our ports, as in those of Great Britain, he can respond that the armaments ordered by the King are but a necessary consequence of those ordered by the Court of London; that His Majesty will halt them as soon as England is prepared to do likewise without wounding her dignity and without sacrificing her interests, and that there is so much the more reason to hope that the disarmament will be effected, since the hostile measures of the two Courts no longer have any purpose; that as it is nevertheless impossible to foresee events, and even less so to rely on the intentions and the good faith of the Court of London, one can have no certainty in France of maintaining the peace; that the King calculates in advance that if it is broken, the Americans will hold to a conduct analogous to the ties that bind them to France, and that they will not allow themselves to be seduced by the insidious language that it is probable the King of Great Britain will pursue toward them. This matter is particularly commended to the Zeal and vigilance of the King's Minister: but he will himself perceive how much discretion, dexterity, and prudence he should employ in his language and in his conduct.

As for affairs in the Levant, the Comte de Moustier will observe to persons who speak to him of them that despite the declaration of war made by the Turks, the King still has some hope of recalling matters to the path of reconciliation; that it is the desire of the Empress of Russia, and that the King is awaiting the effect which the steps that he has stipulated to His Ambassador will have produced. The Comte de Moustier may add that in the event that the Porte should persist in wanting war, it is impossible to foresee, with regard to the present, what influence it might have on the political System of Europe.

The Comte de Moustier will have seen in his predecessor's correspondence and in that of M. Otto that the King is a creditor of the United States for twenty-four millions, and that His Majesty is their guarantor for ten millions with the United Provinces. Copies of the instruments relative to these two loans are herewith enclosed. Congress is too destitute of means for one to be able to press it for payment of the first capital with hope of success; the King does not even expect to recover this sum so soon: in spite of this, it will be useful to remind the Americans of it so that they do not think we have lost sight of it. It is especially appropriate that the King's Minister press them for regular payment of the interest: this article is particularly recommended to him; he will especially insist on the interest which the King pays in Holland for the relief of Congress.

The Comte de Moustier knows the details relative to the quarrel existing between the United States and Spain concerning the navigation of the Mississippi. He is to presume that the sane party in Congress views this dispute with anxiety, and wishes to forestall it: but the Colonies that have been established along the banks of the Ohio are becoming so important that Congress will henceforth be unable to contain them, and that they will undertake, without its consent, to open a passage to the Gulf of Mexico. If they speak to the Comte de Moustier of this subject, he will limit himself to observing that the King would view with anxiety that the United States become embroiled with Spain over a matter regarding which the principles are in favor of that power, and that it would be strongly desired that things be arranged amicably. In addition, the Comte de Moustier will offer neither means for conciliation nor His Majesty's good offices: the question is too delicate for it to be appropriate for the King to interfere therein: his intervention would probably serve only to compromise him with all the interested parties.

The Comte de Moustier will have seen in the correspondence of M. Otto that the Americans are busy with a new Constitution. This matter only weakly affects the King's policy. His Majesty thinks, on one hand, that the deliberations will be unsuccessful because of the diversity of affections, principles, and interests of the various provinces, and on the other, that it suits France that the United States continue in their present condition, because if they achieve the stability of which they are capable, they would ere long acquire a strength and a power of which they would probably be most eager to take advantage. Notwithstanding this last reflection, the King's Minister will take care to maintain the most passive deportment, to appear neither for nor against the new arrangements on which they are employed, and when he is challenged, to speak only of the King's wishes and of his own personal wishes for the prosperity of the United States.

The Comte de Moustier will find his Letters of credence enclosed. He will deliver them to Congress in the accustomed form. He will repeat orally to that assembly the sentiments expressed therein, and he will neglect no occasion to renew the assurance thereof. In New York he will find the ciphers that should be employed in his ordinary correspondence. Regarding political affairs, as regarding those of commerce, he will deal only with the Minister having the Department of Foreign Affairs: however, when the service of the King seems to him to require that he write to other Ministers, he will address his letters under flying seal to the political Department.

Done at Versailles the tenth of October one thousand seven hundred and eighty-seven.   Louis

FFAA: Pol. Corr., U.S., Supplement, v. 1, f. 421-426 (LS); LC Acc. 19022, microfilm reel 1.

Congressional Ratification of the June 1787 Dutch Loan

[New York] October 11th 1787. –

On motion, Resolved That the Contract made by John Adams Esquire Minister Plenipotentiary in behalf of the United States of America on the first day of June 1787 for the Loan of one million of Guilders be and it is hereby ratified. –

Resolved That three fair Copies of the Contract with a Ratification in the form of that agreed to on the first of February 1785 *mutatis mutandis,*[1] endorsed on each Copy be made out and duly attested, and that the Secretary for the department of foreign affairs transmit the same by several conveyances to M[r] J. Adams Minister plenipotentiary aforesaid –

Cha[s] Thomson Sec[y]

NA: PCC, *item 122, p. 103 (LBkC); M247, reel 140.*

[1] *after making the necessary changes*

John Jay to Don Diego de Gardoqui

D[r] Sir   [New York] Office for foreign Affairs 11th October 1787

I have the honor of transmitting to you herewith enclosed, an Act of Congress on the subject of your Letter of the 28th day of August last. Permit me to observe, that in a Country where such extensive License is given to the press, the Sentiments of the People at large cannot be collected from anonymous publications, which often originate in the particular & interested views of the individuals who make them. The official Acts of the Government only merit regard, and I flatter myself that the one in question will be considered as affording strong evidence of the respect and attachment which the United States entertain for his Catholic Majesty. I have the honor to be with very sincere Esteem and Regard &[c]

John Jay

NA: PCC, *item 120, v. 3, p. 290 (LBkC); M40, reel 3.*

Congressional Resolutions on the Redemption of American Captives in Algiers

[New York] October 12th 1787

On a Report of the Board of Treasury in consequence of an Act of 18th of July,

Resolved That the balance of the appropriation for the Barbary Treaties of the 14th of February 1785 not hitherto applied to that object be and it is hereby constituted a fund for redeeming the American Captives now at Algiers, and that the same be for this purpose, subject to the direction of the Minister of the United States at the Court of Versailles.

That the Acts of Congress of the 14ᵗʰ of February 1785, and such part of the Resolves of the 18ᵗʰ of July 1787 as directs provision to be made for the above object be and they are hereby Repealed. –

Chaˢ Thomson Secʸ

NA: PCC, item 122, p. 104 (LBkC); M247, reel 140.

Congressional Resolution Renewing Thomas Jefferson's Commission as Minister to France

[New York] Friday Oct 12. 1787

On motion of Mʳ King seconded by Mʳ H Lee[1]

Resolved That Congress proceed to the election of a Minister plenipotentiary to reside at the Court of France and that his commission commence from the expiration of the present commission of the honᵇˡᵉ Thomas Jefferson and continue in force for the term of three years unless sooner revoked by Congress

Congress accordingly proceeded to the election and the ballots being taken

The honorable Thomas Jefferson was elected.

NA: PCC, item 5, p. 1674 (Journal); M247, reel 19.

[1] *Lee, Henry (1756-1818). Military leader, Virginia political figure. Known as Light-Horse Harry for his exploits in command of elements of the First Continental Dragoons. Member, Continental Congress, 1786-1788. Governor, 1791-1794. As major general, commanded U.S. forces in suppressing Whiskey Rebellion, 1794. Member, U.S. House of Representatives, 1799-1801.*

John Jay's Report on Thomas Barclay's Arrest

[New York] Office for foreign Affairs, 12ᵗʰ October 1787

The Secretary of the United States for the Department of foreign Affairs, to whom was referred a Letter of 21ˢᵗ June last from Mʳ Jefferson, respecting the Arrest of the american Consul General in France,...

Reports. –

That his Report of the 26ᵗʰ September last on the Petition of Messʳˢ French & Nephew, at whose Suit the Consul was arrested, expresses the Opinion of your Secretary on the Legality of that Arrest; and he still thinks, that no Consuls should be exempted from Suits and Arrests for their own proper Debts. –

But as the Arrest and Imprisonment of an american Consul General is a Circumstance which must hurt the Feelings of the United States, and in some Degree wound their Dignity, it may be proper to enquire what Measures it would be proper to take on this Occasion. –

He thinks it would be adviseable to pass the Resolution recommended in the abovementioned Report, declaring that all american Consuls in foreign Ports and all foreign Consuls here, are liable to Arrests &ca: –

That your Secretary should in an informal Manner intimate to the Consul General in Question, that his Arrest and Imprisonment have given Congress much Concern, both on his Account and that of the United States. That they wish he would endeavor so to settle with his Creditors, as that he may return to France early in the Spring, without any Risque of the like Treatment in future. That although his Character and Services will always induce Congress to regret every Circumstance that may hurt either his Feelings or his Fortune, yet that the Respect due to the Dignity of the United States has also strong Claims to their Attention and Care. –

Your Secretary thinks it his Duty to inform Congress that, as well from the Opinion of Mr Jefferson as from other Circumstances, he has Reason to believe that the Conduct of the Consul respecting his Creditors has not merited the harsh Treatment he has received from them. –

.   .   .   .   .

All which is submitted to the Wisdom of Congress. –

John Jay –

read. 15 Oct. 1787

NA: PCC, item 81, v. 3, pp. 27-30 (DS); M247, reel 107.

Congressional Resolution Regarding John Sullivan and Relations with Spain

[New York] Saturday Oct. 13. 1787

On a report of the Secretary at War

Whereas a certain John Sullivan, stiling himself "late captain 4 Regiment American light dragoons" has written an inflammatory & unwarrantable letter to the encargado de negocios of his Catholic Majesty bearing date the first day of March 1787 tending to interrupt and injure the peace and mutual confidence which so happily subsist between the United States and his said Catholic Majesty therefore

Resolved That the Secretary at War direct the Commanding Officer of the troops of the United States on the Ohio that, if the said John Sullivan come within the federal territory, he cause the said J. Sullivan to be seized and confined in order that he may be legally tried and punished according to the nature and degree of his crime.

A motion being made by Mr Butler[1] seconded by Mr Kean[2] that it be Resolved That Congress entertain the highest sense of the friendly disposition of his Catholic Majesty towards the United States and that it is their Ardent desire and fixed intention to preserve uninterrupted that good understanding at present subsisting between the United States and his Catholic Majesty And that Congress should have given evidence of their friendship for his Catholic Majesty and his subjects by entering on an Adjustment of every unsettled matter subsisting between them were they not prevented for the present by pressing domestic concerns which engross the whole of their attention at this time.

NA: PCC, item 5, v. 3, pp. 1662-1664 (Journal); M247, reel 19.

[1] Butler, Pierce (1744-1822). South Carolina planter and political figure. Member, Continental Congress, 1787. Delegate, Constitutional Convention, 1787. U.S. Senator, 1789-1796, 1802-1804.

[2] Kean, John (1756-1795). South Carolina merchant and political figure. Captured at Charleston, 1780. Member, Continental Congress, 1785-1787. Cashier, Bank of the United States, 1791-1795.

Congressional Resolutions Regarding Most-Favored Nation Treatment

[New York, October 13, 1787]

On a report of the Secretary for foreign Affairs to whom was referred a letter to him from the Minister of the United Netherlands enclosing a Note of the same date complaining of an Act of the Legislature of the Commonwealth of Virginia exempting French Brandies imported in French and American Vessels from Certain duties to which the like Commodities imported in Dutch Vessels are left liable, as being contrary to the Second Article in their Treaty with the United States, Stipulating that they shall be treated as the most favoured Nation.

Resolved That whenever any of these States shall think proper to grant a favor to any foreign Nation such State ought to extend it to such other foreign Nations as by Treaties with the United States are to be treated as the most favored Nation. –

Resolved That a Copy of the above Resolution and of the Representation of the Minister of the United Netherlands be transmitted to the Commonwealth of Virginia to the end that the Legislature of that Commonwealth may take the earliest opportunity of Revising the Act of which the said Minister Complains and rendering the same perfectly consistent with the Treaty subsisting between the United States and the United Netherlands and of causing to be repaid whatever extra duties may in Virtue of the said Act be exacted on the Brandies there imported in Dutch Vessels during the Operation of the same. –

Chas Thomson Sec^y

NA: PCC, *item 122, p. 106 (LBkC); M247, reel 140.*

Comte de Montmorin to Comte de Moustier

[Translation]

Versailles, 13 October 1787

United States

I have the honor, Sir, to send you your instructions. They make mention of a Memoir concerning Commerce. I shall send you this document as soon as it is sent to me by the Controller General; you know that it is supposed to comprise the report of a Committee that had the task of determining the advantages which France can accord to American Commerce. As for the obligations of which mention is also made in your instructions, you will find them in the Correspondence of the Chevalier de la Luzerne.

The political subject, Sir, which I have recommended the most to you, is the conduct of England, and the sentiment that predominates in America with regard to that Power. I imagine that if war broke out, the Americans would wish to remain neutrals. The King would probably agree willingly to this arrangement, provided that it was executed in good faith, but this is not the moment to expound on that question, because circumstances could thwart our principles; moreover, it seems to me that it would be up to the Americans to court us regarding a matter that would be an exception to our Treaty of Alliance. Thus, Sir, if you are sounded on this subject, you will respond with the greatest circumspection, and you will take care to say nothing that might bind or constrain His Majesty. Moreover, I still retain hope that war may yet be prevented.

I have the honor to be most perfectly Sir, your most humble and most obedient Servant Le cte De Montmorin – it is not possible for me to write anything more today.*

* Autograph sentence

FFAA: *Pol. Corr., U.S., Supplement, v. 1, f. 419-419vo.* (LS); LC Acc. 19022, *microfilm reel 1.*

Marquis de Lafayette to John Jay

Sir   Paris October the 15 1787

The Present State of Politics Having Been Laid Before Congress I Shall the Less intrude on their time With Repetitions, as the Late Transactions in Holland Have Nothing Pleasing to dwell Upon – that the Republican Party Have Been disUnited in Many Respects and Blinded in the Choice of a General that our Cabinet Have Been treacherously deceived are true, But insufficient Apologies. the Ottomans, Roused By England, Will probably Pay [for] their folly with one Half of their Empire. it Now Lies With England Whether a Maritime War is to Break out, which Must involve the Continent and Connect france With the two imperial Courts. france is Sincere in Her Politics and Moderate in Her Pretentions as it is the Ardent Wish of the King Ministers, and Nation, to Devote themselves to internal improvement. But the Affairs of Holland, those in the East the Giddiness of the King of Prussia's Head and British Rancour for the assistance Given to America Are Causes Of war Which Notwithstanding the disposition of their Ministry May Probably Be Blown up in Great Britain

it is Natural for A Citizen and servant of the United States to Consider what effect a Maritime War Would Have Upon them. and I am Happy to find in their indulgence and long Experienced Confidence Every Encouragement to Offer my Opinion.

A Cooperation Against a Proud and Rancourous Ennemy Would equally please my Politics as a french Man my feelings as an American my Views as an individual. I was Nine Year[s] Ago Honoured With the Choice of Congress to Command an Army into Canada and Never Have I Ceased to Enjoy the Prospect of its Enfranchisement. a Successfull War too Might divide the fisheries Between france and America. But Are Not the United States so Circumstanced for the present as to Render a War too Expensive for them and too dangerous to their Commerce?

Convinced as I am that it is the Case, I think Myself Bound in duty and Love for them, not to indulge My Ambition farther than a Neutrality Useful to them and favourable to their Allies. Every American Harbour will offer a shelter for the french ships a Market for their prizes and all the Conveniences of Repair and Victualling. all which, Being Consistent with treaties, Gives No Ground of Complaint. Altho the trade is Going on Between England and America it does not Hinder the french Colonies from Being Supplied with all their Wants. Privateering itself, if Under french Colors does no Harm – and so may the United States Enrich themselves with a free trade with both Nations, at the same time that they Maintain their own tranquillity and Help their Allies – and Should they be forced into a War, I would Wish at Least it Was delaied as Long as possible and postponed for Obvious Reasons, to the next Campaign.

it is to be Confessed that france Might Lay Some Claims on more decisive Measures, But Sensible as She is of the Unavoidable Situation of Affairs in America I Have Reasons to Believe She Would Not Hurry Her into a War and will be Satisfied with Such a friendly Helping Neutrality

But I Consider the present time as a proper one to Obtain the Restoration of the forts, and Perhaps the Navigation of the Mississipi two points which I Confess I Could Never Submit to the idea of Giving Up. the one is ours by the Laws of Nations, the other by the Laws of Nature, and May I be permitted to add that Either Concession Would be inconsistent with the Character of the United States

Mr Jefferson Gives an Account of the Measures He Has taken Respecting the Commerce Between this Kingdom and America. I wish that Affair Had Been terminated in time for the departure of Count De Moustier a Gentlemen whose personal Character will I trust, deserve the Confidence and Approbation of Congress

We are Anxiously Awaiting for the Result of the Convention in Philadelphia as an Event which being Engrafted in the present disposition of the people will probably add a Lustre, and a proper Weight to the Affairs of America in Europe, and While it Ensures Internal Happiness and Prosperity, Will Baffle the insidious Wishes and Anihilate the Absurd Reports of her Ennemies

the Next Month is the Appointed time for the Session of All Provincial Assemblies. An Establishment Which Will be productive of the Best Consequences.

the Liberty I Have taken to Express My Opinion on an Event not certain – it is true But Not Improbable Cannot Be Apologized for on Any Particular of Vanity or Self Sufficiency, But on those of the Gratitude So Well Grounded and the Unbounded Zeal Which Shall ever Rank me Among the Most devoted Servants of the United States.

With Every Sentiment of....   Lafayette

NA: PCC, item 156, pp. 462-465 (ALS); M247, reel 176.

John Jay to John Adams

D^r· Sir   Office for Foreign Affairs 16th October 1787

· · · · · ·

I have at length the Pleasure of transmitting to you, herewith enclosed, an Act of Congress complying with your Request to return, and expressing their Sentiments of, and their Thanks for the important Services you have rendered your Country. They have not yet come to any Decision respecting a Minister or a Chargé des Affaires at London, nor directed me to convey to you any Instructions relative to any Matters within the Department of your Legation. –

. . . . .

The public Mind is much occupied by the Plan of foederal Government recommended by the late Convention – many expect much Good from its Institution, and others will oppose its Adoption – the Majority seems at present to be in its Favor. For my part I think it much better than the one we have, and therefore that we shall be Gainers by the Exchange; especially as there is Reason to hope that Experience and the good Sense of the People, will correct what may prove to be inexpedient in it. A Compact like this, which is the Result of Accommodation and Compromise, cannot be supposed to be perfectly consonant to the Wishes and Opinions of any of the Parties. It corresponds a good Deal with your favorite and I think just Principles of Government, whereas the present Confederation seems to have been formed without the least Attention to them. –

Congress have thought it best to pass a Requisition for the Expences of the ensuing Year, but like most of their former ones it will produce but little. –

. . . . .

I wish it may be convenient to you to return in some Vessel bound to this Port, that I may have the Pleasure of taking you by the Hand, and personally assuring you of the sincere Esteem and Regard with which I am Dr Sir Your most ob$^{t.}$ and hble: Serv$^{t.}$ John Jay –

MHS: *The Adams Papers, microfilm reel 370* (ALS).

Hendrik Fagel to John Adams

Sir,   Hage 18th Octr 1787. –

I have had the Honor of receiving duly your Letter of the 1st Instant, in which you have sent a Memorial to their High Mightinessess on the Subject of Mr Dumas's Situation – This Memorial not being in French as is the Custom, but in English, could not be taken into formal Deliberation; but as it has nevertheless been communicated to their High Mightinessess by me, I am authorized to write to you in Answer, – that by a Note transmitted to me by said Dumas, dated the 28th of last Month, & presented by me to their High Mightinesses the Lords Deputies of the Province of Holland & West Friesland, they have already been prayed to have an

Eye to the Security of his Person – that their High Mightinesses were unwilling that the said Dumas should be more embarrassed than any of their own Inhabitants, but that they cannot conceal from you Sir, that the said Dumas little Merits their Protection, since he has conducted himself in a Manner, which, in many Respects, is altogether improper. It is for this Reason, that in the Name of their H. Mightinesses I request you, Sir, (a thing which is also expected from your Discretion) that you will employ him no longer here, but that you will appoint another Person for chargé des Affaires here during your Absence. I acquit myself of these Orders, in having the Honor to be &c. –   H. Fagel[1] –

NA: PCC, item 84, v. 6, pp. 553-554 (translation); M247, reel 113.
   [1] Fagel, Hendrick (1706-1790). Dutch political figure. Griffier (secretary) of the States General in the 1780s. A strong supporter of the pro-British House of Orange.

Congressional Resolution Recognizing George Miller as Consul

[New York] October 20th 1787 –
On a report of the Secretary of the United States for the department of foreign Affairs to whom was referred a letter of the Second of this present month October from P. Bond Esquire, enclosing a Commission from his Britannic Majesty constituting George Miller Esquire his Consul and deputy Commissary in the States of North Carolina, South Carolina and Georgia.–
   Whereas George Miller Esquire has communicated to the United States in Congress Assembled a Commission in due form bearing date the 5th day of January 1787 from his Britannic Majesty constituting him the Consul of his Said Majesty in the States of North Carolina South Carolina and Georgia. And although no Commercial Treaty or Convention subsists between his Majesty and the United States, whereby either have a perfect Right to establish Consuls or Commissiaries in the Dominions of the other; yet as the United States are disposed by every proper mark of liberality and attention to promote a good Correspondence between the two Countries, and particularly as amicable Negociations are now depending between them therefore
   Resolved That the said George Miller be, and he is hereby received and Recognized as the Consul of his Britannic Majesty throughout the States of North Carolina South Carolina and Georgia, and that his Commission be recorded in the Secretary's Office –
   Resolved That all the privileges pre-eminences and authority which the Laws of Nations and of the Land give a Consul received by the United States from any Nation with whom they have no Commercial Treaty or

Convention are due and shall be enjoyed by the said George Miller as Consul for the three States above mentioned and that Certified Copies of these Resolutions be transmitted to the Executives thereof for their information. –   Cha⁴ Thomson Sec⁷

NA: PCC, item 122, p. 108 (LBkC); M247, reel 140.

Louis Guillaume Otto to Comte de Montmorin

[Translation]

N⁰· 101   New York, 20 October 1787.

My Lord

When I had the honor to send You the translation of the new System of Government proposed by the Philadelphia Convention, I could not permit myself, without much presumption, the least remark regarding a document, the composition of which has occupied the most enlightened and most able men of this continent for several months. I impose upon myself today the difficult task of indicating the perfections and the inconveniences of this new plan, of which I already had the honor to give You a summary in my Despatch N⁰· 91 before the Convention had commenced its sessions. The gazettes that I have the honor to send You will sufficiently apprise You of all that the spirit of party produces daily on both sides in order to propagate the alliance or to solicit public praise. It is my duty to present to You, under a less illusory point of view, the true state of affairs.

On one hand, *strength and national reputation*, on the other, *civil and political liberty*, give to the new Constitution a favorable or alarming aspect.

A President, invested with the most extensive executive powers, commander in chief of the land and sea forces, disposing in concert with the Senate of the most important Offices both civil and military, elected for four years and capable of being reelected for life – a Congress composed of two chambers, enjoying the *exclusive* right to impose taxes, excises, to contract loans, to establish Courts of Appeal and even inferior tribunals in the various States, to call out the militia and to have it march from one end of the Continent to the other, to raise an army, to fit out fleets – A Government that can efficaciously control the irregular proceedings of inferior Legislatures, prevent the creation of paper money and the legal injustices of debtor States, unite in one center the interests and the force of this great empire, regulate Commerce as much with foreign nations as between individual States, make the national flag respected abroad, repay the public creditors, and restore to the full the good faith, the justice, the probity of the United States – This Government should excite the enthusiasm of all those who desire only the aggrandizement and prosperity of their native land. In fact, Congress will be able, without exacting great sacrifices from the people, to pay the public debts and to render itself formidable in America and in Europe; it will be able to conclude infinitely advantageous treaties with foreign nations, and especially to protect the property of individuals, which it has never been able to do since the revolution, and if liberty consists not only of obeying only the law, but of obeying only just and equitable laws, the proposed Government appears to lead more immediately to liberty. All those who have some property, and this number is very considerable in America, ardently desire the establishment of the new Constitution; they represent it as the only means to remedy the present anarchy; they appear to have no doubt of seeing it adopted by the people, and they are already speaking of General Washington as the only man capable of fulfilling with dignity the important office of President of the United States.

While admiring the wisdom, the foresight, and the talents of those who have projected this new plan, while even agreeing with them that nothing could give more renown to the United States at this moment, I cannot prevent myself, My Lord, from submitting to You the reflections of those who consider this plan only from the point of view of the *public liberty*.

"They think they have sufficiently balanced," they say, "the powers between the President, the Senate, and the House of Representatives by making them like the King of England, the House of Lords, and the House of Commons; but the latter are political personages essentially different in their birth, their rights, their riches, and especially in public opinion, while in America the difference will ever be only nominal and, very far from balancing each other, the three bodies will shortly combine, either to maintain their positions, to have their friends named thereto, to enrich themselves at the expense of the public, or to encroach upon the liberty of their Fellow Citizens. To move an immense mass they will need immense means, and what will become of these means when they are all concentrated in one single body? — It is true that the President will only be elected for four years, the Senator only for six, the Representative only for two, but they will still be *eligible*; might not the elections be bought, as in England, especially when one may dispose of the public treasury at one's pleasure? – The appointments of the President, of the Senate, of the lower Chamber will be fixed by themselves; who can prevent them from augmenting them to infinity? – Congress will have the right to indicate the place of elections; will it not give preference to a city that is particularly devoted to it? – The lower Chamber has the right to impeach a public officer before the Senate, that is to say, before his equals, before men equally interested in destroying all those who are opposed to usurpation! Another poor imitation of the English Constitution. In Great Britain, a coalition between the Lords and the Commons is almost impossible; in America, it will be completely natural between the Senators and the Representatives. – Each House will judge the qualifications of its Members and of the elections; it can therefore reject all those who do not share its views; would it wish to admit a Doria?[1] – Congress will be able to raise armies and fit out fleets; will it not be as interested as the Roman Senate in instigating wars in order to support many troops and to employ them later in the destruction of liberty? – Congress will establish such a tax as it judges appropriate; it will levy imposts, it will contract loans; will not the sums raised serve to corrupt elections? To whom will an accounting of the sums raised be rendered? To the people? It will have a good part of the spoils. – Congress will suspend the act of *habeas corpus* in case of rebellion; but if this rebellion is only a resistance to usurpation, who will be the judge of it? The usurper. – The Constitution is not even accompanied by a *Declaration of rights*, so that there remains to the citizen no recourse against oppression. It is the same with the States; since the Constitution does not permit them to conclude treaties, to be in league among themselves, to issue paper money, to raise troops or levy imposts without the consent of Congress. In England, the right of resistance is part of the constitution, here it is not even mentioned. – All civil cases will be decided in the Supreme Court without the participation of Juries; but the Judges will be named by Congress; what a way to unjustly apply unjust laws! – Congress will have an independent territory of ten thousand *quarrés*,[2] it can establish forts, magazines, dockyards there, it can purchase neighboring territories in order to construct other forts &c[a.] There the President will have all the trappings of a sovereign; at the end of four years, it will be difficult for him to descend into the common herd, to abandon the command of a fleet and an army, all the officers of which have been appointed and commissioned by him, and who consequently will be considered as attached to his person. He will receive and appoint Ambassadors, he will conclude treaties with the consent of two-thirds of the Senate, he will convoke Congress at least once a year; but if he does not convoke it, if like Cromwell[3] he chooses a certain number of his creatures to govern tyrannically; where is the remedy?"

Several of these objections, My Lord, evidently contradict themselves. Some imply a coalition among the three branches, others a decided preponderance by the President or by Congress. As for the two chambers, the balance is really ideal, and their interests should always be the same, unless one thinks that the Senate will lean rather to the side of the President, with whom it is more directly in correspondence. But what will give a surprising vigor to the new Government is that Congress reserves to itself the right to establish supreme courts of appeal, which will take cognizance in the first instance of all cases relative to the law of nations or to the public law of the United States, and in general of *all cases that may arise under this Constitution*; they will even have the right to endorse the laws passed in the various States. The power of individual Legislatures will therefore be limited to regulating their internal police; they will resemble corporations rather than sovereign assemblies. Several persons are even of the opinion that they have still been allowed too much authority and that the people cannot be prevented from regarding them as more direct and more faithful representatives than those who are in Congress.

It would perhaps be interesting to examine whether, in the midst of peace and without any urgent necessity, it is prudent for the confederated republics to unite all their rights and powers in one center and to elect as powerful an officer as the President of the United States will be. I must leave this task, which is foreign to me, to more capable pens.

I am with a profound respect My Lord Your most humble and most obedient servant   Otto.

FFAA: Pol. Corr., U.S., v. 32, f. 375-380 (LC transcription).

¹ *Doria, Andrea (1468?-1560). Genoese admiral and political figure. Commanded French fleet against that of Charles V, 1524-1528. Transferred allegiance to Charles V, 1528. Captured Genoa, 1528, and set up new form of government, in which he held the title of Doge. Defeated Turks at Patras, 1532. Captured Tunis, 1535.*

² *An obsolete French unit of land measurement. The District of Columbia, as originally laid out, comprised ten miles square or 100 square miles.*

³ *Cromwell, Oliver (1599-1658). British military leader and political figure. Protector, 1653-1658.*

Louis Guillaume Otto to Comte de Montmorin

[Translation]

Nᵒ· 102.   New York, 23 October 1787.

My Lord

The dissolution of the General Convention having caused a great number of members of Congress to return to New York, that Assembly has again taken up its sessions. It began by debating the plan of the new Government, but perceiving that the opposition was very strong, it limited itself to sending that plan to the various States without either approving or disapproving it. It is a surprise to see that Congress itself is not agreed on the great powers that it is a question of giving to it. Mr. Richard Henry Lee, the former President, is at the head of the opposition. Although elected a member of the Philadelphia Convention, he continually refused to go there. He does not find the situation of the United States to be so desperate that one needs to have recourse to violent remedies; he disapproves especially that an immense power has been accorded to the Government without having the Constitution preceded by a *Declaration of rights*, which has always been regarded as the palladium of a free people: "If", he says, "instead of a virtuous and patriotic President we are given a William V,[1] what will become of liberty? How prevent usurpation? Where is the Contract between the nation and the Government? The Constitution makes mention only of those who govern, never of the rights of the people governed." – This new Gracchus,[2] My Lord, has all the talents necessary to make an impression; he has against him men equally distinguished by their merit, their knowledge, their services; but he pleads the cause of the people.

Whatever may be the determination of the States, My Lord, the present Congress continues its ordinary occupations. It has just sent the States new requisitions for the Sum of three million piastres, it particularly mentions the interest due in Holland, and it prohibits the funds that are destined for there to be employed in any other manner. The Continental Treasury is so exhausted that the Commissioners do not know how to satisfy the most pressing needs. The moment of efficaciously presenting His Majesty's letters of credence has still not come; from that point of view, the proposed Government would certainly be more favorable to us.

General St. Clair, the current President of Congress, has just been named Governor of the western regions; the other civil Officers have also been elected and are on the point of going to their destinations. Several army officers and a great number of Adventurers are eager to form settlements there; the excess population of the Northern States and all the malcontents are repairing thence in crowds, and the banks of the Ohio will soon be covered with plantations. The authority of Congress will be upheld there by a body of troops that the proximity and the depredations of the Savages render indispensable, and this Assembly will probably be more respected there than in its own homes.

I am with a profound respect My Lord Your most humble and most obedient servant.   Otto.

FFAA: Pol. Corr., U.S., v. 32, f. 381-382vo. (LC transcription).
   [1] A reference to *Willem V, Prince of Orange and Nassau (1748-1806), who was Stadhouder of the United Provinces of the Netherlands, 1751-1795, and whom the Prussians 1787 supported in suppressing the pro-French Patriot party.*

² *Gracchus, Tiberius Sempronius (163-133 BC), and Gaius Sempronius (153-121 BC). Roman political figures. Tiberius, as tribune of the people, in 133 BC, tried to restore the class of small farmers by limiting the amount of public land a citizen might occupy and sponsoring a greater subdivision of lands. Gaius, as tribune of the people, in 123-122 BC, proposed to replace the existing aristocratic government with a democratic one, and advocated the extension of Roman citizenship to the Latins. Both brothers were killed in riots.*

John Jay to Thomas Jefferson

Dʳ Sir   [New York] Office for foreign Affairs 24ᵗʰ October 1787

.   .   .   .   .

Although the Opinion of the most judicious and well informed seems to be that France and Britain will avoid War, and unite their Councils and their Efforts to preserve Peace, yet as great Events are often produced by latent and little Circumstances, especially between Courts who distrust each other, I should not be surprized if notwithstanding their Wishes to the contrary, something should happen to frustrate their pacific Designs. –

You will receive herewith enclosed, two Letters from me dated the 27ᵗʰ July concerning the Consular Convention, with a Commission to you to form one; and also a certified Copy of an Act of Congress of the 23ᵈ July on the Subject of the Morocco Treaty & Papers. The want of a safe and private Conveyance has until now delayed the Transmission of these Letters and this Act....

.   .   .   .   .

The Number of States represented in Congress almost daily diminishes, and I much fear will soon be so reduced as not to leave them in Capacity to despatch any Business requiring nine. –

Congress has been pleased to comply with the Request of Mʳ Adams to return, and I enclose a Copy of their Act on that Head. –

As yet I am not authorized to say any Thing relative to the proposed Post-Office Convention. A Report on that Subject has lain for many Months before Congress, and still remains undecided. –

What will be the Fate of the new Constitution, as it is called, cannot easily be conjectured – at present the Majority seems to be in Favor of it; but there will probably be a strong Opposition in some of the States, particularly in this and Pensylvania. –

I have the Honor to be with great Esteem & Regard &c.

John Jay.–

NA: PCC, *item 121, pp. 285-288 (LBkC); M61, reel 1.*

John Adams to Hendrik Fagel

Sir.   London october 25. 1787.

I have received the Letter you did me the honor to write me on the eighteenth of october instant, and am extreamly sorry to learn, that the Conduct of Mʳ Dumas has not the approbation of their High Mightinesses.

As Mʳ Dumas has not that I recollect, been employed in any business by me, since my residence in England and as he has neither given me any Account of his proceedings nor transmitted his dispatches to Congress through my hands, I am ignorant of the particulars of his Conduct, which are not approved by their High Mightinesses.

I have had so large experience of the friendship of their High Mightinesses to the United States of America my sovereign, and of their Candour and Goodness towards myself, that I should not hesitate to comply with whatever I should know to be their inclination in any thing within my power, and consistent with my honor and my duty but as all the authority by which Mʳ Dumas acts, under the United States is derived directly from Congress and not from me, and as he carries on his Correspondence with that August Body by means of their Ministers at New York and not with me, it is not in my power to do more at this time, in Complyance with the requisition of their High Mightinesses, signified to me in your Letter, than to transmit a Copy of it to Congress, which shall be done by the earliest opportunity.

With great regard I have the honor to be Sir – Your most obedient & most Humble Servant   John Adams

NA: PCC, *item 84, v. 6, pp. 555-556 (C); M247, reel 113.*

Louis Guillaume Otto to Comte de Montmorin

[Translation]

Nᵒˑ 103.   New York, 25 October 1787
My Lord.

In my Despatch Nᵒˑ 89 I had the honor to submit to You a question that was raised concerning exemption from the *right of Escheat** in the French Colonies. I have since received a letter from the Administrators of St. Domingue, an Extract of which I have the honor to enclose here. It leaves no doubt regarding the law established there, but it does not satisfy the Americans who pursue Commerce there. As the Right of Escheat is unknown among them, they could not offer an equivalent for the exemption that His Majesty might judge appropriate to grant them, but the example of several free ports, such as Marseilles and Dunkirk, which have obtained this exemption at different times in favor of all Nations, makes them hope that the same principles could be applied to the ports of deposit that have been opened to them in our Islands. It does not behoove me, My Lord, to discuss this question, but I think I must submit it to Your consideration.

I am with a profound respect My Lord Your most humble and most obedient servant   Otto.
* Droit d'Aubaine

FFAA: Pol. Corr., U.S., v. 32, f. 383-383vo. (LC transcription).

John Adams to Thomas Jefferson

Dear Sir   London Oct. 28. 1787

. . . . .

I can tell you nothing of Politicks. All the World is astonished at the Secrecy of Mr. Pitt. – Great Preparations for War, yet the World can find no Ennemy nor Object. Carmarthen "hopes the Scudd will blow over, and even that the Quarrell between the Port and Russia will be made up. While a Fire is burning in any quarter of Europe, no one can tell when or where it may Spread." The General Understanding is that the U.S. are to be let alone, and they have given general orders to the Navy, to let American Vessells and Seamen alone. They will have their hands full, I believe, and there is little Plunder to be made of Americans, So that We may be quiet, – as long as they will let Us. – But our Countrymen will do well to think of the Possibility of Danger and of the means of Defence. a War would cost Us more than We have of Cash or Credit, but if We Should be attacked We must defend, Money or no Money, Credit or no Credit. – Whether John Bull, has Command enough of his Passions to See Us punctually fullfill our Treaties, as We must do, without being transported with rage, you who know him can tell as well as I. – We know this Gentlemans hasty Temper so well that I think We may very Safely wish for the Continuance of Peace, between France and him, even upon Selfish Principles, tho our Commerce & Navigation would be greatly promoted by a War, if We can keep out of it.

I tremble and agonize for the Suffering Patriots in Holland. You may judge to what L[en]gths the Spirit extends against them by a formal Compl[aint] of their High Mightinesses against Dumas, and a Requisi[ti]on to me, to employ him no longer but to appoint Some other Person in my Absence. it is not, I am well persuaded as Agent for the United States, but as a Friend of France or of the Patriotic Party against the Statholder, that he has unfortunately incurred this Censure & Displeasure. Yet as Mr Dumas holds not his Character or Authority from me, I can do nothing, but transmit the Papers to Congress.

With great Esteem, I have the honour to be dear Sir, your most obedient Servant   John Adams

LC: Jefferson Papers, microfilm reel 8 (ALS).

John Jay to Thomas Jefferson

Dʳ Sir   [New York] Office for foreign Affairs 3ᵈ November 1787
                        .   .   .   .

Advices from Georgia represent that State as much distressed by the Indians. It is said that the Apprehensions of the People there are so greatly alarmed that they are even fortifying Savannah. There doubtless is Reason to fear that their frontier Settlements will be ravaged. The Indians are numerous and they are exasperated, and will probably be put to no Difficulties on Account of military Stores. These Embarrassments result from want of a proper Government, to guard good Faith and punish Violations of it. –

With very sincere Esteem and Regard I have the Honor to be &ca:
                                                    John Jay.–
NA: PCC, item 121, p. 291 (LBkC); M61, reel 1.

Thomas Jefferson to John Jay

Sir   Paris Nov. 3. 1787.
                        .   .   .   .

...I am satisfied the king of England beleives the mass of our people to be tired of their independance, & desirous of returning under his government: and that the same opinion prevails in the ministry & nation. they have hired their newswriters to repeat this lie in their gazettes so long that they have become the dupes of it themselves. but there is no occasion to recur to this in order to account for their arming. a more rational purpose avowed, that purpose executed, and, when executed, a solemn agreement to disarm, seem to leave no doubt that the reestablishment of the Stadtholder was their object. yet it is possible that, having found that this court will not make war in this moment for any ally, new views may arise; and they may think the moment favorable for executing any < * > purpose they may have in our quarter. add to this that reason is no aid in calculating their movements. we are therefore never safe till our magazines are filled with arms. the present season of truce or peace should in my opinion be improved without a moment's respite to effect this essential object, & no means be omitted by which money may be obtained for the purpose. I say this however with due deference to the opinion of Congress, who are better judges of the necessity & practicability of the measure.

I mentioned to you in a former letter the application I had made to the Dutch Ambassadors and Prussian envoy for the protection of mr Dumas. the latter soon after received an assurance that he was put under the protection of the states of Holland: and the Dutch Ambassador called on me a few days ago to inform me by instruction from his consituents "that the States General had received a written application from mr Adams, praying their protection of Dumas: that they had instructed their greffier Fagel to assure mr Adams by letter that he was under the protection of the states of Holland, but to inform him at the same time that mr Dumas's conduct, out of the line of his office, had been so extraordinary, that they would expect *de l'honnetete de* M. Adams,[1] that he would charge some other person with the affairs of the United States, during his absence."

. . . . .

I have the honour to inclose you a letter from Obrian to me containing information from Algiers, and one from mr Montgomery at Alicant. the purpose of sending you this last is to shew you how much the difficulties of ransom are increased since the Spanish negotiations. the Russian captives have cost about 8000 livres a peice on an average. I certainly have no idea that we should give any such sum: and therefore if it would be the sense of Congress to give such a price, I would be glad to know it by instruction. my idea is that we should not ransom but on the footing of the nation which pays least, that it may be as little worth their while to go in pursuit of us as any nation. this is cruelty to the individuals now in captivity, but kindness to the hundreds that would soon be so, were we to make it worth the while of those pyrates to go out of the streights in quest of us. as soon as money is provided I shall put this business into train. I have taken measures to damp at Algiers all expectations of our proposing to ransom at any price. I feel the distress which this must occasion to our countrymen there, & their connections: but the object of it is their ultimate good, by bringing down their holders to such a price as we ought to pay: instead of letting them remain in such expecations as cannot be gratified. the gazettes of France & Leyden accompany this. I have the honour to be,with sentiments of the most...
                                                                    Th: Jefferson

LC: *Jefferson Papers, microfilm reel 8 (press copy).*
  [1] *as a courtesy from Mr. Adams.*

Thomas Jefferson to John Jay

Private   Paris Nov. 3. 1787.
Sir

I shall take the liberty of confiding sometimes to a private letter such details of the small history of the court or cabinet as may be worthy of being known, and yet not proper to be publicly communicated. I doubt whether the administration is yet in a permanent form. the Count de Monmorin & Baron de Breteuil are I believe firm enough in their places. it was doubted whether they would wait for the count de la Luzerne, if the war had taken place: but at present I suppose they will. I wish it also; because M de Hector,[1] his only competitor, has on some occasions shewn little value for the connection with us. Lambert, the Comptroller general is thought to be very insecure. I should be sorry also to lose him. I have worked several days with him, the M. de la Fayette, and Monsr duPont[2] (father of the young gentleman[3] gone to America with the Count de Moustier) to reduce into one arret whatever concerned our commerce. I have found him a man of great judgment & application, possessing good general principles on subjects of commerce, & friendly dispositions towards us. he passed the arret in a very favorable form, but it has been opposed in the council, & will I fear suffer some alteration in the article of whale oil. that of tobacco, which was put into a separate instrument, experiences difficulties also, which do not come from him. Mr duPont has rendered us essential services on these occasions. I wish his son could be so well noticed as to make a favorable report to his father; he would I think be gratified by it, & his good dispositions be strengthened, & rendered further useful to us. whether I shall be able to send you these regulations by the present packet, will depend on their getting thro' the council in time....

.   .   .   .   .

I have the honour to be with very sincere esteem & respect, Dear Sir, your most obedient & most humble servant   Th: Jefferson

LC: *Jefferson Papers, microfilm reel 8 (press copy).*
[1] *Hector, Jean Charles, Comte d'. Not further identified.*
[2] *Du Pont de Nemours, Pierre Samuel (1739-1817). French economist; a disciple of François Quesnay, and a leading Physiocrat. Assisted Vergennes in peace negotiations of 1782-1783; involved in financial aspects of Franco-American commerce in the last years of the Old Regime. Member, Estates-General, 1789. Imprisoned for reactionary views, 1792. Emigrated to the United States, 1799; returned to France, 1802. Secretary to provisional government, 1814. Again emigrated to the United States, 1815.*

[3] Du Pont, Victor Marie (1767-1827). French diplomat. Attached to the Comte de Moustier's legation in the United States, 1787-1789. Aide-de-camp to Lafayette, 1789-1791. Second secretary of French legation in the United States, 1791-1792; first secretary, 1795-1796. Settled in United States, 1800.

Peter Allaire: Occurrences
from 5 October to 6 November 1787

New York 6 November 1787

. . . . .

The Ship *Columbia* Burthen 220 Tons, and Sloop *Lady Washington* Burthen 90 Tons, Commanded by Captain John Kendricks,[1] and Cap[n] R. Gray[2] Sail'd the 10th October from Boston, with Letters from Congress for a Trading Voyage to the North West part of America & Kamshatka

Congress have appointed Arthur S[t] Clair, (the late President of Congress) Governor of the Western Territory & Samuel Holmes Parsons[3] Cheif Justice.

Also that a General Treaty be held with the Tribes of Indians, within the Limits of the United States Inhabiting the Country, N W of the Ohio, and About Lake Irie as soon after the first of April next as conveniently may be, and at such place, and at such particular time as the Governor of the Western Territory shall Appoint, for the purposes of knowing the Causes of uneasiness amongst the said Tribes, and hearing their Complaints, of Regulating Trade, and Amicably setling all Affairs concerning Lands & Boundaries, between them and the United States.

That the said Governor of the Western Territory, hold the said Treaty, Agreeable to such Instructions as shall be given him for that purpose.

All the Tribes of Indians, inhabiting the back part of Georgia South & North Carolina & Virginia, have Declared War against the United States, the Militia of Georgia, and out against them to the Numbers of Eight Hundred, the Militia of the Carolinas have sent about Seven hundred & the Virginia Volunteers, under the Command of General Cook & General Kennedy[4] are upwards of 1700, the Indians have killed & destroyed upwards of One Hundred Families and their Plantations and taken away their Cattle, they have Murthered Major Holland his Son and thirty Men, Cap Davenport and five Men; the different Parties of Militia & Volunteers have killed 29 Indians and supposed to have wounded thirty: they fell in with a large party of Indians, who were defeated & left on the field of Battle, 2. Guns, 32 Brass Kettles, 87 large Packs of Blankets 100 Bridles & Halters, but they had carried off the dead & wounded.

The People of the Western Territories, having made Repeated complaints to Congress of the Grievances they sustained from the Spaniards without any notice having been taken, the State of Franklin have come to the following Resolution, that having made frequent complaints of the hostile behaviour of his Catholick Majestys Subjects in the Floridas & Louisiana, towards the good Citizens of this State, by Credible Evidences & Authentic papers, by Persons Acting under Authority of his Catholick Majesty's Governor, and notwithstanding many & Repeated Remonstrances have been made both to Congress and his Catholick Majesty's Governors to remove those Grievances, they have remained deaf to our just demands, therefore the Assembly have thought proper to put a stop to those depredations, and have Ordered Twelve hundred Men to be Embodied; (previous to this Resolution they had procured Arms, Amunition & Clothing.)

．　　．　　．　　．

Mr Van Berckell Minister from the United Netherlands has delivered to Congress a Memorial, complaining of an Act of the Common Wealth of Virginia, exempting French Brandies, imported in French & American Bottoms from certain duties, to which the like commodities imported in Dutch Vessells are left liable, as being Contrary to the second Article in their Treaty with the United States, stipulating that they should be treated as the most favoured Nation.

In Congress Resolved that a Copy of the Representation of the Minister of the United Netherlands be transmitted to the Commonwealth of Virginia, to the end that the Legislature of that commonwealth may take the earliest Oppertunity of revising the Act of which the said Minister complains & rendering the same perfectly consistent with the Treaty subsisting between the United States & the United Netherlands and of Causing to be repaid, whatever extra duties may in Virtue of the said Act have been exacted on the Brandies there imported in Dutch Vessells during the Operation of the same.

Resolved That whenever any State shall think proper to grant a favor to any Foreign Nation, such State ought to extend it to such other Foreign Nations, as by Treaties with the United States, are to be treated as the most favoured Nation.

．　　．　　．　　．

I have the honor to be Genl Your Most Ob^t Servt　　　　PA
R. 8th Decr 1787.

PRO: FO 4/5, pp. 677-692 (LC transcription).

[1] Kendrick, John (ca. 1740-1794). Massachusetts navigator and trader. Commanded privateers Fanny, 1777; Count D'Estaing, 1778; and Marianne, 1780. Commanded the expedition of the Columbia and the Lady Washington which left Boston in September

1787 and reached Nootka Sound in 1788. Exchanging ships with Robert Gray, July 1789, Kendrick proceeded to lay the foundations for a triangular trade between Boston, the Northwest Coast, and China, based upon the sale of sea-otter pelts at Canton.

² *Gray, Robert (1755-1806). Navigator, fur trader, discover. Captain of the sloop Lady Washington, which left Boston in September 1787 in company with the ship Columbia, captained by John Kendrick, on a voyage of trade and discovery to the Northwest Coast. In July 1789, Gray took command of the Columbia and proceeded to Canton to sell the expedition's sea-otter skins, returning to Boston in August 1790. After a short refit, Gray again sailed for the Northwest Coast, reaching Vancouver Island in June 1791. In May 1792, he sailed the Columbia into the river which bears her name, also discovering Gray's Harbor. After another visit to Canton, he returned to Boston in July 1793.*

³ *Parsons, Samuel Holden (1737-1789). Connecticut lawyer and military figure. Member, Connecticut general assembly, 1762-1774. Colonel, 6th Connecticut Regiment, 1775-1776. Brigadier general, Continental Army, August 1776. Commander, Connecticut division, 1779-1782, with secret service responsibilities. Major general, October 1780. Appointed commissioner to resolve Indian claims to the territory northwest of the Ohio River, September 1785. First judge of the Northwest Territory, 1787-1789.*

⁴ *Not further identified.*

Louis Guillaume Otto to Comte de Montmorin

[Translation]

Nᵒ· 104.   New York, 10 Nov. 1787.

My Lord.

In consequence of the Treaty of peace which assures the United States all the territory on this side of the Mississippi to the 31ˢᵗ· degree, the Georgians believe themselves authorized to take possession of a part of the territory of the Creeks, one of the most powerful nations of the interior, and whose proximity to the Spaniards has rendered them more daring, and although they have concluded boundary treaties with these savages, they have not been very scrupulous in observing them. Congress, wishing to prevent the disorder that these encroachments must necessarily occasion, and regarding the territory in dispute as belonging to the confederation, proposed to the Georgians at various times to settle the differences that have arisen with the Creeks itself, and with this in view recently sent a Commissioner to the Creeks, who was received in the most amicable manner. The Chiefs of these Savages declared to him "that they entrusted their interests with confidence to the decision of the Great Council of the thirteen fires of America, that according to agreements made previously with England the Georgians could only claim from the coast up to the point in the Savannah River reached by the tide; that a claimed cession made by Great Britain in the last treaty of peace was alleged in vain, since the lands in question had never belonged to the King their father, who was far from trespassing against his dear children on this point; that Twenty-four nations had held a general Assembly at Detroit, and that they had resolved there not to permit the encroachments of the *Long Knives*." The Commissioner of Congress assured them of the good intentions and of the protection of the United States and exhorted them to peace. But after his departure, hostilities began again on the frontier. The Georgians will regard the interposition of Congress as unconstitutional or at least as useless; they believed themselves strong enough to subjugate the Creeks, but they are beginning to perceive the unfortunate consequences of their presumption. Their former territory has been devastated in large part, and it is to be feared that the savages will seize their negroes and send them to be sold in Florida, as they have already done on other occasions.

This State, My Lord, also finds itself somewhat in conflict with the Government of East Florida. One of its Delegates has addressed himself to M. de Gardoqui to represent to him that the inhabitants of that Colony protected and encouraged runaway negroes from Georgia. That Minister replied to him that he had received complaints of the same nature from the Governor of St. Augustine; but that these difficulties could not be removed unless by an amicable arrangement between the two nations. "It is for this salutary result," he continued, "that I am come to this country, that I have spent two and a half years here, and You should know perfectly well that it is not I who has delayed success."

Some persons have observed that an individual Delegate has no right to deal with a foreign Minister accredited to Congress and that M. de Gardoqui could have dispensed with replying to him.

Although the circumspection and the justice of Congress have earned it the friendship of most of the savage nations, it has just renewed the engagements of the 700 men posted on the Ohio to protect the new settlements. Several companies have been formed, particularly in New England, which purchase entire districts of several million acres from Congress; they admit shareholders on all sides, and as the payments must be made in Continental loan paper, several French owners of these bills are associated with them. An acre sells for a Sum equivalent to three Livres tournois. A very large settlement is going to be established on the Mississippi between the Illinois River and that of the Kaskaskias; they plan to build a town almost across from the Missouri, whither they reckon to attract all the fur Trade that descends that great river. There is always a little of the miraculous in these plans, but there is perhaps no civilized nation that changes place of residence more easily than the Americans, and that establishes settlements more rapidly. A society that has just been incorporated in Massachusetts to send missions among the Savages cannot but facilitate the first clearings for these new Colonies. It has been remarked in Pennsylvania that Quaker Savages became good citizens, industrious and sedentary, and by expanding Christianity among these tribes one can always expect to soften their manners.

By encouraging these new settlements, My Lord, a great service is no doubt rendered to humanity, but it would perhaps have been more politic of the United States to make itself as compact as possible by tightening its borders on the West. The System of taxation that is necessarily linked to the new Constitution which it is a question of introducing will gradually induce the inhabitants to breathe a freer air on the banks of the Ohio, where the richness and the abundance of the lands will easily repay the costs and difficulties of clearing it. Moreover, it is only in these Regions that they will be entirely sheltered from all foreign invasion, and that the greatest revolutions in other parts of the world can only touch them feebly. This state of affairs would certainly be very desirable if the United States wanted to limit themselves to following their natural intention, which is Agriculture; but this constant emigration toward the western Regions accords little with the principles of a nation which aspires to play a distinguished role from this moment on, to fit out fleets, to extend its commerce to the extremities of Asia, to found manufactories, and to share with the European nations the benefits which they extract from their Colonies.

I am with a profound respect My Lord Your most humble and most obedient Servant   Otto
rec. 21 Jan.ʳ 1788

FFAA: Pol. Corr., U.S., v. 32, f. 394-397 (LC transcription).

Sir John Temple to John Jay

Sir.   New York 10ᵗʰ Novemʳ 1787.
The inclosed petition with the documents annexed to it, from Richard Lawrence an American loyalist to the King my Sovereign, I had the honour to receive by the last packet from England, together with his Majesty's commands, signified to me by one of his principal secretaries of State, that I should make enquiry into the circumstances of said petitioner's case; and, if I should find him justly entitled to the benefit he claims, under the stipulation of the sixth article of the definitive treaty between his Majesty, and the United States of America, I should make the strongest representations to Congress for his being immediately set at liberty, and full restitution made to him of such property as he may have been unjustly

deprived of, together with such further satisfaction as the nature of his case may justify me in soliciting: To which purpose, Sir, will you permit me to request, that the said petition, together with his Majesty's commands so signified to me, may be laid before Congress as soon as may be after that honourable body shall re-assemble to do business? In the mean time I am so confident of your humanity, as well as of your justice, that I have not even the least doubt you will do all that may be in your power, during the present recess of Congress, to mitigate the distresses of the said petitioner now or late a prisoner in the Jail of this city.

I have the honour to be, with very great regard and esteem, Sir, Your most Obedient and most humble Servant   J. Temple

NA: PCC, *item 92, pp. 524-525 (LS); M24, reel 120.*

Martin Oster to
Governor Edmund Randolph of Virginia

Sir   Norfolk, 11th Novem[r.] 1787
The 2[d] of last month I had the honor of giving you an Account of the motives which determined me to act with Severity against a French Captain named Joseph Marie Anne Ferrier & as this criminal had accomplices, that it was my duty to search them out: I at the same time requested that Your Excellency would be pleased to grant me the necessary orders to claim them & arrest them in whatever district of the State they might be found.

My letter to Y[r] Excel[y] on this Subject being still unanswered, not knowing whether the Honorable Council have any reasons why they should not grant my request; & it being necessary on this occasion to justify my Conduct, I once more take the liberty Sir to request that you will be so good as to grant me the order mentioned in my aforesaid letter & if there is no objection against its being made out for me, I beg that you will include therein Cap[t.] Ferrier who was taken from his prison by Surprize & liberated the 7th instant by virtue of a Simple Writ obtained by a person called Breton, on an ill-founded claim for 50 pounds.

This Surprize having happened on board a French Vessel & thro' a frivolous pretext, it cannot be dissembled that it is absolutely contrary to good order, to the confidence, & security of commerce which nations closely united by solemn treaties are interested in supporting & encouraging in their respective possessions. It is accordingly in consequence of these principles that in quality of His Majestys Vice Consul in the Republic of Virginia I take the first oppertunity of complaining to Your Excellency on this Subject & of claiming in the strongest terms Your good offices & authority, that on such occasions in future, measures may be adopted as will not counteract the functions entrusted to me respecting the French Subjects depending on my Vice Consulate & particularly Such as are criminal & within my power, as was Captain Ferrier.

"Agreable to all publications on the Subject of Rights of nations allied in a double point of view, such as France & the U^d States happily are, Capt. Ferrier ought never to have been entirely withdrawn from under my dependance. As a Criminal & publicly acknowledged such, the Sheriff who took him instead of giving him his liberty with Bail & without any particular reason, ought to have held him a prisoner in the prison of the Country & to have kept him there untill he had satisfied his engagements & afterwards returned him to me. This Officer should the rather have acted in this manner as he knew that I had obtained permission from the chief Magistrate in Norfolk to apprehend the criminal.

This Opinion which arises from the principles of that Justice which nations ought to cultivate & which is the Basis of all Society, as well as the safest bond of Commerce; I am persuaded that Y^r Excell^y will think so likewise & grant that without this Virtue which ought to be respected – Human Society w^d degenerate to a Band of Ruffians.

Such Sir are the reasons on which I found the claim which I take the liberty of now making on your Authority & influence in order to prevent in future thro' frivolous pretexts, that the Law respecting debtors be not used in favor of French transgressors who shall be found amenable to the ordinances of his Majesty, without infringing those of the Republic over which You with so much wisdom preside:

I have the honor &c^a   Oster
Faithfully translated from the Original by John Pintard.

NA: PCC, item 96, pp. 462-464 (translation); M247, reel 124.

Thomas Jefferson to John Adams

Dear Sir   Paris Nov. 13. 1787.

.   .   .   .   .

How do you like our new constitution? I confess there are things in it which stagger all my dispositions to subscribe to what such an assembly has proposed: the house of federal representatives will not be adequate to the management of affairs either foreign or federal. their President seems a bad edition of a Polish king. he may be reelected from 4. years to 4. years for life. reason & experience prove to us that a chief magistrate, so continuable, is an officer for life. when one or two generations shall have proved that this is an office for life, it becomes on every succession worthy of intrigue, of bribery, of force, & even of foreign interference. it will be of great consequence to France & England to have America governed by a Galloman or Angloman. once in office, & possessing the military force of the union, without either the aid or check of a council, he would not be easily dethroned, even if the people could be induced to withdraw their votes from him. I wish that at the end of the 4. years they had made him for ever ineligible a second time. indeed I think all the good of this new constitution might have been couched in three or four new articles to be added to the good, old, & venerable fabrick; which should have been preserved even as a religious relique....accept yourself assurances of the sincere esteem & respect with which I have the honour to be, Dear Sir, your friend & servant   Th: Jefferson

·   ·   ·   ·

MHS: *The Adams Papers, microfilm reel 370 (ALS).*

Thomas Jefferson to William Stephens Smith

Dear Sir   Paris Nov. 13. 1787.
...wonderful is the effect of impudent & persevering. lying. the British ministry have so long hired their gazetteers to repeat and model into every form lies about our being in anarchy, that the world has at length believed them, the English nation has believed them, the ministers themselves have come to believe them, & what is more wonderful, we have believed them ourselves. yet where does this anarchy exist? where did it ever exist, except in the single instance of Massachusets? and can history produce an instance of a rebellion so honourably conducted? I say nothing of it's motives. they were founded in ignorance, not wickedness. god forbid we should ever be 20. years without such a rebellion. the people can not be all, & always, well informed. the part which is wrong < * > will be discontented in proportion to the importance of the facts they misconceive; if they remain quiet under such misconceptions it is a lethargy, the forerunner of death to the public liberty. we have had 13. states independant 11. years. there has been one rebellion. that comes to one rebellion in a century & a half for each state. what country before ever existed a century & half without a rebellion? & what country can preserve it's liberties if their rulers are not warned from time to time that their people preserve the spirit of resistance? let them take arms. the remedy is to set them right as to facts, pardon & pacify them. what signify a few lives lost in a century or two? the tree of liberty must be refreshed from time to time with the blood of patriots & tyrants. it is it's natural manure. our Convention has been too much impressed by

the insurrection of Massachusets: and in the spur of the moment they are setting up a kite to keep the henyard in order. I hope in god this article will be rectified before the new constitution is accepted....present my respects to mrs. Smith, and be assured of the sincere esteem of Dear Sir Your friend & servant   Th: Jefferson

LC: *Jefferson Papers, microfilm reel 8 (press copy).*

Henry Knox to Josiah Harmar

Sir   [New York] 14th November 1787

My last Letter to you was dated on the 26th Ult. and enclosed a duplicate of mine to you of the 16th Ult., and also a Copy of a resolve of Congress of the 13th of the same Month directing you to apprehend John Sullivan styling himself late Captain 4th Regiment of light Dragoons, should he come within the federal Territory.

I now enclose a Copy of a Letter said to be written by John Sullivan to Major William Brown dated Charleston 24th September 1787. How far it may be practicable to execute the threats therein contained respecting New Orleans it is difficult, or rather impossible to judge at this distance and with the slender information I possess on the subject.

It has been reported generally that the inhabitants west of the Allegany Mountains have been highly irritated by the circulation of the idea that Congress were about to relinquish the navigation of the Missisippi for a number of years. Other reports also have been received that the inhabitants of Cumberland have talked in a vague manner of the practicability of seizing the Natches and New Orleans, and some unauthenticated publications have stated that there have been consultations on the subject by the inhabitants of Kentucky and Cumberland during the summer past. But nothing has been received that had the appearance of reducing these indistinct accounts to a probability, or of any system being formed to carry them into execution until Mr Sullivan's Letter was received. Indeed his Letter can be regarded only as an indication of his disposition, & not as an evidence of any fixed design on the subject. Such an enterprize would be in defiance of the Laws of Nations, disgraceful and perhaps ruinous to the Country by whose Citizens it should be attempted.

Although I cannot persuade myself that there can be any just foundation to apprehend that such a design is seriously entertained excepting by an insignificant banditti, yet circumstanced as the reports are, it becomes necessary that such precautions be taken on the part of the United States as the nature of the case may require and their means admit.

You will therefore on receiving this Letter endeavour to ascertain,

1st. Whether there is any plan formed or forming of the nature mentioned in Mr Sullivans Letter.

2d If so the numbers of the party and the names and characters of the most influential persons who are concerned in, or abet the design

3d When the design is intended to be executed and by what mode or route, and what means they can obtain for the purpose.

4th. How they are armed, accoutred, and supplied with Ammunition, and whether they have Cannon and the necessary apparatus.

5th. Endeavour particularly to discover whether any british Agents or means are employed on this occasion.

In order to obtain a satisfactory result to your enquiries, it may be necessary to send an officer or two, or other confidential persons to Franklin and Kentucky under the idea of exploring the Country, or you may adopt any other mode you may think proper.

Should such a design actually exist, suppose from an examination of the maps, that the easiest means of executing it would be by water. To prepare the Boats and Stores on the Cumberland river, and thence proceed into the Ohio and down the Missisippi. Were they to proceed from the bent of the Tenessee across by land, they would encouter difficulties from the nature of the Country (if my information be just) as well as from the powerful Tribes of the Choctows and Chickesaws.

I am desirous to have the tract of Country at the mouth of the Ohio surveyed agreeably to the enclosed resolution of Congress. The Officers and Soldiers of the late Army being exceedingly anxious to receive the Lands to which they are entitled. In order that the surveyors be completely protected in the execution of this business it will be necessary that you should station an adequate body of Troops in that vicinity. On this occasion you may think proper to post the greater part of the Troops employed in this service, at the place where Fort Massac stood below the junction of the Tenessee with the Ohio, or some other convenient spot not above the mouth of the Tenessee.

In case you shall receive such information on the subject as to remove all doubt that the design to which Mr Sullivan alludes is on the point of execution, you will form your post *below the Tenessee* of such strength if in your power, as will be able by force to prevent the passage of the party *down the Ohio.*

Previously to exerting actual force you will represent, on behalf of the United States, to the persons conducting the enterprize, the criminality of their conduct, and the obligations of the Sovereign authority to prevent at every hazard such audacious proceedings. Should however persuasions or other mild methods be ineffectual, you will then have recourse to the means in your power to prevent their proceeding in the execution of their design.

I am well aware that I am placing you in a delicate predicament. But there are points of duty which must be accomplished without regarding the consequences. I conceive my duty and my respect to the justice and dignity of the United States, oblige me to give you these orders which will be your justification. I am pursuaded you will conceive it to be your duty to execute them as far as it may be practicable.

But should you find from your enquiries that the design is still in embryo, and that the period of its accomplishment is at a distance, you will transmit me a full account of every circumstance relative to the subject, in order to be submitted to Congress.

It is unfortunate that Congress are not now in session. As soon as they assemble I shall submit a copy of this letter to them, together with any other papers which may be received relative to the subject.

Henry Knox[1]

• • • • •

NA: PCC, item 120, v. 3, pp. 436-440 (LBkC); M40, reel 3.

[1] Knox, Henry (1750-1806). Military leader and political figure. Initially a Massachusetts bookseller and self-trained artillerist, he directed the transfer of ordnance from Fort Ticonderoga to Boston in the winter of 1775-1776. As colonel, brigadier general, and major general, officer in charge of the Continental Army's artillery, 1775-1783. Massachusetts commissioner to treat with Penobscot Indians, 1784. Secretary at War, 1785-1794. Founder, Society of the Cincinnati, 1783.

William Carmichael to Thomas Jefferson

My Dear Sir   Sⁿ· Lorenzo 15 Novʳ 1787.

...I have had an oppertunity of seeing a letter written by Mʳ Eden to the British Minister here, breathing the most pacific Sentiments & Insinuating that G.B. was Sincerely disposed to contribute its Efforts with those of France & this court to pacify the Dispute in the North. Many Handsome things were said of the Cᵗ de Montmorin in this Letter, which were Intended to be conveyed to him thro me – You see that I take the hint. At the same time, altho' I feel the truth of the handsome things written on this Subject, I somewhat doubt the Sincerity of the Writer, as well on this point, as on the Intentions of his nation to cooperate with France in arranging the differences between the Russians & Turks. I know Mʳ Listons[1] Manner of thinking & mode of acting tolerably well. Indeed I beleive no one here knows him so well. This knowledge has been acquired by a particular coincidence of Circumstances, of a Nature not to be committed to paper, but which gave me an Oppertunity of seeing him under the various agitations of passions which developped his heart the weaknesses of which put him of[f] his guard – Late Conversations which I have had with him to which he gave the Lead & which he has renewed without appearing to intend it, have excited suspicions which may appear Groundless to those, to whom it is impossible to convey the many little circumstances which contribute to excite them. But last night He was more clear & explicit than I expected from his character. I had dined with the Sardinian Ambassador & played After Dinner, of course I staid much longer than I usually do. In the Afternoon he had been twice at my lodgings to look for me & left with my servant an Invitation to sup with him, which on returning home I declined, as I had some writing to occupy me. At near Eleven he came to me, And told me that as I would not Sup with him, he had come to eat his bread & cheese with me, & desired that we should be Alone. In a very short time with many professions of personal Friendship for me – He began on the present situation of Affairs, the probability & improbability of the duration of the Late Established Harmony – The designs of France by gaining over Holland to tye up the hands of that Country, which were rendered evident by their Attempts to engage this Country to acceed to their Treaty < *** > with the States & what think you, added he suddenly, of the article of their Treaty with you which excludes us from your ports in case of our being at War with France? To his remarks & his questions I gave such replies as I thought would contribute to a continuance of them. He then proceeded & said He knew the C^t· de Montmorin was an Able Minister, that Mr Eden perhaps had been deceived by him – that he knew the Former had very adroitly availed himself of *circumstances* to conciliate still more the Confidence of the King & Ministry here – That His C.M. had rec^d a Letter from the King of France expressive of his acknowledgements of the great services which the prudent counsels given by the Latter had rendered him, That this Language was held by the C^t· de Montmorin in the direct correspondence which he had with the C^t· de F.B. & added that I must be too well acquainted with the C^t· de Montmorins character & with what passed here not to know that this was the Line of his conduct. In my answers I continued to guard the same rule that I had laid down to myself, with as little deviation as possible, but by assenting or contradicting, provoking further explanations – You will please to observe, that what I have mentioned is the Substance of what I collected from his conversation, For it was carried on with much art on his part & very little on mine, for having no secrets to betray, I had nothing to apprehend. It became however more interesting – He has often mentioned to me how & where he would be probably employed when another replaces him here. His last Object was Russia – He now told me that as Mr Eden would not arrive here until the month of March & as of course he could not Leave this court until the others arrival, it was probable, that in the present critical Situation of Affairs at the Court of Petersburgh another would be sent thither – that he had rec^d hints that he might probably be sent to N. America, cited Mr Eden & shewed me a Letter from Mr Fraser which indicated Mr Pits intentions on this Subject – Some weeks ago he mentioned to me Mr Pits intentions of sending a Minister to America – He expressed his fears of not being well rec^d on acc^t of his being a Scotsman. These Apprehensions I removed; as I could easily do, for tho' Born in America, My Countrymen well knew that I was educated at Edinburgh – that his personal reception would depend on his own conduct & that his public would not certainly be influenced by any narrow or illiberal prejudices. I added that he knew that he might depend on all that I could do to render his personal residence agreable, but at the Same time I told him in a good humored manner that I should put Mr Jay on his guard, if I supposed that his instructions corresponded with the disposition which his Cabinet seamed to have manifested since the peace, which disposition I attributed to bad counsels & mistaken Interests. He returned to the Subject of the Article in our treaty with France before mentioned & said that while that subsisted he did not know how it was possible G.B. & A[merica] could be on Cordial terms. I replyed that as by the Letter he had shewn me, it Appeared that G.B. had the most pacific Intentions and As France by relinquishing what he supposed their designs upon Holland, manifested the same views, the Article ought to give no alarm. That England enjoyed the greatest Share of our Commerce Actually & that its own Interests well considered. they ought to give an extention to our Commerce instead of cramping it for such Conduct on their part would facilitate our payments for the produce which we rec^d from them & in proportion as that Commerce increased our Demands for the Manufactures & even Luxuries of England would augment. I made use of these Observations, because on many Occasions he himself had broached them. from France the Transition was not difficult to Spain. Our Treaty with this country was brought in question. He endeavoured to know whether Spain wished to Obtain an article in their Treaty with us of the same Nature as that in ours with France. on this Subject He could gain nothing from me. For altho' I am paid by the United states to serve them here I have never had any official Information since I have been their Chargé Des Affaires of the propositions made on [one] part or the Other, except what I have gathered by my own Application or if you please Address. I therefore entered into the history of Mr Gardoquis Nomination to America, of his being authorised to treat on the Spot, that of course his propositions were made to Congress thro' M^r· Jay – That he had seen himself how long the Treaty had been in agitation, without being concluded, & of course might draw his own consequences from this delay, one of which would surely meet his reflections, that the late menacing aspect of Affairs would rather accelerate than retard its conclusion. He seemed or appeared to seem Startled at this remark, but consoled himself with the Lenteurs of this court & the little share of capacity possessed as he insinuated by Gardoqui – He spoke in a different Style of the Minister named by France to replace the Chevalier de la Luzerne. In the course of this Conversation, which lasted till near three in the Morning, He inquired About the principal Characters in America, the Mode of Living &c &c and more than once seemed apprehensive that unless Speedy measures were taken by G.B to cultivate a good understanding between the two Countries, the Rising generation in America would be so prejudiced by their mode of Education & the remembrance of the recent horrors of the war, that an Effort for this purpose would become every day more difficult, if not Impracticable. I have judged it necessarey to submit to your consideration this Conversation which appears to me singular & which perhaps would equally Strike you, if I could as well convey the Manner as the Substance of it. Some things may have escaped my recollection, but I think you have the most material. There is an object which however it may be necessary to add. Speaking of our former trade in the Mediterranean, the profits of which I asserted, were ultimately vested in G.B. I could not refrain from reminding him of the conduct of a person Employed by the Court of G.B. who endeavoured by an Information given to the Dey, to have Mess⁺⁺ Lamb & Randall seized as well as the property they carried with them to Algiers. He with great Warmth denied that the British Government had ever countenanced such procedure & to convince me of his own Manner of thinking offered to shew me a copy of a Letter which he had written in the year 1785 [?] endeavouring to persuade the Ministry to favor our peace with the Emperor of Morrocco & thus to prevent the merit which Spain might claim from the Conduct he foresaw it would take in procuring us a treaty with that Country. I also discovered that the *Foreign Minister* whom you saw at Versailles & whom you recommended to me, has been artfully employed, without adverting to the consequences, to repeat to the C. de F B as an *impartial* Person, what Mͬ L—n suggested in favor of his Court & its conduct on the Late Occasion – He has been listened to with apparent Attention & marks of satisfaction & Approbation. As I am on Intimate terms with him, I have this night been informed by him of the Nature of his Late Conferences with the Minister which perfectly coincide with what I had learned from Mr. L—n –

.   .   .   .   .

With great esteem & Respect I have the honor to be Your Excellencys Obliged & Humble Serᵗ   Wᵐ Carmichael

LC: *Jefferson Papers*, microfilm reel 8 (ALS).
[1] Liston, Robert (1742-1836). *British diplomat. Minister to Spain, 1783-1788. Envoy to Sweden, 1789-1793. Ambassador to Turkey, 1794-1795. Minister to the United States, 1796-1800. Minister to the Batavian Republic, 1802-1803. Minister to Denmark, 1803-1804. Ambassador to Turkey, 1812-1820. Knighted, 1816.*

George Miller to Lord Carmarthen

My Lord   Charleston, S° Carolina 17 Novem 1787

. . . . .

This being the first opportunity to London, since receipt of the Constitution formed for these States by the late Foederal Convention, I have the honour to inclose to your Lordship a Copy of the same, 'though I can have no doubt You are before now in possession of it. –

If it is approved of, and should be adopted, it promises, I think, to rescue Congress from that Inefficient situation in which they have long stood, as it grants sufficient powers to comply with, and enforce their Treaties and other National Engagements, without submitting to the Controul of State Legislatures, who, on most occasions, have paid no farther regard to the recommendations of Congress, than as the same did not operate against their own particular and local Interests. – The last to the different States, inforcing the propriety and necessity; that each should make the Treaty of Peace part of the Law of the Land, has met with greater attention and respect than many others; as I believe it has been adopted by most of the Legislatures which have met since it was circulated: And I would hope the true Policy of faithfully adhering to Treaties, will be more and more felt and understood, particularly those with His Majesty, as this Country cannot long be so blind to its own Interests, as not to perceive that the advantages it already derives from a Commercial Intercourse with Great Britain, are superiour to those held out to it by every other nation in Europe. That the people of America are desirous to obtain still greater, by a Commercial Treaty, is not, I presume, to be doubted; but the equivalent they can hold out to Britain, for any relaxation in the Navigation Act, by which only, they can expect benefits in a Commercial view beyond these they already enjoy, is a matter they will, I fear, find it difficult to establish. The rapid settlement of the Western Territory, and the attempts which in all probability will in a few years be made, in consequence thereof, to compel Spain to grant them the free Navigation of the River Missisippi, occasions their perhaps looking forward with an eye of hope to a future Connexion of a different kind, with Great Britain, which might afford them assistance and protection. Whether these conjectures may be founded, time only can determine, I considered it my duty, however, to submit these hints to Your Lordship, as it is obvious the Americans look with much Jealousy at the possessions of Spain in the two Florida's, and it is probable their views may not terminate even there....

.   .   .   .   .

I have the honour to be, with the highest Respect My Lord Your Lordship's most Obedient and most humble Servant   Geo: Miller R. 21ˢᵗ Janʳʸ

PRO: FO 4/5, pp. 717-720 (LC trasncription).

Phineas Bond to Lord Carmarthen

My Lord,   Philadelphia 20ᵗʰ· Nov 1787
    I have the honor to enclose to your Ldp. the affidavit of two persons, natives of England who with great resolution, and no small personal risque purchased here and reshipped to Liverpool three machines for spinning cotton and a machine for carding cotton for spinning. These machines your Ldp. will find were clandestinely shipped from Liverpool to Philadᵃ· packed in Queen's ware crates and casks, to elude discovery: – Their utility in the manufacturing of cotton induced these men to endeavor to prevent their being established here, which they effectually accomplished by returning them to the country, from whence they were fraudulently exported.
    This transaction, my Lord, has been much canvassed and greatly censured here. It has given birth to the introduction of an Act of Assembly to prevent the seducing artists to quit this State and the sending abroad models for manufactories – the immediate necessity for such a bill has been warmly urged in the House of Assembly; and it is now in a train of being passed as soon as the forms of the House will admit; the urgency of the subject is assigned as a reason for passing the bill the same sessions in which it originates: – in ordinary cases, Acts of Assembly are published for consideration and referred to the discussion of a future session – Endeavors have been and certainly will be used, my Lord, to inveigle manufacturers from Gt. Britain and Ireland, and tho' from the smallness of their capitals, the people here may not be able suddenly, to engage in extensive manufactures, the very wants of the country will e'er long point to speculations of that sort; and many material articles may gradually advance towards perfection and interfere essentially with the manufactures of Gt. Britain –
    The Society instituted here for the encouragement of manufactures and the useful arts are very anxious to detain every artist in the country, whose skill may have a tendency to promote the purposes of the institution.

Lately, my Lord, this Society has offered to confer premiums on such persons as may exhibit the most useful engine to be moved by water, fire, etc. by which the ordinary labor of manufacturing cotton, wool, flax, or hemp may be saved – to such persons as shall raise and clean the greatest quantity of hemp, of flax and of cotton: – to such persons as shall exhibit the most approved set of specimens or patterns of printed linen and cotton goods – for the best specimen of letter press, executed by types made in Pennsylvania, – for the best specimen of earthen-ware, approaching nearest to delf, white stone or queen's ware – for the greatest variety of flint glass ware – for the greatest quantity of glass bottles – for the best specimen of sheet glass – for the greatest quantity of pot ashes and pearl ashes, wool and bleached wax for discovering and producing the greatest variety of specimens of painters' colors drawn from the fossils and earths of the United States and for the greatest number of Smith's anvils equal to those imported from England –

I do not apprehend, my Lord, that any of the manufactures for which premiums are offered will be speedily brought to a State of Rivalship with those of Gt. Britain, but when matters of this sort are in agitation, it is fit to guard against an evil, which tho' at present in its infancy may by perseverance and management progressively arrive at such a pitch as to interfere essentially with the interests of the British manufacturers –

The persons, my Lord, who made the enclosed affidavit assured me they had every reason to believe that Joseph Hague therein mentioned was very lately at a place called Simmontly near Hayfield in Derbyshire.

The ideas I had the honor to communicate to your Ldp. respecting the China trade have been confirmed by information I have had that it is now in contemplation to ship teas in casks covered with Indian corn etc from hence to the W. India Islands. This traffic will no doubt, my Lord, thro' some other medium of deception be extended to Gt. Britain and Ireland particularly to the latter.

Several vessels are about to sail from hence to Ireland, and the complexion of the owners justifies the apprehension that they will attempt every means to run teas as well as tobaccos into that country, Guernsey and Jersey too, my Lord, have been found to afford convenient store houses for the tobacco of Virginia and Maryland; and several vessels belonging to those islands have lately been laden with that article, for the purpose of sale to those who convey it clandestinely to England from thence.

I have communicated to some of his Majesty's governors in the W. Indies my apprehensions respecting the export of teas etc, from hence to the islands, and should hope such illicit attempts may be frustrated.

Had I been honored, my Lord, with your Ldp's directions as to the assist-ance I am to afford to British subjects desiring to return home, I could have

extended beneficial relief to some useful manufacturers who wish to revisit England; – at this time, my Lord, any supply on my part may incur the jealousy of the States, if not personal risque; and having no particular instructions, by which I am regulated, the measure, as well as the manner of relief must depend upon my own judgment, until I know your Ldp's decision upon this matter – I have the honor to be, my Lord, your Ldp's most faith: and most obed: servt.   P. Bond.
R.12th. Jan:

AHA 1896, v. 1, pp. 552-555.

Governor Edmund Randolph of Virginia to Martin Oster

Sir,   Richmond Nov. 22. 1787.
   As soon as the Council had decided on Your application of the 2^d ultimo for aid in the execution of Your authority upon a french Subject charged with an offence against the Laws of France, I did myself the honor by *a private hand* of informing You of the Result. I now find by Your Letter of the 11th instant, received late last Evening that my Letter had not reached You. I therefore now repeat that it is the opinion of the Executive, that they cannot interfere or lend assistance in the case which You mentioned. This opinion proceeds not from any disinclination to support the Consular power, but from the *fixed principle* of our Government that no authority can be exercised by any body of men, to whom it has not been duly delegated. The only Law existing on this Subject is one passed in 1780. and of which You have a full Knowledge. I must therefore refer You to it and doubt not that You will discover from thence that it would not justify us in granting the process, which You wish.   Edmund Randolph

NA: PCC, item 96, pp. 466-467 (C); M247, reel 124.

Louis Guillaume Otto to Comte de Montmorin

[Translation]
N°. 105.   New York, 26 Nov. 1787.
My Lord,
   I received the Despatch N°. 4 that You did me the honor to write me on 31 August last. The indulgence with which You have deigned to receive my last reports can only encourage me to redouble my zeal and application.

The debates, My Lord, for and against the new Constitution still absorb public attention, and while the States prepare to appoint individual conventions to adopt or to reject this new plan, the two parties vilify each other in the public papers with an obstinacy that sometimes does not spare even insults and personal remarks. As in these sorts of political commotions, men and things are ordinarily disguised in a manner to become unrecognizable, the partisans of innovation call themselves *federalists* and the others more commonly *Whigs*, although none of these names has a direct connection with the subject in question. This spirit of discussion is even pushed to intolerance with regard to foreigners, and it is arbitrarily wished that we take a position for or against the new constitution. Some politicians, wishing to be more impressive than others, have even suggested that this constitution is bad because it is approved by the foreign Ministers. According to some, Despotism will be the necessary result of the proposed Constitution; according to others, the United States will attain the summit of glory and power with this same Constitution. Indifferent Spectators agree that the new form of Government, well executed, can produce good results; but they also think that if the States really had the desire to be united, the present Confederation would suffice for all their needs. However, they cannot conceal from themselves that after having excited this general fermentation, there is no longer any means of stopping it; that the old edifice is almost pulled down, and that they have to substitute some fabrication or other for it. In fact, it was impossible to deal a blow more violent to the authority of Congress than by saying to all America, to the entire Universe, that this body is insufficient for the needs of the Confederation, and that the United States have become the laughingstock of all the powers. This principle, repeated again and again by all the Innovators, appears as false as their spirits are exalted; the United States hold among the nations the place that their youth and their means assign to them; they are neither rich enough nor populated enough, nor sufficiently well established to appear with more renown, and perhaps they should be reproached only for the impatience of wishing to anticipate their future grandeur.

The new Congress is not yet formed, My Lord; the Delegates are arriving very slowly, and their deliberations can scarcely be important before the various States have given their opinion on the proposed Government. The task of this Assembly will then become very delicate; it should consider without prejudice the opinions and the modifications of the individual States, judge whether nine members of the Confederation have virtually consented to it, and fix the time of the Elections for the new sovereign body. This operation can only take place towards the middle of next year however if one can hope to unite the votes of nine States.

. . . . .

Whatever may happen, My Lord, it still appears that there is only one foreign impetus that can give strength to the federal Government, under whatever form it is considered appropriate to reproduce it. The allocation of taxes and imposts will be the stumbling block that will cause the most discussed plans to fail unless the sudden appearance of an Enemy and an imminent danger rekindles that spirit of unanimity that formerly produced such great effects. But as this revolution is not absolutely necessary, it would be unfortunate to purchase possible advantages by real calamities.

I am with a profound respect My Lord Your most humble and most obedient servant   Otto

rec. 21 Jany. 1788

FFAA: Pol. Corr., U.S., v. 32, f. 401-404 (LC transcription).

John Adams to John Jay

Dear Sir   Grosvenor Square Nov. 30. 1787

. . . . .

...The Interposition of Prussia in the Affairs of Holland cannot be justified upon the Principles of the Law of Nations: and if Truth and Justice are not lost out of the World will be marked by the impartial, both in the present and future Ages with severe Censure. But the Speeches of Mr Fox and Mr Pitt appear to me to have Set every Tie that can bind Mankind, every Principle which ought to be held Sacred at open Defiance. it is openly avowed by both, that a Treaty of Alliance is in Agitation between England and Holland, at this moment when a Treaty recently made between France and Holland is in full force, and when there is no Pretence of a Violation of it. Is not this a most outragious Insult, in the Face of the whole World, for the Debates in Parliament are known to be published all over Europe upon the Law of Nations, upon the Faith of Treaties, and national Honour. Is it the Intention of the Speech and of the Addresses which will eccho it back to the Throne, to force the House of Bourbon into a War? To me, it Seems manifest. – If France should bear it patiently, what are we to think? The Fermentation in that Kingdom, occasioned by the Ruin brought upon it, by that Administration of whose Merits you have long since formed an accurate Judgment, and by the Exertions to obtain provincial and national Assemblies threatens much Confusion. It is not possible to foresee, what the Effect will be. I own myself afraid that the Patriots in France will prove as Unskillful and Unsuccessful Asserters of a free Government as those in Holland have been. a tedious Relaxation if not the most serious divisions are to be apprehended. If however the House of Bourbon is unable to assert her Dignity upon this Occasion, I am clearly convinced that the Pride and Arrogance of England will rise so high, as to demand the Demolition of Cherbourg, and attempt to Sever South America from Spain. nor will this be all: She will demand the Annihilation of Several Articles at least of the Treaties between France and the United States of America. Nor will they Stop here. if they can bind Holland in their Shackles, and France by her internal distractions is unable to interfere, She will make War immediately against Us. they are at present both at Court, and in the Nation at large much more respectful to me, and much more tender of the United States than they Ever have been before. but depend upon it, this will not last. – They will aim at recovering back the Western Lands at taking away our Fisheries and at the total Ruin of our Navigation at least.

The United States of America, therefore, had never more Reason to be upon their Guard: to compleat their Constitution of Government: to Unite as one Man to meet with Courage and Constancy, the severe Tryal, which in all probability they will be called to undergo in a very few years.

...With great Respect I had the Honour to be Dear Sir, your most obedient and most humble Servant   John Adams
February 14. 1788 Referred to the Sec^{y.} for foreign Affairs to report. –

NA: PCC, *item 84, v. 6, pp. 574-578* (ALS); *M247, reel 113.*

Antoine René Charles Mathurin de la Forêt to Comte de Montmorin

[Translation]
My Lord   New York, 5 December 1787.
I had the honor on the 10th of February last to inform My Lord the Marshal de Castries of the exemptions from duties which the State of Virginia had granted to the wines and Brandies of France imported directly by French or American vessels. The legislation had in view discouraging the great importation of Rum from the English Islands. It thought to accomplish this purpose by new duties at the same time that privileges on the Brandies served as compensation for those which His Majesty had just granted in France on several products of the United States imported by French or American vessels.

The Minister Plenipotentiary of the United Provinces immediately presented a memorandum to Congress in which he complained of the distinction established in Virginia between French and Dutch vessels for the importation of Brandies and demanded most favored nation treatment for his nation. The Delegates from the State of Virginia observed that this demand was not admissible, since the privilege granted on the Brandies imported by French vessels was not gratuitous, and that in consequence the Dutch had a right to the terms of their Treaty of Commerce only by offering the compensations on which the privilege was based. Congress acted with regard to this Memorandum only last month. This Senate, which still views with anxiety the instability, incoherence, and inefficacy of the local Regulations which each State makes for its Commerce, has formulated a System of continually objecting to them.

It therefore requested the State of Virginia to review the Act of which the Minister of the United Provinces is complaining, to render it conformable to the treaty existing between the two powers, and to have the duties that might have been collected on brandies imported by Dutch vessels returned.

As we should desire the greatest importation possible of products of the Realm into the United States by whatever vessels, it was in our interest that the State of Virginia extend the execution of its Act. But I understand, Sir, that this state is on the verge of providing a new example of the instability of the commercial Regulations of Members of the union. A powerful party in the present legislature, seeing that the importation of English beers and Rums is little diminished, wishes to put an end to it entirely, and proposes to *proscribe absolutely all spirituous and fermented liquors that are not extracted from materials produced in the United States.* This Bill has passed into the House of Delegates and is being sent by it for the consideration of the People, in order to be taken up again at the first Session. United States Rums extracted from our molasses are indirectly included in the proposed prohibition, those from our Islands share the Fate of those from the English Islands, and our Brandies, a considerable Branch of Commerce in Virginia, are especially mentioned therein.

It appeared important to me to seek to have this Bill modified before it has the force of Law. I enclose herewith a copy of a letter which I wrote on this Subject to the King's Vice Consul in Virginia. I indicate to him the considerations that appeared to me to arise from the stated principles upon which the Bill was presented, and I venture to hope that you will be so good as to approve that we are making use of them.

I am &c.   La Forêt

FFAA: Pol. Corr., U.S., v. 32, f. 405-406 (LC transcription).

John Adams to Thomas Jefferson

Dear Sir   London. Decr 6. 1787
    The Project of a new Constitution, has Objections against it, to which
I find it difficult to reconcile myself, but I am So unfortunate as to differ
Somewhat from you in the Articles, according to your last kind Letter.
    You are afraid of the one – I, of the few. We agree perfectly that the
many should have a full fair and perfect Representation. – You are
Apprehensive of Monarchy, I of Aristocracy. – I would therefore have
given more Power to the President and less to the Senate. The Nomination
and Appointment to all offices I would have given to the President, assisted
only by a Privy Council of his own ~~appointment~~ Creation, but not a Vote
or Voice would I have given to the Senate or any Senator, unless he were
of the Privy Council. Faction and Distraction are the sure and certain
Consequence of giving to a Senate a Vote in the distribution of Offices.
You are apprehensive that the President when once chosen, will be chosen
again and again as long as he lives. So much the better as it appears to me.
– You are apprehensive of foreign Interference, Intrigue, Influence. – So
am I. – But, as often as Elections happen, the danger of foreign Influence
renews. the less frequently they happen the less danger. – and if the Same
Man may be chosen again, it is probable he will be, and the danger of
foreign Influence will be less. Foreigners, Seeing little Prospect will have
less Courage for Enterprize.
    Elections, my dear Sir, Elections to Offices which are great Objects of
Ambition, I look at with terror. – Experiments of this kind have been So
often tryed, and So universally found productive Horrors, that there is great
Reason to dread them. <**********>
    Mr. Littlepage[1] who will have the Honour to deliver this will tell you all
the News. I am, my dear Sir, with great Regard   John Adams.

LC: *Jefferson Papers, microfilm reel 8 (ALS).*
[1] *Littlepage, Lewis (1762-1802). Virginia-born soldier of fortune. A member of John
Jay's household while the latter was in Spain, 1780-1782, he attached himself to the Duc
de Crillon, who commanded the Spanish forces that captured Minorca, 1782, and besieged
Gibraltar. Had major dispute with Jay, 1785-1786, over money the latter had loaned him
in Spain. Chamberlain to King Stanislaus Augustus of Poland, 1786-1798.*

Thomas Jefferson to the Comte de Montmorin

Sir   Paris Dec. 6. 1787.

. . . . .

The Comptroller general having been so good as to explain to me in a conversation that he wished to know what duties were levied in England on American whale oil, I have had the honor of informing him by letter that the antient duties on that article are 17$^£$ 6$^{s.}$ 6^d sterling the ton, & that some late additional duties make them amount to about 18. £ sterling. that the common whale oil sells there but for about 20 £ sterling the ton, & of course the duty amounts to a prohibition. this duty was originally laid on all foreign fish oil, with a view to favor the British & American fisheries. when we became independent & of course foreign to Great Britain, we became subject to the foreign duty. no duty therefore which France may think proper to lay on this article can drive it to the English market. it could only oblige the inhabitants of Nantucket to abandon their fishery. but the poverty of their soil offering them no other resource, they must quit their country, & either establish themselves in Nova Scotia, where, as British fishermen, they may participate of the British premium, in addition to the ordinary price of their whale oil; or they must accept the conditions which this government offers for the establishment they have proposed at Dunkirk. Your Excellency will judge what conditions may counterbalance in their minds the circumstances of the vicinity of Nova Scotia, sameness of language, laws, religion, customs & kindred. remaining in their native country to which they are most singularly attached, excluded from commerce with England, taught to look to France as the only country from which they can derive sustenance, they will, in case of war, become useful Rovers against it's enemies. their position, their poverty, their courage, their address, & their hatred will render them formidable scourges on the British commerce. it is to be considered then on the one hand that the duty which M. de Calonnes had proposed to retain on their oil may endanger the shifing this useful body of seamen out of our joint scale into that of the British; & also may suppress a considerable subject of exchange for the productions of France. on the other hand that it may produce an addition to his majesty's revenue. What I have thus far said, is on the supposition that the duty may operate a diminution of the price received by the fisherman. if it act in the contrary direction, & produce an augmentation of price to the consumer, it immediately brings into competition a variety of other oils vegetable & animal, a good part of which France receives from abroad; & the fisherman thus losing his market, is compelled equally to change either his calling or country. when M. de Calonne first agreed to reduce the duties to what he has declared, I had great hopes the commodity could bear them, & that it would become a medium of commerce between France & the United States. I must confess however that my expectations have not been fulfilled, & that but little has come here as yet. this induces me to fear that it is so poor an article, that any duty whatever will suppress it. should this take place, & the spirit of emigration once seize those people, perhaps an abolition of all duty might then come too late to stop what it would now easily prevent. I fear there is danger in the experiment; & it remains for the wisdom of his majesty & his ministers to decide whether the prospect of gain to the revenue, or establishing a national fishery may compensate this danger. if the government should decide to retain the duty, I shall acquiesce in it chearfully, and do every thing in my power to encourage my countrymen still to continue their occupation.

.   .   .   .   .

I have the honour to be with sentiments of the most profound esteem & respect, Your Excellency's most obedient & most humble servant

Th: Jefferson

LC: *Jefferson Papers, microfilm reel 8 (press copy).*

Peter Allaire: Occurrences from 6 November to 6 December 1787

New York 6 December 1787

Congress have at last found out, that there is no Treating and keeping Peace with the Indians, without paying them, and the Southern Indians, having taken up the hatchet, & Northern ones shew every hostile intention, have compelled them to come to the following Resolutions.

in Congress, Resolved that the Sum of Twenty Thousand Dollars be Appropriated for the Indian Department, for the purposes of holding Treaties with the Tribes of Indians inhabiting the N W of the United States, and that the Governor of the Western Territory appoint such time & place as he shall judge most necessary for holding the same, and that he may apply for such number of Men, as he shall think requisite, to the Commanding Officer of the Troops of the United States, as may be sufficient to protect and Guard the Stores & Goods necessary for holding the said treaty.

Resolved That the States of Georgia, South & North Carolina that the Legislatures if in Session, or Executive, be, and they are hereby Authorized to appoint one Commissioner, who shall in conjunction with the Superintendant of Indian Affairs for the Southern department, negotiate a Treaty of Peace between the United States & those Indians, and their decision be final and Conclusive

That the Sum of Six thousand Dollars be appropriated for holding the said Treaty, in addition to the goods in the hands of the Superintendant, and that the Aforesaid Sum, be in full of all charges of Whatsoever Nature that may be relating to the said Treaty, including the pay of the Commissioners, & such Militia as may be necessary to guard & protect the Goods & that the States of Georgia, South & North Carolina be called on to furnish the aforesaid Sum in Equal proportions, to be passed to the Credit of each State, on Requisitions of Congress.

Martial Law has been proclaimed throughout the State of Georgia, the City of Savan[n]ah to be strongly fortified, as the Indians have committed depredations within 36 Miles of it

In Congress Resolved. That the Executive of the Commonwealth of Virginia be requested to give Orders, to the Militia in the district of Kentucky, to hold themselves in readiness to join the Federal Troops, not exceeding One thousand Men to be Immediately Embodied, to act in Conjunction, as the Commanding Officer of the Federal Troops may judge Necessary, to protect and defend the frontier Settlements. That the State of Pensilvania furnish one thousand Men, on like Conditions &c.

.   .   .   .   .

Georgia & North Carolina have applyed to Congress for a federal Force to go against the Indians, according to the Articles of Confederation those two States have not ceded to Congress their Western Lands, all the others have; they have therefore wrote those two States, that if they do not ceed those lands, they do not hold themselves bound to make Peace or War at the Option and Instigation of any State and that the Assistance they have applyed for from the united States, cannot be complyed with, but when those States Act on Liberal principals & adopt measures founded on Sound policy in granting their lands to be disposed of, for the General good, and payment of the debts of the United States, that then they shall hold themselves bound to protect them from all Domestick & foreign Enemies.

.   .   .   .   .

Our Commerce has increased with the English West Indies greatly this Year, owing to the price of Lumber, such as Staves, heading, Shingles, Boards, Hoops & Joice, having fell from 20 to 30 p Cent: Wheat, Flour, Bread, Pease, fish, nearly in the same proportion, we have had one fourth more English Vessells this Year in our harbours & have Imported more Rum than any preceeding Year since the Peace, your navigation Act having deprived us of being Carriers to your Islands we have no other Market open but Portugal, Spain being too near the Algerines, we have sent but three

Vessells to Lisbone with Wheat at the Rate of 3/6 St^d the Winchester Bushell, I make not the least doubt Wheat will be at 2/6 & all other produce 10 p Cent lower next Year then at present, You may at all times command our Markets by forbiding the Exportation of Rum from your Islands for without that Article, I do not know what we should do, as the french Rum bears no price, in comparison with the English, the former Sells at 2/9 the latter 4/6, the Negroes Refuse it & none but Distillers now purchase it, the consumption of that Article must increase rapidly every Year, should you put any more Restraints on it, you will compell us to make Spiritous liquors from Grain, as you have Already deprived us of being partakers of the Exportation of our own produce to your Islands.

.   .   .   .   .

I Remain with Respect Your V H Serv   P A
R. 18$^{th:}$ Jan^{ry}

PRO: FO 4/5, pp. 767-778 (LC transcription).

Louis Guillaume Otto to Comte de Montmorin

[Translation]

N$^{o.}$ 106.   New York, 7 December 1787.

My Lord

If, in the matter of a political Constitution, the United States are still quite backward, they can be compared to the oldest and most enlightened nations in all that may tend to make the arts and practical sciences flourish among them. It is not for me to enter into any detail on the great number of Societies which have been formed in America either to oversee the education of youth, or to guarantee the property of individuals against the ravages of fire, or to encourage immigrants who are poor and without resources, to come to the aid of the drowning, to solace prisoners, to spread Christianity among the Savages, to abolish the slavery of negroes or at least to render their chains less weighty. This spirit of benevolence and humanity is widespread in all American institutions, and I sometimes regret not being able to present these people to You from this touching point of view, which is the most favorable to them. However, it is also not alien to my task to submit to You the encouragements given to some cultivations and factories, the progress of which could one day interest the Commerce of Europe, either because it will lose a branch of its former Commerce there, or because it will find a new market of raw materials there for its own manufactures.

Several States of the union already include, My Lord, respectable Societies for encouraging some objects of cultivation that are peculiar to them, but that which appears to have the greatest means and the broadest views is the Society of Philadelphia. As the high Cost of Manual labor has hitherto been the greatest obstacle to the establishment of manufactures, the Society offers a prize to anyone who invents a machine which, by means of fire, of water, or of any other Agent, can diminish the manual labor on cotton, wool, linen, or hemp, and render the fabrication thereof less expensive than in Europe. It is offering considerable prizes to those of its Fellow Citizens who, in the course of the year 1788, shall have grown and processed the greatest quantities of hemp, linen, and cotton, to those who shall have produced the most beautiful Calico or linen prints; who shall have printed the most handsome book from type and on paper made in Pennsylvania; who shall have made the most beautiful pottery equal to that of Delft or of England; who shall have created the most beautiful glassware; finally, to those who shall offer for sale the greatest quantity of potash and pearl ash, who shall shear the richest wool in their own flocks, or who shall produce the greatest quantity of beeswax candles for export. The Society offers a still more considerable prize to those who can prove in an incontestable manner that they have extracted from the mines and the soil of Pennsylvania the greatest quantity of pigments suitable for paints, as well as to those who, prior to the 1st of January 1789, shall have forged the greatest number of anvils of the best quality, and comparable to those that have hitherto been imported from England.

When one adds to these efforts, My Lord, those of the Societies which have been formed to render the Potowmac, the Susquehannah, and other important rivers navigable, to construct bridges in order to send Colonies into the western lands, to establish countinghouses in China, in India, & at Mogador, for whaling in the Falkland Islands, or for following in the wake of Cook to the Bering Strait, one cannot help but admire their courage, their industry, and that intelligence which makes them conceive and execute the vastest projects with limited means.

The disposition of the United States, My Lord, to throw off the commercial yoke of Europe cannot but affect Great Britain, which loses each year a certain portion of its Commerce in America.

The conformity of language and manners may, I acknowledge, facilitate these connections, but it has the singular consequence that discoveries made in England immediately become common in the United States, that Workers easily transport themselves, and produce in Philadelphia or in Boston works as perfect as in London. It is not the same with the objects that France can furnish to these States. Wines, brandies, Silks appear fated to assure us a considerable sale there for a very long time.

The reflections that I have just had the honor to submit to You, My Lord, scarcely conform to the vague and exaggerated reports regarding the situation of the United States with which nearly all European and American publications are inundated. There they confuse the uncertainty of a people which has not yet chosen a stable and permanent form of Government with disorder and internal anarchy; but this uncertainty makes itself felt only abroad or in political debates, without affecting in any way the tranquility and industry of the Citizen. The partisans which England still has in America, and of whom several are infatuated enough to hope for a reunion between the two countries, hasten to Confirm these false reports; perhaps England too, having more to fear from emigrations, is interested in representing this country from the most disadvantageous point of view; but however little one examines the general prosperity, the affluence of the individual, the almost inconceivable growth of all parts of the republic, one is tempted to think that of all countries in the world, this one has taken the greatest steps to become opulent and formidable.

I am with a profound respect My Lord Your most humble and most obedient servant. Otto.

rec. 21 Jan^y· 1788

FFAA: Pol. Corr., U.S., v. 32, f. 407-410 (LC transcription).

Thomas Jefferson to John Adams

Dear Sir   Paris Dec. 12. 1787.

In the month of July I received from Fiseaux & co.[1] of Amsterdam a letter notifying me that the principal of their loan to the United States would become due the first of January. I answered them that I had neither powers nor information on the subject, but would transmit their letter to the Board of treasury. I did so by the packet which sailed from Harve Aug. 10. the earliest answer possible would have been by the packet which arrived at Havre three or four days ago. but by her I do not receive the scrip of a pen from any body. this makes me suppose that my letters are committed to Paul Jones who was to sail a week after the departure of the packet: & that possibly he may be the bearer of orders from the treasury to repay Fiseaux' loan with the money you borrowed. but it is also possible he may bring no order on the subject. the slowness with which measures are adopted on our side the water, does not permit us to count on punctual answers: but on the contrary renders it necessary for us to suppose in the present case that no orders will arrive in time, and to consider whether any thing, and what should be done? as it may be found expedient to transfer all our foreign debts to Holland by borrowing there, & as it may always be prudent to preserve a good credit in that country because we may [be] forced into wars whether we will or no, I should supppose it very imprudent to suffer our credit to be annihilated by so small a sum as 51,000 guilders. the injury will be greater too in proportion to the smallness of the sum: for they will ask 'How can a people be trusted for large sums who break their faith for such small ones?' you know best what effect it will have on the minds of the money lenders of that country should we fail in this payment. you know best whether it is practicable and prudent for us to have this debt paid without orders. I refer the matter therefore wholly to your consideration, willing to participate with you in any risk, & any responsability which may arise. I think it one of those cases where it is a duty to risk one's self. you will preceive, by the inclosed, the necessity of an immediate answer, and that if you think any thing can & should be done all the necessary authorities from you should accompany your letter. in the mean time should I receive any orders from the Treasury by P. Jones, I will pursue them, and consider whatever you shall have proposed or done, as *non avenue.*[2] I am with much affection Dear Sir your most obedient & most humble serv^t   Th: Jefferson

MHS: *The Adams Papers, microfilm reel 370 (ALS).*
[1] *The Amsterdam banking house of Henri Fizeaux and Company was a corporate partner in Fizeaux, Grand, and Company, the Amsterdam office of the Paris banking house of Ferdinand Grand, who handled the accounts of the United States in France. Fizeaux and Company was probably trying to get its accounts in order prior to the January 1788 retirement of Henri Fizeaux; the assets of the Fizeaux firm were acquired by the successor house of Hogguer, Grand and Company.*
[2] *void*

Thomas Jefferson to William Carmichael

Dear Sir   Paris Dec 15, 1787.
...about the same time of Linton's conversation with you, similar ones were held with me by mr Eden. he particularly questioned me on the effect of our treaty with France in the case of a war, and what might be our dispositions. I told him without hesitation that our treaty obliged us to receive the armed vessels of France with their prizes into our ports, & to refuse admission to the prizes made on her by her enemies: that there was a clause by which we guarantied to France her American possessions, and which might perhaps force us into the war if these were attacked. "and it is certain, said he, they would have been attacked." I added that our

dispositions would have been to be neutral, & that I thought it the interest of both those powers that we should be so, because it would relieve both from all anxiety as to the feeding their West Indian islands, and England would moreover avoid a heavy land war on our continent which would cripple all her proceedings elsewhere. he expected these sentiments from me personally, and he knew them to be analogous to those of our country. we had often before had occasions of knowing each other: his peculiar bitterness towards us had sufficiently appeared, & I had never concealed from him that I considered the British as our natural enemies, and as the only nation on earth who wished us ill from the bottom of their souls. and I am satisfied that were our continent to be swallowed up by the ocean, Great Britain would be in a bonfire from one end to the other....

. . . . . .

I have the honor to be with very great respect & esteem, Sir, your most obedient & most humble servant   Th: Jefferson

LC: *Jefferson Papers, microfilm reel 8 (press copy).*

Louis Guillaume Otto to Comte de Montmorin

[Translation]

Nº· 107.   New York, 15 December 1787.

My Lord

Rumors of war that have been given out for some ten days, and which come to us not only from the islands, but from Halifax and Ireland, have induced the Captain of His Majesty's packet boat to request from M. de Crevecoeur,[1] the Consul of France, additional men, Cannon, and Gunpowder. That Consul, after having received the advice of the vice consul general and myself, thought he should authorize this expenditure, which is of little consideration when it is compared to the risk of seeing one of His Majesty's Ships seized by the smallest armed shallop. I hope, My Lord, that you will not disapprove of a measure which zeal has dictated to us, even though the news conveyed to us from all parts should be without foundation. We learn, chiefly from Nova Scotia, that great preparations are being made to put it in a State of defense, and that the Government has ordered a most rigorous press there, from which even the American crews that find themselves in Halifax are not exempt. In order to sound out the dispositions of the Americans in regard to England, it has been proclaimed here that that power proposes to station a fleet in Rhode Island in order to facilitate its provisioning and that of the Islands.

There are, My Lord, in the United States men selfish enough and citizens wicked enough to desire a general war in Europe. They hope to derive therefrom great advantages not only for the sale of their commodities, but for their navigation and their Commerce with the Antilles. But they do not consider that they have no means to make their flag respected by the belligerent powers, that it will be difficult for a Government as passive as that of the United States to restrain its citizens within the limits of a scrupulous neutrality, that the benefits of privateering will be too attractive to some restless spirits from New England, and that the least offense could induce Great Britain or any other armed nation to ravage a coast entirely unprotected and deprived of any defense. On the other hand, true patriots and persons more informed and farseeing dread a war in Europe as the greatest calamity for their new-born republic; they understand that the smallest privateer could insult their cities with impunity, that the Conduct of a great number of individuals and perhaps of some States would be imprudent enough to offer a pretext for reprisals; and that they are not even in condition to prevent hostilities in their ports between foreign vessels; hostilities which could have most unfortunate consequences for the United States. It therefore appears, My Lord, that it is with one point of view only that a general war could be useful to America; it is that it would necessarily bring together the incoherent parties of the Confederation, and that it would make felt the necessity of a general Government, active and efficacious to protect and to render respectable the whole mass of States.

· · · · ·

The news from Georgia, My Lord, continues to be very alarming. The Creeks are practicing unprecedented cruelties on the inhabitants, half of the militia has received orders to muster, and the State is endeavoring to call up four regiments of 750 men each. Fifteen hundred citizens of the small State of Frankland have been persuaded to make common cause with the Georgians. The latter have sent a commissioner to the Spanish Governors to ask them not to give Assistance to their enemies. This measure is so much the wiser, as it is only from the two Floridas that the Creeks can get their weapons and their munitions of war. McGillivray,[2] a violent Royalist whose properties were confiscated by the State of Georgia during the Revolution, is the chief of these Savages; he governs them as a Sovereign, and combines the intrepidity of a Savage with the education and Attainments of a Statesman.

· · · · ·

I am with a profound respect My Lord Your most humble and most obedient Servant.   Otto
rec. 21 Jany. 1788

FFAA: Pol. Corr., U.S., v. 32, f. 411-414vo. (LC transcription).

¹ Crèvecoeur, Michel Guillaume Jean de (1735-1813). Essayist, French consular official. After serving under Montcalm during the French and Indian War, during which he explored the lands near the Great Lakes and the Ohio River, he settled in New York, 1759, becoming a naturalized citizen in 1765. During the 1770s, he wrote most of the essays published in Letters from an American Farmer, 1782, which appeared under the nom de plume J. Hector St. John. He spent the years 1780-1783 in France, returning to New York as French Consul, 1783-1790.

² McGillivray, Alexander (ca. 1759-1793). Creek Indian chief. A loyalist in the American Revolution, during which Georgia confiscated the family's properties, he sent out war parties along the frontier and served as agent of the British trading firm of Panton, Leslie & Company. Spanish commissary to enforce Spain's monopoly of trade with the Creeks, 1784-1793. Sought to form confederation of Southern Indians to restore the line of white settlement of 1773. Opposed incursions by Georgia settlers upon Creek lands, 1785-1790. Signed peace treaty with the United States, 1790, but repudiated it in convention with Spain, 1792.

John Adams to John Jay

Dear Sir   Grosvenor Square Decʳ 16. 1787

Two Days ago, I received the Letter, you did me the Honour to write me, on the 16. of Octʳ with its Enclosures.

The Approbation of my Conduct in Europe expressed in the Resolution of Congress of the fifth of October, does me honour, and demands my Acknowledgment. The Permission to return to America and the termination of my Commission in Holland, having removed all Difficulties, It is my Intention, to embark with my Family in the Month of March. It would give me great Pleasure, Sir to accept of your polite and friendly Invitation to New York: but as the health of my Family is very tender, and their Apprehensions of the Sea very great, it will be necessary for me to imbark for Boston. – Mʳ Smith and his Family will embark for New York. As Congress have not transmitted him any Orders, relative to another Minister, or to a Chargé des Affaires at this Court, the Presumption is that it is either the Intention of Congress, to have no Diplomatick Character here, or that other Persons are destined to fill it. in either Case Mʳ Smiths Road is as clear as mine to return home.

· · · · ·

The Public Mind cannot be occupied about a nobler Object than the proposed Plan of Government. it appears to be admirably calculated to cement all America in Affection and Interest as one great Nation. A Result of Accommodation and Compromise, cannot be supposed, perfectly to coincide with any ones Ideas of Perfection. But as all the great Principles necessary to order, Liberty and Safety are respected in it, and Provision is made for Corrections and Amendments as they may be found necessary, I confess I hope to hear of its Adoption by all the States.

.   .   .   .   .

most perfectly do I agree with you that America has nothing to fear, but a Want of Union and a Want of Government. The United States now stand in an elevated Situation, and they must and will be respected and courted, not only by France and England, but by all other Powers of Europe, while they keep themselves neutral.

.   .   .   .   .

...With invariable affection and Esteem I have the Honour to be, Sir, your most obedient and most humble Servant   John Adams Read 2. May 1788

NA: PCC, *item 84, v. 6, pp. 590-594 (ALS); M247, reel 113.*

John Adams to Thomas Jefferson

Dear Sir   London Dec.ʳ· 18 1787
    Last night I received your Letter of the 12. Mʳ Jarvis[1] and Commodore Jones are arrived here from New York both charged with large Dispatches for you....
    As my Dismission from the Service arrived at the Same time, not a Word has been Said to me. Nevertheless *Nil Americanium Alienum,*[2] and I have the honour to agree with you in Your opinion of the Propriety of keeping good our Credit in Holland. I should advise therefore that the Interest on Mʳ Fizeaux's Loan at least Should be paid, and the Creditors requested to wait for their Capitals till further orders can be obtained from Congress. if they will not consent to that, I would pay them Principal and Interest, provided there is Money enough in the hands of our Bankers and neither you nor they have received contrary orders. No Authorities from me will be necessary. Your own Letter to Messrs Willinks and Vanstaphorst will be Sufficient. But if they make any difficulty, which I cannot conceive for Want of any orders from me, I will Send them.
    You have recᵈ Authority to negotiate the Redemption of our unfortunate Countrymen in Algiers. To you therefore I Send a Petition which I received from them a few days ago. With the highest Regard, I am Dear Sir, your most obedient and most humble Servant   John Adams

.   .   .   .   .

LC: *Jefferson Papers, microfilm reel 8 (ALS).*
[1] Jarvis, James. *New York merchant who traveled in Europe, 1785.*
[2] *Nothing American is alien.*

Pieter Johan van Berckel to John Jay

Sir   New York. 18th December 1787
I find myself indispensably obliged to inform you, that this morning a certain John Wessel, calling himself a Constable, endeavoured to seize, carry off & imprison one my domestics; which he pretended to do by virtue of a warrant signed & issued against him by John Wiley, Alderman of New York.

This attempt against the rights & prerogatives of a Foreign Minister, has been greatly aggravated by the insolent conduct of the aforesaid Constable, who was not satisfied with executing the orders he received, but moreover added Abusive & insulting expressions to the repeated efforts to carry off my domestic out of my house by force, nothwithstanding the friendly counsel that was given him to release his prisoner, & retire untill he should receive fresh instructions; which advice he was at last obliged to follow.

As this Process alone, against any one belonging to me, without mentioning the manner in which they endeavoured to execute it, which is a most atrocious injury, is a most notorious & direct violation of the rights of Nations, I conceived that I ought to communicate it to you Sir, requesting that you will grant me Your official aid to obtain the satisfaction due to my Character by virtue of the Laws of Nations which assure to me the protection of Government, as well as the security & inviolability both for my own person & my whole family.

I have the honor of subscribing myself with esteem & respect Sir Your m° hum. & ob. Serv[t.]   P. J. Van Berckel.

NA: PCC, item 99, pp. 289-290 (translation); M247, reel 126.

Thomas Jefferson to James Madison

Dear Sir   Paris Dec. 20. 1787.
. . . . . .
The season admitting only of operations in the Cabinet, and these being in a great measure secret, I have little to fill a letter. I will therefore make up the deficiency by adding a few words on the Constitution proposed by our Convention. I like much the general idea of framing a government which should go on of itself peaceably, without needing continual recurience to the state legislatures. I like the organization of the government into Legislative Judiciary & Executive. I like the power given the Legislature to levy taxes, and for that reason solely approve of the greater house

being chosen by the people directly. for tho' I think a house chosen by them will be very illy qualified to legislate for the Union, for foreign nations &c. yet this evil does not weigh against the good of preserving inviolate the fundamental principle that the people are not to be taxed but by representatives chosen immediately by themselves. I am captivated by the compromise of the opposite claims of the great & little states, of the latter to equal, and the former to proportional influence. I am much pleased too with the substitution of the method of voting by persons, instead of that of voting by states: and I like the negative given to the Executive with a third of either house, though I should have liked it better had the Judiciary been associated for that purpose, or invested with a similar and separate power. there are other good things of less moment. I will now add what I do not like. first the omission of a bill of rights providing clearly & without the aid of sophism for freedom of religion, freedom of the press, protection against standing armies, restriction against monopolies, the eternal & unremitting force of the habeas corpus laws, and trials by jurys in all matters of fact triable by the laws of the land & not by the law of Nations. to say, as mr Wilson[1] does that a bill of rights was not necessary because all is reserved in the case of the general government which is not given, while in the particular ones all is given which is not reserved, might do < *** > for the Audience to whom it was < * > addressed, but is surely a *gratis dictum,*[2] opposed by strong inferences from the body of the instrument, as well as from the omission of the clause of our present confederation which had declared that in express terms. it was a hard conclusion to say because there has been no uniformity among the states as to the cases triable by jury, because some have been so incautious as to abandon this mode of trial < **** >, therefore the more prudent states shall be reduced to the same level of calamity. it would have been much more just & wise to have < * > concluded the other way that as most of the states had judiciously preserved this palladium those who had wandered should be brought back to it, and to have established general right instead of general wrong. let me add that a bill of rights is what the people are entitled to against every government on earth, general or particular, & what no just government should refuse, or rest on inference. the second feature I dislike, and greatly dislike, is the abandonment in every instance of the necessity of rotation in office, and most particularly in the case of the President. experience concurs with reason in concluding that the first magistrate will always be re-elected if the constitution permits it. he is then an officer for life. this once observed it becomes of so much consequence to certain nations to have a friend or a foe at the head of our affairs that they will interfere with money & with arms. a Galloman or an Angloman will be supported by the nation he befriends. if once elected, and ~~and~~ at a second or third election outvoted by one or two votes, he will pretend false votes, foul play, hold possession of the reins of government, be supported by the states voting for him, especially if they are the central ones lying in a compact body themselves & separating their opponents: and they will be aided by one nation in Europe while the majority are aided by another. the election of a President of America some years hence will be much more interesting to certain nations of Europe than ever the election of a king of Poland was. reflect on all the instances in history antient & modern, of elective monarchies, and say if they do not give foundation for my fears. the Roman emperors, the popes, while they were of any importance, the German emperors till they became hereditary in practice, the kings of Poland, the Deys of the Ottoman dependancies. it may be said that if elections are to be attended with these disorders, the seldomer they are renewed the better. but experience shews that the only way to prevent disorder is to render them uninteresting by frequent changes. an incapacity to be elected a second time would have been the only effectual preventative. the power of removing him every fourth year by the votes of the people is a power which will not be exercised. the king of Poland is removeable every day by the Diet, yet they never removed. – smaller objections are the Appeal in fact as well as law, and the binding all persons Legislative Executive & Judiciary by oath to maintain that constitution. I do not pretend to decide what would be the best method of procuring the establishment of the manifold good things in this contitution, and of getting rid of the bad. whether by adopting it in hopes of future amendment, or, after it has been duly weighed & canvassed by the people, after seeing the parts they generally dislike, & those they generally approve, to say to them 'We see now what you wish. send together your deputies again, let them frame a constitution for you omitting what you have condemned, & establishing the powers you approve. even these will be a great addition to the energy of your government. – at all events I hope you will not be discouraged from other trials, if the present one should fail of it's full effect. – I have thus told you freely what I like & dislike merely as a matter of curiosity, for I know your own judgment has been formed on all these points after having heard every thing which could be urged on them. I own I am not a friend to a very energetic government. it is always oppressive. the late rebellion in Massachusets has given more alarm than I think it should have done. calculate that one rebellion in 13 states in the course of 11 years, is but one for each state in a century & a half. no country should be so long without one. nor will any degree of power in the hands of government prevent insurrections. France with all it's despotism, and two or three hundred thousand men always in arms has had three insurrections in the three years I have been here in every one of which greater numbers were engaged than in Massachusets, & a great deal more blood was spilt. in Turkey, which Montesquieu[3] supposes more despotic, insurrections are the events of every day. in England, where the head of power is lighter than here, but heavier than with us they happen every half dozen years. compare again the ferocious depredations of their insurgents with the order, the moderation & the almost self extinguishment of ours. – after all, it is my principle that the will of the Majority should always prevail. if they approve the proposed Convention in all it's parts, I shall concur in it chearfully, in hopes they will amend it whenever they shall find it work wrong. I think our governments will remain virtuous for many centuries; as long as they are chiefly agricultural; and this will be as long as there shall be vacant lands in any part of America. when they get piled upon one another in large cities, as in Europe, they will become corrupt as in Europe. above all things I hope the education of the common people will be attended to; convinced that. on their good sense we may rely with the most security for the <*> preservation of a due degree of liberty. I have tired you by this time with my disquisitions & will therefore only add assurances of those sincerity of those sentiments of esteem & attachment with which I am Dear Sir your affectionate friend & servant   Th: Jefferson

P.S. the instablilty of our laws is really an immense evil. I think it would be well to provide in our constitutions that there shall always be a twelvemonth between the ingrossing a bill & passing it: that it should then be offered to it's passage without changing a word: and that if circumstances should be thought to require a speedier passage, it should take two thirds of both houses instead of a bare majority.

LC: *Madison Papers, microfilm reel 3 (ALS).*
[1] *Wilson, James (1742-1798). Pennsylvania lawyer, jurist and political figure. Member, Continental Congress, 1775-1777, 1783, 1785-1786. Member, Constitutional Convention, 1787. Associate justice of the U.S. Supreme Court, 1789-1798.*
[2] *an unsubstantiated assertion*
[3] *Montesquieu, Charles de Secondat, Baron de la Brede et de (1689-1755). French political philosopher and man of letters. Author of L'Esprit des Lois, 1748.*

James Madison to Thomas Jefferson

Dear Sir   New York Dec[r.] 20 1787

Mr[.] De la Forest the Consul here called on me a few days ago and told me he had information that the farmers general & <**> Mr[.] Morris having found their contract mutually advantageous are evading the resolutions of the committee by tacit arrangements for it's continuance. He observed that the object of the farmers was singly profit that of the government twofold revenue & commerce. It was consequently the wish of the latter to render the monopoly as little hurtful to the trade with America as possible. He suggested as an expedient that farmers should be required to divide the contract among six or seven houses French & American who should be required to ship annually to America a reasonable proportion of goods. This he supposed would produce some competition in the purchases here and would introduce a competition also with British goods here. The latter condition he said could not be well required of, or executed by a single contractor and the government could not abolish the farm. These ideas were meant for you.

       .   .   .   .   .

...I remain D^r· Sir Y^m· Affectly   J^s· Madison J^r·

LC: *Madison Papers, microfilm reel 3 (ALS).*

Samuel Shaw to John Jay

Sir   Canton in China 21st Decr 1787.

    Having in the letter which I did myself the honor of addressing to you towards the close of the last season, mentioned the several matters which came within my observation, relative to the Commerce which the Europeans carry on with this part of the world, I have only to remark generally on this subject, that a detail of it at present, such is its uniformity, would be to involve merely a repetition of the greater part of what was then written. I shall therefore confine myself rather to the quantity, if I may be allowed the expression, than to the manner, of the commerce for the current year.

    Since the Year 1784 the trade here has been constantly tending to the disadvantage of the Europeans. The imports collectively taken, hardly defray the first costs, and the exports have increased in a ratio beyond all possible conjecture. By an average, at the most moderate computation, the price of every sort of Tea, bohea only excepted, is advanced more than forty per cent, nor is it yet at the highest. Such is the demand for this Article, that the Chinese hardly know *how much* to ask for it, and should the rage of purchasing continue only another year, it is not improbable that it may double its price. I shall for your information annex a list of the shipping at Wampo; and though the number for the English does not exceed that of the last year, yet from the size of the ships, the quantity of tonnage is greatly increased. In the opinion of judicious observers, the English seem to be aiming not only at a monopoly of the tea trade for Europe, but appear to have in view the exclusive Commerce of this division of the Globe. The new plan of Government for Bengal and its dependencies – their late establishments both to the eastward and westward – the prohibition to their subjects in India against selling their ships to foreigners – And in short their whole conduct strongly favour the suspicion. This object, and to be sure it is no trifling one, is now considered as the great idol of the English Nation; and in consequence of it the current of popular opinion carries rapidly along every measure which the Company think fit to adopt. How far our republican friends the Dutch, whom it most nearly concerns, will suffer any attempts of this kind, a few years must determine. The settlement of the English at Pulo Pinang, which enables them to command the whole of the navigation from the Peninsula of India, that of Malaya, and of the Island of Sumatra, has not a little alarmed them; and the settlement at Botany Bay on the south east coast of New Holland, has increased their apprehensions. I say nothing of the opposition the English might expect from the Swedes and Danes, who certainly find their advantage in this Commerce; or from the French invariably their Enemies. Perhaps a commercial confederation of these Nations, for their mutual benefit, not unlike the armed neutrality during the late war, may be adopted, as the best means of checking and defeating such exorbitant pretentions.

With respect to our own Commerce this way yet in its infancy, I shall only observe that inconsiderable as it has hitherto been and is this year especially, it is viewed with no small degree of jealousy by our late mother Country. Gentlemen in all parts of the World, of whatever nation they may be, can esteem and sometimes love one another. But Englishmen and Americans merely as such, in any place, as at Canton, where the former have the ascendency, can barely treat each other with civility. It is to national prejudices only, not yet done away, that I have reference, for I have found among them men who are an honor to their species. No national civility on their part have been offered us at Canton, either last year or the present; but at Macao, in the interval, there was a full tender of them made me, with a general invitation to their table. These however I thought proper to decline without assigning a reason, as circumstances rendered any explanation unnecessary. In my own particular I have no cause of complaint. The usual compliment of a visit has been mutually paid and returned, and we frequently meet at other tables, and also at the Danish Concert. They have themselves a public weekly concert, but for the reasons mentioned I never attend it. After saying thus much concerning the English, I should be guilty of the highest ingratitude were I to omit testifying on this occasion, my entire satisfaction in the reception and treatment I have met with from the Chiefs and Gentlemen of the other nations, not only at Canton, but during a residence of six months at Macao. It has been and continues to be in all respects proper, and in many instances really friendly.

Though little can ever be known of China by persons restricted to such narrow limits as are the foreigners who trade here, yet we see enough to give us very unfavourable ideas of its government. The laws may be good, but its police is extremely defective. It would shock your humanity were I to give a sketch of the misery which is here daily exhibited; and what excites the indignation of every foreigner, is that the number of these wretched objects not being considerable, it is evidently in the power of the Magistracy amply to provide for them. This is not the only instance which contradicts the generally received idea of the excellence of the Chinese Government. At present there are great disturbances in many parts of the Empire, and the insurrections in the Island of Formosa, and the adjacent Country threaten consequences of a serious nature. The war in that quarter has raged upwards of a twelvemonth – and its issue is yet doubtful. The oppressions exercised by Government have reduced the inhabitants of those parts to a state of desperation, which has had the most pernicious effects on the agriculture and commerce, not only of that but of the neighbouring Provinces.

From this painful view of the effects of despotism, I turn with pleasure to the contemplation of that happiness which an American enjoys, under the Government of equal laws and a mild administration. Surely, if we avail ourselves of the experience of other nations, and make a proper use of the advantages with which heaven hath blessed us, we cannot fail in due time of becoming a great and a happy people.

In addition to the observations in my former letter respecting the article of Genseng, I shall only observe that the sales of it this Season confirm me in the opinion of the great advantages which our Country may derive from it. The annexed list will shew the quantity brought here, and the price for the best has been from one hundred thirty to two hundred dollars the pecul, (133 1/3 lbs. English) at which it now stands, though probably it will rise twenty or thirty dollars before the departure of the last ships.

It was my intention after dispatching our ship last season to have gone to Bengal, but the vessel in which I had engaged my passage lost so much time at Macao that her destination was changed for Manilla, and I was reduced to the necessity of remaining behind. I am now making a second attempt, have engaged my passage and expect to sail the first week in January. On my return here in August next I hope to meet Mr Randall from America, by whom I flatter myself I shall have the honor of receiving your

Commands. The Commercial engagements I have made, in behalf of Mr Randall and my self, will involve the necessity for me if not for us both, to return at the close of the ensuing season to America. I therefore take the liberty of begging you will be pleased to communicate this circumstance to Congress; and I humbly hope that honorable body will not be offended that I take this step without their permission previously obtained. The loss of time which the waiting for such permission must involve would be prejudicial to us in the extreme, and this with the consideration that the office of Consul at Canton is rather honorary to the person vested with it, than essential to the Commerce of our Country, I presume to flatter myself will be admitted as my excuse.

Be pleased Sir, to do me the honor to accept my acknowledgments for the favours I have received from you, and to believe me most respectfully, with the highest esteem and regard &^c.   Samuel Shaw

NA: PCC, item 120, v. 3, pp. 381-386 (LBkC); M40, reel 3.

George Miller to Lord Carmarthen

My Lord.   Charleston, 24 December 1787.
Five days after the date of the last letter I had the honour to address to Your Lordship, (of the 17th Ultimo, duplicate of which I beg leave now to inclose;) my Commission was returned by Mr Bond with an Act of Congress thereupon of the 20th October, Recognizing me as His Majesty's Consul, only, the other part being suspended on the same grounds as that of Mr Bond: and on the 27th of same month it was made public in this State, in the form which I take the liberty to inclose. – I have also sent copies thereof to the Governours of North Carolina and Georgia, requesting to be announced in the States over which they respectively preside, which I have no doubt will be complied with.

How far this restricted acknowledgment of my Commission, may operate against the principles on which I was placed in my present situation, I cannot properly judge 'till the meeting of the Assembly; I can still, however, willing to indulge a hope, that such representations as I may find it particularly necessary to make to the Legislature, in consequence of Your Lordships commands, will meet with some regard and attention, as they shall be drawn up in a form not calculated to give offence, which at this particular time, when the British Merchants who are interested in the Trade to these States, have a very deep stake depending, it is the more necessary to avoid, especially as the exclusion of Vessels under American Colours from the trade to the Free ports lately established in the West

Indies and the Bahama Islands, has given umbrage to some of the leading men in this State, although they have no shadow of right to expect a participation therein, and might eventually tend to check their readiness to adopt and pursue a line of policy more favourable than the past, to the Commercial interests of Great Britain, from which the advantages they derive are manifest – I would even hope, that after the business of the new Constitution is discussed, – and in South Carolina I have little doubt but that it will be received, – the Recommendation of Congress to make the Treaty of Peace a part of the Law of the Land, will be made binding on this State, in which event, these representations will be confined within narrower bounds than the various heads, against which the Commerce of Britain connected with the trade to the States of North America, has had just right to complain: –

. . . . .

I have the honour to be, with the highest Respect, My Lord, Your Lordships most obedient, and most humble Servant   Geo: Miller

PRO: FO 4/5, pp. 791-793 (LC transcription).

Dutch Bankers to John Adams

Amsterdam 25 December, 1787

Being without any of your Excellency's esteemed favors unreplied to, the Purport of the present is to acquaint you, that on the 22nd Inst. we received a Letter from His Excellency Thos Jefferson Esqr Minister from the United States at the Court of Versailles, notifying to us that Mess$^{rs.}$ H. Fizeaux & Co of this City, had applied to him for f. [florins] 51,000 to pay off so much borrowed by them for account of the United States reimbursable the First Proximo, Punctuality in the discharge whereof M$^r.$ Jefferson conceiving to be highly interesting to the Honor & Credit of the United States, He presses us in the most energetic Stile to furnish the Money, informing us he had wrote your Excellency to join in enforcing his warm Sollicitation; So that we expect to hear from Your Excellency on the subject p[er] the British Mail detained by contrary Winds.

We sincerely regret the Application has been so late, that We are called to determine upon this matter without the necessary time to weigh its Consequences with the requisite Attention. Besides we are deprived of any Communication from the Board of Treasury respecting it, the official Channel thro which ought to issue the directions for Payments of such a Nature. This Remissness on the Part of the Commissioners, even had we plenty of Money of the United States, places us in the ever disagreeable

Predicament of assuming unnecessary Responsibility. Wherefore we request Your Excellency, to second our reiterated strong Representations, to have greater Punctuality shewn us in future on similar occasions. –

The funds we have in hand of the United States, will suffice to face the Interest that will be payable by them the 1ˢᵗ February next, and leave a small Surplus to discharge Your & Mʳ· Jefferson's monthly Drafts for a short time; Thus the Payment of the f. 51,000 would be an actual Advance of our own Cash, there being but little or no probability the Bonds of the last Loan for the U.S. will sell, While there are so many Loans open here for different Countries, whose Governments are firmly established & Punctuality has been long experienced. Our Zeal and Wish to serve the United States, will however prompt us to do all that can be expected on the occasion, and we shall not fail giving you the earliest Intelligence of our determination. In the mean time We must entreat Your Excellency, to desist for the present from accepting any further drafts for account of the United States, and to confine your disposals of Money to your personal Wants, as we might otherwise be exposed to greater Advances, than the Circumstances of the Times incline us to. The disagreeableness this Intimation is to Us, is greatly modified, by our intimate persuasion, that your Excellency's truly patriotic Principles, will induce your Acquiesence without reluctance, to any Measure dictated by a Regard for the Honor and Interest of your Country.

We are very respectfully Your Excellency's Most obedient and very humble Servants   Wilhem & Jan Willink
                              Nic. & Jacob van Staphorst.

MHS: *The Adams Papers, microfilm reel 370 (LS)*.

Claude Guillaume Lambert II to Thomas Jefferson

Versailles, December 29. 1787.

I have the honour, Sir, to send you a copy of an Arret passed in Council, for encouraging the Commerce of the United States of America in France. I shall furnish you with a number of others as soon as they shall be printed.

You will therein see that several considerable favors, not before promised to the American Commerce, have been added to those which the king announced to you, in the letter addressed to you on the 22ᵈ of october of the last year.

If in the mean time any duties have been levied, contrary to the intentions of that letter, they shall be repaid on sight of the vouchers.

I have also ordered a verification of the facts whereon it was represented to you, that the decision of the 24 of may 1786, relative to the Commerce of tobacco, had not been fully executed. Be assured that if it shall appear that engagements have been evaded, which were taken under the sanction of the king, effectual provision shall be made for their scrupulous fulfillment.

You will learn also with pleasure that the measures I have taken to prevent the interruption of the Commerce of tobacco, have had full success.

This commodity shall not be excepted from among those to which the right of entrepot is given. The farmers general shall have no preference in the purchases, the proprietors shall be perfectly masters of their speculations, and free to export their tobaccoes by sea to foreign countries.

Measures only must be taken to prevent those frauds to which the entrepot might serve as a pretext; and the chambers of commerce for the ports shall be consulted, in order that the precautions necessary for this purpose, may not be in a form incompatible with that liberty which Commerce ought to enjoy in its operations.

Although the present stock of the farmers general amounts to about three years consumption I have engaged that company to continue to purchase yearly from the 1st day of january 1788. to the end of their lease fourteen thousand hogsheads of tobacco brought directly into the ports of France in French or American bottoms, and to shew at the end of every four months that their purchases amount to four thousand six hundred and sixty six hogsheads.

As to the prices, you have been sensible yourself of the necessity of leaving them free; and this freedom of price was the principal object of the applications of the American and French merchants when they complained of the contract of M. Morris.

The determination then taken to force the purchases of tobacco, tho at high prices, insomuch that the farmers general now find themselves possessed of three years provision, shews that the interests of the planters and merchants of the United States of America have ever been precious to the King.

The arret of Council herein inclosed, and the other regulations which I have the honour of communicating to you, are a further confirmation of a truth tending so much to strengthen the bands which unite the two nations.

I have the honour to be with a very sincere and inviolable attachment, Sir, you most humble and most obedient servant.

Lambert.

NA: PCC, item 87, v. 2, pp. 35-38 (printed translation); M247, reel 115.

Enclosure: An Act of the French Council of State

An Act of the King's Council of State, For the encouragement of the Commerce of France with the United States of America.

[Paris] December 29. 1787.

Extract from the records of the Council of State.

The King desirous of encouraging the commerce of his subjects with the United States of America and of facilitating between the two Nations connections reciprocally useful: Having heard the report of the Sieur Lambert, Counsellor of State and of the Royal Council of finance and commerce, Comptroller general of finance, His Majesty being in his Council, has ordained, and does ordain as follows:

Article First.

Whale-Oils and spermaceti, the produce of the fisheries of the citizens & inhabitants of the United States of America, which shall be brought into France directly in French vessels or in those of the United States shall continue to be subjected to a duty only of seven livres ten sols the barrel of five hundred and twenty pounds weight, & whale fins shall be subject to a duty of only six livres thirteen sols four deniers the quintal with the ten sols per livre on each of the said duties; which ten sols per livre shall cease on the last day of December one thousand seven hundred & ninety; His Majesty reserving to himself to grant further favors to the produce of the whale fisheries carried on by the fishermen of the United States of America which shall be brought into France in French vessels or in those of the United States, if, on the information which His Majesty shall cause to be taken thereon, he shall judge it expedient for the interest of the two Nations.

II.

The other fish-oils and dry or salted fish, the produce in like manner of the fisheries of the citizens & inhabitants of the United States, & brought also directly into France, in their, or in French Vessels, shall not pay any other nor greater duties than those to which the oils & fish of the same kind, the produce of the fisheries of the Hanseatic towns, or of other the most favored Nations, are or shall be subject in the same case.

III.

The manufacture of candles and tapers of spermaceti shall be permitted in France, as that of other candles & tapers.

IV.

Corn, wheat, rye, rice, peas, beans, lentils, flax-seed and other seeds, flour, trees and shrubs, pot-ash and pearl-ash, skins and fur of beaver, raw hides, furs and peltry, and timber brought from the United States directly

into France, in French vessels or in those of the United States, shall not be
subject but to a duty of one eighth per cent on their value.

V.

Vessels built in the United States and sold in France, or purchased by
Frenchmen shall be exempt from all duties on proof that they were built in
the United States.

VI.

Turpentine, tar and pitch the produce of the United States of America
and brought directly into France in French vessel[s] or in those of the
United States shall pay only a duty of two and a half per cent on their
value, and as well the duties mentioned in this as in the fourth article shall
be exempt from all addition of sous per livre.

VII.

The exportation of arms of all sorts, and of gun powder for the United
States of America, shall be always permitted in French vessels or in those
of the United States, paying for the arms a duty of one eighth per cent on
their value: and gunpowder in that case shall be exempt from all duty on
giving a cautionary bond.

VIII.

Papers of all sorts, even paper hangings and coloured papers, pasteboard
and books shall be exempt from all duties on their embarcation for the
United States of America, in French vessels or in those of the United
States, and shall be entitled in that case to a restitution of the fabrication
duties on paper and pasteboard.

IX.

The Admiralty duties on the vessels of the United States entering into,
or going out of the ports of France, shall not be levied but conformably
with the Edict of the month of june last in the cases therein provided for,
and with the Letters-patent of the tenth of january one thousand seven
hundred and seventy for the objects for which no provision shall have been
made by the said Edict: his Majesty reserving to himself moreover to make
known his intentions as to the manner in which the said duties shall be
levied, whether in proportion to the tonnage of the vessels or otherwise, as
also to simplify the said duties of the Admiralty and to regulate them as far
as shall be possible on the principle of reciprocity, as soon as the orders
shall be completed which were given by his Majesty according to the
twenty-sixth article of the said Edict of the month of june last.

X.

The entrepot (or storing) of all the productions and merchandize of the
United States shall be permitted for six months in all the ports of France
open to the Commerce of her Colonies; and the said entrepot shall be
subject only to a duty of one eighth per cent.

XI.

To favour the exportation of arms, hardware, jewellery bonnetery (*), of wool and of cotton, coarse woollens, small draperies and stuffs of cotton of all sorts, and other merchandizes of French fabric, which shall be sent to the United States of America, in French vessels or in those of the United States, His Majesty reserves to himself to grant encouragements which shall be immediately regulated in his Council, according to the nature of each of the said merchandizes.

XII.

As to other merchandizes not mentioned in this act, brought directly into France from the United States in their or in French vessels, or carried from France to the said United States in French vessels or in those of the United States, and with respect to all commercial conventions whatsoever His Majesty wills and ordains that the citizens of the United States enjoy in France the same rights, privileges and exemptions with the subjects of His Majesty: saving the execution of what is provided in the ninth article hereof.

XIII.

His Majesty grants to the citizens and inhabitants of the United States all the advantages which are enjoyed or which may be here after enjoyed by the most favored nations in his Colonies of America and moreover His Majesty assures to the said citizens and inhabitants of the United States all the privileges and advantages which his own subjects of France enjoy or shall enjoy in Asia and in the scales leading thereto: provided always that their vessels shall have been fitted out and dispatched in some port of the United States.

His Majesty commands and orders M. le duc de Penthievre,[1] Admiral of France, the Intendants and commissaries de parti in the provinces, the commissaries de parti for the observation of the ordinances in the admiralties, the officers of the admiralties masters of the ports, judges des traites, and all others to whom it shall belong to be aiding in the execution of the present regulation which shall be registered in the offices of the said admiralties read published and posted wherever shall be necessary.

Done in the King's council of State, His Majesty present, held at Versailles the twenty ninth of december one thousand seven hundred and eighty seven.   Le Cte de la Luzerne.

(*) This term includes: bonnets stockings, socks underwaist coats, drawers gloves and mitaines as sold by the Bonnetiers.

NA: PCC, item 87, v. 2, pp. 39-46 (printed translation); M247, reel 115.
[1] Penthièvre, Louis Jean Marie de Bourbon, Duc de. Grand Admiral of France.

Phineas Bond to Lord Carmarthen

My Lord,   Philad[a.] Dec. 29[th.] 1787.

I have the honor to enclose to your Ldp a letter for the Rt. Hon. the Lord's Com. of the admiralty, and another for the Hon. the Com. of the Customs forwarding ship's papers; and I am happy to inform your Ldp, that I have discovered a fraud practiced by some traders of this place, to evade the Acts of Navigation, by obtaining British papers, for a vessel, the property of subjects of the United States; the particulars of which I have communicated to the Lords of the Admiralty by this mail. –

Since I had the honor of writing to your Ldp. two ships have sailed from hence to China; one the *Asia*, Capt. Barry,[1] a fine new ship of about 320 tons – the other the *Canton* ship, Capt. Truxton[2] of about 260 tons; the latter of which has already been one voyage.

The ships my Lord are chiefly laden with [   ] rum and other spirits, and British goods of particular kinds, suited to the China markets, most of these goods, my Lord, the too liberal faith of British merchants intrusted to dealers here, who are now speculating and sporting with the property of their creditors and screening themselves under a most relaxed system of laws: There is some specie on board, my Lord, about 57000 dollars in the *Asia* and about 46000 dollars in the *Canton* but this article was not so easily obtainable as British goods; indeed it was found so scarce that many of the company interested in these ships found it extremely difficult to make up their respective quotas; even now, my Lord, the money and goods exported in these ships will not be adequate to the necessary investments in China, to render the voyage a productive one. Recourse will therefore be had to the borrowing on bottomry and respondentia Bonds, from those, who finding it difficult to send their fortunes home, adopt this circuitous mode of remittance; or are perhaps tempted by high premiums to incur an extraordinary risque. – I have heretofore, my Lord, given your Ldp. all the information I was possessed of, on this subject; and the languid manner in which the outfits of these ships have been made here confirms the opinion I presumed to offer to your Ldp, that a very little matter by way of check would perfectly unhinge this trade and completely derange all the plans of those engaged in it.

The ship called the *"Grand Turk,"* Capt Derby[3] sailed again from Salem in New England to the isle of France, on the 8[th.] inst. –

A small brigantine belonging to this port of about 110 tons burden sailed within these few days, hence for Batavia

I have the honor to enclose your Ldp. a direction respecting one of the persons who lately made the affidavit to prove the fraudulent shipping of manufacturing utensils and the decoying manufacturers from Gt. Britain and Ireland; I advanced him a small sum of money, and he is now on his way, with his family to Cork and Liverpool; if your Ldp. should think it proper to have him examined, he may probably furnish very material information respecting those who are engaged in this business –

    I have the honor to be, my Lord, your Ldp's most faithful and obed: servant   P. Bond
R. Jan: 29$^{th.}$

              ·   ·   ·   ·

AHA 1896, v. 1, pp. 555-557.

[1] *Barry, John (1745-1803). U.S. naval officer. Before the revolution, a wealthy Philadelphia shipmaster and shipowner. Commanded brig* Lexington, *1776; frigate* Effingham, *1776-1777; frigate* Raleigh, *1778; and frigate* Alliance, *1781-1783. Named senior captain, 1794, and given command of frigate* United States. *Given charge of all naval forces in the West Indies, 1798. Commanded Guadeloupe station, 1799-1801.*

[2] *Truxtun, Thomas (1755-1822). U.S. naval officer, seafarer. Successful privateersman during Revolutionary War. Captain of the ship* Canton, *the first Philadelphia vessel sent to China, 1786. Appointed captain, U.S. Navy, 1794. Commanded frigate* Constellation *in victorious actions against French frigates* L'Insurgente *and* La Vengeance, *1799-1800.*

[3] *Derby, Elias Hasket (1766-1826). Merchant and seafarer. Captain,* Grand Turk, *on voyage to Isle de France, 1787-1790, during which he established the Derby firm as the major American merchant house on the island.*

Thomas Jefferson to John Jay

Sir   Paris, Dec. 31. 1787.
    Since the receipt of the letter of Monsieur de Calonne of Octob. 22. 1786. I have several times had the honour of mentioning to you that I was endeavouring to get the substance of that letter reduced into an arrêt, which, instead of being revocable by a single letter of a comptroller general, would require an arrêt to repeal or alter it, and of course must be discussed in full council and so give time to prevent it. this has been pressed as much as it could be with prudence. one cause of delay has been the frequent changes of the Comptroller general; as we had always our whole work to begin again with every new one. Monsieur Lambert's continuance in office for some months has enabled us at length to get through the business; and I have just received from him a letter and arrêt duly authenticated; of which I have the honour to send you a number of printed copies. you will find that the several alterations and additions are made, which on my visit to the seaports I had found to be necessary, and which my letters of June 21. and Aug. 6. particularly mentioned to you. besides these we have obtained some new articles of value, for which openings arose in the course

of the negociation. I say *we* have done it; because the Marquis de la Fayette has gone hand in hand with me through this business, and has been a most invaluable aid. I take the liberty of making some observations on the articles of the arrêt severally, for their explanation as well as for the information of Congress.

Article 1. In the course of our conferences with the Comptroller general we had prevailed on him to pass this article with a suppression of all duty. when he reported the arrêt however to the council, this suppression was objected to, and it was insisted to reestablish the duties of 7^L 10^s and of 10^s the livre reserved in the letter of Monsr de Calonne. the passage of the arrêt was stopped, and the difficulty communicated to me. I urged every thing I could, in letters, & in conferences to convince them that whale oil was an article which could bear no duty at all. that if the duty fell on the consumer, he would chuse to buy vegetable oils; if on the fisherman, he could no longer live by his calling, remaining in his own country: and that if he quitted his own country, the circumstances of vicinity, sameness of language, laws, religion, & manners, & perhaps the ties of kindred would draw him to Nova Scotia, in spite of every encouragement which could be given at Dunkirk: and that thus those fishermen would be shifted out of a scale friendly to France, into one always hostile. nothing however could prevail. it hung on this article alone for two months, during which we risked the total loss of the arret on the stability in office of M. Lambert: for if he had gone out, his successor might be less favorable; & if mr Neckar were the successor, we might lose the whole, as he never set any store by us, or the connection with us. about ten days ago it became universally believed that mr Lambert was to go out immediately. I therefore declined further insisting on the total suppression, and desired the arret might pass leaving the duties on whale oil as M. de Calonne had promised them; but with a reservation which may countenance our bringing on this matter again at a more favourable moment.

Article 2. the other fish oils are placed in a separate article; because whatever encouragement we may hereafter obtain for whale oils, they will not be extended to those which their own fisheries produce.

Article 3. A company had silently and by unfair means obtained a monopoly for the making & selling spermaceti candles: as soon as we discovered it, we sollicited it's suppression, which is effected by this clause.

Article 4. the duty of an eighth per cent is merely to oblige the masters of vessels to enter their cargoes for the information of government; without inducing them to attempt to smuggle.

Article 6. Tar, pitch, & turpentine of America coming in competition with the same articles produced in Southwestern parts of France, we could obtain no greater reduction than to 2 1/2 percent. the duties before were from 4. to 6. times that amount.

Article 10. The right of Entrepot given by this article is almost the same thing as the making all their ports, free ports for us. the ships are indeed subject to be visited & the cargoes must be reported in ports of Entrepot, which need not be done in the Freeports. but the communication between the entrepot and the country is not interrupted by continual search of all persons passing into the country, which has proved so troublesome to the inhabitants of our freeports as that a considerable preportion of them have wished to give back the privilege of their freedom.

Article 13. This article gives us the privileges & advantages of native subjects in all their possessions in Asia, and in the *scales leading thereto.* this expression means at present the isles of France and Bourbon, and will include the Cape of good hope should any future event put it into the hands of France. it was with a view to this that I proposed the expression, because we were then in hourly expectation of a war, and it was suspected that France would take possession of that place. it will in no case be considered as including any thing Westward of the Cape of good hope. – I must observe further on this article that it will only become valuable on the suppression of their East India company; because as long as their monopoly continues, even native subjects cannot enter their Asiatic ports for the purposes of commerce. it is considered however as certain that this company will be immediately suppressed.

The article of tobacco could not be introduced into the Arrêt, because it was necessary to consider the Farmers general as parties to that arrangement. it rests therefore of necessity on the basis of a letter only. you will perceive that this is nothing more than a continuation of the order of Berni, only leaving the prices unfixed; & like that it will require a constant and vexatious attention to have it's execution enforced.

The states which have much to carry, & few carriers, will observe perhaps that the benefits of these regulations are somewhat narrowed by confining them to articles brought hither in French or American bottoms. but they will consider that nothing in these instruments moves from us. the advantages they hold out, are all given by this country to us, and the givers will modify their gifts as they please. I suppose it to be a determined principle of this court not to suffer our carrying business, so far as their consumption of our commodities extends, to become a nursery for British seamen. nor would this perhaps be advantageous to us, considering the dispositions of the two nations towards us. the preference which our shipping will obtain on this account may counterpoise the discouragements it experiences from the aggravated dangers of the Barbary states. nor is the idea unpleasing which shews itself in various parts of these papers, of naturalising American bottoms, and American citizens in France, and in it's foreign possessions. once established here, and in their Eastern settlements, they may revolt less at the proposition to extend it to those Westward. they are not yet however at that point; we must be contented to go towards it a step at a time, and trust to future events for hastening our progress.

.   .   .   .   .

...I have the honour to be with sentiments of the most perfect & respect, Sir, your most obedient & most humble servant   Th: Jefferson

LC: *Jefferson Papers, microfilm reel 8 (press copy).*

George Washington to Thomas Jefferson

Dear Sir,   Mount Vernon [January 1, 1788]

.   .   .   .   .

Altho' the finances of France and England were such as led you to suppose, at the time you wrote to me, would prevent a Rupture between those two powers, yet, if we credit the concurrent acc^{ts} from every quarter, there is little doubt but that they have commenced hostilities before this. – Russia & the Porte have formally began the contest, and from appearances (as given to us) it is not improbable but that a pretty general war will be kindled in Europe. should this be the case, we shall feel more than ever the want of an efficient general Government to regulate our Commercial concerns, to give us a National Respectability, and to connect the political views and interests of the several States under one head in such a manner as will effectually prevent them from forming seperate, improper, or indeed any connection, with the European powers which can involve them in their political disputes. – For our situation is such as makes it not only unnecessary, but extremely imprudent for us to take a part in their quarrels; and whenever a contest happens among them, if we wisely & properly improve the advantages which nature has given us, we may be benefitted by their folly – provided we conduct < * > ourselves, with circumspection, & under proper Restrictions, for I perfectly agree with you, that an extensive speculation, – a spirit of gambling, – or the introduction of any thing which will divert our attention from Agriculture, must be extremely prejudicial, if not ruinous to us. but I conceive under an energetic general Government such regulations might be made, and such measures taken, as would render this Country the asylum of pacific and industrious characters from all parts of Europe – Would encourage the cultivation of the Earth by the high price which its products would command – and would draw the wealth, and wealthy men of other Nations, into our own bosom, by giving security to property, and liberty to its holders.

I have the honor to be With great esteem & regard Dear Sir Y^r most Obed. & most H^{ble} Servt·   G$^{o:}$ Washington

LC: *Jefferson Papers, microfilm reel 8 (ALS)*.

Sir John Temple to Lord Carmathen

N^o· 27.   New York 2^d Jan: 1788:

My Lord,

Inclosed is duplicate of the Letter I had the honor of writing to your Lordship on the 5th of December, by the *Antilope* Packet; since which, no Mail hath arrived from England, nor hath any thing occurred in these states deserving your Lordships particular notice or attention. The Deligates to Congress have not yet reassembled to do business, & probably will not until the Spring, when the sense of the several states will have been collected upon the proposed New Constitution: It now seems most probable that it will be adopted, though with a very considerable & obstinate Minority in opposition to it.

The uncertainly of Peace continuing between his Majesty & the french King, keeps the people of this Country in a state of much anxiety for the arrival of the November Packet, now hourly expected; the latest accounts we have from England, were, on Saturday last, by way of Glasgow, up to the 20th of October; from those Accounts, the people here almost *conclude* that War hath commenced before this time; for my own part I cannot but still think & hope, that france, considering her present embarrassed condition, surrounded with difficulties & distress, may, by complying with his Majestys just and honorable requisition, have saved the expence & trouble of compelling them to it, and that, all may be yet Peace and commercial intercourse between the two Nations.

Sh^d it however be otherwise, France will most probable exert her usual Art & influence to procure partiality in these states! and to this Object, I shall, to the utmost of my Ability & influence, pay all attention, and as far as possible, counteract such their designs. A French Minister is, I am informd, expected in the Next Packet from france, and he will not, I dare, say come with Empty Pocketts, no bad policy to these indigent states; but, it is with pleasure I can perceive, that all uncorrupted sensible Americans behold with dislike, & even detestation, the part that faithless Court, have, for a long time, Acted in the Netherlands; &, after all their incendiary projects, have left those ignorant Wrongheaded Dutchmen to shift for themselves!

Sh^{d:} there be War between England & france, it appears to me more than probable that Privateers, from several of these states, will be fitted out on both sides the question! and I believe more of them against the french, than against the English! and such Adventurers will probably bring on Battles in these Ports or harbours, & perhaps on shore, for these states have not a Gun on float, nor a Cannon mounted, to command respect to a Neutral flag! therewith I have the honor of inclosing to your Lordship my tenth Letter, under a flying seal, to the Lords Commrs of the Admiralty, covering a List of such Ships & Vessells as have arrived & departed this Port of New York, with Mediteranean Passes, between the 7th of Novemb^{r} the date of my last returns to that Board, and this present 2^{d} of January 1788. and I have the honor to remain, with all deference, My Lord, Your Lordships most faithful and Obedient Servant   J. Temple.

R. 29^{th:}

PRO: FO 4/6, pp. 1-4 (LC transcription).

Peter Allaire: Occurrences
from 6 December 1787 to 2 January 1788

New York 3 January 1787 [1788]

The State of Delaware have Ratified & Confirmed the New federal Constitution, unanimously, the 6^{th:} December last,

The State of Pensilvania, after a debate of three Weeks on the same Subject, have Confirmed it by a Majority of 46 to 23: 12^{th:} Dec^{r·}

The Federal Constitution is at present under Consideration of the States of New Hampshire, Boston (by the Choice of their Members there is not the least doubt but they will Acceed) New Jersey, and Virginia (who have given full powers to their delegates, not Only to Reject & amend any of the Articles, but to add & improve the same) the other States are not in session, but will be in the Course of this Month, by the present Appearances of the Times, there is little doubt but what the New Federal Constitution will be Adopted by Nine States at least, which will compell the other four to agree to it, or form another Republick, as the New System will certainly take Effect as soon as the Nine States have Ratified it.

The State of Pensilvania have sent to China this Year One Ship, the *Canton* Capt Truxton, New York, One Ship the *Jay*, Capt Randal & a Brig:

Boston, One Ship & a Brig: Amounting in all to About 1100 or 1200 Tons.

The Southern States of Georgia, South & North Carolina & Virginia are at War with the Southern Indians, & they have drafted five thousand Militia to go against them, & are now on their March towards their fron-tiers, (for particulars, see Copy of Lord Dorchesters Letter herewith.) Congress are in so little Credit that the three Southern States of Georgia South & North Carolina, have refused to comply with a Requisition of theres of the 20th October last for two thousand Dollars each, and that those States should be Credited that Sum in the next general Requisition, being intended to be appropriated to the satisfying and quieting the Indians and preventing an Indian War; they Refuse declaring, that Congress are by the Articles of Confederation, bound to protect them against all foreign and Domestick Enemies, and that all Expences attending any Expidition against the Indians, the Common Enemy, ought to be paid out of the Publick Treasury, and not by Individual States, that their proportion of the general Requisition, when call for, shall be paid, but that those States are not at present in a Condition to advance money for the Benefit of the United States.

Their Recommendations & Resolves, with Respect to precuniary Affairs are at present of little Value, the People at large complaining loudly of their Incapability of keeping up the Credit of Congress, on its present plans of paying of part of the principal as well as Interest of the National Debt, and the delegates of Several States have represented the same to Congress. In Jersey as soon as the Receiver General of the County has Received the Taxes, he is sure to be Robbed, three of those Roberies were committed between the 10th & 17 December last in Virginia, they Rob the publick Offices & distroy the Records in several Counties in this Stay [State], they Refuse paying Taxes and when their Goods & Chattles are put up to Sale, no bidders are to be found, & the Collectors are obliged to return their goods to the Original proprietors

Without the new federal Constitution, or some Solid and Coersive Government is soon Adopted, it will certainly end in a general Insurrection of the People for abolish all Taxes. Congress are Convinced that the Credit of the United States cannot be kept up, on its present Systim, nor was it in their power to fullfill their Engagements with their foreign Creditors for the Year 1788, but by the procuring a temporary loan, which was Accom-plished by Mr Adams at Amsterdam the 4 June last for One Million of Guilders, in hopes that the New Constitution may be Established before the next general Requisition; that money is Ordered to be appropriated to the payment of the Interest of the Dutch Loans, the Money lenders of Holland having sent Over a Person fully Impowered to demand of Congress their Interest due According to their Engagements.

The Embassadore at Versailles having represented the present State of Affairs of the United States &c & The King of France has been graciously pleased &c to forgive & Relinquish all the Interest due to him from the United States to November last on Conditions, that the said United States, pay him in fifteen Years, in Equal Instalments with Interest at 5 p Cent the Amount of his Debt being 34 Million of Livres Tournois or About One Million five hundred thousand pounds Sterling, he has Also forgiven them a Debt of Nine Million of Livres, furnished them at the commencement of the War.

His Excellency Lord Dorchester
My Lord
    The States of Georgia, & North Carolina & Virginia have drafted five thousand of their Militia, to go against the Creeks Chiksaws & Chickesaws Indians, they having got in their Crops of Corn have Attacked the frontier settlements of those States, Murdered upwards of Sixty families, and have drove all the frontier Setlers into the forts and home settlements, they are in large parties, some as Numerous as four hundred and have Committed depredations within 36 Miles of Savanah, which has occasioned Martial Law being proclaimed in that State, those States have Applied to Congress to take those forces into pay of the Untied States, on the same footing as the Continental Troops, And to make use of such Stores & Ammunition as they may stand in need of, to be found at their Forts &c, which Congress has Complyed with, on Condition, that all Militia & Forces raised by any of said States, be under the Imediate direction & Command of Coll: Harman, or the Commanding Officer of the Troop of the United States; Franklin, Kentucky & Fayett States have sent an Express to the Governor of the Spanish Settlements on the Mississippi to inform him that they Indians have made War against them & desiring him not to furnish any of those Tribes with any Warlike Stores, or Ammunition, if he does they shall look upon it as a breach of the peace, & a declaration of hostilities.

    The Board of Treasury are now Ordering, provisions, Cloths and Ammunition to be Imediately sent to the frontier forts, for use of those Troops, with the utmost Expedition, Congress has given Orders to Augment their Forces from 750, to 1250 Men for the protection of the frontier Inhabitants, for three Years, unless sooner discharged: they have appointed Arthur St Clair, (late President of Congress) Governor & Commander in Chief of the Western Territory and Superintendant of Indian Affairs for the Northern department with full powers to call Imediately a general meeting of all the Tribes of Indians inhabiting the North West of the Ohio, to settle all differences, enquire fully into the Causes of their Complaints and uneasiness that may have Arisen between the frontier inhabitants and said Indians, to explain & Confirm all former treaties, to fix the line Circumscribing the Indians hunting ground, to use every means in his power to settle in an Amicable manner all complaints & Injuries that may have been committed by any of the Subjects of the United States, and to Endeavour to prevent a general Indian War by every concession (not inconsistant With the dignity of Congress,) and to Assure them of the friendship & good faith of Congress towards them – he has also Orders to draw on the Continental Treasury for fourteen thousand Dollars in Specie, and takes up with him in goods to the Value of Six thousand Dollars, Also Orders to take what Troops from the frontier post with him he shall judge necessary for the protection of the Stores &c, the Indians claims large tracts of Land; which has been Surveyed & Already sold by Congress they dread a general Indian War, and will do every thing in their power to prevent One, a Committee of Congress has Reported, that the Indians do not complain without just cause, that there is Reasons to Apprehend the Indians are Meditating a serious blow against the frontier Setlements of the United States, that many of the White People have taken possession of Indian Lands under false pretences of Indian Grants, that an Avaricious disposition in some of our People to acquire large Tracts of Land & Often by unfair means appear to be the principal Cause of discontent, that the Superintendant of Indian Affairs for the Southern department, to inform those Indians, that Congress has given to hear and adjust all differences between them & the United States, that they have given Orders to supply them with what goods they may want, and as a proof of their friendship, they have Ordered the amount of Six thousand Dollars in goods to be distributed amongst them. should they Order any of their Troops to the Northward towards your frontier post, I shall Imediately obey your private Instructions & waite on your Excellency in Person. Congress has granted to the Canada Refugees setled on Lake Champlain adjoining your posts One Years Rations, to the Aged & infirm who are incapable of providing for themselves, Except Rum, Soap, & Candles;

By the October Packet from England, there is great appearance of a War between England & France, both having fitted out large fleets and were ready to Sail, should a declaration take place I shall take the first Oppertunity of informing your Excellency

I have the honor to be &c

New York 20ᵗʰ December 1787.

The Above Letter containing part of the last Month's Occurrences, induced me to Insert it.

. . . . . .
I Remain with Respect Your Most Obe^t H^e Ser^t   PA
R: 6^{th:} Febry 1788

PRO: FO 4/6, pp. 95-110 (LC transcription).

John Jay to Pieter Johan van Berckel

Sir   New York 10th Jany 1788
The letter you did me the honor to write on the 18th day of December last was transmitted to me whilst in the Country.
On my return to Town I wrote a Letter on the subject of it to the honorable Mr Duane,¹ and enclosed a translation of your Letter; for as the aggression complained of was committed in this City, it appeared to me proper that the circumstances should be made known to its first Magistrate, in order that measures might be immediately taken both for your satisfaction, and to prevent the like improprieties in future.
The Mayor received the application in the manner becoming his Character and Office; but his whole time being engaged by the Mayors Court which is now sitting, a day or two must elapse before it will be in my power to give you any more particular information on the subject.
I exceedingly regret that you should experience the least cause of complaint from any of our Citizens. The present instance doubtless originated in ignorance, not in design, but still as your official rights were infringed, it is highly proper not only that you should assert them, but that proper satisfaction be given you on that head. I have the honor to be with great respect and consideration &^{c.}   John Jay

NA: PCC, item 120, v. 3, pp. 312-313 (LBkC); M40, reel 3.
¹ *Duane, James (1733-1797). New York political figure and jurist. Member, Continental Congress, 1774-1783. Mayor of New York City, 1784-1789. U.S. district judge for the district of New York, 1789-1794.*

Comte de la Luzerne to Comte de Montmorin

[Translation]
Versailles, 10 January 1788.
I have seen, Sir, by the enclosed Letter that M. Otto, the King's Chargé des Affaires in New York, sent you, that some Merchants of Boston, informed that someone wishes to assert the right of escheat regarding the

Estate of one of his Relatives deceased in St. Domingue, observe that this would be to act counter to Article 11 of the Treaty of Commerce between France and the United States, by which the abolition of the right of escheat in France was stipulated in favor of Subjects of the United States. They further claim that the words *in France* sufficiently designate all the French possessions, and that moreover, the free ports which have been granted to Foreigners in our Colonies render necessary the abolition of the right of escheat there, since Foreigners whom we want to attract thither will refrain from going there if we do not allow them the right to dispose of their effects, or the hope of passing them on, *ab intestato*,[1] to their natural heirs.

These arguments in favor of the abolition of the right of escheat in our Colonies are only illusory. It is true that Article 11 of the Treaty, which is invoked, specifies this Abolition in france, but by those indefinite words *in France*, one could not mean the Colonies, where the right of escheat is exercised towards all the friendly or allied powers with which the abolition of the right of escheat has been stipulated. Those of these powers which have Colonies also exercise the same right there towards Frenchmen. This right, moreover, could never have been, and can never be exercised on the chattels, or the proceeds from the chattels, which a foreigner brings to the Islands, as long as the Vessel in which he arrived remains there, and he is occupied in the operations of his voyage. He therefore has only to fear for the Consequences of an Establishment that he may have judged appropriate to make in the Islands, but in this regard, he has no right to complain, since he cannot be unaware that the invariable practice of the powers that have Colonies has been, and still is, to send away Foreigners. The opening of free ports cannot provide grounds for any exception in this regard, because that Action was not intended to induce Foreigners to come there and take up residence, but only to bring goods there that the national Commerce cannot yet furnish, such as Wood, Codfish, Livestock, and other articles of small value, for the sale of which permanent Establishments are not necessary. I am convinced, Sir, that you, like me, will embrace these principles regarding the exercise of the right of escheat in the Colonies, and I beg you to be so good as to transmit them to M. Otto.

I have the honor to be with a most sincere and perfect affection, Sir, your most humble and most obedient Servant.   La Luzerne
Sent Copy to M. Otto, 29 Feb. 1788.

FFAA: Pol. Corr., U.S., v. 33, f. 6-7 (LC transcription).
[1] *by rule of law*

Louis Guillaume Otto to Comte de Montmorin

[Translation]
My Lord,   New York, 18 Jan^{ry}· 1788.
I profit from the departure of a merchant Ship going to Bordeaux to announce to You the happy arrival of M. le Comte de Moustier after a crossing of Sixty-five days. This Minister has been received by the inhabitants of New York with all the demonstrations of respect and affection due to the representative of a nation that has rendered such essential services to the United States. Unfortunately, the health of M. le Comte de Moustier has been much impaired by this long crossing, and he will have need of several weeks' rest to regain his strength.

The news that this Minister brings to America concerning the peace and the affairs of Holland could not be more suitable to contradict the false reports that several persons attached to England have endeavored to give out in the United States.

I am with a profound respect My Lord Your most humble and most obedient servant   Otto.
rec. 30 March

FFAA: Pol. Corr., U.S., v. 33, f. 11-11vo. (LC transcription).

John Wylley to James Duane

Dr Sir   New York Jan^{ry} 19. 1788
In answer to your Letter of the 7th instant on the subject of a Complaint exhibited against me by the Minister of the United Netherlands I beg leave to inform you substantially of the whole of my conduct in that Business, from which you will be enabled to judge whether I have in the least been guilty of a violation of the Priviledge of an Ambassador.

On Thursday the 15th December last I issued a warrant against a certain James Van Antwerp, at the suit of John Van Gelder for a Debt, which warrant by a mistake I dated the 14th instead of 13th· That on Tuesday following I received two Messages from His Excellency M^r van Berkel desiring me to wait on him immediately, I accordingly left my Business and went to His Excellencys Residence when after waiting in a cold Room for about a quarter of an Hour his Excellency appeared and asked me my Name. I answered, John Wylley, he then charged me with having issued a Writ against his Servant, which I denied. I then asked him, the Name of his Servant and on his answering Van Antwerp, I said I had issued a

Warrant against a Young Man of that Name, not knowing him to be an Ambassadors Servant but supposing him to be in the service of a M[r] Stevens as I was informed by M[r] Van Gelder the Plaintiff at the time of issuing the warrant. His Excellency then said I should be made to know his Servants. I replied that I did not know that I was obliged to know him or his Servants but in the way that was Right. He then directed me to go home and mind my Tayloring, that I had no Business to be an Alderman! I replied that I had supported myself and family many Years by the Taylors Business and hoped for the continuance of the favors of many good friends who had employed me in that way; That as to the Office of Alderman, the People had been pleased to elect me and I placed my hope in a higher power than that of His Excellency for support in the execution of my Office. He then said I should be punished as falling under his Notice. I replied, I asked no favor of him – He then asked me if I did not know his Person was sacred I replied I did and had done him no Injury. He then repeated the Threat that he would punish me and I again answered I asked him no favor – Then seating himself in the Window He asked me if I thought him a Fool – I answered that the People of the States of Holland would be wanting in their Duty if they should send a Fool on so important an Embassy. I then asked him if he had any further Commands and on receiving no answer I wished his Excellency a good Morning – On my leaving the Room he repeated the Threat of Punishment and I repeated the answer that I asked no favor. –

I have the Honor to be Sir Your Most Obed[t] Serv[t]

John Wylley

NA: PCC, *item 80, v. 3, pp. 392-393 (C); M247, reel 106.*

Henry Knox to the President of Congress

[New York] 25th January 1788.

I have the honor to transmit to your Excellency the Copy of a Letter said to have been written by a certain M[r] John Sullivan, together with the evidence of its authenticity.

This Letter was delivered to me by the Secretary of foreign Affairs to whom it was enclosed from Philadelphia. The strong intimations contained in it of an audacious and unjustifiable design which might involve the United States in a war with a foreign Nation, seemed to require that some measures should be immediately taken thereon. Accordingly I conceived it my duty in the recess of Congress to transmit to Brigadier General Harmer the commanding Officer of the Troops on the frontiers, the directions contained in the enclosed Letter to him, which I humbly hope may be conformable to the judgment of Congress.

I have hitherto considered this Letter as a secret of State, and it is with all possible deference that I take the liberty of suggesting to Congress the propriety of its still being considered in that light.

It is a fact well ascertained that reports have been circulated on the frontiers, that Congress were about to obtain advantages for the marine States at the expence of some of the rights of the inhabitants of the western waters. If to the existing opinions and prejudices on this subject fresh matter heightened probably by misrepresentation should be added, the result might be greatly pernicious to the public interests.

No report has been received in consequence of my directions of the 14ᵗʰ of November, indeed sufficient time has not yet elapsed to expect any.

I have lately been informed that Brigᵗ General Harmer returned to the Muskinghum on the 20ᵗʰ of Nov. from the expedition to Post Vincennes on the Wabash. That he had transmitted to me a particular report of the operation of the Troops, and of the treaties he had formed with several Indian Tribes at that Post. That the person to whom the letters were entrusted had been detained on the road by accident, but that he might be daily expected in this City. As soon as he shall arrive all the material intelligence in the public dispatches will be submitted to Congress.

. . . . . .

Henry Knox

NA: PCC, item 120, v. 3, pp. 434-436 (LBkC); M40, reel 3.

John Adams to the States General

London January 25, 1788

A Memorial

High and mighty Lords

The Subscriber, Minister Plenipotentiary from the United States of America, has the Honour to communicate to your High Mightinesses, a Resolution of the United States of America, in Congress assembled, on the fifth day of October 1787, by which, he is permitted, agreably to his Request, to return to America, at any time, after the Twenty fourth day of February 1788, and by which his Commission and Credentials to your High Mightinesses are, on that day to terminate.

Nothing would have been more agreable to the Inclinations of the Subscriber than to have passed over to the Hague in order to have paid his final Respects and to have taken Leave of your High Mightinesses, had not, the Shortness of the time, the Severity of the Season and the tender State of his Health, been opposed to his Wishes.

The Magnanimity and Wisdom with which your High Mightinesses in 1782 manifested your Friendship to the United States of America, contributed to accellerate the general Peace of the World which has lasted so long. And the Candour and Goodness of your High Mightinesses and of the whole Republick, to the Subscriber as well as to his Country, have made Impressions on his Mind which neither Time Place or Circumstance can ever efface.

In finishing his Course in Europe and in taking a respectful Leave of your High Mightinesses, he begs leave to express his ardent Wishes for the Happiness and Prosperity of your High Mightinesses and your Families: and his Sincere Assurances, that in whatever Country he may be, he shall never cease to pray for the Liberty, the Independance and the Universal Happiness and Prosperity of the whole Republick of the United Netherlands

Done at London this twenty fifth Day of January A.D. 1788

John Adams.

NA: PCC, item 84, v. 6, pp. 619-621 (ACS); M247, reel 113.

Georgia Assembly Resolution Regarding Fugitive Slaves in East Florida

Georgia   House of Assembly Wednesday the 30th Jan[y] 1788

On a motion made by M[r] William Fell [Few][1] the house came to the following resolution.

Whereas authentic information has been laid before this House, that sundry negro Slaves belonging to Citizens of this State, have absconded from their masters and gone to East Florida, where they are protected and detained from their rightful owners, by the Government of his most Catholic Majesty, to the great injury of the Citizens of this State, contrary to the usage of nations in amity, and those principles of friendship which this state wishes to preserve with the subjects of his most Catholic Majesty—

Resolved that the Letter of Governor de Zespedes,[2] dated the 12th of December 1784 be transmitted to the Delegates of this State in Congress, and that the said Delegates or either of them be and they are hereby instructed and required to lay a statement of the case before the United States in Congress Assembled, and to move that such measures may be taken on the occasion as will redress the injured Citizens of this State and remove the cause of such Complaints.

NA: PCC, item 124, v. 3, pp. 186-187 (LBkC); M247, reel 141.
[1] Few, William (1748-1828). Georgia political figure. Member, Continental Congress, 1780-1782, 1786-1788, and Constitutional Convention, 1787. U.S. Senator, 1789-1793.
[2] Zespedes, Vizente Manuel de. Spanish governor of East Florida.

Comte de Moustier to John Jay

Sir   New York 4 February 1788
My Health being considerably reestablished I have the pleasure of addressing to you the annexed Copy of my Letter of Credence in Quality of Minister Plenipotentiary of his Majesty to the Congress of the United States. I request the favour of you to communicate it to that Assembly to the End that they may fix a day which shall appear to them the most convenient to give me a public Audience.
I greatly regret Sir, that the fatigues of a long voyage have retarded the request which I have the honor now to make to you. I dare to flatter myself that the United States will not be the less convinced of the Zeal which animates me, and of the Sincerity of the Assurances of friendship which I shall give them in the name of his Majesty.
I ought to suppose Sir, that on this Occasion the same Ceremonial will be followed which was observed at the Reception of my Predecessors, but as I have not received any official Communication on this subject I request the favour of you previously to communicate to me the intentions of Congress.
I have the honor to be &c.ᵃ·
                                                    The Count de Moustier
NA: PCC, item 96, pp. 376-377 (translation); M247, reel 124.

Thomas Jefferson to John Jay

Sir   Paris Feb. 5. 1788.
· · · · ·
...a violent opposition is raised against the Arret for the encouragement of our commerce enclosed in my last. all the chambers of commerce have remonstrated against it and the ministers are alarmed. the Count de la Luzerne, on whose friendly dispositions it was supposed we might rely, does not manifest any partialities for us. the instability of the laws in this country is such that no merchant can venture to make any speculation on the faith of a law. I hope however that no material alteration will be permitted in the present instance. therefore I should think it better not to alarm our merchants with any doubts about the continuance of it. –

Commodore Jones set off this day for Copenhagen to settle the demands for prize money against that court. – I have lately seen a person just come from Algiers, who knew well all our captives there. Capt. Coffyn is dead of a consumption two have died of the plague & one of the small pox. he thinks that since the price given by the Spaniards & Neapolitans for the redemption of captives, they will never sell another of any nation for less than from five to six hundred chequins. he supposes that exclusively of the redemption of our captives, it would have cost us a million of dollars to make peace when mr Lamb arrived there. the Spaniards Neapolitans & Portuguese were then all sueing for peace. this has increased excessively the pride of those pyrates. as soon as money is provided I shall set the business of redemption afoot....I have the honour to be with the most perfect esteem & respect, Sir, your most obedient & most humble servant

Th: Jefferson

NA: PCC, *item 87, v. 2, pp. 47-49 (ALS); M247, reel 115.*

Thomas Jefferson to the Board of Treasury

Gentlemen   Paris February 7. 1788.
    Your favors of Nov. 10. & 13. and Dec. 5. have been duly received. Commodore Jones left this place for Copenhagen the 5th. instant to carry into execution the resolution of Congress of Oct. 25. whatever monies that court shall be willing to allow, shall be remitted to your bankers either in Amsterdam or Paris as shall be found most beneficial, allowing previously to be withdrawn < * > Commodore Jones's proportion which will be necessary for his subsistence. I desired him to endeavor to prevail on the Danish minister to have the money paid in Amsterdam or Paris by their banker in either of those cities if they have one.
    Mr. Ast[1] (secretary to the Consulate) is at Lorient. whether he comes up with the papers or sends them, they shall be received, sealed up & taken care of. I will only ask the favor of you that I may never be desired to break the seals unless very important cause for it should arise.
    I have just received from Messrs. Willinks & Van Staphorsts a letter of Jan. 31. in which are these words. "the official communication we have of the actual situation & prospect of the finances of the U.S. would render such a partial paiment as that to Fizeaux's house of no avail towards the support of the public credit unless effectual measures shall be adopted to provide funds for the 270,000 florins interest that will be due the 1st. of June next, a single day's retard in which would ground a prejudice of long duration." they informed me at the same time that they have made to you

the following communication, that mr Stanitski,[1] our principal broker &
holder of 1,340,000 dollars of certificates of our domestic debt, offers to
have our loan of a million of gilders (of which 622,840 are still unfilled)
immediately made up, on condition that he may retain thereout 180,000
gilders being one year's interest on his certificates, allowing a deduction of
10 percent from his said interest as a compensation for his receiving it in
Amsterdam instead of America, & not pretending that this shall give him
any title to ask any <*> paiment of <*> future interest in Europe. they
observe that this will enable them to face the demands of Dutch interest
till the 1st. of June 1789. pay the principal of Fizeaux's debt, & supply the
current expences of your legations in Europe. on these points it is for you
to decide. I will only take the liberty to observe that if they shall receive
your acceptance of the proposition, some days credit will still be to be given
for producing the cash, and that this must be produced 15. days before it
is wanting, because that much previous notice is always given to the
creditors that their money is ready. it is therefore but three months from
this day before your answer should be in Amsterdam. it might answer a useful purpose also could I receive a communication of that answer <*> ten
days earlier than they. the same stagnation <*> attending our passage
from the old to the new form of government which stops the feeble channels of money hitherto flowing towards our treasury, has suspended also
what foreign credit we had. so that at this moment we may consider the
progress of our loan as stopped. tho' much an enemy to the system of
borrowing, yet I feel strongly the necessity of preserving the power to
borrow. without this we might be overwhelmed by another nation merely
by the force of it's credit. however you can best judge whether the paiment
of a single year's interest on Stanitski's certificates in Europe instead of
America may be more injurious to us than the shock of our credit in
Amsterdam which may be produced by a failure to pay our interest. I have
only to offer any services which I can render in this business either here or
by going to Holland at a moment's warning, if that should be necessary.

I have the honour to be with sentiments of the most perfect esteem &
respect, Gentlemen Your most obedient & most humble serv^t

Th: Jefferson

LC: *Jefferson Papers, microfilm reel 8 (press copy).*
[1] *Ast, William Frederick. Secretary to Thomas Barclay in his role as U.S. Consul in
France. Later employed by the L'Orient mercantile house of Lanchon Brothers & Co.*
[2] *Stadnitski (Stadnitzky), Pieter. Dutch financier.*

Don Diego de Gardoqui to Congress

New York 8th February 1788
The underwritten Encargado de Negocios of his Catholic Majesty has the Honor to inform the Honorable Congress of the United States, that his Majesty observes with Pain the Differences which have for some Time subsisted between certain southern States and some neigbouring Nations of Indians. –
That they have at sundry Times complained of the Injustice with which they have been treated by some Americans, and have applied to the Governors of the Possessions of his Majesty in that Quarter, for the Protection which had for a long Time past been granted to them. –
That although his Majesty could not but be sensible of this, yet the Friendship which he professed to the United States has induced him to give the most positive Orders, not only to restrain them from committing Hostilities against any of the United States, but to use their Influence to dissuade them, and dispose them to Peace on reasonable Terms. –
The King's Love for Justice induces him to desire and hope that the same good Disposition on the Part of the Honorable Congress, will provide that those Nations of Indians be not molested in the compleat and peaceable Enjoyment of all their Rights. –
The Underwritten is happy in being able to communicate to the Honorable Congress this irrefragable Proof of his Majesty's Friendship for the United States, which cannot but greatly promote mutual Confidence and good Correspondence between the two Nations, while as he hopes it will be consolidated by Facts more evident. –   Diego de Gardoqui. –
read 12 Feb[y] 1788

NA: PCC, *item 97, pp. 212-213 (translation); M247, reel 125.*

Comte de Moustier to Comte de Montmorin

[Translation]
N[o.] 1   New York 8 Feb[y.] 1788.
My Lord,
The packet boat, the departure of which from this city is fixed by decree of the Council for the 25th of January, not even having arrived at this time, I have profited from this delay to acquire some preliminary information on the present situation in this country. Despite the advantage that I have had of receiving an infinity of interesting and instructive information

in the correspondence of M. le Chevalier de la Luzerne, of M. de Marbois and of M. Otto, matters here present so many different aspects and are subject to variations so singular and so rapid, that it is difficult to form a perfectly accurate idea of them, if one wishes to encompass them in a single whole. The more distant one is, the more difficult it is to judge them well, as I have had reason to convince myself in comparing my opinion regarding these people in Europe to that which I am beginning to form of them now that I am examining them in the country, where it seems to me that one can know them singularly well. I shall not hasten to form my judgment regarding a subject as complicated as that of assessing the present situation and the future fate of these States, nor regarding their true interests and the relations they may have with the powers of Europe, and principally with France.

Congress was not in session when I arrived. As soon as the number of States represented was sufficient to form a Congress, they hastened to name a President. The choice fell on Mr. Griffin,[1] a Deputy from Virginia. It is believed that this haste was caused by the arrival of the King's Minister, for whom Congress wanted to place itself in condition to give audience; at present it is made up of only seven States. The Deputies from the others are not making haste to arrive. The State of Rhode Island has not even named them. The indifference of the members who compose or should compose this Assembly causes a great delay in the expedition of affairs.

Congress, which has owed its importance and its consideration only to the circumstances which made the united Americans feel the necessity for an extended and active power, has lost the little that it had retained, since it is perceived that it has no means of exercising the rights which the confederation seemed to have assured it. Also, this Assembly can no longer be regarded as more than the shadow of a Sovereign power. It can deliberate and prescribe, but cannot compel obedience. Its inadequacy is generally recognized throughout the United States. Despite the opinion of persons who think that these States are not exposed to the influence of movements that could agitate and trouble the powers of Europe, one would soon be convinced that the same weakness which renders Congress inadequate to govern at home, would render it equally incapable of taking any efficacious measure abroad, if the King's wisdom and firmness had not prevented the war which seemed on the verge of breaking out between France and England. In the present situation, Congress cannot be useful to the allies of the United States, and is not in condition to harm their enemies. Without a navy, without troops, without fortifications, without coercive force to support them, it could not prevent its most important posts from falling to the power of the first occupier.

Without examining here whether the division or the consolidation of these States is acceptable to the powers of Europe, and to which one or other it would be most acceptable, I think that it is impossible that the present form of Government can survive. Opinions are not divided on the necessity of establishing another. The diversity of interests thereon causes a great [diversity] in the ideas that various parties have regarding the method that it is proper to adopt. You have been informed, My Lord, by M. Otto of all that has happened to bring about this revolution. I do not doubt that his reportage has appeared very satisfactory to You and has aroused all Your attention.

The Constitution proposed by the general Convention of Philadelphia has already been accepted by five States in the following order: Delaware, Pennsylvania, Jersey, Georgia, Connecticut. The States of New Hampshire, Carolina, Virginia, Maryland and New York have fixed the times of their individual conventions to examine the Constitution in accordance with the invitation of Congress. That of Massachusetts is currently deliberating. The first appearances there were against its adoption; today it appears that the number of its partisans will carry it. The decision of that State is infinitely important, because it seems to have an influence on the decision of New Hampshire and Rhode Island, and probably on that of some other States. It may, in consequence, determine the fate of the new Constitution, since to establish it, it is sufficient that it be adopted by nine of them.

It is possible, My Lord, that the revolution will have been achieved when this Despatch reaches You. The powers of Europe are no longer in time either to favor or to thwart the adoption of the new Constitution. What it seems should occupy them now is adjusting their political conduct regarding an event which would procure for the United States the toughness and vigor of a solid and powerful Government by the union of several opposing powers into a single body, which will be the source and the dispenser thereof. One may presume that England is awaiting the moment of decision of the present crisis to take a definitive stand with regard to the United States. Without having a representative here, it has retained so many partisans, and takes care to maintain so many Emissaries, that it can give all the attention that its interests require to the changes in these States without appearing to do so.

The effect thereof is shown in the scope of the advantageous Commerce that it conducts here in furnishing most of the manufactured goods consumed by the United States without being obliged to take from them as many commodities as before the revolution. We have become the principal consumers of these, either in Europe, or in the Colonies. The result of this is that it is with our money that they pay in England for the merchandise which they import therefrom. The administration will no doubt realize the designs it has formed to remedy this inconvenience, which It has already recognized. I shall wait to present to You, My Lord, my observations on the Commerce of this new nation, until I have had the time to prove them thoroughly.

There remains one matter that I think should not be postponed from submission to You. I regard it as of extreme importance to direct particular attention in France to the appearance, the quality, the prices of consumer goods suitable for united America, so that we can counterbalance the sales of England. It seems to me that by relying in this regard solely on the activity and industry of Merchants, our Commerce courts the risk of being as passive with the Americans for a long time as it is today. Some of our commodities may acquire more sales by the favors which will be granted them in return for those which the King has given theirs. But as for our merchandise, if we wish to assure the sale thereof, we must necessarily furnish the Americans therewith according to their tastes. I would think that without granting an exclusive privilege, it would be infinitely advantageous to be able to form a Company of merchants who would pursue, with regard to Commerce with the United States, the principles which the Chamber of Commerce of Marseilles follows with regard to that with the Levant. Without making regulations, the administration could arouse the Kingdom's various chambers of Commerce to give particular attention to this objective. If it were remarked today that some manufactures are awaiting delivery in consequence of some treaties of commerce in which the interest of the kingdom, taken as a whole, does not prevent the losses of some particular branches, one means of restoring them would be to give them an encouragement sufficient to enable them to adopt appropriate forms and to give the necessary qualities to their works to be susceptible to sale in this country. In order to distinguish them, it suffices to examine in England and in Ireland all the goods that are fabricated there for America. It should be easier to change the habits of the manufacturers than those of an entire people, especially since it is more natural that it be the manufacturer who conforms to the taste of the consumer than that the latter be subject to the caprice or the routine of the former.

Several individual States have endeavored to establish manufactories in order to free themselves to a degree from the tribute which they pay England. As great as their efforts are, and as considerable as the encouragements which they give to these establishments are, the manufactures from Europe should still surpass theirs for a long time. Too many factors oppose themselves to the success of those of this country, at least as to their number. The taste for property preponderates too much among this new people, and the ease of acquiring it is too great for them to devote themselves to work in manufactories. The cultivation of land offers a field more vast and more attractive to their industry. An impetus is given to the inhabitants of the old States to move to the rich territories of the West. The rapid growth of the population there is as prodigious as the fertility of this vast stretch of land. These reasons will long prevent the manufactories there from experiencing a great development, just as the ease of emigration from the old States is a hindrance to those they have endeavored to establish there, since a surplus of hands will not be found there that could be employed therein, as long as men who have no land of their own to cultivate can acquire it easily elsewhere. The advantage which the Europeans will have in the sale of their manufactures should therefore last as long as there are lands to settle in the vast extent of territory of the United States; those who will not take advantage of this can only blame themselves.

I think, My Lord, that on presenting to the Royal Council of Finance and Commerce the unfavorable situation of our relations with this country, where England exercises a de facto monopoly on an infinity of merchandise that we could also furnish, it will look with success for means to remedy so disadvantageous a situation, one so far from the hopes that could be framed after having expended such enormous sums and shed so much blood in order to decide a revolution from which we have hitherto gained only glory, abandoning the profit that it should procure.

I am with respect, My Lord Your most humble and most obedient servant,   Le Cte. de Moustier.
rec. 24 March

FFAA: Pol. Corr., U.S., v. 33, f. 16-21vo. (LC transcription).
[1] *Griffin, Cyrus (1743-1810). Virginia lawyer and political figure. Member, Virginia house of delegates, 1777-1778, 1786-1787. Member, Continental Congress, 1778-1780, 1787-1788; president, 1788. Commissioner to the Creek Nation, 1789. Judge, U.S. District Court of Virginia, 1789-1810.*

John Jay's Report Regarding
the Reception of the Comte de Moustier

[New York] Office for foreign Affairs 12th February 1788
The Secretary of the United States for the Department of foreign Affairs, to whom was referred a Letter of the 4th Instant from the Count de Moustier enclosing a Copy of his Letter of Credence, requesting that a Day be fixed for his *public* Audience, and intimating an Expectation that the Ceremonial will be the same as in the Cases of his Predecessors. –

Reports.

That in his Opinion it would be proper to name as early a Day as may consist with the Convenience of Congress, for receiving the Count. –

That he has perused and considered the Ceremonials heretofore used on such Occasions, and that they appear to him to put much less Distinction between an Ambassador and a Minister, than the Laws and the actual Practice of civilized Nations have established. –

That considering the past and present State of american Affairs, he thinks it might not be so adviseable to correct Mistakes relative to Matters of Ceremony and Etiquette at this Period, as when the proposed Plan of Government shall begin to operate. He therefore is of Opinion that it would be best to receive this Minister, in the same Manner as his Predecessor and the dutch Minister were received.

All which is submitted to the Wisdom of Congress.
Read Feby 13th 1788 – John Jay –

NA: PCC, item 81, v. 3, pp. 39-40, 42 (DS); M242, reel 107.

John Adams to Thomas Jefferson

Dear Sir London Feb. 12. 1788

I have received your Letter of the 6$^{th.}$ and had before received the Same Information from Amsterdam.

I know not how to express to you, the Sense I have of the disingenuity of this Plott. – The Difficulty of Selling the Obligations I believe to be mere Pretence, and indeed the whole appears to me to be a concerted Fiction, in consequence of Some Contrivance or Suggestion of Mr Parker,[1] the great Speculator in American Paper, who, though I love him very well, is too ingenious for me. – I feel myself obliged to write this in Confidence to you, and to put You on your Guard against the immeasurable Avarice of Amsterdam as well as the ungovernable Rage of Speculation. – I feel no Vanity in Saying that this Project never would have been Suggested, if it had not been known, that I was recalled. if I was to continue in Europe and in office I would go to Amsterdam and open a new Loan with John Hodshon[2] before I would Submit to it. – The Undertakers are bound in Honour, as I understand it, to furnish the Money on the new Loan. They agreed to this upon Condition that I would go to Amsterdam to sign the Obligations. The Truth is that Messrs Willinks and Vanstaphorsts have been purchasing immense Quantities of American Paper, and they now Want to have it acknowledged and paid in Europe. – it appears to me totally impossible that You or I should ever agree to it, or approve it, and as far as I can comprehend it is equally impossible for the Board of Treasury or Congress to consent to it. You and I however cannot answer for them: but I think We cannot countenance any hopes that they will ever comply with it. - The Continental Certificates & their Interest are to be paid <*> in America at the Treasury of the United States. if a Precedent is Set of paying them in Europe, I pretend not to Sufficient foresight to predict the Consequences. They appear however to me to be horrid. - if the Interest of one Million Dollars is paid this Year in Europe, you will find the Interest of Ten Millions demanded next year. - I am very sorry to be obliged at this moment of my Retirement to give opinions which may be misrepresented and imputed to Motives that my Soul despizes: but I cannot advise you by any means to countenance this Project: but it is my Serious Opinion that the Judgment of Congress or the Board of Treasury, ought to be waited for, at all hazards. - if the brokers, Undertakers and Money lenders will take Such Advantages of Us, it is high time to have done with them; pay what is due as fast as We can, but never contract another farthing of Debt with them. - if a little Firmness is shewn in adhering to the Resolution of waiting the orders of Congress, it is my opinion, Care will be taken in Amsterdam that our Credit shall not suffer. The Interest of our Commissioners, of the Brokers, Undertakers and Money Lenders, all conspire to induce them to prevent a failure. But in my Judgment a failure had better take Place than this Project. - I shall not write with the Same frankness to Willinks, but I shall give them my opinion that the Judgment of Congress must be waited for. -

My dear Friend farewell. I pity you, in your Situation. dunned and teazed as you will be, all your Philosophy will be wanting to support you. - But be not discouraged, I have been constantly vexed with Such terrible Complaints and frightened with such long Faces these ten years. depend upon it, the Amsterdammers love Money too well, to execute their Threats. They expect to gain too much by American Credit to destroy it. - I am with Sincere Affection and great Esteem, Your Friend & Servant

John Adams.

LC: *Jefferson Papers, microfilm reel 8 (ALS).*

[1] *Parker, Daniel. Massachusetts merchant and speculator. With John Holker (former French Consul General) and William Duer (Assistant Secretary of the Treasury, 1789-1790), partner in providing supplies to the French expeditionary force and the Continental Army, 1781-1783. Member, Embarkation Commission, April-November 1783. With Robert Morris, financed the voyage of the Empress of China, the first United States ship sent to China. Fled to Europe to escape his creditors, 1784. In Europe, speculated in American domestic securities in partnership with Robert Morris, Gouverneur Morris, and the Dutch and French bankers who handled U.S. accounts. Attempted to purchase U.S. debt to France, 1788-1789.*

Adams' opinion appears to have been that the slow subscription rate for the current U.S. loan from the Dutch bankers was connected with Parker's endeavor to purchase the U.S.

debt to France, probably in an effort to drive down the value of these securities in order to increase his profits.

2 Hodshon (Hodson), John. Amsterdam merchant and banker whose firm, John Hodshon and Zoon, which supported the Stadhouder's position in Dutch politics, had American interests.

Hendrik Fagel to John Adams

Sir   Hague the 12th February 1788

I have this Day been honored with your Letter, dated London the 25th January of the present Year, accompanied with a Memorial to their High Mightinesses, and another to his Highness, with a Request to deliver the same. I have ever experienced so many Proofs of your Friendship and good Will, that I should have accounted it an Honor and Pleasure immediately to have complied with your Wishes, altho' I rather wished that you had not taken Leave, and always entertained Hopes to have seen you here once more. Permit me however to inform you that when I communicated your Letter, addressed to their High Mightinesses, to the President and other Members, they did not put any unfavorable Constructions upon the Memorial of taking Leave, which in every Respect was found obliging and satisfactory, excepting that no Letter of Recall from Congress to their High Mightinesses accompanied the same, which is customary; for as a Minister is credited by a Letter of Credence, (such an one as was received by their High Mightinesses on the 22d April 1782, dated the 1st January 1781) so in like Manner a Minister is recalled by a Letter of Recall, upon which a Letter of Recredence is returned. Perhaps this may have been occasioned by an Omission of the Secretary of Congress; and this prevents my making Use of your Memorial, which ought to be delivered with a Letter of Recall from Congress – and your Excellency will I trust not be displeased that I find myself obliged to return to you the Letter and Memorial. –

Your Excellency's Affairs not permitting you to come and take a personal Leave, it will be satisfactory that a Letter of Recall from Congress be transmitted with your Memorial. –

It will ever give me Pleasure to learn of your Welfare and those connected with you, and to find Opportunities of giving you Proofs of the particular Regard with which I have the Honor to be Sir Your Excellency's most humble & obt Servant   H. Fagel. –

P.S. His Highness being in the same Predicament with their High Mightinesses, nothing can be done but to wait for a Letter of Recall from Congress. –

Faithfully translated from the Original by Henry Rensen

NA: PCC, item 84, v. 6, pp. 607-609 (translation); M247, reel 113.

Comte de Moustier to Comte de Montmorin

[Translation]

N°· 3.   New York, 12 Febr. 1788.
My Lord,

. . . . .

One portion of the people of the United States might think that the revolution that is brewing in their federal Government must have excited the King's attention, and that the arrival of His Majesty's Minister is proof of it. I even know that several partisans of the new Constitution, who are without contradiction the most accredited and the most considerable personages of the United States, expect to see me take sides in this event. On the one hand, my instructions stipulate passive conduct and the greatest circumspection for me in that regard; on the other hand, the Constitution gains more favor each day and, it appears, should be adopted by the majority and perhaps by most of the States. I have sought to comply both with my instructions and with what the present circumstances, which the King's council could not foresee, seem to require, in order to avoid giving too much Credit to the opinion, already strongly established, that the King has withdrawn all his interest in the American republic, that he is not only indifferent to its successes, but that they would even give umbrage to him, and finally that His Majesty has never had another goal than to see these States detach themselves from Great Britain, without desiring in any manner to see them prosper: Mr. Jay has spoken to me on this subject with much frankness. He claims to have proofs that this opinon is well-founded, but he has added as a corrective that he thinks that this policy with regard to the United States was particularly that of the Comte de Vergennes, against whom he has evinced to me the strongest suspicion. At the same time, My Lord, he was infinitely pleased with the sentiments and favorable dispositions that he told me he had recognized in You at the time when he had the honor to see You.

If the new Constitution is adopted, as it appears that it soon will be, and if Congress, by virtue of its new form, acquires a power sufficient to give solidity and efficacy to its political ties, it would, I think, be of the most unfortunate consequence to allow the opinion to exist and prevail that the King is not really interested in the prosperity of the United States. The effect of it would be to see given to England the confidence that would be withdrawn from France, to make of the former an ally and to regard the latter as a jealous power. I desire that the terms of my speech, to which I have nonetheless avoided giving too much force, may serve to change this opinon and to become susceptible of the interpretation most appropriate to the King's interests, according to future circumstances. I have drawn the import of it as much from my letters of credence as from my instructions, in which it is expressly noted *that His Majesty attaches a great price to the maintenance of his alliance with the United States.*

However, it was upon the term *Alliance* only that I observed that Mr. Jay stopped in reading my speech, of which I have given him communication confidentially before making it officially. He appeared to me to doubt that the Alliance between the King and the United States has existed since the peace, judging, he told me, that such was also the sentiment of my Court, and that the treaty of 1778 had only been considered as a means of insuring the independence of the United States. It is in this manner that the conversation was entered into, the substance of which I have just reported. Until I can be informed of the opinon of the King and his Council with regard to the Alliance, I think I should appear not to doubt that it exists in its entirety, and to appear convinced that the King has never ceased to interest himself in the prosperity of the United States. As soon as I have received confirmation of the advantages that His Majesty is disposed to grant to their Commerce, I will make use of it to destroy, as much as I can, suspicions that can only be regarded as very harmful.

In some conversations that I have had with various persons relative to Commerce between the two nations, I have remarked how much this subject interested a great number of Americans. It does not concern the merchants alone, but the planters who have need of outlets for their produce. The Antilles appear to them to offer the most convenient one. Assuredly, they cannot legitimately lay claim to a Commerce that would dry up for us the source of an immense public revenue; but until circumstances are favorable to their desires and the interests of the King, the Kingdom's Commerce, the Colonists, and the Americans can all be reconciled together, the latter will find means to conduct an immense contraband trade in our islands, as much of imports as of exports. Experience seems to have convinced the French Government and that of England that when Contraband is incited to a certain degree, and it has become in some measure impossible to stop it, it is prudent to make Commercial regulations in order to authorize under certain restrictions what one cannot prevent. It is according to this principle that I think that the desire that the united Americans show to obtain more facilities to trade with the French Antilles could again attract the attention of the administration. Perhaps it would be possible to find compensation in the duties collected in the islands for what would be the less collected in the Kingdom's customshouses. Probably commercial favors would be obtained from the Americans, by virtue of which the Merchants would be in shape to pursue new branches that would compensate them for what they would think they had lost by a new system adopted for the Commerce of the Islands. I propose to treat this important question at more length, especially on the eve of the revolution that is taking effect in the federal Government. It will be the subject of the observations that I shall take care to assemble on the Commerce of the United States.

I am with respect, My Lord, Your most humble and most obedient servant   Le Cᵗᵉ· de Moustier
rec. 24 March

FFAA: Pol. Corr., U.S., v. 33, f. 30-34vo. (LC transcription).

Congressional Resolution and Order
Regarding Reception of Comte de Moustier

[New York] February 14ᵗʰ 1788
The Secretary for Foreign Affairs having transmitted to Congress a Letter from the Count de Moustier together with a Copy of a Letter of Credence, by which it appears that His Most Christian Majesty has appointed the Count to succeed the Chevalier de la Luzerne in quality of his Minister Plenipotentiary to the United States of America and the said Minister having requested that this may be communicated to Congress, that they may fix a day which shall appear to them the most convenient to give him a Public Audience –

Resolved, That the said Count de Moustier be received as Minister Plenipotentairy from His Most Christain Majesty, and that agreeably to his request he be admitted to a Public Audience on Tuesday the 26ᵗʰ of the present Month in the Room where Congress Assembles –

Ordered, That the Secretary for Foreign Affairs inform the honᵇˡᵉ the Minister of the United Netherlands and his Most Catholic Majesty's Encargado de Negocios of the Public Audience to be given to the honᵇˡᵉ the Minister Plenipotentiary of his Most Christain Majesty –

·   ·   ·   ·   ·

Chaˢ Thomson Secʸ
NA: PCC, item 122, pp. 112-113 (C); M247, reel 140.

John Adams to John Jay

Dear Sir   Grosvenor Square Feb. 14. 1788
I yesterday received Mʳ Remsens Letter of the 14. of December, with the Journals and Gazettes inclosed.

At the last Conferences at White hall which were last Thursday, Lord Carmarthen thought proper to express a Wish that this Country had some sort of Treaty of Commerce with the United States of America, that it might be no longer necessary to take new Measures from time to time which looked hard. This Observation his Lordship made alluding to Mr Grenvilles[1] Motion in the House of Commons, for making the Regulation of the Intercourse between America and the West India Islands, perpetual. His Lordship then, immediately said, "I presume Mr Adams that the States will all immediately adopt the new Constitution. I have read it with Pleasure. it is very well drawn up." All this oracular Utterance, was to signify to me what has all along been insinuated, that there is not as yet any national Government, but that as soon as there shall be one, the British Court will vouchsafe to treat with it. – You will see, by the Morning Chronicle of the 12 of Feb. inclosed that Mr Grenville's Speech is in the same Strain: so that we may conclude it to be the concerted Language of the Cabinet. – it is unnecessary for me to make any Reflections upon it. The Argument that arises out of it, in favour of the new Constitution and a prompt Acceptance of it, is but one among many. – France and Holland furnish as many Reasons as England. Mr Jefferson must soon follow my Example and return to America, if that Constitution is not accepted by all the States: and what will be the Consequence of the Clamours of all the Officers in France, who are Creditors; of all the Notables who may be pleased to cast Reflections; and of all our Creditors in Holland; for want of Payment of Interest and Principal as they become due, must be left to every American Citizen Seriously to consider.

In preparing for my departure, I have been personally treated with the same uniform Tenour of dry Decency and cold Civility, which appears to have been the premeditated Plan from the beginning: and Opposition as well as Administration appear to have adopted the same Spirit. Mr Fox and Mr Burke,[2] Lord Cambden[3] and the Duke of Richmond,[4] Lord Hawkesbury[5] and Lord North[6] and Lord Stormont,[7] have all behaved alike. If this Country can make such arrangements that the King of Prussia may make a Diversion of the French Forces by Land, and the native Indians or discontented Subjects, another, of those of Spain in South America, you may easily believe that England will be eager for War. Let not our Countrymen flatter themselves that they shall be able to maintain Peace. Lord Carmarthen indeed said to me that he did not see a possibility of a Misunderstanding in Europe, and that he even hoped that Peace would be made between Russia and the Porte. His Lordship is in profound Ignorance of it, I presume, if there is really any Probability of an Alliance of France with the Emperor or Empress. Mr Jefferson has informed you, of his Conjectures as well as his Intelligence on that Point. The Marquis de la

Luzerne[8] is now Ambasador at this Court from France, and has already met with Humiliations, not easily borne by Ambassadors. Monsieur De Calonne, appears at the Levee and Drawing Room, and even at the Table of the Marquis of Carmarthen on the Queens Birth Day, with the French Ambassador. The Chevalier De Ternant[9] was presented by the French Ambassador, to the King and Queen, and treated with the most marked Disgust by both. These Things are hard to bear. I have had some Conversations with this Minister, with whom I made a Voyage in 1777 from L'Orient to Boston in the *Sensible*, and could wish to have resided longer with him for he will Certainly be attentive and able. But my Embarkation is fixed to the Month of March, and I hope to be in Boston in May. With great Esteem and Regard I have the Honour to be, dear Sir your most obedient and most humble Servant   John Adams

NA: PCC, item 84, v. 6, pp. 595-598 (ALS); M247, reel 113.

[1] *Grenville, William Wyndham, (1759-1834). British political figure. Member of Parliament, 1782-1790. Vice president, Committee on Trade, 1786-1789. Special mission to the United Provinces of the Netherlands, summer 1787. Special mission to France on Dutch affairs, September 1787-January 1788. Speaker, House of Commons, January-June 1789. Secretary of State for Home Affairs, 1789-1791. Created Baron Grenville, November 1790. Secretary of State for Foreign Affairs, 1791-1801. Prime Minister and First Lord of the Treasury, 1806-1807.*

[2] *Burke, Edmund (1719-1797). British political figure and philosopher. Member of Parliament, 1765-1794, initially as a Rockingham Whig. Favored reconciliation with the American colonies. Later, opponent of the French revolution.*

[3] *Camden, Charles Pratt, Lord (1714-1794). British political figure. Attorney general, 1757-1762. Chief justice of the court of common pleas, 1762-1766. Lord chancellor, 1766-1770. Opposed Lord North's American policy. President of the council under Rockingham and Shelburne, 1782-1783, and under William Pitt, 1784-1794.*

[4] *Richmond, Charles Lennox, Duke of (1735-1806). British political figure. Vociferous opponent of the North Ministry's American policy and of the American war. Master general of the ordinance in Rockingham and Shelburne cabinets, 1782-1783, and in Pitt's administration, 1784-1795.*

[5] *Jenkinson, Charles (1727-1808). British political figure. Member of Parliament, 1761-1786. Undersecretary of state, 1761-1763. Joint secretary to the treasury, 1763-1765. After Lord Bute's retirement, leader of the "King's Friends" in the House of Commons. A Lord of the Admiralty in Grafton's administration. A lord of the treasury, 1767-1772. Secretary at war under Lord North, 1778-1782. After the war, primarily interested in commercial affairs. President, council for trade and the plantations, 1786. Named Baron Hawkesbury, 1786. Played a principal part in negotiation of the Jay Treaty. Named Earl of Liverpool, May 1796.*

[6] *North, Frederick, Lord (1732-1792). King George III's chief minister (North rejected the title of prime minister as unconstitutional), 1770-1782, serving as Chancellor of the Exchequer, 1767-1782, and First Lord of the Treasury, 1770-1782. Resigned March*

1782 after the House of Commons turned against the war in America. Served, in coalition ministry with Charles James Fox, as Secretary of State for Home Affairs, April-December 1783.

⁷ *Stormont, David Murray, Lord (1727-1796). British diplomat and political figure. Envoy extraordinary to the court of Saxony, 1756-1761. Envoy extraordinary to Austria, 1763-1772. Envoy extraordinary to France, 1772-1778. Secretary of state for the southern department, 1779-1782. President of the council, April-December 1783, 1794-1796. From 1793, Lord Mansfield.*

⁸ *The Chevalier de la Luzerne had been made a marquis prior to his appointment as French Ambassador to Great Britain.*

⁹ *Ternant, Jean Baptiste, Chevalier de. French military officer and diplomat. Associated with the Continental Army in various capacities, held rank of colonel. Captured at Charleston, May 1780; exchanged, January 1782. Envoy, special mission to the princes of Baden, Hesse-Darmstadt, and Pfalz-Zweibrücken, June 1790. Minister to the United States, August 1791-May 1793.*

Comte de Moustier to Comte de Montmorin

[Translation]

N⁰· 4.   New York, 14 February 1788.

My Lord.

In order to prepare to pursue with exactitude all that is stipulated for me in my instructions, as well as matters that were recommended to M. Otto and that cannot yet be concluded, I was again enlightened by the reading of my instructions, and I then brought my attention to bear on subjects that are not mentioned there. I propose to make a short recapitulation of them here. The objective that I have sought to fulfill by my speech to Congress, which by publication in a multitude of gazettes may be considered as addressed to all the assembled Americans, has been what was recommended to me. My individual speeches are always directed by the same spirit. You can see, My Lord, from my preceding Despatch, that the Americans' opinion on Commerce with our Islands is growing stronger and stronger, and that although it is prohibited, it does not exist less through Contraband, in which these people are more enterprising and more intelligent than any other.

There is reason to fear that the Americans retain long-held habits in their Commerce with England. It will nonetheless be possible to divert them therefrom and to make them adopt others that are favorable to us, when the administration wishes to encourage and aid Commerce, which at the outset will have need to be particularly protected and enlightened. I submitted to you some ideas on this subject in my despatch N⁰· 1. It is very probable, at least to judge it by effects, that England will not neglect the means to maintain the advantages which its Commerce enjoys in this country. It can also be thought to be occupied with weakening the sentiments that should bind the United States to France. The success of the new Constitution nevertheless proves that it is vain for it to hope for a rapprochement with the mother country.

The proceedings of its Agents for the most part are conducted secretly. The most apparent is Chevalier Temple, appointed Consul General by his Court and recognized here as such, although there exists no treaty of Commerce. Without having functions to exercise by virtue of his Commission, he does nothing but serve as a rallying point for the great number of inhabitants of this city whom interest or affection attaches to Great Britain. All the same, he is not limited to secret plots, but he also employs remarks in conversation and has inserted several paragraphs in the gazettes to exaggerate the forces and the resources of Great Britain and to disparage France. This method, of which he does not make very adroit use, can and should turn against him by a simple exposé of the truth of the facts. Without devoting oneself absolutely to this small war of gazettes, it is however necessary to destroy what can be found that is disadvantageous, false, or injurious. The influence of the American people requires that its opinion be enlightened and won over. Open to prejudices, eager to read gazettes and political writings, it is necessary to conform oneself a little to the customs of this people, whom one is interested in influencing.

The news of the cessation of the armaments that were being made in Europe had preceded my arrival here. I have already mentioned what the difficulties would have been that I would have encountered in treating with Congress in compliance with my instructions. If the new Constitution is adopted, it will be possible to give more solidity and effect to the negotiations that one would like to open with this body, which would become Sovereign in fact, instead of being so in name only. At the present time, they are scarcely occupied with the matters that have agitated the United Provinces and those that agitate Eastern Europe. The United States are in a kind of anarchy, but without experiencing very great inconveniences from it, since they are perfectly tranquil with regard to foreign powers.

The quarrel that has arisen between the States interested in the navigation of the Mississippi and Spain appears in some measure assuaged, although the new Colonists on the banks of the Ohio and its tributary rivers do not lose sight of their claims, which they become from day to day more capable of sustaining. If interest in this affair were to revive, I would conduct myself according to what my instructions stipulate. It appears that Spain has not lost it from sight, if I were not mistaken in the conjecture that I have formed regarding the sudden appearance of a M. de Argès,[1] who arrived here by the packet boat that the King of Spain sends here from time to time solely for his service, without accepting any passengers, nor letters from individuals, so that all is mysterious in these expeditions, which do not take place at regular times. One must think, moreover, that they are of great importance to the King of Spain, since they are made at such great expense. The individual who recently arrived is a Frenchman, and decorated with the cross of St. Louis. After having served in the war for Canada, he lived for a long time in the country between that Colony and the State of New York. Then he went to Martinique and made several voyages successively to Europe and to this Continent. Before going to Europe last year, he had visited all the Western settlements and had sojourned in the most important, which he examined for three years. Although I found him very reserved, and I did not wish to appear to press him, I learned from him several interesting details, and among others that he had established by surveys that 20,000 emigrants had passed towards the Ohio between 1786 and 1787 through only two points from the center, without including those who may have come from the Eastern States, where the mania for emigration has also spread. M. d'Argès will depart on the Spanish packet boat, which will take him to Havana. This shuttle from Spain here, and from here to Havana, combined with M. Gardoqui's affectation not to know him, may allow us to presume that the Court of Spain will have taken steps relative to the Mississippi that she intends to keep very secret. I have entered into this detail only to let You know where this matter stands, which happily does not appear to have to occupy us actively for a long time, although it offers much of interest to observers of the progress of this new people, whose views are so bold and so astonishing.

One need not expect any practicable arrangement relative to reimbursement of public debts under the present system of the American Government. I shall nevertheless make appropriate representations to Congress to establish the lawful rights of the King and of Holland and to insist on the necessity of measures on the part of the United States to satisfy its engagements. Although there is less hope today than ever of any success in proceedings of this kind, I shall nonetheless endeavor to obtain all that circumstances may permit. On the other hand, I think that You will not disapprove, My Lord, that I do not show too marked an eagerness, which moreover would not be more efficacious, in order not to give this people cause to think that the King's Minister has for a principal object the reimbursement of a debt, which at this time is more onerous to him than it will be in the future if the Government acquires more vigor and solidity.

I think I should above all dispose tempers favorably towards our nation, help to restore confidence, reanimate affection, and then ascribe much to time and circumstances, in a country where for several years the operations of the Government have been, despite the desire of the most upright and enlightened minds, subject to variations and inevitable disappointments by the weakness of its Constitution.

If I propose to employ so great a reserve in the pursuit of reimbursements due to the King, I shall use it to greater effect with regard to the claims made by His Majesty's subjects. I think that in such a case all that a King's Minister can do is to aid them particularly by Counsels and to reserve himself to act officially when the difficulties that they encounter clearly counteract stipulations made by treaties in favor of the King's subjects and when they affect the general cause. Nevertheless, I am preparing to present a note of the various recommendations that have been made by the Ministry in favor of various individuals.

The necessity of giving our Commerce all the encouragement and support of which it is susceptible appears to require that the Consular Convention may be put into operation promptly. Indecision in this regard could not produce any good effect. At this point, it seems that one can no longer return to some article in particular without being liable to give rise to a new negotiation on a subject that has already occasioned much discussion. The way to reconcile the differing views of each side would perhaps be to accede to the proposition of Congress to stipulate a limited duration for this convention. During this time, the new form of the American Government would have acquired solidity, and we would have obtained from one side or the other more exact and extensive notions on the nature of Commerce between the two nations and on the means of reconciling mutual interests in compliance with the laws and customs recognized in each State.

I am with Respect My Lord Your most humble and most obedient servant, Le Cte· de Moustier
rec. 24 March

FFAA: Pol. Corr., U.S., v. 33, f. 37-42 (LC transcription).

[1] Argès, Pierre Wouves, Chevalier d'. French adventurer and double agent. Served in Canada during French and Indian War, after which he lived near the Canadian-New York border and travelled in the west. Spent three years residing in or near Kentucky, reporting to Vergennes on developments there. Returned to France in 1787, where he proposed to Aranda, the Spanish ambassador, that Spain should win over the American frontiersmen by allowing them to settle in Spanish territory. Floridablanca, who distrusted him, sent him to New York with a new treaty proposal for Gardoqui, who shared his superior's opinion. D'Argès proceeded to New Orleans, where he spent a fruitless year before returning to France in 1789. For additional information, see Boyd, Jefferson, v. 14, pp. 387-388.

John Adams to John Jay

Dear Sir.   Grosvenor Square, Feb. 16. 1788
There is no Maxim more clearly Settled in all Courts, and in all
Negotiations between Nations, than that Sovereign Should always Speak
to Sovereign and Minister to Minister. I am not at all Surprised therefore,
although I am much mortified at having my Memorials to their High
Mightinessess and to His most Serene Highness returned to me, with the
Letter inclosed from Mᴿ Fagel. I should have had a Letter of Recall, Signed
by the President of Congress by their order, and addressed to their High
Mightinesses. There is a Similar Irregularity, in my recal from the British
Court, for, although my Commission is limited to three Years, yet my Letter
of Credence to His Majesty, has no limits at all, if the omission of a Letter
from Congress to the King, upon this occasion should not be taken as an
offence, it will not be because it is not observed, but from Motives too
humiliating to Congress as well as to their Minister here to be explained.
There is no Alternative now left for me. Home, I must go, and leave all
Europe to conjecture, that I have given Offence in Holland, and in
England, that I have misbehaved abroad, though ~~I am~~ my Conduct has
been approved at home. When the Public shall hear that I am gone home,
without taking leave, there will be no End of Criticisms, Conjectures and
Reflections.
All that now remains for me, is humbly to request that Congress would
be pleased to Send me regular Letters of Recall after my Arrival in America
that I may then transmit my Memorials to Europe and take Leave in Form.
To a Man who has taken the utmost Pains to do his Duty and to fulfill
every Obligation to the Smallest Punctilio nothing can be more disagreable,
than such disappointments, especially as in all my Letters I have so
expressly and repeatedly requested, regular Letters of Recall. With great
Respect, and Esteem I have the Honour to be, dear Sir, your most obedient
and most humble Servant   John Adams.

NA: PCC, item 84, v. 6, pp. 599-601 (ALS); M247, reel 113.

Thomas Earle to Lord Sydney

My Lord,   Liverpool 20ᵗʰ February 1788.
I have made Enquiry concerning the two Chests containing Spinning
Machines, mentioned in the Letter which I had the Honor to receive from
Your Lordship, and I find that they were really sent back from Philadelphia,

and were deposited in this Custom House, but released from thence on the Duty being paid and sent to Manchester.

I have reason to believe that all the Circumstances contained in the Affidavit of which your Lordship sent me a Copy are true, for I have seen one of the deponents "Henry Royle" who is lately returned from America and who related to me the whole Transaction: this Man is gone to Stockport but has left me his Address. I think he is very deserving of some Reward for his Zeal on this Occasion, and it may be an Encouragement to him to be further useful in giving Information of Manufacturers who may have a design of going to America. He mentioned a person of this description to me, and I am using means to discover whether it be really his Intention to emigrate or not.

I am well aware My Lord, of the Efforts making by the Americans to entice the Manufacturers from this Country, and Your Lordship may rely on my best Exertions to prevent that Evil, and to detect the Promoters of it.

I am with the greatest Respect &ᶜ   Thoˢ Earle Mayor.

PRO: FO 4/6, pp. 141-142, 144 (LC transcription).

John Jay's Report Regarding Comte de Moustier's Proposed Speech to Congress

[New York] Office for foreign Affairs 21ˢᵗ February 1788
The Secretary of the United States for the Department of foreign Affairs having received a Copy of the Speech which Count de Moustier purposes to make on Tuesday the 26ᵗʰ February instant, reported the following Answer to it Vizᵗ

Sir,
It will always give us pleasure to acknowledge the friendship and important good Offices which we have experienced from his most christian Majesty, and your generous Nation; and we flatter ourselves that the same principles of magnanimity and regard to mutual Convenience which dictated the connections between us, will continue to operate, and to render them still more extensive in their benefits to the two Countries.

We consider the Alliance as involving engagements highly interesting to both parties, and we are persuaded that they will be observed with entire and mutual good faith.

We are happy in being so explicitly assured of the continuance of his Majesty's freindship and attachment; and in this opportunity of expressing the high sense we entertain of their sincerity and value. It is with real Satisfaction Sir, that we receive you as his Minister plenipotentiary, especially as your Character gives us reason to expect that the harmony and interests of both Nations will not be less promoted by your Talents, Candor and Liberality, than they were by those which distinguished your Predecessor and recommended him to our Esteem and Regard.

All which is submitted to the Wisdom of Congress   John Jay

NA: PCC, item 124, v. 3, pp. 161-162 (LBkC); M247, reel 141.

John Adams to John Jay

Dear Sir   Grosvenor Square Feb. 21. 1788

Yesterday I had my Audience of Leave of His Majesty. I shall not trouble you with any Particulars, of the previous Steps to obtain this audience (which you know are always troublesome enough); nor with any detail of the Conversation, farther than the Publick is immediately interested in it. The Substance of my Address to His Majesty was no more than, a Renewal of assurances in Behalf of the United States, of their friendly Dispositions, and of their continued desire to cultivate a liberal Intercourse of Commerce and good Offices with his Majestys Subjects and States; Thanks for the Protection and Civilities, of His Court; and good Wishes of Prosperity to His Majesty, His Royal Family, His Subjects and Dominions. The Kings Answer to me, was in these Words "Mr Adams You may, with great Truth assure the United States that whenever they shall fulfil the Treaty, on their Part, I, on my Part will fullfil it, in all its Particulars." "As to Yourself, I am Sure I wish you a Safe and pleasant Voyage, and much Comfort with your Family and Friends."

This was the Answer in Ceremony. His Majesty was then pleased to ask me many Questions, about myself and my Family; how long I had been absent from them &c which were intended I suppose to be very gracious and flattering, but are of no Consequence to the Publick, and therefore will be here omitted....

.   .   .   .   .

With much Affection and Esteem your most humble and obedient Servant   [John Adams]

NA: PCC, item 84, v. 6, pp. 627-629 (AL); M247, reel 113.

John Jay to Sir John Temple

Sir   [New York] Office for foreign Affairs 23ᵈ Febʸ 1788
A tedious fit of sickness which commenced soon after the receipt of your Letter of the 10ᵗʰ November last, prevented my answering it in season for you to have mentioned it in your despatches by the last Packet.

When I consider the nature of this application and that of your Commission, I am inclined to think it more adviseable to manage it informally, than to lay your Letter and the papers which accompanied it before Congress, especially as Mʳ Lawrence's Petition contains expressions which are not unexceptionable, and but little calculated to inspire Congress with a desire to comply with his wishes further than mere justice might dictate.

Mʳ Lawrence complains that in manifest violation of the Treaty of Peace, "several actions at Law were commenced against him by the proprietors of Estates at Morisania and Staten Island for the damages they sustained by their Timber being cut down &ᶜ·" "That altho' he pleaded the said Treaty in bar of such actions, yet Judgment was given against him, and he was confined in Gaol &ᶜ" "That he had Petitioned Congress, and the Governor and Assembly of the State of New York, but that no attention has been given to his Petitions &c."

It appears to be true that certain actions of Trespass had been commenced and prosecuted to judgment against Mʳ Lawrence, but Sir, it also appears on inquiry that no such pleas were ever made, and therefore that his assertions on that head are not supported by facts. I herewith enclose copies of the three Records of the only three Causes in which I can find Judgments given against him, and in which you will perceive that his pleas were *not Guilty*.

It is possible that there may have been other Actions prosecuted to Judgment against him if so, I will, on being informed of the Plaintiffs names, search the Records and ascertain whether in any and which of them he pleaded the Treaty, or attempted in any manner to avail himself of it.

How it happened that Mʳ Lawrence omitted to plead the Treaty in either of the three Actions before mentioned, whether through neglect, or because not applicable to his particular Case, I am uninformed; – but as it did not come into question before the Court in those Causes, his complaint against the justice and Government of the Country for violating it in those instances does not appear to be well founded.

I have the honor to be &c: John Jay

NA: PCC, *item 120, v. 3, pp. 331-332 (LBkC); M40, reel 3.*

Comte de Moustier's Speech to Congress

Gentlemen of the Congress   [New York, February 26, 1788]
The relations of friendship and Affection which subsist between the King my Master and the United States, have been established on a basis which cannot but daily acquire a new degree of solidity. It is satisfactory to be mutually convinced that an Alliance formed for obtaining a glorious peace, after efforts directed by the greatest wisdom, and sustained with admirable constancy, must always be conformable to the common interests, and that it is a fruitful source of infinite advantages to both Nations whose mutual confidence and intercourse will encrease in proportion as they become better known to each other.

The King who was the first to connect himself with the United States as a sovereign Power, to second their efforts and favour their interests, has never ceased since that memorable period, to turn his attention to the means of proving to them his Affection. This sentiment directs the vows which his Majesty forms for their prosperity. Their success will always interest him sensibly, and there is reason to hope for it from the wisdom of the measures which they will adopt.

To this solemn assurance of interest and attachment on the part of the King, to the unanimous sentiment of the Nation and to the fervent wishes of a great number of my Countrymen, who have had the advantage to be associated in the military Toils and success of the United States, permit me to add those which I in particular entertain for the growth and glory of these States. I at length enjoy the satisfaction of having it in my power here to testify the profound veneration, with which I have been constantly penetrated for a people, who have been able to fix from their birth, the attention of the most considerable powers in Europe; and whose Courage and Patriotism have astonished all Nations. My happiness will be compleat, Gentlemen, if I could succeed by my Zeal and most constant cares, to merit your esteem, your confidence and your Approbation.

The task which I have to accomplish appears to me to be the more difficult, as in succeeding a Minister who held the place near you, Gentlemen, with which I am now honored, I am far from enjoying the advantages which he derived from his Talents, his knowledge and those Circumstances which placed him in the most intimate relations to you. I will endeavour to resemble him at least, by the greatest attention to promote and give success to whatever may contribute to the satisfaction, the glory and the prosperity of the United States.   The Count de Moustier

NA: PCC, item 96, pp. 420-421 (translation); M247, reel 124.

Comte de Montmorin to Louis Guillaume Otto

[Translation]
Nᵒ· 5   Versailles, 26 Feb. 1788.

         .   .   .   .   .

From your reporting to me, Sir, on the state of our affairs in America, I have seen that Congress has left in oblivion the ratification of a convention relative to the functions of the respective Consuls. I request you to remind Mr. Jay, and to make this Minister understand, that it is time for Congress finally to conclude, in some manner or other, a matter that has been outstanding, for no reason, for several years.

         .   .   .   .   .

Whatever happens, I am relying on your exactness to send me what is enacted in this regard. The King recently published an edict concerning the commerce of the United States; but I postpone sending it to you because an error has slippped into it that must be rectified. It has been discussed with Mr. Jefferson....   Montmorin

         .   .   .   .   .

FFAA: Pol. Corr., U.S., v. 33, f. 111-112vo. (LC transcription).

Peter Allaire: Occurrences from 2 January to 27 February 1788

[New York February 27, 1788]

         .   .   .   .   .

Governour Pierse[1] of Georgia, has made Official Complaints to Don Diego Gardoqui, the Spanish Charge des Affairs respecting the Encouragement given by the Governour of East Florida to Runaway Negroes, and his Refusing to deliver them up, when applied to, by Citizens of the United States, And that the Governour Refuses the free Navigation of the River Mississipi, contrary to the Treaty of Peace with great Britain, to all American Subjects. Don Gardoqui, has had Similar complaints from the Spanish Governour of East Florida for some time past, concerning the Encouragement of Spanish Runaway Negroes, which the Inhabitants of the Southern provinces, sent to the North, and there disposes of, and almost impossible ever to Recover them. And that the Citizens of the United States claims a free Navigation of the River Mississipi. That by the Treaty of Peace made between Spain & America, no mention whatever is made of the free Navigation of the Mississipi. That the Treaty of Peace between Great Britain and the United States cannot bind his Catholic Majesty to grant a free Navigation on that River, that East Florida was a Conquered Country by the Spaniards at the time of the Peace, Consequently Great Britain had no Right to grant a Priveledge in a Country where they had no Jurisdiction, that the King his Master had sent him here to Cultivate harmony and a good understanding between them, that he would write the Governour of Florida with Respect to the Runaway Negroes, and adopt some plan for their mutual benefit; but with Respect to the free Navigation of the River Mississipi, if they intended Navigating thereon, they must Apply to the Court of Spain for permission.

R. 19ᵗʰ March 1788

PRO: FO 4/6, pp. 155-167, 170 (LC transcription).
¹ Georgia had no governor named Pierse in the late 1780s. George Mathews served in that capacity in 1787, George Handley in 1788. Allaire may be referring to William Pierce, a member of the Continental Congress from Georgia in 1787 and a delegate to the Constitutional Convention.

Thomas Jefferson to John Adams

Dear Sir   Paris Mar. 2. 1788. Sunday
    I received this day a letter from mrs Adams, of the 26ᵗʰ ult. informing me you would set out on the 29ᵗʰ for the Hague. our affairs at Amsterdam press on my mind like a mountain. I have no information to go on but that of the Willinks & Van Staphorsts, & according to that something seems necessary to be done. I am so anxious to confer with you on this, & to see you & them together, & get some effectual arrangement made in time that I determine to meet you at the Hague. I will set out the moment some repairs are made to my carriage. it is promised me at 3. oclock tomorrow; but probably they will make it night, & that I may not set out till Tuesday morning. in that case I shall be at the Hague Friday night. in the meantime you will perhaps have made all your bows there. I am sensible how irksome this must be to you in the moment of your departure. but it is a great interest of the U.S. which is at stake and I am sure you will sacrifice to that your feelings & your interest. I hope to shake you by the hand, within 24. hours after you receive this, and in the mean time am with much esteem & respect Dear Sir your affectionate friend & humble sert   Th: Jefferson

LC: Jefferson Papers, microfilm reel 9 (press copy).

Phineas Bond to Lord Carmarthen

My Lord, Philadelphia Mar. 3. 1788
I have the honor to enclose to your Ldp a letter to the Rt. Hon. the Lords Com.ᵐ· of the Admiralty containing a Mediterranean pass, the term for which it was granted being expired and the vessel having undergone a very considerable alteration since the pass was obtained, the master deposited it in my hands for the purpose of transmitting it to England.

The Convention of Massachusetts Bay, having ratified the federal constitution, six States have now adopted it, every other State, my Lord, Rhode Island alone excepted has nominated a Convention, and there seems every prospect at present of a recognition of 12 states of the 13.

It will be a fortunate thing for this country and for those whose interests are connected with it to enjoy a system of Government whose energy may correct the present relaxed situation of the laws and restore public faith and private credit –

In some parts of America, my Lord, particularly in the Southern States, the rights of British subjects are most severely oppressed; and no means of immediate redress presents itself –

I take the liberty of forwarding to your Ldp, two American papers, – one (of the 14ᵗʰ· Jan. last) containing an act of assembly of Virginia passed in consequence of the recommendation of Congress to the different States to repeal all laws inconsistent with the treaty of peace, the other (of the 29ᵗʰ· Jan: last) containing the opinion of the superior court of N. Carolina upon the great question of alienage.

The Act of the Legislature of Virginia, my Lord, too plainly evinces the disposition of that country to evade that article of the Treaty which provides for the mutual recovery and security of debts. What that State has done in that respect amounts to a nullity, as the condition upon which the Act is to take effect cannot possibly be complied with, the caution with which the amendment is passed affords but an unfavorable prospect to those whose interests are at stake.

It would have been too great a risque, my Lord to have noted the condition which was to give operation to the Act upon the adoption of the recommendatory resolve of Congress, by all the other States of the Union; because they might *all* possibly adopt it; – a proviso therefore is substituted by way of amendment, which precludes all apprehension of inconvenience from the operation of the Act; for England, at least in the present state of public affairs here, can have no reliance upon the Faith of Treaties and can not in policy relinquish the only security left to compel the observance of solemn stipulations. –

The decision of the superior court of Carolina, my Lord, goes infinitely further than either the principles of law applied to the circumstances of the case, or the terms of the treaty will justify – Tho' an alien cannot hold real property, the term is improperly applied to the subjects of Gt. Britain, who were competent to hold lands before the Revolution – and it is a very harsh interpretation of the laws of alienage to say that the subjects of a common prince, possessed of a real property in a part of his dominions dismember'd from the Empire shall forfeit that property by reason of the Revolution which occasioned the dismemberment. – But the Treaty of Peace, my Lord, positively provides that no future confiscations shall be made and it is difficult to say to what the 6th article of the treaty applies, if it be not the security and confirmation of the title of lands held by British Subjects in the United States: – For my Lord, persons who had committed treason against the States were attainted and their lands of course forfeited from the period of committing the treason; which must have been antecedent to the Peace; and if every British subject possessed of lands in America forfeited those lands, upon the Declaration of Independence, the terms of the 6th article are vain and nugatory because there is no object existing to which it specifically applies.

My Lord, I have presumed to mention these things to your Lordship that Government may be informed how materially the Spirit and Meaning of the Treaty of Peace is violated and to suggest with great deference and respect the expediency of adopting some measures, which may tend to place the property of British subjects upon some footing of certainty – I have the honor to be, my Lord Your Ldp's most faithful and obed: servant

P. Bond.

R. 29th.

AHA 1896, v. 1, pp. 559-561.

Comte de Moustier to Comte de Montmorin

[Translation]

Nº. 7.   New York, 5 March 1788.

My Lord.

Two events have taken place in this port under my eyes that, being of a nature to recur, have made me decide to submit to You some observations on which it appears interesting to me to obtain a decision that will serve as guide and rule in all similar or analogous cases.

The first was the undertaking of a trial that an American passenger, who arrived here aboard Packet Boat Nº. 1, wished to instigate against the

Captain for various injustices, of which none seemed susceptible of the least dispute. An Attorney was already prepared to second the passenger in his pursuit. It was only on the representation of another Attorney that the individual voluntarily desisted therefrom.

When the captain discussed it with me, the subject appeared to me so ridiculous that I could only answer him that I regarded his adversary as a fool of whom a knavish Attorney wished to take advantage, and I counselled him not to trouble himself about it. In fact, I thought that there was no motive that could authorize a lawsuit before the American tribunals against an Officer of the King's Navy, commanding a Ship that should enjoy the same immunities as the ships of the Royal Navy. I even thought that in such a case as the one that had taken place, a merchant Captain would not be subjected to this jurisdiction. I have since had reason to understand that the Magistrates' claims were much opposed to my opinion. The enclosed letter from the Mayor of New York proves it clearly.

It was written on the occasion of an actual lawsuit brought by an American individual against a Gunner from the Frigate *Aigrette* concerning the theft of a watch. This individual had previously complained to the Commandant of the frigate, who had answered him that if the witnesses that he claimed to have wished to swear to have seen the theft committed, or if he could produce some convincing proofs of it, he would be reimbursed the price of the watch, and that moreover the gunner would receive the punishment due him. The individual, being able to produce neither witnesses nor proofs, waited until two days before the departure of the frigate to bring his complaint to a Justice of the Peace. The Magistrate did not hesitate to grant a *Warrant* to arrest the accused, who was on board the frigate. A *Constable* having presented himself before the frigate, which was moored at the City quay, in order to execute his *Warrant*, he was refused entry. Upon demanding the Captain, he was told that he was at my residence. Upon a third request to at least see the Frigate, he was answered, but without mistreating him, as he claimed, that there was an order from the Captain not to allow anyone on board. It was probably the Constable's report to the Mayor that caused that Magistrate to decide to write the enclosed letter to the King's Consul. The latter having consulted me regarding the response that he should make, I answered him that he should conduct himself according to his instructions. He told me that he had nothing that could guide him in the present case. The Commandant of the Frigate maintained that the Constable's conduct and the Mayor's claim were contrary to the immunity of the flag, but a degree of uncertainty on his part and a diversity of opinions among the other Officers hampered me with regard to the advice that I should give the Consul. The worst appeared to me to yield too much. I consequently took the position of likening the

King's ship to the house of a foreign Minister, and of presuming that it should enjoy the same immunity. It was on this principle that I advised the Consul to recriminate by charging the Justice of the Peace with having violated the Law of Nations, and the Mayor himself with advancing a claim that was entirely contrary to it. In consequence, the Consul wrote the enclosed letter to the Mayor that very day, and went to see him the following day on the pretext that he must not have understood his letter very well, but in fact to convince him of the irregularity of the steps taken concerning the accused Gunner. The Mayor, a man well-intentioned towards the French and of a tranquil character, at first admitted that he had been wrong to issue a *Warrant* before having appealed to the Captain for the extradition of the accused, but he did not the less maintain that the Jurisdiction of the Mayor of the City extended over all its territory, of which the port was a part to the middle of the river, and that no foreigner could escape from the law. He proposed only to endeavor to induce the plaintiff to convert his lawsuit to a civil matter. The Consul, fearing the consequences, took it upon himself to consent to this arrangement and to obtain bail, which still leaves unresolved the question of the immunity of the flag, of which I am convinced, although I do not think that it extends to allowing a warship to serve as an asylum for a Criminal. The Americans who have debated the question of immunity deny it entirely, and go so far as to claim that the Commandant of a foreign Warship cannot exercise any kind of jurisdiction on board it as long as it is within the territory of the United States, so much the more reason that a Consul has none regarding merchant ships. Indeed, it is according to this principle that they conduct themselves on all occasions. Their laws are their sole guides, and they give them so considerable a scope concerning foreigners that they scarcely recognize the law of nations with regard to foreign ministers. The proof of it is in a resolution of Congress to order the Secretary of foreign affairs to make his report on this subject, in order then to be able to recommend to the Legislatures of the States to pass laws in consequence. Mr. Jay, who is charged with making this report, continually postpones it. I do not know for what reason, but it seems to me that the foreign Ministers who are here should unite to insist before this Officer of Congress that the decision that must be made should no longer be postponed. I shall neither induce nor countenance this step unless You authorize me to do so.

Meanwhile, the Americans are still acting according to their principle of following the law, a principle from which no Magistrate can in fact withdraw. Consequently, we have already seen a Constable present himself twice at the residence of the Minister of the States General to arrest that Minister's people for debts in pursuance of a *Warrant*. The complaint against the first measure had not prevented the second. Although neither the one nor the other produced their effect, M. Van Berkel did not regard them the less as an insult to his character, all the more since the second time the Constable insisted, and only withdrew on the threat being made to chase him away with violence. In consequence, the Minister of the States General has requested satisfaction and demanded that an exemplary punishment be made of the Judge who had signed the Warrant and the Constable who had intended to execute it. He was promised that his request would be taken into consideration, but he is waiting, before insisting any further, for the order of his Masters regarding his subsequent conduct. It is doubtful that he will obtain the satisfaction that he requests here, all the more since there are Americans who claim that the privileges and the immunities of foreign Ministers do not extend further in this country than they extended in England before the Parliament of that Kingdom had made a law to determine them. According to American judiciary principle, the letter of the law is the sole guide that one can follow, and since none exists expressly in favor of Foreigners, of whatever rank and status they may be, they must be subject, strictly and without any exception, to the law of the land.

I would like to believe that those same Jurists would find ways to prevent, by a sage interpretation of American Laws, all extremity with regard to the person of a foreign Minister because he would always have in his favor the act of the Parliament of England cited above. The consequence of the principle is more certain with regard to our merchant Ships, our sailors, our merchants, finally in all cases where it would be appropriate that there be a Consular jurisdiction. In accepting the principle of the Americans, which cannot be denied, and which should have its effect for less than a convention that formally acts contrary to the law of the land, we should not claim any navigation in the United States. Our shipowners will be exposed there to continual insults and consumed by expenses. Finally, it will still strictly be possible for any ill-disposed person to instigate an action against a Captain, the effect of which would be to place an embargo on his ship. It is with such a measure that the Mayor threatened the King's frigate when he says in his letter that he hopes that the request made to him to send on board the Constable of the port called *Silver Oar*, because he is armed with a small *oar of silver*, which he uses to touch a ship, an operation by which that ship is detained unless the Captain gives satisfaction or at least sufficient bond, will be rendered unnecessary. It is still worse if an ill-disposed Captain maliciously does damage to his ship in order to have the pretext of dispersing his crew, of selling his ship and its cargo, all of it with impunity, since Consular jurisdiction is not recognized. This circumstance occurred recently in Virginia, and must occur again if a remedy is not produced. One can add to so many inconveniences that of desertion, favored by our sailors, who do not fear being reclaimed or arrested. The frigate *Aigrette* has lost three sailors in this manner during its stay in this port.

My instructions not making any mention of a Consular Convention stipulated as early as 1778 by the treaty of Commerce with the United States, I have searched the correspondence of my predecessors and examined everything that can have a bearing on this subject. I have seen that the most favorable moment to sign the first draft of the convention miscarried in 1781 for reasons that it would have probably been difficult to avoid, and that since then the Americans had made some objections, which have hitherto prevented the execution of an act that I regard as indispensable, if we claim to conduct some Commerce with the Americans, and especially to navigate in their ports.

What is enjoined upon me expressly by my instructions is to communicate to You, My Lord, my observations on Commerce with the United States. In this sense, I believe myself obligated to observe to You that the first operation is to procure for it the necessary protection without which it can never exist. The conclusion or the execution of a Consular Convention appears to me too urgent to postpone it at a time when I could have brought together assembled in one and the same report all that concerns the Commerce of these States.

I take the liberty of submitting to You in consequence some particular observations concerning the projected Convention. I hope by this means to go beyond the demands that You could make on me in this regard after the above explanation. At such a great distance as I find myself, it is excusable seemingly to go a little beyond the bounds of one's instructions, when one can presume that the intention of the King's Ministry can be fulfilled by a step that it would probably have authorized in advance if it had been possible to foresee the reasons that have given rise to it. In addition, my observations will be without effect until You have spoken.

I am with respect My Lord Your most humble and most obedient servant,

Le Cte. de Moustier

rec. 25 May

FFAA: Pol. Corr., U.S., v. 33, f. 124-130vo. (LC transcription).

John Adams to the States General

[March 6, 1788]
To their High Mightinesses, the Lords the States General of the United
Netherlands
A Memorial
High and Mighty Lords
The Subscriber; Minister Plenipotentiary from the United States of
America, has the honour to communicate to your High Mightinesses, a
~~Resolution~~ an Act of the United States of America in Congress assembled,
by which he is recalled from his Mission to your High Mightinesses &
permitted to revisit his native Country.
The Wisdom and Magnanimity, with which your High Mightinesses
manifested your Friendship to the United States of America in the Year,
one Thousand, Seven Hundred and Eighty two, contributed to accellerate
that general Peace of the World which has lasted So long: and the Candour
and Goodness of your High Mightinesses, and of the whole Republick to
the Subscriber, as well as to his Country, have made Impressions on his
Mind, which neither Time nor Place can ever oblitterate.
In terminating his Residence in Europe and in taking a respectful Leave
of your High Mightinesses, he begs leave to express his Thanks for all
Indulgences and Attentions to himself, and his ardent Wishes for the
Happiness of your High Mightinesses and your Families and his Sincere
Assurances, that in whatever Country he may be, he Shall never cease to
pray for the Liberty the Independence and the Universal Prosperity of the
whole Republick of the United Netherlands
Done at the Hague this   Day of March A.D. 1788.

John Adams.

MHS: *The Adams Papers, microfilm reel 371 (ACS).*

Resolution of the States General
of the United Netherlands

[Translation]
Thursday, 6 March 1788
Mr. De Wassenaer Catwyck, president of the Assembly, brought forward
and made known to Their High Mightinesses that Mr. Adams, Minister
Plenipotentiary of the United States of America, had been at his residence
this morning, & had delivered to him a sealed Resolution passed on 5
October 1787 by the United States in Congress assembled, by which it

permitted the said Mr. Adams, in consequence of his request, to return to America, & to conclude his Commission as Minister Plenipotentiary near Their High Mightinesses; & that he had at the same time presented a Memorial by which he takes leave of Their High Mightinesses, which Memorial follows herewith:

fiat Insertio

Whereupon, it having been deliberated, it was found good & resolved by these presents to bid adieu to the said Mr. Adams by declaring that his Person & Conduct have been agreeable to Their High Mightinesses, & that the customary Present of a Chain & Medal of gold, of the value of 1300 florins, be transmitted to him, the Goldsmith De Koning being charged with making it forthwith.

And an Extract of this resolution of Their High Mightinesses will be delivered to the said Mr. Adams by the Agent Slicker.

W.F.H. van Wassenaer
A true Copy. H. Fagel.

MHS: *The Adams Papers, microfilm reel 371 (C).*

John Bondfield to Thomas Jefferson

Sir   Bordeaux 7 Mars 1788

.   .   .   .   .

...Our Tobaccos are all sold not a hogshed remains for Sale, the farmers have purchased about 1000 hog^d that was on hand, the first that comes in will arrive to a good market. the Smugglers that resorted to Lorient of late found it their advantage to come here. this has caused a considerable decrease of Trade at Lorient. but what Lorient has lost Bord^{x} has gain'd, which to the nation becomes the same.

.   .   .   .   .

Administration appears fixt in their Ideas of the National advantages that will result from the Trade of America. The Indulgences granted and protection given will bring it about. England sets every Engine to work to counter Act the Measures, their Agents, factors, and private Subjects settled in the Ports of the Kingdom form societies which with their conections with England form chains and preserve within their Circle the Trade discourageing all in their Power the Introduction of conections between of the Americans with the french. In this they Act their part it is for others to act theirs.

france has very lucretif foreign branches of Trade her West Indies are inexhaustable Resourses, they Aliment a Navigation the most profitable known, the Imports and Exports are extraordinaryly extensive, so long as they can retain their Exclusive Monopoly, they hold tributary the other Powers. England, by forced & fictious resourses supports a Numerous Navigation. The supply of Coals from Newcastle to London < **** > the great nursery of her Seamen is a forced Trade. there are Coal Mines within 10 Miles of London that would amply supply that demand. was france to Cast her Views in the same line she has ample measures. the supply of firewood from New England for the supply of Paris would employ more Shiping and the price paid by the Parisiens for their firewood would allow to the Ships employ'd in that Navigation a greater freight than the Coliers obtain.

As a Cityzen of America, foreign Navigation in the present state of the Country is it the Interest of the States to be pursued to a certain (degre) extent other employm^{ts} do they not offer more substantial advantages. The situations of Europe and America are very diferent. In Europe every Empire Kingdom and State are surrounded by powerful Neighbours who with unremiting attention watch the moment to improve the least relaxation. the Cord of Industry is perpetually stretchd. Power, show, Luxery, under Thousand Shapes by Silent progression are become no longer fictious wants, but indispensable. America has not a neighbour, by the feoderal Convention the parts form the Body. Canada the only people on the Continent to exite attention whenever the States judge it her Interest to incorporate that Province has only to intimate her intentions to work the revolution America having no cause to exert forced measures which in Politics as in Mecanicks are but tempory resources and frequently weaken the Machine. By giving to the different branches and departments protection every nessessary success will timely be brought about

It is incumbent on france to watch the motions of the Rival powers and addopt every measure to draw to her Ports the westren [western] Trade which in every light merrits her pursuit by rendring the Northern Nations tributary and encreasing her Navigation. No Expense or pains ought to be spared on her side even Sacrifices by bounties would be prof[itable] and they appear to Act in Consiquence. The Mercantile Body in General are not indowed with Mercantil spirrit or Intelig[ence.] the next race now Springing will make some progress a different System of Education which is at present carefully inculcated will influence much in favor of Trade and Navigation.

...with Respect I have the Honor to be Sir your most Obedient Humble Servt John Bondfield

LC: *Jefferson Papers, microfilm reel 9* (ALS).

John Jay's Report on Relations with Portugal

[New York] Office for foreign Affairs 12th March 1788
The Secretary of the United States for the Department of foreign
Affairs, to whom was referred a Letter from Col¹ Smith of the 12th
Septemʳ last with the Papers that accompanied it,
Reports. –
That they contain a Detail of Occurrences and Observations in the
Journey he made to Lisbon, to deliver the Letter of Congress to the Queen
of Portugal. It appears from them that he was well received by the Court
of Madrid, and favored by the Minister with a polite and friendly Letter of
Introduction to the Spanish Resident at Lisbon.
That he received particular Marks of Attention from the Queen and her
Minister for foreign Affairs, with whom he had much Conversation
respecting the Treaty negociating between that Country and this. –
That the Queen "was not much pleased that she had not been noticed
by Congress in the Way that her Friends and neighbouring Nations had."–
That she was desirous of receiving a Minister from the United States, and
of sending one to them of any Rank or Degree most agreeable to them; but
she did not wish that only a Chargé des Affaires should be appointed. –
That the Queen would rather negociate for a Treaty at Lisbon than at
London; and that this Disposition rendered it probable that in such an
Event the Obstacles which now retard it might be more easily removed. –
Your Secretary thinks it adviseable for the United States to conclude a
Treaty of Commerce of limited Duration with Portugal, and that a Minister
plenipotentiary should be sent to that Court in Case adequate Provision can
be made for the Expence. –
He further reports, that the Conduct of Col¹ Smith appears to him to
have been proper; and therefore in his Opinion that it would be well to
permit your Secretary to insert the following Paragraph in the next Letter
which he may write to the Colonel. –
"Your Letter of the 12th September last together with the Papers which
accompanied it have been communicated to Congress, and in Obedience
to their Orders I have the Pleasure of informing you that they are pleased
with the Manner in which you appear to have treated the Affairs to which
those Dispatches relate." –
All which is submitted to the Wisdom of Congress. –   John Jay –
read 13 March 1788

NA: PCC, item 81, v. 3, pp. 43-44, 46 (DS); M247, reel 107.

Thomas Jefferson to John Jay

Sir   Amsterdam Mar. 13. 1788
   M[r] Adams having announced to our bankers here his approaching
departure from Europe, & referred them to me for counsel on our affairs in
their hands, they sent me a state of them, & of the difficulties which were
pressing at the moment, and impending more seriously for the month of
June. They were urging me by almost every post on this subject. In this
situation information of mr Adams's journey of leave to the Hague reached
me on the day of his arrival there. I was sensible how important it was to
have the benefit of his interference in a department which had been his
peculiarly from the beginning and with all the details of which he was as
intimately acquainted as I was little so. I set out therefore in the instant,
joined him at the Hague, & he readily concurred with me in the necessity
of our coming here to confer with our bankers on the measures which
might be proper & practicable. we are now engaged on this object & the
result together with a full explanation of the difficulties which commanded
our attention, shall be the subject of a letter which I shall do myself the
honor of writing you by mr Adams to be forwarded by Col° Smith who will
go in the English packet. I avoid further particulars in the present letter
because it is pass thro the different post offices to Paris. it will be forwarded
thence by mr Short, whom I have desired to do himself the honour of
writing to you any occurrences since my departure which may be worthy of
being communicated, by the French packet of this month.
   I have the honor to be with sentiments of the most perfect respect &
esteem, Sir, Your most obedient & most humble servant   Th: Jefferson

NA: PCC, item 87, v. 2, pp. 51-52 (ALS); M247, reel 115.

Thomas Jefferson to John Jay

Sir   Amsterdam Mar 16. 1788
   In a letter of the 13th Inst which I had the honor of addressing you from
this place, I mentioned in general terms the object of my journey hither &
that I should enter into more particular details by the confidential conveiance which would occur thro mr Adams and Col° Smith.
   The board of Treasury had in the month of December, given notice to
our bankers here that it would be impossible for them to make any remittances to Europe for the then ensuing year & that they must therefore rely
altogether on the progress of the late loan, but this in the mean time after

being about one third filled had ceased to get forward. the bankers, who had been referred to me for advice by mr Adams, stated these circumstances & pressed their apprehensions for the ensuing month of June when 270,000 florins would be wanting for interest. In fine, they urged an offer of the holders of the former bonds to take all those now remaining on hand, provided they might retain out of them the interest on a part of our domestic debt, of which they had also become the holders. this would have been 180,000 florins. to this proposition I could not presume any authority to listen. thus pressed between the danger of failure on one hand, & an impossible proposition on the other, I heard of mr Adams's being gone to the Hague to take leave. his knoledge of the subject was too intimate to be neglected under the present difficulty, & it was the last moment in which we could be availed of it. I set out therefore immediately for the Hague & we came on to this place together, in order to see what could be done. it was easier to discover, than to remove, the causes which obstructed the progess of the loan. our affairs here, like those of other nations are in the hands of particular bankers. these employ particular brokers, & they have their particular circle of money lenders. these money lenders, as I have before mentioned, while placing a part of their money in our foreign loans, had at the same time employed another part in a joint speculation to the amount of 840,000 dollars of our domestic debt. a years' interest was becoming due on this, & they wished to avail themselves of our want of money for the foreign interest, to obtain paiment of the domestic. our first object was to convince our bankers that there was no power on this side the Atlantic which could accede to this proposition, or give it any countenance. they at length therefore, but with difficulty receded from this ground, & agreed to enter into conferences with the brokers & lenders, & to use every exertion to clear the loan from the embarrassment in which this speculation had engaged it. what will be the result of these conferences is not yet known. we have hopes however that it is not desperate, because the bankers consented yesterday to pay off, & did actually pay off the capital of 51,000 florins which had become due to the house of Fizeaux and company on the first day of January, & which had not yet been paid.

We have gone still further. the Treasury board gives no hope of remittances till the new government can procure them. for that government to be adopted, it's legislature assembled it's system of taxation & collection arranged the money gathered from the people into their treasury, & then remitted to Europe, must enter us considerably into the year 1790. to secure our credit then for the present year only, is but to put off the evil day to the next. what remains of the last even when it shall be filled up, will little more than clear us of present demands, as may be seen by the estimate inclosed. we thought it better therefore to provide at once for the years

1789. & 1790 also; & thus to place the government at it's ease & our credit in security during that trying interval. the same estimate will shew that another million of florins will be necessary to effect this. we stated this to our bankers, who concurred in our views, & that to ask the whole sum at once would be better than to make demands from time to time so small as that they betray to the money holders the extreme feebleness of our own resources. mr Adams therefore has executed bonds for another million of florins: which however are to remain unissued till Congress shall have ratified the measure, so that this transaction is something or nothing at their pleasure. we suppose it's expediency so apparent as to leave little doubt of it's ratification. in this case much time will have been saved by the execution of the bonds at this moment, & the proposition will be presented here under a more favorable appearance according to the opinion of the bankers. Mr Adams is under a necessity of setting out tomorrow morning, but I shall stay two or three days longer, to attend to & to encourage the efforts of the bankers to judge & to inform you whether they will ensure us a safe passage over the month of June.

> I have the honor to be with sentiments of sincere esteem & respect, Sir, Your most obedient & most humble serv^t   Th: Jefferson

Read 22 May 1788

NA: PCC, item 87, v. 2, pp. 55-59, 66 (ALS); M247, reel 115.

Comte de Moustier to Comte de Montmorin

[Translation]

N°· 8.   New York, 16 March 1788.
My Lord.

The general expectation has been singularly disappointed by the resolution that the Convention of the State of New Hampshire has passed to adjourn until the third Tuesday of the month of June, which will be the 17th· The majority of the votes against the new Constitution had been 70 to 40. It appeared certain that most of the members of the Convention who have voted against the Constitution were bound by instructions from their constituents that forced them to vote counter to the persuasion, which the federalists have subsequently inspired in them, of the necessity and the utility of the new plan. It is only in this manner that one can explain the adhesion of the greatest number to the proposition of the minority to adjourn in order to reconsider the proposed Constitution, after having left the people time to give new instructions to their representatives. This motion passed by the plurality of 53 to 51.

The State of Rhode Island, which has long distinguished itself from the others by the singularity of its conduct, and in which the common people dominate entirely, has passed a very singular resolution. Instead of taking counsel of the people there by the channel of its representatives in a general Convention, the Legislature has submitted the examination of the new federative Constitution to Conventicles formed in each district. The majority of the districts must decide on its adoption. The Demagogues, who govern the people by flattering them, doubtless hope by this means to cause a Constitution, the aim of which is to curb their excesses, to be rejected. However, they may be mistaken in their expectation if the Quakers, who are very numerous in that State, range themselves with the federalists through fear of the abuse of paper money, a terrible weapon by which the demagogues attack and subvert property rights in general.

The fear of lack of security in their property agitates all those who possess any; the avidity of acquiring some or of being freed from their debts excites a great number of those opposing the new Constitution. Those who form this party find in paper money a means of liberating or enriching themselves by forcing the acceptance of this unreal money, which they create and rescind at will when they can prevail in the Legislatures of the States. Thus one can count among the federalists most of the property owners, and among the Antifederalists the bankrupts, the people of bad faith, the paupers, and the men who can only exercise any power in their States as long as no general Government exists. The generality of the people divides its support among its Chiefs. Hitherto more moderation has been seen in the federalists than in their adversaries. But each day it becomes more perplexing to judge what will be the outcome of this contest of power. Just as there may arise a solid, united, durable Government, it is equally possible that we may see the body that hitherto has appeared invested with the power of the Confederation waste away to a shadow. The dissolution of Congress is an event that may happen, as well as that of its regeneration. Interested observers consequently cannot refrain from speculating on these two hypotheses.

It would be principally with regard to politics that the difference would be felt between the consolidation and the division of the American Confederation. With regard to Commerce with the States that compose it, it will always be interesting to adopt the most appropriate measures to extend it. It would no longer be a question of negotiating with a single body that would unite a general power, or with as many Sovereigns as there would be States, which would wish to exist by themselves, or of confederations formed by several individual States. At this point, I see no motive for lessening the ardor with which I continue my research on the Commerce of these States. The great means of making what the King's Subjects could do there prosper are already indicated in my preceding Despatches. The price and the quality of the French merchandise will determine their sales. The ratification of the Consular establishment will assure the necessary protection to the navigation of Frenchmen in America.

These measures are not connected in any manner to the changes that the Government of these States may experience. It would perhaps be more troublesome to negotiate with them if they were divided, but it would also be possible to draw more advantages therefrom. While awaiting the result, I am endeavoring to employ the most circumspection possible in my conduct. However, since there exist no visible leaders of any party, there is less difficulty at present in restraining oneself to generalities. It seems the conduct of a foreign Minister here in the present circumstances should be purely passive. One need not pretend to merit a tolerably lively affection on the part of this people in order that it may influence their resolutions. Everything is calculated, they seek their own interest, the essential thing is to be able to prove it united with ours and not to grant them gratuitous favors.

I am with respect My Lord Your most humble and most obedient servant

Le Cte. de Moustier

rec. 25 May

FFAA: Pol. Corr., U.S., v. 33, f. 152-153vo. (LC transcription).

John Jay's Report Regarding the Arrest of the Dutch Minister's Servant

[New York] Office for foreign Affairs 24th March 1788
The Secretary of the United States for the Department of foreign Affairs, to whom was referred a Letter to him of the 18th December last from the Minister plenipotentiary of the United Netherlands,

Reports.

That in this Letter the Minister complains, that one of his Domestics had been arrested by a Constable of this City named John Wessel, in pursuance of a Warrant issued by John Wiley Esqr one of the Alderman [sic] of the same. –

That on the 4th January last he wrote the following Letter on the Subject to the Mayor of the City, Viz$^{t.}$ –
"Sir   "Office for foreign Affairs 4th January 1788
"The Paper herewith enclosed is a Translation of a Letter in french dated the 18th Ult; which I received from the Minister of the United Netherlands shortly before I returned to Town, the Day before Yesterday. –
"As the Aggression of which he complains, is not the first of the kind which that Minister has experienced during his Residence here, he feels it very sensibly. –
"I think it my Duty, Sir, to lay this Matter before you that proper Measures may be taken to satisfy the Minister, and to prevent the like Improprieties in future. –
"I have the honor to be &ca: "John Jay. –
"The Honorable James Duane Esqr
"Mayor of the City of New York"
That in Answer to this he received the following, Viz^t
"Sir,   "Office of Mayoralty 7th January 1788
"Yesterday I had the Honor of your Favor, enclosing a Copy of the Honorable Mr Van Berckel's Complaint of a Violation of his Privileges, as the Minister at this Court for the United Netherlands. I am now engaged in the Mayor's Court which fully employs my Time and Attention, the Recorder who only could relieve me being absent. As soon as the Term ends I shall hope for a Conference with you on the Subject. In the mean Time I shall apprize Alderman Wiley of the Accusation, and recommend to him Conciliation, that we may be extricated from a Controversy which, if it becomes serious, cannot fail of proving highly disagreeable – perhaps disgraceful to a City with the Police of which I am so intimately connected.–
"I have the Honor to be &ca: "Ja: Duane. –
"Honorable John Jay Esqr
"Secretary for foreign Affairs"
That on the 10th of the same Month he wrote to the Minister as follows, Viz$^{t.}$ –
"Sir   "New York 10th January 1788
"The Letter you did me the Honor to write on the 18th Day of December last was transmitted to me whilst in the Country. –
"On my Return to Town I wrote a Letter on the Subject of it to the Honorable Mr Duane, and enclosed a Translation of your Letter; for as the Aggression complained of was committed in this City, it appeared to me proper that the Circumstances should be made known to its first Magistrate, in Order that Measures might be immediately taken, both for your Satisfaction and to prevent the like Improprieties in future.

"The Mayor received the Application in the Manner becoming his Character and Office; but his whole Time being engaged by the Mayor's Court, which is now sitting, a Day or two must elapse before it will be in my Power to give you any more particular Information on the Subject. –

"I exceedingly regret that you should experience that Cause of Complaint from any of our Citizens. The present Instance doubtless originated in Ignorance, not in Design; but still as your official Rights were infringed, it is highly proper not only that you should assert them, but that proper Satisfaction be given you on that Head.

"I have the Honor to be &ca: "John Jay –
"The Honorable the Minister
"of the United Netherlands"

That he has since had sundry Conferences with the Mayor on the Subject, and that the Mayor appeared willing and desirous to do what might be right on the Occasion.

That the necessary Absence of the Mayor and Recorder, who were obliged to attend the Legislature at Poughkeepsie, has subjected the Progress of this Business to Delays, which he explained to the Minister in a Manner which he had Reason to think satisfactory. –

That he was induced to be at the Trouble of these informal Measures, in Hopes of being able to conclude the Business without the Interference of the national Government, which in his Opinion would tend to give it a greater Degree of Importance than it appeared to him to merit. –

That he nevertheless conceived it to be his Duty to inform Congress precisely of what had happened and been done, and therefore made the written Communications to them, which form the Subject of the Reference in Question. –

That the foederal Government does not appear to him to be vested with any judicial Powers competent to the Cognizance and Judgment of such Cases, and therefore in his Opinion Congress can in the first Place only

Resolve that a Copy of the said Letter be transmitted to his Excellency the Governor of the State of New York, to the End that such judicial Proceedings may be had on the Complaint stated in it, as Justice and the Laws of Nations may require. –

All which is submitted to the Wisdom of Congress –   John Jay –
Read March 25ᵗʰ 1788

NA: PCC, item 81, v. 3, pp. 51-55, 58 (DS); M247, reel 107.

James Duane to John Jay

Sir –   New York Office of Mayoralty 25th March 1788.
I have already acknowledged the receipt of your favor transmitting and stating a Complaint of the Honourable the Minister of the United Netherlands at this Court against a Magistrate and Constable of this City for a breach of his priviledges. I then promised agreeable to your request, to institute an enquiry and to take such measures as the the Law enabled me for obtaining satisfaction and redress. A communication of my proceedings hath been necessarily retarded by my attendance on the Legislature in a distant part of the State from whence I returned but last night.

I lost no time on calling on the accused Magistrate Mr Alderman Wylly for his answer to the Complaint. It is stated in the Paper enclosed for your Consideration. I apprehend no fault can be imputed to him if at the time of issuing the warrant van Antwerp the defendant was not actually retained in the Ministers Service. This fact he affirms and I have every reason to believe with Truth. Upon enquiry I learned that van Antwerp not long after the arrest had been discharged from the service of the Minister, and it was with some difficulty that he could be found. On his Deposition I issued a Warrant for apprehending John Wessell the Constable whose Conduct appears to be highly reprehensible. He now stands bound with sufficient Sureties to appear and take his Trial at the May Sessions. Van Antwerp is also bound to appear and give Evidence. The offence shall then be laid before the Grand Jury and the Indictment tried there or transmitted to the Surpeme Court of Judicature, as shall be thought most adviseable. From this detail you will perceive that all the dispatch has been used for bringing the accused to Justice which Circumstances and the Terms for holding criminal Courts within this Jurisdiction admitted.

I need not remind you, Sir that neither Congress or our internal Legislature have yet passed any Act respecting a breach of the priviledges of Ambassadors so that the nature and degree of Punishment depend on the Common Law the Crime on the Law of nations which is a breach of the common Law. I consider the arrest as an illegal assault and breach of the peace highly aggravated by the violation of the Minister's priviledges and the Circumstances of Insolence which accompanied it, and in this view punishable by fine and imprisonment, for I trust you will agree with me that the provisions of the Statute of Anne, occasioned by the arrest of a Russian Ambassador and the loud remonstrances of his Court never extended to the Colonies before nor to these States since the Revolution.

The necessity of preserving inviolably the Priviledges of Ambassadors is so indispensable that the want of a Tribunal competent to punish aggressors with due promptness and severity is greatly to be regretted, but permit me to assure you that as far as my Authority extends it shall always be chearfully exerted for their Security and Tranquillity.

I have the Honor to be with the greatest Consideration and respect, Sir Your Most Obedient Humble Servant   Ja⁺ Duane

NA: PCC, item 80, v. 3, pp. 391-391/2 (LS); M247, reel 106.

Claude Guillaume Lambert II to Comte de Montmorin

[Translation]

Paris, 25 March 1788.

I have the honor, Sir, to send you a copy of a letter from M. de la Forêt, Consul of France in New York, addressed to M. le Chevalier de la Luzerne. You will see that the State of Virginia proposes to stop the importation of English Beer and Rum, to proscribe absolutely all spirituous or fermented liquors that would not be extracted from raw materials of the country. If this State passed such an act, it would be entirely gratuitously that the King would have granted the Americans the advantages stated in the Decree of 29 December last. I presume that you will judge it appropriate to make observations to Mr. Jefferson thereon, or to charge the King's Minister near Congress with making the strongest representations on this point. I entreat you to be so good as to inform me of what you have decided.

I have the honor to be with a sincere and perfect affection, Sir, your most humble and most obedient Servant   Lambert

FFAA: Pol. Corr., U.S., v. 33, f. 155 (LC transcription).

Thomas Jefferson to the Board of Treasury

Gentlemen   Amsterdam Mar. 29. 1788.
        .   .   .   .   .

I cannot close my letter without some observations on the transfer of our domestic debt to foreigners. this circumstance together with the failure to pay off Fizeaux loan were the sole causes of the stagnation of our late loan. for otherwise our credit would have stood on more hopeful grounds than heretofore. there was a condition in the last loan that the lenders furnishing one third of the money, the remaining two thirds of the bonds should remain 18. months unsold, & at their option to take or not, & that in the mean time the same bankers should open no other loan for us. these same lenders became purchasers of our domestic debt, and they were disposed to avail themselves of the power they had thus acquired over us as to our foreign demands, to make us pay the domestic ones. should the present necessities have obliged you to comply with their proposition for the present year, I should be of opinion it ought to be the last instance. if the transfer of these debts to Europe meet with any encouragement from us, we can no more borrow money here let our necessities be what they will. for who will give 96: percent for the foreign obligations of the same nation whose domestic ones can be bought at the same market for 55 per cent? the former too bearing an interest of only 5. percent while the latter yields 6. if any discouragements can be honestly thrown on this transfer, it would seem adviseable, in order to keep the domestic debt at home. it would be a very effectual one, if, instead of the title existing in our treasury books alone, it was made to exist in loose papers, as our loan office debts do. the European holder would then be obliged to risque the title paper of his capital, as well as his interest in the hands of his agent in America whenever the interest was to be demanded, whereas at present he trusts him with the interest only. this single circumstance would put a total stop to all future sales of domestic debt at this market. whether this or any other obstruction can or should be thrown in the way of these operations is not for me to decide, but I have thought the subject worth your consideration.

I have the honour to be with sentiments of the most perfect esteem & respect Gentlemen Your most obedient & most humble servant

Th: Jefferson

LC: *Jefferson Papers, microfilm reel 9 (press copy).*

Phineas Bond to Lord Carmarthen

My Lord,   Philadelphia Mar. 30. 1788.

I beg leave to inform your Ldp. the recom.ᵛˑ resolve of this congress was lately taken into consideration by a committee of the house of assembly of Pennsylvania; who reported thereon that there were no laws, in this State, repugnant to the Treaty of Peace: – While this matter was in agitation, one of the members of the council informed me, any suggestions I had to make on this subject would be received by the Council. Well knowing, my Lord, from the conversations I had with the Secretary for Foreign affairs, that in my character as consul, I was not deemed competent to make representations to the legislatures of the individual States and yet unwilling to lose this favorable opportunity of stating some points of considerable consequence to the interests of the British merchants I considered myself justified in availing myself of the disposition of the Council to receive any suggestions I might offer; intending to propose them rather in the shape of a private communication than of an official application: – For this purpose my Lord, I addressed a letter of the 7th of March to his Excellency Dr. Franklin, president of the State of Pennsylvania, a copy of which I have the honor to forward to your Ldp: – in consequence of which the council were pleased to fix the 12th of March to hear me on the subject of my letter: – I accordingly attended my Lord, and was favored with a very patient and attentive hearing: – and I have great satisfaction in informing your Ldp. that the disposition of the council seemed strongly inclined to promote every measure which affected national justice. – After I had stated those points which occurred to me as requiring particular reform, his Excell^y· the Pres^t· was pleased to request me to furnish him with any observations in writing, which I did with as much expedition as the nature of the thing would permit; I have now also the honor to enclose your Ldp a copy of those observations. – I trust, my Lord, some legislative interposition will follow, calculated to reach the extent of the grievances complained of.

I was the more anxious my Lord to endeavor to obtain an adoption of the recommendatory resolve in some shape or other by the legislature of Pennsylvania, because its consequence as one of the States of the union might inspire other States with an idea of the necessity of the adoption, besides, my Lord, as the original proviso of the law, brought into the assembly of Virginia restrained the adoption of the recom^y resolve 'till the other States of the union should pass similar laws, it was natural to suppose individual States might have recourse to the same proviso, and the effect of the recom^y· resolve of Congress might be, if not defeated considerably delayed, 'till the adoption became uniform thro'out the States.

I have now my Lord the honor to enclose the Act of Assembly of Virginia, as it really passed the house, the condition upon which the operation of the law now depends is considerably changed. It is unnecessary for me to remark upon it, at this time, having lately presumed to offer my sentiments thereon to your Ldp. well knowing the just ground upon which Government delays the delivery of the posts stipulated to be given up by the Treaty of Peace, I consider the operation of this law as depending upon an impossible condition, so that the law is rendered a compleat nullity –

The state of Virginia, my Lord, in October 1779 passed a law for the protection and encouragement of the commerce of nations, acknowledging the independence of the U.S.A., which Act prescribed a mode of process, by which suits wherein foreigners were parties against subjects of the State should be accelerated. Lately, my Lord, one of the courts in Virginia determined that British subjects were equally comprehended within the provision of that act with subjects of other Empires, who had acknowledged the independence of the United States; as Gt. Britain had now, also, made that recognition the courts of that Commonwealth were open to British subjects on contracts made subsequent to the Treaty of Peace: at the same time two of the judges took occasion to observe, my Lord, that whenever the other question "How far the courts were open to British subjects on contracts made previous to the Peace," should come before them, they would give their opinion to the best of their abilities, unbiassed by party prejudice and uninfluenced by popular clamors.

This conduct of the court, my Lord, most probably gave birth to the Act passed Dec 31$^{st.}$ last, by which the advantage of proceeding in a summary way by foreigners ag$^{st.}$ subjects of the State, is done away: This appeal, my Lord, most essentially affects the rights of the British merchants. and is most probably levelled at them, since their demands greatly surpass those of all other nations: – they are now, my Lord, in this Predicament – it is doubtful whether contracts made anterior to the Peace can be recovered at all, and those made after that event are subject to the common delays of the law, which are grevious and oppressive beyond description.

Some endeavors have lately been made in the assembly of S. Carolina to extend the periods described in the Instalment law of that State: by which law, my Lord, all debts contracted previous to the 1st Jan. 1787 were payable by annual proportions of the 1/3$^{rd.}$, the first 3$^{rd.}$ payable on the 1$^{st.}$ March 1788. – on the 21st of February the house of assembly resumed the consideration of the proposition for altering the installment law which was fortunately negatived, by a very large majority: This endeavor was followed my Lord by a bill brought into the house for the purpose of compelling creditors to take estates and property, seized in Execution, as payment for debts at a valuation and appraisement: but it is hoped, my Lord, this attempt will also be defeated.

The adoption of the recommendatory resolve of Congress to repeal all the repugnant laws, has not yet taken place in S. Carolina, nor is it probable it will; a declaratory law has passed in New York – the assembly of both these states, has been sitting for some time.

A tender law, my Lord, has existed in the State of Massachusetts Bay which enables debtors to pay their debts in property at a valuation – this law being nearly expired a motion was lately made in the Senate to prolong it – but this motion was negatived, from hence my Lord, some degree of confidence results, that the legislators of that State are inspired with a due sense of the value and importance of public faith and the necessity of adopting a system of energy to rescue the country from the difficulties in which it is involved.

It must give cause of great concern to every humane mind to observe the opposition which is growing apace to the confederal constitution.

In this State, my Lord, petitions have been presented to the Assembly signed by a great number of people in the Western parts of Pennsylvania remonstrating against the Constitution proposed by the late federal convention for the government of the United States.

In New Hampshire the State Convention met and adjourned, till June next, a step which is deemed very unfavorable to the adoption of the New Constitution – All the States in the Union have acceded to the measure of appointing Conventions to ratify the New Constitution except Rhode Island: – in that State the mode of ratification is singular – the freemen and freeholders are to convene in their respective towns in town meetings, assembled to deliberate and resolve by poll whether the Constitution shall be adopted or negatived.

.   .   .   .

I have the honor to be my Lord, your Ldp's Most faithful and most obed: servant.   P. Bond.

AHA 1896, v. 1, pp. 561-565.

Sir John Temple to Lord Carmarthen

N° 30. –   New York the 3ᵈ of April 1788.
My Lord,

.   .   .   .

The States which have not yet, in Convention, deliberated upon the proposed New Constitution, continue in great party heats, and those which have, by small Majorities, ratified the same, have violent Minorities raging against it, which leaves it a Matter still of doubt, whether the said Constitution will ever take place to any purpose, if at all, in this distracted Country.

Observing the Number of ships & Vessells that have made Voyages from these States, to India; and the many more that are preparing to Import Tea and Other Articles from the East, I lately desired a Gentleman in whom I have great confidence, to take a suitable Opportunity of asking one of the Principal Merchants of this City who is largely concerned in India Voyages, Whether he was not apprehensive, that the Markets of this Country would be overdone with Tea and other India Articles? the Answer was, "By no means, for, whatever we Import from India more than is wanted here, we can readily dispose of in England & Ireland: I sent, said the Merchant, 250 Chests of Tea last Octobʳ to England, and they sold very well." – of the fact I now have no doubt, though I was much surprized at hearing it! if thus the Sending of Tea & other India Articles, brought from thence in American bottoms, be detrimental, and I sh^d think it must be so, to our India Company, to the Navigation, & to the general Commerce of the Nation, it would not, I apprehend, be difficult to prevent such Importations from this Country, but however that may be, I think it my duty to lay the Annecdote before your Lordship.

...I have the honor to remain, with all deference & Respect, My Lord Your Lordships most faithful, and Obedient Servant.   J. Temple R 14$^{th.}$ May

PRO: FO 4/6, pp. 227-228, 230 (LC transcription).

Peter Allaire: Occurrences from 7 March to 2 April 1788

New York 3^d March [April] 1788

The States of Georgia, South Carolina & North, finding that Congress would not support them in the War they had made against the Indians, have Appointed Commissioners to Treat with the Indians on their frontiers, and desire them to meet at the grand Indian Council to be held in May at Mushingham, under the direction of Mr Sinclair Governor of the Western Territory to settle and adjust all their differences & to Assertain the Boundaries of the hunting ground of the different Tribes. Luke Day, who was Confined in Boston jail, the late Cheif insurgent has been Acquitted by the Assembly of that State by a Majority of Twenty Seven and restored to the Rights of Citizenship.

South Carolina will be the next State that will Adopt the federal Constitution.

The Members Antifederalists of New Hampshire proposed the adjournment, as they had been elected on Conditions, and had promised to oppose the federal Constitution, that they might inform their constituents of their being fully convinced of the propriety of the adopting of the Constitution as Recommended.

.   .   .   .   .

these last three months past Trade has declined both here and at Philadelphia surprizingly, and the want of money is the Universal complaint the greatest proof, that can be given is the low price of our Produce, Flour now sells at 9/6 Sterling p hundred, all other Grain in proportion, the Reason is, we are now obliged to waite, until Foreigners come here to purchase instead of going to them, or seeking a Market amongst the West India Islands a difference loudly complained of by all Mercantile men.

Our Congress are in a State of inaction, looking up in hopes of the adoption of the New federal Constitution, tho laterly the Spirit of the people seem averst to the adoption, but the distresses of the Country for want of a well Regulated Goverment & Trade, will (in my Opinion) compel them to Adopt it, as the heavy Taxation they are compelled to pay will either unite them, or bring on another Revolution.

.   .   .   .

I Remain with Respect,   [PA]
In Sir George Yonge's May14th 1788.

PRO: FO 4/6, pp. 277-280 (LC transcription).

States General to Congress

Our Friends and Allies   The Hague 7th April 1788
     We have seen by your Letter of 12th February last that Mr Adams your Minister Plenipotentiary to our State having made known his Wishes to return to his native Country, you was pleased to grant his Request, and had directed him to take his Leave of us by Letter; which he has complied with in a very polite Manner. –
     Mr Adams during his Residence here has given us so many Proofs of his Capacity, of his Wisdom and of his Experience, and particularly of his laudable Zeal to promote the maintaining and strengthening the good Friendship and Intelligence subsisting between us; that his Person has been extremely agreeable to us; and we doubt not but that he will on his Return with the Candor he has in every Circumstance evinced, report to you the friendly Disposition and good Will in which he found us, and also has left us, more and more to cultivate the mutual Harmony and Confidence between us, and that nothing will be more agreeable to us than to hear from Time to Time of your Welfare and Prosperity, and to find Occasions to convince you of the Esteem we entertain for your Republic and of our Readiness to render you the most agreeable Services. With which we conclude Our Friends and Allies, recommending you to Gods holy Protection.
     Your well wishing good Friends, The States General of the United Netherlands.   H. Tjassons[1]
                               By Order of the same. H. Fagel
Faithfully translated from the Original by Henry Remsen

NA: PCC, item 84, v. 6, pp. 639-640 (translation); M247, reel 113.
[1] Tjassens, Herman, president of the States General.

John Lamb to John Jay

Sir   New York 10th April 1788
    Shall be much obliged if your Excellency will inform the honorable
Congress, that I am here and pray for a settlement of my mission to Algiers.
Your Excellency's most obedt hble Servt   John Lamb

NA: PCC, item 120, v. 3, p. 345 (LBkC); M40, reel 3.

Comte de Moustier to Comte de Montmorin

[Translation]
Nº 10.   New York, 21 April 1788.
My Lord.
    The Council's Decree and the Controller General's letter relative to the
Commerce of the United States with the Kingdom having reached me, I
have rendered these two documents public by way of the gazettes. According to the information I have received, they have made an agreeable impression here, but less great by reason of the general expectation regarding
this decree, the object of which was already known from M. de Calonne's
letter to Mr. Jefferson. Moreover, the Americans are accustomed to exaggerate their importance a little and to think that they can claim greater favors
on the king's part without even reflecting upon the difficulty of offering
advantages that might constitute compensation. Starting from this principle,
it is scarcely but among the enlightened people, who form the smallest
number, that one can find either real gratitude or at least demonstrations
for the services rendered to the Americans since their union with the
nation. The greatest number mean, moreover, to ask for more, rather than
to give thanks for what is granted. In general, all do not cease to declare
their views regarding a greater freedom of commerce with the Antilles, to
which they would like American flour to be admitted, and from which they
would like to receive sugar and Coffee directly. This desire will be more
vigorously expressed on their part accordingly as the supervision of the
superintendents of the customshouses of the Antilles is more efficacious. At
times one would think, in listening to them, that all that they have obtained was owed to them, and that any refusal to grant more is an injustice.
    Here I am not in the District interested in the tobacco trade, but to
judge by the sentiment of the Southern Delegates, the interested parties will
still have claims to make.

I shall not encroach here on the observations which I propose, My Lord, to have the honor to submit to You regarding the Commerce of the United States. I recognize more and more the necessity of not hastening my report. Besides, it appears to me that with regard to French Merchants, there cannot be any inconvenience if they act slowly and with great circumspection. As to the Americans, so long as their propensities in favor of English merchandise hold good, the principal rule for favoring importation of their commodities will be the measure of need that we have of them in the Kingdom. In the present situation, Commerce between the two nations does not contribute to the growth of French navigation, nor to the sale of the Kingdom's manufactures.

It is interesting for us that the American States are emerging from their political indecision. Whether the new Constitution is adopted or the Confederation, already much enfeebled, ceases entirely, we will at least know with whom they will have to deal. Today they preserve a trace of regard for Congress, which on its part still has a trace of the appearance of a federal body. From it they can receive only requests, for which it has only passed *resolutions*, *requisitions*, and *recommendations*, without any means to give them weight or to ensure their effect. You will judge from this, My Lord, that the contest is not equal between us, and what advantage Mr. Jefferson has, who can always request and solicit, but who can promise positively nothing. This Minister is without doubt an excellent American Citizen, and one of the number of those who think that it is in the interest of his nation to be very much united with ours, which I also think, but as the facts prove that this opinion is not generally established by a great deal in America, it seems to me that there can be no reason to grant the Americans with too much facility, nor for some time, any additional favor that is purely gratuitous.

If the new Government is established, we can treat with it, I presume, with security and advantage. If Congress is dissolved, or if it remains in its present condition of weakness, I think that we shall be obliged to treat with each State in particular regarding matters of Commerce, because each ventures to make laws in this regard without consulting or listening to Congress. It is impossible in the present circumstances to undertake anything with this absolutely inert body. In the meantime, I put forward, as much as I can, the favors granted by the King, His Majesty's good intentions, our nation's affection for the United States, and I do my best to support the favorable dispositions which I remark in some Americans; a conduct which I shall take care to observe during the travels which I propose to make into the interior during this summer, and from which I foresee every utility in present and eventual circumstances.

Following the offers of service which General Washington made me, I sent him some questions relative to the Commerce of this country, upon which he promises me clarifications. He then adds: "It seems to me that the public taste for French merchandise is increasing. There are, however, three points which give English Merchants an advantage over all others: 1$^{st.}$, the extended credits which they grant and which I would like to see abolished. 2$^{nd.}$, a storehouse of all the goods one could desire, concentrated in the same city; 3$^{rd.}$, a perfect knowledge of the manufactured objects which suit Americans. Reflection and experience will place French merchants in a position to surmount these obstacles." These observations have served to confirm me in the like opinion, which I already held on the same points.

I am with respect, My Lord, Your most humble and most obedient Servant,   Le C$^{te.}$ de Moustier.

rec. 25 May

FFAA: Pol. Corr., U.S., v. 33, f. 162-165 (LC transcription).

John Jay to Thomas Jefferson

Dr Sir   New York 24th April 1788

. . . . .

The late commercial Arrangements of France relative to the United States, will tend to render the Connection between the two Countries more intimate – they bear Marks of Wisdom and Liberality, and cannot fail of being very acceptable. It is to be regretted that the mercantile People in France oppose a System, which certainly is calculated to bind the two Nations together, and from which both would eventually derive commercial as well as political Advantages. –

It appears to me that France has not a single Ally in Europe on which she can fully depend, and it doubtless would be wise in her to endeavor so to blend her Interests with ours as if possible to render them indissoluble. This in my Opinion can only be done by giving us all the Privileges of Frenchmen, and accepting in Return all the Privileges of Americans. If they could bring themselves to adopt this Idea, their Schemes of Policy respecting us would be greatly simplified; but the Spirit of Monopoly and Exclusion has prevailed in Europe too long to be done away at once, and however enlightened the present Age may appear when compared with former ones, yet whenever ancient Prejudices are touched, we find that we only have Light enough to see our Want of more. Toleration in Commerce like Toleration in Religion gains Ground it is true; but I am not sanguine in my Expectations that either will soon take place in their due Extent. – I have the honor to be &c: John Jay. –

NA: PCC, item 121, pp. 296-298 (LBkC); M61, reel 1.

Report of Lieutenant John Armstrong to Major John P. Wyllys

Sir[1] Garrison Rapids of the Ohio 28th April 1788. Agreeably to your instructions I proceeded on the 19th of March, for the settlement in North Carolina called the State of Franklin, and was detained at Danville ten days waiting for company, it being dangerous travelling through the Wilderness without a considerable Party, who set out on the 2[d] instant for the Block House, where I arrived on the 8th; from whence I proceeded to Sullivan Court House, the Metropolis of the new State, and from thence to Washington and Greene Counties, calling on the most intelligible men on my way, and at each place; And from the inquiries made, agreeably to my instructions, am convinced there is not nor has there been any design formed or forming, of the nature mentioned in the Letter signed John Sullivan, nor has he ever been in that settlement.

I could not learn that any British Agents had been in the settlement of Holston, but that several were during the last summer on the frontiers of Georgia, and among the Indian Nations in the South.

The settlers at Holston are at present divided into two parties – one contending for a new State, the other in opposition thereto. The contending parties headed by John Severe[2] and John Typton,[3] had an engagement on the 29th February in which there was four killed and several wounded. From the circumstances of this dispute, had any such design been on foot as mentioned in my instructions, I should have been informed from the one party or the other, and am of opinion the interposition of the United States will be necessary to put a stop to the effusion of blood in that quarter.

I saw a Letter from the Governor of Georgia, and one from General Clark of that State to John Severe, on the subject of an Indian war; those Letters were dated the 15th and 19th of March. I also saw General Martin,[4] (late Indian Agent for the southern department) – this informant says that on the 19th February a party of Indians to the number of three hundred mounted on Horseback with Colours displayed, drums beating &[c] encamped on the bank of Flint River. While the Militia Commanded by General

Clark were marching to oppose this party, one of equal force went to a settlement on Rack River, where they killed several families, drove off all the Horses and Cattle in the settlement. On the 8th of June last a general Council was held by the Indians both North and South on the Mobile River; the result of which was, that a war was this summer to be carried on against the frontiers in every part of the United States. While the bloody tomhawk was conveyed from one Nation to the other, the Cherokees determined to wait the return of the hatchet from the Northern Indians, which was expected early this Spring, and the Creek Indians conducted by a Mr Gillivray, determined on making excursions as soon as the Season would admit. Enclosed you have an Account of my expences. I hope Sir that my conduct while on this tour will meet your approbation.

· · · · ·

NA: PCC, item 120, v. 3, pp. 440-442 (LBkC); M40, reel 3.

[1] Wyllys, John Plasgrave. Military officer. Served in Connecticut units of Continental Army, 1776-1783, reaching rank of major. Killed in action against Indians, 22 October 1790. Armstrong, John. Military officer. Served in Pennsylvania units of Continental Army, 1776-1783, advancing in rank from sergeant to brevet captain. Served in United States infantry units, 1784-1793, advancing in rank from ensign to major. Resigned, 1793.

[2] Sevier, John (1745-1815). Pioneer, soldier, Tennessee political figure. Settled along the Holston River in the Watauga country of North Carolina, December 1773. County clerk and district judge, 1777-1780. A leader of the Patriot forces at the Battle of King's Mountain, 1780, and in actions in South Carolina, 1781. Governor of Franklin, 1785-1788. A feud between the Sevier and Tipton factions ended in defeat of the former in a "battle" fought near John Tipton's Jonesboro home in February 1788. Member, U.S. House of Representatives, from North Carolina, 1790-1791, and from Tennessee, 1811-1815. Governor of Tennessee, 1796-1801, 1803-1809. State senator, 1810-1811.

[3] Tipton, John (1730-1813). Pioneer, soldier, Virginia, North Carolina, and Tennessee political figure. One of the founders of Woodstock, Virginia. Served in Dunmore's War, 1774. Member, Virginia House of Burgesses, 1774-1776; state assembly, 1776-1781. Moved to the Watauga country of North Carolina, 1783. Opposed John Sevier and state of Franklin. Member, North Carolina assembly, 1785. Colonel, North Carolina-authorized militia. Won "battle" with Sevier faction at his home near Jonesboro, February 1788. Member, Tennessee territorial assembly, 1793-1795. State senator, 1796-1799.

[4] Martin, Joseph (1740-1808). Born in Virginia, he served as an agent to the Cherokee and Chickasaw Indians during the Revolutionary War, at the close of which he moved to western North Carolina. Member, North Carolina assembly, 1783. Indian Commissioner for the Southern Department, 1785-1787. Returned to Virginia, 1789. Member, Virginia assembly, 1791-1799.

William Carmichael to John Jay

Sir   Aranjuez 29th April 1788

On the 23^d instant I came to this place & on the 26th had an opportunity of speaking to his Exc^y the C^t de Flordia Blanca on the subject of
the reports which have been assiduously circulated for sometime past among
the Corps Diplomatique & in the Capital of hostilities having been commenced by the Inhabitants on the Western Waters against Lousiana which
hostilities were said to be secretly excited & encouraged by the United
States: In reply to what I took the Liberty of mentioning on this head his
Exc^y assured me that he had not rec^d any official acc^{ts} which warranted such
rumors & that he was so far from entertaining a suspicion of Congress's
encouraging any Enterprize of that Nature, that he beleived the negotiation
was now in a train of conciliating the interests & claims of the two
Countries to their mutual Satisfaction: That the reports to which I alluded
had come from England & that the Person most active in exciting the
Americans on the Western Waters to Hostilities was an Englishman whose
name he did not then recollect but would mention to me hereafter. After
expressing my Satisfaction with those assurances, which I observed annihilated the suggestions which had been made of his Exc^m having spoke of this
affair with some degree of Chagrin to Several of the Corps Diplomatique,
I reminded him of the Amicable procedure of Congress in having taken the
earliest opportunity of communicating to Mr Gardoqui intercepted Letters
which argued an Intention of some turbulent Spirits of exciting a hostile
disposition in the minds of the People beforementioned. He acquiesced to
what I said & spoke with apparent Satisfaction of the Conduct of Congress
& their Minister on that Occasion.

I must be permitted to observe that I have rec^d no official information
from you relative to the Abovementioned communication, but having obtained by the means of a Correspondent Copies of these intercepted letters
& not having an immediate opportunity of speaking to the Minister, I mentioned to the Chevalier de Otamende now Principal under-Secretary in the
Department for Foreign affairs & particularly charged with the correspondence to the United States that I had copies of such Letters, altho they
had not reached me officially. That Gentleman told me that the C^t de
Florida Blanca had Already received them from Mr Gardoqui to whom they
had been officially communicated. Not having any information but what I
have accidentally learnt of the train in which our Negotiation has been
with Spain for some time past, I did not chuse to put any direct question
to the Minister. It appears to me now, as it has long done, that they think
here, a free Port on the Missisippi will satisfy the wishes of the Americans

& on that idea Ground their expectations that the instructions sent in Autumn last to Mr Gardoqui will enable that Gentleman to bring the Negotiations to a Speedy termination. Perhaps this concession is not their Ultimatum This Idea I communicated to you more fully in November last from the Escurial.

I found the Minister so exceedingly fatigued by conversations of several hours with the French & other Ambassadors & Ministers previous to my admittance (the Etiquette being such that Ambassadors have their audience before the Ministers & the latter the preference of Chargés des Affaires) that he was constrained to sit down to repose himself & to beg me to be seated....I permitted myself however the Liberty of remarking to his Exc^y that I understood the English were disposed to claim a right of trading by the Waters of the Missisippi with our Settlements & I did this in consequence of the Language held by the British Minister here to others. The C^t de F. Blanca rose from his chair & laying his hand on the Table declared "They never shall." The manner & warmth with which he said this marks that Frankness in his character which I have experienced of his possessing whenever he can act entirely in Conformity to his own Ideas, but I believe he is sometimes obliged to combat ancient & rooted prejudices, which cost him as much if not more trouble to eradicate, than the execution of projects which he meditates to render to his country its proper respectability & to immortalize his Administration. Thinking that the Count might have late Intelligence from Mr Gardoqui, I begd to know the date of that Gentlemans last Letters & was informed that they are of the 19th or 20th of Feb$^{y.}$ The C^t de F. Blanca complained to me much of the precariousness of Conveyance from Europe & informed me that this Consideration joined to Others had induced him to establish pacquet-Boats to sail from *Corunna* or Ferrol 5 or six times a year for New York when there to be at the disposition of Mr Gardoqui and that the Chevalier de Otamende would regularly Advise me of the time of their Sailing, – This is a circumstance very Agreeable to me as I shall now have a regular & sure conveyance for writing, altho' if Curiosity is indiscreet They will not escape inspection for notwithstanding my various representations I am still without a Cypher an Inconvenience too striking to render any remark of mine necessary

. . . . .

With great respect I have the honor to be Your Most Obed^t & H^{ble} Servt

W$^{m.}$ Carmichael

read 7 July 1788

NA: PCC, *item* 88, *pp. 504-509, 511 (C); M247, reel 116.*

Thomas Jefferson to George Washington

Sir,   Paris May 2. 1788:

. . . . .

The affairs of Europe are in such a state still that it is impossible to say
what form they will take ultimately. France & Prussia, viewing the Emperor
as their most dangerous & common enemy had heretofore seen their common safety as depending on a strict connection with one another. this had
naturally inclined the Emperor to the scale of England, and the Empress
also, as having views in common with the Emperor against the Turks. but
these two powers would at any time have gladly quitted England to coalesce
with France, as being the power which they met every where opposed as a
barrier to all their schemes of aggrandizement. when therefore the present
king of Prussia took the eccentric measure of bidding defiance to France by
placing his brother in law on the throne of Holland, the two empires immediately seized the occasion of solliciting an alliance with France. the
motives for this appeared so plausible that it was believed the latter would
have entered into this alliance, and that thus the whole political system of
Europe would have taken a new form. what has prevented this court from
coming into it, we know not. the unmeasurable ambition of the Emperor
& his total want of moral principle & honour are suspected. a great share
of Turkey, the recovery of Silesia, the consolidation of his dominions by the
Bavarian exchange, the liberties of the Germanic body, all occupy his mind
together, and his head is not well enough organised to pursue so much only
of all this as is practicable. still it was thought that France might safely
have coalesced with these powers, because Russia & her, holding close
together, as their interests would naturally dictate, the emperor could never
stir but with their permission. France seems however to have taken the
worst of all parties, that is, none at all. she folds her arms, lets the two
empires go to work to cut up Turkey as they can, and holds Prussia aloof
neither as a friend nor foe. this is withdrawing her opposition from the two
empires without the benefit of any condition whatever. in the mean time
England has clearly overreached herself. she excited the war between the
Russians & Turks, in hopes that France, still supporting the Turks, would
be embarrassed with the two empires. she did not foresee the event which
has taken place of France abandoning the Turks, and that which may take
place of her union with the two empires. she has allied herself with
Holland, but cannot obtain the alliance of Prussia. this latter power would
be very glad to close again the breach with France, and therefore, while
their remains an opening for this, holds off from England, whose fleets
could not enter into Silesia to protect that from the Emperor. – thus you

see that the old system is unhinged, and no new one hung in it's place. probabilities are rather in favour of a connection between the two empires, France & Spain. several symptoms shew themselves of friendly dispositions between Russia & France, unfriendly ones between Russsia & England, and such as are barely short of hostility between England & France. but to real hostilities this country would with difficulty be driven. her finances are too deranged, her internal union too much dissolved, to hazard a war. the nation is pressing on fast to a fixed constitution. such a revolution in the public opinion has taken place that the crown already feels it's powers bounded, and is obliged by it's measures to acknowlege limits. a states general will be called at some epoch not distant. they will probably establish a civil list, and leave the government to temporary provisions of money, so as to render frequent assemblies of the national representative necessary. how that representative will be organised is yet incertain. among a thousand projects, the best seems to me that of dividing them into two houses of commons & nobles, the commons to be chosen by the provincial assemblies who are chosen themselves by the people, & the nobles by the body of noblesse as in Scotland. but there is no reason to conjecture that this is the particular scheme which will be preferred. The war between the Russians & Turks has made an opening for our Commodore Paul Jones. the Empress has invited him into her service. she ensures to him the rank of rear-admiral, will give him a separate command and it is understood that he is never to be commanded. I think she means to oppose him to the Captain Pacha on the black sea. he is by this time probably at St. Petersburg. the circumstances did not permit his awaiting the permission of Congress, because the season was close at hand for opening the campaign. but he has made it a condition that he shall be free at all times to return to the orders of Congress whenever they shall please to call for him, and also that he shall not in any case be expected to bear arms against France. I believe Congress had it in contemplation to give him the grade of Admiral from the date of his taking the *Serapis*. such a measure now would greatly gratify him, second the efforts of fortune in his favor, and better the opportunities of improving him for our service < * > whenever the moment shall come in which we may want him.

The danger of our incurring something like a bankruptcy in Holland, which might have been long, and even fatally felt in a moment of crisis, induced me to take advantage of Mr. Adam's journey to take leave at the Hague, to meet him there, get him to go on to Amsterdam, and try to avert the impending danger. the moment of paying a great sum of annual interest was approaching. there was no money on hand; the board of treasury had notified that they could not remit any, and the progress of the loan which had been opened there, had absolutely stopped. our bankers there gave me notice of all this, and that a single day's failure in the paiment of interest would have the most fatal effect on our credit. I am happy to inform you that we were able to set the loan a going again, and that the evil is at least postponed. indeed I am tolerably satisfied that if the measures we proposed are ratified by Congress, all European calls for money (except the French debt) are secure enough till the end of the year 1790. by which time we calculated that the new government might be able to get money into their treasury. much conversation with the bankers, brokers, & money holders gave me insight into the state of national credit there which I had never before been able satisfactorily to get. the English credit is the first, because they never open a loan without laying & appropriating taxes for the paiment of interest, and there has never been an instance of their failing one day in that paiment. the Emperor & Empress have good credit, because they use it little, and have hitherto been very punctual. this country is among the lowest in point of credit. ours stands in hope only. they consider us as the surest nation on earth for the repaiment of the capital. but as the punctual paiment of interest is of absolute necessity in their arrangements, we cannot borrow but with difficulty and disadvantage. the monied men however look towards our new government with a great degree of partiality & even anxiety. if they see that set out on the English plan, the first degree of credit will be transferred to us. a favourable occasion will arise to our new government of asserting this ground to themselves. the transfer of the French debt, public & private, to Amsterdam is certainly desireable. an act of the new government therefore for opening a loan in Holland for this purpose, laying taxes at the same time for paying annually the interest & a part of the principal will answer the two valuable purposes of ascertaining the degree of our credit, and of removing those causes of bickering & irritation which should not be permitted to subsist with a nation with which it is so much our interest to be on cordial terms as with France. a very small portion of this debt, I mean that part due to the French officers, has done us an injury of which those in office in America cannot have an idea. the interest is unpaid for the last three years, and these creditors, highly connected, & at the same time needy, have felt & communicated hard thoughts of us. borrowing as we have done 300. thousand florins a year to pay our interest in Holland, it would have been worth while to have added 20 thousand more to suppress those clamours. I am anxious about every thing which may affect our credit. my wish would be to possess it in the highest degree, but to use it little. were we without credit we might be crushed by a nation of much inferior resources but possessing higher credit. the present system of war renders it necessary to make exertions far beyond the annual resources of the state, and to consume in one year the efforts of many. and this system we cannot change. it remains then that we cultivate our credit with the utmost attention. – I had intended to have written a word to your Excellency on the subject of the new constitution, but I have already spun out my letter to an immoderate length. I will just observe therefore that according to my ideas there is a great deal of good in it. there are two things however which I dislike strongly. 1. the want of a declaration of rights. I am in hopes the opposition of Virginia will remedy this, & produce such a declaration. 2. the perpetural re-eligibility of the President. this I fear will <*> make that an office for life first, & then hereditary. I was much an enemy to monarchy before I came to Europe. I am ten thousand times more so since I have seen what they are. there is scarcely an evil known in these countries which may not be traced to their king as it's source, nor a good which is not derived from the small fibres of republicanism existing among them. I can further say with safety there is not a crowned head in Europe whose talents or merit would entitle him to be elected a vestryman by the people of any parish in America. however I shall hope that before there is danger of this change taking place in the office of President, the good sense & free spirit of our countrymen will make the changes necessary to prevent it. under this hope I look forward to the general adoption of the new constitution with anxiety, as necessary for us under our present circumstances.

I have so much trespassed on your patience already by the length of this letter that I will add nothing further than those assurances of sincere esteem & attachment with which I have the honor to be Your Excellency's most obedient & most humble servant   Th: Jefferson

LC: *Washington Papers, microfilm reel 97 (ALS).*

Thomas Jefferson to John Jay

Sir   Paris May 4. 1788
I had the honor of addressing you in two letters of the 13th & 16th of March from Amsterdam, and have since received mr Remsen's of Feb. 20. I staid at Amsterdam about 10 or 12 days after the departure of mr Adams in hopes of seeing the million of the last year filled up. this however could not be accomplished on the spot. but the prospect was so good as to have dissipated all fear; and since my return here I learn (not officially from our bankers but) through a good channel that they have received near four hundred thousand florins since the date of the statement I sent you in my letter of Mar. 16. and I presume we need not fear the completion of that loan, which will provide for all our purposes of the year 1788. as stated in that paper. I hope therefore to receive from the treasury orders in con-

formity thereto that I may be able to proceed to the redemption of our captives. the purposes of the year 1789. & 1790 as stated in the same paper will depend on the ratification by Congress of mr Adams's bonds of this year for another million of florins. but there arises a new call from this govern-ment for its interest at least. their silence hitherto has made it to be believed in general that they consented to the nonpaiment of our interest to them, in order to accomodate us. you will perceive in the 75[th.] & 76[th.] pages of the *Compte rendu*[1] which I have the honour to send you that they call for this interest & will publish whether it be paid or not; and by N[o.] 25 page 81. that they count on it's regular receipt for the purposes of the year. these calls for the 1[st.] days of January 1789. & 1790 will amount to about a million & a half of florins more, and if to be raised by loan, it must be for two millions, as well to cover the expences of the loan, as that loans are not opened for fractions of millions. this publication seems to render a provision for this interest as necessary as for that of Amsterdam.

I had taken measures to have it believed at Algiers that our government withdrew it's attention from our captives there. this was to prepare their captors for the ransoming them at a reasonable price. I find however that Cap[t] Obrian is apprised that I have received some authority on this subject. he writes me a cruel letter, supposing me the obstacle to their redemption. their own interest requires that I should leave them to think thus hardly of me. were the views of government communicated to them they could not keep their own secret, and such a price would be demanded for them as Congress probably would think ought not to be given lest it should be the cause of involving thousands of others of their citizens in the same condition. the moment I have money the business shall be set into motion.—

·   ·   ·   ·   ·

...I have the honour to be with sentiments of the most perfect esteem & respect, Sir, your most obedient & most humble servant   Th: Jefferson

NA: PCC, *item 87, v. 2, pp. 77-81 (ALS); M247, reel 115.*
[1] report

Sir John Temple to Lord Carmarthen

N[o.] 31. –   New York 7[th.] May 1788.
My Lord,
      Herewith is duplicate of the Letter I had the honor of writing to your Lordship by the *Prince William Henry*, on the 3[d] of last Month, since which the *Antilope* with the March Mail hath arrived from England, but I had not the honor of receiving any Commands from your Lordship by her; nor hath

anything Occurred in this Country, since that date, deserving your Lordships particular notice or attention, except that another state, Mariland, last
week ratified the proposed New Constitution.

There is now a large ship of more than 500 tons burden, lately built at
or near Boston, and designed purposely for the East India trade! this ship
is, I am wel[l] informed, owned principally if not altogether, by Lane &
Fraser Merchants of London, a house well known to have been greatly
favoured by Government during the baneful Administration of Lord North.
Lane one of the partners is now at Boston; the other *Fraser*, said to be a
very cunning Merchant, does the business in London; and great advantages
are expected to be derived from this ship's being an American bottom at
the same time that she is owned by British Merchants! It is only fit and
proper for me to mention the fact to your Lordship, any comment would
not become me.[⊗]

With all deference and Respect, I have the honor to be, My Lord, Your
Lordships most faithful, and Obedient Servant,   J. Temple.
[⊗] Extract sent to the India Board.

R. 25th June.

PRO: FO 4/6, pp. 265-266, 268 (LC transcription).

States General to Congress

At the Hague the 8th. May 1788. –
To the United States of America in Congress Assembled
Our Friends and Allies

Various Reasons conducive to our Interest, have induced us to recall M^{r.}
Van Berckel Home, who has resided some Time with you as our Minister
Plenipotentiary. We trust that his Conduct during his Residence with you,
has merited your Approbation, as it has fully merited ours, and that you will
have the Goodness to part with him in a friendly Manner. –

We have charged him, previous to his Departure, to assure you of our
continued Regard for your Persons and Government, and of our Disposition
to maintain with you good Friendship and Intercourse. We request that you
will please to give full Faith to the Assurances he shall make you relative
thereto on our Behalf, and of the Continuance of our Affection, wherewith
we conclude

Our Friends and Allies, recommending you to Gods holy Protection. —
The State General of the United Netherlands
W. N. Pesters[vt]
By Order   H. Fagel
Faithfuly translated from the Original by Henry Remsen

NA: PCC, *item* 122, *p.* 118 1/2 *(translation); M247, reel* 140.

Comte de Moustier to Comte de Montmorin

[Translation]

N[o.] 11.   New York, 11 May 1788.
My Lord.

.   .   .   .

However, emigrations would slow down if the difficulties and the dangers
were capable of balancing the anxiety of spirit and the avidity of men. The
savages seem more disposed than ever to defend their possessions. Reports
of their incursions and their successes are received from various sides. They
recently attacked two bateaus that were descending the Ohio to enter the
Kentucky. Several Frenchmen were aboard one of these bateaus; two have
been victims of their Zeal for the Sciences; one was a Botanist and the
other a Mineralogist; their plan was not to settle in these savage and distant
lands. One is alarmed to see such hostile dispositions in the savages at the
moment when [commissioners] are ready to open Conferences with them
on the part of Congress to ensure the peace. It is feared that they are being
excited by the Government of Canada. The Americans are very inclined
to think that the Savages could not form combinations to attack or to resist
without foreign help. It is for this reason that they presume that the Creeks
are excited and sustained by the Government of Louisiana. Be that as it
may, this Savage nation renders itself very formidable to the Georgians,
who fear even for Savannah. The Creeks are led by a Scotsman named
MacGillivray, whose possessions were confiscated by the State of Georgia,
which has already offered to return them to him while adding concessions
thereto. His lot appears preferable to him than what he could hope for in
Georgia. He directs all the Commerce of the Creeks with the Spanish, he
possesses large tracts of land, numerous herds, comfortable habitations,
where he keeps women, enjoys a Library, and even has his own Band of
music. He has accustomed the Creeks to regular attacks and to hold firm,
contrary to the usage of the Savages. He has armed them well, and makes
them fight on foot and on horseback. If all the Savage nations who are still

within the boundaries of the territory which the United States claim had
such leaders, the Americans could not regard themselves as its possessors for
a long time.

I am with respect My Lord Your most humble and most obedient servant.

Le Cte. de Moustier

rec. 27 June

FFAA: Pol. Corr., U.S., v. 33, f. 166-168vo. (LC transcription).

Thomas Digges to Thomas Jefferson

Dublin May 12 1788 –

Sir   N° 30 Essex Street

A Cotton manufactory having been lately set up in Virginia, not only
patronizd by the State but encourag'd by some of the leading Gentlemen
in it, some artists from England as well as this Country are wishing to get
to it; And altho I have been a little hurt since my arrival in Ireland
through my endeavours to get some useful mechanicks to my home near
Alexandria, (two or three of whom are *now* under rigourous trial in the
Courts here for attempting to ship themselves with their Tools implements
&c^a &c^a) I cannot refrain from troubling Your Excellency with this letter
– merely introductory of M^r. Henry Wild now the leading mover of the late
Major Brookes's Cotton Manufactory at Prosperous near Naas in this
County. This Gentleman about the year 1782 made an effort, thro' the
direction & advice of Doctor Franklyn, to whom He is well known, (and
in which he was somewhat aided by me) to move with His Family &c^a &c^a
to Philadelphia; but on the point of his Embarkation he was forcibly &
openly stoppd by an order from the Secretary of State, and M^r. Brookes
above mentiond obtain a large premium for getting M^r. Wild fixd at
Prosperous as director & conductor of the principal & still most flourishing
Cotton Manufactury in this Kingdom.

Mr Wild, who is not only at the head of His trade as an Artist but an
excellent scholar & man of genius, has long & still ardently wishes to settle
in a Country, which from his principles in politicks & love of liberty, He
looks to as far above his own, has brought his affairs to nearly that Crisis
as to enable him to move from Ireland; And stands only in need of that
advice & proper direction in his attempt which I would wish every honest
& good Tradesman to possess before he wildly sets down in America.

You will oblige him very much Sir, and it will be rendering our State an
acquisition to get such an able & accomplished artist to settle in it, if You

will favour myself, or Him, with a line mentioning what State the Cotton Manu^y is in – at what particular spot in Virginia it is fixd – what Engines or implements are most immediatley necesary for him to take – The tradesmen such as Spinners or Weavers most wanted – who are the directors or patrons of the Work – where & to whom to apply on his landing – or any other directions which may strike You as most useful for Him. M^r· Wild is not only a perfect master, but can construct *every article of machinery* neccesary for the Cotton Manufactory. I not only wish him success in it, but most ardently request You to add Your advice & aid to Him in the further progress of His Plan.

I am with the highest Esteem Your Excellencys Mos Obed^t· & very H^le·
Servant   Thos· Digges[1]

·   ·   ·   ·   ·

LC: *Jefferson Papers, microfilm reel 9 (ALS).*
    [1] *Digges, Thomas Attwood (1742-1821). Maryland expatriate who lived in London and Lisbon during the American war. Accused of being a liar, a speculator, a trader with the enemy, and a secret agent for the British. Embezzled charitable funds entrusted to him for the relief of American prisoners, for which he earned the condemnation of Benjamin Franklin.*

Thomas Jefferson to John Jay

Sir   Paris May 23. 1788.

·   ·   ·   ·

In my letter of Feb. 5. I had the honour of informing you of the discontent produced by our Arret of Dec. 29. among the merchants of this country & of the deputation from the chambers of commerce to the minister on that subject. the articles attacked were the privileges on the sale of our ships, and the *entrepôt* for codfish. the former I knew to be valuable: the latter I supposed not so; because during the whole of the time we have had four freeports in this kingdom, we have never used them for the smuggling of fish. I concluded therefore the ports of entrepot would not be used for that purpose. I saw that the minister would sacrifice something to quiet the merchants & was glad to save the valuable article relative to our ships by abandoning the useless one for our codfish. it was settled therefore in our conferences that an arret should be passed abridging the former one only as to the entrepot of codfish. I was in Holland when the Arret came out, and did not get a copy of it till yesterday. surprised to find that fish oil was thereby also excluded from the entrepot I have been to-day to make some enquiry into the cause: and from what I can learn, I conclude it must have been a meer error in the clerk who framed the arret, & that it escaped ~~his~~ attention on its passage. the entrepot of whale oil was not objected to by a single deputy at the conferences, and the excluding it is contrary to the spirit of encouragement the ministers have shewn a disposition to give. I trust therefore I may get it altered on the first occasion which occurs, & I believe one will soon occur. in the mean time we do not store a single drop for reexportation, as all which comes here is needed for the consumption of this country; which will alone, according to appearances, become so considerable as to require all we can produce.

By a letter of the 8th. instant from our bankers I learn that they had disposed of bonds enough to pay our June interest and to replace the temporary advances made by mr Grand, & from a fund placed here by the state of Virginia. I have desired them accordingly to replace these monies, which had been lent for the moment only & in confidence of immediate repaiment. they add that the paiment of the June interest, & the news from America will, as they trust, enable them to place the remaining bonds of the last year's million. I suppose indeed that there is no doubt of it, and that none would have been expressed if those two houses could draw better together than they do. in the mean time I hope the treasury board will send an order for so much as may be necessary for executing the purpose of Congress as to our captives at Algiers.

· · · · ·

...I have the honour to be Sir, your most Obedient & most humble serv^t

Th: Jefferson

· · · · ·

NA: PCC, *item 87, v. 2, pp. 103-110 (ALS); M 247, reel 115.*

John Jay's Report on Richard Lawrence

[New York] Office for foreign Affairs 26th. May 1788
The Secretary of the United States for the Department of foreign Affairs, to whom was referred his Letter of 20th March last together with the Letter and Papers from Sir John Temple that were enclosed with it,

Reports .

That the Letter and Papers in question relate to the Case of Richard Lawrence, a Ship Carpenter in the british Service in the late War. –

Among the Papers is a Copy of his Petition to his britannic Majesty, stating, that he was an Inhabitant of Staten Island, and joined the King's Troops on their landing there. –

That he was employed by the british Commander in chief; and in pursuance of Orders, did seize and take several Boats and Vessels, and Ship

Timber and naval Stores, and cause large Quantities of Timber to be cut
and used in the said King's Service. –

That after the Peace, Actions at Law were commenced against him in
this State by the Proprietors of the Timber and other Articles abovementioned – that he pleaded the Treaty in Bar of the said Actions; but that
Judgment was nevertheless given against him, and that he was confined in
Gaol &c: – that he had petitioned Congress, and the Governor and
Assembly of the State of New York; but that no Attention had been given
to his Petitions.

Sir John's Letter states, that he had received his Majesty's Commands to
enquire into M$^{r.}$ Lawrence's Case, and if he should find him entitled to the
Benefit he claims under the 6$^{th.}$ Article of the Treaty of Peace, to make the
strongest Representations to Congress for his being immediately set at
Liberty, and full Restitution made to him &ca. "To which Purpose Sir John
(in his Letter) requested that the said Petition, together with his Majesty's
Commands so signified to him, might be laid before Congress as soon as
might be after that Honorable Body should reassemble to do Business." –

Your Secretary has taken much Pains to acquire an accurate State of the
Facts relative to this Business – He has conversed on this Subject with M$^{r.}$
Lawrence and others, and procured certified Copies of the Records of the
Causes alluded to, which Copies are hereunto annexed. –

One of these Records is of the Proceedings in an Action of Trover
brought against him by Jonathan Morrel. M$^{r.}$ Lawrence plead "*that he was
not guilty of the Premises above laid to his Charge.*" The Jury who tried the
Issue found that he was guilty, and assessed the Damages of the Plaintif at
£230, and the Court gave Judgment accordingly. –

Another of these Records is of the Proceedings in an Action of Trespass
brought and prosecuted against him by Samuel Broome. M$^{r.}$ Lawrence plead
"*that he was not guilty thereof.*" The Jury who tried the Issue found that he
was guilty, and assessed the Plaintif's Damages at £425, and the Court gave
Judgment accordingly. –

The third Record is of the Proceedings of an Action of Trespass
commenced and prosecuted against him by John Broome. M$^{r.}$ Lawrence
plead "*that he was not guilty thereof.*" The Jury who tried the Issue found that
he was guilty, and assessed the Plaintif's Damages at £280, and the Court
gave Judgment accordingly. –

The Word Treaty is not to be found in either of these three Records, so
that M$^{r.}$ Lawrence's Assertions on that Head are not well founded. –

Your Secretary is however informed, and believes that in the Course of
the Trials, the Treaty was urged to the Jury as affording just Cause for their
deciding in Favor of the Defendant, and that the Court charged the Jury on
that Subject, with great Fairness and Impartiality; but whether the Juries

did not conceive that the Treaty applied to those particular Causes, or from what other Cause is not certain; but the Fact is that they found the Verdicts in Favor of the Plaintifs in the Manner beforementioned. –

Your Secretary has been informed and is assured [that] there has not as yet been a single Adjudication in any of [the] Courts of this State against any Article of the Treaty. W[her]ever the Treaty has been specially pleaded, and the Point [there]by brought fairly before the Judges for Decision, there is not a[n] Instance of a Determination against it; but on the other H[and] there is Reason to suspect that some Causes in which the De[fend]ants have been so unwary as to permit them to go to Juri[es] on the general Issue, proper Respect has not in every Insta[nce] been paid to the Treaty. –

There is another Point which seems to deserve A[tten]tion, and that is how far Remonstrances of this kind can [be] made with Propriety to Congress on behalf of any Sovereig[n] by a Person not charged by that Sovereign with such Affairs, [in] the Manner accustomed among Nations.–

Sovereigns should be on equal Terms in all th[eir] Transactions with one another; but that would not be the Case if one was always bound and the other always loose. As Sir John has no Commission nor Letter of Credence which would render his King responsible for any Thing which Sir John may (in Virtue of private Instructions) say or do in his Name Prudence requires that with Respect to all Affairs beyond his Consular Department, he be considered as a private Gentleman.

Your Secretary thinks it adviseable that the Court of London should perceive clearly that Congress will not negociate in this unsafe and improper Way, and also that the Complaints in question against the Justice of this Country are ill founded. For both these Reasons it would in his Opinion be well to permit him to write the following Letter to his britannic Majesty's Minister for foreign Affairs, Viz$^{t.}$ –

My Lord

As there is no Person here properly charged with the Affairs of his britannic Majesty, nor at London with those of the United States, no Communications can be made in that Channel. Occasions however will occur on which some Correspondence may be expedient, especially as mutual Silence might otherwise permit Mistakes to prevail, which friendly Explanations would easily correct. –

Your Lordship will find herewith inclosed a Copy of a Letter to me from Sir John Temple, and a Copy of the Petition of Richard Lawrence which was transmitted with it. They have both been laid before Congress, and by their Order the Facts stated by M$^{r.}$ Lawrence have been investigated.

I have also the Honor of conveying to your Lordship herewith enclosed, Office Copies of the Records of the three Causes to which his Petition alludes. They contain no such Pleas as his Petition describes, nor is the Word Treaty to be found in either of them. He plead the general Issue in each of those Causes, and the three Juries who tried those Issues having found Verdicts for the Plaintiffs, Judgments were given accordingly.

Why Mr Lawrence omitted to plead the Treaty if applicable to his Case, or why his Defence was not so conducted as to give him every Advantage in Error which the Nature of it might admit of, or eventually require, are Questions not interesting to the Design of this Letter. Your Lordship will easily perceive that his Representations are at least not accurate, that the Judgments contained in those Records must operate until legally reversed, and that they cannot be reversed but in the *ordinary* Course of judicial Proceedings, which is as open to Mr Lawrence as to any other Person. –

All which is submitted to the Wisdom of Congress. –   John Jay

NA: PCC, *item 81, v. 3, pp. 63-68, 70 (DS); M247, reel 107.*

Congressional Committee Report
Approving a New Dutch Loan

[New York May 28, 1788]

The Committee &c – to whom was Referred a Letter &c. beg leave to Report

That from the Ideas suggested in the two late Letters of Mr Jefferson, and due Consideration had thereon, it appears to them that the Adoption of the Measure pursued by Mr Adams relative to a new Loan in the United Netherlands of one Million of Florins < * > at this important and critical Juncture of American Affairs would be a wise one, especially as < * > the almost ascertained inability of this Country to make Remittances provisional for the future payment of the foreign Interest, for Some time, yet to come evident[l]y appears to your Committee – They further observe that as the Loan contracted for appears to be from every implication upon the same principles with ~~the last Loan~~ that of Last Year for One Mill^n of Florins which was Ratified by Congress in October last – They therefore submit the follow^g Resolution. –

That Congress will agree. – and Ratify the Contract lately entered into by the Hon. J. Adams for the Loan of one Mill^n of Florins should the Same appear to be made on principles the Same, or equally advantageous to the United States with the Loan of 1787 – for the same Sum –

All which &c –

NA: PCC, *item 25, v. 2, p. 489 (D); M247, reel 32.*

Comte de Moustier to Congress

New York 28th. May. 1788
Note

The undersigned minister Plenip°· of France has the honor of informing the U^d States in Congress Assembled, that he has received an order from his Court to demand the delivery of a French Captain who has been guilty of a crime, the punishment of which is equally interesting to every commer-cial nation.

Joseph Marie Anne Ferrier, a native of Cette in Languedoc Commanding the Brig *David*, was dispatched from the Cape in the Island of S^t· Domingo for Nantz the 1st· July 1787 with a Cargo of 100 thousand Weight of Coffee, belonging to different persons. Under pretence of some leaks which were discovered in his vessel, He directed his course for Norfolk in Virginia where he arrived the 26th· of the Same month.

The Sieur Oster the Kings Vice Consul having gone on board to visit the Vessel & appoint Inspectors in order to prove her condition in conformity with His Majestys ordonnances, found from the depositions of some pas-sengers that the said Ferrier had not intended to go to France as he had only taken in provisions for 15 days, that the evening before he left the Cape he clandestinely Sold a part of his Cargo, that in order for a pretext to Stop at Virginia & there sell his Vessel he had Several leaks made on purpose in the Hold, by which means 12,000^wt· Coffee was damaged, which the Sieur Oster was obliged to order to be sold at Auction; that he had wickedly thrown overboard an Anchor of 750^wt· a large Cable of 120 fathoms, some topmasts & other things belong to his Brig, In short to conceal his misdemeanors he kept at Sea a false Journal which he signed himself & caused his Mate & Crew to do the same in order to make it appear that he had been obliged to renounce his Voyage to Nantz & Stop at the Chesapeake.

Captain Ferrier being informed of these depositions & fearing the consequences of his crime deserted with his Mate & the other accomplices, but he was taken by the inhabitants & brought back to the Sieur Oster who sent him prisoner on board the French Ship the *Jason* after permission obtained from the Mayor of Norfolk. The culprit underwent an interogatory on the 8th [?] December, & confessed the Crime of which he was accused. The process being finished the Sieur Oster called an Assembly of the Merchants belonging to his Nation, in which it was resolved that Ferrier sh^d· be sent to Nantz to be judged by the Officers of the Admiralty. He wrote at the same time to the Governor of Virginia < * > giving him an Account of all these particulars & requesting the consent of the Council to send the said Ferrier to France in the Vessel which he had commanded. He received No answer to this letter w^h· was dated the 2^d· October copy of which (N^o· 1) is annexed: But on the 7th· Novem^r· a Sheriff went on board the French Ship with a Writ to arrest the said Ferrier as a Debtor for £50 to a *Frenchman* resident in Norfolk. the criminal was accordingly liberated after giving bail to appear at the first County Court. The Sieur Oster wrote a second time to the Governor complaining of this irregular procedure, & reclaiming not only the Captain but the other Criminals. He received No other Answer but the ones Annexed (N^o· 2. 3.)

After these particulars, the undersigned has the honor to represent, that it is very surprizing, that notwithstanding the official information which had been given the 2^d· October concerning the crime, of which Capt· Ferrier had been convicted, he should be liberated the 7th· Novem^r· under pretence of a civil Action Of 50 pounds. That condemned in irons on board a French Vessel by the Consul of his Nation & With the consent of the Mayor of Norfolk he was taken away on a suit brought by a *Frenchman* who ought to have acknowledged the Jurisdiction & Authority of his Consul, but who very likely was in concert with the criminal to effect his escape; in short that the Magistrates have facilitated this escape without any regard to the complaints which were made by his Majestys Vice Consul, a conduct the more extraordinary as by a law of 1779 the State of Virginia authorizes the Consuls of Power[s] which have acknowledged the independance of the U^d States to claim the Deserters from the Vessels of their Nation to judge differences between their subjects agreable to the Laws of that country, & to execute their Sentences, provided they do not pronounce corporal punishment. It was in Consequence of this law that the Sieur Oster obtained full & entire satisfaction in August 1784 in a case similar to the one in question.

But even were this Vice Consul unsupported by any particular law, he might [have] found[ed] his claim on the common righ[ts] of nations, on the mutual ties between allied powers, on the Treaty of Commerce & the Consular Convention which was a consequence of it, on the procedure which took place in a similar Case in 1784, on the reciprocity invariably established in France, on the interests of every commercial nation, that a crime of this nature should not remain unpunished, in short on the dignity of Virginia which would be particularly exposed, if one could suspect that State of encouraging & protecting Villains proscribed by the laws of every polished Nation.

In consequence of these observations the undersigned Minister has received orders to claim the criminal & if by a connivance which is not very likely & which would be very wide of the principles of Justice & moderation which Virginia has so often displayed Capt· Ferrier has found means of escaping, he demands to be informed of the motives that determined the Magistrates to pay no respect to the well founded & pressing claims of the Vice Consul of France, & to elude not only the Law which was passed in 1779 but the principles which form the Basis of every Consular establishment, which are formally adopted by the Convention between His Majesty & the U^d States signed by the respective Plenipo^{s.} & which have been hitherto religiously observed in the Kingdom with respect to the Citizens of the U^d States.

The undersigned Minister has the honor of reminding on this occasion the U^d States in Congress assembled agreable to an express order received from his Court, of the necessity of concluding as speedily as possible the last formalities which may have been neglected, in order to give every suitable effect to the aforesaid Convention & to represent to them the propriety of giving definitive instructions on this head to their Minister Plenip^{o.} with his Majesty.

The interest which the King has always taken in the prosperity of the Commerce between the Kingdom & the U^d States, is manifested on every occasion too evidently for His Majesty not to expect on their part every necessary step to secure a perfect reciprocity, the only Solid Basis, on which the advantages granted by His Majesty to the Commerce of the U^d States can < * > exist.   The Count De Moustier.

Faithfully translated from the Original by John Pintard

NA: PCC, item 96, pp. 442-446 (translation); M247, reel 124.

Comte de Moustier to Comte de Montmorin

[Translation]

N°. 12.   New York, 28 May 1788.

My Lord.

M. Otto has confided to me the Despatch N°. 5 that You sent him on 26 Febr. last. I am eager to respond to the article relative to the delay with which the ratification of the Consular Convention has met, of which I have already had the honor to inform You in my Despatch N°. 7 and in the observations enclosed therewith. M. Otto was very active in 1786, and above all made the best of his connections with several members of Congress in order to obtain a definitive response in spite of the delays and the opposition of Mr. Jay and the Northern Delegates. This Secretary of foreign affairs was finally obliged to present to Congress a second report, less unfavorable than the first, and to admit the ratification of the Consular

Convention as it was sent to Mr. Franklin in 1782, with a clause limiting its operation to a certain number of years. This modification was adopted by Congress, and in consequence Mr. Jay received the order to inform Mr. Jefferson of it and to stipulate to him to terminate this negotiation definitively at Versailles. M. Otto only learned these details by private ways, and although he officially requested communication of the resolution of Congress, Mr. Jay answered him that, this Assembly having a Minister Plenipotentiary in France, it found it expedient to deliver its communications by that channel. From that moment, M. Otto conceived some suspicions regarding Mr. Jay's secret intentions, and he did not doubt that he had directed Mr. Jefferson to protract the negotiation under pretext that his correspondence had been lost in transit, a pretext which had already been used to justify the delays of the Congress. To remedy this inconvenience, M. Otto placed the parcel destined for Mr. Jefferson in the packet boat's mail and sent it directly to M. le Comte de Vergennes with a particular letter dated 15 October 1786, in which he explained the reasons for this measure. A short while later, he received Despatch N°· 3, by which M. le Comte de Vergennes charged him "to apprise Mr. Jay that he had received no order to renew his solicitations, and that he should, on the contrary, declare to him that we would wait most peacefully until it pleases Congress to put this affair in order." He conformed to these orders with all the more punctuality, as he had reason to think that this affair no longer depended only upon the negotiations of Mr. Jefferson at Versailles.

According to these details, My Lord, You will easily judge my surprise at Despatch N°· 5, by which it appears that this Minister has not taken any step for nearly eighteen months in consequence of the resolution of Congress that was sent to him on 15 October 1786, and that M. Otto's suspicions regarding Mr. Jay's instructions were only too well founded. I have therefore seized an occasion which naturally presented itself for submitting to Congress the irregular conduct of the Government of Virginia in the affair of Captain Ferrier, pursuit of whom You ordered in the Despatch of 19 February last, in order to request of this Assembly a definitive response regarding the Consular Convention.

I have the honor to send You enclosed, My Lord, a copy of the Note that I sent on this subject. The affair of Captain Ferrier was already known to me through the correspondence of M. Oster, the Vice Consul in Virginia; it is accompagnied by several circumstances that render the conduct of the Governor very odious. Mr. Randolph, who fills that position, was a member of the Committee charged with discussing the various articles of the Consular Convention with M. le Chevalier de la Luzerne in 1782, and he proved infinitely difficult regarding the powers that it was a question of granting. It is according to the same principles that he has thwarted M.

Oster in the exercise of his functions. Congress is less than ever able to render us justice, but the note that I sent will at least convince the various members of the Union that His Majesty is sensitive to the irregularities that are committed with regard to his subjects, and that they should fear reprisals if they do not take measures to remedy them as soon as possible. I indeed think, My Lord, that in case the proposed new Government did not enjoy, more than does the present Congress, all the powers necessary to make our treaties and our flag respected, it could be useful to employ reprisals towards some individual States of which we would have reason to complain. Their mutual jealousy and their own interest would soon lead them to set limits to their egoism and to respect the ties that can only affirm their happiness and render them some consideration in foreign countries.

As for the Bill proposed in Virginia to place an extraordinary duty on our spirituous liquors, on which M. Otto reported to You at the time, it has been rejected by a great majority, but they will perhaps profit from the organization of another legislative Assembly in order to present it again with more success. The democratic spirit of these States gives to all measures an instability that never permits one to foresee the jolts that Commerce will suffer, and it is only in the event that Congress will exclusively have the right to regulate Commerce that we can count on a permanent arrangement and grant favors on the principle of reciprocity.

M. Otto has sent me, My Lord, the letter that You wrote to him on 29 February, as well as the decision of the Minister of the Navy regarding the manner in which one must explain the article of our treaty of commerce relative to exemption from the right of Escheat. I shall emphasize the principles that are contained therein each time the occasion presents itself to do so.

I am with respect, My Lord, Your most humble and most obedient servant,   Le Cte. de Moustier

rec. 10 July

FFAA: Pol. Corr., U.S., v. 33, f. 170-172vo. (LC transcription).

Comte de Moustier to Comte de Montmorin

[Translation]

N°· 13.
My Lord.

New York, 29 May 1788.

.   .   .   .

Since the publication of the Act of the Parliament of England concerning the Commerce of the British Colonies with the United States, it is expected, My Lord, that Virginia and other States that appeared opposed to the new Constitution will feel the necessity of adopting it in order to devise means to avenge themselves for the severity with which they are treated in this act. It could not reach here at a more favorable moment; on the one hand, it indicates the little value that is placed on the friendship or the hatred of the United States in England, and the great importance of the establishment of a more respectable and more vigorous Government; on the other hand, it makes a striking contrast with the generosity that has dictated the decree of 29 December, which had already appeared in the gazettes without authority, and which has since been published by order of Congress. The Americans are indignant to see that after all the fine hopes that Mr. J. Adams had given touching the conclusion of a favorable treaty of commerce, that Minister returns here with an act that renders permanent the regulations that heretofore had been made annually to exclude the flag of the United States from the navigation of the Antilles and to permit them only the exportation of Salt from the Turks Islands under the most humiliating conditions. In order to render this Act still more odious, it was accompagnied by an Ordinance from Lord Dorchester, the Governor of Canada, which, in spite of the encouragements that it gives to the importation of all the products of the interior of the United States, contains the most severe prohibitions concerning the fur trade, a commerce that, by the surrender of the posts in conformity with the Treaty of Peace, should have belonged almost exclusively to these States, and that is prohibited to them for reasons that England could easily justify, but that the Americans are hardly disposed to admit.

Great Britain, My Lord, follows in this regard a policy that essentially keeps to its advantageous situation. Without making any sacrifice, without seeking the friendship of a people deprived of principles of system, of Government, she sees herself in possession of almost all their active and passive Commerce, she reserves to herself the right to take from the Americans all that is indispensable to her Colonies and to carry to them all the foodstuffs that she cannot do without; little content with dictating the law to the Atlantic States, she extends her influence into the interior by diverting into the St. Lawrence River all the products of the border territories of Canada and by paying for them in merchandise manufactured in England. One can say that by the revolution this power has lost only the right to appoint the Governors; but that the United States are still fertile and profitable colonies for her. This state of affairs will certainly change if the new Government is established, but the more Great Britain will have confined the Americans, the more she will be able to offer compensations when it is a question of purchasing favors. These considerations have much influence on the spirit of those who are at the head of the various Conventions, and they are perhaps as strong as the rich men's fear of losing their property through the greed and the bad faith of the populace. Whatever may happen, My Lord, one can still doubt the efficacy of this new Government as to the interior administration, although it should inspire more confidence and consideration in foreign powers. Power is rarely given by unanimous consent; it is due more often to happy circumstances, to genius, to a well-struck blow.

I am with respect My Lord Your most humble and most obedient servant,

Le Cᵗᵉ· de Moustier

P.S. Since my written Despatch, My Lord, Chevalier Temple, the Consul from England, has shown to M. Otto a letter by which Lord Carmarthen requests from him a detailed account of all the extraordinary duties paid by foreign Commerce, and especially by the French and the English, in the different ports of the United States. The Court of London perhaps intends to make them experience in its ports the rigorous treatment that foreigners are subjected to in almost all the States of the union, which would very much conform to the system that it has adopted with regard to the Americans, and which it will maintain until other circumstances induce it to treat them with more discretion.

rec. 10 July

FFAA: Pol. Corr., U.S., v. 33, f. 178-181vo. (LC transcription).

Sir John Temple to Lord Carmarthen

Nᵒ· 32.

My Lord,

New York 4ᵗʰ· of June 1788.

.   .   .   .   .

The Kings order in Council, of the 19ᵗʰ· of March, mentioned in your Lordships Letter of the 2ᵈ· of April, was, by some mistake or accident, omitted to be inclosed, but the Act of Parliament for governing the intercourse of trade, between his Majesty's dominions & these states, I obtained from a Gentleman who came Passenger in the Packet from England, & I caused it to be published in these New York papers. The Kings Proclamation of the 22^d. of March, for recalling & prohibiting his Majestys Seamen from serving foreign Princes & States, I also caused to be publised in these News papers, and shall do every thing that may be in my power to induce his Majestys Subjects & Seamen here, to decline all other, & return to Employment in his Majestys dominions.

. . . . .

This being his Majestys Birthday: The Congress, The Foreign Ministers, The Great officers of state, and all his Majestys officers of Army & Navy who reside here, or happen to be here casually (and they are not few in Number) dine with me, as hath been usual ever since my arrival, on both their Majestys birthdays!...

. . . . .

I am with all deference and Respect, My Lord, Your Lordships most faithful, and Obedient Servant   J. Temple
R. 6th. July
(N°. 32.)

PRO: FO 4/6, pp. 309-312 (LC transcription).

Peter Allaire: Occurrences from 5 April to 6 May 1788

New York 4 June 1788.
Georgia, South & North Carolina, finding Congress would not support them in the War they had declared against the Indians, have agreed to send Commissioners to endeavour to treat with them for a Suspension of Hostilities, and to persuade them to be at the grand Indian meeting to be held in May, at the Miskinham, by Order of Congress, under the direction & Inspection of Arthur Sinclair Esq. Governor of the Western Territory, to conclude a Solid & permanent Treaty of Peace, to Assertain & Limit to each Indian Nation the bounds of their Hunting Grounds, and marking out the Boundaries between them and the United States, to prevent all future, Doubts, dificulties, Altercations, Claims, or disputes.

. . . . .

On the 14th. April we had a Riot here (almost Similar to that of Lord George Gordons)[1] for three days, owing to the indelicacy inattention & Negligence of the Surgeons in disecting. they had put a Mans Arm, to keep the Sash of the window up, which drew the Attention of the passengers a Mob soon gathered: they demanded entrance, the Surgeons Refused: the Mob broke open the Hospital beat the Surgeons, threw all the Anatomical preparations into the Street, with nearly twenty Subjects untouched; every person who had recently lost a friend or Relation, found a resemblance the whole City was in an uproar, they insisted on killing all the Surgeons, the Mayor with great dificulty, got them into Jail. the next Day, a larger Mob, waited on the Mayor and Demanded the Surgeons to be delivered up, he Refused, they proceeded to the Jail & Attempted to pull it down & break in, but in Vain, the Governor, Mayor, Judges & all the Civil Officers endeavoured to persuade them to Return home, but in Vain, they beat the Governor, bruised the Mayor & made the whole party Run for it. The Governor Returned with about 15 of the Militia, they in one Minute, disarmd them, broke their Muskets beat the Men & hauld the Governor through the Kennel, & beat him Severely, he then got together about 150 Men and about 20 of the light horse, he Ordered them to retire, they saluted him with a Shower of stones, he Ordered his Men to fire, killed four & wounded Ten, the light horse soon dispersed the Rest. the next day the Mob went to all the Surgeons houses and distroyed every Skeleton they could meet with & then returned quietly home on the Magistrates assuring them that the Surgeons should be Answerable for whatever insults or damage they had done, the Grand jury was then Seting they have found a Bill & they are to be tryed next Sessions they are bailed at £1000 Surety.

Orders has already been Received from Portugal for the shiping of One hundred & fifty thousand Bushels Wheat, limitted price four Shillings Ster^g. to be drawn for on *London* the present price is about 3/3 Sterling; (no faith but in English Merchants & English bills) without whose Assistance we could not exist.

Richard Lawrence the Person so long Confined who I mentioned in one of my former Occurrences, has been liberated on givin up all his property to his pretended Creditors, and goes to England by this Packet, he will undoubtedly inform your friends, the *very spirited* part Sir J– T–ple took on that Affair.

June 3^d. A Vessell this day from Charles Town South Carolina, that General Sumner[2] on the 22^d May made a Motion in the Convention, that the house pospone the further Consideration of the New Constitution until the 20th. October next, After a debate of 8 hours, they divided Ayes 89, Noes 135, Majority 46, General Gadson[3] moved an adjournment until 9 the next morning, then to take up the Question for Ratifying the New

Constitution, there is no doubt of at least a Majority of 60, the People made loud Rejoicing &c. The Treaty with the Indians is posponed until the middle of July, then to be held by Gov.ʳ Sinclair.

. . . . .

...I Remain with the Greatest Respect Sir Your Very Humb. Serv. PA R. 8ᵗʰ· July 1788.

PRO: FO 4/6, pp. 281-290, 292 (LC transcription).
[1] *Gordon, Lord George (1751-1793). British political figure. Member of Parliament, 1774-1781. Headed Protestant associations formed to seek repeal of Act of Parliament removing certain restrictions on the activities of British Catholics. Led mob in the No-Popery or Gordon Riots of June 2-8, 1780, which destroyed Roman Catholic chapels. Acquitted of treason, but excommunicated. Convicted of libelling Marie Antoinette, 1787, he spent his last years in Newgate Prison, where he converted to Judaism.*
[2] *Sumter, Thomas (1734-1832). Military officer, South Carolina political figure. Fought with Virginia troops in French and Indian War and in campaigns against the Cherokees before moving to South Carolina, 1765. Rose to rank of colonel in Continental Army; resigned, 1778. Led state resistance forces, 1780-1781. Served several terms in state assembly. Member, U.S. House of Representatives, 1789-1793, 1797-1801. U.S. Senator, 1801-1810.*
[3] *Gadsden, Christopher (1724-1805). South Carolina merchant and political figure. Member, state assembly, 1757-1784. Member, Stamp Act Congress, 1765. Member, Continental Congress, 1774-1776. Continental Army officer, 1776-1783. Lieutenant governor, 1778-1780.*

Peter Allaire: Occurrences
from 6 May to 5 June 1788

New York 6 May [June 5] 1788
The Southern Indians have committed and still continue to commit more depredations, then ever was known, they have distroyed upwards of forty families, drove off a large Number of Slaves, Cattle, hogs &c and burnt all the buildings on those farms, have Attacked the federal Troops, and drove them into their fort with the loss of Nine Men and their Captain, Wood, and Lieutenant Hogan, surrounded the fort for Several days. the Command-ing Officer has wrote to Congress for Reinforcements, or will be compelled to abandone that Fort, (Kemp's fort Garrisoned with One hundred & Seven Men Officers Included) the Commissioners from the Southern States have not as yet, tho Nominated by their Legislators, been able to persuade them to be at the grand meeting, to be held by Governor Sinclair, if they do not,

we shall have a general Indian War, & Congress will be obliged to Levy forces to go against them, or at least to gaurd the frontiers, until our New Government can be Consolidated & Organized.

Our present Situation is, Seven States have already Confirmed the New Constitution, Delaware, Philadelphia Jersey, Connecticut, Massachusets, Georgia and Maryland, South Carolina, meet the 14ᵗʰ May, and Virginia the 28ᵗʰ· May: South Carolina are Federalists three to one, and by the best information from Virginia they will have a Majority of upwards of forty, those two States, adopting the Constitution, forms the federal Union. New York meets the 17ᵗʰ· June but it is doubtfull wether it will be adopted, (however, the Southern Counties, by far the most numerous & Richest have determined, to Join the Confederation, and leave the back Country to shift for themselves.

New Hampshire also meets the 17ᵗʰ· June & North Carolina the 4ᵗʰ· July: as for Rhode Island they have not Complyed with the Order of Congress in ordering their Counties to nominate Members for the Convention, but have desired the people to meet in Each County, and give their Votes, for or against the New Constitution; and their appears, seven to one against it.

My Opinion is, that when South Carolina & Virginia have adopted it, the other States must comply, or form another Republick on their own plan, and those States, not being near each other, but on the Contrary, the most distant apart, and surrounded by Federal Government, have no Alternative. I make not the least doubt but the New Federal Constitution will be finally adjusted, and will Act in their Legislative Capacity in the course of this Year.

. . . . .

Our Trade is Brisk, & have the pleasure to inform you, that upwards of one half is Carried on by British Vessells, the demand from Portugal and Spain for Wheat, has been very great this Year, we have several Vessells now loading for Falmouth for a Market, from whence they proceed either to Holland, Spain, or Portugal, all under English Colours.

. . . . .

The Indians continue hostile, nor have we any Accounts wether they have been at the General Treaty, now held by Governor Sinclair, they are in strict freindship with your Canada factor, who trades with safety amongst them & who has gained their Confidence, I write him Regularly on the Subject, which assists him in his Commerce.

You will learn also with pleasure, that the measures I have taken to prevent the interruption of the Commerce of Tobacco have had full success.

This Commodity shall not be accepted from amongst those that the right of Entrepot is given. The Farmers General shall have no preference in the purchases, the Proprietors shall be perfectly master of their speculations and free to Export their Tobacco by Sea to Foreign Countries

Measures must be taken to prevent those frauds to which the Entrepot might serve as a pretext, and the Chambers of Commerce for the Ports shall be consulted, in Order that the precations necessary for this purpose may not be incompatable with that liberty which commerce ought to Enjoy in its Operations. Although the present Stock of the Farmers General amount to above three Years Consumption, I have engaged that Company to continue to purchase Yearly from 1st. January 1788 to the End of their lease fourteen thousand hogshead of Tobacco brought directly into the ports of France in any French or American bottoms, and to shew at the end of every four months that their purchases amount to 4666 hogsheads.

As to the prices, you are sensible of the necessity of leaving them free, and this fredom of price was the principal object of the Application of the American & French Merchants when they complained of the Contract of Mr. Morris.

The determination then taken to force the purchasers of Tobacco, tho at high prices, insomuch that the farmers General now find themselves possessed of three Years provision, shews, that the Interest of the Planters & Merchants of the United States, have ever been precious to the King.

. . . . .

May 1. Congress have Received the following information, that the Indians had attacked a Fort, but were Repulsed: After they way layd three Boats full of Men (between 30 & forty) two Men Escaped & Report: that finding they could not get away: a Frenchman on Board held up a White hankercheif: to which they paid no regard but Tomahawked him & fired at the Rest: they jumped over Board & got safe on shore while the Indians were butchering the Rest, that the next day they saw the two Boats Bottoms upwards on the Mussle Shoals, but knows nothing of the people, wether they are Prisoners or no, this Affair happened on the Meame, we expect a General Indian War, if Sinclair Gov of the Western Territories does not make a firm & lasting peace: but we have not the principal ingredient for making a firm Peace with the Indians Namely: *Cash* without which, or Presents nothing can be depended on with any of them.

May 3d. Accounts from Maryland, that the Convention of that State had Adopted the federal Constitution 63 to 11 Majority 52 – Virgina are become federalist & South Carolina: Virginia we expect will Adopt it this Month: & S: Carolina Early in June, which will form the Confederacy, Seven having Ratified & Confirmed it.

Congress are become a mere Cypher, they do verry little business, not making a house above once a forthnight, they wait with Impatiency the Adoption of the Federal Constitution.

I Remain with Respect   PA
R. 25ᵗʰ· June 1788

PRO: FO 4/6, pp. 315-331, 334 (LC transcription).

John Jay to Thomas Jefferson

Dʳ· Sir   [New York] Office for foreign Affairs 9ᵗʰ· June 1788

· · · · ·

By the Newspapers herewith sent you will perceive that South Carolina has adopted the proposed Constitution. The Convention of this State will convene on Tuesday at Poughkeepsie; and as this City and County has elected me one of their Deputies to it, I shall be absent from hence until it rises. There is Reason to believe that the Majority of this Convention are decidedly opposed to the Constitution, so that whether they will venture to reject it, or whether they will adjourn and postpone a Decision on it is uncertain. –

Accounts from Virginia and New Hampshire render it probable that those States will adopt it, and if so it may be presumed that North Carolina and even this State will follow the Example....

With great and sincere Esteem and Regard, I am &ca: John Jay –

NA: PCC, item 121, pp. 300-302 (LBkC); M61, reel 1.

Congressional Resolution on Informing the State of Virginia of the Need to Apprehend Captain Joseph M. A. Ferrier

Friday June 13. 1788

The Committee consisting of Mʳ Hamilton[1] Mʳ Dane[2] Mʳ Dayton[3] Mʳ Otis[4] & Mʳ Carrington[5] to whom was referred a report of the Secretary for foreign Affairs on a Note from the Minister plenipotentiary of France of the 28 May report

That it appears by the said note and the papers which accompany it that the person mentioned therein to ~~which~~ wit: Joseph Marie Anne Ferrier – commander of the brig David is in substance charged with betraying his trust and running away with a cargo of Coffee; that the execution of this design is alledged to have been begun at the cape, continued by certain acts on the high seas and completed in the commonwealth of Virginia: Whereupon

Resolved That the Secretary for foreign Affairs be and he is hereby directed to transmit the said note of the Minister plenipotentiary of France of the 28 of May last to the executive of the commonwealth of Virginia to the end that the said Executive may communicate to Congress the necessary information on the subject; and also to signify to the said Executive that it is the sense of Congress that the said Joseph Marie Anne Ferrier – ought to be apprehended in order to be dealt with according to the nature of the case. And That the said Secretary be and he is hereby directed to inform the said Minister plenipotentiary, that instructions have already been given to the minister of the United States at the court of France concerning the consular Convention referred to in his note. –

NA: PCC, item 5, v. 3, pp. 1684-1685 (Journal); M247, reel 19.

[1] Hamilton, Alexander (1757-1804). Soldier, lawyer and New York political figure. Aide-de-camp to General Washington, 1777-1781. Member, Continental Congress, 1782-1783, 1788. Member, Constitutional Convention, 1787. Author, with John Jay and James Madison, of The Federalist. Secretary of the Treasury, 1789-1795.

[2] Dane, Nathan (1752-1835). Massachusetts lawyer and political figure. Member, state assembly, 1782-1785. Member, Continental Congress, 1785-1788. State senator, 1790-1791, 1794-1797. Member, Hartford Convention, 1814. Primary author of Northwest Ordinance 1787.

[3] Dayton, Jonathan (1760-1824). Soldier, lawyer, New Jersey land speculator and political figure. Continental Army, 1776-1783, with final rank of captain. Member, state assembly, 1786-1787, 1790; speaker, 1790. Delegate, Constitutional Convention, 1787. Member, Continental Congress, 1787-1788. Member, state council, 1790. Member, U.S. House of Representatives, 1791-1799; speaker, 1795-1799. U.S. Senator, 1799-1805.

[4] Otis, Samuel A. (1740-1814). Massachusetts merchant and political figure. Member, State house of representatives, 1776, 1784-1787; speaker, 1784. Member, Continental Congress, 1787-1788. Secretary of the U.S. Senate, 1789-1814.

[5] Carrington, Edward (1748-1810). Soldier, Virginia lawyer and political figure. Continental Army artillery officer, 1776-1781. Member, Continental Congress, 1786-1788. U.S. Marshal of Virginia, 1789. Jury foreman for Aaron Burr's treason trial, 1807.

John Jay to Lord Carmarthen

My Lord,   New York 13[th.] June 1788.

As there is no Person here properly charged with the Affairs of his Britannic Majesty, nor at London with those of the United States, no Communications can be made in that Channel. Occassions however will occur on which some Correspondence may be expedient, especially as mutual Silence might otherwise permit Mistakes to prevail, which friendly Explanations could easily correct. –

Your Lordship will find, herewith enclosed a Copy of a Letter to me from Sir John Temple, and a Copy of the Petition of Richard Lawrence which was transmitted with it. They have both been laid before Congress, and by their Order the Facts stated by Mʳ· Lawrence have been investigated

I have also the Honor of conveying to your Lordship herewith enclosed, Office Copies of the Records of the three Causes to which his Petition alludes. They contain no such Pleas as his Petition describes, nor is the word Treaty to be found in either of them. He plead the general Issue in each of those Causes, and the three Juries who tried these Issues having found Verdicts for the Plantifs, Judgments were given accordingly.

Why Mʳ· Lawrence omitted to plead the Treaty if applicable to his Case, or why his Defence was not so conducted as to give him every Advantage in Error, which the Nature of it might admit of, or eventually require, are Questions not interesting to the Design of this Letter. Your Lordship will easily perceive that his Representations are at least not accurate, that the Judgements contained in those Records must operate until legally reversed, and that they cannot be reversed but in the *ordinary* Course of judicial Proceedings, which is as open to Mʳ· Lawrence as to any other Person.

I have the Honour to be with great Respect Your Lordships most obᵗ· & very hble Servᵗ·   John Jay –
R. 18ᵗʰ· Augˢᵗ⁚

PRO: FO 4/6, pp. 339-344 (LC *transcription*).

Thomas Jefferson to Comte de Montmorin

Sir   Paris June 20. 1788.

Having had the honor of mentioning to Your Excellency the wish of Congress that certain changes should be made in the articles for a consular convention which had been sent to them, I have now that, conformably to the desire you expressed, of giving a general idea of the alterations to be proposed

the IVᵗʰ· article gives to consuls the immunities of the law of nations. it has been understood however that the laws of France do not admit of this: & that it might be desirable to expunge this article. in this we are ready to concur, as in every other case where an article might call for changes in the established laws either inconvenient or disagreable. After establishing in favour of consuls the general immunities of the law of nations, one consequence of which would have been that they could not have been called upon to give testimony in courts of justice the Vth. article requires that, after the observance of certain formalities which imply very high respect, they shall make a declaration; but *in their own houses* (chez eux) as may be pretended, if not justly inferred, from the expressions in the article. but our laws require indispensably a personal examination of witnesses in the presence of the parties, of their counsel, the jury & judges, each of whom has a right to ask of them all questions pertinent to the fact. the first & highest officers of our government are obliged to appear personally to the order of a court to give evidence. The court takes care that they are treated with respect. it is proposed therefore to omit this article for these particular reasons as well as for the general one that the IVth. being expunged, this, which was but an exception to that, falls of course.

the VIIth. VIIIth X^th. & XIVth. articles extend their pre-eminences far beyond those which the laws of nations would have given. these articles require that the declarations made in the presence of consuls, & certified by them, shall be received in evidence in all courts whatever: & in some instances give to their certficates a credibility which excludes all other testimony. the cases are rare in which our laws admit written evidence of facts: & such evidence when admitted, must have been given in the presence of both parties & must contain the answers to all the pertinent questions which they may have desired to ask of the witness. & to no evidence of whatever nature, written or oral, do our laws give so high credit as to exclude all counter proof.

these principles are of such antient foundation in our system of jurisprudence, & are so much valued & venerated by our citizens, that perhaps it would be impossible to execute articles which should contravene them. nor is it imagined that these Stipulations can be so interesting to this country as to balance the inconvenience & hazard of such an innovation with us. perhaps it might be found that the laws of both countries require a modification of this article, as it is inconcievable that the certificate of an American consul in France could be permitted by one of its courts to establish a fact the falsehood of which should be notorious to the court itself.

the VIIIth. article gives to the consuls of either nation a jurisdiction in certain cases over foreigners of any other. on a dispute arising in France between an American & a Spaniard or an Englishman, it would not be fair to abandon the Spaniard or Englishman to an American consul. on the contrary the territorial judge, as neutral, would Seem to be the most impartial. probably therefore it will be thought convenient for both parties to correct this Stipulation.

A dispute arising between two subjects of France, the one being in France & the other in the United States, the regular tribunals of France would seem entitled to a preference of jurisdiction. yet the XII$^{th.}$ article gives it to their consul in America, & to a Consul of the United States in France, in a like case between their citizens.

the power given by the X$^{th.}$ article of arresting & sending back a vessel its captain & crew is a very great one indeed, and in our opinion more safely lodged with the territorial judge. we would ourselves trust the tribunals of France to decide when there is just cause for so high-handed an act of authority over the persons & property of So many of our citizens, to all of whom these tribunals will stand in a neutral & impartial relation, rather than any single person whom we may appoint as Consul, who will seldom be learned in the laws, & often Susceptible of influence from private interest & personal pique. with us, applications for the arrest of vessels & of their masters are made to the Admiralty courts. these are composed of the most learned & virtuous characters in the several states, & the Maritime laws common to all nations, is the rule of their proceeding. the exercise of foreign jurisdiction within the pale of their own laws, in a very high case, in a case wherein those laws have made honorable provision, would be a phenomenon never yet seen in our country, & which would be Seen with great jealousy & uneasiness. on the contrary to leave this power with the territorial judge, will inspire confidence & friendship, & be really at the Same time more secure against abuse.

the power of arresting deserted seamen seems necessary for the purposes of navigation & commerce, & will be more attentively & effectually exercised by the Consul than by the territorial judge. to this part of the X$^{th.}$ article therefore, as well as to that which requires the territorial judge to assist the consul in the exercise of this function, we can accede. but the extension of the like power to passengers seems not necessary for the purposes either of navigation or commerce. it does not come therefore within the functions of the consul whose institution is for those two objects only, nor within the powers of a commissioner authorized to treat & conclude a convention solely for regulating the powers, privileges & duties of Consuls. the arrest & detention of passengers moreover would often be in contradiction to our bills of rights, which being fundamental, cannot be obstructed in their operation by any law or convention whatever.

Consular institutions being entirely new with us, Congress think it wise to make their first convention probationary & not perpetual. they propose therefore a clause for limiting its duration to a certain term of years. if after the experience of a few years it should be found to answer the purposes intended by it, both parties will have sufficient inducements to renew it, either in its present form, or with such alterations & amendments as time, experience & other circumstances may indicate.

the Convention as expressed in the French language will fully answer our purposes in France, because it will there be understood. but it will not equally answer the purposes of France in America, because it will not there understood. in very few of the courts wherein it may be presented, will there be found a single judge or advocate capable of translating at all, much less of giving to all its terms legal and technical their exact equivalent in the law & language of that country. should any translation which Congress would undertake to publish for the use of our courts, be concieved on any occasion not to render fully the idea of the French original, it might be imputed as an indirect attempt to abridge or extend the terms of a contract at the will of one party only. at no place are there better helps than here for establishing an Englsih text equivalent to the French in all its phrases: no persons can be supposed to know what is meant by these phrases better than those who form them, & no time more proper to ascertain their meaning in both languages than that at which they are formed. I have therefore the honor to propose that the Convention shall be faithfully expressed in English as well as in French, in two columns, side by side, that these columns be declared each of them to be text & to be equally orginal & authentic in all courts of justice.

this, Sir, is a general sketch of the alterations which our laws & our manner of thinking render necessary in this convention, before the faith of our country is engaged for its execution. some of its articles in their present form, could not be executed at all, & others would produce embarassments & ill humour to which it would not be prudent for our government to commit itself. inexact execution on the one part would naturally beget dissatisfaction & complaints on the other, & an instrument intended to strengthen our connecion might thus become the means of loosening it. fewer articles, better observed, will better promote our common interests. as to ourselves, we do not find the institution of Consuls very necessary. its history commences in times of barbarism & might well have ended with them. during these they were perhaps useful, & may still be so in countries not yet emerged from that condition. but all civilized nations at this day understand so well the advantages of commerce, that they provide protection & encouragement for merchant strangers & vessels coming among them. so extensive too are commercial connecions now become, that every mercantile house has correspondents in almost every port. they address their vessels to these correspondents, who are found to take better care of their interests & to obtain more effectually the protection of the laws of the country for them than the consul of their nation can. he is generally a foreigner, unpossessed of the little details of knowlege of greatest use to them. he makes national questions of all the difficulties which arise; the correspondent prevents them. we carry on commerce with good success in all parts of the world: yet we have not a consul in a single port, nor a complaint for the want of one, except from the persons who wish to be Consuls themselves. tho' these considerations may not be strong enough to establish the absolute inutility of Consuls, they may make us less anxious to extend their privileges & jurisdictions so as to render them objects of jealousy & irritation in the places of their residence. that this government thinks them useful, is sufficient reason for us to give them all the functions & facilities which our circumstances will admit. instead therefore of declining every article which will be useless to us, we accede to every one which will not be too inconvenient. had this nation been alone concerned, our desire to gratify them might have tempted us to press still harder on the laws & opinions of our country. but Your Excellency knows that we stand engaged in treaties with some nations which will give them occasion to claim whatever privileges we yield to any other. this renders circumspection more neccessary. permit me to add one other observation. the English allow to foreign Consuls scarcely any functions within their ports. this proceeds in a great measure from the character of their laws, which eye with peculiar jealousy every exemption from their controul. ours are the same in their general character, & rendered still more unpliant by our having thirteen parliaments to relax instead of one.

Upon the whole I hope Your Excellency will See the causes of the delay which this convention has met with, in the difficulties it presents, & our desire to Surmount them: & will be Sensible that the alterations proposed are dictated to us by the necessity of our circumstances, & by a caution which cannot be disapproved, to commit ourselves to no engagements which we foresee we might not be able to fulfill.

these alterations, with some other smaller ones which may be offered on the sole principle of joint convenience, shall be the subject of more particular explanation whenever Your Excellency shall honour me with a conference thereon. I shall then also point out the verbal changes which appear to me necessary to accomodate the instrument to the views before expressed. In the mean time I have the honour to be, with Sentiments of the most perfect respect & attachment   Th: Jefferson

FFAA: Pol. Corr., U.S., v. 33, f. 196-199 (LC transcription).

Rayneval's Observations on Jefferson's Letter to Montmorin

[Translation]

Extract
from Mr. Jefferson's letter
1°

The IVth. article gives to consuls the immunities of the law of nations. it has been understood however that the laws of France do not admit of this: & that it might be desirable to expunge this article.

Observations
on Mr. Jefferson's letter
of 20 June 1788.

This article gives only a slight immunity from the law of nations. it only exempts consuls from personal matters which, if he were subjected thereto, would make him like nationals. the Consul remains a private person; he is obliged to recognize local jurisdiction. The sole prerogatives he should enjoy are set forth in the 2^{d.} paragraph of Article 4. All nonresident aliens enjoy them in France; the consuls also enjoy them: they do not even pay the poll tax, although it is paid even by the heir presumptive to the Throne. In order to salve scruples in America, and in order to determine the prerogatives attached to consular functions in a precise manner, one need only begin the 2^{d.} paragraph of Article 4 with the word "thus".

The article's Suppression would have disadvantages, because the condition of Consuls would remain uncertain; they would be exposed to arbitrary & vexatious demands, and one would be harassed on all sides by eternal complaints on their part.

2^{d.}

After establishing...indispensably....

This observation is concluded by recalling that Article 4, of which Suppression is proposed today, is in the counterdraft resolved upon by Congress on 25 January 1782. it is the 5th.

Article V, to which Mr. Jefferson objects, is Article VII in the counterdraft of Congress. How came this Stipulation to have been admitted in 1782 and rejected *in 1788?* In France, as in America, the most qualified persons are obliged to present themselves to justice when they are summoned; however, American consuls are not obliged to do so: this would be an exception to our public law, and it would not do any injury to the Sovereign authority, because it would be by treaty. The disposition in question takes place between France and Spain.

8. art 2.

FFAA: Pol. Corr., U.S., v. 33, f. 204-205 (LC transcription).

Comte de Montmorin to Comte de Moustier

[Translation]

N°. 1st.   Versailles, 23 June 1788.

M. le Cte. de Moustier

.   .   .   .   .

It would be, Sir, to indulge in a useless discussion to examine whether the change that this constitution occasions will suit us or not, and whether we should or should not take steps to prevent it in the present situation. We should be content with the result, which is: that if the new constitution is introduced, the American confederation will acquire a strength and an energy that it has not had, and that it could not have had until now;

and that if the old constitution is maintained, the Republic of the 13 United States will be only a phantom, Congress only a creature of reason, and, as you observe, we will be forced to treat from our interests with each individual State.

The reserve that has been stipulated for you regarding this matter, Sir, has as its purpose the King's invariable resolution not to interfere in the internal affairs of the United States: this reserve is an homage that His Majesty renders to their independence, and not a proof of indifference on his part. If, as I do not doubt, you explained yourself in this Sense with Mr. Jay, you will surely have recalled him from the error in which he appeared to you to be. Moreover, Sir, I am not surprised by the suspicions of that American Minister with regard to M. le Comte de Vergennes. I know that Mr. Jay has been very demanding, and that he vented his temper against whoever showed himself opposed to his demands; moreover, he has always been suspected of having a trace of Anglomania, or at least little affection for France, and his predominant Sentiment was his jealousy of Mr. Franklin. With such dispositions, it is not surprising that Mr. Jay has been, and that he still is, unjust with regard to M. le Comte de Vergennes, in spite of the important Services that the latter rendered to the Americans. As for me, I was never in the situation of having discussions with Mr. Jay during my Sojourn in Spain; I made him welcome; I seconded his proceedings as much as that could depend on me; from that, it is rather natural that he does not complain of me: but I doubt that he does the same with regard to M. le Comte de Florida Blanca. Moreover, Sir, all these observations are for you alone, and you will make no use of them with anyone, whoever it may be.

The King and his council, Sir, have been singularly astonished by Mr. Jay's opinion that the alliance between the King and the United States no longer exists. This Minister has therefore forgotten the terms in which this alliance was conceived: If he would be so good as to reread the treaty of 6 Feby 1778, he will be convinced that it is perpetual, or does he indeed suppose that the King has acted contrary to it. However, on the part of His Majesty, I am aware only of an accumulation of favors for American commerce. It is true that they wish that we would sacrifice our most precious interests to this commerce, and it is probably because we do not have the weakness to yield to so many unreasonable demands that we are accused not only of indifference but even of having abandoned the alliance. It is appropriate, Sir, that you rectify Mr. Jay's ideas on these various subjects: you will assure him that the King regards his alliance with the United States as unalterable; that His Majesty has always taken, and that he will not cease to take, a true interest in their prosperity, and that His Majesty will continue to contribute thereto as much as he can without prejudicing his own interests. That, Sir, is the doctrine that you should make develop, and that the King's Council was surprised to see so poorly established. As for the new constitution, you will abstain from judging it, but you may say that the King will view with Satisfaction all arrangements that will be proper to assure and consolidate the political existence, the tranquility, and the happiness of the United States.

Your observations, Sir, on our reports of commerce with the Americans are very just: it is up to the manufacturer to yield to the taste of the consumer, and not for the latter to receive the law from the manufacturer. One must hope that this truth will be understood more and more: the administration will do what it can to make it productive. I see with pleasure, Sir, that you are already occupied with so important a matter, and I will have no less thereof in receiving the observations than it will furnish you.

As for the convention relative to Consuls, it is experiencing difficulties that are only due to Mr. Jay's bad will and to his desire to destroy Mr. Franklin's reputation. I think I should observe to you, Sir, that you are in error in supposing that this same convention could have been concluded in America in 1782, and that the Seat of the negotiation was in Philadelphia: M. de la Luzerne was only charged with sounding the disposition of minds, and it was never the King's intention to treat otherwise than under his eyes. Congress has passed resolutions in vain. They will not force our hand regarding the step that we think it appropriate to take in this business. The regulation of consular functions is of a common advantage; it is appropriate to do it by article   of the treaty of friendship and of commerce; it was natural to discuss it at Versailles, and not in America, where these sorts of matters are not yet understood. Whatever happens, Sir, it is time to terminate this tedious discussion; and I think that the simplest way will be to preserve the convention by declaring, on both sides, that it will only last for 10 years. I shall explain myself in this sense with Mr. Jefferson, requesting him to solicit a definitive resolution on the part of his superiors. It is of as much interest to the Americans as to us to secure our respective commerce against vexations and abuses of authority; thus the convention in question interests them as much as us; that is what I request you to observe to Mr. Jay; you will also observe to him that, all the stipulations of the convention being reciprocal, we do not see how it can wound the dignity of the absolute Sovereignty of the United States: if that were so, it would likewise wound the Sovereignty of His Majesty; and this Sentiment has in no way ever affected it.

I presume, Sir, that the Consul will have reported to M. le Comte de la Luzerne the incident in which the theft of a watch by a sailor of the *Aigrette* took place.

I will devise with that minister the instructions that will be appropriate to give you on that subject, and on similar matters that could still present themselves. I think that it would have been well to prevent all discussion in hastening to satisfy the civil party.   De Montmorin

P.S. Mr. Jefferson has just communicated to me the full powers that have been sent to him to settle the affair of the Consuls; we will not delay in dealing with this subject.

FFAA: Pol. Corr., U.S., v. 33, f. 208-213 (LC transcription).

Comte de Moustier to Comte de Montmorin

[Translation]

N°· 15.   New York, 25 June 1788.
My Lord.

· · · · ·

In the event that one of the two abovementioned States,[1] or both of them, detach themselves from the general Confederation, combinations with the American States, which would no longer be the United States, would be of a different nature than in the present situation, in which foreign powers still recognize only a single representative body of general Sovereignty. Those of the King would be essentially the same, for everything is reduced to purchasing from the American States, united or not, commodities that may be appropriate, and to furnishing them with merchandise that may serve as exchange for these commodities. In times of crisis, American ports would be still more exposed than they are today, and would belong to the first occupant, as I had the honor to inform You, My Lord, by my Despatch N°· 2.

The King's Minister in America would be separately accredited to each of the States or particular confederations, and would consequently experience, according to the circumstances, more facilities or more difficulties in his negotiations.

The reimbursement of the debt due to the King would be a particular subject that would fall under a new agreement; but His Majesty could henceforth regard all the States as jointly and separately liable, and the dissolution of the Confederation would change nothing with regard to His Majesty's rights. I am still waiting for the resolution of the present crisis to remind the United States, whatever form their Government takes, of the necessity of concerning themselves with what they owe the King. It is probable that by themselves they would scarcely think of this interesting subject. Their impotence is real, but if they were not treated tactfully, there would be ways to take advantage of this debt. The English are today in possession of the forts that they were supposed to have restored at the peace, under the pretext that the Americans have not satisfied the engagement to pay their debts to the subjects of the British crown. Queen Elizabeth formerly had held places in the united provinces as deposits in trust to guarantee the Sums which this Queen had loaned them. There are on this continent ports that would be useful to His Majesty in certain conjunctures, principally those of New York and Newport. They could perhaps be seized, half by agreement, half by force, and kept as long as that would be useful to the King's interests in consequently coming to terms regarding the debt of the United States to His Majesty. It is in part to facilitate this operation that I thought that it would be advantageous to accustom the United States to seeing the King's Squadrons frequent their ports regularly and alternatively. I abstain from further reflections on the situation of the American States in the event of a schism, until the great question that is currently about to be decided is settled in some manner or other.

Meanwhile, Congress does as much as possible with the weak means at its disposal. It has had the President invite all the States to send the Delegates necessary to represent them in these circumstances. They have taken this into consideration, even that of Rhode Island, so that if the Delegates were individually as zealous for the public business as it seems they should be, Congress could be complete from this moment on, in the same way as it is thought that it will be shortly, which has not been seen for several years. Some members are absent at this moment solely for their pleasure. Nothing constrains them to exactitude. Such is the vicious organization of Congress, independently of its lack of authority, that a single member can, by his absence or by withdrawing at the moment of voting, cause a matter even of the greatest consequence to fail. We had a striking example of this last year. Congress was deliberating whether it would leave New York, nine States were represented, that of Jersey had only two members on whom they relied. At the moment of decision, one of the members rose, took his cane and his hat; they tried in vain to detain him, he left, went straight to the *ferry*, and crossed the river to return to his home. However, it is to a body thus organized that one must go for all requests and all treaties.

Besides, it put more promptitude into the response to the memorial that I sent it by means of Mr. Jay than into any business that may have presented itself in a long time. Mr. Jay himself proceeded with his ordinary slowness. On this occasion, I thought I should abstain from any other step than the sending of my Memorial to the Secretary of foreign affairs, to whom I have not even spoken of what I was discussing therein; my object being to make known to Congress and to Mr. Jay that the King had reason to be dissatisfied. I limited myself to saying laconically to two members from Virginia and to another that I had sent a Memorial to Congress on an abominable matter, and that it was necessary to take measures in order that nothing similar could happen again. By that I meant the conclusion of the Consular Convention, regarding which I did not wish to enter into any explanation, in order that from my Memorial it would appear that I regarded it as concluded, with the exception of some formalities. If there were today in America a body really Sovereign, or if we were in the situation of treating with each State, which are all singly truly Sovereign, well-directed fear could produce good effects regarding the measures that they would take with regard to France, but in the present situation of things, this method works only imperfectly. However, it is to it that I attribute the prompt resolution of Congress. I enclose a copy of the response that I have received from Mr. Jay. I hope that the instructions sent to Mr. Jefferson are satisfactory. I imagine that this American Minister will have had the vigilance to inform Congress that the decree of the Council which grants particular favors to the Americans is not a treaty, but an administrative regulation which the King can revoke or modify at his pleasure. I think that it is useful that they be impressed by this verity. Hitherto they were rather inappropriately persuaded that we had a very great interest in treating them well, and that we could not grant them too much. They still have to recover from many errors regarding their importance in the political balance of Europe. It is troublesome to recognize that they are very susceptible to claims, while they could not be less interested in that regard. If a new Government is established, and enlightened and restrained men are at its head, a more just system could be formed regarding the true relations among the powers, of the United States with Europe in general, and with France in particular.

I am with respect, My Lord, Your most humble and most obedient servant,   Le C$^{te.}$ de Moustier.

P.S. We learn at this moment that New Hampshire has acceded to the new Constitution....
rec. 26 Sept$^{ber.}$

FFAA: Pol. Corr., U.S., v. 33, f. 214-218vo. (LC transcription).
^{1} Virginia and New York.

John Paul Jones to Marquis de Lafayette

On Board the Imperial Ship Wolodimer
at Anchor in the Liman before Ochakoff June 15/26 1788.
My Dear General and Dear Friend,

. . . . .

I went through Sweeden to S^t· Petersburg. The advanced season did not permit my return to Paris, the distance would have been too long through Germany, and Elliot[1] had influenced the English to put difficulties in the way of my Passage by the Baltic. I found the Gulph of Bothnia barred with Ice, and after making several fruitless attempts to Cross it in a small open boat (about 30 feet long) I compelled the Sweedish Peasants to steer as I directed them for the Gulph of Finland. After about 4 or 500 Miles of Navigation I landed at Reval, and having paid the Peasants to their Satisfaction, I gave them a good Pilot with some Provision, to reconduct them to their Homes. My Voyage was looked upon as a kind of Miracle; being what never had been attempted before, unless in large Vessels. –

The Empress received me with a distinction the most flattering that perhaps any Stranger can boast of, on entering into the Russian Service. her Majesty conferred on me immediately the Grade of Rear Admiral. I was detaind against my will a fortnight, and continually feasted at Court and in the first Society. This was a Cruel grief to the English, and I own that their Vexation, which I believe was General in the about S^t· Petersburg, gave me no pain.

I presented the Empress with a Copy of the new American Constitution. Her Majesty spoke to me often about the United States, and is persuaded that *the American Revolution cannot fail to bring about others, and to influence every other Government.* I mentioned the Armed Neutrality, so honorably Patronized by Her Majesty; and I am persuaded that no difficulty will be made about admitting the United-States into that Illustrious Association, so soon as America shall have built some Ships of War. I spoke of it to the Danish Minister of Foreign Affairs, who seemed pleased with the Idea.

The United States have some Commerce with Russia, wch perhaps we may be able to increase. I should think Whale Oil, dry'd fish, Spermaceti & Rice may be articles to suit the Russia Market; If the Mediterranean was not Shut to the American Flag, many articles might be supplied to the Russian Fleet now destined for the Archipelago. I certainly wish to be useful to a Country I have so long served. – I love the People and their cause, and shall always rejoice when I can be useful to promote their Happiness. I am glad that the new Consitution will be, as you tell me, adopted by more than Nine States. I hope however they will alter some parts of it and particularly that they will divest the President of all Military Rank and command; for though General Washington might be safely trusted with such tempting power as the Chief Command of the Fleet and Army, yet depend on it, in some other Hands it could not fail to Overset the libertys of America. The President should be only the first Civil Magistrate, let him command the Military *with the Pen*, but deprive him of the power to draw his Sword and lead them, under some plausible pretext; or under any Circumstances whatever, to cut the throats of a part of his fellow Citizens and to make him the Tyrant of the rest. These are not my Apprehensions alone, for I have mentioned them to many Men of sense and learning since I saw you, and I have found them all of the same Sentiment.

.   .   .   .   .

...I am my Dear General, Your Affectionate & Obliged Friend and most Humble Servant   Paul Jones

.   .   .   .   .

LC: *John Paul Jones microfilm, reel 8 (LS).*
   [1] *Elliot, Hugh (1752-1830). British diplomat. Minister to Bavaria and the German Diet at Regensburg, 1774-1776. Envoy to Prussia, 1777-1782. Envoy to Denmark, 1783-1789. Secret mission in France, 1791. Minister to Saxony, 1792-1802. Minister to the Kingdom of the Two Sicilies, 1803-1806. Governor, Leeward Islands, 1809-1813. Governor of Madras, 1814-1820.*

Lord Carmarthen to Sir John Temple, Phineas Bond, and George Miller

Sir,   Whitehall, June 26th 1788
   Your Letters have been received and laid before The King.
   I send You inclosed Copy of an Order made by His Majesty in Council, prohibiting for a short Time, until his Majesty's Pleasure shall be further signified, the Entry into any Part of this Kingdom, of Wheat, the Produce of the Countries belonging to the United States of America: And I also send You inclosed a Minute of the Enquiry made in Consequence of Information received from North America, of the Injuries done to the Wheat in that Country, by the Insect called the Hessian Fly, representing the Danger which there is Reason to apprehend from permitting the Importation of Grain into Great Britain from America at present, and on which the Order in Council is founded. I am to signify to You His Majesty's Pleasure that You procure and transmit to me the fullest and most particular Information that can be obtained respecting the abovementioned Insect, and the Damage done thereby to the Wheat; and particularly whether,

during the last 30 or 40 Years, any Quantity of Wheat has been exported for Great Britain, from any Part of America, which are now known to have been infected with the Insect at the Time of Shipping the Wheat or other Grains

Carmarthen

PRO: FO 4/6, pp. 401-404 (LC transcription).

Phineas Bond to Lord Carmarthen

My Lord.   Philad[a] June 28[th.] 1788
    I have the honor to inform your Ldp. that accounts have been received here that the State of New Hampshire has adopted the Federal Constitution: – this being the 9[th.] State that has recognized the new Government it is presumed immediate measures will be taken to convene a Congress, in the mode prescribed therein. As no steps have hitherto been taken in consequence of the recent adoption of New Hampshire, it is yet uncertain where the 1[st.] federal establishment will be convened – but it is generally supposed this will be the place of meeting –
    It is at this moment very uncertain, my Lord, whether Virginia and New York will adopt the New Constitution: – the Conventions of both these States are now sitting – it is presumed the majority of the former tho' but very small will be in favor of the adoption but the members returned to the Convention of the latter are chiefly against the new Government: It is hoped however the proceedings of New Hampshire may have some effect to influence the conduct of Virginia and New York: – at any rate, my Lord, in the present circumstances of this country, it will require no short period of time to organize any form of Constitution which has for its object the government of such an extent of territory – where so many clashing interests and local prejudices prevail.
    The wretchedness of the mass of people here occasioned by the reduced and precarious state of all property has inspired a spirit of emigration very detrimental to the consequence and increase of the United States: the settlement on the Mississippi draws off yearly a prodigious number of inhabitants and perhaps there never was a more favorable period, my Lord, to encourage the introduction of settlers into Canada from hence: to which country a number of sober well-disposed persons among the Quakers have already directed their views: – they would probably, my Lord, have carried their intentions into effect but that apprehensions prevailed among them that the French clergy were entitled to some contribution from the land-holders in the nature of tithes; with which the religious principles of these

people are at variance: – It was also conceived, my Lord, that the allot-
ment of new lands was confined only to the frontier of Canada; and as
these people are of a peaceable and quiet disposition, the locality of such
a position might subject them to the attacks of an enemy whom they could
not resist, and who, by availing themselves of this circumstance, might
thereby, in case of war, gain a footing in the interior part of the province.

I have endeavored to dissipate these objections, my Lord, as far as my
situation would justify my taking any part in a business of this nature; – but
I beg leave to observe to your Ldp. I am convinced if favorable terms of
settlement were held out from Canada a vast number of good and useful
inhabitants might be drawn from hence thither.

I have the honor to be, my Lord, yr Ldp's most faithful and most obedt.
servant   P. Bond.
R. Aug. 18ᵗʰ·

AHA 1896, v. 1, pp. 567-568.

Governor Edmund Randolph of Virginia
to John Jay

Sir   Richmond 2ᵈ· July 1788
The Executive of Virginia have reviewed every instance of their intercourse with the representatives and subjects of his most Christian Majesty:
But after the most accurate and unbiased inquiry they are yet unable to
discover, in what respect their friendship for the great Ally of the United
States has justly been brought into suspicion. Judge then Sir, how much
their sensibility has been roused, when they read the Note of the Count de
Moustier, concerning Joseph Marie Anne Ferrier, intimating in terms
poignant, though polite, that positive Laws, the common rights of Nations,
mutual ties between allied powers, the treaty of Commerce, a Consular
Convention, and an established precedent had been violated, to cover from
punishment an enemy to human Society. They will not however refuse an
explanation of the motives by which they have been influenced.

It is still the firm opinion of the Executive that it transcended their
powers to gratify Mʳ· Oster in his request of the 2ᵈ· of October, and 11ᵗʰ· of
November 1787. Our Constitution describes their functions to consist in
"the exercise of the executive powers of Government according to the Laws of the
Commonwealth;" and forbids them "under any pretence to exercise any power
or prerogative by virtue of any Law, Statute or Custom of England," thus
excluding implied powers. Our bill of rights too particularly warns us in

favour of Liberty, by declaring that *"no man shall be deprived of it, except by the Law of the Land or the judgment of his peers."*

In no other Law than that of October 1779 (see N°· 1) do we find even a glimpse of the Authority, the exertion of which has been solicited by the Vice Consul. But even under that Act the Governor cannot order any Sheriff or Military Officer whatsoever to arrest for an Offence against the Laws of France; and thus could not command the Arrest of Joseph Marie Anne Ferrier, in order that he might be transported for such a Crime to France for trial. Nay its context and language confine the interposition of the Executive to *determinations* of differences, controversies, and litigations arising between subjects or Citizens of a foreign State, not extending to life or limb; and to the taking and conveying of a sailor, seaman or marine to his vessel.

Could *"the mutual ties between allied powers"* permit an unlimited indulgence of our respect to the wishes of his Christian Majesty or his Minister, we might perhaps have yielded to the importunities of M^{r·} Oster. But in the use of Official discretion we are bound to discard considerations not warranted by duty – we are bound to deny every obligation not arising from the Law of Nations, the treaty of Commerce or some Consular Convention.

We shall not question the right of the Minister to demand Ferrier under the Law of Nations; although it is not perhaps indisputably certain, that in every Nation in Europe a demand of such a Culprit would be obeyed. Nor shall we discuss the idea of an allegiance, unalterably due from him to his Christian Majesty; and a perpetual amenability to his edicts, although the genius of our Government seems not to distinguish, in the present case, with regard to *"personal protection"* between foreigners owing a temporary fidelity, commensurate only with their stay in our Country, and established Citizens – Still less are we inclined to deny the power of Congress to enforce a surrender of Ferrier; altho' we are yet to learn in what page of the Confederation it is *expressly* delegated to them. But we rather grant for the sake of avoiding every appearance of equivocation, that these positions correspond in truth with the sentiments and pretensions of the Minister. Even with this powerful train of concessions, it will not follow that the Executive of Virginia, possessing certain defined powers under a Constitution, can usurp others, upon no other or better ground, than that there is a national right for the protection of which no Constitutional or legislative provision has yet been made.

That the admission of Consuls is stipulated in the treaty of Commerce is true: but it is equally well founded that not being public Ministers, they enjoy no immunities or authorities (except a certain degree of inviolability in their persons) which are not marked out by treaty or Custom; and that

none such are marked out by the treaty of Commerce. "Custom then (we
are taught by a celebrated Civilian) is to be the rule; for a Prince receiving
a Consul without express conditions, is supposed to receive him on the
footing of Custom." The existence of an American Custom on the subject
of Consuls is to us unknown nay the possibility of its existence, so recently
after the birth of the American Governments, and in derogation of State
Constitutions is not perhaps free from doubt. Believing too, that the french
Customs with regard to Consuls are not conformable with the genius of
Virginia, and have never in a single example been announced by Congress
as conformable with *their* views; recollecting, that for the specification of
Consular functions, which according to the treaty of Commerce were to be
settled by particular agreement, a Convention was begun in the year 1781
between Congress and his Christian Majesty; and never having heard of its
completion, we cannot acknowledge the Sufficiency of the Ministers
complaint on this head.

We have said Sir, that the Completion of the Convention, if it has taken
place, has not been promulged to us. This fact will acquit us of a designed
infraction of it.

The Minister recurs to a precedent an extract from which is now sent.
But neither that nor any other Act, which appears on our files, has authorized any Officer of Virginia to assist the Vice Consul in arresting for an
offence against the Laws of France. If aid has been given in a case wherein
such an Offence was an ingredient, we must have proceeded on imperfect
information. see N°· 3.

The foregoing observations are intended as an answer to M^r· Oster's
Letter of the 2^d of October 1787. In a great measure it will serve as a reply
to that of November the 11th· 1787, by shewing the defect of our Authority
to restore Ferrier to his Custody. But we beg leave to subjoin, that if the
Act of the public Officer in withdrawing Ferrier from the *Jason* was un-
lawful, it belonged to the Judiciary, not the Executive to declare it so: that
if it was lawful the Executive could not wrest him from the hands of that
Officer; especially as M^r· Oster might have reclaimed him, after his discharge, and caused a mulct to be imposed on the Sheriff if that discharge
was improper.

It is our sincere hope that this explanation may prove satisfactory to the
Minister of his Christian Majesty. But should we be disappointed, we have
a thorough persuasion that the relief sought by M^r· Oster, was far beyond
the scope of our powers. I have the honor Sir to be &^c

                                                        Edm: Randolph

NA: PCC, item 120, v. 3, pp. 401-405 (LBkC); M40, reel 3.

Comte de Moustier to Comte de Montmorin

[Translation]

N⁰· 17   New York, 5 July 1788.

My Lord.

I have learned by a secure channel that Congress decided to send Mr. Jefferson new instructions relative to the Consular Convention only from fear of too expressly displeasing the King. The System that this Assembly has adopted relative to the establishment of Consuls is still the same. It finds it contrary to its interests; that is to say that it perceives the utility it has for nations that wish to trade in the United States, where many people think that they should create an act of navigation appropriate to encourage American navigation and to repulse that of foreigners.

Mr. Jefferson's instructions are directed in such a way that he can temporize if he finds an opening, and that he is not pressed. He should not anticipate anything, and cede only what he cannot retain. However, I think that he has orders to do whatever will satisfy the King. Thus, in the event that You should insist on concluding the Convention, even for an indefinite term, the American Plenipotentiary would consent to it. You will judge better than I, My Lord, if it would not be more advantageous to yield in this regard to the desires of Congress by limiting the duration of the Convention. Everything depends on the hope, which we may have, that during the time stipulated a new Convention will be obtained in which clauses are inserted that are desired in principle by our side, and that have since been omitted. Perhaps You could stipulate "that the Convention will be in effect for the space of ten years, at the end of which time the changes that it appears appropriate to make in it will be examined from all sides, but that in the meantime it is agreed that it will continue in effect as it is set forth in its full extent."

But I am persuaded, My Lord, that if You do not call upon Mr. Jefferson, he will avoid occasions to speak to You of the Consular Convention, so that I think that it is necessary that You assign him a day to conclude this affair with him in a single session, regarding which he has orders to accept because You wish it, if he discovers that the Court of France is well resolved to have satisfaction.

It will be infinitely useful that this affair be entirely ended when the new Government begins to function. It appears very interesting to me early to oppose a great firmness to the extravagant claims that one can expect to see advanced in the new Congress by the Delegates of several States in which the mercantile spirit entirely dominates. The great number of traders and merchants who influence the deliberations of these States already imagine that they will have only to ask or to request in order to obtain from foreign powers advantages which they are deprived of today only because the United States did not know how to render themselves sufficiently respect-able to be *in great demand*, sought after by these same powers, which according to them will hasten to anticipate their wishes. These wishes are still principally a free commerce with the Antilles and particular favors in Europe.

These ideas, which are generally spread about and which are found in all the public papers, are more warmly cherished in the Eastern States, where they have the power to weaken all others. There has come to me a letter from a Delegate in Congress from the State of Massachusetts that contains the substance of the dominant opinions with regard to France and England. It is possible that it expresses only the particular way of thinking of this Delegate, but I see in it too much of the spirit of system not to regard it as the result of what has been deliberated and adopted by a great part of Congress, and especially by the leading characters in the Northern States.

The Delegate at first contradicts the false report that has circulated concerning Congress' design to abolish the debt of the union, but he does not see the possibility of paying either interest or capital on the French debt for a long time. He thinks that if ever the present Congress or another should be so weak or perverse as to cancel this debt by indirect measures, the injured party would be justified in the eyes of the universe in seizing American ships on the high seas and in securing their ports as mortgage. If there have not been any requisitions made, it is because they have not wished to compromise the Government or animate minds at a moment of general fermentation, and because it was thought that if the people were in a disposition to pay, there still existed old requisitions regarding which they could exercise it.

You can [see] by this language, My Lord, whether the opinion that I have already had the honor of indicating to You of the incapacity of Congress was well-founded. Moreover, it is so visible from so many sides that it was necessary that Congress be annihilated entirely if it could not regenerate itself under the new form that it will receive.

I translate here word for word the expressions of the Delegate from Massachusetts regarding France and England:

"In France they are thinking, among other things, of discontinuing the packet boats to America on principles of economy.

"The last decree for the encouragement of the Commerce of France with the United States excites cries from the Chambers of Commerce, and the Parliaments are refusing its registration, without which one can only regard it as uncertain. – Someone wants to form a fishing enterprise at Dunkirk, and the Directors are persuading the French Government that they will be capable of doing great things. According to this idea, our fishing is discouraged in the hope of increasing theirs, which will end in smoke.

"With regard to England, it is supposed that sooner or later they will succeed in concluding a treaty of commerce. Interest, the guide of men and of nations, will dictate it. Interest, which dispels all personal animosity and changes national hatred into friendship, indicates it, and whatever may be the present sentiments of the two nations, they will one day be united by this powerful connection. Meanwhile, it is indiscrete on the part of our Printers to season their papers with national reflections. It is equally unfortunate to see public writings reproach and injure Fellow States; the union is our sole hope; this connection once broken, the tragedies of ancient Greece and modern Italy would be repeated in our homeland, today happy."

The movements of interest are those that the leaders of this people listen to today, as they have almost always rather openly done. The people themselves will not be so quick to forget the gratitude that they owe to France and the insults that they have received from England. Among these leaders there are in fact very few who have suffered; many have gained by the revolution; but they are still too far from the pleasures for which they hope. Their desires are only more irritated, and their impatience is extreme. As they wished to play a role, they persuaded the American people that it should play that of a great nation, and it is on this idea that the whole system of consolidation is carried. It is clear that it gives the Americans as a people more resources than they have hitherto had, but the European powers are very far from having more motives than previously to sacrifice their interests to those of the Americans.

· · · · ·

I am with respect My Lord Your most humble and most obedient servant,

Le Cte. de Moustier.

rec. 26 Sept^{ber.}

FFAA: Pol. Corr., U.S., v. 33, f. 227-231vo. (LC transcription).

British Lords of Admiralty to Lord Carmarthen

My Lord.   Admiralty Office 10th. July 1788.

Your Lordship having transmitted to Us, in your Letter of the 25th. of January last, a Letter from Mr. Adams Minister Plenipotentiary from the United States of America, with the Original Protest and Certificate of the Vice Admiralty Court at Barbadoes, referred to therein, complaining of the

Seizure of the *Jane & Elizabeth* an American Brigantine at Barbadoes, by Cap.[t] Nelson[1] of His Majestys Ship the *Boreas*; And your Lordship having signified to Us His Majestys pleasure that We should give Orders for an Enquiry to be made into the reasons on which this Seizure was founded, and that We should acquaint you with the result of such Enquiry in order that you may return an Answer to the American Minister; We are to inform Your Lordship, That in July 1786 We received Letters from Rear Admiral Sir Richard Hughes then Commander in Chief of His Majestys Ships & Vessels at Barbadoes and the Leeward Islands, representing that Cap.[t] Nelson had seized the Vessel mentioned in M.[r] Adams's Letter in Carlisle Bay upon the ground of his having been trading to the British Colonies contrary to the Act of Navigation; And that in pursuance of the directions therein contained, she had been regularly libelled in the Kings Name in the Vice Admiralty Court at Barbadoes by His Majestys Attorney General and Advocate General there, but that the Judge of that Court had refused to receive the Informations so filed against the Vessel, insisting that Cap.[t] Nelson should join in the prosecution, That in December following We received a Memorial from M.[r] Weekes, Judge of the Vice Admiralty Court at Barbadoes, stating the ground upon which he refused proceedings against the said Vessel, and at the same time complaining that in consequence of his refusal, Captain Nelson had taken the Vessel out of the Jurisdiction of the Court at Barbadoes, and carried her to Nevis, in the Admiralty Court of which Island she had been prosecuted & condemned; And that having upon the receipt of the Papers above mentioned directed the Proctor for the Admiralty to prepare from them a full State of the Case, and to lay the same before the Kings Advocate, the Attorney General, and the Advocate of the Admiralty; We take leave to send Your Lordship the inclosed Copies of the Opinions they have given thereupon, By which it appears that the Judge of the Vice Admiralty Court at Barbadoes acted improperly in refusing to permit the Information filed by the Attorney General of the Island of Barbadoes to proceed in His Majestys Name; that Cap.[t] Nelsons Conduct in carrying the Vessel to another Jurisdiction was not regular, but under the Circumstances in which he stood not such as called for Reprehension; and that as the Ship was condemned by a Court having Jurisdiction, they did not think fit to advise any farther proceedings to be had respecting that Affair.

We are, My Lord, Your Lordships most humble Servants   Howe[2]

Cha Brett[3]

Arden.[3]

PRO: FO 4/6, pp. 433-435 (LC transcription).
[1] *Nelson, Horatio (1758-1805). British naval officer. Captain, H.M.S. Boreas, March*

1784-December 1787. Rear admiral, 1797. Destroyed French fleet in Battle of the Nile, 1798. Vice admiral, 1801. Attacked Copenhagen, 1801. Created Viscount Nelson, 1801. Killed in Battle of Trafalgar, 1805.

² Howe, Richard Lord (1726-1799). British admiral. Brother of General Sir William Howe. Appointed naval commander-in-chief in North America, February 1776. With his brother, commissioned to treat with the American rebels and to attempt a conciliation with the American colonies, May 6, 1776; Congress refused to treat on these terms. Provided naval support for British army maneuvers, 1776-1778. Fought indecisive engagement with French squadron off Newport, August 1778; returned to England, October 1778, and resigned his command. Commander-in-chief in the Channel, April-July 1782. Commanded British fleet tha relieved Gibraltar, October 1782. First Lord of the Admiralty, 1783-1788. Commanded British fleet in its victory over the French, 1794.

³ Not further identified.

Thomas Jefferson to Comte de Montmorin

Sir   Paris July 30. 1788.

I have the pleasure to inform your Excellency that the new Constitution proposed for the United States is finally established by the vote of nine States. New Hampshire acceded to it certainly on the 24ᵗʰ· of June, and I have great reason to conclude that Virginia had done it some days before, in which case the vote of New Hampshire would be the tenth.

I have the honour to be with sentiments of the most perfect esteem & respect your Excellency's most obedient & most humble Servant   .

Th: Jefferson

FFAA: Pol. Corr., U.S., v. 33, f. 235 (LC transcription).

Charles W. F. Dumas to John Jay

Sir   The Hague 1ˢᵗ· Augᵗ· 1788

.   .   .   .   .   .

I am again advised to caution the Uᵈ States to be on their Guard in case of a War between France & her Rival against every surprize & incursion as well ~~on the side of~~ with respect to their Navigation & Fisheries as to their Forts which ought to be evacuated & delivered up agreable to the Treaty of peace which is not the case. The person who gives this advice has my promise not to mention him. I cannot however refrain from mentioning this circumstance which lays heavy on my mind & which appears the more probable from the daily conduct of this rival, requesting at the same time that Y. Excellʸ· will be pleased to protect by existence honor & interests under the new Congress as You have already kindly done under the old.

I am with great respect Y꙳ Excell꙳ &c꙳   C. W. F. Dumas

Faithfully translated from the Original by John Pintard.

NA: PCC, item 115B, pp. 105-106 (translation); M247, reel 137.

States General to Congress

In the Hague the 1ˢᵗ· of August 1788. –
To the United States of America in Congress assembled.
Our Friends and Allies.

After having for Reasons relating to our Service thought proper to recall M꙳ Peter John VanBerckel, who has hitherto officiated as our Minister plenipotentiary with you, it was our first Care to find another proper Person to manage our Affairs with you, for which we could find no one more suitable than M꙳ Peter Francis Van Berckel,[1] Son of the said Minister, in whose Abilites we place full Confidence, and to whom we have given the Character of our Resident. We flatter ourselves that he will not be disagreeable to you, particularly when by our Order, he will give you renewed Assurances of our high Respect for your Republic, and of our Anxiety and Desire to cultivate, and more and more to establish with you good Harmony and Correspondence, which will prove beneficial to the Subjects and Citizens of both Countries. We request therefore for that Purpose, that you will be pleased to grant the said M꙳ Van Berckel a favorable Audience, and to give the same Credit to all what he in our Name, and on our Behalf shall represent to you, as if the same was done by ourselves, for which we shall conceive ourselves obliged to you, and on all Occasions will endeavor to prove how much we are disposed to render you essential Services. Wherewith concluding

Our Friends and Allies – Recommending you to God's holy Protection....
Your well disposed good Friends
The States General of the United Netherlands.
Jˢ· Mossel Sᵗ·[2]
By order of the same.
H. Fagel. –

NA: PCC, item 129, pp. 81-82 (translation); M247, reel 143.

[1] *Van Berckel, Pieter Franco. Dutch diplomat. Minister to the United States, May 1789-September 1795.*

[2] *President of the States General.*

Thomas Jefferson to John Jay

Sir   Paris Aug. 3. 1788.

. . . . .

News of the accession of nine states to the new form of federal government has been received here about a week. I have the honour to congratulate you sincerely on this event. of it's effect at home you are in the best
situation to judge. on this side the Atlantic it is considered as a very wise
reformation. in consequence of this, speculations are already begun here to
purchase up our domestic liquidated debt. indeed I suspect that orders may
have been previously lodged in America to do this as soon as the new constitution was accepted effectually. if it is thought that this debt should be
retained at home, there is not a moment to lose, and I know of no means
of retaining it but those I suggested to the Treasury board in my letter to
them of March 29. the transfer of these debts to Europe will excessively
embarrass, & perhaps totally prevent the borrowing any money in Europe
till these shall be paid off. this is a momentous object, and in my opinion
should receive instantaneous attention....

I have the honour to be with sentiments of the most perfect esteem &
respect, Sir your most obedient & most humble servant   Th: Jefferson

NA: PCC, *item 87, v. 2, pp. 183-190 (ALS); M247, reel 115.*

John Brown Cutting to Thomas Jefferson

Sir   London 3ᵈ August 1788.

. . . . .

There is such a rooted aversion to us grown up in the court that if we
cou'd be smitten without the hazard of a general war – or a risk of shaking
the present ministry from their places – hostilities wou'd be recommenced
against the United States – if it were only to gratify the irascible feelings
of the monarch. Happily for both countries perhaps insuperable obstacles
at present forbid the renewal of a war the embers of which tho' they are
covered are by no means extinguish'd. Yet I am told by very moderate
politicians who are not anti-american [in] their theories – that if our new
government form a navigation act – and attempt to accellerate a commercial treaty with Britain by heavy impositions upon her Shipping and
manufactures – and at the same time demand an evacuation of the western
posts – she will not endure our measures. At such opinions and semi-

menaces I smile – still I own in the present moment of british insolence
and royal hatred – a fresh conflict with us may not be very distant.

.   .   .   .   .

...I have the honor to be with much respect and attachment Your
Excellency's obliged And Most Obed^t Servt John Brown Cutting[1]

.   .   .   .   .

LC: *Jefferson Papers, microfilm reel 9 (ALS).*
[1] *Cutting, John Brown(e). Physician and lawyer. Apothecary General in the Continental
Army's Middle District. Studied law in London, 1786-1787, after which he pursued a
career there as an attorney. Heavily involved in defense of impressed American seamen,
1790.*

Robert Montgomery to John Jay

Dear Sir   Alicante 5$^{th.}$ August 1788 –
     I had the honour of Addressing your Excellency under the   Since
which am deprived of your favours.
     by late Advices from Algiers we learn that the first Minister of that
Regency having formed a plot against the Life of the Dey was discover'd
and Immediately put to death, the Minister of Marine to whom the Dey
owes this discovery is now first Minister of State and a Creature of that
Minister appointed to that of Marine or Miquilhaj in his place. I thought
it prudent to give you the Earlayist Information possible of this Circumstance as he that is now first Minister and who from his tallents and
Activity in A great meashure governs the State, has allways Shewn a
decided partiality for America and Indeed is the Only Friend we Seemed to
have in that Country. Should your Excellency after having Inform'd
Congress of those Circumstances Judge this a favourable Juncture for
Receiving an offer of treating for a peace with the Regency a Person of
Confidence might be Sent Over in a private Character who with prudence
might learn how far the Minister of State Sustained his former Sentiments
for the United States and you Could Judge from thence what new Overtures Could be made with propriety. Should your Excellency think my going
to Algiers Could be of any use in the Manner Already mentioned Y[ou
have] Only to Signify your desire to that Effect and I Shall Imedia[tely]
Embark for that place on Business of Commerce which I shall make of
Sufficient Consequence for my Sojourn there the Necessary [Time.] I have
also friends there of Importance and good Influence in [the] Divan so that
I Can be well introduced to the Minister, and anything I might say on the
Subject of a Concilliation might be Rejected or Approved as the wisdom
of Congress might dictate, my Appearing [there] as a Merchant on business

of Commerce only having nothing to do with Affairs of the States and the expence attending this [Journey] would be Very Inconsiderable and I trust that the advantages m[ight] be of the greatest utillity to Our Trade in the Mediterranean, [as is] Evident from Our present inability to Supply this Coast with f[lour] from America in Our Own Vessels in this Season of Scarcity Exclusive of the Constant Supplys of dry Fish that might be Sent hither from the Northern States

With wishing you every happyness and prosperity I have the honor to be with Sincere Repect Sir Your Excellency's most Obedient and most Humble Servant   Rob[t.] Montgomery.[1]

NA: RG59, *Consular Despatches, Alicante, v. 1; National Archives Microfilm Publication T357, reel 1.*

[1] *Montgomery, Robert. American merchant residing in Alicante, Spain, who involved himself in American relations with Morocco and Algiers throughout the 1780s. Appointed U.S. Consul at Alicante, 1793.*

Verdict in State of New York v. John Wessells

[New York, August 8, 1788]

City and County of New York

The People of the State of New York Versus John Wessells

At a Court of General Sessions of the Peace holden at the City Hall in and for the City and County of New York, before James Duane Esquire Mayor, Richard Varick Esquire Recorder and William W. Gilbert Esquire Alderman of the City of New York and their Associates, Justices of the People of the State of New York, assigned to keep the Peace within the said City and County, on Friday the eighth Day of August 1788. –

The Defendant having at the last Sessions been indicted for assaulting and falsely imprisoning James Van Antwerp, a Servant of his Excellency the Minister of the United Netherlands, contrary to the Law of Nations and the Privileges of Ambassadors, and the Defendant having then plead thereto not guilty, comes now into Court and prays Leave to retract his Plea, pleads guilty and submits to the Mercy of the court. Whereupon It is ordered that he be committed to the common Gaol of this City and

County, there to remain for the Space of three
calendar Months.

Extract from the Minutes

Rob$^{t.}$ Benson, Cl$^{k.}$ –

NA: PCC, item 80, v. 3, pp. 412-413 (C); M247, reel 106.

Thomas Jefferson to John Jay

Sir   Paris Aug. 11. 1788.

.   .   .   .   .

I am informed from Algiers, of the 5$^{th.}$ of June, that the Plague is raging
there with great violence, that one of our captives was dead of it and
another ill, so that we have there, in all, now only 15. or 16; that the
captives are more exposed to it's ravages than others: that the great
redemptions by the Spaniards, Portuguese & Neapolitans, & the havock
made by the plague had now left not more than 400. slaves in Algiers, so
that their redemption was become not only exorbitant but almost inadmissible; that common sailors were held at 400 £ sterling, and that our 15. or
16. could probably not be redeemed for less than from 25. to 30,000
Dollars....I have the honour to be with sentiments of perfect esteem and
respect, Sir, Your most obedient & most humble serv^t

Th: Jefferson

NA: PCC, item 87, v. 2, pp. 207-209 (ALS); M247, reel 115.

John Jay's Report Regarding
Fugitive Slaves in East Florida

[New York] Office for foreign Affairs 14$^{th.}$ August 1788
The Secretary of the United States for the Department of foreign
Affairs, to whom was referred a Resolution of the House of
Assembly of Georgia of the 30$^{th.}$ January last, with a letter from
Governor Zespedes, dated at St Augustin in Florida 12$^{th.}$ Decem$^{r.}$
1784, Reports.

That from these papers it appears that sundry negroe Slaves belonging to
Citizens of Georgia had fled to East Florida, and were there protected and
detained. –

That Application had been made on the Subject to the Governor of East
Florida, and that although he has permitted those Fugitives to be apprehended and put in the keeping of Persons named by their Masters, yet that

he cannot deliver them up without Instructions from his Court, which he has solicited, it having heretofore been the Practice of Florida not to deliver such Fugitives to Georgia, because the latter while under the british Government had refused to observe a reciprocal Conduct in that Respect.–

That although in his Opinion these and similar Matters cannot be conveniently regulated but by Treaty, yet that for the present it would be proper to send Copies of these Papers to the Chargé des Affaires of the United States at Madrid, and instruct him to represent to his Catholic Majesty the Inconveniences which the States bordering on his Dominions experience from the Asylum afforded to their fugitive Slaves, to solicit his Orders to his Governors to permit and facilitate their being apprehended and delivered to their Owners or to Persons authorized to receive them, and to assure his Majesty that the said States will observe the like Conduct respecting all such Slaves belonging to his Subjects as may be found therein. –

That it also appears to him expedient to communicate these Papers to the Encargado de Negocios of Spain, and that it be signified to him by your Secretary, that his Interposition to obtain proper Regulations to be made on this Head, would be very agreeable to Congress. –

All which is submitted to the wisdom of Congress. –   John Jay – read Aug. 15. 1788

NA: PCC, *item 81, v. 3, pp. 79-80, 82 (DS); M247, reel 107.*

Louis Guillaume Otto to Comte de Montmorin

[Translation]

N⁰· 20.   New York, 16 August 1788.
My Lord.

· · · · ·

New hostilities committed by the Ohio Savages come to the support of the efforts of the Federalists and favor the Consolidation. If, in imitation of the Roman Senate, and by adopting a more profound policy than Congress can have in its current composition, this Assembly succeeded in exciting a general war with these turbulent neighbors, there would infallibly result from it a coalition of all the parties, and the clamor of arms would smother the impotent cries of the Democrats, who do not cease to agitate in the popular Conventicles, and who perceive only too well that the Government that is proposed to them must serve as a brake to their ambition by removing from the people an excessive power that they have abused. – The anxiety, the perfidies, the ferocity of the Savages and the imprudent intrigues of England will perhaps sooner or later produce this salutary effect. The treaty that the Governor of the West was to conclude with these tribes has just been delayed by an accident that was not expected; a party of Savages has carried off by force the presents that were destined for them and massacred those who were carrying them. By this means they have avoided concluding a treaty that did not suit them, but without losing the presents, to which they are very attached. It is certain that if these barbarians understood their true interests they would oppose with all their forces the numerous settlements that the Americans are establishing on the Ohio. At the same time, they would render an essential service to the confederation not only by furnishing it with a pretext to raise troops, but by putting an end to the emigrations that constantly weaken the United States. The Savages will finish by being victims of their little foresight; the Colony of Muskingum is composed of the most courageous and enterprising men from New England. When it succeeds in entrenching itself in its new settlements, the united efforts of all the savage nations will be insuffficient to dislodge it, and it can easily drive these former inhabitants back beyond the Lakes. Congress has just given the most extensive powers to its Governor without considering that he cannot be strengthened from that side without weakening the union by dispersing over an immense surface a small population, the totality of which, according to the most favorable summaries, does not yet reach three million, and by encouraging settlements that in less than 20 years will throw off the yoke of the United States and govern themselves according to their own laws.

I am with a profound respect My Lord Your most humble and most obedient Servant.   Otto.
rec. 26 Sept[ber.]

FFAA: Pol. Corr., U.S., v. 33, f. 249-252 (LC transcription).

Louis Guillaume Otto to Comte de Montmorin

[Translation]
N[o.] 21.   New York, 17 August 1788.
My Lord.

.   .   .   .   .

But although we may have reason to be content with this procedure,[1] we are not equally content with the conduct observed towards our merchant Vessels. In the absence of a Consular Convention, they are ceaselessly exposed to vexations discouraging to the Kingdom's Commerce. The Captain of a Vessel from S^t· Domingue who put in here in distress, who is supposed to depart tomorrow, and who will be charged, My Lord, with carrying to You this Despatch and those of M. le Comte de Moustier, since we have been so long without packet boats, has just received a subpoena to respond before an American Judge to the complaint of three of his sailors who, in defiance of His Majesty's ordinances, demand to be paid and discharged. There are a Vice Consul General and a Consul here, but as their powers have not yet been determined by a Convention, the local jurisdiction extends over all the ships, and in almost all cases favors the breaking up of the crews. It is only by dint of negotiations that we will succeed in keeping these sailors and in facilitating the departure of the Captain. Cases of this kind present themselves so often that the functions of the Consuls are becoming very laborious and often useless. – Foreign vessels are subject here to several other vexations. Such is, among others, the obligation to have guards on board to watch over the interests of the insurers. Over a long stay, these guards become very expensive, as well as embarrassing for the Captains, and often apply themselves to debauching the crew. Wherever there is a consul of His Majesty, precautions of this kind are absolutely useless, and serve only to restrain commerce.

Given these new proofs of the indispensable necessity of the ratification of our Consular Convention, You will perhaps not disapprove, My Lord, that I recall here the requests that M. le Comte de Moustier has made to finish with Mr. Jefferson and to ensure by this Convention the property of our merchants, the Jurisdiction of our Consuls, and the preservation of our crews. Without these essential conditions, it is impossible for our Commerce ever to make any progress in America.

I am with a profound respect My Lord Your most humble and most obedient servant   Otto.

rec. 26 Sept^ber·

FFAA: Pol. Corr., U.S., v. 33, f. 253-254vo. (LC transcription).
[1] *The previous paragraph describes the efforts of New York City officials to appease the Dutch Minister in connection with violations of the law of nations committed during the arrest of one of his servants.*

Joseph Ste. Marie to John F. Hamtramck

Sir[1]   Post Vincents 23^d· Aug^t· 1788. –

In pursuance to the ancient Usage and Custom of this Country I in the month of November last applied for and obtained Leave of absence on a trading Voyage, In consequence of which, and of my rights as a Freeman and Citizen of the United States of America I loaded a Petty Augur [?] with several Goods & Merchandises, to the Amount of Five Thousand and Nine Hundred & Forty one Livres and Fifteen sous in Peltry currency of this place equal to One Thousand Nine Hundred and Eighty Dollars and Forty two Ninetieths of a Dollar, and sent them under the care and Management of my Clerk M^r· Swimmer, with directions to proceed down the Mississippi River and trade them off with the Indian Nations Living within the Boundaries of the United States of America.

M^r· Swimmer accordingly set out, and went down that River to a place called the Chicasaw Lake, which is situated about Ninety leagues down from the River Ohio, about Twenty Leagues higher than where the English Fort of the Arquancas formerly stood, and in about 34.° 40.' of north Latitude according to Hutchin's Map,[2] where he pitched his Camp on the East or American Side of the Mississippi in the neighbourhood of some friendly Indians who were there hunting. Here after a few days Stay he was taken up by an Order from Monsr· Valliere the Spanish Commandant at the post of the Arquancas by a party of Spanish Soldiers sent from that Fort, who at the same time, seized the Petty Augur and the goods, and carried them together with my Clerk and the other hands in the Boat to the Spanish Fort, where Monsr· Valliere the Commandant seized and confiscated the Property for the use of the Spanish King, at the same time informing the Men that his Orders from the Governor of Louisiana at New Orleans were express to seize and confiscate all Property which might be found on the Mississippi or on either of its shores any where below the mouth of the Ohio and to send the Persons of those found with such goods Prisoners to him at New Orleans. – Being very soon after informed of this Transaction I went myself to the Arquancas and applied to the Spanish Commandant for a Restoration of my Property who in very peremptory terms refused giving them up, alledging his before mentioned Orders, and adding that I might take it as a great favour that my Clerk & hands as well as myself were not confined and sent in Irons to Orleans as Prisoners – When I reasoned on my Right as an American Subject to traffic in the American Dominions, and that my Property was Seized in the Territory to which I conceived America had an undoubted Right he stopped me short, by informing me that the Country on both sides of the River Mississippi as high up as the mouth of the River Ohio belonged to Spain, and that the whole of the Country on the East side of the Mississippi from the mouth of Ohio downwards was then under the Spanish Government. – Surprised at this Information and not being satisfied that the Governor had really given such orders I went to New Orleans and on or about the 20th· day of May last obtained an Audience of the Governor Don Mero,[3] who as soon as informed of my name asked me in very haughty terms how I could have the audacity to appear before him on the Subject of the Seizure of my Property. That altho' I was a Frenchman born, yet that I then was an American Subject, and that if he the Governor was to follow his Orders from the Court of Spain he would send me Prisoner to the mines of Brazil, and then concluded in a threatening manner with bidding me depart from thence and be no more seen, which last Orders I was glad to obey and withdrew myself as soon as far as possible from such Despots, without receiving any Satisfaction. –

Thus circumstanced my only and last Resource is to the Honorable the Congress of the United States of America as Guardians of the Rights and Liberties of her Subjects, whose Persons have been Seized and Properties confiscated on her acknowledged Territory by an Armed Force in Pursuance to the orders of a foreign Prince.

From the Time that the American name has been known in this Country, I have been a Subject of the United States; I have fought in the defence of that Country whose subjects a Spanish Commandant is hardy enough to oppress; I am now unless Government interferes, without any Remedy for a Loss which will reduce me with a Wife and a numerous Family to the Utmost Distress.

I must beg of you Sir to make known my Case to Congress in such manner as you shall think proper, and as Speedy as possible, As in me the Rights of Sovereignty of America as well to a very extensive Territory, as to the navigation of the Mississippi, any where below the mouth of the River Ohio, has been invaded; my Cause is become a Public Cause, and will in its Consequences determine a grand National Question. I dare hope and trust that as an Ancient Inhabitant of this Country and as one of the first Subjects of America in it, I shall be thought worthy the Protection of Congress, & that they will adopt some means to give Satisfaction and Recompence for my Losses. – To convince you and the world of the Justice of my Cause, I propose to make Oath before a Magistrate of the Truth of the whole of the Case as before Stated and shall whenever called upon produce proper Vouchers & Proofs to authenticate the Same.

I am Sir Your most Obedient and very humble Servant.

Joseph St. Marie[4]

. . . . .

NA: PCC, item 150, v. 3, pp. 519-520 (LS); M247, reel 165.

[1] *Hamtramck (Hamtranck), John Francis (d. 1803). Military officer. Born in Canada, he ended the Revolutionary War as captain of a company in a New York regiment. As a major, commanded Post Vincennes. As a lieutenant colonel, commanded the left wing in the Battle of Fallen Timbers, 1794, in which he played a conspicuous part.*

² *Hutchin's Map.* Presumably a reference to a map prepared by Thomas Hutchins (1730-1789), who served as Geographer of the United States, 1781-1789.

³ Miró, Esteban Rodríguez (1744-1795). Spanish colonial official. Aide-de-camp to Bernardo de Gálvez, 1776-1782. Colonel commanding the regular Louisiana regiment and acting governor of Louisiana, 1782-1785. Governor of Louisiana, 1785-1791. Assumed additional duties of intendant, 1788. Promoted to brigadier general, 1789.

⁴ Not further identified.

Pieter Johan van Berckel to Congress

New York 25ᵗʰ August 1788

The undersigned Minister plenipotentiary of the States General of the United Netherlands, has the Honor to inform Congress, that he has received a Resolution by which their High Mightinesses have been pleased to recall him. He thinks it his Duty to deliver the Letters which his Masters have addressed to him on this Subject, and thereby perform without Delay the last Function he has to fulfil. –

It is with the highest Satisfaction that he perceives himself authorized to repeat the Assurances of Friendship and good Will, which he made at the Commencement of his Ministry; and to declare in the Name of his Masters, that they constantly desire to promote and confirm the Harmony and good Understanding which so happily subsist between the two Nations.

Could their High Mightinesses have been apprized of the important Change made by the United States in their Government, they would probably have ordered the undersigned Minister to testify how ardently they wish, that this Revolution may conduce to the Grandeur, the Prosperity and Duration of a Republic, whose Success cannot fail to be exceedingly dear to them. –

To these Assurances of Attachment and good Will on the part of his Masters, the undersigned Minister cannot forbear to add Expressions of the lively Gratitude with which he is impressed, by the gracious Reception he has experienced during his Residence for several Years near Congress. He has been a Witness to the Efforts made by this Assembly, to establish the Government confided to them on a solid and permanent Basis. His Communications to his Masters have always been calculated to impress them with the Importance of this Object, and to cherish the friendly Dispositions of their High Mightinesses. –

He flatters himself that his Conduct has been such as to leave no Doubts respecting the Purity of his Intentions, and his Attachment to the reciprocal Interests of the two Powers. It would give him the highest Satisfaction to be ascertained, that his Exertions have conduced to confirm the Connection, and to strengthen the commercial and political Relations which one of the most happy and important of Revolutions had formed between them. –

May the great Arbiter of Events be propitious to the Measures now pursuing by all the Members of the Confederacy – and may the Government about to be established ensure Prosperity to a Nation who from their Origin have astonished Europe, and whose Situation internal Resources and political Constitution, as well as the Moderation and Patriotism of their Counsels, destine to become one of the most great, most powerful and most happy in the World.   P. J. Van Berckel

NA: PCC, *item 99, pp. 304-305 (translation); M247, reel 126.*

Congressional Resolution

Tuesday Aug. 26. 1788

On the report of the com^ee· consisting of Mr Hamilton Mr Sedgwick[1] & Mr Madison to whom was referred a report of the Secretary for the department of foreign Affairs of the 14th Instant.

Resolved, That the Secretary for the department of foreign Affairs be directed to transmit copies of the papers referred to in his said report to the Chargé des Affaires of the United States at Madrid and instruct him to represent to his Catholic Majesty the inconveniencies which the States bordering on his dominions experience from the Asylum afforded to fugitive negroes belonging to the citizens of the said States; and that Congress have full confidence that orders will be given to his Governors to permit, and facilitate their being apprehended and delivered to persons authorised to receive them; assuring his Majesty that the said States will observe the like conduct, respecting all such negroes belonging to his Subjects as may be found therein. –

Resolved, That the said Secretary be also directed to communicate the said papers to the Encargado de Negocios of Spain, and to signify to him, that his interposition to obtain proper regulations to be made on the subject, would be very agreeable to Congress –

NA: PCC, *item 5, v. 3, p. 1698 (Journal); M247, reel 19.*
[1] *Sedgwick, Theodore (1746-1813). Massachusetts lawyer and political figure. Member, state house of representatives, 1780, 1782-1783, 1787-1788; speaker, 1788. State senator, 1784-1785. Member, Continental Congress, 1785-1786, 1788. Member, U.S. House of Representatives, 1789-1796, 1799-1801; speaker, 1799-1801. U.S. Senator, 1796-1799. Judge, state supreme court, 1802-1813.*

George Washington to Thomas Jefferson

Dear Sir, Mount Vernon Aug.ᵗ· 31ˢᵗ· 1788.

. . . . .

I am much obliged by the information you give respecting the credit of different Nations among the Dutch Money-holders; & fully accord with you with regard to the manner in which our own ought to be used. – I am strongly impressed with the expediency of establishing our National faith beyond imputation, and of having recourse to loans only on critical occasions. – Your proposal for transfering the whole foriegn debt to Holland is highly worthy of consideration. – I feel mortyfied that there should have been any just gr[oun]ᵈ for the clamour of the foreign Officers who served with us; but, having received a quarter of their whole debt in specie & their interest in the same for sometime, they have infinitely less reason for complaint than our native Officers, of whom the suffering and neglect have only been equalled by their patience & patriotism. – A great proportion of the Officers & Soldiers of the American Army have been compelled by indigence to part with their securities for one eighth of the nominal value. Yet their conduct is very different from what you represent that of the French Officers to have been. –

The merits and defects of the proposed Constitution have been largely & ably discussed. – For myself, I was ready to have embraced any tolerable compromise that was competent to save us from impending ruin; and I can say, there are scarcely any of the amendments which have been suggested to which I have *much* objection, except that which goes to the prevention of direct taxation – and that, I presume, will be more strenuously advocated and insisted upon hereafter than any other. – I had indulged the expectation, that the New Government would enable those entrusted with its Administration to do justice to the public creditors and retrieve the National character. – But if no means are to be employed but requisitions, that expectation was vain and we may as well recur to the old Confederation. – If the system can be put in operation without touching much the Pockets of the People, perhaps, it may be done; but, in my judgment, infinite circumspection & prudence are yet necessary in the experiment. – It is nearly impossible for any body who has not been on the Spot to conceive (from any description) what the delicacy and danger of our situation have been. – Though the peril is not passed entirely; thank God! the prospect is somewhat brightening. – You will probably have heard before the receipt of this letter, that the general government has been adopted by eleven States; and that the actual Congress have been prevented from issuing their Ordinance for carrying it into execution, in consequence of a dispute about the place at which the future Congress shall meet. – It is probable that Philadelphia or New York will soon be agreed upon. –

I will just touch on the bright side of our national State, before I conclude: and we may perhaps rejoice that the People have been ripened by misfortune for the reception of a good government. – They are emerging from the gulf of dissipation & debt into which they had precipitated themselves at the close of the war. – OEconomy & industry are evidently gaining ground. – Not only Agriculture, but even Manufactures are much more attended to than formerly. – Notwithstanding the shackles under which our trade in general labours; commerce to the East Indies is prosecuted with considerable success: salted provisions and other produce (particularly from Massachusetts) have found an advantageous market there. – The Voyages are so much shorter & the Vessels are navigated at so much less expence, that we hope to rival & supply (at least through the West Indies) some part of Europe, with commodities from thence. – This year the exports from Massachusets have amounted to a great deal more than their imports. – I wish this was the case every where. –

On the subject of our Commerce with France, I have received several queries from the Count de Moustiers – besides the information he desired relative to articles of importation from & exportation to France – he wished to know my opinion of the advantage or detriment of the Contract between M$^{r.}$ Morris & the Farm; as also what emoluments we had to give in return for the favors we solicited in our intercourse with the Islands. – As I knew that these topics were also in agitation in France, I gave him the most faithful & satisfactory advice I could: but in such a cautious manner as might not be likely to contradict your assertions or impede your negotiations in Europe. –

With sentiments of highest regard & esteem I have the honor to be Dear Sir Your Most Obed^t H^{ble} Ser^t G$^{o.}$ Washington

LC: Jefferson Papers, microfilm reel 9 (ALS).

Deposition of Leonard White Outerbridge Regarding the Schooner *William Henry*

[New York September 1, 1788]

Leonard White Outerbridge, a Native of the Island of Bermuda, and at present Mate of the Schooner *William Henry* now in this Port, being sworn on the holy Evangelists of Almighty God, deposes and says – That being at the Island of New Providence on or about the 19th. Day of July last past, he then and there shipped himself before the mast on board the said Schooner *William Henry*, whereof William Thompson (who said he was of New Haven in Connecticut) was Captain, on a Voyage from thence to Baltimore in Maryland; That he sailed on the twentieth of the said Month in the said Schooner, and with the said Captain from New Providence aforesaid, bound to Baltimore, and having no other Cargo on Board but four Sticks of Maghogany, and about twenty five Passengers – That he understood and believes it to be true, having heard it from the said Captain and from the said Passengers, and from Inhabitants at Providence, that they the said Passengers had come from Dublin in a Brig commanded by one Captain Stafford, who landed them the Evening before Christmas last on the Island of Heneaugua, from whence they were brought to new Providence by one Captain Thomas Thompson who had been there a wrecking. And this Deponent further saith, that on his Passage to Baltimore he heard his Captain, vizt. William Thompson, say, that the Schooner's Owners at New Providence had received from Lord Dunmore[1] the Governor of the Island, two Guineas a Head for transporting the said Passengers from thence to Baltimore – That before he sailed as aforesaid from Providence, he heard the said Passengers spoken of among the People there as being Convicts.

That he arrived in the said Schooner at Baltimore about the Beginning of August last – That the Captain landed there about six of the said Passengers, he being ordered by the Magistrates there not to land any more of them, but to carry the Rest out of the State of Maryland – That they departed accordingly and went up Rapahannock River, and there landed all the Rest except four – That from thence the said Schooner proceeded to New York and arrived here in the Night, but the Captain for Reasons unknown to this Deponent, hoisted sail the next Morning and went to Blandford near New Haven in Connecticut. – That there the Captain took out his Chest and Bedding and went to New Haven, saying that he did not intend to return to the Schooner, but would take his Passage in the Schooner *Fair Abiconian* – Captain Thurston, who was soon to sail from New Haven to the Island of New Providence – That Captain Thompson before his Departure gave up the Schooner's Papers to a Mr Kelso, who came on Board at Providence as Supercargo. – That the said Kelso thereupon took the Command of the Schooner, and directed this Deponent and the Mariners to navigate the said Schooner back to this City – That they did so, and arrived here on Friday last, but that in the Course of the Passage, vizt. on Tuesday last on the Long Island Side of the Sound, nearly opposite to New Haven, the said Kelso being in Liquor, accidentally fell over board and was drowned – That this Deponent being much at a Loss

what to do, and not thinking it proper to open Kelso's Chest (which was locked) to look therein for Papers, applied for Advice to M.ʳ Shedden a Merchant of this City, in whose Employ this Deponent had formerly sailed – That by M.ʳ Shedden he was sent to others, and finally to Sir John Temple the british Consul General, who desired him to go and relate the whole Matter to M.ʳ Jay. – And this Deponent also saith, that while at Baltimore the Mate of the Schooner left her, and that thereupon Captain Thompson made this Deponent Mate of her: – And further this Deponent saith not.   Leonard White Outerbridge
Sworn the first Day of September 1788 – Before me. R[ichard] Morris

NA: PCC, *item 78, v. 17, pp. 405-408 (LS); M247, reel 100.*
¹ *Dunmore, John Murray, Lord (1732-1809). British colonial official. Governor of New York, 1770-1771. Governor of Virginia, 1771-1776. Governor of the Bahamas, 1787-1796.*

John Jay's Report Regarding
Navigation of the Mississippi River

[New York] Office for foreign Affairs, 2.ᵈ September 1788
The Secretary of the United States for the Department of foreign Affairs, to whom was referred a Motion of the Honorable the Delegates of North Carolina in the Words following, Viz.ᵗ: "Whereas many Citizens of the United States who possess Lands on the Western Waters, have expressed much Uneasiness from a Report *that Congress are disposed to treat with Spain for the Surrender of their Claim to the Navigation of the River Missisippi*, in Order therefore to quiet the Minds of our fellow Citizens by removing such ill founded Apprehensions, Resolved that the United States have a clear, absolute and unalienable Claim to the free Navigation of the River Missisippi, which Claim is not supported by the express Stipulations of Treaties, but by the great Law of Nature." – Reports. –
      That the Report mentioned in the said Motion, is not warranted by any part of the Negociations between the United States and Spain, and therefore that in his Opinion, it would be expedient so far to rescind the Orders of Secrecy relative to those Negociations, as that the Delegates of North Carolina & others be at Liberty to contradict the said Report in the most explicit and positive Terms. –
      That as divers Events which ought to have an Influence on those Negociations, have taken place since the Commencement of them, and parti-

cularly the Institution of a new Form of national Government for the United States, which is speedily to be established, it would be prudent to suspend all further Progress therein, and refer the same with all the Papers and Documents respecting it to the new Government. Wherefore he thinks it should be

Resolved, that the Report mentioned to Congress by the Delegates of North Carolina, as prevailing and causing Uneasiness in the Western Country, Viz.ᵗ· *"that Congress are disposed to treat with Spain for the Surrender of their Claim to the Navigation of the River Missisippi,"* is not founded in Fact; and that the Delegates in Congress be authorized (their former Injunctions of Secrecy notwithstanding) to contradict the same in the most explicit and unequivocal Terms. –

Resolved, that no further Progress be made in the said Negociations by the Secretary for foreign Affairs; but that the same in the State they now are, be referred to the foederal Government about to be established and organized. –

Your Secretary further reports that if the aforegoing Resolutions should be deemed expedient, He much doubts the Propriety of adopting the one contained in the Motion under Consideration.

1. Because although it does impliedly, yet it does not expressly, deny the Truth of the Report, which has created the Apprehensions intended to be removed.

2. Because if the Report be destroyed, by being positively contradicted, the Uneasinesses flowing from it must cease; which is all that appears to him necessary to be done at present, provided Congress should think it proper to suspend the Progress of the Negociation, and refer it to the new Government. –

As to declaring and resolving that the United States have a clear, absolute and unalienable Right to the Navigation of the River, he thinks no Objections can be derived from the Nature of their Right to declaring it to be clear and absolute. Authentic Documents now among the Papers of Congress shew that he has uniformly been of Opinion, that the United States possess a perfect Right to that Navigation, and ought never to cede it. –

Whether it would be wise in the United States to consent, in Consideration of equivalent Advantages, to any and what Modifications of the Use of that Right, is a Question on which his Opinion communicated to Congress in Writing is well known. The Modifications then contemplated, appeared to him at that Time adviseable; but he confesses that Circumstances and Discontents have since interposed to render it more questionable than it then appeared to be. How far the Resolution proposed by North Carolina, which declares the Right to be unalienable, as well as absolute, would tend to exclude all Modifications, however temporary and adapted to present Circumstances and Convenience, merits Consideration, nor is it clear to him that such Exclusion would be a Measure which however supported by Right, would also be warranted by good Policy. Whether that Right be unalienable or not does not depend on the Nature of the Title; but on the Extent of the Powers constitutionally vested in Government. How far the present or ensuing Government may be restrained or authorized in these Respects, is a Question of too great Magnitude to be decided without deliberate and mature Investigation. He knows the Prejudices and Opinions prevailing in the Western Country respecting whatever may concern that Navigation, and he knows also that groundless though not unnatural Jealousies are also entertained of him respecting it; but as personal considerations ought not to influence his public Conduct, he thinks it his Duty to report in plain Terms, that any Resolution calculated to exclude the Possibility of such Modifications, and without impairing the Right, might be advantageous to the United States, and satisfactory to their Citizens, would not in his Opinion be wise. Whether such Modifications could be formed, he will not attempt to conjecture. Certain it is that the Probability of it will become greater and encrease, as the Population of those Countries advances, and as the Respectability of the United States rises in the Estimation of Spain and other foreign Nations. –

He therefore thinks it best to let these Negociations pass over in their present State to the new Government, which will undoubtedly be tenacious of the public Rights, and *may* be enabled *by Circumstances not yet developed*, to terminate these Negociations with Spain, in a Manner perfectly consistent with the Right in Question, and with the Interests and Wishes of their Constituents –

All which is submitted to the Wisdom of Congress   John Jay –
Read Sep^t 3^d 1788

NA: PCC, *item 81, v. 3, pp. 147-151, 154 (DS); M247, reel 107.*

John Jay to the President of Congress

Sir   [New York] Office for foreign Affairs 3 Sepr 1788
I have the Honor of transmitting to your Excellency herewith enclosed, an affidavit of Leonard White Outerbridge, respecting the Importation of Convicts into the United States by a british Vessel. For this Information I am indebted to Sr John Temple. a gentle Remonstrance on this Subject

to the Court of London, would probably prevent such an improper Practice
in future – as to the present Case, there is Reason to suppose that it arose
from the unauthorized Interference of Lord Dunmore. –
With great Respect & Esteem I have the Honor to be Your Excellency's
most ob^t· & h'ble Servt·   John Jay –

NA: PCC, *item 80, v. 3, p. 565 (ALS); M247, reel 106.*

Lord Carmarthen to John Jay

Sir,   Whitehall September 4th· 1788.
I had the Honor to receive Your Letter dated the 13th· of June, with it's
several Inclosures, by the last New York Mail.
I cannot at present enter into the Particulars of the Case of Richard
Lawrence, farther than to say, that it appears to me that he has been ill-
advised by his Counsel, and that the Plea on which he would probably have
obtained a favourable Verdict, had been omitted. – If by the Laws of the
United States an Appeal, or a fresh Trial can be allowed, I am persuaded
You will afford him such Countenance and Support as You shall judge
proper, in any farther Attempt he may make to obtain Justice; I, at the
same Time, take the Opportunity to assure You, Sir, that you will always
find me disposed to give the most friendly Attention to any Representations
you may be authorized to make on Behalf of the Subjects of the United
States, who may have Claims depending here.   Carmarthen

PRO: FO 4/6, *pp. 533-534, 536 (LC transcription).*

John Jay to Don Diego de Gardoqui

D^r· Sir   [New York] Office for foreign Affairs 5th Sept^r· 1788
In obedience to the orders of Congress I have the honor of transmitting
to you, herewith enclosed the following papers Viz^t· N^o· 1. containing an
extract of a Letter of 25th· January last from the Secretary at War to
Congress – N^o· 2 containing extracts from a Letter of 14th· November last
to Brigadier General Harmar from the Secretary at War – N^o· 3 an extract
of a Letter of 15th· June 1788 to the Secretary at War from General Harmar
– and N^o· 4 Lieut^t· Armstrong's report to Major John P. Wyllys dated 28th·
April last.
These papers will unfold to you the measures that were taken in
pursuance of the discovery of the Letter written by John Sullivan to Major

Wm Brown in Philadelphia dated at Charleston 24th· September 1787, and I flatter myself that these measures will be considered as affording strong proof of the attention of this Government to whatever may affect the friendship which so happily subsists between his Catholic Majesty and the United States.

With great respect and esteem &^c   John Jay

NA: PCC, item 120, v. 3, p. 434 (LBkC); M40, reel 3.

John Jay to William Carmichael

Sir   [New York] Office for foreign Affairs 9th· September 1788

You will receive herewith enclosed, a certified Copy of an Act of Congress of the 26th· Ult: together with a Copy of a Resolution of the Assembly of Georgia of the 30th· January last, and of a Letter from Governor de Zespedes dated the 12th· December 1784. These Papers I have the Honor of transmitting to you by Order of Congress: They respect the Inconveniences which the States bordering on the Floridas, experience from the Asylum afforded to their fugitive Slaves, in those Provinces of his Catholic Majesty. Although this is a Practice not consistent with good Neighbourhood, yet it seems from the Letter of Governor Zespedes that without Instructions from his Court, it will not be in his Power to prevent it. It is the Pleasure of Congress therefore, that you make to his Catholic Majesty the Representations and Assurances specified in the before-mentioned Act; and it will be useful that they be informed as speedily & precisely as possible, of the Answer that may be given to you. It certainly is of much Importance to both Countries, that the Harmony at present subsisting between them be preserved, and that their Conduct towards each other give no cause of Disgust or Complaint to either. –

I have the Honor to be &ca: John Jay. –

NA: PCC, item 121, pp. 304-305 (LBkC); M61, reel 1.

Memorial of Paul R. Randall to Congress

[New York September 10, 1788]

To the Honorable the United States of America in Congress assembled.

The Memorial of Paul R. Randall

Respectfully sheweth

That your Memorialist being in London about the first day of October in the year one thousand seven hundred and eighty five was solicited by their

Excellencies John Adams and Thomas Jefferson Esquires to go with John
Lamb Esquire to the Court of Algiers in the quality of Secretary and was
offered one hundred and fifty guineas as a salary for that service – That
your Memorialist flattered with a hope of serving his country in that
negotiation as well as impressed with a deep sense of the sufferings of the
American Captives which he expected to be instrumental in relieving
accepted the honor with alacrity and set off on that unfortunate business
and hath not received any part of his said salary. –
      Wherefore your Memorialist most humbly prays that your Honorable
body will give him the salary so stipulated to be paid. –
      And your Memorialist shall ever pray &c   P R Randall –
Read Sep$^{r.}$ 10$^{th.}$ 1788 –

NA: PCC, *item 41, v. 8, pp. 357-358 (LS); M247, reel 51.*

Louis Guillaume Otto to Comte de Montmorin

[Translation]
N$^{o.}$ 24.   New York, 10 September 1788.
My Lord
      Mr. Van Berkel, Minister Plenipotentiary of the States General, has just
presented his letters of recall to Congress. Brother of the pensioner,
declared enemy of England and of the Stathouder, a great partisan of
France, today he shares the fate of other *patriots*, and he is chagrined to see
himself betrayed by his own son, who is going to replace him in the quality
of Resident. In his letters of recall, mention is made only of reasons of
economy. Instead of requesting a public audience, he has limited himself to
sending Congress a memorandum accompagnied by his letters of recall. This
assembly answered him through Mr. Jay without departing from the Style
employed in such cases, although it may have recollected that Mr. Van
Berkel had been sacrificed to the Stathouder and to the enemies of the
United States, and that this minister was in part a victim of his family's old
affection for the Americans. At the time of the departure of M. le Marquis
de la Luzerne, the President himself wrote to him, but this time they were
content to charge the Secretary of foreign Affairs therewith. Mr. Van
Berkel was pained by this lack of attention, but the response of Congress
to the States General, in which it expressed itself in a manner most
flattering to that Minister, gave him more satisfaction.
      M. le Comte de Moustier is now the sole Minister Plenipotentiary
resident near Congress, Mr. Gardoqui having only the title of chargé

d'affaires Plenipotentiary; the little success that the latter has had in the negotiation of his treaty of commerce makes him desire to be recalled.

I am with a most profound respect My Lord Your most humble and most obedient Servant   Otto.

FFAA: Pol. Corr., U.S., v. 33, f. 261-261vo. (LC transcription).

John Jay to the President of Congress

Sir   [New York] Office for foreign Affairs 12[th.] September 1788

On the 12[th.] October last Congress was pleased, on a Report from the Board of Treasury, to resolve that the Balance of the Appropriation for the Barbary Treaties of the 14[th.] February 1785 not then applied to that Object, be constituted a Fund for *redeeming* the american Captives at Algiers, and that the same be *for that* Purpose subject to the Direction of the Minister of the United States at the Court of Versailles. –

As neither this Act nor any other I recollect provides for the *Subsistence* of these Captives, whose Situation claims from their Country such Aids and Supplies as may be necessary to render their Condition as comfortable as the Pains and Rigours of Slavery may permit; I take the Liberty of submitting to Congress the Propriety of directing their Minister at Versailles out of the beforementioned Fund, to make such Provision for the Maintenance and comfortable Subsistence of the american Captives at Algiers, and to give such Orders touching the same, as shall to him appear right and proper. –

M[r.] Jefferson indeed instructed M[r.] Lamb to supply as well as to redeem them; but M[r.] Lamb is now in this Country – and M[r.] Jefferson observes in his Letter that his giving such Instructions "must rest for *Justification* on the Emergency of the Case," and that "it would be a Comfort to know that Congress does not disapprove of this Step." On this Letter I reported, Viz[t.] 11[th.] May 1786, a Resolution importing such Approbation; but I am not informed that it was ever agreed to.

M[r.] Jefferson has found it necessary in order to facilitate their Redemption, to let it be reported and believed at Algiers that Congress would not redeem them. That Intelligence has greatly added to their Distress; but it would not be expedient that they should at present be undeceived. Little Supplies may however be conveyed in so indirect a Manner as not to be traced either by them or by the Algerines, and would tend greatly to the Comfort of these unhappy People. –

With great Respect and Esteem I have the Honor to be Your Excellency's
Most ob^t· and very hble: Servt·   John Jay –

NA: PCC, item 80 v. 3, pp. 577-579 (LS); M247, reel 106.

James Madison's Motion Regarding
the American Captives at Algiers

[New York September 13, 1788]
That out of the fund appropriated for the redemption of the American
Captives at Algiers or any other monies belonging to the United States in
Europe the Minister plenipotentiary of the United States at the Court of
Versailles be and he is hereby Authorised to make such provision for the
maintenance & comfortable subsistence of the American captives at Algiers
and to give such Orders touch^g the same as shall to him appear right &
proper
        That Congress approve the instructions heretofore given to Mr Lamb by
Mr Jefferson their Minister at the Court of France for supplying the s^d·
Captives

NA: PCC, item 25, v. 2, p. 505 (D); M247, reel 32.

Congressional Resolution Implementing
the Federal Constitution

[New York] September 13th· 1788 –
Whereas the Convention assembled in Philadelphia, pursuant to the
Resolution of Congress of the 21st of February 1787, did on the 17th of
September in the same year Report to the United States in Congress
Assembled a Constitution for the people of the United States; whereupon
Congress on the 28th of the same September did Resolve Unanimously
"That the said report with the Resolutions and Letter accompanying the
same be transmitted to the several Legislatures, in order to be submitted to
a Convention of Delegates chosen in each State by the people thereof in
conformity to the Resolves made and provided in that case." And whereas
the Constitution so reported by the Convention, and by Congress transmitted to the several Legislatures has been ratified in the manner therein
declared to be sufficient for the establishment of the same, and such
ratifications duly Authenticated have been received by Congress and are

filed in the Office of the Secretary – therefore Resolved That the first Wednesday in January next be the day for appointing Electors in the several States which before the said day shall have ratified the said Constitution, that the first Wednesday in February next be the day for the Electors to assemble in their respective States and vote for a President; and that the first Wednesday in March next be the time, and the present seat of Congress the place for commencing proceedings under the said Constitution. –

Cha⁸ Thomson Sec^y

NA: PCC, *item 122, p. 137 (DS); M247, reel 140.*

John Jay's Report Regarding Transportation of British Convicts to the United States

[New York] Office for foreign Affairs 13th. September 1788
The Secretary of the United States for the Department of foreign Affairs, to whom was referred his letter of 3^{d.} Instant with the Affidavit of Leonard White Outerbridge, respecting the Importation of Convicts from the Island of New Providence to Maryland &c:

Reports.

That the Facts stated in this Affidavit render it in his Opinion highly probable, that the Persons brought to and landed at Baltimore and other Places by the Schooner *William Henry*, of which William Thompson was Captain, were Convicts, and that Lord Dunmore the Governor of New Providence, was instrumental in their being transported to those Places. –

That it does not become the Court of Great Britain to countenance, nor the United States to tolerate so nefarious a Practice; and although there is no Reason to presume that the Transportation in Question, was made by the Orders or Desire of the british Government, yet he thinks it would be proper that he should be permitted to send a Copy of the said Affidavit, enclosed in a Letter of the following Tenor, to his britannic Majesty's Secretary for foreign Affairs.

My Lord

It will sometimes happen that Individuals without being authorized by the Orders or encouraged by the Connivance of Government, do Things that are not only disreputable to their own Nation, but also offensive to others. –

The Facts stated in an Affidavit of which I have the Honor to enclose you a Copy, afford Reason to presume that the Truth of this Observation has been confirmed by a recent Instance.

To insist on the Impropriety of the Practice which that Affidavit will explain, would seem to imply Doubts of its being considered in that Point of Light; I forbear therefore to enlarge on that Topic, nor can it be necessary to hint that the same Principles of Honor and Delicacy should obtain between Nations, as between private Gentlemen. –

I am directed, My Lord, just to make known this Business to you – Congress being well persuaded that his Majesty will, on receiving the Information, give such Orders on the Occasion, as the Nature of the Case may require. –

I ought not to omit mentioning to your Lordship, that Sir John Temple's Conduct relative to this Case, has been such as receives the Approbation of Congress; for instead of endeavoring to retard, he promoted the Investigation. –

All which is submitted to the Wisdom of Congress. –   John Jay –
Read Sep^t 16th 1788 –

NA: PCC, *item 81, v. 3, pp. 91-92, 94 (DS); M247, reel 107.*

Congressional Committee Report Regarding Navigation of the Mississippi River

[New York September 15, 1788]
The Committee to whom was committed the Report of the Secretary for Foreign affairs founded on a referred motion of the Delegates of N.Carolina, stating the uneasiness produced by a Report "that Congress are disposed to treat with Spain for the surrender of their claim to the navigation of the River Mississippi" and proposing a resolution intended to remove such apprehensions, submit the following Resolutions:

1. Resolved that the said report not being founded in fact the Delegates be at liberty to communicate all such circumstance as may be necessary to contradict the same & <*> to remove misconceptions –

2. ~~That the United States have a clear and ab~~ That the free navigation of the River Mississippi is a clear and essential right of the ~~salute right to the free navigation of the river Mississipi; and~~ United States, and that the same ought to ~~that the same right in no manner whatsoever to be invalid~~ be considered and supported as such.

3. Resolved that no further progress be made in the negotiations with Spain by the Secretary for foreign affairs but that the subject to which they relate be referred to the Foederal Government which is to assemble in March next.
Passed Sep^t 16th 1788 –

NA: PCC, item 25, v. 2, pp. 503-504 (D); M247, reel 32.

Congressional Resolution Regarding Transportation of Foreign Convicts to the United States

[New York] September 16th 1788 –
On Motion, Resolved That it be and it is hereby recommended to the several States to pass proper laws for preventing the transportation of Convicted Malefactors from Foreign Countries into the United States. –
Chas Thomson Sec^y
NA: PCC, item 122, p. 138 (DS); M247, reel 140.

John Jay to Don Diego de Gardoqui

Sir   [New York] Office for foreign Affairs 16$^{th.}$ Sept$^{r.}$ 1788
In obedience to the orders of Congress I have the honor of transmitting to you herewith enclosed copies of the following papers vizt of an extract from the minutes of the House of Assembly of the State of Georgia of 30$^{th.}$ January 1788 & of a Letter from Governor Zespedes of Florida, dated 12$^{th.}$ December 1784.

These papers respect the inconveniences which the States bordering on his Catholic Majesty's Dominions experience from the asylum there afforded to fugitive negroes belonging to the Citizens of those States.

The American Chargé des Affaires at Madrid is instructed to represent these inconveniences to his Majesty, and Congress are persuaded from his Justice and friendship, that proper orders will be given to his Governors on the subject.

These inconveniences cause much uneasiness among the people affected by them, and it being the interest and the wish of both Countries that the rights of good neighbourhood be constantly preserved, an early attention to matters of this kind is always expedient. Your endeavours to obtain convenient regulations to be made on this head, would doubtless tend greatly to promote that end, and would be very agreeable to Congress. They are desirous that orders be given to his Majesty's Governoi s to permit and facilitate such fugitive negroes being apprehended and delivered to persons authorized to receive them; and the United States will on their part observe the like conduct respecting all such negroes belonging to his Majesty's subjects, as may be found within their Jurisdiction.

With great respect and esteem &ᶜ·   John Jay

NA: PCC, item 120, v. 3, pp. 444-445 (LBkC); M40, reel 3.

Don Diego de Gardoqui to John Jay

Sir,   New York 19ᵗʰ· September 1788.

My late Indisposition has prevented my answering your Favor of the 5ᵗʰ· of this Month with usual Punctuality, but I embrace the Moment to acknowledge its Receipt with the Extracts Nᵒ· 1. 2. 3. & 4. which you was pleased to enclose to me by Order of the Honorable Congress.

I shall take particular Care to transmit them to his Majesty by the first Opportunity, as Proofs of the Attention of this Government to the Continuance of the Friendship which so happily subsists between his Majesty and the United States.

Permit me nevertheless to add, that it may be represented to Congress, that I have sufficient Reasons to believe, that there still remains many of the same illdisposed Associates who have given Occasion to the said Extracts, and who have held repeated private Meetings in the Place called The North Fork, which I believe is in North Carolina, and although, according to my Advices, I regard them as contemptible, I cannot forbear to feel the Force of the just Reasons which I have to suspect that there are some respectable Citizens in those Neighbourhoods, who if they do not assist, at least countenance them.

I profit at the same Time of this Opportunity to acknowledge the Receipt of your Favor of the 16ᵗʰ· of this Month, in which you inclose me Copies of an Extract from the Assembly of Georgia of the 30ᵗʰ· January of this Year, and of the Letter from our Governor of Florida of the 12ᵗʰ· December 1784, and in which, among other Things, you desire me to promote the remedying of the Inconveniences, which happen on that Frontier.

What you mention to me, and what you observe more below, are so many Proofs of what I have represented to Congress in my various Communications respecting the Necessity of not deferring the Regulation of the Rights of both Nations on Principles of Equity and Justice; For which purpose the King my Master, with the most generous Disposition towards the United States, was pleased to Commission me – And you know that for my Part, I have always been ready to apply to a Work, which is as important as it is commendable.

Notwithstanding this Delay greatly injures the Subjects of his Majesty, particularly the Commercial Part, whose Balance is against Spain, yet without the least Necessity, his royal Benevolence not only permits the Introduction of all the Productions of the United States without altering the Regulations which existed before the War, but also in Addition to the many former ones, he has lately given this new Proof of his Liberality, by prevailing by his powerful Influence on the Creek Indians, who are under his royal Protection, to agree to a Cessation of Hostilities, for treating about an Accommodation of their Differences with the State of Georgia – so that he can assure the United States that they owe to the express Orders given by his Majesty to the Commandants on that Frontier, the ceasing of that Effusion of Blood, which was caused by a nation warlike and embittered with Georgia.

I am so well persuaded of the Generosity and Rectitude with which the King my Master desires to maintain the Rights of good Neighbourhood, which you assure me of on the Part of the Honorable the Congress, that provided they assure to me Reciprocity, I shall be encouraged to contract in the Name of his Majesty, that there shall not be protected nor countenanced in the Dominions of the one nor of the other, the Male-factors who have fled or retired from the one or the other, & that their Persons shall be apprehended and delivered as soon as demanded, with all their Effects, Goods, Money or Vessels, which they may have taken with them their own or other's, without Delay or any Difficulty and without other Deduction than that of the Charges they may have occasioned by their being apprehended and delivered; proceeding in all Things with the greatest good Faith.

Considering that this is the only Way to check the continual Calamities which happen on those Frontiers, I request you to represent to the Honorable Congress, and to add another deplorable one, of which I am just informed, in the atrocious Murder committed by certain Lodewyck and William Ashely, on the Person of Henry O'Neille, commissioned for our Governor of Florida in the Spanish Part of the River St Mary, as well as another not less horrible, committed, according to my Information, by two of the Name of Murees, on one John Hartley, also a Resident under the Protection of Spain, for which Acts I hope that the Honorable Congress will cause that Satisfaction to be given, which an Injury so notorious as well as iniquitous demands.[1]

Confiding that you will promote the Remedying of such Evils, and desirous that the United States will on their Part contribute that the Zeal

of his Majesty for the good of Humanity may have its due Effect without
Delay
I remain, with all Esteem & Respect, &c.   Diego de Gardoqui.

NA: PCC, item 97, pp. 230-232 (translation); M247, reel 125.
[1] *No further information is available on these alleged felonies.*

Comte de Montmorin to Comte de Moustier

[Translation]
N⁰· 2.   Versailles, 23 September 1788.
Mʳ· le Comte de Moustier
   I have received, Sir, the despatch that you did me the honor to write me
under N⁰· 11, as well as the 2 without numbers of 2 and 25 July.
   It seems, Sir, that the new constitution can be regarded as definitively
adopted: but it remains to be seen whether the modifications that the new
Congress will be obliged to make in it will give rise to debates of which it
is impossible to foresee the result. And when everything is arranged, there
will be the question of providing for a permanent public revenue: this
article, as you foresee it, will surely cause a great commotion, and will meet
with great resistance on the part of the inhabitants of the countryside.
   We are not surprised, Sir, at the conduct of the Savages: from all sides
they seek to encroach on their territory; and it is easy to conceive that they
are aroused to resistance, and even that they are furnished with the means.
I think that Congress will finish by having many regrets of not having put
a stop to their encroachments, for there will be ceaseless emigrations
towards the Ohio, and sooner or later a nation will be formed there that
will cause difficulties and anxieties to the thirteen States. Moreover, Sir,
these reflections are for you alone; for you would try in vain to make the
Americans recant their penchant to extend their boundaries and the idea
that nothing can stop them.

                   ·   ·   ·   ·   ·

   They probably also, Sir, have their eyes fixed on our internal difficulties,
and it must be presumed that the English agents are most careful to exaggerate them. If you are furnished the occasion to speak of it, or rather if you
are placed in that necessity, you will observe that the evil is not such that
one is pleased to spread it; that it is larger in opinion than in reality; that
the King is occupied at this moment with appeasing the parliamentary
fermentation, and that there is every reason to hope that the session of the

Estates General fixed for the month of January next will finish by restoring calm, by causing our financial difficulties to cease. De Montmorin

FFAA: Pol. Corr., U.S., v. 33, f. 275-276vo. (LC transcription).

John Jay to
Governor Edmund Randolph of Virginia

Sir [New York] Office for foreign Affairs 24[th.] Sept[r.] 1788
I have had the honor of receiving and communicating to Congress, your Letters of the 30[th.] June and 2[d] July last. The receipt of them should have been sooner acknowledged, had I not flattered myself with being shortly enabled to give you some information on the subject. My attendance in the Convention of this State, and Count de Moustier's excursion to Albany &[c.] left me no opportunity of discussing these matters with him. He returned last Week, but the very day afterwards set out for Boston. I saw him just before his departure and mentioned the affair to him. He was satisfied that it should be left in the state it was until his return.

The Consular Convention mentioned by your Excellency never was ratified, and consequently cannot yet have operation in the United States. The foreign Consuls here have no other authority than what they may derive from the Laws of Nations, and the Acts of particular States. The propriety of these Acts appears to me to be questionable, especially as National objects should be regulated by national Laws. When the Consul returns I promise myself the pleasure of writing to you more at large on this subject. With great respect and Consideration I have the honor to be &[c.]

John Jay

NA: PCC, item 120, v. 3, pp. 453-454 (LBkC); M40, reel 3.

Peter Allaire: Occurrences
from 5 September to 2 October 1788

New York October 2[d] 1788.
Congress have Issued their Proclamation to the different States, requesting the Inhabitants who are Electors, to meet and Nominate their Representatives the first Wednesday in January next to Represent them in the New Constitution, to Vote for them the first Wednesday in february, and to meet at the City of New York the first Wednesday in March, to Organize and put in force the said Constitution.

Our Election is Singular, it is not the different Counties that send a Member, but the whole State Votes, Names are put up in every County and the Six Names that have the most Votes, from all the Counties are duely Elected, The Elected of all the different States then meet who choose out of their own Body, Ten Names for President, those Ten choose Three, those Three–One, who is to be the happy Man, therefore I think their can be no bribery & Corruption in this mode of proceedings, as all the business is finally setled amongst themselves, before they brake up, After they have first met. The General Opinion is that M^r· George Washington will be Nominated President, Boston have Nominated John Adams (late at your Court) if Washington will Accept it, there is little doubt of his success.

The Governors of the Different States are now in Treaty with the different Tribes, bordering on their Respective frontiers, previous to the Indians going to the Grand General Meeting, held by Governor Sinclair at the Muskingham River (his Capital) this month in hopes to make a lasting peace. (I have sent word to your Canada Agent) during the above Negotiation with the Indians, the Inhabitants of Hodgston County, State of South Carolina went out in a large Party, killed Ninety Indians amongst which are five Chiefs, and burnt Eight Indian Towns, the Party lost Sixty Men besides above forty Wounded.

The State of Pensilvania have Authorised their Commissioners to purchase from the Indians at the Grand meeting as much Land as the Indians will dispose of adjoining their State. (would it not be good policy in your house to make Similar purchases.)

One of our Ships of Two hundred & fifty Tons is Arrived from India at Philadelphia, loaded chiefly with Bohea Tea, not having capital to purchase a better Cargoe, she Arrived 10th· September

The State of Boston, Connecticut, New York and Pensilvania have again Applyed to Congress, Relating the furr Trade, they sent one of their Officers to Lord Dorchester to know the Reasons of his Encroachments & on the State of New York, and prohibition of the Subjects of the united States from the Fur Trade, Answer, his Orders were such, and nothing but a superiour force should compel them to give them up, the States of New York & Pensilvania are loosers at least of One hundred thousand a Year it will be one of the first Objects of the New Constitution, however you will enjoy it peaceably these two Years.

.   .   .   .   .

Party Spirit, is at an End in this City, on the 15th· September the Merchants met, and having fully considered & pointed out the Evil, Attending being Governed by low Illiterate Men, they came to a resolution of proposing Men of the first Character and fortune as Majestrates, both (Wiggs & Tories are in the Nomination) their is not the least doubt of their being chosen, this is a final and fatal Stab to the Violent hot Wigg Party, who have been the Instigators Abettors and makers of those infamous Laws that has disgraced this State, they being Men in needy Circumstances and profiting by their own Nefarious Acts, to the prejudice of Publick and private property

The Cherokees have sent some of their head Men to Congress praying protection Against the people of Hodgston & Kentucky Counties they have given Orders to Coll Harman to protect them and to drive those people of[f] their Lands (their Orders will be disregarded, as there are at least Twenty thousand setlers on those Lands claimed by the Indians, who will only part with their property, by parting with their Lives.

Our present Government is so weak and inervated, that they have not the power of Compeling any deliquent State or set of Insurgents to due Obedience, nor have they the least Credit in any of the United States.

I Remain with Respect Yours &C   P A
R. 10$^{th:}$ Nov$^{r.}$ 1788

PRO: FO 4/6, pp. 617-624 (LC transcription).

Phineas Bond to Lord Carmarthen

My Lord.   Philadelphia Oct. 2$^{nd.}$ 1788
I have the honor to inform your Ldp. that the French fleet under the command of M. de Sanville arrived at Boston on the 22$^{nd.}$ day of August, consisting of two 74^s· *Superbe* and *Achille*, frigates, *Proserpine*, *Fine*, *Mignione*, *Modeste* and sloop *Favorite*: – their purpose is to remain there during the hurricane months. –

About the 20$^{th.}$ of Aug. my Lord, the ship *Light Horse* Capt. Nicholls sailed from Salem in New England, bound for China –

On the 17$^{th.}$ of this month the ship *Alliance*, Thos Read[1] master arrived here from China: – I have the honor to enclose your Ldp. a manifest of her cargo the value of which is computed to be little short of £100000 sterling: the teas are *said* to be the same in quality as those purchased this year by the B. East India Co.

This ship my Lord completed the voyage in about 15 months – it is asserted she passed the South cape of New Holland, and being again on the passage, to the Northward towards Canton between the Lat. of 7 and 4 degrees South, and 156 and 162 degrees E. Long: they discovered many islands the inhabitants of which were black; and in Lat. 8° N Long: 160° E: they discovered what they call two new islands fertile and much cultivated, the natives of which were brown, with straight black hair: – and

Capt. Read begin induced to think himself the 1ˢᵗ· discoverer has given these islands names, Morris I. and Alliance I, it will however, my Lord, very probably turn out, that these islands have already been observed among the great number of islands in those seas by other navigators, tho' perhaps 'till the present moment they were not favored with a name –

It is probable, my Lord, the new Federal Constitution will be put in motion in the course of the spring: – the nature of the extensive duty, to which I shall have occasion to attend when the federal court is established will render my absence from hence indispensible and I therefore trust your Ldp. will be pleased to honor me with instructions as to the establishing deputies here and elsewhere within my district, to whom the super-intendence of the different ports may be committed.

I have the honor to be, my Lord, your Ldp's most faithful and most obed: servant.   P. Bond.

AHA 1896, v. 1, pp. 578-579.
¹ Read, Thomas (1740?-1788). Seafarer, naval officer, and privateer. Made voyage to China in former frigate Alliance, June 1787-September 1788.

John Jay to Don Diego de Gardoqui

Sir   [New York] Office of foreign Affairs 17ᵗʰ· October 1788

I have the honor of informing you that Congress have deemed it expedi-ent in the present situation of affairs, to refer their negociations with his Catholic Majesty to the federal Government, which is to assemble in march next. The dissolution of one Government and the establishment of another, form a period little adapted to negociations, especially in a popular Govern-ment. The inconveniences which thence arise are obvious, and need not be enumerated, especially as you are well apprized that the term of the present Congress is nearly expired, & that a succeeding Congress adequate to such business, will not probably convene during the winter.

As these facts render the measure in question proper, I am persuaded you will so represent and explain it to his Catholic Majesty, as that it may be ascribed to the peculiar situation of our national Government and not to any desire or disposition to postpone a business which it is the interest of both parties to have speedily and satisfactorily settled.

I have the honor to be &ᶜ   John Jay

NA: PCC, item 120, v. 4, pp. 6-7 (LBkC); M40, reel 4.

John Brown Cutting to Thomas Jefferson

Sir,   London 17th Oct$^{r.}$ 1788.

. . . . .

The motives of ministers are sometimes inscrutable; but in England whenever I am at a loss to assign a motive rationally political for any portion of any law or proclamation touching the interests of our country – I resolve it into the obvious principle of a hatred personally or nationally inextinguishable: an envious malignant disposition that is gratified in puny efforts to fetter the commerce and check the prosperity of a country whom it cannot forgive because it cou'd not subdue; a temper that policy < ** > does not mask, time ameliorate nor experience correct. And which I believe nothing will correct but such arrangements on the part of the government of the United States as will make any future correction of it quite immaterial to America and unbeneficial to Britain. In those arrangements I know, and I rejoice that You will assist. Hence it is that I am sedulous to communicate to You every Scrap of information that I can collect, wishing nothing so much as that some portion of it may be rendered useful to our common country – of whose solid greatness and superior elevation to the puerile politics of Europe – I fully expect within the fourth part of a century to be a proud, < * > living witness. Among other strong and natural foundations of the western empire, I rank the faculties of our citizens in the most hazardous naval enterprizes. In their spirit and expertness they stand alone. The skill and intrepidity which they have heretofore exhibited in the most difficult and dangerous of the whale fisheries – are still unrival'd. Nor have the seamen of this nation yet ventured to imitate their undaunted habits – in any one instance. No notwithstanding the affluent bounties which this government have expended in augmenting and cherishing the british whale fisheries. They have not yet struck the Swift Sperma Caeti whale in the open Sea and pursued him in his desperate track till he yielded. They but fish coldly around the Islands of ice and harpoon his more unwieldy Cousin. Hence perhaps it is that so many of their Ships are lost. Depend upon it that compar'd with our Nantucket people – they carry on their whale fisheries most clumsily....

. . . . .

I have the honor to be with sentiments equally affectionate and respectful Your obliged & mo obed^t Sert$^{t.}$ John Brown Cutting

LC: *Jefferson Papers*, microfilm reel 10 (ALS).

Comte de La Luzerne to Comte de Montmorin

[Translation]

Versailles, 19 October 1788.

The last draft of the Convention, Sir, that is destined to fix the functions and prerogatives of the respective Consuls and Vice Consuls of France and the United States of America, just as you had it sent to me, no longer appears to me susceptible of any observation on my part. I have the honor to return it to you enclosed herein, so that you may take the King's orders for the Conclusion and the Signature of this Convention. If you judge it appropriate to have it printed, I request you to send me a large enough number of copies so that I can provide them to the Kingdom's Admiralties and to our Consuls in America, who will be charged with watching over its execution. About a hundred to a hundred and fifty would be needed.

I have the honor to be, with a most sincere affection Sir, your most humble and most obedient Servant.   La Luzerne

FFAA: Pol. Corr., U.S., v. 33, f. 297 (LC transcription).
¹Luzerne, César Henri, Comte de la. Minister of Marine, 1787-1789.

St. John de Crevecoeur to Thomas Jefferson

Sir   New York Oct^r· 20th· 1788

. . . . .

After a long & melancholy interval, there are at last well-grounded hopes, that the new Constitution will take place & bind every part of this Continent into a firm & solid political compact; I shall greatly rejoice to see this auspicious event; The murmers of partial discontent, cloak'd under what is called here antifederalism, seems now greatly to abate; there remains but one wish, which is, that those country partys may not preponderate in the choice of federal Senators & Delegates; if a majority of federalists can be obtained in those two bodies, everything will go smoothly on. Their first session which is to begin in March, will put the finishing hand to the great organisation: but an amazing task when one considers the extent of all the departments. What a cool & exploring [sa]gacity will be wanted in the discussion & acceptation of those numberless amendments, which a few of the States insist upon, in order to please every body, & yet to discriminate the useful from the needless &c^a· In contemplating this great event I see with pleasure the happy & immediate consequences which will result to this country from this atchievement of reason, for hitherto no other weapon has been made use of; if the natural order of causes & effects is not interrupted by untoward circumstances, by those fatal accidents which are so apt to start up, the transient evils which this country labors under, will gradually disappear, to lead the people to gradual & substantial happiness. Experience will prevent & correct past errors; the inhabitants of this Country will awake from their delusive dreams of credit, of unlimitted trade, from those motley expedients which have been so often made use of by several of the States, in which dignity, national honor, justice & law have been perverted; the destructive jealousy, the fatal influence of local preposessions, will be partly extinguished; one great national prevailing sentiment will operate throughout the whole. Never was so great a change in the opinion of the best people, as has happened these five years; almost every body feels the necessity of coercive laws, Government, Union, Industry & labor. I hope the small differences entertained by some people about the mode of regeneration, will no longer be a barrier. Such will be the foundations of America's future peace, opulence & power....

. . . . .

With sentiments of the most unfeigned esteem & respect, I am Sir Your most Obedient humble Servant   S^(t.) Jn^(o.) de Crevecoeur.

. . . . .

LC: *Jefferson Papers, microfilm reel 10 (LS).*

George Miller to Thomas Pinckney

Sir[1]   Meeting Street 20^(th.) October 1788. –
    Having this day seen the Copy of a Bill now before The Honourable the Assembly of this State, which if passed into a Law will, I conceive, be highly repugnant to the Treaty of Peace between the King of Great Britain, and the United States; And having Instructions to make proper Representations against such Laws or Ordinances as may tend to Counteract the endeavours of his Majesty's Subjects, in the Recovery of their Debts, in conformity to the Fourth Article of the said Treaty; I therefore beg leave, with the utmost respect, to lay before Your Excellency the following Remarks on this Bill, with my humble request that the same may be communicated to the Honourable The Legislature –
    Treaties of Peace between Nations at war with each other, imply mutual concessions on principles of Reciprocal advantage and convenience, and are entered into, to relieve the Subjects or Citizens of either Power, from the Calamities and distress inseparable from a State of Hostility. – In Return for very considerable and important matters, conceded on the part of Great Britain to The United States, it was solemnly agreed to, and became an

Article in the Treaty between the two Countries – "That Creditors on either side should meet with no lawful impediment to the Recovery of the full value in Sterling Money, of all bonâ fide debts Theretofore Contracted"–

The Bill now before the Honble. the Assembly, I humbly conceive to be expressly contrary to the letter, as well as the Spirit, true intent, and meaning of the fore-recited Article; since in one instance it obliges the Creditor, instead of Sterling money, to take in payment of his just claim, a property which can be no use to him; or in another, reduces him to the necessity of waiting twelve Months after obtaining Judgment, before he can recover his legal demand. –

But exclusive of these objections to the Bill now under consideration, there are others of still greater weight and consequence, to which I with much deference solicit the attention of Your Excellency, and that of the Honourable The Legislature.

Experience affords the justest grounds to believe, that by far the greater part of the value of property seized in Execution under the operation of this Bill, if passed into a Law, would consist in Lands. – In many instances the Creditor in order to save himself, and to secure at some period, the full value of his Debt, might be induced to become the purchaser, since the depreciated value of Property at public Sale, so much, and I believe so justly complained of, would operate so as to oblige him to accept of what may be termed a composition of his claim, but for such interference. –

The Class of Creditors in whose behalf I have the honor to make this representation, are British Subjects, who by the Law of Alienage cannot hold or possess such property, therefore a Law that in any case, or by any means whatever, makes Lands a Tender in payment, would, to them, be an effectual denial of Justice: and though it may be urged, that Titles might be taken in the name of a third Person, in Trust, Yet that expedient would not prevent the consequences of a Forfeiture, on it being discovered that such property was held for the use and benefit of a Foreigner. –

The fourth Article of the Treaty of Peace extends the Priviledge it conveys to Creditors on either side, but there cannot remain a doubt that it was intended chiefly for the security of the British Creditor, there being so great a disparity between the amount of the private claims of the two Nations: – Yet in Great Britain this Article has been so scrupulously adhered to, that there are instances of Loyalists, whose confiscated property in America was by Law made liable to the payment of their American Debts, and afforded funds for that purpose, who have had actions brought against them in England, by Citizens of America, since the Peace, and the full amount of the demand recovered. –

These observations, Sir, I have the Honour to submit to the considera-
tion of Your Excellency, and The Honourable The Legislature, in the full
trust & confidence, that they will be deemed of sufficient weight, to
prevent *any farther interference* between British Creditors, claiming under the
Fourth Article of the Treaty of Peace, and their debtors in this State. –
To the Justice and Liberty of the Legislature, and its regard to National
Engagements, I made this Representation; and with every Sentiment of
Respect for Your Excellency, and for both Houses of Assembly, I have the
Honour to be, Sir, Your Excellency's Most Obedient and most humble
Servant   Geo: Miller

PRO: FO 4/6, pp. 625-628 (LC transcription).
¹ Pinckney, Thomas (1750-1828). *Military officer, South Carolina political figure and
diplomat. Served at Fort Moultrie, 1776-1777, in East Florida campaign, 1778, at
Savannah, 1779, at Charleston and Camden, 1780, and at Yorktown, 1781. Governor,
1787-1789. U.S. Minister to Great Britain, 1792-1796, and Envoy to Spain, 1794-1795.
Member, U.S. House of Representatives, 1797-1801. Served as major general during War
of 1812.*

Full Powers for Comte de Montmorin to Sign
the Consular Convention with the United States

[Translation]
Versailles, 22 October 1788.
Louis by the grace of God King of France and of Navarre to all those
who shall see these present Letters Greeting. By Article 29 of the treaty of
amity and Commerce which we have concluded with the thirteen States of
North America, we and the said States have agreed that the two Powers
shall have the liberty of maintaining in their respective States and Ports
Consuls, Vice Consuls, Agents, and Commissioners, and that their
functions and prerogatives shall be determined by a particular Convention.
These Causes and other good considerations moving us to this, we, fully
confiding in the Capacity and experience, zeal and fidelity for our Service
of our very dear and Well-Loved Comte de Montmorin de Sᵗ-Herem,
marshal of our camps and Armies, Chevalier of our orders and of the
Golden Fleece, our Counselor in all our Councils, Minister and Secretary
of State and of our Commands and Finances, having the Department of
Foreign Affairs, we have appointed, empowered, and deputed him, and by
these presents, Signed by our hand, we do appoint, empower, and depute
him our Minister plenipotentiary, giving him power and Special mandate,
in our name, to settle, conclude, and Sign with the Plenipotentiary of the

United States, furnished alike with their powers in good form, such Convention and articles relative to the functions and prerogatives of the said Consuls, vice Consuls, Agents, and Commissioners, as he shall perceive to be good, desiring that he may act with the same authority as we would or could do if we were present in person, even if there were something that requires a more Special mandate than that which is contained in these presents, Promising &ᵃ...done at Versailles the first Day of the month of July in the year of grace &ᵃ·   Louis

FFAA: Pol. Corr., U.S., v. 33, f.298-298vo. (LC transcription).

Thomas Jefferson to Comte de Montmorin

Sir: Paris Octob. 23. 1788.

I take the liberty of troubling your Excellency on the subject of the Arrêt which has lately appeared for prohibiting the importation of Whale oils and Spermaceti, the produce of foreign fisheries. this prohibition being expressed in general terms, seems to exclude the Whale oils of the United States of America, as well as of the nations of Europe. the uniform disposition however which his Majesty & his ministers have shewn to promote the commerce between France and the United states, by encouraging our productions to come hither, & particularly those of our fisheries, induces me to hope that these were not within their view at the passing of this Arrêt. I am led the more into this opinion when I recollect the assiduity employed for several months; in the year 1785, by the Committee appointed by government to investigate the objects of commerce of the two countries, and to report the encouragements of which it was susceptible – the result of that investigation which his Majesty's Comptroller general did me the honor to communicate in a letter of the 22ᵈ of October 1786. stating therein the principles which should be established for the future regulation of that commerce, and particularly distinguishing the article of Whale oils, by an abatement of the duties on them for the present, & a promise of farther abatement after the year 1790. – the thorough re-investigation with which Monsieur de Lambert honoured this subject when the letter of 1786. was to be put into the form of an Arrêt, – that Arrêt itself, bearing date the 29ᵗʰ· of December last, which ultimately confirmed the abatements of duty present & future, & declared that his majesty reserved to himself to grant other favors to that production, if, on further information, he should find it for the interest of the two nations; – and finally, the letter in which Monsieur Lambert did me the honor to inclose the Arrêt, and to assure me that the duties which had been levied on our

Whale oils contrary to the intention of the letter of 1786 should be restored. On a review then of all these circumstances, I cannot but presume that it has not been intended to reverse, in a moment, views so maturely digested and uniformly pursued; & that the general expressions of the Arrêt of Sep. 28. had within their contemplation the *nations* of Europe only. this presumption is further strengthened by having observed that in the treaties of commerce, made since the epoch of our independance, the *jura gentis amicissimae*[1] conceded to other nations are expressly restrained to those of the 'most favored European nation:' his Majesty wisely foreseeing that it would be expedient to regulate the commerce of a nation, which brings nothing but raw materials to employ the industry of his subjects, very differently from that of the European nations, who bring mostly, what has already passed thro' all the stages of manufacture.

On these considerations, I take the liberty of asking information from your Excellency, as to the extent of the late Arrêt; and if I have not been mistaken in supposing it did mean to abridge that of Decemb. 29. I would sollicit an explanatory Arrêt, to prevent the misconstructions of it which will otherwise take place. it is much to be desired too, that this explanation could be given as soon as possible, in order that it may be handed out with the Arrêt of Septemb. 28. great alarm may otherwise be spread among the merchants and adventurers in the fisheries; who, confiding in the stability of regulations, which his majesty's wisdom had so long and well matured, have embarked their fortunes in speculations in this branch of business.

The importance of the subject to one of the principal members of our Union induces me to attend with great anxiety a reassurance from your Excellency that no change has taken place in his majesty's views on this subject; and that his dispositions to multiply, rather than diminish the combinations of interest between the two people continue unaltered.

Commerce is slow in changing it's channel. that between this country & the United States, is as yet but beginning; and this beginning has received some checks. the Arrêt in question would be a considerable one, without the explanation I have the honour to ask. I am persuaded that a continuation of the dispositions which have been hitherto manifested towards us will ensure effects, political & commercial, of value to both nations.

I have had too many proofs of the friendly interest your Excellency is pleased to taken [sic] in whatever may strengthen the bands, and connect the views of the two countries to doubt your patronage of the present application; or to pretermit any occasion of repeating assurances of those sentiments of high respect and esteem with which I have the honour to be Your Excellency's Most obedient & most humble servant   Th: Jefferson

FFAA: Pol. Corr., U.S., v. 33, f. 303-305 (ALS); LC microfilm reel 20.

[1] *The right of the most friendly nation.*

Thomas Jefferson to John Jay

Sir   Paris Nov. 14. 1788.
    In my letter of Dec. 21. 1787. I had the honour of acknoledging the
receipt of your two favours of July 27. 1787. which had come to my hands
Dec. 19. & brought with them my full powers for treating on the subject
of the Consular convention. being then much engaged in getting forward
the Arret which came out the 29th· of Dec. & willing to have some interval
between that act, & the sollicitation of a reconsideration of our Consular
convention, I had declined mentioning it for some time, & was just about
to bring it on the carpet, when it became necessary for me to go to
Amsterdam. immediately after my return, which was about the last of April,
I introduced the subject to the Count de Montmorin, & have followed it
unremittingly from that time. the office of Marine, as well as that of foreign
affairs, being to be consulted in all the stages of the negociation, has
protracted it's conclusion till this time. it is at length signed this day, & I
have now the honour to inclose the original for the ratification of Congress.
the principal changes effected are the following:
    The clauses of the Convention of 1784, cloathing Consuls with the
privileges of the law of Nations, are struck out, & they are expressly
subjected, in their persons & property, to the laws of the land.
    That giving the right of Sanctuary to their houses is reduced to a
protection of their Chancery room & it's papers.
    Their coercive powers over passengers are taken away: and over those
whom they might have termed deserters of their nation, are restrained to
deserted seamen only.
    The clause allowing them to arrest & send back vessels is struck out, &
instead of it they are allowed to exercise a police over the ships of their
nation generally.
    So is that which declared the indelibility of the character of subject, &
the explanation & extention of the 11th article of the treaty of Amity.
    The innovations in the Laws of evidence are done away.
    And the Convention is limited to 12 years duration.
    Convinced that the fewer examples, the better, of either persons or
causes inamenable to the laws of the land, I could have wished still more
had been done. but more could not be done with good humor. the
extensions of authority given by the Convention of 1784 were so
homogeneous with the spirit of this government, that they were prized here.
Monsieur de Rayneval has had the principal charge of arranging this
instrument with me; &, in justice to him, I must say I could not have

desired more reasonable & friendly dispositions than he demonstrated through the whole of it.

I inclose herewith the several schemes successively proposed between us, together with copies of the written observations given in with them, & which served as texts of discussion in our personal conferences. they may serve as a commentary on any passage which may need it, either now or hereafter, and as a history how any particular passage comes to stand as it does. N$^{o.}$ 1. is the Convention of 1784. N$^{o.}$ 2 is my first scheme. N$^{o.}$ 3 theirs in answer to it. N$^{o.}$ 4. my next, which brought us so near together, that, in a conference on that, we arranged it in the form in which it has been signed. I add N$^{o.}$ 5. the copy of a translation which I have put into their hands, with a request that, if they find any passages in which the sense of the original is not faithfully rendered they will point them out to me. otherwise we may consider it as having their approbation. this, and the Convention of 1784. (marked N$^{o.}$ 1.) are placed side by side so as to present to the eye, with less trouble, the changes made; and I inclose a number of printed copies of them for the use of the members who will have to decide on the ratification. it is desireable that the ratification should be sent here for exchange as soon as possible.[1]

With respect to the Consular appointments, it is a duty on me to add some observations which my situation here has enabled me to make. I think it was in the Spring of 1784. that Congress (harrassed by multiplied applications from foreigners, of whom nothing was known but on their own information, or on that of others as unknown as themselves) came to a resolution that the interest of America would not permit the naming any person, not a citizen, to the office of Consul, vice consul, agent, or commissary. this was intended as a general answer to that swarm of foreign pretenders. it appears to me that it will be best still to preserve a part of this regulation. Native citizens, on several valuable accounts, are preferable to Aliens, & to citizens alien born. they possess our language know our laws, customs, & commerce: have generally acquaintance in the U.S. give better satisfaction, and are more to be relied on in the point of fidelity. their disadvantages are, an imperfect acquaintance with the language of this country, & an ignorance of the organisation of it's judicial & executive powers, & consequent awkwardness whenever application to either of these is necessary, as it frequently is. but it happens that in some of the principal ports of France there is not a single American (as in Marseilles, Lorient & Havre) in others but one (as in Nantes & Rouen) and in Bordeaux only are there two or three. fortunately for the present moment, most of these are worthy of appointments. but we should look forward to future times when there may happen to be no native citizens in a port but such as, being bankrupt, have taken asylum in France from their creditors, or young ephemeral adventurers in commerce without substance or conduct, or other descriptions which might disgrace the consular office, without protecting our commerce. to avail ourselves of our good *native citizens*, when we have one in a port, &, when there are none, to have yet some person to attend to our affairs, it appears to me adviseable to declare, by a standing law, that no person but a native citizen shall be capable of the office of *Consul*; & that the Consul's presence in his port should suspend for the time the functions of the Viceconsul. this is the rule of 1784 restrained to the office of *Consul* and to *native* citizens. the establishing this by a standing law will guard against the effect of particular applications, & will shut the door against such applications, which will otherwise be numerous. this done, the office of Viceconsul may be given to the best subject in the port, whether citizen of alien, and that of Consul be kept open for any native citizen of superior qualifications, who might come afterwards to establish themselves in the port. the functions of the Viceconsul would become dormant during the presence of his principal, come into activity again on his departure, & thus spare us & them the painful operation of revoking & reviving their commissions perpetually. add to this that during the presence of the Consul, the Viceconsul would not be merely useless, but would be a valuable counsellor to his principal, new in office, the language, laws & customs of the country. every Consul & viceconsul should be restrained in his jurisdiction to the post for which he is named and the territory nearer to that than to any other Consular or Viceconsular port, and no idea permitted to arise that the grade of consul gives a right to any authority whatever over a viceconsul, or draws on any dependance.

To these general facts & observations I will add some local, and of the present moment.

Marseilles. there is no native. Stephen Cathalan, the father, has had the agency, by appointment either of Doct^r. Franklin or mr Barclay. but his son, of the same name, has solely done the duties & is best capable of them. he speaks our language perfectly is familiar with our customs, as having lived in a counting house in London, is sensible, active, & solid in his circumstances. both the port & person merit a Viceconsulate.

Bordeaux. mr John Bondfield, a native citizen, has hitherto acted by appointment from Doct^r. Franklin. he is well known in America; is of a <*> higher degree of information than is usually to be found, and unexceptionable in every point of view. his circumstances, indeed, have, at one time, been perplexed; but I suppose them to be otherwise now. he is likely to remain long at Bordeaux, and is so much respected, that we cannot expect a better subject there. I think him proper for a *Consular* commission.

Nantes. we have but one native citizen there, mr Burrell Carnes,[3] who has acted by appointment from mr Barclay, and acted well as far as I am able to judge. he is young, & beginning businesss only, would be proper for the viceconsulate at present, & for the Consulate when time shall have added experience & firm establishment to his present qualifications.

Lorient. no citizen at all. mr Loreilhé, a Frenchman and very worthy man, acted for some time: but failing in his affairs, he removed to the neighborhood of Bordeaux. after that, I wrote occasionally to Wilt & Delmestre: but they too are become bankrupt. there is lately gone there from Paris a Monsieur Vernés, an uncommonly sensible well informed man, speaking our language well, connected in commerce with the wealthy house of Berard & co. & particularly engaged in the American commerce. I suppose him proper for a Vice-consulate.

Havre. there is no native. Mr. André Limosin has acted by appointment of Doct^{r.} Franklin. he is a very solid merchant, speaks & writes our language, is sensible, experienced, & very zealous. his services hitherto have been so assiduous as to entitle him to the viceconsulate, in preference to any other person in that port.

Rouen. there is but one citizen there, mr Thomas Appleton, son of Nathaniel Appleton of Boston. he is young, & just beginning business. he is sensible, active, & fit for the viceconsulate, with a view to the Consulate at some future day, as in the case of mr Carnes.

The preceding are the only ports worthy of either Consular or Viceconsular establishment. to multiply would be to degrade them, and excite jealousy, in the government. at the following I should suppose Agents sufficient.

Dunkirk. Francis Coffyn, an American, & good man, appointed by Doct^{r.} Franklyn.

Dieppe. Mr Cavalier, a Frenchman appointed by mr Barclay.

Bayonne. Louis Alexander has meddled for us of his own accord. I know neither good nor harm of him. he writes a broken English, but I do not know whether he speaks the language. tho' a free-port there had entered there but one or two ships from the peace to the autumn of 1787. I have no account since.

Cette. Nicholas Guirrard, named by Dr. Franklin. he is of the mercantile house of Guirrard & Portas. I saw one of the partners when at Cette, who spoke English well, is familiar with English usages in commerce, is sensible, & has the apperance of being a good man. but I do not recollect whether the person I describe was Guirrard, or Portas. the other partner does not speak English. mr Barclay can probably fix this uncertainty, as well as give fuller information on all the other persons named. this one, whichever he be, is fittest for the Agency.

Besides these I would take the liberty of recommending the appointment
of Agents at Toulon, Rochefort, Brest, & Cherburg, merely for the purposes
of intelligence. they are king's ports, & it is in them that the symptoms of
a maritime war will always first shew themselves. such a correspondence
therefore, will be always proper for your minister here, and in general the
consuls & viceconsuls should be instructed to correspond with him for his
information. it does not appear to me proper that he should have any power
of naming or removing them. it might lead to abuse.

.　.　.　.　.

I have the honour to be with sentiments of the most perfect esteem &
respect, Sir, Your most obedient & most humble servant

Th: Jefferson

NA: PCC, *item 87, v. 2, pp. 291-300 (ALS); M247, reel 115.*
  [1] *Enclosures include the signed official text of the Consular Convention and copies of
the numbered documents mentioned above. See PCC, item 87, v. 2, pp. 303-399. For a
full explanation of these documents, see* Boyd, Jefferson Papers, v, 14, pp. 127-180.
  [2] *Carnes (Cairnes),* Burrill. *American merchant who, upon his arrival in France, settled
first in L'Orient, then in Nantes. Thomas Barclay made him U.S. consular agent at
Nantes in February 1786. There he opened the firm of Burrill Carnes & Co. in July
1787. That summer Thomas Jefferson entrusted him with verifying the accounts of French
merchants who sold prizes captured by U.S. naval vessels during the war.*

Franco-American Consular Convention
of 1788 as Ratified

[14 November 1788]

Convention between His most Christian Majesty and the United States of
America, for the purpose of defining and establishing the functions and
privileges of their respective Consuls and vice-Consuls.

His Majesty the most Christian King and the United States of America
having by the 29th article of the Treaty of amity and commerce concluded
between them, mutually granted the liberty of having, in their respective
States and Ports, Consuls, vice-Consuls, Agents and Commissaries, and
being willing in consequence thereof to define and establish in a reciprocal
and permanent manner the functions and privileges of Consuls and vice-
Consuls, which they have judged it convenient to establish of preference.
His M. C. Majesty has nominated the Sieur Count of Montmorin of St.
Herent, Marechal of his Camps and Armies, Knight of his Orders and of
the Golden Fleece, his Counsellor in all his Councils, Minister and
Secretary of State and of his Commandments and Finances, having the
Department of foreign affairs, and the United States have nominated the

Sieur Thomas Jefferson, Citizen of the United States of America and their Minister Plenipotentiary near the King, who after having communicated to each other their respective full powers, have agreed on what follows:

Art. I. The Consuls and vice-Consuls named by the M.C.K. and the U.S. shall be bound to present their commissions according to the forms which shall be established respectively by the M.C.K. within his dominions, and by the Congress with the U.S. There shall be delivered to them, without any charges, the Exequatur necessary for the exercise of their functions; and on exhibiting the said Exequatur, the Governors, Commanders, Heads of justice, bodies corporate, Tribunals and other Officers having authority in the ports and places of their consulates, shall cause them to enjoy immediately, and without difficulty, the preeminencies, authority and privileges, reciprocally granted, without exacting from the said Consuls and vice-Consuls any fee, under any pretext whatever.

Art. II. The Consuls and vice-Consuls and persons attached to their functions that is to say, their Chancellors and Secretaries, shall enjoy a full and entire immunity for their Chancery and the papers which shall be therein contained: they shall be exempt from all personal service, from soldiers billets, militia, watch, guard, guardianship, trustee-ship, as well as from all duties, taxes, impositions, and charges whatsoever, except on the estate real and personal of which they may be the proprietors or possessors, which shall be subject to the taxes imposed on the estates of all other individuals: and in all other instances they shall be subject to the laws of the land as the natives are.

Those of the said Consuls and vice-Consuls who shall exercise commerce shall be respectively subject to all taxes, charges and impositions established on other merchants.

They shall place over the outward door of their house the arms of their Sovereign: but this mark of indication shall not give to the said house any privilege of asylum for any person or property whatsoever.

Art. III. The respective Consuls and vice-Consuls may establish Agents in the different ports and places of their departments where necessity shall require. These Agents may be chosen among the merchants either national or foreign, and furnished with a commission from one of the said Consuls: they shall confine themselves respectively to the rendering to their respective merchants, navigators, and vessels all possible service, and to inform the nearest Consul of the wants of the said merchants, navigators and vessels, without the said Agents otherwise participating in the immunities, rights and privileges attributed to Consuls and vice-Consuls, and without power under any pretext whatever to exact from the said merchants any duty or emolument whatsoever.

Art. IV. The Consuls and vice-Consuls respectively may establish a chancery, where shall be deposited the Consular determinations, acts and proceedings as also testaments, obligations, contracts, and other acts done by, or between persons of their nation, and effects left by deceased persons or saved from shipwreck.

They may consequently appoint fit persons to act in the said chancery, receive and swear them in, commit to them the custody of the seal, and authority to seal commissions, sentences and other consular acts, and also to discharge the functions of notary and register of the Consulate.

Art. V. The Consuls and vice-Consuls respectively shall have the exclusive right of receiving in their chancery, or on board of vessels, the declarations and all the other acts, which the captains, masters, crews, passengers, and merchants of their nation may chuse to make there, even their testaments and other disposals by last will: and the copies of the said acts, duly authenticated by the said Consuls or vice-Consuls, under the seal of their consulate shall receive faith in law, equally as their originals would, in all the tribunals of the dominions of the M. C. King and of the United States.

They shall also have, and exclusively, in case of the absence of the testamentary executor, administrator or legal heir, the right to inventory, liquidate and proceed to the sale of the personal estate left by subjects or citizens of their nation, who shall die within the extent of their consulate: they shall proceed therein with the assistance of two merchants of their said nation, or, for want of them, of any other at their choice, and shall cause to be deposited in their chancery, the effects and papers of the said estates; and no officer military, judiciary, or of the police of the country shall disturb them or interfere therein, in any manner whatsoever: but the said Consuls and vice-Consuls shall not deliver up the said effects, nor the proceeds thereof to the lawful heirs or to their order, till they shall have caused to be paid all debts which the deceased shall have contracted in the country; for which purpose the creditor shall have a right to attach the said effects in their hands as they might in those of any other individual whatever, and proceed to obtain sale of them till payment of what shall be lawfully due to them. When the debts shall not have been contracted by judgment, deed or note, the signature whereof shall be known, payment shall not be ordered but on the creditor's giving sufficient surety resident in the country, to refund the sums he shall have unduly received, principal, interest and costs: which surety nevertheless shall stand duly discharged after the term of one year in time of peace, and of two in time of war, if the demand in discharge cannot be formed before the end of the term against the heirs who shall present themselves.

And in order that the heirs may not be unjustly kept out of the effects of the deceased the Consuls and vice-Consuls shall notify his death in some one of the gazettes published within their consulate, and that they shall retain the said effects in their hands four months to answer all just demands which shall be presented: and they shall be bound after this delay to deliver to the persons succeeding thereto what shall be more than sufficient for the demands which shall have been formed.

Art. VI. The Consuls and vice-Consuls respectively shall receive the declarations, protests and reports of all captains and masters of their respective nation on account of average losses sustained at sea: and these captains and masters shall lodge in the chancery of the said Consuls and vice-Consuls, the acts which they may have made in other ports on account of the accidents which may have happened to them on their voyage. If a subject of the M.C.K. and a citizen of the U.S. or a foreigner are interested in the said cargo, the average shall be settled by the tribunals of the country and not by the Consuls or vice-Consuls; but when only the subjects or citizens of their own nation shall be interested, the respective Consuls or vice-Consuls shall appoint skilful persons to settle the damages and average.

Art. VII. In cases where by tempest, or other accident, French ships or vessels shall be stranded on the coasts of the U.S. and ships or vessels of the U. S. shall be stranded on the coasts of the dominions of the M.C.K. the Consul or vice-Consul nearest to the place of shipwreck shall do whatever he may judge proper, as well for the purpose of saving the said ship or vessel, its cargo and appurtenances, as for the storing and the security of the effects and merchandise saved. He may take an inventory of them, without the intermedling of any officers of the military, of the customs, of justice, or of the police of the country, otherwise than to give the Consuls, vice-Consuls, captain and crew of the vessel shipwrecked or stranded all the succour and favour which they shall ask of them, either for the expedition and security of the saving and of the effects saved, as to prevent all disturbance.

And in order to prevent all kind of dispute and discussion in the said cases of shipwreck, it is agreed that when there shall be no Consul or vice-Consul to attend to the saving of the wreck, or that the residence of the said Consul or vice-Consul (he not being at the place of wreck) shall be more distant from the said place than that of the competent Judge of the Country, the latter shall immediately proceed therein, with all the dispatch, certainty and precautions prescribed by the respective laws; but the said territorial Judge shall retire, on the arrival of the Consul or vice-Consul, and shall deliver over to him the report of his proceedings, the expences of which the Consul or vice-Consul shall cause to be reimbursed to him, as well as those of saving the wreck.

The merchandise and effects saved shall be deposited in the nearest custom house, or other place of safety, with the inventory thereof which shall have been made by the Consul or vice Consul, or by the Judge who shall have proceeded in their absence, that the said effects and merchandise may be afterwards delivered (after levying therefrom the costs) and without form of process, to the owners, who being furnished with an order for their delivery from the nearest Consul or vice-Consul, shall reclaim them by themselves, or by their order, either for the purpose of reexporting such merchandise, in which case they shall pay no kind of duty of exportation, or for that of selling them in the Country, if they be not prohibited there, and in this last case, the said merchandise, if they be damaged, shall be allowed an abatement of entrance duties proportioned to the damage they have sustained, which shall be ascertained by the affidavits taken at the time the vessel was wrecked or struck.

Art. VIII. The Consuls or vice-Consuls shall exercise Police over all the vessels of their respective Nations and shall have on board the said vessels all power and Jurisdiction in Civil Matters, in all the disputes which may there arise. They shall have an entire inspection over the said vessels, their crew and the changes and substitutions there to be made. For which purpose they may go on board the said vessels whenever they may judge it necessary. Well understood that the functions hereby allowed shall be confined to the interior of the vessels, and that they shall not take place in any case which shall have any interference with the Police of the ports where the said vessels shall be.

Art. IX. The Consuls and vice-Consuls may cause to be arrested the Captains, Officers, Mariners, Sailors, and all other persons being part of the crews of the vessels of their respective Nation who shall have deserted from the said vessels in order to send them back and transport them out of the Country. For which purpose the said Consuls and vice-Consuls shall address themselves to the courts, Judges and Officers competent, and shall demand the said deserters in writing, proving by an exhibition of the registers of the vessel or ship's roll that those men were part of the said crews: and on this demand so proved (saving however where the contrary is proved) the delivery shall not be refused; and there shall be given all aid and assistance to the said Consuls and vice-Consuls for the search, seizure and arrest of the said deserters, who shall even be detained and kept in the prisons of the Country, at their request and expence until they shall have found an opportunity of sending them back. But if they be not sent back within three months, to be counted from the day of their arrest they shall be set at liberty, and shall be no more arrested for the same cause.

Art. X. In cases where the respective subjects or citizens shall have committed any crime, or breach of the peace, they shall be amenable to the Judges of the Country.

Art. XI. When the said offenders shall be a part of the crew of a vessel of their Nation, and shall have withdrawn themselves on board the said vessel they may be there seized and arrested by order of the Judges of the Country: these shall give notice thereof to the Consul or vice-Consul, who may repair on board if he thinks proper: but this notification shall not in any case delay execution of the order in question. The persons arrested shall not afterwards be set at liberty until the Consul or vice-Consul shall have been notified thereof; and they shall be delivered to him, if he requires it, to be put again on board of the vessel on which they were arrested, or of others of their Nation, and to be sent out of the Country.

Art. XII. All differences and suits between the subjects of the M.C.K. in the U.S. or between the citizens of the United states within the dominions of the M.C.K. and particularly all disputes relative to the wages and terms of engagement of the crews of the respective vessels, and all differences of whatever nature they be, which may arise between the privates of the said crews, or between any of them and their captains, or between the captains of different vessels of their nation, shall be determined by the respective Consuls and vice-Consuls, either by a reference to arbitrators, or by a summary judgment and without costs.

No Officer of the country, civil or military, shall interfere therein or take any part whatever in the matter: and the appeals from the said consular sentences shall be carried before the tribunals of France or of the U.S. to whom it may appertain to take cognizance thereof.

Art. XIII. The general utility of commerce having caused to be established within the dominions of the M.C.K. particular tribunals and forms for expediting the decision of commercial affairs, the merchants of the U.S. shall enjoy the benefit of these establishments; and the Congress of the U.S. will provide in the manner the most conformable to its laws for the establishment of equivalent advantages in favour of the French merchants, for the prompt dispatch and decision of affairs of the same nature.

Art. XIV. The subjects of the M.C.K. and citizens of the U.S. who shall prove by legal evidence that they are of the said nations respectively shall in consequence enjoy an exemption from all personal service in the place of their settlement.

Art. XV. If any other nation acquires by virtue of any convention whatever, a treatment more favourable with respect to the consular preeminencies, powers, authority and privileges, the Consuls and vice-Consuls of the M.C.K. or of the U.S. reciprocally shall participate therein, agreeable to the terms stipulated by the 2d. 3d. and 4th. articles of the treaty of amity and commerce, concluded between the M.C.K. and the U.S.

Art. XVI. The present Convention shall be in full force during the term of twelve years to be counted from the day of the exchange of ratifications, which shall be given in proper form, and exchanged on both sides within the space of one year, or sooner if possible.

In Faith whereof we Ministers Plenipotentiary have signed the present Convention, and have thereto set the seal of our arms.

Done at Versailles the 14th. of November one thousand seven hundred and eighty eight.

L. C. De Montmorin   Th: Jefferson

Boyd, Jefferson Papers, v. 14, pp. 171-177.

Phineas Bond to Lord Carmarthen

My Lord,   Philad^{a.} Nov. 16th. 1788

I have the honor to enclose your Ldp. a duplicate of my letter of the Nov. Mail and of a recent publication on the subject, the Hessian fly. I also transmit to your Ldp. a report to the board of managers on the state of manufactures in this city; – and another publication on the same subject:–

Your Ldp. will perceive the scale upon which the manufacturing society have hitherto acted in a contracted one, they are essentially deficient in those main sinews of advancement, money, fit artificers, and fit utensils; – Still their exertions are made with great zeal and the improvements tho' small are progressive.

Endeavors have been and certainly will be used to decoy our manufacturers from Gt. Britain and Ireland and to procure such essential utensils as can be procured from thence alone: – Perhaps my Lord, human caution and vigilance are not equal to preventing the success of these endeavors entirely, but from the observations I have made, I think proper regulations might be imposed upon ships engaged in the traffic of carrying passengers, particularly from Ireland, which would tend in a very great degree to correct these evils: – By throwing difficulties in the way of the trade and by reducing the profits perhaps this line of commerce so very oppressive in its nature and pernicious in its tendency might even eventually be destroyed.

The humanity with which Government has interposed in the regulation of the slave trade has excited even the admiration of our enemies: – Something of a similar sort, my Lord, extended to ships which convey passengers from Scotland and Ireland particularly, would be naturally and beneficially applied: – such a regulation would steer clear of a direct restraint upon the will of the subject to migrate; but would as effectually remedy the evil, by destroying the means of migration, under color of a humane provision for the comforts of those who are disposed to quit their native country – If the unfortunate Africans are fit objects of the humane provision of Government, our own fellow subjects may justly claim an equal measure of benevolent attention: –

The plan I now beg leave to submit to your Ldp's consideration is similar to the regulations of the African trade, with some additions to suit the peculiar nature of the case:

I have my Lord, often, heretofore, been witness of the severity experienced by redemptioners and indented servants brought hither from different parts of Europe; numbers crowded in small ships – provisions scarce and bad and the treatment oppressive and cruel.

I have great satisfaction, my Lord, in observing that the spirit of migration has of late years remitted exceedingly: – Still however numbers do arrive upon this continent annually; particularly from Ireland, and the phantoms of freedom and happiness under the new Constitution may tempt greater numbers to follow the example.

In point of policy my Lord, if the rage for emigration can be checked; it must operate as a great national benefit; but it will also be beneficial to numbers who quitting their homes from the force of delusive representations frequently discover when it is too late the misery in which they are involved.

The nature of this traffic in human flesh is this; – passengers who embark are either redemptioners or indented servants; – such as go under the name of redemptioners agree to have a time allowed them for the payment of their passage money, after their arrival, which payment redeems them from their engagements: – but failing in this payment the redemptioners are then reduced to the plight of common indented servants, and, with them are sold, to discharge their passage money, for a term of years.–

It too often happens, my Lord, that the merchants and masters of ships, with a view of clearing their vessels immediately and to save the expenses of maintaining their unfortunate passengers deprive them of the hope of being redeemed by abridging this limited time, and before their friends can receive intimation of their arrival to interpose their relief, they are frequently hurried in droves, under the custody of severe and brutal drivers, (for these are the terms) into the back country to be disposed of as servants–

I was lately an eye-witness of a scene which interested me exceedingly, but I could administer little more than pity, my Lord, for, in me, any interposition would have been construed into an endeavor to discourage the spirit of migration in which the consequence of the United States is so essentially involved, as one means of increasing population.

The vessels engaged in the passenger trade are known very frequently to bring out implements of manufacturing – so that too great attention cannot be paid to these vessels; and every just means of preventing this traffic must be deemed expedient. With sentiments of the most perfect respect, I have the honor to be, my Lord, Your Ldp's, most faith: and most obet. ser^t.

                                                              P. Bond.
R. 17th Jan:

AHA 1896, v. 1, pp. 581-583.

Phineas Bond to Evan Nepean

Dear Sir,[1]   Philadelphia Nov. 16th. 1788
    I am truly thankful to you for your friendly letter, and especially for the very obliging manner in which you hint the circumstances of a late intro- duction into Canada....
    The introduction I had to my Ld. D.[2] thro' your goodness has been suc- ceeded by the most ready attention to the few communi: I have made to him officially; – I look up to him with a sort of reverence; I admire his integrity and his zeal; no man can possibly do higher honor and credit to his appointments. I waited but for an answer to some representations I made to Govern^t. respecting Canada to have entered into a correspondence with his Ldp. upon a very interesting subject (the distracted situation of the United States affords a most favorable opportunity to encourage migrations from hence into Canada) – a general promulgation of the terms and advantages of settlement seems essentially requisite to induce vast bodies of laborious sober people to remove into a country where they can enjoy once again the blessings of his Majesty's Govern^t. and be exempt from those evils which a relaxed system of laws a ruined trade and oppressive taxes have brought upon them: –) the settlements of Kentucky and Muskingum have and will annually draw off vast bodies of the inhabitants from the Middle States, but these are and will be men of desperate fortunes who availing themselves of the facility of an establishment for their families and the shelter which new settlements always afford ag^t. creditors fly thither as to a sanctuary for protection. But there is a class of people in this country who with industry and the competent means of improvement are anxious to direct their speculations to another quarter: – they have observed the times growing daily worse and worse: the produce of their farms and of their labor is so limited and reduced in quantity, as well as price as to restrain them in

the enjoyment of those comforts which habit has rendered essential: – with these disadvantages not a little aggravated by the pressure of taxes, they foresee the impossibility of raising their families respectably: they must change their position and quit the site their fathers first planted and improved; they can look neither to Kentucky nor Muskingum; for in neither place can they expect the protection of laws or safety against invasions; nor does the temper and disposition of the present inhabitants accord with their habits of conduct or modes of thinking: already has the country of Canada presented itself – some have explored it and many others may be induced to follow and accept the terms of colonization there held out. Most of the people I allude to are of the sect called Quakers: – at first the apprehension was general and even now it is by no means done away, that they would be liable to the payment of tithes – that military duties would be required of them and that the locality of their situation would subject them to the attacks of the Indians. – I made particular inquiry as to these facts while the Hon. M^r· Cochrane (Lord Dundonald's brother) was here, and being convinced the apprehension was ill founded, I took the earliest opportunity to remove these obstacles from the minds of some of the leading quakers whose inclinations tended, I knew, thither, they having applied to me on the subject: – as I was circumstanced it was necessary to manage this business with infinite caution, it was a sort of treason against the consequence of the United States, whose jealousy increases with the confusion of the times: Hitherto I had had no direct authority from Government to interfere: M^r· Cochrane wished me to go to Canada to confer with my Lord Dorchester but unless I had been so instructed, it was impossible I could quit the duties of my office here: I however immediately wrote to the Secretary of State.

It will be very important to have the terms of settlement not only fully explained, but promulgated thro' every channel as diffusely as possible, in the varies newspapers in Gt. Britain etc. in the W. Indies in Canada and in Nova Scotia; thro' these channels the information will get fully abroad here: and when known and when the obstacles which arose from the fear of tithes, from the apprehension of military duties and from the danger of attacks by the savages are generally removed, under the sanction of official authority, the benefits of a rapid migration thither will *follow rapidly*: – I presume you have seen M^r· Cochrane, he promised to wait upon the Secy's of State and I assured him I would cheerfully go to Canada or undertake whatever Governt. might direct to promote a very useful purpose –

I am rejoiced to observe prosecutions have been instituted to check the endeavors to seduce artificers from Gt. Britain and Ireland: I agree with you it is almost impossible to prevent it entirely but I am convinced a strict attention to the ships which carry passengers hither, (of which formerly there were numbers in this trade) would lead to the discovery of very indirect schemes practices as well towards artificers as towards other unwary natives in decoying them from their country: They are annexed(?) with the prospect of wealth and happiness and find too late that when they left their homes the door of competence and comfort was shut against them for ever–

The migrations from Ireland hither have of late been much reduced. – I am well convinced scarcely an artificer of any sort can at this time meet a decent support: How far the expectations of a great and rising empire and growing dignity under the Federal Govern⁺· may dazzle weak eyes and promote a fresh spirit of migration, is yet to be determined. I have taken the liberty of suggesting some modifications as to the manner of providing for passengers who are redemptioners or indented servants, which I think will have a good effect, and while such wise and humane provisions made for the wretched natives of Africa [the] extension of similar regulations to relax the rigor of Egyptian taskmasters towards their white slaves will be deemed just and equal; I should be glad to have your opinion of this plan – You will perceive it is founded upon the principles by which the slave trade is to be regulated with some additional provisions to suit the particular nature of the case – the freedom of the English Constitution will not admit of any direct restraints upon the will of Brit: subjects to remove whithersoever they will; but fit restraints may with a real attention to the comfort of the parties be so contrived as to lessen the profit of those who exercise a traffic in human carcasses and by lessening the profits discourage the trade effectually: – a matter of considerable consequence when viewed in a political light as everything must be which tends to check the spirit of migration.

Among several representations I have made I have pointed out the great difficulties which many reputable Artificers and other valuable subjects experience in this country; where failing in the expectation of employment and having expended the means of support they brought hither, are left destitute and distressed: – Numbers constantly apply to me to send them home: – the distance to New York and the charges of travelling from Falmouth often discourage my attempting to send them by that route; and, in many instances I have been obliged to solicit the humanity of British Ship Masters to give some deserving object a passage to the ports, most contiguous to their native places: This is quite a matter of courtesy – the power of sending distressed British seamen home in British vessels upon a certain allowance is confined to that class of men: but it might very aptly reach to all meritorious distressed subjects, and the provision made for seamen, if extended to other subjects would be but a small national expenditure, productive of a great national benefit; – for thus numbers would be reclaimed; and the story of their misery would deter others from engaging in similar adventures; – I might add too, that tho' I have never yet failed in any application I have made to the agent of the British packets to furnish distressed subjects with a passage in the packets, the adopting my recommendation is also a matter of courtesy of the part of the agent and cannot officially be required by me. – Upon the subject which is entirely of a public nature, I have hitherto been favored with no sort of instruction, and am often extremely at a loss how to act. Humanity has been the best beacon by which I could steer, but the frequency of applications and the frequency of relief will essentially abridge my own means of subsistence and such a burden would fall heavy upon an individual, which, as a national provision would not be felt: – a small sum annually might be excellently well applied by a due selection of fit objects whose labor and industry when reclaimed would amply compensate the expenditure.

Your letter gave me reason to expect some communications I had made to Govern.ᵗ˙ respecting the seduction of artificers would be acknowledged by the mail; but hitherto I have not been so fortunate; nor have I often been gratified in this respect, which I lament the more, when I consider the nature of the intelligence, I have from time to time communicated and the critical predicament in which I stand.

You have kindly given me leave to say something about myself, and as I have great reason to complain of total inattention to some representations I have made in my own behalf, I shall consider myself extremely obliged to you to obtain a satisfactory reply to my letters on the following points: – I was encouraged by Govern.ᵗ˙ to expect the nomination of agents or deputies, in my district, as well upon the ground of national policy as of relieving me in part from that constant duty which engages my whole time, I have urged the expediency of such a nomination – shortly I must inevitably be employed in effecting the purposes of my mission by due representations of the grievances under which the kings subjects labor in consequence of local regulations, inconsistent with the Faith of Treaties, or with private compacts. Either my duty as consul, or this important duty must be neglected: – I have applied for authority to name deputies and have pointed out the stations, but hitherto I have had no instructions in the matter. I have requested Govern.ᵗ˙ would annex a sum to my salary, by way of provision for contingent expenses, and in this respect to put me upon a footing with M.ʳ Miller, who I am informed has a gross sum allowed for contingencies – but I have not succeeded in this application tho' my request is reasonable and tho' this is the only mode by which I can be compensated: – I can not make specific demands, the nature of my information and the mode of obtaining it will not admit of a charge upon paper; if a gross sum is allowed for contingencies, in one instance, it is but just to allow it in my case; unless I am less deserving: – I feel however a consciousness of being unremitted in my duty, and I trust I shall be thought entitled to the same provision which has been made elsewhere, I ask no more.

I have more than once requested to know if consulage is of right due and may be demanded: I found this request upon the knowledge of a fact that fees of office are universally required by every consul in the Medit^n etc. who holds the King's commission. In my case I can see no reason why they should be dispensed with since the nature of the appointment subjects me to constant applications for assistance which can not be rendered elsewhere; much too, must be done, which is, in a manner, unconnected with official duty – yet hitherto I have received no fees of any kind:

The expenses of living are enormous as I am circumstanced: perhaps it is a misfortune to be the only commissioned officer here from England – for the same expenses are incurred as would attend the establishment of an officer of higher dignity, and they seem indispensible.

My friend Barclay will converse with you on these points. – I rely upon your goodness to obtain some satisfaction thereon, with this assurance that notwithstanding the friendly professions you have favored me with, I shall be tender upon encroaching upon your time, or your kindness by future applications on my own behalf at least.

With sentiments of the most unfeigned regard, I am dear Sir Your faith. and obed: servant   P. Bond

.   .   .   .   .

AHA 1896, v. 1, pp. 583-589.
^{1} Nepean, Evan (1751-1822). British government official. After an early career as a clerk or purser in the navy, became secretary to the port admiral at Plymouth, 1782. Undersecretary of state for the Home Department, 1782-1789. Made a commissioner of the privy seal, 1784. Undersecretary for War, 1794-1795. Secretary of the Admiralty, 1795-1804. Knighted, 1802. Chief secretary for Ireland, January-September 1804. One of the lords commissioners of the admiralty, 1804-1806. Governor of Bombay, 1812-1819.
^{2} Lord Dorchester.

Comte de Moustier to Comte de Montmorin

[Translation]

N° 26.   New York, 18 November 1788.
My Lord,

The interruption of the Packet Boats has hitherto deprived me entirely of the advantage of receiving some response to the various Despatches that

I have had the honor to send You. I regret all the more that since my arrival on this continent, I have seen a revolution accomplished in the government of the United States that entirely changes the relations under which they have hitherto been envisaged.

I have consequently prepared memoranda to explain to you the various points of view under which the powers of the new American Government can be envisaged; but on the one hand they are a little too extensive to be able to be transcribed in cypher, and on the other I cannot find any sure occasion to send them to you. I still expect with confidence, My Lord, that you will furnish me with one yourself.

I even dare to hope that before the reception of my memoranda, of which one includes a general plan of conduct towards the united Americans, you yourself will have stipulated for me in part to adopt the step that I believe the most appropriate to render useful to the King a revolution from which he has gathered so much glory.

The present moment is critical. It is favorable to us, but it would be possible that too long a delay would make us lose an occasion that would perhaps not be met with again with the same advantages. I should think that England, which since the peace has treated the United States with a disdain founded on their real Situation rather than on that to which one might think them susceptible, will change her conduct towards Them as soon as she has recognized the Stability and regularity of the administration to which the new constitution renders them Susceptible.

I have reason to be well pleased with the dispositions that I have found in several of the principal personages influencing this Country. I have been perfectly satisfied in particular with General Washington, with whom I spent several days. The result of his conversations has been, in proper terms, "that very certainly people in the United States were still animated by a lively and sincere gratitude to the King and the French nation; but that nevertheless interest alone could fix the connections between nations; that it was very easy to recognize that it was owing only to His Majesty's doing that the United States found their interest in being closely united with Him."

This conclusion is all the more remarkable since General Washington will be president of the United States, if he agrees to it, and since his power and his influence in that quality are of the greatest importance according to the new Constitution. I have endeavored on all occasions, without compromising myself, to make people think that if our connections with the Americans have hitherto not been closer, the fault should be attributed only to their vicious constitution, and that the revolution that it has just experienced has always been desired by His Majesty and his Council. This language appears to me useful and even necessary, in thinking that the event is in some manner accomplished, and that it is no longer only a question of endeavoring to make the best of it. It is in the month of March that the new Congress is to assemble; the time is near. If it seems necessary to you, My Lord, that I receive instructions consistent with an order of things that did not exist at my departure from the Kingdom, I think that in the event that the packet boats to communicate with the United States are not yet reestablished, you could nevertheless have them reach me by an aviso.

One particularly regrets the interruption of the packet boats in circumstances that seemed to favor the surest and most regular speculations between the two nations. The Commerce of England is somewhat diminishing. Some American manufactories are furnishing common objects that were previously drawn from Great Britain. The few articles that are beginning to be imported from France have an assured sale. But it is only by feeling their way in some degree that French and American Merchants are resuming a Commerce that was at first undertaken with a boldness that nothing warranted, and that sprang from presumption rather than from real knowledge that the two nations had of their resources and their means. These first assays should be encouraged; they are the seeds of a Commerce that, conducted wisely and gradually, can offer all the more advantages since they are reciprocal. To favor them, one must assure routes of correspondence to the two nations. If Commerce had acquired the full extent of which it is susceptible, it would maintain these routes itself, but it is only nascent and scarcely in its infancy; if the King does not come to its aid, this infancy will be long. I cannot help thinking that the establishment of Packet Boats *for the United States* is certainly considered useful, and that the expense that it may occasion is only a very slight advance made to open the channels that will cause it to return a Hundredfold. Several merchants accustomed to grant and receive Commissions by this route were caught unawares and have suffered by an interruption that took place before they could be warned of it, while many of their speculations have failed because of this event. Some are even obliged to go to France by way of England to regulate their affairs. Today it is spread about that the Kingdom has need of grain as a result of the hailstorm that destroyed a part of the harvest, that the war between the Powers of Northern Europe deprived it of the grain resources of Poland, that the Barbary Coast cannot furnish any this year, and that consequently the United States could meet the Kingdom's need in this circumstance. It is thought that this event will be infinitely favorable to extend the Commerce between the two nations, since the Americans would have the means to pay in foodstuffs for the value of a great quantity of French merchandise which, lacking capital and credit, they are obliged to renounce today.

However, in spite of these flattering appearances, the Americans prefer to limit themselves to their circumscribed operations, the result of which they know in advance, rather than to devote themselves to those that they cannot judge with precision for lack of sufficiently certain or prompt information. I have expatiated a little, My Lord, on one part of the effects of the interruption of the packet boats because in the situation in which I find myself, I am more capable than anyone of perceiving them, and I am persuaded that it suffices to indicate them in order to induce the King's Council to assent to the preservation of a very advantageous, although also inexpensive establishment, which may be that of the packet boats according to the plan that I sent to the Secretary of State of the Navy at the beginning of this year.

. . . . . .

I am with respect, My Lord, Your most humble and most obedient servant,   Le C$^{te.}$ de Moustier.
rec. 11 February 1789

FFAA: Pol. Corr., U.S., v. 33, f. 332-339 (LC transcription).

Thomas Jefferson to John Jay

Sir   Paris. Nov. 19. 1788.

. . . . .

Before this can reach you, you will probably have heard of an Arret passed the 28th of Sep for prohibiting the introduction of foreign whale oils, without exception. the English had glutted the markets of this country with their oils. it was proposed to exclude them, and an Arret was drawn with an exception for us. in the last stage of this Arret, the exception was struck out, without my having any warning or even suspicion of this. I suspect this stroke came from the Count de la Luzerne, minister of marine; but I cannot affirm it positively. as soon as I was apprized of this, which was several days after it passed (because it was kept secret till published in their seaports) I wrote to the count de Montmorin a letter, of which the enclosed is a copy, and had conferences on the subject from time to time with him and the other ministers. I found them possessed by the partial information of their Dunkirk fisherman: and therefore thought it necessary to give them a view of the whole subject in writing, which I did in the piece, of which I inclose you a printed copy. I therein entered into more details than the question between us seemed rigorously to require. I was led to them by other objects. the most important was to disgust mr Neckar, as an economist, of against their new fishery, by letting him foresee it's expence. the particular manufactures suggested to them were in consequence of repeated applications from the shippers of rice & tobacco. other details which do not appear immediately pertinent, were occasioned by circumstances which had arisen in conversation, or an apparent necessity of giving information on the whole matter. at a conference in the presence of M. Lambert on the 16th. (where I was ably aided by the Marquis de la Fayette, as I have been through the whole business) it was agreed to except us from the prohibition. but they will require rigorous assurance that the oils coming under our name, are really of our fishery. they fear we shall cover the introduction of the English oils from Halifax. the arret for excepting us was communicated to me, but the formalities of proving the oils to be American, were not yet inserted. I suppose they will require every vessel to bring a certificate from their consul or vice consul residing in the state from which it comes. more difficult proofs were sometimes talked of. I supposed I might surely affirm to them that our government would do whatever it could to prevent this fraud, because it is as much our interest as theirs to keep the market for the French & American oils only. I am told Massachusets has prohibited the introduction of foreign fish oils into her ports. this law, if well executed will be an effectual guard against fraud; & a similar one in the other states interested in the fishery, would much encourage this government to continue her indulgence to us – tho the Arret then for the re-admission of our oils is not yet passed I think I may assure you it will be so in a few days, and of course that this branch of commerce after so threatening an appearance, will be on a better footing than ever, as enjoying jointly with the French oil a monopoly of their markets. the continuance of this will depend on the growth of their fishery. whenever they become able to supply their own wants, it is very possible they may refuse to take our oils but I do not believe it possible for them to raise their fishery to that unless they can continue to draw off our fishermen from us. their 17 ships this year had 150 of our sailors on board. I do not know what number the English have got into their service. – you will readily perceive that there are particulars in these printed observations which it would not be proper to suffer to become public. they were printed merely that a copy might be given to each minister & care has been taken to let them go into no other hands.

I must now trouble Congress with a petition on my own behalf. when I left my own house in Octob. 1783. it was to attend Congress as a member, & in expectation of returning in five or six months. in the month of May following however I was desired to come to Europe, as member of a commission which was to continue two years only. I came off immediately, without going home to make any other arrangements in my affairs, thinking they would not suffer greatly before I should return to them. before the close of the two years, Doctor Franklin retiring from his charge here,

Congress were pleased to name me to it. so that I have been led on by events to an absence of five years instead of five months. in the mean time, matters of great moment to others as well as myself, & which can be arranged by nobody but myself, will await no longer. another motive of still more powerful cogency on my mind is the necessity of carrying my family back to their friends and country. I must therefore ask of Congress a leave of short absence. allowing three months on the sea, going & coming, and two months at my own house, which will suffice for my affairs, I need not be from Paris but between five & six months....I send you the newspapers to this date, & have the honour to be with the greatest esteem & respect, Sir, your most obedient humble serv^t·   Th: Jefferson

. . . . . .

NA: PCC, item 87, v. 2, pp. 243-250 (ALS); M247, reel 115.

Comte de Montmorin to Comte de Moustier

[Translation]

N^o· 3.   Versailles, 21 November 1788.
M. le Cte· de Moustier
    I have received, Sir, the despatches that you have done me the honor to write me from N^o· 12 to 20, as well as those numbered 21 and 22 that M. Otto sent me.

. . . . .

    Mr. Jefferson asked that it not be mentioned in the convention because it would give umbrage to the American legislatures.[1] We consented to it because, besides the fact that this subject has nothing in common with consuls and commerce, Mr. Jefferson has observed that if the principle of the immunity of the flag of a warship is general, it will be respected in America, that if on the contrary it is only local, a specific decision of the United States would be necessary to authorize it in America.
    The Consular convention, Sir, was finally signed yesterday as you will find it enclosed herewith. I presume that its ratification will not meet with any difficulties. I cannot praise too highly the frank manner and the good will with which Mr. Jefferson has negotiated. I desire that you should, without affectation and without pushing yourself forward too much, expedite the ratification by the present congress.
    We have learned with pleasure, Sir, that Mr. Van Berkel has obtained the Satisfaction that he had demanded in relation to the Seizure of one of his domestics. The judgment that was rendered states the principles of the Americans concerning the immunities of foreign ministers.

You will probably have learned, Sir, that the decree that was rendered in favor of the Americans suffered an attack with regard to whale oil, and I presume that some discontent will have been expressed to you in that regard. Mr. Jefferson has not delayed in lodging complaints. We are occupied at this moment with examining them, and I am persuaded in advance that the King's decision will be as favorable to the Americans as our own circumstances may permit. You may say this to the persons who converse with you on this matter, observing to them that a decree is not a convention.

Congress, Sir, has done all that its feeble authority permits in recommending to the state of Virginia the matter of Captain Ferrier. We shall see what this step will produce. I like to think that the enormity of the crime and the danger of impunity will have prevailed over the silence of the law. Mr. Jefferson has not yet spoken to me of the instructions that he must have received regarding this affair.

It appears, Sir, that the new constitution will finally be adopted, but that it will experience many modifications that will diminish the good effects that were to be expected from it: however, the United States will have at least ameliorated their internal and external existence: the amendments that remain to be desired will probably be the fruit of time and circumstances.

> . . . . .

De Montmorin

> . . . . .

FFAA: Pol. Corr., U.S., v. 33, f. 342-345 (LC transcription).
¹ *The omitted material discusses the immunity of foreign warships from actions under civil law.*

John Jay to Thomas Jefferson

Dʳ· Sir   [New York] Office for foreign Affairs 25ᵗʰ· November 1788

> . . . . .

I enclose a Copy of a Letter of the 5ᵗʰ· of August last from Mʳ· Robert Montgomery at Alicant. I find his Letter was a Copy, the Original never came to my Hands. The Facts stated in this Letter merit Attention, and as the Business it alludes to is in your Department, I take the earliest Opportunity of making this Communication. To me it appears highly probable, that every maritime Nation in Europe is well content that War should subsist between Barbary and the United States, and in my Opinion none of them (execpt perhaps Spain for particular Reasons) will really and sincerely promote any Measures tending to the Establishment of Peace between us. If this be so, it is important that as much Secrecy as possible should be observed in all our Proceedings relative to that Object. I wish the Porte could be sounded on this Subject. Overtures for a Treaty from us to that Court, made at this period, would probably be grateful, and might eventually terminate all our Difficulties with Algiers &ca:, especially as the Emperor of Morocco will promote it. –

Much remains to be done and much to be attemped; but without a competent Goverment and adequate Funds, no national Affairs can be well managed. –

. . . . .

With sincere Esteem and Regard I have the Honor to be &c.

John Jay. –

NA: PCC, item 121, pp. 312-314 (LBkC); M61, reel 1.

John Jay to Thomas Jefferson

Private   NYork 25 Novʳ 1788 –

Dear Sir

. . . . .

The Count de Moustier found in this Country the best Dispositions to make it agreable to him – but it seems he expected more particular and flattering Marks of minute Respect than our People in general entertain Ideas of, or are either accustomed or inclined to pay to anybody. This added as I suspect and believe, to Insinuations from persons who have no Desire that he should be very agreable to us, or we to him, have led him into Errors relative to men and things which naturally dispose him to give and recieve Disgust. Appearances (whether well or ill founded is not important) have created and diffused an Opinion that an improper Connection subsists between him and the Marchioness. You can easily concieve the Influence of such an Opinion on the Minds and Feelings of such a People as ours – For my part I regret it – she seems to be an amiable woman; and I think if left to the Operation of his own Judgmᵗ and Disposition, his Conduct relative to this Country would be friendly and useful. These are things that I have not said or written to any other Person – nor is it pleasant to say or write them – but in the Situation you are in, Information of this Kind may have its uses – With great Esteem and Regard I am Dear Sir Your most obᵗ & hble Servᵗ   John Jay –

LC: Jefferson Papers, microfilm reel 10 (ALS).

Thomas Jefferson to John Jay

Sir   Paris Nov. 29. 1788.
    In the hurry of making up my letter of the 19th. inst. I omitted to inclose
the printed paper on the subject of whale oil. that omission is now supplied
by another conveiance by the way of London. the explanatory Arrêt is not
yet come out. I still take for granted it will pass, tho' there be an opposition
to it in the council. in the mean time orders are given to receive our oils
which may arrive. the apprehension of a want of corn has induced them to
turn their eyes to foreign supplies; and to shew their preference of receiving
them from us, they have passed the inclosed arrêt giving a premium on
wheat and flour from the United States for a limited time. this you will
doubtless think proper to have translated & published....
    I enclose those of Leyden to the present date with the gazettes of France,
and have the honor to be with sentiments of the most perfect esteem &
respect, Sir, Your most obedient humble servant
                                                                Th: Jefferson
NA: PCC, *item 87, v. 2, pp. 275-276 (ALS); M247, reel 115.*

Enclosure
Observations on the Whale-Fishery

[October 1788]
    Whale oil enters, as a raw material, into several branches of manufacture,
as of wool, leather, soap: it is used also in painting, architecture and
navigation. But its great consumption is in lighting houses and cities. For
this last purpose however it has a powerful competitor in the vegetable oils.
These do well in warm, still weather, but they fix with cold, they extinguish easily with the wind, their crop is precarious, depending on the
seasons, and to yield the same light, a larger wick must be used, and greater
quantity of oil consumed. Estimating all these articles of difference together,
those employed in lighting cities find their account in giving about 25 per
cent. more for whale than for vegetable oils. But higher than this the whale
oil, in its present form, cannot rise; because it then becomes more advantageous to the city-lighters to use others. This competition then limits its
price, higher than which no encouragement can raise it, and becomes, as
it were, a law of nature, but, at this low price; the whale fishery is the
poorest business into which a merchant or sailor can enter. If the sailor,
instead of wages, has a part of what is taken, he finds that this, one year
with another, yields him less than he could have got as wages in any other
business. It is attended too with great risk, singular hardships, and long

absences from his family. If the voyage is made solely at the expence of the merchant, he finds that, one year with another, it does not reimburse him his expences. As, for example, an English ship of 300 ton, and 42. hands brings home, communibis annis, after a four months voyage, 25. ton of oil, worth 437 £. 10s. sterl. but the wages of the officers and seamen will be 400 £. The Outfit then and the merchant's profit must be paid by the government. And it is accordingly on this idea that the British bounty is calculated. From the poverty of this business then it has happened that the nations, who have taken it up, have successively abandoned it. The Basques began it. But, tho' the most economical and enterprising of the inhabitants of France, they could not continue it; and it is said they never employed more than 30. ships a year. The Dutch and Hanse towns succeeded them. The latter gave it up long ago tho' they have continued to lend their name to British and Dutch oils. The English carried it on, in competition with the Dutch, during the last, and beginning of the present century. But it was too little profitable for them in comparison with other branches of commerce open to them. In the mean time too the inhabitants of the barren Island of Nantucket had taken up this fishery, invited to it by the whales presenting themselves on their own shore. To them therefore the English relinquished it, continuing to them, as British subjects, the importation of their oils into England duty free, while foreigners were subject to a duty of 18 £. 5s. sterl. a ton. the Dutch were enabled to continue it long, because, 1. They are so near the northern fishing grounds, that a vessel begins her fishing very soon after she is out of port. 2. They navigate with more economy than the other nations of Europe. 3. Their seamen are content with lower wages: and 4. their merchants with a lower profit on their capital. Under all these favorable circumstances however, this branch of business, after long languishing, is at length nearly extinct with them. It is said they did not send above half dozen ships in pursuit of the whale this present year. The Nantuckois then were the only people who exercised this fishery to any extent at the commencement of the late war. Their country, from its barrenness, yielding no subsistence, they were obliged to seek it in the sea which surrounded them. Their economy was more rigorous than that of the Dutch. Their seamen, instead of wages, had a share in what was taken. This induced them to fish with fewer hands, so that each had a greater dividend in the profit. It made them more vigilant in seeking game, bolder in pursuing it, and parcimonious in all their expences. London was their only market. When therefore, by the late revolution, they became aliens in great Britain, they became subject to the alien duty of 18 £. 5s. the ton of oil, which being more than equal to the price of the common whale oil, they were obliged to abandon that fishery. So that this people, who before the war had empoyed upwards of 300 vessels a year in the whale fishery, (while great Britain had herself never employed one hundred) have now almost ceased to exercise it. But they still had the seamen, the most important material for this fishery; and they still retained the spirit of fishing: so that at the reestablishment of peace they were capable in a very short time of reviving their fishery in all its splendor. The British government saw that the moment was critical. They knew that their own share in that fishery was as nothing. That the great mass of fishermen was left with a nation now separated from them: that these fishermen however had lost their ancient market, had no other resource within their country to which they could turn, and they hoped therefore they might, in the present moment of distress, be decoyed over to their establishments, and be added to the mass of their seamen. To effect this they offered extravagant advantages to all persons who should exercise the whale fishery from British establishments. But not counting with much confidence on a long connection with their remaining possesions on the continent of America, foreseeing that the Nantuckois would settle in them preferably, if put on an equal footing with those of great Britain, and that thus they might have to purchase them a second time, they confined their high offers to settlers in Great Britain. The Nantuckois, left without resource by the loss of their market, began to think of removing to the British dominions: some to Nova Scotia, preferring smaller advantages, in the neighbourhood of their ancient country and friends; others to great Britain postponing country and friends to high premiums. A vessel was already arrived from Halifax to Nantucket to take off some of those who proposed to remove; two families had gone on board and others were going, when a letter was received there, which had been written by Monsieur le Marquis de la Fayette to a gentleman in Boston, and transmitted by him to Nantucket. The purport of the letter was to dissuade their accepting the British proposals, and to assure them that their friends in France would endeavour to do something for them. This instantly suspended their design: not another went on board, and the vessel returned to Halifax with only the two families.

In fact the French government had not been inattentive to the views of the British, nor insensible to the crisis. They saw the danger of permitting five or six thousand of the best seamen existing to be transferred by a single stroke to the marine strength of their enemy, and to carry over with them an art which they possesed almost exclusively. The counterplan which they set on foot was to tempt the Nantuckois by high offers to come and settle in France. This was in the year 1785. The British however had in their favour a sameness of language, religion, laws, habits and kindred. 9 families only, of 33 persons in the whole came to Dunkirk; so that this project was

not likely to prevent their emigration to the English establishments, if
nothing else had happened.

France had effectually aided in detaching the U. S. of America from the
force of Great Britain. But as yet they seemed to have indulged only a silent
wish to detach them from her *commerce*. They had done nothing to induce
that event. In the same year 1785, while M. de Calonne was in treaty, with
the Nantuckois, an estimate of the commerce of the U. S. was submitted
to the count de Vergennes, and it was shewn that, of 3. millions of pounds
sterling to which their exports amounted, one third might be brought to
France and exchanged against her productions and manufactures advantageously for both nations, provided the obstacles of prohibition, monopoly,
and duty were either done away or moderated as far as circumstances would
admit. A committee, which had been apponted to investigate a particular
one of these subjects, was thereupon instructed to extend its researches to
the whole, and to see what advantages and facilities the Government could
offer for the encouragement of a general commerce with the United States.
The Committee was composed of persons well skilled in commerce; and,
after labouring assiduously for several months, they made their report: the
result of which was given in the letter of his Majesty's Comptroller General
of the 2d of Octob. 1786. wherein he stated the principles which should be
established for the future regulation of the commerce between France and
the United States. It was become tolerably evident, at the date of this
letter, that the terms offered to the Nantuckois would not produce their
emigration to Dunkirk; and that it would be safest in every event to offer
some other alternative which might prevent their acceptance of the British
offers. The obvious one was to open the ports of France to their oils, so
that they might still exercise their fishery, remaining in their native
country, and find a new market for its produce instead of that which they
had lost. The article of Whale oil was accordingly distinguished, in the
letter of M. de Calonne, by an immediate abatement of duty, and promise
of further abatement after the year 1790. This letter was instantly sent to
America, and bid fair to produce there the effect intended, by determining
the fishermen to carry on their trade from their own homes, with the
advantage only of a free market in France, rather than remove to Great
Britain where a free market and great bounty were offered them. An Arret
was still to be prepared to give legal sanction to the letter of M. de
Calonne. M. Lambert, with a patience and assiduity almost unexampled,
went through all the investigations necessary to assure himself that the
conclusions of the Committee had been just. Frequent conferences on this
subject were held in his presence; the Deputies of the Chambers of
Commerce were heard, and the result was the Arret of Dec. 29. 1787.
confirming the abatements of duty present and future, which the letter of

Octob 1786. had promised, and reserving to his Majesty to grant still further favours to that production, if on further information he should find it for the interest of the two Nations.

The English had now begun to deluge the markets of France with their whale oils: and they were enabled by the great premiums given by their Government to undersell the French fisherman, aided by feebler premiums, and the American aided by his poverty alone. Nor is it certain that these speculations were not made at the risk of the British Government, to suppress the French and American fishermen in their only market. Some remedy seemed necessary. Perhaps it would not have been a bad one to subject, by a general law, the merchandize of every nation and of every nature to pay additional duties in the ports of France exactly equal to the premiums and drawbacks given on the same merchandise by their own government. This might not only counteract the effect of premium in the instance of whale oils, but attack the whole British system of bounties and drawbacks by the aid of which they make London the center of commerce for the whole earth. A less general remedy, but an effectual one, was to prohibit the oils of all *European* nations: the treaty with England requiring only that she should be treated as well as the most favoured *European* nation. But the remedy adopted was to prohibit all oils without exception.

. . . .

A material observation must be added here. Sudden vicissitudes of opening and shutting ports, do little injury to merchants settled on the opposite coast, watching for the opening, like the return of a tide, and ready to enter with it. But they ruin the adventurer whose distance requires 6 months notice. Those who are now arriving from America, in consequence of the Arret of Dec. 29. will consider it as the false light which has led them to their ruin. They will be apt to say that they come to the ports of France by the invitation of that Arret, that the subsequent one of Sept. 28. which drives them from those ports, founds itself on a single principle, viz. "that the prohibition of foreign oils is the most useful encouragement which can be given to that branch of industry." They will say that, if this be a true principle, it was as true on the 29th. of Dec. 1787. as on the 28th. of Sept. 1788. it was then weighed against other motives, judged weaker, and overruled, and it is hard it should be now revived to ruin them.

. . . .

After this review of the whale fishery as a Political institution, a few considerations shall be added on its produce as a basis of Commercial exchange between France and the United States. The discussions it has undergone on former occasions, in this point of view, leaves little new to be now urged.

The United-States not possessing mines of the precious metals, they can purchase necessaries from other nations so far only as their produce is received in exchange. Without enumerating our smaller articles, we have three of principal importance, proper for the French market, to wit, Tobacco, whale oil, and rice. The first and most important is Tobacco. This might furnish an exchange for 8. millions of the productions of this country: but it is under a monopoly, and that not of a mercantile, but a financiering company, whose interest is to pay in money, and not in merchandise; and who are so much governed by the spirit of simplifying their purchases and proceedings, that they find means to elude every endeavour on the part of government to make them diffuse their purchases among the merchants in general. Little profit is derived from this then as an article of exchange for the produce and manufactures of France. Whale oil might be next in importance; but that is now prohibited. American Rice is not yet of great, but it is of growing consumption in France, and being the only article of the three which is free, it may become a principal basis of exchange....The way to encourage purchasers is to multiply their means of payment. Whale oil might be an important one. In one scale is the interest of the millions who are lighted, shod or clothed with the help of it, and the thousands of labourers and manufacturers who would be employed in producing the articles which might be given in exchange for it, if received from America. In the other scale are the interests of the adventurers in the whale fishery; each of whom indeed, politically considered may be of more importance to the state than a simple labourer or manufacturer: but to make the estimate with the accuracy it merits, we should multiply the numbers in each scale into their individual importance, and see which preponderates.

Whether then we consider the Arret of Sep. 28. in a political or a commercial light, it would seem that the U. S. should be excepted from its operation. Still more so when they invoke against it the amity subsisting between the two nations, the desire of binding them together by every possible interest and connection, the several acts in favour of this exception, the dignity of legislation which admits not of changes backwards and forwards, the interests of commerce which require steady regulations, the assurances of the friendly motives which have led the king to pass these acts, and the hope that no cause will arise to change either his motives or his measures towards us.

NA: PCC, *item 87, v. 2, pp. 261-274/4 (printed copy); M247, reel 115.*

David Humphreys to Thomas Jefferson

Dear Sir   Mount Vernon Nov$^{r.}$ 29$^{th.}$ 1788

. . . . .

There has been an extraordinary revolution in the sentiments of men, respecting political affairs, since I came to America; & much more favorable in the result than could then have been reasonably expected. At the close of the war, after the little season of unlimited credit was passed, the people in moderate circumstances found themselves very much embarrassed by the scarcity of money, by debts & taxes. They affected to think that the part of Society composed of men in tbe liberal professions & those who had considerable property, were in combination to distress them, & to establish an Aristocracy. Demagogues made use of these impressions to procure their own elections & to carry their own schemes into execution. Lawyers, in some States, by these artifices, became indiscriminately odious. In others men of the strongest local prejudices & narrowest principles had the whole direction of the affairs of their States. You will feel the force of this assertion the more readily, when you shall have been informed that the same Gen$^{l.}$ Wadsworth,[1] who was in Congress with you at Annapolis became, in conjunction with two or three of his Subalterns the director of every political measure in Connecticut; and prevented, in almost every instance, a compliance with the Requisitions of Congress. On the other part, great numbers of those who wished to see an efficient foederal government prevail, began to fear that the bulk of the people would never submit to it. In short some of them, who had been utterly averse to Royalty, began to imagine that hardly any thing but a king could cure the evil. It was truly astonishing to have been witness to some conversations, which I have heard. Still all the more reasonable men saw that the remedy would be infinitely worse than the disease. In this fluctuating & irritable situation the public mind continued, for some time. The insurrection in Massachusetts was not without its benefits. From a view of the impotence of the general government, of the contempt in which we were held abroad & of the want of happiness at home, the Public was thus gradually wrought to a disposition for receiving a government possessed of sufficient energy to prevent the calamities of Anarchy & civil war; & yet guarded, as well as the nature of circumstances will admit, so as to prevent it from degener-ating into Aristocracy, Oligarchy or Monarchy. True it is, that honest & wise men have differed in sentiment about the kind of checks & balances which are necessary for this purpose: but equally true it is that there is not an honest & wise man who does not see & feel the indispensable necessity of preserving the Union....

. . . . .

...you will ever believe me with the sincerest gratitude & unalterable friendship Dear Sir Your much obliged & very Humble Servant

D. Humphreys

LC: *Jefferson Papers, microfilm reel 10 (ALS).*
[1] *Wadsworth, James (1730-1817). Attorney, militia officer and Connecticut political figure. New Haven town clerk, 1756-1786. Judge, New Haven county court, 1773-1778. Served in state militia, reaching rank of major general. Member, Continental Congress, 1784. Member, state executive council, 1785-1789. State comptroller, 1786-1787.*

George Miller to Lord Carmarthen

Nᵒ· 9.   Charleston 30 November 1788.
My Lord,

. . . . .

The Assembly of this State met on the 7ᵗʰ· Ultᵒ·, pursuant to adjournment. – Several petitions were presented from the interior part of the Country, stating the distress of the people from the want of a sufficient circulating Medium, and praying for a farther interference of the Legislature between Debtor and Creditor. – These petitions were referred to a large Committee of Members of both Houses, who, after enquiring into the different allegations therein specified, unanimously reported "That the interference of the Legislature is become indispensibly necessary," which report was agreed to in both Houses, the members of each, reserving their right to oppose any particular plan of redress which they might disapprove of. Three different methods were proposed – a valuation Law of all property seized in Execution; an extention of the Three years Instalment law, to Five, and a further emission of paper currency. –

The valuation bill was the first brought forward. It was read a first time the 16ᵗʰ· ordered to be read a second time on the 21ˢᵗ·, and to be printed. This Bill was so strongly characteristic of the Sheriffs sale bill, passed in 1785, well known by the name of "the pine barren Law" – leaving nothing optional with the Creditor respecting choice of property, and being expressly contrary to the 4ᵗʰ· Article of the Treaty of Peace, and to the interests of the British Creditors, by that Article secured, that I conceived myself called upon by every principle of Duty to make representations against it. –

The printed copy of the Bill did not come from the Press until the day preceding that appointed for the second reading, which straitened me much in point of time to prepare the representations, of which, a perusal of the copy I have the honour to enclose, will afford too plain a proof; but as they would have been nugatory in any later stage of the business, not a moment was to be lost. I therefore prepared them in the form of a letter to the Governour, having been previously informed that this was the regular method, requesting they might be communicated to the Legislature. This he complied with the following morning; when, on the business of the day being entered upon, and my paper being begun to be read by the Clerk, the Member who brought in the Bill opposed the farther reading, on the principle that, there being no Commercial Treaty between Great Britain and the United States, I had not sufficient power to make Representations. – After some debate, it was carried that my letter should not be read, but that it might lie on the Table, for the information of the Members. –

The debates on this Bill continued two days, and at the close of the second, when the sense of the House was taken on the first clause, there appeared a majority of 44 against it. – I beg leave to inclose a copy of the Bill. – The Member who framed it, gave immediate notice that before the adjournment of the House, he would move for a resolve on the subject of my letter to the Governour. –

This he accordingly did on the 30$^{th.}$ Ulto. as follows; "Resolved, that no Consul residing in this State, has any power or authority to represent to this House, upon any Bill depending or passed the Legislature thereof." A long debate took place on this Resolve, most of the principal speakers insisting that my Representations having been made regularly through the Executive, they could not by any means be construed to influence the freedom of debate. – Others on the same side contended that however cautious Congress might have been in the manner of Recognizing my Commission, yet since it was received, and I was under the Orders of my Sovereign, whose instructions I professed to abide by, my Office would be a mere nullity, if the power were denied me of making representations against any measure which militated against an Article of the Treaty of Peace between the two Countries, or against the rights of His Majesty's subjects, which it was the express intention of my Office to protect. – The House decided against the Resolve, there being only 8 members in the affirmative, and near 100 against it.

This decision is not, however, satisfactory for it was urged, that although in making representations against the infringement of any Article of the Treaty of Peace, I acted strictly within the line of my Duty, Yet Great Britain having in the first instance, as it was said, suffered a Violation of it, in permitting Her Garrisons to take away Negroes without compensation, it lay with the House to determine what degree of respect ought to be paid to them. – Such fallacious arguments, only prove a desire in the people here, whenever it may conspire to their convenience, to make a handle of any thing to avoid a compliance with national Engagements. – I consider it my duty to give Your Lordship this particular account of what has recently passed in the Legislature on this subject, in order to enable Your Lordship to honour me with such Commands as You may think necessary to bring the business to a point, and by which it may be better and more clearly understood in future.

Both houses considering themselves pledged, by their having agreed to the report of the Committee, to adopt one of the modes of redress abovementioned, and the members possessed of the best principles conceiving, that an extension of the Instalment law would be attended with the least distress to the Creditors, that plan was preferred to a farther emission of paper Medium, and was accordingly passed into a Law, (copy of which I have the honor to inclose,) on the 4$^{th.}$ Instant, soon after which the Legislature adjourned to January next; but not before a Member gave notice, that he should, if elected, move for an emission of paper next Sessions, as the only means of giving ample relief, and of prosecuting some public schemes, now at a stand for want of means to carry them on.

Every legislative interference in contracts between individuals, is a disgraceful method of alleviating the real or supposed distress, of a people at large, and in the present instance bears exceedingly hard on British Creditors; yet I cannot help being of opinion, that of the three evils suggested, the one received will be the mildest in its effects, were it for no other reason than that, whenever the new Government is set in motion, and a federal Judicature is appointed, the Treaty of Peace being declared by the Constitution paramount to the Law of the land, the Judges will be constrained to admit and hear all causes brought under the 4$^{th.}$ Article of the Treaty, notwithstanding any partial State laws to the contrary, as the establishment of these Courts will operate as a repeal to such laws, as far as suitors under the Treaty are concerned. –

How long it may be before the Government of this Country shall have acquired a degree of efficacy sufficient to carry its constitution into force, I cannot pretend to judge, but until that is the case, much is the British Creditor to be pitied, whether claiming for debts secured by the Treaty, or contracted since, for little is to be expected from the integrity of individuals, and the present Government is too lax and feeble to carry the Laws into execution, even to the extent they are suffered to operate, which I have little doubt was one reason with many, for acceding to the extension of the Instalment law, as the probable means of preventing serious commotions in the Country.

·   ·   ·   ·   ·

Since the commencement of my Official duties here I have had many applications from British subjects for a passage to their native Country, the expence of which they were themselves unable to defray. – Some of these have been made by people who came out on speculation, with a view to settle here, but finding their expectations disappointed, were desirous to return; and others by Seamen, who from disability or sickness, could not obtain a passage by their labour. These poor people languish not only under the pressure of poverty, and sometimes disease, but are also exposed to a very inhospitable climate, all of which must, in a short time, put a period to lives, that in their own Country might be employed with advantage to the community. – As it is the cause of humanity; and as the return of these unhappy people, who would faithfully declare the failure of their delusive hopes, might have a strong effect in checking that spirit of emigration which prevails to a great degree in some parts of His Majesty's European Dominions, I take the liberty, with much deference, most earnestly to solicit Your Lordships Instructions, whether, and how far, I may be permitted to afford them the relief they petition for, and at what office the Masters of Merchant Vessels may apply for reimbursement of their passage money, none of His Majesty's ships or Packets ever calling here.

.   .   .   .   .

I have the honour to be, with the highest Respect, My Lord Your Lordships most obedient, and most humble Servant   Geo: Miller R, 17 Janry

PRO: FO 4/6, pp. 693-699 (LC transcription).

Peter Allaire: Occurrences
from 6 November to 3 December 1788

New York 3ᵈ· December 1788.

The Inhabitants of the frontier parts of South Carolina have raised by Voluntary Subscription a Troop of Horse of fifty Men Officers included, they took the field the 20ᵗʰ· last month, to protect themselves against the Indians, contrary to the express Orders of the late Congress, which forbad the Molesting of any of the Indian tribes, but the Carolinians alledge, their is no safety but in Arms.

The grand Treaty under Governor Sinclair is not yet concluded tho by the last Accounts, it will end to the satisfaction of all the Parties. like all other Treaties, while they are Drunk & Receive Presents, they are good friends, & the next day Enemies, I am fully convinced nothing but fear can keep them quiet.

Thomas Mifflin,[1] (one of our late Generals) is appointed to the Presedancy of Pensilvania, in the room of Doctor Franklin who declines fast into Childhood.

The States of South Carolina, Maryland, Virginia, Pensilvania, Jersey, & Connecticut have already Nominated their Senators and Assembly Men for the New federal Constitution, Boston & New York are in Session – North Carolina have called another Convention to Reconsider their late resolve in Rejecting the federal Constitution as Recommended by Congress, they are affraid of being left our of the Union.

Rhode Island puts the United States at defiance, they did on the 17th November, again Reject the Constitution, and refuse sending delegates to the New Government. the Voice of the People are still in favor of G: Washington, and Adams as Vice.

. . . . .

Trade brisk with England & Ireland, and the English West Indies, our produce very low, not having any Vent, we live in hopes that the New Constitution will be enabled to enlarge our Commerce.

Our friend & great & good Ally has shut Point Peter of Gaurdeloupe against us, and opened a paltry harbour instead thereof where there is not ten houses.

Van Beckle the Dutch Embassadore has purchased a farm in Jersey about 12 miles from this & is building; he expects his dismission, but I do not think he will return to Holland: the Report is, his Son is to be Consul

. . . . .

I Remain with Respect Sir Your VH Servt   P.A.

PRO: FO 4/6. pp. 653-657 (LC transcription).
  [1] Mifflin, Thomas (1744-1800). Pennsylvania merchant, military leader, political figure. Quartermaster General of the Continental Army, August 1775-March 1778. Member, Continental Congress, 1774-1775, 1782-1784; president, December 1783-June 1784. Member, Constitutional Convention, 1787. President, state supreme executive council, 1788-1790. Governor 1790-1799.

Thomas Jefferson to George Washington

Sir   Paris N̶o̶v̶. Dec. 4. 1788.
   Your favor of Aug. 31. came to hand yesterday; and a confidential conveiance offering by way of London, I avail myself of it to acknolege the receipt. I have seen, with infinite pleasure, our new constitution accepted by 11. states, not rejected by the 12th. and that the 13th. happens to be a state of the least importance. it is true that the minorities in most of the

accepting states have been very respectable, so much so as to render it prudent, were it not otherwise reasonable, to make some sacrifices to them. I am in hopes that the annexation of a bill of rights to the constitution will alone draw over so great a proportion of the minorities, as to leave little danger in the opposition of the residue; and that this annexation may be made by Congress and the assemblies, without calling a convention which might endanger the most valuable parts of the system. calculation has convinced me that circumstances may arise, and probably will arise, wherein all the resources of taxation may be necessary for the safety of the state. for tho I am decidedly of opinion we should take no part in European quarrels, but cultivate peace and commerce with all, yet who can avoid seeing the source of war in the tyranny of those nations who deprive us of the natural right of trading with our neighbors? the produce of the U.S. will soon exceed the European demand. what is to be done with the surplus, when there shall be one? it will be employed, without question, to open by force a market for itself with those placed on the same continent with us, and who wish nothing better. other causes too are obvious which may involve us in war; and war requires every resource of taxation & credit. <*> the power of making war often prevents it <*>, and in our case would give efficacy to our desire of peace. if the new government wears the front which I hope it will I see no impossibility in the availing ourselves of ~~in time of war~~ the wars of others to open the other parts of America to our commerce, as the price of our neutrality.

. . . . .

Your communications to the Count de Moustier, whatever they may have been, cannot have done injury to my endeavors here to open the W. Indies to us. on this head the ministers are invincibly mute, tho' I have often tried to draw them into the subject. I have therefore found it necessary to let it lie till war or other circumstances may force it on. whenever they are in war with England, they must open the islands to us, and perhaps during that war they may see some price which might make them agree to keep them always open. in the mean time I have laid my shoulder to the opening the markets of this country to our produce, and rendering it's transportation a nursery for our seamen. a maritime force is the only one by which we can act on Europe. our navigation law (if it be wise to have any) should be the reverse of that of England. instead confining *importations* to home bottoms or those of the *producing* nation, I think we should confine *exportations* to home bottoms or to those of nations *having treaties with us.* our exportations are heavy, and would nourish a great force of our own, or be a tempting price to the nation to whom we should offer a participation of it in exchange for free access to all their possessions. <*> this is an object to which our government alone is adequate in the [gross]. but I have ventured to pursue it here, so far as the consumption of our productions by this country extends. thus in our arrangements relative to tobacco, none can be received here but in French or American bottoms. this is emploiment for near 2000 seamen, and puts nearly that number of British out of employ. by the arret of Dec. 1787. it was provided that our whale oils should not be received here but in French or American bottoms, and by later regulations all oils but those of France and America are excluded. this will put 100 English whale vessels immediatly out of employ, and 150. ere long: and call so many of French & American into service. we have had 6000 seamen formerly in this business, the whole of whom we have been likely to lose. the consumption of rice is growing fast in this country, and that of Carolina gaining ground on every other kind. I am of opinion the whole of Carolina rice can be consumed here. it's transportation employs 2500 sailors, almost all of them English at present. the rice being deposited at Cowes & brought from thence here. it would be dangerous to confine this transportation to French & American bottoms the ensuing year, because they will be much engrossed by the transportation of wheat & flour hither, and the crop of rice might lie on hand for want of vessels: but I see no objections to the extension of our principle to this article also, beginning with the year 1790....I...assure you of the sentiments of sincere attachment and respect with which I have the honor to be your Excellency's most obed^t. humble servant   Th: Jefferson

LC: *Washington Papers, microfilm reel 98* (ALS).

Arret of the King's Council of State Regarding American Whale Oil

7th. December 1788

Extract from the Registers of the Council of State.

The King having taken information on the Arret pronounced in his Council the 28th December last, prohibiting the importation of Whale Oil and Spermaceti the produce of foreign fisheries into the Kingdom, observing, that Oil made from Sea Calves & other Fish & sea animals not being comprehended in the said Arret, a fraudulent importation of Whale Oil might take place under the name of the aforesaid oils & that on the other hand it might be inferred from the tenor of the said arret that oils the produce of the fisheries of the U.S. were prohibited and His Majesty wishing to remove every doubt on this Head. To provide therefore for the same, having heard the report of the Sieur Lambert Counsellor of State in ordinary & of the Council of Despatches, & Royal Council of Finances & Commerce; The King being present in his Council has ordained & does ordain, that, reckoning from the 1ˢᵗ day of April next, Oil made from Sea Calves & from fish & other Sea animals produced from foreign Fisheries, as well as Whale bone produced in like manner from the said Foreign Fisheries, shall be prohibited from importation into the Kingdom, without permitting the said prohibition nevertheless to extend either to the said kinds of Oils or to the said Whale Oils & Spermaceti or the Whale bone produced from the Fisheries of the Uᵈ States of America, & imported directly into France in French Vessels or those belonging to the Subjects of the said Uᵈ States, which shall continue to be provisionally admitted agreable to the 1ˢᵗ· & 3ᵈ· Articles of the Arret of the 29ᵗʰ· of December last, on condition however that the Captains of the said Vessels belonging to the Uᵈ States bring with them certificates from the Consuls of France residing in the Ports of the said United States, or where these cannot be obtained, from the Magistrates of the places where the embarkation of the said Oil shall be made, for the purpose of proving that the Cargo of the said Vessels is the Produce of the Fisheries carried on by the Citizens of the Uᵈ States which certificates shall be presented to the Officers of the Admiralty also to the Commissioners of the Farms in the ports of France where it shall be landed; to be mentioned in the Report of their arrival. His Majesty commands & orders the Duke de Penthievre, Admiral of France, the Intendants & Commissaries throughout the provinces, the Commissary appointed to observe the Ordinances of the Admiralty, the Officers of the Admiralty, Masters of Ports, Judges of treaties, & all others whom it may concern, to assist in the execution of the present Arret, which shall be registered in the offices of the said Admiralties, read, published & posted wherever it may appear necessary.

Done in the King's Council of State His Majesty being present held at Versailles the 7ᵗʰ of Decʳ· 1788.   La Luzerne

·   ·   ·   ·   ·

Faithfully translated from the original by John Pintard.

NA: PCC, item 87, v. 2, pp. 426-427 (translation); M247, reel 115.

James Madison to Thomas Jefferson

Dear Sir   Philadelphia Decʳ· 8. 1788.

·   ·   ·   ·   ·

...Moutier proves a most unlucky ap[point]ment. He is unsocial proud and niggardly and betrays a sort of fastidiousness toward this country. He suffers also from his illicit connection with Madame de Brehan[1] which is universally known and offensive to American manners. she is perfectly soured toward this country. The ladies of New York (a few within the official circle excepted) have for some time withdrawn their attentions from her. she knows the cause is deeply stung by it views every thing thro the medium of rancor and conveys her impressions to her paramour over whom she exercises despotic sway. Latterly their time < * > has [been] chiefly spent in [travelling]. The first vis[it] was to an indian treaty at Fort Schuyler and thence to the Oneida town. The next to Boston and thence to N. Hampshire. The last to Mount Vernon from which they but lately returned. On their journeys it is said they often neglect the most obvious precautions for veiling their intimacy. – At Boston he imprudently suffered etiquette to prevent even an interview with governor Hancock. The inhabitants taking part with the governor neither visited or invited the count. They were the less apprehensive of a misinterpretation < ** > of the neglect as the most cordial intercourse had just preceded between the town and the French squadron. Both the count and the marchioness are particularly unpopular among their countrymen here. Such of them as are not under restraint make very free remarks and are anxious for a new diplomatic arrangement. It is but right to add to these particulars, that there is reason to believe that unlucky impressions were made on the count at his first [arrival] probably by dela forest the Consul a cunning disciple I take it of marbois' politics and by something in his communications with Jay which he considered as the effect of coldness and sourness toward France....

    .   .   .   .   .

With the sincerest affection & the highest esteem I am Dear Sir yrs.

              Js. Madison Jr.

    .   .   .   .   .

LC: *Madison Papers, microfilm reel 3 (ALS).*
 [1] *Bréhan, Marquise de. Sister-in-law of Comte de Moustier, who accompanied him to the United States allegedly to improve her feeble health and to oversee the education of her son. The Marquis de Bréhan, an army officer, was required to remain at his post; William Short described him as an old gentleman and hard of hearing.*

Arthur St. Clair to John Jay

Sir   Fort Harmar Dec.ʳ 13.ᵗʰ 1788
 I have received Information from Detroit, which I depend upon, that a certain Coll.ˡ Conolly,[1] who came to that place, < * > from Quebec, last

Winter has, not long ago set out for Louisville at the rapids of the Ohio –
he is the Conolly that made himself pretty remarkable during the progress
of the Revolution and was appointed a Lieut.ᵗ· Collonel in one of the
Refugee Corps – he is upon the half pay List, and has lately obtained from
Lord Dorchester an addition of two hundred pounds Sterling pᵉʳ Annum,
and his Expences. The Reason he assigned, at Detroit for his Journey to
Louisville was that he might obtain Certificates of the value of his Property
in that Country which had been confiscated in order to support the Claim
he had made upon the british Government for Compensation. My Information is, that he is sent to tamper with the People of Kentucky and
induce them to throw themselves into the Arms of Great Britain, and to
assure them of protection and Support in that Measure – if that cannot be
brought about, to stimulate them to Hostilities against the Spaniards, and
at rate to detach them from the united States. I have written to Major
Wyllis, who commands at the Rapids, informing him of those Circumstances, and requesting him to have an Eye upon him and, if he finds him
either exciting a Revolt, or tempting the People to Hostilities against
Spain, to make him a Prisoner, and to send him to this Post, with a
transcript of the Testimony against him, and the Names of the Persons who
will support it, that they may be forwarded together to You. I know of no
other Officer of the United States Sir, who could with propriety take
Cognizance of it, but if in that I am mistaken, you will please to inform me
to whom he should be sent in case he should be apprehended. The Offence
I have no doubt is Treasonable, but whether we have any Laws to punish
Treason against the united States, I doubt very much even in that Case as
the Country is within the Limits of Virginia, it will be Treason against that
State, and there he might be punished for it. Since his Arrival at Louisville
he gives out that he has discovered some Flaw in the Act of Assembly, and
means to attempt the recovery of his Estate by a Course of Law, and as that
will detain him in the Country, he has hired a House and taken up his
Residence. It is certain Sir, that in their last Convention, a proposal was
made that the District of Kentucky should set up for itself, not only as
independant of Virginia but of the united States also and was rejected by
a small Majority only – it may possibly be that Overtures have been made
to Lord Dorchester; but it cannot be that my Lord would make Conolly
such an Allowance, or indeed any Allowance for looking after his property
and to bring on a Claim upon his Nation. Conally has also been writing to
many People about Pittsburgh and in that Country, and has intimated an
intention to visit that Place this Winter, and I have heard has opened
himself pretty freely to General Morgan² of Winchester in Virginia – All
there Circumstances put together make it more than probable that he is an
Agent of the British for some sinister purpose – If any other Measures than

those I have directed ought to be pursued, you will oblige me by pointing them out, and they shall be executed without delay.

After the tedious Expectation that has attended the proposed Treaty with the Indians there is now a prospect of its soon beginning, indeed in a few days, as they are now within two short days Journey – it will not however be a very general meeting as Brant,[3] who is also a british Pensioner at four hundred pounds Sterling p^r Annum after coming within sixty Miles of Us, is gone back to Detroit, and has taken with him the whole of the Mohawks, and a part of some other Tribes of the five Nations, and it is to be feared will also prevail with the Shawanese and the western People who were within two days Journey of him, on their way here, to return with him likewise – I do not however consider that as any great Misfortune, because I believe the Consequences will be the Dissolution of the general Confederacy which he and the british have taken so much Pains to form, and hope to be able [to] keep the Frontiers of New York, Pennsylvania and the upper part of Virginia in Peace this Winter – No Treaty I believe will secure the lower frontier of that State at present: If that, and the Possession and Sale of the western Territory is an Object with Congress they must prepare to chastise the western Nations seriously as early in the Summer as possible – The Depredations they commit upon the Inhabitants is intolerable – and it is not confined now to the Inhabitants – they have had the audacity to fall upon the Parties escorting Provisions to the Posts; and those Posts are so weak, so distant from each other, and supplied with so much difficulty that they will either fall into their Hands or be abandoned for want of Provisions, if things remain upon the Foot – It is to be feared that the Indians, at the same Time, will not want for assistance from the British – and it is pretty evident that People have no thought of surrendering the Posts they hold within the Territory of the united States, for Lord Dorchester, who visited them himself this last Summer, has ordered the Town at Detroit to be picketted in, < * > which is compleated, and additional Works to be constructed there, and a Fort they call Castle St Clair, on the american side of the Strait between the Lake of that Name and the Huron, which had been begun during the War and abandoned at the Peace, to be compleated.

It was always my Fear that our western Territory, instead of proving a Fund for paying the national Debt, would be a Source of Mischief and encreasing Expence – but the Expence is not the worst part of it – It has given such a Spring to the Spirit of Emigration, too high before that tho' it is pregnant with the most serious Consequences to the Atlantic States, it cannot now be held back – and the Spaniards are also trying to turn that Spirit, with great Industry, to their Advantage – so that those States not only lose their People and sink the value of their Soil for the present but are laying the foundation of the Greatness of a rival Country. It is a considerable time that the Spaniards have been offering a thousand Acres of Land gratis, to every American who would remove into west Florida – to pay him ten Dollars for every hundred weight of Tobacco he could raise and deliver at New Orleans ~~and~~ an exemption from all Taxes and a proportionate price for Provisions and other Articles the produce of his Farm but they have lately gone a step farther. – If I am well informed Coll⁺ Morgan,[4] who was lately in Treaty with the Board of Treasury for a Tract of Land on the Mississippi, has obtained of Mʳ· Gardoqui a Grant of a very large Tract upon the spanish side opposite to the mouth of the Ohio, which he engages to settle with Americans – they are to have the same Priviledges with those whose remove into Florida – He is now at Fort Pitt, and it is supposed will carry a good many People from that Country – upon Kentucky is however his chief Dependence, for in that Quarter are many Thousands of People who have been tempted by the Accounts published of its amazing fertility to quit their ancient Settlements without having secured a foot of Land there and cannot obtain Lands, but at a Price that is beyond their reach – There is no doubt many of those will readily join him, for they have no Country, and indeed that Attachment to the *natale Solum*[5] that has been so powerful and active a Principle in other Countries is very little felt in America. – I have been casting about for some way to counteract Mʳ· Morgan, and I cannot think of any so likely to succeed, as for Congress to change the mode of disposing of the western Lands in large Tracts – at least to change it for a part of them and lay them open to be taken up by People who settle upon them – The Country upon the Mississippi and between that and the Wabash, would accommodate the People of Kentucky who have no Land, and I believe it would tempt them to remove to it, rather than the spanish side, and it might be disposed of in the manner the Proprietors of Pennsylvania sold the Lands they last purchased of the Indians – It was thus – The Lands were set at five Pounds Sterling pʳ· hundred Acres – no more than three hundred Acres were allowed to be taken up by one Man – he made a Description in writing of the Peice he wanted, bounding it either upon Lands already granted, or some Creek or River, or marked Trees that rendered it sufficiently certain, and carried it to the Office of the Surveyor Genᴸ where it was entered in a Book kept for the purpose – The Surveyor General issued an order for making the Survey, returnable within a certain time to his Office and the Applicant took Possession – The purchase Money run upon Interest from the date of the order of Survey – and was discharged when it was in the Persons power, tho' to make them more industrious a time was fixed within which the Patents should be taken out, but no Advantage was ever taken of their overpassing that time – On the payment of principal and interest the Patent issued – I believe there is not an instance, tho' it was a very extensive Country, at least the Instances are few, where the Patents have not been taken out, and all the Land good and bad has been sold – Altho this mode would not so suddenly extinguish any part of the Debt as that now in Use, yet an Interest equal to the Interest of the Debt as far as the Lands went, would be accruing to the united States, and the principal would come in at last, and the People, who are of infinite value, that will otherwise be worse than lost, will be secured – the present Inhabitants of that Country, when they see it gathering strength by the accession of new Inhabitants will be more inclined to remain in it – The Spaniards are also at work with them to induce them to abandon it, and have succeeded with many of them. Excuse me Sir for troubling you with my Ideas on the Subject – they are crude Ideas, but you will improve upon them and perfect them, if they deserve any attention – the Subject is, in my Opinion an interesting one to the united States.

The Spaniard has also been making Seizures upon the east side of the Mississippi within the Territory of the united States. General Harmar, some time ago, transmitted to the War Office, the Complaint of a Mʳ· McIntosh,[6] and I now enclose you the Deposition of a Monsieur de Sᵗ· Marie on a Like Occasion, and extracts from a Letter of Major Hamtramack the Commandant at Post Sᵗ· Vincennes of the 13ᵗʰ· of October to Genˡ· Harmar.

I ought Sir to beg pardon for troubling you with so long a Letter but I cannot put an end to it without requesting you to present my best Respects to Mʳˢ· Jay, and to believe that I Am with the greatest Respect and Esteem Sir Your most obedient Servant   Aʳ· Sᵗ· Clair

15th. I have mentioned Extracts from Majʳ· Hamtramack's Letter but you will find but one – the other which respects some Depredations and the Murder of some friendly Indians, has been enclosed by Genˡ Harmar in his Despatches to the Secʳʸ· at War, and I have not now time to get another made out.

The Treaty with the Indians is opened, and as far as we have yet gone looks well.

NA: PCC, item 150, v. 3, pp. 509-516 (ALS); M247, reel 165.

¹ Connolly, John (c. 1750-?). Land speculator and loyalist. Held Virginia land grants near Pittsburgh at outbreak of Revolutionary War. Took part in Dunmore's War (1774) as Virginia militia officer, but forced to leave Pittsburgh when his loyalist views became clear. Agent of Lord Dunmore, with commission as lieutenant colonel, to capture Pittsburgh and reconquer Virginia, 1775-1776. After capture in Maryland, imprisoned, 1776-1780. Sent to serve under Cornwallis, 1781. Captured at Yorktown. Released, March 1782, on condition that he leave for England. Spent time in Kentucky, late 1780s,

and plotted to seize New Orleans and gain control of the Mississippi, late 1790s, but without result.

[2] Morgan, Daniel (1736-1802). Military officer, frontiersman. As wagoner, delivered supplies to Virginia frontier posts. Served as officer in Pontiac's War and Dunmore's War. Raised two companies of riflemen for service at Boston, 1775. With Arnold's expedition to Quebec, 1775, where he was captured. Commissioned colonel upon release, and raised a corps of sharpshooters which earned high praise in the Saratoga campaign. Resigned, July 1779, but recalled to service in 1780. Promoted to brigadier general and given command of troops in western North Carolina. Won Battle of Cowpens, January 17, 1781, after which ill health forced his retirement. Commanded Virginia militia in suppression of Whiskey Rebellion, 1794. Extensive land holdings on the Monongahela and Ohio Rivers. Member, U.S. House of Representatives, 1797-1799.

[3] Brant, Joseph (1742-1807). Mohawk chief. Closely linked to Sir William Johnson and to Guy Johnson, British superintendents of Indian affairs, and secretary of the latter. Sought to persuade the Iroquois to aid the British in the Revolution. Given a captain's commission and sent to England, where he was presented at court. Led Indian raids in the Mohawk Valley, southern New York, and northern Pennsylvania. Failed to reach settlement with the United States after the war, but persuaded Governor Haldimand to assign the Mohawks land in Canada. Visited England again in 1785 to obtain funds to indemnify the Iroquois for wartime losses and to buy new lands. Again failed to reach settlement with the United States, but successfully opposed attempts of land speculators to buy up Mohawk lands.

[4] Morgan, George (1743-1810). Land speculator and Indian agent. A trader in the Illinois country before the Revolution, he became secretary-general of the Indiana Company and superintendent of its land office at Ft. Pitt, in 1776. During the Revolutionary War, U.S. Indian agent in the middle department and deputy commissary-general of purchases for the western department, with rank of colonel. Resigned, 1779. As gentleman-farmer, dabbled in scientific research, notably the life of the Hessian fly. With the support of Don Diego de Gardoqui, founded colony of New Madrid in Spanish Louisiana, now Missouri, 1789.

[5] native soil

[6] Not further identified.

Comte de Moustier to Comte de Montmorin

[Translation]

N[o.] 28.

My Lord.

New York, 25 Dec. 1788.

The revolution that has taken place in the form of the Government of the United States will doubtless not produce, at least not immediately, all the effects that have been expected from it by the party that has been distinguished by the name of Federalist, after the principal objective which it appeared to pursue, which was to form a real Union or a true consolidation among all the States, which were *confederated* States rather than *united* States. But whatever may be the consequences that may result from it, they appear perhaps sufficiently important to merit the complete attention of the King and of his Council. I therefore thought it my duty to consider it in all its aspects and to submit to You the results of my reflections. I have divided this work into two memoranda that I have the honor to send You enclosed herewith.

Nᵒ· 1. *The first* is relative *to the probable consequences of the establishment of the new Government with regard to the internal administration of the United States.* Although this question may be irrelevant to us up to a certain point, it appeared to me indispensable to discuss it in detail in order better to fathom the principles that should serve as the basis for examining the *relations of the new Government of the United States with foreign Powers.* The consideration of those relations is the object of the *second* Memorandum.

Nᵒ· 2. The great distance at which I find myself, My Lord, and the difficulty of providing clarifications on several points that might appear doubtful or obscure have obliged me to elaborate on subordinate questions that might be considered superfluous. But I preferred to expose myself to this inconvenience than to neglect a single remark that circumstances might perhaps render interesting.

The new Congress will infallibly regard a close alliance with whatever European Nation will offer it the most resources as one of the principal means of consolidating its authority. There are only two that can attract its attention from this point of view: *France* and *England*: and events may take place that force it to choose between these two Powers. If it decides for our rivals, the object of the war that we undertook solely to detach the United States from Great Britain would be entirely lost, and the *free* Americans would become for us Enemies much more dangerous than the American *Colonists* ever were. In promoting the American revolution, we would have worked against ourselves. – If, on the other hand, these States were closely linked to France, there would result inestimable advantages, which I think I have fully explained in Memorandum *Nᵒ 2.* – But the alternative appears inevitable in any case; the political and unusual situation of Congress will incline it to depend heavily on a foreign Alliance, and if we wait for the event of a war, it will probably be too late to derive any advantage from the Americans, their plan will be formed, England will have taken measures to make use of them by agreement or by force.

It is thus, My Lord, in the firmest persuasion of the utility, the importance, and even the most indispensable necessity of completely dedicating to us the collective body of the United States that I have the honor to submit to You the reflections enclosed herewith. Whatever the point of view from which one wishes to consider these States, no inconvenience can result from the measures that His Majesty will take to strengthen and consolidate their new Government, while indifference will inevitably be a source of the most alarming misfortunes. The sacrifices that it will be necessary to make in order always to have a great majority of Congress on our side are very modest when they are compared to the advantages that could be obtained. The Sums employed in *Politics* will infallibly return, and with interest, through *Commerce*, and as I have had occasion to observe, circumstances will present themselves in which an expense incurred opportunely can be regarded as a real economy.

In order to complete the work that I had intended to do on our relations with the United States, I thought I should enclose Memorandum N° 3 *concerning His Majesty's financial Credit.*

I hope, My Lord, that You will render sufficient justice to my Zeal to be convinced that the observations that I thought I should make regarding the conduct and the full powers of His Majesty's Minister Plenipotentiary or Ambassador are exempt from all personal views, and that I have had as my object only the success of the Negotiations with which he may be charged and the advantage of having a constant and irresistible influence in all the Councils of the United States.

I am with respect My Lord Your most humble and most obedient servant,

Le Cte· de Moustier.

FFAA: Pol. Corr., U.S., v. 33, f. 385-385vo. (LC transcription).

Marquise de Bréhan to Thomas Jefferson

Newyork December the 29th 1788.

Since a long time, Sir, I wish'd to find an opportunity to recall myself to your remembrance, but our travels into the interior part of your country, the suppression of our packets, the want of information when some vessels were going to France (for the most time we learn it at the very moment of their departure;) all these reasons have deprived me of the pleasure of giving you new assurances of my tender friendship. I regret sincerely, your society here, every body in the United States does not think like you, in general they are not fond of candor, simplicity and goodness; I had but those qualifications to offer them, they were not sufficient. You thought that I would be loved by your country men – how much you have been deceived! I see very few Gentlemen and still less Ladies. They have been too *exigents* for my health. I am not able to spend my life in paying visits; it is not possible. Two, or three Ladies are more indulgent and come sometimes without keeping accounts. when Mr Madisson is in Newyork, he comes in a friendly way to visit us, but I do not know if we shall see him in the new Congress; he has not been chosen for one of the Senators; not because he is not the proper man and wanting merits to be elected, but because he is a *federalist*; an excellent reason to which there is no reply.

We have had the pleasure to see Gal Washington at Mountvernon, it is not necessary to tell you, Sir, how much we have been pleased with his person and his settlement, every thing there, is enchanting. In going to Virginia, we had formed a plan to see Monticello, the naturel bridge, and Richmond; but the season was too far advanced, and we had so much suffer'd from the cold in going, that we were obliged to return quickly. we are in hopes to be able to pay a second visit to Virginia next year and to see all the curiosities of that Country.

I pray you, Sir, to give me some particulars about yourself when you will have an opportunity to write to our new world; we are without news from your old one, since eight months; this privation is very distressing. I expect from you some pity and the continuation of your esteem and friendship.[1]

.   .   .   .   .

LC: *Jefferson Papers, microfilm reel 10 (AL).*
[1] *Most of the remainder of this letter was written by the Comte de Moustier.*

Phineas Bond to Lord Carmarthen

My Lord,   Philad^a· Jan. 4th· 1789.
I have the honor of forwarding to your Ldp., letters for the R^t· Hon. the Lords Comm^rs of the Admiralty and for the Hon: the Comm^rs of his Majesty's customs in England and in Scotland, enclosing ship's papers which have been deposited in my hands for the purpose of being transmitted.

The beneficial effects of the new regulations of trade my Lord can not perhaps be better manifested than by the returning British vessels, which constantly enter the ports of the United States; and almost wholly engross the carrying trade of this country: – In the course of the year 1788 no less than 215 sail of British vessels (whose tonnage amounted to upwards of 27000 tons) entered the single port of Philad^a; and I should presume a proportionate number entered other large ports on this continent, particularly Charles Town and New York.

Tho' frauds are still practiced to evade these regulations, and will continue to be practiced as long as the temptation is so powerful, the use of false papers by vessels belonging to this port is by no means so common as heretofore: but some very loose practices prevail, my Lord, in the repairing British vessels, the comparative cheapness of timber and of work being strong inducements to evade the provisions of the new act of Navigation: In the article of repairs the Act seems open to evasion, – by confining the oath of the extent of the damage sustained, and the time of sustaining it to the master of the vessel alone; whereas by requiring the persons who are approved of as surveyors to make oath of their belief as to the probable time the damage was sustained, and the value of the repairs necessary for the safety of the vessel, the intention of the Act would be more likely to be effected.

Repairs may, by connivance with the persons who survey the vessel, be easily brought within the sum limited by the Act, or when the repairs are obviously of such an extent as to exceed in value the limited sum, the master then complies with the requisites prescribed by the Act by swearing the repairs necessary to be made were incurred in consequence of damage sustained in the *last* voyage: – the new Act as it now stands merely calls for this oath from the *master;* – the delivery in writing of the particulars of the damage and the amount of the necessary repairs is all that is required of those who survey. Whereas if their returns were to be sanctioned by an oath on their part, they having neither convenience or interest to influence them it is more probable the real truth of the case would be ascertained, and undue collusions defeated.

Having reason to believe such collusions have been practiced here in repairing vessels whose damage has been the effect of gradual decay and not of recent injury (tho' I have not been able to discover the fraud with certainty) I take the liberty of suggesting these remarks to your Ldp's consideration, as a probable means of providing against future frauds. With sentiments of the most perfect respect, I have the honor to be, my Lord, your Ldp's Most faith: and most obed: servant,   P. Bond.
R. Feb. 4[th.]

AHA 1896, v. 1, pp. 591-592.

Lord Carmarthen to Phineas Bond

Sir,   Whitehall Jan[ry.] [7] 1789.
Your Letters dated the 4th of last Month arrived this Morning, and I would not defer acknowledging the Receipt of them by the Mail of Today as the very clear and able Manner in which you have expressed yourself both with regard to the beneficial Effects of the last Act for the Regulation of Trade and the precarious Situation of the United States with respect to the Formation of a Permanent Constitution, appears to be very deserving of my entire Approbation. If however the New Constitution should finally

be adopted, it appears to me to be very proper that you should present your Commission as His Majesty's Commissary for all Commercial Affairs for Approbation & I am persuaded You will not omit any thing which may be in Your Power to promote the Interests of those Persons who have just Claims on the Subjects of the United States.

. . . . . .

Carmarthen

PRO: FO 4/7, pp. 31-32, 34 (LC transcription).

Sir John Temple to Lord Carmarthen

N$^{o.}$ 40.   New York 7 January 1789
My Lord

. . . . .

I have not yet been able to Obtain, as I expected, the Opinion & Sentiments of the Agricultural Society at Philadelphia concerning the Hessian Fly further mentioned in your Lordships last letter upon that Subject, its delay I apprehend to be from the Absence of Col^o Morgan a principal man in that Society, & who Obligingly furnished me with the Remarks & Observations contained in my letter to your Lordship of the 4$^{th.}$ of Sep$^r.$ Col$^{o.}$ Morgan is at present down the Missisippi engaged in some concern with Mr Gardoqui the Spanish Minister here! but he is expected to return very soon, when I hope to have his further Opinion, with that of the Philadelphia Society, concerning the Hessian Fly, & the Virginia wheat fly.

The Spaniards have lately adopted a Policy which probably will be beneficial to them, they now give great encouragement, by Grants of Lands &c^a, to respectable people of *property* in these states, as well as to common settlers, to become Inhabitans & cultivators, upon that River, down almost to their own settlements! Col$^{o.}$ Morgan is become one of them, others of consequence & importance are also going from several of the states.

I have the honor to remain with all deference & respect, My Lord, Your Lordships most faithful, and Obedient Servant   J. Temple
R. 4$^{th:}$ Febry.

PRO: FO 4/7, pp. 19-20, 22 (LC transcription).

Thomas Jefferson to John Jay

Sir   Paris. Jan. 11. 1789.

. . . . .

Since writing mine of Nov. 29. yours of the 23$^{d.}$ of September came to
hand. as the General of the Mathurins was to be employed in the final
redemption of our captives, I thought that their previous support had better
be put into his hands and conducted by himself in such a way as not to
counterwork his plan of redemption, whenever we can enable him to begin
on it. I gave him full powers as to the amount and manner of subsisting
them. he has undertaken it, informing me at the same time that it will be
on a very low scale, to avoid suspicion of it's coming from the public. he
spoke of but 3. sous a day per man, as being sufficient for their physical
necessaries, more than which he thinks it not adviseable to give. I have no
definitive answer yet from our bankers whether we may count on the whole
million last agreed to be borrowed, but I have no doubt of it, from other
information, tho I have not their formal affirmative. the gazettes of Leyden
& France to this date accompany this. I have the honour to be with sentiments of the most perfect esteem & repect, Sir, your most obedient & most
humble servant   Th: Jefferson

NA: PCC, *item 87, v. 2, pp. 400-407 (ALS); M247, reel 115.*

∞   *Peace with the Algerines*   ∞

*Release of the Americans held captive in Algiers was long in coming.
Early in 1792, Congress appropriated funds to pay for the negotiation of
a peace, and on June 1, John Paul Jones was appointed envoy to treat for
peace and U.S. consul at Algiers. Thomas Pinckney, who was sailing to
Europe to serve as U.S. Minister to Great Britain, took charge of the
commissions and instructions for the Algiers mission. Upon his arrival in
England, he learned that Jones had died in Paris on July 18. Pinckney had
the authority to turn the mission over to Thomas Barclay if Jones could
not serve; unfortunately, Barclay died in Lisbon on January 19, 1793,
while preparing to embark for Algiers.
Congress then appointed Colonel David Humphreys to undertake the
mission to Algiers. Various delays kept Humphreys from reaching Gibraltar*

until the autumn of 1793. In the meantime, Charles Logie, the British Consul at Algiers, succeeded in negotiating a truce in the war between Algiers and Portugal under Great Britain's guarantee. The Portuguese navy, which had protected American merchantmen, no longer was there to do so. Word of the truce had barely reached Iberian ports when Algerine corsairs sailed past the straits, capturing over a hundred American citizens. The Dey of Algiers refused to negotiate with Humphreys, who at once dispatched a vessel to the United States to warn potential victims of the altered situation.

One consequence of the renewed Algerine depredations was the passage of legislation in the spring of 1794 that authorized the construction of four 44-gun and two 36-gun frigates, the first vessels of the new U.S. Navy. On July 19, 1794, Humphreys was authorized to expend $800,000 to obtain peace with Algiers and to ransom the American prisoners there. However, he soon learned from Richard O'Brien that the Dey of Algiers had set the price of peace and ransom at $2,435,000.

Humphreys, who had little desire to continue the mission to Algiers, returned to the United States late in 1794. However, he was prevailed upon to continue, and given additional instructions to proceed to France to secure French government assistance in the negotiations, and to employ Joseph Donaldson, Jr., the U.S. Consul-designate at Tunis and Tripoli, as his agent at Algiers. Humphreys and Donaldson left the United States in April 1795, and Donaldson reached Algiers on September 3.

Thereafter, events proceeded quickly, accompanied by extensive discussions over price and how the funds would be apportioned among the Algerine recipients. On September 5, an agreement was reached by which the United States agreed to pay $642,500 in cash for peace and ransom, plus an annual tribute of $21,600 in naval stores. Richard O'Brien took the treaty to Humphreys in Lisbon for his approval, then proceeded to London in order to collect the cash from Barings Bank.

Unfortunately, the bank was unable to supply the necessary cash. O'Brien returned without the funds, which incensed the Dey. In an effort to placate the Algerine ruler, Joel Barlow,[1] who was assisting Humphreys in the mission, gathered up suitable presents in France and hastened to Algiers. A promise of the additional present of a 36-gun frigate and a larger-than-usual present for the Dey upon the arrival of the first U.S. consul saved the treaty. Barlow also managed to borrow the necessary cash to pay the American obligation to the Dey.

In March 1796, the United States government ratified the treaty with Algiers. That same month, the Americans held captive in Algiers boarded a vessel bound for Marseilles and freedom.

¹ Barlow, Joel (1754-1812). *Poet and diplomat. Contributed to* The Anarchiad, *1786. Author,* The Vision of Columbus, *1787. Land agent of the Scioto Company in France, 1788-1789. Lived as writer in London, 1790-1792; his* Advice to the Privileged Orders *(1792) was suppressed, and he himself proscribed by the British government. Closely associated with Thomas Paine in publication of* The Age of Reason. *Warmly received in revolutionary France, where wise investments made him rich. U.S. Consul at Algiers, 1796-1797; also participated in negotiation of treaties with Tunis and Tripoli. Returned to America, 1805, and published* The Columbiad, *1807. U.S. Minister to France, 1811-1812.*

Jacques Necker to Thomas Jefferson

Sir   Versailles 11$^{th.}$ January 1789
    I have the honor to send you a copy of the Arret which has just been returned to the Council to Explain the one of the 28$^{th.}$ of September last, to except from the prohibitions therein contained, Whale bone, Whale, Spermaceti & Fish Oil arising from the Fisheries of the U^d States of America & imported into France in Vessels belonging to the Subjects of the U^d States or France. These Articles, will continue to be entered, as heretofore, agreable to the dispositions of the Arret of the 29$^{th.}$ December last, that is to say subject to the duty of 7 livres 10$^{s.}$ per Barrel of Oil weighing 520$^{lb.}$ & 6 livres 13$^{s.}$ 4$^{d.}$ per quintal of Whale Bone and Ten sols per livre (over and above both duties) which shall cease on the last of December 1790. His Majesty is always disposed to favor as far as possible the commerce of the United States, but he is bound to give a preference to the national Commerce, & it would be contrary to the spirit of justice which inspires him, were he to allow the importation of Foreign Oils, whenever the national Fishery shall be adequate to the supply of the Kingdom. For this reason therefore His Majestys wisdom could only permit a provisional importation of American Oil & Whale bone untill the national Fishery is capable of supplying the wants of France. But the U^d States are sufficiently acquainted with the equity which regulates all his Majestys inclinations, to be persuaded that whenever the national oils shall be sufficient for the consumption of the Kingdom the American Oil & Whale bone which shall be found embarked at the time of that revocation

shall be admitted into France untill it shall be known in America & he has charged me to acquaint you with it.

I make no doubt but that the U^d States of America will consider this decision of His Majesty as a fresh proof of his desire to keep up the most intimate connexion between the two nations & to give proofs thereof; & on their part he expects they will ~~use every~~ add to the precautions prescribed by this arret, such as may be in their power to prevent the fraudulent importation of Foreign Oil & Whale bone under the name of American.

I have the honor to be with sincere Attachment Sir Your most hum^e· & m^o· ob^d Servant.   Necker.

Faithfully translated from the Original by John Pintard.

NA: PCC, item 87, v. 2, pp. 416-417 (translation); M247, reel 115.

Thomas Jefferson to John Jay

Sir   Paris Jan. 14. 1789.

In my letter of the 11th· I have said nothing of the Arret explanatory of that of Sep. 28. on the subject of whale oils, which my letter of Nov. 19. gave you reason to expect. tho this explanatory arret has been passed so long ago as the 7th· of December it has not been possible for me to obtain an authentic copy of it till last night. I now inclose that to you with a copy of a letter to me from M^r· Necker on the subject. the reception of our oils in the mean time is provided for by an intermediate order. you will observe that in the Arret it is said to be passed "provisoirement," and that mr Necker expressly holds up to us, in his letter, a repeal whenever the national fishery supplies their wants. the Arret however is not limited in it's duration, and we have several chances against it's repeal. it may be questioned whether mr Necker thinks the fishery worth the expence. it may be well questioned whether, with or without encouragement, the nation whose navigation is the least economical of all in Europe, can ever succeed in the whale fishery which calls for the most rigorous economy. it is hoped that a share in the legislation will pass immediately into the hands of the States general, so as to be no longer in the power of the Commis of a bureau, or even of his minister to smuggle a law thro unquestioned; and we may even hope that the national demand for this oil will increase faster than both their & our fisheries together will supply. but in spite of all these hopes, if the English should find means to cover their oils under our name there will be great danger of a repeal. it is essential then that our government take effectual measures to prevent the English from obtaining genuine sea-papers, and that they enable their Consuls in the ports of France (as soon as they shall be named) to detect counterfeit papers, and that we convince this government that we use our best endeavors with good faith, as it is clearly our interest to do. for the rivalship of the English is the only one we have to fear. it had already began to render our oils invendible in the ports of France. you will observe that mr Necker renews the promise of taking off the 10. sous pour livre at the end of the next year.

...I have the honor to be with sentiments of the most perfect esteem & respect, Sir, your most obedient & most humble serv^{t.}

Th: Jefferson

NA: PCC, item 87, v. 2, pp. 408-409 (ALS); M247, reel 115.

Stephen Higginson to John Adams

Sir   Boston 17 Jany. 1789

   You may recollect that the Court of France by an edict, about 2 Years since, opend a trade to the Americans to Mauritius and the french settlements in India upon the same terms as their own subjects pursue it. This permission we soon improved, & for two Years past, many vessels have gone to Port Louis in the Isle of France from different parts of the Continent with cargos of the various exports from the Northern middle & Southern States. We there found a ready, & a good market for Beef, Pork, Butter & Flour, dried & pickled fish, Wheat, Tobacco, Naval Stores &c. all the vessels from this state that have gone there, have carried those with some other small Articles. Those from the middle & Southern States have carried principally their own particular exports. – We have taken in return from thence Coffee, Pepper, Hides, Teas and the manufactures of India; & some of those articles have been again exported to Europe and the West Indies with advantage, as Coffee, Teas, pepper Spices & Nankins &c. As the articles we have carried to the Isle of France, have in a good degree been again exported from thence to the various markets in India &c, where a ready & extensive sale has been found for them; this trade would probably in a short time take off great quantities of our american exports, and give employ to a great number of our men & Ships. We find by calculation that not less than 3,000 tons of Shipping went to Mauritius the last year from America; & this year I think there will be more than 4,000 tons go there, besides those Ships that have been fitted out for China. –

   From these facts, I think that a free trade to the Mauritius, as was at first granted, must be very important to America, for though the markets in

India &c, which have rec^d our exports from thence may be open to us, generally, it is not easy for us at once to Supply them direct, nor till we shall have more knowledge of their navigation & trade – besides which the voyages to the Continent would be too long and tedious, for our common traders of small Capitals to pursue them; those to Mauritius are as much So, as the persons who have sent there can in general bear. – To have that or any other branch of trade so circumstanced, as that none but wealthy Individuals, or companies can pursue it, is not to be desired upon public principles. – But this trade to the Isle of France we are perhaps in danger of losing, or having it so restricted, as, in a good degree, to deprive us of the advantages we have been led to expect from it. The few french Merchants who reside there, have enjoyed exclusively the Supply of that market with some of the same articles which we carry there; & have generally engrossed to themselves the Crops of Coffee, as well as the India Exports, which have been there Sold. by this means they have commanded their own prices, both for their supplies to their planters and transient Traders, and for the produce &c exported from thence. – we have not only undersold them in the articles we have carried; but by going over to Bourbon, where the Coffee is raised, and contracting with the planters for what we wanted, we got it much cheaper than to have bought it at Port Louis, & taught the planters to make more of their crops than they had before done, and deprived the Merchants at Port Louis of a profit they used to make at the Planters expense. – These diminutions of the merchants gains, resulting from our trade, have made them & their connexions at Lorient very uneasy; & they have combined, we are told, to Suppress, or at least to restrain < * > our Trade at that market, by joint representations to the Court of France. – They have, indeed, already prevailed on the Commandant at Port Louis, to prevent our vessels from going to Bourbon to buy & take in Coffee; and we now have to take it from the Merchants at Port Louis, at the advanced price of 2½ to 3 Dollars pC· – This restriction we might perhaps Support but should we be liable to any additional ones of moment, we may be obliged to abandon the Trade. –

If the french Government should not be misled by false representations, I cannot suppose they will subject us to any farther embarrassments; but on the contrary, by considering the Subject in a national & Political view, they must be disposed to encourage our Trade, to the Isle of France in particular, & give us all that freedom which they at first intended, and we enjoyed. The local situation of that Island is peculiarly favourable to annoy the British trade to India & China, and to protect their own. It may indeed be viewed as the Key to both the Chinese & Indian Seas from Europe – No ship can pass for either of them, without being in a great degree Subject to the Cruisers Stationed at the Isle of France; & if a free trade is permitted to us, they certainly will have every Supply, & every advantage for cruising upon the British from thence. that Island will certainly soon become the Place of deposit, for American, Chinese & Indian exports. – we shall carry to them, all the various products of America, that will answer in those Seas, and shall want in return the produce & exports of the east. – Our vessels will lodge the former, and take the latter in return. The french Ships, or the natives from the Continent will bring their exports, & take ours away for other markets. Such a Trade will not only employ the french Ships in carrying our exports to other Markets from Mauritius, & in bringing theirs in return for us to take away; but very great advantages beside must be derived from it. It is impossible but the Settlement must, with such advantages, soon become very wealthy & important; it will certainly be resorted to by other Europeans, and all the various nations inhabiting the Shores in those Seas. It will in this way soon become the general Magazine for Naval Stores, & for provisions of every kind. – In a political view, no event can be more desireable. It will enable the french to operate against the british in any future rupture with amazing advantage. – They will then have an important post filled, not only with Provisions & military Stores, but with Active enterprizing & wealthy inhabitants. –

Should the immediate effect of our trade be to Supplant, or even to ruin the few Merchants now residing at Port Louis, it would be of no moment in a national view, Since it must inevitably establish great numbers in their stead. But even this cannot happen, unless from their own folly & imprudence – for though they may be deprived, by means of our trade, of the profits on the business they before pursued; they certainly may avail themselves in Common with others, of the many new openings for beneficial Commerce which result from it. –

It appears to me that the french Court acted with great wisdom and policy when they open'd those ports to us; & the same principles which induced them to do it, will retain their weight in favour of the measure, while the trade of Europe with India & China, and the relative Interests of France & Britain, in those Seas remain as they now are: and If I am not mistaken, as to the views & Interests of the french Court, upon this Subject, there can be no doubt of Mr Jefferson's being able to prevent any new restrictions upon our vessels, & to obtain for them the same liberty which they at first enjoyed. –

With these sentiments, as to the importance of a free trade to those Seas, I thought it could not be improper to state to you the foregoing facts & observations. Should they have weight in your mind, you may perhaps advance the Interest of America by making some representation to Mr Jefferson on the Subject. –

with much respect I have the honour to be Sir your very humble
Servant. —   Stephen Higginson[1]

LC: *Jefferson Papers, microfilm reel 10 (ALS). Enclosure in John Adams to TJ, March
1, 1789.*
  [1] *Higginson, Stephen (1743-1828). Massachusetts seafarer and merchant. Privateer
during Revolutionary War. Member, state assembly, 1782. Member, Continental
Congress, 1783. Militia officer during suppression of Shays' Rebellion. One of Boston's
wealthiest merchants. Served as U.S. naval agent, late 1790s.*

Comte de Moustier to Comte de Montmorin

[Translation]

N⁰· 1.   New York, 19 Jan. 1789.
My Lord.

           .   .   .   .   .

I would have wished to be able to fall in precisely with the language
which I have been obliged to speak in a country where it is, of course,
necessary to show goodwill at every moment, since the general conversation
turns almost always on public affairs. I hope I have explained myself so as
to justify perfectly the helplessness in which the Americans believed that
France has left them. In general I told them that the past sufficiently proves
to them that the King was very favorable to them, but that since the peace
the weakness and the incoherence of their government, more nominal than
real, have prevented understanding their principles and establishing any
judgment regarding their existence. I cast all the blame on them – no one
denied it, and several blushed.
     The dissolution of a government reprobated by every American, and even
by those who do not approve the form of the new, appeared to me favorable to this language. Moreover, I thought that it was advisable to show
that their weakness was seen by people who are naturally much too inclined
to exaggerate their importance. If the King adopts the path of caution in
their regard, it can be justified in several respects. If, on the contrary, His
Majesty finds it convenient to his interests to favor the new system and to
consolidate it, it appears interesting to me to make known to the
Americans that it is from a great Prince that they receive favors, and that
they should show themselves worthy thereof. They will not know how to
appreciate a gratuitous generosity for a long time, but they should at least
perceive the tone in which it is appropriate for them to request favors.
     I have had occasion to discover by means of a longer stay that Mr. Jay
did not have all the influence he sought to procure for himself. The first

obstacle came from the very impotence of the body in the name of which he acts and speaks. Others arise from the jealousy of various deputations, and then of various members. Lastly, Mr. Jay wished to establish his pre-eminence over the individual members of Congress as chief officer of a department, whereas the majority of the members of Congress, wishing to invest themselves individually with all the consideration of the body, regarded him as their servant, in such a way that Mr. Jay was obliged to have one party in Congress and to play off some against the others. What gave him some importance was the difficulty of replacing him, the per-ception that he is an industrious person (this is in spite of the scantiness of his work), the necessity of transmitting communications through him, the ignorance of the majority of the members of Congress above all regarding affairs abroad, and lastly, the rotation of the members, who are often very young men or men of very little importance in comparison with a man, a former Magistrate in his State, a member of the first Congress, the President of this body, and a Negotiator employed in Europe. He has worked constantly to increase it by another method which directly concerns the foreign Ministers, which is to see to it that there were few direct connections between them and the members of Congress, and to endeavor to give them aversions that obliged them to have recourse to him. This method did not work in my regard in the single instance in which I have had to treat with Congress on the occasion of the request to put an end to the consular convention and of the demand for Captain Ferrier. The course I then took of speaking directly to the Delegates from Virginia produced the effect that I could wish for up to a certain point, which was that Congress come to a decision on it, the end of its power. It was, in consequence, then decided that it would send orders to Mr. Jefferson to conclude the convention, and that Congress would write to the Legislature of Virginia to give the King the satisfaction demanded by His Majesty. But I fear that the secret recommendations of Mr. Jay to Mr. Jefferson were to endeavor to gain time, and to evade as long as he is not absolutely forced to finish. Your despatch of 23 September, My Lord, does not inform me that the Convention has been signed, although You have done me the honor to indicate by that of 23 June that the American Plenipotentiary had just communicated his full powers. One of the dominant traits in the character of the Americans is the ruse. They practice it from a very early age. Their desires being in general above their strengths, they make up the deficiency by the ruse. If Congress were not on the point of vanishing, and we had to leave ourselves open to negotiating with it again, I would beg you, My Lord, to authorize me to request that the Secretary of Congress for Foreign Affairs be obliged to communicate to me in proper terms the resolutions of Congress regarding the matters which I would have had to negotiate, in the same way that is practiced by the States General of the United Provinces, instead of receiving only a very laconic and obscure extract, in the fashion of this Secretary. However, if under the new Government the President of the United States does not think himself authorized to engage the United States by his personal decisions, and it is necessary to join them together with those of the Senate, it seems to me that there could only be real advantage in determining that resolutions passed by the President of the United States and the Senate regarding replies to make to a foreign Minister be communicated to him just as they have been agreed upon.

According to Mr. Jay's method, I have only had knowledge of satisfactory resolutions passed by Congress concerning the Convention and the demand that I made in the King's name that they deliver up Captain Ferrier to His Majesty's Vice Consul in Virginia by a confidential route of the members of Congress. This latter affair is entirely settled, and Mr. Jay probably hopes that it will not be taken up again. The embarrassment of Congress would be extreme if the King insisted sharply and peremptorily on the satisfaction demanded. That body, which has played the role of Sovereign so long without being one, would be obliged to confess its inadequacy, and then the King would have to demand directly from the State of Virginia Satisfaction of an injury which that State's Governor has claimed to justify in some way. Mr. Jay undoubtedly thought the arguments of that Magistrate well-grounded, when he confidentially sent me the Governor of Virginia's response to Congress, apparently with the notion that I would be content with it. I answered him at that time that I saw therein only some sophisticated arguments by an attorney, who claimed to argue from the ambiguous texts of peculiar laws of a recently-formed State, and who had not yet had the time to become acquainted with what are the true relations between nations. Since that time, Congress has occupied itself for only six weeks with the weighty and important question of understanding when it will be necessary to fix the first meeting of the members who will make up the new Congress, and after having finished this great matter it totally dispersed. At present, it is still composed of only a few members, who do not anticipate having any business to conclude, because it does not appear to intend to proceed with that upon which it seems to me it should give me some sort of decision, out of regard for the Sovereign in whose name a demand has been made.

I hope to have succeeded in restoring the idea that the United States should regard the alliance with the King as existent. I have discussed, in the memorandum which I had the honor to send You on 25 December last, the value of the engagements that result therefrom. I limit myself to observing here that according to the hypothesis whereby it would suit the King to make use of the resources and the progressive forces which the United

States can offer, it is necessary to offer them a base of support and a center of union, which is not amongst them. The heart of American policy must necessarily derive from a great foreign Power. In order to reach the place where the Americans are, they had need of a mother's attentions. In order to be in condition to make good use of their emancipation, they need a tutor. Despite the singular suspicion which they have had and, what is more immoderate, which foreigners have entertained of their insights on politics, I do not fear to declare that they are very weak as to domestic policy and extremely narrow-minded as to foreign policy. The numerous and petulant race of lawyers has thought-itself suddenly metamorphosed into a body of Legislators, it has extolled itself, it has attributed to the country where these Jurists were born or had settled innumerable advantages over other nations, and unfortunately their hyperboles have inflamed the thinking of a part of our own nation, which has presumed to determine the rights of nations and the true principles of Governments, because of having been taken over for a few moments by the declamations of the Americans. Reason and reckoning, in reducing the advantages of this new people to their just value, still leaves them a sufficiency, although much below the absurd ideas that the America-manes have conjured up. The new American System is indeed sufficient proof of the weakness of the old, much-vaunted political activities, and the successive variations which it will experience will furnish new proofs of the absurdity of a great Democracy. Likewise, is it not only from lack of sufficient maturity, and because the principles of fermentation are not yet sufficiently combined, that the great inconveniences of this kind of Government are not yet felt more strongly? The question is to know whether the United States will proceed to monarchy by the shortest path, or whether it will reach there after having passed through all the decomposition of anarchy, the formation of a type of feudal system, and the gradual and successive reunion of the members proper to compose a great body solid, energetic, and harmonious. The Americans are ardent, eager to enjoy the execution of their plans, disposed to become discouraged rather by delays than by the magnitude of difficulties. Ambition is only beginning to emerge, a few successes have nourished it; it is to be presumed that a few souls more violent than the others will attempt the shortest way.

They take an interest, or at least claim to have much interest, in the movements that are troubling France. In spite of the want of all direct news from the Kingdom, and not being able to have any ideas of what is taking place there through the inaccurate medium of the English gazettes or from the even more extravagant and at the same time malicious reports of some Frenchmen, and among others, of one named Brissot de Warville,[1] who came here provided with a letter that You had granted him to present to me at the recommendation of M. le Marquis de la Fayette, I have had the good fortune to come upon the true story of how one should envisage the situations in the Kingdom. I have found no one who is not, or does not appear to be, convinced by my talk of the absurdity and the injustice of the claims of certain Provinces, certain Bodies, and certain individuals defending their particular interest on the pretext of the good of the people, whereas all their proceedings tend only to remain forever fixed between these same people and the King, in order to enjoy odious privileges at the expense of the Sovereign's authority and the people's ease. I do not think it doubtful that the majority of Americans is in favor of the good cause and that they do fashion their prayers for the success of a King who appears animated solely by charity and justice. Those Frenchmen who are particularly well-known in America are blamed for the conduct they have pursued in order to show their opposition to His Majesty's views. I present the Kingdom to Americans as a sick lion whose recovery will show him stronger and more respectable than ever.

I am with respect, My Lord, Your most humble and most obedient servant, Le Cᵗᵉ· de Moustier.

rec. 27 June

FFAA: Pol. Corr., U.S., v. 34, f. 4-10vo. (LC transcription).
¹ Brissot de Warville, Jacques Pierre (1754-1793). French publicist and political figure. Briefly imprisoned in the Bastille, 1784, for pamphlets allegedly libelling the Queen and the government. Founded Société des Amis des Noirs, inspired by British anti-slavery movement, 1788. Spent four months in the United States, 1788, from which resulted his New Travels in the United States of America, 1788. Founded newspaper Le patriote français, May 1789. As Paris city official, took delivery of keys to the Bastille, July 1789. Elected to Legislative Assembly, 1791, and involved in diplomatic affairs, including declaration of war against Austria, 1792, and Great Britain and the Netherlands, 1793. Arrested with the other Girondin leaders, June 1793; guillotined October 1793.

Comte de Moustier to Comte de Montmorin

[Translation]

Nᵒ· 2.   New York, 2 Feb. 1789.
My Lord.

The new constitution that is about to be introduced in America gives the President of the United States the right to receive Ambassadors and Ministers of foreign Powers without his needing to assemble the Senate or the representatives for this purpose. However elevated the position of President may be, it is certain that this reception will be much less solemn than heretofore, since it cannot be denied that that Officer is really only one of the three branches of the Sovereignty of the United States, while Congress, the functions of which are about to expire, at least nominally represented the whole confederation. It does not appear that a Sovereign, either in his letters or through his ministers, may treat on a footing of equality with an elective Officer who is charged for only four years with a third part of the administration, and who does not have the right to appoint Ministers or to conclude treaties or conventions with foreign Powers without the consent of the Senate. It results that these Powers would be according to him a prerogative that is refused him by the United States themselves, and that they would be treating as Sovereign a man who is not one. Without elevating the President, they would be abasing themselves. The Americans, always attentive to give their executive Officers consideration abroad rather than power at home, are already occupied with several titles by which they count on enhancing the dignity of their President in the eyes of foreigners. Some have proposed to call him *Your elected Majesty*, others *Your Most Serene Highness* or *Your Most Illustrious Highness*.

It therefore appeared useful to me, My Lord, to submit to You early some doubts regarding the protocol and the etiquette that it might be advisable to adopt with regard to the United States, and since they will probably occupy themselves with this subject from the formation of the new government, I request You to be so good as to direct my language and my conduct by Your instructions. I am the sole resident Minister Plenipotentiary near Congress, and they will not fail to consult me when they propose to make some regulations in this regard. At least my opposition will produce some effect, if they venture to establish an etiquette prejudicial to the foreign Powers.

Since in these discussions examples often succeed better than reasonings, You will perhaps judge it appropriate, My Lord, to have communicated to me the ceremonial used at The Hague, in Venice, and in Genoa, where the chief executives of the republic, at least by their Constitution, have a great resemblance to the President of Congress, who cannot demand to be treated with more distinction than a Stadhouder or a Doge. It seems to me that the protocol of the King's Letters to the United States should be preserved, that it suits His Majesty's dignity to address himself as heretofore to the President and the Members of Congress, and to receive only letters signed by the President in the name of the two Chambers of Congress. Following the example of the Parliament of England, the Senate will often be adjourned. There would be inconvenience in sending memoranda and notes to Congress *assembled*, since it would be necessary to wait too long for the response, and it will be less embarrassing to treat with the President, whose response will be more prompt and often more satisfying than that of an always punctilious Senate, insatiable for debates. But it appears that in the event of a public audience, the King's Minister is to be received by the President and the Senate together, as he is in Holland by the States General. One cannot be too attentive not to compromise the character of a foreign Minister in a democratic country, the leaders of which are most disposed to disparage him. One can judge it by the article of the former ceremonial of Congress which declares that immediately after his audience, the foreign Minister *shall make* the first visit to the members of Congress. Besides the fact that this pretention is set forth a little harshly, it is absurd in itself, and I only conformed to it at the time of my arrival, but since that time I have continually refused to take any step towards the arriving members. It is possible that under the new Government the Senators may have the same pretention. In that event I hope, My Lord, that You will approve that I continue in my refusal, and that I only make the first visit to the President, who is the ostensible leader of the republic. If I should deviate from this rule, it would only be in favor of the chiefs of departments, because it would appear that I would seek them out only as public Officers, with whom I would have business to conduct, rather than as men invested with a dignity of representation. The visits that I would make in this case to the chiefs of departments could be declared as being of no consequence regarding preeminence. Mine could be determined by ruling that in all public ceremonies, His Majesty's Minister will occupy the first place after the President, and that in no event will he yield place either to a Senator or to any other Officer of the United States. In this country, where they keep much to ceremonial, it is important to establish sure and invariable principles early, and not to expose the Minister of the first Sovereign of Europe to lose the consideration that is due him.

Moreover, it cannot be concealed that the grandeur that the Americans claim to establish in their government is still purely ideal, and that the new government itself is only an infant whose existence, and consequently whose future strength, are very uncertain. It is easier for the Americans to disparage a representative of a foreign Power than themselves to raise their nation to the level of powerful nations, to which it would sometimes seem that they would like not to limit themselves to being assimilated.

I shall not make, My Lord, any overture on this subject before having received Your instructions, and I shall continue to concede nothing that cannot be justified by the orders that You have given me. If I am questioned before having received them, I shall limit myself to taking everything *ad referendum* unless I am offered satisfactory distinctions in every respect.

I am with respect My Lord Your most humble and most obedient Servant,   Le Cte. de Moustier.
P.S. of 8 March 1789.

Since the sending of this despatch, part of the Senators and representatives who compose the new Congress have arrived, and the greatest number of them have immediately come to make me the first visit. However, some of those who were in the old Congress continue to hold themselves at a distance and still appear to expect a first step on my part. Whatever, My Lord, may be the conduct of those who are still on the road, and whatever may be the determination of the two chambers when they are formed, I shall only deviate from the principles that I have adopted after having heen particuliarly authorized to do so.   L. C. d. M.
rec. 27 June

FFAA: Pol. Corr., U.S., v. 34, f. 15-18vo. (LC transcription).

Thomas Jefferson to John Jay

Sir   Paris Feb. 4. 1789.
    Your favour of Nov. 25. by Gouverneur Morris is duly recieved. [I must beg you to take the trouble of decyphering yourself what follows, and to communicate it to nobody but the President, at least for the present.] We had before understood thro' different channels that the conduct of the Count de Moustier was politically and morally offensive. it was delicate for me to speak on the subject to the Count de Montmorin. the invaluable mediation of our friend the Marquis de la Fayette was therefore resorted to, & the subject explained tho' not pressed. later intelligence shewing the necessity of pressing it, it was yesterday resumed and represented thro' the same medium to the Count de Montmorin, that recent information proved to us that his minister's conduct had rendered him personally odious in America, and might even influence the dispositions of the two nations, that his recall was become a matter of mutual concern, that we had understood he was instructed to remind the new government of their debt to this country, and that he was in the purpose of doing it in very harsh terms, that this could not increase their desire of hastening paiment, and might wound their affections, that therefore it was much to be desired that his discretion should not be trusted as to the form in which the demand should be made but that the letter should be written here and he instructed to add nothing but his signature; nor was his private conduct omitted. the Count de Montmorin was sensibly impressed. He very readily determined that the letter should be formed here, but said that the recall was a more difficult

business: that as they had no particular fact to allege against the Count de Moustier they could not recall him from that ministry without giving him another, and there was no vacancy at present. however he would hazard his first thoughts on the subject, saving the right of correcting them by further consideration: they were these; that there was a loose expression in one of his letters which might be construed into a petition for leave of absence, that he would give him permission to return to France, that it had been before decided on the request of the Marquis de la Luzerne that Otto should go to him in London, that they would send a person to America as Chargé des Affaires in place of Otto, and that if the President General Washington approved of him he should be afterwards made minister. He had cast his eye on Colonel Ternant and desired the Marquis to consult me whether he would be agreeable. at first I hesitated, recollecting to have heard Ternant represented in America as an hypochondriac discontented man, and paused for a moment between him and Barthelemy at London of whom I have heard a great deal of good. However I concluded it safer to take one we knew and who knows us. The Marquis was decidedly of this opinion. Ternant will see that his predecessor is recalled for unconciliatory deportment and that he will owe his own promotion to the approbation of the President. He established a solid reputation in Europe by his conduct when Generalissimo of one of the United Provinces during their late disturbances and it is generally thought that if he had been put at the head of the principal province instead of the Rhingrave de Salm he would have saved that cause. upon the whole I believe you may expect that the Count de Moustier will have an immediate leave of absence which will soon after become a recall in effect[1]. I will try also to have their consuls admonished as to the line of conduct they should observe.

I shall have the honor of writing you a general letter within a few days: I have now that of assuring you of the sentiments of sincere esteem & respect with which I am Dear Sir your most obedient & most humble serv^t   Th: Jefferson

                                                        Paris March 14.

The operation mentioned in my letter of Feb. 4. is going on. Montmorin has proposed to Ternant to go as Chargé des affaires. Ternant called on me a few days ago to know whether I thought his appointment would be agreeable to us. tho he is obliged to give up his regiment, which is a certainty for life, for this mission which is incertain in it's duration, he will do it. perhaps Otto may be left awhile longer to put Ternant into the train of affairs. I suppose de Moutier will have recieved his leave of absence before you recieve this.

Mar. 18.
Ternant has again seen Montmorin, who told him that in the beginning
of April he would decide finally about his mission.

*Boyd, Jefferson Papers, vol. 14, pp. 520-521; NA: PCC, item 87, v. 2, pp. 438-444
(ALS); M247, reel 115 (original in cypher and plain text).*
¹*Moustier departed the United States in October 1789.*

Comte de Moustier to Comte de Montmorin

[Translation]
N⁰· 3.   New York, 4 Febr. 1789.
My Lord.
   The tranquility which the United States are enjoying at this time is only
apparent; until the new Government takes shape, the parties acquire more
consistency daily. Those from the State of New York do not cease to be
irritated by vexations which are often puerile and always inconsequential.
The cause of Antifederalism has become personal to the Governor and to
his partisans; it is no longer desirous of reasoning, but of men. The federalists are constantly in the minority; no occasion is missed to mortify them,
and the Senate struggles in vain against the petulance of the House of
Representatives, which is almost entirely composed of men of the people.
In the meantime, they are endeavoring to overthrow the Governor, who is
at the head of this majority, and more commotions, animosity, and hatred
than one sees today to render that Officer odious to the multitude have
never been seen in the United States. – Another State of the Union also
continues to show aversion to the new constitution as long as it is not
amended; that is Virginia. The elected Senators are antifederalists, and a
part of its representatives will be so as well. Nevertheless, that party will
evidently have the inferior position in the new Congress, and it will only
serve to contain it within the boundaries that the constitution stipulates for
it. I shall speak neither of Rhode Island nor of North Carolina, since those
States are at this moment separated from the confederation, and if the new
plan succeeds, they are too weak not to desire to be admitted to it. New
Hampshire and Massachusetts are peaceably occupied with the extension of
their navigation and their fisheries, and although there may be parties, they
are hardly violent. Connecticut is unanimous for all public measures, it is
the best constituted and the most industrious State of the union; it is
beginning to manufacture cloth, linen, and other common objects for its
own consumption and even for that of some Southern States. New Jersey
is still poor, and cannot hope for any influence in the general Government.
The war in Northern Europe and the scarcity that is felt in France have

given a new energy to the activity of the Pennsylvanians. That State is making astonishing progress in Agriculture and even in some manufactures of prime necessity. General Mifflin, its current President, is known for his patriotism and his affection for France. Delaware merits the attention of a foreign Power still less than New Jersey. More unanimity has reigned for some time in Maryland; it is all the more disposed toward the new government because by its central situation it hopes to become its residence. South Carolina is beginning to recover from its losses: she has shown herself firm and almost unanimous in the present discussion; she is preserving a perfect neutrality between the Georgians and the Creeks. It is therefore only Georgia that is in a true state of suffering, and which, far from recovering since the peace, has only become more and more entangled while indulging herself in projects of expansion that are beyond her strength. McGillivray, who directs the operations of the Creeks, refuses all negotiation with men who hitherto have scarcely respected the treaties; he only wants to ascribe himself to an accommodation by the interposition of Congress. In order to contain the inhabitants of Frankland, who are allied with the Georgians, he has aroused the Cherokees to fall upon them. Devastations and assassinations succeed one another on the frontiers, and to complete the misfortune, Georgia's paper money is so depreciated that they do not know where to find funds to provide for the most urgent needs.

This brief picture of the current situation of the United States can only be satisfying as long as one considers only the verge that is on the ocean. The districts of the interior generally have various views and opinions concerning the general Government of the United States, but as the federalists are in possession of the ports and the river mouths, they can hope to have the upper hand if they take care to make use of this advantage with moderation.

I am more and more persuaded, My Lord, that it will depend on France to consolidate the work of the federalists and to give energy and vigor to the American confederation at least for some time. I had the honor at the end of last year to submit to You my reflections on this important question, and I dare to think that You have found them worthy of Your attention. However limited may be the needs of the new Congress, they are still above its means, and the more it insists on indispensable contributions, the more it will weaken its popularity. It cannot do without foreign support for several years, and it is to be feared that England will grant it what we will have refused it. The principles and the connections of Mr. J. Adams, who will be Vice President and leader of the Senate, are known; he will do what he can to consolidate the new government without concerning himself with the means and without sparing France, of which he has never been a partisan. Unless Mr. Jay can raise himself still higher, he will probably keep the department of foreign affairs. These two men, closely united by their character, and sustained by a very active and very scheming party, may be able to lay down the law to General Washington himself, whose intentions appear to be favorable to us. After these observations, You will perhaps not disapprove, My Lord, that I reiterate to You my entreaties to give me instructions on the most important points of the memoranda that accompany my despatch of 25 Dec. last.

It seems to me that everything depends on the first moment, and that our influence may be established or lost forever in the United States.

For the little that their dispositions and their habits are examined, it is easy to be convinced that one could not bind them by politics without attaching them at the same time by commerce. This part of my work appeared so important to me, My Lord, that I did not wish to submit the result of it to You before having assembled from various parts of the Continent the clearest and most precise notions. Hitherto I have not had reason to be pleased with the activity of the people to whom I addressed myself for this purpose; I have not been happier with regard to the information that I have requested in France. My task has become more painful, but without discouraging me. I hope to have the honor to submit to You in the course of this year all that I can ascertain regarding the Commerce of these States.

I am with respect, My Lord, Your most humble and most obedient Servant,   Le Cte. de Moustier.
rec. 27 June

FFAA: Pol. Corr., U.S., v. 34, f. 19-22 (LC transcription).

Comte de Moustier to Comte de Montmorin

[Translation]

N°. 4.   New York, 12 Febr. 1789,
My Lord.

While waiting for a suitable occasion to send you my preceding despatches, I am profiting from the departure of an English ship to warn You that we were informed only yesterday by a letter from Mr. Jefferson to Mr. Jay of the terms of the Decree of 23 Nov^ber. to encourage the importation of grain and flour from the United States through premiums. We had hitherto had only vague reports regarding the present needs of the Kingdom, and although several American merchants have hazarded some shipments, this supply effort is very far from being raised to the level that it could have reached if we had had timely news direct from the Kingdom. I cannot refrain from observing to You, My Lord, that this is again one of the unfortunate results of the suppression of the packet boats, the successive news from which could have placed the Americans in a position to make great speculations and to prepare their shipments. I dare even to assert that in this event the supply effort would have been so abundant, that without the lure of a premium the provinces where the scarcity is being felt would have been provided with American flour. The great efforts that are about to be undertaken at this moment on the part of the Pennsylvanians will be retarded by the ice in the Delaware, and a merchant from Philadelphia must cart grain and flour to Virginia to ship them by the Chesapeake. That merchant could earn 75000 livres tournois through the premium alone, which according to the plan which I have had the honor to submit to You regarding the organization of the packet boats, would have been sufficient to maintain those packet boats for more than six months. You will judge from that, My Lord, that the suppression of the packet boats has become, as a result, an economy infinitely onerous to the government, and that a regular communication with the United States could have maintained plenty in the Kingdom without necessitating recourse to extraordinary means to encourage the importation of foreign flour.

I recall also, My Lord, very indirectly that Mr. Jefferson makes mention in his letter of the definitive ratification of the consular Convention. I must presume that the despatch by which You have undoubtedly had the goodness to inform me of this resolution is on its way. It appears above all of interest that the Consuls be informed of it by the Minister of their department so that they set about the execution of a Convention that has been so long suspended. One may think that the persons in America who have had an interest in hindering its conclusion will also do everything possible to keep it secret in order to prevent our consuls from taking advantage of it.

The Electors appointed by the various States to choose the President and the Vice President of the United States assembled on the 4th of this month. Their votes have not yet been made public, but to judge from present reports it appears that Gen. Washington will be President and Mr. John Adams Vice President. It is said that several Electors only voted for the latter because they feared that unless he had a role in the new Government, he would become a redoubtable adversary thereof.

I am with respect, My Lord, Your most humble and most obedient servant   Le Cte· de Moustier.

rec. 12 April

FFAA: Pol. Corr., U.S., v. 34, f. 24-25vo. (LC transcription).

Phineas Bond to Lord Carmarthen

My Lord,   Philad^{a.} 19th. Feb. 1789.
I have the honor to inform your Ldp the Assembly of Penn^{a.} have lately
passed an Act to enable foreigners to hold real estates, a copy of which I
now enclose to your Ldp – The operation of this law in one respect will be
of essential benefit; the British merchants have now an opportunity of
securing their debts by taking land in discharge of them, where all other
means of payment have failed – but my Lord, I well know this regulation
will be used by needy and avaricious men to effect great deceptions in the
sales of lands to foreigners. I have already mentioned to your Ldp. some
practices upon unwary people in Gt. Britain, and Ireland, very successfully
managed by the agents of extensive landholders in America, sent over with
very flattering charts and descriptions to tempt purchasers, and to encourage
migration. In consequence of the passing this act, a renewal of this baneful
practice is now in contemplation, and every artifice and stratagem will be
used to deceive purchasers and to decoy settlers to migrate from Europe –
I have the honor to be my Lord, your Ldp's most faith: and most. obed^{t.}
servant   P. Bond.

AHA 1896, v. 1, p. 594.

Thomas Jefferson to the Dutch Bankers

Gentlemen[1]   Paris Feb. 22. 1789
I have just recieved your joint letter of the 16th. inst. to me, and have
perused that of the same date to the Board of Treasury which you were so
kind as to inclose for my perusal. I shall immediately forward it to them.
you therein state the balance in your hands to be 123,674 florins, to which
will be added the nett produce of 103. bonds, engaged, tho' not yet delivered, and you say there will then be a deficiency of about 100,000 florins for
the June interest. from this an implication arises that you consider this
balance as a deposit for the June interest, and propose again to postpone
the article of 60,000 florins appropriated in the estimate we left you to a
particular purpose as of the last year. but I must observe to you that this
article is of a nature not to admit such postponement. the situations it is
intended to relieve are too cruel to be suffered. that estimate was under the
eyes of Congress when they approved the loan which was to fulfill it's
views. the order of appropriation is as much established by their will as the
sums appropriated; and priority in order gives priority of right. tho' that

article stands among those which should have been furnished in 1788 I said nothing when I found you were postponing it to the interest of Feb. 1789. but I did not expect it would be again proposed to postpone it to that of June; and were I to be silent now it might afterwards be postponed to that of February, & so on without end. besides my instructions from Congress, which do not leave me at liberty to permit this object to lose it's turn; besides the pressing cries of humanity which urge it's right, another reason is superadded. I have asked, & hope to receive leave to go to America in the ensuing spring, and shall not return till the fall. were I to leave Europe without setting this business into motion, it would be suspended till my return, which no consideration will permit. as I expect then to sail about the middle of April, I must draw on you in the course of the month of March for these 60,000 florins, and I hope the same motives will urge you to honor the draught which will oblige me to make it. Besides this, the article of the Medals stands before that of either the February or June interest; & as my departure would render it necessary that these also should be finished, & their execution requires time, I have been obliged to enter into contracts with the several workmen, who are already well advanced in their work, & will finish it by the middle of April. they will soon become entitled to partial paiments; so that I must immediately begin these draughts on you, & make the whole of them between this & the middle of April. with respect to the appropriation for the foreign officers, I have no orders. I presume they will be sent to you. should your two houses concur in sentiments on the subject of this letter, I shall hope to receive your joint answer as usual. should they differ in opinion, I must ask your answers separately. I have the honor to be, gentlemen, your most obed$^{t.}$ s$^{t.}$

Th: Jefferson

NA: PCC, *item 87, v. 2, pp. 458-459 (C); M247, reel 115.*
^{1} *This letter is addressed to Mess$^{rs.}$ Willinks & Van Staphorsts.*

Thomas Jefferson to David Humphreys

Dear Sir   Paris Mar. 18. 1789.

·   ·   ·   ·   ·

The change in this country, since you left it, is such as you can form no idea of. it. the frivolities of conversation have given way entirely to politicks – men, women & children talk nothing else: and all you know talk a great deal. the press groans with daily productions, which in point of boldness make an Englishman stare, who hitherto has thought himself the boldest of men. a complete revolution in this government has, within the space of two years (for it began with the Notables of 1787) been effected merely by the force of public opinion, aided indeed by the want of money which the dissipations of the court had brought on. and this revolution has not cost a single life, unless we charge to it a little riot lately in Bretagne which begun about the price of bread, became <*> afterwards political and ended in the loss of 4. or 5. lives....

The operations which have taken place in America lately, fill me with pleasure. in the first place they realize the confidence I had that whenever our affairs get obviously wrong, the good sense of the people will interpose and set them to rights. the example of changing a constitution by assembling the wise men of the state, instead of assembling armies, will be worth as much to the world as the former examples we had given them. the constitution too which was the result of our deliberations, is unquestionably the wisest ever yet presented to men, and some of the accomodations of interest which it has adopted are greatly pleasing to me who have before had occasions of seeing how difficult those interests were to accomodate. a general concurrence of opinion seems to authorize us to say it has some defects. I am one of those who think it a defect that the important rights, not placed in security by the frame of the constitution itself, were not explicitly secured by a supplementary declaration. there are rights which it is useless to surrender to the government, and which yet, governments have always been fond to invade. these are the rights of thinking, and publishing our thoughts by speaking or writing: the right of free commerce: the right of personal freedom: there are instruments for administering the government, so peculiarly trust-worthy, that we should never leave the legislature at liberty to change them. the new constitution has secured these in the executive & legislative departments; but not in the judiciary. it should have established trials by the people themselves, that is to say by jury. there are instruments so dangerous to the rights of the nation, and which place them so totally at the mercy of their governors, that those governors whether legislative or executive, should be restrained from keeping such instruments on foot but in well defined cases. such an instrument is a standing army. We are now allowed to say <**> such a declaration of rights, as a supplement to the constitution where that is silent, is wanting to secure us in these points. the general voice has legitimated this objection. it has not however authorized me to consider as a real defect, what I thought and still think one, the perpetual re-eligibility of the president. but three states out of 11. having declared against this, we must suppose we are wrong according to the fundamental law of every society, the *lex majoris partis*,[1] to which we are bound to submit. and should the majority change their opinion, & become sensible that this trait in their constitution is wrong, I would wish it to remain uncorrected as long as we can avail ourselves of the services of our great leader, whose talents and whose weight of character I consider as peculiarly necessary to get the government so under way as that it may afterwards be carried on by subordinate characters.

...I hope to receive soon permission to visit America this summer, and to possess myself anew, by conversation with my countrymen, of their spirit & their ideas. I know only the Americans of the year 1784. they tell me this is to be much a stranger to those of 1789. this renewal of acquaintance is no indifferent matter to one acting at such a distance as that instructions cannot be received hot and hot. one of my pleasures too will be that of talking over the old & new with you. in the mean time, & at all times, I have the honor to be with great & sincere esteem Dear Sir Your friend & servant   Th: Jefferson

LC: *Jefferson Papers, microfilm reel 11 (press copy).*
¹ *the law of the majority*

Comte de Moustier to Comte de Montmorin

[Translation]

Nᵒ· 8.   New York, 20 March 1789.
My Lord.

A new epoch in the history of united America is now marked by the expiration of the Congress composed at first of the Delegates of the thirteen Colonies of Great Britain, who came together to deliberate on the means to obtain redress of their grievances against the mother country, who then entered into confederation to act, and who finally declared themselves free and independent States. In these various degrees of power, Congress has never enjoyed any real benefits. In the first period, fear joined together spirits ever inclined, in moments of crisis and suffering, to obey the voice that guides them, the visible deference of a General whom his prudence and good fortune made the first man of the people he defended. The attentions evinced by foreigners also contributed to give a great consideration to Congress.

The distancing of danger, the uselessness of the services of the Savior of the fatherland, the presumption that they no longer have need of foreign assistance have reduced Congress to a true exercise of its functions, which consisted of deliberating without having any means of coercion. Everything tended toward resolutions and recommendations whose execution depended on men whose particular interests were completely in opposition to the public interests. So, although most of the resolutions and recommendations of Congress were dictated by wisdom and generally enough by honor, they have almost always remained without effect.

Its powerlessness having been perceived, several wise men sought to remedy it early on by attributing to Congress the real exercise of certain powers. This first idea was soon expanded into a total reformation concurred in equally by well-intentioned men and by others who saw that in such a great change they would find a way open to their ambition. In the passage from one idea to the other, and during the time employed for the reformation of the federal Government, Congress gradually fell into a kind of contempt, which rendered the most prominent men almost ashamed to enter it. Many others whose occupations were lucrative refused to take seats where there was neither honor nor profit to acquire. A very small number of men of merit were to be found in this body in these last years. The majority of the members who composed it were idlers without station, without occupation, and without talents, or young men scarcely out of college.

The small recompense that was granted them, and the title of *honorable* attached to the character of Delegate, provided for the needs of some and flattered the vanity of others. Congress kept the shadow of the equivocal authority that it had enjoyed and that at a distance still appeared as a phantom of Sovereignty. But it was time that it be replaced, since it could not be reformed. The American union was going to break down if it did not erect a new center more capable of consolidating all the parties that should be brought together therein.

It seems that the former Congress, before ceasing to exist, should have sought to give some sign of life that would have left an honorable memory of its last actions. It could have assembled all the information proper to facilitate the first operations of a body constituted to act, it could have prepared to expedite affairs that have long remained unexecuted, finally, since its pretentions were to figure as a body invested with Sovereignty, it could have made dispositions that would have given its end an appearance of transmutation, instead of an extinction that has characterized the nullity and the somewhat disgraceful weakness of an impotent body. Several Members from the small number of those who have some idea of patriotism had the desire to perform an act of decency and utility, but the greatest number, that of the thoughtless and the incapable, had dispersed, so that Congress could not even assemble, and ceased to be without even having existed since the start of the old federal year, which commenced in November.

It is surprising, after this kind of existence, to see the members who are still here in small numbers still pretend to compose a Body and to induce some of their confreres to come together to form a Congress according to the old federal Constitution, while on the other hand the members of the new Congress have assembled regularly since the day from which the new Government fixes its birth. In this way, there are two suns at once on the

American Continent. One no longer has heat or brilliance, the other is barely on the horizon, one must see it rise in order to judge it. It is not at all certain that it will not be obscured by some clouds before it reaches the elevation towards which it tends. These clouds may conceal and develop more than one storm.

It is a small blemish for a Government announced as more active and energetic than that which it succeeds to find itself at its birth in a state of nullity, for all that the present members can do is to assemble every day in order to adjourn. Their conversations have no weight, they cannot come to any legal resolution so long as they do not form a competent number, which is called a *quorum*, in each chamber. The quorum of the Senate should be 12, which is one vote more than half of the whole. That of the Chamber of representatives of the people should be 30 of 59, which is the whole number for the eleven United States.

It appears that it is not yet agreed what matters the two Chambers can consider before Congress is entirely constituted by the declaration of the election of the President of the United States, who forms the third branch of this body under its new configuration. But that declaration is precisely within their present competence, since it is stipulated by the new Constitution that the election ballots that were sent to the old Congress sealed by the Electors, and which are now under the guard of the Secretary of that Body, must be opened by the Senate in the presence of the representatives. The delay of the members who could have already arrived has hitherto prevented proceeding to so important an operation. One would like to think that bad roads are the cause of this delay, but the great number do not countenance this excuse, as the State of Jersey and that of Delaware are so near this federal residence that there is no plausible pretext to allege in order to justify the absence of the members from those two States. The fact is that the men who compose the new Congress, although generally much better chosen than those of the old one, are feeling the effects of the general indifference for public affairs when it is a question of applying themselves thereto. When no one in particular can be charged with public disgrace, it often happens that public honor and utility are compromised. The United States has had experience of this. It is to be desired that the new government may remedy the old abuses that have disgraced Congress.

The negligence that several States have shown in proceding to the election of new members, either by holding them too late or by not taking care to remove difficulties that could be foreseen, is the reason that all the members of the new Congress are not yet even appointed. The State of New York has no Senators; its Legislature, divided by the spirit of party, and to which belongs the power of determining the mode of election, has broken up without having enacted anything. Congress will attend to this, and that will be the first act of supremacy that it will exercise regarding an individual State, and precisely regarding one of those that have shown the most antipathy to investing Congress with an authority that, if it remains in force, must necessarily weaken that of the individual States. The representatives will be elected, because the mode of Election is determined by the federal Constitution, but the results of the elections will not be known until the end of this month. Jersey and Massachusetts both are incomplete. Georgia is so distant that we are still not exactly informed of the progress of the elections. So much negligence does not augur a unanimous concurrence with the measures from which the regeneration of public prosperity was hoped. It is difficult to judge how a body whose members do not have the same spirit will succeed in effecting the good which the most perfect accord in Congress could only procure with the greatest good fortune.

I thought I should acquaint You, My Lord, with the end of a body that has enjoyed a singular concourse of circumstances and the favor of its great distance from the part of the earth that alone occupied itself before the American revolution with the voice of renown, of a reputation, and of an admiration, to which it has responded very badly. The debut of the body that replaces it has appeared to me no less interesting to ascertain. If this infant Colossus rises, strengthens itself, and maintains itself, its beginnings will be retraced with interest. If the vast hopes of the Americans are not realized, they will not receive the general tribute of admiration that they already give themselves and that, judging from previous events and the fate of their first, so exalted Government, one is well justified in holding in reserve. If the body formed by the American union acquires vigor, I shall say that it was only deranged by curable maladies. If it does not deviate from its languor, I shall regard it as gangrenous, and shall envisage its dissolution. The facts acquaint us with the nature of the evils, the effects of which we see, and make us appreciate the quality of the remedies that one is disposed to employ.

I am with respect My Lord Your most humble and most obedient Servant,   Le Cte. de Moustier.
rec. 27 June

FFAA: Pol. Corr., U.S., v. 34, f. 34-39 (LC transcription).

Comte de Montmorin to Comte de Moustier

[Translation]

Versailles, [22] March 1789.

I have received, Sir, the despatches which you have done me the honor to write me under the N⁰⁶·..., as well as the memoranda that accompanied this last one.

The details which these memoranda contain, Sir, are very interesting, and I have made it my duty to make known near the King the Zeal which made you undertake so useful a task.

Like you, I am convinced, Sir, of the necessity of attending to our relations with the United States: but I think that there is no step to take at this time, and that in preparing materials we should defer putting them to work until the new Constitution has acquired Consistence. The only object to which we should attach ourselves in the present state of affairs is to support the Americans in their friendly dispositions toward France and to relieve them of every doubt of the King's sentiments in their regard and of His Majesty's perseverance in the engagements which exist between him and the united provinces.

As for what advantages, Sir, to grant the Americans in our islands, that is an infinitely delicate matter, and one which requires the most serious reflections. Certainly we shall grant them everything that depends upon us; but it is natural that our interest be considered before that of others; and nothing can make us abandon this maxim, which is the basis of the exaggerated claims of the Americans.

We have just restored the packet boats to America. There will be 6 of them per year; they will call at New York, and go from there to Norfolk. If you have any observations to make on this arrangement, I request you to send them to me.   De Montmorin

FFAA: Pol. Corr., U.S., v. 34, f. 51-52 (LC transcription).

Thomas Jefferson to John Paul Jones

Dear Sir   Paris Mar. 23. 1789.

.   .   .   .   .

Our new constitution was acceded to in the course of the last summer by all the states except N. Carolina and Rhode island. Massachusets, Virginia and New York, tho they accepted unconditionally, yet gave it as a perpetual instruction to their future delegates never to cease urging certain amendments. N. Carolina insisted that the amendments should be made before she would accede. The most important of these amendments will be effected by adding a bill of rights; and even the friends of the Constitution are become sensible of the expediency of such an addition were it only to conciliate the opposition. in fact this security for liberty seems to be demanded by the general voice of America, & we may conclude it will unquestionably be added. N. York, Virginia & N. Carolina have also demanded that a term be fixed after which the president shall be no longer eligible. but the public has been silent on this demand; so we may doubt it's success. in the mean time the elections for the new government were going on quietly at the date of our last letters. we have the names of most of the Senators; but not of the representatives. there was no question but Genl. Washington would be elected President; and we know that he would accept it, tho' with vast reluctance. The new Congress was to meet the 1st. Wednesday in this month, at New York. the tickets of election of the President would then be opened, and I presume that General Washington is now at New York, and the new legislature in a course of business. the only competitors for the Vice presidentship were mr J. Adams and mr Hancock. it was thought the former would be chosen. tho' the new constitution was adopted in 11 states, yet in those of Massachusets, Virginia & New York it was by very small majorities; & the minorities in the two last are far from the laudable acquiescence of that of Massachusets. Govr. Clinton[1] in New York, & mr Henry[2] in Virginia are moving heaven and earth to have a new Convention to make capital changes. but they will not succeed. there has been just opposition enough to produce probably further guards to liberty without touching the energy of the government, and this will bring over the bulk of the opposition to the side of the new government.

...I shall be glad to hear from you as often as possible, and have the honor to be with very great esteem, Dear Sir your most obedient & most humble serv^t

Th: Jefferson

LC: *Jefferson Papers, microfilm reel 10 (press copy).*

[1] *Clinton, George (1739-1812). New York political figure, military officer. Member, Continental Congress, 1775-1776. Appointed brigadier general of militia, 1776-1777, and of Continental Army, 1777-1783. Brevet major general, 1783. Governor of New York, 1777-1795, 1801-1804. Vice President of the United States, 1805-1812.*

[2] *Henry, Patrick (1736-1799). Virginia political figure. Member, Virginia House of Burgesses, 1765-1775. Member, Continental Congress, 1774-1775. Governor of Virginia, 1776-1779 and 1784-1786.*

∞ *Epilogue* ∞

On April 30, 1789, George Washington took the oath of office as the first president of the United States under the federal Constitution. John Adams, who had returned from London in the spring of 1788, having achieved little success in resolving the country's problems with Great Britain, became vice president in the new federal government. Thomas Jefferson remained in France until October 1789, when he returned to Virginia to attend to personal affairs; Washington asked him to accept the post of Secretary of State in the new government, which he agreed to do, taking office on March 22, 1790. John Jay, having previously accepted the post of Chief Justice of the United States, served as acting Secretary of State until Jefferson's arrival in New York.

Benjamin Franklin, whose participation in diplomatic matters had ended with his return from France in 1785, served as a delegate to the Constitutional Convention from Pennsylvania. James Madison recorded Franklin's comments during the formal signing of the United States Constitution as follows:

> Whilst the last members were signing it Doctr. Franklin looking towards the President's Chair, at the back of which a rising sun happened to be painted, observed to a few members near him, that Painters had found it difficult to distinguish in their art a rising from a setting sun. I have said he, often and often in the course of the Session, and the vicisitudes of my hopes and fears as to its issue, looked at that behind the President without being able to tell whether it was rising or setting. But now at length I have the happiness to know that it is a rising and not a setting sun.[1]

That sun rose on a new nation still plagued by restrictions which its largest foreign trading partner, Great Britain, had placed on U.S. commerce with British possessions in the Western Hemisphere. The British also retained the frontier posts which they had pledged themselves to turn over to the United States in the peace treaty, disputed the northeast boundary, demanded the payment of prewar debts owed to British creditors, and expressed concern at the treatment accorded loyalists who attempted to recover property seized and rights denied during the American Revolution. Since the United States derived its primary revenues from an import tariff, however, the maintenance of peace with Great Britain was a major priority.

When tensions over the frontier posts and British treatment of American merchant vessels in the West Indies reached a boiling point in 1794, President Washington sent John Jay to London in an effort to reach an amicable settlement of points in contention. The Jay Treaty, signed in November 1794, brought the transfer of the frontier posts into American hands and established mixed claims commissions to settle other mutual grievances, but was tremendously unpopular in the United States. Approved by the Senate nonetheless, it kept the peace, which allowed the U.S. government to continue strengthening itself through the judicious expenditure of its import duties.

Bourbon France persevered in asserting that the wartime Franco-American alliance remained in effect, although French leaders privately admitted that the best they could hope for was a benevolent American neutrality in any future war they might wage against Great Britain. Despite Jefferson's efforts, Franco-American trade remained a small part of U.S. foreign commerce.

Revolutionary France also held the Franco-American alliance to remain viable. France declared war on Great Britain and the United Provinces on February 1, 1793; Edmond Charles Genet, its new minister to the United States, aroused the ire of President Washington and the leading Federalists by attempting to fit out French privateers in American ports and to influence American political opinion through the formation of Jacobin clubs in major American cities. Washington, who requested Genet's recall, later announced that his purpose was to keep the United States free and independent of political connections with any foreign country.

Relations between the United States and Spain remained correct, although no settlement of outstanding disputes was reached until October 1795, with the Treaty of San Lorenzo, also known as the Pinckney Treaty in honor of Thomas Pinckney, the American negotiator. The Pinckney Treaty settled the southern boundary of the United States, secured navigation of the entire Mississippi River by American vessels, and established New Orleans as a free port for American produce.

The United States secured the release of the American seamen held by Algiers through a treaty of peace and amity signed in September 1795 and ratified by the United States the following March. That treaty required the United States to pay an annual tribute to Algiers in order to maintain the peace. However, the growing strength of the new nation was evident in an act passed by Congress in March 1794, which provided for the establishment of a United States Navy and the construction of six frigates destined for use against the Barbary pirates. The year 1794 also saw the growing United States Army victorious over the Indians at the Battle of Fallen Timbers.

As more and more settlers poured into the Western lands, and more and more American merchant vessels put to sea carrying American produce for sale in foreign lands, the foreign trade status of the United States gradually improved. By March 1797, when President Washington left office, the United States had made significant strides toward an economic independence to match the political freedom won by its first diplomats at the negotiating tables of Paris in 1782 and 1783. The emerging nation was fast becoming sovereign, free, and independent in fact as well as in name.

---

[1] John P. Kaminski and Gaspare J. Saladino, eds., The Documentary History of the Ratification of the Constitution. Volume XIII: Commentaries on the Constitution, Public and Private. Volume 1: 21 February to 7 November 1787 (Madison: State Historical Society of Wisconsin, 1981), p. 215.

Index

ISBN 0-16-048500-2

9 780160 485008

90000